Italian
Dictionary

English-Italiano
Italian-Inglese

Peter F. Ross

BARNES
&NOBLE
BOOKS
NEW YORK

This edition published by Marboro Books Corp.,
a division of Barnes & Noble, Inc.,
by arrangement with Hippocrene books.

1992 Barnes & Noble Books

ISBN 0-88029-937-1

Printed and bound in the United States of America

M 9 8 7 6 5 4

Abbreviations/Abbreviazioni

adj adjective
admin administration
adv adverb
aero aeronautics
agg aggettivo
agric agriculture, agricoltura
anat anatomy, anatomia
arch architecture, architettura
art article, articolo
astrol astrology, astrologia
astron astronomy, astronomia
auto automobilismo
aux auxiliary
avv avverbio
biol biology, biologia
bot botany, botanica
chem chemistry
chim chimica
coll colloquial
comm commerce, commercio
cong congiunzione
conj conjunction
derog derogatory
dir diritto
econ economics, economia
elec electricity
elett elettricità
f feminine, femminile
fam familiar, familiare
ferr ferrovia
fig figurato
filos filosofia
fis fisica
foto fotografia
gastr gastronomia
geog geography, geografia

geol geology, geologia
geom geometry, geometria
gramm grammar, grammatica
impol impolite
inter interiezione
interj interjection
invar invariable, invariabile
m masculine, maschile
mar marina
mat matematica
math mathematics
mec mechanical, meccanica
med medicine, medicina
mil military, militare
n noun
naut nautical
phone telephone
phot photography
pl plural, plurale
pol politics, politica
prep preposition, preposizione
pron pronoun, pronome
psic psicologia, psichiatria
psych psychology, psychiatry
rail railways
rel religion, religione
s sostantivo
sing singular, singolare
spreg spregiativo
tec tecnologia
tech technical
TV television, televisione
v verb, verbo
V vide (see, vedi)
volg volgare
zool zoology, zoologia

Italian pronunciation

As wide variations exist between pronunciations in different parts of Italy, we have favoured the standard accepted in the north as this is rapidly gaining general acceptance.

a sano ['sano]
ε bene ['bεne]
e festa ['festa]
i tinto ['tinto]
ɔ brodo ['brɔdo]
o mondo ['mondo]
u fune ['fune]
b bene ['bεne]
d dito ['dito]
f fine ['fine]
g gallo ['gallo]
j lezione [le'tsjone]
k capo ['kapo]
l legge ['leddʒe]
m mago ['mago]

n nitido ['nitido]
p pulce ['pultʃe]
r rete ['rete]
s sabbia ['sabbja]
t tanto ['tanto]
v via ['via]
w quando ['kwando]
z viso ['vizo]
dz zucchero ['dzukkero]
ts anzi ['antsi]
ʃ sciame ['ʃame]
tʃ cibo ['tʃibo]
dʒ gentile [dʒen'tile]
ʎ figlio ['fiʎo]
ɲ ragno ['raɲo]
ŋ smoking ['zmɔkiŋ]

The symbol ' indicates that the following syllable should be stressed.

Pronuncia inglese

a hat [hat]
e bell [bell]
i big [big]
o dot [dot]
ʌ bun [bʌn]
u book [buk]
ə alone [ə'loun]
a: card [ka:d]
ə: word [wə:d]
i: team [ti:m]
o: torn [to:n]
u: spoon [spu:n]
ai die [dai]
ei ray [rei]
oi toy [toi]
au how [hau]
ou road [roud]
eə lair [leə]
iə fear [fiə]
uə poor [puə]
b back [bak]
d dull [dʌl]
f find [faind]

g gaze [geiz]
h hop [hop]
j yell [jel]
k cat [kat]
l life [laif]
m mouse [maus]
n night [nait]
p pick [pik]
r rose [rouz]
s sit [sit]
t toe [tou]
v vest [vest]
w week [wi:k]
z zoo [zu:]
θ think [θiŋk]
ð those [ðouz]
ʃ shoe [ʃu:]
ʒ treasure ['treʒə]
tʃ chalk [tʃo:k]
dʒ jump [dʒʌmp]
ŋ sing [siŋ]

Il simbolo ' precede la sillaba che ha l'accento tonico principale.
Il simbolo , precede la sillaba che ha l'accento tonico secondario.

Guide to the dictionary

Irregular plural forms are shown at the headword and in the text. The following categories of Italian plural forms are considered regular:

albero	alberi
viale	viali
chiesa	chiese
amica	amiche
lunga	lunghe
città	città
tesi	tesi

In addition, masculine Italian words ending in **-a** are considered regular if they form their plural in **-i**. Masculine words ending in **-co** and **-go** form their plurals in **-chi** and **-ghi** unless the word is of more than two syllables and the **-co** or **-go** preceded by a vowel, in which case the plural is formed in **-ci** and **-gi**. Exceptions to this rule are considered irregular.

Irregular verbs listed in the verb tables are marked with an asterisk in the headword list. Compounds are not listed in the verb tables.

Adverbs are shown only if their formation is irregular. English adverbs are considered regular if they are formed by adding *-ly* or *-ally* to the adjective. Italian adverbs are considered regular if they are formed by adding *-mente* to the feminine form of the adjective.

Guida all'uso del vocabolario

I plurali irregolari dei sostantivi sono indicati sia sotto la voce di partenza sia nel testo stesso. Le seguenti categorie vengono considerate di formazione regolare in inglese:

cat	cats
glass	glasses
fly	flies
half	halves
wife	wives

I verbi irregolari nell'apposita tavola sono contraddistinti con un asterisco nella lista delle voci di partenza. Non sono compresi nella tavola i verbi composti.

Gli avverbi sono indicati con voci proprie solo quando si tratta di formazioni irregolari. Vengono considerati regolari in inglese gli avverbi formati con l'aggiunta di -*ly* o di -*ally* all'aggettivo. Vengono considerati regolari in italiano gli avverbi formati mediante l'aggiunta di -*mente* al femminile dell'aggettivo.

Italian irregular verbs

Infinitive	Present	Past Absolute	Future	Past Participle
addurre	adduco	addussi	addurrò	addotto
affiggere	affiggo	affissi	affiggerò	affisso
affliggere	affliggo	afflissi	affliggerò	afflitto
alludere	alludo	allusi	alluderò	alluso
andare	vado	andai	andrò	andato
annettere	annetto	annessi	annetterò	annesso
apparire	appaio	apparvi	apparirò	apparso
appendere	appendo	appesi	appenderò	appeso
aprire	apro	aprii	aprirò	aperto
ardere	ardo	arsi	ardirò	arso
assistere	assisto	assistetti	assisterò	assistito
assolvere	assolvo	assolsi	assolverò	assolto
assumere	assumo	assunsi	assumerò	assunto
avere	ho	ebbi	avrò	avuto
bere	bevo	bevvi	berrò	bevuto
cadere	cado	caddi	cadrò	caduto
cogliere	colgo	colsi	coglierò	colto
comprimere	comprimo	compressi	comprimerò	compresso
concedere	concedo	concedetti	concederò	concesso
conoscere	conosco	conobbi	conoscerò	conosciuto
correre	corro	corsi	correrò	corso
crescere	cresco	crebbi	crescerò	cresciuto
cuocere	cuocio	cossi	cuocerò	cotto
dare	do	diedi	darò	dato
dire	dico	dissi	dirò	detto
dirigere	dirigo	diressi	dirigerò	diretto
discutere	discuto	discussi	discuterò	discusso
dissuadere	dissuado	dissuasi	dissuaderò	dissuaso
distinguere	distinguo	distinsi	distinguerò	distinto
dolere	dolgo	dolsi	dorrò	doluto
dovere	debbo	dovetti	dovrò	dovuto
emergere	emergo	emersi	emergerò	emerso
erigere	erigo	eressi	erigerò	eretto
esigere	esigo	esigetti	esigerò	esatto
espellere	espello	espulsi	espellerò	espulso
esplodere	esplodo	esplosi	esploderò	esploso
essere	sono	fui	sarò	stato

Infinitive	Present	Past Absolute	Future	Past Participle
estinguere	estinguo	estinsi	estinguerò	estinto
evadere	evado	evasi	evaderò	evaso
fare	faccio	feci	farò	fatto
flettere	fletto	flessi	fletterò	flesso
fondere	fondo	fusi	fonderò	fuso
friggere	friggo	frissi	friggerò	fritto
giacere	giaccio	giacqui	giacerò	giaciuto
godere	godo	godetti	godrò	goduto
incutere	incuto	incussi	incuterò	incusso
infliggere	infliggo	inflissi	infliggerò	inflitto
invadere	invado	invasi	invaderò	invaso
leggere	leggo	lessi	leggerò	letto
mettere	metto	misi	metterò	messo
mordere	mordo	morsi	morderò	morso
morire	muoio	morii	morirò	morto
muovere	muovo	mossi	muoverò	mosso
nascere	nasco	nacqui	nascerò	nato
nascondere	nascondo	nascosi	nasconderò	nascosto
nuocere	nuoccio	nocqui	nuocerò	nociuto
offrire	offro	offersi	offrirò	offerto
parere	paio	parvi	parrò	parso
perdere	perdo	perdetti	perderò	perso
persuadere	persuado	persuasi	persuaderò	persuaso
piacere	piaccio	piacque	piacerò	piaciuto
porgere	porgo	porsi	porgerò	porto
porre	pongo	posi	porrò	posto
potere	posso	potei	potrò	potuto
proteggere	proteggo	protessi	proteggerò	protetto
redimere	redimo	redensi	redimerò	redento
redigere	redigo	redassi	redigerò	redatto
reggere	reggo	ressi	reggerò	retto
rifulgere	rifulgo	rifulsi	rifulgerò	rifulso
rimanere	rimango	rimasi	rimarrò	rimasto
rispondere	rispondo	risposi	risponderò	risposto
rodere	rodo	rosi	roderò	roso
rompere	rompo	ruppi	romperò	rotto
sapere	so	seppi	saprò	saputo
scegliere	scelgo	scelsi	sceglierò	scelto
scindere	scindo	scissi	scinderò	scisso

Infinitive	Present	Past Absolute	Future	Past Participle
sciogliere	sciolgo	sciolsi	scioglierò	sciolto
scoprire	scopro	scoprii	scoprirò	scoperto
scorgere	scorgo	scorsi	scorgerò	scorto
scrivere	scrivo	scrissi	scriverò	scritto
scuotere	scuoto	scossi	scuoterò	scosso
sedere	siedo	sedetti	sederò	seduto
solere	soglio	solei	solerò	solito
sommergere	sommergo	sommersi	sommergerò	sommerso
sorgere	sorgo	sorsi	sorgerò	sorto
spandere	spando	spansi	spanderò	spanto
spargere	spargo	sparsi	spargerò	sparso
spegnere	spengo	spensi	spegnerò	spento
stare	sto	stetti	starò	stato
stringere	stringo	strinsi	stringerò	stretto
struggere	struggo	strussi	struggerò	strutto
svellere	svello	svelsi	svellerò	svelto
tacere	taccio	tacqui	tacerò	taciuto
tenere	tengo	tenni	terrò	tenuto
togliere	tolgo	tolsi	toglierò	tolto
torcere	torco	torsi	torcerò	torto
trarre	traggo	trassi	trarrò	tratto
udire	odo	udii	udirò	udito
ungere	ungo	unsi	ungerò	unto
uscire	esco	uscii	uscirò	uscito
valere	valgo	valsi	varrò	valso
vedere	vedo	vidi	vedrò	visto
venire	vengo	venni	verrò	venuto
vincere	vinco	vinsi	vincerò	vinto
vivere	vivo	vissi	vivrò	vissuto
volere	voglio	volli	vorrò	voluto
volgere	volgo	volsi	volgerò	volto

For verbs ending in:

-cedere see concedere	-nettere see annettere
-durre see addurre	-ngere (except stringere) see ungere
-endere see appendere	-parire see apparire
-figgere see affiggere	-primere see comprimere
-idere or -udere see alludere	-sistere see assistere

Verbi inglesi irregolari

Infinito	Preterito	Participo Passato	Infinito	Preterito	Participo Passato
abide	abode	abode	deal	dealt	dealt
arise	arose	arisen	dig	dug	dug
awake	awoke	awoken	do	did	done
be	was	been	draw	drew	drawn
bear	bore	borne	dream	dreamed	dreamed
		or born		or dreamt	or dreamt
beat	beat	beaten	drink	drank	drunk
become	became	become	drive	drove	driven
begin	began	begun	dwell	dwelt	dwelt
behold	beheld	beheld	eat	ate	eaten
bend	bent	bent	fall	fell	fallen
bet	bet	bet	feed	fed	fed
beware			feel	felt	felt
bid	bid	bidden	fight	fought	fought
		or bid	find	found	found
bind	bound	bound	flee	fled	fled
bite	bit	bitten	fling	flung	flung
bleed	bled	bled	fly	flew	flown
blow	blew	blown	forbid	forbade	forbidden
break	broke	broken	forget	forgot	forgotten
breed	bred	bred	forgive	forgave	forgiven
bring	brought	brought	forsake	forsook	forsaken
build	built	built	freeze	froze	frozen
burn	burnt	burnt	get	got	got
	or burned	or burned	give	gave	given
burst	burst	burst	go	went	gone
buy	bought	bought	grind	ground	ground
can	could		grow	grew	grown
cast	cast	cast	hang	hung	hung
catch	caught	caught		or hanged	or hanged
choose	chose	chosen	have	had	had
cling	clung	clung	hear	heard	heard
come	came	come	hide	hid	hidden
cost	cost	cost	hit	hit	hit
creep	crept	crept	hold	held	held
cut	cut	cut	hurt	hurt	hurt

Infinito	Preterito	Participo Passato	Infinito	Preterito	Participo Passato
keep	kept	kept	say	said	said
kneel	knelt	knelt	see	saw	seen
knit	knitted	knitted	seek	sought	sought
	or knit	or knit	sell	sold	sold
know	knew	known	send	sent	sent
lay	laid	laid	set	set	set
lead	led	led	sew	sewed	sewn
lean	leant	leant			or sewed
	or leaned	or leaned	shake	shook	shaken
leap	leapt	leapt	shear	sheared	sheared
	or leaped	or leaped			or shorn
learn	learnt	learnt	shed	shed	shed
	or learned	or learned	shine	shone	shone
leave	left	left	shoe	shod	shod
lend	lent	lent	shoot	shot	shot
let	let	let	show	showed	shown
lie	lay	lain	shrink	shrank	shrunk
light	lit	lit	shut	shut	shut
	or lighted	or lighted	sing	sang	sung
lose	lost	lost	sink	sank	sunk
make	made	made	sit	sat	sat
may	might		sleep	slept	slept
mean	meant	meant	slide	slid	slid
meet	met	met	sling	slung	slung
mow	mowed	mown	slink	slunk	slunk
must			slit	slit	slit
ought			smell	smelt	smelt
pay	paid	paid		or smelled	or smelled
put	put	put	sow	sowed	sown
quit	quitted	quitted			or sowed
	or quit	or quit	speak	spoke	spoken
read	read	read	speed	sped	sped
rid	rid	rid		or speeded	or speeded
ride	rode	ridden	spell	spelt	spelt
ring	rang	rung		or spelled	or spelled
rise	rose	risen	spend	spent	spent
run	ran	run	spill	spilt	spilt
saw	sawed	sawn		or spilled	or spilled
		or sawed	spin	spun	spun

Infinito	Preterito	Participo Passato	Infinito	Preterito	Participo Passato
spit	spat	spat	**swim**	swam	swum
split	split	split	**swing**	swung	swung
spread	spread	spread	**take**	took	taken
spring	sprang	sprung	**teach**	taught	taught
stand	stood	stood	**tear**	tore	torn
steal	stole	stolen	**tell**	told	told
stick	stuck	stuck	**think**	thought	thought
sting	stung	stung	**throw**	threw	thrown
stink	stank	stunk	**thrust**	thrust	thrust
	or stunk		**tread**	trod	trodden
stride	strode	stridden	**wake**	woke	woken
strike	struck	struck	**wear**	wore	worn
string	strung	strung	**weave**	wove	woven
strive	strove	striven	**weep**	wept	wept
swear	swore	sworn	**win**	won	won
sweep	swept	swept	**wind**	wound	wound
swell	swelled	swollen	**wring**	wrung	wrung
		or swelled	**write**	wrote	written

Glossary of menu terms

Italy is a happy place to eat. Waiters, food store owners, hostesses all urge you to have something good to eat. Italian cuisine is based on the food that is available locally, and it is, therefore, seasonal. A good look at a market will give you an idea of what is most abundant and freshest.

There are three main meals and any number of informal snacks in Italy. **Prima colazione** (breakfast) is usually only coffee and bread for Italians. If you want a more substantial meal, try a café at midmorning, or better yet, shop in a food store or open market the night before. **Colazione** (or **pranzo**) is lunch and **cena** is dinner. These two meals are much alike; choose to have your major meal at whichever time is convenient. (If you plan to have two large meals, include some vigorous sightseeing or sports; you will have consumed a lot of food.)

Traditionally each of the regions of Italy (Tuscany, Latium, Venezia, Apulia, etc.) had its own distinctive cuisine, employing its own particular crops, cheeses, and wines, quite different from that of other regions. Modern standardization is having its effects here as elsewhere, but you will still find dishes on local menus which are not found any place else. Only some of the more famous of these regional specialties could be included here.

The title **ristorante** is used for the larger, more elegant — and more expensive — eating establishments. For every **ristorante**, there are many **trattorie** (singular: **trattoria**), where one might eat in plainer surroundings, and much more cheaply, food at least as good as that in a **ristorante**. In recent years **trattorie** have been disappearing, but a good one is still worth looking for.

Italian eating establishments usually list all or most of the following categories on their menus: **antipasta** (hors d'oeuvre), **minestre** (soups), **pasta** (spaghetti, etc.), **pesce** (seafood), **carne** (meats), **contorni** (vegetables), **insalata** (salads), **uova** (egg dishes), **formaggi** (cheeses), **frutta** (fruits), **dolci** (desserts). A very special Italian meal might include an item from every category, but the waiter (**cameriere**) of today knows that the tourist is not so ambitious.

Most Italian restaurants offer a fixed-price meal (**prezzo fisso**, abbreviation p.f.), a full-course dinner, no substitutions allowed. If you order from the full menu, you may find some dishes marked **piatti del giorno** or **pronti**. These are ready to serve. Others will be **piatti da farsi**, dishes which have to be made up. This may take a far amount of time.

You must ask for the check (**conto**); it is not brought automatically. Law now requires that you be given a legible itemized bill. There will be a fixed percentage added for service (**servizio**), but your waiter will still expect a modest tip in addition.

Antipasti (Hors d'Oeuvre)

Italian hors d'oeuvre may range from a single dish to a wide selection of appetizers. A typical antipasto might include cold cuts: **salami** there are a number of regional varieties, Genovese, Milanese, etc; **prosciutto** thin sliced uncooked ham; **mortadella** similar to U.S. bologna but with more fat; **coppa** pork sausage

fish: **acciughe** anchovies; **tonno** tuna; **sardine** sardines

vegetables done as salads: **fagioli** beans; **carciofi** artichokes; **peperoni** peppers (sweet); **peperoncini** small pickled peppers

pickles: **funghi sott'olio** pickled mushrooms; **caponata** eggplant in sweet and sour sauce

hardcooked eggs: **uova sode coi tonno** eggs stuffed with tuna; **uova sode coi spinachi** eggs stuffed with spinach

Dishes which may be served separately or as part of an antipasto:

prosciutto e melone sliced ham with honeydew melon

prosciutto e fichi sliced ham with figs

crostini di acciughe anchovies on toast

crostini alla napoletana toast with anchovies, cheese, and tomatoes

crostini alla fiorentina chicken livers on toast

mozzarella in carozza fried cheese sandwiches

Minestre (Soups)

Soups are as important a part of the Italian menu as pasta (and the two are never taken at the same meal; generally lunch is accompanied by some form of pasta, dinner by soup). Most soups are either **brodo**, broth of chicken, meat, fish, or vegetables, either plain or with pasta **(pastina in brodo)**; or minestrone (literally "big soup," combinations of several fresh or dried vegetables). All are served with generous helpings of grated cheese **(parmigiana, romana)**. Every region has its own particular version of **minestrone, e.g. minestrone alla Genovese, alla Milanese,** etc.; and the vegetables used will vary according to what is in season. Other famous soups: **zuppa di pesce** Italian equivalent of bouillabaisse, a stew of mixed fish and shellfish (the combination varies according to the area)

zuppa di cozze mussel soup

minestra di pasta e fagioli bean and pasta soup

stracciatella broth with egg strands

zuppa pavese poached egg in broth with toast

Pasta

Pasta is a mainstay of the Italian menu but **not** the principal dish Americans often make of it. Nor is it just spaghetti and macaroni; there are literally hundreds of different sizes and shapes of dried pasta made of the semolina flour in common use in Italy. For example, **vermicelli** (finer than spaghetti); **rigatoni** (ridged tubes); **ziti** (smaller tubes); **linguine** (flat narrow strips); **tagliatelle** (broader than **linguine**); **lasagne** (very broad); **farfalle** (butterfly-shaped bows, used in soups); and many, many more. Also, the same pasta is often called by another name in different regions: what is called **tagliatelle** in Bologna is **fettucine** in Rome. In general, **pasta asciutte** ("dry pasta," even when served swimming in sauce) is distinguished from **pasta in brodo**, soup with some variety of pasta in it.

Pasta with sauces:

al burro dressed with butter

aglio e olio with olive oil and lightly fried garlic

alla Bolognese with rich meat sauce

alle cozze with mussels

alla carbonara with a sauce of bacon and lightly cooked egg

al pesto (Genovese) with a sauce of fresh basil, pine nuts, and cheese pounded to paste (a specialty of Genoa)

Pasta stuffed and baked (usually served as main dishes):

cannelloni tubes of pasta stuffed with meat or cheese and baked in sauce

lasagne layers of flat pasta baked with cheese and tomato sauce

lasagne verde lasagne made with spinach kneaded into the dough giving it a pale green color

gnocchi dumplings made of semolina, potato, or corn meal baked with butter, cheese, or other sauce

ravioli pasta dumplings stuffed with meat, cheese, or various vegetables, served plain or with sauce

Riso (Rice)

Northern Italy is rice country, and there the distinctive rise dish, **risotto**, may take the place of the pasta course on the menu.

risotto alla Milanese rice cooked in chicken stock and wine sauce with a touch of saffron

risotto alla Piemontese rice in a meat sauce with cheese

risotto alla marinara rice cooked in fish stock with shrimp and mussels

risi e bisi risotto with green peas (a specialty of Venice)

arancini "oranges": rice balls stuffed with meat, cheese, and tomato sauce and deep-fried (a specialty of Sicily)

Polenta

Italians don't eat corn on the cob, but they are fond of this corn-meal dish. To call it "corn-meal mush" may discourage those unfamiliar with what the Italian do with it. Every region has its own special way of cooking **polenta**, and it is served with a variety of sauces, meats, and cheeses. Be sure to try it.

Pesce (Fish)

Italian waters are rich in fish, but it is difficult to give the tourist an idea of what is available, for the varieties are so different and names and even types of fish vary from region to region. For example, **cozze** is a common word for mussel, but in Genoa mussels are called **muscoli**; in Venice they are called **peoci**, etc. Some common names are: **acciughe** anchovies; **anguille** eels (small); **calamare** squid; **calamaretti** baby squid; **capitone** eels (large); **cozze** mussels; **merluzzo** cod; **sardine** sardines; **scampi** shrimp; **scungilli** conch; **spigola** bream; **tonno** tunny; **triglie** mullet; **trote** trout

Fish is usually cooked by grilling (**alla griglia**), frying (**fritti**) or roasting (**arrosto**), whole (including the head), or in slices.

Some common fish sauces:

alla marinara sailor style with tomato and herbs

alla pizzaiola tomato sauce

alla Napoletana lemon juice, oil, and herbs

alla Siciliana capers, olives, and herbs

Baccalà is a popular stew of dried cod with tomatoes and herbs.

Carni e Pollame (Meats and Fowl)

Meat, in Italy, almost invariably means veal (**vitello**) — so much so that menus normally carry the seemingly contradictory item **bistecca di vitello** — literally, "veal beefsteak." Some areas offer excellent dishes of lamb (**agnello**) and pork (**maiale**).

Similarly, fowl mainly means chicken (**pollo**); but turkey (**tachino**) is quite common, and game birds like pheasant (**fagiano**) are excellent when avaiable.

Veal is very commonly served in the form of **scallope** (or **scaloppini**), thin slices fried with various sauces: **scallope al Marsala**, wine sauce; **alla piccata**, lemon juice; **alla Bolognese**, topped with cheese.

saltimbocca a Roman specialty, is veal scallops topped with thin slices of ham and cheese, and cooked with sage

costolette breaded veal cutlets; **alla Milanese**, lightly fried and served with lemon wedges; **alla Modenese**, baked in wine and tomato sauce; **alla Parmeggiana**, baked with tomatoes and cheese

arrosto di vitello veal roast

vitello tonnato pot roast of veal in tuna sauce

arista florentina pork roast Florentine style

bistecca alla fiorentina grilled steak (usually cooked well done on the outside and rare on the inside)

bistecca alla pizzaiola fried steak with sauce of tomato and herbs

costoletto di agnello piccante lamb chops fried with herbs and dressed with lemon juice

abbacchio al forno roast leg of lamb

ossobucchi alla Milanese veal shanks with marrow cooked in wine

stufato rich beef stew (meat may vary) with wine and herbs

fritto misto deep-fried pieces of organ meats (liver, heart, brains, etc)

fegato alla Veneziana liver and onions

rognoni trifolati kidneys cooked with anchovies and lemon juice

cervelli fritti calf brains sliced, breaded, and fried

regalo cocks' combs in wine sauce

pollo alla cacciatora chicken stewed with wine, tomatoes, mushrooms, and herbs

pollo alla diavola chicken covered with red pepper flakes and cooked in a light wine sauce

pollo alla Romana chicken stewed with tomatoes, peppers, wine, and herbs

petti di pollo alla Bolognese chicken breasts topped with ham and cheese

petti di pollo al Marsala chicken breasts cooked in wine

fegato di pollo alla salvia chicken livers cooked with sage

Contorni (di verdure) (Vegetables)

In Italian restaurants, while some vegetables may be served with the meat, it is common for vegetables to be eaten as a separate course, often before the main dish. Cooking is usually simple: green vegetables are blanched or steamed briefly and served with olive oil and lemon. Eggplant, tomatoes, and peppers are often stuffed with meat or vegetable mixtures and various spices.

carciofi artichokes (Italian artichokes are usually smaller and tenderer than the American kind and eaten whole)

melanzane eggplant

zucchine zucchini

peperoni sweet peppers

finocchi fennel (rather like celery with an anise flavor)

piselli peas

spinaci spinach

pomidori tomatoes

patate potatoes; **patate fritte** — "French-fried" potatoes

funghi mushrooms

cavalfiore cauliflower

legumi beans

sedani celery

cipolle onions

broccoli broccoli

asparago asparagus

carota carrots

Insalate (Salads)

Salads are an important part of the Italian meal, and may appear as part of the antipasto, as an accompaniment to the main dish, or as a separate course after the meat. Most are very simple with vinegar (or lemon juice) and oil dressing. Restaurants usually set the table with cruets of vinegar and oil so that the diner may make his own dressing. Many of the vegetables listed as hot dishes under **contorni** may also be served cold as salad.

insalata verde green salad, lettuce and other available greens

insalata de pomidori tomato salad

insalata di broccoli broccoli salad (fresh or cooked)

insalata di melanzane eggplant salad

insalata di finocchi fennel salad

fagiolini al tonno salad of green beans and tuna

insalata Nizzarda salad Nicoise: lettuce, tomatoes, green beans, peppers, olives, and anchovies in vinegar and oil.

Uova (Egg Dishes)

Eggs are never served for breakfast in Italy (though a homesick tourist may sometimes coax a dish of scrambled eggs from a sympathetic cook with the phrase **uova strapazzate**). But they are often fare for lunch or a light supper.

uova al tegamino fried eggs served in the cooking pan

frittata the Italian omelet; unlike the French variety, it is turned and browned on both sides, cooked right through; often served with chopped meats, vegetables, fish, as : **frittata coi carcioff** artichoke omelet; **frittata con tonno** omelet with tuna; **frittata con zucchine** omelet with zucchini; **frittata con spinachi** spinach omelet; **uova al piatto coi pomidori** eggs poached in tomato sauce; **uova al piatto coi fegatini** eggs with chicken livers.

Formaggi (Cheeses)

Italy produces many excellent cheeses, and they are an indispensable element in the Italian cuisine. Many are also delicious for eating and form a separate course in the Italian dinner, between the main dish and dessert. Some common eating cheeses:

gorgonzola a blue veined cheese, similar to Roquefort but richer and stronger flavored

bel paese a mild, smooth cheese, excellent for eating and cooking

Parmigiano Parmesan, always served grated with pasta and main dishes, also served for eating

pecorino sheeps' milk cheese, widely used for eating fresh; for grating when aged

provolone a sweet eating cheese when fresh; acquires a sharp flavor when aged and is used for cooking

mozzarella a fresh cheese, rather like cottage cheese; used for cooking and eating

ricotta a creamy fresh cheese eaten and used in desserts

Frutte (Fruits)

It is not unusual for an Italian meal to end with cheese and fruit rather than a formal dessert. Fruits are usually served raw and peeled at the table (an Italian never touches his fruit except with knife and fork; this seems difficult to the un-initiate but can be learned).

mele apples
Arancie oranges
pesche peaches
banane bananas
fragole strawberries
ciliege cherries
pera pears
fichi figs
melone melon
macedonia de frutta mixed fruit salad

Dolci (Desserts)

zabaglione (or zabaione) custard-flavored with Marsala wine

montebianco puréed chestnuts flavored with Marsala and topped with whipped cream

cassata rich cheese cake flavored with liqueurs (a specialty of Sicily)

dolce al rhum rum cake
pan di spagna sponge cake
budino di ricotta ricotta cheese pudding
gelata, spumone ice cream
granite fruit ices

Bevande (Drinks)

Italian restaurants do not usually serve cocktails; the Italian preference is for an aperitif **(aperitivo),** of which there are many. **Vermouth bianco** is probably the most popular. With the meal, it is usually a safe bet to take one of the local wines — every region has its own vintages, and they often have a remarkable affinity for the local dishes. Some wines which are available country-wide are:

Asti spumante the Italian champagne
Bardo a robust full-bodied red **(rosso)**
Valpolicella a light red
Soave one of the best whites **(bianco)**

Chianti real Chianti is a revelation if you have encountered only imitations

Orvieto a superb white: either dry **(secco)** or semi-sweet **(abboccato)**

Est! Est! Est! a white famous since the Middle Ages

Frascati the classic white wine of Rome

Capri and **Ischia** the Neapolitan islands produce good dry reds and whites

Lacrima Christi the famous dessert wine from Mount Vesuvius

Marsala (dolce) the dessert wine of Sicily

Coffee. Most Italians like to end their meal with the strong sweet **espresso. Cappuccino** is strong coffee with milk. **Caffelatte** is coffee and milk half-and-half.

Tea **(te)** is usually available. Nowadays, you can usually order milk with your meal **(bicchiere di latte)** without causing a major sensation. Italians often drink bottled mineral water **(acqua minerale)** with their meal in preference to wine. Many varieties are available nationally.

English—Italiano

A

a, an [ə, ən] *art* un, uno *m*; una *f*.

aback [ə'bak] *adv* be taken aback essere colto di sorpresa.

abandon [ə'bandən] *v* abbandonare. *n* abbandono *m*.

abashed [ə'baʃt] *adj* confuso.

abate [ə'beit] *v* diminuire. **abatement** *n* diminuzione *f*.

abattoir ['abətwaɪ] *n* macello *m*.

abbey ['abi] *n* abbazia *f*. **abbess** *n* badessa *f*. **abbot** *n* abate *m*.

abbreviate [ə'briːvieit] *v* abbreviare. **abbreviation** *n* abbreviazione *f*.

abdicate ['abdikeit] *v* abdicare. **abdication** *n* abdicazione *f*.

abdomen ['abdəmən] *n* addome *m*. **abdominal** *adj* addominale.

abduct [əb'dʌkt] *v* rapire. **abduction** *n* rapimento *m*.

aberration [abə'reiʃən] *n* aberrazione *f*. **aberrant** *adj* aberrante.

abet [ə'bet] *v* favoreggiare. **aid and abet** farsi complice di.

abeyance [ə'beiəns] *n* sospensione *f*. **in abeyance** in sospeso.

abhor [əb'hoɪ] *v* aborrire. **abhorrence** *n* aborrimento *m*. **abhorrent** *adj* aborrevole, odioso.

*abide [ə'baid] *v* (*wait*) aspettare; (*tolerate*) soffrire. **abide by** sostenere, restar fedele a.

ability [ə'biləti] *n* abilità *f*. **to the best of one's ability** come meglio potrà.

abject [,abdʒekt] *adj* abietto.

ablaze [ə'bleiz] *adj* in fiamme, risplendente.

able ['eibl] *adj* capace; (*talented*) abile. **able-bodied** *adj* robusto. **be able** potere, essere in grado di.

abnormal [ab'noɪml] *adj* anormale. **abnormality** *n* anormalità *f*.

aboard [ə'boɪd] *adv*, *prep* a bordo (di). **all aboard!** tutti a bordo! **go aboard** imbarcarsi.

abode [ə'boud] *V* abide. *n* dimora *f*.

abolish [ə'boliʃ] *v* abolire. **abolition** *n* abolizione *f*.

abominable [ə'bominəbl] *adj* abominevole. **abominate** *v* detestare. **abomination** *n* abominazione *f*.

aborigine [abə'ridʒini] *n* indigeno *m*.

abortion [ə'boɪʃən] *n* aborto *m*. **abort** *v* abortire.

abound [ə'baund] *v* abbondare.

about [ə'baut] *adv* (*around*) intorno; (*nearly*) verso, presso; circa; (*concerning*) su. *prep* di, su; intorno a. **be about to** stare per.

above [ə'bʌv] *adv* in alto, di sopra. *prep* sopra, al di sopra di; (*number*) più di; (*rank*) superiore a. **above all** sopratutto. **above-mentioned** *adj* suddetto. **from above** dall'alto.

abrasion [ə'breizən] *n* abrasione *f*. **abrasive** *adj* abrasivo.

abreast [ə'brest] *adv* **keep abreast of** or **with** tenersi al corrente di. **two abreast** due per due.

abridge [ə'bridʒ] *v* abbreviare. **abridgement** *n* abbreviazione *f*.

abroad [ə'broɪd] *adv* all'estero.

abrupt [ə'brʌpt] *adj* brusco.

abscess ['abses] *n* ascesso *m*.

abscond [əb'skond] *v* rendersi latitante.

absent ['absənt] *adj* assente. **absent-minded** *adj* distratto. *v* **absent oneself** assentarsi. **absence** *n* assenza *f*. **absentee** *n* assente *m*. **absenteeism** *n* assenteismo *m*.

absolute ['absəluɪt] *adj* assoluto. **absolutely** *adv* assolutamente, perfettamente. **absolutism** *n* assolutismo *m*.

absolve [əb'zolv] v assolvere. **absolution** n assoluzione f.

absorb [əb'zoɪb] v assorbire. **be absorbed in** essere concentrato in. **absorbent** adj assorbente. **absorbing** adj (coll) molto interessante. **absorption** n assorbimento m.

abstain [əb'stein] v astenersi. **abstention** n astensione f.

abstemious [əb'stiimiəs] adj astemio.

abstinence ['abstinəns] n astinenza f.

abstract ['abstrakt; v ab'strakt] adj astratto. v astrarre. **abstractedly** adv distrattamente. **abstraction** n astrazione f.

absurd [əb'səɪd] adj assurdo, ridicolo. **absurdity** n assurdità f.

abundance [ə'bʌndəns] n abbondanza f. **abundant** adj abbondante.

abuse [ə'bjus; v ə'bjuz] n abuso m; insulto m. v abusare di, maltrattare; insultare, oltraggiare. **abusive** adj offensivo; abusivo.

abyss [ə'bis] n abisso m. **abysmal** adj abissale; profondo.

academy [ə'kadəmi] n accademia f. **academic** n, adj accademico, -a.

accede [ak'siid] v accedere.

accelerate [ək'seləreit] v accelerare. **acceleration** n accelerazione f. **accelerator** n acceleratore m.

accent ['aksənt] n accento m. v accentuare; (gramm) accentare.

accept [ək'sept] v accettare, accogliere. **acceptable** adj (agreeable) gradevole; accettabile. **acceptance** n accettazione f.

access ['akses] n accesso m. **accessible** adj accessibile.

accessory [ək'sesəri] n accessorio m; (law) complice m, f. adj accessorio.

accident ['aksidənt] n accidente m, infortunio m. **by accident** per caso. **accidental** adj fortuito.

acclaim [ə'kleim] v acclamare. n also **acclamation** acclamazione f.

acclimatize [ə'klaimətaiz] v acclimatare.

accolade ['akəleid] n abbraccio m.

accommodate [ə'kɒmədeit] v accomodare; (lodge) ospitare; (provide) provvedere (di). **accommodating** adj cortese, conciliante. **accommodation** n (housing) alloggio m; (hotel) posto m.

accompany [ə'kʌmpəni] v accompagnare. **accompaniment** n accompagnamento m. **accompanist** n accompagnatore, -trice m, f.

accomplice [ə'kʌmplis] n complice m, f.

accomplish [ə'kʌmpliʃ] v compiere, realizzare. **accomplished** adj (talented) compito. **accomplishment** n effettuazione f; talento m.

accord [ə'kɔɪd] v concedere, accordare. n accordo m. **of one's own accord** spontaneamente. **in accordance with** in conformità con. **accordingly** adv pertanto, quindi, di conseguenza. **according to** secondo.

accordion [ə'kɔɪdiən] n fisarmonica f.

accost [ə'kɒst] v rivolgersi a.

account [ə'kaunt] n (report) relazione f, versione f; (status) importanza f; (bank) conto m. **by all accounts** a quanto si dice. **on no account** a nessuna condizione. **on one's own account** per propria iniziativa. **v account** for spiegare la ragione di, giustificare. **accountant** n contabile m, f, ragioniere m.

accrue [ə'kruː] v accrescere.

accumulate [ə'kjuːmjuleit] v accumulare. **accumulation** n ammasso m, accumulamento m.

accurate ['akjurət] adj accurato, preciso. **accuracy** n accuratezza f, precisione f.

accuse [ə'kjuz] v accusare, incolpare. **the accused** n l'imputato, -a m, f. **accusation** n accusa f.

accustom [ə'kʌstəm] v abituare.

ace [eis] nm asso m. **within an ace of** a un dito di.

ache [eik] n dolore m. v far male, dolere.

achieve [ə'tʃiɪv] v concludere, ottenere, compiere. **achievement** n compimento m, successo m.

acid ['asid] nm, adj acido.

acknowledge [ək'nɒlidʒ] v riconoscere, ammettere. **acknowledge receipt of** accusare ricevuta di. **acknowledgement** n riconoscimento m; ricevuta f.

acne ['akni] n acne m.

acorn ['eikɔɪn] n ghianda f.

acoustic [ə'kuɪstik] adj acustico. **acoustics** pl n acustica f sing.

acquaint [ə'kweint] v avvertire, mettere al corrente. **acquaintance** n (knowledge) conoscenza f; (person) conoscente m, f. **become acquainted with** (person) fare la conoscenza di; (thing) informarsi su.

acquiesce [akwi'es] v acconsentire tacitamente. **acquiescence** n acquiescenza f. **acquiescent** adj acquiescente.

acquire [ə'kwaiə] v acquisire, acquistare.
acquisition [akwi'ziʃən] n acquisto m; acquisizione f. **acquisitive** adj avido di guadagno.
acquit [ə'kwit] v esonerare. **acquit oneself** comportarsi. **acquittal** n (law) assoluzione f.
acrid ['akrid] adj acre, pungente.
acrimony ['akriməni] n acrimonia f. **acrimonious** adj acrimonioso, astioso.
acrobat ['akrəbat] n acrobata m, f. **acrobatic** adj acrobatico. **acrobatics** pl n acrobazie f pl.
across [ə'kros] adv per traverso; (crossword) orizzontali. prep al di là di, attraverso.
acrylic [ə'krilik] adj acrilico.
act [akt] v agire; (theatre) recitare; (behave) comportarsi. **act as** fungere da. **act for** agire per conto di. n (deed) azione f; (theatre) atto m; (law) decreto m. **actor** n attore m. **actress** n attrice f.
action ['akʃən] n azione f; (law) processo m; (mil) combattimento m. **out of action** fuori uso.
active ['aktiv] adj attivo, energico. **activate** v attivare. **activist** n attivista m. **activity** n attività f.
actual ['aktʃuəl] adj effettivo, reale. **actually** adv effettivamente.
actuate ['aktjueit] v mettere in atto or moto.
acupuncture ['akjupʌŋktʃə] n acupuntura f.
acute [ə'kjut] adj acuto, perspicace.
adamant ['adəmənt] adj inflessibile.
Adam's apple [adəm'zapl] n pomo d'Adamo m.
adapt [ə'dapt] v adattare, modificare. **adaptability** n adattabilità f. **adaptable** adj adattabile. **adaptation** n adattamento m. **adapter** n (theatre) riduttore m; (elec) raccordo m.
add [ad] v aggiungere. **add to** aumentare. **add up** fare la somma di, sommare. **addition** n addizione f. **additional** adj supplementare.
addendum [ə'dendəm] n aggiunta f.
adder ['adə] n vipera f.
addict [adikt; v ə'dikt] n (drug) drogato, -a m, f, tossicomane m, f. **be addicted to** essere abituato or dedito a. **addiction** n dedizione f; tossicomania f.
additive ['aditiv] n aggiunta f.

address [ə'dres] v (letter) indirizzare; (meeting, etc.) rivolgere la parola a, fare un discorso a. **address oneself to** mettersi a. n (speech) discorso m; (letter) indirizzo m, recapito m. **addressee** n destinatario m.
adenoids ['adənoidz] pl n adenoidi f pl.
adept [ə'dept] nm, adj esperto.
adequate ['adikwət] adj sufficiente, adeguato.
adhere [əd'hiə] v aderire, attaccarsi. **adhesion** n adesione f. **adhesive** nm, adj adesivo.
adherent [əd'hiərənt] n partigiano m, seguace m.
adjacent [ə'dʒeisənt] adj adiacente, contiguo.
adjective ['adʒiktiv] n aggettivo m.
adjoin [ə'dʒoin] v confinare (con). **adjoining** adj adiacente.
adjourn [ə'dʒəːn] v aggiornare, rinviare. **adjournment** n rinvio m.
adjudicate [ə'dʒuːdikeit] v aggiudicare. **adjudicator** n arbitro m.
adjust [ə'dʒʌst] v regolare, mettere a punto. **adjustment** n adattamento m, rettifica f.
ad-lib [ad'lib] v improvvisare.
administer [əd'ministə] v amministrare; (med) somministrare. **administration** n amministrazione f. **administrative** adj amministrativo. **administrator** n amministratore, -trice m, f.
admiral ['admərəl] n ammiraglio m.
admire [əd'maiə] v ammirare. **admirable** adj ammirevole. **admiration** n ammirazione f. **admiringly** adv con meraviglia.
admit [əd'mit] v ammettere; concedere; confessare. **admissible** adj ammissibile. **admission** n ammissione f. **admittance** n ingresso m, entrata f.
adolescence [adə'lesns] n adolescenza f. **adolescent** n(m+f), adj adolescente.
adopt [ə'dopt] v adottare. **adopted** adj (child) adottivo. **adoption** n adozione f.
adore [ə'doɪ] v adorare. **adoration** n adorazione f.
adorn [ə'doɪn] v abbellire, guarnire. **adornment** n ornamento m.
adrenaline [ə'drenəlin] n adrenalina f.
adrift [ə'drift] adv alla deriva.
adroit [ə'droit] adj abile, destro.
adulation [adju'leiʃən] n adulazione f.
adult ['adʌlt] n, adj adulto, -a.

adulterate [ə'dʌltəreit] v adulterare; (wine) sofisticare.

adultery [ə'dʌltəri] n adulterio m. **adulterer** n adultero, -a m, f.

advance [əd'vains] v avanzare, progredire, anticipare. n avanzamento m; (mil) marcia in avanti f; (cash) anticipo m. **book in advance** prenotare.

advantage [əd'vaintidʒ] n vantaggio m, beneficio m. **take advantage of** approfittare di. **advantageous** adj vantaggioso.

advent ['ædvənt] n avvento m.

adventure [əd'ventʃə] n avventura f, impresa rischiosa f. **adventurer** n avventuriero m. **adventurous** adj avventuroso.

adverb ['ædvəːb] n avverbio m.

adversary ['ædvəsəri] n avversario, -a m, f. **adverse** ['ædvəːs] adj avverso. **adversity** n avversità f.

advertise ['ædvətaiz] v annunziare, fare pubblicità a. **advertisement** n annunzio m, inserzione f. **advertising** n pubblicità f.

advise [əd'vaiz] v consigliare, raccomandare. **ill-advised** adj imprudente, inopportuno. **well-advised** adj saggio. **advice** n consiglio m, suggerimento m. **advisable** adj opportuno, consigliabile. **adviser** n consulente m, f. **advisory** adj consultivo.

advocate ['ædvəkeit] v sostenere.

aerial ['eəriəl] adj aereo. n antenna f.

aerodynamics [eərədai'næmiks] n aerodinamica f.

aeronautics [eərə'noitiks] n aeronautica f.

aeroplane ['eərəplein] n aereo m.

aerosol ['eərəsol] n aerosol m.

aesthetic [iis'θetik] adj estetico. **aesthetics** n estetica f.

affair [ə'feə] n affare m. **have an affair** avere una relazione intima.

affect[1] [ə'fekt] v (influence) colpire, toccare.

affect[2] [ə'fekt] v (pretend) fingere, simulare.

affection [ə'fekʃən] n affetto m, affezione f. **affectionate** adj affezionato.

affiliate [ə'filieit] v affiliare. **affiliation** n affiliazione f.

affinity [ə'finəti] n affinità f.

affirm [ə'fəːm] v affermare, confermare. **affirmation** n affermazione f, conferma f. **affirmative** adj affermativo.

affix [ə'fiks] v affiggere.

afflict [ə'flikt] v affliggere, angosciare. **affliction** n afflizione f, dolore m.

affluent ['æfluənt] adj ricco, opulento. **affluence** n affluenza f, ricchezza f.

afford [ə'foid] v avere i mezzi per; (produce) dare, offrire; (allow oneself to) permettersi di.

affront [ə'frʌnt] n affronto m, offesa f. v insultare, offendere.

afloat [ə'flout] adv a galla.

afoot [ə'fut] adv a piedi; (fig) in atto.

aforesaid [ə'foised] adj suddetto, sopranominato.

afraid [ə'freid] adj impaurito, pauroso, spaventato. **be afraid of** temere, aver paura di.

afresh [ə'freʃ] adv da capo, nuovamente.

Africa ['æfrikə] n Africa f. **African** n, adj africano, -a.

aft [aift] adv a poppa.

after ['aiftə] prep dopo, in seguito a. adv dopo, poi. conj dopo che. **after all** dopo tutto, insomma. **afterwards** adv dopo, poi.

afternoon [aiftə'nuin] n pomeriggio m, dopo pranzo m. **good afternoon!** buona sera!

aftershave ['aiftəʃeiv] n dopobarba m invar.

again [ə'gen] adv di nuovo, ancora. **again and again** ripetutamente. **never again** mai più.

against [ə'genst] prep contro, in opposizione a.

age [eidʒ] n età f; era f. **of age** maggiorenne. **old age** vecchiaia f. **under age** minorenne. v invecchiare. **aged** adj vecchio; (seasoned) invecchiato.

agency ['eidʒənsi] n agenzia f, rappresentanza f.

agenda [ə'dʒendə] n ordine del giorno m.

agent ['eidʒənt] n agente m, f; rappresentante m, f.

aggravate ['ægrəveit] v aggravare; (coll) irritare. **aggravation** n aggravamento m; (coll) irritazione f.

aggregate ['ægrigət] nm, adj aggregato.

aggression [ə'greʃən] n aggressione f. **aggressive** adj aggressivo. **aggressor** n aggressore m.

aghast [ə'gaist] adj stupefatto, atterrito.

agile ['ædʒail] adj agile. **agility** n agilità f.

agitate ['ædʒiteit] v agitare, turbare. **agitation** n agitazione f. **agitator** n agitatore, -trice m, f.

agnostic [ag'nostik] *n*, *adj* agnostico, -a. **agnosticism** *n* agnosticismo *m*.

ago [ə'gou] *adv* fa.

agog [ə'gog] *adj* bramoso.

agony [ægəni] *n* agonia *f*, angoscia *f*. **be in agony** soffrire dolori atroci.

agree [ə'griɪ] *v* essere *or* andare d'accordo, convenire, accordarsi. **agreeable** *adj* piacevole, simpatico. **agreement** *n* accordo *m*, patto *m*, contratto *m*.

agriculture [ˈagrikʌltʃə] *n* agricoltura *f*. **agricultural** *adj* agricolo.

aground [ə'graund] *adv* arenato. **run aground** incagliarsi.

ahead [ə'hed] *adv* (in) avanti.

aid [eid] *v* aiutare, sovvenire, soccorrere. *n* aiuto *m*, sussidio *m*. **first aid** pronto soccorso *m*. **in aid of** a favore di.

aim [eim] *v* puntare, prendere di mira; aspirare. *n* mira *f*; (*purpose*) scopo *m*, proposito *m*.

air [eə] *n* aria *f*; (*bearing*) aspetto *m*, contegno *m*. *v* ventilare.

airbed [ˈeəbed] *n* materassino pneumatico *m*.

airborne [ˈeəbɔɪn] *adj* aerotrasportato.

air-conditioned *adj* ad aria condizionata.

aircraft [ˈeəkraft] *n* aereo *m*. **aircraft-carrier** *n* portaerei *m invar*.

airfield [ˈeəfiɪld] *n* campo d'aviazione *m*.

air force *n* aviazione *f*.

air-hostess *n* assistente di volo *f*, hostess *f invar*.

air lift *n* ponte aereo *m*.

airline [ˈeəlain] *n* linea aerea *f*.

airmail [ˈeəmeil] *n* posta aerea *f*.

airport [ˈeəpɔːt] *n* aeroporto *m*.

air-raid *n* incursione aerea *f*. **air-raid shelter** rifugio contraereo *m*.

airtight [ˈeətait] *adj* ermetico, impenetrabile all'aria.

airy [ˈeəri] *adj* arioso, ben ventilato.

aisle [ail] *n* navata *f*.

ajar [ə'dʒaɪ] *adj* socchiuso.

akin [ə'kin] *adj* simile, parente.

alabaster [ˈaləbaistə] *n* alabastro *m*.

alarm [ə'laɪm] *n* allarme *m*. **alarm clock** sveglia *f*. *v* allarmare.

alas [ə'las] *interj* purtroppo!

Albania [al'beinjə] *n* Albania *f*. **Albanian** *n*(*m+f*), *adj* albanese.

albatross [ˈalbətrɔs] *n* albatro *m*.

albino [al'biɪnou] *n*, *adj* albino -a.

album [ˈalbəm] *n* album *m*.

alchemy [ˈalkəmi] *n* alchimia *f*. **alchemist** *n* alchimista *m*, *f*.

alcohol [ˈalkəhɔl] *n* alcool *m*.

alcoholic [alkə'hɔlik] *adj* alcoolico. *n* alcoolizzato, -a *m*, *f*. **alcoholism** *n* alcoolismo *m*.

alcove [ˈalkouv] *n* nicchia *f*.

alderman [ˈɔːldəmən] *n* assessore municipale *m*.

ale [eil] *n* birra *f*.

alert [ə'ləɪt] *adj* vigilante. *v* avvertire. **be on the alert** stare all'erta.

algebra [ˈaldʒibrə] *n* algebra *f*.

alias [ˈeiliəs] *adv* altrimenti detto.

alibi [ˈalibai] *n* alibi *m invar*.

alien [ˈeiliən] *n*, *adj* straniero, -a, forestiero, -a. **alienate** *v* alienare. **alienation** *n* alienazione *f*.

alight¹ [ə'lait] *v* scendere, smontare.

alight² [ə'lait] *adj* acceso, illuminato.

align [ə'lain] *v* allineare.

alike [ə'laik] *adj* simile, somigliante. *adv* ugualmente. **be alike** assomigliarsi.

alimentary canal [ali'mentəri] *adj* alimentare.

alimony [ˈaliməni] *n* alimenti *m pl*.

alive [ə'laiv] *adj* vivo, vivente. **alive to** sensibile a.

alkaline [ˈalkəlain] *adj* alcalino.

all [ɔːl] *adj* tutto. *adv* completamente. *n* tutti *m pl*, tutte *f pl*. **all right!** va bene! **All Saints' Day** Ognissanti *m*. **All Souls' Day** giorno dei morti *m*. **all the same** con tutto ciò. **not at all** niente affatto.

allay [ə'lei] *v* calmare.

allege [ə'ledʒ] *v* allegare, asserire. **alleged** *adj* sedicente.

allegiance [ə'liɪdʒəns] *n* obbedienza *f*, fedeltà *f*.

allegory [ˈaligəri] *n* allegoria *f*.

allergy [ˈalədʒi] *n* allergia *f*. **allergic** *adj* allergico.

alleviate [ə'liivieit] *v* alleviare, attenuare.

alley [ˈali] *n* vicolo *m*.

alliance [ə'laiəns] *n* alleanza *f*, patto *m*.

alligator [ˈaligeitə] *n* alligatore *m*.

alliteration [əlitə'reiʃən] *n* allitterazione *f*.

allocate [ˈaləkeit] *v* assegnare, collocare. **allocation** *n* assegnamento *m*.

allot [ə'lɔt] *v* assegnare. **allotment** *n* (*land*) lotto *m*, pezzo di terreno *m*; (*portion*) parte assegnata *f*.

allow [ə'lau] *v* permettere, concedere. **allow for** tener conto di. **allow me!**

permetta! **allowance** n (*grant*) assegno m; (*reduction*) sconto m.

alloy ['ælɔi; v ə'lɔi] n lega f. v legare, amalgamare.

allude [ə'luud] v riferirsi (a), alludere (a).

allusion [ə'luuʒən] n allusione f, riferimento m.

allure [ə'ljuə] n fascino m. v affascinare. **alluring** adj seducente.

ally ['ælai; v ə'lai] n alleato, -a m, f. v alleare.

almanac ['ɔilmənæk] n almanacco m.

almighty [ɔil'maiti] adj onnipotente. **the Almighty** n il Padreterno m.

almond ['ɑimənd] n (*nut*) mandorla f; (*tree*) mandorlo m.

almost [ɔil'moust] adv quasi.

alms [ɑimz] pl n elemosina f sing. **give alms** fare l'elemosina. **almshouse** n ospizio dei poveri m.

aloft [ə'lɔft] adv in alto.

alone [ə'loun] adj solo. adv solo, da solo; (*only*) solamente. **leave alone** lasciar stare.

along [ə'lɔŋ] prep lungo. **along with** insieme a. **come along!** su! avanti! **alongside** prep accanto a.

aloof [ə'luuf] adj riservato, freddo. adv a distanza.

aloud [ə'laud] adv ad alta voce.

alphabet ['ælfəbit] n alfabeto m.

Alps [ælps] pl n **the Alps** le Alpi f pl. **alpine** adj alpino.

already [ɔil'redi] adv già.

also ['ɔilsou] adv anche, pure, inoltre.

altar ['ɔiltə] n altare m. **altarpiece** n pala d'altare f. **high altar** altare maggiore m.

alter ['ɔiltə] v alterare, cambiare, alterarsi. **alteration** n cambiamento m, mutamento m.

alternate ['ɔiltəneit; adj ɔil'təinət] v alternare, alternarsi, ·succedersi. adj alterno. **alternation** n alternazione f, successione reciproca f.

alternative [ɔil'təinətiv] adj alternativo. n alternativa f.

although [ɔil'ðou] conj sebbene, benché.

altitude ['æltitjuid] n altezza f, altitudine f; (*aircraft*) quota f.

altogether [ɔiltə'geðə] adv complessivamente, nell'insieme.

altruistic [æltru'istik] adj altruistico. **altruism** n altruismo m. **altruist** n altruista m, f.

aluminium [ælju'miniəm] n alluminio m.

always ['ɔilweiz] adv sempre.

am [æm] V be.

amalgamate [ə'mælgəmeit] v amalgamare. **amalgam** n amalgama m.

amass [ə'mæs] v accumulare.

amateur ['æmətə] n dilettante m, f. **amateurish** adj da dilettante.

amaze [ə'meiz] v stupire, meravigliare. **amazement** n stupore m, meraviglia f. **amazing** adj straordinario, stupendo.

ambassador [æm'bæsədə] n ambasciatore, -trice m, f.

amber ['æmbə] n ambra f.

ambidextrous [æmbi'dekstrəs] adj ambidestro.

ambiguous [æm'bigjuəs] adj ambiguo.

ambition [æm'biʃən] n ambizione f. **ambitious** adj ambizioso.

ambivalent [æm'bivələnt] adj ambivalente.

amble ['æmbl] v camminare lentamente.

ambulance ['æmbjuləns] n ambulanza f.

ambush ['æmbuʃ] n imboscata f, agguato m. v tendere un agguato.

ameliorate [ə'miiliəreit] v migliorare.

amenable [ə'miinəbl] adj trattabile, suscettibile.

amend [ə'mend] v emendare, correggere. **amendment** n emendamento m, correzione f. **make amends** fare ammenda.

amenity [ə'miinəti] n amenità f. **amenities** pl n comodità f pl.

America [ə'merikə] n America f. **American** n, adj americano, -a.

amethyst ['æməθist] n ametista f.

amiable ['eimiəbl] adj gentile, amabile.

amicable ['æmikəbl] adj amichevole.

amid [ə'mid] prep fra, tra, in mezzo a.

amiss [ə'mis] adv **take amiss** aversene a male.

ammonia [ə'mouniə] n ammoniaca f.

ammunition [æmju'niʃən] n munizioni f pl.

amnesia [æm'niizjə] n amnesia f.

amnesty ['æmnəsti] n amnistia f.

amoeba [ə'miibə] n ameba f.

among [ə'mʌŋ] prep fra, tra, in mezzo a.

amoral [ei'mɔrəl] adj amorale.

amorous ['æmərəs] adj amoroso.

amorphous [ə'mɔifəs] adj amorfo.

amount [ə'maunt] n quantità f, importo m, somma f. v ammontare, equivalere.

ampere ['æmpeə] n ampere m invar.

amphetamine [æm'fetəmiin] n amfetamina f, anfetamina f.

amphibian [am'fibiən] *nm, adj* anfibio.

amphitheatre ['amfiθiətə] *n* anfiteatro *m*.

ample [ampl] *adj* ampio, abbondante.

amplify ['amplifai] *v* amplificare, ampliare. **amplification** *n* amplificazione *f*. **amplifier** *n* amplificatore *m*.

amputate ['ampjuteit] *v* amputare. **amputation** *n* amputazione *f*.

amuse [ə'mjuz] *v* divertire, dilettare. **amusement** *n* divertimento *m*, svago *m*. **amusing** *adj* divertente, buffo.

anachronism [ə'nakrənizəm] *n* anacronismo *m*.

anaemia [ə'nimiə] *n* anemia *f*. **anaemic** *adj* anemico.

anaesthetic [anəs'θetik] *nm, adj* anestetico. **anaesthesia** *n* anestesia *f*. **anaesthetist** *n* anestesista *m, f*. **anaesthetize** *v* anestetizzare.

anagram ['anəgram] *n* anagramma *m*.

anal ['einl] *adj* anale.

analogy [ə'nalədʒi] *n* analogia *f*. **analogous** *adj* analogo (*pl* -ghi).

analysis [ən'aləsis] *n, pl* -ses analisi *f*. **analyse** *v* analizzare. **analyst** *n* analista *m, f*. **analytical** *adj* analitico.

anarchy ['anəki] *n* anarchia *f*. **anarchic** *adj* anarchico. **anarchist** *n* anarchico, -a *m, f*.

anathema [ə'naθəmə] *n* anatema *m*.

anatomy [ə'natəmi] *n* anatomia *f*. **anatomical** *adj* anatomico. **anatomist** *n* anatomista *m, f*.

ancestor ['ansestə] *n* antenato *m*. **ancestral** *adj* avito. **ancestry** *n* stirpe *f*, lignaggio *m*.

anchor ['aŋkə] *n* ancora *f. v* ancorare.

anchovy ['antʃəvi] *n* acciuga *f*.

ancient ['einʃənt] *adj* antico (*m pl* -chi), anziano.

ancillary [an'siləri] *adj* ausiliario, sussidiario.

and [and] *conj* e, ed.

anecdote ['anikdout] *n* aneddoto *m*.

anemone [ə'neməni] *n* anemone *m*.

anew [ə'nju] *adv* da capo, di nuovo.

angel ['eindʒəl] *n* angelo *m*. **angelic** *adj* angelico.

anger ['aŋgə] *n* rabbia *f*, stizza *f*, ira *f. v* far arrabbiare.

angina [an'dʒainə] *n* (*med*) angina *f*.

angle ['aŋgl] *n* (*corner*) angolo *m*; (*viewpoint*) punto di vista *m*.

angling ['aŋliŋ] *n* pesca all'amo *f*. **angler** *n* pescatore *m*.

angry ['aŋgri] *adj* arrabbiato, stizzito.

anguish ['aŋgwiʃ] *n* angoscia *f*, tormento *m. v* angosciare, tormentare.

anguiar ['aŋgjulə] *adj* angolare.

animal ['animəl] *n* animale *m*, bestia *f. adj* animale.

animate ['animət; *v* 'animeit] *adj* animato, vivente. *v* animare. **animated** *adj* vivace. **animation** *n* animazione *f*.

animosity [ani'mosəti] *n* animosità *f*.

aniseed ['anisid] *n* anice *m*.

ankle ['aŋkl] *n* caviglia *f*.

annals ['anlz] *pl n* annali *m pl*.

annex [ə'neks; *n* 'aneks] *v* annettere. *n* annesso *m*; (*hotel*) dipendenza *f*. **annexation** *n* annessione *f*.

annihilate [ə'naiəleit] *v* annientare. **annihilation** *n* annientamento *m*.

anniversary [ani'vəisəri] *nm, adj* anniversario.

annotate ['anəteit] *v* annotare.

announce [ə'nauns] *v* annunciare, rendere noto. **announcement** *n* annuncio *m*. **announcer** *n* annunciatore, -trice *m, f*.

annoy [ə'noi] *v* dar noia a, disturbare, seccare. **annoyance** *n* fastidio *m*, noia *f*. **annoying** *adj* seccante, fastidioso.

annual ['anjuəl] *adj* annuale, annuo. *n* (*book*) annuario *m*; (*plant*) pianta annuale *f*. **annually** *adv* annualmente.

annuity [ə'njuiəti] *n* annualità *f*. **life annuity** *n* vitalizio *m*.

annul [ə'nʌl] *v* annullare. **annulment** *n* annullamento *m*.

◆Annunciation [ə,nʌnsi'eiʃn] *n* (*rel*) Annunziazione *f*.

anode ['anoud] *n* anodo *m*.

anomaly [ə'noməli] *n* anomalia *f*. **anomalous** *adj* anomalo, irregolare.

anonymous [ə'noniməs] *adj* anonimo.

anorak ['anərak] *n* giacca a vento *f*.

another [ə'nʌðə] *adj, pron* un altro. **one another** l'un l'altro.

answer ['ansə] *v* rispondere (a). **answer for** rispondere di. *n* risposta *f*.

ant [ant] *n* formica *f*. **ant-hill** *n* formicaio *m*.

antagonize [an'tagənaiz] *v* provocare l'ostilità (di). **antagonism** *n* antagonismo *m*. **antagonist** *n* antagonista *m, f*.

antecedent [anti'siidənt] *adj* antecedente. **antecedents** *pl n* precedenti *m pl*; (*forbears*) antenati *m pl*.

antelope ['antəloup] *n* antilope *f.*

antenatal [anti'neitl] *adj* prenatale.

antenna [an'tenə] *n* antenna *f.*

anthem ['anθəm] *n* inno *m.*

anthology [an'θɔlədʒi] *n* antologia *f.*

anthropology [anθrə'pɔlədʒi] *n* antropologia *f.* **anthropologist** *n* antropologo, -a *m, f.*

anti-aircraft [anti'eəkraft] *adj* contraereo.

antibiotic [antibai'ɔtik] *nm, adj* antibiotico.

antibody ['anti,bɔdi] *n* anticorpo *m.*

anticipate [an'tisipeit] *v* anticipare, prevenire. **in anticipation** in anticipo.

anticlimax [anti'klaimaks] *n* conclusione banale *f.*

anticlockwise [anti'klokwaiz] *adj, adv* in senso antiorario.

antics ['antiks] *pl n* buffoneria *f sing.*

anticyclone [anti'saikloun] *n* anticiclone *m.*

antidote ['antidout] *n* antidoto *m.*

antifreeze ['antifriz] *n* antigelo *m.*

antipathy [an'tipəθi] *n* antipatia *f.*

antique [an'tik] *adj* antico (*m pl* -chi). *n* oggetto antico *m.* **antique dealer** *n* antiquario *m.* **antiquity** *n* antichità *f.*

anti-Semitic [antisə'mitik] *n* antisemita *m, f.* **anti-Semitism** *n* antisemitismo *m.*

antiseptic [anti'septik] *nm, adj* antisettico.

antisocial [anti'souʃəl] *adj* antisociale.

anti-tank [anti'taŋk] *adj* anticarro.

antithesis [an'tiθəsis] *n, pl* -ses antitesi *f.*

antler ['antlə] *n* corno *m.*

antonym ['antənim] *n* antonimo *m.*

anus ['einəs] *n* ano *m.*

anvil ['anvil] *n* incudine *f.*

anxious ['aŋkʃəs] *adj* ansioso, preoccupato. **anxiety** *n* ansia *f,* ansietà *f.*

any ['eni] *adj* del, della, etc.; qualche *invar;* alcuno. *pron* alcuno, nessuno, ne. **anybody** *or* **anyone** *pron* qualcuno, alcuno; chiunque. **anyhow** *or* **anyway** *adv* in ogni caso, tuttavia; ad ogni modo. **anything** *pron* qualcosa, qualche cosa; (*everything*) qualunque cosa. **anywhere** *adv* in qualunque luogo, in alcun luogo; (*everywhere*) dovunque.

apart [ə'pɑːt] *adv* a parte, in disparte. **come apart** disfarsi. **tell apart** distinguere l'uno dall'altro.

apartment [ə'pɑːtmənt] *n* appartamento *m,* alloggio *m.*

apathy ['apəθi] *n* apatia *f.* **apathetic** *adj* apatico.

ape [eip] *n* scimmia *f. v* scimmiottare, imitare.

aperitif [əperi'tiːf] *n* aperitivo *m.*

aperture ['apətjuə] *n* apertura *f.*

apex ['eipeks] *n* vertice *m,* apice *m.*

aphid ['eifid] *n* afide *m.*

aphrodisiac [afrə'diziak] *n* afrodisiaco *m.*

apiece [ə'piːs] *adv* a testa, per ciascuno, per uno.

apology [ə'pɔlədʒi] *n* scusa *f,* giustificazione *f.* **apologetic** *adj* apologetico. **apologize** *v* chiedere scusa, scusarsi.

apoplexy ['apəpleksi] *n* apoplessia *f.* **apoplectic** *adj* apoplettico. **apoplectic fit** colpo apoplettico *m.*

apostle [ə'pɔsl] *n* apostolo *m.*

apostrophe [ə'pɔstrəfi] *n* (*punctuation*) apostrofo *m;* (*speech*) apostrofe *f.*

appal [ə'pɔːl] *v* inorridire, sgomentare. **appalling** *adj* terribile, spaventoso.

apparatus [apə'reitəs] *n* apparecchio *m,* apparato *m.*

apparent [ə'parənt] *adj* apparente, evidente, manifesto.

apparition [apə'riʃən] *n* visione *f,* fantasma *m.*

appeal [ə'piːl] *n* appello *m. v* appellarsi, fare appello; (*law*) ricorrere in appello. **appealing** *adj* attraente, commovente.

appear [ə'piə] *v* apparire, sembrare, parere. **appearance** *n* apparenza *f,* aspetto *m.* **put in an appearance** fare atto di presenza.

appease [ə'piːz] *v* calmare, pacificare. **appeasement** *n* pacificazione *f.*

appendix [ə'pendiks] *n* appendice *m.* **appendicitis** *n* appendicite *f.*

appetite ['apitait] *n* appetito *m.* **appetizing** *adj* gustoso, succolento.

applaud [ə'plɔːd] *v* applaudire. **applause** *n* applauso *m.*

apple [apl] *n* (*fruit*) mela *f;* (*tree*) melo *m.*

apply [ə'plai] *v* rivolgersi, fare domanda; (*refer*) riferirsi; (*use*) applicare. **apply oneself** to dedicarsi a. **appliance** *n* apparecchio *m,* strumento *m.* **applicable** *adj* applicabile, idoneo. **applicant** *n* candidato *m.* **application** *n* domanda *f,* richiesta *f.* **application form** modulo di richiesta *m.*

appoint [ə'point] *v* nominare; (*arrange*) fissare. **appointment** *n* (*engagement*) appuntamento *m;* (*post*) nomina *f.*

apportion [ə'pɔːʃən] v distribuire.

appraisal [ə'preizl] n valutazione f. **appraise** v stimare, valutare.

appreciate [ə'priːʃieit] v (esteem) apprezzare, stimare; (be aware of) rendersi conto di; (increase in value) aumentare di valore. **appreciable** adj apprezzabile, sensibile. **appreciation** n apprezzamento m, stima f.

apprehend [apri'hend] v cogliere, arrestare. **apprehension** n arresto m; (worry) timore m. **apprehensive** adj timoroso, preoccupato.

apprentice [ə'prentis] n apprendista m, f. **apprenticeship** n tirocinio m, apprendistato m.

approach [ə'prəutʃ] v avvicinare; (come near) avvicinarsi (a). n avvicinamento m, accesso m.

appropriate [ə'proupriət; v ə'prouprieit] adj adatto, opportuno. v impadronirsi di.

approve [ə'pruːv] v approvare, dare il benestare. **approval** n approvazione f, benestare m. **on approval** in visione, in esame. **approved** adj approvato, convalidato, riconosciuto.

approximate [ə'proksimeit; adj ə'proksimət] v approssimare. adj approssimativo. **approximately** adv approssimativamente, all'incirca, su per giù.

apricot ['eiprikɔt] n (fruit) albicocca f; (tree) albicocco m.

April ['eiprəl] n aprile m.

apron ['eiprən] n grembiule m, grembiale m.

apt [apt] adj atto, adatto. **aptitude** ['aptitjuːd] n abilità f, attitudine f.

aqualung ['akwəlʌŋ] n autorespiratore m.

aquarium [ə'kweəriəm] n acquario m. **Aquarius** [ə'kweəriəs] n Acquario m.

aquatic [ə'kwatik] adj acquatico.

aqueduct ['akwidʌkt] n acquedotto m.

Arab ['arəb] n, adj arabo, -a. **Arabia** n Arabia f. **Arabic** n (language) arabo m.

arable ['arəbl] adj arabile.

arbitrary ['aːbitrəri] adj arbitrario.

arbitrate ['aːbitreit] v arbitrare. **arbitration** n arbitraggio m.

arc [aːk] n arco m. **arc lamp** lampada ad arco f.

arcade [aː'keid] n portico m, galleria f.

arch[1] [aːtʃ] n arco m, volta f. v curvare, arcuare.

arch[2] [aːtʃ] adj (chief) arci-.

archaeology [aːki'ɔlədʒi] n archeologia f. **archaeologist** n archeologo, -a m, f.

archaic [aː'keiik] adj arcaico.

archbishop [aːtʃ'biʃəp] n arcivescovo m. **archduke** [aːtʃ'djuːk] n arciduca m.

archery ['aːtʃəri] n tiro all'arco m. **archer** n arciere m.

archetype ['aːkitaip] n archetipo m.

archipelago [aːki'peləgou] n arcipelago (pl -ghi) m.

architect ['aːkitekt] n architetto, -a m, f. **architecture** n architettura f.

archives ['aːkaivz] pl n archivio m sing.

arctic ['aːktik] adj artico.

ardent ['aːdənt] adj ardente, appassionato.

ardour ['aːdə] n ardore m, fervore m.

arduous ['aːdjuəs] adj arduo, difficile.

are [aː] V be.

area ['eəriə] n area f, superficie f, zona f.

arena [ə'riːnə] n arena f.

argue ['aːgjuː] v argomentare, discutere, disputare. **arguable** adj discutibile. **argument** n argomento m, discussione f. **argumentative** adj polemico.

arid ['arid] adj arido.

Aries ['eəriːz] n Ariete m.

***arise** [ə'raiz] v alzarsi, sorgere.

arisen [ə'rizn] V arise.

aristocracy [ari'stokrəsi] n aristocrazia f. **aristocrat** n aristocratico, -a m, f. **aristocratic** adj aristocratico.

arithmetic [ə'riθmətik] n aritmetica f.

ark [aːk] n arca f. **Noah's Ark** arca di Noè f.

arm[1] [aːm] n (limb) braccio m (pl -a f). **armchair** n poltrona f. **arm in arm** a braccetto. **armpit** n ascella f. **within arm's reach** a portata di mano.

arm[2] [aːm] n (weapon) arma (pl -i) f. **bear arms** essere sotto le armi. **be up in arms against** essere in rivolta contro. **coat of arms** stemma m. v armare.

armistice ['aːmistis] n armistizio m.

armour ['aːmə] n armatura f, corazza f. **armourer** n armiere m. **armour-plated** adj corazzato. **armoury** n arsenale m.

army ['aːmi] n esercito m, armata f.

aroma [ə'roumə] n aroma m.

arose [ə'rouz] V arise.

around [ə'raund] prep attorno a, intorno a. adv intorno. **all around** tutto intorno.

arouse [ə'rauz] v destare, eccitare.

arrange [ə'reindʒ] v accomodare, ordinare; (*music*) adattare; (*meeting, etc.*) organizzare; (*put in order*) sistemare. **arrangement** n combinazione *f*; accomodamento *m*; adattamento *m*. **come to an arrangement** mettersi d'accordo.

array [ə'rei] n schieramento *m*; mostra imponente *f*. v ornare, schierare.

arrears [ə'riəz] pl n arretrati *m pl*. **be in arrears** avere degli arretrati.

arrest [ə'rest] n arresto. **under arrest** in stato d'arresto. v arrestare, sospendere.

arrive [ə'raiv] v arrivare, giungere. **arrival** n arrivo *m*; (*person*) arrivato, -a *m, f*.

arrogant ['ærəgənt] adj arrogante. **arrogance** n arroganza *f*.

arrow ['ærou] n freccia *f*.

arse [ais] n (*vulgar*) culo *m*.

arsenal ['aisənl] n arsenale *m*.

arsenic ['aisnik] n arsenico *m*.

arson ['aisn] n incendio doloso *m*.

art [ait] n arte *f*. **art gallery** galleria d'arte *f*, pinacoteca *f*. **artful** adj astuto.

artefact ['aitifækt] n artefatto *m*.

artery ['aitəri] n arteria *f*.

arthritis [ai'θraitis] n artrite *f*.

artichoke ['aititʃouk] n carciofo *m*.

article ['aitikl] n articolo *m*; oggetto *m*.

articulate [ai'tikjuleit; adj ai'tikjulət] v articolare. adj articolato, distinto.

artifice ['aitifis] n artifizio *m*, astuzia *f*.

artificial [aiti'fiʃəl] adj artificiale, finto. **artificiality** n artificiosità *f*.

artillery [ai'tiləri] n artiglieria *f*.

artisan [aiti'zæn] n artigiano, -a *m, f*.

artist [aitist] n artista *m, f*. **artistic** adj artistico.

as [æz] adv come, quanto. conj come; (*while*) mentre; (*because*) poiché, siccome. **as . . . as** così . . . come, tanto . . . quanto. prep da. **as far as** (*distance*) sino a. **as for** or to per quanto riguarda. **as if** come se. **as long as** finché, purché. **as much** altrettanto. **as soon as** (non) appena. **as well** anche. **as well as** (*in addition to*) oltre a.

asbestos [az'bestos] n asbesto *m*, amianto *m*.

ascend [ə'send] v salire, ascendere. **ascendancy** n ascendente *m*. **ascension** n ascensione *f*. **ascent** n ascesa *f*, salita *f*.

ascertain [asə'tein] v accertarsi di, verificare.

ascetic [ə'setik] adj ascetico. n asceta *m, f*.

ash[1] [aʃ] n (*cinder*) cenere *f*. **ashen** adj cinereo. **ashtray** n portacenere *m*.

ash[2] [aʃ] n (*tree*) frassino *m*.

ashamed [ə'feimd] adj vergognoso. **be ashamed of** vergognarsi di.

ashore [ə'ʃoi] adv a terra, sulla riva.

Ash Wednesday n mercoledì delle Ceneri *m*.

Asia ['eiʃə] n Asia *f*. **Asian** n, adj asiatico, -a.

aside [ə'said] adv da parte, a parte, in disparte. n (*theatre*) parole dette a parte *f pl*.

ask [aisk] v domandare, chiedere. **ask about** informarsi di or su. **ask after** chiedere notizie di.

askew [ə'skjui] adv di traverso.

asleep [ə'sliip] adj addormentato. **fall asleep** addormentarsi.

asparagus [ə'spærəgəs] n asparago *m*.

aspect ['æspekt] n aspetto *m*, apparenza *f*.

asphalt ['æsfælt] n asfalto *m*.

asphyxiate [əs'fiksieit] v

aspire [ə'spaiə] v ambire. **aspiration** n ambizione *f*.

aspirin ['æspərin] n aspirina *f*.

ass [æs] n asino *m*, somaro *m*.

assail [ə'seil] v assalire, aggredire. **assailant** n aggressore *m*.

assassinate [ə'sæsineit] v assassinare. **assassin** n assassino, -a *m, f*. **assassination** n assassinio *m*.

assault [ə'soilt] n assalto *m*, attacco *m*. v assalire, attaccare.

assemble [ə'sembl] v riunire, riunirsi; (*put together*) montare. **assembly** n assemblea *f*, riunione *f*. **assembly line** catena di montaggio *f*.

assent [ə'sent] v assentire, approvare. n assenso *m*, consenso *m*.

assert [ə'soit] v asserire, sostenere. **assert oneself** farsi valere, imporsi. **assertion** n asserzione *f*, rivendicazione *f*.

assess [ə'ses] v valutare, stimare. **assessment** n valutazione *f*, imposizione di tassa *f*. **assessor** n assessore *m*, agente del fisco *m*.

asset ['æset] n bene *m*. **assets** pl n attività *f pl*.

assiduous [ə'sidjuəs] adj assiduo.

assign [ə'sain] v assegnare; (*law*) delegare. **assignee** n mandatario *m*. **assignment** n assegnazione *f*, attribuzione *f*.

assimilate [ə'simileit] *v* assimilare. **assimilation** *n* assimilazione *f*.

assist [ə'sist] *v* assistere, aiutare. **assistance** *n* assistenza *f*, soccorso *m*. **assistant** *n* assistente *m*, *f*, aiutante *m*, *f*; (*shop*) commesso, -a *m*, *f*.

associate [ə'sousieit; *n* ə'sousiət] *v* associare, associarsi. **associate with** frequentare. *n* socio, -a *m*, *f*, collega *m*, *f*. **association** *n* associazione *f*, società *f*; (*club*) circolo *m*.

assorted [ə'sottid] *adj* assortito. **assortment** *n* assortimento *f*.

assume [ə'sjum] *v* assumere; presumere. **assumption** *n* assunzione *f*, supposizione *f*. **assuming that** supposto che.

assure [ə'ʃuə] *v* assicurare. **assurance** *n* assicurazione *f*, certezza *f*, promessa *f*.

asterisk ['astərisk] *n* asterisco *m*.

asthma ['asmə] *n* asma *m*.

astonish [ə'stoniʃ] *v* stupire, meravigliare. **astonishing** *adj* sbalorditivo, sorprendente. **astonishment** *n* sorpresa *f*, stupore *m*.

astound [ə'staund] *v* stupefare, stupire. **astounding** *adj* stupefacente, sbalorditivo.

astray [ə'strei] *adv* fuori strada. **go astray** smarrirsi. **lead astray** sviare, traviare.

astride [ə'straid] *adv* a cavalcioni.

astringent [ə'strindʒənt] *adj* astringente.

astrology [ə'strolədʒi] *n* astrologia *f*. **astrologer** *n* astrologo, -a *m*, *f*.

astronaut ['astrənott] *n* astronauta *m*, *f*.

astronomy [ə'stronəmi] *n* astronomia *f*. **astronomer** *n* astronomo, -a *m*, *f*. **astronomic(al)** *adj* astronomico.

astute [ə'stjut] *adj* astuto, furbo.

asunder [ə'sandə] *adv* a pezzi.

asylum [ə'sailəm] *n* ricovero *m*, rifugio *m*; (*for the insane*) manicomio *m*.

at [at] *prep* a, in, da.

ate [et] *V* eat.

atheism ['eiθiizəm] *n* ateismo *m*. **atheist** *n* ateo, -a *m*, *f*.

Athens ['aθinz] *n* Atene *f*. **Athenian** *n(m+f)*, *adj* ateniese.

athlete ['aθlit] *n* atleta *m*, *f*. **athletic** *adj* atletico. **athletics** *n* atletica *f*.

Atlantic [ət'lantik] *nm*, *adj* atlantico.

atlas ['atləs] *n* atlante *m*.

atmosphere ['atmosfiə] *n* atmosfera *f*; ambiente *m*. **atmospheric** *adj* atmosferico. **atmospherics** *pl n* disturbi atmosferici *m pl*.

atom ['atəm] *n* atomo *m*. **atomic** *adj* atomico.

atone [ə'toun] *v* espiare, fare ammenda. **atonement** *n* espiazione *f*.

atrocious [ə'trouʃəs] *adj* atroce, terribile. **atrocity** *n* atrocità *f*.

attach [ə'tatʃ] *v* attaccare, attribuire. **become attached to** affezionarsi a. **attachment** *n* (*friendship*) affezione *f*; (*law*) sequestro *m*; (*tech*) accessorio *m*.

attaché [ə'taʃei] *n* addetto *m*. **attaché case** *n* valigetta rigida *f*, borsa per documenti *f*.

attack [ə'tak] *v* attaccare, assalire. *n* attacco *m*; offensiva *f*; (*med*) accesso. **attacker** *n* aggressore *m*.

attain [ə'tein] *v* ottenere, raggiungere. **attainment** *n* raggiungimento *m*, conseguimento *m*. **attainments** *pl n* coltura *f sing*.

attempt [ə'tempt] *v* tentare, provare. *n* tentativo *m*, prova *f*; (*crime*) attentato *m*.

attend [ə'tend] *v* (*wait on*) servire, accompagnare; (*listen*) prestar attenzione; (*be present at*) assistere. **attendance** *n* presenza *f*; servizio *m*. **attendant** *n* inserviente *m*, *f*; sorvegliante *m*, *f*, assistente *m*, *f*.

attention [ə'tenʃən] *n* attenzione *f*, cura *f*. **pay attention** far attenzione, stare attento. **attentive** *adj* attento, sollecito, premuroso.

attic ['atik] *n* attico *m*, soffitta *f*.

attire [ə'taiə] *n* abbigliamento *m*. *v* vestire.

attitude ['atitjud] *n* atteggiamento *m*, posa *f*.

attorney [ə'təmi] *n* procuratore *m*. **power of attorney** procura *f*.

attract [ə'trakt] *v* attrarre, attirare; affascinare. **attraction** *n* attrazione *f*; fascino *m*. **attractive** *adj* attraente; affascinante.

attribute [ə'tribjut; *v* ə'tribjut] *n* attributo *m*, qualità *f*. *v* attribuire, ascrivere. **attribution** *n* attribuzione *f*.

attrition [ə'triʃən] *n* attrito *m*.

atypical [ei'tipikl] *adj* atipico.

aubergine ['oubəʒin] *n* melanzana *f*.

auburn ['otbən] *adj invar* color rame.

auction ['oikʃən] *n* asta *f*. *v* vendere all'asta. **auctioneer** *n* venditore all'asta *m*, banditore *m*.

audacious [ot'deiʃəs] *adj* audace, intrepido. **audacity** *n* temerità *f*.

audible ['ɔːdəbl] *adj* udibile. **audibility** *n* udibilità *f.*

audience ['ɔːdjəns] *n* pubblico *m*; *(assembly of spectators)* uditorio *m*; *(formal interview)* udienza *f.*

audiovisual [ɔːdiou'viʒuəl] *adj* audiovisivo.

audit ['ɔːdit] *n* controllo *m*, verifica dei conti *f*, revisione *f*. *v* rivedere, verificare i conti. **auditor** *n* revisore di conti *m*; sindaco *m.*

audition [ɔː'diʃən] *n* audizione *f*. *v* ascoltare in audizione.

auditorium [ɔːdi'tɔːriəm] *n* sala per concerti *f*, auditorio *m.*

augment [ɔːg'ment] *v* aumentare, crescere.

August ['ɔːgəst] *n* agosto *m.*

aunt [ɑːnt] *n* zia *f.*

au pair [ou 'peə] *n* ragazza alla pari *f.*

aura ['ɔːrə] *n* aura *f.*

auspicious [ɔː'spiʃəs] *adj* propizio, di buon augurio.

austere [ɔː'stiə] *adj* austero. **austerity** *n* austerità *f.*

Australia [ɔ'streiljə] *n* Australia *f*. **Australian** *n*, *adj* australiano, -a.

Austria ['ɔstriə] *n* Austria *f*. **Austrian** *n*, *adj* austriaco, -a.

authentic [ɔː'θentik] *adj* autentico. **authenticate** *v* convalidare. **authenticity** *n* autenticità *f.*

author ['ɔːθə] *n* autore, -trice *m*, *f.*

authority [ɔː'θɔrəti] *n* autorità *f*; *(influence)* ascendente *m*; *(accepted source)* fonte autorevole *f*. **on good authority** da fonte autorevole. **authoritative** *adj* autorevole. **authoritarian** *adj* autoritario. **authorize** ['ɔːθəraiz] *v* autorizzare. **authorization** *n* autorizzazione *f.*

autobiography [ɔːtoubai'ɔgrəfi] *n* autobiografia *f*. **autobiographical** *adj* autobiografico.

autocratic [ɔːtou'kratik] *adj* autocratico.

autograph ['ɔːtəgrɑːf] *n* autografo *m*. *v* autografare.

automatic [ɔːtə'matik] *adj* automatico. **automation** *n* automazione *f.*

automobile ['ɔːtəməbiːl] *n* automobile *f*; *(fam)* macchina *f.*

autonomous [ɔː'tɔnəməs] *adj* autonomo. **autopsy** ['ɔːtɔpsi] *n* autopsia *f.*

autumn ['ɔːtəm] *n* autunno *m*. **autumnal** *adj* autunnale.

auxiliary [ɔːg'ziljəri] *n*, *adj* ausiliario, -a.

avail [ə'veil] *v* servire, giovare a. **avail oneself of** servirsi di. *n* vantaggio *m*. **be of no avail** non servire a nulla.

available [ə'veiləbl] *adj* disponibile, libero; *(to hand)* sotto mano. **availability** *n* disponibilità *f.*

avalanche ['avəlɑːnʃ] *n* valanga *f.*

avarice ['avəris] *n* avarizia *f*. **avaricious** *adj* avaro.

avenge [ə'vendʒ] *v* vendicare, vendicarsi. **avenger** *n* vendicatore, -trice *m*, *f.*

avenue ['avinjuː] *n* viale *m.*

average ['avəridʒ] *n* media *f*. **on average** in media. *adj* medio. *v* fare la media.

aversion [ə'vɜːʃən] *n* avversione *f*, antipatia *f*. **not be averse to** non aver nulla in contrario a.

avert [ə'vɜːt] *n* *(turn away)* distogliere; *(ward off)* allontanare; *(prevent)* prevenire.

aviary ['eiviəri] *n* uccelliera *f.*

aviation [eivi'eiʃən] *n* aviazione *f.*

avid ['avid] *adj* avido.

avocado [avə'kɑːdou] *n* pera avocado *f.*

avoid [ə'void] *v* evitare, schivare. **avoidance** *n* fuga *f*; l'evitare *m.*

await [ə'weit] *v* aspettare, attendere.

***awake** [ə'weik] *adj* sveglio. *v* svegliare, svegliarsi. **awaken** *v* risvegliare, risvegliarsi. **awakening** *n* risveglio *m.*

award [ə'wɔːd] *n* premio *m*; *(honour)* onorificenza *f*. *v* aggiudicare, premiare, conferire.

aware [ə'weə] *adj* consapevole, conscio. **be aware of** sapere, rendersi conto di. **awareness** *n* consapevolezza *f*, sensibilità *f.*

away [ə'wei] *adv* lontano, via; *(absent)* fuori.

awe [ɔː] *n* timore reverenziale *m*. **awe-struck** *adj* in preda a timore. **awe-inspiring** *adj* che incute rispetto.

awful ['ɔːful] *adj* terribile, spaventoso. **awfully** *adv* terribilmente; *(coll)* molto.

awkward ['ɔːkwəd] *adj* goffo, sgraziato.

awl [ɔːl] *n* lesina *f.*

awning ['ɔːniŋ] *n* tenda *f.*

awoke [ə'wouk] *V* **awake.**

awoken [ə'woukn] *V* **awake.**

axe [aks] *n* ascia *f*, scure *f.*

axiom ['aksiəm] *n* assioma *m.*

axis ['aksis] *n* asse *m.*

axle ['aksl] *n* asse *m*; perno *m.*

B

babble ['babl] v balbettare, ciarlare. n balbettio m.

baby ['beibi] n bimbo, -a m, f, bebè m. **babysitter** n babysitter m, f invar. **babyish** adj bambinesco.

bachelor ['batʃələ] n scapolo m. **Bachelor of Arts/Science** n laureato, -a in lettere/scienze m, f.

back [bak] n (anat) dorso m, schiena f; (chair) schienale m; (reverse) rovescio m. **back to front** a rovescio. adv dietro, indietro, di ritorno. v appoggiare, sostenere; (bet on) scommettere su, puntare su. **back out** ritirarsi.

*****backbite** ['bakbait] v calunniare, sparlare di.

backbone ['bakboun] n spina dorsale f.

backdate [ˌbak'deit] v retrodatare.

backfire [ˌbak'faiə] v far ritorno di fiamma; (coll) andare all'aria.

background ['bakgraund] n sfondo m; (milieu) ambiente m.

backhand ['bakhand] n rovescio m.

backlash ['baklaʃ] n contraccolpo m.

backlog ['baklog] n arretrati m pl.

back pay n arretrati di paga m pl.

backside ['baksaid] n sedere m.

*****backslide** ['bakslaid] v ricadere nell'errore.

backstage ['baksteidʒ] adv dietro le quinte.

backstroke ['bakstrouk] n nuoto sul dorso m.

backward ['bakwəd] adj tardivo, arretrato.

backwards ['bakwədz] adv indietro, all'indietro.

backwater ['bakwoɪtə] n (pool) acqua stagnante f; (place) posto dove non succede mai nulla m.

bacon ['beikən] n pancetta f.

bacteria [bak'tiəriə] pl n batteri m pl.

bad [bad] adj cattivo, malvagio, dannoso, brutto; (serious) grave. **bad language** parolacce f pl. **feel bad** sentirsi male. **go bad** andare a male. **badly** adv male, malamente; (seriously) gravemente.

badge [badʒ] n distintivo m, emblema m.

badger ['badʒə] n tasso m. v molestare.

baffle ['bafl] v sconcertare, confondere. **baffling** adj sconcertante.

bag [bag] n sacco m, borsa f, borsetta f. v insaccare; (coll) impadronirsi di, prendere.

bail¹ [beil] n (law) cauzione f, garanzia f. **grant bail** concedere libertà provvisoria (su cauzione). **stand bail for** rendersi garante per. v dar garanzia per, prestar cauzione a. **bail out** ottenere libertà provvisoria (su cauzione).

bail² or **bale** [beil] v **bail out** (flooded boat) aggottare; (from aircraft) lanciarsi.

bailiff ['beilif] n (law) funzionario incaricato a fare sequestri m; (of estate) fattore m.

bait [beit] n (fishing) esca f; (lure) lusinga f. v adescare; (annoy) tormentare.

bake [beik] v cuocere al forno. **baker** n fornaio panettiere m. **bakery** n panificio m. **baking powder** lievito minerale m, bicarbonato m. **baking tin** teglia f.

balance ['baləns] n equilibrio m, armonia f; (scales) bilancia f; (comm) bilancio m. **balance of payments** bilancia dei pagamenti f. v bilanciare, equilibrare; (comm) fare il bilancio.

balcony ['balkəni] n balcone m; (theatre) balconata f.

bald [boɪld] adj calvo; (naked) nudo, disadorno. **baldness** n calvizie f invar.

bale¹ [beil] n balla f. v imballare.

bale² V **bail²**

baleful ['beilful] adj maligno, distruttivo.

ball¹ [boɪl] n palla f; (inflatable) pallone m; (sphere) sfera f. **ball-bearings** pl n cuscinetti a sfere m pl. **ball-point pen** penna a sfera f.

ball² [boɪl] n (dance) ballo m. **ballroom** n sala da ballo f.

ballad ['baləd] n ballata f; (music) canzone popolare f.

ballast ['baləst] n zavorra f. v zavorrare.

ballet ['balei] n balletto m. **ballet dancer** ballerino, -a m, f.

ballistic [bə'listik] adj balistico. **ballistic missile** proiettile balistico m.

balloon [bə'luɪn] n pallone m, aerostato m; (toy) palloncino m. **balloonist** n aeronauta m.

ballot ['balət] n votazione f, scrutinio m; (paper) scheda f. v ballottare, votare segretamente. **ballot-box** n urna elettorale f.

bamboo [bam'buː] n bambù m.

ban [ban] n proibizione f, bando m, interdizione f. v proibire, interdire.

banal [bə'naːl] adj banale.

banana [bə'naːnə] n (fruit) banana f; (tree) banano m.

band¹ [band] n (troop) banda f, schiera f; (music) banda f, orchestrina f. **bandstand** n palco per banda m. v **band together** legare insieme.

band² [band] n (strip) striscia f, fascia f.

bandage ['bandidʒ] n benda f, fascia f. v bendare, fasciare.

bandit ['bandit] n bandito m.

bandy ['bandi] adj storto, curvo. **bandy-legged** adj a gambe storte. v **bandy words** scambiare parole.

bang [baŋ] n colpo m, botta f. v sbattere.

bangle ['baŋgl] n braccialetto m.

banish ['baniʃ] v bandire, esiliare. **banishment** n bando m, esilio m.

banister ['banistə] n ringhiera f.

banjo ['bandʒou] n banjo m invar.

bank¹ [baŋk] n (edge) sponda f; (river) riva f. v arginare.

bank² [baŋk] n banca f, banco m. **bank account** conto in banca m. **bank holiday** festa legale f. **bank manager** direttore di banca m. v depositare in banca. **bank on** contare su.

bankrupt ['baŋkrʌpt] adj fallito. v far fallire. **bankruptcy** n fallimento m.

banner ['banə] n stendardo m, insegna f.

banquet ['baŋkwit] n banchetto m.

banter ['bantə] v canzonare, prendere in giro. n presa in giro f.

baptize [bap'taiz] v battezzare. **baptism** n battesimo m. **baptismal** adj battesimale. **Baptist** n battista m.

bar [baː] n (metal) sbarra f, stanga f; (line) striscia f; (chocolate) tavoletta f; (law) ordine degli avvocati m; barriera f; (drinks) bar m invar; (music) battuta f. **barmaid** n cameriera al banco f, barista f. **barman** n barista m. v proibire, impedire, escludere. prep eccetto, tranne.

barbarian [baː'beəriən] n, adj barbaro, -a.

barbecue ['baːbikjuː] n arrosto all'aperto m. v arrostire all'aperto.

barb [baːb] n spina f. **barbed** adj pungente. **barbed wire** filo spinato m.

barber ['baːbə] n barbiere m, parrucchiere m.

barbiturate [baː'bitjurət] n barbiturato m.

bare [beə] adj (without covering) scoperto; (simple) semplice; (naked, unadorned) nudo; (just sufficient) appena sufficiente. v denudare, rivelare. **barefoot** adj, adv scalzo, a piedi scalzi. **barely** adv appena.

bargain ['baːgin] n (transaction) affare m; (offer) occasione f. **into the bargain** per giunta, in più. v contrattare, mercanteggiare.

barge [baːdʒ] n barcone m, chiatta f. v **barge in** intervenire a sproposito, irrompere. **barge into** imbattersi per caso.

baritone ['baritoun] n baritono m.

bark¹ [baːk] n (dog) latrato m. v abbaiare, latrare.

bark² [baːk] n (tree) scorza f, corteccia f.

barley ['baːli] n orzo m. **barley sugar** zucchero d'orzo m. **barley water** tisana d'orzo f.

barn [baːn] n granaio m.

barometer [bə'romitə] n barometro m.

baron ['barən] n barone m. **baroness** n baronessa f. **baronet** n baronetto m.

baroque [bə'rok] nm, adj barocco.

barracks ['barəks] pl n caserma f sing.

barrage ['baraːʒ] n sbarramento f.

barrel ['barəl] n (cask) barile m, botte f; (gun, etc.) canna f. **barrel organ** organetto m.

barren ['barən] adj sterile, infecondo.

barricade [bari'keid] n barricata f. v barricare.

barrier ['bariə] n barriera f.

barrister ['baristə] n avvocato m.

barrow ['barou] n carretta f; (archaeol) tumulo m.

barter ['baːtə] v barattare. n baratto m.

base¹ [beis] v fondare, basare. n base f, fondamento m. **baseless** adj infondato.

base² [beis] adj vile, basso. **baseness** n bassezza f.

basement ['beismənt] n sottosuolo m.

bash [baʃ] n colpo violento m. v colpire violentemente.

bashful ['baʃful] adj timido, vergognoso.

basic ['beisik] adj fondamentale; (chem) basico.

basil ['bazl] n basilico m.

basin ['beisin] n bacino m, catino m; (wash-basin) lavabo m.

basis ['beisis] n, pl **-ses** base f, fondamento m.

bask [baːsk] v crogiolarsi.

bee

basket ['bɑːskɪt] n cesto m, paniere m. **basketball** n pallacanestro f.

Basle [bɑːl] n Basilea f.

bas-relief ['bæsrɪˌliːf] n bassorilievo m.

bass¹ [beɪs] n basso m.

bass² [bæs] n (sea) branzino m, spigola f; (freshwater) pesce persico m.

bassoon [bə'suːn] n fagotto m.

bastard ['bɑːstəd] n, adj bastardo, -a.

baste [beɪst] v (cookery) arrosolare; (sewing) imbastire; (beat) bastonare.

bastion ['bæstjən] n bastione m.

bat¹ [bæt] n (cricket, baseball) mazza f; (table tennis) racchetta f. v battere.

bat² [bæt] n (zool) pipistrello m. **blind as a bat** cieco come una talpa.

batch [bætʃ] n lotto m, partita f; (bread) infornata f.

bath [bɑːθ] n bagno m. v fare un bagno; lavare. **bathchair** n carrozzella per invalidi f. **bathmat** n stuoia da bagno f. **bathrobe** n accappatoio m. **bathroom** n stanza da bagno f.

bathe [beɪð] v bagnare, fare un or il bagno. **bather** n bagnante m, f. **bathing cap** cuffia da bagno f. **bathing costume** costume da bagno m. **bathing trunks** calzoncini da bagno m pl.

baton ['bætn] n (mil) bastone m; (music) bacchetta f.

battalion [bə'tæljən] n battaglione m.

batter¹ ['bætə] v percuotere, colpire con violenza. **battering ram** (mil) ariete m.

batter² ['bætə] n (cookery) pastella f.

battery ['bætəri] n batteria f, pila f.

battle ['bætl] n battaglia f, combattimento m. **battlefield** n campo di battaglia m. **battleship** n nave da battaglia f. v combattere, lottare.

bawdy ['bɔːdi] adj licenzioso.

bawl [bɔːl] v urlare, gridare.

bay¹ [beɪ] n (geog) baia f, golfo m, insenatura f.

bay² [beɪ] v (cry) abbaiare. n latrato m. **at bay** a bada.

bay³ [beɪ] n (tree) lauro m.

bayonet ['beɪənɪt] n baionetta f.

bay window n finestra sporgente f.

*__**be**__ [biː] v essere, esistere; (remain) stare.

beach [biːtʃ] n spiaggia f, lido m.

bead [biːd] n grano m; (liquid) goccia f.

beagle ['biːgl] n cane da caccia m.

beak [biːk] n becco m, rostro m.

beaker ['biːkə] n coppa f.

beam [biːm] n (wood) trave f; (light) raggio m; (radio) segnale m; (smile) sorriso m. v irradiare; (smile) sorridere.

bean [biːn] n fava f, fagiolo m; (coffee) chicco m. **French bean** fagiolino m. **full of beans** energico.

*__**bear¹**__ [beə] v (carry) portare; (support weight) reggere; (tolerate) soffrire, sopportare; (give birth to) dare alla luce. **bear oneself** comportarsi. **bear with** aver pazienza con. **bearable** adj sopportabile. **bearer** n portatore, -trice m, f.

bear² [beə] n orso, -a m, f.

beard [biəd] n barba f. v sfidare. **bearded** adj barbuto. **beardless** adj imberbe.

bearing ['beəriŋ] n condotta f, contegno m; (aircraft) rilevamento m; (mech) cuscinetto m. **bearings** pl n orientamento m sing, senso di direzione m sing. **lose one's bearings** disorientarsi.

beast [biːst] n bestia f, animale m. **beastly** adj bestiale; (coll) veramente cattivo.

*__**beat**__ [biːt] v battere; (hit) bastonare; (heart) palpitare; (defeat) sconfiggere; (eggs, etc.) sbattere. n battito m, palpito m; (music) battuta f; (police) ronda f. **beating** n bastonata f, sconfitta f.

beaten ['biːtn] V beat.

beauty ['bjuːti] n bellezza f. **beautiful** adj bello. **beautify** v abbellire.

beaver ['biːvə] n castoro m.

became [bi'keɪm] V become.

because [bi'kɔz] conj perché, poiché. **because of** a causa di.

beckon ['bekən] v chiamare con un cenno.

*__**become**__ [bi'kʌm] v diventare, divenire. **becoming** adj che sta bene; (suitable) conveniente.

bed [bed] n letto m; (sea) fondo m; (coal) giacimento m; (flowers) aiuola f. **bedbug** n cimice m. **bedroom** n camera da letto f. **bedside** n capezzale m. **bedsitter** n camera studio f. **bedspread** n copriletto m. **double bed** letto matrimoniale m. **go to bed** andare a letto. **twin beds** letti gemelli m pl. **bedding** n (sheets) lenzuola f pl; (covers) coperte f pl.

bedevil [bi'devl] v vessare.

bedlam ['bedləm] n confusione f.

bedraggled [bi'dragld] adj fradicio, inzaccherato.

bee [biː] n ape f. **beehive** n alveare m. **bee-keeper** n apicoltore m.

beech [biːtʃ] n faggio m.

beef [biːf] n manzo m. **beefsteak** n bistecca f.

been [biːn] V be.

beer [biə] n birra f.

beetle ['biːtl] n scarabeo m. **black beetle** scarafaggio m.

beetroot ['biːtruːt] n barbabietola f.

before [bi'foː] adv prima, già. prep prima di, davanti a. conj prima che. **beforehand** adv in anticipo.

befriend [bi'frend] v sostenere, mostrarsi amico a.

beg [beg] v implorare, pregare; (for alms) chiedere l'elemosina. **beggar** n mendicante m, f.

began [bi'gan] V begin.

*****begin** [bi'gin] v cominciare, iniziare. **to begin with** anzitutto. **beginner** n principiante m, f. **beginning** n principio m, inizio m.

begrudge [bi'grʌdʒ] v invidiare.

begun [bi'gʌn] V begin.

behalf [bi'haːf] n **on behalf of** a nome di.

behave [bi'heiv] v comportarsi. **behaviour** n condotta f, comportamento m.

behead [bi'hed] v decapitare.

beheld [bi'held] V behold.

behind [bi'haind] adv dietro, indietro; (late) in ritardo. prep dietro a or di, dopo. **behindhand** adv in arretrato, in ritardo. n (coll) sedere m.

*****behold** [bi'hould] v vedere. **beholder** n osservatore, -trice m, f.

beige [beiʒ] adj beige invar.

being [biːŋ] n essere m, creatura f. **for the time being** per il momento.

belated [bi'leitid] adj tardivo.

belch [beltʃ] v ruttare. n rutto m.

belfry [belfri] n campanile m.

Belgium ['beldʒəm] n Belgio m. **Belgian** n(m+f), adj belga (m pl -gi).

believe [bi'liːv] v credere, pensare, aver fede in. **make believe** v far finta. **belief** n, pl -s fede f, credenza f, opinione f. **believable** adj credibile. **believer** n credente m, f, fedele m, f.

bell [bel] n campana f; (door) campanello m. **bellringer** n campanaro m. **bell-tower** n campanile m.

belligerent [bi'lidʒərənt] adj belligerente.

bellow ['belou] v urlare, muggire.

bellows ['belouz] pl n soffietto m sing, mantice m sing.

belly ['beli] n pancia f, ventre m.

belong [bi'loŋ] v appartenere, spettare, far parte (di). **belongings** pl n roba f sing, effetti personali m pl.

beloved [bi'lʌvid] n, adj amato, -a.

below [bi'lou] adv sotto, di sotto, giù. prep sotto, al di sotto di, inferiore a.

belt [belt] n cintura f; (mech) cinghia f; (zone) fascia f. v (coll: hit) picchiare; (coll: rush) precipitarsi.

bench [bentʃ] n (workshop) banco m; (long seat) panchina f, panca f; (law) magistratura f.

*****bend** [bend] v piegare, curvare. n curva f, svolta f.

beneath [bi'niːθ] adv giù, abbasso. prep sotto, al di sotto di.

benefactor ['benəfaktə] n benefattore, -trice m, f. **benefaction** n beneficenza f.

benefit ['benəfit] n beneficio m, vantaggio m, utilità f. v giovare a, far bene a, approfittare. **beneficial** adj vantaggioso, utile. **beneficiary** n, adj beneficiario, -a.

benevolent [bi'nevələnt] adj benevolo, caritatevole. **benevolence** n benevolenza f.

benign [bi'nain] adj benevolo; (med) benigno.

bent [bent] V bend. adj curvato; (determined) risoluto; (dishonest) corrotto. n tendenza f.

bequeath [bi'kwiːð] v lasciare per testamento. **bequest** n lascito m.

bereaved [bi'riːvd] n essere in lutto. **bereavement** n lutto m.

beret ['berei] n beretto m.

berry ['beri] n bacca f, chicco m.

berserk [bə'səːk] adv **go berserk** montare su tutte le furie.

berth [bəːθ] n (sleeping) cuccetta f; (naut) posto d'ormeggio m. **give a wide berth to** evitare. v ancorare.

beside [bi'said] prep accanto a, presso, vicino a. **be beside oneself** essere fuori di sè. **besides** adv d'altronde, inoltre, per di più.

besiege [bi'siːdʒ] v assediare.

best [best] adj il migliore. adv meglio. **as best one can** come meglio si può, il meglio possibile. **come off best** avere la meglio. **do one's best** fare del proprio meglio. **the best** il meglio. **to the best of my knowledge** per quanto ne sappia.

bestial ['bestjəl] adj bestiale.

bestow [bi'stou] v conferire, dare.

bet [bet] n scommessa f. v scommettere.

betray [bi'trei] v tradire, svelare. **betrayal** n tradimento m.

better ['betə] adj meglio, migliore. adv meglio, in modo migliore. v migliorare. **all the better** tanto meglio. **be or feel better** star meglio. **get the better of** aver la meglio su.

between [bi'twiːn] adv in mezzo. prep tra, fra, in mezzo a.

beverage ['bevəridʒ] n bevanda f, bibita f.

*****beware** [bi'weə] v guardarsi da, stare attento a. **beware of the dog!** attenti al cane!

bewilder [bi'wildə] v sconcertare, confondere. **bewildered** adj sconcertato, perplesso. **bewildering** adj sconcertante. **bewilderment** n disorientamento m.

beyond [bi'jond] adv oltre, più in là. prep oltre, al di là di.

bias ['baiəs] n inclinazione f, pregiudizio m, preconcetto m. **on the bias** (tailoring) per sbieco. **biased** adj prevenuto.

bib [bib] n bavaglino m.

Bible ['baibl] n bibbia f. **biblical** adj biblico.

bibliography [bibli'ogrəfi] n bibliografia f. **bibliographer** n bibliografo, -a m, f. **bibliographical** adj bibliografico.

biceps ['baiseps] n bicipite m.

bicker ['bikə] v litigare, bisticciare. **bickering** n bisticciarsi m invar.

bicycle ['baisikl] n bicicletta f.

*****bid** [bid] n offerta f; (cards) dichiarazione f. v (order) comandare; (auction) offrire; (cards) dichiarare. **bidder** n offerente m, f; (auction) dichiaratore, -trice m, f. **bidding** n ordine m; dichiarazione f.

bide [baid] v **bide one's time** aspettare il momento propizio.

bidet ['biːdei] n bidè m.

biennial [bai'eniəl] adj biennale.

bifocals [bai'foukəlz] pl n lenti bifocali f pl.

big [big] adj grande, grosso, importante.

bigamy ['bigəmi] n bigamia f. **bigamist** n bigamo m. **bigamous** adj bigamo.

bigot ['bigət] n bigotto m, fanatico, -a m, f. **bigoted** adj bigotto, fanatico. **bigotry** n bigotteria f, fanatismo m.

bikini [bi'kiːni] n bikini m invar.

bilateral [bai'latərəl] adj bilaterale.

bilingual [bai'liŋgwəl] adj bilingue.

bilious ['biljəs] adj (med) biliare; (irritable) collerico; (sickly) nauseante. **bile** n bile f. **biliousness** n travaso di bile m.

bill[1] [bil] n (hotel, restaurant) conto m; (shop, invoice) fattura f; (pol) progetto di legge m, atto m; (poster) affisso m; (theatre) cartellone m. **bill of fare** menù m. v fatturare; (poster) affiggere; (theatre) mettere in programma.

bill[2] [bil] n (beak) becco m, rostro m.

billiards ['biljədz] n biliardo m.

billion ['biljən] n (10^{12}) bilione m, mille miliardi m pl; (10^9) miliardo m.

billow ['bilou] n onda f; (smoke) ondata f. v (sail) gonfiarsi; (smoke) emanare.

bin [bin] n recipiente m; (dustbin) pattumiera f.

binary ['bainəri] adj binario.

*****bind** [baind] v legare, attaccare; (book) rilegare; (force) costringere. n (slang) scocciatura f.

binding ['baindiŋ] n legatura f, legame m; (book) rilegatura f. adj impegnativo, obbligatorio.

binoculars [bi'nokjuləz] pl n binocolo m sing.

biography [bai'ogrəfi] n biografia f. **biographer** n biografo, -a m, f. **biographical** adj biografico.

biology [bai'olədʒi] n biologia f. **biological** adj biologico. **biologist** n biologo, -a m, f.

birch [bəːtʃ] n betulla f.

bird [bəːd] n uccello m. **bird's-eye view** veduta a volo d'uccello f.

birth [bəːθ] n nascita f; (origin) f; discendenza f. **birth certificate** atto di nascita m. **birth control** controllo delle nascite m. **birthday** n compleanno m. **birthmark** n voglia f. **birthplace** n luogo di nascita m. **birth rate** natalità f, indice demografico m. **give birth to** mettere al mondo, dare alla luce.

biscuit ['biskit] n biscotto m.

bishop ['biʃəp] n (church) vescovo m; (chess) alfiere m.

bison ['baisən] n bisonte m.

bit[1] [bit] V **bite**. n (horse) morso m; (drill) punta f, morsa f.

bit[2] [bit] n (morsel) boccone m; (small piece) pezzo m, pezzetto m. **bit by bit** poco a poco. **do one's bit** fare la propria parte. **wait a bit!** aspetta un po'!

bitch [bitʃ] n cagna f; (slang) antipatica f. **bitchy** adj malvagio.

*bite [bait] *n* morso *m*; (*insect*) puntura *f*; (*fish*) l'abboccare *m*; (*food*) boccone *m*. *v* mordere, addentare. **biting** *adj* pungente, mordente.

bitten ['bitn] *V* **bite**.

bitter ['bitə] *adj* amaro, aspro, accanito. **bitter-sweet** *adj* agrodolce. **to the bitter end** ad oltranza. **bitterness** *n* amarezza *f*, rancore *m*.

bizarre [bi'zɑː] *adj* bizzarro, strano.

black [blak] *adj* nero. **things look black** le cose si mettono male. *n* (*colour*) nero *m*; (*person*) negro, -a *m, f*. **blacken** *v* annerire.

blackberry ['blakbəri] *n* (*fruit*) mora *f*; (*bush*) rovo *m*.

blackbird ['blakbəːd] *n* merlo *m*.

blackboard ['blakbɔːd] *n* lavagna *f*.

blackcurrant [ˌblak'kʌrənt] *n* ribes nero *m invar*.

blackhead ['blakhed] *n* comedone *m*.

blackleg ['blakleg] *n* crumiro *m*.

blackmail ['blakmeil] *n* ricatto *m*. *v* ricattare. **blackmailer** *n* ricattatore, -trice *m, f*.

black market *n* borsa nera *f*.

blackout ['blakaut] *n* oscuramento *m*; (*med*) svenimento *m*.

blacksmith ['blaksmiθ] *n* fabbro *m*.

blackshirt ['blakʃəːt] *n* camicia nera *f*.

bladder ['bladə] *n* vescica *f*.

blade [bleid] *n* lama *f*; (*oar, propeller*) pala *f*; (*grass*) filo d'erba *m*.

blame [bleim] *n* biasimo *m*, responsabilità *f*. *v* biasimare, incolpare, rimproverare. **blameless** *adj* innocente.

blanch [blaːntʃ] *v* (*cookery*) sbollentare; (*go pale*) impallidire.

bland [bland] *adj* blando.

blank [blaŋk] *adj* vuoto, in bianco; (*puzzled*) perplesso. *n* spazio vuoto *m*; (*cartridge*) cartuccia a salve *f*. **point blank** a bruciapelo.

blanket ['blaŋkit] *n* coperta *f*. *v* ricoprire.

blare [bleə] *v* squillare, sonare con tutta forza. *n* (*trumpet*) squillo *m*; (*loud noise*) chiasso *m*.

blaspheme [blas'fiːm] *v* bestemmiare. **blasphemous** *adj* blasfemo, empio. **blasphemy** *n* bestemmia *f*.

blast [blaːst] *n* (*wind*) raffica *f*; esplosione *f*. *v* far esplodere, far saltare. **blast-furnace** *n* altoforno (*pl* altiforni) *m*.

blatant ['bleitənt] *adj* vistoso, evidente.

blaze [bleiz] *n* (*flame*) fiamma *f*; (*sudden outburst of fire*) vampata *f*. *v* ardere, divampare. **blazer** *n* giacca sportiva *f*.

bleach [bliːtʃ] *v* scolorire, candeggiare. *n* candeggina *f*.

bleak [bliːk] *adj* (*desolate*) triste; (*dreary*) squallido; (*depressing*) deprimente.

bleat [bliːt] *v* belare.

bled [bled] *V* **bleed**.

*bleed [bliːd] *v* sanguinare, perder sangue. **bleeding** *n* emorragia *f*, perdita di sangue *f*.

blemish ['blemiʃ] *n* difetto *m*, imperfezione *f*. *v* sfigurare, macchiare.

blend [blend] *v* mescolare, combinare. *n* miscela intima *f*.

bless [bles] *v* benedire. **be blessed with** godere di, essere dotato di. **bless you!** salute! **blessing** *n* benedizione *f*.

blew [bluː] *V* **blow**.

blind [blaind] *adj* cieco. **blind drunk** ubriaco fradicio. **blind spot** punto cieco *m*. **turn a blind eye to** chiudere gli occhi davanti a. **blindness** *n* cecità *f*. *v* accecare, ingannare. *n* (*window*) tendina *f*, persiana *f*; (*pretence*) finzione *f*.

blindfold ['blaindfould] *n* benda (agli occhi) *f*. *v* bendare gli occhi.

blink [bliŋk] *v* battere le palpebre; (*wink*) ammiccare.

bliss [blis] *n* beatitudine *f*. **blissful** *adj* beato.

blister ['blistə] *n* bolla *f*, vescica *f*. *v* far venire vesciche; coprirsi di vesciche.

blizzard ['blizəd] *n* tormenta *f*, bufera *f*.

blob [blob] *n* macchia *f*.

bloc [blok] *n* blocco *m*.

block [blok] *v* bloccare, sbarrare. *n* blocco *m*, ceppo *m*; (*large building*) palazzo *m*; (*obstacle*) ostacolo *m*. **block letter** stampatello *m*; (*capital*) maiuscola *f*. **blockade** [blo'keid] *n* blocco *m*, assedio *m*. *v* bloccare.

bloke [blouk] *n* (*coll*) tipo *m*.

blond [blond] *adj* biondo. **blonde** *n* bionda *f*.

blood [blʌd] *n* sangue *m*; (*descent*) stirpe *f*. **blood clot** coagulo di sangue *m*. **bloodcurdling** *adj* raccapricciante. **blood group** gruppo sanguigno *m*. **bloodhound** *n* segugio *m*. **blood poisoning** setticemia *f*. **blood pressure** pressione sanguigna *f*. **bloodshed** *n* carneficina *f*. **bloodshot** *adj* arrossato. **bloodthirsty** *adj* assetato di sangue. **bloody** *adj* macchiato di sangue; (*slang*) maledetto.

boost

bloom [bluːm] v fiorire. n fiore m, fioritura f.

blot [blɒt] n macchia f, sgorbio m. v macchiare. **blot out** cancellare. **blotting paper** carta assorbente f.

blouse [blauz] n blusa f, camicetta f.

blow¹ [blou] n colpo m; (fist) pugno m; (stick) bastonata f. **come to blows** venire alle mani.

*blow² [blou] v soffiare; (trumpet, etc.) suonare. **blow away** spazzar via. **blow one's nose** soffiarsi il naso. **blow out** spegner. **blow up** (explode) far saltare; (inflate) gonfiare.

blown [bloun] V **blow²**.

blubber [ˈblʌbə] n (whale) grasso di balene m. v (weep) piangere singhiozzando.

blue [bluː] nm, adj azzurro; (pale) celeste; (dark) blu. **bluebell** n giacinto selvatico m. **blueprint** n progetto m.

bluff [blʌf] v ingannare; (cards) bluffare. n vanteria infondata f; (poker) bluff m invar.

blunder [ˈblʌndə] n errore m, papera f. v commettere un errore.

blunt [blʌnt] adj (not sharp) ottuso, spuntato; (frank) brusco. v smussare, ottundere.

blur [bləː] v rendere confuso, oscurare. n offuscamento m, macchia f.

blush [blʌʃ] v arrossire. n rossore m.

boar [boː] n cinghiale m.

board [boːd] v (ship, etc.) abbordare, imbarcarsi. n (wood) asse m, tavola f; (food) vitto m; (examiners) commissione f. **board of directors** consiglio d'amministrazione m. **full board** pensione completa f. **half board** mezza pensione f. **on board** a bordo. **boarding house** pensione f. **boarding school** collegio m.

boast [boust] n vanto m. v vantare. **boastful** adj millantatore, vanaglorioso.

boat [bout] n barca f, battello m. **boat race** gara di canottaggio f. **boating** n canottaggio m.

bob [bɒb] v **bob up** (come to surface) venire a galla. **bob up and down** muoversi in su e in giù.

bobbin [ˈbɒbin] n bobina f.

bodice [ˈbɒdis] n busto m, liseuse f.

body [ˈbɒdi] n corpo m; entità f; gruppo m; (corpse) cadavere m; (organization) ente m. **bodyguard** n guardia del corpo f.

bog [bɒg] n palude f, pantano m.

bogus [ˈbougəs] adj falso.

bohemian [ouˈhiːmiən] adj da artista.

boil¹ [bɔil] v bollire, far bollire, lessare. **boiler** n caldaia f. **boiler suit** tuta f. **boiling point** punto d'ebollizione m.

boil² [bɔil] n (swelling) foruncolo m.

boisterous [ˈbɔistərəs] adj chiassoso, impetuoso.

bold [bould] adj audace, ardito, sfacciato. **boldness** n audacia f, coraggio m.

bolster [ˈboulstə] n capezzale m, cuscino m. v **bolster up** sostenere.

bolt [boult] n (for nut) bullone m; (door) catenaccio m; (arrow) freccia f. v (bar) sprangare; (run away) scappare. **a bolt from the blue** un fulmine a ciel sereno. **bolt upright** diritto come un fuso.

bomb [bɒm] n bomba f. v bombardare. **bombing** n bombardamento m.

bond [bɒnd] n (tie) legame m, vincolo m; (agreement) impegno m; (comm) titolo m; (law) cauzione f. **bonded warehouse** magazzino doganale m. **bondage** n schiavitù f.

bone [boun] n osso m (pl -a f). v disossare. **bony** adj ossuto.

bonfire [ˈbɔnfaiə] n falò m.

bonnet [ˈbɔnit] n (hat) cappellino m; (car) cofano m.

bonus [ˈbounəs] n gratifica f, premio m.

booby trap [ˈbuːbi] n mina nascosta f, trappola esplosiva f; (pitfall) trabocchetto m.

book [buk] n libro m. v (reserve) prenotare.

bookcase [ˈbukkeis] n scaffale m.

booking [ˈbukin] n prenotazione f.

bookkeeping [ˈbukˌkiːpin] n contabilità f. **bookkeeper** n contabile m, f.

booklet [ˈbuklit] n opuscolo m.

bookmaker [ˈbukmeikə] n bookmaker m invar, allibratore m.

bookmark [ˈbukmaːk] n segnalibro m.

bookseller [ˈbukselə] n libraio m.

bookshop [ˈbukʃɒp] n libreria f.

bookstall [ˈbukstɔːl] n edicola f.

boom [buːm] v (noise) rimbombare, tuonare; (econ) essere in gran voga. n rimbombo m, tuono m; (econ) boom m invar.

boorish [ˈbuəriʃ] adj grossolano.

boost [buːst] n pressione f, spinta f. v aumentare, spingere.

boot [buːt] n (shoe) stivale m; (car) portabagagli m.

booth [buːð] n baracca f, cabina f.

booze [buːz] (coll) n bevanda alcoolica f. v ubriacarsi, sbronzarsi.

border ['bɔːdə] n orlo m, limite m, frontiera f. v (embroidery) orlare; (geog) confinare (con). **borderline case** caso limite m.

bore¹ [bɔː] n (hole) buco m, foro m; (gun) calibro m. v forare, trapanare; (mech) alesare.

bore² [bɔː] v (weary) seccare, annoiare. n (person) seccatore, -trice m, f; (matter) seccatura f; noia f.

bore³ [bɔː] V **bear¹**.

born [bɔːn] adj nato. **be born** nascere.

borne [bɔːn] V **bear¹**.

borough ['bʌrə] n comune m, borgo m.

borrow ['borou] v prendere a prestito, farsi prestare.

bosom ['buzəm] n petto m, seno m.

boss [bos] n capo m, direttore m. v comandare. **bossy** adj prepotente.

botany ['botəni] n botanica f. **botanical** adj botanico. **botanist** n botanico, -a m, f.

both [bouθ] adj, pron ambedue, entrambi, tutti e due.

bother ['boðə] n seccatura f, noia f. v seccare, preoccuparsi.

bottle ['botl] n bottiglia f. v imbottigliare. **bottleneck** n ingorgo m. **bottle-opener** n apribottiglie m invar.

bottom ['botəm] n fondo m. adj ultimo, inferiore. **bottomless** adj senza fondo.

bough [bau] n ramo m.

bought [bɔːt] V **buy**.

boulder ['bouldə] n macigno m, masso roccioso m.

bounce [bauns] v (far) rimbalzare. n balzo m, rimbalzo m.

bound¹ [baund] v saltare, rimbalzare. n salto m, balzo m. **by leaps and bounds** a passi da gigante.

bound² [baund] n confine m, restrizione f. v porre limiti a, confinare. **boundary** n limite m, frontiera f. **boundless** adj illimitato.

bound³ [baund] adj **bound for** diretto per, con destinazione per.

bound⁴ [baund] V **bind**.

bouquet [buːkei] n mazzo m.

bourgeois ['buəʒwaɪ] n(m+f), adj borghese.

bout [baut] n periodo d'attività m; (illness) attacco m; (match) ripresa f.

bow¹ [bau] n (greeting) saluto m; (bend) inchino m. v inchinarsi, salutare, chinare.

bow² [bou] n (archery) arco m; (violin, etc.) archetto m; (ribbon) fiocco m. **bow-legged** adj dalle gambe storte. **bow-tie** n cravatta a farfalla f.

bow³ [bau] n (naut) prua f, prora f.

bowels ['bauəlz] pl n viscere f pl.

bowl¹ [boul] n (basin) scodella f, ciotola m.

bowl² [boul] n (ball) boccia f. v far rotolare, servire la palla. **bowls** n gioco delle bocce m. **bowler** n (hat) bombetta f.

box¹ [boks] n scatola f, cassetta f; (theatre) palco m. **box number** casella postale f. **box office** botteghino m.

box² [boks] v fare a pugni, fare del pugilato, fare la boxe. **boxing** n pugilato m, boxe f.

Boxing Day n giorno di San Stefano m.

boy [boi] n ragazzo m. **boyhood** n fanciullezza f. **boyish** adj da ragazzo.

boycott ['boikot] n boicottaggio m. v boicottare.

bra [braː] n reggipetto m, reggiseno m.

brace [breis] v fortificare, rinvigorire. n sostegno; (tool) trapano m; (pair) coppia f. **braces** pl n bretelle f pl.

bracelet ['breislit] n braccialetto m.

bracken ['brakən] n felce f.

bracket ['brakit] n mensola f, braccio m; (printing) parentesi f invar. **put in brackets** mettere fra parentesi. **bracket together** accoppiare.

brag [brag] v vantarsi. **braggart** n fanfarone m.

brain [brein] n cervello m. **brainwashing** n lavaggio del cervello m. **brainwave** n idea geniale f. **brainy** adj intelligente.

braise [breiz] v brasare, cuocere a stufato.

brake [breik] n freno m. v frenare, serrare il freno.

bramble ['brambl] n (bush) rovo m; (fruit) mora f.

bran [bran] n crusca f.

branch [braːntʃ] n ramo m; (office) succursale f. **branch off** biforcarsi. **branch out** estendersi.

brand [brand] n (trademark) marchio m; (grade, make) marca f; (marking) marchio m, stigma m; (burning wood) tizzone m. **brand-new** adj nuovo di zecca.

nuovo fiammante. v marchiare, stigmatizzare.

brandish ['brandiʃ] v brandire.

brandy ['brandi] n cognac m, acquavite f.

brass [brɑːs] n ottone m. **brassy** adj d'ottone; (impudent) sfacciato.

brassiere ['brasiə] V **bra**.

brave [breiv] adj prode, coraggioso, ardito. v sfidare, affrontare. **bravery** n audacia f, coraggio m.

brawl [brɔːl] n rissa f, zuffa f. v rissare, azzuffarsi.

brawn [brɔːn] n (strength) forza muscolare f; (meat) testina f.

brazen ['breizn] adj sfacciato, impudente; (brass) di ottone.

breach [briːtʃ] n violazione f, rottura f; (mil) breccia f. v far una breccia in, rompere.

bread [bred] n pane m. **breadcrumbs** pl n briciole di pane f pl.

breadth [bredθ] n larghezza f, ampiezza f; (cloth) altezza f.

*__break__ [breik] n rottura f, frattura f; interruzione f, pausa f; (chance) opportunità f. v rompere, spezzare, infrangere; (record) battere. **at breakneck speed** a rompicollo. **break away** fuggire, distaccarsi. **break off** mandare a monte. **break out** (war) scoppiare. **breakthrough** n scoperta f, innovazione f. **breakable** adj fragile. **breakage** n rottura f.

breakdown ['breikdaun] n crollo m; (car) panna f; (nerves) esaurimento nervoso m. v **break down** demolire; analizzare; (car) avere una panna; (nerves) avere un esaurimento nervoso.

breakfast ['brekfəst] n prima colazione f.

breast [brest] n petto m, seno m. **breastbone** n sterno m. **breast-stroke** n nuoto a rana m.

breath [breθ] n respiro m, fiato m, soffio m. **breathless** adj ansimante. **breathtaking** adj sorprendente.

breathalyser ['breθəlaizə] n analizzatore del fiato m.

breathe [briːð] v respirare, prender fiato; (sigh) sospirare. **breathing** n respirazione f.

bred [bred] V **breed**.

*__breed__ [briːd] v generare, allevare. n razza f, stirpe f. **breeding** n (animals) allevamento m; (manners) educazione f.

breeze [briːz] n brezza f. **breezily** adv con disinvoltura.

brew [bruː] v (beer) far fermentare; (tea) preparare; (storm) essere nell'aria. n miscela f. **brewer** n birraio m. **brewery** n birreria f.

bribe [braib] v corrompere, allettare. n dono a scopo di corruzione m; (coll) bustarella f. **bribery** n corruzione f.

brick [brik] n mattone m. **bricklayer** n muratore m. **drop a brick** fare una gaffe.

bride [braid] n sposa f, sposina f. **bridal** adj nuziale. **bridegroom** n sposo m. **bridesmaid** n damigella d'onore della sposa f.

bridge[1] [bridʒ] n ponte m. v congiungere. **bridge a gap** colmare una lacuna.

bridge[2] [bridʒ] n (cards) bridge m.

bridle ['braidl] n briglia f, freno m. v risentirsi. **bridle-path** n sentiero percorribile a cavallo m.

brief [briːf] adj breve. n riassunto m; istruzioni m pl; lettera f. v riassumere per sommi capi; (law) affidare una causa. **brief-case** n borsa f.

brigade [bri'geid] n brigata f.

bright [brait] adj lucido, risplendente; (lively) vivace; (clever) intelligente. **brighten** v rendere più brillante, illuminare. **brightness** n luminosità f, splendore m.

brilliant ['briljənt] adj brillante.

brim [brim] n orlo m, bordo m; (hat) falda f. **brimful** adj colmo.

brine [brain] n acqua salata f.

*__bring__ [briŋ] v portare, condurre. **bring about** causare. **bring back** riportare; restituire. **bring up** educare; vomitare.

brink [briŋk] n orlo m.

brisk [brisk] adj vivace, arzillo.

bristle ['brisl] n (human) pelo duro m; (animal) setola f. v rizzarsi.

Britain ['britn] n Gran Bretagna f. **British** adj britannico. **Briton** n britannico, -a m, f.

brittle ['britl] adj fragile.

broach [brəutʃ] v (subject) intavolare un discorso su.

broad [brɔːd] adj (wide) largo, ampio; (overall) generale. **broad bean** fava f. **broad-minded** adj di larghe vedute. **broaden** v allargare.

*__broadcast__ ['brɔːdkɑːst] v trasmettere alla radio. adj radiodiffuso. n trasmissione radio f.

broccoli ['brokəli] n broccolo m.

brochure ['brouʃuə] n opuscolo m.

broke [brouk] V break. adj (coll) al verde, rovinato.

broken ['broukn] V break.

broker ['broukə] n agente m, commissionario m, sensale m.

bronchitis [broŋ'kaitis] n bronchite f.

bronze [bronz] n bronzo m. v abbronzare.

brooch [broutʃ] n spilla f.

brood [bruid] n covata f, figliolanza f. v covare; (think) meditare.

brook [bruk] n ruscello m. v ammettere.

broom [brum] n (brush) scopa f; (plant) ginestra f.

broth [broθ] n brodo m.

brothel ['broθl] n bordello m.

brother ['brʌðə] n fratello m. **brother-in-law** n cognato m. **brotherhood** n fratellanza f, fraternità f. **brotherly** adj fraterno.

brought [brott] V bring.

brow [brau] n fronte f; (hill) cima f. **browbeat** v intimidire.

brown [braun] nm, adj bruno, marrone, castano. v abbrunire, abbronzare; (cooking) rosolare.

browse [brauz] v brucare, scartabellare.

bruise [bruiz] v ammaccare, intaccare. n livido m, contusione f. **bruised** adj (person) contuso; (fruit) ammaccato.

brunette [bru'net] nf, adj bruna, brunetta.

brush [brʌʃ] n spazzola f; spazzolino m; (paint) pennello m; (encounter) scontro m. v spazzolare. **brush against** sfiorare. **brush aside** ignorare. **brush up** (revise) ripassare.

brusque [brusk] adj brusco.

Brussels ['brʌsəlz] n Brusselle f. **Brussels sprouts** cavoli di Brusselle m pl.

brute [bruit] nm, adj bruto. **brutal** adj brutale.

bubble ['bʌbl] n bolla f. v formar bolle, gorgogliare.

buck [bʌk] n maschio m; (deer) daino m. **buck-tooth** n dente sporgente m. **pass the buck** scaricare la responsabilità. v **buck up** (rear up) impennarsi; (coll: cheer up) rallegrarsi.

bucket ['bʌkit] n secchio m, secchia f.

buckle ['bʌkl] n fibbia f, fermaglio m. v affibbiare.

bud [bʌd] n bocciolo m, gemma f. v

germogliare, sbocciare. **nip in the bud** troncare sul nascere.

budge [bʌdʒ] v scostarsi.

budget ['bʌdʒit] n bilancio preventivo m. v fare un bilancio preventivo.

buffalo ['bʌfəlou] n bufalo, -a m, f.

buffer ['bʌfə] n (trains) respingente m. **buffer state** stato cuscinetto m.

buffet[1] ['bʌfit] v (hit) schiaffeggiare. n schiaffo m.

buffet[2] ['bufei] n (cafeteria) buffet m, caffè ristoratore m; (sideboard) credenza f. **cold buffet** cibi freddi m pl.

bug [bʌg] n cimice f; (coll) piccolo insetto m.

bugger ['bʌgə] (impol) n sodomita m; (fellow) tizio m; (derog) brutto ceffo m. v inculare. **bugger off** svignarsela. **bugger off!** va a quel paese! va al diavolo! **buggery** n sodomia f, pederastia f.

bugle ['bjuɪgl] n tromba f.

*build [bild] v costruire, fabbricare. n corporatura f. **building** n edificio m, costruzione f. **building society** n società immobiliare f, credito edilizio m.

built [bilt] V build.

bulb [bʌlb] n (plant) bulbo m; (light) lampadina f.

Bulgaria [bʌl'geəriə] n Bulgaria f. **Bulgarian** n, adj bulgaro, -a.

bulge [bʌldʒ] n protuberanza f, gonfiore m. v gonfiarsi, sporgere.

bulk [bʌlk] n massa f, volume m. **the bulk** la maggior parte f. **bulky** adj massiccio, voluminoso.

bull [bul] n toro m; (papal) bolla f. **bulldog** n mastino m. **bulldozer** n livellatrice f. **bullfight** n corrida f. **bull's eye** centro (del bersaglio) m.

bullet ['bulit] n pallottola f. **bullet-proof** adj blindato, corazzato.

bulletin ['bulətin] n bollettino m.

bullion ['buliən] n lingotto (di metallo prezioso) m.

bully ['buli] n prepotente m. v tiranneggiare, maltrattare.

bum [bʌm] (coll) n sedere m. adj scadente. v **bum around** vagabondare.

bump [bʌmp] v urtare. n protuberanza f, bernoccolo m. **bump into** (collide) andare a sbattere contro; (meet) incontrare per caso. **bumpy** adj irregolare.

bumper ['bʌmpə] n (mot) paraurti m. adj abbondante.

bun [bʌn] *n* (*cake*) focaccia *f*; (*hair*) crocchia *f*.

bunch [bʌntʃ] *n* fascio *m*, mazzo *m*, gruppo *m*; (*grapes*) grappolo d'uva *m*. *v* riunire, raggruppare.

bundle ['bʌndl] *n* fagotto *m*, involto *m*. *v* mettere insieme alla rinfusa, fare un involto di, affastellare.

bungalow ['bʌŋɡəlou] *n* bungalow *m*, villino ad un piano *m*.

bungle ['bʌŋɡl] *v* sciupare, lavorar male. *n* lavoro malfatto *m*. **bungler** *n* confusionario *m*, guastamestieri *m*.

bunion ['bʌnjən] *n* protuberanza callosa *f*.

bunk [bʌŋk] *n* cuccetta *f*.

bunker ['bʌŋkə] *n* (*coal*) carbonaia *f*; (*mil*) ricovero militare seminterrato *m*; (*golf*) ostacolo *m*.

buoy [bɔi] *n* gavitello *m*, boa *f*. **buoyancy** *n* galleggiabilità *f*. **buoyant** *adj* galleggiante.

burden ['bəːdn] *n* peso *m*, onere *m*. *v* caricare, tassare.

bureau ['bjuərou] *n* (*desk*) scrittoio *m*; (*office*) ufficio *m*.

bureaucracy [bju'rɔkrəsi] *n* burocrazia *f*. **bureaucrat** *n* burocrate *m*, *f*. **bureaucratic** *adj* burocratico.

burglar ['bəːɡlə] *n* scassinatore *m*, ladro *m*. **burgle** *v* scassinare, svaligiare.

***burn** [bəːn] *v* bruciare, scottare, risplendere. **burn down** incendiare. *n* ustione *f*, scottatura *f*. **burner** *n* bruciatore *m*, becco a gas *m*.

burnt [bəːnt] *V* burn.

burrow ['bʌrou] *n* tana *f*, covo *m*. *v* farsi una tana, scavare.

***burst** [bəːst] *n* scoppio *m*, raffica *f*. *v* scoppiare, esplodere.

bury ['beri] *v* seppellire, sotterrare. **burial** *n* sepoltura *f*.

bus [bʌs] *n* autobus *m invar*. **bus station** capolinea (*pl* capilinea) *m*. **bus stop** fermata dell'autobus *f*.

bush [buʃ] *n* (*shrub*) cespuglio *m*; (*woodland*) macchia *f*. **bushy** *adj* folto.

business ['biznis] *n* affare *m*, mestiere *m*. **business-like** *adj* metodico. **businessman** *n* uomo d'affari *m*.

bust¹ [bʌst] *n* (*anat*) busto *m*, petto *m*.

bust² [bʌst] *adj* (*coll*: *bankrupt*) rovinato. *v* rovinare.

bustle ['bʌsl] *n* trambusto *m*, agitazione *f*. *v* agitarsi, affaccendarsi.

busy ['bizi] *adj* occupato, attivo, indaffarato. **busybody** *n* ficcanaso *m*. *v* **busy oneself with** occuparsi di.

but [bʌt] *conj* ma. *adv* (*only*) solo, soltanto. *prep* (*except*) eccetto, tranne.

butane ['bjuːtein] *n* butano *m*.

butcher [butʃə] *n* macellaio *m*. **butcher's shop** macelleria *f*. *v* macellare, massacrare. **butchery** *n* strage *f*, massacro *m*.

butler ['bʌtlə] *n* maggiordomo *m*.

butt¹ [bʌt] *n* (*gun*) calcio *m*, impugnatura *f*; (*cigarette*) mozzicone *m*.

butt² [bʌt] *n* (*laughing-stock*) bersaglio *m*, zimbello *m*.

butt³ [bʌt] *n* (*hit*) cornata *f*, cozzo *m*. *v* cozzare, urtare con la testa. **butt in** interrompere, intromettersi.

butter ['bʌtə] *n* burro *m*. *v* imburrare.

buttercup ['bʌtəkʌp] *n* ranuncolo *m*.

butterfly ['bʌtəflai] *n* farfalla *f*.

buttocks ['bʌtəks] *pl n* natiche *f pl*.

button ['bʌtn] *n* bottone *m*. **buttonhole** *n* occhiello *m*, asola *f*. *v* attaccare un bottone. **button up** abbottonare.

buttress ['bʌtris] *n* sostegno *m*, sperone *m*. *v* sostenere.

***buy** [bai] *v* acquistare, comprare. *n* acquisto *m*. **buyer** *n* compratore *m*.

buzz [bʌz] *n* ronzio *m*; (*phone*) telefonata *f*. *v* ronzare; telefonare.

by [bai] *adv* vicino. *prep* da, con, a, di, per, entro. **by and large** generalmente parlando. **by the way** a proposito. **by-law** *n* legge locale *f*. **bypass** *n* circonvallazione *f*; deviazione stradale *f*. **by-product** *n* prodotto secondario *m*. **bystander** *n* astante *m*, *f*. **byword** *n* detto *m*.

C

cab [kab] *n* tassì *m*.

cabaret ['kabərei] *n* caffè concerto *m*, cabaret *m invar*.

cabbage ['kabidʒ] *n* cavolo *m*.

cabin ['kabin] *n* cabina *f*, capanna *f*.

cabinet ['kabinit] *n* (*furniture*) armadietto *m*; (*pol*) gabinetto *m*; (*cocktails*) bar *m invar*. **cabinet-maker** *n* ebanista *m*.

cable ['keibl] *n* cavo *m*; telegramma *m*. *v* telegrafare. **cable-car** *n* funivia *f*.

cackle ['kakl] *v* (*hens*) schiamazzare; (*people*) chiacchierare. *n* schiamazzo *m*, chiacchiera *f*.

cactus ['kaktəs] n cactus m.

caddie ['kadi] n (golf) caddie m.

cadence ['keidəns] n cadenza f.

cadet [kə'det] n cadetto m.

café [kafei] n caffè m.

cafeteria [kafə'tiəriə] n bar-ristorante m.

caffeine ['kafim] n caffeina f.

cage [keidʒ] n gabbia f. v ingabbiare. **cagey** adj cauto.

cake [keik] n (sweet) torta f, focaccia f, dolce m; (soap) saponetta f, pezzo di sapone m. v incrostarsi.

calamine ['kaləmain] n calamina f.

calamity [kə'laməti] n calamità f, disgrazia f.

calcium ['kalsiəm] n calcio m.

calculate ['kalkjuleit] v calcolare. **calculation** n calcolo m. **calculator** n calcolatore m, macchina calcolatrice f.

calendar ['kaləndə] n calendario m.

calf¹ [kaif] n (animal) vitello, -a m, f.

calf² [kaif] n (leg) polpaccio m.

calibre ['kalibə] n calibro m, qualità f.

call [koil] n chiamata f, appello m, grido m, visita f. **call-box** n cabina telefonica f. **call-girl** n ragazza squillo f. v chiamare. **call off** annullare. **call on** visitare. **call up** telefonare; (mil) richiamare sotto le armi. **calling** n vocazione f.

callous ['kaləs] adj insensibile. n insensibilità f.

calm [kaim] adj calmo. v calmare. **calm down** calmarsi. n calma f.

calorie ['kaləri] n caloria f.

came [keim] V **come**.

camel ['kaməl] n cammello m.

camera ['kamərə] n macchina fotografica f. (film/television) **cameraman** n operatore (cinematografico/televisivo) m.

camouflage ['kaməflaiʒ] v mimetizzazione f, mascheramento m. v mimetizzare, mascherare.

camp [kamp] n campo m, accampamento m. **camp-bed** n branda f. **campsite** n campeggio m. v accamparsi, campeggiare.

campaign [kam'pein] n campagna f. v fare una campagna.

campus ['kampəs] n campo universitario m.

camshaft ['kamʃaift] n albero a camme or eccentrici m.

°can¹ [kan] v (be able) potere, essere in grado di; (know how) sapere.

can² [kan] n scatola f, recipiente m. **can-opener** n apriscatole m invar. v mettere in scatola.

Canada ['kanədə] n Canadà m. **Canadian** n(m+f), adj canadese.

canal [kə'nal] n canale m.

canary [kə'neəri] n canarino m.

cancel ['kansəl] v annullare, disdire. **cancellation** n annullamento m.

cancer ['kansə] n cancro m. **Cancer** n Cancro m.

candid ['kandid] adj candido, sincero.

candidate ['kandidət] n candidato, -a m, f.

candle ['kandl] n candela f; (church) cero m. **candlelight** n lume di candela m. **candlestick** n candeliere m.

candour ['kandə] n franchezza f.

candy ['kandi] n (US) caramella f. **candied** adj candito.

cane [kein] n canna f, bastone m; (school) verga f. v bastonare.

canine ['keinain] adj canino.

canister ['kanistə] n latta f.

cannabis ['kanəbis] n hascisc m.

cannibal ['kanibəl] n cannibale m. **cannibalism** n cannibalismo m.

cannon ['kanən] n cannone m. **cannonball** n palla di cannone f.

canoe [kə'nui] n canoa f.

canon ['kanən] n canone m, criterio m; (church dignitary) canonico m. **canonical** adj canonico. **canonize** v canonizzare.

canopy ['kanəpi] n baldacchino m.

canteen [kan'tim] n (dining place) mensa f; (cutlery) posateria f.

canter ['kantə] n piccolo galoppo m. v andare al piccolo galoppo.

canvas ['kanvəs] n tela f; (sails) velatura f.

canvass ['kanvəs] v (orders, votes) sollecitare. **canvasser** n sollecitatore, -trice m, f.

canyon ['kanjən] n burrone m.

cap [kap] n (hat) berretto m; (bathing) cuffia f; (mech) coperchio m, cappello m. v coprire; sorpassare.

capable ['keipəbl] adj capace. **capability** n capacità f.

capacity [kə'pasəti] n capacità f, abilità f. **in the capacity of** nella qualità di.

cape¹ [keip] n (cloak) mantellina f.

cape² [keip] n (geog) capo m, promontorio m.

caper[1] ['keɪpə] n (bot) cappero m.

caper[2] ['keɪpə] n capriola f.

capillary [kə'pɪləri] adj capillare. n vaso capillare m.

capital ['kapɪtl] n capitale f; (arch) capitello m; (letter) maiuscola f. adj capitale. **capitalism** n capitalismo m. **capitalist** n(m+f), adj capitalista. **capitalize** v capitalizzare.

Capitol ['kapɪtl] n Campidoglio m.

capitulate [kə'pɪtjuleɪt] v capitolare. **capitulation** n resa f.

capricious [kə'prɪʃəs] adj capriccioso.

Capricorn ['kaprɪkoɪn] n Capricorno m.

capsicum ['kapsɪkəm] n peperone m.

capsize [kap'saɪz] v capovolgere, capovolgersi.

capsule ['kapsjuɪl] n capsula f.

captain ['kaptɪn] n (chief) capo m; (army, team) capitano m; (navy) capitano di vascello m; comandante m. v comandare.

caption ['kapʃən] n didascalia f.

captive ['kaptɪv] n, adj prigioniero, -a; schiavo, -a. **captivate** v cattivare. **captivity** n cattività f, prigionia f.

capture ['kaptʃə] v catturare. n cattura f. **captor** n catturatore m.

car [kaɪ] n macchina f, automobile f. **car park** parcheggio m. **go by car** andare in macchina.

carafe [kə'raf] n caraffa f.

carat ['karət] n carato m.

caravan ['karəvan] n (vehicle) roulotte (pl -s) f; (travelling group) carovana f.

caraway ['karəweɪ] n cumino m.

carbohydrate [kaɪbə'haɪdreɪt] n carboidrato m.

carbon ['kaɪbən] n carbonio m. **carbon paper** carta carbone f.

carbuncle ['kaɪbʌŋkl] n carbonchio m, pustola f.

carburettor ['kaɪbjuretə] n carburatore m.

carcass ['kaɪkəs] n carcassa f.

card [kaɪd] n carta f; (greetings, etc.) cartolina f; (playing) carta da gioco; (visiting) biglietto da visita m; (index) scheda f.

cardboard ['kaɪdboɪd] n cartone m, cartoncino m.

cardiac ['kaɪdiak] adj cardiaco. **cardiac arrest** arresto cardiaco m.

cardigan ['kaɪdɪgən] n golf m, giacca f.

cardinal ['kaɪdɪnl] nm, adj cardinale.

care [keə] v curare; preoccuparsi; interessarsi. n cura f, premura f; ansietà f; responsabilità f. **carefree** adj spensierato. **care of** presso. **caretaker** n custode m, f. **careful** adj attento; (thorough) curato. **careless** adj disattento, trascurato. **carelessness** n trascuratezza f.

career [kə'rɪə] n carriera f.

caress [kə'res] n carezza f. v accarezzare.

cargo ['kaɪgou] n carico (pl -chi) m.

caricature ['karikətjuə] n caricatura f. v mettere in caricatura. **caricaturist** n caricaturista m, f.

carnage ['kaɪnɪdʒ] n strage f.

carnal ['kaɪnl] adj carnale, sensuale.

carnation [kaɪ'neɪʃən] n garofano m.

carnival ['kaɪnɪvəl] n carnevale m.

carnivorous [kaɪ'nɪvərəs] adj carnivoro. **carnivore** n carnivoro m.

carol ['karəl] n cantico m. **Christmas carol** cantico di Natale m.

carpenter ['kaɪpəntə] n falegname m. **carpentry** n falegnameria f, ebanisteria f.

carpet ['kaɪpɪt] n tappeto m, moquette f.

carriage ['karɪdʒ] n (vehicle) carrozza f, vettura f; (bearing) portamento m; (railway) vagone m.

carrier ['karɪə] n portatore, -trice m, f; (comm) trasportatore m; (med) vettore m. **carrier bag** sacchetto per acquisti m. **carrier pigeon** piccione viaggiatore m.

carrot ['karət] n carota f.

carry ['karɪ] v portare, trasportare. **carrycot** n culla portabile f. **carry on** proseguire, gestire. **carry out** eseguire, realizzare. **carry over** riportare.

cart [kaɪt] n carro m, carretta f. **cartload** n carrettata f. **turn cartwheels** fare la ruota. v portar via.

cartilage ['kaɪtɪlɪdʒ] n cartilagine f.

cartography [kaɪ'tografɪ] n cartografia f. **cartographer** n cartografo, -a m, f.

carton ['kaɪtən] n scatola di cartone f; (cigarettes) stecca f.

cartoon [kaɪ'tum] n (drawing) cartone m; (film) cartone animato m; caricatura f. **cartoonist** n disegnatore, -trice m, f; caricaturista m, f.

cartridge ['kaɪtrɪdʒ] n cartuccia f.

carve [kaɪv] v (meat) tagliare, trinciare; (art) scolpire, intagliare. **carving** n intaglio m. **carving knife** trinciante m.

cascade [kas'keɪd] n cascata f. v scrosciare.

case¹ [keis] n (matter) caso m, fatto m, questione f; (case) cosa f; (law) causa f. processo m. **in any case** ad ogni modo. **in case** qualora. **in most cases** in genere. **in that case** allora.

case² [keis] n (box) scatola f; (luggage) valigia f; (glasses, pens) astuccio f.

cash [kaʃ] v incassare, riscuotere. n denaro m; contanti m pl. **cash desk** cassa f. **cash payment** pagamento in contanti m. **petty cash** spese varie f pl.

cashier¹ [kaʃia] n cassiere, -a m, f.

cashier² [kaʃia] v destituire.

cashmere [kaʃmia] n cachemire m invar.

casing [keisiŋ] n copertura f, rivestimento m.

casino [kəsiːnou] n casinò m.

casket [kaiskit] n cofanetto m; (coffin) cassa da morto f.

casserole [kasəroul] n casseruola f. v cucinare in umido.

cassette [kəset] n cassetta f.

cassock [kasək] n tonaca f.

*****cast** [kaist] n (throw) lancio m, getto m; (mould) forma f, calco m; (metal) fusione f; (theatre) complesso m, insieme degli attori m; (plaster) ingessatura f. v lanciare, gettare; (metal) fondere; (theatre) dare la parte. **cast away** gettar via. **cast iron** ghisa f. **cast-off** adj abbandonato.

caste [kaist] n casta f.

castle [kaisl] n castello m.

castor [kaistə] n (furniture) rotella al piede di mobili f; (condiments) ampolliera f. **castor oil** olio di ricino m. **castor sugar** zucchero semolato m.

castrate [kəstreit] v castrare. **castration** n castratura f.

casual [kaʒuəl] adj casuale, fortuito, disinvolto.

casualty [kaʒuəlti] n vittima f; (accident) incidente m; (hospital) pronto soccorso m.

cat [kat] n gatto, -a m, f. **cat's eye** catarifrangente m. **catty** adj malevolo.

catalogue [katələg] n catalogo (pl -ghi) m, elenco m. v elencare.

catalyst [katəlist] n catalizzatore m. **catalysis** n, pl -ses catalisi f.

catamaran [katəmə'ran] n catamarano m.

catapult [katəpʌlt] n catapulta f, fionda f. v scagliare.

cataract [katərakt] n cateratta f.

catarrh [kə'taɪ] n catarro m.

catastrophe [kə'tastrəfi] n catastrofe f. **catastrophic** adj catastrofico.

*****catch** [katʃ] n preda f, cattura f; (door) spranga f. v prendere, acchiappare; (fish) pescare. **catch-phrase** n frase fatta f. **catch up with** raggiungere. **catchword** n slogan m. **catching** adj (med) contagioso, infettivo.

category ['katəgəri] n categoria f. **categorical** adj categorico.

cater ['keitə] v provvedere cibo. **cater for** provvedere a. **caterer** n approvvigionatore, -trice m, f. **catering** n approvvigionamento m.

caterpillar ['katəpilə] n bruco m.

cathedral [kə'θiːdrəl] n cattedrale f.

catheter ['kaθitə] n catetere m.

cathode ['kaθoud] n catodo m.

catholic [kaθəlik] n, adj cattolico, -a. **catholicism** n cattolicesimo m.

catkin ['katkin] n gattino m.

cattle ['katl] n bestiame m.

caught [kɔːt] V **catch**.

cauliflower ['kɔliflauə] n cavolfiore m.

cause [kɔːz] n causa f, ragione f, motivo m. v causare, provocare, suscitare.

causeway ['kɔːzwei] n strada rialzata f; (main highway) strada maestra f.

caustic ['kɔːstik] adj caustico.

caution ['kɔːʃən] n cautela f, circospezione f; (law) diffida f, ammonimento m. v ammonire, mettere in guardia. **cautious** adj cauto, prudente.

cavalry ['kavəlri] n cavalleria f.

cave [keiv] n caverna f, grotta f.

caviar ['kaviaː] n caviale m.

cavity ['kavəti] n cavità f, buco m.

cease [siːs] v cessare, smettere. **cease-fire** n tregua f, cessate il fuoco m invar. **ceaseless** adj continuo, incessante.

cedar ['siːdə] n cedro m.

ceiling ['siːliŋ] n soffitto m.

celebrate ['seləbreit] v celebrare, festeggiare, far festa. **celebration** n festa f, commemorazione f. **celebrity** n celebrità f.

celery ['seləri] n sedano m.

celestial [si'lestiəl] adj celestiale, celeste.

celibate ['selibət] n, adj celibe m. **celibacy** n celibato m.

cell [sel] n (room) cella f; (biol) cellula f; (elec) pila f.

cellar ['selə] n cantina f, sottosuolo m.

cello ['tʃelou] n violoncello m. **cellist** n violoncellista m, f.

cellular ['seljulə] adj cellulare.

cement [sə'ment] n cemento m. v cementare, consolidare.

cemetery ['semətri] n cimitero m, camposanto m.

censor ['sensə] n censore m. v censurare. **censorious** adj ipercritico. **censorship** n censura f.

censure ['senʃə] n censura f.

census ['sensəs] n censimento m.

cent [sent] n centesimo m, soldo m.

centenary [sen'tiinəri] nm, adj centenario.

centigrade ['sentigreid] adj centigrado.

centimetre ['sentimiitə] n centimetro m.

centipede ['sentipiid] n millepiedi m invar.

centre ['sentə] n centro m. v centrare, accentrare. **central** adj centrale. **central heating** riscaldamento centrale m. **centralization** n centralizzazione f. **centralize** v centralizzare.

centrifugal [sen'trifjugəl] adj centrifugo (m pl -ghi). **centrifuge** n centrifuga f.

century ['sentʃuri] n secolo m.

ceramic [sə'ramik] adj ceramico. **ceramics** n ceramica f.

cereal ['siəriəl] nm, adj cereale.

cerebral ['serəbrəl] adj cerebrale.

ceremony ['serəməni] n cerimonia f, funzione f. **stand on ceremony** far complimenti. **ceremonial** adj solenne, rituale. **ceremonious** adj formalista, cerimonioso.

certain ['səːtn] adj certo, sicuro. **certainly** adv certo, certamente, senza dubbio. **certainty** n certezza f, sicurezza f.

certificate [sə'tifikət] n certificato m, atto m, diploma m. **certify** v certificare, attestare, vidimare; (declare insane) classificare come pazzo.

cervix ['səːviks] n cervice f.

cesspool ['sespuːl] n cloaca f.

chafe [tʃeif] v irritarsi.

chaffinch ['tʃafintʃ] n fringuello m.

chain [tʃein] n catena f. **chain-smoke** v fumare ininterrottamente. **chain store** magazzino a catena m. v incatenare.

chair [tʃeə] n sedia f, seggio m; (university) cattedra f. **chairlift** n seggiovia f. **chairman** n presidente m. v presiedere.

chalk [tʃɔːk] n gesso m. **chalky** adj gessoso; pallido.

challenge ['tʃalindʒ] n sfida f, provocazione f. v sfidare, opporsi a, provocare. **challenging** adj stimolante, provocatorio.

chamber ['tʃeimbə] n camera f. **chambermaid** n cameriera f. **chamber music** musica da camera f.

chameleon [kə'miliən] n camaleonte m.

chamois ['ʃamwaː] n camoscio m; (leather) pelle di camoscio f.

champagne [ʃam'pein] n champagne m.

champion ['tʃampiən] n campione, -essa m, f. **championship** n campionato m. v difendere, sostenere.

chance [tʃaːns] n caso m, fortuna f, opportunità f, rischio m. **by chance** per caso. v (risk) arrischiare; (happen) capitare. adj fortuito.

chancellor ['tʃaːnsələ] n cancelliere m; (university) rettore titolare m.

chandelier [ʃandə'liə] n lampadario m.

change [tʃeindʒ] n cambio m, mutamento m; (money) resto m, spiccioli m pl. v cambiare, mutare, cambiarsi. **changeable** adj variabile, mutevole. **changeability** n variabilità f. **changeless** adj immutevole, costante.

channel ['tʃanl] n canale m. **English Channel** Manica f. v incanalare.

chant [tʃaːnt] n canto m, salmodia f. v cantare, salmodiare.

chaos ['keios] n caos m.

chap[1] [tʃap] v screpolare, screpolarsi. n fessura f.

chap[2] [tʃap] n (fellow) tipo m, tizio m.

chapel ['tʃapəl] n cappella f.

chaperon ['ʃapəroun] n chaperon f. v accompagnare.

chaplain ['tʃaplin] n cappellano m.

chapter ['tʃaptə] n capitolo m.

char[1] [tʃaː] v carbonizzare, bruciare.

char[2] [tʃaː] v fare i lavori di casa. **charwoman** n donna di servizio f, donna a mezzo servizio f.

character ['karəktə] n carattere m, indole f, qualità f; (acting) personaggio m. **characterization** n caratterizzazione f. **characterize** v caratterizzare.

characteristic [,karəktə'ristik] adj caratteristico. n caratteristica f.

charcoal ['tʃaːkoul] n carbone di legna m.

charge [tʃaːdʒ] n spesa f, costo m; cura f, custodia f; (law) accusa f; (mil) carica f. **free of charge** gratis, gratuito. **in charge**

addetto, incaricato. **take charge of** incaricarsi di. v addebitare; caricare. **chargeable** adj addebitabile.

charity ['tʃærəti] n carità f, elemosina f. **charitable** adj caritatevole.

charm [tʃɑːm] n fascino m, incantesimo m; (trinket) portafortuna m invar. v affascinare, incantare. **charming** adj incantevole, affascinante.

chart [tʃɑːt] n mappa f, diagramma f, grafico m, quadro m. v tracciare un diagramma o grafico di.

charter ['tʃɑːtə] n carta f, documento m; (flight) volo charter m; (document) istituire; (hire) noleggiare. **chartered accountant** ragioniere diplomato m.

chase [tʃeis] n caccia f, inseguimento m. v cacciare, inseguire; (jewellery) incastonare; (metal) cesellare.

chasm ['kazəm] n abisso m.

chassis ['ʃæsi] n telaio m.

chaste [tʃeist] adj casto, austero. **chastity** n castità f, purezza f.

chastise [tʃas'taiz] v castigare, punire. **chastisement** n castigo (pl -ghi) m, punizione f.

chat [tʃat] n chiacchiera f, chiacchierata f. v chiacchierare.

chatter ['tʃatə] v chiacchierare; (teeth) battere. n chiacchiera f.

chauffeur ['ʃoufə] n autista m, f.

chauvinism ['ʃouvinizəm] n sciovinismo m. **chauvinist** n(m+f), adj sciovinista.

cheap [tʃiːp] adj economico, a buon mercato, poco caro; (derog) spregevole. **cheapen** v abbassare il prezzo di, screditare.

cheat [tʃiːt] n imbroglione, -a m, f, truffatore, -trice m, f; (cards) baro, -a m, f. v imbrogliare, truffare; barare. **cheating** n imbroglio m, truffa f.

check [tʃek] n controllo m, pausa f, ostacolo m; (chess) scacco m. v controllare, verificare, fermare; (chess) dare scacco. **check in** registrare all'arrivo. **check up on** informarsi su.

check [tʃek] n assegno m. **check book** n. libretto d'assegni m.

cheek [tʃiːk] n guancia f; (insolence) faccia tosta f. **cheeky** adj sfacciato, sfrontato.

cheer [tʃiə] n (shout) applauso m; (mood) allegria f, buonumore m. **cheerio!** interj ciao! arrivederci! v applaudire. **cheer up**

rallegrare, rallegrarsi. **cheerful** adj allegro, di buonumore. **cheerless** adj triste.

cheese [tʃiːz] n formaggio m. **cheesecloth** n garza f. **cheese-paring** adj tirchio.

chef [ʃef] n capocuoco (pl -chi) m.

chemical ['kemikl] n prodotto chimico m. adj chimico.

chemistry ['kemistri] n chimica f. **chemist** n chimico, -a m, f, farmacista m, f. **chemist's shop** farmacia f.

cherish ['tʃeriʃ] v tener caro, nutrire, amare.

cherry ['tʃeri] n (fruit) ciliegia f; (tree) ciliegio m.

chess [tʃes] n scacchi m pl. **chessboard** n scacchiera f.

chest [tʃest] n cassa f; (anat) petto m, torace m. **chest of drawers** cassettone m.

chestnut ['tʃesnʌt] n (fruit) castagna f; (tree) castagno m. adj castano.

chew [tʃuː] v masticare. **chew over** meditare. **chewing-gum** n chewing gum m invar, gomma da masticare f.

chicken ['tʃikin] n pollo m; (chick) pulcino m. **chicken-coop** n pollaio m. **chicken-pox** n varicella f.

chicory ['tʃikəri] n cicoria f, indivia f.

chick-pea ['tʃik,piː] n cece m.

chide [tʃaid] v sgridare.

chief [tʃiːf] nm, pl -s, adj capo, principale.

chilblain ['tʃilblein] n gelone m.

child [tʃaild] n, pl **children** bambino, -a m, f; ragazzo, -a m, f; (offspring) figlio, -a m, f. **childbirth** n parto m. **childhood** n infanzia f. **childish** adj puerile, infantile. **childlike** adj da bambino, semplice, innocente.

chill [tʃil] v raffreddare, agghiacciare. adj freddo, gelido. n freddo m, brivido m; (illness) raffreddore m. **catch a chill** buscarsi un raffreddore. **take the chill off** intiepidire. **chilly** adj freddo, fresco, freddoloso.

chilli ['tʃili] n peperone m, pepe rosso m.

chime [tʃaim] v suonare, scampanare. n scampanio m, rintocco m.

chimney ['tʃimni] n camino m, caminetto m. **chimney-pot** n ciminiera f, fumaiolo m. **chimney-sweep** n spazzacamino m.

chimpanzee [tʃimpən'ziː] n scimpanzè m.

chin [tʃin] n mento m. **chin-strap** n sottogola m invar.

china ['tʃainə] n porcellana f, ceramica f. **china clay** caolino m.

China ['tʃainə] *n* Cina *f*. **Chinese** *n*(*m+f*), *adj* cinese.

chink¹ [tʃiŋk] *n* (*fissure*) fessura *f*, crepa *f*.

chink² [tʃiŋk] *n* (*sound*) tintinnio *m*. *v* tintinnare.

chip [tʃip] *n* scheggia *f*, frammento *m*, truciolo *m*; (*gambling*) cip (*pl* -s) *m*, gettone *m*. **chips** *pl n* (*cookery*) patatine fritte *f pl*. *v* scheggiare. **chip in** intervenire; (*contribute money*) contribuire.

chiropodist [ki'rɔpədist] *n* pedicure *m*, *f invar*.

chirp [tʃəːp] *v* cinguettare, pigolare. *n* cinguettio *m*, pigolio *m*. **chirpy** *adj* allegro.

chisel ['tʃizl] *n* cesello *m*, bulino *m*. *v* cesellare.

chivalry ['ʃivəlri] *n* galanteria *f*. **chivalrous** *adj* galante.

chive [tʃaiv] *n* erba cipollina *f*.

chlorine ['klɔːriːn] *n* cloro *m*.

chlorophyll ['klɔrəfil] *n* clorofilla *f*.

chocolate ['tʃokələt] *n* cioccolato *m*, cioccolatino *m*; (*drink*) cioccolata *f*. *adj* cioccolato *invar*.

choice [tʃois] *n* scelta *f*, assortimento *m*. *adj* scelto, di prima qualità.

choir ['kwaiə] *n* coro *m*.

choke [tʃouk] *v* soffocare, strozzare. *n* (*motor*) valvola dell'aria *f*, diffusore *m*.

cholera ['kɔlərə] *n* colera *m*.

******choose** [tʃuːz] *v* scegliere, eleggere, preferire.

chop¹ [tʃop] *n* (*meat*) braciola *f*; (*blow*) colpo *m*. *v* (*split*) spaccare; (*mince*) tagliuzzare, tritare. **chop down** abbattere. **chopper** *n* accetta *f*. **chopping-block** *n* tagliere *m*. **choppy sea** maretta *f*.

chop² [tʃop] *v* **chop and change** fare e disfare. **chop logic** cavillare.

chops [tʃops] *pl n* mascelle *f pl*. **lick one's chops** leccarsi i baffi.

chord [kɔːd] *n* corda *f*, accordo *m*.

chore [tʃɔː] *n* (*task*) lavoro *m*, compito *m*. **household chores** lavori domestici *m pl*.

choreography [kɔri'ɔgrəfi] *n* coreografia *f*. **choreographer** *n* coreografo, -a *m*, *f*.

chorus ['kɔːrəs] *n* coro *m*. **choral** *adj* corale. **chorister** *n* corista *m*, *f*.

chose [tʃouz] *V* **choose**.

chosen ['tʃouzn] *V* **choose**.

Christ [kraist] *n* Cristo *m*.

christen ['krisn] *v* battezzare; (*name*) chiamare. **christening** *n* battesimo *m*.

Christian ['kristʃən] *n*, *adj* cristiano, -a. **Christian Democrat** democriziano, a *m*, *f*. **Christian name** nome di battesimo *m*. **Christendom** *n* cristianesimo *m*. **Christianity** *n* cristianità *f*.

Christmas ['krisməs] *n* Natale *m*. *adj* di Natale; natalizio.

chromatic [krə'matik] *adj* cromatico.

chromium ['kroumiəm] *n* cromo *m*. **chromium-plate** *v* cromare. **chromium-plating** *n* cromatura *f*.

chromosome ['krouməsoum] *n* cromosoma *m*.

chronic ['kronik] *adj* cronico.

chronicle ['kronikl] *n* cronaca *f*. *v* narrare, fare la cronaca di.

chronological [kronə'lodʒikəl] *adj* cronologico.

chrysalis ['krisəlis] *n* crisalide *f*.

chrysanthemum [kri'sanθəməm] *n* crisantemo *m*.

chubby ['tʃʌbi] *adj* paffuto, grassoccio.

chuck [tʃʌk] *v* gettare, buttare. **chuck out** buttar fuori.

chuckle ['tʃʌkl] *v* ridacchiare, ridere di soppiatto.

chunk [tʃʌŋk] *n* grosso pezzo *m*; (*food*) fetta *f*.

church [tʃəːtʃ] *n* chiesa *f*. **church-goer** *n* praticante *m*, *f*. **churchyard** *n* cimitero *m*, camposanto *m*.

churlish ['tʃəːliʃ] *adj* burbero.

churn [tʃəːn] *n* zangola *f*. *v* agitare, sbattere.

chute [ʃuːt] *n* (*slide*) scivolo *m*; (*waterfall*) cascata *f*.

cider ['saidə] *n* sidro *m*.

cigar [si'gaː] *n* sigaro *m*.

cigarette [sigə'ret] *n* sigaretta *f*. **cigarette-end** *n* mozzicone *m*. **cigarette-lighter** *n* accendino *m*.

cinder ['sində] *n* tizzone *m*, cenere *f*. **burnt to a cinder** carbonizzato.

cine camera ['sini] *n* macchina da presa *f*.

cinema ['sinəmə] *n* cinema *m*.

cinnamon ['sinəmən] *n* cannella *f*.

circle ['səːkl] *n* cerchio *m*, circolo *m*; (*theatre*) galleria *f*; (*environment*) cerchia *f*, ambiente *m*. *v* girare attorno a, accerchiare; (*aeroplane*) volteggiare. **circular** *adj* circolare. *n* volantino *m*. **circulate** *v* circolare, mettere in circolazione, girare. **circulation** *n* (*movement*) circolazione *f*; (*distribution*) tiratura *f*.

circuit ['sɔːkit] n circuito m, giro m.
circumcise ['sɔːkəmsaiz] v circoncidere.
circumcision n circoncisione f.
circumference [sɔːˈkʌmfərəns] n circonferenza f.
circumscribe ['sɔːkəmskraib] v circoscrivere.
circumstance ['sɔːkəmstəns] n circostanza f, condizione f. circumstantial adj particolareggiato. circumstantial evidence prove indiziarie indirette f pl.
circus ['sɔːkəs] n circo m; (convergence of streets) largo m.
cistern ['sistən] n cisterna f, serbatoio m.
cite [sait] v citare. citation n citazione f; (mil) encomio m.
citizen ['sitizn] n cittadino, -a m, f. citizenship n cittadinanza f.
citrus fruits [sitrəs] pl n agrumi m pl.
city ['siti] n città f; (business centre) centro degli affari m. city hall municipio m.
civic ['sivik] adj civico, municipale.
civil ['sivl] adj civile; (polite) cortese, educato. civil engineer ingegnere civile m. civil engineering ingegneria civile f. civil servant funzionario, -a statale m, f. Civil Service amministrazione dello Stato f. civil war guerra civile f.
civilian [səˈviljən] n(m+f), adj civile, borghese. in civilian clothes in borghese.
civilization [ˌsivilaiˈzeiʃən] n civiltà f, civilizzazione f. civilize v civilizzare, incivilire. civilized adj civilizzato.
clad [klad] adj vestito.
claim [kleim] n (right) diritto m; (title) titolo m; (complaint) reclamo m; (insurance) rivendicazione f; asserzione f. v chiedere, esigere; rivendicare; asserire.
clairvoyant [kleəˈvoiənt] n chiaroveggente m, f.
clam [klam] n vongola f.
clamber ['klambə] v arrampicarsi.
clammy ['klami] adj viscido.
clamour ['klamə] n clamore m, schiamazzo m. v strepitare, vociferare. clamorous adj clamoroso, strepitoso.
clamp [klamp] n morsa f, morsetto m. v tener fermo, stringere. clamp down on far smettere.
clan [klan] n tribù f, famiglia f. clannish adj imbevuto di spirito di parte.
clandestine [klanˈdestin] adj clandestino.
clang [klaŋ] n suono metallico m, strepito m. v strepitare.

clap [klap] n (blow, noise) colpo m, scoppio m; applauso m, battimano m. v applaudire. clap hands battere le mani. clap into prison sbattere in prigione.
clapper n (bell) battaglio m. claptrap n sproloquio m.
claret ['klarət] n chiaretto m.
clarify ['klarəfai] v chiarire, raffinare.
clarinet [klarəˈnet] n clarinetto m. clarinettist n clarinettista m, f.
clash [klaʃ] n (noise) strepito m; (collision) urto m; (conflict) scontro m, contrasto m; (colours, sounds) stonatura f. v urtare, urtarsi; scontrarsi; stonare.
clasp [klaːsp] n (device) fermaglio m; (grasp) stretta f; (embrace) abbraccio m. v agganciare, stringere, abbracciare. clasp-knife n coltello a serramanico m.
class [klas] n classe f, categoria f, qualità f. class-mate n compagno, -a di classe m, f. classroom n aula f. v also classify classificare. classy adj di classe.
classic ['klasik] nm, adj classico.
clatter ['klatə] n fracasso m. v far fracasso.
clause [klɔːz] n clausola f, proposizione f, articolo m.
claustrophobia [klɔːstrəˈfoubiə] n claustrofobia f. claustrophobic adj claustrofobico.
claw [klɔː] n artiglio m; (tool) raffio m. v (seize) aggraffare; (scratch) graffiare.
clay [klei] n argilla f, creta f.
clean [kliːn] adj pulito, nitido. clean-shaven adj sbarbato. make a clean breast confessare tutto. v pulire; (remove stains) smacchiare. cleanliness n pulizia f, nettezza f.
cleanse [klenz] v pulire, depurare.
clear [kliə] adj chiaro, limpido; ovvio; libero. keep clear of tenersi lontano da. v chiarire, chiarificare; (empty) vuotare; (overcome) superare; (law) assolvere; (comm) sdoganare. clear away portar via; (table) sparecchiare. clear off andarsene. clear up chiarire, mettere in chiaro; (weather) rasserenarsi; (tidy) rassettare. clearance n (customs) sdoganamento m; (sale) liquidazione f; (distance) gioco m. clearing n (land) radura f; (bank) clearing m; (emptying) sgombro m.
clef [klef] n chiave f.
clench [klentʃ] v stringere. with clenched fists a pugni stretti.

clergy ['klɜːdʒi] n clero m. **clergyman** n ecclesiastico m, pastore m, prete m.

clerical ['klerikəl] adj (church) clericale; (office) d'ufficio, impiegatizio. **clerical error** n errore materiale m, errore di trascrizione m.

clerk [klaːk] n impiegato, -a m, f; commesso, -a m, f.

clever ['klevə] adj abile, ingegnoso, bravo. **cleverness** n abilità f, ingegnosità f, intelligenza f.

cliché ['kliːʃei] n espressione stereotipata f, frase fatta f.

click [klik] n scatto m, schiocco m. v scattare, schioccare.

client ['klaiənt] n cliente m, f.

cliff [klif] n scoglio m.

climate ['klaimət] n clima m.

climax ['klaimæks] n apice m, apogeo m.

climb [klaim] v scalare, salire, arrampicarsi. n scalata f, salita f. **climb down** scendere; (withdraw) tirarsi indietro. **climb over** scavalcare.

*cling [kliŋ] v aggrapparsi, aderire.

clinic ['klinik] n clinica f, ambulatorio m. **clinical** adj clinico.

clip[1] [klip] n (cut) taglio m; (slap) scappellotto m. v tagliare, tosare. **clip the wings of** tarpare le ali a.

clip[2] [klip] n (fastener) fermaglio m, graffa f.

clipper ['klipə] n (boat) clipper m, goletta f.

clitoris ['klitəris] n clitoride f.

cloak [klouk] n (garment) mantello m, cappa f; (mask) maschera f; (pretext) pretesto m, scusa f. v (conceal) celare. **cloak and dagger** cappa e spada. **cloakroom** n guardaroba m.

clock [klɔk] n orologio m. **clockmaker** n orologiaio m. **clockwork** n meccanismo d'orologeria m. **clockwise** adv in senso orario.

clog [klɔg] n (shoe) zoccolo m. v intasare.

cloister ['klɔistə] n chiostro m. v rinchiudere in convento.

close[1] [klouz] v chiudere, concludere. **close down** (shop) chiudere bottega. **close ranks** serrare le file. n (end) fine f.

close[2] [klous] n (place) recinto m. adj vicino, stretto; intimo. **close by** vicino.

closet ['klɔzit] n gabinetto m, studio m. v rinchiudere.

clot [klɔt] n grumo m, coagulo m; (coll) scemo, -a m, f. v raggrumare, coagulare,

coagularsi, rapprendersi. **clotted cream** panna rappresa f.

cloth [klɔθ] n panno m, stoffa f, tessuto m; (for dishes) strofinaccio m.

clothe [klouð] v vestire, abbigliare; (dress) vestirsi. **clothes** pl n vestiti m pl, abiti m pl, indumenti m pl. **clothes line** corda per il bucato f. **clothes peg** molletta f. **clothing** n vestiario m, abbigliamento m.

cloud [klaud] n nuvola f. **cloudburst** n acquazzone m. v annuvolare; (obscure) offuscare. **cloud over** annuvolarsi. **cloudy** adj nuvoloso; (liquid) torbido.

clove[1] [klouv] n (plant) garofano m; (spice) chiodo di garofano m.

clove[2] [klouv] n (part of bulb) spicchio m.

clover ['klouvə] n trifoglio m.

clown [klaun] n pagliaccio m, buffone, -a m, f. v fare il pagliaccio. **clownery** n pagliacciata f. **clownish** adj pagliaccesco.

club [klʌb] n (stick) mazza f, randello m; (golf) bastone da golf m; (social) circolo m, club m; (cards) fiore m. v picchiare, bastonare. **club together** associarsi, riunirsi.

clue [kluː] n indizio m, chiave f.

clump [klʌmp] n gruppo m, cespo m.

clumsy ['klʌmzi] adj maldestro, goffo. **clumsiness** n goffaggine f, malaccortezza f.

clung [klʌŋ] V **cling**.

cluster ['klʌstə] n gruppo m; (bunch) grappolo m.

clutch [klʌtʃ] n presa f; (mot) frizione f. **fall into the clutches of** cadere nelle grinfie di. v afferrare, aggrapparsi a.

clutter ['klʌtə] n ingombro m, confusione f. v ingombrare.

coach [koutʃ] n carrozza f; (bus) corriera f, torpedone m; (tutor) ripetitore, -trice m, f; (sport) allenatore, -trice m, f. **coachbuilder** n carrozziere m. **coachwork** n carrozzeria f. v (teach) dare lezioni private; (sport) allenare.

coagulate [kou'agjuleit] v coagulare, coagularsi, accagliarsi. **coagulant** n coagulante m.

coal [koul] n carbone m. **coal-tar** n catrame m. **coalmine** n miniera di carbone f.

coalition [kouə'liʃən] n coalizione f.

coarse [kɔːs] adj (rude) grossolano, rozzo; (rough) ruvido. **coarseness** n volgarità f, ruvidezza f.

coast [koust] *n* costa *f*, litorale *m*. *v* (*cycling*) scendere a ruota libera; (*motoring*) andare in folle. **coastal** *adj* costiero.

coat [kout] *n* soprabito *m*, cappotto *m*; (*jacket*) giacca *f*; (*animal*) pelame *m*, pelliccia *f*; (*paint*) mano *f*. **coat-hanger** *n* attaccapanni *m*. **coat-of-arms** *n* stemma *m*. **coating** *n* rivestimento *m*. *v* coprire, rivestire.

coax [kouks] *v* blandire, lusingare.

cobbler ['koblə] *n* ciabattino *m*, calzolaio *m*.

cobra ['koubrə] *n* cobra *m*.

cobweb ['kobweb] *n* ragnatela *f*.

cocaine [kə'kein] *n* cocaina *f*.

cock[1] [kok] *n* (*male bird*) uccello maschio *m*; (*chicken*) gallo *m*; (*tap*) rubinetto *m*; (*gun*) cane *m*; (*vulgar*) cazzo *m*. **cocky** *adj* impertinente, pieno di sè.

cock[2] [kok] *v* (*gun*) armare; (*ears*) drizzare. **cock a snook** fare marameo.

cockle ['kokl] *n* cardio *m*. **cockle-shell** *n* conchiglia *f*.

cockpit ['kokpit] *n* (*plane*) carlinga *f*, cabina di guida *f*; (*naval*) cassero *m*.

cockroach ['kokroutʃ] *n* scarafaggio *m*.

cocktail ['kokteil] *n* cocktail *m*.

cocoa ['koukou] *n* cacao *m*.

coconut ['koukənʌt] *n* noce di cocco *f*.

cocoon [kə'kun] *n* bozzolo *m*.

cod [kod] *n* merluzzo *m*. **cod-liver oil** olio di fegato di merluzzo *m*.

code [koud] *n* cifrario *m*, codice *m*.

codeine ['koudiin] *n* codeina *f*.

coeducation [kouedju'keiʃən] *n* scuola mista *f*.

coerce [kou'əis] *v* costringere, forzare.

coexist [kouig'zist] *v* coesistere. **coexistence** *n* coesistenza *f*.

coffee ['kofi] *n* caffè *m*. **coffee bean** chicco di caffè *m*. **coffee pot** caffettiera *f*.

coffin ['kofin] *n* cassa da morto *f*, bara *f*, feretro *m*.

cog [kog] *n* dente *m*.

cohabit [kou'habit] *v* coabitare.

coherent [kou'hiərənt] *adj* coerente. **cohesion** *n* coesione *f*.

coil [koil] *n* rotolo *m*, bobina *f*. *v* avvolgere, attorcigliare, ravvolgere.

coin [koin] *n* moneta *f*.

coincide [kouin'said] *v* coincidere. **coincidence** *n* coincidenza *f*.

colander ['koləndə] *n* colabrodo *m*, colino *m*.

cold [kould] *adj* freddo, gelido; (*unfriendly*) riservato. **be cold** (*person*) aver freddo; (*weather*) far freddo. *n* freddo *m*; (*illness*) raffreddore *m*. **catch a cold** prendere un raffreddore, raffreddarsi. **have a cold** essere raffreddato.

colic ['kolik] *n* colica *f*.

collaborate [kə'labəreit] *v* collaborare. **collaboration** *n* collaborazione *f*. **collaborator** *n* collaboratore, -trice *m, f*.

collapse [kə'laps] *v* crollare, afflosciarsi. *n* crollo *m*, collasso *m*, rovina *f*.

collar ['kolə] *n* colletto *m*, bavero *m*; (*animal*) collare *m*; (*mech*) manicotto *m*. *v* afferrare per il collo; (*take possession*) appropriarsi di.

colleague ['koliig] *n* collega (*m pl* -ghi) *m, f*.

collect [kə'lekt] *v* raccogliere, riunire; (*take delivery*) prendere in consegna, ricuperare; (*make collection of*) far collezione di; (*meet*) radunarsi. **collect call** *n* (*US*) chiamata rovesciata *f*. **collected** *adj* calmo, padrone di sè. **collection** *n* collezione *f*, raccolta *f*; (*charity*) colletta *f*. **collective** *adj* collettivo. **collector** *n* collezionista *m*.

college ['kolidʒ] *n* collegio *m*, istituto *m*, università *f*.

collide [kə'laid] *v* scontrarsi, investire. **collision** *n* urto *m*, scontro *m*, investimento *m*.

colloid ['koloid] *n* colloide *m*.

colloquial [kə'loukwiəl] *adj* familiare. **colloquialism** *n* espressione familiare *f*.

colon ['koulon] *n* (*biol*) colon *m invar*; (*gramm*) due punti.

colonel ['kəinl] *n* colonnello *m*.

colonnade [kolə'neid] *n* colonnata *f*, portico *m*.

colony ['koləni] *n* colonia *f*. **colonial** *n, adj* coloniale. **colonize** *v* colonizzare.

colossal [kə'losəl] *adj* colossale, enorme.

colour ['kʌlə] *n* colore *m*, tinta *f*. **colour bar** discriminazione razziale *f*. **colourblind** *adj* daltonico. *v* colorare, tingere, colorire. **coloured** *adj* colorato, colorito, a colori; (*person*) di colore. **colourful** *adj* pittoresco, a tinte vivaci. **colouring** *n* colorito *m*.

colt [koult] *n* puledro *m*.

column ['koləm] *n* colonna *f*; (*newspaper*) rubrica *f*, cronaca *f*. **columnist** *n* cronista *m, f*, giornalista *m, f*.

coma ['koumə] n coma m invar.

comb [koum] n pettine m; (horse) striglia f; (birds) cresta f. v pettinare, strigliare. comb one's hair pettinarsi.

combat ['kombat] n combattimento m, lotta f. v combattere, lottare. combatant n combattente m, f.

combine [kəm'bain] n 'kombain] v combinare, unire, abbinare, combinarsi. n associazione f, consorzio m. combineharvester n mietitrebbiatrice f. combination n combinazione f.

combustion [kəm'bʌstʃən] n combustione f. internal combustion engine motore a combustione interna m.

*come [kʌm] v venire, arrivare, giungere. come about accadere. come across incontrare per caso, trovare per caso. come in entrare. come into force entrare in vigore. come off (succeed) riuscire. come to blows venire alle mani. come to light venire alla luce. come up salire; (to the surface) venire a galla.

comedy ['komədi] n commedia f. comedian n commediante m, f, comico, -a m, f. comet ['komit] n cometa f.

comfort ['kʌmfət] n agio m, conforto m, consolazione f, agiatezza f. v consolare, confortare.

comic ['komik] n comico, -a m, f; (periodical) giornaletto a fumetti m. adj comico. comic opera opera buffa f. comic strip fumetto m. comical adj comico.

comma ['komə] n virgola f. in inverted commas fra virgolette.

command [kə'maind] n comando m, ordine m. v comandare; (mil) ordinare, avere il comando di. commander n comandante m, f, capo m. commanding position posizione dominante f. commandment n comandamento m, precetto m.

commandeer [komən'diə] v requisire.

commando [kə'maindou] n truppe d'assalto f pl, commando m invar.

commemorate [kə'meməreit] v commemorare. commemoration n commemorazione f.

commence [kə'mens] v cominciare, iniziare. commencement n inizio m, principio m.

commend [kə'mend] v raccomandare, lodare. commendable adj lodevole, encomiabile. commendation n lode f, encomio m.

comment ['koment] n commento m, osservazione f, rilievo m. v commentare, fare delle osservazioni. commentary n commentario m, cronaca f. commentator n commentatore, -trice m, f; cronista m, f; radiocronista m, f.

commerce ['komɔis] n commercio m, scambi m pl. commercial adj commerciale.

commiserate [kə'mizəreit] v commiserare, compiangere.

commission [kə'miʃən] n commissione f, delegazione f; (authority) incarico m; (comm) provvigione f; (mil) brevetto da ufficiale m. v incaricare, dare una carica; nominare ufficiale; (ship) armare. commissionaire n portiere m. commissioned officer ufficiale m. non-commissioned officer sottufficiale m. commissioner n commissario m.

commit [kə'mit] v commettere; affidare, rimettere. commit oneself impegnarsi. commit to memory imparare a memoria. commitment n impegno m. committed adj impegnato.

committee [kə'miti] n comitato m, commissione f.

commodity [kə'modəti] n merce f, derrata f.

common ['komən] adj comune, ordinario, volgare. n parco demaniale m. commonplace adj ordinario, banale. common sense buonsenso m.

commotion [kə'mouʃən] n agitazione f, confusione f.

commune¹ [kə'mjuun] v intrattenersi, discutere.

commune² ['komjuun] n comune m, comunità f. communal adj comunale, in comune.

communicate [kə'mjuunikeit] v comunicare, informare, trasmettere. communicate with essere in comunicazione con. communication n comunicazione f, informazione f, rapporto m.

communion [kə'mjuunjən] n comunione f.

communism ['komjunizəm] n comunismo m. communist n(m+f), adj comunista.

community [kə'mjuunəti] n comunità f.

commute [kə'mjuut] v commutare; (travel) fare il pendolare. commuter n pendolare m, f.

compact¹ [kəm'pakt; n 'kompakt] adj compatto, serrato. n (powder) portacipria m invar.

compact[1] ['kɔmpakt] n (*agreement*) patto m, accordo m.

companion [kəm'panjən] n compagno, -a m, f. **companionship** n compagnia f, cameratismo m, amicizia f.

company ['kʌmpəni] n compagnia f, comitiva f; (*comm*) ditta f, società f; (*ship*) equipaggio m. **in the company of** accompagnato da. **part company with** separarsi da.

compare [kəm'peə] v paragonare, confrontare, essere paragonabile a. **comparable** adj paragonabile, comparabile. **comparative** adj comparativo, relativo. **compared with** rispetto a, di fronte a. **comparison** n confronto m, paragone m.

compartment [kəm'pɑːtmənt] n compartimento m, casella f; (*railway*) scompartimento m.

compass ['kʌmpəs] n bussola f. **compasses** pl n compasso m sing. v cingere, circondare.

compassion [kəm'paʃən] n compassione f, pietà f, misericordia f. **compassionate** adj misericordioso, pieno di compassione.

compatible [kəm'patəbl] adj compatibile. **compatibility** n compatibilità f.

compel [kəm'pel] v costringere, obbligare, forzare. **compel respect** farsi rispettare. **compelling** adj irresistibile.

compensate ['kɔmpənseit] v compensare, ricompensare, indennizzare. **compensation** n compenso m, ricompensa f; (*comm*) compensazione f.

compete [kəm'piːt] v concorrere, fare concorrenza a, gareggiare. **competition** n (*contest*) gara f; (*rivalry*) concorrenza f; (*exam*) concorso m. **competitive** adj competitivo. **competitor** n concorrente m, f; rivale m, f.

competent ['kɔmpətənt] adj competente, capace. **competence** n competenza f, capacità f.

compile [kəm'pail] v compilare. **compilation** n compilazione f.

complacent [kəm'pleisnt] adj soddisfatto di sè.

complain [kəm'plein] v lamentarsi, lagnarsi. **complaint** n (*discontent*) lamentela f; (*merchandise*) reclamo m; (*illness*) malattia f.

complement ['kɔmpləmənt] n complemento m. v completare, fare da complemento a. **complementary** adj complementare.

complete [kəm'pliːt] adj completo, intero. v completare, finire. **completion** n fine f, compimento m.

complex ['kɔmpleks] nm, adj complesso.

complexion [kəm'plekʃən] n (*skin*) colorito m; (*nature*) aspetto m.

complicate ['kɔmplikeit] v complicare. **complicated** adj complicato, complesso. **complication** n difficoltà f.

complicity [kəm'plisəti] n complicità f.

compliment ['kɔmpləmənt] n complimento m. v congratularsi con. **complimentary** adj (*flattering*) lusinghiero; (*free*) di favore.

comply [kəm'plai] v ubbidire, acconsentire. **in compliance with** conforme a.

component [kəm'pəunənt] nm, adj componente.

compose [kəm'pəuz] v comporre. **composed** adj calmo. **composer** n compositore, -trice m, f. **composite** adj composto, misto. **composition** n composizione f.

compost ['kɔmpost] n concime m.

composure [kəm'pəuʒə] n compostezza f, calma f.

compound[1] [kəm'paund; n 'kɔmpaund] v (*compose*) comporre; (*mix*) mescolare; (*settle*) regolare. n composto m, miscela f. adj composto.

compound[2] ['kɔmpaund] n (*enclosure*) campo m, accampamento m.

comprehend [kɔmpri'hend] v comprendere, capire. **comprehensible** adj comprensibile. **comprehension** n comprensione f. **comprehensive** adj comprensivo, esauriente.

compress [kəm'pres; n 'kɔmpres] v comprimere. n compressa f. **compression** n compressione f.

comprise [kəm'praiz] v includere.

compromise ['kɔmprəmaiz] n compromesso m. v giungere a un compromesso; (*endanger*) compromettere. **compromising** adj compromettente, imbarazzante.

compulsion [kəm'pʌlʃən] n costrizione f, obbligo m. **compulsive** adj coercitivo. **compulsory** adj obbligatorio.

compunction [kəm'pʌŋkʃən] n rimorso m.

computer [kəm'pjuːtə] n computer (*pl* -s) m, elaboratore elettronico m.

comrade ['kɔmrid] n compagno, -a m, f; camerata m, f. **comradeship** n cameratismo m.

concave [kɒnˈkeiv] *adj* concavo.

conceal [kənˈsiːl] *v* celare, nascondere.

concede [kənˈsiːd] *v* concedere, ammettere, riconoscere.

conceit [kənˈsiːt] *n* vanità *f*, presunzione *f*. **conceited** *adj* vanitoso, presuntuoso.

conceive [kənˈsiːv] *v* concepire; immaginare. **conceivable** *adj* concepibile, immaginabile.

concentrate [ˈkɒnsəntreit] *v* concentrare. *n* concentrato *m*. **concentration** *n* concentrazione *f*. **concentration camp** campo di concentramento *m*.

concentric [kɒnˈsentrik] *adj* concentrico.

concept [ˈkɒnsept] *n* concetto *m*, nozione *f*.

conception [kənˈsepʃən] *n* concezione *f*, idea *f*.

concern [kənˈsəːn] *n* (*care*) sollecitudine *f*, preoccupazione *f*; (*business*) affare *m*, faccenda *f*; interesse *m*; (*firm*) azienda *f*, ditta *f*. *v* riguardare, toccare. **concerned** *adj* in questione; (*anxious*) preoccupato. **concerning** *prep* riguardo a, in merito a, inerente a.

concert [ˈkɒnsət] *n* concerto *m*. **concerted** *adj* predisposto, stabilito d'accordo con altri.

concertina [kɒnsəˈtiːnə] *n* fisarmonica *f*.

concerto [kənˈtʃəːtou] *n* concerto *m*.

concession [kənˈseʃən] *n* concessione *f*.

conciliate [kənˈsilieit] *v* conciliare. **conciliation** *n* conciliazione *f*. **conciliatory** *adj* conciliatorio.

concise [kənˈsais] *adj* conciso, breve.

conclude [kənˈkluːd] *v* concludere, dedurre. **conclusion** *n* conclusione *f*, fine *f*. **in conclusion** *adv* in fine, insomma. **conclusive** *adj* conclusivo.

concoct [kənˈkɒkt] *v* (*contrive*) inventare. **concoction** *n* intruglio *m*, pasticcio *m*.

concrete [ˈkɒnkriːt] *adj* concreto. *n* calcestruzzo *m*, cemento *m*. **concrete mixer** betoniera *f*. **reinforced concrete** cemento armato *m*. *v* cementare, rivestire di calcestruzzo.

concussion [kənˈkʌʃən] *n* commozione cerebrale *f*.

condemn [kənˈdem] *v* condannare. **condemnation** *n* condanna *f*.

condense [kənˈdens] *v* condensare. **condensation** *n* condensazione *f*.

condescend [kɒndiˈsend] *v* degnarsi. **condescending** *adj* condiscendente. **condescension** *n* condiscendenza *f*.

condition [kənˈdiʃən] *n* condizione *f*. *v* condizionare. **conditional** *adj* condizionale.

condolence [kənˈdouləns] *n* condoglianza *f*. **express condolences** fare le condoglianze.

condom [ˈkɒndɒm] *n* preservativo *m*.

condone [kənˈdoun] *v* perdonare.

conducive [kənˈdjuːsiv] *adj* contribuente.

conduct [kənˈdʌkt; *n* ˈkɒndʌkt] *v* condurre; (*music*) dirigere. **conduct oneself** comportarsi. *n* condotta *f*, comportamento *m*.

conductor [kənˈdʌktə] *n* (*transport*) bigliettario, -a *m, f*; (*music*) direttore d'orchestra *m*; (*physics*) conduttore *m*.

cone [koun] *n* cono *m*; (*fir*) pigna *f*.

confectioner [kənˈfekʃənə] *n* pasticciere, -a *m, f*. **confectioner's shop** *n* pasticceria *f*.

confederate [kənˈfedərət] *adj* confederato, alleato. *v* confederarsi, allearsi.

confer [kənˈfəː] *v* conferire, consultarsi. **conference** *n* conferenza *f*. **conferment** *n* conferimento *m*.

confess [kənˈfes] *v* confessare, ammettere; (*rel*) confessarsi. **confession** *n* confessione *f*, professione *f*. **confessor** *n* confessore *m*.

confetti [kənˈfeti] *n* coriandoli *m pl*.

confide [kənˈfaid] *v* confidare. **confidant, -e** *n* confidente *m, f*. **confidence** *n* fiducia *f*; sicurezza di sè *f*. **have confidence in** aver fiducia in. **in confidence** in confidenza. **confident** *adj* fiducioso, sicuro. **confidential** *adj* riservato.

confine [kənˈfain] *n* confine *m*. *v* relegare; (*to barracks*) consegnare. **be confined** (*childbirth*) partorire. **confinement** *n* imprigionamento *m*, segregazione *f*; (*childbirth*) parto *m*.

confirm [kənˈfəːm] *v* confermare; (*statement*) ribadire; (*rel*) cresimare; (*law*) omologare. **confirmation** *n* conferma *f*; (*law*) ratifica *f*; (*rel*) confermazione *f*, cresima *f*. **confirmed** *adj* confermato; (*belief*) convinto, impenitente.

confiscate [ˈkɒnfiskeit] *v* confiscare.

conflict [ˈkɒnflikt; *v* kənˈflikt] *n* conflitto *m*, lotta *f*, contrasto *m*. *v* **conflict with** essere in disaccordo *or* contrasto con. **conflicting** *adj* (*evidence*) contraddittorio; (*interests*) contrastante.

conform [kən'fɔːm] v conformare, adattarsi. **conformist** n conformista m, f. **conformity** n conformità f. **in conformity with** conforme a, conformemente a.

confound [kən'faund] v sconcertare, sconvolgere.

confront [kən'frʌnt] v affrontare; (law) mettere a confronto. **confrontation** n confronto m.

confuse [kən'fjuːz] v confondere, sconcertare, disorientare, scambiare. **confusing** adj sconcertante, che rende perplesso. **confusion** n confusione f, disordine m.

congeal [kən'dʒiːl] v (freeze) congelare, congelarsi; coagulare, coagularsi.

congenial [kən'dʒiːniəl] adj congeniale.

congenital [kən'dʒenitl] adj congenito, innato.

congested [kən'dʒestid] adj congestionato. **congestion** n congestione f.

conglomeration [kəngloməˈreiʃən] n conglomerazione f.

congratulate [kən'grætjuleit] v congratularsi con, felicitare, felicitarsi con. **congratulation** n felicitazione f. **congratulations!** interj auguri!

congregate [ˈkɔŋgrigeit] v congregare, riunirsi. **congregation** n (rel) comunità f, adunanza dei fedeli f.

congress [ˈkɔŋgres] n congresso m.

conical [ˈkɔnikəl] adj conico.

conifer [ˈkɔnifə] n conifera f.

conjecture [kən'dʒektʃə] v supporre. n supposizione f.

conjugal [ˈkɔndʒugəl] adj coniugale.

conjugate [ˈkɔndʒugeit] v coniugare. **conjugation** n coniugazione f.

conjunction [kən'dʒʌŋkʃən] n congiunzione f.

conjunctivitis [kəndʒʌŋkti'vaitis] n congiuntivite f.

conjure [ˈkʌndʒə; (invoke) kən'dʒuə] v fare giochi di prestigio; (invoke) scongiurare. **conjure up** v evocare. **conjurer**, **-trice** m, f. **conjuring trick** gioco di prestigio m.

connect [kə'nekt] v connettere, congiungere; associare; (trains) far coincidenza. **connection** n connessione f, rapporto m; coincidenza f. **in connection with** in merito a.

connoisseur [kɔnə'səː] n intenditore, -trice m, f.

connotation [kɔnə'teiʃən] n significato implicito m.

conquer [ˈkɔŋkə] v conquistare, vincere. **conqueror** n conquistatore, -trice m, f; vincitore, -trice m, f. **conquest** n conquista f, vittoria f.

conscience [ˈkɔnʃəns] n coscienza f.

conscientious [kɔnʃi'enʃəs] adj coscienzioso, diligente. **conscientious objector** obiettore di coscienza m.

conscious [ˈkɔnʃəs] adj conscio, cosciente; (deliberate) intenzionale. **consciousness** n coscienza f.

conscript [ˈkɔnskript] v chiamare alle armi, arruolare. n soldato di leva m. **conscription** n leva f.

consecrate [ˈkɔnsikreit] v consacrare. **consecration** n consacrazione f.

consecutive [kən'sekjutiv] adj consecutivo.

consensus [kən'sensəs] n consenso m, assenso m.

consent [kən'sent] v consentire, acconsentire. n consenso m, benestare m, accordo m.

consequence [ˈkɔnsikwəns] n conseguenza f, effetto m, importanza f. **consequently** adv di conseguenza, quindi, perciò.

conserve [kən'səːv] v conservare, preservare. n conserva f. **conservation** n preservazione f. **conservative** adj conservativo, cauto; (pol) conservatore. **conservatoire** n (music) conservatorio m. **conservatory** n serra f.

consider [kən'sidə] v considerare, giudicare, ritenere, pensare. **considerable** adj notevole. **considerate** adj sollecito, riguardoso. **consideration** n considerazione f, riflessione f; (feeling, regard) riguardo m, sollecitudine f, delicatezza f.

consign [kən'sain] v consegnare, affidare. **consignee** n destinatario, -a m, f. **consignor** n mittente m, f. **consignment** n spedizione f, invio m; (goods) partita di merce f.

consist [kən'sist] v consistere (in), essere composto. **consistency** n consistenza f. **consistent** adj regolare, costante, coerente.

console[1] [kən'soul] v confortare. **consolation** n consolazione f, conforto m.

console[2] [ˈkɔnsoul] n (arch) mensola f; (furniture) mobile m; (tech) quadro di comando m.

consolidate [kən'sɔlideit] *v* consolidare. **consolidation** *n* consolidazione *f*.

consommé [kən'sɔmei] *n* brodo *m*.

consonant ['kɔnsənənt] *n* consonante *f*.

consortium [kən'sɔːtiəm] *n* consorzio *m*.

conspicuous [kən'spikjuəs] *adj* cospicuo, evidente.

conspire [kən'spaiə] *v* complottare. **conspiracy** *n* complotto *m*, congiura *f*.

constable ['kʌnstəbl] *n* vigile *m*, poliziotto *m*.

constant ['kɔnstənt] *adj* costante, invariabile. *n* costante *f*.

constellation [kɔnstə'leiʃən] *n* costellazione *f*.

constipation [kɔnsti'peiʃən] *n* stitichezza *f*. **constipated** *adj* stitico.

constitute ['kɔnstitjuːt] *v* costituire, creare. **constituent** *nf, adj* costituente. **constituency** *n* collegio elettorale *m*. **constitution** *n* costituzione *f*; statuto *m*; (*health*) salute *f*.

constraint [kən'streint] *n* (*restriction*) costrizione *f*; (*embarrassment*) imbarazzo *m*.

constrict [kən'strikt] *v* stringere, restringere, comprimere. **constriction** *n* restringimento *m*; (*tight feeling*) oppressione *f*.

construct [kən'strʌkt] *v* costruire. **construction** *n* costruzione *f*; (*building*) edificio *m*; (*meaning*) senso *m*. **constructive** *adj* costruttivo, positivo.

consul ['kɔnsəl] *n* console. **consulate** *n* consolato *m*.

consult [kən'sʌlt] *v* consultare; (*consider*) tener conto di. **consultant** *n* consulente *m, f*, esperto, -a *m, f*. **consultation** *n* consultazione *f*; (*med*) consulta *f*. **consulting room** (*med*) studio *m*.

consume [kən'sjuːm] *v* consumare. **consumer** *n* consumatore, -trice *m, f*. **consumer goods** generi di consumo *m pl*.

contact ['kɔntakt] *n* contatto *m*; (*acquaintance*) conoscenza *f*. *v* mettere in contatto con, mettersi in contatto. **contact lens** *n* lente a contatto *f*.

contagious [kən'teidʒəs] *adj* contagioso.

contain [kən'tein] *v* contenere, includere. **container** *n* recipiente *m*.

contaminate [kən'taməneit] *v* contaminare, inquinare. **contamination** *n* contaminazione *f*, inquinamento *m*.

contemplate ['kɔntəmpleit] *v* contemplare, meditare; (*intend to*) proporsi,

aver intenzione di. **contemplation** *n* contemplazione *f*.

contemporary [kən'tempərəri] *n, adj* contemporaneo, -a; coetaneo, -a.

contempt [kən'tempt] *n* disprezzo *m*. **contempt of court** oltraggio alla corte *m*. **contemptible** *adj* spregevole. **contemptuous** *adj* sprezzante, altezzoso.

contend [kən'tend] *v* contendere, sostenere, affermare. **bone of contention** pomo della discordia *m*.

content[1] ['kɔntent] *n* contenuto *m*.

content[2] [kən'tent] *adj* contento, soddisfatto. *v* accontentare.

contest ['kɔntest; *v* kən'test] *n* gara *f*, lotta *f*. *v* contestare, impugnare.

context ['kɔntekst] *n* contesto *m*.

continent ['kɔntinənt] *nm, adj* continente. **continental** *adj* continentale.

contingency [kən'tindʒənsi] *n* contingenza *f*.

continue [kən'tinjuː] *v* continuare, proseguire. **continual** *or* **continuous** *adj* continuo, ininterrotto. **continuation** *n* seguito *m*. **continuity** *n* continuità *f*; (*film*) sceneggiatura *f*.

contort [kən'tɔtt] *v* contorcere. **contortion** *n* contorcimento *m*. **contortionist** *n* contorsionista *m, f*.

contour ['kɔntuə] *n* contorno *m*. **contour map/line** carta/curva ipsometrica *f*.

contraband ['kɔntrəband] *n* contrabbando *m*.

contraception [kɔntrə'sepʃən] *n* pratiche antifecondative *f pl*. **contraceptive** *nm, adj* anticoncezionale, anticoncettivo, antifecondativo.

contract ['kɔntrakt; *v* kən'trakt] *n* patto *m*, accordo *m*, contratto *m*. *v* (*draw together*) contrarre, restringere; (*acquire, take on*) contrarre; (*enter into*) contrattare. **contraction** *n* contrazione *f*.

contradict [kɔntrə'dikt] *v* contraddire, smentire. **contradiction** *n* contraddizione *f*, smentita *f*.

contralto [kən'traltou] *n* contralto *m*.

contraption [kən'trapʃən] *n* congegno *m*, aggeggio *m*.

contrary ['kɔntrəri] *nm, adj* contrario, opposto. **contrary to** contrariamente a. **on the contrary** al contrario, anzi.

contrast ['kɔntrast; *v* kən'traist] *n* contrasto *m*, antitesi *f invar*. *v* contrastare, confrontare, mettere in contrasto.

contravene [kɒntrə'viːn] v contravvenire a.

contribute [kən'trɪbjut] v contribuire. **contributor** n contributore, -trice m, f; (writer) collaboratore, -trice m, f. **contribution** n contributo m; (writing) articolo m.

contrive [kən'traɪv] v riuscire a, escogitare.

control [kən'troul] v controllare, dominare. n controllo m, autorità f. **controls** pl n comandi m pl. **remote control** controllo a distanza m, telecontrollo m.

controversy [kən'trɒvəsi] n controversia f. **controversial** adj controverso.

convalesce [kɒnvə'les] v rimettersi in salute. **convalescence** n convalescenza f. **convalescent home** convalescenziario m.

convector [kən'vektə] nm, adj convettore.

convenience [kən'viːnjəns] n comodo m, comodità f, convenienza f. **at the earliest convenience** alla prima occasione. **public convenience** gabinetto pubblico m. **convenient** adj conveniente, comodo.

convent ['kɒnvənt] n convento m.

convention [kən'venʃən] n convenzione f; (meeting) adunata f; (agreement) accordo m. **convene** v convocare, adunare. **conventional** adj convenzionale.

converge [kən'vɜːdʒ] v convergere.

converse [kən'vɜːs; n, adj 'kɒnvɜːs] v conversare. nm, adj contrario, opposto. **conversation** n conversazione f.

convert [kən'vɜːt; n 'kɒnvɜːt] v convertire, trasformare. n convertito, -a m, f. **convertible** n (car) auto decapottabile f.

convex ['kɒnveks] adj convesso.

convey [kən'veɪ] v trasportare; (impart) esprimere. **conveyance** n mezzo di trasporto m; (law) atto di cessione m. **conveyor belt** nastro trasportatore m.

convict [kən'vɪkt; n 'kɒnvɪkt] v condannare. n carcerato, -a m, f; prigioniero, -a m, f.

conviction [kən'vɪkʃən] n (sentence) condanna f; persuasione f, convinzione f.

convince [kən'vɪns] v convincere, persuadere.

convivial [kən'vɪvɪəl] adj allegro.

convoy ['kɒnvoɪ] n convoglio m, scorta f. v convogliare, scortare.

convulsion [kən'vʌlʃən] n convulsione f. v **be convulsed (with laughter)** contorcersi (dalle risa).

cook [kuk] n cuoco, -a m, f. v cuocere,

cucinare, far la cucina. **cook the books** falsificare i registri. **cooker** n fornello m. **cookery** or **cooking** n cucina f, arte culinaria f.

cool [kuːl] adj fresco, calmo. v rinfrescare, raffreddare. **cooler** n refrigerante m; (slang) gattabuia f.

coop [kuːp] n stia f. v **coop up** stipare, pigiarsi.

cooperate [kou'ɒpəreɪt] v cooperare. **cooperation** n cooperazione f, collaborazione f. **cooperative** adj cooperativo. **cooperator** n collaboratore, -trice m, f.

coordinate [kou'ɔːdɪneɪt] v coordinare. n coordinata f. adj coordinato. **coordination** n coordinazione f.

cop [kɒp] n (slang) poliziotto m. v pescare. **cop it** prenderle.

cope¹ [koup] v riuscire. **cope with** far fronte a.

cope² [koup] n cappa f.

Copenhagen [koupən'heɪgən] n Copenhagen f.

copious ['koupiəs] adj abbondante.

copper¹ ['kɒpə] n rame m. adj color rame.

copper² ['kɒpə] n (slang) poliziotto m.

copulate ['kɒpjuleɪt] v accoppiarsi. **copulation** n accoppiamento m, copulazione f.

copy ['kɒpi] v copiare; ricopiare, riprodurre; imitare. n copia f, trascrizione f, imitazione f; (book) esemplare m. **copyright** n diritti d'autore m pl.

coral ['kɒrəl] n corallo m.

cord [kɔːd] n corda f; (string) spago m; (elec) filo m, cavo m.

cordial ['kɔːdɪəl] adj cordiale, caloroso.

cordon [kɔːdn] n cordone m. **cordon off** fare cordone intorno a, isolare.

corduroy ['kɔːdəroɪ] n fustagno m.

core [kɔː] n centro m; (fruit) torsolo m; (mech) anima f.

cork [kɔːk] n (bark) sughero m; (stopper) tappo m, turacciolo m. **corkscrew** n cavatappi m invar. v turare. **corked** adj (wine) che sa di turacciolo.

corn¹ [kɔːn] n (grain) grano m; (wheat) frumento m; (maize) mais m invar, granturco m. **cornflour** n farina finissima di granturco f. **corny** adj banale.

corn² [kɔːn] n (toe) callo m.

corner ['kɔːnə] n angolo m; (football) corner m invar, calcio d'angolo m. v (prevent escape) mettere alle strette; (stock) accaparrare; (drive) fare una curva.

cornet ['kɔɪnit] *n* (*music*) cornetta *f*; (*ice-cream*) cono *m*.

coronary ['kɔrənəri] *adj* coronario. **coronary thrombosis** trombosi coronaria *f*.

coronation [kɔrə'neiʃən] *n* incoronazione *f*.

corporal[1] ['kɔɪpərəl] *adj* (*bodily*) corporale; (*material*) corporeo.

corporal[2] ['kɔɪpərəl] *n* caporale, -a *m, f*.

corporation [kɔɪpə'reiʃən] *n* corporazione *f*, ente *m*.

corps [kɔɪ] *n* corpo *m*.

corpse [kɔɪps] *n* cadavere *m*.

correct [kə'rekt] *v* correggere. *adj* corretto, giusto, esatto. **correction** *n* correzione *f*, rettifica *f*.

correlate ['kɔrəleit] *v* mettere in correlazione. **correlated** *adj* correlativo. **correlation** *n* correlazione *f*.

correspond [kɔrə'spɔnd] *v* corrispondere, equivalere; (*letters*) essere in corrispondenza, scambiare lettere. **correspondence** *n* corrispondenza *f*, scambio di lettere *m*. **correspondent** *n* corrispondente *m, f*. **corresponding** *adj* corrispondente.

corridor ['kɔridɔɪ] *n* corridoio *m*.

corrode [kə'roud] *v* corrodere, corrodersi. **corrosion** *n* corrosione *f*. **corrosive** *adj* corrosivo.

corrupt [kə'rʌpt] *v* corrompere. *adj* corrotto. **corruption** *n* corruzione *f*.

corset ['kɔɪsit] *n* busto *m*; (*orthopaedic*) corsetto *m*.

Corsica ['kɔɪsikə] *n* Corsica *f*. **Corsican** *n*, *adj* corso, -a.

cosh [kɔʃ] *n* randello *m*.

cosmetic [koz'metik] *nm, adj* cosmetico. **cosmetics** *pl n* prodotti di bellezza *m pl*.

cosmic ['kozmik] *adj* cosmico. **cosmonaut** *n* cosmonauta *m, f*.

cosmopolitan [kozmə'politən] *nm, adj* cosmopolitano.

***cost** [kost] *n* costo *m*, prezzo *m*. *v* costare. **costly** *adj* costoso, caro.

costume ['kostjuɪm] *n* costume *m*, abito *m*; (*suit*) tailleur *m*.

cosy ['kouzi] *adj* comodo, intimo, accogliente.

cot [kot] *n* lettino *m*, culla *f*.

cottage ['kotidʒ] *n* villino *m*, casetta *f*.

cotton ['kotn] *n* cotone *m*. **cotton-wool** *n* bambagia *f*, ovatta *f*; (*med*) cotone idrofilo *m*.

couch [kautʃ] *n* divano *m*, canapè *m*.

cough [kof] *n* tosse *f*. **cough mixture** sciroppo per la tosse *m*. *v* tossire.

could [kud] *V* **can**[1]

council ['kaunsəl] *n* consiglio *m*; (*rel*) concilio *m*. **councillor** *n* consigliere *m*, membro del consiglio *m*.

counsel ['kaunsəl] *n* (*advice*) consiglio *m*; (*lawyer*) avvocato *m*. *v* raccomandare, consigliare. **counsellor** *n* consigliere, -a *m, f*; (*consultant*) consulente *m, f*.

count[1] [kaunt] *v* contare, includere. **count on** contare su, fare affidamento su. *n* conto *m*, calcolo *m*; (*law*) capo d'accusa *m*.

count[2] [kaunt] *n* conte *m*. **countess** *n* contessa *f*.

countenance ['kauntinəns] *n* espressione *f*. *v* tollerare.

counter[1] ['kauntə] *n* (*token*) gettone *m*; (*table top*) banco *m*; (*device*) calcolatore *m*.

counter[2] ['kauntə] *v* opporsi a, controbattere. *adj* contrario, opposto.

counteract [kauntə'rakt] *v* neutralizzare, invalidare, mandare a vuoto.

counter-attack *n* contrattacco *m*. *v* contrattaccare.

counterfeit ['kauntəfit] *adj* falsificato, falso. *v* falsificare.

counterfoil ['kauntəfoil] *n* matrice *f*, figlia *f*.

counterpart ['kauntəpaɪt] *n* contropartita *f*, complemento *m*.

country ['kʌntri] *n* (*countryside*) campagna *f*; (*state*) paese *m*; (*homeland*) patria *f*.

county ['kaunti] *n* provincia *f*, regione *f*.

coup [kuɪ] *n* coup de grace colpo di grazia *m*. **coup d'état** colpo di stato *m*.

couple ['kʌpl] *n* coppia *f*, paio *m* (*pl* -a *f*). *v* accoppiare, abbinare.

coupon ['kuɪpon] *n* tagliando *m*, scontrino *m*.

courage ['kʌridʒ] *n* coraggio *m*. **courageous** *adj* coraggioso.

courgette [kuə'ʒet] *n* zucchina *f*, zucchino *m*.

courier ['kuriə] *n* accompagnatore, -trice *m, f*; messaggero, -a *m, f*.

course [kɔɪs] *n* corso *m*, percorso *m*, linea *f*; (*food*) piatto *m*; (*aircraft*) rotta *f*. **in due course** a tempo debito. **in the course of** durante, nel corso di. **of course** naturalmente, beninteso.

court [kɔɪt] n corte f; (law) tribunale m; (tennis) campo m. **court-martial** n corte marziale f. **courtyard** n cortile m. v corteggiare, far la corte a.

courteous ['kɔːtiəs] adj cortese, gentile. **courtesy** n cortesia f, gentilezza f.

cousin ['kʌzn] n cugino, -a m, f.

cove [kouv] n insenatura f.

cover ['kʌvə] n coperta f, copertura f; (shelter) riparo m; (book) copertina f. v coprire, ricoprire; (travel) percorrere; (journalism) riferire. **covering** n copertura f. **covering letter** lettera d'accompagnamento f.

cow [kau] n vacca f, mucca f. v intimidire.

coward ['kauəd] n vigliacco, -a m, f; vile m, f. **cowardly** adj vigliacco, vile. **cowardice** n vigliaccheria f.

cower ['kauə] v accovacciarsi, rannicchiarsi.

cowl [kaul] n (chimney) comignolo m; (hood) cappa f; (car) cofano m.

coy [kɔi] adj ritroso, timido.

crab [krab] n granchio m.

crack [krak] n (opening) screpolatura f, fessura f; (whip) schiocco m; (rifle) scoppio m; (noise) schianto m. **have a crack at** provare a fare. v spaccare, schioccare, screpolare.

cracker ['krakə] n (biscuit) cracker (pl -s) m, gallettina f. (firework) mortaretto m.

crackle ['krakl] v crepitare, scricchiolare. n crepitio m, scricchiolio m.

cradle ['kreidl] n culla f. v cullare.

craft [krɑːft] n mestiere m, professione f; (cunning) astuzia f; (boat) imbarcazione f. **crafty** adj astuto.

cram [kram] v ficcare, cacciare.

cramp [kramp] n (med) crampo m. v paralizzare, bloccare.

cranberry ['kranbəri] n mirtillo rosso m.

crane [krein] n gru f invar. v **crane one's neck** allungare il collo.

crank [krank] n (mech) gomito m, manovella f; (eccentric) eccentrico, -a m, f. **crank up** avviare.

crap [krap] n (vulgar) merda f; (impol: nonsense) scemenze f pl, stupidaggini f pl. v (vulgar) cacare.

crash [kraʃ] n (collision) scontro m; (noise) fracasso m; (collapse) crollo m; (aircraft) caduta f. **crash-helmet** n casco paraurti m. **crash-landing** n atterraggio di

fortuna m. v (clash) scontrarsi; fracassare; crollare; precipitare.

crate [kreit] n cassa f. v imballare.

crater ['kreitə] n cratere m.

crave [kreiv] v ambire, bramare. **craving** n smania f, brama f.

crawl [krɔːl] v trascinarsi, strisciare. n (swimming) crawl m invar.

crayfish ['kreifiʃ] n gambero (di fiume) m.

crayon ['kreiən] n pastello m, matita colorata f.

craze [kreiz] n mania f, pazzia f. **crazy** adj pazzo, matto. **drive crazy** far impazzire.

creak [kriːk] v cigolare, scricchiolare. n cigolio m, scricchiolio m.

cream [kriːm] n panna f, crema f. v scremare. **creamy** adj cremoso; (soft) morbido.

crease [kriːs] n piega f, grinza f. v sgualcirsi, raggrinzarsi. **creased** adj raggrinzato; (clothes) sgualcito.

create [kri'eit] v creare, provocare. **creation** n creazione f. **creative** adj creativo, originale. **creativity** n potenza creativa f, originalità f. **creator** n creatore, -trice m, f. **creature** n creatura f.

credentials [kri'denʃəlz] pl n credenziali f pl.

credible ['kredəbl] adj credibile. **credibility** n credibilità f.

credit ['kredit] n credito m; (trustworthyness) fiducia f, considerazione f; (bank) attivo m. **credit balance** saldo attivo m. **credit card** carta di credito f. v (comm) accreditare; (have faith in) credere, prestar fede a; (ascribe) attribuire. **creditable** adj degno di lode, che fa onore. **creditor** n creditore, -trice m, f.

credulous ['kredjuləs] adj credulo, ingenuo.

creed [kriːd] n credo m, professione di fede f.

*****creep** [kriːp] v strisciare, insinuarsi; (plants) arrampicarsi. **creeper** n (plant) pianta rampicante f. **creepy** adj che dà i brividi.

cremate [kri'meit] v cremare. **cremation** n cremazione f. **crematorium** n crematorio m.

crept [krept] V creep.

crescent ['kresnt] n mezzaluna f.

cress [kres] n crescione m. **mustard and cress** crescione inglese m, agretto m. **watercress** n crescione d'acqua m.

crest [krest] n cresta f, ciuffo m; (heraldry, helmet) cimiero m. **crestfallen** adj mortificato.

crevice ['krevis] n crepa f, fessura f.

crew [kruː] n equipaggio m, squadra f.

crib [krib] n (rel) presepio m; (bed) lettino m; (manger) mangiatoia f; (coll) bigino m. v plagiare.

cricket¹ ['krikit] n (insect) grillo m.

cricket² ['krikit] n (sport) cricket m.

crime [kraim] n delitto m, reato m. **criminal** n(m+f), adj criminale.

crimson ['krimzn] adj cremisi.

cringe [krindʒ] v comportarsi in modo servile.

crinkle ['krinkl] n grinza f. v raggrinzare.

cripple ['kripl] n storpio, -a m, f; invalido, -a m, f. v storpiare, mutilare, paralizzare.

crisis ['kraisis] n, pl **-ses** crisi f invar.

crisp [krisp] adj (lively) nitido; (bracing) invigorante; (firm, fresh) fresco; (brittle) croccante; (crinkled) crespo. **crisps** pl n patatine fritte croccanti f pl.

criterion [krai'tiəriən] n, pl **-ria** criterio m.

criticize ['kritisaiz] v criticare, esprimere un giudizio su. **critic** n critico m. **critical** adj critico. **criticism** n critica f; (philosophy) criticismo m. **critique** n saggio critico m.

croak [krouk] v gracchiare, gracidare; (grumble) brontolare. n gracchiare m, gracchio m, gracidio m.

crochet ['krouʃei] v lavorare all'uncinetto.

crockery ['krɔkəri] n vasellame m, stoviglie f pl.

crocodile ['krɔkədail] n coccodrillo m.

crocus ['kroukəs] n croco m.

crook [kruk] n (hook) uncino m; (bishop's) pastorale m; (shepherd's) bastone da pastore m; (criminal) truffatore, -trice m, f. v piegare, curvare.

crooked ['krukid] adj (bent) piegato, storto; disonesto.

crop [krɔp] n (produce) raccolto m; (riding) frusta f; (gullet) gozzo m. v (clip hair) tagliar corto; (trees) mozzare; (cut grain, etc.) mietere. **come a cropper** far fiasco.

croquet ['kroukei] n croquet m invar.

cross [krɔs] n croce f. adj arrabbiato. **be cross** arrabbiarsi. v incrociare; (street, etc.) attraversare; (threshold) varcare; (cheque) sbarrare; (annoy) ostacolare. **cross oneself** segnarsi. **cross one's mind** venire in mente a uno. **cross out** cancellare. **cross-examine** v sottoporre a interrogatorio. **cross-examination** n interrogatorio m. **cross-eyed** adj strabico. **crossfire** n fuoco incrociato m **cross-legged** adj a gambe accavallate. **cross-reference** n richiamo m. **crossroads** n crocevia m, incrocio m. **crossword** n cruciverba m invar, parole incrociate f pl. **crossing** n traversata f.

crotchet ['krɔtʃit] n (music) semiminima f; (hook) uncinetto m. **crotchety** adj irritabile.

crouch [krautʃ] v rannicchiarsi.

crow¹ [krou] n (bird) corvo m, cornacchia f. **as the crow flies** in linea diretta. **crow's nest** coffa f. **crow's foot** ruga f, zampa di gallina f.

crow² [krou] v cantare, esultare; (boast) vantarsi, trionfare.

crowd [kraud] n folla f, massa f, compagnia f. v affollare, ammassare. **crowded** adj affollato, stipato, pieno zeppo.

crown [kraun] n corona f; (hat) cocuzzolo m; (head) calotta f; (road) colmo m. **crown-prince** n principe ereditario m. v incoronare; (reward) ricompensare; (tooth) mettere una corona a. **to crown it all** come se non bastasse.

crucial ['kruːʃəl] adj decisivo, critico.

crucify ['kruːsifai] v crocifiggere, mettere in croce; tormentare, mortificare. **crucifix** n crocifisso m. **crucifixion** n crocifissione f.

crude [kruːd] adj (rough, vulgar) grossolano, rozzo, volgare; (unrefined) grezzo.

cruel ['kruːəl] adj crudele. **be cruel to** maltrattare. **cruelty** n crudeltà f.

cruise [kruːz] n crociera f. v go on a **cruise** fare una crociera.

crumb [krʌm] n briciola f.

crumble ['krʌmbl] v sgretolare; (collapse) crollare. **crumbly** adj friabile.

crumple ['krʌmpl] v sgualcire, sgualcirsi; (collapse) sfasciarsi, accasciarsi.

crunch [krʌntʃ] v sgretolare, sgranocchiare. n scricchiolio m; (critical point) momento di crisi m.

crusade [kruː'seid] n crociata f. **crusader** n crociato m.

crush [krʌʃ] v schiacciare, frantumare; (destroy) annientare. n calca f, ressa f. **have a crush on** prendersi una cotta per. **crusher** n frantoio m.

crust [krʌst] n crosta f, corteccia f. **crusty** adj crostoso; (surly) burbero.

crutch [krʌtʃ] n gruccia f, stampella f.

crux [krʌks] n **the crux of the matter** il nodo della questione m.

cry [krai] n urlo m, strillo m, lamento m. v urlare, gridare; (weep) piangere.

crypt [kript] n cripta f. **cryptic** adj ambiguo, misterioso.

crystal ['kristl] n cristallo m. **crystallization** n cristallizzazione f. **crystallize** v cristallizzare.

cub [kʌb] n cucciolo m.

cube [kjuːb] n cubo m. v elevare al cubo. **cubic** adj cubico.

cubicle ['kjuːbikl] n stanzino m; (changing-room) spogliatoio m.

cuckold ['kʌkould] n cornuto m. v fare le corna a.

cuckoo ['kukuː] n cuculo m, cucù m.

cucumber ['kjuːkʌmbə] n cetriolo m.

cuddle ['kʌdl] v coccolare, abbracciare teneramente. n abbraccio tenero m.

cue¹ [kjuː] n (theatre) battuta d'entrata f; (hint) spunto m.

cue² [kjuː] n (billiards) stecca f.

cuff¹ [kʌf] n (shirt) polsino m. **cuff-links** pl n gemelli m pl.

cuff² [kʌf] n (hit) schiaffo m, sberla f. v schiaffeggiare.

culinary ['kʌlinəri] adj culinario, gastronomico.

culminate ['kʌlmi,neit] v concludersi. **culmination** n culmine m.

culprit ['kʌlprit] n colpevole m, f.

cult [kʌlt] n culto m.

cultivate ['kʌltiˌveit] v coltivare. **cultivation** n coltivazione f, coltura f.

culture ['kʌltʃə] n cultura f; (land, plants) coltura f. **cultural** adj culturale. **cultured** adj colto.

cumbersome ['kʌmbəsəm] adj ingombrante.

cunning ['kʌniŋ] adj scaltro, astuto. n astuzia f, scaltrezza f.

cup [kʌp] n tazza f; (sport) coppa f.

cupboard ['kʌbəd] n armadio m, credenza f. **cupboard love** amore interessato m.

curate ['kjuərət] n curato m, parroco m.

curator [kjuə'reitə] n direttore, -trice di museo m, f; curatore, -trice m, f.

curb [kəːb] v frenare.

curdle ['kəːdl] v cagliare, cagliarsi; (blood) gelare.

cure [kjuə] n cura f, rimedio m. v sanare,

guarire; (food) conservare; (salt) **salare**; (smoke) affumicare.

curfew ['kəːfjuː] n coprifuoco m.

curious ['kjuəriəs] adj (odd) strano, curioso, insolito; (inquisitive) curioso.

curl [kəːl] n ricciolo m. v arricciare, arrotolare; (lip) torcere. **curl up** rannicchiarsi; (animal) accucciarsi. **curler** n bigodino m.

currant ['kʌrənt] n ribes m invar; (dried) uva passa f, uvetta f.

currency ['kʌrənsi] n decorrenza f; (money) valuta f, moneta legale f.

current ['kʌrənt] n corrente f. adj corrente, comune.

curry ['kʌri] n curry m invar. v **curry favour** ingraziarsi.

curse [kəːs] n (oath) bestemmia f; (evil) maledizione f. v bestemmiare, maledire. **be cursed with** essere afflitto da.

curt [kəːt] adj brusco.

curtail [kəː'teil] v limitare, ridurre.

curtain ['kəːtn] n cortina f; (cloth) tenda f, tendina f; (theatre) sipario m.

curtsy ['kəːtsi] n inchino m. v inchinarsi.

curve [kəːv] n curva f, svolta f. v curvare, svoltare.

cushion ['kuʃən] n cuscino m; (billiards) sponda f. v smorzare, assorbire.

custody ['kʌstədi] n custodia f, guardia f. **take into custody** arrestare. **custodian** n guardiano m, custode m, f.

custom ['kʌstəm] n costume m, usanza f, abitudine f. **customs** n dogana f. **customs officer** doganiere, -a m, f. **customary** adj abituale, solito. **customer** n cliente m, f.

*****cut** [kʌt] n taglio m, incisione f; (wound) ferita f. v tagliare, incidere; (wound) ferire; (cards) alzare le carte. **cut down** ridurre; (fell) abbattere. **cut off** tagliar via; (suspend) sospendere. **cut out** ritagliare; omettere; (elec) interrompere. **cut it out!** piantala! **cut price** prezzo ridotto m. **cut-throat** adj spietato.

cute [kjuːt] adj grazioso, ingegnoso.

cutlery ['kʌtləri] n posate f pl, posateria f; (knives) coltelleria f.

cutlet ['kʌtlit] n costoletta f, cotoletta f.

cutting ['kʌtiŋ] adj tagliente. n (newspaper) ritaglio m; (plant) margotta f; (railway) trincea f.

cycle ['saikl] n ciclo m, periodo m; (bicycle) bicicletta f. v andare in bicicletta. **cyclic** adj ciclico. **cycling** n ciclismo m. **cyclist** n ciclista m, f.

cyclone ['saikloun] *n* ciclone *m*.

cylinder ['silində] *n* cilindro *m*; (*revolver*) tamburo *m*; (*printing*) rullo *m*; (*gas*) bombola *f*.

cymbal ['simbəl] *n* cembalo *m*.

cynic ['sinik] *n* cinico, -a *m*, *f*. **cynical** *adj* cinico. **cynicism** *n* cinismo *m*.

cypress ['saiprəs] *n* cipresso *m*.

Cyprus ['saiprəs] *n* Cipro *m*. **Cypriot** *n*(*m+f*), *adj* cipriota.

cyst [sist] *n* cisti *f*.

Czechoslovakia [ˌtʃekəslo'vakiə] *n* Cecoslovacchia *f*. **Czech** *n*, *adj* ceco, -a, cecoslovacco, -a.

D

dab [dab] *v* toccare leggermente; applicare. *n* (*small quantity*) tocco *m*; (*light blow*) colpetto *m*.

dabble ['dabl] *v* (*dip, paddle*) guazzare. **dabble in** dilettarsi a; fare da dilettante.

dad [dad] *n* babbo *m*, papà *m*.

daffodil ['dafədil] *n* narciso *m*.

daft [daːft] *adj* scemo, sciocco.

dagger ['dagə] *n* pugnale *m*, stiletto *m*. **be at daggers drawn** essere ai ferri corti.

daily ['deili] *adj* giornaliero, quotidiano. *n* giornale *m*; (*maid*) domestica a giornata *f*. *adv* ogni giorno, quotidianamente.

dainty ['deinti] *adj* delicato, squisito.

dairy ['deəri] *n* latteria *f*. **dairy produce** latticini *m pl*.

daisy ['deizi] *n* margherita *f*.

dam [dam] *n* diga *f*, argine *m*. *v* sbarrare, arginare.

damage ['damidʒ] *n* danno *m*, guasto *m*; (*law*) indennizzo *m*. *v* danneggiare, guastare, nuocere. **damaging** *adj* dannoso.

damn [dam] *v* dannare, maledire. *interj* maledizione! *n* (*negligible amount*) bel niente *m*.

damp [damp] *adj* umido, madido. *n* umido *m*. *v* *also* **dampen** (*moisten*) inumidire; (*dull*) smorzare, deprimere. **damper** *n* (*furnace*) valvola di tiraggio *f*; (*elec*) smorzatore *m*; (*music*) sordina *f*.

damson ['damzən] *n* (*fruit*) susina selvatica *f*; (*tree*) susino selvatico *m*.

dance [daːns] *n* danza *f*, ballo *m*. *v* danzare, ballare. **dancer** *n* danzatore, -trice *m*, *f*; ballerino, -a *m*, *f*.

dandelion ['dandiˌlaiən] *n* dente di leone *m*.

dandruff ['dandrəf] *n* forfora *f*.

danger ['deindʒə] *n* pericolo *m*. **dangerous** *adj* pericoloso.

dangle ['dangl] *v* (far) ciondolare *or* dondolare.

Danish ['deiniʃ] *nm*, *adj* danese. **Dane** *n* danese *m*, *f*.

dare [deə] *v* (*be bold*) osare; (*challenge*) sfidare. **I dare say** suppongo; probabilmente; (*not deny*) non nego.

daring ['deəriŋ] *adj* audace. *n* audacia *f*.

dark [daːk] *n* *also* **darkness** buio *m*, oscurità *f*. *adj* buio, oscuro, cupo. **darken** *v* scurire, offuscare, rabbuiarsi.

darling ['daːliŋ] *n* tesoro *m*, gioia *f*, favorito, -a *m*, *f*. *adj* carissimo, amatissimo.

darn [daːn] *v* rammendare. *n* rammendo *m*, rammendatura *f*.

dart [daːt] *n* dardo *m*, freccia *f*. *v* (*move swiftly*) balzare, slanciarsi, precipitarsi; (*throw*) lanciare.

dash [daʃ] *v* buttare, urtare; (*spoil*) frustrare; (*rush*) scappare. *n* spruzzo *m*; (*rush*) slancio *m*; (*drink*) goccio *m*; (*pinch*) pizzico *m*; (*printing*) lineetta *f*. **dashboard** *n* cruscotto *m*.

data ['deitə] *pl n* dati *m pl*, elementi *m pl*. **data processing** elaborazione di dati *f*.

date[1] [deit] *n* (*calendar*) data *f*; (*appointment*) appuntamento *m*. *v* datare, fare appuntamento con. **date from** risalire a. **out of date** fuori moda, antiquato. **up to date** aggiornato.

date[2] [deit] *n* (*fruit*) dattero *m*.

daughter ['dɔːtə] *n* figlia *f*, figliola *f*. **daughter-in-law** *n* nuora *f*.

daunt [dɔːnt] *v* intimidire.

dawdle ['dɔːdl] *v* sprecar tempo, bighellonare. **dawdler** *n* fannullone, -a *m*, *f*; bighellone, -a *m*, *f*.

dawn [dɔːn] *n* alba *f*, aurora *f*; (*beginning*) inizio *m*. *v* albeggiare; (*appear*) apparire, manifestarsi.

day [dei] *n* giorno *m*, giornata *f*. **by day** di giorno. **daybreak** *n* alba *f*, spuntar del giorno *m*. **daylight** *n* luce del giorno *f*. **every other day** un giorno sì e uno no. **the day before yesterday** ieri l'altro. **the day after tomorrow** dopodomani.

daydream ['deidriːm] *v* sognare ad occhi aperti; fantasticare. *n* sogno ad occhi aperti *m*, fantasticheria *f*.

daze [deiz] *v* stordire, sbalordire. *n* stupore *m*.

dazzle ['dazl] *v* abbagliare.

dead [ded] *adj* morto, defunto; (*coll: absolute*) assoluto, completo. **dead drunk** ubriaco fradicio. **deadline** *n* scadenza *f*. **deadlock** *n* punto morto *m*; incaglio *m*. **dead slow** a passo d'uomo. **deaden** *v* attutire. **deadly** *adj* mortale.

deaf [def] *adj* sordo. **turn a deaf ear** fare orecchi da mercante. **deaf-mute** *n* sordomuto, -a *m, f*. **deafen** *v* rendere sordo, intontire. **deafness** *n* sordità *f*.

***deal** [diil] *v* (*cards*) dare le carte. **deal in** commerciare in. **deal with** occuparsi di; (*things*) trattare di; (*people*) avere rapporti con. *n* (*business*) affare *m*; (*agreement*) accordo *m*; (*amount*) quantità *f*. **dealer** *n* commerciante *m, f*; (*retail*) dettagliante *m, f*; (*wholesale*) grossista *m, f*. **dealt** [delt] *V* **deal**.

dean [diin] *n* (*university*) preside di facoltà *m, f*; (*rel*) decano *m*.

dear [diə] *adj* caro. **oh dear!** ahimè! Dio mio!

death [deθ] *n* morte *f*. **death certificate** certificato di morte *m*. **death duties** tassa di successione *f sing*. **death warrant** sentenza di morte *f*. **deathly** *adj, adv* mortale; cadaverico.

debase [di'beis] *v* degradare, svalutare.

debate [di'beit] *v* dibattere, discutere. *n* dibattito *m*, discussione *f*.

debit ['debit] *n* debito *m*; (*accounts*) dare *m*. *v* addebitare.

debris ['deibri] *n* detrito *m*, macerie *f pl*.

debt [det] *n* debito *m*; (*obligation*) obbligo *m*. **debt collector** *n* esattore, -trice *m, f*. **debtor** *n* debitore, -trice *m, f*.

decade ['dekeid] *n* decennio *m*.

decadent ['dekədənt] *adj* decadente.

decant [di'kant] *v* travasare. **decanter** *n* caraffa *f*.

decay [di'kei] *v* deperire, putrefare, putrefarsi, andare in rovina; (*teeth*) cariare. *n* sfacelo *m*, rovina *f*, deperimento *m*.

deceased [di'siist] *n, adj* defunto, -a. **decease** *n* decesso *m*.

deceit [di'siit] *n* inganno *m*, truffa *f*. **deceitful** *adj* falso, perfido.

deceive [di'siiv] *v* ingannare, imbrogliare, illudersi.

December [di'sembə] *n* dicembre *m*.

decent ['diisənt] *adj* (*proper*) decente; (*fitting*) decoroso; (*fair*) discreto; (*respectable*) bravo. **decency** *n* decenza *f*, decoro *m*.

deceptive [di'septiv] *adj* ingannevole, illusorio. **deception** *n* inganno *m*, imbroglio *m*.

decibel ['desi,bel] *n* decibel *m invar*.

decide [di'said] *v* decidere, decidersi. **decided** *adj* deciso, risoluto.

decimal ['desiməl] *nm, adj* decimale.

decipher [di'saifə] *v* decifrare.

decision [di'siʒən] *n* decisione *f*. **decisive** *adj* decisivo.

deck [dek] *n* (*naut*) ponte *m*, coperta *f*; (*cards*) mazzo *m*. *v* ornare. **deck-chair** *n* sedia a sdraio *f*.

declare [di'kleə] *v* dichiarare, proclamare. **declaration** *n* dichiarazione *f*, proclama *m*.

decline [di'klain] *v* (*refuse*) rifiutare; (*gramm*) declinare; (*deteriorate*) deperire. *n* (*gradual loss*) declino *m*; deterioramento *m*; decadenza *f*.

decompose [,diikəm'pouz] *v* decomporre. **decomposition** *n* decomposizione *f*, putrefazione *f*.

decorate ['dekə,reit] *v* decorare, ornare; (*house*) verniciare. **decoration** *n* decorazione *f*, ornamento *m*. **decorator** *n* (*interior*) arredatore, -trice *m, f*; (*building*) decoratore, -trice *m, f*, pittore, -trice *m, f*. **decorous** *adj* decoroso. **decorum** *n* decoro *m*.

decoy ['diikoi] *n* richiamo *m*, uccello da richiamo *m*, esca *f*; (*person*) adescatore, -trice *m, f*.

decrease [di'kriis] *v* diminuire. *n* diminuzione *f*, ribasso *m*.

decree [di'krii] *n* decreto *m*, ordinanza *f*. *v* decretare.

decrepit [di'krepit] *adj* decrepito.

dedicate ['dedi,keit] *v* dedicare. **dedication** *n* dedicazione *f*; (*book*) dedica *f*.

deduce [di'djuis] *v* dedurre, inferire. **deduction** *n* (*inference*) deduzione *f*.

deduct [di'dʌkt] *v* dedurre, sottrarre. **deduction** *n* (*subtraction*) sottrazione *f*.

deed [diid] *n* fatto *m*, azione *f*; (*law*) atto notarile, strumento *m*; (*undertaking*) impresa *f*. **good deed** buona azione *f*.

deep [diːp] *adj* profondo, alto; *(colour)* scuro, cupo. **deep-rooted** *or* **deep-seated** *adj* radicato. **deepen** *v* approfondire.

deep-freeze *v* surgelare. *n* congelatore *m*, freezer *m invar*.

deer [diə] *n (roe)* capriolo *m*; *(fallow)* daino *m*.

deface [diˈfeis] *v* sfregiare, mutilare.

defamatory [diˈfamətəri] *adj* diffamatorio. **defamation** *n* diffamazione *f*, calunnia *f*.

default [diˈfɔːlt] *v* rendersi contumace. **by default** in contumacia. **in default of** in difetto di.

defeat [diˈfiːt] *n* sconfitta *f*, disfatta *f*. *v* sconfiggere. **defeatism** *n* disfattismo *m*. **defeatist** *n* disfattista *m, f*.

defect [ˈdiːfekt] *n* difetto *m*, mancanza *f*. **defective** *adj* difettoso, imperfetto; *(gramm)* difettivo.

defect² [diˈfekt] *v* disertare. **defection** *n* diserzione *f*, defezione *f*.

defend [diˈfend] *v* difendere, proteggere. **defence** *n* difesa *f*. **defenceless** *adj* indifeso, senza difesa. **defendant** *n* imputato, -a *m, f*. **defender** *n* difensore *m*.

defensive [diˈfensiv] *adj* difensivo. *n* difensiva *f*. **be on the defensive** stare sulla difesa.

defer¹ [diˈfəː] *v (put off)* rimandare, rinviare.

defer² [diˈfəː] *v (yield to)* sottoporsi. **deferential** *adj* rispettoso, deferente.

deficient [diˈfiʃənt] *adj* deficiente, incompleto, insufficiente. **deficiency** *n* deficienza *f*, mancanza *f*, carenza *f*.

deficit [ˈdefisit] *n* deficit *m invar*, disavanzo *m*.

define [diˈfain] *v* definire, precisare. **definition** *n* definizione *f*.

definite [ˈdefinit] *adj* definito, determinato, preciso.

deflate [diˈfleit] *v* sgonfiare; *(comm)* deflazionare. **deflation** *n* sgonfiamento *m*, deflazione *f*.

deflect [diˈflekt] *v* deviare. **deflection** *n* deviazione *f*.

deform [diˈfɔːm] *v* deformare. **deformity** *or* **deformation** *n* deformazione *f*.

defraud [diˈfrɔːd] *v* frodare, defraudare.

defray [diˈfrei] *v* **defray expenses** rimborsare le spese.

defrost [diˈfrɔst] *v* scongelare.

deft [deft] *adj* destro, lesto. **deftness** *n* destrezza *f*, agilità *f*.

defunct [diˈfʌŋkt] *adj* defunto.

defy [diˈfai] *v* sfidare, provocare. **defiance** *n (resistance)* sfida *f*; dispetto *m*. **in defiance of** a dispetto di. **defiant** *adj* ribelle, ricalcitrante.

degenerate [diˈdʒenərit; *v* diˈdʒenəreit] *adj* degenerato, perverso. *v* degenerare. **degeneracy** *or* **degeneration** *n* degenerazione *f*.

degrade [diˈgreid] *v* degradare. **degrading** *adj* degradante.

degree [diˈgriː] *n* grado *m*; *(diploma)* titolo di studio *m*, laurea *f*.

dehydrate [diːˈhaidreit] *v* disidratare. **dehydration** *n* disidratazione *f*.

de-icer [diːˈaisə] *n* dispositivo antighiaccio *m*.

deign [dein] *v* degnarsi.

deity [ˈdiːiti] *n* divinità *f*, deità *f*.

dejected [diˈdʒektid] *adj* avvilito, abbattuto.

delay [diˈlei] *n* ritardo *m*, indugio *m*. *v* ritardare, differire.

delegate [ˈdeligit; *v* ˈdeligeit] *n* delegato, -a *m, f*. *v* delegare, autorizzare. **delegation** *n* delegazione *f*.

delete [diˈliːt] *v* espungere. **deletion** *n* cancellatura *f*, espunzione *f*.

deliberate [diˈlibərət; *v* diˈlibəreit] *adj (intentional)* voluto; *(unhurried)* misurato; *(carefully considered)* ponderato. *v* deliberare, riflettere. **deliberation** *n* riflessione *f*, deliberazione *f*.

delicate [ˈdelikət] *adj* delicato, fine; *(sensitive)* sensibile. **delicacy** *n* delicatezza *f*; sensibilità *f*; *(food)* leccornia *f*.

delicious [diˈliʃəs] *adj* delizioso; *(food)* squisito.

delight [diˈlait] *n* delizia *f*, diletto *m*. *v* dilettare. **delight in** rallegrarsi di. **delighted** *adj* ben lieto. **delightful** *adj* delizioso, incantevole, simpaticissimo.

delinquency [diˈliŋkwənsi] *n* delinquenza *f*. **delinquent** *n(m+f)*, *adj* delinquente.

delirious [diˈliriəs] *adj (feverish)* delirante; *(wildly excited)* ebbro.

deliver [diˈlivə] *v (hand over)* recapitare, consegnare; *(set free)* liberare; *(save)* salvare; *(speech)* pronunciare. **deliverance** *n* liberazione *f*. **delivery** *n* consegna *f*; *(birth)* parto *m*; *(diction)* dizione *f*.

delta [ˈdeltə] *n* delta *m*.

delude [diˈluːd] *v* deludere, deludersi. **delusion** *n* delusione *f*.

deluge ['dɛljuːdʒ] n diluvio m. v diluviare.

delve [dɛlv] v (dig) scavare; (research) far ricerche.

demand [di'maɪnd] v esigere, pretendere. n pretesa f, richiesta f. **in demand** ricercato. **on demand** su richiesta. **demanding** adj esigente.

demented [di'mentid] adj demente, impazzito.

democracy [di'mɔkrəsi] n democrazia f. **democrat** n democratico, -a m, f. **democratic** adj democratico.

demolish [di'mɔliʃ] v demolire, abbattere. **demolition** n demolizione f.

demon ['diːmən] n demonio m, diavolo m.

demonstrate ['demənstreit] v dimostrare. **demonstrable** adj dimostrabile. **demonstration** n dimostrazione f; (proof) prova f; (meeting) manifestazione f. **demonstrative** adj dimostrativo; (feeling) espansivo.

demoralize [di'mɔrəlaiz] v demoralizzare, scoraggiare.

demure [di'mjuə] adj modesto, schivo.

den [dɛn] n tana f.

denial [di'naiəl] n (contradiction) smentita f; (negation) diniego m; (refusal) rifiuto m.

denim ['denim] n tela pesante f.

Denmark ['denmɑːk] n Danimarca f.

denomination [di,nɔmi'neiʃən] n denominazione f; (belief) setta f, religione f; (money) taglio m. **denominator** n denominatore m.

denote [di'nout] v denotare, indicare.

denounce [di'nauns] v denunciare; (openly accuse) inveire contro.

dense [dɛns] adj denso, fitto. **density** n densità f.

dent [dɛnt] n tacca f, ammaccatura f. v intaccare, ammaccare.

dental ['dɛntl] adj dentale; (of dentistry) dentistico.

dentist ['dɛntist] n dentista m, f. **dentistry** n odontoiatria f.

denture ['dɛntʃə] n dentiera f.

denude [di'njuːd] v denudare, privare.

denunciation [dinʌnsi'eiʃən] n denuncia f.

deny [di'nai] v negare, smentire. **deny oneself** privarsi di, fare a meno di.

deodorant [diː'oudərənt] nm, adj deodorante.

depart [di'pɑːt] v (leave) partire; (diverge) deviare. **departure** n partenza f, deviazione f.

department [di'pɑːtmənt] n reparto m. **department store** grande magazzino m.

depend [di'pɛnd] v dipendere, fare assegnamento. **depend on** dipendere da, fare assegnamento su. **dependable** adj fidato. **dependence** n dipendenza f. **dependent** n(m+f), adj dipendente.

depict [di'pikt] v rappresentare, descrivere.

deplete [di'pliːt] v esaurire, vuotare.

deplore [di'plɔː] v biasimare, disapprovare. **deplorable** adj riprensibile, biasimevole.

deport [di'pɔːt] v deportare, espellere. **deportation** n deportazione f, espulsione f.

depose [di'pouz] v (dismiss) deporre; (witness) testimoniare. **deposition** n deposizione f, testimonianza f.

deposit [di'pɔzit] v depositare, posare. n deposito m; (security) cauzione f, pegno m. **deposit account** conto vincolato m.

depot ['depou] n deposito m, magazzino m, parco m.

deprave [di'preiv] v corrompere, depravare.

depreciate [di'priːʃieit] v deprezzare; (money) svalutare; (belittle) screditare, denigrare. **depreciation** n deprezzamento m, svalutazione f; discredito m, denigrazione f.

depress [di'pres] v deprimere. **depressed** adj depresso, abbattuto; (market) basso. **depressing** adj deprimente, triste. **depression** n depressione f; (comm) crisi f invar.

deprive [di'praiv] v privare. **deprivation** n privazione f.

depth [depθ] n profondità f, altezza f. **be out of one's depth** non essere all'altezza.

deputy ['depjuti] n delegato m, deputato m. **deputation** n deputazione f.

derail [di'reil] v uscire dalle rotaie, deragliare. **derailment** n deragliamento m.

derelict ['derilikt] adj derelitto, abbandonato.

deride [di'raid] v deridere, schernire. **derision** n derisione f, scherno m. **derisive** or **derisory** adj irrisorio, derisivo.

derive [di'raiv] v derivare, provenire. **derivation** n derivazione f, provenienza f, origine f.

derogatory [di'rogətəri] adj sprezzante, diffamante.

descend [di'send] v scendere; (come from) derivare, discendere. **descent** n discesa f; (ancestry) discendenza f, lignaggio m. **descendant** n discendente m, f.

describe [di'skraib] v descrivere. **description** n descrizione f.

desert[1] ['dezət] n deserto m.

desert[2] [di'zərt] v disertare, abbandonare. **deserter** n disertore m. **desertion** n diserzione f, abbandono m.

desert[3] [di'zərt] n get one's just deserts ricevere quel che si merita.

deserve [di'zərv] v meritare, essere degno di.

design [di'zain] v (plan) progettare; (intend) destinare. n disegno m, progetto m; (intention) proposito m. **have designs on** avere delle mire su. **designer** n progettista m, f, modellista m, f.

designate ['dezigneit] v designare. adj designato.

desire [di'zaiə] v desiderare, bramare. n (wish) desiderio m; (craving) brama f; passione f. **desirable** adj desiderabile.

desk [desk] n scrivania f; (school) banco m; (cash) cassa f.

desolate ['desələt] adj desolato; (barren) deserto; (lonely) solitario; (sad) afflitto, rattristato.

despair [di'speə] n disperazione f. v disperare.

desperate ['despərət] adj disperato; (hopeless) senza speranza. **desperation** n disperazione f.

despise [di'spaiz] v disprezzare.

despite [di'spait] prep malgrado.

despondent [di'spondənt] adj accasciato, depresso.

despot ['despot] n despota m, f.

dessert [di'zərt] n dessert m invar.

destine ['destin] v destinare. **destination** n destinazione f, recapito m. **destiny** n destino m, sorte f.

destitute ['destitjut] adj indigente.

destroy [di'stroi] v distruggere. **destruction** n distruzione f.

detach [di'tatʃ] v staccare, distaccare. **detached** adj staccato; (house) isolato; (aloof) distaccato; (objective) obiettivo. **detachment** n distacco m; (army) distaccamento m; indifferenza f; obiettività f.

detail ['diːteil] n particolare m, dettaglio m. v dettagliare, descrivere minutamente.

detain [di'tein] v detenere; (delay) trattenere. **detainee** n detenuto, -a m, f; carcerato, -a m, f.

detect [di'tekt] v scoprire, individuare. **detection** n scoperta f. **detective** n detective m invar, investigatore, -trice m, f. **detective novel** romanzo poliziesco m, romanzo giallo m.

détente [dei'tɑ̃mt] n distensione f.

detention [di'tenʃən] n detenzione f.

deter [di'tər] v dissuadere, scoraggiare. **deterrent** n deterrente m.

detergent [di'tərdʒənt] nm, adj detergente, detersivo.

deteriorate [di'tiəriəreit] v deteriorare, peggiorare. **deterioration** n deterioramento m, peggioramento m.

determine [di'tərmin] v determinare, stabilire; decidere. **determination** n determinazione f, risolutezza f. **determined** adj determinato, risoluto.

detest [di'test] v detestare, odiare. **detestable** adj detestabile, odioso.

detonate ['detəneit] v detonare, esplodere. **detonation** n detonazione f, esplosione f. **detonator** n detonatore m.

detour ['diːtuə] n deviazione f.

detract [di'trakt] v detrarre.

detriment ['detrimənt] n to the detriment of a scapito di.

deuce [djuːs] n (cards) due m; (tennis) quaranta pari.

devalue [diːˈvaljuː] v svalutare. **devaluation** n svalutazione f.

devastate ['devəsteit] v devastare, rovinare. **devastating** adj devastante; (highly effective) schiacciante.

develop [di'veləp] v sviluppare; elaborare; (land) usare come terreno da costruzione. **develop into** diventare. **developer** n (phot) sviluppatore m; (land) persona che apporta migliorie f. **development** n sviluppo m; evoluzione f; (land) valorizzazione di terreno f.

deviate ['diːviəit] v deviare. **deviation** n deviazione f.

device [di'vais] n (contrivance) congegno m; (crafty scheme) schema m, espediente m; (heraldry) motto m, divisa f.

devil ['devl] n diavolo m, demonio m. **devilish** adj diabolico, infernale.

devious ['diːviəs] adj indiretto, tortuoso.

devise [di'vaiz] v escogitare, progettare.

devoid [di'void] adj privo.

devolution [diːvəˈluːʃən] n devoluzione f.

devote [di'vout] v dedicare, consacrare. **devoted** adj devoto, affezionato. **devotion** n devozione f; (prayer) preghiere f pl.

devour [di'vauə] v divorare.

devout [di'vaut] adj devoto, pio, fervente.

dew [djuː] n rugiada f.

dextrous ['dekstrəs] adj destro, abile. **dexterity** n destrezza f.

diabetes [‚diəə'biːtiːz] n diabete m. **diabetic** nm, adj diabetico.

diagnose [‚diəəg'nouz] v fare la diagnosi. **diagnosis** n, pl -ses diagnosi f. **diagnostic** adj diagnostico.

diagonal [dai'agənəl] nf, adj diagonale.

diagram ['daiəgram] n diagramma m.

dial ['daiəl] n (watch) quadrante m; (telephone) disco combinatore m. v (number) comporre.

dialect ['daiəlekt] n dialetto m.

dialogue ['daiəlog] n dialogo (pl -ghi) m.

diameter [dai'amitə] n diametro m.

diamond ['daiəmənd] n diamante m. **diamonds** pl n (cards) quadri m pl.

diaper ['daiəpə] n (US) pannolino (per neonati) m.

diaphragm ['daiə‚fram] n diaframma m.

diarrhoea [‚daiə'riə] n diarrea f.

diary ['daiəri] n diario m, agenda f.

dice [dais] n dado m.

dictate [dik'teit] v dettare, imporre. n (order) comando m; (rule) regola f. **dictation** n dettato m. **dictator** n dittatore m. **dictatorial** adj dittatorio, dittatoriale. **dictatorship** n dittatura f.

dictionary ['dikʃənəri] n dizionario m, vocabolario m.

did [did] V **do**.

die [dai] v morire. **die away** scomparire. **die down** spegnersi lentamente.

diehard ['daihaid] n(m+f), adj tradizionalista, intransigente.

diesel ['diːzəl] n **diesel engine** motore diesel m. **diesel oil** gasolio m, nafta f.

diet ['daiət] n dieta f; (food) alimentazione f, vitto m. **be on a diet** stare a dieta, stare o essere a regime. **dietary** adj dietetico.

differ ['difə] v essere diverso, differire; (disagree) dissentire. **difference** n differenza f. **different** adj differente, diverso.

difficult ['difikəlt] adj difficile; (troublesome, tricky) difficoltoso. **difficulty** n difficoltà f.

diffident ['difidənt] adj timido.

*dig [dig] v scavare; (agric) vangare. n (archaeol) scavi m pl.

digest [dai'dʒest; n 'daidʒest] v digerire, assimilare. n sommario m, selezione f. **digestible** adj digeribile. **digestion** n digestione f.

digit ['didʒit] n (figure) numero semplice m, cifra f; (finger, toe) dito m. **digital** adj digitale.

dignified ['digni‚faid] adj dignitoso, nobile.

dignity ['dignəti] n dignità f.

digress [dai'gres] v digredire, deviare. **digression** n digressione f.

digs [digz] pl n alloggio m sing.

dilapidated [di'lapi‚deitid] adj decrepito.

dilate [dai'leit] v dilatare.

dilemma [di'lemə] n dilemma m.

diligent ['dilidʒent] adj diligente, assiduo.

dilute [dai'luːt] v diluire, allungare. adj diluito.

dim [dim] v attenuare, affievolire. adj fioco, tenue; (stupid) poco intelligente.

dimension [di'menʃən] n dimensione f.

diminish [di'miniʃ] v diminuire, ridurre.

diminutive [di'minjutiv] adj diminutivo, minuscolo.

dimple ['dimpl] n fossetta f.

din [din] n fracasso m, baccano m.

dine [dain] v pranzare. **dining car** vagone ristorante m. **dining room** sala da pranzo f.

dinghy ['dingi] n barca f.

dingy ['dindʒi] adj squallido.

dinner ['dinə] n pranzo m, cena f.

dinosaur ['dainə‚soːt] n dinosauro m.

diocese ['daiəsis] n diocesi f invar.

dip [dip] v abbassare, tuffare, immergere. n immersione f; (swim) nuotata f; inclinazione f.

diphthong ['difθon] n dittongo m.

diploma [di'ploumə] n diploma m.

diplomacy [di'plouməsi] n diplomazia f. **diplomat** n diplomatico m. **diplomatic** adj diplomatico.

dipstick ['dipstik] n asta di livello f.

dire [daiə] adj **dire need** bisogno urgente m. **dire straits** miseria squallida f sing.

direct [di'rekt] adj diretto, immediato; sincero. v dirigere, amministrare. **direction** n direzione f; (management) amministrazione; (address) indirizzo m; (stage) didascalia f. **director** n (comm) amministratore, -trice m, f; (theatre) regista *m, f*. **directory** *n* annuario *m*, guida *f*; *(phone)* elenco telefonico *m*.

dirt [dɜːt] *n* sporcizia *f*. **dirty** *adj* sporco, sudicio. **dirty word** parolaccia *f*.

disability [ˌdisəˈbiləti] *n* incapacità *f*, inabilità *f*. **disabled** *nm, adj* invalido, mutilato.

disadvantage [ˌdisədˈvantidʒ] *n* svantaggio *m*.

disagree [ˌdisəˈgriː] *v* non andar d'accordo, non essere d'accordo. **disagree with** *(food)* far male a. **disagreeable** *adj* sgradevole, antipatico. **disagreement** *n* disaccordo *m*, dissenso *m*.

disappear [ˌdisəˈpiə] *v* sparire, scomparire. **disappearance** *n* scomparsa *f*.

disappoint [ˌdisəˈpoint] *v* deludere. **disappointed** *adj* deluso, scontento. **disappointment** *n* delusione *f*.

disapprove [ˌdisəˈpruːv] *v* disapprovare, riprovare. **disapproval** *n* disapprovazione *f*.

disarm [disˈaːm] *v* disarmare. **disarmament** *n* disarmo *m*.

disaster [diˈzaːstə] *n* disastro *m*, disgrazia *f*; calamità *f*. **disastrous** *adj* disastroso.

disband [disˈband] *v* sbandare, sciogliere, congedare.

disc *or US* **disk** [disk] *n* disco *m*.

discard [disˈkaːd] *v* scartare.

discern [diˈsəːn] *v* discernere, scorgere. **discerning** *adj* avveduto, accorto. **discernment** *n* discernimento *m*, giudizio *m*.

discharge [disˈtʃaːdʒ] *v* scaricare; *(dismiss)* licenziare; *(law)* assolvere; *(radiation)* emettere; *(med)* suppurare; *(a duty)* adempiere; *(a debt)* saldare. *n* scarico *m*; licenziamento *m*; assoluzione *f*; emissione *f*; suppurazione *f*; *(elec)* scarica *f*.

disciple [diˈsaipl] *n* discepolo, -a *m, f*.

discipline [ˈdisiplin] *n* disciplina *f*. *v* disciplinare. **disciplinary** *adj* disciplinare.

disclaim [disˈkleim] *v* ripudiare, sconfessare, smentire. **disclaimer** *n* ripudio *m*, smentita *f*; denunzia di un contratto *f*.

disclose [disˈklouz] *v* svelare, rivelare. **disclosure** *n* rivelazione *f*.

discolour [disˈkʌlə] *v* scolorire, sbiadire.

discomfort [disˈkʌmfət] *n* disagio *m*. *v* mettere a disagio.

disconcert [ˌdiskənˈsəːt] *v* sconcertare. **disconcerting** *adj* sconcertante.

disconnect [ˌdiskəˈnekt] *v* sconnettere; *(mech)* disinnestare.

disconsolate [disˈkonsələt] *adj* sconsolato, desolato.

discontinue [ˌdiskənˈtinjuː] *v* sospendere, interrompere, terminare.

discord [ˈdiskoːd] *n* discordia *f*, dissenso *m*; *(music)* dissonanza *f*, disarmonia *f*. **discordant** *adj* discorde; *(noise)* discordante; dissonante.

discotheque [ˈdiskoˌtek] *n* discoteca *f*.

discount [ˈdiskaunt] *v* *(disregard)* non badare a. *n* sconto *m*, ribasso *m*.

discourage [disˈkʌridʒ] *v* scoraggiare. **discouragement** *n* scoraggiamento *m*. **discouraging** *adj* scoraggiante.

discover [disˈkʌvə] *v* scoprire. **discovery** *n* scoperta *f*.

discredit [disˈkredit] *v* screditare, mettere in dubbio.

discreet [diˈskriːt] *adj* discreto, riservato. **discretion** *n* discrezione *f*; prudenza *f*; *(judgment)* giudizio *m*. **discretionary** *adj* discrezionale.

discrepancy [diˈskrepənsi] *n* divario *m*, disaccordo *m*.

discrete [diˈskriːt] *adj* separato, distinto, discreto.

discriminate [diˈskrimiˌneit] *v* discriminare, differenziare. **discriminating** *adj* penetrante, giudizioso. **discrimination** *n* discriminazione *f*, distinzione *f*.

discus [ˈdiskəs] *n* disco *m*.

discuss [diˈskʌs] *v* discutere, dibattere. **discussion** *n* discussione *f*, dibattimento *m*.

disease [diˈziz] *n* malattia *f*. **diseased** *adj* malato, ammalato.

disembark [ˌdisimˈbaːk] *v* sbarcare.

disengage [ˌdisinˈgeidʒ] *v* disimpegnare, liberare; *(mech)* disinnestare. **disengaged** *adj* libero.

disfigure [disˈfigə] *v* sfigurare, deturpare.

disgrace [disˈgreis] *n* disonore *m*, vergogna *f*, scandalo *m*, ignominia *f*. *v* disonorare, screditare. **disgraceful** *adj* vergognoso.

disgruntled [disˈgrʌntld] *adj* di cattivo umore, scontento.

disguise [disˈgaiz] *v* camuffare, mascherare. *n* maschera *f*, travestimento *m*.

disgust [disˈgʌst] *n* disgusto *m*, ribrezzo *m*, schifo *m*. *v* disgustare, far schifo, nauseare. **disgusting** *adj* disgustoso, schifoso.

dish [diʃ] *n* piatto *m*. **dishcloth** *n*

strofinaccio per i piatti *m*. **dishwasher** *n* lavapiatti *m*.

dishearten [dis'ha:tn] *v* scoraggiare.

dishevelled [di'ʃevəld] *adj* scapigliato, arruffato.

dishonest [dis'ɔnist] *adj* disonesto. **dishonesty** *n* disonestà *f*.

dishonour [dis'ɔnə] *v* disonorare. *n* disonore *m*, infamia *f*. **dishonourable** *adj* disonorevole.

disillusion [disi'luːʒən] *v* disilludere, disingannare. *n* disillusione *f*, disinganno *m*.

disinfect [disin'fekt] *v* disinfettare. **disinfectant** *nm*, *adj* disinfettante.

disinherit [disin'herit] *v* diseredare.

disintegrate [dis'intigreit] *v* disintegrare, disgregare, disfare, disfarsi. **disintegration** *n* disfacimento *m*, sfacelo *m*, disintegrazione *f*.

disinterested [dis'intristid] *adj* disinteressato.

disjointed [dis'dʒɔintid] *adj* sconnesso, incoerente.

dislike [dis'laik] *v* detestare, sentire antipatia per. *n* antipatia *f*, avversione *f*.

dislocate [dislə'keit] *v* dislocare; *(joint)* lussare. **dislocation** *n* dislocazione *f*; lussazione *f*.

dislodge [dis'lɔdʒ] *v* sloggiare, scacciare.

disloyal [dis'lɔiəl] *adj* sleale, infedele. **disloyalty** *n* slealtà *f*, infedeltà *f*.

dismal [dizməl] *adj* triste, lugubre, malinconico.

dismantle [dis'mantl] *v* smantellare.

dismay [dis'mei] *v* costernare, sgomentare. *n* costernazione *f*, sgomento *m*.

dismiss [dis'mis] *v (send away)* respingere; *(discard)* scartare; *(discharge)* licenziare. **dismissal** *n* licenziamento *m*.

dismount [dis'maunt] *v* smontare.

disobey [disə'bei] *v* disubbidire, disobbedire. **disobedience** *n* disubbidienza *f*. **disobedient** *adj* disubbidiente.

disorder [dis'ɔtdə] *n* disordine *m*, confusione *f*; *(med)* disturbo *m*. **disorderly** *adj* disordinato.

disorganized [dis'ɔtgənaizd] *adj* disorganizzato. **disorganization** *n* disorganizzazione *f*.

disown [dis'oun] *v* ripudiare, rinnegare.

disparage [dis'paridʒ] *v* denigrare, screditare.

disparity [dis'pariti] *n* disparità *f*.

dispassionate [dis'paʃənit] *adj* spassionato, obiettivo.

dispatch [dis'patʃ] *v* spedire, inviare; *(settle)* sbrigare; *(kill)* spacciare. *n* spedizione *f*; *(mil)* dispaccio *m*; *(speed)* prontezza *f*, sollecitudine *f*.

dispel [dis'pel] *v* dissipare, scacciare.

dispense [dis'pens] *v* dispensare, distribuire; *(justice)* amministrare. **dispense with** fare a meno di. **dispensary** *n* dispensario *m*, farmacia *f*.

disperse [dis'pəts] *v* disperdere, spargliare, dileguarsi. **dispersion** *n* dispersione *f*, diffusione *f*.

displace [dis'pleis] *v* spostare; *(take place of)* soppiantare. **displaced person** profugo *(pl* -ghi*) m*, -a *f*. **displacement** *n* spostamento *m*.

display [dis'plei] *v* mostrare, esibire, ostentare, manifestare. *n* mostra *f*, manifestazione *f*, esposizione *f*.

displease [dis'pliz] *v* spiacere, dispiacere, scontentare. **displeasure** *n* dispiacere *m*, ira *f*.

dispose [dis'pouz] *v* disporre, sistemare. **dispose of** sbarazzarsi di, eliminare. **disposal** *n (control)* disposizione *f*; *(act of disposing)* sistemazione *f*. **disposed** *adj* disposto, intenzionato. **disposition** *n* disposizione *f*, tendenza *f*; *(character)* indole *f*.

disprove [dis'pruːv] *v* confutare.

dispute [dis'pjuːt] *n* disputa *f*, vertenza *f*; *(quarrel)* lite *f*. *v* contestare.

disqualify [dis'kwɔli,fai] *v (sport)* squalificare; *(render unfit)* incapacitare; *(law)* interdire. **disqualification** *n* squalifica *f*, incapacità *f*, interdizione *f*.

disregard [disrə'gaːd] *v* non far caso a, ignorare. *n* noncuranza *f*, inosservanza *f*.

disreputable [dis'repjutəbl] *adj* malfamato, vergognoso.

disrespect [disrə'spekt] *n* mancanza di rispetto *f*, irreverenza *f*. **disrespectful** *adj* poco rispettoso, che non mostra rispetto.

disrupt [dis'rʌpt] *v* scompigliare, mettere in confusione. **disruption** *n* scompiglio *m*.

dissatisfy [di'satisfai] *v* scontentare. **dissatisfaction** *n* insoddisfazione *f*.

dissect [di'sekt] *v* sezionare; *(corpse)* dissecare; *(analyse)* analizzare. **dissection** *n* sezionamento *m*; dissezione *f*; analisi *f*.

dissent [di'sent] *n* dissenso *m*. *v* dissentire.

dissident ['disidənt] *n(m+f)*, *adj* dissidente.

dissimilar [di'similə] *adj* dissimile.

dissipated ['disipeitid] *adj* dissoluto.

dissociate [di'sousieit] *v* dissociare, sdoppiare. **dissociation** *f* dissociazione *f*, sdoppiamento *m*.

dissolve [di'zolv] *v* sciogliere, sciogliersi, dissolvere. **dissolute** *adj* dissoluto, licenzioso.

dissuade [di'sweid] *v* dissuadere, distogliere. **dissuasion** *n* dissuasione *f*, distoglimento *m*.

distance ['distəns] *n* distanza *f*, lontananza *f*; (*reserve*) riserbo *m*. **distant** *adj* distante, lontano, remoto; riservato.

distaste [dis'teist] *n* avversione *f*. **distasteful** *adj* sgradevole.

distemper [dis'tempə] *n* (*paint*) intonaco *m*; (*canine*) cimurro *m*. *v* intonacare.

distended [dis'stendid] *adj* dilatato.

distil [di'stil] *v* distillare. **distillation** *n* distillazione *f*. **distillery** *n* distilleria *f*.

distinct [di'stiŋkt] *adj* differente, diverso; distinto; (*clear*) chiaro. **distinction** *n* distinzione *f*; differenza *f*. **distinctive** *adj* caratteristico, distintivo.

distinguish [di'stiŋgwiʃ] *v* distinguere, differenziare, individuare. **distinguish oneself** farsi notare. **distinguishable** *adj* distinguibile. **distinguished** *adj* distinto, insigne.

distort [di'stɔtt] *v* deformare, alterare. **distortion** *n* deformazione *f*, alterazione *f*.

distract [di'strakt] *v* distrarre; (*disturb*) turbare. **distraction** *n* distrazione *f*.

distraught [di'strott] *adj* turbato.

distress [di'stres] *n* (*anxiety*) angoscia *f*; (*poverty*) miseria *f*; (*ship*) pericolo *m*; (*worry*) preoccupazione *f*. *v* angosciare, affliggere, preoccupare. **distressed** *adj* dolente, angosciato. **distressing** *adj* penoso, doloroso.

distribute [di'stribjut] *v* distribuire. **distribution** *n* distribuzione *f*. **distributor** *n* distributore *m*.

district ['distrikt] *n* distretto *m*, quartiere *m*, zona *f*.

distrust [dis'trʌst] *v* diffidare di, sospettare, non aver fiducia in. *n* sospetto *m*, sfiducia *f*, diffidenza *f*.

disturb [di'stəɪb] *v* disturbare, incomodare. **disturbance** *n* disturbo *m*; (*breach of peace*) sommossa *f*.

ditch [ditʃ] *n* fossa *f*, fossato *m*. *v* (*abandon*) piantare.

ditto ['ditou] *adv* idem.

divan [di'van] *n* divano *m*.

dive [daiv] *v* tuffarsi, fare un tuffo, sommergersi. *n* (*plunge*) tuffo *m*; (*coll*) taverna *f*, bettola *f*. **diver** *n* palombaro *m*. **diving board** trampolino *m*. **diving suit** scafandro *m*.

diverge [dai'vɔtdʒ] *v* divergere.

diversify [dai'vəisifai] *v* diversificare, differenziare.

divert [dai'vɔtt] *v* deviare; distrarre; (*amuse*) divertire. **diversion** *n* (*distraction*) diversivo *m*, distrazione *f*; (*mil*) diversione *f*; deviazione *f*.

divide [di'vaid] *v* dividere, separare. **divided** *adj* diviso. **dividers** *pl n* compasso *m sing*. **division** *n* divisione *f*.

dividend ['dividend] *n* dividendo *m*.

divine [di'vain] *adj* divino, sacro. *n* teologo *m*, sacerdote *m*. *v* scoprire, indovinare; (*prophesy*) pronosticare. **diviner** *n* (*soothsayer*) indovino, -a *m*, *f*; (*user of divining rod*) rabdomante *m*. **divinity** *n* divinità *f*.

divorce [di'vɔɪs] *n* divorzio *m*. *v* divorziare, divorziarsi.

divulge [dai'vʌldʒ] *v* divulgare, diffondere.

dizzy ['dizi] *adj* vertiginoso. **feel dizzy** avere il capogiro; sentirsi girare la testa. **dizziness** *n* capogiro *m*, vertigine *f*.

*do [duɪ] *v* fare; (*suffice*) bastare; (*achieve*) compiere; (*carry out*) eseguire. **do away with** abolire; (*kill*) uccidere. **do-it-yourself** *adj* da fare da soli. **do out of** deprivare di. **do up** (*clothes, etc.*) abbottonare. **do without** fare a meno di. **how do you do?** come sta? (*polite*) come stai? **make do** arrangiarsi.

docile ['dousail] *adj* docile, mansueto.

dock[1] [dok] *n* (*wharf*) banchina *f*; (*waterway*) bacino *m*; (*port area*) zona portuale *f*. *v* attraccare. **docker** *n* portuale *m*. **dockyard** *n* cantiere navale *m*.

dock[2] [dok] *v* mozzare, troncare.

dock[3] [dok] *n* (*law*) banco degli imputati *m*.

docket ['dokit] *n* bolletta *f*.

doctor ['doktə] *n* dottore, -essa *m*, *f*; (*med*) medico, -chessa *m*, *f*. **doctorate** *n* dottorato *m*.

doctrine ['doktrin] *n* dottrina *f*. **doctrinal** *adj* dottrinale.

document ['dokjumənt] *n* documento *m*. *v* documentare. **documentary** *n* documentario *m*. **documentation** *n* documentazione *f*.

dodge [dodʒ] v schivare, scansare. n sotterfugio m, stratagemma f.

doe [dou] n selvaggina femmina f; (deer) daina f; (rabbit) femmina del coniglio f; (hare) lepre femmina f.

dog [dog] n cane m. **dog-eared** adj (page) accartocciato, con le orecchie. **dogrose** n rosa canina f. **dog-tired** adj stanco morto. **dogtooth** n dente canino m. v pedinare. **be dogged by** essere perseguitato da. **dogged** adj ostinato, accanito.

doge [doudʒ] n doge m.

dogma ['dogmə] n dogma m. **dogmatic** adj dogmatico.

dole [doul] n sussidio di disoccupazione m. v **dole out** distribuire.

doll [dol] n bambola f, pupa f. v **doll up** agghindarsi, abbellirsi.

dollar ['dolə] n dollaro m.

dolphin ['dolfin] n delfino m.

domain [də'mein] n (land) proprietà f; (law) demanio m; (control, sphere of activity) dominio m.

dome [doum] n cupola f.

domestic [də'mestik] adj domestico; (not foreign) nazionale. n domestico, -a m, f. **domesticate** v addomesticare. **domesticity** n domesticità f.

domicile ['domisail] n domicilio m.

dominate ['domi,neit] v dominare. **dominant** adj dominante.

domineer [,domi'niə] v signoreggiare. **domineering** adj imperioso; (overbearing) prepotente.

dominion [də'minjən] n dominio m; autorità f.

domino ['dominou] n domino m.

don¹ [don] v vestire, indossare.

don² [don] n (Spanish title) don m invar; (scholar) docente universitario, -a m, f.

donate [də'neit] v donare. **donation** n dono m, donazione f. **donor** n donatore, -trice m, f.

done [dʌn] V do.

donkey ['donki] n asino, -a m, f; somaro, -a m, f.

doom [duːm] n destino m, sorte f; (ruin) rovina f. v destinare, condannare. **doomed** adj condannato. **doomsday** n giorno del giudizio m.

door [doː] n porta f, uscio m. **doorbell** n campanello m. **door-handle** n maniglia f. **door-keeper** n portiere, -a m, f; portinaio, -a m, f. **door-knocker** n battiporta m,

batacchio m. **doormat** n zerbino m, stoino m. **doorstep** n soglia f. **doorway** n entrata f, portone m.

dope [doup] n (slang: drug) stupefacente m, droga f; (slang: information) notizie f pl. v drogare. **dopey** adj inebetito.

dormant ['doːmənt] adj addormentato, latente.

dormitory ['doːmitəri] n dormitorio m.

dormouse ['doː,maus] n ghiro m.

dose [dous] n dose f. v dosare.

dot [dot] n punto m. v punteggiare. **on the dot** in orario. **dotty** adj (coll) picchiatello.

dote [dout] v **dote on** essere infatuato di.

double ['dʌbl] v raddoppiare. **double up** piegare or piegarsi in due; contorcersi. adj doppio. n doppio m; (person) sosia m invar. **at the double** a passo di corsa. **double-barrelled** adj a doppia canna. **double bass** contrabbasso m. **double bed** letto matrimoniale m. **double-breasted** adj a doppio petto. **double-cross** v fare il doppio gioco, tradire.

doubt [daut] n dubbio m, incertezza f. v dubitare, mettere in dubbio. **doubtful** adj dubbio, incerto, problematico. **doubtless** adv senza dubbio.

dough [dou] n pasta f; (slang) quattrini m pl. **doughnut** n ciambella f, krapfen m invar.

dove [dʌv] n colomba f. **dovecot** n colombaia f. **dovetail** v (carpentry) incastrare a coda di rondine; (fit exactly) combaciare, far combaciare.

dowdy ['daudi] adj sciatto, trasandato.

down¹ [daun] adv giù, di sotto, per terra. adj depresso, abbattuto. **down and out** ridotto in miseria. v **down tools** abbandonare il lavoro.

down² [daun] n (plumage) piumino m, lanugine f; (soft hair) peluria f.

downcast ['daun,kaːst] adj abbattuto, depresso.

downfall ['daun,foːl] n rovina f, caduta f.

downhearted [,daun'haːtid] adj depresso, scoraggiato.

downhill [,daun'hil] adv in discesa.

downpour ['daun,poː] n acquazzone m.

downright ['daun,rait] adv categoricamente, nettamente.

downstairs [,daun'steəz] adv da basso, al piano inferiore. **go downstairs** scendere le scale.

downstream [ˌdaun'striːm] *adv* a valle, seguendo la corrente.

downtrodden [ˌdaun'trɔdn] *adj* oppresso.

downward ['daunwəd] *adj* discendente.

downwards ['daunwədz] *adv* in giù, verso il basso.

dowry ['dauəri] *n* dote *f.*

doze [douz] *v* sonnecchiare, fare un pisolino. **doze off** assopirsi. **dozy** *adj* sonnolento.

dozen ['dʌzn] *n* dozzina *f.*

drab [drab] *adj* squallido, scialbo.

draft [drɑːft] *n* (*sketch*) abbozzo *m*; (*preliminary copy*) brutta copia *f*; (*conscription*) leva *f*; (*written order*) tratta *f*, cambiale *f*; (*bank*) assegno circolare *m*. *v* abbozzare, delineare; (*conscript*) chiamare sotto le armi, arruolare.

drag [drag] *v* trascinare; (*search*) dragare; (*extract*) strappare. *n* trazione *f*. **in drag** vestito da donna.

dragon ['dragən] *n* drago *m*; (*woman*) megera *f*. **dragon-fly** *n* libellula *f.*

drain [drein] *n* fogna *f*, tubo di scarico *m*. *v* (*draw off*) scolare, prosciugare; (*med*) drenare; (*exhaust*) esaurire; (*drink up*) bere fino all'ultimo. **drainage** *n* scarico *m*, fognatura *f*, drenaggio *m*. **draining board** scolatoio *m*. **drainpipe** *n* grondaia *f.*

drama ['drɑːmə] *n* dramma *m*. **dramatic** *adj* drammatico, impressionante. **dramatist** *n* drammaturgo, -a *m*, *f*. **dramatize** *v* drammatizzare.

drank [drank] *V* **drink**.

drape [dreip] *v* drappeggiare.

draper ['dreipə] *n* negoziante di tessuti *m*, *f*. **drapery** *n* tessuti *m pl*; tendaggio *m.*

drastic ['drastik] *adj* drastico.

draught *or US* **draft** [drɑːft] *n* (*air current*) corrente d'aria *f*; (*drink*) sorso *m*; (*pull*) tiro *m*; (*fishing*) retata *f*. **draughts** *n* gioco della dama *m*. **draughtsman** *n* disegnatore, -trice *m*, *f*, progettista *m*, *f*; (*of documents*) compilatore, -trice *m*, *f*. **it's draughty** c'è una corrente d'aria.

*****draw** [drɔː] *v* (*pull*) tirare; (*attract*) attirare, attrarre; (*picture*) disegnare; (*sport*) pareggiare; (*extract*) estrarre. **draw back** ritirarsi. **drawback** *n* inconveniente *m*. **drawbridge** *n* ponte levatoio *m*. **draw near** avvicinarsi. **draw on** (*funds*) attingere (a). *n* (*sport*) pareggio *m*. **drawing** *n* disegno *m*. **drawing-board** *n* tavola

da disegno *f*. **drawing-pin** *n* puntina da disegno *f*. **drawing-room** *n* salotto *m.*

drawer ['drɔːə] *n* cassetto *m*. **chest of drawers** cassettone *m*. **drawers** *pl n* (*underclothes*) mutandine *f pl.*

drawl [drɔːl] *v* strascicare le parole.

drawn [drɔːn] *V* **draw**.

dread [dred] *v* aver paura di. *n* timore *m*, paura *f*, fobia *f*. **dreadful** *adj* spaventoso.

*****dream** [driːm] *n* sogno *m*; visione *f*. *v* sognare; immaginare. **dreamer** *n* sognatore, -trice *m*, *f*; visionario, -a *m*, *f*. **dreamy** *adj* (*vague*) vago.

dreamt [dremt] *V* **dream**.

dreary ['driəri] *adj* triste; (*boring*) noioso. **dreariness** *n* tristezza *f.*

dredge [dredʒ] *v* dragare.

dregs [dregz] *pl n* feccia *f sing*; (*coffee*) fondo *m sing.*

drench [drentʃ] *v* inzuppare, bagnare.

dress [dres] *v* (*clothe*) vestire; (*salad, etc.*) condire; (*wounds*) bendare. *n* abito *m*, vestito *m*. **dress circle** prima galleria *f*. **dressmaker** *n* sarta *f*. **dressmaking** *n* confezione di abiti da donna *f*. **dress rehearsal** prova generale *f*. **dressing** *n* condimento *m*; benda *f*. **dressing down** rimprovero *m*. **dressing-gown** *n* vestaglia *f*. **dressing-room** *n* camerino *m*. **dressing-table** *n* toilette (*pl* -s) *f.*

dresser[1] ['dresə] *n* (*furniture*) credenza *f.*

dresser[2] ['dresə] *n* (*theatre*) vestiarista *m*, *f*; (*med*) assistente medico, -a *m*, *f.*

drew [druː] *V* **draw**.

dribble ['dribl] *v* sbavare; (*trickle*) gocciolare; (*ball*) palleggiare. *n* bava *f*; gocciolamento *m*; palleggio *m.*

drier ['draiə] *n* (*clothes*) asciugatrice *f*; (*hair*) asciugacapelli *m.*

drift [drift] *v* andare alla deriva; (*wander aimlessly*) lasciarsi andare. **drift apart** perdersi di vista. *n* tendenza *f*, direzione *f*; (*movement*) deriva *f*; (*current*) corrente *f.*

drill[1] [dril] *n* trivella *f*, sonda *f*, trapano *m*. *v* trapanare, sondare.

drill[2] [dril] *n* esercitazioni *f pl*, addestramento *m*. *v* esercitarsi, fare esercitazioni, addestrare.

*****drink** [drink] *v* bere. *n* bibita *f*, bevanda *f*. **drinkable** *adj* bevibile, potabile. **drinking fountain** *n* fontanella *f*. **drinking water** acqua potabile *f.*

drip [drip] *v* gocciolare. *n* gocciolio *m*, gocciolatura *f*; (*slang*) persona insulsa *f.*

dripping n stillicidio m; (fat) grasso colato m.

*drive [draiv] v condurre; (car) guidare; (push) spingere. **drive away** scacciare. n (road) viale m; (trip) corsa f, giro m, energia f, iniziativa f; (golf) colpo forte m. **driver** n guidatore, -trice m, f. **driving-licence** n patente di guida f. **driving-test** n esame di guida m.

drivel ['drivl] n (nonsense) sciocchezze f pl. v dir sciocchezze.

driven ['drivn] V **drive**.

drizzle ['drizl] n pioggerella f. v piovigginare.

drone [droun] n (bee) fuco m, pecchione m; (idler) fannullone m; (hum) ronzio m. v (hum) ronzare. **droning** adj ronzante, monotono.

droop [druːp] v afflosciarsi, accasciarsi. n accasciamento m. **drooping** adj piegato in giù, floscio.

drop [drop] n goccia f; (fall) caduta f. v (fall) cadere; (let fall) far cadere; (lower) calare; diminuire, abbassarsi. **dropper** n contagocce m. **droppings** pl n sterco m sing.

dropout ['dropaut] n emarginato, -a m, f. v **drop out** ritirarsi, rinunciare.

drought [draut] n siccità f.

drove [drouv] V **drive**.

drown [draun] v annegare, affogare.

drowsy ['drauzi] adj sonnolento, assopito.

drudge [drʌdʒ] v sfacchinare, sgobbare. n sgobbone, -a m, f. **drudgery** n sfacchinata f.

drug [drʌg] n medicinale m, droga f, stupefacente m. **drug-addict** n drogato, -a m, f, tossicomane m, f. v narcotizzare, drogare.

drum [drʌm] n tamburo m, timpano m; (cylinder) cilindro m, rullo m. **drumstick** n bacchetta da tamburo f; (chicken) coscia di pollo f. v suonare il tamburo; (beat) tamburellare. **drummer** n tamburo m.

drunk [drʌŋk] V **drink**. adj ubriaco (m pl -chi), sbronzo. **get drunk** ubriacarsi. **drunkard** n ubriacone, -a m, f; sbronzo, -a m, f. **drunkenness** n ubriachezza f.

dry [drai] adj asciutto, secco; (uninteresting) monotono; (caustic) mordace. v asciugare, seccare. **dry-clean** v lavare a secco. **dry-cleaning** n lavaggio a secco m. **dry rot** carie del legno f.

dual ['djuəl] adj doppio, duplice.

dubbed ['dʌbd] adj (film) doppiato; (name) qualificato.

dubious ['djuːbiəs] adj dubbio, equivoco, incerto. **dubiousness** n incertezza f.

duchess ['dʌtʃis] n duchessa f.

duck[1] [dʌk] n (zool) anitra f. **duckling** n anatroccolo m.

duck[2] [dʌk] v (plunge) tuffare, immergere; (dodge) schivare; (lower the head) chinarsi di colpo.

dud [dʌd] adj inutile. n (explosive) proiettile che non esplode m.

due [djuː] adj (owing) da pagarsi; (rightful, proper) debito; (attributable) dovuto; (expected) atteso, in arrivo. adv direttamente. **due to** a causa di. **dues** pl n dazio m sing, diritti m pl.

duel ['djuəl] n duello m, lotta f.

duet [dju'et] n duetto m.

duffel bag ['dʌfəl] n sacca da viaggio f.

duffel coat ['dʌfəl] n montgomery m invar.

dug [dʌg] V **dig**.

duke [djuːk] n duca m.

dull [dʌl] adj (unintelligent) ottuso; (boring) noioso; (slow) lento; monotono; (not sharp) non tagliente; (weather) grigio. v attutire, attenuare, intorpidire. **dullness** n lentezza f; noia f.

duly ['djuːli] adv debitamente.

dumb [dʌm] adj muto, reticente; (slang: foolish) scemo. **dumbfound** v sbalordire, stupire.

dummy ['dʌmi] adj falso, finto. n (man of straw) uomo di paglia m; (cards) morto m; (baby's) biberon m invar, poppatoio m; (model) manichino m.

dump [dʌmp] n (tip) luogo di scarico m; (coll) posto triste m. v (get rid of) scartare, disfarsi di; (unload) scaricare.

dunce [dʌns] n ignorante m, f.

dune [djuːn] n duna f.

dung [dʌŋ] n letame m, sterco m.

dungarees [ˌdʌŋgə'riːz] pl n (overalls) tuta f sing.

dungeon ['dʌndʒən] n segreta f, cella sotterranea f.

duplicate ['djuːplikət; v 'djuːplikeit] adj duplice, doppio. n duplicato m, duplice copia f, doppione m. v duplicare.

durable ['djuərəbl] adj durevole, duraturo.

duration [dju'reiʃən] n durata f.

during ['djuriŋ] *prep* durante, nel corso di.

dusk [dʌsk] *n* crepuscolo *m*.

dust [dʌst] *n* polvere *f*. *v* (*clean*) spolverare; (*sprinkle*) cospargere. **dustbin** *n* pattumiera *f*. **dustman** *n* spazzino *m*. **dustpan** *n* paletta per la spazzatura *f*. **duster** *n* spolverino *m*, strofinaccio *m*. **dusty** *adj* polveroso.

Dutch [dʌtʃ] *adj* olandese. **Dutch person** olandese *m*, *f*. **go Dutch** fare *or* pagare alla romana.

duty ['djuːti] *n* dovere *m*; (*customs*) dogana *f*.

duvet ['duːvei] *n* piumino *m*.

dwarf [dwoːf] *n* nano *m*. *v* (*make appear small*) far sembrar piccolo; (*render insignificant*) sminuire.

dwell [dwel] *v* (*reside*) dimorare. **dwell on** soffermarsi su. **dwelling** *n* dimora *f*, abitazione *f*.

dwelt [dwelt] *V* **dwell**.

dwindle ['dwindl] *v* diminuire; (*decline*) deperire.

dye [dai] *n* colorante *m*, tintura *f*. *v* colorare, tingere. **dyed in the wool** inveterato, radicato. **dyer** *n* tintore *m*.

dyke [daik] *n* diga *f*, argine *m*.

dynamic [dai'namik] *adj* dinamico. **dynamics** *n* dinamica *f*.

dynamite ['dainə,mait] *n* dinamite *f*.

dynamo ['dainə,mou] *n* dinamo *f invar*.

dynasty ['dinəsti] *n* dinastia *f*.

dysentery ['disəntri] *n* dissenteria *f*.

dyslexia [dis'leksiə] *n* dislessia *f*.

dyspepsia [dis'pepsiə] *n* dispepsia *f*.

E

each [iːtʃ] *adj* ogni, ciascuno. *pron* ognuno. *adv* (*apiece*) l'uno, l'una. **each other** l'un l'altro.

eager ['iːgə] *adj* avido, premuroso; impaziente. **eagerness** *n* impazienza *f*; zelo *m*; brama *f*.

eagle ['iːgl] *n* aquila *f*.

ear¹ [iə] *n* orecchio *m*. **be up to one's ears in** ... aver ... fin sopra i capelli. **earache** *n* mal d'orecchi *m*. **eardrum** *n* timpano *m*. **earmark** *v* contrassegnare; (*set aside*) mettere da parte; (*money*) stanziare. **ear-plug** *n* tappo per orecchi *m*. **ear-ring** *n* orecchino *m*. **ear-splitting**

adj assordante. **within earshot** a portata d'orecchio.

ear² [iə] *n* spiga *f*.

earl [əːl] *n* conte *m*.

early ['əːli] *adv* presto, di buon'ora. *adj* primo; (*morning*) mattiniero, mattutino; (*before time*) prematuro; (*ancient*) antico (*m pl* -chi).

earn [əːn] *v* guadagnare, meritare. **earnings** *pl n* guadagni *m pl*, stipendio *m*.

earnest ['əːnist] *adj* serio, coscienzioso. **be in earnest** fare sul serio. **earnestness** *n* serietà *f*.

earth [əːθ] *n* terra *f*; (*world*) mondo *m*; (*soil*) terreno *m*. **earthquake** *n* terremoto *m*. *v* (*elec*) mettere a terra. **earthenware** *n* terraglia *f*. **earthly** *adj* terrestre. **earthy** *adj* (*coarse*) grossolano; robusto.

earwig ['iəwig] *n* forbicina *f*.

ease [iːz] *n* agio *m*, comodo *m*. **at ease** tranquillo. **ill at ease** a disagio. *v* agevolare, alleggerire.

easel ['iːzl] *n* cavalletto m.

east [iːst] *adj* orientale, dell'est. *n* oriente *m*, est *m*. **Middle/Near/Far East** medio/prossimo/estremo oriente *m*. **eastward** *adv*, *adj* verso est, ad est, verso oriente.

Easter ['iːstə] *n* Pasqua *f*.

easy ['iːzi] *adj* facile, semplice; (*informal*) disinvolto; (*compliant*) accomodante. **easy chair** poltrona *f*. **easy-going** *adj* (*placid*) bonaccione, pacione; indolente; tollerante.

eat [iːt] *v* mangiare. **eatable** *adj* mangiabile, mangereccio.

eaten ['iːtn] *V* **eat**.

eavesdrop ['iːvzdrop] *v* origliare.

ebb [eb] *n* riflusso *m*; declino *m*. *v* rifluire; declinare.

eccentric [ik'sentrik] *nm*, *adj* eccentrico. **eccentricity** *n* eccentricità *f*.

ecclesiastical [ikliːzi'astikl] *adj* ecclesiastico.

echo ['ekou] *v* echeggiare, far eco a. *n* eco *f*, *m* (*pl* -i *m*).

eclair [ei'kleə] *n* bignè *m invar*.

eclipse [i'klips] *n* eclissi *f*. *v* eclissare.

ecology [i'kolədʒi] *n* ecologia *f*.

economy [i'konəmi] *n* economia *f*. **economical** *or* **economic** *adj* economico, a buon prezzo; (*thrifty*) frugale. **economics** *n* economia *f*, scienze economiche *f pl*. **economist** *n* economista *m*, *f*. **economize** *v* economizzare, fare economia.

ecstasy ['ekstəsi] *n* estasi *f*. **ecstatic** *adj* estatico.

eczema ['eksimə] *n* eczema *m*.

edge [edʒ] *n* orlo *m*, margine *m*; (*blade*) filo *m*; (*road*) ciglio *m*; (*river*) sponda *f*. **be on edge** avere i nervi. *v* orlare.

edible ['edəbl] *adj* mangereccio, mangiabile.

Edinburgh ['edinbərə] *n* Edimburgo *f*.

edit ['edit] *v* curare, redigere, dirigere. **editor** *n* redattore, -trice *m*, *f*; (*newspaper*) direttore, -trice *m*, *f*. **editorial** *n* articolo di fondo *m*. **edition** *n* edizione *f*.

educate ['edjukeit] *v* educare, istruire. **educated** *adj* colto, istruito. **education** *n* educazione *f*, istruzione *f*; (*teaching*) insegnamento *m*, pedagogia *f*.

eel [iil] *n* anguilla *f*.

eerie ['iəri] *adj* (*strange*) misterioso; (*causing fear*) pauroso.

effect [i'fekt] *n* effetto *m*; conseguenza *f*, risultato *m*; impressione *f*. **take effect** entrare in vigore. **with effect from** a partire da. *v* effettuare, realizzare. **effective** *adj* efficace, efficiente.

effeminate [i'feminət] *adj* effeminato.

effervescent [,efə'vesnt] *adj* effervescente.

efficient [i'fiʃnt] *adj* efficiente, capace. **efficiency** *n* efficienza *f*, capacità *f*; (*machine*) rendimento *m*.

effigy ['efidʒi] *n* effigie *f*.

effort ['efət] *n* sforzo *m*, fatica *f*. **make an effort** sforzarsi, fare di tutto. **effortless** *adj* senza sforzo.

egg [eg] *n* uovo *m* (*pl* -a *f*). **egg-cup** *n* portauovo *m*. **egg-shaped** *adj* ovale. **eggshell** *n* guscio d'uovo *m*. **egg-whisk** *n* frullino *m*. *v* **egg on** aizzare.

ego ['iigou] *n* ego *m*. **egocentric** *adj* egocentrico. **egoism** *n* egoismo *m*. **egoist** *n* egoista *m*, *f*. **egoistic(al)** *adj* egoista, egoistico. **egotism** *n* egoismo *m*. **egotist** *n* egoista *m*, *f*. **egotistic(al)** *adj* egoista.

Egypt ['iidʒipt] *n* Egitto *m*. **Egyptian** *n* Egiziano, -a; *adj* egiziano, -a; (*ancient*) egizio, -a.

eiderdown ['aidədaun] *n* piumino *m*.

eight [eit] *nm*, *adj* otto. **eighth** *nm*, *adj* ottavo.

eighteen [ei'tiin] *nm*, *adj* diciotto. **eighteenth** *nm*, *adj* diciottesimo.

eighty ['eiti] *nm*, *adj* ottanta. **eightieth** *nm*, *adj* ottantesimo.

either ['aiðə] *pron*, *adj* l'uno o l'altro; (*each*) ciascuno dei due, tutti e due. *adv* nemmeno, neppure, neanche. *conj* **either ... or ...**, o ... o ..., sia ... che ..., sia ... sia ...

ejaculate [i'dʒakjuleit] *v* eiaculare; esclamare. **ejaculation** *n* eiaculazione *f*, esclamazione *f*.

eject [i'dʒekt] *v* espellere, gettar fuori. **ejector seat** sedile eiettabile *m*.

eke [iik] *v* **eke out** supplire. **eke out a living** sbarcare il lunario.

elaborate [i'labreit; *adj* i'labərət] *v* elaborare, sviluppare. *adj* elaborato, minuzioso.

elapse [i'laps] *v* passare, decorrere.

elastic [i'lastik] *nm*, *adj* elastico.

elated [i'leitid] *adj* giubilante, euforico.

elbow ['elbou] *n* gomito *m*. **elbow-room** *n* libertà di movimento *f*. *v* (*jostle*) dar gomitate.

elder[1] ['eldə] *adj* più vecchio, maggiore. *n* anziano, -a *m*, *f*. **elderly** *adj* di una certa età, anziano.

elder[2] ['eldə] *n* sambuco (*pl* -chi) *m*. **elderberry** *n* bacca di sambuco *f*.

eldest ['eldist] *adj* più vecchio, maggiore, primogenito.

elect [i'lekt] *v* eleggere, scegliere. *adj* eletto, scelto. **election** *n* elezione *f*. **electioneering** *n* campagna elettorale *f*. **electorate** *n* elettorato *m*. **elector** *n* elettore, -trice *m*, *f*.

electricity [elek'trisəti] *n* elettricità *f*. **electric** *adj* elettrico. **electric appliances** elettrodomestici *m pl*. **electrician** *n* elettricista *m*. **electrify** *v* elettrificare. **electrocution** *n* elettroesecuzione *f*. **electrode** *n* elettrodo *m*. **electrolysis** *n* elettrolisi *f*. **electron** *n* elettrone *m*. **electronic** *adj* elettronico. **electronics** *n* elettronica *f*.

elegant ['eligənt] *adj* elegante, fine. **elegance** *n* eleganza *f*, finezza *f*.

elegy ['elidʒi] *n* elegia *f*. **elegiac** *adj* elegiaco.

element ['eləmənt] *n* elemento *m*, fattore *m*. **elemental** *adj* fondamentale. **elementary** *adj* elementare.

elephant ['elifənt] *n* elefante *m*. **elephantine** *adj* elefantesco.

elevate ['eliveit] *v* elevare, innalzare; (*exalt*) esaltare. **elevated** *adj* elevato, eminente. **elevation** *n* (*altitude*) altezza *f*; (*drawing*) proiezione ortogonale *f*; (*grandeur*) elevatezza *f*. **elevator** *n* (*lift*) ascensore *m*.

eleven [i'levn] *nm, adj* undici. **eleventh** *nm, adj* undicesimo.

elf [elf] *n* elfo *m*, folletto *m*.

eligible ['elidʒəbl] *adj* eleggibile; desiderabile.

eliminate [i'limineit] *v* eliminare, scartare. **elimination** *n* eliminazione *f*.

elite [ei'liːt] *n* élite (*pl* -s) *f*, fior fiore *m invar*.

ellipse [i'lips] *n* ellisse *f*.

elm [elm] *n* olmo *m*.

elocution [elə'kjuːʃən] *n* elocuzione *f*.

elope [i'loup] *v* fuggire. **elopement** *n* fuga *f*.

eloquent ['eləkwənt] *adj* eloquente, rettorico. **eloquence** *n* eloquenza *f*, rettorica *f*.

else [els] *adv, pron* altro, altrimenti. **elsewhere** *adv* altrove.

elucidate [i'luːsideit] *v* chiarire, spiegare.

elude [i'luːd] *v* eludere, evitare. **elusive** *adj* evasivo, elusivo.

emaciated [i'meisieitid] *adj* scarno, emaciato.

emanate ['eməneit] *v* emanare, emettere, scaturire. **emanation** *n* emanazione *f*, emissione *f*.

emancipate [i'mansipeit] *v* emancipare. **emancipation** *n* emancipazione *f*.

embalm [im'baɪm] *v* imbalsamare.

embankment [im'baŋkmənt] *n* argine *m*, lungofiume *m*.

embargo [im'baɪgou] *n* embargo *m*, sanzioni *f pl*, proibizione *f*.

embark [im'baɪk] *v* imbarcare. **embark on** intraprendere.

embarrass [im'barəs] *v* mettere in imbarazzo. **embarrassment** *n* imbarazzo *m*.

embassy ['embəsi] *n* ambasciata *f*.

embellish [im'beliʃ] *v* abbellire, ornare. **embellishment** *n* abbellimento *m*.

ember ['embə] *n* tizzone *m*. **embers** *pl n* brace *f pl*.

embezzle [im'bezl] *v* appropriarsi indebitamente. **embezzlement** *n* appropriazione indebita *f*, malversazione *f*. **embezzler** *n* malversatore, -trice *m, f*.

embitter [im'bitə] *v* rendere amaro, amareggiare.

emblem ['embləm] *n* emblema *m*, simbolo *m*.

embody [im'bodi] *v* incorporare; (*comprise*) comprendere; incarnare; concretare.

emboss [im'bos] *v* sbalzare, fare in rilievo, scolpire in rilievo.

embrace [im'breis] *v* abbracciare. *n* abbraccio *m*.

embroider [im'broidə] *v* ricamare; (*embellish*) abbellire. **embroidery** *n* ricamo *m*.

embryo ['embriou] *n* embrione *m*. **embryonic** *adj* embrionale.

emerald ['emərəld] *n* smeraldo *m*.

emerge [i'məːdʒ] *v* emergere.

emergency [i'məːdʒənsi] *n* emergenza *f*, caso imprevisto *m*. **emergency exit** uscita di sicurezza *f*. **in case of emergency** in caso di urgenza.

emigrate ['emigreit] *v* emigrare. **emigration** *n* emigrazione *f*.

eminent ['eminənt] *adj* eminente, distinto.

emit [i'mit] *v* emettere, emanare. **emission** *n* emissione *f*.

emotion [i'mouʃən] *n* emozione *f*, sentimento *m*, commozione *f*. **emotional** emotivo; impressionabile.

empathy ['empəθi] *n* empatia *f*, immedesimazione *f*.

emphasis ['emfəsis] *n, pl* -ses enfasi *f*, veemenza *f*, rilievo *m*. **emphasize** *v* dare rilievo a, mettere in evidenza. **emphatic** *adj* enfatico, risoluto, intenso.

empire ['empaiə] *n* impero *m*. **emperor** *n* imperatore *m*. **empress** *n* imperatrice *f*.

empirical [im'pirikal] *adj* empirico.

employ [im'ploi] *v* impiegare; (*use*) adoperare, usare. **employee** *n* impiegato, -a *m, f*. **employer** *n* padrone, -a *m, f*; datore, -trice di lavoro *m, f*. **employment** *n* impiego (*pl* -ghi) *m*, lavoro *m*. **employment agency** ufficio di collocamento *m*.

empower [im'pauə] *v* autorizzare.

empty ['empti] *adj* vuoto. *v* vuotare, scaricare. **empty-handed** *adj* a mani vuote.

emulate ['emjuleit] *v* emulare. **emulation** *n* emulazione *f*.

emulsion [i'mʌlʃən] *n* emulsione *f*.

enable [i'neibl] *v* mettere in grado di, permettere; (*law*) abilitare.

enact [i'nakt] *v* (*ordain*) ordinare; (*decree*) decretare; (*put into operation*) promulgare; (*theatre*) recitare.

enamel [i'naməl] *n* smalto *m*. *v* smaltare.

enamoured [i'naməd] *adj* innamorato.

enchant [in'tʃaint] *v* incantare, affascinare, ammaliare. **enchanting** *adj* incantevole. **enchantment** *n* incanto *m*, incantesimo *m*, fascino *m*.

encircle [in'sətkl] v cingere, accerchiare. **encirclement** n accerchiamento m.

enclose [in'klouz] v rinchiudere; (letter) allegare. **enclosure** n recinto m; (letter) allegato m; (rel) clausura f.

encore ['oŋkɔː] nm, interj bis.

encounter [in'kauntə] v incontrare, affrontare. n incontro m; (battle) lotta f.

encourage [in'kʌridʒ] v incoraggiare, favorire, stimolare. **encouragement** n incitamento m, stimolo m.

encroach [in'kroutʃ] v **encroach on** abusare di; (intrude on) invadere.

encumber [in'kʌmbə] v ingombrare, impacciare; (burden) sopraffare. **encumbrance** n (hindrance) impaccio m; (burden) carico m (pl -chi) m.

encyclopedia [insaiklə'piːdiə] n enciclopedia f.

end [end] n fine f, termine m; (purpose) scopo m; (result) conclusione f. **in the end** infine. **make ends meet** sbarcare il lunario. v finire, concludere, terminare. **endless** adj interminabile, senza fine.

endanger [in'deindʒə] v mettere in pericolo, compromettere.

endear [in'diə] v rendere caro. **endearing** adj simpatico, amabile.

endeavour [in'devə] v cercare, tentare. n sforzo m, tentativo m.

endemic [en'demik] n endemico.

endive ['endiv] n indivia f, cicoria f.

endorse [in'dɔːs] v approvare; (sign) vistare; (cheque) girare; (record infringement) annotare le infrazioni commesse. **endorsement** n visto m, girata f, annotazione delle infrazioni commesse f.

endow [in'dau] v dotare, fornire. **endowment** n dotazione f, donazione f.

endure [in'djuə] v tollerare, sopportare; (last) durare; resistere. **endurance** n resistenza f.

enema ['enəmə] n clistere m, enteroclisma m.

enemy ['enəmi] n nemico, -a m, f; avversario, -a m, f.

energy ['enədʒi] n energia f. **energetic** adj energico.

enfold [in'fould] v avvolgere.

enforce [in'fɔːs] v imporre, far valere, far rispettare. **enforced** adj obbligatorio, imposto. **enforcement** n imposizione f, applicazione f.

engage [in'geidʒ] v (employ) assumere, impiegare; (occupy) impegnare,

occupare; (mil) attaccare; (interlock) ingranare, innestare; (reserve) prenotare. **engaged** adj (busy) occupato; (betrothed) fidanzato. **get engaged** fidanzarsi. **engagement** n fidanzamento m; (employment) impiego (pl -ghi) m; (obligation) impegno m; (appointment) appuntamento m.

engine ['endʒin] n motore m, macchina f; (rail) locomotiva f.

engineer [endʒi'niə] n ingegnere, -a m, f; meccanico, -a m, f; tecnico, -a m, f; (mil) geniere m. v (construct) costruire; (contrive) macchinare, tramare. **engineering** n costruzione f; (study, science) ingegneria f.

England ['iŋglənd] n Inghilterra f. **English** n(m+f), adj inglese.

engrave [in'greiv] v incidere, intagliare; (printing) imprimere. **engraver** n incisore m, intagliatore m. **engraving** n incisione f.

engrossed [in'groust] adj preso (da), immerso.

engulf [in'gʌlf] v ingolfare.

enhance [in'hɑːns] v intensificare, aumentare, migliorare.

enigma [i'nigmə] n enigma m. **enigmatic** adj enigmatico, misterioso.

enjoy [in'dʒɔi] v godere, apprezzare. **enjoy oneself** divertirsi. **enjoyable** adj divertente, piacevole. **enjoyment** n piacere m, godimento m, gioia f, divertimento m.

enlarge [in'lɑːdʒ] v ingrandire. **enlarge on** dilungarsi su. **enlargement** n ingrandimento m; (med) ipertrofia f.

enlighten [in'laitn] v illuminare, chiarire. **enlightenment** n schiarimento m, delucidazione f; (history) illuminismo m.

enlist [in'list] v arruolare; (obtain) ottenere. **enlistment** n arruolamento m.

enliven [in'laivn] v animare, ravvivare.

enmity ['enmiti] n ostilità f.

enormous [i'nɔːməs] adj enorme, immenso.

enough [i'nʌf] adv abbastanza, sufficientemente. adj sufficiente, abbastanza, bastante. **be enough** bastare. interj basta!

enquire [in'kwaiə] V inquire.

enrage [in'reidʒ] v far arrabbiare. **enraged** adj arrabbiato, furioso.

enrich [in'ritʃ] v arricchire, abbellire.

enrol [in'roul] v (mil) arruolare; (college, etc.) iscrivere. **enrolment** n arruolamento m; iscrizione f.

enslave [in'sleiv] *v* far schiavo, assoggettare. **enslavement** *n* schiavitù *f*.

ensue [in'sju:] *v* seguire, risultare.

ensure [in'ʃuə] *v* assicurare, garantire.

entail [in'teil] *v* comportare, implicare.

entangle [in'tangl] *v* impigliare, aggrovigliare; (*involve*) coinvolgere. **entanglement** *n* impiccio *m*, imbroglio *m*.

enter ['entə] *v* entrare (in); penetrare; (*join*) iscriversi a; (*record*) notare.

enterprise ['entə,praiz] *n* impresa *f*, iniziativa *f*. **enterprising** *adj* intraprendente, pieno d'iniziativa.

entertain [,entə'tein] *v* (*amuse*) divertire; (*receive guests*) ricevere ospitare; (*consider*) concepire, prendere in considerazione. **entertainer** *n* (*actor*) attore, -trice *m*, *f*; (*singer*) cantante *m*, *f*. **entertaining** *adj* divertente, piacevole. **entertainment** *n* divertimento *m*, spettacolo *m*.

enthral [in'θrɔːl] *v* affascinare.

enthusiasm [in'θuːziˌazəm] *n* entusiasmo *m*. **enthusiast** *n* entusiasta *m*, *f*; (*fam*) tifoso, -a *m*, *f*. **enthusiastic** *adj* entusiastico, appassionato.

entice [in'tais] *v* sedurre, allettare. **enticement** *n* seduzione *f*, allettamento *m*.

entire [in'taiə] *adj* intero, completo, assoluto. **in its entirety** nel suo insieme.

entitle [in'taitl] *v* dar diritto a, qualificare, autorizzare; (*name*) intitolare. **entitlement** *n* diritto *m*, titolo *m*.

entity ['entəti] *n* entità *f*.

entrails ['entreilz] *pl n* viscere *f pl*.

entrance[1] ['entrəns] *n* entrata *f*, ingresso *m*, ammissione *f*.

entrance[2] [in'trains] *v* incantare, estasiare.

entrant ['entrənt] *n* candidato, -a *m*, *f*; concorrente *m*, *f*.

entreat [in'triːt] *v* supplicare, implorare. **entreaty** *n* supplica *f*, preghiera *f*.

entrée ['ontrei] *n* (*main course*) piatto principale *m*, secondo piatto *m*; (*first course*) primo piatto *m*.

entrench [in'trentʃ] *v* trincerare, rafforzare. **entrenched** *adj* (*set*) radicato.

entrepreneur [,ontrəprə'nəi] *n* imprenditore, -trice *m*, *f*.

entrust [in'trʌst] *v* affidare.

entry ['entri] *n* entrata *f*; (*book-keeping*) partita *f*; annotazione *f*.

entwine [in'twain] *v* intrecciare.

enumerate [i'njuːm/ vorwait]   *ereit] *v* annoverare, elencare.

enunciate [i'nʌnsiˌeit] *v* enunciare; articolare.

envelop [in'veləp] *v* avvolgere.

envelope ['envə,loup] *n* busta *f*.

environment [in'vaiərənmənt] *n* ambiente *m*.

envisage [in'vizidʒ] *v* contemplare, immaginare.

envoy ['envoi] *n* inviato, -a *m*, *f*.

envy ['envi] *n* invidia *f*. *v* invidiare. **envious** *adj* invidioso.

enzyme ['enzaim] *n* enzima *m*.

ephemeral [i'femərəl] *adj* effimero, passeggero.

epic ['epik] *adj* epico. *n* epopea *f*.

epicure ['epikjuə] *n* epicureo *m*; (*gourmet*) buongustaio, -a *m*, *f*.

epidemic [epi'demik] *n* epidemia *f*. *adj* epidemico.

epilepsy ['epilepsi] *n* epilessi *f*. **epileptic** *nm*, *adj* epilettico.

epilogue ['epilog] *n* epilogo (*pl* -ghi) *m*.

Epiphany [i'pifəni] *n* Epifania *f*.

episcopal [i'piskəpəl] *adj* vescovile.

episode ['episoud] *n* episodio *m*, incidente *m*.

epitaph ['epi,taːf] *n* epitaffio *m*.

epitome [i'pitəmi] *n* epitome *f*, compendio *m*.

epoch ['iːpok] *n* epoca *f*.

equable ['ekwəbl] *adj* equanime, sereno, uniforme.

equal ['iːkwəl] *adj* eguale, uguale, pari. *v* uguagliare; (*in calculations*) fare. **equality** *n* uguaglianza *f*, parità *f*. **equalize** *v* ragguagliare; (*sport*) pareggiare.

equanimity [ekwə'nimiti] *n* equanimità *f*, serenità *f*.

equate [i'kweit] *v* uguagliare, paragonare. **equation** *n* equazione *f*.

equator [i'kweitə] *n* equatore *m*.

equestrian [i'kwestriən] *adj* equestre.

equilateral [,iːkwi'lætərəl] *adj* equilatero.

equilibrium [,iːkwi'libriəm] *n* equilibrio *m*. **equilibrate** *v* equilibrare, bilanciare.

equinox ['ekwinoks] *n* equinozio *m*.

equip [i'kwip] *v* (*array*) allestire; (*furnish*) attrezzare, fornire (di), dotare (di). **equipment** *n* equipaggiamento *m*, attrezzatura *f*.

equity ['ekwəti] *n* giustizia *f*; imparzialità *f*; (*property*) valore netto *m*; (*securities*) azioni ordinarie *f pl*.

equivalent [i'kwivələnt] *nm*, *adj* equivalente.

era ['iərə] n era f, epoca f.
eradicate [i'rædi,keit] v sradicare, estirpare.
erase [i'reiz] v cancellare.
erect [i'rekt] v erigere, costruire. adj eretto, dritto. **erection** n erezione f.
ermine ['əːmin] n ermellino m.
erode [i'roud] v erodere. **erosion** n erosione f.
erotic [i'rotik] adj erotico.
err [əː] v errare; (make mistakes) sbagliare; (sin) peccare.
errand ['erənd] n commissione f. **errand-boy** n fattorino m.
erratic [i'rætik] adj erratico.
error ['erə] n errore m, sbaglio m, torto m. **erroneous** adj erroneo.
erudite ['erudait] adj erudito, dotto. **erudition** n erudizione f.
erupt [i'rʌpt] v (volcano) eruttare; (burst out) erompere. **eruption** n eruzione f.
escalate ['eskə,leit] v intensificare. **escalation** n intensificazione f. **escalator** n scala mobile f.
escalope ['eskə,lop] n scaloppina f.
escape [is'keip] v fuggire, sfuggire; (avoid) evitare. n fuga f, evasione f. **escapism** n evasione dalla realtà f.
escort [es'kɔːt; n 'eskɔːt] n scorta f. v scortare.
esoteric [esə'terik] adj esoterico.
especial [i'speʃəl] adj notevole, particolare. **especially** adv specie, specialmente.
espionage ['espiə,naːʒ] n spionaggio m.
esplanade [,esplə'neid] n spianata f; lungomare m.
essay ['esei] n saggio m, tema m.
essence ['esns] n essenza f; (gist) nocciolo m.
essential [i'senʃəl] adj essenziale, indispensabile.
establish [i'stæbliʃ] v stabilire, fondare; (ascertain) constatare; (set up) istituire, instaurare; (fix) determinare. **established** adj (set) radicato; (beyond question) indubbio. **establishment** n costituzione f, fondazione f; (house) casa f; (organization) personale effettivo m.
estate [i'steit] n (property) tenuta f; (possessions) beni m pl, patrimonio m. **estate agent** agente immobiliare m. **estate car** giardinetta f. **housing estate** quartiere residenziale m.
esteem [i'stiːm] n stima f, considerazione f. v stimare, apprezzare.

estimate ['esti,meit; n 'estimət] v (value) valutare; (judge) stimare; (assess cost) preventivare. n preventivo m; valutazione f. **estimation** n valutazione f; considerazione f.
estrange [i'streindʒ] v alienare. **estrangement** n alienazione f; allontanamento m.
estuary ['estjuəri] n estuario m.
eternal [i'təːnl] adj eterno. **eternity** n eternità f.
ether ['iːθə] n etere m.
ethereal [i'θiəriəl] adj etereo, evanescente.
ethical ['eθikl] adj etico, morale. **ethics** pl n etica f sing, morale f sing.
ethnic ['eθnik] adj etnico. **ethnology** n etnologia f.
etiquette ['eti,ket] n etichetta f, comportamento m, cerimoniale m.
etymology [,eti'molədʒi] n etimologia f. **etymological** adj etimologico.
Eucharist ['juːkərist] n eucaristia f.
eunuch ['juːnək] n eunuco (pl -chi) m.
euphemism ['juːfə,mizəm] n eufemismo m. **euphemistic** adj eufemistico.
euphoria [ju'fɔːriə] n euforia f. **euphoric** adj euforico.
Europe ['juərəp] n Europa f. **European** n, adj europeo, -a. **European Economic Community** Comunità Economica Europea f.
euthanasia [,juːθə'neiziə] n eutanasia f.
evacuate [i'vækju,eit] v evacuare, sfollare. **evacuation** n evacuazione f, sfollamento m.
evade [i'veid] v evadere, evitare, eludere. **evasion** n evasione f. **evasive** adj evasivo, elusivo.
evaluate [i'vælju,eit] v valutare. **evaluation** n valutazione f.
evangelical [,iːvan'dʒelikəl] adj evangelico. **evangelist** n evangelista m.
evaporate [i'væpə,reit] v evaporare, far evaporare. **evaporation** n evaporazione f.
eve [iːv] n vigilia f.
even ['iːvən] adj (flat) piano, piatto; (regular) uniforme, regolare; (not odd) pari. adv (still) ancora; (indeed) perfino. **even if** benché, sebbene, quantunque. v livellare, uguagliare.
evening ['iːvniŋ] n sera f, serata f. **evening class** classe or scuola serale f. **evening dress** abito da sera m.
evensong ['iːvən,soŋ] n vespro m.

event [i'vent] *n* avvenimento *m*, evento *m*; (*outcome*) eventualità *f*; (*sport*) gara *f*. **eventful** *adj* ricco di vicende, memorabile. **eventual** *adj* finale, contingente. **eventually** *adv* alla fine, ultimamente.

ever ['evə] *adv* sempre, mai. **ever since** da quando, da allora. **evergreen** *nm*, *adj* sempreverde. **everlasting** *adj* eterno, perpetuo, perenne. **hardly ever** quasi mai.

every ['evri] *adj* ogni, ognuno, ciascuno. **everybody** or **everyone** *pron* ognuno, tutti *pl*. **everyday** *adj* quotidiano, normale. **every now and then** di tanto in tanto. **every other day** un giorno sì un giorno no. **everything** *pron* tutto, ogni cosa. **everywhere** *adv* dovunque, dappertutto.

evict [i'vikt] *v* sfrattare. **eviction** *n* sfratto *m*.

evidence ['evidəns] *n* prova *f*, evidenza *f*; (*law*) testimonianza *f*, deposizione *f*. **give evidence** (*law*) deporre, testimoniare. **evident** *adj* evidente, manifesto, ovvio.

evil ['iːvl] *adj* cattivo, malvagio. *n* male *m*, peccato *m*. **evil-doer** malfattore, -trice *m*, *f*. **evil eye** malocchio *m*. **evil-looking** *adj* losco. **evil-minded** *adj* malintenzionato.

evoke [i'vouk] *v* evocare.

evolve [i'volv] *v* evolvere, sviluppare. **evolution** *n* evoluzione *f*.

ewe [juː] *n* pecora (femmina) *f*.

exacerbate [ig'zasə,beit] *v* esacerbare, inasprire, irritare.

exact [ig'zakt] *adj* esatto, preciso. *v* esigere, richiedere. **exacting** *adj* esigente, impegnativo. **exactitude** *n* esattezza *f*, precisione *f*.

exaggerate [ig'zadʒə,reit] *v* esagerare. **exaggeration** *n* esagerazione *f*.

exalt [ig'zolt] *v* esaltare; (*praise*) vantare, lodare. **exaltation** *n* esaltazione *f*.

examine [ig'zamin] *v* esaminare; verificare; (*med*) visitare; (*law*) interrogare. **examination** *n* esame *m*; verifica *f*; visita medica *f*; (*law*) interrogatorio *m*. **examiner** *n* ispettore, -trice *m*, *f*.

example [ig'zaːmpl] *n* esempio *m*; (*specimen*) esemplare *m*. **for example** per esempio.

exasperate [ig'zaːspə,reit] *v* esasperare; esacerbare; irritare. **exasperating** *adj* esasperante. **exasperation** *n* esasperazione *f*.

excavate ['ekskə,veit] *v* scavare. **excavation** *n* scavo *m*.

exceed [ik'siːd] *v* eccedere, superare. **exceedingly** *adv* estremamente.

excel [ik'sel] *v* eccellere.

excellent ['eksələnt] *adj* eccellente, ottimo. **excellence** *n* eccellenza *f*, superiorità *f*. **Excellency** *n* Eccellenza *f*.

except [ik'sept] *prep* eccetto, salvo, tranne, all'infuori di. *v* escludere, eccettuare.

excerpt ['eksəːpt] *n* estratto *m*, brano *m*.

excess [ik'ses] *n* eccesso *m*, sovrabbondanza *f*. **excess baggage** eccedenza di bagaglio *f*. **excess weight** soprappeso *m*. **excessive** *adj* eccessivo, smoderato.

exchange [iks'tʃeindʒ] *n* cambio *m*, scambio *m*; (*phone*) centralino *m*. **rate of exchange** cambio *m*. *v* cambiare, scambiare.

exchequer [iks'tʃekə] *n* tesoro *m*, erario *m*.

excise ['eksaiz] *n* imposta di consumo *f*. *v* recidere, tagliar via.

excite [ik'sait] *v* eccitare, stimolare, provocare. **excitable** *adj* eccitabile, impressionabile. **excitement** *n* eccitamento *m*, agitazione *f*, emozione *f*.

exclaim [iks'kleim] *v* esclamare. **exclamation** *n* esclamazione *f*. **exclamation mark** punto esclamativo *m*.

exclude [iks'kluːd] *v* escludere. **excluding** *prep* escluso, eccetto. **exclusion** *n* esclusione *f*. **exclusive** *adj* esclusivo. **exclusivity** *n* esclusiva *f*.

excommunicate [ekskə'mjuːni,keit] *v* scomunicare. **excommunication** *n* scomunica *f*.

excrement ['ekskrəmənt] *n* sterco *m*, feci *f pl*. **excrete** *v* defecare. **excretion** *n* escrezione *f*.

excruciating [ik'skruːʃieitiŋ] *adj* atroce.

excursion [ik'skəːʃən] *n* escursione *f*, gita *f*.

excuse [ik'skjuːz] *n* scusa *f*, pretesto *m*. **make excuses** scusarsi. *v* scusare, perdonare; giustificare. **excuse from** esentare da. **excuse me!** scusi!

execute ['eksi,kjuːt] *v* eseguire, mettere in esecuzione, effettuare; (*kill*) giustiziare. **execution** *n* esecuzione *f*; (*death*) esecuzione capitale *f*. **executioner** *n* boia *m invar*.

executive [ig'zekjutiv] *adj* esecutivo. *n* (*body*) esecutivo *m*; (*person*) funzionario,

-a m, f. **executor** n esecutore, -trice m, f. testamentario, -a m, f.

exemplify [ig'zempli,fai] v esemplificare, illustrare.

exempt [ig'zempt] v esentare, esonerare. adj esente. **exemption** n esenzione f, dispensa f.

exercise ['eksə,saiz] n esercizio m, uso m; (task) compito m; (mil) manovra f. v esercitare, usare. **exercise-book** n quaderno m.

exert [ig'zəːt] v esercitare. **exert oneself** sforzarsi. **exertion** n sforzo m.

exhale [eks'heil] v emanare; (breathe out) esalare.

exhaust [ig'zɔːst] v stancare, esaurire, estenuare. n scarico m (pl -chi) m, scappamento m. **exhausted** adj sfinito, esausto. **exhausting** adj faticoso, estenuante. **exhaustion** n esaurimento m.

exhibit [ig'zibit] v esibire, esporre. n oggetto per mostra m; (law) oggetto di appoggio m. **exhibition** n mostra f, esposizione f. **exhibitionism** n esibizionismo m. **exhibitionist** n esibizionista m, f. **exhibitor** n esibitore, -trice m, f.

exhilarating [ig'zilareitiŋ] adj esilarante, rallegrante.

exigency [ig'zidʒənsi] n esigenza f, necessità f.

exile ['eksail] n (expulsion) esilio m; (person) esule m, f, esiliato, -a m, f. v esiliare, mettere al bando.

exist [ig'zist] v esistere, vivere. **existence** n esistenza f, vita f. **existentialism** n esistenzialismo m. **existing** adj esistente, attuale.

exit ['egzit] n uscita f. v uscire.

exodus ['eksədəs] n esodo m.

exonerate [ig'zonə,reit] v esonerare, assolvere.

exorbitant [ig'zɔːbitənt] adj esorbitante, esagerato.

exorcize ['eksɔːsaiz] v esorcizzare. **exorcism** n esorcismo m. **exorcist** n esorcista m, f.

exotic [ig'zotik] adj esotico; (strange) strano.

expand [ik'spænd] v espandere, estendere. **expansion** n espansione f.

expanse [ik'spæns] n spazio m, distesa f.

expatriate [eks'peitrieit; n, adj eks'peitriət] v espatriare, emigrare. n, adj espatriato, -a.

expect [ik'spekt] v (await) aspettare; anticipare; (believe) credere. **expectant** adj in attesa. **expectation** n aspettativa f, attesa f, prospettiva f.

expedient [ik'spiːdiənt] n espediente m, accorgimento m. adj opportuno, conveniente.

expedition [,ekspi'diʃən] n spedizione f. **expeditious** adj sbrigativo.

expel [ik'spel] v espellere, scacciare.

expenditure [ik'spenditʃə] n spesa f, consumo m.

expense [ik'spens] n spesa f. **expense account** conto spese m. **expensive** adj caro, costoso.

experience [ik'spiəriəns] v provare, subire. n esperienza f; incidente m, avventura f.

experiment [ik'speriment] n esperimento m, prova f. v sperimentare, provare, fare esperimenti. **experimental** adj sperimentale.

expert ['ekspəːt] adj esperto, perito, competente. n esperto, -a m, f, perito, -a m, f; conoscitore, -trice m, f. **expertise** [,ekspəː'tiːz] n perizia f, maestria f.

expire [ik'spaiə] v scadere, terminare; (die) morire. **expiry** n termine m, scadenza f.

explain [ik'splein] v spiegare, chiarire. **explanation** n spiegazione f, chiarimento m. **explanatory** adj esplicativo.

expletive [ek'spliːtiv] n (profanity) bestemmia f.

explicit [ik'splisit] adj esplicito, chiaro.

explode [ik'sploud] v esplodere, far saltare, scoppiare; (discredit) screditare. **explosion** n esplosione f.

exploit[1] ['eksploit] n impresa f. **exploits** pl n gesta f pl.

exploit[2] [ik'sploit] v sfruttare, valorizzare. **exploitation** n sfruttamento m, valorizzazione f.

explore [ik'splɔː] v esplorare; studiare. **exploration** n esplorazione f; studio m. **exploratory** adj esploratorio.

exponent [ik'spounənt] n esponente m, f; (representative) interprete m, f, rappresentante m, f. **exponential** adj esponenziale.

export ['ekspɔːt; v ik'spɔːt] n esportazione f. v esportare.

expose [ik'spouz] v esporre, mostrare; (reveal) svelare; (unmask) smascherare. **exposition** n spiegazione f; mostra f.

exposure n esposizione f; smascheramento m; rivelazione f; (phot) posa f.

express [ik'spres] adj espresso, esplicito. express train direttissimo m, rapido m. v esprimere. expression n espressione f; manifestazione f; (phrase) modo di dire m. expressionless adj impassibile. expressway (mot) n autostrada

expulsion [ik'spʌlʃən] n espulsione f.

expurgate ['ekspəgeit] v espurgare.

exquisite ['ekswizit] adj squisito; (intense) vivo, acuto.

extend [ik'stend] v estendere, prolungare. extension n estensione f; (time) proroga f; (phone) telefono interno m. extensive adj esteso, vasto.

extent [ik'stent] n estensione f; limite m.

extenuating [ik'stenjueitiŋ] adj attenuante.

exterior [ik'stiəriə] nm, adj esterno.

exterminate [ik'stəmineit] v sterminare, annientare. extermination n sterminio m, annientamento m.

external [ik'stəml] adj esterno.

extinct [ik'stiŋkt] adj estinto.

extinguish [ik'stiŋgwiʃ] v estinguere, spegnere. fire extinguisher n estintore m.

extol [ik'stoul] v esaltare, lodare.

extort [ik'stott] v estorcere, strappare. extortion n estorsione f. extortionate adj esorbitante, esagerato.

extra ['ekstrə] adj extra invar, straordinario, supplementare, in più. n (theatre) comparsa f; (additional charge) spesa extra f. adv in più.

extract [ik'strakt] v estrarre; (tooth) cavare. extraction n estrazione f; origine f.

extradite ['ekstrədait] v estradare. extraditable adj passibile di estradizione. extradition n estradizione f.

extramural [ekstrə'mjuərəl] adj fuori le mura; (university) al di fuori dell'università. extramural course corso libero m.

extraneous [ik'streiniəs] adj estraneo.

extraordinary [ik'strɔtdənəri] adj straordinario, eccezionale, fenomenale.

extravagant [ik'stravəgənt] adj stravagante; (wasteful) prodigo, spendereccio; (exaggerated) esagerato. extravagance n stravaganza f, prodigalità f.

extreme [ik'stritm] adj estremo, ultimo. n estremo m. extremist n estremista m, f. extremity n estremità f.

extricate ['ekstri,keit] v extricate oneself districarsi, tirarsi d'impaccio, liberarsi.

extrovert ['ekstrəvətt] nm, adj estroverso.

exuberant [ig'zjubərənt] adj esuberante. exuberance n esuberanza f.

exude [ig'zjud] v emanare.

exult [ig'zʌlt] v esultare. exultant adj esultante, trionfante. exultation n esultazione f, trionfo m.

eye [ai] n occhio m; (needle) cruna f. see eye to eye (with) vederla allo stesso modo (di). v adocchiare, osservare.

eyeball ['aiboul] n bulbo oculare m.

eyebrow ['aibrau] n sopracciglio m.

eyelash ['ailaʃ] n ciglio m (pl -a f).

eyelet ['ailit] n occhiello m.

eyelid ['ailid] n palpebra f.

eye-opener n fatto rivelatore m.

eye shadow n bistro m, ombretto m.

eyesight ['aisait] n vista f, visione f.

eyesore ['aisot] n pugno in un occhio m.

eyewitness ['ai,witnis] n testimonio oculare m.

F

fable ['feibl] n favola f.

fabric ['fabrik] n (cloth) tessuto m, stoffa f; (structure) struttura f.

fabricate ['fabrikeit] v (make up) inventare; (fake) falsificare; (construct) fabbricare. fabrication n costruzione f, invenzione f.

fabulous ['fabjuləs] adj favoloso.

façade [fə'saud] n facciata f.

face [feis] n faccia f, volto m, viso m; (clock) quadrante m; (type) carattere m. v (look towards) fronteggiare; (confront) affrontare; (cover) rivestire. face-cloth n pezzuola per lavarsi f. face-lift n plastica facciale f; (restyling) restauro m. face-pack n maschera di bellezza f. face value valore nominale m. lose face perdere prestigio.

facet ['fasit] n (small plane) faccetta f; (aspect) aspetto m.

facetious [fə'siːʃəs] adj arguto, spiritoso.

facial ['feiʃəl] adj facciale.

facile ['fasail] adj (glib) superficiale, pronto; (easy) facile.

facilitate [fə'sili,teit] v facilitare, agevolare.

facility [fə'siləti] n facilità f; (help) facilitazione f, agevolazione f; opportunità f. **facilities** pl n servizi m pl.

facing ['feisiŋ] n (covering) rivestimento m; (dress) risvolto m.

facsimile [fak'siməli] n facsimile m invar.

fact [fakt] n fatto m, verità f. **as a matter of fact** in effetti. **fact-finding** adj di inchiesta. **in fact** infatti. **factual** adj effettivo.

faction [fakʃən] n fazione f, dissenso m. **factious** adj fazioso, partigiano.

factor ['faktə] n fattore m; agente m, f.

factory ['faktəri] n fabbrica f, stabilimento m.

faculty ['fakəlti] n facoltà f.

fad [fad] n capriccio m; (fashion) moda f.

fade [feid] v (colour) sbiadire; (lose freshness) appassire; (disappear) svanire. **fade away** affievolirsi.

fag [fag] v sfacchinare. n (hard work) sgobbata f; (slang) sigaretta f. **fag-end** n cicca f. **fagged out** stanco morto.

fail [feil] v fallire; (fall short) mancare; (not pass) bocciare, essere respinto. **without fail** senza fallo. **failure** n insuccesso m, mancanza f.

failing ['feiliŋ] n debole m, difetto m. adj debile. prep salvo.

faint [feint] v svenire. adj fiacco, tenue, appena percettibile. **feel faint** sentirsi venir meno. **not have the faintest idea** non avere la più pallida idea.

fair¹ [feə] adj (colouring) biondo, chiaro; (unbiased) giusto, imparziale; (moderately good) discreto. **fair copy** bella copia f. **fair play** comportamento leale m. adv secondo le regole. **fairly** adv (moderately) abbastanza; (properly) giustamente. **in all fairness** in tutta franchezza.

fair² [feə] n fiera f, mercato m.

fairy ['feəri] n fata f. **fairy-tale** n fiaba f.

faith [feiθ] n (belief) fede f; (confidence) fiducia f. **faith-healer** n guaritore, -trice per suggestione m, f. **faithful** adj fedele. **faithless** adj che non ha fede, sleale.

fake [feik] v contraffare, fingere. n (object) contraffazione f; (person) impostore, -a m, f.

falcon ['fɔilkən] n falco m, falcone m.

*fall [fɔil] v cadere, cascare; (collapse) crollare; (lower) abbassarsi. **fall asleep** addormentarsi. **fall back** ricorrere a. **fall behind** rimanere indietro; (fig) essere in arretrato. **fall ill** ammalarsi. **fall-out** n pioggia radioattiva f. **fall through** fallire.

n caduta f; crollo m, rovina f; abbassamento m; (autumn) autunno m.

fallacy ['faləsi] n falsità f. **fallacious** adj fallace, falso.

fallen ['fɔilən] V **fall**.

fallible ['faləbl] adj fallibile. **fallibility** n fallibilità f.

fallow ['falou] adj a maggese.

false [fɔils] adj falso, artificiale, finto. **false alarm** falso allarme m. **false pretences** (law) millantato credito m. **false teeth** denti artificiali m pl. **falsehood** n menzogna f. **falseness** n perfidia f. **falsify** v falsificare.

falsetto [fɔil'setou] n falsetto m.

falter ['fɔiltə] v (waver) vacillare, titubare; (speak hesitatingly) balbettare. **faltering** adj titubante.

fame [feim] n fama f, rinomanza f. **famed** adj rinomato.

familiar [fə'miljə] adj familiare; intimo; (impudent) sfacciato; (well-known) noto. **be on familiar terms with** aver dimestichezza con. **familiarity** n familiarità f; intimità f; (impertinence) sfacciataggine f.

family ['faməli] n famiglia f. **family allowance** assegni familiari m pl. **family tree** albero genealogico m.

famine ['famin] n carestia f.

famished ['famiʃt] adj affamato.

famous ['feiməs] adj famoso, celebre.

fan¹ [fan] n ventaglio m; (mechanical) ventilatore m. **fan-belt** n cinghia per ventilatore f. v (flames) soffiare su; (excite) aizzare. **fan oneself** farsi vento.

fan² [fan] n (admirer) tifoso, -a m, f.

fanatic [fə'natik] n, adj fanatico, -a; (sport) tifoso, -a. **fanaticism** n fanatismo m; tifo m.

fancy ['fansi] adj elaborato, raffinato, di fantasia. **fancy-dress** n costume m. **fancy-dress ball** ballo in maschera m. n immaginazione f, fantasia f, capriccio m. v desiderare, immaginare. **fanciful** adj fantasioso, capriccioso.

fanfare ['fanfeə] n fanfara f.

fang [faŋ] n zanna f.

fantastic [fan'tastik] adj fantastico, strano.

fantasy ['fantəsi] n fantasia f, capriccio m.

far [faɪ] adv, adj lontano, distante; (much) molto. **as far as** (place) fino a. **as far as I know** a quanto sappia. **far-fetched** adj improbabile, forzato. **far-reaching** adj di gran portata. **far-sighted** adj (prudent) previdente. **so far** (up to this point) fin qui.

farce [faɪs] n farsa f.

fare [feə] n tariffa f, prezzo del biglietto m; (person) viaggiatore, -trice m, f; (food) vitto m. v vivere, trovarsi.

farewell [feəˈwel] n addio m, congedo m. interj addio!

farm [faɪm] n fattoria f, podere m. **farmhouse** n casa colonica f. v coltivare, fare l'agricoltore. **farm out** dare in appalto. **farmer** n agricoltore, contadino, -a m. f. **farming** n agricoltura f, coltivazione f.

fart [faɪt] (vulgar) n scoreggia f. v fare scoregge.

farther [ˈfaɪðə] adj, adv più lontano; ulteriore. **farthest** adj il più lontano.

fascinate [ˈfasiˌneit] v affascinare, incantare. **fascinating** adj affascinante, avvincente. **fascination** n fascino m, attrattiva f.

fascism [ˈfaʃizəm] n fascismo m. **fascist** n(m+f), adj fascista.

fashion [ˈfaʃən] n (manner) modo m, maniera f; (dress) moda f; (style) stile m; (vogue) voga f. **after a fashion** in un certo modo. **in fashion** alla moda. **out of fashion** fuori moda. v foggiare, modellare. **fashionable** adj elegante, di moda.

fast¹ [faɪst] adj rapido, veloce; (firmly held) fisso, saldo; (colour) solido. adv presto, rapidamente. **the clock is ... fast** l'orologio va avanti di ....

fast² [faɪst] n digiuno m. v digiunare.

fasten [ˈfaɪsn] v legare, fissare, agganciare, attaccare. **fastener** or **fastening** n chiusura f, fermaglio m.

fastidious [faˈstidiəs] adj meticoloso, schifiltoso.

fat [fat] adj, nm grasso. **fatten** v ingrassare. **fatty** adj grasso, untuoso.

fatal [ˈfeitl] adj fatale, ineluttabile. **fatalism** n fatalismo m. **fatalist** n fatalista m, f. **fatality** n fatalità f.

fate [feit] n fato m, destino m. **fated** adj destinato. **fateful** adj decisivo.

father [ˈfaɪðə] n padre m; (coll) babbo m. v procreare, originare. **fatherhood** n paternità f. **father-in-law** n suocero m. **fatherland** n patria f. **fatherly** adj paterno.

fathom [ˈfaðəm] v (understand) indovinare, penetrare; (depth) sondare. n braccio m.

fatigue [fəˈtiɪg] n stanchezza f, esaurimento m. v stancare.

fatuous [ˈfatjuəs] adj fatuo, frivolo, vuoto.

fault [foɪlt] n (flaw) difetto m, imperfezione f; (cause for blame) colpa f; (geol) faglia f; (tennis) fallo m. **be at fault** essere colpevole. **find fault with** criticare, biasimare. **faultless** adj senza colpa. **faulty** adj difettoso.

favour [ˈfeivə] n favore m, piacere m. v favorire, favoreggiare, preferire. **favourable** adj favorevole, vantaggioso.

favourite [ˈfeivrit] adj preferito. n favorito, -a m, f.

fawn¹ [foɪn] n (zool) daino m, cerbiatto m. adj (colour) fulvo.

fawn² [foɪn] v **fawn on** adulare.

fear [fiə] v temere, aver paura di. n timore m, paura f. **fearful** adj terribile, spaventoso. **fearless** adj intrepido.

feasible [ˈfiɪzəbl] adj fattibile, realizzabile. **feasibility** n praticabilità f.

feast [fiɪst] n festa f, banchetto m.

feat [fiɪt] n impresa f, azione f.

feather [ˈfeðə] n penna f, piuma f. **feather-bed** n letto di piume m. **feathered** adj pennuto.

feature [ˈfiɪtʃə] n caratteristica f, tratto distintivo m; (newspaper) elzeviro m; (geog) configurazione f. **features** pl n (anat) lineamenti m pl. v dar rilievo a; (theatre) presentare. **featureless** adj scialbo.

February [ˈfebruəri] n febbraio m.

fed [fed] V **feed**.

federal [ˈfedərəl] adj federale. **federation** n federazione f.

fee [fiɪ] n onorario m, parcella f; (school) retta f; (entrance fee) tassa d'iscrizione f.

feeble [ˈfiɪbl] adj debole, fiacco. **feeble-minded** adj cretino, debole di mente. **feebleness** n debolezza f.

*****feed** [fiɪd] v nutrire; (supply) alimentare; (eat) mangiare, nutrirsi. n mangime m, nutrimento m; (baby) poppata f. **feedback** n retroazione f, feedback m invar; (response) reazione f. **fed up** (coll) stufo.

*****feel** [fiɪl] v (touch) tastare, toccare; (emotion) sentire. **feel like** sentirsi disposto a. **feeler** n tentacolo m; (proposal) sondaggio m. **feeling** n (physical) senso m, sensazione f; (emotion) sensibilità f, suscettibilità f; (affection) affetto m.

feet [fiːt] V **foot**.

feign [fein] v fingere, simulare, far finta.

feline ['fiːlain] adj felino.

fell[1] [fel] V **fall**.

fell[2] [fel] v (*cut down*) abbattere; (*strike down*) atterrare.

fellow ['felou] n individuo m, tipo m; (*companion*) compagno m, collega m, f; (*member*) membro m, socio m. **fellow-countryman** n compatriota m, f. **fellowship** n (*companionship*) cameratismo m; (*rel*) comunità f; (*allowance*) borsa di studio f.

felony ['feləni] n crimine m. **felon** n delinquente m, f.

felt[1] [felt] V **feel**.

felt[2] [felt] n feltro m.

female ['fiːmeil] n femmina f. adj also **feminine** femminile.

feminism ['feminizəm] n femminismo m. **feminist** n femminista m, f.

fence [fens] n (*barrier*) steccato m, palizzata f; (*receiver of stolen goods*) ricettatore, -trice m, f. v (*sport*) tirar di scherma. **fence in** recintare. **fencing** n recinto m; (*sport*) scherma f.

fend [fend] v **fend for oneself** provvedere a sè stesso, arrangiarsi. **fend off** parare, schivare.

fender ['fendə] n paracenere m invar; (*US*) paraurti m.

fennel ['fenl] n finocchio m.

ferment ['fəːment; v fə'ment] n fermento m. v fermentare. **fermentation** n fermentazione f.

fern [fəːn] n felce f.

ferocious [fə'rouʃəs] adj feroce. **ferocity** n ferocia f.

ferret ['ferit] n furetto m. v **ferret out** scovare.

ferry ['feri] n traghetto m. v traghettare.

fertile ['fəːtail] adj fertile, fecondo. **fertility** n fertilità f, fecondità f. **fertilize** v (*enrich*) fertilizzare; fecondare. **fertilizer** n fertilizzante m, concime m.

fervent ['fəːvənt] adj fervente, fervido. **fervour** n fervore m, ardore m.

fester ['festə] v suppurare; (*rankle*) bruciare.

festival ['festəvəl] n festival m invar, festa f.

festoon [fə'stuːn] v decorare con festoni. n festone m.

fetch [fetʃ] v andare a prendere; (*call*)

chiamare; (*a price*) realizzare. **fetching** adj attraente.

fête [feit] n festa f. v festeggiare.

fetid ['fiːtid] adj fetido, puzzolente.

fetish ['fetiʃ] n feticcio m, idolo m.

fetter ['fetə] n catena f. v incatenare.

feud [fjuːd] n lite f. v essere in lotta.

feudal ['fjuːdl] adj feudale. **feudalism** n feudalesimo m.

fever ['fiːvə] n febbre f. **feverish** adj febbricitante; (*restless*) febbrile.

few [fjuː] pron, adj pochi, -e. **a few** alcuni, -e. **quite a few** parecchi, parecchie. **fewer** adj meno invar. **fewest** adj meno invar.

fiancé [fi'onsei] n fidanzato m. **fiancée** n fidanzata f.

fiasco [fi'askou] n fiasco m.

fib [fib] n (*coll*) frottola f. v raccontar frottole.

fibre ['faibə] n fibra f. **fibreglass** n fibra di vetro f. **fibrous** adj fibroso.

fickle ['fikl] adj volubile. **fickleness** n volubilità f.

fiction ['fikʃən] n (*invention*) finzione f; (*novels, etc.*) novellistica f, narrativa f. **fictional** or **fictitious** adj fittizio, immaginario.

fiddle ['fidl] n violino m; (*coll: fraud*) imbroglio m, truffa f. v suonare il violino; (*coll: cheat*) truffare, imbrogliare. **fit as a fiddle** sano come un pesce.

fidelity [fi'deləti] n fedeltà f.

fidget ['fidʒit] v muoversi irrequietamente, dimenarsi. **fidgety** adj irrequieto, nervoso.

field [fiːld] n campo m; (*of knowledge, etc.*) settore m. **field glasses** binoccolo m sing. **field marshal** maresciallo m.

fiend [fiːnd] n demonio m. **fiendish** adj infernale, diabolico.

fierce [fiəs] adj feroce, intenso.

fiery ['faiəri] adj focoso, ardente.

fifteen [fif'tiːn] nm, adj quindici. **fifteenth** nm, adj quindicesimo.

fifth [fifθ] nm, adj quinto.

fifty ['fifti] nm, adj cinquanta. **fiftieth** nm, adj cinquantesimo.

fig [fig] n fico m.

*****fight** [fait] v lottare, combattere. n lotta f, combattimento m; (*scuffle*) zuffa f.

figment ['figmənt] n **figment of the imagination** finzione f.

figure ['figə] n (*numeral*) cifra f; (*shape*) forma f; (*pictorial*) figura f; (*character*) personaggio m; (*bodily form*) linea f.

figurehead n (naut) polena f; (derog) uomo di paglia m. **figure of speech** modo di dire m. v (appear) apparire. **figure out** calcolare.

filament ['filəmənt] n filamento m.

file¹ [fail] n (dossier) pratica f; archivio m; (for papers) cartella f; (card with details) scheda f; (row) fila f. v archiviare, mettere in ordine, registrare. **filing** n schedare m. **filing cabinet** schedario m. **single file** fila indiana f.

file² [fail] n (tool) lima f. v limare, levigare.

filial ['filiəl] adj filiale.

fill [fil] v riempire; (tooth) otturare. **fill in** completare, inserire. **fill up** (mot) fare il pieno. **filling** n (cookery) ripieno m; (tooth) otturazione f. **filling station** stazione di rifornimento f.

fillet ['filit] n (meat) filetto m. v disossare.

film [film] n pellicola f; (phot, cinema) film m invar. **film star** divo, -a del cinema m, f. v girare un film.

filter ['filtə] n filtro m. **filter-tip** n filtro m. v filtrare.

filth [filθ] n sudiciume m, sporcizia f; oscenità f. **filthy** adj sudicio, sporco; lurido, osceno.

fin [fin] n pinna f.

final ['fainl] adj finale, ultimo. n finale f. **finalist** n finalista m, f. **finally** adv infine.

finance [fai'nans] n finanza f. v finanziare. **financial** adj finanziario. **financier** n finanziere m, finanziatore m.

finch [fintʃ] n fringuello m.

***find** [faind] v scoprire, trovare. **find out** scoprire.

fine¹ [fain] adj (high quality) pregiato, raffinato; (minute) fine; (accomplished) bravo; (beautiful) bello. adv bene.

fine² [fain] n (penalty) multa f. v multare.

finesse [fi'nes] n finezza f.

finger ['fiŋgə] n dito m (pl dita f). **cross one's fingers** toccar ferro. **finger bowl** lavadita m invar. **finger-mark** n ditata f. **fingernail** n unghia f. **fingerprint** n impronta digitale f. **fingertip** n punta delle dita f. v (touch) palpare.

finish ['finiʃ] v finire, concludere. n fine f, conclusione f; (surface) finitura f; (textile) appretto m.

finite ['fainait] adj limitato, circoscritto; (math) finito.

Finland ['finlənd] n Finlandia f. **Finn** n finlandese m, f. **Finnish** nm, adj finlandese.

fir [fəː] n abete m.

fire ['faiə] n fuoco m; (conflagration) incendio m; (heater) stufa f. **catch fire** prender fuoco. **hang fire** indugiare. **set fire to** appiccare il fuoco a, incendiare. v (shoot) sparare; (dismiss) licenziare, silurare; (inflame) eccitare, infiammare; (inspire) ispirare.

fire alarm n allarme d'incendio m.

firearm ['faiəˌaːm] n arma da fuoco f.

fire brigade n corpo dei vigili del fuoco m.

fire door n esercitazione antincendio f.

fire drill n pompa antincendio f.

fire engine n uscita di sicurezza f.

fire escape n uscita di sicurezza f.

fire extinguisher n estintore m.

firefly ['faiəflai] n lucciola f.

fire-guard n parafuoco m, paracenere m invar.

fireman ['faiəmən] n pompiere m, vigile del fuoco m.

fireplace ['faiəˌpleis] n focolare m, camino m, caminetto m.

fireproof ['faiəˌpruːf] adj incombustibile, resistente al fuoco.

fireside ['faiəˌsaid] n focolare m.

fire station n caserma dei pompieri f.

firewood ['faiəˌwud] n legna da ardere f.

fireworks ['faiəˌwəːks] pl n fuochi d'artifizio m pl.

firing squad n plotone d'esecuzione m.

firm¹ [fəːm] adj fermo; (steady) saldo; (steadfast) risoluto; solido; stabile. **stand firm** tener duro. **firmness** n fermezza f; saldezza f; risolutezza f.

firm² [fəːm] n (comm) ditta f, azienda f.

first [fəːst] adj primo. adv prima; in primo luogo; anzitutto. **first aid** pronto soccorso m. **first-class** adj ottimo, di prima qualità, eccellente; (rail, etc.) di prima classe. **first floor** primo piano m. **first-hand** adj, adv di prima mano. **first name** nome di battesimo m.

fiscal ['fiskəl] adj fiscale.

fish [fiʃ] n pesce m. v pescare. **fishy** adj (coll) losco.

fishbone ['fiʃˌboun] n lisca f.

fisherman ['fiʃəmən] n pescatore m.

fish fingers pl n bastoncini di pesce m pl.

fishing ['fiʃiŋ] n pesca f. **fishing boat** peschereccio m. **fishing rod** canna da pesca f.

fishmonger ['fiʃ,mʌŋgə] n pescivendolo, -a m, f.

fishpond ['fiʃ,pond] n vivaio m.

fission ['fiʃən] n fissione f.

fissure ['fiʃə] n fessura f.

fist [fist] n pugno m.

fit¹ [fit] adj (suitable) adatto; competente; (healthy) sano. **keep fit** mantenersi in forma, mantenersi in forma. n misura f. v (clothes, etc.) star bene; (suit) adeguare, convenire. **fit in** incastrare. **fitting** adj conveniente, adatto. **fittings** pl n suppellettili m pl, arredi m pl.

fit² [fit] n accesso m, attacco m. **fitful** adj intermittente.

five [faiv] nm, adj cinque.

fix [fiks] v fissare, stabilire. **fix up** sistemare, mettere a posto. n (coll) difficoltà f, guaio m. **fixation** n fissazione f. **fixed** adj fisso, stabile. **fixture** n (accessory) attrezzatura f; (sport) avvenimento sportivo m.

fizz [fiz] v frizzare. n spumante m. **fizzy** adj effervescente, frizzante.

fizzle ['fizl] v fizzle out far cilecca.

flabbergast ['flæbəgɑːst] v sbalordire.

flabby ['flæbi] adj floscio, flaccido.

flag¹ [flæg] n (banner) bandiera f. **flag-pole** n asta di bandiera f. **flagship** n nave ammiraglia f. v **flag down** intimare di fermarsi.

flag² [flæg] v (tire) indebolirsi, accasciarsi.

flag³ [flæg] n (stone) lastra (di pietra) f.

flagon ['flægən] n bottiglione m.

flagrant ['fleigrənt] adj flagrante.

flair [fleə] n intuito m, inclinazione f.

flake [fleik] v sfaldare, sfaldarsi. n falda f, scaglia f. **flaky** adj a scaglie. **flaky pastry** sfoglia f.

flamboyant [flæm'bɔiənt] adj sgargiante.

flame [fleim] n fiamma f. v fiammeggiare, risplendere. **burst into flames** divampare. **flaming** adj fiammeggiante, violento.

flamingo [flə'miŋgou] n fiammingo m.

flan [flæn] n sformato m, torta f.

flank [flæŋk] v fiancheggiare. n fianco m, lato m.

flannel ['flænl] n (fabric) flanella f; (facecloth) pezzuola per lavarsi f. v (slang) abbindolare con le chiacchiere.

flap [flæp] v agitare; (wings) battere; (coll) agitarsi. n lembo m; (wings) colpo m; panico m.

flare [fleə] n fiammata f, bagliore m; (rocket) razzo m. v brillare; (clothes) svasare. **flare up** divampare; (anger, etc.) arrabbiarsi.

flash [flæʃ] n baleno m, lampo m. v balenare. **flashback** n scena retrospettiva f, flashback m invar. **flash bulb** lampadina flash f. **flashlight** n fotolampo m, flash m invar.

flask [flɑːsk] n flacone m, borraccia f.

flat¹ [flæt] adj piatto, piano; (tyre) a terra; (net) netto; (stale) svanito, insipido. n (music) bemolle m. **flat-footed** adj con i piedi piatti. **flat out** a briglia sciolta. n (music) bemolle m. **flatten** v appiattire, livellare.

flat² [flæt] n appartamento m.

flatter ['flætə] v adulare, lusingare. **flatterer** n adulatore, -trice m, f. **flattering** adj lusinghiero. **flattery** n lusinghe f pl, adulazione f.

flatulence ['flætjuləns] n flatulenza f. **flatulent** adj flatulento.

flaunt [flɔːnt] v ostentare, pavoneggiarsi.

flautist ['flɔːtist] n flautista m, f.

flavour ['fleivə] n sapore m, gusto m. v condire. **flavouring** n condimento m.

flaw [flɔː] n tacca f, difetto m. **flawed** adj difettoso. **flawless** adj perfetto.

flax [flæks] n lino m. **flaxen** adj di lino; (colour) biondissimo.

flea [fliː] n pulce f.

fleck [flek] n chiazza f, macchia f. v chiazzare, macchiare.

fled [fled] V **flee**.

***flee** [fliː] v fuggire, scappare.

fleece [fliːs] n vello m. v (coll) pelare, derubare.

fleet [fliːt] n flotta f; (of cars) parco m.

fleeting ['fliːtiŋ] adj fugace, transitorio.

Flemish ['flemiʃ] nm, adj fiammingo.

flesh [fleʃ] n carne f; (fruit) polpa f.

flew [fluː] V **fly¹**.

flex [fleks] v flettere. n filo o cavo elettrico m. **flexible** adj flessibile. **flexibility** n flessibilità f.

flick [flik] n colpetto m. v dare un colpetto a.

flicker ['flikə] v tremolare. n tremolio m.

flight¹ [flait] n (flying) volo m; (steps) rampa f. **flighty** adj frivolo.

flight² [flait] n (fleeing) fuga f.

flimsy ['flimzi] adj tenue, fragile; (inadequate) insufficiente.

flinch [flintʃ] v (wince) sussultare; (shrink from) sottrarsi a. **without flinching** senza batter ciglio.

*fling [fliŋ] v lanciare, scagliare, buttare. n have one's fling godersela.

flint [flint] n selce f.; (lighter) pietrina f.

flip [flip] n colpetto m. v dare un colpetto a. **flip a coin** fare testa e croce. **flip through** sfogliare, dare una scorsa a.

flippant ['flipənt] adj poco serio, frivolo. **flippancy** n mancanza di serietà f.

flirt [flɜːt] v flirtare. n dongiovanni m; civetta f.

flit [flit] v svolazzare; (disappear) squagliarsela.

float [flout] v galleggiare, stare a galla. n galleggiante m; (angling) sughero m; (procession) carro m.

flock¹ [flok] n (animals) branco m; (birds) stormo m; (sheep) gregge m; (crowd) folla f. v accorrere in massa, affluire. **flock together** radunarsi.

flock² [flok] n fiocco m; (mattress filling) borra f.

flog [flog] v bastonare, frustare; (sell) spacciare.

flood [flʌd] v inondare, allagare. n inondazione f, alluvione f, diluvio m; (outpouring) torrente m, ondata f. **floodlight** n riflettore m. **floodlit** adj illuminato a giorno.

floor [flɔː] n pavimento m; (storey) piano m. **floorboard** n tavola di pavimento f. **take the floor** (speak) prendere la parola; (dance) ballare. v pavimentare; (knock down) atterrare.

flop [flop] n tonfo m; (coll) fiasco m. v cader di schianto; (coll) fallire.

Florence ['florəns] n Firenze f. **Florentine** n, adj fiorentino, -a.

florist ['florist] n fioraio, -a m, f; fiorista m, f.

flotsam ['flotsəm] n relitti m pl. **flotsam and jetsam** (people) relitti umani m pl.

flounce¹ [flauns] v dimenare.

flounce² [flauns] n balza f.

flounder ['flaundə] v dibattersi, dimenarsi; (speech) impappinarsi. n passera di mare f.

flour [flauə] n farina f. **floury** adj farinoso.

flourish ['flʌriʃ] v (prosper) fiorire; (brandish) brandire. n (fanfare) squillo di tromba m; (writing) ghirigoro m; (speech) fioretta f; (gesture) largo gesto m.

flout [flaut] v sprezzare, schernire.

flow [flou] n corrente f, flusso m. v scorrere, circolare.

flower [flauə] n fiore m. **flower-bed** n aiuola f. **flower-pot** n vaso da fiori m. v fiorire, essere in fiore. **flowering** adj in fiore. **flowery** adj fiorito.

flown [floun] V **fly¹**.

flu [fluː] n influenza f.

fluctuate ['flʌktjueit] v fluttuare. **fluctuation** n fluttuazione f.

flue [fluː] n gola del camino f.

fluent ['fluːənt] adj corrente, scorrevole. **speak fluently** parlare correntemente.

fluff [flʌf] n lanugine f, peluria f.

fluid ['fluːid] nm, adj fluido, liquido.

fluke [fluːk] n (lucky chance) colpo fortunato m.

flung [flʌŋ] V **fling**.

fluorescent [fluəˈresnt] adj fluorescente.

fluoride ['fluəraid] n fluoruro m. **fluoridation** n fluorizzazione f.

flush¹ [flʌʃ] n (colouring) rossore m; (rush of liquid) flusso m; (blushing) vampa f; (poker) flush m invar. v (wash out) pulire con un getto d'acqua; (lavatory) vuotare; (redden) arrossire, avvampare.

flush² [flʌʃ] adj (level) a livello, rasente; (slang: rich) ben fornito.

fluster ['flʌstə] v turbare, confondere.

flute [fluːt] n flauto m.

flutter ['flʌtə] v battere; agitare, confondere; (fly) svolazzare. n battito m, agitazione f; (bet) scommessa f.

flux [flʌks] n flusso m.

*fly¹ [flai] v volare; (flutter) svolazzare; (flag) sventolare; (flee) fuggire, scappare. **fly away** or **off** volar via. **flyleaf** n risguardo m. **flyover** n cavalcavia m invar. **flysheet** n volantino m. **flywheel** n volano m. **flying squad** squadra mobile f.

fly² [flai] n (insect) mosca f.

foal [foul] n puledro m.

foam [foum] n schiuma f. **foam rubber** gomma piuma f. v spumeggiare.

focus ['foukəs] n fuoco m, centro m. v concentrare; (bring into focus) mettere a fuoco. **focal** adj focale.

fodder ['fodə] n mangime m, foraggio m.

foe [fou] n nemico, -a m, f; avversario, -a m, f.

foetus ['fiːtəs] n feto m.

fog [fog] n nebbia f. **fog-bound** adj fermo per la nebbia. **fog-horn** n sirena da nebbia f. **foggy** adj nebbioso.

foible ['foibl] n debole m.

foil¹ [foil] v frustrare, sventare.

foil² [foil] n lamina (di metallo) f; (tinfoil) stagnolo m; (contrast) contrappeso m.

foist [foist] v rifilare, affibbiare.

fold¹ [fould] v piegare; (envelop) avvolgere. **fold one's arms** incrociare le braccia. **fold (up)** (collapse) chiudere, cessare l'esercizio. n piega f, ripiegatura f. **folder** n cartella f. **folding** adj pieghevole.

fold² [fould] n (enclosure) ovile m.

foliage ['fouliidʒ] n fogliame m.

folk [fouk] n gente f, popolo m. **folk dance** danza rustica f. **folklore** n folclore m. **folk song** canto popolare m.

follicle ['folikl] n follicolo m.

follow ['folou] v seguire, succedere; (understand) capire; (result) risultare, conseguire. **follower** n seguace m, f. **following** adj seguente, successivo.

folly ['foli] n follia f.

fond [fond] adj affettuoso, affezionato. **become fond of** affezionarsi a. **be fond of** voler bene a; (person) amare.

fondle ['fondl] v accarezzare, coccolare.

font [font] n fonte battesimale f.

food [fuːd] n cibo m, vitto m; (foodstuffs) generi alimentari m pl.

fool [fuːl] n sciocco, -a m, f; cretino, -a m, f; (jester) buffone, -a m, f, pagliaccio m. **foolhardy** adj temerario. **foolproof** adj sicurissimo. v (deceive) ingannare. **foolish** adj sciocco, insensato. **foolishness** n sciocchezza f.

foolscap ['fuːlskap] n carta protocollo f.

foot [fut] n, pl **feet** piede m; (birds, animals) zampa f. v **foot the bill** saldare il conto. **on foot** a piedi. **put one's foot down** farsi valere. **put one's foot in it** fare una gaffe.

football ['futbɔːl] n football m invar, pallone m. **footballer** n calciatore m.

foot-bridge ['futbridʒ] n passerella f.

foothold ['futhould] n punto d'appoggio m.

footing ['futiŋ] n (foundation) base f; (mutual standing) relazioni f pl.

footlights ['futlaits] pl n luci della ribalta f pl.

footnote ['futnout] n postilla f, nota in calce f.

footpath ['futpaːθ] n sentiero m.

footprint ['futprint] n orma f.

footstep ['futstep] n passo m.

footwear ['futweə] n calzatura f.

for [fɔ] prep per, a favore di, a, di, da. conj poiché.

forage ['foridʒ] v foraggiare. n foraggio m.

forbade [fɔ'bad] V forbid.

*****forbear** [fɔ'beə] v astenersi da, pazientare.

*****forbid** [fɔ'bid] v proibire, vietare. **forbidding** adj austero, formidabile.

forbidden [fɔ'bidn] V forbid.

force [fɔs] n forza f. **in force** in vigore. v forzare; (compel) costringere. **forceful** adj energico.

forceps ['fɔseps] pl n forcipe m sing.

ford [fɔd] n guado m. v guadare.

fore [fɔ] adj anteriore. **come to the fore** venire alla ribalta.

forearm ['fɔraːm] n avambraccio m.

forebear ['fɔbeə] n antenato, -a m, f.

foreboding [fɔ'boudiŋ] n presagio m.

*****forecast** ['fɔkaːst] n previsione f, pronostico m. v prevedere.

forecourt ['fɔkɔːt] n cortile m.

forefather ['fɔfaːðə] n antenato m, avo m.

forefinger ['fɔfiŋgə] n indice m.

forefront ['fɔfrʌnt] n prima linea f.

foreground ['fɔgraund] n primo piano m.

forehand ['fɔhand] nm, adj (tennis) diritto.

forehead ['forid] n fronte f.

foreign ['forən] adj straniero, forestiero; (trade, etc.) estero; (not belonging) estraneo. **foreigner** n straniero, -a m, f; forestiero, -a m, f.

foreleg ['fɔleg] n zampa anteriore f.

foreman ['fɔmən] n caposquadra (pl capisquadra) m, capo operaio m; (jury) presidente m.

foremost ['fɔmoust] adj principale, primo. adv in primo luogo. **first and foremost** anzitutto.

forename ['fɔneim] n nome di battesimo m.

forensic [fə'rensik] adj forense. **forensic medicine** medicina legale f.

forerunner ['fɔrʌnə] n precursore m.

*****foresee** [fɔ'siː] v prevedere. **foreseeable** adj prevedibile.

foreshadow [fɔ'ʃadou] v adombrare.

foreshorten [fɔ'ʃɔtn] v scorciare. **foreshortened** adj di scorcio.

foresight ['fɔsait] n (prevision) preveggenza f; (care for future) previdenza f.

foreskin ['fɔ:skin] *n* prepuzio, *m*.

forest ['fɔrist] *n* foresta *f*. **forester** *n* guardia forestale *f*. **forestry** *n* selvicoltura *f*.

forestall [fɔ:'stɔ:l] *v* anticipare, prevenire.

foretaste ['fɔ:teist] *n* pregustazione *f*.

***foretell** [fɔ:'tel] *v* predire, pronosticare.

forethought ['fɔ:θɔːt] *n* premeditazione *f*, previdenza *f*.

forever [fɔ'revə] *adv* per sempre.

foreword ['fɔ:wəd] *n* prefazione *f*.

forfeit ['fɔːfit] *n* (*pawn*) pegno *m*; (*fine*) multa *f*. *v* (*give up*) dover abbandonare; pagare il fio.

forgave [fɔ'geiv] *V* **forgive**.

forge[1] [fɔːdʒ] *v* (*counterfeit*) falsificare, contraffare; (*metal*) forgiare. *n* fucina *f*. **forger** *n* falsario, -a *m*, *f*. **forgery** *n* contraffazione *f*, falso *m*.

forge[2] [fɔːdʒ] *v* avanzare. **forge ahead** farsi strada; (*take lead*) distanziarsi, staccarsi.

***forget** [fɔ'get] *v* dimenticare, scordare, non ricordarsi di. **forget-me-not** *n* nontiscordardimè *m*. **forget oneself** lasciarsi andare. **forgetful** *adj* smemorato.

***forgive** [fɔ'giv] *v* perdonare, rimettere. **forgiveness** *n* perdono *m*, indulgenza *f*. **forgiving** *adj* clemente, indulgente.

forgiven [fɔ'givn] *V* **forgive**.

***forgo** [fɔ'gou] *v* rinunciare a.

forgot [fɔ'gɔt] *V* **forget**.

forgotten [fɔ'gɔtn] *V* **forget**.

fork [fɔːk] *n* (*cutlery*) forchetta *f*; (*agriculture*) forca *f*, forcone *m*; (*road*) bivio *m*; (*branching*) biforcazione *f*. *v* forcare; biforcarsi. **fork out** (*slang: pay*) metter mano alla borsa.

forlorn [fɔ'lɔ:n] *adj* disperato, desolato.

form [fɔ:m] *n* forma *f*; (*document*) modulo *m*; (*bench*) banco *m*; (*school*) classe *f*. *v* formare. **formation** *n* formazione *f*. **formative** *adj* formativo.

formal ['fɔ:məl] *adj* formale, esplicito. **formality** *n* formalità *f*, cerimonia *f*.

format ['fɔ:mæt] *n* formato *m*.

former ['fɔ:mə] *adj* precedente, anteriore. **the former** il primo. **formerly** *adv* in passato, già, in altri tempi.

formidable ['fɔ:midəbl] *adj* formidabile, spaventoso, terribile.

formula ['fɔ:mjulə] *n*, *pl* **-ae** formula *f*.

formulate ['fɔ:mjuleit] *v* formulare. **formulation** *n* formulazione *f*.

***forsake** [fə'seik] *v* abbandonare.

forsaken [fə'seikn] *V* **forsake**.

forsook [fə'suk] *V* **forsake**.

fort [fɔ:t] *n* fortezza *f*, forte *m*.

forth [fɔ:θ] *adv* avanti; (*out of concealment*) fuori. **and so forth** e così via. **forthcoming** *adj* imminente, prossimo. **forthright** *adj* franco, schietto. **forthwith** *adv* immediatamente.

fortify ['fɔ:tifai] *v* fortificare, rafforzare, dar forza a; (*wine*) alcolizzare. **fortification** *n* fortificazione *f*.

fortitude ['fɔ:titjuːd] *n* forza d'animo *f*; (*virtue*) fortezza *f*.

fortnight ['fɔ:tnait] *n* quindicina *f*, due settimane *f pl*. **fortnightly** *nm*, *adj* quindicinale, bimensile.

fortress ['fɔ:tris] *n* fortezza *f*.

fortuitous [fɔ:'tjuːitəs] *adj* fortuito.

fortune ['fɔ:tʃən] *n* fortuna *f*; (*riches*) ricchezza *f*; futuro *m*. **fortune-teller** *n* chiromante *m*, *f*. **fortune-telling** *n* chiromanzia *f*. **fortunate** *adj* fortunato.

forty ['fɔ:ti] *nm*, *adj* quaranta. **fortieth** *nm*, *adj* quarantesimo.

forum ['fɔ:rəm] *n* foro *m*; (*court*) tribuna *f*.

forward ['fɔ:wəd] *adj* avanzato; presuntuoso. *adv also* **forwards** avanti, in avanti. **look forward to** anticipare con piacere. **put forward** proporre. *v* spedire, inoltrare; (*mail*) rispedire.

fossil ['fɔsl] *n* fossile *m*. **fossilized** *adj* fossilizzato.

foster ['fɔstə] *v* (*child*) allevare; incoraggiare; nutrire, alimentare. **foster-child** *n* figlio adottivo *m*. **foster-parents** *pl n* genitori adottivi *m pl*.

fought [fɔ:t] *V* **fight**.

foul [faul] *adj* lurido, schifoso; (*weather*) pessimo. **foul play** (*crime*) delitto *m*; (*sport*) gioco falloso *m*.

found[1] [faund] *V* **find**.

found[2] [faund] *v* fondare, istituire, basare. **foundation** *n* fondazione *f*; istituto *m*; (*base*) fondamento *m*, base *f*. **founder** *n* fondatore, -trice *m*, *f*.

founder ['faundə] *v* (*sink*) colare a picco.

foundry ['faundri] *n* fonderia *f*.

fountain ['fauntin] *n* fontana *f*. **fountain pen** penna stilografica *f*.

four [fɔ:] *nm*, *adj* quattro. **foursome** *n* quattro *m*. **on all fours** (a) carponi.

fourth *nm*, *adj* quarto.

fourteen [for'tim] nm, adj quattordici. **fourteenth** nm, adj quattordicesimo.

fowl [faul] n pollame m; (chicken) pollo m.

fox [foks] n volpe f; (sly person) furbacchione m, furbo, -a m, f. **foxglove** n digitale f. **fox-hound** n bracco m. v (coll) ingannare. **foxed** adj perplesso.

foyer ['foiei] n ridotto m.

fraction ['frakʃən] n frazione f.

fracture ['fraktʃə] n frattura f, rottura f. v rompere, fratturare.

fragile ['fradʒail] adj fragile; (delicate) gracile.

fragment ['fragmənt] n frammento m.

fragrant ['freigrənt] adj fragrante, profumato. **fragrance** n profumo m.

frail [freil] adj fragile, gracile.

frame [freim] n struttura f; (skeleton) ossatura f; (picture) cornice f; (machine) telaio m. **frame of mind** disposizione d'animo, umore m. **framework** n (mech) intelaiatura f; (outline) abbozzo m. v incorniciare, costruire; (compose) redigere; (fabricate evidence) calunniare.

France [frams] n Francia f.

franchise ['frantʃaiz] n (privilege) franchigia f; (comm) concessione f.

frank [fraŋk] adj sincero, schietto. **frankness** n sincerità f, schiettezza f.

frantic ['frantik] adj frenetico.

fraternal [frə'tətnl] adj fraterno. **fraternity** n fratellanza f; (friendship) fraternità f. **fraternize** v fraternizzare.

fraud [frod] n (deceit) frode f, inganno m; (deceiver) impostore, -a m, f, truffatore, -trice m, f. **fraudulent** adj fraudolento, doloso.

fraught [frot] adj (tense) nervoso. **fraught with** pieno or denso di.

fray[1] [frei] v (unravel) logorare, consumare. **frayed** adj (clothes, etc.) logoro dall'uso, liso. **frayed nerves** nervi scoperti m pl.

fray[2] [frei] n (brawl) mischia f.

freak [frik] n fenomeno m; figura grottesca f, mostro m.

freckle ['frekl] n lentiggine f. **freckled** adj lentigginoso.

free [fri] adj libero; (without payment) gratis, gratuito; (unconstrained) disinvolto, sciolto; (lavish) generoso. **free from** esente da. **freehold** n proprietà fondiaria assoluta f. **freelance** adj indipendente. **Freemason** n massone m.

free speech libertà di parola f. **free trade** libero scambio m. **free will** libero arbitrio m. v liberare. **freedom** n libertà f.

freesia ['frizia] n fresia f.

*****freeze** [friz] v gelare, congelare; (block) bloccare. n gelo m. **freezer** n congelatore m, freezer m invar. **freezing** adj gelido. **below freezing** sotto zero. **freezing point** punto di congelamento m.

freight [freit] n (cargo) carico m; (charge) nolo m; (conveyance) trasporto m. **freight train** treno merci m. v trasportare. **freighter** n nave da carico f.

French [frentʃ] nm, adj francese. **French bean** n fagiolino verde m, cornetto m. **French horn** corno (a pistoni) m. **Frenchman/woman** n francese m, f. **french fries** pl n patatine fritte f pl

frenzy ['frenzi] n frenesia f. **frenzied** adj frenetico.

frequent ['frikwənt; v fri'kwent] adj frequente. v frequentare. **frequency** n frequenza f.

fresco ['freskou] n affresco m.

fresh [freʃ] adj fresco; (water) dolce; (brisk) vigoroso; (cheeky) insolente. **fresh from** appena venuto da. **freshman** n matricola f. **freshen** v rinfrescare, rinnovare. **freshness** n freschezza f, vigore m.

fret[1] [fret] v inquietarsi. **fretful** adj irritabile.

fret[2] [fret] n (pattern) fregio m. v ornare con fregi, traforare. **fretwork** n lavoro di traforo m.

friar ['fraiə] n frate m. **friary** n convento di frati m.

friction ['frikʃən] n attrito m; (conflict) dissenso m.

Friday ['fraidei] n venerdì m.

fridge [fridʒ] n (coll) frigorifero m.

fried [fraid] adj fritto.

friend [frend] n amico, -a m, f. **make friends** fare amicizia. **friendless** adj senza amici. **friendliness** n amichevolezza f, cordialità f. **friendly** adj amichevole, cordiale, gentile. **be friendly with** essere amico di. **friendship** n amicizia f.

frieze [friz] n fregio m.

frigate ['frigit] n fregata f.

fright [frait] n spavento m. **frighten** v spaventare, allarmare. **be frightened** aver paura. **frightening** adj spaventevole, terribile. **frightful** adj terribile.

frigid ['frɪdʒɪd] *adj* freddo; (*woman*) frigido. **frigidity** *n* freddezza *f*; frigidità *f*.

frill [frɪl] *n* fronzolo *m*. **frilly** *adj* carico di fronzoli.

fringe [frɪndʒ] *n* (*border*) orlo *m*; limite *m*; (*ornamental border, hair*) frangia *f*; periferia *f*. *v* ornare di frange.

frisk [frɪsk] *v* saltellare; (*search*) perquisire. **frisky** *adj* vivace.

fritter[1] ['frɪtə] *v* fritter away sprecare.

fritter[2] ['frɪtə] *n* (*cookery*) frittella *f*.

frivolity [frɪ'vɒlɪtɪ] *n* frivolezza *f*. **frivolous** *adj* superficiale, frivolo.

frizz [frɪz] *v* arricciare. *n* ricciolo *m*. **frizzy** *adj* ricciuto.

fro [frou] *adv* **to and fro** avanti e indietro.

frock [frɒk] *n* vestito *m*.

frog [frɒg] *n* rana *f*. **frogman** *n* uomo rana *m*.

frolic ['frɒlɪk] *v* trastullarsi, scherzare. *n* scherzo *m*.

from [frɒm] *prep* da, per, da parte di.

front [frʌnt] *n* parte anteriore *f*; (*mil, pol*) fronte *m*; (*arch*) facciata *f*; (*seaside*) lungomare *m*. *adj* primo, anteriore. **front door** portone *m*. **in front of** davanti a.

frontier [frʌn'tɪə] *n* frontiera *f*, confine *m*.

frost [frɒst] *n* gelo *m*. **frost-bite** *n* gelone *m*. *v* brinare; (*cookery*) glassare. **frosted glass** vetro smerigliato *m*. **frosty** *adj* (*weather*) gelido; (*manner*) freddo.

froth [frɒθ] *n* schiuma *f*. *v* spumare, schiumare.

frown [fraun] *v* aggrottare le ciglia, corrugare la fronte. **frown at** guardare in cagnesco. *n* cipiglio *m*, viso arcigno *m*.

froze [frouz] *V* **freeze**.

frozen ['frouzn] *V* **freeze**. *adj* gelato, congelato; bloccato.

frugal ['fruːgəl] *adj* frugale, sobrio.

fruit [fruːt] *n* frutto *m*; (*collectively*) frutta *f*; (*result*) risultato *m*. **fruit salad** macedonia di frutta *f*. *v* (*bear fruit*) fruttare. **fruiterer** *n* fruttivendolo, -a *m, f*. **fruitful** *adj* fecondo; (*profitable*) redditizio. **fruition** *n* realizzazione *f*. **fruitless** *adj* infruttuoso; inutile. **fruity** *adj* saporito; di frutta; (*wine*) dal gusto d'uva.

frustrate [frʌ'streit] *v* frustrare. **frustration** *n* frustrazione *f*.

fry [frai] *v* friggere. **frying pan** padella *f*.

fuchsia ['fjuːʃə] *n* fucsia *f*.

fuck [fʌk] *v* (*vulgar*) fottere, chiavare.

fuel ['fjuəl] *n* combustibile *m*; (*mot*) carburante *m*. **fuel oil** gasolio *m*, nafta *f*. *v* alimentare.

fugitive ['fjuːdʒitiv] *adj* (*runaway*) fuggitivo, fuggiasco; (*fleeting*) effimero, fugace. *n* fuggiasco, -a *m, f*; profugo, -a *m, f*.

fugue [fjuːg] *n* fuga *f*.

fulcrum ['fulkrəm] *n* fulcro *m*.

fulfil [ful'fil] *v* adempiere, compiere, soddisfare. **fulfilment** *n* adempimento *m*, realizzazione *f*.

full [ful] *adj* pieno; completo; intero. **full-length** *adj* di lunghezza normale; (*portrait*) in piedi. **full moon** luna piena *f*. **full-sized** *adj* di grandezza naturale. **full stop** punto *m*. **full-time** *adj* a tempo intero, a orario completo. **fully** *adv* completamente.

fumble ['fʌmbl] *v* brancolare.

fume [fjuːm] *v* emettere fumo; (*coll: rage*) arrabbiarsi, imperversare. *n* fumo *m*, esalazione *f*.

fumigate ['fjuːmigeit] *v* suffumicare.

fun [fʌn] *n* spasso *m*, divertimento *m*, scherzo *m*. **funfair** *n* luna park *m invar*. **in fun** per ridere. **make fun of** prendere in giro.

function ['fʌŋkʃən] *n* funzione *f*; (*purpose*) scopo *m*; (*duty*) mansione *f*; (*ceremony*) cerimonia *f*. *v* funzionare. **functional** *adj* funzionale.

fund [fʌnd] *n* fondo *m*, riserva *f*, capitale *m*. **funds** *pl n* soldi *m pl*.

fundamental [fʌndə'mentl] *adj* fondamentale, basilare.

funeral ['fjuːnərəl] *n* funerale *m*. *adj* funebre. **funereal** *adj* funereo.

fungus ['fʌŋgəs] *n, pl* **-gi** fungo *m*. **fungicide** *n* anticrittogamico *m*.

funnel ['fʌnl] *n* imbuto *m*; (*ship*) ciminiera *f*.

funny ['fʌni] *adj* divertente, comico; (*odd*) strano. **funny story** barzelletta *f*. **the funny thing** is il bello è.

fur [fəː] *n* (*skin*) pelo *m*; pelliccia *f*. *v* incrostarsi. **furrier** *n* pellicciaio *m*. **furry** *adj* peloso.

furious ['fjuəriəs] *adj* furibondo, arrabbiatissimo.

furnace ['fəːnis] *n* fornace *f*.

furnish ['fəːniʃ] *v* (*supply*) fornire, dotare; (*house, etc.*) arredare, ammobiliare.

furniture ['fəːnitʃə] *n* mobilio *m*, mobili *m pl*; (*fittings*) attrezzatura *f*.

furrow ['fʌrou] n solco m; (brow) ruga f, grinza f.

further ['fɜːðə] adj ulteriore, più lontano. adv più lontano, oltre. **furthermore** adv inoltre. **further on** più avanti. **further up** più in su. v favorire, promuovere.

furthest ['fɜːðist] adj in più lontano, estremo.

furtive ['fɜːtiv] adj furtivo, di soppiatto.

fury ['fjuəri] n furia f.

fuse¹ [fjuːz] n (elec) valvola f, fusibile f. **blow a fuse** saltare la corrente. v (melt) fondere; (blend) amalgamare, unire. **fusion** n fusione f.

fuse² [fjuːz] n (bomb) detonatore m.

fuselage ['fjuːzəlaːʒ] n fusoliera f.

fuss [fʌs] v lamentarsi, agitarsi. **fuss over** affaccendarsi attorno a. n scalpore m, trambusto m. **make a fuss** fare un gran chiasso. **fussy** adj pignolo, meticoloso.

futile ['fjuːtail] adj vano, inutile. **futility** n inutilità f.

future ['fjuːtʃə] n futuro m, avvenire m. adj futuro.

fuzz [fʌz] n lanugine f, peluria f. **fuzzy** adj peloso; (unclear) sfocato.

G

gabble ['gabl] v borbottare. n borbottio m.

gaberdine [gabə'diːn] n gabardina f.

gable ['geibl] n pigna f, frontone m.

gadget ['gadʒit] n congegno m, dispositivo m.

gag¹ [gag] n bavaglio m. v imbavagliare.

gag² [gag] n (joke) battuta f.

gaiety ['geiəti] n allegria f.

gaily ['geili] adv allegramente.

gain [gein] n guadagno m, profitto m. v guadagnare; (obtain) ottenere.

gait [geit] n andatura f, passo m.

gala ['gaːlə] n festa f.

galaxy ['galəksi] n galassia f.

gale [geil] n bufera f, burrasca f.

gallant ['galənt] adj (courageous) prode; (courtly) galante. n cavaliere m. **gallantry** n valore m, coraggio m; galanteria f.

gall-bladder ['gɔːlˌbladə] n cistifellea f, vescica biliare f.

galleon ['galiən] n galeone m.

gallery ['galəri] n galleria f; (theatre) loggione m.

galley ['gali] n (naut) galea f; (kitchen) cambusa f.

gallop ['galəp] n galoppo m; galoppata f. v galoppare, andare al galoppo.

gallows ['galouz] n patibolo m.

gallstone ['gɔːlstoun] n calcolo biliare m.

galore [gə'lɔː] adv in quantità.

galvanize ['galvənaiz] v galvanizzare. **galvanometer** n galvanometro m.

gambit ['gambit] n gambetto m.

gamble ['gambl] v (risk) rischiare, arrischiare; (game) giocare. n impresa rischiosa f, speculazione f. **gambler** n giocatore, -trice m, f. **gambling** n gioco d'azzardo m.

game [geim] n gioco m; (match) partita f; (hunting) selvaggina f. **gamekeeper** n guardacaccia m. adj (plucky) che ha del fegato.

gammon ['gamən] n prosciutto m.

gander ['gandə] n papero m.

gang [gaŋ] n squadra f, gruppo m; (youths, thieves, etc.) banda f. v **gang up** allearsi. **gangster** n gangster m invar, bandito m.

gangling ['gaŋgliŋ] adj allampanato.

gangrene ['gaŋgriːn] n cancrena f.

gangway ['gaŋwei] n passaggio m, corsia f; (naut) barcarizzo m.

gaol V **jail**.

gap [gap] n (breach) breccia f; (opening) apertura f; (hole) buco m; (vacant space) vuoto m; intervallo m; (divergence) distacco m.

gape [geip] v stare a bocca aperta; (open wide) spalancare.

garage ['garaːʒ] n garage m invar; (repairs) autorimessa f.

garbage ['gaːbidʒ] (US) n rifiuti m pl. **garbage can** bidone della spazzatura m.

garble ['gaːbl] v mutilare.

garden ['gaːdn] n giardino m. v fare del giardinaggio. **gardener** n giardiniere, -a m, f. **gardening** n giardinaggio m.

gargle ['gaːgl] v gargarizzare. n gargarismo m.

garish ['geəriʃ] adj vistoso.

garland ['gaːlənd] n ghirlanda f. v inghirlandare.

garlic ['gaːlik] n aglio m.

garment ['gaːmənt] n indumento m, capo di vestiario m.

garnish ['gaːniʃ] v guarnire, adornare. n ornamento m, guarnizione f.

garret ['gærət] n soffitta f.

garrison ['gærisn] n guarnigione f, presidio m. v presidiare.

garrulous ['gærələs] adj loquace.

garter ['gɑːtə] n giarrettiera f.

gas [gæs] n gas m invar; (US: petrol) benzina f. **gas cooker** fornello a gas m. **gas fire** stufa a gas f. **gas mask** maschera antigas f. v asfissiare.

gash [gæʃ] n sfregio m, squarcio m. v sfregiare, squarciare.

gasket ['gæskit] n guarnizione f.

gasoline ['gæsəˌliːn] n (US) benzina f.

gasp [gɑːsp] v boccheggiare, ansimare. n rantolo m.

gastric ['gæstrik] adj gastrico.

gastronomy [gə'strɒnəmi] n gastronomia f. **gastronomic** adj gastronomico.

gate [geit] n cancello m, porta f. **gatecrash** v fare il portoghese, entrare senza invito or pagare. **gatepost** n montante del cancello m. **gateway** n entrata f, portone m.

gateau ['gætou] n pasticcino m, gateau m.

gather ['gæðə] v cogliere; (bring together) raccogliere; (infer) dedurre; (assemble) radunarsi. **gathering** n riunione f, adunata f.

gaudy ['gɔːdi] adj vistoso.

gauge [geidʒ] n (measure) misura f; (instrument) calibro m; (rail) scartamento m. v misurare, calibrare.

gaunt [gɔːnt] adj emaciato, desolato.

gauze [gɔːz] n garza f.

gave [geiv] V give.

gay [gei] adj vivace, allegro; (slang) omosessuale.

gaze [geiz] v mirare, guardare fissamente. **gaze at** fissare. n sguardo fisso m.

gazelle [gə'zel] n gazzella f.

gazette [gə'zet] n gazzetta ufficiale f.

gazetteer [gæzə'tiə] n dizionario geografico m.

gear [giə] n (mot) marcia f, velocità f; (equipment, tools) arnesi m pl, attrezzatura f; (belongings) roba f. **change gear** cambiare velocità. **gearbox** n scatola del cambio f. **gear lever** leva del cambio f. v preparare, adattare.

gelatine ['dʒelə,tiːn] n gelatina f.

gelignite ['dʒelig,nait] n gelatina esplosiva f.

gem [dʒem] n gemma f.

Gemini ['dʒemini] n Gemelli m pl.

gender ['dʒendə] n genere m, sesso m.

gene [dʒiːn] n gene m.

genealogy [dʒiːni,alədʒi] n genealogia f. **genealogical** adj genealogico.

general ['dʒenərəl] nm, adj generale. **general practitioner** medico generico m. **generalization** n generalizzazione f. **generalize** v generalizzare.

generate ['dʒenəreit] v generare, produrre. **generation** n generazione f. **generator** n generatore m.

generic [dʒi'nerik] adj generico.

generous ['dʒenərəs] adj generoso. **generosity** n generosità f.

genetic [dʒi'netik] adj genetico. **geneticist** n genetista m, f. **genetics** n genetica f.

Geneva [dʒi'niːvə] n Ginevra f.

genial ['dʒiːniəl] adj gioviale, simpatico.

genital ['dʒenitl] adj genitale. **genitals** pl n organi genitali m pl.

genius ['dʒiːnjəs] n genio m.

Genoa ['dʒenouə] n Genova f. **Genoese** n(m+f), adj genovese.

genteel [dʒen'tiːl] adj signorile. **gentility** n signorilità f.

gentle ['dʒentl] adj tenero; (mild) mite; (not steep) dolce. **gentleman** n signore m; (of good breeding, etc.) gentiluomo m. **gentlemanly** adj signorile. **gentleness** n dolcezza f. **gently** adv dolcemente; adagio, piano.

gentry ['dʒentri] n piccola nobiltà f.

gents [dʒents] n (sign) uomini, signori.

genuine ['dʒenjuin] adj genuino, autentico; sincero. **genuinely** adv (really) veramente.

genus ['dʒiːnəs] n genere m.

geography [dʒi'ogrəfi] n geografia f. **geographer** n geografo, -a m, f. **geographical** adj geografico.

geology [dʒi'olədʒi] n geologia f. **geological** adj geologico. **geologist** n geologo, -a m, f.

geometry [dʒi'omətri] n geometria f. **geometric** adj geometrico.

geranium [dʒə'reiniəm] n geranio m.

geriatric [dʒeri'atrik] adj geriatrico. **geriatrics** n geriatria f.

germ [dʒəːm] n germe m.

Germany ['dʒəːməni] n Germania f. **German** n, adj tedesco, -a. **German measles** rosolia f, rubeola f.

germinate ['dʒəːmineit] v germinare. **germination** n germinazione f.

gerund ['dʒərənd] *n* gerundio *m*.
gesticulate [dʒe'stikju‚leit] *v* gesticolare. **gesticulation** *n* gesticolazione *f*.
gesture ['dʒestʃə] *n* gesto *m*. *v* gesticolare, fare gesti.
*****get** [get] *v* (*obtain*) ottenere, procurare; (*fetch*) andare a prendere; (*receive*) ricevere; (*understand*) capire; (*become*) diventare; (*reach*) arrivare. **get across** attraversare; (*make understand*) far capire. **get along with** andare d'accordo con. **get at** (*reach*) raggiungere; (*hint*) alludere. **getaway** *n* fuga *f*. **get off** scendere. **get out** uscire. **get up** alzarsi.
geyser ['gizə] *n* (*geog*) geyser *m*; (*water-heater*) scaldabagno *m*.
ghastly ['gaistli] *adj* orrendo; (*pale*) spettrale.
gherkin ['gəikin] *n* cetriolino *m*.
ghetto ['getou] *n* ghetto *m*.
ghost [goust] *n* fantasma *m*, spettro *m*. **ghostly** *adj* spettrale.
giant ['dʒaiənt] *n* gigante, -essa *m, f. adj* gigantesco, gigante.
gibberish ['dʒibəriʃ] *n* discorso incomprensibile *m*.
gibe [dʒaib] *n* beffa *f*; scherno *m*. *v* **gibe at** beffarsi di, beffare.
giblets ['dʒiblits] *pl n* rigaglie *f pl*, frattaglie *f pl*.
giddy ['gidi] *adj* (*flighty*) incostante, volubile; (*dizzy*) preso da vertigini; (*height*) vertiginoso. **feel giddy** avere il capogiro. **giddiness** *n* capogiro *m*, vertigini *f pl*.
gift [gift] *n* dono *m*, regalo *m*. **gifted** *adj* dotato.
gigantic [dʒai'gantik] *adj* gigantesco.
giggle ['gigl] *v* ridere sciccamente. *n* risatina sciocca *f*. **have the giggles** avere la ridarella.
gill [gil] *n* (*fish*) branchia *f*; (*mushroom*) lamella *f*.
gilt [gilt] *n* doratura *f. adj* dorato.
gimmick ['gimik] *n* (*coll: device*) congegno *m*; stratagemma *m*.
gin [dʒin] *n* gin *m invar*.
ginger ['dʒindʒə] *n* zenzero *m. adj* fulvo.
gingerly ['dʒindʒəli] *adj* cauto.
gipsy ['dʒipsi] *n* zingaro, -a *f*.
giraffe [dʒi'raif] *n* giraffa *f*.
girder ['gəidə] *n* trave maestra *f*, putrella *f*.
girdle ['gəidl] *n* busto *m*, cintura *f. v* cingere.

girl [gəil] *n* ragazza *f*. **girlfriend** *n* amica *f*. **girlish** *adj* da ragazza.
giro ['dʒairou] *n* giroconto *m*, postagiro *m*.
girth [gəiθ] *n* circonferenza *f*.
gist [dʒist] *n* nocciolo *m*.
*****give** [giv] *v* dare; (*present*) regalare; (*relinquish*) cedere. **give away** regalare; (*betray*) tradire; (*secret*) rivelare. **give back** restituire. **give in** cedere. **give oneself up** costituirsi. **give out** distribuire. **give rise to** risultare in. **give up** abbandonare; (*cease*) smettere. *n* elasticità *f*.
given ['givn] *V* **give**.
glacier ['glasiə] *n* ghiacciaio *m*.
glad [glad] *adj* lieto, contento. **gladden** *v* rallegrare. **gladly** *adv* con piacere.
glamour ['glamə] *n* fascino *m*. **glamorous** *adj* affascinante.
glance [glams] *n* sguardo *m*. **at a glance** a prima vista. *v* dare un'occhiata.
gland [gland] *n* ghiandola *f*. **glandular** *adj* ghiandolare.
glare [gleə] *n* (*light*) bagliore *m*; (*fierce look*) sguardo torvo *m*. *v* **glare at** guardare con cipiglio, guardare con occhio torvo.
glass [glais] *n* vetro *m*; (*container*) bicchiere *m*. **glasses** *pl n* occhiali *m pl*. **glassy** *adj* vitreo.
glaze [gleiz] *n* smalto *m*, patina *f. v* smaltare, verniciare; (*fit with glass*) fornire di vetri.
gleam [gliim] *v* luccicare. *n* barlume *m*, luccichio *m*.
glean [gliin] *v* racimolare.
glee [glii] *n* gioia *f*. **gleeful** *adj* pieno di gioia.
glib [glib] *adj* facondo.
glide [glaid] *v* scivolare, scorrere; (*aero*) planare. **glider** *n* aliante *m*. **gliding** *n* volo a vela *m*.
glimmer ['glimə] *v* luccicare; (*of dawn*) albeggiare. *n* barlume *m*, luccichio *m*.
glimpse [glimps] *n* occhiata *f*, visione *f. v* intravedere.
glint [glint] *n* luccichio *m. v* luccicare, scintillare.
glisten ['glisn] *v* luccicare, brillare.
glitter ['glitə] *v* brillare, scintillare. *n* lucentezza *f*.
gloat [glout] *v* gongolare (malignamente).

globe [gloub] n globo m. **global** adj globale.

gloom [gluːm] n (darkness) oscurità f; (depression) malinconia f, tristezza f. **gloomy** adj malinconico, triste.

glory ['glɔːri] n gloria f, splendore m. **glorify** v glorificare. **glorious** adj illustre, splendido.

gloss¹ [glos] n (lustre) lucentezza f; (appearance) apparenza f. **glossy** adj lucido.

gloss² [glos] n (explanation) chiosa f. v chiosare, commentare.

glossary ['glosəri] n lessico m.

glove [glʌv] n guanto m.

glow [glou] v risplendere; ardere. n rossore m; (colour) luminosità f. **glowing** adj acceso, ardente; fervente.

glucose ['gluːkous] n glucosio m.

glue [gluː] n colla f. v incollare.

glum [glʌm] adj tetro, cupo.

glut [glʌt] n sovrabbondanza f. v saturare.

glutton ['glʌtən] n ghiottone, -a m, f; goloso, -a m, f. **gluttonous** adj ghiotto, goloso. **gluttony** n golosità f.

gnarled [nɑːld] adj nodoso.

gnash [naʃ] v **gnash one's teeth** digrignare i denti.

gnat [nat] n zanzara f.

gnaw [nɔː] v rodere, rosicchiare. **gnawing** adj rosicante.

gnome [noum] n gnomo m.

go [gou] v andare; (become) diventare. **go away** andarsene. **go back** ritornare. **go-between** n intermediario m. **go by** passare; (be guided by) regolarsi su. **go down** scendere; (sink) affondare. **go in** entrare. **go off** esplodere; (spoil) guastarsi; (leave) andarsene. **go on** continuare. **go out** uscire. **go up** salire. **go without** fare a meno di. n energia f; (try) colpo m. **on the go** molto attivo.

goad [goud] n pungolo m. v incitare.

goal [goul] n (aim) meta f; (sport) porta f, rete f. **goalkeeper** n portiere m. **goal-post** n palo della porta m.

goat [gout] n capra f.

gobble ['gobl] v inghiottire.

goblin ['goblin] n folletto m.

god [god] n dio (pl dei) m. **goddaughter** n figlioccia f. **godfather** n padrino m. **godmother** n madrina f. **godson** n figlioccio m. **goddess** n dea f.

goggles ['goglz] pl n occhiali di protezione m pl.

gold [gould] n oro m. **goldfinch** n cardellino m. **goldfish** n pesce dorato or rosso m. **gold mine** miniera d'oro f. **goldsmith** n orefice m. **golden** adj d'oro; (colour) aureo. **golden rule** regola d'oro f.

golf [golf] n golf m. **golf course** campo di golf m. **golfer** n giocatore, -trice di golf m, f.

gondola ['gondələ] n gondola f.

gone [gon] V **go**.

gong [gon] n gong m invar.

gonorrhoea [gonə'riə] n gonorrea f.

good [gud] adj buono; valido; (well-behaved, clever) bravo. **good afternoon** buon giorno; (later) buona sera. **goodbye** interj addio; arrivederci; (coll) ciao. **good-for-nothing** n buono a nulla m. **good-looking** adj bello. **good morning** buon giorno. **goodnight** interj buona notte. **goodwill** n benevolenza f; (comm) avviamento m. **n be no good** non servire. **for good** per sempre. **goodness** n bontà f, gentilezza f, virtù f.

Good Friday n Venerdì Santo m.

goods [gudz] pl n merce f pl, beni m pl. **goods train** treno merci m.

goose [guːs] n, pl **geese** oca f.

gooseberry ['guzbəri] n uva spina f.

gore [gɔː] v trafiggere.

gorge [gɔːdʒ] n (geol) gola f. v rimpinzarsi (di).

gorgeous ['gɔːdʒəs] adj splendido.

gorilla [gə'rilə] n gorilla m invar.

gorse [gɔːs] n ginestrone m.

gory [gɔːri] adj cruento.

gosling ['gozlin] n papero, -a m, f.

gospel ['gospəl] n vangelo m; (coll: truth) verità implicita f.

gossip ['gosip] n ciarla f, pettegolezzo m; (person) ciarlone, -a m, f, chiacchierone, -a m, f. v ciarlare, chiacchierare.

got [got] V **get**.

Gothic ['goθik] adj gotico.

gourd [guəd] n zucca f.

gourmet ['guəmei] n buongustaio, -a m, f.

gout [gaut] n gotta f.

govern ['gʌvən] v governare f; (gramm) reggere. **governess** n governante f. **government** n governo m. **governor** n governatore m; (coll: boss) capo m.

gown [gaun] n (dress) veste f; (robe) toga f.

grab [grab] v arraffare. n strappo m.

grace [greis] n grazia f, eleganza f. v adornare. **graceful** adj grazioso. **gracious** adj benigno.

grade [greid] n grado m; (level) livello m; classe f. v classificare.

gradient ['greidiənt] n gradiente m; (slope) pendio m.

gradual ['grad̩uəl] adj graduale. **gradually** adv poco a poco.

graduate ['grad̩uət; v 'grad̩ueit] n laureato, -a m, f. v laurearsi.

graft[1] [graft] n (bot) innesto m; (med) trapianto m; (hard work) sgobbata f. v innestare; trapiantare; sgobbare.

graft[2] [graft] n (bribery) corruzione f. v corrompere.

grain [grein] n (seed) chicco m, granello m; (wheat) grano m; (wood) venatura f; (leather) grana f. **against the grain** contro pelo.

gram [gram] n grammo m.

grammar ['gramə] n grammatica f. **grammatical** adj grammaticale.

gramophone ['graməfoun] n grammofono m.

granary ['granəri] n granaio m.

grand [grand] adj (imposing) grandioso; (first rate) splendido. **grandchild** n nipote m, f; nipotino, -a m, f. **grandfather** n nonno m. **grandmother** n nonna f. **grand piano** pianoforte a coda m. **grandstand** n tribuna coperta f. **grand total** somma f. **grandeur** n grandiosità f.

granite ['granit] n granito m.

grant [grant] v (confer) concedere, accordare; (give) dare; (admit) ammettere. **take for granted** ritenere per certo. n (student) borsa di studio f; concessione f.

granule ['granjul] n granello m.

grape [greip] n acino m, chicco d'uva m. **grapes** pl n uva f sing. **grapevine** n vite f; (coll) canali confidenziali m pl.

grapefruit ['greipfrut] n pompelmo m.

graph [graf] n (math) grafico m; diagramma m. **graphic** adj grafico. **graph paper** carta millimetrata f.

grapple ['grapl] v afferrare; (understand) capire. n stretta f. **grasping** adj avaro.

grasp [grasp] v afferrare; (understand) capire. n stretta f. **grasping** adj avaro.

grass [gras] n erba f; (lawn) prato m. **grasshopper** n cavalletta f. **grassy** adj erboso.

grate[1] [greit] n graticola f. **grating** n inferriata f.

grate[2] [greit] v grattugiare; (sound harshly) stridere; (irritate) dare sui nervi.

grateful ['greitful] adj riconoscente, grato.

gratify ['gratifai] v appagare.

gratitude ['gratitjud] n gratitudine f.

gratuitous [grə'tjuitəs] adj (free) gratuito; (unsolicited gift) ingiustificato.

gratuity [grə'tjuəti] n (tip) mancia f; (unsolicited gift) gratifica f.

grave[1] [greiv] n tomba f, sepolcro m. **gravedigger** n becchino m. **gravestone** n lapide funeraria f. **graveyard** n cimitero m.

grave[2] [greiv] adj grave.

gravel ['gravəl] n ghiaia f.

gravity ['gravəti] n gravità f. **gravitate** v gravitare.

gravy ['greivi] n sugo di carne m; salsa f.

graze[1] [greiz] v (touch) sfiorare; (scrape) scalfire. n scalfittura f, lesione superficiale f.

graze[2] [greiz] v (animal) pascolare.

grease [gris] n grasso m, unto m. **greaseproof paper** carta oleata f. v ungere, ingrassare. **greasy** adj grasso, unto; (slippery) scivoloso.

great [greit] adj grande; (very good) magnifico; (very large) grandissimo. **Great Britain** Gran Bretagna f. **greatly** adv molto. **greatness** n grandezza f.

Greece [gris] n Grecia f. **Greek** n, adj greco (pl -ci), -a.

greed [grid] n ingordigia f. **greedy** adj ingordo.

green [grin] adj verde. n verde m; (land) prato m; (golf) green m. **greenfly** n afide m. **greengage** n prugna verde f. **greengrocer** n erbivendolo, -a m, f, fruttivendolo, -a m, f. **greenhouse** n serra f. **green light** luce verde f. **greens** pl n verdura f sing.

Greenland ['grinlənd] n Groenlandia f. **Greenlander** n groenlandese m, f.

greet [grit] v salutare. **greeting** n saluto m.

gregarious [gri'geəriəs] adj gregario, socievole.

grenade [grə'neid] n granata f.

grew [gru] V grow.

grey [grei] adj grigio.

grid [grid] n (network) rete f; (map) reticolo m; (grating) grata f.

grief [griːf] n dolore m, afflizione f. **come to grief** far fiasco or cilecca.

grieve [griːv] v (upset) affliggere, addolorare; (sorrow) affliggersi. **grievance** n (injustice) ingiustizia f; (complaint) lamentela f. **grievous** adj doloroso, atroce.

grill [gril] n (cookery) graticola f, gratella f; (grilled meat) carne ai ferri f. v (cookery) cucinare ai ferri; (question severely) sottoporre a un interrogatorio severo.

grille [gril] n inferriata f, grata f.

grim [grim] adj (unrelenting) insorabile; (fierce) feroce; (forbidding) arcigno. **grimly** adv con severità.

grimace [gri'meis] n smorfia f. v fare smorfie.

grime [graim] n sudiciume m. **grimy** adj sudicio.

grin [grin] v fare un largo sorriso. n largo sorriso m.

*__**grind**__ [graind] v (pulverize) macinare; (sharpen) affilare; (teeth) digrignare. n (coll: hard work) sgobbata f.

grip [grip] v stringere; (hold interest) avvincere; (take firm hold) far presa. n presa f, stretta f; (control) padronanza f. **come to grips with** venire alle prese con.

gripe [graip] n colica f. v (coll) lagnarsi.

grisly ['grizli] adj orribile, macabro.

gristle ['grisl] n cartilagine f. **gristly** adj cartilaginoso.

grit [grit] n (sand) sabbia f; (mech) graniglia f; (coll: courage) fegato m. v (teeth) digrignare. **gritty** adj sabbioso.

groan [groun] n gemito m, lamento m. v gemere, lamentarsi.

grocer ['grousə] n droghiere, -a m, f. **grocer's** n (shop) drogheria f. **groceries** pl n generi coloniali m pl.

groin [groin] n inguine m.

groom [gruːm] n stalliere m; (bridegroom) sposo m. v preparare; (horse) strigliare.

groove [gruːv] n solco m. v scanalare.

grope [group] v brancolare. **grope for** cercare a tentoni, brancolare in cerca di.

gross [grous] adj grossolano, volgare; (not net) lordo. v (income) avere un introito lordo di. n grossa f.

grotesque [grə'tesk] adj fantastico; (incongruous) grottesco.

grotto ['grotou] n grotta f.

ground[1] [graund] V **grind**.

ground[2] [graund] n (soil) terreno m;

(earth, floor) terra f; (sport) campo m; (reason) motivo m; (bottom) fondo m. **ground floor** pianterreno m. **grounds** pl n (sediment) deposito m sing; (dregs) fondi m pl. v (base) fondare; (teach) insegnare i primi elementi; (aircraft) impedire di volare. **grounding** n base f. **groundless** adj infondato.

group [gruːp] n gruppo m. v raggruppare, disporre.

grouse[1] [graus] n (bird) urogallo m.

grouse[2] [graus] (coll) v brontolare, lamentarsi. n lagnanza f.

grove [grouv] n boschetto m.

grovel ['grovl] v umiliarsi; (cringe) strisciare.

*__**grow**__ [grou] v crescere; (thrive) prosperare; (become) diventare. **grown-up** n, adj adulto, -a. **grow on** piacere sempre più. **grow up** crescere, sorgere. **grower** n coltivatore, -trice m, f. **growth** n crescita f, progresso m; (med) escrescenza f, tumore m.

growl [graul] v ringhiare; (rumble) brontolare. n ringhio m; brontolio m.

grown [groun] V **grow**.

grub [grʌb] n (insect) larva f, bruco m; (coll) roba da mangiare f. v ripulire; (uproot) sradicare.

grubby ['grʌbi] adj (dirty) sudicio; (contemptible) abietto.

grudge [grʌdʒ] n rancore m. **bear a grudge against** nutrire rancore verso. v (give reluctantly) dare malvolentieri; (resent) invidiare. **grudgingly** adv malvolentieri.

gruelling ['gruːliŋ] adj faticoso.

gruesome ['gruːsəm] adj raccapricciante.

gruff [grʌf] adj (surly) burbero; (hoarse) rauco; (harsh) aspro.

grumble ['grʌmbl] v (complain) lagnarsi; (growl) brontolare. n lagnanza f, brontolio m.

grumpy ['grʌmpi] adj scontroso.

grunt [grʌnt] v grugnire. n grugnito m.

guarantee [garən'tiː] v garantire, rispondere di. n garanzia f.

guard [gaːd] v (keep safe) custodire; (watch over) sorvegliare; (keep watch) stare in guardia. **guard against** badare a. n guardia m, f; (appliance) protezione f; (railway) capotreno m. **guarded** adj cauto. **guardian** n custode m; (legal) tutore m.

guerrilla [gə'rilə] n guerrigliero m. **guerrilla warfare** guerriglia f.

guess [ges] n congettura f, supposizione f. **at a rough guess** a occhio e croce. v indovinare.

guest [gest] n ospite m, f; (of hotel) cliente m, f. **guest-house** n pensione f.

guide [gaid] n guida f; (of tourists) cicerone m. **guidebook** n guida f. v guidare; (advise) consigliare; (direct) dirigere. **be guided by** seguire il consiglio di. **guidance** n (leadership) guida f; (instruction) norma f.

guild [gild] n corporazione f.

guile [gail] n astuzia f. **guileless** adj ingenuo.

guillotine ['gilətiin] n ghigliottina f.

guilt [gilt] n colpa f. **guiltless** adj innocente. **guilty** adj colpevole. **have a guilty conscience** avere la coscienza sporca or cattiva.

guinea-pig ['ginipig] n cavia f.

guitar [gi'tar] n chitarra f. **guitarist** n chitarrista m, f.

gulf [gʌlf] n (geog) golfo m; (wide separation) abisso m.

gull [gʌl] n gabbiano m.

gullet ['gʌlit] n (throat) gola f; (oesophagus) esofago m.

gullible ['gʌləbl] adj credulo. **gullibility** n credulità f.

gully ['gʌli] n (canyon) burrone m; (ditch) cunetta f.

gulp [gʌlp] n (food) boccone m; (drink) sorso m. v (food) ingoiare; (drink) tracannare; (choke) soffocare.

gum[1] [gʌm] n (secretion) gomma f; (glue) colla f. v ingommare; incollare.

gum[2] [gʌm] n (mouth) gengiva f.

gun [gʌn] n fucile m; cannone m. **gunfire** n sparatoria f. **gunman** n bandito armato m. **gunner** n artigliere m. **gunpowder** n polvere da sparo f. **gunshot** n colpo di fucile m.

gurgle ['gəːgl] v gorgogliare. n gorgoglio m.

gush [gʌʃ] n sgorgo m; (language) torrente m. v (liquid) scaturire; (speech) parlare con effusione.

gust [gʌst] n raffica f.

gusto ['gʌstou] n fervore m.

gut [gʌt] n budello m (pl -a f). **guts** pl n (coll) fegato m sing. v sbudellare.

gutter ['gʌtə] n (house) grondaia f; (street) cunetta f; (conduit) condotto m. **guttersnipe** n scugnizzo m.

guy[1] [gai] n tipo m, individuo m.

guy[2] [gai] n (rope) tirante m.

gymnasium [dʒim'neiziəm] n palestra f. **gymnast** n ginnasta m, f. **gymnastics** n ginnastica f.

gynaecology [gainə'kolədʒi] n ginecologia f. **gynaecological** adj ginecologico. **gynaecologist** n ginecologo, -a m, f.

gypsum ['dʒipsəm] n gesso m.

gyrate [dʒai'reit] v girare, roteare.

gyroscope ['dʒairəskoup] n giroscopio m.

H

haberdasher ['habədaʃə] n merciaio, -a m, f. **haberdashery** n merceria f.

habit ['habit] n abitudine f; (dress) tonaca f. **habitual** adj abituale. **habitually** adv di solito.

habitable ['habitəbl] adj abitabile.

habitat ['habitat] n ambiente m.

hack[1] [hak] v tagliare, troncare. **hacksaw** n seghetto m.

hack[2] [hak] n (horse) ronzino m; (writer) scribacchino m.

hackneyed ['haknid] adj trito, comune.

had [had] V **have**.

haddock ['hadək] n eglefino m.

haemorrhage ['hemoridʒ] n emorragia f.

haemorrhoids ['heməroidz] pl n emorroidi f pl.

hag [hag] n vecchiaccia f, strega f.

haggard ['hagəd] adj smunto, scarno.

haggle ['hagl] v mercanteggiare.

Hague [heig] n l'Aia f.

hail[1] [heil] n grandine f. **hailstone** n chicco di grandine m. v grandinare.

hail[2] [heil] v salutare; (call) chiamare. **hail from** essere oriundo di. interj salve! m saluto m.

hair [heə] n capelli m pl; (single strand) capello m; (of animals) pelo m. **split hairs** cercare il pelo nell'uovo. **hairy** adj capelluto; peloso.

hairbrush ['heəbrʌʃ] n spazzola per capelli f.

haircut ['heəkʌt] n taglio dei capelli m. **have a haircut** farsi tagliare i capelli.

hairdresser ['heə,dresə] n parrucchiere, -a m, f.

hair-dryer ['heə,draiə] *n* asciugacapelli *m invar.*

hairpin ['heəpin] *n* forcina *f.*

hair-raising ['heə,reiziŋ] *adj* raccapricciante.

hake [heik] *n* nasello *m.*

half [haif] *adj* mezzo. *n* mezzo *m,* metà *f;* (*sport: period*) tempo *m.* **in half** in due.

half-and-half *adj, adv* metà e metà.

half-back ['haifbak] *n* mediano *m.*

half-baked [,haif'beikt] *adj* (*coll*) inesperto, immaturo.

half-breed ['haifbriid] *nm, adj* ibrido.

half-brother ['haifbrʌðə] *n* fratellastro *m.*

half-hearted [,haif'haitid] *adj* esitante, poco entusiasta.

half-hour [,haif'auə] *n* mezz'ora *f.*

half-mast [,haif'maist] *n* **at half-mast** a mezz'asta.

half-moon [,haif'muin] *n* mezzaluna *f.*

half-sister ['haifsistə] *n* sorellastra *f.*

half-time [,haif'taim] *n* intervallo *m.*

half-tone ['haiftoun] *n* mezzatinta *f,* fotoriproduzione *f.*

halfway [,haif'wei] *adj, adv* a metà strada. **meet halfway** giungere a un compromesso.

half-witted [,haif'witid] *adj* scemo, deficiente.

halibut ['halibət] *n* halibut *m invar,* ippoglosso *m.*

hall [hoil] *n* (*entrance*) entrata *f;* (*room*) sala *f,* salone *m;* (*building*) villa *f,* casa signorile *f.*

hallmark ['hoilmaik] *n* marchio d'autenticità *m;* elemento caratteristico *m.* *v* marcare.

hallowed ['haloud] *adj* venerato.

hallucination [hə,luisi'neiʃən] *n* allucinazione *f.*

halo ['heilou] *n* aureola *f;* (*astron*) alone *m.*

halt [hoilt] *n* fermata *f;* (*temporary*) sosta *f.* *v* sostare, fermare, fermarsi. *interj* alt!

halter ['hoiltə] *n* capestro *m;* cavezza *f.*

halve [haiv] *v* dimezzare, ridurre della *or* alla metà.

ham [ham] *n* prosciutto *m.*

hamburger ['hambəigə] *n* hamburger *m invar.*

hammer ['hamə] *n* martello *m.* *v* martellare.

hammock ['hamək] *n* amaca *f.*

hamper[1] ['hampə] *v* intralciare, ostacolare.

hamper[2] ['hampə] *n* paniere *m.*

hamster ['hamstə] *n* criceto *m.*

hand [hand] *n* mano (*pl* -i) *f;* (*clock*) lancetta *f;* (*worker*) operaio, -a *m, f.* **at hand** a portata di mano. **by hand** a mano. **hands down** completamente, con facilità. **hands off!** via le mani! **hands up!** alto le mani! **in hand** (*under control*) sotto controllo; (*available*) a disposizione; (*being dealt with*) in corso. **on hand** presente; (*available*) disponibile. **on the other hand** d'altra parte. *v* (*give*) dare, porgere. **hand down** trasmettere, tramandare. **hand in** *or* **over** consegnare. **hand out** distribuire. **handful** *n* manata *f;* piccolo gruppo *m.*

handbag ['handbag] *n* borsetta *f.*

handbill ['handbil] *n* volantino *m.*

handbook ['handbuk] *n* manuale *m.*

handbrake ['handbreik] *n* freno a mano *m.*

handcuff ['handkʌf] *n* manetta *f.* *v* ammanettare.

handicap ['handikap] *n* svantaggio *m,* impedimento *m;* (*sport*) handicap *m invar.* *v* impedire.

handicraft ['handikraift] *n* artigianato *m;* (*trade*) mestiere *m.*

handiwork ['handiwəik] *n* (*personal work*) opera *f.*

handkerchief ['haŋkətʃif] *n* fazzoletto *m.*

handle ['handl] *n* manico *m;* (*door*) maniglia *f;* (*crank*) manovella *f.* *v* (*manipulate*) maneggiare; (*deal with*) trattare. **handlebar** *n* manubrio *m.*

handmade [,hand'meid] *adj* fatto a mano.

hand-out ['handaut] *n* comunicato *m,* campione pubblicitario *m.*

hand-pick [hand'pik] *v* scegliere a mano.

handrail ['handreil] *n* ringhiera *f.*

handshake ['handʃeik] *n* stretta di mano *f.*

handsome ['hansəm] *adj* bello; generoso, considerevole.

handstand ['hand,stand] *n* posata verticale sulle mani *f.*

hand-towel ['hand,tauəl] *n* asciugamano *m.*

handwriting ['hand,raitiŋ] *n* calligrafia *f.*

handy ['handi] *adj* (*accessible*) a portata di mano; (*deft*) destro, abile; (*convenient*) comodo.

•hang [haŋ] *v* pendere, appendere, sospendere; (*execute*) impiccare. **hang around** bazzicare. **hanger** *n* (*clothes*) attaccapanni *m invar*. **hanger-on** *n* scroccone *m*. **hangman** *n* boia *m invar*. **hang on** persistere, indugiare; (*phone*) restare in linea. **hangover** *n* postumi di una sbornia *m pl*.

hangar ['haŋə] *n* hangar *m invar*; aviorimessa *f*.

hanker ['haŋkə] *v* **hanker after** bramare. **hankering** *n* forte desiderio *m*, brama *f*.

haphazard [,hap'hazəd] *adj* casuale.

happen ['hapən] *v* (*take place*) accadere, succedere. **as it happens** per caso. **happening** *n* avvenimento *m*.

happy ['hapi] *adj* felice, contento, lieto; (*in greetings*) buono. **happy-go-lucky** *adj* spensierato. **happiness** *n* felicità *f*, contentezza *f*.

harass ['harəs] *v* molestare, tormentare, irritare. **harassment** *n* tormento *m*, molestia *f*.

harbour ['haːbə] *n* porto *m*. *v* (*shelter*) dare asilo a.

hard [haːd] *adj* duro; difficile; severo. *adv* molto; (*solidly*) sodo. **hard and fast** immutabile. **hard-boiled** *adj* (*egg*) sodo; (*person*) duro. **hard core** nucleo *m*. **hard-headed** *adj* accorto, pratico. **hard-hearted** *adj* insensibile. **hard up** al corto di quattrini. **hardware** *n* ferramenta *f pl*; (*computer*) meccanismo *m*. **hard-wearing** *adj* duraturo, durevole. **hard work** lavoro faticoso *m*. **try hard** provare assiduamente. **work hard** lavorar sodo. **hardness** *n* durezza *f*. **hardship** *n* privazione *f*.

hardly ['haːdli] *adv* (*not quite*) non esattamente; (*barely*, *almost not*) quasi, appena; (*with difficulty*) a stento.

hardy ['haːdi] *adj* robusto, resistente; (*courageous*) coraggioso.

hare [heə] *n* lepre *f*. **hare-brained** *adj* scervellato.

harm [haːm] *n* male *m*, danno *m*. *v* nuocere a, far male a. **harmful** *adj* nocivo, dannoso. **harmless** *adj* innocuo, inoffensivo.

harmony ['haːməni] *n* armonia *f*, accordo *m*. **harmonic** *adj* armonico, armonioso. **harmonize** *v* armonizzare.

harness ['haːnis] *n* briglia *f*. *v* imbrigliare.

harp [haːp] *n* arpa *f*. **harpist** *n* arpista *m*, *f*.

harpoon [haː'puːn] *n* rampone *m*. *v* ramponare.

harpsichord ['haːpsi,koːd] *n* clavicembalo *m*.

harrowing ['harouiŋ] *adj* straziante.

harsh [haːʃ] *adj* aspro, duro. **harshness** *n* asprezza *f*, durezza *f*.

harvest ['haːvist] *n* raccolto *m*. *v* raccogliere, mietere.

has [haz] *V* **have**.

hash [haʃ] *n* carne tritata *f*; (*coll*: *mess*) confusione *f*, pasticcio *m*. **make a hash of** sciupare, mandare a rotoli.

hashish ['haʃiːʃ] *n* (h)ascisc *m invar*.

haste [heist] *n* fretta *f*. **hasten** *v* precipitare, affrettarsi. **hasty** *adj* frettoloso.

hat [hat] *n* cappello *m*.

hatch[1] [hatʃ] *v* (*bring forth*) covare; (*contrive*) tramare.

hatch[2] [hatʃ] *n* (*naut*) boccaporto *m*; (*opening*) portello *m*, sportello *m*.

hatchet ['hatʃit] *n* accetta *f*.

hate [heit] *v* odiare. *n also* **hatred** odio *m*. **hateful** *adj* odioso.

haughty ['hoːti] *adj* altezzoso, arrogante.

haul [hoːl] *n* tiro *m*; (*fish*) retata *f*; (*coll*: *booty*) bottino *m*. *v* tirare.

haunch [hoːntʃ] *n* anca *f*.

haunt [hoːnt] *v* perseguitare, ossessionare. *n* ritrovo *m*. **haunting** *adj* ossessionante.

*****have** [hav] *v* avere. **have to** avere da, dovere. **have it in for** avercela con. **have on** (*wear*) portare; (*have planned*) aver intenzione di fare, aver da fare; (*coll*: *tease*) prendere in giro.

haven ['heivn] *n* (*harbour*) porto *m*; (*shelter*) rifugio *m*.

haversack ['havəsak] *n* bisaccia *f*.

havoc ['havək] *n* **play havoc with** rovinare, far strage di.

hawk[1] [hoːk] *n* falco *m*, falcone *m*.

hawk[2] [hoːk] *v* spacciare; fare il venditore ambulante.

hawthorn ['hoːθoːn] *n* biancospino *m*.

hay [hei] *n* fieno *m*. **go haywire** perdere le staffe. **hay fever** raffreddore del fieno *m*. **haystack** *n* fienile *m*.

hazard ['hazəd] *n* (*danger*) pericolo *m*; (*risk*) rischio *m*. *v* azzardare. **hazardous** *adj* pericoloso, rischioso.

haze [heiz] *n* foschia *f*. **hazy** *adj* nebuloso, indistinto.

hazel ['heizl] *n* (*tree*) nocciolo *m*. **hazelnut** *n* nocciola *f*. *adj* color nocciola *invar*.

he [hiː] *pron* egli, lui. **he who** colui che.

head [hed] *n* testa *f*; (*leader*) capo *m*. *v* (*lead*) essere a capo di; (*direct*) dirigere.

headache ['hedeik] *n* mal di testa *m*; (*coll*) preoccupazione *f*.

headdress ['heddres] *n* copricapo *m*.

heading *n* (*title*) intestazione *f*; (*topic*) voce *f*.

headlamp ['hedlamp] *n* also **headlight** (*mot*) faro *m*, fanale *m*.

headland ['hedlənd] *n* promontorio *m*.

headline ['hedlain] *n* titolo *m*. **headlines** *pl n* (*news*) sommario *m sing*.

headlong ['hedloŋ] *adv* a capofitto.

headmaster [‚hed'maistə] *n* preside *m*.

headphones ['hedfounz] *pl n* cuffia *f sing*.

headquarters [‚hed'kwɔːtəz] *n* (*mil*) quartiere generale *m*; (*office*) sede *f*, direzione *f*.

headrest ['hedrest] *n* appoggiatesta *m invar*.

headscarf ['hedskaɪf] *n* foulard *m invar*.

headstrong ['hedstroŋ] *adj* testardo, cocciuto.

headway ['hedwei] *n* progresso *m*. **make headway** far strada.

heady ['hedi] *adj* impetuoso; (*intoxicating*) che dà alla testa.

heal [hiːl] *v* guarire, sanare.

health [helθ] *n* salute *f*. **healthy** *adj* (*person*) sano; (*climate, etc.*) salubre.

heap [hiːp] *n* mucchio *m*. *v* ammucchiare.

*****hear** [hiə] *v* udire, sentire; (*be informed of*) venire a sapere. **hear about** aver notizie di. **hear from** aver notizie da. **hearing** *n* udito *m*; (*audience*) udienza *f*. **hearsay** *n* voce *f*.

heard [həːd] *V* **hear**.

hearse [həːs] *n* carro funebre *m*.

heart [haːt] *n* cuore *m*; (*feeling*) animo *m*; (*essential part*) parte centrale *f*, centro *m*. **by heart** a memoria. **hearts** *pl n* (*cards*) cuori *m pl*. **take to heart** prendersi a cuore.

heart attack *n* attacco cardiaco *m*.

heartbeat ['haːtbiːt] *n* battito del cuore *m*.

heart-breaking ['haːtbreikiŋ] *adj* straziante. **heart-broken** *adj* accorato, affranto.

heartburn ['haːtbəːn] *n* bruciore di stomaco *m*.

heartening ['haːtniŋ] *adj* incoraggiante.

heartfelt ['haːtfelt] *adj* sincero.

hearth [haːθ] *n* focolare *m*.

heartless ['haːtlis] *adj* spietato, insensibile.

hearty ['haːti] *adj* (*warm-hearted*) caloroso; sincero; vigoroso.

heat [hiːt] *n* calore *m*, caldo *m*; (*sport*) batteria *f*; (*oestrum*) estro *m*. **heat wave** calura *f*. *v* scaldare, riscaldare. **heated** *adj* animato. **heater** *n* riscaldatore *m*; stufa elettrica *f*. **heating** *n* riscaldamento *m*.

heath [hiːθ] *n* brughiera *f*.

heathen ['hiːðn] *n, adj* pagano, -a.

heather ['heðə] *n* erica *f*.

heave [hiːv] *v* sollevare; (*retch*) avere i conati di vomito. **heave a sigh** tirare un sospiro. *n* sollevamento *m*.

heaven ['hevn] *n* cielo *m*, paradiso *m*. **for heaven's sake!** per l'amor del cielo! **good heavens!** santo cielo! **heavenly** *adj* divino, delizioso.

heavy ['hevi] *adj* pesante, forte. **heavyweight** *n* peso massimo *m*.

Hebrew ['hiːbruː] *n* (*language*) ebraico *m*; (*person*) ebreo, -a *m, f*. *adj* ebraico; ebreo.

heckle ['hekl] *v* interrompere con domande imbarazzanti.

hectare ['hektaɪ] *n* ettaro *m*.

hectic ['hektik] *adj* febbrile.

hedge [hedʒ] *n* siepe *f*; (*bet*) copertura *f*. *v* (*bet*) coprire dai rischi. **as a hedge against** per mettersi al riparo contro.

hedgehog ['hedʒhog] *n* riccio *m*.

heed [hiːd] *v* badare a, dar retta a. **heedless** *adj* noncurante.

heel [hiːl] *n* (*anat*) calcagno *m*; (*shoe*) tacco *m*. **Achilles' heel** tallone d'Achille *m*.

hefty ['hefti] *adj* robusto.

heifer ['hefə] *n* giovenca *f*.

height [hait] *n* altezza *f*; (*hill*) collina *f*; (*highest degree*) colmo *m*; (*highest point*) culmine *m*. **heighten** *v* intensificare.

heir [eə] *n* erede *m, f*.

held [held] *V* **hold'**.

helicopter ['helikɔptə] *n* elicottero *m*.

hell [hel] *n* inferno *m*. **hellish** *adj* infernale.

hello [hə'lou] *interj* (*on meeting*) ciao! (*phone*) pronto!

helm [helm] *n* timone *m*.

helmet ['helmit] *n* elmo *m*, elmetto *m*; (*motorcyclist, airman*) casco *m*.

help [help] *n* aiuto *m*, assistenza *f*; (*remedy*) rimedio *m*. *v* aiutare, assistere. **helpful** *adj* utile, vantaggioso. **helping** *n* porzione *f*. **helpless** *adj* impotente, indifeso.

hem [hem] *n* orlo *m*. *v* orlare. **hem in** rinchiudere, accerchiare.

hemisphere ['hemi‚sfiə] *n* emisfera *f*.

hemp [hemp] *n* canapa *f*.

hen [hen] *n* gallina *f*.

hence [hens] *adv* quindi.

henna ['henə] *n* tintura di henna *f*.

her [həː] *pron* (*direct object*) la; (*indirect object*) le; (*after prep*) lei. *adj* (il) (la) sua; (*pl*) (i) suoi, (le) sue.

herald ['herəld] *n* araldo *m*, messaggero *m*.

heraldry ['herəldri] *n* araldica *f*.

herbs [həːbz] *pl n* erbe aromatiche *f pl*.

herd [həːd] *n* gregge *m*, mandria *f*; (*people*) massa *f*. **herd together** raggruppare, radunare.

here [hiə] *adv* qui, qua; (*emphasizing*) ecco. **here I am!** eccomi qua!

hereabouts ['hiərə'bauts] *adv* qui vicino.

hereafter [.hiər'aːftə] *adv* d'ora innanzi, in futuro. *n* the hereafter l'al di là *m*.

hereby [.hiə'bai] *adv* così, con questo.

hereditary [hi'reditri] *adj* ereditario.

heredity [hi'redəti] *n* eredità *f*.

heresy ['herəsi] *n* eresia *f*. **heretic** *n* eretico, -a *m*. **heretical** *adj* eretico.

herewith [.hiə'wið] *adv* con questo; (*correspondence*) con la presente.

heritage ['heritidʒ] *n* patrimonio *m*.

hermit ['həːmit] *n* eremita *m*.

hernia ['həːniə] *n* ernia *f*.

hero ['hiərou] *n* eroe *m*; (*principal character*) protagonista *m*. **heroic** *adj* eroico. **heroine** *n* eroina *f*; protagonista *f*.

heroin ['herouin] *n* eroina *f*.

heron ['herən] *n* airone *m*.

herring ['heriŋ] *n* aringa *f*. **herring-bone** *adj* a lisca di pesce.

hers [həːz] *pron* il suo, la sua; (*pl*) i suoi, le sue.

herself [həː'self] *pron* lei stessa; (*after prep*) sè (stessa); (*reflexive*) si; (*emphatic*) proprio lei.

hesitate ['heziteit] *v* esitare. **hesitant** *adj* esitante. **hesitation** *n* esitazione *f*. **without hesitation** decisamente.

heterogeneous [hetərə'dʒiːniəs] *adj* eterogeneo.

heterosexual [hetərə'sekʃuəl] *adj* eterosessuale.

hexagon ['heksəgən] *n* esagono *m*. **hexagonal** *adj* esagonale.

heyday ['heidei] *n* (*prime*) fiore *m*; più bel periodo *m*; (*splendour*) fulgore *m*.

hiatus [hai'eitəs] *n* (*med*) interruzione *f*; iato *m*.

hibernate ['haibəneit] *v* svernare; (*of animals*) ibernare.

hiccup ['hikʌp] *n* singhiozzo *m*. *v* singhiozzare. **have hiccups** avere il singhiozzo.

hid [hid] *V* **hide¹**.

hidden ['hidn] *V* **hide¹**.

*hide¹ [haid] *v* nascondere, nascondersi. **hide-out** *n* nascondiglio *m*.

hide² [haid] *n* (*raw*) pelle *f*; (*dressed*) cuoio *m*. **hidebound** *adj* gretto, di mentalità ristretta.

hideous ['hidiəs] *adj* orrendo, ripugnante.

hiding¹ ['haidiŋ] *n* **be in hiding** essere or tenersi nascosto. **go into hiding** nascondersi, darsi alla macchia.

hiding² ['haidiŋ] *n* (*beating*) batosta *f*.

hierarchy ['haiəraːki] *n* gerarchia *f*.

high [hai] *adj* alto, elevato; (*of meat*) andato a male. **it's high time** è ora. **leave high and dry** piantare in asso. *adv* in alto. *n* culmine *f*; (*weather*) anticiclone *m*. **highness** *n* altezza *f*.

highbrow ['haibrau] *n*(*m+f*), *adj* intellettuale.

high chair *n* seggiolina *f*.

high-fidelity *adj* ad alta fedeltà.

high frequency *adj* ad alta frequenza.

high jump *n* salto in alto *m*.

highlight ['hailait] *v* mettere in rilievo. *n* clou *m invar*, culmine *m*.

high-pitched [hai'pitʃd] *adj* acuto.

high point *n* culmine *m*.

high-powered *adj* potente, dinamico.

high pressure *n* alta pressione *f*. **high-pressure** *adj* ad alta pressione; (*coll*) aggressivo.

high-rise block *adj* a molti piani.

high-spirited [.hai'spiritid] *adj* vivace. **high spirits** *pl n* buonumore *m sing*.

high street *n* corso *m*.

highway ['haiwei] *n* strada maestra *f*. **highway code** codice della strada *m*.

hijack ['haidʒak] *v* (*goods*) rubare in transito; (*aero*) dirottare. **hijacker** *n* dirottatore *m*, pirata dell'aria *m*. **hijacking** *n* dirottamento *m*.

hike [haik] *n* gita a piedi *f*. *v* fare una gita *or* escursione a piedi.

hilarious [hi'leəriəs] *adj* divertente, allegro.

hill [hil] *n* colle *m*, collina *f*; (*slope*) salita *f*.

him [him] *pron* (*direct object*) lo; (*indirect object*) gli; (*after prep*) lui.

himself [him'self] *pron* lui stesso; (*after prep*) sè (stesso); (*reflexive*) si; (*emphatic*) proprio lui.

hinder ['hində] *v* (*make difficult*) intralciare; (*make impossible*) impedire.

Hindu [hin'du:] *n*(*m+f*), *adj* indù *invar.* **Hinduism** *n* induismo *m*.

hinge [hindʒ] *n* cardine *m*, perno *m*. *v* (*depend*) dipendere (da).

hint [hint] *n* cenno *m*, allusione *f*; (*clue*) suggerimento *m*; (*slight amount*) traccia *f*. *v* far capire, accennare, alludere.

hip [hip] *n* fianco *m*, anca *f*.

hippopotamus [hipə'potəməs] *n* ippopotamo *m*.

hire [haiə] *v* prendere a nolo, noleggiare. **hire out** dare a nolo, noleggiare. *n* nolo *m*, noleggio *m*. **hire purchase** vendita a rate *f*.

his [hiz] *adj* (il) suo, (la) sua; (*pl*) (i) suoi, (le) sue. *pron* il suo, la sua; (*pl*) i suoi, le sue.

hiss [his] *v* sibilare. *n* sibilo *m*. **hissing** *adj* sibilante.

history ['histəri] *n* storia *f*; (*past*) passato *m*. **historian** *n* storico *m*. **historic** *adj* storico; memorabile.

*hit [hit] *n* colpo *m*, botta *f*; successo *m*. *v* colpire, battere. **hit on** scoprire. **hit-or-miss** *adv* alla buona.

hitch [hitʃ] *v* attaccare. **hitch-hike** *v* fare l'autostop. **hitch up** tirar su. *n* (*obstacle*) intoppo *m*; (*knot*) nodo *m*.

hitherto [,hiðə'tu:] *adv* finora.

hive [haiv] *n* alveare *m*.

hoard [ho:d] *n* scorta *f*, mucchio *m*. *v* ammucchiare.

hoarding ['ho:diŋ] *n* (*billboard*) tabellone *m*.

hoarse [ho:s] *adj* rauco. **hoarseness** *n* raucedine *f*.

hoax [houks] *n* beffa *f*.

hobble ['hobl] *v* zoppicare.

hobby ['hobi] *n* passatempo *m*, hobby *m* *invar.*

hock¹ [hok] *n* (*joint*) garretto *m*.

hock² [hok] *n* (*wine*) vino bianco del Reno *m*.

hockey ['hoki] *n* hockey *m* *invar.*

hoe [hou] *n* zappa *f*. *v* zappare.

hog [hog] *n* maiale *m*, porco *m*. *v* (*coll*) monopolizzare.

hoist [hoist] *n* montacarichi *m* *invar.* *v* sollevare.

*hold¹ [hould] *n* presa *f*, stretta *f*; (*dominating influence*) ascendente *m*. **get hold of** (*grasp*) afferrare; (*obtain*) ottenere. *v* tenere; contenere; esser valido. **hold back** trattenere. **hold out** resistere. **hold up** (*delay*) ostacolare; (*stop by force*) fermare per derubare; (*exhibit*) esibire. **hold-up** *n* intoppo *m*; (*robbery*) rapina a mano armata *f*. **holder** *n* supporto *m*; detentore *m*. **holding** *n* (*land*) tenuta *f*; (*shares*) pacchetto (di azioni) *m*.

hold² [hould] *n* (*naut*) stiva *f*.

hole [houl] *n* buco *m*; (*in the ground*) buca *f*; (*burrow*) tana *f*; (*predicament*) guaio *m*.

holiday ['holədi] *n* (*day*) giorno festivo *m*, festa *f*; (*period*) vacanza *f*. **go on holiday** andare in vacanza *or* villeggiatura. **holiday-maker** *n* villeggiante *m*, *f*.

Holland ['holənd] *n* Olanda *f*.

hollow ['holou] *adj* cavo; concavo; (*not solid*) vuoto; (*of sound*) cupo; falso. *n* buca *f*, cavità *f*; (*anat*) cavo *m*.

holly ['holi] *n* agrifoglio *m*.

holster ['houlstə] *n* fondina *f*.

holy ['houli] *adj* santo, sacro.

homage ['homidʒ] *n* omaggio *m*. **pay homage to** rendere omaggio a.

home [houm] *n* (*house*) casa *f*, domicilio *m*; (*land*) patria *f*; (*institution*) ricovero *m*, rifugio *m*; (*habitat*) ambiente naturale *m*. **at home** a casa. **feel at home** sentirsi a proprio agio. **leave home** lasciare la casa paterna. *adj* domestico, casalingo. *adv* a casa; in patria; (*all the way*) a fondo. **strike home** colpire nel vivo.

homecoming ['houm,kʌmiŋ] *n* ritorno in casa *or* patria *m*.

home-grown [houm'groun] *adj* nostrano.

homeless ['houmləs] *adj* senza tetto.

homely ['houmli] *adj* semplice, senza pretese; (*unattractive*) brutto.

home-made [,houm'meid] *adj* fatto in casa.

homesick ['houmsik] *adj* nostalgico.

homework ['houmwə:k] *n* compiti di casa *m pl.*

homicide ['homisaid] *n* (*crime*) omicidio *m*; (*murderer*) omicida *m*, *f*. **homicidal** *adj* micidiale.

homogeneous [homə'dʒi:niəs] *adj* omogeneo.

homosexual [homə'seksuəl] *n*(*m+f*), *adj* omosessuale.

honest ['ɔnist] *adj* onesto. **honestly!** *interj* davvero! **honesty** *n* onestà *f*.

honey ['hʌni] *n* miele *m*. **honeycomb** *n* favo *m*. **honeymoon** *n* luna di miele *f*.

honeysuckle ['hʌnisʌkl] *n* caprifoglio *m*.

honour ['ɔnə] *n* onore *m*; (*respect*) stima *f*. *v* onorare; (*comm*) far onore a. **honours** *pl n* (*titles*) onorificenza *f sing*. **honorary** *adj* onorario. **honourable** *adj* onorevole, stimato, probo.

hood [hud] *n* cappuccio *m*; (*mot*) cappotta *f*.

hoof [huːf] *n* zoccolo *m*.

hook [huk] *n* gancio *m*; (*fishing*) amo *m*. *v* agganciare.

hooligan ['huːligən] *n* teppista *m*.

hoop [huːp] *n* cerchio *m*.

hoot [huːt] *v* (*car*) suonare il clacson; (*shriek*) stridere; (*hiss*) fischiare. **hooter** *n* sirena *f*; (*car*) clacson *m invar*.

hop¹ [hop] *v* saltellare *n* salterello *m*.

hop² [hop] *n* (*bot*) luppolo *m*.

hope [houp] *n* speranza *f*. *v* sperare. **hopeful** *adj* pieno di speranza, fiducioso; (*promising*) promettente. **hopeless** *adj* senza speranza, disperato; (*not resolvable*) irrimediabile.

horde [hoːd] *n* banda *f*.

horizon [hə'raizn] *n* orizzonte *m*. **horizontal** *adj* orizzontale.

hormone ['hoːmoun] *n* ormone *m*.

horn [hoːn] *n* corno (*pl* -a) *m*; (*mot*) clacson *m invar*.

hornet ['hoːnit] *n* calabrone *m*.

horoscope ['horəskoup] *n* oroscopo *m*.

horrible ['horibl] *adj also* **horrid** orribile, orrendo.

horrify ['horifai] *v* inorridire, raccapricciare. **horrifying** *adj* raccapricciante.

horror ['horə] *n* orrore *m*, spavento *m*.

hors d'oeuvre [oːˈdəːvr] *n* antipasto *m*.

horse [hoːs] *n* cavallo *m*. **on horseback** a cavallo.

horseback ['hoːsbak] *n*

horse-chestnut *n* ippocastano *m*.

horse-fly *n* tafano *m*.

horseman ['hoːsmən] *n* cavaliere *m*.

horsepower ['hoːs,pauə] *n* cavallo vapore *m*.

horse-race *n* corsa ippica *f*.

horseradish ['hoːs,radiʃ] *n* cren *m invar*; (*plant*) barbaforte *m*.

horseshoe ['hoːʃ,ʃuː] *n* ferro di cavallo *m*.

horsewoman ['hoːs,wumən] *n* cavallerizza *f*.

horticulture ['hoːtikʌltʃə] *n* orticultura *f*.

hose [houz] *n* (*stocking*) calza *f*, calzino *m*; (*pipe*) tubo flessibile *m*, manichetta *f*. *v* **hose** (**down**) dare una lavata a, annaffiare.

hosiery ['houʒiəri] *n* calzetteria *f*.

hospitable [ho'spitəbl] *adj* ospitale.

hospital ['hospitl] *n* ospedale *m*. **hospitalize** far ricoverare in ospedale.

hospitality [,hospi'taliti] *n* ospitalità *f*.

host¹ [houst] *n* oste *m*, ospite *m*. **hostess** *n* ospite *f*, ostessa *f*.

host² [houst] *n* moltitudine *f*, gran numero *m*.

host³ [houst] *n* (*rel*) ostia *f*.

hostage ['hostidʒ] *n* ostaggio *m*.

hostel ['hostəl] *n* ostello *m*, alloggio *m*.

hostile ['hostail] *adj* ostile. **hostility** *n* antagonismo *m*. **hostilities** *pl n* ostilità *f pl*.

hot [hot] *adj* caldo; ardente, impetuoso; (*pungent, peppery*) forte, piccante. **be hot** aver caldo. **hot-blooded** *adj* dal sangue caldo. **hot-headed** *adj* impetuoso. **hot-house** *n* serra *f*. **hotplate** *n* scaldavivande *m invar*; (*hob*) fornello *m*. **hot-tempered** *adj* irascibile.

hotel [hou'tel] *n* albergo *m*. **hotel-keeper** *n* albergatore, -trice *m*, *f*.

hound [haund] *n* bracco *m*.

hour ['auə] *n* ora *f*. **hours** *pl n* (*time spent*) orario *m sing*. **kilometres/miles per hour** chilometri/miglia all'ora.

hourly ['auəli] *adj* orario. *adv* (*every hour*) ogni ora; (*hour by hour*) d'ora in ora, continuamente.

house [haus; *v* hauz] *n* casa *f*; (*theatre attendance*) sala *f*; (*audience*) pubblico *m*; (*dynasty*) dinastia *f*, famiglia *f*; (*comm*) ditta *f*. *v* (*shelter*) alloggiare; (*put in safe place*) mettere al sicuro.

houseboat ['hausbout] *n* casa galleggiante *f*. **houseboat** *f invar*.

housebound ['hausbaund] *adj* costretto a stare a casa.

housebreaking ['haus,breikiŋ] *n* scasso *m*.

household ['haushould] *n* famiglia *f*, casa *f*. *adj* casalingo, domestico.

housekeeper ['haus,kiːpə] *n* massaia *f*, governante *f*, famiglia *f*. **housekeeping** *n* economia domestica *f*.

housemaid ['hausmeid] *n* domestica *f*, cameriera *f*.

house-to-house adj di porta in porta.
housewife ['hauswaif] n massaia f, casalinga f.
housework ['hauswə:k] n lavori di casa m pl.
housing ['hauziŋ] n alloggio m. **housing estate** quartiere residenziale m.
hovel ['hɔvəl] n tugurio m.
hover ['hɔvə] v librarsi. **hovercraft** n hovercraft m invar.
how [hau] adv come, in che modo; (to what extent) quanto. **how are you?** come sta? **how do you do** (after introduction) piacere; buon giorno. **how much** quanto. **how many** quanti. **how often** quante volte. conj che.
however [hau'evə] adv comunque, tuttavia. conj nonostante, tuttavia.
howl [haul] v ululare, lamentarsi. n ululato m, lamento m.
hub [hʌb] n parte centrale f; (of wheel) mozzo m. **hub cap** coppa f.
hubbub ['hʌbʌb] n baccano m.
huddle ['hʌdl] v **huddle together** affollarsi, accalcarsi.
hue [hju:] n colore m, tinta f.
huff [hʌf] n stizza f, risentimento m. **in a huff** offeso.
hug [hʌg] v abbracciare. n abbraccio m.
huge [hju:dʒ] adj enorme, immenso.
hulk [hʌlk] n carcassa f. **hulking** adj goffo.
hull [hʌl] n (shell) guscio m; (husk) buccia f; (of nuts) mallo m; (pod) baccello m; (naut) scafo m.
hum [hʌm] v ronzare; cantare a bocca chiusa, canterellare. n ronzio m.
human ['hju:mən] adj umano. **human being** essere umano m.
humane [hju'mein] adj umanitario, umano, compassionevole.
humanism ['hju:mənizəm] n umanesimo m. **humanist** n umanista m, f.
humanitarian [hju:mæni'tɛəriən] adj filantropico. n filantropo, -a m, f.
humanity [hju'manəti] n umanità f; compassione f.
humble ['hʌmbl] adj umile, modesto. v umiliare.
humdrum ['hʌmdrʌm] adj monotono, noioso.
humid ['hju:mid] adj umido. **humidity** n umidità f.
humiliate [hju'milieit] v umiliare.
humility [hju'miləti] n umiltà f.

humour ['hju:mə] n (mood) umore m; stato d'animo m, disposizione f; (comic quality) comicità f. v compiacere, accontentare. **humorist** n umorista m, f. **humorous** adj divertente, spiritoso.
hump [hʌmp] n gobba f; (hill) cresta f.
hunch [hʌntʃ] n gobba f. **have a hunch** (coll) avere un sospetto. **hunchback** n gobbo m. **hunchbacked** adj gobbo.
hundred ['hʌndrəd] nm, adj cento. **hundredth** nm, adj centesimo.
hung [hʌŋ] V **hang**.
Hungary ['hʌŋgəri] n Ungheria f. **Hungarian** n(m+f), adj ungherese.
hunger ['hʌŋgə] n fame f, appetito m. **hungry** adj affamato. **be hungry** aver fame.
hunt [hʌnt] n caccia f; (pursuit) inseguimento m; (search) ricerca affannosa f. v andare a caccia di; inseguire; cercare affannosamente. **hunter** n cacciatore m.
hurdle ['hə:dl] n ostacolo m. v fare la corsa a ostacoli.
hurl [hə:l] v scagliare, scaraventare.
hurrah [hu'ra:] interj evviva!
hurricane ['hʌrikən] n uragano m. **hurricane lamp** lanterna controvento f.
hurry ['hʌri] n fretta f. **be in a hurry** aver fretta. v affrettare. **hurry up** sbrigarsi.
***hurt** [hə:t] v far male a, nuocere a; (wound) ferire; (feel painful) dolere. n dolore m, male m; ferita f; offesa f. **feel hurt** rimanere offeso.
husband ['hʌzbənd] n marito m.
hush [hʌʃ] n silenzio m. interj zitto! v far tacere. **hush-hush** adj (coll) segretissimo. **hush up** nascondere, dissimulare; (suppress) soffocare.
husk [hʌsk] n guscio m, baccello m.
husky ['hʌski] adj (of voice) rauco, fioco; (burly) grande e grosso.
hustle ['hʌsl] n spintone m. v spingere, sbrigarsi.
hut [hʌt] n capanna f, baracca f.
hutch [hʌtʃ] n conigliera f.
hyacinth ['haiəsinθ] n giacinto m.
hybrid ['haibrid] nm, adj ibrido.
hydrant ['haidrənt] n idrante m.
hydraulic [hai'drɔ:lik] adj idraulico.
hydrocarbon [,haidrou'ka:bən] n idrocarburo m.
hydro-electric [,haidroui'lektrik] adj idroelettrico.
hydrofoil ['haidroufɔil] n aliscafo m.

hydrogen ['haidrədʒən] n idrogeno m.
hyena [hai'iːnə] n iena f.
hygiene ['haidʒiːn] n igiene f. hygienic adj
igienico.
hymn [him] n inno m, canto sacro m.
hyphen ['haifən] n lineetta f.
hypnosis [hip'nousis] n ipnosi f. hypnotic
adj ipnotico. hypnotism n ipnotismo m,
ipnosi f. hypnotist n ipnotizzatore, -trice
m, f.
hypochondria [haipə'kondriə] n ipocondria f. hypochondriac n, adj ipocondriaco, -a.
hypocrisy [hi'pokrəsi] n ipocrisia f. hypocrite n ipocrita m, f. hypocritical adj
ipocrita.
hypodermic [haipə'dəːmik] adj
ipodermico.
hypotenuse [hai'potənjuːz] n ipotenusa f.
hypothesis [hai'poθəsis] n, pl -ses ipotesi
f. hypothetical adj ipotetico.
hysterectomy [histə'rektəmi] n ister-
ectomia f.
hysteria [his'tiəriə] n isterismo m. hysterical adj isterico. hysterics pl n crisi isteri-
ca f sing.

I

I [ai] pron io.
ice [ais] n ghiaccio m. iceberg n iceberg m
invar. ice-cold adj freddo come il
ghiaccio, glaciale, gelido. ice cream
gelato m. ice lolly ghiacciolo m. ice rink
pista di pattinaggio f. v (cookery) glassare; (cover with ice) ghiacciare. icing n
glassa f. icy adj glaciale, gelido.
Iceland ['aislənd] n Islanda f. Icelander n
islandese m, f. Icelandic adj islandese.
icicle ['aisikl] n ghiacciolo m.
icon ['aikon] n icona f. iconoclast n ico-
noclasta m, f.
idea [ai'diə] n idea f, concetto m, impressione f.
ideal [ai'diəl] nm, adj ideale. idealist n
idealista m, f. idealistic adj idealistico.
idealize v idealizzare.
identical [ai'dentikəl] adj identico.
identify [ai'dentifai] n identificare. identification n identificazione f.
identity [ai'dentiti] n identità f. identity
card carta d'identità f. identity parade

confronto all'americana m. mistaken
identity errore di persona m.
ideology [aidi'olədʒi] n ideologia f. ideological adj ideologico.
idiom ['idiəm] n (expression) frase idiomatica f; (language) idioma m.
idiosyncrasy [idiə'siŋkrəsi] n idiosincra-
sia f.
idiot ['idiət] n idiota m, f; cretino, -a m, f.
idiotic adj idiota, cretino, imbecille.
idle ['aidl] adj (lazy) pigro; (doing nothing) disoccupato; (machine) fermo;
(worthless) vano. v stare senza far nulla;
(machine) girare a folle. idler n fannullone, -a m, f.
idol ['aidl] n idolo m. idolatry n idolatria
f. idolize v idoleggiare.
idyllic [i'dilik] adj idillico.
if [if] conj se. as if come se. if not se no. if
you please per piacere.
ignite [ig'nait] v accendere, dar fuoco a;
(catch fire) prender fuoco.
ignition [ig'niʃən] n accensione f. ignition
key interruttore dell'accensione m.
ignorant ['ignərənt] adj ignorante. be
ignorant of ignorare. ignorance n
ignoranza f.
ignore [ig'noː] v (disregard) non badare a,
trascurare; (refrain from see-
ing/recognizing/hearing) fingere di non
vedere/riconoscere/sentire.
ill [il] adj (sick) malato; (bad) cattivo. nm,
adv male. ill-advised adj malavveduto. ill-
bred or ill-mannered adj maleducato. ill-
treat v maltrattare. illness n malattia f.
illegal [i'liːgəl] adj illegale.
illegible [i'ledʒəbl] adj illeggibile.
illegitimate [ili'dʒitimit] adj illegittimo.
illicit [i'lisit] adj illecito.
illiterate [i'litərit] n(m+f), adj analfabeta.
illogical [i'lodʒikəl] adj illogico.
illuminate [i'luːmineit] v illuminare, rischiarare. illuminating adj illuminante.
illumination n illuminazione f.
illusion [i'luːʒən] n illusione f.
illustrate [i'ləstreit] v illustrare. illustration n illustrazione f.
illustrious [i'lʌstriəs] adj illustre, celebre.
image ['imidʒ] n immagine f, ritratto m.
imagery n immagini f pl.
imagine [i'madʒin] v farsi un'idea di,
immaginarsi; (suppose) supporre;
(believe) credere. imaginary adj
immaginario. imagination n immaginazione f, fantasia f.

imbalance [im'baləns] n squilibrio m.
imbecile ['imbə,siil] n(m+f), adj imbecille.
imitate ['imi,teit] v imitare, contraffare. **imitation** n imitazione f, copia f, contraffattura f.
immaculate [i'makjulit] adj immacolato.
immaterial [,imə'tiəriəl] adj (unimportant) di nessuna importanza.
immature [,imə'tjuə] adj immaturo. **immaturity** n immaturità f.
immediate [i'miidiət] adj immediato. **immediately** adv immediatamente, subito.
immense [i'mens] adj immenso.
immerse [i'məɪs] v immergere. **immersion** n immersione f. **immersion heater** riscaldatore a immersione m.
immigrate ['imi,greit] v immigrare. **immigrant** n(m+f), adj immigrante. **immigration** n immigrazione f.
imminent ['iminənt] adj imminente.
immobile [i'moubail] adj immobile, fermo. **immobilize** v immobilizzare.
immoral [i'morəl] adj immorale. **immorality** n immoralità f.
immortal [i'mottl] adj immortale. **immortality** n immortalità f. **immortalize** v immortalare.
immovable [i'muɪvəbl] adj inamovibile, fisso.
immune [i'mjuɪn] adj immune. **immunity** n immunità f. **immunization** n immunizzazione f. **immunize** v immunizzare.
imp [imp] n folletto m.
impact ['impakt] n urto m, scontro m; (effect) impressione f.
impair [im'peə] v danneggiare, menomare.
impale [im'peil] v impalare.
impart [im'paɪt] v impartire.
impartial [im'paɪʃəl] adj imparziale. **impartiality** n imparzialità f.
impasse [am'pais] n impasse m, intoppo m.
impatient [im'peiʃənt] adj impaziente. **get impatient** impazientirsi. **impatience** n impazienza f.
impeach [im'piitʃ] v accusare; (call in question) mettere in dubbio, imputare.
impeccable [im'pekəbl] adj impeccabile.
impede [im'piid] v ostacolare, impedire.
impediment [im'pedimənt] n impedimento m, ostacolo m. **speech impediment** difetto or impedimento di lingua m.
impel [im'pel] v spingere, impellere.

impending [im'pendiŋ] adj imminente.
imperative [im'perətiv] nm, adj imperativo.
imperfect [im'pɔɪfikt] nm, adj imperfetto.
imperial [im'piəriəl] adj imperiale. **imperialism** n imperialismo m.
imperil [im'peril] v mettere in pericolo, compromettere.
impersonal [im'pəɪsənl] adj impersonale, comune.
impersonate [im'pəɪsə,neit] v impersonare; (theatre) interpretare.
impertinent [im'pəɪtinənt] adj impertinente. **impertinence** n impertinenza f.
impervious [im'pəɪviəs] adj impervio; impermeabile; (fig) sordo.
impetuous [im'petjuəs] adj impetuoso.
impetus ['impitəs] n impeto m, slancio m.
impinge [im'pindʒ] v **impinge on** colpire.
implement ['implimənt; v 'impliment] n attrezzo m, utensile m. v adempiere. **implementation** n adempimento m.
implicate ['impli,keit] v implicare, coinvolgere. **implication** n implicazione f.
implicit [im'plisit] adj implicito.
implore [im'ploɪ] v supplicare.
imply [im'plai] v (mean) significare; (suggest) far pensare a.
impolite [impə'lait] adj scortese, sgarbato.
import [im'poɪt] v importare. n (comm) importazione f; importanza f. **importer** n importatore m.
importance [im'poɪtəns] n importanza f. **important** adj importante.
impose [im'pouz] v imporre. **impose on** abusare di. **imposing** adj imponente. **imposition** n imposizione f.
impossible [im'posəbl] adj impossibile. **impossibility** n impossibilità f.
impostor [im'postə] n impostore m.
impotent ['impətənt] adj impotente. **impotence** n impotenza f.
impound [im'paund] v confiscare.
impoverish [im'povəriʃ] v impoverire.
impractical [im'praktikəl] adj (person) privo di senso pratico; (thing) inservibile, non pratico.
impregnate [im'pregneit] v impregnare. **impregnation** n impregnazione f.
impress [im'pres] v colpire, fare impressione su; (urge) raccomandare; (print) imprimere, stampare. **impression** n impressione f; (print) stampa f, ristampa f. **impressive** adj impressionante.

imprint ['imprint] *n* impronta *f*.

imprison [im'prizn] *v* carcerare. **imprisonment** *n* carcerazione *f*.

improbable [im'probabl] *adj* improbabile. **improbability** *n* improbabilità *f*.

impromptu [im'promptju] *adj* improvvisato. *adv* all'improvviso.

improper [im'propa] *adj* (*inappropriate*) improprio; (*unseemly*) indecente, indecoroso.

improve [im'pruv] *v* migliorare; (*increase value*) valorizzare; (*get better*) star meglio. **improve on** perfezionare. **improvement** *n* miglioramento *m*; (*making more valuable*) miglioria *f*.

improvise ['impravaiz] *v* improvvisare. **improvisation** *n* improvvisazione *f*.

impudent ['impjudant] *adj* sfacciato. **impudence** *n* sfacciataggine *f*.

impulse ['impʌls] *n* impulso *m*, stimolo *m*. **impulsive** *adj* impulsivo.

impure [im'pjuə] *adj* impuro. **impurity** *n* impurità *f*.

in [in] *prep* in; (*within*) tra, entro. *adv* dentro, a casa, in sede.

inability [,inə'biləti] *n* incapacità *f*.

inaccessible [,inak'sesəbl] *adj* inaccessibile.

inaccurate [in'akjurət] *adj* inesatto. **inaccuracy** *n* inesattezza *f*.

inactive [in'aktiv] *adj* inattivo, passivo.

inadequate [in'adikwit] *adj* inadeguato, insufficiente, inetto. **inadequacy** *n* inadeguatezza *f*.

inadmissible [inəd'misəbl] *adj* inammissibile.

inadvertent [,inəd'vəitənt] *adj* involontario.

inane [in'ein] *adj* insensato, futile.

inanimate [in'animit] *adj* (*not animate*) inanimato; (*lifeless*) esanime.

inarticulate [,inar'tikjulit] *adj* (*person*) che non sa esprimersi; inarticolato.

inasmuch [,inəz'mʌtʃ] *conj* dacché, poiché.

inaudible [in'ɔːdəbl] *adj* inaudibile.

inaugurate [i'nɔːgjureit] *v* inaugurare. **inaugural** *adj* inaugurale. **inauguration** *n* inaugurazione *f*.

inauspicious [inɔr'spiʃəs] *adj* infausto.

inbred [,in'bred] *adj* (*inborn*) innato; (*resulting from inbreeding*) endogamo. **inbreeding** *n* endogamia *f*.

incalculable [in'kalkjuləbl] *adj* incalcolabile, imprevedibile.

incapable [in'keipəbl] *adj* incapace, inetto.

incendiary [in'sendiəri] *adj* incendiario.

incense[1] ['insens] *n* incenso *m*.

incense[2] [in'sens] *v* irritare, provocare.

incentive [in'sentiv] *n* incentivo *m*.

incessant [in'sesənt] *adj* continuo.

incest ['insest] *n* incesto *m*. **incestuous** *adj* incestuoso.

inch [intʃ] *n* pollice *m*. **inch by inch** gradatamente. *v* **inch forward** avanzare poco alla volta.

incident ['insidənt] *n* caso *m*, episodio *m*; (*event with serious consequences*) incidente *f*. **incidental** *adj* incidentale. **incidentally** *adv* tra parentesi, a proposito.

incinerator [in'sinəreitə] *n* inceneritore *m*. **incinerate** *v* incenerire.

incisive [in'saisiv] *adj* acuto.

incite [in'sait] *v* incitare, spronare. **incitement** *n* incitamento *m*.

incline [in'klain] *v* inclinare, chinare. **be inclined to** essere propenso *or* disposto a. *n* piano inclinato *m*, pendio *m*. **inclination** *n* inclinazione *f*; propensione *f*.

include [in'kluːd] *v* includere. **inclusion** *n* inclusione *f*. **inclusive** *adj* compreso.

incoherent [,inkə'hiərənt] *adj* incoerente.

income [inkʌm] *n* entrata *f*, reddito *m*. **income tax** imposta sull'entrata *f*. **incoming** *adj* in arrivo.

incompatible [inkəm'patəbl] *adj* incompatibile. **incompatibility** *n* incompatibilità *f*.

incompetent [in'kompitənt] *adj* incompetente. **incompetence** *n* incompetenza *f*.

incomplete [inkəm'pliːt] *adj* incompleto.

incomprehensible [in,kompri'hensəbl] *adj* incomprensibile.

inconceivable [inkən'siːvəbl] *adj* inconcepibile.

inconclusive [inkən'kluːsiv] *adj* inconcludente.

incongruous [in'koŋgruəs] *adj* incongruo.

inconsiderate [,inkən'sidərit] *adj* sconsiderato; (*person*) che manca di riguardo.

inconsistent [,inkən'sistənt] *adj* inconsistente. **inconsistency** *n* inconsistenza *f*.

incontinence [in'kontinəns] *n* incontinenza *f*. **incontinent** *adj* incontinente.

inconvenience [inkən'viːnjəns] *n* sconvenienza *f*. *v* sconvenire, disturbare. **inconvenient** *adj* sconveniente, scomodo.

incorporate [in'kɔːpəˌreit] v incorporare.

incorrect [ɪnkə'rekt] adj scorretto.

increase [in'kriːs] v aumentare, ingrandirsi, crescere. n aumento m. **increasingly** adv sempre più.

incredible [in'kredəbl] adj incredibile.

incredulous [in'kredjuləs] adj incredulo.

increment ['iŋkrəmənt] n incremento m, aumento m.

incriminate [in'krimineit] v incolpare.

incubate ['iŋkjuˌbeit] v incubare. **incubation** n incubazione f. **incubator** n incubatrice f.

incumbent [in'kʌmbənt] adj be incumbent on spettare a.

incur [in'kəɪ] v incorrere in.

incurable [in'kjuərəbl] adj incurabile.

indebted [in'detid] adj (owing money) indebitato; (under obligation) riconoscente.

indecent [in'diːsnt] adj indecente. **indecency** n indecenza f; (law) oltraggio al pudore m.

indeed [in'diːd] adv infatti, effettivamente, proprio. interj davvero!

indefatigable [indi'fatigəbl] adj indefesso.

indefinite [in'definit] adj indefinito, vago, illimitato.

indelible [in'deləbl] adj indelebile; (memory) indimenticabile.

indemnity [in'demnəti] n indennità f; (sum paid) indennizzo m. **indemnify** v indennizzare.

indent [in'dent] v (notch) dentellare; (make recess) incavare. **indentation** n incavo m, dentellatura f, rientranza f; (printing) capoverso m.

independent [ˌindi'pendənt] adj indipendente. **independence** n indipendenza f.

index ['indeks] n indice m. **index card** scheda f. **index finger** indice m.

India ['indjə] n India f. **India rubber** gomma f. **Indian** n, adj indiano, -a. **Indian ink** inchiostro di china m.

indicate ['indikeit] v indicare.

indict [in'dait] v accusare. **indictment** n accusa f; (law) atto d'accusa m.

indifferent [in'difrənt] adj indifferente. **indifference** n indifferenza f.

indigenous [in'didʒinəs] adj indigeno.

indigestion [ˌindi'dʒestʃən] n indigestione f.

indignant [in'dignənt] adj sdegnato. **feel indignant** indignarsi, sdegnarsi (contro).

indignity [in'dignəti] n indegnità f.

indirect [ˌindi'rekt] adj indiretto.

indiscreet [ˌindi'skriːt] adj indiscreto. **indiscretion** n indiscrezione f.

indiscriminate [ˌindi'skriminit] adj indiscriminato.

indispensable [ˌindi'spensəbl] adj indispensabile.

indisposed [ˌindi'spouzd] adj indisposto.

individual [ˌindi'vidjuəl] n individuo m. adj individuale, particolare.

indoctrinate [in'doktriˌneit] v indottrinare. **indoctrination** n indottrinamento m.

indolent ['indələnt] adj indolente. **indolence** n indolenza f.

indoor ['indɔː] adj di or da casa. **indoors** adv in casa, all'interno, dentro.

induce [in'djuːs] v indurre.

indulge [in'dʌldʒ] v (gratify) appagare, soddisfare; essere indulgente verso. **indulge in** abbandonarsi a, dedicarsi a. **indulgence** n indulgenza f. **indulgent** adj indulgente.

industry ['indəstri] n industria f; diligenza f, zelo m. **industrial** adj industriale. **industrialize** v industrializzare. **industrious** adj diligente, operoso.

inebriated [i'niːbrieitid] adj ubriaco.

inedible [in'edibl] adj immangiabile.

inefficient [ˌini'fiʃnt] adj inefficiente. **inefficiency** n inefficienza f.

inept [i'nept] adj inetto, incapace.

inequality [ˌini'kwoləti] n ineguaglianza f.

inert [i'nəːt] adj inerte. **inertia** n inerzia f.

inevitable [in'evitəbl] adj inevitabile.

inexcusable [ˌinik'skjuːzəbl] adj imperdonabile, ingiustificabile.

inexhaustible [ˌinig'zɔːstəbl] adj inesauribile.

inexpensive [ˌinik'spensiv] adj a buon mercato, poco caro.

inexperienced [ˌinik'spiəriənst] adj inesperto.

inexplicable [inik'splikəbl] adj inspiegabile.

infallible [in'faləbl] adj infallibile. **infallibility** n infallibilità f.

infamous ['infəməs] adj infame. **infamy** n infamia f.

infancy ['infənsi] n infanzia f.

infant ['infənt] n infante m, bambino, -a m, f. **infantile** adj infantile, puerile. **infant prodigy** bambino prodigio m.

infantry ['infəntri] n fanteria f.

infatuated [in'fætjueitid] adj infatuato. **be infatuated** prendere una cotta.

infect [in'fekt] v infettare. **infection** n infezione f. **infectious** adj infettivo.

infer [in'fəː] v dedurre, desumere. **inferable** adj deducibile. **inference** n inferenza f, deduzione f.

inferior [in'fiəriə] n(m+f), adj inferiore. **inferiority** n inferiorità f.

infernal [in'fəːnl] adj infernale.

infest [in'fest] v infestare.

infidelity [infi'deliti] n infedeltà f.

infiltrate [in'filtreit] v infiltrare. **infiltration** n infiltrazione f.

infinite ['infinit] nm, adj infinito. **infinity** n infinità f, infinito m.

infinitive [in'finitiv] nm, adj infinito.

infirm [in'fəːm] adj infermo. **infirmity** n infermità f.

inflame [in'fleim] v infiammare. **inflammable** adj infiammabile. **inflammation** n infiammazione f.

inflate [in'fleit] v gonfiare. **inflation** n inflazione f.

inflection [in'flekʃən] n inflessione f.

inflexible [in'fleksəbl] adj inflessibile.

inflict [in'flikt] v infliggere.

influence ['influəns] n influenza f, ascendente m. v influire su, influenzare. **influential** adj autorevole, importante.

influenza [influ'enzə] n influenza f.

influx ['inflʌks] n afflusso m, affluenza f.

inform [in'fɔːm] v informare, far sapere a. **inform against** or **on** (denounce) denunziare. **informant** n informatore, -trice m, f. **informer** n spia f, delatore, -trice m, f.

informal [in'fɔːml] adj alla buona, senza cerimonia, non ufficiale. **informality** n mancanza di formalità f.

information [infə'meiʃən] n informazioni f pl, notizie f pl. **for your information** a titolo di informazione.

infra-red [infrə'red] adj infrarosso.

infrequent [in'friːkwənt] adj raro.

infringe [in'frindʒ] v violare, trasgredire. **infringement** n violazione f.

infuriate [in'fjuərieit] v fare arrabbiare. **be infuriated** essere furibondo or arrabbiatissimo.

ingenious [in'dʒiːnjəs] adj ingegnoso. **ingenuity** n ingegnosità f.

ingot ['ingət] n lingotto m.

ingredient [in'griːdjənt] n ingrediente m.

inhabit [in'hæbit] v abitare, vivere, dimorare. **inhabitant** n abitante m, f.

inhale [in'heil] v inalare.

inherent [in'hiərənt] adj inerente.

inherit [in'herit] v ereditare. **inheritance** n eredità f.

inhibit [in'hibit] v inibire. **inhibition** n inibizione f.

inhuman [in'hjuːmən] adj inumano. **inhumanity** n inumanità f.

iniquity [i'nikwəti] n iniquità f. **iniquitous** adj iniquo.

initial [i'niʃl] nf, adj iniziale. v siglare. **initiate** [i'niʃieit] v iniziare, istituire. **initiation** n iniziazione f, inizio m.

initiative [i'niʃiətiv] n iniziativa f.

inject [in'dʒekt] v iniettare; (introduce) immettere. **injection** n iniezione f.

injure ['indʒə] v (damage) danneggiare; (hurt) far male a; (wound) ferire; (law) ledere. **injurious** adj dannoso, nocivo. **injury** n male m; danno m; torto m; ferita f.

injustice [in'dʒʌstis] n ingiustizia f.

ink [ink] n inchiostro m. **ink-well** n calamaio m.

inkling ['inklin] n sospetto m, sentore m.

inland ['inlənd; adv in'lænd] adj interno. adv all' or nell'interno.

in-laws ['inlɔːz] pl n (coll) parenti acquisiti m pl.

*****inlay** ['inlei] v intarsiare. n intarsio m.

inlet ['inlet] n (geog) insenatura f.

inmate ['inmeit] n (of hospital, etc.) ricoverato, -a m, f; (of prison) carcerato, -a m, f.

inn [in] n locanda, osteria f, albergo m. **innkeeper** n locandiere, -a m, f; oste, -essa m, f; albergatore, -trice m, f.

innate [i'neit] adj innato.

inner ['inə] adj interno, interiore; (thoughts, etc.) intimo. **inner tube** camera d'aria f.

innocent ['inəsnt] n(m+f), adj innocente. **innocence** n innocenza f.

innocuous [i'nokjuəs] adj innocuo.

innovation [inə'veiʃən] n innovazione f, novità f. **innovate** v innovare. **innovator** n innovatore, -trice m, f.

innuendo [inju'endou] n insinuazione f.

innumerable [i'njuːmərəbl] adj innumerevole.

inoculate [i'nokjuleit] v inoculare. **inoculation** n inoculazione f.

inorganic [ˌinɔːˈganik] *adj* inorganico.

input ['input] *n* (*elec*) alimentazione *f*; (*computer*) input *m invar*.

inquest ['inkwest] *n* inchiesta *f*, istruttoria *f*.

inquire [inˈkwaiə] *v* chiedere, domandare.

inquiry *n* domanda *f*, informazione *f*, inchiesta *f*.

inquisition [ˌinkwiˈziʃən] *n* inquisizione *f*, inchiesta *f*.

inquisitive [inˈkwizətiv] *adj* curioso.

insane [inˈsein] *adj* pazzo, matto. **insanity** *n* pazzia *f*, follia *f*.

insatiable [inˈseiʃəbl] *adj* insaziabile.

inscribe [inˈskraib] *v* (*enrol*) inscrivere; (*engrave*) incidere. **inscription** *n* iscrizione *f*, dedica *f*.

insect ['insekt] *n* insetto *m*. **insecticide** *n* insetticida *m*.

insecure [ˌinsiˈkjuə] *adj* malsicuro, instabile. **insecurity** *n* incertezza *f*, instabilità *f*.

inseminate [inˈsemineit] *v* inseminare. **insemination** *n* inseminazione *f*.

insensible [inˈsensəbl] *adj* insensibile; (*unconscious*) privo di sensi.

insensitive [inˈsensətiv] *adj* insensibile, indifferente.

inseparable [inˈsepərəbl] *adj* inseparabile.

insert [inˈsəːt; *n* 'insəːt] *v* inserire. *n* also **insertion** inserzione *f*.

inshore [ˌinˈʃoː] *adj* costiero. *adv* verso la riva.

inside [ˌinˈsaid] *adv* dentro, internamente. *prep* dentro, all'interno. *adj* interno, interiore; (*confidential*) riservato. *n* interno *m*; (*soccer*) mezzala *f*. **inside out** a rovescio.

insidious [inˈsidiəs] *adj* insidioso, perfido.

insight ['insait] *n* discernimento *m*, intuito *m*.

insignificant [ˌinsigˈnifikənt] *adj* insignificante.

insincere [ˌinsinˈsiə] *adj* insincero.

insinuate [inˈsinjueit] *v* insinuare, dare ad intendere. **insinuation** *n* insinuazione *f*.

insipid [inˈsipid] *adj* insipido.

insist [inˈsist] *v* insistere. **insistence** *n* insistenza *f*. **insistent** *adj* insistente.

insolent ['insələnt] *adj* impertinente. **insolence** *n* impertinenza *f*.

insoluble [inˈsoljubl] *adj* insolubile; (*not solvable*) insolvibile.

insomnia [inˈsomniə] *n* insonnia *f*. **insomniac** *n* insonne *m, f*.

inspect [inˈspekt] *v* ispezionare, verificare; (*troops*) passare in rivista. **inspection** *n* ispezione *f*, verifica *f*; rivista *f*. **inspector** *n* ispettore, -trice *m, f*; (*bus, train*) controllore, -a *m, f*; (*police*) commissario *m*.

inspire [inˈspaiə] *v* ispirare, infondere. **inspiration** *n* ispirazione *f*.

instability [ˌinstəˈbiləti] *n* instabilità *f*.

install [inˈstoːl] *v* installare. **installation** *n* installazione *f*.

instalment [inˈstoːlmənt] *n* (*comm*) rata *f*; (*serial*) puntata *f*.

instance ['instəns] *n* esempio *m*. **for instance** per esempio.

instant ['instənt] *adj* immediato; urgente; (*comm*) corrente; (*of food*) istantaneo. *n* istante *m*, momento *m*. **instantaneous** *adj* istantaneo.

instead [inˈsted] *adv* invece.

instep ['instep] *n* (*anat*) collo del piede *m*; (*shoe*) collo della scarpa *m*.

instigate ['instigeit] *v* istigare. **instigation** *n* istigazione *f*.

instil [inˈstil] *v* instillare, infondere.

instinct ['instiŋkt] *n* istinto *m*. **instinctive** *adj* istintivo.

institute ['institjuːt] *n* istituto *m*. *v* istituire, iniziare. **institution** *n* istituzione *f*.

instruct [inˈstrʌkt] *v* (*teach*) istruire; (*direct*) dare istruzioni *or* disposizioni a. **instruction** *n* istruzione *f*, disposizioni *f pl*. **instructive** *adj* istruttivo. **instructor** *n* istruttore, -trice *m, f*, insegnante *m, f*.

instrument ['instrəmənt] *n* strumento *m*; (*tool*) arnese *m*; (*law*) titolo *m*, atto *m*. **instrumental** *adj* strumentale. **be instrumental in** essere utile a.

insubordinate [ˌinsəˈboːdənət] *adj* insubordinato. **insubordination** *n* insubordinazione *f*.

insufficient [ˌinsəˈfiʃənt] *adj* insufficiente.

insular ['insjulə] *adj* insulare; (*outlook*) gretto.

insulate ['insjuleit] *v* isolare. **insulating tape** nastro isolante *m*. **insulation** *n* isolamento *m*.

insulin ['insjulin] *n* insulina *f*.

insult [inˈsʌlt; *n* 'insʌlt] *v* insultare, offendere. *n* insulto *m*, offesa *f*.

insure [inˈʃuə] *v* assicurare. **insurance** *n* assicurazione *f*.

intact [inˈtakt] *adj* intatto.

intake ['inteik] n (consumption) consumo m; (employment) assunzione f; (people newly taken on) reclute f pl.

intangible [in'tandʒəbl] adj intangibile.

integral ['intigrəl] adj integrale.

integrate ['intigreit] v integrare. **integration** n integrazione f.

integrity [in'tegrəti] n integrità f.

intellect ['intilekt] n intelletto m. **intellectual** [‑ +f], adj intellettuale.

intelligent [in'telidʒənt] adj intelligente. **intelligence** n intelligenza f; informazioni f pl. **intelligentsia** n intellighenzia f.

intelligible [in'telidʒəbl] adj intelligibile.

intend [in'tend] v intendere, aver l'intenzione di. **intended** adj premeditato, voluto.

intense [in'tens] adj intenso, profondo.

intent[1] [in'tent] n intento m, proposito m, intenzione f. **to all intents and purposes** a tutti gli effetti.

intent[2] [in'tent] adj intento, assorto. **intent on** deciso a.

intention [in'tenʃən] n intenzione f, proposito m. **intentional** adj intenzionale.

inter [in'təi] v seppellire. **interment** n sepoltura f.

interact [intər'akt] v esercitare un'azione reciproca, interagire. **interaction** n azione reciproca f.

intercede [intə'siid] v intercedere.

intercept [intə'sept] v intercettare. **interception** n intercettazione f.

interchange [intə'tʃeindʒ] v scambiare. **interchangeable** adj intercambiabile, scambievole.

intercom ['intəkom] n citofono m.

intercourse ['intəkois] n rapporti m pl.

interest ['intrist] v interessare. **be interested in** interessarsi di. n interesse m. **interesting** adj interessante.

interfere [intə'fiə] v interferire, immischiarsi. **interference** n interferenza f.

interim ['intərim] n interim m. adj provvisorio, temporaneo.

interior [in'tiəriə] nm, adj interno. **interior decorator** arredatore, ‑trice m, f.

interjection [intə'dʒekʃən] n interiezione f.

interlude ['intəlud] n interludio m.

intermediary [intə'miidiəri] n intermediario m.

intermediate [intə'miidiət] adj intermedio.

interminable [in'təiminəbl] adj senza fine.

intermission [intə'miʃən] n interruzione f.

intermittent [intə'mitənt] adj intermittente.

intern [in'təim] v internare. **internment** n internamento m.

internal [in'təinl] adj interno, interiore.

international [intə'naʃənl] adj internazionale.

interpose [intə'pouz] v frapporre.

interpret [in'təiprit] v interpretare. **interpretation** n interpretazione f. **interpreter** n interprete m, f.

interrogate [in'terəgeit] v interrogare. **interrogation** n interrogazione f. **interrogative** adj, nm interrogativo.

interrupt [intə'rʌpt] v interrompere. **interruption** n interruzione f.

intersect [intə'sekt] v intersecare. **intersection** n intersezione f.

intersperse [intə'spəis] v cospargere.

interval ['intəvəl] n intervallo m.

intervene [intə'vim] v intervenire. **intervention** n intervento m.

interview ['intəvjui] n intervista f, colloquio m. v intervistare.

intestine [in'testin] n intestino m. **intestinal** adj intestinale.

intimate[1] [in'timeit] adj intimo, familiare. **intimacy** n intimità f.

intimate[2] [in'timeit] v intimare, suggerire. **intimation** n intimazione f.

intimidate [in'timideit] v intimidire, intimorire. **intimidation** n intimidazione f.

into ['intu] prep in, dentro.

intolerable [in'tolərəbl] adj insopportabile, intollerabile.

intolerant [in'tolərənt] adj intollerante. **intolerance** n intolleranza f.

intonation [intə'neiʃən] n intonazione f.

intoxicate [in'toksikeit] v intossicare; (with drink) ubriacare; (excite) esaltare. **intoxicated** adj ubriaco, eccitato.

intransigent [in'transidʒənt] adj intransigente.

intransitive [in'transitiv] adj intransitivo.

intravenous [intrə'viməs] adj endovenoso.

intrepid [in'trepid] adj intrepido.

intricate ['intrikət] adj complicato, complesso. **intricacy** n complicazione f.

intrigue ['intriig; v in'triig] n intrigo (pl

-ghi) m. v (plot) intrigare; (excite curiosity) incuriosire. **intriguing** adj interessante, affascinante.

intrinsic [in'trinsik] adj intrinseco.

introduce [,intrə'djus] v introdurre; (people) presentare. **introduction** n introduzione f, presentazione f. **introductory** adj introduttorio, introduttivo.

introspective [,intrə'spektiv] adj introspettivo. **introspection** n introspezione f.

introvert ['intrə,vət] adj, n introverso, -a.

intrude [in'trud] v intrudere. **intrusion** n intrusione f.

intuition [,intju'iʃən] n intuito m; (psychol, etc.) intuizione f. **intuitive** adj intuitivo.

inundate ['inʌndeit] v inondare, allagare. **inundation** n allagamento m.

invade [in'veid] v invadere. **invader** n invasore m. **invasion** n invasione f.

invalid[1] [in'valid] n, adj invalido, -a; malato, -a.

invalid[2] [in'valid] adj (not valid) invalido, senza validità, nullo. **invalidate** v invalidare, annullare.

invaluable [in'valjuəbl] adj inestimabile, incalcolabile.

invariable [in'veəriəbl] adj invariabile, costante.

invective [in'vektiv] n invettiva f.

invent [in'vent] v inventare. **invention** n invenzione f.

inventory ['invəntri] n inventario m.

invert [in'vət] v invertire; (inside out) rovesciare; (upside down) capovolgere. **inverted commas** virgolette f pl. **inversion** n inversione f, rovesciamento m.

invertebrate [in'vətibrət] nm, adj invertebrato.

invest [in'vest] v investire. **investment** n investimento m.

investigate [in'vestigeit] v investigare, svolgere indagini. **investigation** n indagine f.

invigorating [in'vigəreitiŋ] adj che invigorisce, fortificante.

invincible [in'vinsəbl] adj invincibile.

invisible [in'vizəbl] adj invisibile. **invisibility** n invisibilità f.

invite [in'vait] v invitare; provocare; (lay oneself open to) esporsi a. **invitation** n invito m. **inviting** adj attraente, seducente.

invoice ['invois] n fattura f. v fatturare.

invoke [in'vouk] v invocare. **invocation** n invocazione f.

involuntary [in'voləntəri] adj involontario.

involve [in'volv] v (imply) implicare; (implicate) coinvolgere; (entail) comportare. **involvement** n implicazione f.

inward ['inwəd] adj interno, intimo. **inwardly** adv interiormente. **inwards** adv verso il centro.

iodine ['aiədiin] n iodio m.

ion ['aiən] n ione m.

irate [ai'reit] adj arrabbiato.

Ireland ['aiələnd] n Irlanda f. **Irish** n(m+f), adj irlandese.

iris ['aiəris] n (anat) iride f; (bot) giaggiolo m.

irk [ə:k] v infastidire, dar noia a. **irksome** adj seccante, noioso.

iron ['aiən] n ferro m; (for pressing) ferro da stiro m. **iron curtain** cortina di ferro f. **ironmonger's** n ferramenta f. v stirare. **ironing board** tavola da stiro f.

irony ['aiərəni] n ironia f. **ironic** adj ironico.

irrational [i'raʃənl] adj irrazionale.

irregular [i'regjulə] adj irregolare. **irregularity** n irregolarità f.

irrelevant [i'reləvənt] adj non pertinente.

irreparable [i'repərəbl] adj irreparabile.

irresistible [,iri'zistəbl] adj irresistibile.

irrespective [,iri'spektiv] adj **irrespective of** senza riguardo a, senza tener conto di.

irresponsible [,iri'sponsəbl] adj irresponsabile. **irresponsibility** n irresponsabilità f.

irrevocable [i'revəkəbl] adj irrevocabile.

irrigate ['irigeit] v irrigare. **irrigation** n irrigazione f.

irritate ['iriteit] v irritare. **irritating** adj irritante. **irritation** n irritazione f.

Islam ['izlam] n Islam m. **Islamic** adj islamico.

island ['ailənd] n isola f.

isolate ['aisəleit] v isolare. **isolation** n isolamento m.

issue ['iʃu] n questione f, problema m; (outcome) conclusione f, edizione f; (shares, etc.) emissione f. v pubblicare; emettere; uscire.

isthmus ['isməs] n istmo m.

it [it] pron (subject) esso, -a; (direct object) lo, la; (indirect object) gli, le.

italic [i'talik] adj (handwriting) italico;

(*printing*) corsivo. **in italics** in (carattere) corsivo.

Italy ['itəli] *n* Italia *f*. **Italian** *n, adj* italiano, -a; (*language*) italiano *m*.

itch [itʃ] *n* (*sensation*) prurito *m*; (*desire*) gran voglia *f*. *v* sentire prurito.

item ['aitəm] *n* voce *f*, capo *m*, pezzo *m*.

itinerary [ai'tinərəri] *n* itinerario *m*.

its [its] *adj* (il) suo, (la) sua; (*pl*) (i) suoi, (le) sue.

itself [it'self] *pron* (*reflexive*) si; (*after prep*) sè; (*emphatic*) se esso, -a, se stesso, -a.

ivory ['aivəri] *n* avorio *m*.

ivy ['aivi] *n* edera *f*.

J

jab [dʒab] *n* puntura *f*. *v* pungere, punzecchiare.

jack [dʒak] *n* (*car*) cricco *m*; (*cards*) fante *m*; (*bowls*) boccino *m*. *v* **jack up** alzare.

jackdaw ['dʒakdɔt] *n* taccola *f*.

jacket ['dʒakit] *n* giacca *f*; (*of book*) copertina *f*; (*boiler, etc.*) rivestimento *m*. **jacket potato** patata in camicia *f*.

jack-knife ['dʒaknaif] *n* coltello a serramanico *m*.

jackpot ['dʒakpot] *n* posta intera *f*, monte premi *m*. **hit the jackpot** avere un colpo di fortuna.

jade [dʒeid] *n* giada *f*.

jaded ['dʒeidid] *adj* stracco, spossato.

jagged ['dʒagid] *adj* scabro, intaccato, dentellato.

jaguar ['dʒagjuə] *n* giaguaro *m*.

jail *or* **gaol** [dʒeil] *n* prigione *f*, carcere *m*. *v* incarcerare, mettere in prigione.

jam[1] [dʒam] *v* (*block*) bloccare; (*cause to stop functioning*) intralciare; (*squeeze*) pigiare; (*radio*) disturbare; (*traffic*) intasare. **jam on the brakes** bloccare i freni. *n* (*traffic*) intasamento *m*. **get into a jam** mettersi nei pasticci.

jam[2] [dʒam] *n* marmellata *f*, conserva di frutta *f*.

janitor ['dʒanitə] *n* portinaio, -a *m, f*.

January ['dʒanjuəri] *n* gennaio *m*.

Japan [dʒə'pan] *n* Giappone *m*. **Japanese** *n* (*m+f*), *adj* giapponese.

jar[1] [dʒɑː] *n* (*vessel*) brocca *f*; (*usually with lid*) barattolo *m*.

jar[2] [dʒɑː] *v* vibrare; produrre un suono aspro. **jarring** *adj* discorde.

jargon ['dʒɑːgən] *n* gergo *m*.

jasmine ['dʒazmin] *n* gelsomino *m*.

jaundice ['dʒɔːndis] *n* itterizia *f*. **jaundiced** *adj* distorto, invelenito.

jaunt [dʒɔːnt] *n* gita *f*.

jaunty ['dʒɔːnti] *adj* vivace, disinvolto.

javelin ['dʒavəlin] *n* giavellotto *m*.

jaw [dʒɔː] *n* (*upper*) mascella *f*; (*lower*) mandibola *f*.

jay [dʒei] *n* ghiandaia *f*.

jazz [dʒaz] *n* jazz *m invar*.

jealous ['dʒeləs] *adj* geloso. **become jealous** ingelosirsi. **make jealous** ingelosire. **jealousy** *n* gelosia *f*.

jeans [dʒiːnz] *pl n* jeans *m pl*.

jeep [dʒiːp] *n* jeep *f invar*.

jeer [dʒiə] *v* schernire, canzonare. *n* derisione *f*, scherno *m*.

jelly ['dʒeli] *n* gelatina *f*, budino di gelatina *m*.

jeopardize ['dʒepədaiz] *v* mettere a repentaglio, arrischiare. **jeopardy** *n* repentaglio *m*.

jerk [dʒəːk] *n* (*shock*) scossa *f*; (*pull*) strappo *m*; (*sudden start*) scatto *m*. *v* scuotere; dare uno strappo; scattare.

jersey ['dʒəːzi] *n* (*fabric*) jersey *m invar*; (*garment*) maglione *m*.

jest [dʒest] *n* scherzo *m*, burla *f*. *v* scherzare. **jester** *n* buffone *m*.

Jesuit ['dʒezjuit] *adj, nm* gesuita. **Jesuitical** *adj* gesuitico.

Jesus ['dʒiːzəs] *n* Gesù *m*. **Jesus Christ** Gesù Cristo.

jet [dʒet] *n* getto *m*, zampillo *m*; (*spout*) becco *m*; (*aero*) aviogetto *m*, aeroplano a reazione *m*. **jet-black** *adj* (nero) ebano *invar*. **jet engine** motore a reazione *m*.

jettison ['dʒetisn] *v* buttar via, disfarsi di.

jetty ['dʒeti] *n* molo *m*, banchina *f*.

Jew [dʒuː] *n* ebreo, -a *m, f*. **Jewish** *adj* (*person*) ebreo; (*thing*) ebraico.

jewel ['dʒuːəl] *n* gioiello *m*; (*watch*) rubino *m*; (*treasure*) tesoro *m*. **jeweller** *n* gioielliere *m*. **jewellery** *n* gioielleria *f*.

jib[1] [dʒib] *n* (*sail*) fiocco *m*; (*crane*) braccio *m*.

jib[2] [dʒib] *v* **jib at** essere restio *or* ritroso a.

jig [dʒig] *n* (*machine tool*) maschera di montaggio *f*. *v* lavorare con maschere.

jig' *n* (*dance*) giga *f*. *v* ballare la giga. **jig up and down** salterellare su e giù.

jiggle ['dʒigl] v dondolare, muoversi in qua e in là.

jigsaw ['dʒigsɔ:] n sega da traforo f. **jig-saw puzzle** puzzle m.

jilt [dʒilt] v piantare in asso.

jingle ['dʒingl] n (sound) tintinnio m; (song) ritornello m, cantilena f. v tintinnare.

jinx [dʒiŋks] n malocchio m.

job [dʒɔb] n impiego (pl -ghi) m, lavoro m; (coll) affare m, mestiere m.

jockey ['dʒɔki] n fantino m. v maneggiare.

jocular ['dʒɔkjulə] adj faceto.

jodhpurs ['dʒɔdpəz] pl n calzoni da equitazione m pl.

jog [dʒɔg] v (sport) fare il footing; (horse) andare al piccolo trotto. **jog the memory** richiamare alla memoria. n (push) spinta f; (nudge) colpetto m; (elbowing) gomitata f; (trot) piccolo trotto m.

join [dʒɔin] n giuntura f. v unire, congiungere, unirsi a; (become member) iscriversi a, entrare. **join in** entrare a far parte di.

joiner ['dʒɔinə] n falegname m.

joint [dʒɔint] n (join) giuntura f; articolazione f; (plant) nodo m; (meat) taglio (di carne) m; (coll: bar, etc.) bettola f. adj comune, collettivo.

joist [dʒɔist] n trave f, travicello m.

joke [dʒɔuk] n scherzo m, barzelletta f. **no joke** un affare serio m. v scherzare.

joker ['dʒɔukə] n burlone m; (cards) jolly m invar, matta f.

jolly ['dʒɔli] adj divertente, ameno, gaio. adv molto.

jolt [dʒɔult] v scuotere, far sobbalzare. n scossa f, sobbalzo m.

jostle ['dʒɔsl] n (push) spinta f; (elbowing) gomitata f. v fare a gomitate, spingersi avanti.

journal ['dʒə:nl] n periodico m; (daily record) diario m, giornale m; (day-book) brogliaccio m. **journalism** n giornalismo m. **journalist** n giornalista m, f.

journey ['dʒə:ni] n viaggio m. v viaggiare. **go on a journey** andare or mettersi in viaggio.

jovial ['dʒɔuviəl] adj gioviale, lieto.

jowl [dʒaul] n (jaw) mascella f; (flesh) gota f.

joy [dʒɔi] n gioia f, allegrezza f, allegria f. **joyful** or **joyous** adj gioioso.

jubilant ['dʒu:bilənt] adj giubilante.

jubilee ['dʒu:bili:] n giubileo m.

Judaism ['dʒu:dei,izəm] n giudaismo m.

judge [dʒʌdʒ] n giudice m; (of competition) arbitro m; (expert) intenditore, -trice m, f. v giudicare, considerare. **judgment** n giudizio m; (law) sentenza f; (opinion) parere m. **Last Judgment** giudizio universale m.

judicial [dʒu:'diʃəl] adj giudiziario; legale.

judiciary [dʒu:'diʃiəri] n magistratura f.

judicious [dʒu:'diʃəs] adj giudizioso, prudente.

judo ['dʒu:dou] n judo m invar, giudò m.

jug [dʒʌg] n brocca f, caraffa f.

juggernaut ['dʒʌgənɔ:t] n (lorry) grosso autotreno m.

juggle ['dʒʌgl] v giocolare, prestigiare; (trick) truffare. **juggle with** svisare, travisare. **juggler** n giocoliere, -a m, f; prestigiatore, -trice m, f.

jugular ['dʒʌgjulə] adj giugulare.

juice [dʒu:s] n succo m, sugo m. **juicy** adj sugoso, succolento.

jukebox ['dʒu:kbɔks] n jukebox m invar.

July [dʒu:'lai] n luglio m.

jumble ['dʒʌmbl] n miscuglio m, confusione f. **jumble sale** bazar di beneficenza m invar.

jump [dʒʌmp] n salto m; (sudden rise) balzo m; (nervous) sussulto m. **long/high jump** salto in lungo/alto m. v saltare, fare un salto; sussultare; (of prices) rincarare. **jump at** accettare con entusiasmo. **jump off** lanciarsi da. **jump over** scavalcare.

jumper ['dʒʌmpə] n (pullover) maglione m, pullover m invar; (jacket) casacca f; (person) saltatore, -trice m, f.

junction ['dʒʌŋkʃən] n congiunzione f; (rail) nodo ferroviario m.

juncture ['dʒʌŋkʃə] n frangente m, momento (critico) m.

June [dʒu:n] n giugno m.

jungle ['dʒʌŋgl] n giungla f.

junior ['dʒu:njə] adj minore, più giovane.

juniper ['dʒu:nipə] n ginepro m.

junk[1] [dʒʌŋk] n (rubbish) roba vecchia f, robaccia f, rifiuti m pl.

junk[2] [dʒʌŋk] n (boat) giunca f.

junta ['dʒʌntə] n giunta f.

jurisdiction [dʒuəris'dikʃən] n giurisdizione f.

jury ['dʒuəri] n giuria f. **juror** n giurato, -a m, f.

just [dʒʌst] *adj* giusto, preciso. *adv* giusto, per l'appunto, proprio; (*barely*) appena; (*not more than*) soltanto.

justice ['dʒʌstis] *n* giustizia *f*; (*judge*) giudice *m*, magistrato *m*. **do justice to** (*show appreciation*) far onore a; (*concede what is due*) apprezzare, stimare.

justify ['dʒʌstifai] *v* giustificare, scusare. **justifiable** *adj* giustificabile, scusabile, legittimo. **justification** *n* giustificazione *f*, scusa *f*.

jut [dʒʌt] *v* sporgere, protendere (in fuori).

jute [dʒuːt] *n* giuta *f*.

juvenile ['dʒuːvənail] *adj* giovanile, per ragazzi, minorenne.

juxtapose [dʒʌkstə'pouz] *v* giustapporre. **juxtaposition** *n* giustapposizione *f*.

K

kaleidoscope [kə'laidəskoup] *n* caleidoscopio *m*.

kangaroo [kaŋgə'ruː] *n* canguro *m*.

karate [kə'raːti] *n* karatè *m invar*.

keel [kiːl] *n* chiglia *f*. **v keel over** capovolgersi.

keen [kiːn] *adj* (*cutting*) tagliente; (*sharp*) aguzzo; (*perceptive*) vivo, perspicace; (*biting*) mordace; (*eager*) appassionato, entusiasta. **keenness** *n* passione *f*, entusiasmo *m*, intensità *f*; (*eagerness*) ardore *m*.

*****keep** [kiːp] *v* tenere; mantenere; conservare; (*hold in custody*) custodire; (*manage*) gestire; (*observe*) osservare, rispettare. **keep at** persistere, continuare a fare. **keep back** (*stay behind*) stare indietro; (*withhold*) trattenere. **keep down** reprimere. **keep good time** (*watch*) funzionare bene. **keep in with** mantenersi in buoni rapporti con. **keep on** continuare. **keep out** non lasciar entrare; restar fuori. **keep to** aderire a. **n earn one's keep** mantenersi. **for keeps** per sempre.

keeper ['kiːpə] *n* guardiano, -a *m, f*; custode *m, f*.

keeping ['kiːpiŋ] *n* custodia *f*. **in keeping with** conforme *or* consono a.

keepsake ['kiːpseik] *n* ricordo *m*.

keg [keg] *n* barilotto *m*.

kennel ['kenl] *n* canile *f*.

kept [kept] *V* keep.

kerb [kəːb] *n* banchina *f*.

kernel ['kəːnl] *n* nocciolo *m*, nucleo *m*.

kerosene [kerə'siːn] *n* cherosene *m*.

kettle ['ketl] *n* bollitore *m*, pentola *f*.

kettledrum ['ketldrʌm] *n* timpano *m*.

key [kiː] *n* chiave *f*; (*part of keyboard*) tasto *m*. **keyboard** *n* tastiera *f*. **keyhole** *n* buco della chiave *m*. **keynote** *n* nota determinante *f*.

khaki ['kaːki] *adj* cachi.

kick [kik] *v* dare un calcio a, dare una pedata a; protestare. **kick off** iniziare. **kick out** buttar fuori. **kick up** scatenare, provocare. **n** calcio *m*, pedata *f*; (*force*) forza *f*.

kid[1] [kid] *n* (*child*) bimbo, -a *m, f*; (*goat*) capretto *m*. **handle with kid gloves** trattare coi guanti.

kid[2] [kid] *v* (*coll*) prendere in giro.

kidnap ['kidnap] *v* rapire. **kidnapper** *n* rapitore, -trice *m, f*.

kidney ['kidni] *n* (*organ*) rene *m*; (*food*) rognone *f*. **kidney bean** fagiolo *m*.

kill [kil] *v* uccidere, ammazzare. **killer** *n* assassino, -a *m, f*.

kiln [kiln] *n* forno *m*.

kilo ['kiːlou] *n* chilo *m*. **kilogram** *n* chilogrammo *m*.

kilometre ['kiləmiːtə] *n* chilometro *m*.

kilt [kilt] *n* gonnellino scozzese *m*.

kin [kin] *n* parenti *m pl*; (*kinship*) parentela *f*. **kinsman** *n* parente *m*. **next of kin** parente prossimo *m*.

kind[1] [kaind] *adj* gentile, cortese, buono; (*well-meant*) cordiale. **kind-hearted** *adj* benevolo. **kindly** *adv* gentilmente; (*please*) per cortesia, per favore. **kindness** *n* gentilezza *f*, cortesia *f*.

kind[2] [kaind] *n* genere *m*, specie *f*, razza *f*.

kindergarten ['kindəgaːtn] *n* giardino d'infanzia *m*, asilo (infantile) *m*.

kindle ['kindl] *v* accendere; (*excite*) eccitare.

kindred ['kindrid] *n* parentela *f*. *adj* affine, simile. **kindred spirit** anima gemella *f*.

kinetic [kin'etik] *adj* cinetico.

king [kiŋ] *n* re *m invar*. **kingdom** *n* regno *m*.

kingfisher ['kiŋˌfiʃə] *n* martin pescatore *m*.

kink [kiŋk] *n* attorcigliamento *m*, piega *f*; (*whim*) ghiribizzo *m*. **kinky** *adj* (*odd*) strambo; (*coll*) pervertito.

kiosk ['kiːɒsk] n chiosco m; (newsagent) edicola f.

kipper ['kɪpə] n aringa affumicata f.

kiss [kɪs] n bacio m. v baciare.

kit [kɪt] n (tools) attrezzi m pl, utensili m pl; (outfit) corredo m. v attrezzare. **kit out** equipaggiare.

kitchen ['kɪtʃɪn] n cucina f.

kite [kaɪt] n aquilone m; (bird) nibbio m.

kitten ['kɪtn] n micio m, gattino m.

kitty ['kɪtɪ] n (joint pool) fondo comune m; (cards) posta f.

kleptomania [klɛptə'meɪnɪə] n cleptomania f. **kleptomaniac** n cleptomane m, f.

knack [nak] n destrezza f, bernoccolo m.

knapsack ['napsak] n zaino m.

knave [neɪv] n furfante m; (cards) fante m.

knead [niːd] v impastare.

knee [niː] n ginocchio m (pl -a f). **kneecap** n rotula f, patella f. **knee-deep** adj che arriva fino al ginocchio; (submerged) sommerso.

*****kneel** [niːl] v inginocchiarsi, mettersi in ginocchio.

knelt [nɛlt] V kneel.

knew [njuː] V know.

knickers ['nɪkəz] pl n mutandine f pl.

knife [naɪf] n coltello m. v accoltellare.

knight [naɪt] n cavaliere m.

*****knit** [nɪt] v lavorare a maglia, fare la calza; (join together) unire. **knit one's brows** aggrottare le ciglia. **knitting needle** ferro da calza m. **knitwear** n maglieria f.

knob [nɒb] n pomo m, manopola f; (protuberance) bitorzolo m. **knobbly** adj bitorzoluto, nodoso.

knock [nɒk] v (at door) bussare; (hit) colpire, battere; (of motor engine) battere in testa. **knock about** (mistreat) malmenare; (wander aimlessly) fare vita randagia. **knock down** (strike) abbattere; demolire; (lower) abbassare. **knock-kneed** adj dalle gambe a X. **knock off** (stop work) tralasciare, smettere; (deduct) dedurre; (coll: steal) far man bassa, portar via; (complete hurriedly) buttar giù. **knock out** (stun) far perdere i sensi a; (put out of action) mettere fuori combattimento. **knock together** (make hurriedly) acciabattare. **knock up** (wake) svegliare; (tennis) fare del palleggio. n colpo m; bussata f; (blow) batosta f. **knocker** n battiporta m invar, picchiotto m.

knot [nɒt] n nodo m. v annodare. **knotted** adj nodoso, annodato, pieno di nodi. **knotty** adj pieno di nodi; difficile, complesso.

*****know** [nou] v (facts) sapere; (be acquainted with) conoscere; (understand) capire; (recognize) riconoscere. **as far as is known** per quanto si sappia. **know about** essere informato su, essere al corrente di. **know how to** sapere. n **in the know** (coll) al corrente di. **knowing** adj accorto, intelligente. **known** adj noto, conosciuto. **make known** far sapere or conoscere, divulgare, render noto.

knowledge ['nɒlɪdʒ] n cognizione f, conoscenze f pl.

known [noun] V know.

knuckle ['nʌkl] n nocca f. **knuckle down** applicarsi. **knuckle under** sottomettersi, piegarsi.

kosher ['kouʃə] adj kasher, cascer.

L

label ['leɪbl] n etichetta f; (strip of paper) cartellino m; definizione f. v etichettare, qualificare.

laboratory [lə'bɒrətəri] n laboratorio m.

labour ['leɪbə] n (toil) lavoro m; (hard work, task) fatica f; (effort) sforzo m; (workforce) manodopera f; (childbirth) doglie del parto f pl, travaglio del parto m. **Labour Party** partito laburista m. **labour-saving** adj che risparmia fatica. v faticare, lavorare. **labour** under essere vittima di. **laborious** adj laborioso, faticoso.

laburnum [lə'bəːnəm] n laburno m.

labyrinth ['labərinθ] n labirinto m.

lace [leɪs] n pizzo m, merletto m, brina f; (string, cord) laccio m; (braid) gallone m. v (fasten) allacciare; (trim with lace) ornare di pizzi; (add to drink) correggere. **lacemaker** n trinaia f.

lacerate ['lasəreɪt] v lacerare.

lack [lak] n mancanza f, insufficienza f. v mancare (di).

lackadaisical [,lakə'deizikəl] adj svogliato, infingardo.

lacquer ['lakə] n lacca f. v laccare.

lad [lad] n ragazzo m, giovanotto m.

ladder ['lædə] n scala f; (stocking) smagliatura f. v smagliarsi. **ladder-proof** adj indemagliabile.

laden ['leidn] adj carico (m pl -chi).

ladle ['leidl] n (dish-shaped) mestolo m; (cup-shaped) ramaiuolo m, cucchiaione m. v scodellare.

lady ['leidi] n signora f. **lady of the house** padrona di casa f.

ladybird ['leidibəːd] n coccinella f.

lag¹ [læg] v avanzare lentamente. **lag behind** rimanere indietro. n ritardo m, intervallo m.

lag² [læg] v (cover) rivestire di materiale isolante, isolare. **lagging** n rivestimento isolante m.

lager ['lɑːgə] n birra (chiara) f.

lagoon [lə'guːn] n laguna f.

laid [leid] V **lay¹**.

lain [lein] V **lie¹**.

lair [leə] n tana f.

laity ['leiəti] n **the laity** i laici m pl.

lake [leik] n lago m.

lamb [læm] n agnello m.

lame [leim] adj zoppo, storpio; (poor) debole, insufficiente. **lame duck** fallito m.

lament [lə'ment] n lamento m. v lamentare, compiangere. **lamented** adj compianto.

laminate ['læmineit] v laminare.

lamp [læmp] n lampada f, lume m; (of car, ship) fanale m. **lamp-holder** n portalampada m. **lamp-post** n lampione m. **lampshade** n paralume m.

lance [lɑːns] n lancia f. v incidere col bisturi. **lancet** n bisturi m invar.

land [lænd] n terra f; (country) paese m; (agricultural area) campagna f; (site, soil) terreno m. v (put on shore) sbarcare, approdare; (from the air) atterrare; (obtain) ottenere. **landing** n sbarco m; atterraggio m; (of stairs) pianerottolo m.

landlady ['lændleidi] n padrona di casa f, proprietaria f.

landlord ['lændloːd] n padrone di casa m, proprietario m; (of inn) oste m.

landmark ['lændmɑːk] n punto di riferimento m.

landscape ['lændskeip] n paesaggio m.

landslide ['lændslaid] n frana f.

lane [lein] n (between houses) vicolo m; (track) sentiero m; (part of road, sports track) corsia f.

language ['læŋgwidʒ] n (of a nation) lingua f; (means of expression) linguaggio m.

languish ['læŋgwiʃ] v languire.

lanky ['læŋki] adj alto e magro.

lantern ['læntən] n lanterna f.

lap¹ [læp] n (anat) grembo m; (loose fold) falda f, piega f; (circuit) giro m; (part of journey) tappa f.

lap² [læp] v lambire. **lap up** lappare; (coll) ascoltare or accettare con avidità.

lapel [lə'pel] n risvolto m.

Lapland ['læplænd] n Lapponia f. **Lapp** n(m+f), adj lappone.

lapse [læps] n svista f, errore m; (time) corso m, periodo m; (law) scadenza f; decadenza f. v (become void) scadere; (decline) decadere; (time) trascorrere. **lapsed** adj (law) decaduto; (rel) apostata.

larceny ['lɑːsəni] n furto m.

larch [lɑːtʃ] n larice m.

lard [lɑːd] n strutto m.

larder ['lɑːdə] n dispensa f.

large [lɑːdʒ] adj grande, ampio. **at large** in libertà; (in general) in complesso.

lark¹ [lɑːk] n (bird) allodola f.

lark² [lɑːk] n (coll) burla f. v **lark about** divertirsi.

larva ['lɑːvə] n, pl **larvae** larva f.

larynx ['læriŋks] n laringe f. **laryngitis** n laringite f.

laser ['leizə] n laser m invar.

lash [læʃ] n sferzata f; (eye) ciglio m (pl -a f). v (whip) sferzare; (tie) legare. **lash out** menar colpi; (coll: money) non badare a spese. **lash out at** inveire contro.

lass [læs] n fanciulla f, giovane f.

lassitude ['læsitjuːd] n stanchezza f.

lasso [lə'suː] n lasso m, laccio m. v catturare al lasso or laccio.

last¹ [lɑːst] adj finale, ultimo; (past) scorso, passato. **last but one** penultimo. **last night** ieri sera. adv (after all others) per ultimo; (most recently) l'ultima volta; finalmente. **at last** alla fine, finalmente.

last² [lɑːst] v durare. **lasting** adj durevole.

latch [lætʃ] n saliscendi m invar, chiavistello m. v chiudere con saliscendi. **latch on to** afferrare.

late [leit] adj tardo; recente; (former) precedente; (dead) defunto, fu. adv (not on time) in ritardo; (not early) tardi. **lately** adv recentemente. **lateness** n ritardo *m.* **later** *adv* più tardi, dopo. **see you later!** a più tardi! **latest** *adj* ultimo; recentissimo. **at the latest** al più tardi.

latent ['leitənt] *adj* latente.

lateral ['lætərəl] *adj* laterale.

lathe [leið] *n* tornio *m.*

lather ['laːðə] *n* schiuma *f.* *v (of soap)* far schiuma.

Latin ['latin] *nm, adj* latino.

latitude ['latitjuːd] *n* latitudine *f.*

latrine [lə'triːn] *n* latrina *f.*

latter ['latə] *adj* secondo, ultimo. **the latter** il secondo, questo.

lattice ['latis] *n* traliccio *m*, grata *f.*

laugh [laːf] *v* ridere. **laugh at** ridere per o di. *n* risata *f*; *(coll)* spasso *m.* **have a laugh** fare una risata. **laughable** *adj* ridicolo, risibile. **laughing stock** zimbello *m.* **laughter** *n* riso *m (pl -a f)*, risata *f.*

launch¹ [lɔːntʃ] *v* varare; *(give a start)* lanciare; *(attack)* sferrare.

launch² [lɔːntʃ] *n (naut)* lancia *f.*

launder ['lɔːndə] *v* fare il bucato, lavare e stirare. **launderette** *n* lavanderia automatica *f*, lavanderia a gettoni *f.* **laundry** *n (place)* lavanderia *f*; *(clothes, etc.)* bucato *m.*

laurel ['lɔrəl] *n* alloro *m*, lauro *m.*

lava ['laːvə] *n* lava *f.*

lavatory ['lavətəri] *n* gabinetto *m*, ritirata *f.*

lavender ['lavində] *n* lavanda *f.*

lavish ['laviʃ] *adj* prodigo, generoso. *v* dispensare *or* spendere largamente.

law [lɔː] *n* legge *f*; *(profession)* diritto *m*; *(rule)* norma *f*, regola *f.* **law-abiding** *adj* ligio alla legge. **lawsuit** *n* causa *f*, processo *m.* **lawful** *adj* legittimo, lecito. **lawyer** *n* avvocato, -essa *m, f.*

lawn [lɔːn] *n* prato rasato *m.* **lawn-mower** *n* falciatrice *or* tosatrice per prati *f.*

lax [laks] *adj* rilassato; negligente.

laxative ['laksətiv] *nm, adj* lassativo.

***lay¹** [lei] *v* posare, mettere; *(eggs)* deporre; *(table)* apparecchiare. **lay-by** *n* area *or* piazzola di sosta *or* parcheggio *f.* **lay down** posare per terra; stabilire. **lay off** *(workers)* sospendere. **lay on** disporre, installare. **layout** *n* disposizione *f*; *(sketch)* tracciato *m*, pianta *f.* **lay out** *(spread)* stendere; *(coll: spend)* sborsare. **be laid up** essere costretto di rimanere a letto.

lay² [lei] *adj* laico; non professionale. **layman** *n* laico, -a *m, f*; profano, -a *m, f.*

lay³ [lei] *V* **lie¹**.

layer ['leiə] *n* strato *m.*

lazy ['leizi] *adj* pigro, indolente. **laziness** *n* pigrizia *f.*

***lead¹** [liːd] *v* condurre; influenzare; *(bring)* portare; *(be at head of)* essere in testa di, essere al comando di; *(act as guide)* guidare; *(make go)* indurre. *n* direzione *f*, comando *m*; *(for dog)* guinzaglio *m*; *(theatre)* primo attore, prima attrice *m, f.* **be in the lead** *(sport)* essere in testa. **take the lead** *(sport)* passare in testa. **leader** *n* capo *m*, dirigente *m, f*; *(newspaper)* articolo di fondo *m.* **leadership** *n* direzione *f*, comando *m.* **leading** *adj* principale, primo.

lead² [led] *n* piombo *m.* **leaden** *adj* di piombo.

leaf [liːf] *n (plant)* foglia *f*; *(paper)* foglio *m*; *(table)* asse *f.* **v leaf through** sfogliare. **leaflet** *n* volantino *m*, manifestino *m.*

league [liːg] *n* lega *f*; classe *f.*

leak [liːk] *n (escape)* fuga *f*; *(crack)* fessura *f*; *(boat)* falla *f*; *(news)* trapelamento *m.* *v* perdere; *(boat)* far acqua; trapelare.

***lean¹** [liːn] *v* appoggiare, inclinare, pendere. **lean against** appoggiarsi a. **lean out** sporgersi. **lean towards** tendere verso. **leaning** *n* inclinazione *f*, propensione *f.*

lean² [liːn] *adj* magro, scarno; *(poor)* povero.

leant [lent] *V* **lean¹**.

***leap** [liːp] *n* salto *m*, balzo *m.* **by leaps and bounds** a passi da gigante. *v* saltare, balzare. **leap-frog** *n* cavallina *f.* **leap year** anno bisestile *m.*

leapt [lept] *V* **leap**.

***learn** [lɔːn] *v* imparare, studiare; *(become informed)* sentire, apprendere. **learned** *adj* dotto, erudito, colto. **learner** *n (beginner)* principiante *m, f*; allievo, -a *m, f*; apprendista *m, f.* **learning** *n* cultura *f*, erudizione *f.*

learnt [lɔːnt] *V* **learn**.

lease [liːs] *n* affitto *m*, contratto d'affitto *m.* *v* affittare.

leash [liːʃ] *n* guinzaglio *m.*

least [liːst] *adj* minimo. *pron, adv* (il) meno. **at least** almeno. **not in the least** per nulla, affatto.

leather ['leðə] *n* cuoio *m*, pelle *f.* **leather goods** pelletteria *f sing.*

***leave¹** [liːv] *v* lasciare; abbandonare; *(go out from)* uscire da; *(depart)* partire. **leave alone** lasciar stare, lasciare in pace.

leave home andar via. **leave out** omettere. **be left** rimanere. **be left over** avanzare.

leave² [liːv] n permesso m; (holiday) licenza f, congedo m.

lecherous ['letʃərəs] adj lussurioso, lascivo. **lecher** n libertino m. **lechery** n lascivia f.

lectern ['lektən] n leggio m.

lecture ['lektʃə] n lezione f, conferenza f; (reprimand) ramanzina f, sgridata f. v tenere una conferenza; dare un corso di lezioni; (rebuke) predicare, fare una paternale a. **lecturer** n conferenziere, -a m, f; (university) docente m, f.

led [led] V **lead¹**.

ledge [ledʒ] n (window) davanzale m; (projecting part) sporgenza f.

ledger ['ledʒə] n (libro) mastro m.

lee [liː] n (shelter) riparo m; (naut) sottovento m. **leeward** adj, adv sottovento.

leech [liːtʃ] n sanguisuga f.

leek [liːk] n porro m.

leer [liə] v guardare di sbieco. n sguardo sbieco m.

leeway ['liːwei] n (naut) deriva f. **make up leeway** recuperare lo svantaggio.

left¹ [left] V **leave¹**.

left² [left] adj sinistro. n sinistra f. **the Left** (pol) la Sinistra. adv a sinistra, verso sinistra, sulla sinistra. **left-hand** adj sinistro. **left-handed** adj mancino.

leg [leg] n gamba f; (furniture) piede m; (lap) tappa f; (poultry) coscia f; (meat) cosciotto m.

legacy ['legəsi] n lascito m, eredità f.

legal ['liːgəl] adj lecito, legittimo, legale. **legality** n legalità f. **legalize** v legalizzare, legittimare.

legend ['ledʒənd] n leggenda f. **legendary** adj leggendario.

Leghorn ['leg'hoːn] n Livorno m.

legible ['ledʒəbl] adj leggibile. **legibility** n leggibilità f.

legion ['liːdʒən] n legione f.

legislate ['ledʒisleit] v promulgare leggi. **legislation** n legislazione f.

legitimate [lə'dʒitimət] adj legittimo, lecito. v legittimare. **legitimacy** n legittimità f.

leisure ['leʒə] n agio m, tempo libero m. **leisurely** adj fatto con comodo.

lemon ['lemən] n limone m. adj color limone invar. **lemonade** n limonata f. **lemon juice** succo di limone m.

*lend [lend] v prestare, dare in prestito.

length [leŋθ] n lunghezza f; (time) durata f; (cloth) taglio m. **at length** per disteso.

lengthen v allungare. **lengthy** adj lungo.

lenient ['liːmiənt] adj benigno, indulgente. **leniency** n indulgenza f.

lens [lenz] n lente f; (camera) obiettivo m.

lent [lent] V **lend**.

Lent [lent] n quaresima f.

lentil ['lentil] n lenticchia f.

Leo ['liːou] n Leone m.

leopard ['lepəd] n leopardo m.

leotard ['liːətaːd] n calzamaglia (pl calzemaglie) f.

leper ['lepə] n lebbroso, -a m, f. **leprosy** n lebbra f.

lesbian ['lezbiən] n lesbica f.

less [les] adj minore, meno, meno. nm, adv, prep meno. **lessen** v diminuire. **lesser** adj minore, inferiore.

lesson ['lesn] n lezione f.

lest [lest] conj per paura che.

*let [let] v lasciare, permettere; (rent) affittare. **let down** (lower) calare; (hair) sciogliere; (disappoint) deludere; (dress) allungare. **let in** fare entrare. **let know** far sapere. **let out** far uscire, liberare; (dress) allargare; (secret) lasciar sfuggire; (emit) fare.

lethal ['liːθəl] adj letale.

lethargy ['leθədʒi] n letargia f. **lethargic** adj letargico.

letter ['letə] n lettera f; (character) carattere m. **letter-box** n buca delle lettere f. **lettering** n iscrizione f.

lettuce ['letis] n lattuga f.

leukaemia [luː'kiːmiə] n leucemia f.

level ['levl] n livello m, piano m; (height, position) altezza f. v livellare, spianare. adj piano, uniforme; (equal) pari. **be level with** essere a livello di. **level crossing** passaggio a livello m. **level-headed** adj equilibrato.

lever ['liːvə] n leva f. **leverage** n leva f, stimolo m.

levy ['levi] n imposta f, contributo m. v imporre, esigere.

lewd [luːd] adj lascivo, osceno.

liable ['laiəbl] adj responsabile. **liable to** soggetto a, passibile di. **liability** n obbligo m, responsabilità f; (comm) passività f, deficit m invar.

liaison [li'eizon] n legame m; (sexual) relazione amorosa f.

liar ['laiə] n bugiardo, -a m, f.

libel ['laibl] n diffamazione f, calunnia f. v diffamare, calunniare. **libellous** adj diffamatorio, calunnioso.

liberal ['libərəl] adj liberale, generoso. n liberale m, f. **liberalism** n liberalismo m.

liberate ['libəreit] v liberare, mettere in libertà. **liberation** n liberazione f.

liberty ['libəti] n libertà f.

Libra ['librə] n Libra f.

library ['laibrəri] n biblioteca f. **librarian** n bibliotecario, -a m, f.

libretto [li'bretou] n libretto m.

lice [lais] V **louse**.

licence ['laisəns] n licenza f, permesso m; (driving) patente (di guida) f; (arms) porto d'armi m. **license** v autorizzare. **licensee** n gestore autorizzato m, concessionario m.

lichen ['laikən] n lichene m.

lick [lik] v leccare. n leccata f.

lid [lid] n coperchio m.

***lie**[1] [lai] v giacere, stare sdraiato. **lie down** coricarsi, sdraiarsi. **lie in** (stay in bed) restare a letto; (consist of) consistere di. **lie with** spettare a.

lie[2] [lai] n (untruth) bugia f, menzogna f. v mentire, dire una bugia.

lieu [luː] n **in lieu of** invece di.

lieutenant [ləf'tenənt] n tenente m.

life [laif] n vita f. **lifeless** adj esanime.

lifebelt ['laifbelt] n salvagente m.

lifeboat ['laifbout] n scialuppa di salvataggio f.

life insurance n assicurazione sulla vita f.

life-jacket n cintura di salvataggio f.

lifeline ['laiflain] n linea di communicazione vitale f.

lifelong ['laifloŋ] adj di tutta la vita.

lifetime ['laiftaim] n vita f, durata della vita f.

lift [lift] n ascensore m; (coll: ride) autostop m. v sollevare, alzare.

***light**[1] [lait] n luce f, lume m; illuminazione f. **switch on/off the light** accendere/spegnere la luce. adj chiaro. **light bulb** ampolla f. **lighthouse** n faro m. **light-year** n anno luce m. v accendere. **lighten** v rischiarare, illuminare. **lighter** n (for cigarette) accendino m. **lighting** n illuminazione f.

light[2] [lait] adj leggero. **light-headed** adj

frivolo; (giddy) preso da vertigini. **light-hearted** adj gaio. **lighten** v alleggerire, alleviare. **lightness** n leggerezza f.

***light**[3] [lait] v **light upon** imbattersi in.

lightning ['laitniŋ] n fulmine m, lampo m. **lightning conductor** n parafulmine m.

like[1] [laik] adj simile, uguale. prep come. **be** or **look like** rassomigliare a. **liken** v paragonare. **likeness** n somiglianza f; (portrait) ritratto m. **likewise** adv parimenti, altrettanto.

like[2] [laik] v gradire; (want) volere. **I like ... mi piace ... . likeable** adj simpatico. **liking** n simpatia f, gusto m. **have a liking for** trovar simpatico or gradevole.

likely ['laikli] adj probabile, verosimile. adv probabilmente. **likelihood** n probabilità f.

lilac ['lailək] nm, adj lilla invar.

lily ['lili] n giglio m. **lily-of-the-valley** n mughetto m.

limb [lim] n arto m, membro m (pl -a f).

limbo ['limbou] n limbo m.

lime[1] [laim] n calce f. **limestone** n calcare m.

lime[2] [laim] n (fruit) limetta f; (linden) tiglio m.

limelight ['laimlait] n luci della ribalta f pl. **be in the limelight** essere alla ribalta.

limit ['limit] n limite m, ambito m. v limitare. **limitation** n limitazione f. **limitless** adj illimitato.

limousine ['liməziin] n berlina f, limousine f invar.

limp[1] [limp] v zoppicare. n zoppicamento m.

limp[2] [limp] adj floscio; (weak) debole.

limpet ['limpit] n patella f.

line [lain] n linea f; (row) fila f; (string) corda f; (wrinkle) ruga f; (of letters) riga f. v rigare; (clothes) foderare; (border) fiancheggiare. **line up** allineare. **linear** adj lineare.

linen ['linin] n lino m; (sheets, etc.) biancheria f. adj di lino.

liner ['lainə] n (naut) transatlantico m; (aero) aereo di linea m.

linger ['liŋgə] v indugiare, soffermarsi. **lingering** adj protratto.

lingerie ['læʒəriː] n biancheria per signora f.

linguist ['liŋgwist] n linguista m, f; poliglotta m, f. **linguistic** adj linguistico. **linguistics** n linguistica f.

lining ['lainiŋ] n (clothes) fodera f; rivestimento interno m.

link [liŋk] n (of chain) anello m; (bond) legame m; (mech) collegamento m. v collegare, congiungere.

linoleum [li'nouliəm] n linoleum m invar.

linseed ['lin,siid] n semi di lino m pl. **linseed oil** olio di semi di lino m.

lint [lint] n filaccia (di lino) f.

lion ['laiən] n leone m. **lioness** n leonessa f.

lip [lip] n labbro m (pl -a f). **lip-read** v capire dal movimento delle labbra. **lipstick** n rossetto m.

liqueur [li'kjuə] n liquore m.

liquid ['likwid] nm, adj liquido. **liquidate** v liquidare; eliminare. **liquidation** n liquidazione f.

liquor ['likə] n bevanda alcoolica f.

liquorice ['likəris] n liquirizia f.

lisp [lisp] v essere o parlar bleso. n blesità f.

list[1] [list] n lista f, elenco m. v elencare, registrare.

list[2] [list] v (naut) sbandare. n sbandamento m.

listen ['lisn] v ascoltare; (heed) badare. **listener** n ascoltatore, -trice m, f.

listless ['listlis] adj languido, svogliato.

lit [lit] V **light**.

litany ['litəni] n litania f.

literal ['litərəl] adj letterale. **literally** adv alla lettera, letteralmente.

literary ['litərəri] adj (writing) letterario; (people) letterato.

literate ['litərət] adj che sa leggere e scrivere. **literacy** n il saper leggere e scrivere m.

literature ['litrətʃə] n letteratura f.

litigation [liti'geiʃən] n lite f, causa f. **litigate** v essere in causa.

litre ['liitə] n litro m.

litter ['litə] n rifiuti m pl, immondizia f; (zool) figliata f; (bed, etc.) lettiga f. v sparpagliare, lasciare in disordine.

little ['litl] adj piccolo, piccino; (not much) un po' di, poco; (short) breve. nm, adv poco. **little by little** a poco a poco.

liturgy ['litədʒi] n liturgia f.

live[1] [liv] v vivere; (reside) abitare, stare. **live by** or **on** vivere di. **live down** v dimenticare. **live up to** mettere in pratica, giustificare.

live[2] [laiv] adj vivo; (broadcast) dal vivo, in ripresa diretta; (coal, etc.) ardente; (wire) sotto tensione.

livelihood ['laivlihud] n vita f.

lively ['laivli] adj vivace, animato. **liveliness** n vivacità f.

liven ['laivn] v **liven up** animare.

liver ['livə] n fegato m.

livestock ['laivstok] n bestiame m.

livid ['livid] adj livido.

living ['liviŋ] adj vivente, vivo. n vita f. **living room** stanza di soggiorno f.

lizard ['lizəd] n lucertola f.

load [loud] n carico (pl -chi) m; (weight) peso m; (quantity carried) portata f; (elec) carica f. v caricare. **loaded** adj caricato, carico; (question) insidioso; (slang) ricco.

loaf[1] [louf] n pane m.

loaf[2] [louf] v oziare, girellare, stare con le mani in mano. **loafer** n bighellone, -a m, f; fannullone, -a m, f.

loan [loun] n prestito m. v prestare, dare in prestito.

loathe [louð] v aborrire, detestare. **loathing** n disgusto m. **loathsome** adj disgustoso.

lob [lob] (sport) n pallonetto m. v fare un pallonetto.

lobby ['lobi] n atrio m, anticamera f; (theatre) ridotto m. v influenzare con manovre di anticamera.

lobe [loub] n (anat) lobo m.

lobster ['lobstə] n aragosta f.

local ['loukəl] adj locale, del luogo. **locality** n località f. **localize** v circoscrivere, delimitare.

locate [lə'keit] v individuare; determinare la posizione di; situare. **location** n posizione f, sito m; (cinema) set m invar.

lock[1] [lok] n serratura f; (canal) conca f. **locksmith** n magnano m. **lock, stock, and barrel** barca e barattini. **under lock and key** sotto chiave. v serrare, chiudere a chiave; (mech) bloccare. **lock away** mettere al sicuro. **lock in** rinchiudere. **lock out** chiudere fuori; (workers) fare una serrata. **lock up** chiudere a chiave, mettere sotto chiave.

lock[2] [lok] n (of hair) ciocca f, ricciolo m.

locker ['lokə] n armadietto m.

locket ['lokit] n medaglione m.

locomotive [,loukə'moutiv] n locomotiva f.

locust ['loukəst] n cavalletta f.

lodge [lodʒ] n capanna f; (porter's) portineria f. v alloggiare; (put in place, deposit) deporre, collocare; (report) presentare. **lodge a complaint** sporgere querela. **lodger** n pensionante m, f. **lodging** n alloggio m.

loft [loft] n solaio m, soffitta f. **lofty** adj alto; (style) nobile.

log [log] n ceppo m, tronco m. **logbook** n registro m; (naut) giornale di bordo m; (mot) libretto di circolazione m. v registrare.

logarithm ['logəriðəm] n logaritmo m.

loggerheads ['logəhedz] n **be at loggerheads** prendersi per i capelli, essere ai ferri corti.

logic ['lodʒik] n logica f. **logical** adj logico.

loin [loin] n (cookery) lombata f. **gird up one's loins** apprestarsi.

loiter ['loitə] v bighellonare, passare oziando.

lollipop ['lolipop] n lecca lecca m invar.

London ['landən] n Londra f.

lonely ['lounli] adj solitario, solo. **loneliness** n solitudine f.

long[1] [loŋ] adj lungo. adv a lungo. **as long as** finquanto. **long-distance** adj a lunga distanza; (phone) interurbano. **long-playing record** disco microsolco m. **long-range** adj (distance) a lunga portata; (time) a lunga scadenza. **long-sighted** adj presbite; (having foresight) previdente. **long-standing** adj di vecchia data. **longwave** adj (radio) a onde lunghe. **longwinded** adj prolisso.

long[2] [loŋ] v bramare, aver gran desiderio (di). **longing** n brama f, desiderio ardente m.

longevity [lon'dʒevəti] n longevità f.

longitude ['londʒitjuud] n longitudine f.

loo [luu] n (coll) gabinetto m.

look [luk] n sguardo m, occhiata f; (appearance) aspetto m; espressione f. v guardare; (appear, seem) sembrare, parere. **look after** (care for) occuparsi di, badare a. **look at** guardare, considerare. **look down on** guardare con disprezzo. **look for** cercare. **look forward to** aspettare con impazienza. **look out** guardar fuori, affacciarsi; (be on guard) stare attento. **look over** ripassare, riesaminare.

loom[1] [luum] v apparire (indistintamente), intravedere; (be imminent) incombere.

loom[2] [luum] n telaio m.

loop [luup] n cappio m, laccio m, anello m. v fare un cappio o laccio, allacciare.

loophole ['luuphoul] n scappatoia f.

loose [luus] adj sciolto, libero; (tooth) caduco. **come** or **get loose** allentarsi. **let loose** liberare. **loose-fitting** adj ampio. **loose-leaf** adj a fogli staccati. **loosely** adv scioltamente; in senso lato. **loosen** v sciogliere, allentare.

loot [luut] n bottino m. v far man bassa, saccheggiare. **looting** n saccheggio m.

lop [lop] v potare. **lop off** mozzare.

lopsided [,lop'saidid] adj sbilenco, asimmetrico.

lord [lord] n signore m; (English title) lord m invar. **lordship** n signoria f.

lorry ['lori] n autocarro m, camion m invar. **lorry-driver** n camionista m.

lose [luz] v perdere, smarrire; (clock) ritardare. **lose interest** non interessarsi più. **lose one's temper** arrabbiarsi.

loss [los] n perdita f, danno m. **be at a loss** non sapere cosa fare, essere disorientato.

lost [lost] V lose. adj perso, smarrito. **lost cause** causa persa f. **lost property** oggetti smarriti m pl.

lot [lot] n (destiny) sorte f; (of land) lotto m; (method of decision) sorteggio m; (comm) partita f; (coll: large amount) grande quantità f. **a lot of** molto. **lots of** tanti. **the whole lot** tutto quanto. **what a lot of** quanto.

lotion ['louʃən] n lozione f.

lottery ['lotəri] n lotteria f.

lotus ['loutəs] n loto m.

loud [laud] adj forte, alto; (gaudy) vistoso. adv forte. **loud-mouthed** adj sguaiato. **loudspeaker** n altoparlante m. **loudness** n forza f, altezza di voce f.

lounge [laundʒ] n salotto m; sala di ritrovo f. v oziare, dondolarsi.

louse [laus] n, pl **lice** pidocchio m. **lousy** adj pidocchioso; (slang: bad) schifoso.

love [lʌv] n amore m; (tennis) zero m. **fall in love (with)** innamorarsi (di). **love affair** relazione amorosa f. **make love (to)** fare all'amore (con). **with love** (in letter) affettuosamente. v amare, voler bene a. **lovable** adj amabile, simpatico. **lovely** adj bello, grazioso, incantevole. **lover** n amante m, f; (enthusiast) appassionato, -a m, f. **loving** adj affettuoso.

low [lou] adj basso; (coll) depresso; volgare. adv basso, in basso. **lowbrow** adj incolto, popolare. **low-lying** adj situato in pianura. **low-necked** adj scollato. **lowly** adj umile, dimesso.

lower ['louə] adj più basso, inferiore. v abbassare, ridurre; (flag) ammainare; degradare.

loyal ['loiəl] adj fedele, devoto, leale. **loyalty** n fedeltà f, devozione f, lealtà f.

lozenge ['lozindʒ] n pastiglia f, pasticca f.

lubricate ['lubrikeit] v lubrificare. **lubricant** nm, adj lubrificante. **lubrication** n lubrificazione f.

lucid ['lusid] adj (easily understood) chiaro; (clear) limpido; (bright) lucido.

luck [lʌk] n fortuna f; (chance) sorte f. **bad luck** sfortuna f. **be in/out of luck** essere fortunato/sfortunato. **good luck** buona fortuna f. **lucky** adj fortunato.

lucrative ['lukrətiv] adj lucroso, redditizio.

ludicrous ['ludikrəs] adj ridicolo, irrisorio.

lug [lʌg] v tirare, trascinare.

luggage ['lʌgidʒ] n bagaglio m. **hand luggage** bagaglio a mano m. **left luggage** deposito bagagli m. **luggage rack** n (rail) rete portabagagli f.

lukewarm ['lukwoːm] adj tiepido.

lull [lʌl] n momento di calma m; (truce) tregua f. v (put to sleep) far addormentare; calmare.

lumbago [lʌm'beigou] n lombaggine f.

lumber¹ ['lʌmbə] n legname m; (useless articles) cianfrusaglie f pl. v (encumber) ingombrare, accatastare. **lumberjack** n boscaiolo m.

lumber² ['lʌmbə] v (move clumsily) muoversi pesantemente o goffamente.

luminous ['luminəs] adj luminoso.

lump [lʌmp] n massa f; (swelling) gonfiore m. **lump sum** somma globale f. **lump together** mettere insieme. **lumpy** adj grumoso.

lunacy ['lunəsi] n pazzia f.

lunar ['lunə] adj lunare.

lunatic ['lunətik] n, adj pazzo, -a, matto, -a. **lunatic asylum** n manicomio m.

lunch [lʌntʃ] n colazione f, pranzo m. v far colazione, pranzare.

lung [lʌŋ] n polmone m.

lunge [lʌndʒ] v scagliarsi. n rapido movimento in avanti m.

lurch¹ [ləːtʃ] v barcollare, sbandare. n barcollamento m, sbandamento m.

lurch² [ləːtʃ] n **leave in the lurch** piantare in asso.

lure [luə] n (bait) esca f; (fascination) fascino m. v adescare, attirare, affascinare.

lurid ['luərid] adj raccapricciante.

lurk [ləːk] v (be in hiding) nascondersi; (lie in wait) stare in agguato.

luscious ['lʌʃəs] adj succulento.

lush [lʌʃ] adj lussureggiante.

lust [lʌst] n brama f; (sexual) libidine f; concupiscenza f. v **lust after** aver brama or sete di.

lustre ['lʌstə] n splendore m.

lute [luːt] n liuto m.

Luxembourg ['lʌksəmˌbəːg] n Lussemburgo m.

luxury ['lʌkʃəri] n lusso m. **luxuriant** adj lussureggiante, rigoglioso. **luxurious** adj lussuoso, di lusso.

lynch [lintʃ] v linciare.

lynx [liŋks] n lince f.

lyre [laiə] n lira f.

lyrical ['lirikəl] adj lirico.

lyrics ['liriks] pl n parole (di una canzone) f pl.

M

mac [mak] n (coll) impermeabile m.

macabre [mə'kaːbr] adj macabro.

macaroni [makə'rouni] n maccheroni m pl.

mace¹ [meis] n (club) mazza f.

mace² [meis] n (spice) macis f invar.

machine [mə'ʃiːn] n macchina f. **machine-gun** n mitragliatrice f. **machine tool** macchina utensile f. v lavorare a macchina. **machinery** n macchinario m; meccanismo m; (system) organizzazione f. **machinist** n macchinista m, f.

mackerel ['makrəl] n sgombro m.

mackintosh ['makinˌtoʃ] n impermeabile m.

mad [mad] adj matto, pazzo; furioso. **drive mad** far impazzire. **go mad** impazzire. **madden** v far impazzire. **madness** n pazzia f.

madam ['madəm] n signora f.

made [meid] V **make**.

magazine [magə'ziːn] n (publication) rivista f, periodico m; (phot) magazzino m; (rifle) caricatore m.

maggot ['magət] n larva f.

magic ['madʒik] adj magico. n magia f, incanto m. **magician** n mago m, stregone m; (conjurer) illusionista m.

magistrate ['mædʒistreit] n magistrato m, pretore m. **magistrature** n magistratura f, pretura f.

magnanimous [mag'naniməs] adj magnanimo. **magnanimity** n magnanimità f.

magnate ['magneit] n magnate m.

magnet ['magnət] n magnete m, calamita f. **magnetic** adj magnetico. **magnetism** n magnetismo m. **magnetize** v magnetizzare.

magnificent [mag'nifisnt] adj magnifico, splendido. **magnificence** n magnificenza f.

magnify ['magnifai] v magnificare, ingrandire. **magnifying glass** lente d'ingrandimento f. **magnification** n ingrandimento m.

magnitude ['magnitjud] n grandezza f.

magnolia [mag'noulia] n magnolia f.

magpie ['magpai] n gazza f.

mahogany [mə'hogəni] n mogano m.

maid [meid] n domestica f, donna di servizio f. **old maid** vecchia zitella f.

maiden ['meidən] n fanciulla f. adj primo; (journey) inaugurale. **maiden lady** signorina f. **maiden name** nome da ragazza m.

mail[1] [meil] n posta f. **mail order** vendita per catalogo f. v imbucare, mandare per posta.

mail[2] [meil] n (armour) maglia di ferro f. **mailed fist** pugno di ferro m.

maim [meim] v mutilare, storpiare.

main [mein] adj principale, essenziale. **mainland** n terra ferma f. **mainspring** (of watch) molla principale f; (impelling cause) movente principale m. **mainstay** n (chief support) sostegno m, braccio destro m. **mainstream** n tendenza dominante f. n (gas, water, etc.) conduttura principale f. **in the main** nel complesso, in genere. **mainly** adv soprattutto; in genere.

maintain [mein'tein] v mantenere; (support) sostenere; (assert) affermare. **maintenance** n mantenimento m; (machinery, etc.) manutenzione f; (alimony) alimenti m pl.

maisonette [meizə'net] n casetta f.

maize [meiz] n mais m invar, granturco m invar.

majesty ['mædʒəsti] n maestà f. **majestic** adj maestoso.

major ['meidʒə] nm, adj maggiore. **majority** n maggioranza f; (age) maggiore età f.

make [meik] v fare; produrre. **make believe** dare da intendere, far finta di. **make-believe** n finzione f, illusione f. **make do** arrangiarsi. **make out** preparare; decifrare; (understand) capire. **make up** costituire, costruire; inventare; compensare; (cosmetics) truccare. **make-up** n trucco m, truccatura f; (composizione f; costituzione f. **maker** n creatore, -trice m, f; fabbricante m, f.

makeshift ['meikʃift] adj di fortuna, improvvisato. n espediente m.

maladjusted [malə'dʒʌstid] adj disadattato.

malaise [ma'leiz] n malessere m.

malaria [mə'leəriə] n malaria f.

male [meil] n maschio m. adj maschio, maschile.

malevolent [mə'levələnt] adj malevolo. **malevolence** n malevolenza f.

malfunction [mal'fʌŋkʃən] n funzionamento difettoso m.

malice ['malis] n malizia f, malignità f. **with malice aforethought** con premeditazione maliziosa. **malicious** adj malizioso, maligno.

malignant [mə'lignənt] adj maligno. **malignancy** n malignità f.

malinger [mə'liŋgə] v darsi malato, scansar fatiche. **malingerer** n scansafatiche m, f invar.

mallet ['malit] n maglio m, martello (di legno) m. **malleable** adj malleabile.

malnutrition [malnju'triʃən] n malnutrizione f.

malt [molt] n malto m.

Malta ['moltə] n Malta f. **Maltese** n(m+f), adj maltese.

maltreat [mal'trit] v maltrattare. **maltreatment** n maltrattamento m.

mammal ['maməl] n mammifero m.

mammoth ['maməθ] n mammut m. adj enorme, mastodontico.

man [man] n, pl **men** uomo (pl uomini) m. v equipaggiare, presidiare. **manly** adj virile.

manage ['manidʒ] v dirigere, amministrare; (cope) farcela. **manage to** riuscire a, fare in modo da. **manage without** fare a meno di. **manageable** adj (people) trattabile, docile; (things) maneggevole. **management** n amministrazione f, direzione f. **manager** n direttore m. **manageress** n direttrice f. **managing director** consigliere delegato m.

mandarin ['mandərin] n mandarino m.
mandate ['mandeit] n mandato m. **mandatory** adj mandatario.
mandolin ['mandəlin] n mandolino m.
mane [mein] n criniera f.
mange [meindʒ] n rogna f. **mangy** adj rognoso.
mangle[1] ['mangl] v (disfigure) deformare, mutilare.
mangle[2] ['mangl] n (wringer) mangano m. v manganare.
manhandle [man'handl] v manovrare a mano; (treat harshly) malmenare.
manhole ['manhoul] n botola f. **manhole cover** tombino m.
mania ['meiniə] n mania f. **maniac** n maniaco, -a m, f. **maniacal** adj maniaco.
manicure ['manikjuə] n manicure f invar.
manifest ['manifest] adj evidente, palese. v manifestare, dimostrare. n (comm) manifesto (di bordo) m, nota di carico f.
manifesto [mani'festou] n manifesto m, proclama m.
manifold ['manifould] adj molteplice, vario. n (tech) collettore m.
manipulate [mə'nipjuleit] v maneggiare. **manipulation** n maneggio m. **manipulative** adj manipolatore.
mankind [man'kaind] n umanità f, genere umano m.
man-made [,man'meid] adj artificiale, sintetico.
manner ['manə] n modo m, maniera f; stile m; sorta f, specie f. **manners** pl n maniere f pl, educazione f sing. **mannerism** n affettazione f, manierismo m.
manoeuvre [mə'nuːvə] n manovra f. v manovrare, maneggiare.
manor ['manə] n castello m, maniero m.
manpower ['man,pauə] n manodopera f; forze di lavoro f pl; capacità lavorativa f.
mansion ['manʃən] n palazzo m, casa signorile f.
mantelpiece ['mantlpiːs] n mensola (del caminetto) f.
manual ['manjuəl] nm, adj manuale. **manually** adv a mano.
manufacture [manju'faktʃə] n manifattura f, fabbricazione f, confezione f. v fabbricare. **manufacturer** n fabbricante m.
manure [mə'njuə] n concime f, fertilizzante m.
manuscript ['manjuskript] nm, adj manoscritto.

many ['meni] adj, pron molti, -e. **as many** altrettanti, -e. **how many** quanti, -e. **so many** tanti, -e. **too many** troppi, -e.
map [map] n mappa f, carta geografica f; (of town) pianta f. **off the map** remoto. v **map out** tracciare.
maple ['meipl] n acero m.
mar [maː] v guastare, rovinare.
marathon ['marəθən] n maratona f.
marble ['maːbl] n marmo m; (glass ball) bilia f. adj di marmo, marmoreo.
march [maːtʃ] n marcia f. v marciare. **march-past** n sfilata f.
March [maːtʃ] n marzo m.
marchioness [maːʃə'nes] n marchesa f.
mare [meə] n cavalla f.
margarine [maːdʒə'riːn] n margarina f.
margin ['maːdʒin] n margine m. **marginal** adj marginale.
marguerite [maːgə'riːt] n margherita f.
marigold ['marigould] n calendola f.
marijuana [mari'wɑːnə] n marijuana f invar, canapa indiana f.
marina [mə'riːnə] n porticciuolo m.
marinade [mari'neid] n marinata f. v marinare.
marine [mə'riːn] adj marino, marittimo. n (fleet) marina f; (soldier) soldato di marina m.
marital ['maritl] adj coniugale.
maritime ['maritaim] adj marittimo.
marjoram ['maːdʒərəm] n maggiorana f.
mark[1] [maːk] n segno m; (brand) marchio m; (rating) voto m; (trace) traccia f. **marksman** n tiratore scelto m. v segnare; notare; osservare; (correct, grade) dare i voti a. **mark off** delimitare. **mark out** tracciare. **marking** n marchio m. **markings** pl n segni caratteristici m pl.
mark[2] [maːk] n (money) marco m.
market ['maːkit] n mercato m. **market garden** orto m. **market research** ricerca di mercato f. v mettere in vendita. **marketing** n marketing m invar.
marmalade ['maːməleid] n marmellata f.
maroon[1] [mə'ruːn] nm, adj (colour) marrone rossastro.
maroon[2] [mə'ruːn] v abbandonare.
marquee [maː'kiː] n grande tenda f; padiglione m.
marquess ['maːkwis] n marchese m.
marriage ['maridʒ] n matrimonio m. **marriage licence** dispensa di matrimonio f.

marrow ['marou] n zucca f.

marry ['mari] v sposare. **married** adj sposato. **get married** sposarsi.

Mars [maiz] n Marte m. **Martian** n, adj marziano, -a.

marsh [maif] n palude f. **marshy** adj paludoso.

marshal ['maifəl] v disporre; (mil) schierare. n maresciallo m.

martial ['maifəl] adj marziale.

martin ['martin] n balestruccio m.

martyr ['maitə] n martire m, f. v martirizzare. **martyrdom** n martirio m.

marvel ['marvəl] n meraviglia f. v meravigliarsi. **marvel at** stupirsi di, ammirare.

marvellous ['marvələs] adj meraviglioso.

marzipan [mazzi'pan] n marzapane m.

mascara [ma'skairə] n mascara m invar.

mascot ['maskət] n portafortuna m invar, mascotte f.

masculine ['maskjulin] adj maschile, virile. **masculinity** n mascolinità f, virilità f.

mash [maf] v ridurre in polpa, schiacciare; (cookery) fare un purè di. n (cookery) passata f, purè m.

mask [maisk] n maschera f. v mascherare; (hide) nascondere.

masochist ['masəkist] n masochista m, f. adj masochistico. **masochism** n masochismo m.

mason ['meisn] n muratore m; (freemason) massone m. **masonic** adj massonico. **masonry** n muratura f.

masquerade [maskə'reid] n mascherata f. v **masquerade as** mascherarsi da, farsi passare per.

mass[1] [mas] n massa f, (bulk) mole f; (great number) gran numero m; (large amount) grande quantità f. **masses** pl n (coll) mucchio m sing. **mass meeting** adunata popolare f. **mass-produced** adj prodotto in serie. **mass-production** n produzione in serie or massa f.

mass[2] [mas] n (rel) messa f.

massacre ['masəkə] n massacro m, strage f. v massacrare, far strage di.

massage ['masaiʒ] n massaggio m. v massaggiare. **masseur** n massaggiatore m. **masseuse** n massaggiatrice f.

massive ['masiv] adj massiccio, solido.

mast [maist] n albero m.

mastectomy [ma'stektəmi] n mastectomia f.

master ['maistə] n padrone m, signore m; (of ship) capitano m; (school) professore m. **masterpiece** n capolavoro m. v dominare, impadronirsi di; (learn) conoscere a perfezione. **masterly** adj magistrale.

masturbate ['mastəbeit] v masturbarsi. **masturbation** n masturbazione f.

mat [mat] n (covering) tappeto m; (for floor) stuoia f; (at door) zerbino m; (on table) sottopiatto m.

match[1] [matf] n (light) fiammifero m. **matchbox** n scatola da fiammiferi f.

match[2] [matf] v (clothes, colours, etc.) andare bene insieme; corrispondere; (oppose) opporre; (equal) uguagliare. n (equal) uguale m, f, pari m, f; (contest, partner) partita f. **matchmaker** n sensale di matrimoni. **meet one's match** trovare un degno avversario.

mate [meit] n compagno, -a m, f; (help) aiuto m, assistente m, f; (naut) secondo m.

material [mə'tiəriəl] n (substance) sostanza f, materia f; materiale m; (fabric) stoffa f. adj materiale, essenziale. **materialize** v realizzarsi, prender corpo.

maternal [mə'təinl] adj materno. **maternity** n maternità f.

mathematics [maθə'matiks] n matematica f. **mathematical** adj matematico. **mathematician** n matematico, -a m, f.

matinee ['matinei] n rappresentazione diurna f.

matins ['matinz] n mattutino m.

matriarch ['meitriaik] n matrona f. **matriarchal** adj matriarcale.

matrimony ['matriməni] n matrimonio m. **matrimonial** adj matrimoniale.

matrix ['meitriks] n matrice f.

matron ['meitrən] n (hospital) capoinfermiera f; (institution) direttrice f.

matt [mat] adj matto, opaco.

matter ['matə] v importare. n materia f; (thing, affair) cosa f, affare m; (of book, etc.) argomento m, questione f. **as a matter of fact** in realtà, fatto sta che. **matter-of-fact** adj pratico. **what's the matter?** cosa c'è?

mattress ['matris] n materasso m.

mature [mə'tjuə] v maturare; (become due) scadere. **maturity** n maturità f.

maudlin ['moidlin] adj lamentevole, querulo.

maul [mɔːl] v dilaniare.

mausoleum [mɔːsə'liəm] n mausoleo m.

mauve [mouv] adj (color) malva invar.

maxim ['maksim] n massima f.

maximum ['maksiməm] n, adj massimo.

*may [mei] v potere. **maybe** può darsi, forse.

May [mei] n maggio m.

mayonnaise [ˌmeiə'neiz] n maionese f.

mayor [meə] n sindaco m.

maze [meiz] n labirinto m.

me [miː] pron mi; (after prep) me. **it's me** sono io.

meadow ['medou] n prato m.

meagre ['miːgə] adj scarso.

meal[1] [miːl] n (food) pasto m.

meal[2] [miːl] n (grain) farina f.

*mean[1] [miːn] v significare, voler dire; intendere; destinare.

mean[2] [miːn] adj gretto; (miserly) avaro; (shabby) meschino; (low) basso. **meanness** n grettezza f; avarizia f.

mean[3] [miːn] n (average) media f. adj medio.

meander [mi'andə] v divagare.

meaning ['miːniŋ] n significato m, senso m. adj significativo.

means [miːnz] n mezzi m pl. **by means of** per mezzo di. **by no means** niente affatto. **by some means or other** in qualche modo.

meant [ment] V mean[1].

meanwhile ['miːnwail] adv also **in the meantime** nel frattempo, intanto.

measles ['miːzlz] n morbillo m. **German measles** n rosolia f, rubeola f. **measly** adj (wretched) miserabile.

measure ['meʒə] n misura f; (action) provvedimento m. **made to measure** fatto su misura. v misurare; (estimate) valutare. **measurement** n misura f. **measurements** pl n dimensioni f pl.

meat [miːt] n carne f. **meaty** adj sostanzioso.

mechanic [mi'kanik] n meccanico m. **mechanical** adj meccanico. **mechanism** n meccanismo m. **mechanized** adj meccanizzato.

medal ['medl] n medaglia f.

meddle ['medl] v immischiarsi, intromettersi. **meddler** n ficcanaso m invar.

media ['miːdiə] pl n mezzi di comunicazione m pl.

median ['miːdiən] adj mediano. n mediana f.

mediate ['miːdieit] v fare da mediatore or intermediario. **mediation** n mediazione f. **mediator** n mediatore, -trice m, f.

medical ['medikəl] adj medico. n (examination) esame medico m. **medication** n medicazione f. **medicinal** adj medicinale. **medicine** n (science) medicina f; (substance) medicinale m, farmaco m.

medieval [medi'iːvəl] adj medievale.

mediocre [miːdi'oukə] adj mediocre. **mediocrity** n mediocrità f.

meditate ['mediteit] v meditare. **meditation** n meditazione f.

Mediterranean [ˌmeditə'reiniən] n Mediterraneo m. adj mediterraneo.

medium ['miːdiəm] n (spiritualist) medium m, f invar; (biology) brodo (di coltura) m; (agency) mezzo m. **happy medium** giusto mezzo m. adj medio.

medley ['medli] n miscuglio m, pasticcio m.

meek [miːk] adj mansueto, mite. **meekness** n mansuetudine f.

*meet [miːt] v incontrare; (by arrangement) trovare; (gather) riunirsi. **meeting** n incontro m; riunione f.

megaphone ['megəfoun] n megafono m.

melancholy ['melənkəli] n malinconia f. adj also **melancholic** malinconico.

mellow ['melou] adj maturo; (wine) amabile; (soft) morbido. v maturare; (person) intenerirsi.

melodrama ['melədrɑːmə] n melodramma m. **melodramatic** adj melodrammatico.

melody ['melədi] n melodia f. **melodious** adj melodioso.

melon ['melən] n melone m.

melt [melt] v fondere, sciogliere; (feeling) intenerire. **melt down** fondere. **melting point** punto di fusione m. **melting pot** crogiuolo m.

member ['membə] n membro m; (of society, club, etc.) socio, -a m, f; (of parliament) deputato, -a m, f. **membership** n (number) numero dei soci m; (condition) l'essere socio m.

membrane ['membrein] n membrana f.

memento [mə'mentou] n ricordo m.

memo ['memou] n appunto m.

memoirs ['memwɑːz] pl n memorie f pl.

memorandum [memə'randəm] n appunto m, promemoria m invar; (document) memorandum m invar.

memorial [mi'motriəl] *n* monumento *m*. *adj* commemorativo.

memory ['meməri] *n* (*faculty*) memoria *f*; (*recollection*) ricordo *m*. **memorable** *adj* memorabile. **memorize** *v* imparare a memoria.

men [men] *V* **man**.

menace ['menis] *n* minaccia *f*. *v* minacciare. **menacing** *adj* minaccioso.

menagerie [mi'nadʒəri] *n* serraglio *m*.

mend [mend] *v* riparare, aggiustare; (*get better*) migliorare. **mend one's ways** ravvedersi. *n* **be on the mend** stare rimettendosi. **mending** *n* rammendo *m*.

menial ['miniəl] *adj* servile, umile.

meningitis [,menin'dʒaitis] *n* meningite *f*.

menopause ['menəpoːz] *n* menopausa *f*.

menstrual ['menstruəl] *adj* mestruale. **menstruate** *v* mestruare. **menstruation** *n* mestruazione *f*.

mental [mentl] *adj* mentale; (*home, hospital*) psichiatrico. **mentality** *n* mentalità *f*.

menthol ['menθol] *n* mentolo *m*.

mention ['menʃən] *v* accennare a, parlare di, citare. **don't mention it!** prego! *n* menzione *f*, cenno *m*; citazione *f*.

menu ['menjuː] *n* menu *m invar*, lista dei cibi *f*.

mercantile ['məːkəntail] *adj* mercantile.

mercenary ['məːsinəri] *nm*, *adj* mercenario.

merchandise ['məːtʃəndaiz] *n* merce *f*.

merchant ['məːtʃənt] *n* commerciante *m*, *f*. **merchant navy** marina mercantile *f*.

mercury ['məːkjuri] *n* mercurio *m*.

mercy ['məːsi] *n* pietà *f*, carità *f*. **at the mercy of** alla mercè di. **merciful** *adj* pietoso, caritatevole.

mere [miə] *adj* puro, mero.

merge [məːdʒ] *v* fondere, amalgamare. **merger** *n* fusione *f*.

meridian [mə'ridiən] *n* meridiano *m*.

meringue [mə'raŋ] *n* meringa *f*.

merit ['merit] *n* merito *m*, valore *m*. *v* meritare.

mermaid ['məːmeid] *n* sirena *f*.

merry ['meri] *adj* allegro; (*coll*) brillo. **merry-go-round** *n* carosello *m*. **merry-making** *n* festa *f*.

mesh [meʃ] *n* maglia *f*; (*net*) rete *f*. **in mesh** ingranato.

mesmerize ['mezməraiz] *v* ipnotizzare; affascinare.

mess [mes] *n* confusione *f*, pasticcio *m*; (*eating place*) mensa *f*. **be in a mess** (*of things*) essere in disordine; (*of people*) trovarsi nei guai. **make a mess of** rovinare. *v* **mess about** perdersi in cose inutili; (*inconvenience*) disturbare. **mess up** rovinare. **messy** *adj* confuso, disordinato; (*dirty*) sporco.

message ['mesidʒ] *n* messaggio *m*. **messenger** *n* messaggero *m*; (*errand boy*) fattorino *m*.

met [met] *V* **meet**.

metabolism [mi'tabolizm] *n* metabolismo *m*. **metabolic** *adj* metabolico.

metal ['metl] *n* metallo *m*. **metallic** *adj* metallico. **metallurgy** *n* metallurgia *f*.

metamorphosis [,metə'moːfəsis] *n* metamorfosi *f invar*.

metaphor ['metəfə] *n* metafora *f*. **metaphor(ic)al** *adj* metaforico.

metaphysics [,metə'fiziks] *n* metafisica *f*. **metaphysical** *adj* metafisico.

meteor ['miːtiə] *n* meteora *f*. **meteoric** *adj* meteorico; rapidissimo.

meteorology [,miːtiə'rolədʒi] *n* meteorologia *f*. **meteorological** *adj* meteorologico. **meteorologist** *n* meteorologo, -a *m*, *f*.

meter ['miːtə] *n* contatore *m*; (*parking*) parchimetro *m*. *v* misurare.

methane ['miːθein] *n* metano *m*.

method ['meθəd] *n* metodo *m*, modo *m*. **methodical** *adj* metodico, sistematico.

methylated spirits ['meθileitid] *n* alcool denaturato *m*.

meticulous [mi'tikjuləs] *adj* meticoloso.

metre ['miːtə] *n* metro *m*. **metric** *adj* metrico.

metronome ['metrənoum] *n* metronomo *m*.

metropolis [mə'tropəlis] *n* metropoli *f*. **metropolitan** *adj* metropolitano.

mettle ['metl] *n* **put someone on his mettle** mettere qualcuno alla prova.

mews [mjuːz] *n* vicolo *m*.

miaow [mi'au] *n* miagolare.

mice [mais] *V* **mouse**.

microbe ['maikroub] *n* microbo *m*.

microfilm ['maikrəfilm] *n* microfilm *m invar*.

microphone ['maikrəfoun] *n* microfono *m*.

microscope ['maikrəskoup] *n* microscopio *m*. **microscopic** *adj* microscopico. **microscopy** *n* microscopia *f*.

mid [mid] *adj* **in mid ... a metà ...**, in mezzo a ..., in pieno .... **midday** *n* mezzogiorno *m*. **midnight** *n* mezzanotte *f*. **mid-ocean** *n* alto mare *m*. **midsummer** *n* mezza estate *f*. **midway** *adv* a metà strada.

middle ['midl] *n* mezzo *m*, centro *m*. *adj* medio. **middle-aged** *adj* di mezza età. **Middle Ages** Medio Evo *m sing*. **middleclass** *adj* borghese. **middle man** *n* intermediario *m*.

midge [midʒ] *n* zanzara *f*.

midget ['midʒit] *n* nano *m*.

midst [midst] *n* mezzo *m*, centro *m*. **in the midst of** nel mezzo di, in mezzo a, fra.

midwife ['midwaif] *n* levatrice *f*. **midwifery** *n* ostetricia *f*.

might[1] [mait] *V* may.

might[2] [mait] *n* (*power*) forza *f*, potenza *f*. **mighty** ['maiti] *adj* forte, potente. *adv* (*coll*) estremamente.

migraine ['miːgrein] *n* emicrania *f*.

migrate [mai'greit] *v* migrare. **migrant** *n*, *adj* migratore, -trice. **migration** *n* migrazione *f*. **migratory** *adj* migratorio.

Milan [mi'lan] *n* Milano *f*. **Milanese** *n*(*m*+*f*), *adj* milanese.

mild [maild] *adj* mite. **mildness** *n* mitezza *f*.

mildew ['mildjuː] *n* muffa *f*. **mildewy** *adj* ammuffito.

mile [mail] *n* miglio *m* (*pl* -a *f*). **mileage** *n* distanza percorsa in miglia, chilometraggio *m*. **mileometer** *n* contachilometri *m invar*.

militant ['militənt] *n*(*m*+*f*), *adj* militante, attivista.

military ['militəri] *adj* militare. **militarism** *n* militarismo *m*. **militate** *v* militare. **militia** *n* milizia *f*.

milk [milk] *n* latte *m*. **milkman** *n* lattaio *m*. *v* mungere; (*exploit*) sfruttare.

mill [mil] *n* (*flour*) mulino *m*; (*textiles*) stabilimento *m*; (*tech*) fresa *f*; (*coffee*) macinino *m*. **millstone** *n* macina *f*; (*burden*) macigno *m*. *v* macinare; (*metal*) laminare; (*crowd*) circolare. **milling** *n* (*corn*) macinatura *f*; (*metal*) laminatura *f*; (*tech*) fresatura *f*; (*coins*) zigrinatura *f*.

millennium [mi'leniəm] *n* millennio *m*.

millet ['milit] *n* miglio *m*.

milligram ['miligram] *n* milligrammo *m*.

millilitre ['mili,liːtə] *n* millilitro *m*.

millimetre ['mili,miːtə] *n* millimetro *m*.

milliner ['milinə] *n* modista *f*.

million ['miljən] *n* milione *m*. **millionaire** *n* milionario, -a *m*, *f*. **millionth** *nm*, *adj* milionesimo.

mime [maim] *n* (*art*) mimica *f*; (*artist*) mimo, -a *m*, *f*. *v* mimare.

mimic ['mimik] *v* contraffare; (*ape*) scimmiottare. *n* imitatore, -trice *m*, *f*; contraffattore, -trice *m*, *f*. **mimicry** *n* mimica *f*; (*zool*) mimetismo *m*.

mimosa [mi'mouzə] *n* mimosa *f*.

minaret [minə'ret] *n* minareto *m*.

mince [mins] *v* tritare, tagliuzzare. **not mince one's words** parlare apertamente. *n* (*meat*) carne tritata *f*. **make mincemeat of** (*coll*) demolire. **mincer** *n* tritatutto *m invar*.

mind [maind] *n* mente *f*, intelletto *m*, spirito *m*; (*reason*) ragione *f*; (*opinion*) parere *m*. **bear in mind** tenere a mente. **make up one's mind** decidersi. **peace of mind** serenità *f*. **piece of one's mind** (*reprimand*) rimprovero *m*. **speak one's mind** parlar chiaro. **state of mind** stato d'animo *m*. *v* badare a, occuparsi di; (*watch out*) far attenzione. **do you mind if ... ?** ti dispiace se ... ? **never mind!** non importa! **mindful** *adj* attento. **mindless** *adj* (*heedless*) sbadato; (*senseless*) insensato.

mine[1] [main] *pron* il mio, la mia; (*pl*) i miei, le mie.

mine[2] [main] *n* miniera *f*; (*explosive*) mina *f*. *v* (*dig*) scavare; (*extract*) estrarre; (*mil*) minare. **mine-detector** *n* rilevatore di mine *m*. **minefield** *n* campo minato *m*. **minesweeper** *n* dragamine *m invar*. **miner** *n* minatore *m*.

mineral ['minərəl] *nm*, *adj* minerale.

mingle ['miŋgl] *v* mescolare, mischiarsi.

miniature ['miniʧə] *n* miniatura *f*. *adj* in miniatura.

minim ['minim] *n* (*music*) minima *f*.

minimum ['miniməm] *n* minimo *m*. **minimal** *adj* minimo. **minimize** *v* minimizzare.

mining ['mainiŋ] *n* estrazione *f*, scavo *m*; (*mil*) posa di mine *f*. *adj* minerario.

minister ['ministə] *n* (*pol*) ministro, -a *m*, *f*; (*rel*) sacerdote *m*; (*diplomat*) incaricato, -a *m*, *f*. *v* **minister to** soccorrere. **minister to the needs of** provvedere ai bisogni di. **ministerial** *adj* ministeriale. **ministry** *n* ministero *m*; (*clergy*) clero *m*.

mink [miŋk] *n* visone *m*.

minor ['mainə] *adj* minore, più piccolo, meno importante. *n* minorenne *m, f.*

minority *n* minoranza *f;* (*age*) minorità *f,* età minore *f.*

minstrel ['minstrəl] *n* menestrello *m,* cantante *m.*

mint[1] [mint] *n* (*bot*) menta *f.*

mint[2] [mint] *n* zecca *f.* **be in mint condition** essere nuovo di zecca. **have a mint of money** avere un mucchio di soldi. *v* coniare.

minuet [minju'et] *n* minuetto *m.*

minus ['mainəs] *prep* meno.

minute[1] ['minit] *n* minuto *m;* momento *m.* **minutes** *pl n* (*of meeting*) verbale *m sing. v* (*record*) prendere nota; (*enter in minutes*) mettere agli atti.

minute[2] [mai'njuːt] *adj* minuto *m;* (*detailed*) minuzioso.

minx [minks] *n* (*coll*) civetta *f.*

miracle ['mirəkl] *n* miracolo *m.* **miraculous** *adj* miracoloso.

mirage ['mirɑːʒ] *n* miraggio *m.*

mirror ['mirə] *n* specchio *m. v* riflettere, rispecchiare.

mirth [məːθ] *n* ilarità *f,* allegria *f.*

misadventure [misəd'ventʃə] *n* infortunio *m,* disavventura *f.*

misanthropist [miz'anθrəpist] *n* misantropo, -a *m, f.* **misanthropic** *adj* misantropico. **misanthropy** *n* misantropia *f.*

misapprehension [misapri'henʃən] *n* equivoco *m,* malinteso *m.* **misapprehend** *v* fraintendere.

misbehave [misbi'heiv] *v* comportarsi male. **misbehaviour** *n* cattiva condotta *f.*

miscalculate [mis'kalkjuleit] *v* calcolar male. **miscalculation** *n* calcolo errato *m.*

miscarriage [mis'karidʒ] *n* (*med*) aborto *m.* **miscarry** *v* abortire.

miscellaneous [misə'leiniəs] *adj* miscellaneo.

mischance [mis'tʃɑːns] *n* sventura *f.*

mischief ['mistʃif] *n* (*harm*) danno *m;* (*of child, etc.*) fastidi *m pl;* (*teasing*) malizia *f.* **be up to mischief** combinare un brutto tiro. **make mischief** creare discordia. **mischief-maker** *n* attaccabrighe *m invar.* **mischievous** *adj* malizioso; (*of child*) birichino.

misconception [miskən'sepʃən] *n* malinteso *m.*

misconduct [mis'kondʌkt] *n* cattiva condotta *f.*

misdeed [mis'diːd] *n* misfatto *m,* delitto *m.*

misdemeanour [misdi'miːnə] *n* (*misbehaviour*) cattiva condotta *f;* (*crime*) delitto *m.*

miser ['maizə] *n* avaro, -a *m, f.* **miserly** *adj* avaro.

miserable ['mizərəbl] *adj* (*unhappy*) infelice, triste; (*pitiful*) pietoso; (*painful*) penoso; depresso.

misery ['mizəri] *n* miseria *f;* sofferenze *f pl.*

misfire [mis'faiə] *v* fare cilecca *or* fiasco.

misfit ['misfit] *n* (*person*) spostato, -a *m, f.*

misfortune [mis'fɔːtʃən] *n* sfortuna *f,* disgrazia *f.*

misgiving [mis'givin] *n* dubbio *m.*

misguided [mis'gaidid] *adj* fuori posto, sviato.

mishap ['mishap] *n* disgrazia *f,* contrattempo *m.*

misjudge [mis'dʒʌdʒ] *v* farsi un'idea sbagliata di, giudicare male.

*****mislay** [mis'lei] *v* smarrire.

*****mislead** [mis'liːd] *v* ingannare. **misleading** *adj* ingannevole.

misnomer [mis'noumə] *n* termine improprio *m.*

misplace [mis'pleis] *v* mettere fuori posto.

misprint ['misprint] *n* errore tipografico *m.*

miss[1] [mis] *n* colpo mancato *m. v* mancare (a); (*not catch*) perdere; (*skip*) saltare; (*not find*) non trovare; (*regret absence of*) sentire la mancanza di. **miss out** omettere. **be missing** mancare.

miss[2] [mis] *n* signorina *f.*

missile ['misail] *n* missile *m.*

mission ['miʃən] *n* missione *f.* **missionary** *n, adj* missionario, -a.

mist [mist] *n* caligine *f,* foschia *f. v* offuscare. **misty** *adj* caliginoso, fosco.

*****mistake** [mis'teik] *n* errore *m,* sbaglio *m.* **by mistake** per errore. **make a mistake** sbagliare, fare un errore. *v* (*confuse*) confondere, scambiare. **mistaken** *adj* sbagliato, falso.

mistletoe ['misltou] *n* vischio *m.*

mistress ['mistris] *n* padrona *f;* (*school*) insegnante *f;* (*lover*) amante *f.*

mistrust [mis'trʌst] *v* diffidare di, non aver fiducia in. *n* diffidenza *f,* sfiducia *f.* **mistrustful** *adj* diffidente.

*****misunderstand** [misʌndə'stand] *v*

fraintendere, capir male. **misunderstanding** n malinteso m, equivoco m. **misunderstood** adj incompreso.

misuse [mis'juːs; v mis'juːz] n abuso m; uso incorretto m. v abusare; (ill-treat) maltrattare; (use badly) adoperare male.

mitigate ['mitigeit] v mitigare; (law) attenuare. **mitigation** n (law) attenuante f.

mitre ['maitə] n (rel) mitra f; (carpentry) ugnatura f. v ugnare.

mitten ['mitn] n mezzo quanto m, muffola f.

mix [miks] v mescolare, mischiare; combinare. **mix up** confondere. **mix-up** n confusione f. **mixed** adj misto. **mixer** n (tech) agitatore m. **be a good mixer** essere socievole. **mixture** n miscela f; miscuglio m.

moan [moun] n (complaint) lamento m; (groan) gemito m. v lamentarsi; gemere.

moat [mout] n fosso m, fossato m.

mob [mob] n folla f, marmaglia f, plebaglia f. v moiestare, assalire.

mobile ['moubail] adj mobile. **mobility** n mobilità f. **mobilization** n mobilitazione f. **mobilize** v mobilitare.

moccasin ['mokəsin] n mocassino m.

mock [mok] v deridere, canzonare. adj finto, falso. **mockery** n presa in giro f, derisione f. **mocking** adj beffardo. **mocking-bird** n mimo m.

mode [moud] n modo m, maniera f.

model ['modl] n modello m; (art) modello, -a m, f; (fashion) indossatore, -trice m, f. adj modello, esemplare. v modellare, fare l'indossatore.

moderate ['modərət; v 'modəreit] adj misurato, moderato; (price) modico. v moderare. **moderation** n misura f, moderazione f. **in moderation** moderatamente.

modern ['modən] adj moderno. **modernization** n rimodernamento m. **modernize** v rimodernare.

modest ['modist] adj modesto. **modesty** n modestia f.

modify ['modifai] v modificare. **modification** n modifica f.

modulate ['modjuleit] v modulare. **modulation** n modulazione f.

module ['modjuːl] n modulo m.

mohair ['mouheə] n mohair m invar.

moist [moist] adj umido. **moisten** v inumidire; (surface) umettare. **moisture** n umidità f. **moisturize** v umidificare.

molar ['moulə] nm, adj molare.

molasses [mə'lasiz] n melassa f.

mold (US) V **mould**.

mole¹ [moul] n (on skin) neo m.

mole² [moul] n (zool) talpa f.

molecule ['molikjuːl] n molecola f. **molecular** adj molecolare.

molest [mə'lest] v molestare.

mollify ['molifai] v placare.

mollusc ['moləsk] n mollusco m.

mollycoddle ['molikodl] v coccolare.

molt (US) V **moult**.

molten ['moultən] adj fuso.

moment ['moumənt] n momento m, istante m. **at the moment** attualmente. **momentary** adj momentaneo. **momentous** adj grave, importante. **momentum** n impeto m, slancio m.

Monaco ['monəkou] n Monaco f.

monarch ['monək] n monarca m, f. **monarchist** n, adj monarchico, -a. **monarchy** n monarchia f.

monastery ['monəstəri] n monastero m. **monastic** adj monastico.

Monday ['mʌndi] n lunedì m.

money ['mʌni] n denaro m, soldi m pl. **money-box** n salvadanaio m. **money-lender** n usuraio m. **money order** vaglia m invar. **monetary** adj monetario.

mongol ['mongəl] adj mongolo; (med) mongoloide. **Mongolia** n Mongolia f.

mongrel ['mʌngrəl] nm, adj bastardo.

monitor ['monitə] n (radio) ascoltatore m; (tech) monitor m invar. v (radio) ascoltare; controllare. **monitoring service** n servizio d'ascolto m.

monk [mʌŋk] n monaco m, frate m.

monkey ['mʌŋki] n scimmia f.

monogamy [mə'nogəmi] n monogamia f. **monogamous** adj monogamo.

monogram ['monəgram] n monogramma m.

monograph ['monəgraːf] n monografia f.

monolithic [,monə'liθik] adj monolitico.

monologue ['monəlog] n monologo (pl -ghi) m.

monopolize [mə'nopəlaiz] v monopolizzare. **monopoly** n monopolio m.

monosyllable ['monəsiləbl] n monosillabo m. **monosyllabic** adj monosillabico, monosillabo.

monotony [mə'notəni] n monotonia f. **monotone** n tono uniforme m. **monotonous** adj monotono.

monsoon [mon'suːn] n monsone m.

monster ['monstə] n mostro m. **monstrosity** n mostruosità f. **monstrous** adj mostruoso.

month [mʌnθ] n mese m.

monthly ['mʌnθli] n (periodical) rivista mensile f. adj mensile. adv al mese, mensilmente.

monument ['monjument] n monumento m. **monumental** adj monumentale.

mood[1] [muːd] n umore m, stato d'animo m. **feel in the mood** to sentirsi disposto a, aver voglia di. **moodiness** n malumore m; volubilità f. **moody** adj capriccioso; (sulky) di malumore.

mood[2] [muːd] n (gramm) modo m.

moon [muːn] n luna f. **moonlight** n chiaro di luna m.

moor[1] [muə] n brughiera f. **moorhen** n gallinella d'acqua f.

moor[2] [muə] v ormeggiare, ancorare. **mooring** n ormeggio m, ancoraggio m.

moose [muːs] n alce m.

moot [muːt] adj discutibile.

mop [mop] n scopa di cotone per lavaggio f; (of hair) zazzera f. v **mop one's brow** asciugarsi la fronte. **mop up** asciugare; rastrellare.

mope [moup] v fare il broncio, immusonirsi.

moped ['mouped] n ciclomotore m.

moral ['morəl] nf, adj morale. **morals** pl n morale f sing. **morale** n morale m. **moralist** n moralista m, f. **morality** n moralità f, buon costume m.

morbid ['moːbid] adj morboso, patologico.

more [moː] adv più, di più; (again) ancora. nm, adj più. **more and more** sempre più. **more than** più di o che.

moreover [moː'rouvə] adv inoltre, per di più.

morgue [moːg] n obitorio m.

morning ['moːniŋ] n mattina m, mattinata f. **this morning** stamane. **tomorrow morning** domattina. adj del mattino, mattutino.

moron ['moːron] n deficiente m, f. **moronic** adj deficiente, scemo.

morose [mə'rous] adj scontroso.

morphine ['moːfiːn] n morfina f.

Morse code [moːs] n alfabeto Morse m.

morsel ['moːsəl] n boccone m.

mortal ['moːtl] n(m+f), adj mortale. **mortality** n mortalità f.

mortar ['moːtə] n (vessel, arms) mortaio m; (building) malta f.

mortgage ['moːgidʒ] n ipoteca f. v ipotecare, impegnare.

mortify ['moːtifai] v mortificare. **mortification** n mortificazione f.

mortuary ['moːtʃuəri] n camera ardente or mortuaria f.

mosaic [mə'zeiik] n mosaico m.

Moscow ['moskou] n Mosca f.

mosque [mosk] n moschea f.

mosquito [mə'skiːtou] n zanzara f.

moss [mos] n muschio m, musco m. **mossy** adj muscoso.

most [moust] adj (majority) la maggior parte di, il più di; (greatest) il più grande, il maggiore. n il più m; (greatest part) la maggior parte f; (majority) la maggioranza f; il più m pl. adv il più; (very) molto, assai.

motel [mou'tel] n motel m invar, autostello m.

moth [moθ] n lepidottero m. **clothes moth** tarma f. **mothball** n pallina antitarmica f.

mother ['mʌðə] n madre f; (coll) mamma f. v aver cura di come una madre. **mother-in-law** n suocera f. **mother-of-pearl** n madreperla f. **mother tongue** madrelingua f. **motherly** adj materno.

motion ['mouʃən] n moto m, movimento m; (proposal) mozione f; (law) istanza f. **go through the motions** far finta. **set in motion** avviare, mettere in moto. v accennare a, far cenno a. **motionless** adj immobile.

motivate ['moutiveit] v motivare, spingere. **motivation** n spinta f, stimolo m.

motive ['moutiv] n motivo m, ragione f.

motor ['moutə] nm, adj motore. **motorboat** n motoscafo m. **motor car** automobile f, macchina f. **motorcycle** n motocicletta f. **motorcyclist** n motociclista m, f. **motorway** n autostrada f. v andare in macchina. **motoring** n automobilismo m. **motorist** n automobilista m, f. **motorize** v motorizzare.

mottled ['motld] adj chiazzato.

motto ['motou] n motto m, massima f.

mould[1] or US **mold** [mould] n stampo m, forma f. v formare, foggiare, modellare.

mould[2] or US **mold** [mould] n muffa f. **mouldy** adj ammuffito. **go mouldy** ammuffire.

moult or US **molt** [moult] v mutare, fare la muta.

mound [maund] n tumulo m; (heap) mucchio m.

mount¹ [maunt] v montare. n (setting) montatura f.

mount² [maunt] n monte m.

mountain ['mauntən] n montagna f. **mountaineer** n alpinista m, f. **mountaineering** n alpinismo m. **mountainous** adj montuoso, alpestre.

mourn [mɔːn] v rimpiangere, essere in lutto per. **mourning** n lutto m, cordoglio m. **mournful** adj triste; lugubre.

mouse [maus] n, pl **mice** topo m. **mousetrap** n trappola (per topi) f. **mousy** adj (colour) grigio topo; timido.

mousse [muːs] n mousse f, spuma f.

moustache [məˈstɑːʃ] n baffi m pl.

mouth [mauθ] n bocca f; (of river) foce f. **mouth organ** armonica f. **mouthpiece** n (spokesman) portavoce m invar; (of pipe) bocchino m. v declamare. **mouthful** n boccone m.

move [muːv] v muovere, spostare; (house) traslocare; (arouse feelings) commuovere; (propose) proporre. **move away** or **off** allontanare; (depart) partire. **move back** indietreggiare; (return) tornare. **move forward** avanzare. **move in** occupare. **move out** uscire, sgombrare. **move up** (raise) salire; (get closer) avvicinarsi. n mossa f, passo m; (house) trasloco m. **movable** adj movibile. **movement** n movimento m; (sign) cenno m; (tech) meccanismo m. **moving** adj commovente; (in motion) in moto.

movie ['muːvi] n (US) film m invar.

*mow [mou] v falciare.

mown [moun] V **mow**.

Mr ['mistə] n signor m.

Mrs ['misiz] n signora f.

much [mʌtʃ] pron, adj molto, assai. adv molto, assai. **as much as** (tanto) quanto. **how much** quanto. **so much** tanto. **too much** troppo.

muck [mʌk] n letame m; (coll: filth) porcheria f. v **muck about** (coll) bighellonare. **muck up** (coll) rovinare.

mucus ['mjuːkəs] n muco m. **mucous membrane** mucosa f.

mud [mʌd] n fango m. **mudguard** n parafango m. **mudslinger** n maldicente m, f. **muddy** adj fangoso, inzaccherato.

muddle ['mʌdl] n confusione f, pasticcio

m. v **muddle through** arrabattarsi. **muddle up** confondere. **muddler** n confusionario, -a m, f.

muff [mʌf] n manicotto m. v mancare, sbagliare.

muffle ['mʌfl] v smorzare, attutire.

mug [mʌg] n (cup) tazza f; (coll: face) muso m, ceffo m; (slang: fool) gonzo m. v assalire.

mulberry ['mʌlbəri] n (fruit) mora di gelso f; (tree) gelso m.

mule¹ [mjuːl] n (zool) mulo m. **mulish** adj (stubborn) duro.

mule² [mjuːl] n (slipper) ciabatta f, pianella f.

mullet ['mʌlit] n (grey) muggine m; (red, triglia f.

multicoloured [ˌmʌltiˈkʌləd] adj multicolore.

multimillionaire [ˌmʌltimiljəˈnɛə] n multimilionario, -a m, f.

multiple ['mʌltipl] adj multiplo, molteplice. n multiplo m.

multiply ['mʌltiplai] v moltiplicare. **multiplication** n moltiplicazione f. **multiplicity** n varietà f.

multiracial [ˌmʌltiˈreiʃəl] adj multirazziale.

multitude ['mʌltitjuːd] n moltitudine f, massa f.

mum [mʌm] adj **keep mum** star zitto.

mumble ['mʌmbl] v borbottare.

mummy¹ ['mʌmi] n (corpse) mummia f. **mummify** n mummificare.

mummy² ['mʌmi] n (coll: mother) mamma f, mammina f.

mumps [mʌmps] n orecchioni m pl.

munch [mʌntʃ] v sgranocchiare.

mundane [mʌnˈdein] adj mondano.

municipal [mjuːˈnisipəl] adj municipale. **municipality** n comune m.

mural ['mjuərəl] n pittura murale f.

murder ['məːdə] n assassinio m. v assassinare, ammazzare; (coll) massacrare. **murderer** n assassino m. **murderess** n assassina f. **murderous** adj micidiale.

murmur ['məːmə] n mormorio m. v mormorare.

muscle ['mʌsl] n muscolo m.

muse¹ [mjuːz] n musa f.

muse² [mjuːz] v meditare, riflettere.

museum [mjuːˈziəm] n museo m.

mushroom ['mʌʃrum] n fungo m. v (gather) raccogliere funghi; (spread) dilagare, svilupparsi rapidamente.

music ['mjuːzik] n musica f. **musician** n musicista m, f.

musical ['mjuːzikl] adj musicale; (gifted) dotato per la musica. n musical m invar.

musk [mʌsk] n (zool) muschio m.

musket ['mʌskit] n moschetto m.

Muslim ['mʌzlim] n, adj musulmano, -a.

muslin ['mʌzlin] n mussola f.

mussel ['mʌsl] n mitilo m, cozza f.

*must¹ [mʌst] v dovere. n (coll) cosa essenziale f.

must² [mʌst] n (wine) mosto m.

mustard ['mʌstəd] n senape f, mostarda f.

muster ['mʌstə] v radunare. **muster up courage** farsi coraggio. n **pass muster** essere accettabile.

mute [mjuːt] adj muto, taciturno. n muto, -a m, f; (music) sordina f.

mutilate ['mjuːtileit] v mutilare, mozzare. **mutilation** n mutilazione f.

mutiny ['mjuːtini] n ammutinamento m, ribellione f. v ammutinarsi, ribellarsi. **mutinous** adj ammutinato, ribelle.

mutter ['mʌtə] v brontolare, borbottare.

mutton ['mʌtn] n carne ovina f, castrato m. **dead as mutton** morto stecchito.

mutual ['mjuːtʃuəl] adj mutuo, reciproco; comune.

muzzle ['mʌzl] n (gun) imboccatura f; (animal) muso m; (device) museruola f. v mettere la museruola a; (silence) far tacere.

my [mai] adj (il) mio, (la) mia; (pl) (i) miei, (le) mie.

myself [mai'self] pron io stesso; (after prep) me stesso; (reflexive) mi.

myopia [mai'oupiə] n miopia f. **myopic** adj miope.

mystery ['mistəri] n mistero m, segreto m. **mysterious** adj misterioso, strano.

mystic ['mistik] n mistico, -a m, f. **mystical** adj mistico, misterioso. **mysticism** n misticismo m, mistica f.

mystify ['mistifai] v mistificare, disorientare.

mystique [mi'stiːk] n mistica f.

myth [miθ] n mito m. **mythical** adj mitico. **mythological** adj mitologico. **mythology** n mitologia f.

N

nag¹ [nag] v rimbrottare, brontolare. **nagging** adj bisbetico.

nag² [nag] n ronzino m.

nail [neil] n (anat) unghia f; (metal) chiodo m. **nail-brush** n spazzolino per le unghie m. **nail-file** n lima per le unghie f. **nail polish** smalto per le unghie m. **nail-scissors** pl n forbici per le unghie f pl.

naive [naiˈiːv] adj ingenuo. **naivety** n ingenuità f.

naked ['neikid] adj nudo, scoperto. **strip naked** spogliare. **nakedness** n nudità f.

name [neim] v chiamare. n nome m. **go by the name of** chiamarsi. **my name is** . . . mi chiamo . . . . **namesake** n omonimo m. **nameless** adj anonimo. **namely** adv cioè.

nanny ['nani] n bambinaia f.

nap¹ [nap] n (doze) pisolino m. v fare or schiacciare un pisolino.

nap² [nap] n (cloth) pelo m.

nape [neip] n nuca f.

napkin ['napkin] n tovagliolo m.

nappy ['napi] n pannolino m.

narcotic [naːˈkɔtik] n, adj narcotico.

narrate [nəˈreit] v narrare, raccontare. **narration** n racconto m. **narrative** n narrativa f. **narrator** n narratore, -trice m, f.

narrow ['narou] adj stretto; limitato; (person, mind, etc.) ristretto. **narrow-gauge** adj (railway) a scartamento ridotto. **narrow-minded** adj gretto, di mente ristretta. v restringere, limitare. **narrowly** adv per un pelo, a stento.

nasal ['neizəl] adj nasale.

nasturtium [nəˈstəːtʃəm] n nasturzio m.

nasty ['naːsti] adj (filthy) disgustoso; (offensive) ripugnante; (unpleasant) cattivo, sgradevole. **nastiness** n cattiveria f.

nation ['neiʃən] n nazione f. **national** adj nazionale. **national insurance** assicurazione sociale f. **nationalism** n nazionalismo m. **nationalist** n(m+f), adj nazionalista. **nationality** n nazionalità f. **nationalization** n nazionalizzazione f. **nationalize** v nazionalizzare.

native ['neitiv] n, adj (original inhabitant) indigeno, -a; (of town, etc.) nativo, -a, oriundo, -a.

nativity [nəˈtivəti] n natività f.

natural ['natʃərəl] adj naturale; normale;

istintivo. **naturalization** n naturalizzazione f. **naturalize** v naturalizzare.

nature ['neitʃə] n natura f; (condition) indole f; disposizione f.

naught [nɔtt] n nulla m. **come to naught** ridurre a zero.

naughty ['nɔtti] adj cattivo; (mischievous) birichino; indecente, spinto.

nausea ['nɔziə] n nausea f; fastidio m. **nauseous** adj nauseabondo, disgustoso.

nautical ['nɔttikəl] adj nautico.

naval ['neivəl] adj navale, marittimo.

nave¹ [neiv] n (of church) navata f.

nave² [neiv] n (hub) mozzo m.

navel ['neivəl] n ombelico m.

navigate ['nævigeit] v navigare, pilotare. **navigable** adj navigabile. **navigation** n navigazione f. **navigator** n navigatore m; (officer) ufficiale di rotta m.

navy ['neivi] n marina militare f. **navy blue** adj blu marino.

near [niə] adj vicino. prep vicino a, accanto a. adv vicino. v avvicinare. **near at hand** a portata di mano. **near-sighted** adj miope. **nearby** adj, adv, prep vicino (a). **nearly** adv quasi.

neat [niːt] adj (orderly) ordinato, accurato; elegante; (undiluted) liscio. **neatness** n ordine m; eleganza f.

nebulous ['nebjuləs] adj vago, nebuloso.

necessary ['nesisəri] adj necessario, indispensabile. **necessity** n necessità f, bisogno m.

neck [nek] n (anat) collo m; (of dress) scollatura f. **have a stiff neck** avere il torcicollo. **neck and neck** testa a testa. **necklace** n collana f. **necktie** n cravatta f.

nectar ['nektə] n nettare m. **nectarine** n pesca noce f.

née [nei] adj nata.

need [niːd] n bisogno m, necessità f; (poverty) miseria f. **if need be** caso mai, se c'è bisogno. v aver bisogno di; (require) richiedere. **needed** adj necessario. **needless** adj inutile, superfluo. **needy** adj indigente, bisognoso.

needle ['niːdl] n ago m; (knitting) ferro m; (gramophone) puntina f. **needlework** n (sewing) cucitura f; (embroidery) ricamo m. v (coll) punzecchiare.

negative ['negətiv] adj negativo. n negativa f. **answer in the negative** rispondere di no.

neglect [ni'glekt] n negligenza f, trascuratezza f. v trascurare. **neglect to** mancare di. **negligent** adj negligente. **negligible** adj trascurabile.

negligée ['negliʒei] n negligé m invar, vestaglia f.

negotiate [ni'gouʃieit] v trattare, negoziare; (obstacle, etc.) superare. **negotiable** adj negoziabile. **negotiation** n trattativa f, negoziato m.

Negro ['niːgrou] nm, adj negro. **Negress** n negra f.

neigh [nei] v nitrire. n nitrito m.

neighbour ['neibə] n vicino, -a m, f. **next-door neighbour** vicino di casa m. **neighbourhood** n vicinanza f, paraggi m pl. **neighbouring** adj adiacente, vicino. **neighbourly** adj socievole, da buon vicino.

neither ['naiðə] adj nè l'uno nè l'altro. adv **neither ... nor ...** nè ... nè .... pron nessuno, nè l'uno nè l'altro.

neon ['niːon] n neon m.

nephew ['nefjuː] n nipote m.

nepotism ['nepətizəm] n nepotismo m.

nerve [nəːv] n nervo m; coraggio m; (coll: cheek) sfacciataggine f, faccia tosta f. **get on the nerves of** dare sui nervi a. **nerve-racking** adj snervante. **nervous** adj nervoso; apprensivo. **get nervous** inquietarsi. **nervous breakdown** esaurimento nervoso m.

nest [nest] n nido m. **nest egg** gruzzolo m. v annidarsi.

nestle ['nesl] v annidarsi, accoccolarsi.

net¹ [net] n rete f. **network** n rete f. v (enclose) cintare con reti; (catch) prendere con reti; (ball) mandare in rete. **netting** n reticolato m.

net² [net] adj netto.

Netherlands ['neðələndz] pl n Paesi Bassi m pl.

nettle ['netl] n ortica f. **nettle-rash** n orticaria f. v irritare.

neurosis [nju'rousis] n nevrosi f. **neurotic** n, adj nevrotico, -a.

neuter ['njuːtə] adj neutro. v castrare.

neutral ['njuːtrəl] adj neutro; (tech) neutro. n neutrale m, f. **neutrality** n neutralità f. **neutralize** v neutralizzare. **neutron** n neutrone m.

never ['nevə] adv (non ...) mai. **never-ending** adj interminabile.

nevertheless [nevəðə'les] adv, conj ciononostante, tuttavia.

new [njuː] *adj* nuovo. **new-born** *adj* neonato. **newcomer** *n* nuovo venuto, nuova venuta *m, f.*

news [njuːz] *n* novità *f pl,* notizie *f pl,* informazioni *f pl.* **news agency** agenzia d'informazioni *f.* **newsagent** *n* giornalaio *m.* **news bulletin** notiziario *m;* (*radio*) giornale radio *m.* **news item** notizia *f.* **newspaper** *n* giornale *m.* **newsprint** *n* carta da giornale *f.* **newsreel** *n* cinegiornale *m.*

newt [njuːt] *n* tritone *m.*

New Year *n* Anno nuovo *m.* **Happy New Year!** Buon Anno! **New Year's Day** il Capodanno *m.* **New Zealand** *n* Nuova Zelanda *f.* **New Zealander** neozelandese *m, f.*

next [nekst] *adj* prossimo; (*nearest*) più vicino; (*following*) successivo, seguente. *adv* (*after*) dopo, poi; (*later*) in seguito. **next-of-kin** *n* parente prossimo *m, f.*

nib [nib] *n* pennino *m.*

nibble [ˈnibl] *n* (*morsel*) bocconcino *m. v* rosicchiare.

nice [nais] *adj* bello; piacevole, simpatico; (*subtle*) sottile; delicato; (*refined*) elegante, fine. **nicely** *adv* proprio bene. **nicety** *n* esattezza *f.* **niceties** *pl n* finezze *f pl,* sfumature *f pl.*

niche [nitʃ] *n* nicchia *f.*

nick [nik] *v* intaccare; (*slang: steal*) arraffare; (*slang: catch*) acchiappare. *n* tacca *f.* **in the nick of time** all'ultimo momento.

nickel [ˈnikl] *n* nichel *m;* (*US: coin*) nichelino *m.*

nickname [ˈnikneim] *n* nomignolo *m,* soprannome *m. v* soprannominare.

nicotine [ˈnikətiːn] *n* nicotina *f.*

niece [niːs] *n* nipote *f.*

niggling [ˈniglin] *adj* insignificante.

night [nait] *n* notte *f;* (*evening*) sera *f.* **have a good/bad night** dormir bene/male. **night-club** *n* night *m invar.* **nightdress** *n* camicia da notte *f.* **nightfall** *n* tramonto *m.* **nightmare** *n* incubo *m.* **nightmarish** *adj* opprimente, spaventoso. **stay the night** pernottare.

nightingale [ˈnaitiŋgeil] *n* usignolo *m.*

nightly [ˈnaitli] *adj* notturno; (*every night*) di tutte le sere. *adv* ogni notte *or* sera.

nil [nil] *n* nulla *m,* niente *m,* zero *m.*

nimble [ˈnimbl] *adj* agile, svelto. **nimbleness** *n* agilità *f.*

nine [nain] *nm, adj* nove. **ninepins** *n* birilli *m pl.* **ninth** *nm, adj* nono.

nineteen [nainˈtiːn] *nm, adj* diciannove. **nineteenth** *adj* diciannovesimo.

ninety [ˈnainti] *nm, adj* novanta. **ninetieth** *nm, adj* novantesimo.

nip¹ [nip] *v* pizzicare; (*bite*) morsicare. **nip in** intromettersi, entrare lestamente. **nip in the bud** stroncare sul nascere. **nip out** fare un salto. *n* (*frost*) gelo *m;* (*bite*) morso *m.* **nippy** *adj* (*speedy*) svelto; (*cold*) frizzante.

nip² [nip] *n* (*drop*) bicchierino *m,* sorso *m.*

nipple [ˈnipl] *n* capezzolo *m;* (*tech*) rubinetto *m.*

nit [nit] *n* lendine *m;* (*coll*) stupido, -a *m, f.*

nitrogen [ˈnaitrədʒən] *n* azoto *m.*

no [nou] *adj* nessuno, neppure uno; (*forbidden*) vietato. *adv* no; (*with comparative*) non. *n* no *m invar.*

noble [ˈnoubl] *n(m+f), adj* nobile. **nobility** *n* nobiltà *f.*

nobody [ˈnoubodi] *pron* nessuno. *n* zero *m,* sconosciuto, -a *m, f.*

nocturnal [nokˈtəːnl] *adj* notturno.

nod [nod] *n* cenno col capo *m. v* fare un cenno col capo; (*doze*) sonnecchiare; (*assent*) annuire; (*greet*) salutare. **nodding acquaintance** conoscenza superficiale *f.*

noise [noiz] *n* rumore *m;* (*loud*) baccano *m.* **background noise** rumori di fondo *m pl.* **big noise** (*coll*) pezzo grosso *m.* **noiseless** *adj* silenzioso. **noisy** *adj* rumoroso, chiassoso.

nomad [ˈnoumad] *n(m+f), adj* nomade.

nominal [ˈnominl] *adj* nominale; simbolico.

nominate [ˈnomineit] *v* nominare; (*propose*) proporre. **nomination** *n* nomina *f.*

nominative [ˈnominətiv] *nm, adj* nominativo.

nonchalant [ˈnonʃələnt] *adj* indifferente, noncurante. **nonchalance** *n* indifferenza *f,* noncuranza *f.*

nonconformist [nonkənˈfoːmist] *n(m+f), adj* dissidente, anti-conformista.

nondescript [ˈnondiskript] *adj* inclassificabile, qualunque.

none [nʌn] *pron* nessuno, nulla, niente. *adv* affatto, punto. **none other than** nientedimeno che.

nonentity [non'entəti] n nullità f, zero m.
nonetheless [ˌnʌnðə'les] adv ciononostante, tuttavia.
nonsense ['nonsəns] n nonsenso m, assurdo m; (coll) sciocchezze f pl. **nonsensical** adj assurdo, sciocco. **talk nonsense** dire sciocchezze.
non-stop [non'stop] adj continuo, ininterrotto.
noodles ['nuːdlz] pl n tagliatelle f pl, taglierini m pl.
nook [nuk] n cantuccio m, angolo m.
noon [num] n mezzogiorno m.
no-one ['nouwʌn] pron nessuno.
noose [nuːs] n nodo scorsoio m, laccio m.
nor [noː] conj nè, neppure, nemmeno.
norm [noːm] n norma f, modello m. **normal** adj normale, regolare. **normally** adv di solito.
north [noːθ] n nord m, settentrione m. adj also **northern** del nord, settentrionale. **northerly** adj di nordo; da nordo; a nordo. **north-east** n nordest m. **north-eastern** del nordest. **north-west** n nordovest m. **north-western** del nordovest.
Norway ['noːwei] n Norvegia f. **Norwegian** n(m+f), adj norvegese.
nose [nouz] n naso m; (of animal, aeroplane, etc.) muso m. v fiutare. **nose around** esplorare. **nosy** adj (coll) curioso.
nostalgia [no'stældʒə] n nostalgia f, rimpianto m. **nostalgic** adj nostalgico.
nostril ['nostrəl] n narice f.
not [not] adv non. **not at all** niente affatto. **not even** neppure, neanche.
notable ['noutəbl] adj notevole, degno di nota.
notary ['noutəri] n notaio m.
notch [notʃ] n tacca f, intaglio m. v intaccare.
note [nout] n nota f, appunto m, commento m; (money) biglietto m. **note-book** n taccuino m. **notepaper** n carta da lettere or scrivere. **noteworthy** adj degno di nota, notevole. **take note of** prendere atto di. **take notes** prendere appunti.
notation n notazione f. v notare; osservare. **noted** adj noto, rinomato.
nothing ['nʌθiŋ] n niente m, zero m. adv per nulla, niente (affatto). **next to nothing** quasi nulla. **nothing but** null'altro che. **nothing less than** semplicemente.
notice ['noutis] n avviso m, annuncio m;

(advance warning) preavviso m; (criticism) recensione f. **give notice** (dismiss) licenziare. **notice-board** n tabellone m. **take notice of** fare attenzione a. v notare, rilevare. **noticeable** adj apparente, percettibile.
notify ['noutifai] v notificare, avvertire. **notification** n notifica f.
notion ['nouʃən] n nozione f, idea f.
notorious [nou'toːriəs] adj notorio, famigerato. **notoriety** n notorietà f.
notwithstanding [notwið'standiŋ] prep nonostante, malgrado. adv ciononostante, con tutto ciò.
nougat ['nuːgaː] n torrone m.
nought [noːt] n zero m.
noun [naun] n nome m, sostantivo m.
nourish ['nʌriʃ] v nutrire, alimentare. **nourishing** adj nutriente. **nourishment** n cibo m, alimento m.
novel[1] ['novəl] n romanzo m. **novelist** n romanziere, -a m, f.
novel[2] ['novəl] adj nuovo, originale; (unusual) insolito. **novelty** n novità f.
November [nə'vembə] n novembre m.
novice ['novis] n novizio, -a m, f.
now [nau] adv ora, adesso. **from now on** d'ora in poi. **just now** or ora. **nowadays** adv oggigiorno, al giorno d'oggi. **now and again** ogni tanto, di quando in quando. **until now** finora.
nowhere ['nouweə] adv in nessun luogo.
noxious ['nokʃəs] adj nocivo, malefico.
nozzle ['nozl] n (spout) becco m; (tech) ugello m.
nuance ['njuːãs] n sfumatura f.
nuclear ['njuːkliə] adj nucleare.
nucleus ['njuːkliəs] n nucleo m.
nude ['njuːd] n, adj nudo, -a. **nudism** n nudismo m. **nudist** n nudista m, f. **nudity** n nudità f.
nudge [nʌdʒ] n colpetto m. v dare un colpetto a.
nugget ['nʌgit] n pepita f.
nuisance ['njuːsns] n fastidio m, seccatura f; (law) infrazione f. **make a nuisance of oneself** seccare tutti.
null [nʌl] adj nullo. **null and void** senza validità legale.
numb [nʌm] adj intorpidito; (stunned) intontito. v intorpidire, paralizzare. **numbness** n torpore m.
number ['nʌmbə] n numero m; (numeral) cifra f; quantità f. **number plate** targa f. v

numerare, contare. **numberless** adj innumerevole.

numeral ['njuːmərəl] n cifra f.

numerical [njuːˈmerɪkl] adj numerico.

numerous ['njuːmərəs] adj numeroso.

nun [nʌn] n monaca f, suora f. **become a nun** prendere il velo. **nunnery** n convento m.

nurse [nəːs] v curare, fare l'infermiere; (suckle) allattare; (hope, grievance, etc.) nutrire, covare. n infermiere, -a m, f; (children's) balia f, bambinaia f. **nursing** n professione d'infermiere f. **nursing home** casa di cura f, clinica f.

nursery ['nəːsəri] n (children's) camera dei bambini f; (plants, etc.) vivaio m, serra f. **day nursery** asilo infantile m. **nursery rhyme** filastrocca f. **nursery school** giardino d'infanzia m.

nurture ['nəːtʃə] v (feed) nutrire; (rear) allevare. n nutrimento m; allevamento m.

nut [nʌt] n noce f; (tech) dado m; (coll: head) zucca f. **be nuts** (coll) essere matto. **in a nutshell** in poche parole. **nutcrackers** pl n schiaccianoci m invar. **nutmeg** n noce moscata f. **nut-tree** n noce m.

nutrient ['njuːtriənt] adj nutriente. n nutrimento m.

nutrition [njuːˈtrɪʃən] n alimentazione f. **nutritious** adj nutriente.

nuzzle ['nʌzl] v accucciolarsi, rannicchiarsi.

nylon ['naɪlon] n nailon m.

nymph [nɪmf] n ninfa f. **nymphomaniac** n ninfomane f.

O

oak [ouk] n quercia f.

oar [oɪ] n remo m.

oasis [ouˈeisis] n, pl -ses oasi f invar.

oath [ouθ] n (promise) giuramento m; (profanity) bestemmia f.

oats [outs] pl n avena f sing. **oatmeal** n farina d'avena f.

obedient [əˈbiːdiənt] adj ubbidiente, obbediente. **obedience** n ubbidienza f, obbedienza f.

obese [əˈbiːs] adj obeso. **obesity** n obesità f.

obey [əˈbei] v ubbidire, obbedire.

obituary [əˈbitjuəri] n necrologia f.

object ['obʒikt; v əbˈʒekt] n oggetto m; (aim) scopo m. v obiettare, protestare. **objection** n obiezione f, protesta f. **have no objection to** aver nulla in contrario a. **objectionable** adj offensivo, sgradevole, riprensibile. **objective** nm, adj obiettivo.

oblige [əˈblaidʒ] v costringere, obbligare; fare un favore a. **be obliged to** (have to) dovere; (be grateful to) essere riconoscente a. **obligation** n (law) obbligazione f; (binding promise) obbligo (pl -ghi) m; (duty) dovere m. **obligatory** adj obbligatorio. **obliging** adj cortese, accomodante.

oblique [əˈbliːk] adj obliquo; indiretto.

obliterate [əˈblitəreit] v obliterare, cancellare; (destroy) distruggere. **obliteration** n distruzione f.

oblivion [əˈbliviən] n oblio m. **oblivious** adj dimentico (m pl -chi).

oblong ['oblon] adj bislungo.

obnoxious [əbˈnokʃəs] adj odioso, offensivo.

oboe ['oubou] n oboe m. **oboist** n oboista f.

obscene [əbˈsiːn] adj osceno. **obscenity** n oscenità f.

obscure [əbˈskjuə] adj (not clear) ambiguo, oscuro; (inconspicuous) vago. v offuscare, velare. **obscurity** n oscurità f.

observe [əbˈzəːv] v (see) osservare; notare, rilevare; (rel) praticare. **observance** n osservanza f. **observant** adj osservante. **observation** n osservazione f, attenzione f. **keep under observation** tenere in osservazione. **observatory** n osservatorio m. **observer** n osservatore, -trice m, f.

obsess [əbˈses] v ossessionare. **obsession** n ossessione f.

obsolescent [obsəˈlesnt] adj che sta cadendo in disuso.

obsolete ['obsəliːt] adj caduto in disuso; antiquato.

obstacle ['obstəkl] n ostacolo m.

obstetrics [obˈstetriks] n ostetricia f. **obstetrician** n ostetrico, -a m, f.

obstinate ['obstinət] adj ostinato. **obstinacy** n ostinatezza f.

obstreperous [əbˈstrepərəs] adj ribelle.

obstruct [əbˈstrʌkt] v impacciare, ostacolare. **obstruction** n impaccio m, ostacolo m.

obtain [əbˈtein] v ottenere, procurare. **obtainable** adj ottenibile, raggiungibile.

obtrusive [əb'truːsɪv] *adj* importuno; invadente. **obtrusion** *n* invadenza *f*.

obtuse [əb'tjuːs] *adj* ottuso.

obverse ['ɒbvɜːs] *n* faccia *f*, diritto *m*; (*counterpart*) inverso *m*.

obvious ['ɒbvɪəs] *adj* ovvio, evidente.

occasion [ə'keɪʒən] *v* causare. *n* (*time*) occasione *f*, volta *f*; (*cause*) motivo *m*, ragione *f*. **rise to the occasion** mostrarsi all'altezza. **occasional** *adj* saltuario, sporadico. **occasionally** *adv* ogni tanto.

occult ['ɒkʌlt] *adj* occulto. *n* forze occulte *f pl*.

occupy ['ɒkjupaɪ] *v* occupare. **occupant** *or* **occupier** *n* occupante *m*, *f*. **occupation** *n* occupazione *f*; (*trade*) mestiere *m*, professione *f*. **occupational** *adj* del lavoro, professionale.

occur [ə'kɜː] *v* succedere, capitare; (*come to mind*) venire in mente. **occurrence** *n* avvenimento *m*, caso *m*.

ocean ['əuʃən] *n* oceano *m*.

ochre ['əukə] *n* ocra *f*. *adj* (*color*) ocra.

o'clock [ə'klɒk] *adv* **one o'clock** l'una. **two/three/etc. o'clock** le due/tre/etc.

octagon ['ɒktəgən] *n* ottagono *m*. **octagonal** *adj* ottagonale.

octane ['ɒkteɪn] *n* ottano *m*.

octave ['ɒktɪv] *n* ottava *f*.

October [ɒk'təubə] *n* ottobre *m*.

octopus ['ɒktəpəs] *n* polpo *m*.

oculist ['ɒkjulɪst] *n* oculista *m*, *f*.

odd [ɒd] *adj* (*not even*) dispari; (*not paired*) scompagnato; (*strange*) strano, bizzarro; casuale; (*approximately*) circa. **oddity** *n* stranezza *f*; (*person*) eccentrico, -a *m*, *f*. **oddments** *pl n* rimasugli *m pl*, scampoli *m pl*.

odds [ɒdz] *pl n* probabilità *f pl*, differenza *f sing*; (*betting*) posta *f sing*. **be at odds with** essere in disaccordo con. **lay odds** scommettere. **odds and ends** cosette varie *f pl*, rimasugli *m pl*.

ode [əud] *n* ode *f*.

odious ['əudɪəs] *adj* odioso.

odour ['əudə] *n* odore *m*. **odourless** *adj* inodoro.

oesophagus [iː'sɒfəgəs] *n* esofago *m*.

of [ɒv] *prep* di.

off [ɒf] *adv* via, distante. *prep* lontano da, fuori (di). *adj* (*holiday*) libero; (*food*) marcio, non buono. **be off** (*cancelled*) non aver luogo.

offal ['ɒfəl] *n* frattaglie *f pl*.

offend [ə'fend] *v* offendere. **offence** *n* offesa *f*; (*law*) infrazione alla legge *f*. **take offence** offendersi. **offender** *n* colpevole *m*, *f*; trasgreditore, -trice *m*, *f*.

offensive [ə'fensɪv] *adj* offensivo; (*disagreeable*) sgradevole; insolente. *n* offensiva *f*.

offer ['ɒfə] *v* offrire, presentare, dare. *n* offerta *f*, proposta *f*.

offhand [ɒf'hand] *adj* noncurante. *adv* all'improvviso.

office ['ɒfɪs] *n* (*place*) ufficio *m*; (*post, function*) carica *f*. **head office** *n* sede (centrale) *f*. **officer** *n* funzionario, -a *m*, *f*; (*mil, etc.*) ufficiale *m*.

official [ə'fɪʃəl] *adj* ufficiale. *n* funzionario, -a *m*, *f*.

officious [ə'fɪʃəs] *adj* inframmettente, invadente.

offing ['ɒfɪŋ] *n* **in the offing** in vista.

off-load [ɒf'ləud] *v* scaricare.

off-peak [ɒf'piːk] *adj* non di punta.

off-putting ['ɒf,putɪŋ] *adj* sconcertante, che lascia perplesso.

off-season [ɒf'siːzn] *adj* fuori stagione.

offset [ɒf'set; *n* 'ɒfset] *v* compensare, controbilanciare. *n* (*print*) offset *m invar*.

offshoot ['ɒfʃuːt] *n* ramo *m*.

offshore ['ɒfʃɔː] *adv* al largo. *adj* di terra.

offside [ɒf'saɪd] *adv*, *adj* fuori gioco.

offspring ['ɒfsprɪŋ] *n* prole *f*; frutto *m*.

offstage [ɒf'steɪdʒ] *adv*, *adj* fuori scena.

often ['ɒfn] *adv* spesso, sovente, molte volte. **how often** quante volte. **too often** troppe volte.

ogre ['əugə] *n* orco *m*.

oil [ɔɪl] *n* olio *m*; petrolio *m*; gasolio *m*. **oilfield** *n* giacimento petrolifero *m*. **oil-fired** *adj* a gasolio *or* nafta. **oil-painting** *n* pittura a olio *f*. **oilskin** *n* tela impermeabile *f*. **oil-well** *n* pozzo petrolifero *m*. *v* ungere, lubrificare. **oily** *adj* oleoso, untuoso.

ointment ['ɔɪntmənt] *n* unguento *m*.

old [əuld] *adj* vecchio, antico (*m pl* -chi); (*not new*) usato. **old age** vecchiaia *f*. **old-fashioned** *adj* fuori moda. **old man** vecchio *m*. **old people** vecchi *m pl*. **old woman** vecchia *f*. **oldish** *adj* vecchiotto.

olive ['ɒlɪv] *n* oliva *f*. **olive green** *adj* verde oliva. **olive grove** oliveto *m*. **olive oil** olio d'oliva *m*. **olive-tree** *n* olivo *m*.

Olympic [ə'lɪmpɪk] *adj* olimpico. **Olympic Games** olimpiadi *f pl*.

omelette ['omlit] *n* frittata *f*.

omen ['oumən] *n* presagio *m*, segno *m*.

ominous ['ominəs] *adj* sinistro, minaccioso.

omit [ou'mit] *v* omettere, tralasciare. **omission** *n* omissione *f*.

omnipotent [om'nipətənt] *adj* onnipotente. **omnipotence** *n* onnipotenza *f*.

on [on] *prep* su, sopra; a. *adv* su. *adj* (*gas, elec, etc.*) acceso; (*tap*) aperto.

once [wʌns] *adv* una volta. **all at once** ad un tratto. **at once** subito.

one [wʌn] *n, adj* uno, -a. *pron* uno; (*impersonal*) si. **oneself** *pron* sè (stesso); (*reflexive*) si. **one by one** a uno a uno. **one-sided** *adj* unilaterale; parziale; ineguale. **one-way street** senso unico *m*. **the one** quello, -a. **which one?** quale?

onion ['ʌnjən] *n* cipolla *f*.

onlooker ['onlukə] *n* spettatore, -trice *m, f*.

only ['ounli] *adj* solo, unico. *conj* ma. *adv* solo, soltanto. **only just** appena.

onset ['onset] *n* inizio *m*.

onshore ['onʃoː] *adv* a terra.

onslaught ['onsloːt] *n* attacco *m*, assalto *m*.

onus ['ounəs] *n* onere *m*, obbligo (*pl* -ghi) *m*.

onward ['onwəd] *adj* che progredisce *or* avanza. **onwards** *adv* (in) avanti.

onyx ['oniks] *n* onice *m*.

ooze [uz] *v* colare, trasudare.

opal ['oupəl] *n* opale *m*.

opaque [ə'paik] *adj* opaco (*m pl* -chi). **opacity** *n* opacità *f*.

open ['oupən] *v* aprire; iniziare; inaugurare. **open wide** spalancare. *nm, adj* aperto. **lay oneself open** to esporsi a. **open-handed** *adj* generoso. **open-hearted** *adj* sincero. **open-minded** *adj* spregiudicato, libero da preconcetti. **open-mouthed** *adj, adv* a bocca aperta.

opening ['oupəniŋ] *adj* introduttivo, inaugurale. *n* apertura *f*; inaugurazione *f*.

opera ['opərə] *n* opera *f*. **opera glasses** binocolo da teatro *m pl*. **opera house** teatro dell'opera *m*. **opera singer** cantante lirico, -a *m, f*. **operetta** *n* operetta *f*.

operate ['opəreit] *v* operare. **operation** *n* operazione *f*; (*activity*) attività *f*; (*surgical*) intervento (chirurgico) *m*. **come into operation** entrare in vigore. **operative** *adj*

operativo; attivo; (*surgical*) operatorio. **operator** *n* operatore, -trice *m, f*; (*phone*) telefonista *m, f*.

ophthalmic [of'θalmik] *adj* oftalmico.

opinion [ə'pinjən] *n* opinione *f*, parere *m*, giudizio *m*. **in the opinion of** secondo. **opinionated** *adj* dogmatico, intransigente.

opium ['oupiəm] *n* oppio *m*.

opponent [ə'pounənt] *n* avversario, -a *m, f*.

opportune [opə'tjuːn] *adj* opportuno, giusto.

opportunity [opə'tjuːnəti] *n* occasione *f*.

oppose [ə'pouz] *v* opporre, combattere; contrastare. **opposed** *adj* opposto, contrario. **opposition** *n* opposizione *f*.

opposite ['opəzit] *nm, adj* opposto, contrario. **opposite to** di fronte a, dirimpetto a.

oppress [ə'pres] *v* opprimere. **oppression** *n* oppressione *f*. **oppressive** *adj* oppressivo, opprimente. **oppressor** *n* oppressore *m*.

opt [opt] *v* optare. **opt out** decidere di non partecipare.

optical ['optikl] *adj* ottico. **optician** *n* ottico *m*. **optics** *n* ottica *f*.

optimism ['optimizəm] *n* ottimismo *m*. **optimist** *n* ottimista *m, f*. **optimistic** *adj* ottimistico.

optimum ['optiməm] *n* optimum *m*, meglio *m*. *adj* migliore.

option ['opʃən] *n* opzione *f*, scelta *f*. **optional** *adj* facoltativo.

opulent ['opjulənt] *adj* opulento. **opulence** *n* opulenza *f*.

or [oː] *conj* o, oppure. **either ... or ...** o ... o ... **or else** altrimenti.

oracle ['orəkl] *n* oracolo *m*.

oral ['oːrəl] *adj* orale.

orange ['orindʒ] *n* (*fruit*) arancia *f*; (*tree, colour*) arancio *m*. *adj* (*colour*) arancio, arancione. **orange juice** succo d'arancio *m*; (*drink*) spremuta d'arancio *f*. **orange squash** aranciata *f*.

orator ['orətə] *n* oratore, -trice *m, f*. **oration** *n* orazione *f*.

orbit ['oːbit] *n* orbita *f*.

orchard ['oːtʃəd] *n* frutteto *m*.

orchestra ['oːkəstrə] *n* orchestra *f*. **orchestral** *adj* orchestrale. **orchestrate** *v* orchestrare. **orchestration** *n* orchestrazione *f*.

orchid ['oːkid] *n* orchidea *f*.

ordain [oː'dein] *v* ordinare.

ordeal [oː'diːl] *n* dura prova *f*, travaglio *m*.

order ['ɔːdə] n ordine m; comando m; classe f, grado m; (commission) ordinazione f. in order that affinché, perché. in order to per, allo scopo di. out of order guasto. v ordinare. order about mandar qua e là.

orderly ['ɔːdəli] adj ordinato, regolare. n attendente m, inserviente m.

ordinal ['ɔːdinl] adj ordinale.

ordinary ['ɔːdinəri] nm, adj ordinario, solito, comune.

ore [ɔː] n minerale m.

oregano [ori'gɑːnou] n origano m.

organ ['ɔːgən] n organo m. **organ-pipe** n canna d'organo f. **organic** adj organico. **organist** n organista m, f.

organism ['ɔːgənizəm] n organismo m.

organize ['ɔːgənaiz] v organizzare. **organization** n organizzazione f. **organizer** n organizzatore, -trice m, f.

orgasm ['ɔːgəzəm] n orgasmo m.

orgy ['ɔːdʒi] n orgia f.

orient ['ɔːriənt] n oriente m. v orientare. **oriental** adj orientale. **orientate** v orientare. **orientation** n orientamento m.

origin ['ɔridʒin] n origine f. **originate** v originare. **originate from** derivare or provenire da. **originator** n creatore, -trice m, f; originatore, -trice m, f.

original [ə'ridʒinl] adj originale; (authentic, primitive) originario. n originale m. **originality** n originalità f. **originally** adv in origine.

ornament ['ɔːnəmənt] n ornamento m; (music) abbellimento m; (object, fitting) suppellittile f. v abbellire. **ornamentation** n abbellimento m.

ornate [ɔː'neit] adj ornato.

ornithology [ɔːni'θɔlədʒi] n ornitologia f. **ornithologist** n ornitologo, -a m, f.

orphan ['ɔːfən] n orfano, -a m, f. v rendere orfano. **be orphaned** rimanere orfano. **orphanage** n orfanotrofio m.

orthodox ['ɔːθədɔks] adj ortodosso. **orthodoxy** n ortodossia f.

orthopaedic [ɔːθə'piːdik] adj ortopedico. **orthopaedics** n ortopedia f. **orthopaedist** n ortopedico, -a m, f.

oscillate ['ɔsileit] v (far) oscillare; (fluctuate) vacillare. **oscillation** n oscillazione f.

ostensible [o'stensəbl] adj ostensibile.

ostentatious [osten'teiʃəs] adj ostentato, ostentoso.

osteopath ['ostiəpæθ] n osteologo, -a m, f.

ostracize ['ostrəsaiz] v osteggiare, mettere al bando.

ostrich ['ostritʃ] n struzzo m.

other ['ʌðə] adj altro, diverso. **on the other hand** d'altra parte. **other people** gli altri. pron altro. **each other** l'un l'altro.

otherwise ['ʌðəwaiz] adv altrimenti.

otter ['ɔtə] n lontra f.

*****ought** [ɔːt] v dovere.

our [auə] adj (il) nostro, (la) nostra; (pl) (i) nostri, (le) nostre.

ours [auəz] pron il nostro, la nostra; (pl) i nostri, le nostre.

ourselves [auə'selvz] pron noi (stessi); (reflexive) ci.

oust [aust] v espellere, soppiantare.

out [aut] adj (not alight) spento. adv via, fuori; (to the end) alla fine. **feel out of it** sentirsi a disagio. **out of** (without) senza. **out of action** fuori servizio, guasto. **out of date** antiquato; (ticket, etc.) scaduto. **out of doors** all'aperto. **out of place** inopportuno. **out of pocket** in perdita. **out of print** esaurito, fuori stampa. **out of tune** stonato. **out of work** disoccupato.

outboard ['autbɔːd] adj fuoribordo.

outbreak ['autbreik] n scoppio m; (riot) sommossa; eruzione f; epidemia f.

outbuilding ['autbildiŋ] n edificio annesso m, dipendenza f.

outburst ['autbəːst] n scoppio m; (invective) tirata f.

outcast ['autkɑːst] n, adj proscritto, -a, reietto, -a.

outcome ['autkʌm] n esito m, risultato m.

outcry ['autkrai] n grido m, scalpore m.

*****outdo** [aut'duː] v sorpassare.

outdoor ['autdɔː] adj all'aperto.

outer ['autə] adj esterno, esteriore.

outfit ['autfit] n corredo m, equipaggiamento m; (coll) equipaggiamento m.

outgoing ['autgouiŋ] adj uscente, in partenza; (person) estroverso, espansivo. **outgoings** pl n spese f pl.

*****outgrow** [aut'grou] v (grow taller than) sorpassare in altezza; (clothes) diventare troppo grande per.

outhouse ['authaus] n fabbricato annesso m.

outing ['autiŋ] n gita f, scampagnata f.

outlandish [aut'landiʃ] adj esotico.

outlast [aut'lɑːst] v durare più a lungo di, sopravvivere a.

outlaw ['autlɔ] n fuorilegge m, f invar. v mettere al bando, proscrivere.

outlay ['autlei] n spesa f, dispendio m.

outlet ['autlit] n sfogo m, sbocco m.

outline ['autlain] v delineare; (draft) abbozzare. n contorno m; (general sketch) abbozzo m. **outlines** pl n elementi m pl.

outlive [aut'liv] v sopravvivere a.

outlook ['autluk] n (view) veduta f; (future prospect) prospettiva f; (mental view) modo di vedere m, vedute f pl.

outlying ['autlaiiŋ] adj periferico, lontano.

outnumber [aut'nʌmbə] v superare in numero.

outpatient ['autpeiʃənt] n paziente esterno or ambulatoriale m, f.

outpost ['autpəust] n avamposto m.

output ['autput] n produzione f; (yield) rendimento m.

outrage ['autreidʒ] n oltraggio m. v oltraggiare.

outrageous [aut'reidʒəs] adj (disgraceful) vergognoso; offensivo; (excessive) esagerato.

outright ['autrait; adv aut'rait] adj completo, categorico. adv (at once) subito; (entirely) completamente; (openly) apertamente.

outset ['autset] n **at the outset** al principio.

outside [aut'said; adj 'autsaid] n esterno, esteriore; (extraneous) estraneo. adv fuori, all'aperto. prep fuori di; (except) all'infuori di. n esterno m. **at the outside** (coll) tutt'al più. **outsider** n estraneo m; (sport) outsider m invar.

outsize ['autsaiz] adj di taglia forte, fuori misura.

outskirts ['autskəːts] pl n dintorni m pl, periferia f sing.

outspoken [aut'spəukən] adj franco, esplicito, schietto.

outstanding [aut'standiŋ] adj (striking) eminente, notevole; (unpaid) in sospeso, arretrato.

outstrip [aut'strip] v distanziare.

outward ['autwəd] adj esterno, esteriore, superficiale; (journey) d'andata. **outwardly** adv in apparenza.

outweigh [aut'wei] v superare in importanza.

outwit [aut'wit] v superare in astuzia.

oval ['əuvəl] nm, adj ovale.

ovary ['əuvəri] n ovaia f.

ovation [əu'veiʃən] n ovazione f.

oven ['ʌvn] n forno m.

over ['əuvə] adv oltre, al di sopra; (in excess) in più; (finished) finito. prep su, sopra; (across) al di là di; (more than) più di. **over here** qui, da questa parte. **over there** là, laggiù.

overall ['əuvərɔːl] adj globale, completo. n (workman's) tuta f; (scientist's) camice m; (woman's) grembiulone m. adv in complesso.

overbalance [əuvə'baləns] v sbilanciare, perdere l'equilibrio.

overbearing [əuvə'beəriŋ] adj prepotente, altezzoso.

overboard ['əuvəbɔːd] adv in mare or acqua.

overcast [əuvə'kɑːst] adj coperto, nuvoloso.

overcharge [əuvə'tʃɑːdʒ] v far pagare troppo.

overcoat ['əuvəkəut] n cappotto m, soprabito m.

*****overcome** [əuvə'kʌm] v superare. adj sopraffatto, commosso.

overcrowded [əuvə'kraudid] adj sovraffollato. **overcrowding** n sovraffollamento m.

*****overdo** [əuvə'duː] v esagerare; (overcook) stracuocere.

overdose ['əuvədəus] n dose eccessiva f.

overdraft ['əuvədrɑːft] n scoperto (di conto) m.

*****overdraw** [əuvə'drɔː] v andare allo scoperto.

overdrive ['əuvədraiv] n marcia sovramoltiplicata f.

overdue [əuvə'djuː] adj in ritardo, tardivo; (bill) scaduto.

overestimate [əuvə'estimeit] v sopravvalutare.

overexpose [əuvəik'spəuz] v sovraesporre. **overexposure** n sovraesposizione f.

overflow [əuvə'fləu; n 'əuvəfləu] v (flood) inondare; (river) straripare; (vessel) traboccare. n (outlet) troppopieno m. **overflow pipe** scarico del troppopieno m.

overgrown [əuvə'grəun] adj ricoperto di vegetazione.

*****overhang** [əuvə'haŋ; n 'əuvəhaŋ] v sporgere sopra; (impend) incombere su, minacciare. n aggetto m; (mountaineering) strapiombo m.

overhaul [ouvə'hɔːl] v (*investigate*) esaminare; (*repair*) ripassare, riparare. n esame minuzioso m.

overhead [ouvə'hed] adv in alto, di sopra. adj di sopra, aereo. **overheads** pl n spese generali f pl.

*overhear** [ouvə'hiə] v udire per caso; (*eavesdrop*) origliare.

overheat [ouvə'hiːt] v surriscaldare.

overjoyed [ouvə'dʒɔid] adj felicissimo, colmo di gioia.

overland [ouvə'lænd] adj, adv per terra.

overlap [ouvə'læp] v sovrapporre, accavallare; coincidere or corrispondere in parte con.

*overlay** ['ouvəlei; v ouvə'lei] n copertura f. v ricoprire; incrostare.

overleaf [ouvə'liːf] adv see **overleaf** vedi retro.

overload [ouvə'loud; n 'ouvəloud] v sovraccaricare. n sovraccarico m.

overlook [ouvə'luk] v (*miss*) lasciarsi sfuggire, non rilevare; condonare; (*ignore*) non tener conto di, trascurare; (*house, etc.*) dare su.

overnight [ouvə'nait] adv di notte; (*suddenly*) d'un tratto. **stay overnight** pernottare.

overpower [ouvə'pauə] v sopraffare, dominare. **overpowering** adj irresistibile.

overrate [ouvə'reit] v sopravvalutare.

overreach [ouvə'riːtʃ] v **overreach oneself** sopravvalutare le proprie forze.

overriding [ouvə'raidiŋ] adj di primaria importanza.

overrule [ouvə'ruːl] v (*decision*) annullare; (*plea*) respingere.

*overrun** [ouvə'rʌn] v invadere, infestare.

overseas [ouvə'siːz] adv oltremare. adj d'oltremare, straniero.

overseer [ouvə'siə] n ispettore, -trice m, f, sorvegliante m, f.

overshadow [ouvə'ʃadou] v oscurare; (*render insignificant*) eclissare.

*overshoot** [ouvə'ʃuːt] v (*miss*) fallire; (*go beyond*) oltrepassare. **overshoot the mark** passare il segno. **overshoot the runway** atterrare lungo.

oversight ['ouvəsait] n svista f, inavvertenza f.

*oversleep** [ouvə'sliːp] v dormire troppo a lungo, dormire oltre all'ora stabilita.

overspill ['ouvəspil] n sovrappiù m.

overt [ou'vəːt] adj manifesto, overto.

*overtake** [ouvə'teik] v sorpassare.

*overthrow** [ouvə'θrou; n 'ouvəθrou] v rovesciare, sconfiggere. n rovesciamento m.

overtime ['ouvətaim] n ore straordinarie f pl.

overtone ['ouvətoun] n (*implication*) sfumatura f.

overture ['ouvətjuə] n (*music*) ouverture f, preludio m; (*proposal*) proposta f; (*political*) apertura f.

overturn [ouvə'təːn] v rovesciare, capovolgere.

overweight [ouvə'weit] adj be overweight pesare troppo.

overwhelm [ouvə'welm] v (*defeat*) sopraffare; (*crush*) schiacciare; (*with kindness, etc.*) colmare. **overwhelmingly** adv in modo schiacciante.

overwork [ouvə'wəːk] v (far) lavorar troppo. n eccesso di lavoro m.

overwrought [ouvə'rɔt] adj teso, turbato, agitato.

ovulate ['ovjuleit] v ovulare. **ovulation** n ovulazione f.

owe [ou] v dovere. **owing** adj dovuto. **owing to** dovuto a, grazie a.

owl [aul] n gufo m, civetta f.

own [oun] adj proprio. **get one's own back** rendere pan per focaccia. **on one's own** da solo. v possedere; (*recognize*) riconoscere; confessare. **owner** n proprietario, -a m, f. **ownership** n proprietà f, possesso m.

ox [oks] n, pl **oxen** bue (pl buoi) m. **oxtail** n coda di bue f.

oxygen ['oksidʒən] n ossigeno m.

oyster ['ɔistə] n ostrica f.

ozone ['ouzoun] n ozono m.

P

pace [peis] n passo m; (*speed*) velocità f. **keep pace with** (*walking*) camminare di pari passo con; (*keep up to date*) tenersi al corrente di. v **pace off** misurare a passi. **pace up and down** andare su e giù.

Pacific [pə'sifik] nm, adj pacifico.

pacifism ['pasifizəm] n pacifismo m. **pacifist** n pacifista m, f.

pacify ['pasifai] v pacificare.

pack [pak] n (*parcel*, *package*) pacco m; (*of goods*) imballo m; (*rucksack*) zaino m; (*cards*) mazzo m; (*thieves*) banda f;

(*hounds*) muta *f*. **pack of lies** tessuto di bugie *m*. v imballare; (*suitcases*) fare (le valige); (*cram*) pigiare. **packed** adj (*full*) pieno zeppo. **packing** *n* confezione *f*, imballaggio *m*; (*tech*) guarnizione *f*. **do one's packing** fare le valige, fare i bagagli.

package ['pakidʒ] *n* pacco *m*. *adj* (*deal, etc.*) comprensivo.

packet ['pakit] *n* pacchetto *m*.

pact [pakt] *n* patto *m*.

pad[1] [pad] *n* (*cushion*) cuscinetto *m*, tampone *m*; (*notepaper*) taccuino *m*; (*paw*) zampa *f*. v imbottire. **pad out** (*speech, essay, etc.*) infarcire. **padding** *n* imbottitura *f*; infarcimento *m*.

pad[2] [pad] v camminare a passo felpato.

paddle[1] ['padl] *n* (*of boat*) pagaia *f*; (*tech*) spatola *f*; (*zool*) pinna *f*. **paddle-boat** *n* piroscafo a ruote *m*. v remare piano.

paddle[2] ['padl] v sguazzare (nell'acqua). **paddling pool** piscina per bambini *f*.

paddock ['padək] *n* recinto *m*; (*racing*) paddock *m invar*.

paddy-field ['padifiːld] *n* risaia *f*.

padlock ['padlok] *n* lucchetto *m*. v chiudere col lucchetto.

paediatric [piːdi'atrik] *adj* pediatrico. **paediatrician** *n* pediatra *m, f*. **paediatrics** *n* pediatria *f*.

pagan ['peigən] *n, adj* pagano, -a.

page[1] [peidʒ] *n* (*book*) pagina *f*.

page[2] [peidʒ] *n also* **page-boy** paggio *m*; (*hotel*) piccolo *m*. v (*coll*) chiamare.

pageant ['padʒənt] *n* corteo storico *m*. **pageantry** *n* fasto *m*.

paid [peid] *V* pay.

pain [pein] *n* dolore *m*, sofferenza *f*. **be at pains to** sforzarsi di. **on pain of** sotto pena di. **painkiller** *n* analgesico *m*. **painstaking** adj laborioso. v addolorare, far male a. **painful** adj dóloroso. **painless** adj indolore.

paint [peint] v dipingere, pitturare; (*decorate*) verniciare. *n* colore *m*, vernice *f*. **paint-box** *n* scatola di colori *f*. **paintbrush** *n* pennello *m*. **painter** *n* pittore, -trice *m, f*; decoratore *m*. **painting** *n* quadro *m*, pittura *f*.

pair [peə] *n* paio *m* (*pl* -a *f*), coppia *f*. v accoppiare.

pal [pal] *n* (*coll*) compagno, -a *m, f*.

palace ['paləs] *n* palazzo *m*. **palatial** adj sontuoso.

palate ['palit] *n* palato *m*. **palatable** adj saporito.

pale[1] [peil] adj pallido. v impallidire. **paleness** *n* pallore *m*.

pale[2] [peil] *n* (*stake*) palo *m*. **beyond the pale** adj (*coll*) impossibile.

palette ['palit] *n* tavolozza *f*. **palette knife** spatola *f*.

pall[1] [poːl] v smettere *or* cessare di interessare; (*weary*) stancare.

pall[2] [poːl] *n* drappo funebre *m*.

palm[1] [paːm] *n* (*of hand*) palmo *m*. v **palm off** affibbiare. **palmist** *n* chiromante *m, f*. **palmistry** *n* chiromanzia *f*.

palm[2] [paːm] *n* (*tree*) palma *f*. **Palm Sunday** Domenica delle Palme *f*.

palpitation [ˌpalpi'teiʃən] *n* palpitazione *f*.

pamper ['pampə] v viziare.

pamphlet ['pamflit] *n* opuscolo *m*; (*polemical*) libello *m*.

pan [pan] *n* pentola *f*, casseruola *f*, padella *f*. **pancake** *n* frittella *f*. **Pancake Tuesday** martedì grasso *m*.

pancreas ['pankriəs] *n* pancreas *m invar*. **pancreatic** adj pancreatico.

panda ['pandə] *n* panda *m invar*.

pander ['pandə] v **pander to** favorire, andare incontro a.

pane [pein] *n* vetro *m*.

panel ['panl] *n* pannello *m*; (*jury*) lista *f*; (*instruments*) cruscotto *m*. **panelling** *n* rivestimento a pannelli *m*.

pang [paŋ] *n* dolore acuto *m*, spasimo *m*.

panic ['panik] *n* panico *m*, allarme *m*. **panic-stricken** adj colto dal panico. v essere in preda al panico. **panicky** adj apprensivo.

panorama [ˌpanə'raːmə] *n* panorama *m*.

pansy ['panzi] *n* (*flower*) viola del pensiero *f*; (*coll: homosexual*) finocchio *m*.

pant [pant] v anelare, sbuffare.

panther ['panθə] *n* pantera *f*.

pantomime ['pantəmaim] *n* pantomina *f*; (*Christmas*) spettacolo di Natale *m*.

pantry ['pantri] *n* dispensa *f*.

pants [pants] *pl n* mutande *f pl*.

papal ['peipl] adj papale. **papacy** *n* papato *m*.

paper ['peipə] *n* carta *f*; documento *m*; (*treatise*) discorso *m*; (*news*) giornale *m*. **paperback** *n* edizione economica *f*. **paper-clip** *n* fermaglio *m*, agrafe *f*. **papermill** *n* cartiera *f*. **paperweight** *n* fermacarte *m invar*. **paperwork** *n* lavoro d'ufficio *m*; documenti *m pl*. *v* tappezzare.

paprika ['pæprikə] *n* paprica *f*.

par [pɑː] *n* above/below par sopra/sotto la pari. feel below par sentirsi (un po') giù. on a par with alla pari con.

parable ['pærəbl] *n* parabola *f*.

parabola [pə'ræbələ] *n* parabola *f*.

parachute ['pærəʃuːt] *n* paracadute *m invar*. *v* scendere col paracadute. **parachutist** *n* paracadutista *m*, *f*.

parade [pə'reid] *n* (*display*) sfoggio *m*; (*mil*) sfilata *f*; (*sea-front*) lungomare *m*. *v* ostentare, sfoggiare; sfilare.

paradise ['pærədais] *n* paradiso *m*.

paradox ['pærədɒks] *n* paradosso *m*. **paradoxical** *adj* paradossale.

paraffin ['pærəfin] *n* paraffina liquida *f*; (*oil*) cherosene *m*, petrolio da illuminazione *m*.

paragraph ['pærəgrɑːf] *n* paragrafo *m*; (*news item*) trafiletto *m*.

parallel ['pærəlel] *adj* parallelo. **parallel line** parallela *f*. *n* parallelo *m*; (*comparison*) paragone *m*.

paralyse ['pærəlaiz] *v* paralizzare. **paralysis** *n*, *pl* -ses paralisi *f*. **paralytic** *n*, *adj* paralitico, -a.

parameter [pə'ræmitə] *n* parametro *m*.

paramilitary [,pærə'militəri] *adj* paramilitare.

paramount ['pærəmaunt] *adj* sommo, supremo.

paranoia [,pærə'nɔiə] *n* paranoia *f*. **paranoiac** *or* **paranoid** *n*, *adj* paranoico, -a.

parapet ['pærəpit] *n* parapetto *m*.

paraphernalia [,pærəfə'neiliə] *n* oggetti vari *m pl*, cianfrusaglie *f pl*.

paraphrase ['pærəfreiz] *n* parafrasi *f*. *v* parafrasare.

paraplegic [,pærə'pliːdʒik] *n*, *adj* paraplegico, -a. **paraplegia** *n* paraplegia *f*.

parasite ['pærəsait] *n* parassita *m*, *f*. **parasitic** *adj* parassita, parassitico.

parasol ['pærəsɒl] *n* parasole *m*.

paratrooper ['pærə,truːpə] *n* (soldato) paracadutista *m*.

parcel ['pɑːsl] *n* pacco *m*, pacchetto *m*. **by parcel post** a mezzo pacco postale. **part and parcel of** parte integrale di. *v* **parcel up** impacchettare.

parched [pɑːtʃt] *adj* riarso. **be parched with thirst** morire dalla sete.

parchment ['pɑːtʃmənt] *n* pergamena *f*,

cartapecora *f*. **parchment paper** carta pergamenata *f*.

pardon ['pɑːdn] *n* perdono *m*; (*law*) grazia *f*; (*for minor fault*) scusa *f*. **I beg your pardon** mi scusi. *v* scusare; perdonare; graziare. *interj* prego? **pardonable** *adj* perdonabile.

pare [peə] *v* sbucciare, pelare. **pare down** ridurre.

parent ['peərənt] *n* padre, madre *m*, *f*. **parents** *pl n* genitori *m pl*. **parental** *adj* dei genitori. **parenthood** *n* l'essere genitori *m*.

parenthesis [pə'renθəsis] *n*, *pl* -ses parentesi *f*.

pariah [pə'raiə] *n* paria *m invar*.

Paris ['pæris] *n* Parigi *f*. **Parisian** *n*, *adj* parigino, -a.

parish ['pæriʃ] *n* parrocchia *f*; (*civil*) comune *m*. **parish priest** parroco (*pl* -chi) *m*. **parishioner** *n* parrocchiano, -a *m*, *f*.

parity ['pærəti] *n* parità *f*.

park [pɑːk] *n* parco *m*. *v* parcheggiare, posteggiare. **parking** *n* posteggio *m*, parcheggio *m*. **parking meter** parchimetro *m*.

parliament ['pɑːləmənt] *n* parlamento *m*. **member of parliament** deputato *m*. **parliamentary** *adj* parlamentare.

parlour ['pɑːlə] *n* salotto *m*. **parlour game** gioco di società *m*.

Parmesan [,pɑːmi'zæn] *n* (*cheese*) (formaggio) parmigiano *m*, grana *m invar*.

parochial [pə'roukiəl] *adj* provinciale.

parody ['pærədi] *n* parodia *f*. *v* parodiare.

parole [pə'roul] *v* rilasciare sulla parola. *n* rilascio sulla parola *m*.

paroxysm ['pærəksizəm] *n* parossismo *m*, accesso *m*.

parrot ['pærət] *n* pappagallo *m*.

parsley ['pɑːsli] *n* prezzemolo *m*.

parsnip ['pɑːsnip] *n* pastinaca *f*.

parson ['pɑːsn] *n* prete *m*, parroco *m*. **parsonage** *n* casa parrocchiale *f*, presbiterio *m*.

part [pɑːt] *n* parte *f*; (*theatre*) ruolo *m*; (*district*) quartiere *m*. **part-time** *adv*, *adj* a mezzo tempo. **spare part** pezzo di ricambio *m*. **take part** prender parte. *v* separare, spartire; (*hair*) dividere. **part with** rinunciare a. **parting** *n* separazione *f*, addio *m*; (*hair*) divisa dei capelli *f*, riga *f*.

***partake** [pɑː'teik] *v* **partake of** consumare.

partial ['pɑːʃəl] adj parziale. **be partial to** avere un debole per. **partiality** n preferenza f. **partially** adv in parte.

participate [pɑː'tisipeit] v partecipare. **participant** n partecipante m, f. **participation** n partecipazione f.

participle ['pɑːtisipl] n participio m.

particle ['pɑːtikl] n particella f.

particular [pə'tikjulə] adj particolare, speciale; (exacting) esigente. n particolare m, dettaglio m. **particularly** adv in particolare, specie.

partisan [pɑːti'zan] n, adj partigiano, -a.

partition [pɑː'tiʃən] n spartizione f; (of room) tramezzo m. v spartire; tramezzare.

partly ['pɑːtli] adv in parte.

partner ['pɑːtnə] n (comm) socio m; compagno, -a m, f, partner (pl -s) m, f. v far da compagno a, associarsi a. **partnership** n società f, associazione f.

partridge ['pɑːtridʒ] n pernice f.

party ['pɑːti] n (group) compagnia f, gruppo m; (entertainment) festa f, trattenimento m; (pol) partito m; (law) parte f. **third party** terzi m pl.

pass [pɑːs] n (mountain) passo m, valico (pl -chi) m; (permit) permesso m; (mil) libera uscita f; (school) promozione f; (sport) allungo m. v passare, superare; promuovere; allungare. **pass by** (disregard) non curarsi di; (in front of) passare davanti a. **pass off** far passare (per). **pass on** trasmettere; (die) morire. **pass out** (faint) svenire.

passage ['pɑːsidʒ] n passaggio m; (in book) brano m.

passenger ['pɑːsindʒə] n viaggiatore, -trice m, f. **passenger train** treno viaggiatori m.

passer-by [pɑːsə'bai] n passante m, f.

passing ['pɑːsiŋ] adj passeggero, transitorio; casuale. **in passing** di passaggio or sfuggita; (by the way) tra parentesi.

passion ['pɑːʃən] n passione f, entusiasmo m. **passionate** adj appassionato, ardente.

passive ['pɑːsiv] nm, adj passivo. **passivity** n passività f.

Passover ['pɑːsouvə] n Pasqua degli ebrei f.

passport ['pɑːspɔːt] n passaporto m.

password ['pɑːswəːd] n parola d'ordine f.

past [pɑːst] prep al di là di, oltre; (after) dopo. **five past six** le sei e cinque. adj passato, scorso; (former) ex. adv davanti, oltre. n passato m.

pasta ['pɑːstə] n pasta f, pastasciutta f.

paste [peist] n pasta f; (adhesive) colla f. v incollare.

pastel ['pɑːstəl] n pastello m.

pasteurize ['pɑːstʃəraiz] v pastorizzare. **pasteurization** n pastorizzazione f.

pastime ['pɑːstaim] n passatempo m.

pastoral ['pɑːstərəl] adj pastorale.

pastry ['peistri] n pasta f. **pastry-cook** n pasticciere, -a m, f.

pasture ['pɑːstʃə] n pascolo m, pastura f. v pascolare.

pasty[1] ['peisti] adj pallido; (consistency) pastoso.

pasty[2] ['pɑːsti] n (pie) pasticcio m.

pat[1] [pat] adj pronto, apposito. adv (aptly) a proposito; (exactly) precisamente.

pat[2] [pat] n (light blow) colpetto m; (of butter) pezzetto m. v dare un colpetto a.

patch [patʃ] n (material) pezza f, toppa f; (land) pezzo m. **go through a bad patch** attraversare un momento brutto. v rattoppare. **patch up** rattoppare, accomodare; (quarrel) comporre. **patchy** adj rattoppato; (not uniform) variabile.

pâté ['patei] n pasticcio m, pâté m invar.

patent ['peitənt] adj manifesto, ovvio. **patent leather** pelle verniciata f. **patent medicine** specialità medicinale f. n brevetto m. v brevettare.

paternal [pə'təːnl] adj paterno. **paternity** n paternità f.

path [pɑːθ] n sentiero m; (course, way) via f, strada f.

pathetic [pə'θetik] adj patetico, commovente.

pathology [pə'θolədʒi] n anatomia patologica f. **pathological** adj patologico. **pathologist** n anatomo patologo, anatoma patologa m, f.

patient ['peiʃənt] adj paziente. n paziente m, f, malato, -a m, f. **be patient** pazientare, aver pazienza. **patience** n pazienza f.

patio ['patiou] n patio m invar.

patriarchal ['peitriɑːkl] adj patriarcale. **patriarch** n patriarca m.

patriot ['patriət] n patriota m, f. **patriotic** adj patriottico. **patriotism** n patriottismo m.

patrol [pə'troul] n pattuglia f. v andare in pattuglia, ispezionare.

patron ['peitrən] n patrono m, protettore m; (customer) cliente abituale m, f, avventore, -a *m, f.* **patronage** *n* protezione *f*, auspici *m pl.* **patronize** *v* favorire, proteggere; frequentare. **patronizing** *adj* condiscendente.

patter[1] ['patə] *v (sound)* picchiettare. *n* picchiettio *m.*

patter[2] ['patə] *n (speech)* cicalata *f*, ciancia *f. v* cicalare, cianciare.

pattern ['patən] *n* modello *m*, tipo *m*; disegno *m. v* modellare.

paunch [pɔintʃ] *n* pancia *f.* **paunchy** *adj* panciuto.

pauper ['pɔipə] *n* povero, -a *m, f*; mendicante *m, f.* **pauperize** *v* impoverire.

pause [pɔiz] *n* pausa *f*; esitazione *f. v* fare una pausa; esitare.

pave [peiv] *v* pavimentare. **pave the way** preparare il terreno. **pavement** *n* marciapiede *m.* **paving stone** lastra da selciato *f.*

pavilion [pə'viljən] *n* padiglione *m.*

paw [pɔi] *n* zampa *f. v (ground)* scalpitare; *(handle)* palpeggiare.

pawn[1] [pɔin] *n (deposit)* pegno *m.* **pawnbroker** *n* prestatore su pegno *m.* **pawnshop** *n* monte di pietà *m. v* pignorare, dare in pegno.

pawn[2] [pɔin] *n (chess)* pedina *f.*

*****pay** [pei] *n* paga *f*, stipendio *m.* **in the pay of** al servizio di. **pay-roll** *n* organico *m. v* pagare; *(settle)* saldare; *(profit)* rendere; *(attention, etc.)* fare. **pay back** rimborsare, restituire. **pay in** versare. **pay off** liquidare. **payable** *adj* pagabile. **payee** *n* beneficiario, -a *m, f.* **payment** *n* pagamento *m*, versamento *m.*

pea [pii] *n* pisello *m.*

peace [piis] *n* pace *f*; tranquillità *f.* **breach of the peace** violazione dell'ordine pubblico *f.* **peace-loving** *adj* pacifico. **peace offering** dono propiziatorio *m.* **peace-time** *n* tempo di pace *m.* **peaceful** *adj* pacifico.

peach [piitʃ] *n (fruit)* pesca *f*; *(tree)* pesco *m.*

peacock ['piikɔk] *n* pavone *m.* **peacock blue** *nm, adj.* blu pavone. **peahen** *n* pavona *f.*

peak [piik] *n* cima *f*, vetta *f*; *(highest point)* massimo *m*; *(on cap)* visiera *f.* **peak hours** ore di punta *f pl.* **peak load** carico massimo *m. v* raggiungere il massimo.

peal [piil] *n (bells)* scampanio *m*; *(thunder, laughter)* scoppio *m*, scroscio *m. v* scampanare; *(thunder)* rimbombare.

peanut ['piinʌt] *n* arachide *f.*

pear [peə] *n (fruit)* pera *f*; *(tree)* pero *m.*

pearl [pəil] *n* perla *f.* **pearly** *adj (like pearl)* perlaceo; *(adorned with pearls)* perlato.

peasant ['peznt] *n* contadino, -a *m, f.*

peat [piit] *n* torba *f.*

pebble ['pebl] *n* ciottolo *m.* **pebbly** *adj* ciottoloso.

peck [pek] *v* beccare; *(food)* mangiucchiare; *(kiss)* dare un bacetto a, baciucchiare. *n* beccata *f*; baciucchio *m.*

peckish ['pekiʃ] *adj* **feel peckish** sentirsi vuoto *or* affamato.

peculiar [pi'kjuiljə] *adj* strano, particolare. **peculiarity** *n* particolarità *f*, stranezza *f.*

pedal ['pedl] *n* pedale *m. v* pedalare.

pedantic [pi'dantik] *adj* pedante. **pedant** *n* pedante *m, f.* **pedantry** *n* pedanteria *f.*

peddle ['pedl] *v* spacciare.

pedestal ['pedistl] *n* piedistallo *m.*

pedestrian [pi'destriən] *adj* pedonale; *(commonplace)* pedestre. *n* pedone *m.* **pedestrian precinct** zona pedonale *f.*

pedigree ['pedigrii] *n* genealogia *f*; *(of animals)* pedigree *m invar. adj* di razza.

pedlar ['pedlə] *n (salesman)* venditore ambulante *m.*

peel [piil] *n* buccia *f. v* sbucciare; *(paint, skin)* staccarsi. **peeler** *n* sbucciatore *m.* **peelings** *pl n* bucce *f pl.*

peep [piip] *n* occhiata *(furtiva)* *f*, sguardo furtivo *m. v* dare un'occhiatina, spiare. **peep-hole** *n* spiraglio *m.* **peep out** mostrarsi appena.

peer[1] [piə] *v* **peer at** scrutare, guardare da presso.

peer[2] [piə] *n* pari *m.* **peerage** *n* nobiltà *f.*

peevish ['piiviʃ] *adj* permaloso, scontroso.

peg [peg] *n* piolo *m*; *(violin, etc.)* bischero *m*; *(washing)* molletta *f.* **off the peg** *adj* pronto. *v (prices)* stabilire. **peg out** *(coll: die)* crepare.

pejorative [pə'dʒɔrativ] *adj* peggiorativo.

Peking [pii'kiŋ] *n* Pechino *f.* **Pekingese** *n (dog)* *(cane)* pechinese *m.*

pelican ['pelikən] *n* pellicano *m.*

pellet ['pelit] *n* pallottola *f*, pallina *f*; *(pill)* pillola *f.*

pelmet ['pelmit] *n* mantovana *f.*

pelt[1] [pelt] *v* scagliare; *(rain)* piovere

dirottamente, diluviare. *n* **at full pelt** a piena velocità.

pelt² [pelt] *n* pelliccia *f*.

pelvis ['pelvis] *n* pelvi *f*, bacino *m*. **pelvic** *adj* pelvico.

pen¹ [pen] *n* (*for writing*) penna *f*. *v* scrivere.

pen² [pen] *n* recinto *m*; (*for sheep*) ovile *m*; (*for pigs*) porcile *m*. *v* **pen in** rinchiudere.

penal ['piːnl] *adj* penale. **penalize** *v* punire. **penalty** *n* pena *f*; (*fine*) multa *f*. **penalty kick** (*sport*) calcio di rigore *m*.

penance ['penəns] *n* penitenza *f*.

pencil ['pensl] *n* matita *f*. **pencil-sharpener** *n* temperamatite *m invar*.

pendant ['pendənt] *n* ciondolo *m*.

pending ['pendiŋ] *adj* in sospeso. *prep* in attesa di.

pendulum ['pendjuləm] *n* pendolo *m*. **pendulum clock** orologio a pendolo *m*.

penetrate ['penitreit] *v* penetrare. **penetration** *n* penetrazione *f*.

pen-friend *n* amico. **-a** per corrispondenza *m*, *f*.

penguin ['pengwin] *n* pinguino *m*.

penicillin [peni'silin] *n* penicillina *f*.

peninsula [pə'ninsjulə] *n* penisola *f*. **peninsular** *adj* peninsulare.

penis ['piːnis] *n* pene *m*.

penitent ['penitənt] *n(m+f)*, *adj* penitente. **penitence** *n* penitenza *f*, pentimento *m*. **penitentiary** *n* (*prison*) penitenziario *m*; (*church dignitary*) penitenziere *m*.

penknife ['pennaif] *n* temperino *m*.

pen-name *n* pseudonimo *m*.

pennant ['penənt] *n* pennello *m*.

penniless ['peniləs] *adj* al verde, senza un soldo.

pension ['penʃən] *n* pensione *f*. *v* **pension off** mettere a riposo, mettere in pensione. **pensioner** *n* pensionato, **-a** *m*, *f*.

pensive ['pensiv] *adj* pensoso, pensieroso, preoccupato.

pentagon ['pentəgən] *n* pentagono *m*. **pentagonal** *adj* pentagonale.

penthouse ['penthaus] *n* attico *m*.

pent-up ['pent'ʌp] *adj* represso.

penultimate [pi'nʌltimit] *adj* penultimo.

people ['piːpl] *n* popolo *m*, nazione *f*. *pl* **gente** *f sing*; (*coll: family*) i suoi *m pl*. *v* popolare.

pepper ['pepə] *n* pepe *m*. **peppercorn** *n* grano di pepe *m*. **pepper-mill** *n*

macinapepe *m invar*. **peppermint** *n* (*herb*) menta piperita *f*; (*sweet*) mentina *f*. **pepper-pot** *n* pepaiola *f*. *v* (*season*) pepare; (*dot*) cospargere; (*hit*) tempestare.

per [pəː] *prep* a. as per secondo. **per cent** percento. **percentage** *n* percentuale *f*.

perceive [pə'siːv] *v* rilevare, scorgere, accorgersi di.

perceptible [pə'septibl] *adj* percettibile; visibile. **perceptibility** *n* percettibilità *f*; visibilità *f*.

perception [pə'sepʃən] *n* percezione *f*. **perceptive** *adj* percettivo, sensibile.

perch¹ [pəːtʃ] *n* posatoio *m*. *v* posarsi.

perch² [pəːtʃ] *n* (*fish*) pesce persico *m*.

percolate ['pəːkəleit] *v* filtrare. **percolator** *n* percolatore *m*.

percussion [pə'kʌʃən] *n* percussione *f*.

perennial [pə'reniəl] *adj* perenne; perpetuo. *v* pianta perenne *f*.

perfect ['pəːfikt; *v* pə'fekt] *adj* perfetto, ideale; (*real*) vero. *v* perfezionare. **perfection** *n* perfezione *f*.

perforate ['pəːfəreit] *v* perforare. **perforation** *n* perforazione *f*.

perform [pə'fɔːm] *v* eseguire, compire; (*music, theatre*) recitare. **performance** *n* esecuzione *f*; recita *f*; (*show*) spettacolo *m*. **performer** *n* artista *m*, *f*.

perfume ['pəːfjuːm] *n* profumo *m*. *v* profumare. **perfumery** *n* profumeria *f*.

perfunctory [pə'fʌŋktəri] *adj* fatto alla buona, meccanico, indifferente.

perhaps [pə'haps] *adv* forse, magari.

peril ['peril] *n* rischio *m*. **perilous** *adj* rischioso, pericoloso.

perimeter [pə'rimitə] *n* perimetro *m*.

period ['piəriəd] *n* periodo *m*; (*full stop*) punto fermo *m*; (*med*) mestruazione *f*. *adj* antico (*m pl* -chi), storico. **periodic** *adj* periodico. **periodical** *nm*, *adj* periodico.

peripheral [pə'rifərəl] *adj* periferico. **periphery** *n* periferia *f*.

periscope ['periskoup] *n* periscopio *m*.

perish ['periʃ] *v* perire; (*food, etc.*) guastarsi, deperire. **perishable** *adj* deperibile.

perjure ['pəːdʒə] *v* spergiurare. **perjurer** *n* spergiuro, **-a** *m*, *f*. **perjury** *n* spergiuro *m*, giuramento falso *m*.

perk [pəːk] *v* **perk up** rianimarsi, ravvivarsi. **perky** *adj* vispo.

perm [pəːm] *n* permanente *f*. **have a perm** farsi fare la permanente.

permanent ['pɔ:mənənt] *adj* permanente.
permeate ['pɔ:mieit] *v* permeare.
permit ['pɔ:mit; *v* pə'mit] *n* permesso *m*, licenza *f*. *v* permettere. **permissible** *adj* permissibile. **permission** *n* permesso *m*. **permissive** *adj* permissivo.
permutation [pɔ:mju'teiʃən] *n* permutazione *f*.
pernicious [pə'niʃəs] *adj* pernicioso.
pernickety [pə'nikəti] *adj* pignolo.
perpendicular [,pɔ:pən'dikjulə] *nf*, *adj* perpendicolare.
perpetrate ['pɔ:pitreit] *v* commettere. **perpetration** *n* perpetrazione *f*. **perpetrator** *n* perpetratore, -trice *m*, *f*.
perpetual [pə'petʃuəl] *adj* perpetuo. **perpetuate** [pə'petʃueit] *v* perpetuare. **perpetuation** *n* perpetuazione *f*. **in perpetuity** in perpetuo.
perplex [pə'pleks] *v* confondere, rendere perplesso. **perplexed** *adj* perplesso, confuso. **perplexing** *adj* imbarazzante. **perplexity** *n* perplessità *f*, imbarazzo *m*.
persecute ['pɔ:sikjut] *v* perseguitare. **persecution** *n* persecuzione *f*.
persevere [,pɔ:si'viə] *v* perseverare. **perseverance** *n* perseveranza *f*, assiduità *f*. **persevering** *adj* perseverante, assiduo.
persist [pə'sist] *v* persistere, ostinarsi, perseverare. **persistence** *n* perseveranza *f*, persistenza *f*, ostinazione *f*. **persistent** *adj* ostinato, persistente.
person ['pɔ:sn] *n* persona *f*, individuo *m*. **personage** *n* personaggio *m*. **personal** *adj* personale; (*disparaging*) offensivo, di carattere personale. **personality** *n* personalità *f*; carattere *m*; celebrità *f*. **personify** [pə'sonifai] *v* personificare. **personification** *n* personificazione *f*.
personnel [,pɔ:sə'nel] *n* personale *m*, impiegati *m pl*.
perspective [pə'spektiv] *n* prospettiva *f*.
perspire [pə'spaiə] *v* sudare. **perspiration** *n* sudore *m*.
persuade [pə'sweid] *v* persuadere. **persuasion** *n* persuasione *f*. **persuasive** *adj* persuasivo.
pert [pɔ:t] *adj* (*lively*) vispo; impudente, insolente.
pertain [pə'tein] *v* **pertain to** riguardare, appartenere a. **pertinent** *adj* pertinente, a proposito. **pertinence** *n* pertinenza *f*.
perturb [pə'tɔ:b] *v* turbare, sconcertare.
peruse [pə'ru:z] *v* leggere attentamente.

pervade [pə'veid] *v* pervadere. **pervasive** *adj* penetrante.
perverse [pə'vɔ:s] *adj* perverso. **perversity** *n* perversità *f*.
pervert ['pɔ:vɔ:t; *v* pə'vɔ:t] *n* pervertito, -a *m*, *f*. *v* pervertire. **perversion** *n* perversione *f*, pervertimento *m*.
pessimism ['pesimizəm] *n* pessimismo *m*. **pessimist** *n* pessimista *m*, *f*. **pessimistic** *adj* pessimista, pessimistico.
pest [pest] *n* animale *or* parassita nocivo *m*; (*coll: nuisance*) seccatore *m*. **pest control** disinfestazione *f*. **pesticide** *n* pesticida *m*.
pester ['pestə] *v* seccare.
pet [pet] *n* animale favorito *m*; (*favourite*) cocco, -a *m*, *f*. *adj* prediletto. **pet aversion** avversione spiccata *f*. **pet name** nomignolo *m*. *v* coccolare. **petting** *n* (*slang*) carezze amorose *f pl*.
petal ['petl] *n* petalo *m*.
petition [pə'tiʃən] *n* petizione *f*, supplica *f*. *v* presentare una petizione *or* supplica.
petrify ['petrifai] *v* pietrificare, paralizzare. **petrified** *adj* allibito, pietrificato.
petrol ['petrəl] *n* benzina *f*. **petrol-tank** *n* serbatoio *m*.
petroleum [pə'trouliəm] *n* petrolio *m*.
petticoat ['petikout] *n* sottana *f*.
petty ['peti] *adj* insignificante; (*mean*) meschino. **petty cash** piccola cassa *f*, fondo per le piccole spese *m*. **petty officer** capo *m*. **pettiness** *n* piccolezza *f*, meschinità *f*.
petulant ['petjulənt] *adj* scontroso, irritabile. **petulance** *n* scontrosità *f*, irritabilità *f*.
pew [pju:] *n* banco (di chiesa) *m*.
pewter ['pju:tə] *n* peltro *m*.
phantom ['fantəm] *n* fantasma *m*.
pharmacy ['fa:məsi] *n* farmacia *f*. **pharmaceutical** *adj* farmaceutico. **pharmacist** *n* farmacista *m*, *f*.
pharynx ['farinks] *n* faringe *f*.
phase [feiz] *n* fase *f*.
pheasant ['feznt] *n* fagiano *m*.
phenomenon [fə'nomənən] *n*, *pl* **-ena** fenomeno *m*. **phenomenal** *adj* fenomenale.
phial ['faiəl] *n* fiala *f*.
philanthropy [fi'lanθrəpi] *n* filantropia *f*. **philanthropic** *adj* filantropico. **philanthropist** *n* filantropo, -a *m*, *f*.
philately [fi'latəli] *n* filatelia *f*. **philatelist** *n* filatelico, -a *m*, *f*.

philosophy [fi'losəfi] *n* filosofia *f*. **philosopher** *n* filosofo, -a *m, f*. **philosophical** *adj* filosofico.

phlegm [flem] *n* (*mucus*) muco *m*; (*sluggishness*) flemma *f*.

phlegmatic [fleg'matik] *adj* flemmatico.

phobia ['foubiə] *n* fobia *f*.

phone [foun] *n* (*coll*) telefono *m*. *v* telefonare (a).

phonetic [fə'netik] *adj* fonetico. **phonetics** *n* fonetica *f*.

phoney ['founi] (*coll*) *adj* falso, fasullo. *n* ipocrita *m, f*; impostore *m*.

phosphate ['fosfeit] *n* fosfato *m*.

phosphorescence [fosfə'resəns] *n* fosforescenza *f*. **phosphorescent** *adj* fosforescente.

phosphorus ['fosfərəs] *n* fosforo *m*.

photo ['foutou] *n* (*coll*) foto *f*.

photocopy ['foutou,kopi] *n* fotocopia *f*. *v* fotocopiare.

photogenic [,foutou'dʒenik] *adj* fotogenico.

photograph ['foutəgraif] *n* fotografia *f*. *v* fotografare. **photographer** *n* fotografo *m*. **photographic** *adj* fotografico. **photography** *n* fotografia *f*.

phrase [freiz] *n* frase *f*, modo di dire *m*. *v* esprimere, formulare.

physical ['fizikəl] *adj* fisico.

physician [fi'ziʃən] *n* medico *m*.

physics ['fiziks] *n* fisica *f*. **physicist** *n* fisico, -a *m, f*.

physiology [,fizi'olədʒi] *n* fisiologia *f*. **physiological** *adj* fisiologico. **physiologist** *n* fisiologo, -a *m, f*.

physiotherapy [,fiziou'θerəpi] *n* fisioterapia *f*. **physiotherapist** *n* fisioterapista *m, f*.

physique [fi'ziːk] *n* fisico *m*.

piano [pi'anou] *n* pianoforte *m*. **pianist** *n* pianista *m, f*.

pick¹ [pik] *v* (*choose*) scegliere; (*pluck*) cogliere. **pick out** scegliere. **pickpocket** *n* borsaiolo *m*. **pick up** raccogliere; (*recover*) star meglio; (*passenger*) far salire; (*learn*) imparare. **pick-up** *n* pick-up *m*. *n* (*choice*) scelta *f*; (*best*) fior fiore *m*.

pick² [pik] *n* piccone *m*.

picket ['pikit] *n* picchetto *m*. *v* picchettare.

pickle ['pikl] *v* marinare; (*in vinegar*) mettere sott'aceto. *n* (*coll: predicament*) pasticcio *m*. **pickles** *pl n* sottaceti *m pl*. **pickled** *adj* sottaceto.

picnic ['piknik] *n* picnic *m invar*, colazione all'aperto *f*.

pictorial [pik'toːriəl] *adj* illustrato.

picture ['piktʃə] *v* immaginare, figurare. *n* (*painting*) quadro *m*; foto *f*; (*image*) immagine *f*; film *m*. **be in the picture** essere informato. **pictures** *n* (*coll*) cinema *m*. **put in the picture** mettere al corrente.

picturesque [piktʃə'resk] *adj* pittoresco.

pidgin ['pidʒən] *n* linguaggio bastardo *or* maccheronico *m*.

pie [pai] *n* pasticcio *m*; (*sweet*) crostata *f*.

piece [piːs] *n* pezzo *m*. **piecemeal** *adv* gradualmente, un po' alla volta. **piecework** *n* lavoro a cottimo *m*. *v* rappezzare. **piece together** aggiustare, mettere assieme.

Piedmont ['piːdmənt] *n* Piemonte *m*.

pier [piə] *n* molo *m*, banchina *f*.

pierce [piəs] *v* forare, penetrare. **piercing** *adj* acuto, penetrante; (*wind*) pungente.

piety ['paiəti] *n* devozione religiosa *f*.

pig [pig] *n* maiale *m*, porco (*pl* -ci) *m*. **pigheaded** *adj* ostinato, testardo. **pigheadedness** *n* testardaggine *f*. **pig-iron** *n* ghisa *f*. **piglet** *n* porcellino *m*. **pigskin** *adj* cinghiale. **pigsty** *n* porcile *m*. **pigtail** *n* codino *m*.

pigeon ['pidʒən] *n* piccione *m*. **carrier pigeon** piccione viaggiatore *m*. **clay pigeon** piattello *m*.

pigeon-hole *n* casella *f*. *v* incasellare.

pigment ['pigmənt] *n* pigmento *m*.

pike [paik] *n* (*fish*) luccio *m*.

pilchard ['piltʃəd] *n* sardina *f*, sarda *f*.

pile¹ [pail] *n* (*heap*) mucchio *m*; (*building*) fabbricato *m*. *v* accumulare. **pile on** (*coll*) esagerare. **pile up** accatastare.

pile² [pail] *n* (*post*) palo *m*. **pile-driver** *v* battipalo *m*.

pile³ [pail] *n* (*of carpet, etc.*) pelo *m*.

piles [pailz] *pl n* (*med*) emorroidi *f pl*.

pilfer ['pilfə] *v* rubacchiare. **pilferer** *n* ladruncolo *m*.

pilgrim ['pilgrim] *n* pellegrino *m*. **pilgrimage** *n* pellegrinaggio *m*.

pill [pil] *n* pillola *f*. **pillbox** *n* scatoletta per pillole *f*; (*mil*) casamatta *f*.

pillage ['pilidʒ] *n* saccheggio *m*. *v* saccheggiare.

pillar ['pilə] n pilastro m, colonna f. **pillar-box** n buca delle lettere f.

pillion ['piljən] n sella posteriore f, sedile posteriore m. **ride pillion** viaggiare sul sedile posteriore.

pillow ['pilou] n guanciale m. **pillowslip** n federa f.

pilot ['pailət] n pilota m, f. v pilotare.

pimento [pi'mentou] n (allspice) pimento m; (capsicum) peperone m.

pimp [pimp] n ruffiano m.

pimple ['pimpl] n pustoletta f, foruncolo m.

pin [pin] n spillo m; (brooch) spilla f. **pincushion** n portaspilli m invar. **pinpoint** v determinare con precisione. **pinprick** n (annoyance) seccatura f. v puntare. **pin down** inchiodare. **pin-up** n (girl) ragazza da copertina f, pin-up f invar.

pinafore ['pinəfo] n grembiulino m.

pincers ['pinsəz] pl n pinza f sing, tenaglia f sing.

pinch [pintʃ] v pizzicare; (hurt) far male a; (coll: steal) rubare; (coll: catch) acchiappare. n (nip) pizzicotto m; (small quantity) pizzico (pl -chi) m. **at a pinch** caso mai.

pine[1] [pain] n (tree) pino m. **pine-cone** n pigna f.

pine[2] [pain] v languire. **pine for** desiderare ardentemente.

pineapple ['painapl] n ananas m.

pinion[1] ['pinjən] n (tech) pignone m.

pinion[2] ['pinjən] v (shackle) legare.

pink [piŋk] adj rosa invar. n (colour) rosa m invar; (flower) garofano m. **in the pink of condition** in ottima forma.

pinnacle ['pinəkl] n cima f, colmo m; (arch) pinnacolo m.

pioneer [paiə'niə] n pioniere, -a m, f. v aprire la strada a.

pious ['paiəs] adj pio, devoto.

pip[1] [pip] n (seed) seme m, granello m.

pip[2] [pip] n (phone) segnale acustico m.

pipe [paip] n tubo m, condotto m; (for smoking) pipa f. **pipe-cleaner** n nettapipe m invar. **pipedream** n illusione f. **pipeline** n oleodotto m; linea di comunicazione f. **v pipe down!** sta zitto! **pipe up** farsi sentire. **piping** n (sewing) cordonetto m. **piping hot** caldo bollente.

piquant ['pikənt] adj piccante, mordace.

pique [pik] n dispetto m. v **feel piqued** risentirsi.

pirate ['paiərət] n pirata m. **pirate radio** radiopirata f. v (radio) servirsi abusivamente di; (book) plagiare. **piracy** n pirateria f.

pirouette [piru'et] n piroetta f. v piroettare.

Pisces ['paisiz] n Pesci m pl.

piss [pis] n (vulgar) piscia f. v pisciare. **pissed** adj sbronzo.

pistachio [pi'staʃiou] n pistacchio m.

pistol ['pistl] n pistola f.

piston ['pistən] n pistone m.

pit [pit] n fossa f; (theatre) platea f; (scar) buttero m. v **pit against** opporre.

pitch[1] [pitʃ] n lancio m; (degree) grado m; (music) tono m, registro m; (sport) campo m, terreno m. v lanciare; (tent) piantare; (fix) fissare; (ship) beccheggiare. **pitchfork** n forcone m.

pitch[2] [pitʃ] n pece f. **pitch-dark** adj buio pesto.

pitfall ['pitfoːl] n trappola f, tranello m.

pith [piθ] n midollo m. **pithy** adj succinto.

pittance ['pitəns] n somma irrisoria f.

pituitary [pi'tjuitəri] n ipofisi f, glandola pituitaria f.

pity ['piti] n pietà f, compassione f; (shame) peccato m. **what a pity!** che peccato! v avere pietà di, compatire. **pitiful** adj (wretched) pietoso; (contemptible) miserabile. **pitiless** adj spietato.

pivot ['pivət] n perno m, fulcro m. v imperniare.

placard ['plakaːd] n cartellone m.

placate [plə'keit] v placare, conciliare.

place [pleis] n luogo m, posto m. **out of place** inopportuno. **put in one's place** umiliare. **take place** aver luogo, accadere. v mettere, posare, porre; (order) piazzare.

placenta [plə'sentə] n placenta f.

placid ['plasid] adj placido.

plagiarize ['pleidʒəraiz] v plagiare. **plagiarism** n plagio m. **plagiarist** n plagiario, -a m, f.

plague [pleig] n (disease) peste f; (calamity) piaga f. v tormentare, affliggere.

plaice [pleis] n passera di mare f.

plaid [plad] n plaid m invar.

plain [plein] adj (clear) chiaro; (simple) semplice; (frank) schietto; (not patterned) a tinta unita; (unattractive) brutto. **in plain clothes** in borghese. **plain cooking** cucina semplice or casalinga f. n pianura f.

plaintiff ['pleintif] *n* querelante *m*, *f*; attore, -trice *m*, *f*.

plaintive ['pleintiv] *adj* querulo, lamentoso.

plait [plat] *n* (*braid*) treccia *f*; (*pleat*) piega *f*. *v* intrecciare; piegare.

plan [plan] *n* piano *m*, progetto *m*; intenzione *f*; (*drawing*) disegno *m*; (*map*) pianta *f*. *v* progettare; intendere; (*econ*) pianificare.

plane¹ [plein] *n* (*flat surface*) piano *m*, livello *m*; (*coll*) aereo *m*. *adj* piano.

plane² [plein] *n* (*tool*) pialla *f*. *v* piallare.

plane³ [plein] *n* (*tree*) platano *m*.

planet ['planit] *n* pianeta *m*. **planetarium** *n* planetario *m*. **planetary** *adj* planetario.

plank [plaŋk] *n* asse *f*, tavola *f*.

plankton ['plaŋktən] *n* plancton *m invar*.

plant [plaint] *n* (*bot*) pianta *f*; (*manufacturing*) impianto *m*, stabilimento *m*. *v* piantare. **plantation** *n* piantagione *f*.

plaque [plaik] *n* placca *f*.

plasma ['plazmə] *n* plasma *m*.

plaster ['plaistə] *n* intonaco *m*; (*med*) impiastro *m*; (*for wound*) cerotto *m*. **plaster of Paris** gesso *m*. *v* intonacare; impiastrare; ingessare.

plastic ['plastik] *adj* plastico. *n* plastica *f*.

plate [pleit] *n* (*dish*) piatto *m*; (*of metal*) lamiera *f*, lastra *f*; (*denture*) dentiera *f*; (*metallic ware*) argenteria *f*; (*in book*) tavola *f*, illustrazione *f*. **plate-glass** *n* cristallo *m*. *v* galvanizzare; (*silver*) argentare.

plateau ['platou] *n* altipiano *m*.

platform ['platfoim] *n* piattaforma *f*; (*rail*) binario *m*.

platinum ['platinəm] *n* platino *m*.

platonic [plə'tonik] *adj* platonico.

platoon [plə'tuin] *n* plotone *m*.

plausible ['ploizəbl] *adj* ammissibile, credibile.

play [plei] *v* giocare; (*musical instrument*) suonare; (*act*) recitare. **play down** minimizzare. **play fair** comportarsi lealmente. **play truant** marinare la scuola. *n* gioco *m*, divertimento *m*; (*theatre*) spettacolo *m*. **playboy** *n* playboy *m*, buontempone *m*. **playground** *n* cortile di scuola *m*. **playmate** *n* compagno, -a di gioco *m*, *f*. **play-pen** *n* recinto per bambini *m*, box *m invar*. **play-school** *n* asilo *m*. **playwright** *n* commediografo, -a *m*, *f*; drammaturgo, -a *m*, *f*. **player** *n* giocatore, -trice *m*, *f*; (*music*) suonatore, -trice *m*, *f*; (*theatre*) attore, -trice *m*, *f*. **playful** *adj* scherzoso, giocoso. **playing card** carta da gioco *f*. **playing field** campo sportivo *m*.

plea [pliː] *n* difesa *f*, supplica *f*; (*excuse*) scusa *f*.

plead [pliid] *v* implorare; perorare. **plead guilty/innocent** dichiararsi colpevole/innocente. **plead with** intercedere presso. **pleading** *n* perorazione *f*.

please [pliiz] *v* piacere (a), contentare, soddisfare. **please oneself** fare il proprio comodo. *adv* per favore, per cortesia. **pleased** *adj* contento, lieto, soddisfatto. **pleasing** *adj* piacevole, gradevole. **pleasure** *n* piacere *m*, favore *m*.

pleat [pliit] *n* piega *f*. *v* pieghettare.

pledge [pledʒ] *n* promessa solenne *f*; (*undertaking*) impegno *m*. *v* impegnare, garantire; promettere solennemente.

plenty ['plenti] *n* abbondanza *f*. **in plenty** in abbondanza. **plenty of** abbastanza. **plentiful** *adj* abbondante.

pleurisy ['pluərisi] *n* pleurite *f*.

pliable ['plaiəbl] *adj* flessibile. **pliability** *n* flessibilità *f*.

pliers ['plaiəz] *pl n* pinza *f sing*, tenaglia *f sing*.

plight [plait] *n* stato *m*.

plimsoll ['plimsəl] *n* scarpa da tennis *f*.

plod [plod] *v* **plod along** tirare avanti. **plodder** *n* sgobbone, -a *m*, *f*.

plonk [ploŋk] *n* (*coll*) vino comune *m*.

plot¹ [plot] *n* (*story*) trama *f*, intreccio *m*; (*secret plan*) congiura *f*, complotto *m*. *v* tramare, complottare; (*trace*) tracciare. **plotter** *n* cospiratore, -trice *m*, *f*.

plot² [plot] *n* (*land*) lotto *or* pezzo di terreno *m*.

plough [plau] *n* aratro *m*. *v* arare; (*coll: fail exam*) trombare. **plough back** riinvestire. **plough through** (*book, etc.*) leggere con fatica.

pluck [plʌk] *v* cogliere; (*feathers*) spennare; (*tug at*) strappare. **pluck up courage** farsi coraggio. *n* (*courage*) fegato *m*. **be plucky** aver fegato.

plug [plʌg] *n* tappo *m*; (*elec*) spina *f*; (*mot*) candela *f*. *v* tappare.

plum [plʌm] *n* (*fruit*) prugna *f*, susina *f*; (*tree*) prugno *m*, susino *m*. *adj* (*colour*) prugna.

plumage ['pluːmidʒ] *n* piumaggio *m*.

plumb [plʌm] *adj* verticale. *adv* **a** piombo; (*absolutely*) proprio. *n* piombo *m*, scandaglio *m*. *v* sondare; (*naut*) scandagliare. **plumber** *n* idraulico *m*.

plume [plum] *n* penna *f*, piuma *f*; (*on helmet*) pennacchio *m*.

plummet ['plʌmit] *v* piombare.

plump¹ [plʌmp] *adj* (*fat*) grassoccio, paffuto.

plump² [plʌmp] *v* **plump for** scegliere.

plunder ['plʌndə] *n* bottino *m*. *v* spogliare, depredare.

plunge [plʌndʒ] *n* tuffo *m*. *v* tuffare; immergere; (*rush*) lanciarsi. **plunger** *n* (*tech*) stantuffo *m*.

pluperfect [plur'pəfikt] *n* trapassato remoto *m*.

plural ['pluərəl] *nm*, *adj* plurale. **in the plural** al plurale.

plus [plʌs] *adj* addizionale. *prep* più.

plush [plʌʃ] *n* felpa *f*. *adj* lussuoso.

plutocrat ['pluːtəkrat] *n* plutocrate *m*, *f*.

ply¹ [plai] *v* (*travel*) viaggiare regolarmente; (*trade*) esercitare.

ply² [plai] *n* (*layer*) strato *m*; (*wool*) filo *m*. **plywood** *n* legno compensato *m*.

pneumatic [nju'matik] *adj* pneumatico.

pneumonia [nju'mouniə] *n* polmonite *f*.

poach¹ [poutʃ] *v* (*game*) cacciare di frodo; (*fish*) pescare di frodo; (*encroach on*) usurpare. **poacher** *n* bracconiere *m*.

poach² [poutʃ] *v* (*cookery*) lessare. **poached egg** uovo affogato *m*, uovo in camicia *m*.

pocket ['pokit] *n* tasca *f*, taschino *m*; (*billiards*) buca *f*. **be out of pocket** rimetterci. *v* intascare. *adj* tascabile. **pocketbook** *n* taccuino *m*. **pocket-knife** *n* temperino *m*. **pocket-money** *n* soldi per le piccole spese *m pl*.

pod [pod] *n* baccello *m*.

podgy ['podʒi] *adj* grassotto, paffuto.

poem ['pouim] *n* poesia *f*.

poet ['pouit] *n* poeta *m*. **poetess** *n* poetessa *f*. **poetic** *adj* poetico. **poetry** *n* poesia *f*.

poignant ['poinjənt] *adj* intenso, vivo, commovente.

point [point] *n* punto *m*; (*sharp end*) punta *f*; (*elec*) presa *f*. **be on the point of** stare per. **make a point of** insistere su. **point-blank** *adv* a bruciapelo; (*coll*) di punto in bianco. *v* indicare; (*aim*) puntare; (*brickwork*) affilettare. **pointed** *adj* acuto. **pointer** *n* (*hint*) indicazione *f*; (*dog*) pointer *m*. **pointing** *n* affilettatura *f*. **pointless** *adj* inutile.

poise [poiz] *n* equilibrio *m*, compostezza *f*, portamento *m*. *v* equilibrare, essere in equilibrio.

poison ['poizən] *n* veleno *m*. *v* avvelenare. **poisonous** *adj* velenoso.

poke [pouk] *n* spinta *f*, gomitata *f*. *v* (*stick into*) ficcare; (*thrust*) cacciare; (*fire*) attizzare. **poke about** frugare. **poke fun at** beffarsi di. **poker** *n* attizzatoio *m*. **poky** *adj* meschino, piccolo.

poker ['poukə] *n* (*cards*) poker *m*. **poker-faced** *adj* impassibile.

Poland ['pouland] *n* Polonia *f*. **Pole** *n* polacco, -a *m*, *f*. **Polish** *nm*, *adj* polacco.

polar ['poulə] *adj* polare. **polar bear** orso bianco *m*. **polarize** *v* polarizzare. **polarity** *n* polarità *f*.

pole¹ [poul] *n* (*post*) palo *m*, asta *f*. **polevault** *n* salto all'asta *m*.

pole² [poul] *n* (*geog*) polo *m*.

police [pə'lis] *n* polizia *f*. **policeman** *n* carabiniere *m*, poliziotto *m*, vigile *m*. **police station** questura *f*. *v* mantenere l'ordine, sorvegliare, vigilare.

policy¹ ['poləsi] *n* politica *f*, linea di condotta *f*.

policy² ['poləsi] *n* (*insurance*) polizza *f*.

polio ['pouliou] *n* poliomielite *f*.

polish ['poliʃ] *n* (*for shoes, etc*.) lucido *m*; (*for nails*) smalto *m*; raffinatezza *f*. *v* lucidare, lustrare. **polish off** (*dispose of quickly*) sbrigare; liquidare. **polish up** ripassare.

polite [pə'lait] *adj* cortese, garbato. **politeness** *n* cortesia *f*, garbo *m*.

politics ['politiks] *n* politica *f*. **politic** *adj* espediente. **political** *adj* politico. **politician** *n* uomo politico *m*.

polka ['polkə] *n* polca *f*.

poll [poul] *n* elezione *f*; (*casting of votes*) votazione *f*; (*votes cast*) voti *m pl*. **opinion poll** sondaggio d'opinioni *m*. *v* ottenere voti. **polling booth** cabina elettorale *f*.

pollen ['polən] *n* polline *m*. **pollinate** *v* impollinare. **pollination** *n* impollinazione *f*.

pollute [pə'luːt] *v* inquinare. **pollution** *n* inquinamento *m*.

polo ['poulou] *n* polo *m*. **polo-neck** *n* collo ciclista *m*. **polo-neck sweater** ciclista *f*.

polygamy [pə'ligəmi] *n* poligamia *f*. **polygamist** *n* poligamo *m*. **polygamous** *adj* poligamo.

polygon ['poligən] n poligono m. **polygonal** adj poligonale.

polytechnic [poli'teknik] n politecnico m.

polythene ['poliθin] n politene m.

pomegranate ['pomigranit] n melagrana f.

pomp [pomp] n pompa f, sfarzo m. **pompous** adj pomposo, ampolloso.

pond [pond] n stagno m.

ponder ['pondə] v ponderare; valutare. **ponderous** adj ponderoso, pesante.

pontiff ['pontif] n pontefice m, papa m. **pontifical** adj pontificio. **pontificate** v pontificare.

pontoon [pon'tum] n pontone m; (cards) ventuno m.

pony ['pouni] n pony m.

poodle ['puːdl] n cane barbone m.

poof [puf] n (derog) finocchio m.

pool¹ [puːl] n (pond) stagno m; (puddle) pozzanghera f; (swimming) piscina f.

pool² [puːl] v mettere in comune. n fondo comune m; (football) totocalcio m.

poor [puə] adj povero; mediocre; (meagre) magro; (not good) cattivo.

poorly ['puəli] adj malaticcio. adv male. feel poorly non sentirsi troppo bene.

pop¹ [pop] v schioccare, saltare. pop in fare una breve visita. pop out saltar fuori. pop up apparire. n schiocco m; (drink) bibita gassata f.

pop² [pop] adj popolare. pop-art n pop-art f. pop music musica pop f.

pope [poup] n papa m.

poplar ['poplə] n pioppo m.

poppy ['popi] n papavero m.

popular ['popjulə] adj popolare; (favourite) ben visto. **popularity** n popolarità f. **popularize** v divulgare.

population [popju'leiʃən] n popolazione f. **populate** v popolare.

porcelain ['poːslin] n porcellana f.

porch [poːtʃ] n portico m.

porcupine ['poːkjupain] n porcospino m.

pore¹ [poː] n (opening) poro m.

pore² [poː] v pore over meditare su, essere assorto in.

pork [poːk] n carne suina f, carne di maiale f.

pornography [poː'nogrəfi] n pornografia f. **pornographic** adj pornografico.

porous ['poːrəs] adj poroso.

porpoise ['poːpəs] n focena f.

porridge ['poridʒ] n pappa di fiocchi d'avena f.

port¹ [poːt] n (harbour) porto m.

port² [poːt] n (naut: left) sinistra f, babordo m.

port³ [poːt] n (wine) porto m invar.

portable ['poːtəbl] adj portatile.

portent ['poːtent] n (omen) presagio m; (marvel) portento m. **portentous** adj prodigioso, portentoso; grave.

porter ['poːtə] n (janitor) portinaio, -a m, f; (carrier) facchino m.

portfolio [poːt'fouliəu] n (pol) portafoglio m; (case) cartella f.

porthole ['poːthoul] n oblò m.

portion ['poːʃən] n porzione f. v ripartire.

portrait ['poːtrət] n ritratto m. **portrait-painter** n ritrattista m, f.

portray [poː'trei] v rappresentare.

Portugal ['poːtjugl] n Portogallo m. **Portuguese** n(m+f), adj portoghese.

pose [pouz] n posa f; (posture) atteggiamento m. v posare, atteggiarsi (a); (propound) porre.

posh [poʃ] adj elegante.

position [pə'ziʃən] n posizione f, situazione f; (employment) posto m. v collocare, piazzare.

positive ['pozətiv] adj positivo; (certain) sicuro. n (phot) positiva f; (gramm) positivo m.

possess [pə'zes] v possedere, avere. **possessed** adj ossesso, frenetico. **possession** n possesso m. **possessions** pl n (goods) beni personali m pl. **possessive** nm, adj possessivo. **possessor** n possessore m, posseditrice f.

possible ['posəbl] adj possibile. **possibility** n possibilità f. **possibly** adv (perhaps) forse, può darsi; (if possible) possibilmente.

post¹ [poust] n (pole) palo m. v affiggere.

post² [poust] n (job) posto m. v collocare.

post³ [poust] n (mail) posta f. post-box n buca da lettere f. postcard n cartolina f. postman n postino m. postmark n timbro postale m. postmarked adj timbrato. post office posta f, ufficio postale m. post office box casella postale f. v imbucare; (book-keeping) registrare. keep posted tenere al corrente. postage n tariffa postale f. postage stamp francobollo m. postal adj postale. postal order vaglia postale m invar.

poste restante [poust'restãt] adv fermo posta.

poster ['pousta] n cartellone m, manifesto m, avviso pubblicitario.

posterior [po'stiaria] adj posteriore.

posterity [po'sterati] n posterità f.

postgraduate [poust'grædjuit] adj di perfezionamento or specializzazione. n laureato, -a che continua gli studi universitari m, f.

posthumous ['postjumas] adj postumo.

post-mortem [poust'mɔːtəm] n autopsia f.

postpone [pous'poun] v posporre, rinviare. **postponement** n rinvio m.

postscript ['pousskript] n poscritto m.

postulate ['postjuleit; n 'postjulət] v postulare. n postulato m.

posture ['postʃə] n posizione f; (attitude) atteggiamento m. v assumere una posa.

pot [pot] n vaso m; (pan) pentola f; (container) recipiente m. v (plant) piantare in vaso; (billiards) mandare in buca. **pot-belly** n pancione m. **pot-bellied** adj panciuto. **take pot luck** mangiare alla buona.

potassium [pə'tasjəm] n potassio m. **potash** n potassa f.

potato [pə'teitou] n patata f.

potent ['poutənt] adj potente, forte. **potency** n potenza f.

potential [pə'tenʃəl] adj, nm potenziale.

pot-hole ['pothoul] n (cave) spelonca f; (in road) buca f. **pot-holer** n speleologo, -a m, f. **pot-holing** n speleologia f.

potion ['pouʃən] n pozione f.

potter[1] ['potə] v **potter about** lavoricchiare.

potter[2] ['potə] n ceramista m, f, vasaio, -a m, f.

pottery ['potəri] n (ware) ceramica f; (workshop) laboratorio di ceramiche m.

potty[1] ['poti] adj (coll) matto.

potty[2] ['poti] n (coll) vaso da notte m, pitale m.

pouch [pautʃ] n borsa f, tasca f, sacchetto m.

poultice ['poultis] n cataplasma m.

poultry ['poultri] n pollame m. **poulterer** n pollivendolo, -a m, f.

pounce [pauns] n sbalzo m. v balzare. **pounce on** piombare su, saltare addosso a.

pound[1] [paund] v (hit) pestare, battere. n colpo m.

pound[2] [paund] n (weight) libbra f; (sterling) lira sterlina f.

pound[3] [paund] n (enclosure) recinto m.

pour [pɔ] v versare, riversarsi; (rain) scrosciare.

pout [paut] v fare il broncio. n broncio m.

poverty ['povəti] n povertà f, miseria f. **poverty-stricken** adj bisognoso, indigente.

powder ['paudə] n polvere f; (cosmetic) cipria f. **powder compact** portacipria m invar. **powder puff** piumino per la cipria m. v polverizzare, incipriare. **powdery** adj polveroso.

power ['pauə] n potere m; (pol, phys, etc.) potenza f; (tech) energia f, forza f. **powers** pl n facoltà f pl. **power station** centrale elettrica f. **powerful** adj potente. **powerless** adj impotente, incapace.

practicable ['praktikəbl] adj fattibile.

practical ['praktikəl] adj pratico. **for practical purposes** in pratica. **practical joke** beffa f. **practically** adv in effetto, quasi.

practice ['praktis] n pratica f; esercizio m; clientela f; (sport) allenamento m. **normal practice** regola f. **out of practice** fuori esercizio.

practise ['praktis] v praticare, esercitare; (music) esercitarsi; (sport) allenarsi. **practised** adj esperto, pratico. **practising** adj (rel) praticante.

practitioner [prak'tiʃənə] n **general practitioner** medico generico m.

pragmatic [prag'matik] adj grammatico; (officious) inframmettente; dogmatico. **pragmatism** n pragmatismo m; dogmatismo m.

Prague [praig] n Praga f.

prairie ['prɛəri] n prateria f.

praise [preiz] n lode f, elogio m. v lodare, elogiare. **praiseworthy** adj lodevole.

pram [pram] n carrozzella f.

prance [prains] v pavoneggiarsi; (child) saltellare; (horse) impennarsi.

prank [praŋk] n burla f, tiro m. **play a prank** on fare un tiro a.

prattle ['pratl] v cianciare, ciarlare.

prawn [prɔin] n gambero m, palemone m.

pray [prei] v pregare. **prayer** n preghiera f. **prayer-book** n libro di preghiere m; (missal) messale m.

preach [priitʃ] v predicare. **preach a sermon** fare una predica. **preacher** n predicatore m.

preamble [pri'ambl] n preambolo m.

prearrange [priiə'reindʒ] v predisporre.

precarious [pri'keəriəs] *adj* precario, incerto.

precaution [pri'kɔ:ʃən] *n* precauzione *f*.

precede [pri'si:d] *v* precedere. **precedence** *n* precedenza *f*. **precedent** *n* precedente *m*.

precinct ['pri:siŋkt] *n* (*area*) zona *f*; ambito *m*.

precious ['preʃəs] *adj* prezioso.

precipice ['presipis] *n* precipizio *m*.

precipitate [pri'sipiteit; *adj* pri'sipitət] *v* precipitare; (*hurry up*) affrettare. *n* precipitato *m*. *adj* precipitoso.

précis ['preisi] *n* sunto *m*.

precise [pri'sais] *adj* preciso, esatto; (*strict*) puntiglioso. **precision** *n* precisione *f*, esattezza *f*.

preclude [pri'klu:d] *v* precludere.

precocious [pri'kouʃəs] *adj* precoce. **precociousness** *n* precocità *f*.

preconceive [,pri:kən'si:v] *v* avere preconcetti su. **preconception** *n* preconcetto *m*.

precursor [pri'kə:sə] *n* precursore *m*.

predatory ['predətəri] *adj* predatore, rapace.

predecessor ['pri:disesə] *n* predecessore *m*.

predestine [pri'destin] *v* predestinare. **predestination** *n* predestinazione *f*.

predicament [pri'dikəmənt] *n* situazione imbarazzante *f*, pasticcio *m*.

predicate ['predikət] *n* predicato *m*.

predict [pri'dikt] *v* predire, pronosticare. **predictable** *adj* prevedibile. **prediction** *n* predizione *f*.

predispose [pri:di'spouz] *v* predisporre. **predisposition** *n* predisposizione *f*.

predominate [pri'domineit] *v* predominare, prevalere. **predominance** *n* predominio *m*, ascendente *m*.

pre-eminent [pri:'eminənt] *adj* preminente, per eccellenza. **pre-eminence** *n* preminenza *f*.

preen [pri:n] *v* **preen oneself** (*bird*) lisciarsi le penne; (*person*) agghindarsi.

prefabricate [pri:'fabrikeit] *v* prefabbricare. **prefab** *n* (*coll*) casa prefabbricata *f*.

preface ['prefis] *n* prefazione *f*. *v* premettere.

prefect ['pri:fekt] *n* prefetto *m*; (*school*) capoclasse *m*.

prefer [pri'fə:] *v* preferire. **preferable** *adj* preferibile. **preference** *n* preferenza *f*. **preference shares** azioni privilegiate *f pl*. **preferential** *adj* preferenziale, di favore.

prefix ['pri:fiks] *n* prefisso *m*. *v* prefiggere.

pregnant ['pregnənt] *adj* incinta; (*animal*) gravida. **pregnancy** *n* gravidanza *f*.

prehistoric [,pri:hi'storik] *adj* preistorico. **prehistory** *n* preistoria *f*.

prejudice ['predʒədis] *n* pregiudizio *m*, prevenzione *f*. **have a prejudice against** esser prevenuto contro. *v* pregiudicare, compromettere. **prejudiced** *adj* prevenuto.

preliminary [pri'liminəri] *nm*, *adj* preliminare.

prelude ['prelju:d] *n* preludio *m*.

premarital [pri:'maritl] *adj* prematrimoniale.

premature [premə'tʃuə] *adj* prematuro.

premeditate [pri:'mediteit] *v* premeditare. **premeditation** *n* premeditazione *f*.

premier ['premiə] *adj* primo, primario. *n* primo ministro *m*.

premiere ['premieə] *n* prima (rappresentazione) *f*.

premise ['premis] *n* premessa *f*. **premises** *n* locali *m pl*. **off the premises** fuori. **on the premises** sul posto.

premium ['pri:miəm] *n* premio *m*; (*finance*) aggio *m*. **at a premium** (*econ*) sopra la pari.

premonition [,premə'niʃən] *n* premonizione *f*.

preoccupied [pri:'okjupaid] *adj* preoccupato. **preoccupation** *n* preoccupazione *f*.

prepare [pri'peə] *v* preparare. **preparation** *n* preparazione *f*. **preparatory** *adj* preparatorio.

preposition [,prepə'ziʃən] *n* preposizione *f*.

preposterous [pri'postərəs] *adj* assurdo.

prerequisite [pri:'rekwizit] *n* requisito (principale) *m*.

prerogative [pri'rogətiv] *n* prerogativa *f*.

prescribe [pri'skraib] *v* prescrivere. **prescription** *n* prescrizione *f*; (*med*) ricetta medica *f*.

presence ['prezns] *n* presenza *f*; (*appearance*) aspetto *m*.

present¹ ['preznt] *adj* presente, attuale. *n* (*time*) presente *m*. **at present** attualmente. **for the present** per ora. **presently** *adv* quanto prima.

present² [pri'zent; *n* 'preznt] *v* presentare, offrire. *n* (*gift*) regalo *m*. **presentable** *adj* presentabile. **presentation** *n* presentazione *f*.

preserve [pri'zəiv] *v* conservare, preservare; (*appearances*) salvare. *n* (*food*) conserva *f*; (*reserve*) riserva *f*.
preservation *n* preservazione *f*. **preservative** *nm, adj* preservativo.
preside [pri'zaid] *v* **preside over** presiedere a.
president ['prezidənt] *n* presidente *m*. **presidency** *n* presidenza *f*. **presidential** *adj* presidenziale.
press [pres] *v* premere; (*squeeze*) comprimere, schiacciare; far pressione su; insistere su; (*iron*) stirare. **press-button** *n* pulsante *m*. **press-stud** *n* bottone automatico *m*. *n* (*newspapers*) stampa *f*; (*printing*) macchina da stampa *f*; (*publishing house*) casa editrice *f*; (*tech*) torchio *m*. **press cutting** ritaglio (di giornale) *m*. **pressing** *adj* urgente.
pressure ['preʃə] *n* pressione *f*. **pressure-cooker** *n* pentola a pressione *f*. **pressurize** *v* pressurizzare; (*force*) far pressione su.
prestige [pre'stiʒ] *n* prestigio *m*.
presume [pri'zjum] *v* presumere, supporre. **presumption** *n* presunzione *f*, supposizione *f*; arroganza *f*. **presumptuous** *adj* presuntuoso. **presumptive** *adj* presuntuo.
pretend [pri'tend] *v* pretendere; (*feign*) fingere, far finta. **pretence** *n* pretesa *f*; (*pretext*) pretesto *m*. **pretension** *n* pretensione *f*. **pretentious** *adj* pretenzioso, pieno di pretese.
pretext ['priitekst] *n* pretesto *m*.
pretty ['priti] *adj* carino, simpatico. *adv* (*quite*) piuttosto, abbastanza; (*moderately*) quasi.
prevail [pri'veil] *v* prevalere. **prevail upon** persuadere, indurre. **prevalent** *adj* prevalente.
prevent [pri'vent] *v* impedire. **prevention** *n* prevenzione *f*; (*med*) profilassi *f*.
preview ['priivjuu] *n* anteprima *f*.
previous ['priivias] *adj* precedente, anteriore. **previously** *adv* prima.
prey [prei] *n* preda *f*. **be/fall a prey to** essere/cadere in preda a. *v* **prey on** predare; (*fear, etc.*) rodere.
price [prais] *n* prezzo *m*. **price-list** *n* listino dei prezzi *m*. *v* valutare, fare il prezzo di. **priceless** *adj* impagabile; (*very amusing*) divertentissimo.
prick [prik] *v* pungere, punzecchiare.

prick up one's ears drizzare le orecchie. *n* puntura *f*.
prickle ['prikl] *n* spina *f*. **prickly** *adj* spinoso; (*sensitive*) difficile. **prickly pear** fico d'India *m*.
pride [praid] *n* orgoglio *m*, amor proprio *m*; (*best part*) fiore *m*. *v* **pride oneself on** essere orgoglioso di.
priest [priist] *n* prete *m*, sacerdote *m*. **priesthood** *n* sacerdozio *m*.
prig [prig] *n* borioso, -a *m, f*. **priggish** *adj* borioso.
prim [prim] *adj* affettato, compassato; (*formal*) cerimonioso.
primary ['praiməri] *adj* primario, fondamentale, primo. **primary school** scuola elementare *f*.
primate ['praimət] *n* primate *m*. **primacy** *n* primato *m*.
prime [praim] *adj* primo; di prima qualità. *n* fiore *m*, primavera *f*. *v* (*arms*) innescare; (*paint*) mesticare; (*information*) mettere al corrente; (*pump*) adescare. **primer** *n* (*book*) testo elementare *m*; (*paint*) mestica *f*.
primitive ['primitiv] *adj* primitivo.
primrose ['primrouz] *n* primula *f*.
primus stove ['praiməs] *n* fornello a petrolio *m*.
prince [prins] *n* principe *m*. **princess** *n* principessa *f*.
principal ['prinsəpəl] *adj* principale, primo. *n* (*of business*) principale *m, f*; (*of school*) direttore, -trice *m, f*; (*comm*) capitale *m*.
principle ['prinsəpəl] *n* principio *m*.
print [print] *v* stampare, imprimere; (*handwriting*) scrivere a stampatello. *n* stampa *f*; impressione *f*; (*phot*) copia *f*. **out of print** esaurito. **printer** *n* tipografo *m*. **printing** *n* tipografia *f*; (*edition*) tiratura *f*.
prior¹ ['praiə] *adj* precedente, anteriore. **prior to** prima di. **priority** *n* precedenza *f*.
prior² ['praiə] *n* priore *m*. **prioress** *n* priora *f*. **priory** *n* convento *m*, monastero *m*.
prise [praiz] *v* far leva su. **prise open** forzare.
prism ['prizm] *n* prisma *m*.
prison ['prizn] *n* prigione *f*. **prisoner** *n* prigioniero, -a *m, f*. **take prisoner** far prigioniero.
private ['praivət] *adj* privato, personale. *n* soldato semplice *m*. **privacy** *n* intimità *f*.

privet ['privət] n ligustro m.

privilege ['privəlidʒ] n privilegio m.

privy ['privi] adj privato. **be privy to** essere a conoscenza di.

prize [praiz] n (reward) premio m. **prize-fighter** n pugile m. **prize-giving** n distribuzione dei premi f. **prizewinner** n vincitore, -trice m, f. v apprezzare, valutare.

probable ['probəbl] adj probabile. **probability** n probabilità f.

probation [prə'beiʃən] n (law) libertà condizionata f; (for job, etc.) periodo di prova m. **probationary** adj di prova.

probe [proub] v esplorare, sondare. n (investigation) sondaggio m, inchiesta f; (instrument) sonda f.

problem ['probləm] n problema m. **problematic** adj problematico.

proceed [prə'siid] v procedere, proseguire. **proceeds** pl n ricavo m sing, incasso m sing. **procedure** n procedura f; (proceeding) procedimento m.

process ['prouses] n processo m, andamento m; (procedure) procedimento m. v trattare, trasformare. **processed cheese** formaggio fuso m.

procession [prə'seʃən] n processione f, sfilata f.

proclaim [prə'kleim] v proclamare. **proclamation** n proclama m.

procrastinate [prə'krastineit] v procrastinare.

procreate ['proukrieit] v procreare. **procreation** n procreazione f.

procure [prə'kjuə] v procurare. **procurement** n approvvigionamento m.

prod [prod] v (incite) sollecitare; (push) spingere.

prodigy ['prodidʒi] n prodigio m.

produce [prə'djuus; n 'prodjuus] v produrre; (pull out) tirar fuori; (theatre) mettere in scena. n prodotti or generi agricoli m pl. **producer** n produttore, -trice m, f; (theatre, etc.) regista m, f. **product** n prodotto m, frutto m. **production** n produzione f; messa in scena f. **productive** adj produttivo; fertile. **productivity** n produttività f.

profane [prə'fein] adj profano. **profanity** n profanità f; (language) bestemmia f.

profess [prə'fes] v professare, manifestare; (practise) esercitare; (imply) pretendere di. **professed** (avowed)

dichiarato. **profession** n professione f; dichiarazione f.

professional [prə'feʃənl] n professionista m, f. adj professionale. **professionalism** n professionismo m.

professor [prə'fesə] n professore, -essa m, f.

proficient [prə'fiʃənt] adj competente, provetto. **proficiency** n perizia f, competenza f.

profile ['proufail] n profilo m.

profit ['profit] n profitto m, guadagno m. v (be of benefit to) giovare a, essere utile a. **profit from** approfittare di, trarre profitto da. **profitable** adj vantaggioso; lucroso.

profound [prə'faund] adj profondo.

profuse [prə'fjuus] adj abbondante, prodigo. **apologize profusely** profondersi in scuse. **profusion** n abbondanza f.

prognosis [prog'nousis] n prognosi f.

programme ['prougram] n programma m. v programmare.

progress ['prougres] v progredire, avanzare. n progresso m, andamento m. **progression** n progressione f. **progressive** adj progressivo.

prohibit [prə'hibit] v proibire, vietare. **prohibition** n proibizione f, divieto m; (of alcohol) proibizionismo m.

project ['prodʒekt; v prə'dʒekt] n progetto m, disegno m. v (plan) progettare; (math, screen) proiettare; (protrude) sporgere. **projectile** n proiettile m. **projection** n proiezione f; sporgenza f. **projector** n proiettore m.

proletariat [proulə'teəriət] n proletariato m. **proletarian** n, adj proletario, -a.

proliferate [prə'lifəreit] v proliferare. **prolific** [prə'lifik] adj prolifico.

prologue ['proulog] n prologo (pl -ghi) m.

prolong [prə'loŋ] v prolungare.

promenade [promə'naid] v fare una passeggiata. n passeggiata f; (sea-front) lungomare m.

prominent ['prominənt] adj prominente; eminente, importante. **prominence** n prominenza; eminenza f. **give prominence to** dar risalto a.

promiscuous [prə'miskjuəs] adj indiscriminato. **promiscuity** n promiscuità f.

promise ['promis] v promettere, assicurare. n promessa f, assicurazione f. **promising** adj che promette bene.

promontory ['promǝntǝri] *n* promontorio *m*.

promote [prǝ'mout] *v* promuovere; (*comm*) lanciare. **promotion** *n* promozione *f*; lancio *m*.

prompt [prompt] *adj* pronto, sollecito. *v* ispirare, suggerire.

prone [proun] *adv* bocconi. **be prone to** essere disposto *or* propenso a.

prong [proŋ] *n* rebbio *m*. *v* infilzare.

pronoun ['prounaun] *n* pronome *m*.

pronounce [prǝ'nauns] *v* pronunciare; dichiarare. **pronounced** *adj* pronunciato, spiccato. **pronouncement** *n* dichiarazione *f*. **pronunciation** *n* pronuncia *f*.

proof [pruːf] *n* prova *f*; (*printing*) bozza *f*. *adj* impenetrabile, resistente (a). *v* impermeabilizzare.

prop[1] [prop] *n* appoggio *m*, sostegno *m*; (*building*) puntello *m*. *v* **prop up** sorreggere, appoggiare; puntellare.

prop[2] [prop] *n* (*coll*) oggetto teatrale *m*.

propaganda [propǝ'gandǝ] *n* propaganda *f*.

propagate ['propǝgeit] *v* propagare. **propagation** *n* propagazione *f*.

propel [prǝ'pel] *v* spingere avanti, azionare. **propellant** *n* propellente *m*. **propeller** *n* elica *f*.

proper ['propǝ] *adj* proprio; (*right*) particolare; (*good*) buono. **properly** *adv* come si deve; correttamente; (*well*) bene.

property ['propǝti] *n* proprietà *f*; possesso *m*, beni *m pl*.

prophecy ['profǝsi] *n* profezia *f*. **prophesy** *v* fare il profeta, predire.

prophet ['profit] *n* profeta *m*. **prophetess** *n* profetessa *f*. **prophetic** *adj* profetico.

propitious [prǝ'piʃǝs] *adj* propizio, favorevole.

proportion [prǝ'poːʃǝn] *n* proporzione *f*. **out of proportion** sproporzionato, smisurato. **proportional** *adj* proporzionale.

propose [prǝ'pouz] *v* proporre, intendere; fare una proposta di matrimonio. **proposal** *n* proposta *f*; offerta di matrimonio *f*. **proposition** *n* proposta *f*; (*gramm*) proposizione *f*.

proprietor [prǝ'praiǝtǝ] *n* proprietario *m*, padrone *m*. **proprietress** *n* proprietaria *f*, padrona *f*.

propriety [prǝ'praiǝti] *n* decoro *m*, decenza *f*.

propulsion [prǝ'pʌlʃǝn] *n* propulsione *f*.

prose [prouz] *n* prosa *f*. **prosaic** *adj* prosaico, banale.

prosecute ['prosikjuːt] *v* citare in giudizio, processare. **prosecution** *n* processo *m*. **prosecutor** *n* procuratore *m*, pubblico ministero *m*.

prospect ['prospekt; *v* prǝ'spekt] *n* prospettiva *f*, aspettativa *f*; (*view*) prospetto *m*. *v* esplorare. **prospective** *adj* futuro.

prospectus [prǝ'spektǝs] *n* prospetto *m*.

prosper ['prospǝ] *v* prosperare. **prosperity** *n* prosperità *f*. **prosperous** *adj* prospero, benestante.

prostitute ['prostitjuːt] *v* prostituire. *n* prostituta *f*, puttana *f*. **prostitution** *n* prostituzione *f*.

prostrate [pro'streit; *adj* 'prostreit] *v* prostrare, prosternare. *adj* abbattuto.

protagonist [prou'tagǝnist] *n* protagonista *m*, *f*.

protect [prǝ'tekt] *v* proteggere. **protection** *n* protezione *f*. **protective** *adj* protettivo. **protector** *n* protettore, -trice *m*, *f*. **protectorate** *n* protettorato *m*.

protégé [prou'teʒei] *n* protetto, -a *m*, *f*.

protein ['proutiːn] *n* proteina *f*.

protest [prǝ'test; *n* 'proutest] *v* protestare. *n* protesta *f*; (*comm*) protesto *m*; (*pol*) contestazione *f*. **under protest** protestando.

Protestant ['protistǝnt] *n*(*m*+*f*), *adj* protestante. **Protestantism** *n* protestantesimo *m*.

protocol ['proutǝkol] *n* protocollo *m*.

proton ['prouton] *n* protone *m*.

protoplasm ['proutǝplazǝm] *n* protoplasma *m*.

prototype ['proutǝtaip] *n* prototipo *m*.

protract [prǝ'trakt] *v* protrarre, prolungare.

protractor [prǝ'traktǝ] *n* goniometro *m*.

protrude [prǝ'truːd] *v* sporgere.

proud [praud] *adj* orgoglioso, fiero.

prove [pruːv] *v* dimostrare, confermare.

proverb ['provǝːb] *n* proverbio *m*.

provide [prǝ'vaid] *v* provvedere, fornire. **provide against** premunirsi contro. **provided that** purché. **providence** *n* provvidenza *f*.

province ['provins] *n* provincia *f*. **provincial** *adj* provinciale.

provision [prǝ'viʒǝn] *n* provvedimento *m*. **provisions** *pl n* viveri *m pl*, provviste *f pl*. **provisional** *adj* provvisorio.

proviso [prǝ'vaizou] *n* stipulazione *f*, condizione *f*.

provoke [prə'vouk] v provocare, irritare. **provocation** n provocazione f. **provocative** adj provocativo.

prow [prau] n prua f, prora f.

prowess ['prauis] n (ability) bravura f; (bravery) prodezza f, valore m.

prowl [praul] v girare furtivamente, vagare.

proximity [prok'siməti] n prossimità f.

proxy ['proksi] n (agency, authorization) procura f; (person) procuratore, -trice m, f.

prude [pruːd] n persona che affetta pudore, puritano, -a m, f. **prudish** adj che affetta pudore, puritano.

prudent ['pruːdənt] adj prudente, cauto. **prudence** n prudenza f, avvedutezza f.

prune[1] [pruːn] v sfrondare; (tree) potare.

prune[2] [pruːn] n prugna secca f.

pry [prai] v curiosare, ficcare il naso (in).

psalm [saːm] n salmo m.

pseudonym ['sjuːdənim] n pseudonimo m.

psychedelic [saikə'delik] adj psichedelico.

psychiatry [sai'kaiətri] n psichiatria f. **psychiatric** adj psichiatrico. **psychiatrist** n psichiatra m, f.

psychic ['saikik] adj psichico.

psychoanalysis [saikouə'naləsis] n psicanalisi f. **psychoanalyse** v psicanalizzare. **psychoanalyst** n psicanalista m, f. **psychoanalytic** adj psicanalitico.

psychology [sai'kolədʒi] n psicologia f. **psychological** adj psicologico. **psychologist** n psicologo, -a m, f.

psychopath ['saikəpaθ] n psicopatico, -a m, f.

psychosis [sai'kousis] n psicosi f. **psychotic** n, adj psicotico, -a.

psychosomatic [saikəsə'matik] adj psicosomatico.

psychotherapy [saikə'θerəpi] n psicoterapia f. **psychotherapist** n psicoterapista m, f.

pub [pʌb] n bar m invar.

puberty ['pjuːbəti] n pubertà f.

pubic ['pjuːbik] adj pubico.

public ['pʌblik] nm, adj pubblico. **public holiday** festa civile f. **public library** biblioteca comunale f. **public school** collegio privato m. **public-spirited** adj dotato di senso civico. **publican** proprietario del bar m, oste m.

publication [pʌbli'keiʃən] n pubblicazione f.

publicity [pʌb'lisəti] n pubblicità f. **publicist** n pubblicista m, f.

publicize ['pʌblisaiz] v divulgare; (advertise) fare la pubblicità a.

publish ['pʌbliʃ] v pubblicare. **publisher** n (person) editore m; (firm) casa editrice f.

pucker ['pʌkə] v corrugare, raggrinzare.

pudding ['pudin] n budino m, dolce m.

puddle ['pʌdl] n pozzanghera f.

puerile ['pjuərail] adj puerile.

puff [pʌf] n (of wind) soffio m; (of smoke) buffata f; (of breath) alito m; (powder) piumino m; (pipe, cigarette) boccata f. **puff pastry** pasta sfoglia f. v sbuffare.

pull [pul] n tirata f, strappo m; (influence) ascendente m. v tirare; (haul) trascinare. **pull back** tirare indietro, trattenere. **pull down** tirar giù; demolire. **pull in** (train) entrare in stazione. **pull oneself together** riprendere animo. **pull up** tirar su; (plant, etc.) strappare; (stop) fermarsi.

pulley ['puli] n puleggia f.

pullover ['pul,ouvə] n pullover m invar.

pulp [pʌlp] n polpa f. v ridurre in polpa.

pulpit ['pulpit] n pulpito m.

pulsate [pʌl'seit] v palpitare, pulsare. **pulsation** n pulsazione f.

pulse[1] [pʌls] n (beat) polso m; (elec) impulso m; vitalità f. v pulsare.

pulse[2] [pʌls] n (vegetables) legumi m pl.

pulverize ['pʌlvəraiz] v polverizzare.

pump [pʌmp] n pompa f. **petrol pump** distributore di benzina m. v pompare; (bullets) scaricare.

pumpkin ['pʌmpkin] n zucca f.

pun [pʌn] n gioco di parole m. v fare giochi di parole.

punch[1] [pʌntʃ] v (hit) picchiare, dare un pugno or cazzotto a. n pugno m; (coll) cazzotto m; (energy) forza f. **punch-drunk** adj stordito.

punch[2] [pʌntʃ] n (drink) ponce m.

punch[3] [pʌntʃ] n (tool) punzone m. v (tickets) forare; (tech) punzonare; (stamp) timbrare.

punctual ['pʌŋktʃuəl] adj puntuale. **punctuality** n puntualità f.

punctuate ['pʌŋktʃueit] v interrompere ripetutamente; (sentence) mettere la punteggiatura. **punctuation** n punteggiatura f.

puncture ['pʌŋktʃə] n puntura f; (tyre) foratura f. **have a puncture** avere una gomma a terra. v forare, bucare.

pungent ['pʌndʒənt] *adj* pungente, aspro; caustico.

punish ['pʌniʃ] *v* punire, castigare. **punishment** *n* punizione *f*, castigo (*pl* -ghi) *m*. **punitive** *adj* punitivo.

punt[1] [pʌnt] *n* (*boat*) barchino *m*.

punt[2] [pʌnt] *v* (*bet*) puntare. **punter** *n* giocatore d'azzardo *m*, scommettitore *m*.

puny ['pjuːni] *adj* sparuto, debole.

pupil[1] ['pjuːpl] *n* (*school*) allievo, -a *m*, *f*, alunno, -a *m*, *f*.

pupil[2] ['pjuːpl] *n* (*anat*) pupilla *f*.

puppet ['pʌpit] *n* burattino *m*.

puppy ['pʌpi] *n* cagnolino *m*.

purchase ['pəːtʃəs] *v* acquistare, comprare. *n* acquisto *m*; (*tech*) presa *f*. **purchaser** *n* compratore, -trice *m*, *f*.

pure ['pjuə] *adj* puro. **purify** *v* purificare, depurare. **purity** *n* purezza *f*.

purée ['pjuərei] *n* puré *m*.

purgatory ['pəːgətəri] *n* purgatorio *m*.

purge [pəːdʒ] *v* (*purify*) purgare; (*pol*) epurare. *n* purga *f*, epurazione *f*.

puritan ['pjuəritən] *n*, *adj* puritano, -a. **puritanism** *n* puritanesimo *m*.

purl [pəːl] *v* (*knitting*) lavorare a punto rovescio; (*edge*) smerlare. *n* punto rovescio *m*; punto smerlo *m*.

purple ['pəːpl] *n* porpora *f*. *adj* purpureo; (*of face*) paonazzo.

purpose ['pəːpəs] *n* scopo *m*, proposito *m*. **on purpose** apposta.

purr [pəː] *n* fusa *f pl*. *v* far le fusa.

purse [pəːs] *n* borsa *f*; (*for money*) borsellino *m*. *v* contrarre.

purser ['pəːsə] *n* commissario di bordo *m*.

pursue [pə'sjuː] *v* (*seek to attain*) perseguire; (*follow closely*) perseguitare; (*continue*) seguire, proseguire. **pursuit** *n* (*quest*) ricerca *f*; (*chase*) inseguimento *m*; (*activity*) impiego *m* (*pl* -ghi) *m*.

pus [pʌs] *n* pus *m*, materia *f*.

push [puʃ] *n* spinta *f*; (*effort*) sforzo *m*, energia *f*; (*idea*) esprimere. *adj* energico, aggressivo.

put [put] *v* mettere, porre; (*question*) rivolgere; (*idea*) esprimere. **put about** (*rumour*) diffondere. **put across** (*explain*) spiegare. **put aside** *or* by mettere da parte, risparmiare. **put down** (*suppress*) sopprimere; (*land*) atterrare; (*ascribe*)
attribuire. **put forward** proporre, nominare. **put off** rinviare; (*get rid of*) sbarazzarsi di; (*cause to dislike*) ripugnare. **put out** (*extinguish*) spegnere; (*inconvenience*) disturbare. **put up** (*lodge*) offrire alloggio a; (*stay*) prendere alloggio; (*raise*) alzare; (*notice, etc.*) affiggere. **put up with** sopportare.

putrid ['pjuːtrid] *adj* putrido.

putt [pʌt] *v* colpire leggermente, fare il putting. *n* colpo leggero *m*, putting *m* invar.

putty ['pʌti] *n* stucco *m*. *v* stuccare.

puzzle ['pʌzl] *n* indovinello *m*; enigma *m*. *v* confondere, rendere perplesso. **puzzled** *adj* perplesso.

pygmy ['pigmi] *n*, *adj* pigmeo, -a.

pyjamas [pə'dʒɑːməz] *pl n* pigiama *m sing*.

pylon ['pailən] *n* pilone *m*.

pyramid ['pirəmid] *n* piramide *f*.

python ['paiθən] *n* pitone *m*.

Q

quack[1] [kwak] *v* (*duck*) schiamazzare.

quack[2] [kwak] *n* (*med*) ciarlatano *m*, medicastro *m*.

quadrangle ['kwodraŋgl] *n* (*math*) quadrangolo *m*; (*arch*) corte quadrangolare *f*.

quadrant ['kwodrənt] *n* quadrante *m*.

quadrilateral [kwodrə'latərəl] *nm*, *adj* quadrilatero.

quadruped ['kwodruped] *n* quadrupede *m*.

quadruple [kwod'ruːpl] *adj* quadruplo.

quagmire ['kwagmaiə] *n* pantano *m*.

quail[1] [kweil] *n* (*bird*) quaglia *f*.

quail[2] [kweil] *v* aver paura, sgomentarsi.

quaint [kweint] *adj* interessante *or* pittoresco in un modo insolito.

quake [kweik] *v* tremare; (*person*) fremere. *n* (*coll: earthquake*) terremoto *m*.

Quaker ['kweikə] *n* quacchero, -a *m*, *f*.

qualify ['kwolifai] *v* qualificare; (*define*) precisare. **qualification** *n* qualifica *f*; (*limitation*) riserva *f*. **qualified** *adj* qualificato, idoneo; (*limited*) condizionato.

quality ['kwoləti] *n* qualità *f*.

qualm [kwɑːm] n scrupolo m, apprensione f.

quandary ['kwondəri] n situazione difficile f, imbarazzo m.

quantify ['kwontifai] v quantificare.

quantity ['kwontəti] n quantità f.

quantum ['kwontəm] n quanto m.

quarantine ['kwɔrəntiin] n quarantena f. v mettere in quarantena.

quarrel ['kworəl] n lite f, bisticcio m. **pick a quarrel** attaccar briga. v litigare, bisticciare. **quarrelsome** adj litigioso.

quarry[1] ['kwori] n (prey) preda f.

quarry[2] ['kwori] n (mining) cava f. v scavare.

quarter ['kwɔːtə] n quarto m; (three months) trimestre m; (district, mercy) quartiere m. **at close quarters** da vicino. **quarters** pl n (mil) accantonamento m sing. v dividere in quattro; (mil) acquartierare. **quarterly** nm, adj trimestrale.

quartet [kwɔr'tet] n quartetto m.

quartz [kwɔːts] n quarzo m.

quash [kwoʃ] v sopprimere; (law) annullare, cassare.

quaver ['kweivə] n (music) croma f; (shaky voice) tremolio m. v tremolare.

quay [kiː] n banchina f.

queasy ['kwizi] adj che sente nausea.

queen [kwiːn] n regina f.

queer [kwiə] adj strambo, bizzarro. **feel queer** sentirsi male. n (coll: homosexual) finocchio m.

quell [kwel] v reprimere, sopprimere.

quench [kwentʃ] v spegnere. **quench one's thirst** dissetarsi.

query ['kwiəri] n domanda f, quesito m. v chiedersi; (raise doubt) mettere in dubbio.

quest [kwest] n ricerca f.

question ['kwestʃən] n questione f, domanda f; (gramm) interrogazione f; problema m. **question mark** punto interrogativo m. v interrogare; (query) mettere in dubbio.

queue [kjuː] n coda f. v fare la coda, mettersi in coda.

quibble ['kwibl] n cavillo m. v cavillare.

quick [kwik] adj rapído, veloce; (lively) vivace. **quicksand** n sabbia mobile f. **quicksilver** n argento vivo m. **quick-tempered** adj impulsivo. **quick-witted** adj sveglio. adv presto. n **cut to the quick**

toccare sul vivo. **quicken** v affrettare, accelerare.

quid [kwid] n (coll) sterlina f.

quiet ['kwaiət] adj tranquillo, quieto. **keep quiet** tacere, star zitto. n quiete f, tranquillità f; silenzio m. **on the quiet** di nascosto. **quieten** v calmare, acquietare.

quill [kwil] n penna f.

quilt [kwilt] v trapuntare. n trapunta f; (duvet) piumino m.

quince [kwins] n cotogna f.

quinine [kwi'nin] n chinino m.

quinsy ['kwinzi] n angina f.

quintet [kwin'tet] n quintetto m.

quirk [kwəːk] n ticchio m, vezzo m.

*⚫**quit** [kwit] v lasciare, abbandonare; (depart) partire.

quite [kwait] adv perfettamente, bene, affatto, proprio; (somewhat) abbastanza.

quits [kwits] adj pari. **call it quits** far pari e patta. **double or quits** lascia o raddoppia.

quiver[1] ['kwivə] v fremere; (voice) tremolare. n fremito m; tremolio m.

quiver[2] ['kwivə] n (arrows) faretra f.

quiz [kwiz] n quiz m invar. v interrogare. **quizzical** adj (odd) curioso; (ridiculing) beffardo.

quota ['kwoutə] n quota f, rata f; (trade) contingente m.

quote [kwout] v citare; (price) quotare. **quotation** n citazione f. **quotation marks** virgolette f pl.

quotient ['kwouʃnt] n quoziente m.

R

rabbi ['rabai] n rabbino m.

rabbit ['rabit] m coniglio m.

rabble ['rabl] n plebaglia f.

rabies ['reibizz] n rabbia f. **rabid** adj (med) idrofobo; furioso; fanatico.

race[1] [reis] n (sport) corsa f, gara f. **racecourse** n ippodromo m. **racehorse** n cavallo da corsa m. **race-track** n pista f. v correre; (compete) gareggiare con. **racing** adj da corsa. **racy** adj vivace, piccante.

race[2] [reis] n razza f. **racial** adj razziale. **racialism** or **racism** n razzismo m. **racialist** or **racist** n(m+f), adj razzista.

rack[1] [rak] n rastrelliera f; (for plates) scolapiatti m invar; (tech) cremagliera f;

(*for luggage*) rete *f.* v **rack one's brains** scervellarsi, lambiccarsi il cervello.

rack² [rak] *n* **go to rack and ruin** andare in malora.

racket¹ ['rakit] *n* (*bat*) racchetta *f.*

racket² ['rakit] *n* (*noise*) baccano *m*, chiasso *m*; (*dishonest scheme*) truffa *f.*

radar ['reidɑ] *n* radar *m.*

radial ['reidiəl] *adj* radiale.

radiant ['reidiənt] *adj* raggiante; splendido; (*joyful*) esultante; (*phys, tech*) radiante. **radiance** *n* splendore *m.*

radiate ['reidieit] *v* irradiare, raggiare. **radiation** *n* irradiazione *f*; (*phys*) radiazione *f*. **radiator** *n* (*car*) radiatore *m.*; (*central heating*) termosifone *m.*

radical ['radikəl] *n*(*m+f*), *adj* radicale.

radio ['reidiou] *nf invar, adj* radio.

radioactive [reidiou'aktiv] *adj* radioattivo. **radioactivity** *n* radioattività *f.*

radiography [reidi'ogrɑfi] *n* radiografia *f.*

radiology [reidi'olədʒi] *n* radiologia *f.* **radiologist** *n* radiologo, -a *m, f.*

radish ['radiʃ] *n* ravanello *m.*

radium ['reidiəm] *n* radio *m.*

radius ['reidiəs] *n* raggio *m.*

raffia ['rafiə] *n* rafia *f.*

raffle ['rafl] *n* riffa *f.*

raft [rɑft] *n* zattera *f.*

rafter ['rɑftə] *n* trave *f.*

rag¹ [rag] *n* (*cloth*) straccio *m*, cencio *m*; (*derog: newspaper*) giornalaccio *m*. **ragged** *adj* lacero, cencioso.

rag² [rag] (*coll*) *v* prendere in giro. *n* baldoria *f.*

rage [reidʒ] *n* rabbia *f*, collera *f*; (*enthusiasm*) passione *f*, moda *f*. **be in a rage** essere furioso *or* arrabbiato. **fly into a rage** infuriarsi. *v* montare su tutte le furie, infuriarsi; (*storm, etc.*) imperversare. **rage against** inveire contro. **raging** *adj* furioso, violento.

raid [reid] *n* incursione *f*, razzia *f*. *v* fare un'incursione in, razziare, invadere. **raider** *n* razziatore *m.*

rail [reil] *n* (*bar*) sbarra *f*; (*barrier*) ringhiera *f*; (*handrail*) corrimano *m invar*; (*for train*) rotaia *f*, binario *m*. **by rail** col treno. **go off the rails** perdere le staffe. **railway** *n* ferrovia *f.*

railings ['reiliŋz] *pl n* cancellata *f sing*, inferriata *f sing.*

rain [rein] *n* pioggia *f*. **rainbow** *n* arcobaleno *m*. **raincoat** *n* impermeabile *m*. **raindrop** *n* goccia di pioggia *f*. *v*

piovere. **rain cats and dogs** piovere a catinelle. **rainy** *adj* piovoso.

raise [reiz] *v* (*lift up*) alzare; (*rear*) allevare; (*bring up*) sollevare; (*increase*) aumentare; (*cause*) suscitare.

raisin ['reizən] *n* uva secca *f.*

rake [reik] *n* (*tool*) rastrello *m*. *v* rastrellare. **rake up the past** rivangare il passato.

rally ['rali] *n* (*meeting*) raduno *m*; (*mot*) rally *m invar*; (*recovery*) ricupero di forze *m*, ripresa *f*; (*tennis, etc.*) scambio di colpi *m*. *v* radunare; riprendersi.

ram [ram] *n* montone *m*. *v* ficcare; (*of ships*) speronare.

ramble ['rambl] *n* gita *f*, giro *m*. *v* vagare, girovagare; (*speech*) divagare; (*mind*) delirare. **rambling** *adj* (*unconnected*) sconnesso, sconclusionato. **rambling rose** rosa rampicante *f.*

ramp [ramp] *n* rampa *f.*

rampage [ram'peidʒ] *n* **go on the rampage** andare su tutte le furie.

rampant ['rampənt] *adj* (*unchecked*) sfrenato; (*heraldry*) rampante.

rampart ['rampɑt] *n* bastione *m.*

ramshackle ['ramʃakl] *adj* cadente.

ran [ran] *V* **run.**

ranch [rɑntʃ] *n* fattoria (per l'allevamento di bestiame) *f*, ranch *m invar.*

rancid ['ransid] *adj* rancido.

rancour ['raŋkə] *n* amarezza *f*, rancore *m.*

random ['randəm] *adj* casuale, fortuito. *n* **at random** a casaccio.

randy ['randi] *adj* lascivo.

rang [raŋ] *V* **ring².**

range [reindʒ] *n* (*assortment*) gamma *f*; (*mountains*) catena *f*; (*scope*) portata *f*; (*for shooting*) campo di tiro *m*; (*of voice*) estensione *f*; (*stove*) fornello *m*. **out of range** fuori tiro. **range-finder** *n* telemetro *m*. **within range** a portata; (*of gun*) a tiro. *v* (*arrange*) disporre; (*set in order*) schierare; (*between limits*) estendersi, variare.

rank¹ [raŋk] *n* (*class*) grado *m*; (*row*) fila *f*. **ranks** *pl n* truppe *f pl*. *v* (*arrange*) schierare; classificare; considerare.

rank² [raŋk] *adj* (*excessive*) rigoglioso; (*utter*) assoluto; (*smell*) puzzolente.

rankle ['raŋkl] *v* bruciare; (*cause bitterness*) amareggiare.

ransack ['ransak] *v* mettere sossopra, rovistare.

ransom ['ransəm] *n* riscatto *m*. *v* riscattare.

rap [rap] *v* picchiare, colpire. **rap over the knuckles** rimproverare. *n* colpetto *m*. **take the rap** accollarsi il biasimo.

rape [reip] *n* stupro *m*, violenza carnale *f*; (*abduction*) rapimento *m*. *v* violentare, stuprare; rapire.

rapid ['rapid] *adj* rapido, veloce. **rapidity** *n* rapidità *f*.

rapier ['reipiə] *n* spada *f*, stocco *m*.

rapture ['raptʃə] *n* estasi *f*. **rapturous** *adj* estatico.

rare¹ ['reə] *adj* (*scarce*) raro. **rarity** *n* rarità *f*.

rare² ['reə] *adj* (*meat*) al sangue.

rascal ['raiskəl] *n* briccone *m*, mascalzone *m*.

rash¹ [raʃ] *adj* avventato, sconsiderato. **rashness** *n* avventatezza *f*, imprudenza *f*.

rash² [raʃ] *n* (*med*) eruzione *f*.

rasher ['raʃə] *n* fetta (di prosciutto) *f*.

raspberry ['razbəri] *n* lampone *m*. **blow a raspberry** (*coll*) fare una pernacchia.

rat [rat] *n* ratto *m*; (*coll: traitor*) traditore *m*. **smell a rat** (*coll*) avere dei sospetti.

rate [reit] *n* (*charge*) tasso *m*; (*speed*) velocità *f*, passo *m*; (*degree*) grado *m*. **at any rate** comunque. **at this rate** così, a questo passo. **ratepayer** *n* contribuente *m*, *f*. **rates** *pl n* imposta *f sing*. *v* stimare, valutare, considerare.

rather ['raiðə] *adv* piuttosto, anzi. *interj* certo! altro che! **I would rather ...** preferirei ....

ratify ['ratifai] *v* ratificare. **ratification** *n* ratifica *f*.

ratio ['reiʃiou] *n* rapporto *m*, proporzione *f*.

ration ['raʃən] *n* razione *f*. **rations** *pl n* viveri *m pl*. *v* razionare.

rational ['raʃənl] *adj* razionale.

rattle ['ratl] *v* sbatacchiare; (*disconcert*) sconcertare. *n* sbatacchio *m*; (*toy, instrument*) raganella *f*; (*in throat*) rantolo *m*.

raucous ['rotkəs] *adj* rauco.

ravage ['ravidʒ] *v* devastare. *n* devastazione *f*.

rave [reiv] *v* delirare. **rave about** andar pazzo di.

raven ['reivən] *n* corvo *m*.

ravenous ['ravənəs] *adj* vorace. **be ravenous** avere una fame da lupo.

ravine [rə'vin] *n* burrone *m*.

ravish ['raviʃ] *v* (*delight*) incantare; (*rape*) violentare. **ravishing** *adj* incantevole.

raw [rot] *adj* (*not cooked*) crudo; (*not refined*) greggio; (*untrained*) inesperto. **raw material** materia prima *f*. **touch on the raw** toccare sul vivo.

ray¹ [rei] *n* raggio *m*.

ray² [rei] *n* (*fish*) razza *f*.

rayon ['reion] *n* raion *m*.

razor ['reizə] *n* rasoio *m*. **razor blade** lametta *f*.

reach [riitʃ] *n* portata *f*; (*continuous stretch*) tratto *m*. **out of reach** fuori mano. **within reach** a portata di mano. *v* (*get to*) raggiungere; (*hand*) porgere.

react [ri'akt] *v* reagire. **reaction** *n* reazione *f*. **reactionary** *n, adj* reazionario, -a. **reactor** *n* reattore *m*.

*read [riid] *v* leggere; studiare. **well-read** *adj* istruito. **readable** *adj* leggibile. **reader** *n* lettore, -trice *m*, *f*. **readership** *n* lettori *m pl*. **reading** *n* lettura *f*; interpretazione *f*.

readjust [riiə'dʒʌst] *v* raggiustare.

ready ['redi] *adj* pronto, preparato; (*willing*) disposto. **get ready** preparare, prepararsi. **ready-made** *adj* confezionato. **ready money** contanti *m pl*.

real [riəl] *adj* reale, effettivo, genuino. **real estate** beni immobili *m pl*. **realism** *n* realismo *m*. **realist** *n* realista *m*, *f*. **realistic** *adj* realistico. **reality** *n* realtà *f*.

realize ['riəlaiz] *v* realizzare. **realization** *n* realizzazione *f*.

really ['riəli] *adv* effettivamente; (*before adj*) proprio. *interj* davvero.

realm [relm] *n* dominio *m*; (*special field*) campo *m*.

reap [riip] *v* mietere; (*profit, etc.*) raccogliere.

reappear [riiə'piə] *v* riapparire. **reappearance** *n* ricomparsa *f*.

rear¹ [riə] *n* (*back*) dietro *m*, parte posteriore *f*; (*mil*) retroguardia *f*. **at the rear of** di dietro. **rear-view mirror** retrovisore *m*. **stay in the rear** restare per ultimo. *adj* posteriore.

rear² [riə] *v* (*raise*) allevare; (*horse, etc.*) impennarsi; (*elevate*) innalzare.

rearm [ri'aim] *v* riarmare. **rearmament** *n* riarmo *m*.

rearrange [riiə'reindʒ] *v* riordinare. **rearrangement** *n* riordinamento *m*.

reason ['riːzn] n ragione f, causa f; (judgment) ragionevolezza f. **it stands to reason** è evidente. v ragionare. **reasonable** adj ragionevole, giusto. **reasoning** n modo di ragionare m.

reassure [riːə'ʃuə] v rassicurare. **reassurance** n rassicurazione f.

rebate ['riːbeit] n sconto m.

rebel ['rebl] v ribellarsi. n ribelle m, f. **rebellion** n ribellione f. **rebellious** adj ribelle.

rebound [ri'baund; n 'riːbaund] v rimbalzare. n rimbalzo m.

rebuff [ri'bʌf] v respingere, rifiutare. n scacco m, rifiuto m.

*rebuild [riː'bild] v ricostruire. **rebuilding** n ricostruzione f.

rebuke [ri'bjuːk] n rimprovero m. v rimproverare.

recall [ri'koːl] v richiamare; (remember) rievocare, ricordare. n richiamo m, memoria f. **past recall** irrevocabile.

recap ['riːkap] (coll) v ricapitolare. n ricapitolazione f.

recede [ri'siːd] v recedere, inclinarsi all'indietro.

receipt [ri'siːt] v quietanzare. n ricevuta f. **receipts** pl n incasso m sing, entrate f pl.

receive [ri'siːv] v ricevere; (sustain) sostenere, riportare; (stolen goods) ricettare. **receiver** n ricettatore, -trice m, f; (bankruptcy) curatore fallimentare m; (phone) ricevitore m.

recent ['riːsnt] adv recente. **recently** adv di recente, poco fa.

receptacle [rə'septəkl] n recipiente m; (bot) ricettacolo m.

reception [ri'sepʃən] n ricevimento m; (radio) ricezione f. **receptionist** n segretaria f, receptionist f invar. **receptive** adj ricettivo.

recess [ri'ses] n nicchia f; pausa f; (holiday) vacanza f. **recesses** pl n (of mind, etc.) recessi m pl.

recession [rə'seʃən] n recessione f.

recharge [riː'tʃɑːdʒ] v ricaricare.

recipe ['resəpi] n ricetta f.

recipient [rə'sipiənt] n destinatario, -a m, f. adj ricevente.

reciprocate [rə'siprəkeit] v contraccambiare, reciprocare; (tech) alternarsi. **reciprocal** adj reciproco. **reciprocity** n reciprocità f.

recite [rə'sait] v recitare. **recital** n (narrative) racconto m; (entertainment) recital m invar. **recitation** n recitazione f.

reckless ['rekləs] adj imprudente, avventato. **recklessness** n avventatezza f.

reckon ['rekən] v contare; (consider) giudicare. **reckon on** contare su. **reckon with** prendere in considerazione. **reckoning** n (bill) resa dei conti f.

reclaim [ri'kleim] v redimere; (land) bonificare; (material) ricuperare. **reclamation** n bonifica f.

recline [ri'klain] v appoggiarsi.

recluse [rə'kluːs] n eremita m.

recognize ['rekəgnaiz] v riconoscere. **recognition** n riconoscimento m. **recognizable** adj riconoscibile.

recoil [rə'koil] v rinculare. **recoil from** rifuggire da. n rinculo m.

recollect [rekə'lekt] v rammentarsi di. **recollection** n memoria f, ricordo m.

recommence [riːkə'mens] v ricominciare.

recommend [rekə'mend] v raccomandare, consigliare. **recommendation** n raccomandazione f.

recompense ['rekəmpens] v compensare, risarcire. n indennizzo m, risarcimento m.

reconcile ['rekənsail] v mettere d'accordo, riconciliare. **reconcile oneself to** rassegnarsi a. **reconciliation** n rappacificazione f.

reconnoitre [rekə'noitə] v fare un sopralluogo; (mil) fare una ricognizione. **reconnaissance** n esplorazione f, sopralluogo m (pl -ghi) m; (mil) ricognizione f.

reconstruct [riːkən'strʌkt] v ricostruire. **reconstruction** n ricostruzione f.

record [rə'koːd; n 'rekoːd] v registrare; notare; (as document) mettere a verbale. n nota f, registro m; (court report) verbale m; (sport) record m invar; disco m; (dossier) stato di servizio m. **keep a record of** prendere nota di. **off the record** ufficiosamente. **record-player** n giradischi m invar. **recorder** n (music) flautino m. **recording** n registrazione f.

recount [ri'kaunt] v riferire, raccontare.

recoup [ri'kuːp] v rifarsi di, compensare.

recourse [rə'koːs] n **have recourse to** ricorrere a. **without recourse** senza rivalsa.

recover [rə'kʌvə] v (get back) riprendere, ricuperare; (regain health) rimettersi.

recovery n ricupero m; (health) guarigione f.

recreation [rekri'eiʃən] n ricreazione f, passatempo m, svago m.

recrimination [rəkrimi'neiʃən] n recriminazione f.

recruit [rə'kruːt] n recluta f. v arruolare. **recruitment** n reclutamento f.

rectangle ['rektaŋgl] n rettangolo m. **rectangular** adj rettangolare.

rectify ['rektifai] v rettificare; (elec) raddrizzare.

rectum ['rektəm] n retto m.

recuperate [rə'kjuːpəreit] v ricuperare; (get well again) rimettersi. **recuperation** n ricupero m.

recur [ri'kəː] v ricorrere, ritornare. **recurrence** n ricorrenza f; (of illness) ricaduta f. **recurrent** adj ricorrente.

red [red] adj rosso. **go red** (person) arrossire; (thing) diventar rosso. **redcurrant** n ribes m invar. **red-handed** adj in flagrante. **red herring** diversivo m. **red-hot** adj rovente. **Red Indian** n pellerossa (pl pellirosse) m, f. **n in the red** scoperto. **reddish** adj rossastro.

redeem [rə'diːm] v redimere, estinguere, svincolare. **redeeming feature** particolare che salva m. **redeemable** adj redimibile. **redemption** n redenzione f; salvezza f; liberazione f.

redress [rə'dres] n riparazione f, soddisfazione f. v soddisfare, correggere.

reduce [rə'djuːs] v ridurre. **reduced** adj ridotto. **reduction** n riduzione f.

redundant [rə'dʌndənt] adj superfluo. **make redundant** (employee) mettere in cassa d'integrazione.

reed [riːd] n canna f; (of musical instrument) linguetta f.

reef [riːf] n scogliera f.

reek [riːk] v puzzare. n puzzo m.

reel¹ [riːl] n rocchetto m; (fishing) mulinello m; (film) rotolo m. v arrotolare. **reel off** rifilare.

reel² [riːl] v (sway) barcollare; (of head) girare.

refectory [rə'fektəri] n refettorio m.

refer [rə'fəː] v (report, ascribe) riferire; (consult) ricorrere, rivolgersi; (send back) rimandare. **referring to** con riferimento a. **reference** n riferimento m; (testimonial) referenza f, attestato m.

referee [refə'riː] n arbitro m. v arbitrare.

referendum [refə'rendəm] n referendum m.

refill ['riːfil] n refill m invar, pezzo di ricambio m.

refine [rə'fain] v raffinare. **refined** adj raffinato, squisito. **refinement** n (tech) raffinazione f; (manners) raffinatezza f. **refinery** n raffineria f.

reflation [rə'fleiʃn] n reflazione f.

reflect [rə'flekt] v riflettere; (manifest) rispecchiare. **reflection** n riflessione f. **on reflection** a pensarci su. **reflector** n riflettore m; (of vehicle) catarifrangente m.

reflex ['riːfleks] nm, adj riflesso. **reflexive** adj riflessivo. c

reform [rə'fɔːm] n riforma f. v riformare, correggere. **reformation** n riforma f. **reformatory** n riformatorio m. **reformer** n riformatore, -trice m, f.

refract [rə'frakt] v rifrangere. **refraction** n rifrazione f.

refractory [rə'fraktəri] adj refrattario; (stubborn) ostinato.

refrain¹ [rə'frein] v astenersi, trattenersi.

refrain² [rə'frein] n ritornello m, ripresa f.

refresh [rə'freʃ] v rinfrescare, ristorare. **refresher course** corso di aggiornamento m. **refreshments** pl n rinfreschi m pl.

refrigerator [rə'fridʒəreitə] n frigorifero m.

refuel [riː'fjuəl] v rifornirsi di carburante.

refuge ['refjuːdʒ] n rifugio m. **take refuge** rifugiarsi. **refugee** n profugo, -a m, f.

refund [ri'fʌnd; n 'riːfʌnd] v rimborsare. n rimborso m.

refuse¹ [rə'fjuːz] v rifiutare, dire di no; (deny) negare, respingere; (prohibit) vietare. **refusal** n rifiuto m; (option) diritto di opzione m.

refuse² ['refjuːs] n rifiuti m pl, immondizia f.

refute [ri'fjuːt] v confutare.

regain [ri'gein] v riacquistare, riprendere. **regain consciousness** riprendere i sensi, rianimarsi.

regal ['riːgəl] adj regale.

regard [rə'gaːd] v (consider) stimare; (concern) riguardare. n riguardo m; rispetto m; considerazione f; deferenza f. **with regard to** riguardo a, per quanto riguarda. **regardless of** senza badare or riguardo a.

regatta [rə'gatə] n regata f.

regent ['riːdʒənt] n reggente m. **regency** n reggenza f.

regime [rei'ʒim] *n* regime *m*.
regiment ['redʒimənt] *n* reggimento *m*. *v* irreggimentare. **regimental** *adj* reggimentale. **regimentation** *n* irreggimentazione *f*.
region ['riːdʒən] *n* regione *f*, zona *f*. **regional** *adj* regionale.
register ['redʒistə] *n* registro *m*; (*voting*) lista elettorale *f*; (*professional*) albo *m*. *v* registrare; (*show*) indicare; (*enter formally*) iscriversi. **registered letter** (*lettera*) raccomandata *f*. **registered office** sede legale *f*. **registrar** *n* segretario *m*; ufficiale di stato civile *m*. **registration** registrazione *f*; iscrizione *f*. **registry office** ufficio di stato civile *m*.
regress [ri'gres] *v* regredire. **regression** *n* regressione *f*. **regressive** *adj* regressivo.
regret [rə'gret] *n* dispiacere *m*, rammarico *m*. **regrets** *pl n* (*sorrow*) rimorsi *m pl*; (*excuses*) scuse *f pl*. *v* rimpiangere, rammicarsi di. **regretful** *adj* spiacente. **regrettable** *adj* spiacevole.
regular ['regjulə] *adj* regolare. **regularity** *n* regolarità *f*.
regulate ['regjuleit] *v* regolare. **regulation** *n* regolamento *m*; (*rule*) regola *f*.
rehabilitate [riːhə'biliteit] *v* riabilitare. **rehabilitation** *n* riabilitazione *f*.
rehearse [rə'həːs] *v* (*theatre*) provare; (*enumerate*) ripetere, recitare. **rehearsal** *n* prova *f*. **dress rehearsal** prova generale *f*.
reign [rein] *n* regno *m*. *v* regnare; prevalere.
reimburse [riːim'bəːs] *v* rimborsare. **reimbursement** *n* rimborso *m*.
rein [rein] *n* redine *f*, briglia *f*. **give free rein to** dare libero sfogo a. *v* **rein in** frenare.
reincarnation [riːinkaː'neiʃən] *n* reincarnazione *f*.
reindeer ['reindiə] *n* renna *f*.
reinforce [riːin'fɔːs] *v* rinforzare. **reinforced concrete** cemento armato *m*. **reinforcement** *n* rinforzo *m*.
reinstate [riːin'steit] *v* reintegrare. **reinstatement** *n* reintegrazione *f*.
reinvest [riːin'vest] *v* rinvestire.
reissue [riː'iʃuː] *n* nuova emissione *f*, ristampa *f*. *v* emettere di nuovo, ristampare.
reject [rə'dʒekt; *n* 'riːdʒekt] *v* rifiutare, respingere; (*discard*) scartare. *n* scarto *m*. **rejection** *n* rifiuto *m*.

rejoice [rə'dʒois] *v* rallegrarsi, gioire. **rejoicing** *n* allegrezza *f*, allegria *f*.
rejoin [rə'dʒoin] *v* (*join again*) ricongiungere; (*come back to*) tornare a; (*answer*) rispondere; (*law*) replicare. **rejoinder** *n* risposta *f*, replica *f*.
rejuvenate [ri'dʒuːvəneit] *v* ringiovanire. **rejuvenation** *n* ringiovanimento *m*.
relapse [rə'laps] *v* ricadere; (*med*) riammalarsi. *n* ricaduta *f*.
relate [rə'leit] *v* (*tell*) narrare; (*refer*) riferire, riguardare; (*be connected*) aver rapporto. **related** *adj* associato, congiunto; (*family*) parente.
relation [rə'leiʃn] *n* (*family*) parente *m, f*; (*connection*) rapporto *m*; (*narration*) racconto *m*. **relationship** *n* parentela *f*, rapporto *m*.
relative ['relativ] *adj* relativo. **relative to** (*concerning*) riguardante. *n* parente *m, f*. **relativity** *n* relatività *f*.
relax [rə'laks] *v* rilassare, allentare; (*rest*) riposarsi. **relaxation** *n* distensione *f*, riposo *m*; (*entertainment*) svago *m*.
relay ['riːlei; *v* ri'lei] *n* (*shift*) turno *m*; (*elec*) relè *m invar*, soccorritore *m*; (*radio*) trasmissione *f*. **relay race** (corsa a) staffetta *f*. *v* trasmettere.
release [rə'liːs] *v* liberare, rimettere in libertà; (*launch*) lanciare; (*let go*) mollare; (*publication*) mettere in circolazione. *n* liberazione *f*; lancio *m*; (*press*) comunicato stampa *m*.
relent [rə'lent] *v* placarsi, cedere. **relentless** *adj* inesorabile, spietato.
relevant ['relavant] *adj* pertinente, a proposito. **relevance** *n* pertinenza *f*.
reliable [ri'laiəbl] *adj* fidato; sicuro; (*information*) attendibile. **reliability** *n* sicurezza *f*; (*person*) fidatezza *f*; attendibilità *f*.
relic ['relik] *n* reliquia *f*.
relief [rə'liːf] *n* (*alleviation*) sollievo *m*; (*help*) soccorso *m*; (*prominence*) rilievo *m*. **relief map** *n* plastico *m*, levata topografica *f*.
relieve [rə'liːv] *v* alleviare; (*help*) soccorrere. **feel relieved** sentirsi sollevato.
religion [rə'lidʒən] *n* religione *f*. **religious** *adj* religioso, devoto.
relinquish [rə'liŋkwiʃ] *v* abbandonare, rinunziare a.
relish ['reliʃ] *v* apprezzare, godere. *n* piacere *m*, godimento *m*.

reluctant [rə'lʌktənt] *adj* restio, riluttante. **reluctance** *n* riluttanza *f.* **reluctantly** *adv* di malavoglia, a malincuore.

rely [rə'lai] *v* contare, fare assegnamento, fidarsi (di).

remain [rə'mein] *v* rimanere, restare. **remainder** *n* resto *m*, avanzo *m.* **remains** *pl n* resti *m pl*; (*mortal*) spoglie *f pl.*

remand [rə'maind] *v* rinviare. *n* rinvio *m.*

remark [rə'maːk] *n* nota *f*, osservazione *f*, commento *m.* *v* notare, osservare. **remarkable** *adj* notevole.

remarry [riː'mari] *v* risposarsi.

remedy ['remədi] *n* rimedio *m.* *v* rimediare, correggere; (*heal*) curare. **remedial** *adj* (*school*) correttivo, (*law*) riparatore.

remember [riː'membə] *v* ricordare, ricordarsi (di), rammentare. **remembrance** *n* memoria *f*, ricordo *m.*

remind [rə'maind] *v* ricordare, rammentare, richiamare alla mente. **reminder** *n* promemoria *m invar*, ricordo *m.*

reminiscence [remə'nisəns] *n* reminiscenza *f.* **reminiscent** *adj* che rammenta.

remiss [rə'mis] *adj* negligente, disattento.

remit [rə'mit] *v* (*transmit*) rimettere; (*abate*) mitigare; (*send back*) rinviare; perdonare. **remittance** *n* rimessa *f.*

remnant ['remnənt] *n* scampolo *m*, resto *m.*

remorse [rə'mɔːs] *n* rimorso *m.* **remorseful** *adj* preso *or* tormentato dal rimorso. **remorseless** *adj* spietato.

remote [rə'mout] *adj* remoto, lontano; (*faint*) pallido. **remote control** telecomando *m.*

remove [rə'muːv] *v* (*take off*) togliere; (*do away with*) eliminare; (*withdraw*) ritirare; (*move house*) traslocare. **removal** *n* (*house*) trasloco *m*; (*med*) ablazione *f*; (*act of removing*) rimozione *f.*

remunerate [rə'mjuːnəreit] *v* ricompensare. **remuneration** *n* ricompensa *f*, rimunerazione *f.* **remunerative** *adj* rimunerativo.

renaissance [rə'neisəns] *n* rinascimento *m.*

rename [riː'neim] *v* rinominare.

render ['rendə] *v* rendere; rappresentare; (*give back*) restituire; (*cookery*) struggere; (*building*) incalcinare.

rendezvous ['rondivuː] *n* appuntamento *m*, convegno *m.*

renegade ['renigeid] *n*, *adj* rinnegato, -a.

renew [rə'njuː] *v* rinnovare. **renewal** *n* rinnovamento *m.*

renounce [ri'nauns] *v* rinunciare a, ripudiare. **renouncement** *or* **renunciation** *n* rinunzia *f.*

renovate ['renəveit] *v* rinnovare, ripristinare; (*buildings*) restaurare. **renovation** *n* ripristinamento *m*; restauro *m.*

renown [rə'naun] *n* fama *f.* **renowned** *adj* rinomato, famoso, celebre.

rent[1] [rent] *v* affittare; (*take, occupy*) prendere in affitto; (*let out*) dare in affitto. *n* affitto *m.*

rent[2] [rent] *n* (*tear*) strappo *m*, rottura *f.*

reopen [riː'oupən] *v* riaprire. **reopening** *n* riapertura *f.*

reorganize [riː'ɔːgənaiz] *v* riorganizzare. **reorganization** *n* riorganizzazione *f.*

rep[1] [rep] *n* (*coll*) teatro stabile, compagnia stabile *f.*

rep[2] [rep] *n* (*coll*) rappresentante *m, f.*

repair [ri'peə] *v* riparare, aggiustare. *n* riparazione *f.* **beyond repair** irreparabile. **in good/bad repair** in buono/cattivo stato. **repairer** *n* riparatore, -trice *m, f.*

repartee [repa'tiː] *n* battuta di spirito *f.*

repatriate [riː'patrieit] *v* rimpatriare. **repatriation** *n* rimpatrio *m.*

*repay [ri'pei] *v* ripagare; (*refund*) rimborsare. **repayment** *n* rimborso *m*; ricompensa *f.*

repeal [rə'piːl] *v* revocare, annullare. *n* revoca *f*, annullamento *m.*

repeat [rə'piːt] *v* ripetere; (*food*) tornare a gola. *n* ripetizione *f*; (*music*) ripresa *f.*

repel [rə'pel] *v* respingere. **repellent** *adj* repellente.

repent [rə'pent] *v* pentirsi. **repentance** *n* penitenza *f*; (*regret*) pentimento *m.*

repercussion [riːpə'kʌʃən] *n* ripercussione *f.*

repertoire ['repətwaɪ] *n* repertorio *m.*

repertory ['repətəri] *n* teatro stabile *m.* **repertory company** compagnia stabile *f.*

repetition [repə'tiʃn] *n* ripetizione *f.* **repetitive** *adj* che si ripete.

replace [rə'pleis] *v* rimpiazzare; (*put back*) rimettere a posto; sostituire. **replaceable** *adj* sostituibile. **replacement** *n* sostituzione *f.*

replay ['riːplei] *v* ri'pleiː] *n* rivincita *f.* *v* fare la rivincita.

replenish [rə'pleniʃ] *v* rifornire. **replenishment** *n* rifornimento *m.*

replica ['replikə] n facsimile m invar, copia f.

reply [rə'plai] n risposta f. v rispondere.

report [rə'pɔɪt] n rapporto m, relazione f; (school) pagella f; (rumour) voce f; (noise) scoppio m. v (relate) riferire, fare un rapporto; denunciare; presentarsi. **reporter** n cronista m, f; reporter m invar.

repose [rə'pouz] n riposo m. v riposarsi.

reprehensible [repri'hensəbl] adj biasimevole, riprensibile.

represent [repri'zent] v rappresentare; (depict) raffigurare. **representation** n rappresentazione f.

representative [reprə'zentətiv] adj rappresentativo, caratteristico. m rappresentante m, f; (pol) deputato, -a m f.

repress [rə'pres] v reprimere. **repressed** adj represso. **repression** n repressione f. **repressive** adj repressivo.

reprieve [rə'priɪv] v graziare. n grazia f.

reprimand ['reprimaɪnd] v rimproverare, sgridare. n rimprovero m, predica f.

reprint [riɪ'print; n 'riɪprint] v ristampare. n ristampa f.

reprisal [rə'praizəl] n rappresaglia f.

reproach [rə'proutʃ] v rimproverare, biasimare. n rimprovero m, biasimo m.

reproduce [riɪprə'djuɪs] v riprodurre. **reproduction** n riproduzione f. **reproductive** adj riproduttivo.

reprove [rə'pruɪv] v rimproverare, sgridare. **reproof** n rimprovero m.

reptile ['reptail] n rettile m.

republic [rə'pʌblik] n repubblica f. **republican** n, adj repubblicano, -a.

repudiate [rə'pjuɪdieit] v ripudiare; (disown) disconoscere; (reject) respingere. **repudiation** n ripudio m.

repugnant [rə'pʌgnənt] adj ripugnante. **repugnance** n ripugnanza f.

repulsion [rə'pʌlʃn] n ripulsione f, ripugnanza f. **repulsive** adj ributtante, schifoso.

repute [rə'pjuɪt] v reputare, stimare. n also **reputation** reputazione f, fama f. **reputable** adj rispettabile, stimabile, onorevole. **reputedly** adv presumibilmente.

request [ri'kwest] n richiesta f, domanda f. v richiedere, domandare, sollecitare.

requiem ['rekwiəm] n requiem m invar.

require [ri'kwaiə] v richiedere; (demand) esigere, pretendere; rendere necessario. **requirement** n esigenza f, bisogno m.

requisite ['rekwizit] adj necessario, indispensabile. n requisito m.

requisition [rekwi'zifən] v requisire. n (mil) requisizione f, ordine m.

re-route [riɪ'ruɪt] v deviare.

resale [riɪ'seil] n rivendita f.

rescue ['reskjuɪ] n salvataggio m, soccorso m. v liberare; soccorrere. **rescuer** n liberatore, -trice m, f; soccorritore, -trice m, f.

research [ri'səɪtʃ] n ricerca f, indagine f. v fare or compiere ricerche, indagare. **researcher** n ricercatore, -trice m, f.

resemble [rə'zembl] v somigliare, rassomigliare. **resemblance** n somiglianza f, rassomiglianza f.

resent [ri'zent] v risentirsi di, offendersi or sdegnarsi per. **resentful** adj offeso, sdegnoso. **resentment** n risentimento m, sdegno m, rancore m.

reserve [ri'zəɪv] v riservare. n riserva f; (manner) riserbo m; (circumspection) riservatezza f. **reservation** n riserva f; (booking) prenotazione f.

reservoir ['rezəvwaɪ] n cisterna f, serbatoio m; (artificial lake) lago artificiale m, bacino di riserva m.

reside [rə'zaid] v dimorare, risiedere. **residence** n residenza f, dimora f. **residence permit** permesso di soggiorno m. **resident** n(m+f), adj residente. **residential** adj residenziale.

residue ['rezidjuɪ] n residuo m. **residual** adj residuo, rimanente.

resign [rə'zain] v dimettersi, rassegnare le dimissioni; (surrender) rinunciare a. **resign oneself** to rassegnarsi a. **resignation** n dimissioni f pl, rassegnazione f. **resigned** adj rassegnato.

resilient [rə'ziliənt] adj flessibile. be **resilient** (person) aver capacità di ricupero. **resilience** n flessibilità f, resilienza f; capacità di ricupero f.

resin ['rezin] n resina f. **resinous** adj resinoso.

resist [ri'zist] v resistere (a). **resistance** n resistenza f. **resistant** adj resistente.

***resit** [riɪ'sit] v ripetere.

resolute ['rezəluɪt] adj deciso, risoluto. **resolution** n risoluzione f; (determination) risolutezza f; decisione f.

resolve [rə'zolv] v risolvere; decidere; (clear up) chiarire. n decisione f.

resonant ['rezənənt] *adj* risonante. **resonance** *n* risonanza *f*.

resort [rə'zɔːt] *v* **resort to** ricorrere a. *n* (*recourse*) ricorso *m*; (*expedient*) risorsa *f*; (*holiday, etc.*) luogo di soggiorno *m*, stazione di villeggiatura *f*.

resound [rə'zaund] *v* risonare, echeggiare.

resource [rə'zɔːs] *n* risorsa *f*. **resourceful** *adj* pieno di risorse, ingegnoso.

respect [rə'spekt] *v* rispettare, aver riguardo per. *n* rispetto *m*; (*esteem*) stima *f*, riguardo *m*; (*detail*) aspetto *m*. **pay one's respects** rendere omaggio a. **with due respect** coi debiti riguardi. **with respect to** riguardo a, quanto a. **respectable** *adj* rispettabile; onesto; considerevole. **respectful** *adj* rispettoso. **respectively** *adv* rispettivamente.

respiration [respə'reiʃn] *n* respirazione *f*. **respirator** *n* (*med*) respiratore *m*; (*gas mask*) maschera antigas *f*. **respiratory** *adj* respiratorio.

respite ['respait] *n* tregua *f*, proroga *f*.

respond [rə'spond] *v* rispondere, reagire. **respondent** *n* (*law*) imputato, -a *m*, *f*. **response** *n* risposta *f*; reazione *f*; (*church*) responsorio *m*. **responsive** *adj* sensibile.

responsible [rə'sponsəbl] *adj* responsabile. **responsibility** *n* responsabilità *f*.

rest¹ [rest] *v* riposarsi; (*place*) posare; (*stay*) stare, fermarsi. *n* riposo; (*support*) appoggio *m*. **restful** *adj* riposante, tranquillo. **restive** *adj* restio. **restless** *adj* inquieto, irrequieto.

rest² [rest] *n* resto *m*.

restaurant ['restront] *n* ristorante *m*, trattoria *f*. **restaurant car** vagone ristorante *m*.

restore [rə'stɔː] *v* ristabilire; (*building, etc.*) restaurare. **restoration** *n* ristabilimento *m*; restauro *m*; (*history*) restaurazione *f*.

restrain [rə'strein] *v* trattenere, reprimere, frenare. **restraint** *n* freno *m*, ritegno *m*; limitazione *f*.

restrict [rə'strikt] *v* restringere, limitare. **restriction** *n* restrizione *f*, limitazione *f*. **restrictive** *adj* restrittivo.

result [rə'zʌlt] *n* risultato *m*, esito *m*. *v* risultare, derivare. **resultant** *adj* risultante.

resume [rə'zjuːm] *v* riprendere; riassumere. **resumption** *n* ripresa *f*.

résumé ['reizumei] *n* riassunto *f*.

resurgence [ri'səːdʒəns] *n* risurrezione *f*, rinascita *f*.

resurrect [rezə'rekt] *v* risuscitare. **resurrection** *n* risurrezione *f*.

resuscitate [rə'sʌsəteit] *v* risuscitare.

retail ['riːteil] *n* vendita al dettaglio *or* minuto *f*. *v* (*sell*) vendere al dettaglio *or* minuto; (*tell*) raccontare, dettagliare. *adv*, *adj* al dettaglio *or* minuto. **retailer** *n* dettagliante *m*.

retain [rə'tein] *v* ritenere, mantenere. **retainer** (*law*) caparra *f*.

retaliate [rə'talieit] *v* contraccambiare, rendere la pariglia. **retaliation** *n* contraccambio *m*, rappresaglia *f*.

retard [rə'taːd] *v* ritardare, ostacolare. **retarded** *adj* tardivo.

retch [retʃ] *v* aver conati di vomito.

reticent ['retisənt] *adj* reticente, riservato, taciturno. **reticence** *n* reticenza *f*, riservatezza *f*, taciturnità *f*.

retina ['retinə] *n* retina *f*.

retinue ['retinjuː] *n* seguito *m*.

retire [rə'taiə] *v* ritirarsi; (*go to bed*) andare a letto; (*give up work*) andare in pensione. **retired** *adj* in pensione, a riposo; (*withdrawn*) ritirato, appartato. **retirement** *n* ritirata *f*; riposo *m*.

retort¹ [rə'tɔːt] *v* ribattere, rimbeccare. *n* (*reply*) ritorsione *f*, rimbecco *m*.

retort² [rə'tɔːt] *n* (*chem*) storta *f*.

retrace [ri'treis] *v* (*follow up*) rintracciare; (*go back over*) ripercorrere; risalire alle origini di.

retract [rə'trakt] *v* (*withdraw*) ritirare, far rientrare; (*disown*) disdire.

retreat [rə'triːt] *n* ritiro *m*; rifugio *m*, asilo *m*; (*mil*) ritirata *f*. *v* ritirarsi, indietreggiare.

retrieve [rə'triːv] *v* ricuperare; riparare; rimediare. **retrieval** *n* ricupero *m*. **retriever** *n* (*dog*) cane da riporto *m*.

retrograde ['retrəgreid] *adj* retrogrado.

retrospect ['retrəspekt] *n* **in retrospect** guardando indietro. **retrospective** *adj* retrospettivo.

return [rə'təːn] *v* tornare, ritornare; (*put back*) rimettere; (*reciprocate*) contraccambiare; (*give back*) restituire; (*send back*) rinviare. *n* ritorno *m*; restituzione *f*; rinvio *m*; (*profit*) utile *m*; (*report*) relazione *f*, rapporto *m*; (*statement*) rendiconto *m*. **by return of post** a giro di posta. **in return for** in cambio di. **return**

match rivincita f. **return ticket** biglietto di andata e ritorno m.

reunite [riju:'nait] v riunire. **reunion** n riunione f.

rev [rev] v (mot) imballare. n giro m. **rev counter** contagiri m invar.

reveal [rə'vi:l] v rivelare, manifestare. **revelation** n rivelazione f.

revel ['revl] v (take pleasure) trovar diletto; (make merry) far baldoria. n also **revelry** baldoria f.

revenge [rə'vendʒ] n vendetta f. v vendicare.

revenue ['revinju:] n (income) rendita f; (yield) reddito m; (of state) erario m; (department) fisco m.

reverberate [rə'və:bəreit] v (sound) risonare, riecheggiare; (heat, light) riverberare. **reverberation** n riverberazione f.

reverence ['revərəns] n riverenza f, venerazione f. **reverend** nm, adj reverendo. **reverent** adj riverente. **reverential** adj reverenziale.

reverse [rə'və:s] v rovesciare; (inside out) rivoltare; (mot) far marcia indietro. **reverse the charges** addebitare al destinatario. adj contrario, rovescio, inverso. n contrario m, rovescio m, inverso m; (mot) retromarcia f. **reversal** n rovesciamento m; (law) revoca f. **reversible** adj reversibile; (law) revocabile; (fabric) a due diritti.

revert [rə'və:t] v ritornare.

review [rə'vju:] n (survey) rassegna f, esame m; critica f, recensione f; (mil, periodical) rivista f. v riesaminare; fare la critica di; passare in rivista. **reviewer** n critico m.

revise [rə'vaiz] v rivedere, correggere. **revision** n revisione f.

revive [rə'vaiv] v rianimare, risvegliare; (restore to use) ripristinare. **revival** n risveglio m; ripristino m; (theatre) ripresa f.

revoke [rə'vouk] v revocare.

revolt [rə'voult] v ribellarsi; (feel disgust) provare orrore; (cause disgust) disgustare. **revolting** adj rivoltante, disgustoso; (rebellious) ribelle.

revolution [revə'lu:ʃən] n rivoluzione f; (turn) giro m. **revolutionary** n, adj revoluzionario, -a.

revolve [rə'volv] v (turn) girare; (depend) basarsi (su), dipendere (da). **revolver** n

rivoltella f. **revolving** adj (door) girevole; (credit) rotativo.

revue [rə'vju:] n rivista f.

revulsion [rə'vʌlʃən] n ripugnanza f, disgusto m; (med) revulsione f.

reward [rə'wo:d] n ricompensa f, compenso m. v ricompensare, rimunerare. **rewarding** adj rimunerativo.

rhetoric ['retərik] n retorica f. **rhetorical** adj retorico.

rheumatism ['ru:mətizəm] n reumatismo m. **rheumatic** adj reumatico.

Rhine [rain] n Reno m.

rhinoceros [rai'nosərəs] n rinoceronte m.

rhododendron [roudə'dendrən] n rododendro m.

rhombus ['rombəs] n rombo m.

rhubarb ['ru:ba:b] n rabarbaro m.

rhyme [raim] n rima f. v rimare, far rima.

rhythm ['riðəm] n ritmo m. **rhythmic** adj ritmico.

rib [rib] n costola f. **ribbed** adj a coste, scanalato.

ribbon ['ribən] n nastro m. **torn to ribbons** ridotto a brandelli.

rice [rais] n riso m.

rich [ritʃ] adj ricco; (full) pieno, abbondante; (food) pesante; (colour) intenso. **riches** pl n ricchezza f sing. **richness** n ricchezza f.

rickety ['rikəti] adj traballante, instabile; (med) rachitico.

***rid** [rid] v liberare, sbarazzare. **get rid of** sbarazzarsi di. **good riddance!** che liberazione!

ridden ['ridn] V ride.

riddle[1] ['ridl] n indovinello m, enigma m. **speak in riddles** parlare per enigmi.

riddle[2] ['ridl] v crivellare.

***ride** [raid] n (on horseback) passeggiata a cavallo f; (on bicycle) passeggiata in bicicletta f; (in vehicle) corsa f, giro m. **take for a ride** (make fun of) prendere in giro; (deceive) imbrogliare. v cavalcare, andare a cavallo. **rider** n (horse) cavallerizzo, -a m, f; ciclista m, f; motociclista m, f; (additional clause) clausola aggiunta f, codicillo m. **riding school** maneggio m.

ridge [ridʒ] n (geog) cresta f; (raised strip) costa f; (roof) colmo m; (meteorology) espansione di alta pressione f. v corrugare, incresparsi.

ridicule ['ridikju:l] v mettere in ridicolo, canzonare. n ridicolo m. **be an object of**

ridicule esser posto in ridicolo. **ridiculous** adj ridicolo, assurdo.

rife [raif] adj diffuso, corrente.

rifle¹ ['raifl] n fucile m. **rifle-range** n poligono di tiro m.

rifle² ['raifl] v svaligiare. **rifle through** rovistare or frugare in.

rift [rift] n crepa f, spacco m; (in relations) disaccordo m, screzio m; (geol) falda f.

rig [rig] n (naut) attrezzatura f; (industry) impianto m; (fraudulent dealing) broglio m, manipolazione f. v attrezzare; (equip) montare; manipolare, manovrare.

right [rait] adj corretto, giusto; (geom) retto; (not left) destro. be right aver ragione. **right-angled** adj ad angolo retto. **right-hand man** braccio destro m. **right wing** (pol) destra f. **right-winger** n persona di destra f. n bene m, giusto m; (law) diritto m; (not left) destra f. right of way (vehicles) precedenza f; (law) servitù di passaggio f; (path) passaggio pubblico m. adv bene; (exactly) proprio; direttamente; completamente; (direction) a destra. right away subito. v (restore to position) raddrizzare; (correct) aggiustare, accomodare, metere a posto; (redress) riparare. **rightful** adj legittimo. **rightly** adv giustamente.

righteous ['raitʃəs] adj retto, giusto. **righteousness** n rettitudine f.

rigid ['ridʒid] adj rigido, inflessibile, rigoroso. **rigidity** n rigidezza f; (stiffness) rigidità f.

rigmarole ['rigmərəul] n (long procedure) trafila f; (nonsense) filastrocca f.

rigour ['rigə] n rigore m. **rigorous** adj rigoroso, rigido.

rim [rim] n orlo m, bordo m; (of wheel) cerchio m; (of spectacles) montatura f.

rind [raind] n (fruit) buccia f, scorza f; (cheese) crosta f.

ring¹ [riŋ] n anello m; (enclosure) recinto m, pista f; (boxing) quadrato m, ring m invar. v cingere, circondare. **ringlet** n (curl) ricciolo m.

*ring² [riŋ] n (sound) suono m, squillo m; (inherent quality) tono m; (coll) telefonata f, colpo di telefono m. v suonare; (echo) risonare, echeggiare; telefonare (a).

rink [riŋk] n pista di pattinaggio f.

rinse [rins] v sciacquare, risciacquare. n risciacquatura f; (hair) cachet m.

riot ['raiət] n rivolta f, sommossa f; (uproar) baccano m, fracasso m; (profusion) orgia f. **riot squad** squadra mobile or volante f. v insorgere, far baccano. **riotous** adj tumultuoso; (noisy) chiassoso, clamoroso; dissoluto.

rip [rip] n strappo m, squarcio m. v strappare, squarciare. let rip (give vent to) dare libero sfogo a.

ripe [raip] adj maturo. **ripen** v (far) maturare. **ripeness** n maturità f. **ripening** n maturazione f.

ripple ['ripl] n increspamento m, crespa f; (sound) mormorio m. v incrspare, mormorare.

*rise [raiz] v sorgere; (get up) alzarsi, levarsi; (increase) aumentare, salire; (swell) gonfiarsi; (rebel) insorgere. n salita f; aumento m. **give rise to** causare.

risen ['rizn] V rise.

risk [risk] v rischiare, arrischiare, correre il rischio di. n rischio m. at the risk of a rischio di. **risky** adj rischioso.

rissole ['risəul] n polpetta f, crocchetta f.

rite [rait] n rito m.

ritual ['ritʃuəl] nm, adj rituale.

rival ['raivəl] n(m+f), adj rivale. v rivaleggiare, competere. **rivalry** n rivalità f.

river ['rivə] n fiume m.

rivet ['rivit] n rivetto m. v rivettare. **riveting** adj affascinante.

road [roud] n strada f, via f. **road-block** n posto di blocco m. **road sign** cartello stradale m. **road-works** pl n lavori stradali m pl. **roadworthy** adj atto a prendere la strada.

roam [roum] v vagare, errare.

roar [ro] v (wild beast) ruggire, urlare; (sea) muggire. **roar with laughter** scoppiare dalle risa. n ruggito m, urlo m; muggito m; (thunder) rombo m; (laughter) scroscio m.

roast [roust] v arrostire; (coffee) tostare. n arrosto m.

rob [rob] v derubare, rapinare; (plunder) svaligiare. **robber** n ladro m, rapinatore m. **robbery** n rapina f. **armed robbery** rapina a mano armata f.

robe [roub] n abito lungo m, toga f.

robin ['robin] n pettirosso m.

robot ['roubot] n automa m.

robust [rə'bʌst] adj robusto.

rock¹ [rok] n (stone) roccia f, scoglio m; (support) rocca f. **on the rocks** (coll: without money) al verde; (coll: with ice) con

ghiaccio. **rock-bottom** adj bassissimo.
rock-crystal n cristallo di rocca m. **rock-salt** n salgemma m. **rocky** adj roccioso.
rock² [rok] v dondolare, oscillare; (baby) cullare. **off one's rocker** (coll) matto. **rocking-chair** n sedia a dondolo f. **rocking-horse** n cavallo a dondolo m.
rocket ['rokit] n razzo m; (reprimand) cicchetto m. v (increase sharply) andare alle stelle.
rod [rod] n bastone m, stecca f; (fishing) canna (da pesca) f; (piston) biella f.
rode [roud] V ride.
rodent ['roudant] nm, adj roditore.
roe¹ [rou] n (deer) capriolo m.
roe² [rou] n (hard) uova di pesce f pl; (soft) latte di pesce m.
rogue [roug] n (dishonest person) mariolo m; (rascal) briccone m, furfante m. **roguery** n bricconeria f. **roguish** adj bricconesco; (mischievous) furbo.
role [roul] n ruolo m, funzione f.
roll [roul] v rullare; (wave) ondeggiare; (rotate) roteare; (ship) rollare. **be rolling in money** guazzare nel denaro. **roll out** (pastry) spianare. **roll up** arrotolare. n rotolo m; (bread) panino m. **roll-call** n appello m. **roller** n cilindro m, rullo m. **roller-skate** n schettino m, pattino a rotelle m. **rolling-pin** n matterello m.
romance [rou'mans] n romanzo (cavalleresco) m; (medieval tale) romanza f; (love affair) idillio m, avventura amorosa f. **romantic** adj romantico; (fanciful) romanzesco.
Romania [ru:'meinjə] n Romania f. **Romanian** n, adj romeno, -a.
Rome [roum] n Roma f. **Roman** n, adj romano, -a. **Roman Catholic** adj cattolico (romano).
romp [romp] v giocare rumorosamente, ruzzare. **romp home** (win easily) vincere facilmente. **romp through** (exam) superare con facilità. n trambusto m; (coll) cagnara f.
roof [ru:f] n, pl -s tetto m. **hit the roof** (coll) andare su tutte le furie. **roof of the mouth** palato m.
rook [ruk] n (bird) corvo m; (chess) torre f; (swindler) truffatore, -trice m, f. v barare, truffare.
room [ru:m] n stanza f, sala f, camera f; (space) posto m, spazio m; opportunità f. **room temperature** temperatura ambiente f. v alloggiare. **roomy** adj spazioso, vasto.

roost [ru:st] n (building) pollaio m; (pole) posatoio m. **rule the roost** fare il gallo del pollaio. v appollaiarsi.
root¹ [ru:t] n radice f; (cause) fondo m. **root and branch** radicalmente. **root cause** causa prima f. **take root** mettere radice. v piantare, abbarbicare; (become fixed) mettere radici, radicare.
root² [ru:t] v (search) frugacchiare. **root for** (slang) sostenere. **root out** scovare.
rope [roup] n corda f, fune f. **know the ropes** esser pratico, saperla lunga. **learn the ropes** familiarizzarsi.
rosary ['rouzəri] n rosario m.
rose¹ [rouz] V rise.
rose² [rouz] n rosa f. **rose-bush** n rosa f, rosaio m. **rosy** adj roseo.
rosé [rouzei] n rosato m.
rosemary ['rouzməri] n rosmarino m.
rosette [rou'zet] n coccarda f, rosetta f.
roster ['rostə] n turno di servizio m; (mil) ruolino m.
rostrum ['rostrəm] n tribuna f, piattaforma f.
rot [rot] v putrefare, marcire; (teeth, wood) cariare. n putrefazione f; (rotten matter) marciume m; (coll: nonsense) sciocchezze f pl; declino m. **rotten** adj marcio; (coll: annoying) seccante.
rota ['routə] n turno (di servizio) m, lista f.
rotate [rou'teit] v rotare; (crops) avvicendare. **rotary** adj (motion) rotatorio; (tech) rotativo. **rotation** n rotazione f; avvicendamento m.
rouge [ru:ʒ] n belletto m, rossetto m.
rough [rʌf] adj (coarse) ruvido; (person) rozzo; (ground) malagevole, irregolare; violento; (sea, weather) agitato, tempestoso; approssimativo; (unrefined) greggio. **rough-and-ready** adj improvvisato. **rough-and-tumble** n zuffa f, mischia f. v **rough it** vivere primitivamente. **rough out** abbozzare. **roughen** v irruvidire. **roughness** n ruvidezza f.
roulette [ru:'let] n roulette f.
round [raund] adj tondo, rotondo; circolare; sferico. prep tutto intorno a. n tondo m, cerchio m; (tour) giro m; (game) partita f; (boxing) ripresa f; (ammunition) scarica f; (applause) salva f. adv in giro. **all year round** tutto l'anno. **show round** fare da guida a. v **round off**

completare. **round up** (*number*) arrotondare.

roundabout ['raundəbaut] *n* anello stradale *m. adj* indiretto, obliquo.

rouse [rauz] *v* destare. **rousing** *adj* stimolante.

route [ruːt] *n* strada *f*, rotta *f*. **en route** per strada.

routine [ruːˈtiːn] *n* uso *m*, abitudine *f*.

rove [rouv] *v* errare, vagabondare.

row¹ [rou] *n* fila *f*.

row² [rou] *v* remare. *n* remata *f*. **rowing boat** barca a remi *f*.

row³ [rau] *n* (*quarrel*) rissa *f*, lite *f*; (*noise*) chiasso *m*, baccano *m. v* litigarsi.

rowdy ['raudi] *adj* chiassoso, turbolento. *n* attaccabrighe *m, f invar*.

royal ['roiəl] *adj* reale, regio, regale. **royalist** *m(n+f), adj* realista. **royalties** *pl n* diritti d'autore *m pl*; (*people*) reali *m pl*; (*status*) regalità *f*, dignità di re *f*.

rub [rʌb] *v* fregare, strofinare. **rub down** (*clean*) pulire fregando; (*dry*) asciugare fregando. **rub out** cancellare. **rub shoulders** venire in contatto.

rubber ['rʌbə] *n* gomma *f*, caucciù *m*.

rubbish ['rʌbiʃ] *n* (*waste*) immondizia *f*; (*derog*) robaccia *f*; (*nonsense*) sciocchezze *f pl*. **rubbish bin** pattumiera *f*.

rubble ['rʌbl] *n* frantumi *m pl*, macerie *f pl*.

ruby ['ruːbi] *n* rubino *m. adj* (*color*) rubino *or* vermiglio.

rucksack ['rʌksak] *n* sacco da montagna *m*, zaino *m*.

rudder ['rʌdə] *n* timone *m*.

rude [ruːd] *adj* (*discourteous*) scortese; (*unmannerly*) rozzo, grossolano; (*sturdy*) robusto. **rudeness** *n* scortesia *f*; grossolanità *f*; robustezza *f*.

rudiment ['ruːdimənt] *n* rudimento *m*.

rueful ['ruːfəl] *adj* triste, lamentevole.

ruff [rʌf] *n* gorgiera *f*.

ruffian ['rʌfiən] *n* ruffiano *m*, farabutto *m*.

ruffle ['rʌfl] *v* arruffare, increspare.

rug [rʌg] *n* tappeto *m*; (*travelling*) coperta da viaggio *f*; (*bedside*) scendiletto *m*.

rugby ['rʌgbi] *n* rugby *m invar*, palla ovale *f*.

rugged ['rʌgid] *adj* irregolare; rude.

ruin ['ruːin] *n* rovina *f. v* rovinare. **ruinous** *adj* rovinoso.

rule [ruːl] *n* regola *f*, norma *f*; (*ruler*)

regolo *m.* **as a rule** di regola *or* solito. *v* regolare, dirigere; decidere, (*mark with lines*) rigare. **rule out** escludere. **ruler** *n* sovrano *m*, governatore *m*; (*school*) regolo *m*. **ruling** *n* direttiva *f*, decisione *f*.

rum [rʌm] *n* rum *m*.

rumble ['rʌmbl] *v* rimbombare, brontolare; (*stomach*) gorgogliare; (*coll: detect*) scoprire. *n* brontolio *m*, gorgoglio *m*.

rummage ['rʌmidʒ] *v* frugare, rovistare.

rummy ['rʌmi] *n* ramino *m*.

rumour ['ruːmə] *n* diceria *f*, voce *f. v* far correre voce.

rump [rʌmp] *n* groppa *f*, culatta *f*. **rump steak** bistecca *f*.

***run** [rʌn] *n* corsa *f*; (*outing*) gita *f*; serie *f invar*; durata *f*. **in the long run** a lungo andare. **on the run** in fuga. *v* correre; (*flow*) scorrere; funzionare; (*colour*) spandere; (*stockings*) smagliare; (*manage*) dirigere. **run away** *or* **off** fuggire. **runaway** *n, adj* fuggiasco, -a. **run down** (*slow*) rallentarsi; (*car, etc.*) investire; (*disparage*) parlar male di; (*find*) trovare. **run in** rodare. **run into** (*encounter*) incontrare per caso, imbattersi; (*collide with*) urtare; (*amount to*) raggiungere. **run out** (*supplies, etc.*) esaurirsi. **run over** (*car, etc.*) investire; (*overflow*) traboccare; (*rehearse*) ripassare. **runway** *n* pista di decollo *or* atterraggio *f*. **runner** *n* corridore *m*; (*messenger*) fattorino *m*; (*carpet*) passatoia *f*; (*plant*) pollone *m*. **runner bean** fagiolo rampicante) *m*. **runner-up** *n* secondo arrivato, seconda arrivata *m, f*.

rung¹ [rʌŋ] *n* piolo *m*.

rung² [rʌŋ] *V* **ring²**.

running ['rʌniŋ] *n* corsa *f*; funzionamento *m*; (*competition*) gara *f*. **be in the running** aver possibilità di vincere. **make the running** fare l'andatura. *adj* funzionante; regolare; consecutivo.

rupture ['rʌptʃə] *n* rottura *f*; (*med*) ernia *f. v* rompere.

rural ['ruərəl] *adj* campestre, rurale.

rush¹ [rʌʃ] *v* precipitarsi, avventarsi; (*convey with haste*) precipitare, spostare in fretta. *n* corsa precipitosa *f*; (*intense activity*) trambusto *m*; (*haste*) fretta e furia *f*; (*sudden coming*) accesso *m*. **rush hour** ora di punta *f*.

rush² [rʌʃ] *n* (*plant*) giunco *m*.

rusk [rʌsk] *n* biscotto (non dolce) *m*.

Russia ['rʌʃə] *n* Russia *f*. **Russian** *n*, *adj* russo, -a.

rust [rʌst] *n* ruggine *f*. **rustproof** *adj* inossidabile. *v* arrugginirsi. **rusty** *adj* arrugginito, rugginoso; (*out of practice*) fuori d'esercizio.

rustic ['rʌstik] *adj* rustico.

rustle ['rʌsl] *n* fruscio *m*. *v* frusciare, stormire.

rut [rʌt] *n* solco *m*, carreggiata *f*; (*fixed habit*) abitudine fissa *f*.

ruthless ['ruːθlis] *adj* spietato, implacabile.

rye [rai] *n* segala *f*.

S

sabbatical [sə'batikəl] *adj* sabbatico.

sable ['seibl] *n* zibellino *m*. *adj* di zibellino.

sabotage ['sabətɑːʒ] *n* sabotaggio *m*. *v* sabotare. **saboteur** *n* sabotatore, -trice *m*, *f*.

sabre ['seibə] *n* sciabola *f*. **sabre-rattling** *n* minaccia di guerra *f*, bravata *f*.

saccharin ['sakərin] *n* saccarina *f*.

sachet ['saʃei] *n* sacchetto profumato *m*.

sack [sak] *n* sacco *m*; (*coll*; *dismissal*) licenziamento *m*. **get the sack** (*coll*) essere mandato a spasso. **v** (*coll*) mandare a spasso.

sacrament ['sakrəmənt] *n* sacramento *m*. **sacramental** *adj* sacramentale.

sacred ['seikrid] *adj* sacro, sacrosanto.

sacrifice ['sakrifais] *n* sacrificio *m*; (*comm*) perdita *f*. *v* sacrificare; (*comm*) vendere sottocosto.

sacrilege ['sakrəlidʒ] *n* sacrilegio *m*. **sacrilegious** *adj* sacrilego (*m pl* -ghi).

sad [sad] *adj* triste. **sadden** *v* rattristare. **sadness** *n* tristezza *f*.

saddle ['sadl] *n* sella *f*. *v* sellare.

sadism ['seidizəm] *n* sadismo *m*. **sadist** *n* sadico, -a *m*, *f*. **sadistic** *adj* sadico.

safe [seif] *adj* sicuro; (*unharmed*) salvo; innocuo. **safe and sound** sano e salvo. **safe-conduct** *n* salvacondotto *m*. **safeguard** *v* salvaguardare; proteggere. **safe keeping** *n* in cassaforte *f*. **safety** *n* sicurezza *f*, salvezza *f*. **safety-belt** *n* cintura di sicurezza *f*. **safety-catch** *n* sicura *f*. **safety-pin** *n* spillo di sicurezza *m*.

saffron ['safrən] *n* zafferano *m*.

sag [sag] *v* incurvarsi, piegarsi.

saga ['sɑːgə] *n* saga *f*.

sage¹ ['seidʒ] *n*, *adj* saggio, -a. **sagacious** *adj* sagace, avveduto.

sage² [seidʒ] *n* (*herb*) salvia *f*.

Sagittarius [sadʒi'teəriəs] *n* Sagittario *m*.

sago ['seigou] *n* sagù *m*.

said [sed] *V* say.

sail [seil] *v* navigare; (*leave*) salpare. *n* vela *f*. **sailcloth** *n* tela olona *f*. **sailing** *n* vela *f*, sport della vela *m*. **sailing boat** barca a vela *f*. **sailor** *n* marinaio *m*.

saint [seint] *n* santo, -a *m*, *f*; *adj* santo. **saintly** *adj* santo, pio.

sake [seik] *n* beneficio *m*, interesse *m*, bene *m*. **for God's sake** per l'amor di Dio. **for the sake of** (*in order to*) tanto per. **for your own sake** per il tuo bene.

salad ['saləd] *n* insalata *f*.

salami [sə'lɑːmi] *n* salame *m*.

salary ['saləri] *n* stipendio *m*.

sale [seil] *n* vendita *f*; (*clearance*) liquidazione *f*, saldo *m*. **for** or **on sale** in vendita. **salesgirl** *n* commessa *f*. **salesman** *n* commesso *m*. **travelling salesman** commesso viaggiatore *m*.

saline ['seilain] *adj* salino. **salinity** *n* salinità *f*.

saliva [sə'laivə] *n* saliva *f*. **salivary** *adj* salivare. **salivate** *v* salivare.

sallow ['salou] *adj* giallastro, olivastro.

salmon ['samən] *n* salmone *m*.

salon ['salon] *n* salone *m*.

saloon [sə'luːn] *n* salone *m*; (*ship*) ritrovo per passeggeri *m*. **saloon car** berlina *f*.

salt [sɒlt] *n* sale *m*. **salt-cellar** *n* saliera *f*. *adj* also **salty** salato, piccante. *v* salare.

salubrious [sə'luːbriəs] *adj* salubre.

salute [sə'luːt] *n* saluto *m*. *v* salutare.

salvage ['salvidʒ] *n* salvataggio *m*, ricupero *m*. *v* salvare, ricuperare.

salvation [sal'veiʃən] *n* salvezza *f*; (*theology*) salvazione *f*.

same [seim] *adj* stesso, medesimo; (*unchanged*) immutato. *pron* lo stesso, il medesimo. **all the same** (*nevertheless*) malgrado tutto. **at the same time** nello stesso tempo; (*notwithstanding*) con tutto ciò, ciononostante. **the same to you!** altrettanto! **sameness** *n* somiglianza *f*, uniformità *f*, monotonia *f*.

sample ['sɑːmpl] *n* campione *m*; (*specimen*) saggio *m*. *v* campionare; (*test*) assaggiare. **sampling** *n* campionatura *f*.

sanatorium [sanə'tɔːrɪəm] n sanatorio m.

sanctify ['saŋktɪfaɪ] v santificare, consacrare.

sanctimonious [saŋktɪ'məunɪəs] adj santocchio, santerello.

sanction ['saŋkʃən] n sanzione f. v sanzionare, sancire.

sanctity ['saŋktətɪ] n santità f.

sanctuary ['saŋktjuəri] n santuario m; (refuge) asilo m, rifugio m.

sand [sand] n sabbia f. v (sprinkle) insabbiare; (smooth) smerigliare. **sand-blast** v pulire con un getto di sabbia. **sandpaper** n carta vetrata f. **sandy** adj (consistency) sabbioso; (colour) biondo rossiccio.

sandal ['sandl] n sandalo m.

sandwich ['sanwɪdʒ] n sandwich m invar, panino imbottito m. v inserire.

sane [seɪn] adj equilibrato, sano di mente. **sanity** n sanità di mente f, equilibrio m.

sang [saŋ] V **sing**.

sanitary ['sanɪtəri] adj igienico, sanitario. **sanitary towel** n pannolino igienico m.

sank [saŋk] V **sink**.

sap¹ [sap] n (plant) linfa f.

sap² [sap] v (undermine) minare, indebolire.

sapphire ['safaɪə] n zaffiro m. adj zaffirino.

sarcasm ['saːkazəm] n sarcasmo m. **sarcastic** adj sarcastico.

sardine [saː'diːn] n sardina f.

Sardinia [saː'dɪnjə] n Sardegna f. **Sardinian** n, adj sardo, -a.

sardonic [saː'dɒnɪk] adj sardonico.

sash¹ [saʃ] n (scarf) sciarpa f.

sash² [saʃ] n (frame) telaio m. **sash-cord** n corda del contrappeso f. **sash-window** n finestra alla ghigliottina f.

sat [sat] V **sit**.

satchel ['satʃəl] n cartella f.

satellite ['satəlaɪt] nm, adj satellite. **satellite town** città satellite f.

satin ['satɪn] nm, adj raso.

satire ['sataɪə] n satira f. **satirical** adj satirico. **satirist** n satirista m, f.

satisfy ['satɪsfaɪ] v soddisfare. **satisfaction** n soddisfazione f. **satisfactory** adj soddisfacente.

saturate ['satʃəreɪt] v saturare. **saturated** adj saturo. **saturation** n saturazione f.

Saturday ['satədɪ] n sabato m.

sauce [sɔːs] n salsa f; (coll) impertinenza f. **saucy** adj impertinente, sfacciato. **sauciness** n impertinenza f, sfacciataggine f.

saucepan ['sɔːspən] n casseruola f, pentola f.

saucer ['sɔːsə] n piattino m, sottocoppa f.

sauerkraut ['sauəkraut] n sarcrauti m pl.

sauna [sɔːnə] n sauna f.

saunter [sɔːntə] v girovagare, andare a passeggio, girare. n giro m.

sausage ['sɒsɪdʒ] n salsiccia f, salame m.

savage ['savɪdʒ] adj selvaggio; feroce, crudele. v assalire, ferire. **savagery** n selvatichezza f; ferocia f, crudeltà f.

save¹ [seɪv] v salvare; (keep) conservare; (put aside) risparmiare. **saver** n risparmiatore, -trice m, f. **saving** n economia f. **savings** pl n risparmi m pl.

save² [seɪv] prep (except) salvo, eccetto.

saviour ['seɪvjə] n liberatore, -trice m, f; (rel) redentore m.

savoury ['seɪvəri] adj (appetizing) saporito, gustoso; (piquant) piccante. n piatto appetitoso m.

***saw¹** [sɔː] n sega f. **sawdust** n segatura f. **sawmill** n segheria f. v segare.

saw² [sɔː] V **see¹**.

sawn [sɔːn] V **saw¹**.

saxophone ['saksəfəun] n sassofono m.

***say** [seɪ] v dire; (declare) dichiarare, affermare. **I say!** senti! guarda un po'! (let's) say (as an estimate) mettiamo, facciamo. n **have no say** non aver voce. **have one's say** dire la sua. **saying** n massima f, motto m, proverbio m.

scab [skab] n crosta f; (biol) scabbia f, rogna f; (derog: non-striker) crumiro, -a m, f. **scabby** adj rognoso, scabbioso.

scaffold ['skafəld] n (execution) patibolo m. **scaffolding** n impalcatura f, ponteggio m; (theatre) palco m.

scald [skɔːld] n scottatura f. v scottare.

scale¹ [skeɪl] n (thin plate) lamina f; (of fish, etc.) scaglia f, squama f; tartaro m; incrostazione f. v squamare; incrostare. **scaly** adj squamoso.

scale² [skeɪl] n (music, math, etc.) scala f. **to scale** in proporzione. v (climb) scalare; (climb over) scavalcare. **scale down** ridurre proporzionalmente.

scales [skeɪlz] pl n bilancia f sing. **tip the scales** dare il crollo alla bilancia.

scallop ['skaləp] n (zool) pettine m; (shell) conchiglia f; (edging) dentellatura f.

scalp [skalp] n scalpo m. v scalpare.

scalpel ['skalpəl] n scalpello m.

scampi ['skampi] *pl n* scampi *m pl.*

scan [skan] *v* scrutare; (*radar, etc.*) analizzare, sondare; (*poetry*) scandire; (*glance at*) dare una scorsa a. **scanner** *n* analizzatore *m*, dispositivo di esplorazione *m.*

scandal ['skandl] *n* scandalo *m*; (*gossip*) maldicenza *f*, diceria *f.* **scandalmonger** *n* maldicente *m, f.* **scandalize** *v* scandalizzare. **scandalous** *adj* scandaloso.

scanty ['skanti] *adj also* **scant** scarso, insufficiente. **scantily dressed** vestito succintamente.

scapegoat ['skeipgout] *n* capro espiatorio *m.*

scar [skaɪ] *n* cicatrice *f*, sfregio *m. v* (*mark*) sfregiare; (*heal*) cicatrizzare. **scarred** *adj* sfregiato.

scarce [skeəs] *adj* scarso, raro. **scarcely** *adv* appena. **scarcity** *n* scarsezza *f.*

scare [skeə] *n* paura *f*, panico *m. v* impaurire, spaventare. **be scared** avere paura. **be scared stiff** avere una paura matta. **scarecrow** *n* spauracchio *m.* **scaremonger** *n* allarmista *m, f.*

scarf [skaɪf] *n* sciarpa *f*; (*square*) foulard *m invar.*

scarlet ['skaɪlit] *adj* scarlatto. **scarlet fever** scarlattina *f.* **scarlet runner** fagiolo di Spagna *m.*

scathing ['skeiðiŋ] *adj* sprezzante, sdegnoso.

scatter ['skatə] *v* spargere, disperdere, diffondere. **scatterbrained** *adj* scervellato, distratto.

scavenge ['skavindʒ] *v* (*streets*) spazzare; (*zool*) nutrirsi di cadaveri. **scavenger** *n* (*street cleaner*) spazzino *m*; (*zool*) animale necrofago *m.*

scene [sim] *n* scena *f*, spettacolo *m.* **scenario** *n* scenario *m.*

scenery ['simari] *n* (*landscape*) paesaggio *m*, veduta *f*; (*theatre*) scenario *m.*

scent [sent] *n* profumo *m*, odore *m*; (*track*) pista *f.* **throw off the scent** far perdere la traccia. *v* (*detect*) fiutare; (*perfume*) profumare.

sceptic ['skeptik] *n* scettico, -a *m, f.* **sceptical** *adj* scettico. **scepticism** *n* scetticismo *m.*

sceptre ['septə] *n* scettro *m.*

schedule ['ʃedjuːl] *n* programma *m*; (*timetable*) orario *m*; lista *f*, specchietto *m.* **according to schedule** secondo il previsto

or programma. *v* programmare; (*list*) elencare.

scheme [skiːm] *n* schema *m*, progetto *m*, piano *m*; intrigo (*pl* -ghi) *m*, trama *f. v* progettare; tramare. **schematic** *adj* schematico.

schizophrenia [ˌskitsəˈfriːniə] *n* schizofrenia *f.* **schizophrenic** *n, adj* schizofrenico, -a.

scholar ['skolə] *n* persona erudita *f*, studioso, -a *m, f*; studente, -essa *m, f.* **scholarly** *adj* erudito, dotto. **scholarship** *n* erudizione *f*; studio *m*; (*award*) borsa di studio *f.*

scholastic [skəˈlastik] *adj* scolastico.

school¹ [skuːl] *n* scuola *f.* **schoolboy** *n* scolaro *m.* **schoolfellow** *n* compagno, -a di scuola *m, f.* **schoolgirl** *n* scolara *f.* **schoolmaster** *n* maestro *m*; insegnante *m.* **schoolmistress** *n* maestra *f*, insegnante *f. v* istruire, ammaestrare.

school² [skuːl] *n* (*of fish*) banco *m*, frotta *f.*

schooner ['skuːnə] *n* goletta *f.*

sciatica [saiˈatikə] *n* sciatica *f.* **sciatic** *adj* sciatico.

science ['saiəns] *n* scienza *f.* **science fiction** fantascienza *f.* **scientific** *adj* scientifico. **scientist** *n* scienziato, -a *m, f.*

scissors ['sizəz] *pl n* forbici *f pl.*

scoff¹ [skof] *v* (*mock*) beffare, schernire. *n* beffa *f.*

scoff² [skof] *v* (*coll: eat*) pappare.

scold [skould] *v* sgridare, rimproverare. **scolding** *n* sgridata *f*, lavata di capo *f.*

scone [skon] *n* focaccia *f.*

scoop [skuːp] *n* (*kitchen*) mestolo *m*; (*dredge*) benna *f*; (*coll*) colpo *m. v* scavare. **scoop out** scodellare. **scoop up** raccogliere, tirar su.

scooter ['skuːtə] *n* motoretta *f*, scooter *m invar*; (*child's*) monopattino *m.*

scope [skoup] *n* (*extent*) portata *f*; opportunità *f*; possibilità *f*; (*space for activity*) campo libero *m.*

scorch [skoːtʃ] *n* scottatura *f. v* abbruciacchiare. **scorcher** *n* (*coll*) giornata caldissima *f.*

score [skoɪ] *n* (*sport*) punteggio *m*; (*account*) conto *m*; (*debt*) debito *m*; (*ground*) causa *f*; (*music*) partitura *f.* **scoreboard** *n* tabellone *m. v* (*sport*) segnare; (*points*) notare; marcare; (*notches*) intaccare; orchestrare. **score off** aver la meglio su.

scorn [skoːn] n disprezzo m, sdegno m. v sdegnare, sprezzare. **scornful** adj sdegnoso, sprezzante.

Scorpio ['skoːpiou] n Scorpione m.

scorpion ['skoːpiən] n scorpione m.

scotch [skotʃ] v sopprimere.

Scotland ['skotlənd] n Scozia f. **Scot** n scozzese m, f. **Scotch** n (whisky) scotch m invar, whisky scozzese m. **Scottish** or **Scots** adj scozzese.

scoundrel ['skaundrəl] n furfante m, mascalzone m.

scour¹ [skauə] v (clean) pulire sfregando; (rub) fregare, forbire.

scour² [skauə] v (search) perlustrare.

scout [skaut] v esplorare, perlustrare. n (mil) vedetta f; (boy) giovane esploratore m; osservatore m.

scowl [skaul] n cipiglio m, guardataccia f. v acciglIarsi.

scramble ['skrambl] v (move hastily) sgambettare; (climb) arrampicarsi; (struggle) azzuffarsi, battagliare; (radio, etc.) disturbare. **scrambled eggs** uova strapazzate f pl. n confusione f, parapiglia f; (struggle) lotta f.

scrap [skrap] n (small piece) pezzetto m, frammento m; (metal) rottame m. **scrapbook** n album m invar. **scraps** pl n rifiuti m pl; (leftovers) avanzi m pl, rimasugli m pl. v scartare, mettere fuori servizio. **scrappy** adj frammentario.

scrape [skreip] v raschiare, grattare. **scrape through** cavarsela; (exam) passare per il buco della serratura. **scrape together** racimolare, raccogliere. n (embarrassing situation) impaccio m.

scratch [skratʃ] v graffiare, grattare; cancellare; (withdraw) ritirarsi. n graffiatura f. **from scratch** da zero. **up to scratch** all'altezza della situazione.

scrawl [skroːl] n scarabocchio m. v scarabocchiare.

scream [skriːm] v strillare. n strillo m; (coll: funny person) spasso m.

screech [skriːtʃ] v stridere, cigolare. n strido m (pl -a f).

screen [skriːn] n paravento m; (shelter) riparo m; (film, etc.) schermo m. v (hide) nascondere; (protect) proteggere; (check) vagliare; (cinema) proiettare.

screw [skruː] n vite f. **screwdriver** n cacciavite m invar. v avvitare. **screw up one's courage** farsi coraggio.

scribble ['skribl] n sgorbio m. v

scribacchiare. **scribbler** n scribacchino, -a m, f.

script [skript] n (handwriting) scrittura f; manuscritto m; (theatre) copione m.

Scripture ['skriptʃə] n Sacra Scrittura f, Bibbia f.

scroll [skroul] n (roll) rotolo m; (ornament) voluta f.

scrounge [skraundʒ] (coll) v scroccare. **scrounger** n scroccone, -a m, f.

scrub¹ [skrʌb] v lavare o pulire fregando forte. **scrubbing brush** spazzola dura f, spazzolone per lavare m.

scrub² [skrʌb] n (bush) macchia f.

scruffy ['skrʌfi] adj trasandato.

scruple ['skruːpl] n scrupolo m. **scrupulous** adj scrupoloso.

scrutiny ['skruːtəni] n esame accurato m. **scrutinize** v esaminare accuratamente.

scuffle ['skʌfl] n tafferuglio m. v azzuffarsi.

scullery ['skʌləri] n retrocucina f.

sculpt [skʌlpt] v scolpire. **sculptor** n scultore m. **sculptress** n scultrice f. **sculptural** adj scultorio. **sculpture** n scultura f.

scum [skʌm] n (on liquids) schiuma f; (on metals) scoria f; (worthless people) feccia f.

scurf [skəːf] n forfora f. **scurfy** adj forforoso.

scurrilous ['skʌriləs] adj scurrile.

scurvy ['skəːvi] n scorbuto m.

scuttle¹ ['skʌtl] n (for coal) secchio da carbone m.

scuttle² ['skʌtl] v (run) scorrazzare.

scuttle³ ['skʌtl] v (sink) affondare.

scythe [saið] n falce f. v falciare.

sea [siː] n mare m. **at sea** in mare; perplesso. **by sea** per mare. **put out to sea** prendere il largo.

sea bed n fondo del mare m.

seafaring ['siːˌfeəriŋ] adj navigatore, -trice; marinaro. **seafarer** n navigatore m.

seafood ['siːfuːd] n frutti di mare m pl.

sea front n marina f.

seagoing ['siːˌgouiŋ] adj d'alto mare.

sea-gull n gabbiano m.

sea-horse n cavalluccio marino m.

seal¹ [siːl] n (stamp) sigillo m; chiusura f. v sigillare; (close) chiudere. **sealing wax** ceralacca f.

seal² [siːl] n (animal) foca f. **sealskin** n pelle di foca f.

sea-level n livello del mare m.

sea-lion n leone marino m.

seam [siːm] n cucitura f, giuntura f; (geol) vena f. v cucire.

seaman ['siːmən] n marinaio m.

search [sɔːtʃ] v frugare, rovistare. n (act) ricerca f; esame minuto m; (for something hidden) perquisizione f. **searchlight** n proiettore m. **search-party** n squadra di ricerca f. **search-warrant** n mandato di perquisizione m. **searching** adj (careful) minuzioso; (observing) indagatore, -trice m, f.

seashore ['siːʃɔː] n spiaggia f, costa f.

seasick ['siːsik] adj be seasick avere il mal di mare. **seasickness** n mal di mare m.

seaside ['siːsaid] n at or to the seaside al mare.

season ['siːzn] n stagione f. **season ticket** abbonamento m. v (wood) stagionare; (spice) condire. **seasonable** adj (timely) opportuno. **seasoning** n condimento m.

seat [siːt] n sedile m; (chair) sedia f; (place) posto m; (coll: behind) sedere m; (location) sede f. **take a seat** accomodarsi. v (cause to sit) far sedere; (provide with seat) provvedere di posti (a sedere).

seaweed ['siːwiːd] n alga f.

seaworthy ['siːwɔːði] adj atto a tenere il mare.

secluded [si'kluːdid] adj isolato, appartato. **seclusion** n isolamento m.

second ['sekənd] n secondo m; (day) due m; (gear) seconda f. adj secondo. on second thoughts ripensandoci bene. **second-hand** adj di seconda mano. **second-rate** adj mediocre. **second sight** chiaroveggenza f.

secondary ['sekəndəri] adj secondario.

secret ['siːkrit] nm, adj segreto. **top secret** adj riservatissimo. **secrecy** n segretezza f.

secretary ['sekrətəri] n segretario, -a m, f. **secretarial** adj segretariale. **secretariat** n segreteria f, segretariato m.

secrete [si'kriːt] v (biol) secernere; (conceal) celare. **secretion** n secrezione f.

sect [sekt] n setta f. **sectarian** adj settario.

section ['sekʃən] n sezione f, parte f.

sector ['sektə] n settore m.

secular ['sekjulə] adj secolare; profano; laico.

secure [si'kjuə] adj sicuro; solido. v mettere al sicuro, assicurare; garantire;

procurarsi. **security** n sicurezza f, garanzia f. **securities** pl n titoli m pl, obbligazioni f pl.

sedate [si'deit] adj pacato, posato. . v calmare, tranquillizzare. **sedative** n sedativo m; calmante m.

sediment ['sedimənt] n sedimento m. **sedimentation** n sedimentazione f.

seduce [si'djuːs] v sedurre. **seducer** n seduttore, -trice m, f. **seduction** n seduzione f. **seductive** adj seducente.

*see[1] [siː] v vedere. **see about** or to occuparsi di. **see home** accompagnare a casa. **see through** penetrare.

see[2] [siː] n (bishop's) diocesi f. **Holy See** Santa Sede f.

seed [siːd] n seme m; (collective) semenza f. **go to seed** (bot) sementire; (decay) scadere, declinare. v seminare. **seedling** n germoglio m, semenzale m. **seedy** adj (shabby) malconcio; indisposto.

*seek [siːk] v cercare.

seem [siːm] v sembrare, parere. **seeming** adj apparente.

seen [siːn] V see[1].

seep [siːp] v infiltrare.

seesaw ['siːsɔː] n altalena (a bilico) f. adj oscillante. v altalenare.

seethe [siːð] v bollire; (be agitated) fremere. **seethe with rage** fremere di rabbia.

segment ['segmənt] n segmento m, sezione f.

segregate ['segrigeit] v segregare. **segregation** n segregazione f.

seize [siːz] v (grasp) afferrare; (by force) impadronirsi di; confiscare. **seize up** grippare, ingranarsi. **seizure** n confisca f; conquista f; (med) attacco m.

seldom ['seldəm] adv raramente, di rado.

select [sə'lekt] adj scelto, distinto. v scegliere. **selection** n selezione f, scelta f. **selective** adj selettivo. **selectivity** n selettività f.

self [self] n io m, persona f.

self-assured adj sicuro di sè. **self-assurance** sicurezza di sè f.

self-centred adj egocentrico, egoista.

self-confident adj sicuro di sè. **self-confidence** n fiducia in sè.

self-conscious adj impacciato. **self-consciousness** n impaccio m.

self-contained adj (not shared) indipendente; (uncommunicative) riservato; (self-sufficient) autosufficiente.

self-critical adj autocritico. **self-criticism** n autocritica f.

self-defence n autodifesa f; (law) legittima difesa f.

self-discipline n autodisciplina f.

self-employed adj **be self-employed** lavorare in proprio.

self-evident adj manifesto, palese.

self-explanatory adj ovvio.

self-expression n espressione della propria personalità f.

self-government n autonomia f.

self-interest n interesse personale m.

selfish ['selfiʃ] adj egoista, egoistico. **selfishness** n egoismo m.

selfless ['selflis] adj altruista, altruistico. **selflessness** n altruismo m.

self-pity n autocommiserazione f.

self-portrait n autoritratto m.

self-possessed adj composto, padrone di sè.

self-preservation n conservazione f.

self-propelled adj che si muove per forza propria.

self-respect n amor proprio m. **self-respecting** adj dignitoso.

self-restraint n autocontrollo m.

self-righteous adj compiaciuto di sè stesso. **self-righteousness** n autocompiacimento m.

self-sacrifice n abnegazione f.

selfsame ['selfseim] adj identico, proprio lo stesso.

self-satisfied adj contento di sè. **self-satisfaction** n autocompiacimento m.

self-service n self-service m invar.

self-styled adj sedicente.

self-sufficient adj autosufficiente. **self-sufficiency** n autosufficienza f.

self-willed adj ostinato; (wilful) caparbio.

*****sell** [sel] v vendere. **seller** n venditore, -trice m, f.

sellotape ® ['seləteip] n scotch ® m invar, nastro autoadesivo m.

semantic [sə'mantik] adj semantico. **semantics** n semantica f.

semaphore ['seməfoɪ] n semaforo m.

semen ['siɪmən] n sperma m.

semibreve ['semibriɪv] n semibreve f.

semicircle ['semisəɪkl] n semicerchio m. **semicircular** adj semicircolare.

semicolon ['semi'koulən] n punto e virgola m.

semifinal [semi'fainl] n semifinale f. **semifinalist** n semifinalista m, f.

seminar ['seminaɪ] n seminario m.

seminary ['seminəri] n seminario m.

semi-precious adj semiprezioso.

semiquaver ['semikweivə] n semicroma f.

semitone ['semitoun] n semitono m.

semolina [,semə'liɪnə] n semolino m.

senate ['senit] n senato m. **senator** n senatore m.

*****send** [send] v mandare; (dispatch) spedire; trasmettere. **send for** (person) mandare a chiamare; (thing) mandare a prendere. **send in** sottoporre. **send on** (readdress) inoltrare. **sender** n mittente m, f.

senile ['siɪmail] adj senile. **senility** n (old age) senilità f; (mental infirmity) senilismo m.

senior ['siɪnjə] adj più anziano, maggiore. n anziano, -a m, f; superiore, -a m, f. **seniority** n anzianità f.

sensation [sen'seiʃən] n sensazione f. **cause a sensation** far sensazione or colpo. **sensational** adj sensazionale, che fa colpo.

sense [sens] n senso m. **take leave of one's senses** perder la ragione. **talk sense** parlare sensatamente. v intuire, capire.

sensible ['sensəbl] adj sensato, ragionevole; (appreciable) sensibile. **sensibility** n sensibilità f.

sensitive ['sensitiv] adj sensibile; delicato; (physiology) sensitivo. **sensitivity** n sensibilità f; suscettibilità f; delicatezza f.

sensual ['sensjuəl] adj sensuale. **sensuality** n sensualità f.

sensuous ['sensjuəs] adj gradevole ai sensi, voluttuoso.

sent [sent] V **send**.

sentence ['sentəns] n (gramm) frase f; (law) condanna f, pena f. **pass sentence** pronunciare (una) sentenza. v condannare.

sentiment ['sentimənt] n sentimento m. **sentimental** adj sentimentale. **sentimentality** n sentimentalità f.

sentry ['sentri] n sentinella f. **stand sentry** fare la guardia.

separate ['sepərət; v 'sepəreit] adj separato; distinto; indipendente. v separare. **separation** n separazione f.

September [sep'tembə] n settembre m.

septic ['septik] adj settico. **septicaemia** n setticemia f.

sequel ['siːkwəl] *n* seguito *m*; conseguenza *f*.

sequence ['siːkwəns] *n* successione *f*; (*math, cards*) sequenza *f*. **in sequence** in ordine successivo.

sequin ['siːkwin] *n* lustrino *m*.

serenade [serə'neid] *n* serenata *f*. *v* fare una serenata a.

serene [sə'riːn] *adj* sereno. **serenity** *n* serenità *f*.

sergeant ['saɪdʒənt] *n* (*mil*) sergente *m*; (*police*) brigadiere *m*.

serial ['siəriəl] *n* (*novel*) romanzo a puntate *m*; (*play*) commedia a puntate *f*. *adj* (*in instalments*) a puntate; (*tech*) di *or* in serie. **serialize** *v* pubblicare *or* trasmettere a puntate.

series ['siəriːz] *n* serie *f*.

serious ['siəriəs] *adj* serio, grave. **are you serious?** dice sul serio? **seriousness** *n* serietà *f*.

sermon ['səːmən] *n* predica *f*.

serpent ['səːpənt] *n* serpente *m*. **serpentine** *adj* serpentino; (*winding*) serpeggiante.

serum ['siərəm] *n* siero *m*.

servant ['səːvənt] *n* domestico, -a *m, f*; servo, -a *m, f*.

serve [səːv] *v* servire. **it serves you right!** ti sta bene! te lo sei meritato!

service ['səːvis] *n* servizio *m*; (*disposal*) disposizione *f*; (*rel*) ufficio divino *m*. **of service** d'aiuto, utile. **service area/station** area/stazione di servizio *f*. *v* provvedere alla manutenzione di, controllare. **serviceable** *adj* pratico, funzionale.

serviette [səːvi'et] *n* tovagliolo *m*.

servile ['səːvail] *adj* servile. **servility** *n* servilità *f*.

session ['seʃən] *n* seduta *f*, sessione *f*.

*****set** [set] *adj* fisso; (*ready*) pronto; prescritto; deciso; preparato; (*prearranged*) stabilito. *n* serie *f*, assortimento *m*; (*theatre, etc.*) set *m invar*, scenario *m*; (*tennis*) set *m invar*, partita *f*. *v* (*place*) mettere, posare; (*fix*) fissare; (*solidify*) indurirsi, rapprendersi; (*sun*) tramontare; (*jewel*) incastonare; (*hair*) mettere in piega; (*bones*) mettere a posto. **set about** (*begin to*) accingersi a; (*attempt*) cercare di; (*coll*) attaccare. **set aside** *or* **by** mettere da parte. **set back** (*hinder*) impedire; (*delay*) ritardare. **set-back** *n* regresso *m*, contrattempo *m*. **set**

free liberare. **set off** far esplodere; (*depart*) mettersi in viaggio; (*intensify*) mettere in risalto; compensare. **set out** partire. **set up** (*erect*) erigere; (*establish*) stabilire, metter su; (*prepare*) allestire.

setting *n* (*environment*) ambiente *m*; (*jewel*) montatura *f*; (*theatre*) scenario *m*, messa in scena *f*; (*music*) messa in musica *f*; (*sun*) tramonto *m*.

settee [se'tiː] *n* canapè *m*, sofà *m*.

settle ['setl] *v* fissare, determinare; (*pay*) regolare, saldare; (*compose*) sistemare; decidere. **settle down** stabilizzarsi; (*live*) stabilirsi. **settlement** *n* decisione *f*; saldo *m*; colonia *f*. **settler** *n* colonizzatore, -trice *m, f*.

seven ['sevn] *nm, adj* sette. **seventh** *nm, adj* settimo.

seventeen [sevn'tiːn] *nm, adj* diciassette. **seventeenth** *adj* diciassettesimo.

seventy ['sevnti] *nm, adj* settanta. **seventieth** *adj* settantesimo.

sever ['sevə] *v* staccare.

several ['sevrəl] *pron* parecchi, diversi. *adj* parecchi, diversi; separato; (*own*) proprio.

severe [sə'viə] *adj* severo; grave; (*weather*) rigido; (*pain, etc.*) violento, vivo. **severity** *n* severità *f*, rigore *m*; violenza *f*.

*****sew** [sou] *v* cucire. **sewing** *n* cucito *m*. **sewing machine** macchina da cucire *f*.

sewage ['sjuidʒ] *n* acque di scolo *or* scarico *f pl*.

sewer ['sjuə] *n* fogna *f*. **sewerage** *n* fognatura *f*.

sewn [soun] *V* sew.

sex [seks] *n* sesso *m*. **sexual** *adj* sessuale. **sexuality** *n* sessualità *f*.

sextet [seks'tet] *n* sestetto *m*.

shabby ['ʃabi] *adj* (*of poor appearance*) malconcio, trasandato; (*badly worn*) logoro, frusto; (*contemptible*) meschino.

shack [ʃak] *n* baracca *f*.

shade [ʃeid] *n* ombra *f*; (*colour*) tinta *f*; (*lamp*) paralume *m*. *v* ombreggiare; (*protect*) proteggere (dalla luce); (*drawing*) sfumare. **shading** *n* sfumatura *f*.

shadow ['ʃadou] *n* ombra *f*. *v* ombreggiare; (*follow*) pedinare. **shady** *adj* ombreggiato; (*dubious*) disonesto, losco.

shaft [ʃaːft] *n* (*pole*) asta *f*; (*passageway*) condotto *m*; (*handle*) manico *m*; (*light*) fascio *m*; (*sarcasm*) frecciata *f*.

shaggy ['ʃagi] *adj* peloso, irsuto.

*shake [ʃeik] n scossa f. **no great shakes** di poco conto. v scuotere; agitare; *(tremble)* tremare; *(disturb)* fremere. **shake hands** stringere la mano. **shake off** liberarsi da. **shake-up** n riorganizzazione f. **shaky** adj tremolante; *(insecure)* malsicuro; precario.

shaken [ʃeikn] V **shake.**

shall [ʃal] aux translated by future tense.

shallot [ʃəˈlot] n scalogno m.

shallow [ˈʃalou] adj poco profondo, basso, superficiale. **shallows** pl n bassofondo (pl bassifondi) m sing.

sham [ʃam] adj finto, falso. n finzione f, inganno m. v fingere, simulare.

shambles [ˈʃamblz] n macello m.

shame [ʃeim] v svergognare. n vergogna f. **bring shame on** recar onta a, disonorare. **shamefaced** adj timido, vergognoso. **what a shame!** che peccato! **shameful** adj vergognoso. **shameless** adj svergognato, spudorato; *(brazen)* sfacciato. **shamelessness** n spudoratezza f, sfacciataggine f.

shampoo [ʃamˈpuː] n shampoo m invar. v **shampoo one's hair** lavarsi i capelli.

shamrock [ˈʃamrɔk] n trifoglio d'Irlanda m.

shanty¹ [ˈʃanti] n *(hut)* capanna f. **shanty town** baraccopoli f, bidonville (pl -s) f.

shanty² [ˈʃanti] n *(song)* canzone marinaresca f.

shape [ʃeip] n forma f; condizione f. **take shape** concretizzarsi, prender forma. v formare, dar forma a; modellare; adattare. **shapeless** adj informe, confuso. **shapely** adj ben fatto, bello.

share [ʃeə] n porzione f, parte f; *(comm)* azione f. **shareholder** n azionista m, f. v dividere; *(jointly)* condividere. **share in** prender parte a. **share out** distribuire.

shark [ʃaːk] n pescecane (pl pescicani) m.

sharp [ʃaːp] adj *(cutting)* tagliente; *(not blunt)* aguzzo; brusco; *(distinct)* netto; *(flavour)* aspro, piccante; acuto; *(alert)* sveglio; *(biting)* mordace; *(shrewd)* scaltro. adv bruscamente; *(punctually)* in punto. n *(music)* diesis m. **sharpen** v affilare; *(pencil)* far la punta a; rendere più acuto.

shatter [ˈʃatə] v *(break into fragments)* frantumare; *(destroy)* rovinare. **shattering** adj *(coll)* schiacciante.

shave [ʃeiv] n rasatura f. **have a close shave** cavarsela per un pelo. v farsi la

barba; *(cut closely)* radere, rasare. **shaving brush/soap** pennello/sapone da barba m. **shaving cream** crema da barba f.

shawl [ʃɔːl] n scialle m.

she [ʃiː] pron ella, lei. **she who** colei che.

sheaf [ʃiːf] n fascio m; *(cereals)* covone m.

*shear [ʃiə] v tosare; *(tech)* spezzarsi; *(deprive)* privare. **shears** pl n cesoie f pl.

sheath [ʃiːθ] n guaina f. **sheathe** v rivestire; *(sword)* ringuainare.

*shed¹ [ʃed] v *(let fall)* versare; *(lose)* perdere. **shed light on** far luce su.

shed² [ʃed] n capannone m; *(outhouse)* capanna f, rimessa f.

sheen [ʃiːn] n lucentezza f.

sheep [ʃiːp] n pecora f. **sheep-dog** n (cane da) pastore m. **sheepish** adj timido.

sheer¹ [ʃiə] adj *(mere)* mero; assoluto; *(steep)* a piombo; trasparente.

sheer² [ʃiə] v cambiar rotta.

sheet [ʃiːt] n *(bedding)* lenzuolo m (pl -a f); *(paper)* foglio m; *(iron, etc.)* lamiera f; *(glass)* lastra f. **sheet lightning** lampeggio m.

shelf [ʃelf] n *(support)* mensola f, ripiano m; *(ledge)* sporgenza f; *(rock)* scogliera f. **set of shelves** scaffale m.

shell [ʃel] n *(of egg, etc.)* guscio m; *(of fish)* conchiglia f; *(mil)* proiettile m; *(hollow casing)* involucro m. **shellfish** n crostaceo m, mollusco m; *(pl: as food)* frutti di mare m pl. **shell-shock** n psicosi traumatica da guerra f. v *(mil)* bombardare; *(eggs, etc.)* sgusciare; *(peas)* sgranare.

shelter [ˈʃeltə] n riparo m, rifugio m; protezione f. **take shelter** ripararsi, rifugiarsi. v proteggere, dare asilo a.

shelve [ʃelv] v *(put aside)* mettere da parte; *(postpone)* rimandare, archiviare.

shepherd [ˈʃepəd] n pastore m. **shepherdess** n pastora f.

sheriff [ˈʃerif] n sceriffo m.

sherry [ˈʃeri] n sherry m invar.

shield [ʃiːld] n schermo m; *(armour)* scudo m. v proteggere.

shift [ʃift] v spostare, trasferire; *(free oneself from)* liberarsi da. **shift for oneself** fare da sè. n turno m; *(change)* cambiamento m; *(artifice)* espediente m. **shifting** adj instabile, mutevole; *(sands)* mobile. **shifty** adj malizioso.

shimmer [ˈʃimə] v luccicare. n luccichio m.

shin [ʃin] *n* stinco *m*.

*****shine** [ʃain] *n* splendore *m*. *v* brillare, risplendere; (*polish*) lustrare.

shingle [ʃiŋgl] *n* (*roof*) lastra di copertura *f*; (*stone*) ciottolo *m*; (*extent of pebbles*) ghiaia *f*.

shingles [ʃiŋglz] *n* erpete *m*; (*coll*) fuoco di Sant'Antonio *m*.

ship [ʃip] *n* nave *f*. **shipowner** *n* armatore *m*. **shipshape** *adv* in ordine perfetto. **shipwreck** *n* naufragio *m*. **be shipwrecked** naufragare. **shipyard** *n* cantiere navale *m*. *v* spedire. **shipper** *n* spedizioniere *m*.

shirk [ʃəːk] *v* evitare, scansare. **shirker** *n* scansafatiche *m f invar*.

shirt [ʃəːt] *n* camicia *f*.

shit [ʃit] (*vulgar*) *n* merda *f*. *v* cacare.

shiver [ʃivə] *v* tremare, rabbrividire. *n* brivido *m*, tremito *m*. **have the shivers** (*cold*) avere i brividi; (*fear*) avere la tremarella.

shoal [ʃoul] *n* frotta *f*; (*fish*) banco *m*.

shock¹ [ʃok] *n* colpo *m*; (*encounter*) scontro *m*; (*elec*) scossa *f*; (*med*) shock *m invar*; impressione *f*. **shock absorber** ammortizzatore *m*. *v* colpire; disgustare; impressionare; dare una scossa a. **shocking** *adj* terribile; ripugnante, disgustoso.

shock² [ʃok] *n* (*hair*) chioma *f*.

shod [ʃod] *V* **shoe**.

shoddy [ʃodi] *adj* scadente.

*****shoe** [ʃuː] *n* scarpa *f*. **shoe-lace** *n* laccio delle scarpe *m*. **shoemaker** *n* calzolaio *m*. *v* (*horse*) ferrare.

shone [ʃon] *V* **shine**.

shook [ʃuk] *V* **shake**.

*****shoot** [ʃuːt] *v* tirare, sparare; (*hit*) ferire; (*kill*) uccidere; (*film*) girare; (*bot*) germogliare. *n* (*plant*) rampollo *m*, germoglio *m*; (*spedizione di*) caccia *f*. **shooting** *n* tiro *m*, caccia *f*; (*firing*) sparatoria *f*. **shooting pain** dolore lancinante *m*. **shooting star** stella filante *f*.

shop [ʃop] *n* negozio *m*, bottega *f*; (*in factory, etc.*) officina *f*. **shopkeeper** *n* negoziante *m*, **shoplifter** *n* taccheggiatore, -trice *m, f*. **shoplifting** *n* taccheggio *m*. **shop-soiled** *adj* sciupato. **shop-window** *n* vetrina *f*. **shut up shop** chiudere bottega. **talk shop** parlare d'affari. *v* fare gli acquisti, fare la spesa. **shopper** *n* acquirente *m, f*. **shopping** *n* acquisti *m pl*. **go shopping** fare la spesa. **shopping bag** borsa per la spesa *f*.

shore¹ [ʃoː] *n* sponda *f*, riva *f*. **on shore a** terra.

shore² [ʃoː] *v* **shore up** puntellare.

shorn [ʃoːn] *V* **shear**.

short [ʃoːt] *adj* (*not long*) corto; breve; (*not tall*) basso; brusco. *adv* bruscamente; (*suddenly*) di botto. **in short** in breve. **nothing short of** addirittura. **run short** scarseggiare. **to cut a long story short** a farla breve. *n* (*film*) short *m invar*, cortometraggio *m*. **shortage** *n* mancanza *f*, carenza *f*. **shorten** *v* accorciare, abbreviare. **shortly** *adv* presto.

shortbread [ʃoːtbred] *n* biscotto di pasta frolla *m*.

short-circuit *n* corto circuito *m*. *v* mettere in corto circuito.

shortcoming [ʃoːtkʌmiŋ] *n* difetto *m*.

short cut *n* scorciatoia *f*.

shorthand [ʃoːthand] *n* stenografia *f*. **shorthand typist** *n* stenodattilografo, -a *m, f*.

short list *n* rosa dei candidati *f*. *v* mettere nella rosa dei candidati.

short-lived *adj* di poca durata.

shorts [ʃoːts] *pl n* shorts *m pl*; calzoncini corti *m pl*.

short-sighted *adj* miope; (*lacking foresight*) imprevidente. **short-sightedness** *n* miopia *f*; imprevidenza *f*.

short story *n* novella *f*.

short-tempered *adj* irascibile.

short-term *adj* a breve scadenza.

short-wave *adj* a onde corte.

shot¹ [ʃot] *V* **shoot**.

shot² [ʃot] *n* sparo *m*, colpo *m*; (*pellet*) pallottola *f*; (*pellets*) pallini di piombo *m pl*; (*person*) tiratore *m*; (*phot*) istantanea *f*; (*film*) ripresa *f*. **off like a shot** via come un bolide. **shotgun** *n* fucile da caccia *m*.

should¹ [ʃud] *aux translated by conditional tense.*

should² [ʃud] *aux translated by conditional tense of* **dovere**.

shoulder [ʃouldə] *n* spalla *f*; (*road*) banchina *f*. **give the cold shoulder** trattare con freddezza. **shoulder-blade** *n* scapola *f*. **shoulder-strap** *n* spallina *f*. *v* caricarsi sulle spalle; (*assume as burden*) addossarsi.

shout [ʃaut] *v* gridare, urlare. *n* grido *m* (*pl* -a *f*), urlo *m* (*pl* -a *f*). **shout at** sgridare, alzar la voce con. **shout down** far tacere a forza di grida.

shove [ʃʌv] *n* spinta *f*. *v* spingere.

shovel [ʃʌvl] *n* pala *f*. **shovelful** *n* palata *f*.

*show [ʃou] *n* (*display*) mostra *f*, esposizione *f*; (*theatre*) spettacolo *m*; apparenza *f*; ostentazione *f*. **give the show away** rivelare tutto. **run the show** essere in controllo. **show business** mondo dello spettacolo *m*. **show-case** *n* vetrina *f*. **show-down** *n* (*final reckoning*) resa dei conti *f*. **showman** *n* (*theatre*) impresario *m*; showman *m invar*. **show-room** *n* sala d'esposizione *f*. *v* mostrare, manifestare, indicare, dimostrare. **show off** ostentare, darsi delle arie. **show up** (*reveal*) svelare; (*display*) far risaltare; (*appear*) presentarsi.

shower [ʃauə] *n* (*bath*) doccia *f*; (*rain*) acquazzone *m*; (*blows*) grandine *f*. **have a shower** fare la doccia. *v* **shower with** tempestare di, inondare di.

shown [ʃoun] *V* show.

shrank [ʃraŋk] *V* shrink.

shred [ʃred] *n* (*piece torn off*) brandello *m*; (*bit*, *scrap*) briciolo *m*. *v* fare a brandelli o pezzetti.

shrew [ʃruː] *n* (*woman*) bisbetica *f*; (*zool*) toporagno *m*.

shrewd [ʃruːd] *adj* accorto, scaltro. **shrewdness** *n* accortezza *f*, scaltrezza *f*.

shriek [ʃriːk] *v* strillare. *n* strillo *m*.

shrill [ʃril] *adj* stridulo, acuto.

shrimp [ʃrimp] *n* gamberetto *m*.

shrine [ʃrain] *n* santuario *m*, reliquario *m*, tempio *m*.

*shrink [ʃriŋk] *v* (*become tight*) restringersi; (*withdraw*) ritirarsi; (*become less*) ridursi. **shrink from** rifuggire da. **shrinkage** *n* restringimento *m*.

shrivel [ʃrivl] *v* raggrinzirsi.

shroud [ʃraud] *n* lenzuolo funebre *m*; (*mist*) velo *m*. *v* avvolgere.

Shrove Tuesday [ʃrouv] *n* martedì grasso *m*.

shrub [ʃrʌb] *n* arbusto *m*.

shrug [ʃrʌg] *v* scrollare (le spalle). **shrug off** (*minimize*) prendere alla leggera; (*shake off*) scrollarsi di dosso. *n* scrollata (di spalle) *f*.

shrunk [ʃrʌŋk] *V* shrink.

shudder [ʃʌdə] *n* brivido *m*, tremito *m*. *v* rabbrividire.

shuffle [ʃʌfl] *v* mettere in disordine; rimaneggiare; (*cards*) mescolare; (*feet*) strascicare.

shun [ʃʌn] *v* scansare, sfuggire (a).

shunt [ʃʌnt] *v* (*rail*) smistare; (*get rid of*) mettere da parte; (*elec*) shuntare. *n* (*rail*) scambio *m*; (*elec*) shunt *m invar*.

*shut [ʃʌt] *adj* chiuso. *v* chiudere. **shut down** (*work*) sospendere l'attività. **shut off** bloccare, sottrarsi a. **shut out** non lasciar entrare. **shut up** star zitto.

shutter [ʃʌtə] *n* (*window*) persiana *f*; (*phot*) otturatore *m*.

shuttle [ʃʌtl] *n* spola *f*, navetta *f*. **shuttlecock** *n* volano *m*. **shuttle service** servizio di spola *m*, servizio pendolare *m*.

shy [ʃai] *adj* timido, schivo. *v* (*horse*) scartare. **shy from** rifuggire da; (*shun*) schivare. **shyness** *n* timidezza *f*, diffidenza *f*.

sick [sik] *adj* malato; (*fed up*) stanco, stufo. **be sick** essere malato, star male; vomitare. **feel sick** sentirsi male, avere la nausea. **make sick** (*infuriate*) mandare in bestia; disgustare; far vomitare. **sick-bay** *n* infermeria *f*. *n* vomito *m*. **sicken** *v* ammalarsi. **sickening** *adj* nauseabondo, disgustante. **sickness** *n* malattia *f*.

sickle [sikl] *n* falce *f*.

side [said] *n* lato *m*, fianco *m*; (*lake*, *etc*.) riva *f*; (*in battle*, *quarrel*, *etc*.) partito *m*, parte *f*. **on the other side** d'altra parte. **sideboard** *n* credenza *f*. **side-issue** *n* questione secondaria *f*. **sidelight** *n* (*mot*) luce di posizione *f*. **sidelong** *adj* di traverso, furtivo. **sidestep** *v* schivare. **side-street** *n* via laterale *f*. **sidetrack** *v* distrarre. **sideways** *adv* lateralmente; obliquamente. *v* **side with** essere dalla parte di. **siding** *n* binario di raccordo *m*.

sidle [saidl] *v* andare a sghembo. **sidle up to** accostarsi furtivamente a.

siege [siːdʒ] *n* assedio *m*. **lay siege** assediare. **raise the siege** togliere l'assedio.

sieve [siv] *n* setaccio *m*. *v* setacciare.

sift [sift] *v* setacciare; (*examine*) vagliare.

sigh [sai] *v* sospirare. *n* sospiro *m*.

sight [sait] *n* vista *f*; (*coll*) spettacolo *m*; (*tech*) mirino *m*. **catch sight of** intravedere. **know by sight** conoscere di vista. **lose sight of** perdere di vista. **sights** *pl n* luoghi d'interesse *m pl*. **sightseeing** *n* turismo *m*.

sign [sain] *n* segno *m*, cenno *m*; (*inscription*) insegna *f*, segnale *m*; (*trace*) traccia *f*. **signpost** *n* indicatore *m*. *v* firmare, ratificare. **sign off** ritirarsi. **sign on** (*employ*) assumere; (*commit oneself*) impegnarsi.

signal ['signəl] n segnale m. v segnalare.

signature ['signətʃə] n firma f. **signatory** n firmatario, -a m, f.

signify ['signifai] v significare; (*mean*) voler dire; (*be of consequence*) importare.

significance n importanza f; (*meaning*) significato m. **significant** adj significativo, espressivo.

silence ['sailəns] n silenzio m. v ridurre al silenzio, far tacere; (*put to rest*) porre fine a. **silencer** n silenziatore m.

silent ['sailənt] adj silenzioso; tacito; muto. **keep silent** tacere, rimaner zitto.

silhouette [silu'et] n silhouette (*pl -s*) f.

silk [silk] n seta f. **silkworm** n baco da seta m. **silken** adj di seta. **silky** adj di seta; (*lustrous*) lucido; (*smooth*) morbido.

sill [sil] n (*window*) davanzale m.

silly ['sili] adj sciocco. **silliness** n sciocchezza f.

silt [silt] n limo m. **silt up** insabbiarsi.

silver ['silvə] n argento m; (*cutlery, etc.*) argenteria f. adj d'argento, argenteo. v argentare.

similar ['similə] adj simile. **similarity** n somiglianza f.

simile ['simili] n (*figure of speech*) similitudine f; (*example*) paragone m.

simmer ['simə] v sobbollire.

simple ['simpl] adj semplice. **simpleton** n sempliciotto, -a m, f. **simplicity** n semplicità f. **simplification** n semplificazione f. **simplify** v semplificare.

simulate ['simjuleit] v simulare, fingere. **simulation** n simulazione f, finzione f.

simultaneous [,siməl'teinjəs] adj simultaneo.

sin [sin] n peccato m. v peccare. **sinful** adj peccaminoso. **sinner** n peccatore, -trice m, f.

since [sins] adv (*from then*) da allora; (*subsequently*) poi; (*ago*) fa. prep da. conj (*period*) da quando; dacchè; (*because*) poichè.

sincere [sin'siə] adj sincero. **sincerity** n sincerità f.

sinew ['sinju] n tendine m; (*force*) nerbo m.

***sing** [siŋ] v cantare. **singer** n cantante m, f. **singing** n canto m.

singe [sindʒ] v strinare; (*scorch*) bruciacchiare.

single ['siŋgl] adj (*one only*) singolo, solo; (*unmarried*) celibe. **single-breasted** adj a un petto. **single file** fila indiana f. **single-handed** adj (*unaided*) solo, senza aiuto. **single-minded** adj deciso, fermo, tenace. **single mindedness** n fermezza f, tenacia f. **single ticket** biglietto di andata solo m. **singolo** m. v **single out** scegliere.

singular ['siŋgjulə] nm, adj singolare.

sinister ['sinistə] adj (*ominous*) di cattivo augurio.

***sink** [siŋk] n lavandino m. v (*submerge, go under*) affondare; (*go down*) calare, abbassarsi.

sinuous ['sinjuəs] adj tortuoso.

sinus ['sainəs] n seno m; (*nasal*) seno paranasale m. **sinusitis** n sinusite f.

sip [sip] n sorso m. v sorseggiare, bere a piccoli sorsi.

siphon ['saifən] n sifone m. v travasare con un sifone.

sir [sə] n signore m.

siren ['saiərən] n sirena f.

sirloin ['sətloin] n lombata f.

sister ['sistə] n sorella f; (*nursing*) infermiera capo sala f; (*rel*) suora f. **sister-in-law** n cognata f.

***sit** [sit] v sedere; posare; (*garment*) cadere; (*exam*) dare; (*be convened*) essere in seduta. **sit down** sedersi, mettersi a sedere. **sit on the fence** non prendere partito. **sit tight** non lasciarsi smuovere. **sitting** n seduta f. **sitting room** salotto m.

site [sait] n posizione f; (*building*) cantiere edile m. v situare.

situation [sitju'eiʃən] n situazione f; (*post*) posizione f. **situated** adj situato.

six [siks] nm, adj sei. **sixth** nm, adj sesto. **sixteen** [siks'tiin] nm, adj sedici. **sixteenth** nm, adj sedicesimo.

sixty ['siksti] nm, adj sessanta. **sixtieth** nm, adj sessantesimo.

size¹ [saiz] n dimensione f, grandezza f; (*garments*) misura f, taglia f. v **size up** valutare. **sizeable** adj notevole.

size² [saiz] n (*glue*) bozzima f. v imbozzimare.

sizzle ['sizl] v sfriggere. n sfrigolio m.

skate¹ [skeit] v pattinare. n pattino m. **skater** n pattinatore, -trice m, f. **skating** m pattinaggio m.

skate² [skeit] n (*fish*) razza f.

skeleton ['skelitn] n scheletro m.

sketch [sketʃ] n abbozzo m; (theatre) bozzetto m. v abbozzare; delineare. **sketchbook** n albo di or per schizzi m. **sketchy** adj impreciso, superficiale.

skewer ['skjuə] n spiedo m.

ski [skiː] n sci m. **ski-lift** n sciovia f. v sciare. **skier** n sciatore, -trice m, f. **skiing** n sci m.

skid [skid] v slittare; (car) sbandare; (plane) derapare. n slittamento m; sbandamento m.

skill [skil] n abilità f, destrezza f. **skilful** adj abile, esperto. **skilled** adj abile, esperto; (worker) specializzato.

skim [skim] v (milk) scremare; (glide over) rasentare. **skim over** sfiorare; (reading) sfogliare.

skimp [skimp] v (food, expense, etc.) lesinare, risparmiare; (person) tenere a stecchetto; (scrimp) fare economia. **skimpy** adj (scanty) scarso; (mean) tirchio.

skin [skin] n pelle f; (fruit) buccia f, scorza f; (film) pellicola f; (colouring) carnagione f. **by the skin of one's teeth** per il rotto della cuffia. **skin-deep** adj superficiale. **skin-diving** n pesca subacquea f. **skinflint** n spilorcio m. **skin-graft** n innesto epidermico m. v sbucciare; (animals) scorticare. **skinny** adj magro, ossuto.

skip [skip] v saltare; (leap) balzellare. n balzo m.

skipper ['skipə] n capitano m.

skirmish ['skəːmiʃ] n scaramuccia f. v scontrarsi.

skirt [skəːt] n gonna f, sottana f. v costeggiare; (edge) orlare. **skirting board** zoccolo m.

skittle ['skitl] n birillo m.

skull [skʌl] n cranio m, teschio m. **skull-cap** n calotta f, papalina f.

skunk [skʌŋk] n moffetta f; (coll) farabutto m.

sky [skai] n cielo m. **blow sky-high** far saltare per aria. **sky-blue** adj celeste. **skylark** n allodola f. **skylight** n lucernario m. **skyline** n profilo m, orizzonte m. **skyscraper** n grattacielo m.

slab [slab] n piastra f; (thick piece) fetta f.

slack [slak] adj (loose) lento; (inactive) fiacco; (negligent) indolente. v (rope) imbando m; (comm) attività ridotta f. v (neglect duty) trascurare. **slacken** v rallentare.

slacks [slaks] pl n calzoni sportivi m pl.

slag [slag] n scoria f.

slalom ['slaːləm] n slalom m.

slam [slam] v sbattere. n (bridge) slam m invar.

slander ['slaːndə] n diffamazione f. v diffamare. **slanderer** n diffamatore, -trice m, f. **slanderous** adj diffamatorio.

slang [slaŋ] n gergo m. v vituperare. **slanging match** battibecco m.

slant [slaːnt] v inclinare, inclinarsi; (news) presentare in modo tendenzioso. n (slope) inclinazione f; (point of view) punto di vista m; (bias) tendenza f.

slap [slap] n schiaffo m; (rebuke) rabbuffo m. **slap in the face** insulto m, umiliazione f. **slap on the back** felicitazione f. v schiaffeggiare. **slap-bang** adv (right) in pieno; (suddenly) di colpo. **slapdash** adj fatto a casaccio, abborracciato. **slap-happy** adj incosciente.

slash [slaʃ] v tagliare, squarciare. n taglio m.

slat [slat] n stecca f, assicella f.

slate [sleit] n lavagna f; (geol) ardesia f. **have a clean slate** aver la fedina pulita. **wipe the slate clean** ricominciare dimenticando il passato.

slaughter ['slɔːtə] n macello m; (massacre) strage f. v macellare, far strage di. **slaughterhouse** n macello m.

slave [sleiv] n schiavo, -a m, f. **slave-driver** n negriero, -a m, f. **slave labour** lavori forzati m pl. v sgobbare.

sledge [sledʒ] n slitta f.

sledgehammer ['sledʒhamə] n mazza f. **sledgehammer blow** mazzata f.

sleek [sliːk] adj (glossy) lucido; (smooth) liscio; (soft) morbido; (unctuous) mellifluo.

*****sleep** [sliːp] n sonno m. **go to sleep** addormentarsi, prendere sonno. **have a good sleep** fare una bella dormita. v dormire; (accommodate) alloggiare. **sleep on** dormirci su. **sleeper** n dormiente m, f; (timber beam) traversina f; (on train) vagone letto m. **be a heavy/light sleeper** avere il sonno pesante/leggero. **sleeping bag** sacco a pelo m. **sleeping partner** (econ) socio accomandante m. **sleeping pill** sonnifero m. **sleepless** adj insonne. **sleepy** adj sonnolento.

sleet [sliːt] n nevischio m.

sleeve [sliiv] *n* manica *f*; (*tech*) manicotto *m*; (*record*) copertina *f*. **up one's sleeve** di riserva.

sleigh [slei] *n* slitta *f*. *v* andare in slitta.

slender ['slendə] *adj* snello; (*small*) esiguo, scarso.

slept [slept] *V* sleep.

slice [slais] *n* fetta *f*; parte *f*, porzione *f*; (*spatula*) paletta *f*. *v* affettare, tagliare a fette; (*sport*) tagliare.

slick [slik] *adj* (*sleek*) lucido; (*coll: smooth*) untuoso; (*coll: shrewd*) spigliato, scaltro.

slid [slid] *V* slide.

*****slide** [slaid] *n* (*inclined plane*) scivolo *m*; (*microscope*) vetrino *m*; (*phot*) diapositiva *f*; (*hair*) fibbia *f*; (*act of sliding*) scivolata *f*. **slide-rule** *n* regolo calcolatore *m*. *v* scivolare. **let slide** lasciar correre. **sliding scale** scala mobile *f*.

slight [slait] *adj* leggero; (*frail*) esile. *n* affronto *m*, dispetto *m*, mancanza di rispetto *f*. *v* mancare di rispetto, ignorare.

slim [slim] *adj* magro, snello; (*poor*) povero; (*scant*) minimo. *v* dimagrare. **slimming** *adj* dimagrante.

slime [slaim] *n* melma *f*; (*secretion*) bava *f*. **slimy** *adj* melmoso; bavoso; (*servile*) untuoso.

*****sling** [sliŋ] *n* (*weapon*) fionda *f*; (*bandage*) benda *f*, fascia *f*; (*rifle*) cinghia *f*; (*hoist*) braca *f*. **have one's arm in a sling** portare un braccio al collo. *v* (*throw*) lanciare, gettare; (*suspend*) sospendere.

*****slink** [sliŋk] *v* sgattaiolare.

slip [slip] *n* errore *m*, svista *f*; (*garment*) sottana *f*; (*skid*) scivolata *f*; (*plant*) rampollo *m*; (*of paper*) pezzetto *m*. **slip of the tongue** lapsus linguae *m invar*. *v* scivolare. **let slip** lasciar scappare. **slip away** andarsene. **slip-knot** *n* nodo scorsoio *m*. **slip-road** *n* raccordo *m*. **slip up** fare uno sbaglio, prendere una papera.

slipper ['slipə] *n* pantofola *f*, ciabatta *f*.

slippery ['slipəri] *adj* scivoloso.

*****slit** [slit] *n* taglio *m*, fessura *f*. *v* tagliare, squarciare.

slither ['sliðə] *v* scivolare.

slobber ['slobə] *v* sbavare.

sloe [slou] *n* (*fruit*) prugnola *f*; (*tree*) prugnolo *m*.

slog [slog] *v* (*walk*) avanzare a fatica; (*toil*) faticare. *n* camminata dura *f*; faticata *f*.

slogan ['slougən] *n* motto *m*, slogan *m invar*.

slop [slop] *v* versare; (*spill over*) traboccare. **slops** *pl n* (*food*) pappa *f sing*; (*dirty water*) lavatura *f sing*.

slope [sloup] *n* pendio *m*. *v* inclinarsi, pendere. **sloping** *adj* inclinato, obliquo.

sloppy ['slopi] *adj* (*wet*) bagnato; (*careless*) abborracciato; (*untidy*) scatto; sentimentale.

slot [slot] *n* fessura *f*, apertura *f*. **slot-machine** *n* (*vending*) apparecchio a gettoni *m*; (*gambling*) slot-machine *m invar*. *v* **slot into** incanalare.

slouch [slautʃ] *v* (*walk*) camminare dinoccolato; (*droop*) languire. *n* andatura dinoccolata *f*.

slovenly ['slʌvnli] *adj* sciatto, trascurato.

slow [slou] *adj* lento; (*late*) tardo; (*clock*) indietro *invar*. *adv* piano, adagio. *v* **slow down** rallentare.

slug [slʌg] *n* lumaca *f*.

sluggish ['slʌgiʃ] *adj* lento, inerte.

sluice [sluis] *n* chiusa *f*. *v* (*flush*) lavare abbondantemente.

slum [slʌm] *n* quartiere povero *or* basso *m*; (*tumbledown house*) tugurio *m*, catapecchia *f*.

slumber ['slʌmbə] *v* sonnecchiare. *n* (*heavy*) dormita *f*; (*light*) dormiveglia *m invar*.

slump [slʌmp] *n* crollo *m*, caduta *f*. *v* cadere, crollare.

slung [slʌŋ] *V* sling.

slunk [slʌŋk] *V* slink.

slur [slə] *v* (*speech*) biascicare; (*disparage*) denigrare; (*music*) legare. **slur over** passar sopra a. *n* affronto *m*; (*blot*) macchia *f*.

slush [slʌʃ] *n* melma *f*. **slushy** *adj* melmoso.

slut [slʌt] *n* (*immoral*) sgualdrina *f*; (*slovenly*) sciattona *f*.

sly [slai] *adj* astuto, scaltro. **on the sly** in sordina.

smack[1] [smak] *n* (*hit*) schiaffo *m*; (*sound*) schiocco *m*; (*kiss*) bacione *m*. **smack in the eye** (*snub*) rabbuffo *m*; (*disappointment*) delusione *f*. *v* schiaffeggiare, schioccare. **smack one's lips** leccarsi i baffi.

smack[2] [smak] *n* sapore *m*. *v* **smack of** (*taste*) sapere di; (*suggest*) ricordare.

small [smoil] *adj* piccolo; (*low*) basso; (*humble*) umile; insignificante. **small change** spiccioli *m pl*. **small fry** persone

171   **snow**

di poco conto *f pl*. **small-minded** *adj* gretto. **smallpox** *n* vaiolo *m*. **small talk** chiacchera *f*, cicaleccio *m*.

smart [smɑːt] *adj* (*sharp*) acuto; intelligente; (*shrewd*) sveglio; elegante; brillante. *v* bruciare, sentire un vivo dolore. **smarten** *v* abbellire, ravvivarsi.

smash [smaʃ] *n* (*collision*) scontro *m*; (*ruin*) rovina *f*, disastro *m*; (*tennis*) smash *m invar*. **smash-and-grab raid** (*coll*) spaccata *f*. *v* (*shatter*) fracassare; (*destroy*) annientare. **smashing** *adj* (*coll*) magnifico.

smear [smiə] *v* (*grease*) ungere; (*daub*) spalmare; (*soil*) macchiare; (*defame*) calunniare. *n* macchia *f*; (*slur*) calunnia *f*.

*****smell** [smel] *n* odore *m*, profumo *m*; (*faculty*) odorato *m*. *v* sentire l'odore di; (*perceive*) fiutare; (*stink*) puzzare. **smell a rat** fiutare un imbroglio. **smell of** aver odore di.

smelt [smelt] *V* **smell**.

smile [smail] *n* sorriso *m*. *v* sorridere.

smirk [smɜːk] *n* sorriso compiaciuto *m*. *v* sorridere con aria compiaciuta.

smock [smok] *n* camiciotto *m*; (*artists'*) blusa *f*. **smocking** *n* nido d'ape *m*, punto smock *m*.

smog [smog] *n* smog *m invar*.

smoke [smouk] *n* fumo *m*. **smoke-screen** *n* cortina di fumo *f*. **smoke-stack** *n* fumaiolo *m*. *v* fumare; (*cure*) affumicare. **smokeless** *adj* senza fumo. **smoker** *n* (*person*) fumatore, -trice *m, f*; (*compartment*) scompartimento per fumatori *m*. **smoky** *adj* fumoso, che sa di fumo.

smooth [smuːð] *adj* (*not rough*) liscio; (*unruffled*) calmo; (*not harsh*) gradevole. *v* lisciare, spianare, facilitare.

smother ['smʌðə] *v* soffocare, sopprimere.

smoulder ['smouldə] *v* covare (sotto la cenere).

smudge [smʌdʒ] *n* sgorbio *m*. *v* sgorbiare.

smug [smʌg] *adj* soddisfatto di sè.

smuggle ['smʌgl] *v* **smuggle in/out** far entrare/uscire di contrabbando. **smuggler** *n* contrabbandiere, -a *m, f*. **smuggling** *n* contrabbando *m*.

snack [snak] *n* (*light meal*) spuntino *m*.

snag [snag] *n* (*impediment*) intoppo *m*. *v* (*stocking*) smagliare.

snail [sneil] *n* chiocciola *f*, lumaca *f*.

snake [sneik] *n* serpente *m*.

snap [snap] *v* (*noise*) schioccare; (*break suddenly*) spezzarsi; (*phot*) scattare. **snap**

out of it riprendersi. **snap up** non lasciarsi sfuggire. *n* schiocco *m*; rottura improvvisa *f*; (*sudden bite*) morsicata *f*; (*phot*) istantanea *f*; (*short spell*) ondata *f*. **snapdragon** *n* bocca di leone *f*. *adj* istantaneo. **snappy** *adj* irritabile; (*lively*) vivace.

snare [sneə] *n* laccio *m*, lacciolo *m*. *v* prendere al laccio; accalappiare.

snarl¹ [snɑːl] *v* (*growl*) ringhiare. *n* ringhio *m*.

snarl² [snɑːl] *n* (*tangle*) groviglio *m*. *v* aggrovigliare.

snatch [snatʃ] *v* ghermire, agguantare. *n* strappo *m*; (*scrap*) frammento *m*.

sneak [sniːk] *v* muoversi furtivamente; (*coll: steal*) squagliarsela; (*slang: tell tales*) spifferare. *n* (*coll*) spifferone, -a *m, f*; (*despicable person*) vigliacco, -a *m, f*. **sneakers** *pl n* scarpe da tennis *or* ginnastica *f pl*.

sneer [sniə] *n* (*derisory*) ghigno *m*; (*contemptuous*) sogghigno *m*. *v* ghignare; sogghignare. **sneer at** canzonare, burlarsi di.

sneeze [sniːz] *n* starnuto *m*. *v* starnutire. **sneeze at** (*coll*) sprezzare.

sniff [snif] *n* annusare, fiutare; aspirare col naso. *n* annusata *f*, fiuto *m*.

snigger ['snigə] *v* ridere sotto i baffi, ridacchiare. *n* ghigno *m*.

snip [snip] *v* tagliuzzare; (*cut off*) spuntare. *n* (*piece*) ritaglio *m*; (*bargain*) occasione *f*.

snipe [snaip] *n* (*bird*) beccaccino *m*. *v* sparare di sorpresa. **sniper** *n* tiratore scelto che spara di soppiatto *m*.

snivel ['snivl] *v* moccicare; (*whine*) frignare. **sniveller** *n* moccioso, -a *m, f*; frignone, -a *m, f*.

snob [snob] *n* snob *m, f invar*.

snoop [snuːp] *v* curiosare.

snooty ['snuːti] *adj* (*coll*) sdegnoso, altezzoso.

snooze [snuːz] *v* sonnecchiare. *n* pisolino *m*.

snore [snɔː] *v* russare, ronfare.

snorkel ['snɔːkl] *n* respiratore a tubo *m*.

snort [snɔːt] *n* sbuffata *f*. *v* sbuffare.

snout [snaut] *n* muso *m*; (*pig*) grugno *m*; (*nozzle*) becco *m*.

snow [snou] *n* neve *f*. **snowball** *n* palla di neve *f*. **snowbound** *adj* bloccato dalla neve. **snow-drift** *n* cumulo *or* banco di neve *m*. **snowdrop** *n* bucaneve *m invar*.

snowfall n nevicata f. **snowflake** n fiocco di neve m. **snowman** n pupazzo di neve m. **snow-plough** n spazzaneve m invar.

snowstorm n tormenta f. v nevicare.

snowy adj nevoso; (colour) niveo, candido.

snub [snʌb] n rabbuffo m, affronto m. v trattare con disprezzo. **snub-nosed** adj camuso.

snuff[1] [snʌf] v fiutare, aspirare. n tabacco da fiuto m. **snuffbox** n tabacchiera f.

snuff[2] [snʌf] v **snuff it** (coll: die) crepare. **snuff out** spegnere.

snug [snʌg] adj (comfortable) comodo; (cosy) intimo; (close-fitting) aderente.

snuggle ['snʌgl] v rannicchiarsi; (cuddle) coccolare.

so [sou] adv così, tanto; (to that extent) talmente. conj perciò, quindi. **and so on** eccetera. **if so** in tal caso. **in so far as** per quanto. **so-called** adj cosiddetto. **so far** finora. **so long as** finché. **so much** tanto. **so-so** adv discretamente, così così. **so to speak** per così dire.

soak [souk] v inzuppare, imbevere. **be soaked through** essere bagnato fradicio. **soak in** penetrare. **soak up** assorbire.

soap [soup] n sapone m. **soap-dish** n portasapone m invar. **soap flakes/powder** sapone in scaglie/polvere m. **soap-suds** n saponata f sing. v insaponare. **soapy** adj (covered with soap) insaponato; (like soap) saponoso.

soar [soɪ] v librarsi; (rise) salire.

sob [sob] n singhiozzo m. v singhiozzare.

sober ['soubə] adj sobrio, calmo. v **sober down** calmarsi. **sober up** smaltire una sbornia. **sobriety** n moderatezza f, serietà f.

soccer ['sokə] n calcio m, football m invar.

sociable ['souʃəbl] adj socievole. **sociability** n socievolezza f.

social ['souʃəl] adj (of a community) sociale; (disposition) socievole; (of polite society) mondano. **social security** previdenza sociale f. **social worker** assistente sociale m. **socialism** n socialismo m. **socialist** n(m+f), adj socialista.

society [sə'saiəti] n società f, compagnia f.

sociology [sousi'olədʒi] n sociologia f. **sociological** adj sociologico. **sociologist** n sociologo, -a.

sock[1] [sok] n (short) calzino m; (long) calza f.

sock[2] [sok] n (slang) n colpo m. v picchiare; (punch) prendere a pugni.

socket ['sokit] n cavità f; (eye) orbita f, occhiaia f; (elec) presa f.

soda ['soudə] n (water) seltz m invar; (sodium carbonate) soda f; **soda caustica** f.

sodden ['sodn] adj fradicio.

sofa ['soufə] n sofà m invar.

soft [soft] adj (not hard) molle; (not rough) morbido, soffice; (pleasant) mite, dolce; (soothing) tenero; (water) dolce. adv piano. **soften** v ammorbidire, intenerirsi. **softly** adv pian piano, adagio, dolcemente.

soggy ['sogi] adj fradicio, inzuppato.

soil[1] [soil] n suolo m, terra f.

soil[2] [soil] v sporcare, insudiciare.

solar ['soulə] adj solare.

sold [sould] V **sell**.

solder ['soldə] n saldatura f. v saldare. **soldering iron** saldatore m.

soldier ['souldʒə] n soldato m. v **soldier on** tirare avanti.

sole[1] [soul] adj solo, unico.

sole[2] [soul] n (foot) pianta f; (shoe, tech) suola f.

sole[3] [soul] n (fish) sogliola f.

solemn ['soləm] adj solenne, serio.

solicitor [sə'lisitə] n avvocato, -essa m, f.

solicitous [sə'lisitəs] adj premuroso.

solid ['solid] adj solido, sodo, compatto; (sound) serio. n (corpo) solido m. **solidarity** n solidarietà f. **solidity** n solidità f; serietà f.

solitary ['solitəri] adj solitario, solo, isolato. **solitary confinement** n reclusione or segregazione cellulare f.

solitude ['solitjuːd] n solitudine f, isolamento m.

solo ['soulou] n assolo m. adj solo, solitario. **soloist** n solista m, f.

solstice ['solstis] n solstizio m.

soluble ['soljubl] adj solubile.

solution [sə'luːʃən] n soluzione f.

solve [solv] v risolvere. **solvent** nm, adj solvente. **solvency** n solvenza f.

sombre ['sombə] adj tetro, fosco.

some [sʌm] adj del, della; (pl) dei, delle; qualche; (certain) alcuni, -e; pron alcuni, -e; (before verb) ne. **somebody** or **someone** pron qualcuno. **somebody else** qualcun altro. **some day** un bel giorno. **somehow**

adv in qualche modo, in un modo o in un altro. **some ... some ... gli uni ... gli altri ....** **something** *pron* qualcosa. **something else** qualcos'altro. **sometime** *adv* un giorno o l'altro, presto o tardi. **sometimes** *adv* qualche volta; *(now and then)* di tanto in tanto. **somewhat** *adv* piuttosto. **somewhere** *adv* in qualche parte. **somewhere else** altrove.

somersault [ˈsʌməsɔːlt] *n* capriola *f*, salto mortale. *m. v* fare una capriola, fare un salto mortale.

son [sʌn] *n* figlio *m*. **son-in-law** *n* genero *m*.

sonata [səˈnɑːtə] *n* sonata *f*.

song [sɒŋ] *n* canzone *f*; *(act of singing)* canto *m*. **for a song** per una sciocchezza.

sonic [ˈsɒnik] *adj* sonico. **sonic bang or boom** boato sonico *m*.

sonnet [ˈsɒnit] *n* sonetto *m*.

soon [suːn] *adv* presto, tra poco. **as soon as** appena. **how soon?** fra quanto tempo? **soon after** subito dopo. **too soon** in anticipo. **very soon** tra breve, quanto prima. **no sooner said than done** detto fatto. **sooner or later** presto o tardi, prima o poi.

soot [sut] *n* fuliggine *f*. **sooty** *adj* fuligginoso.

soothe [suːð] *v* calmare, mitigare.

sophisticated [səˈfistikeitid] *adj* raffinato, sofisticato.

sopping [ˈsɒpiŋ] *adj* fradicio.

soprano [səˈprɑːnou] *n* soprano *m*, *f*.

sordid [ˈsɔːdid] *adj* sordido.

sore [sɔː] *adj* doloroso. **sore throat** mal di gola *m*. **n** piaga *f*, ulcera *f*.

sorrow [ˈsɒrou] *n* dolore *m*, dispiacere *m*; *(cause of regret)* rincrescimento *m*. **sorrowful** *adj* triste, addolorato; *(distressing)* penoso.

sorry [ˈsɒri] *adj* dolente, spiacente, triste; *(wretched)* meschino, miserabile. **feel sorry for** compatire. **I'm sorry** mi dispiace or rincresce. **interj** pardon! scusi! scusate!

sort [sɔːt] *n* sorta *f*, specie *f* invar. **a good sort** una brava persona *f*. **out of sorts** giù di giri. *v* classificare, raggruppare. **sort out** smistare; *(choose)* scegliere.

soufflé [ˈsuːflei] *n* soufflé *m* invar.

sought [sɔːt] *V* **seek**.

soul [soul] *n* anima *f*, spirito *m*.

sound¹ [saund] *n* suono *m*; *(noise)* rumore

m. **sound effect** effetto sonoro *m*. **soundproof** *adj* fonoassorbente, impenetrabile al suono. **sound-track** *n* colonna sonora *f*. *v* suonare; *(seem)* sembrare.

sound² [saund] *adj (not damaged)* sano; valido, legittimo; *(sleep, etc.)* profondo.

sound³ [saund] *n (med)* sonda *f*. *v* sondare; *(naut)* scandagliare.

soup [suːp] *n* minestra *f*; *(broth)* brodo *m*; *(with bread)* zuppa *f*. **be in the soup** trovarsi nei pasticci. **soup-ladle** *n* cucchiaione *m*. **soup-plate** *n* fondina *f*.

sour [sauə] *adj* acido; *(tart, harsh)* acerbo, agro.

source [sɔːs] *n* sorgente *f*, origine *f*.

south [sauθ] *n* sud *m*; *(of country)* meridione *m*. *adj also* **southern, southerly** del sud; meridionale. *adv (direction)* verso sud; *(location)* al sud; *(origin)* dal sud. **south-east** *n* sudest *m*. **South Pole** polo sud *m*. **south-west** *n* sudovest *m*. **southernmost** *adj* il più a sud.

souvenir [suːvəˈniə] *n* ricordo *m*.

sovereign [ˈsɒvrin] *n*, *adj* sovrano, -a. **sovereignty** *n* sovranità *f*.

*sow¹ [sou] *v* seminare; disseminare.

sow² [sau] *n* scrofa *f*.

sown [soun] *V* **sow¹**.

soya [ˈsɔiə] *n* soia *f*.

spa [spɑː] *n* terme *f pl*, stazione termale *f*.

space [speis] *n* spazio *m*. *v* scaglionare; *(printing)* spaziare. **spaceman** *n* astronauta *m*. **spaceship** *n* astronave *f*. **spacious** *adj* ampio, spazioso.

spade [speid] *n* badile *m*, vanga *f*. **call a spade a spade** dire pane al pane.

spades [speidz] *pl n (cards)* picche *f pl*.

Spain [spein] *n* Spagna *f*. **Spaniard** *n* spagnolo, -a *m*, *f*. **Spanish** *nm*, *adj* spagnolo.

span [span] *n (hand)* spanna *f*; *(bridge)* arco *m*; *(extent)* portata *f*; *(time)* durata *f*. *v* stendersi attraverso.

spaniel [ˈspanjəl] *n* spaniel *m* invar.

spank [spaŋk] *v* sculacciare.

spanner [ˈspanə] *n* chiave *f*; *(adjustable)* chiave inglese *f*.

spare [speə] *adj* di riserva or scorta; *(surplus)* in più, disponibile; frugale; *(lean)* magro. **spare part** pezzo di ricambio *m*. **spare room** camera in più *f*. **spare time** tempo disponibile *m*. **spare wheel** ruota di scorta *f*. *v (not harm)* risparmiare; *(do without)* fare a meno di. **spare no**

expense non badare a spese. **sparing** adj parco, sobrio, limitato.

spark [spɑːk] n scintilla f; (gleam) barlume m. v emettere scintille, scintillare; (elec) accendere. **sparking-plug** n candela (d'accensione) f.

sparkle ['spɑːkl] n scintilla f, splendore m. v scintillare, brillare, risplendere. **sparkling** adj brillante; (wine) spumante.

sparrow ['sparou] n passero m.

sparse [spɑːs] adj rado, scarso. **sparsely** adv poco.

spasm ['spazəm] n accesso m; (muscular) spasmo m. **spasmodic** adj spasmodico.

spastic ['spastik] n, adj spastico, -a.

spat [spat] V **spit**¹.

spate [speit] n piena f.

spatial ['speiʃl] adj spaziale.

spatula ['spatjulə] n spatola f.

spawn [spɔːn] n (zool) uova f pl; (brood) progenie f. v deporre uova; (give rise to) generare, produrre (in abbondanza); (derog) figliare.

*****speak** [spiːk] v parlare. **so to speak** per così dire. **speaking of** a proposito di. **speak out** parlare apertamente. **speak up** (loudly) parlare ad alta voce, parlare più forte. **speak up for** parlare a favore di. **strictly speaking** per essere precisi. **speaker** n oratore m; (pol) presidente m; (hi-fi) cassa acustica.

spear [spiə] n lancia f. v trafiggere.

special ['speʃəl] adj speciale, particolare; straordinario. **specialist** n specialista m, f. **speciality** n specialità f. **specialization** n specializzazione f. **specialize** v specializzare.

species ['spiːʃiːz] n specie f invar, genere m.

specify ['spesifai] v specificare, precisare. **specific** adj specifico, preciso. **specification** n specificazione f; (detailed description) specifica f.

specimen ['spesimin] n esemplare m, modello m; (for test) campione m.

speck [spek] n (spot) macchia f; (particle) granello m. **speckle** n macchia f, chiazza f. **speckled** adj chiazzato.

spectacle ['spektəkl] n spettacolo m. **spectacles** pl n occhiali m pl. **spectacled** adj occhialuto.

spectator [spek'teitə] n spettatore, -trice m, f.

spectrum ['spektrəm] n spettro m.

speculate ['spekjuleit] v speculare,

meditare. **speculation** n speculazione f. **speculative** adj speculativo. **speculator** n speculatore, -trice m, f.

sped [sped] V **speed**.

speech [spiːtʃ] n (faculty) parola f; discorso m. **speechless** adj muto, senza parole.

*****speed** [spiːd] n velocità f. **at full speed** a tutta corsa, a velocità massima. **speedboat** n fuoribordo m. **speed limit** limite di velocità m. **speedometer** n tachimetro m. v andare in fretta. **speed up** accelerare. **speedy** adj veloce; (ready) pronto.

*****spell**¹ [spel] v (read) compitare, sillabare; (write) scrivere; significare. **spelling** n ortografia f.

spell² [spel] n (magic) incanto m, incantesimo m; fascino m. **cast a spell** incantare. **spellbind** v affascinare.

spell³ [spel] n periodo m; (work) turno m; (bout) attacco m.

spelt [spelt] V **spell**¹.

*****spend** [spend] v spendere; (employ) impiegare, dedicare; (time) trascorrere, passare; (consume) esaurire. **spendthrift** n, adj prodigo, -a.

spent [spent] V **spend**.

sperm [spɔːm] n sperma m.

spew [spjuː] v vomito m. v vomitare.

sphere [sfiə] n sfera f. **spherical** adj sferico.

spice [spais] n (cookery) spezie f invar; (flavour) gusto m, sapore m. v condire (con spezie); dar gusto or interesse a. **spicy** adj piccante, aromatico; salace.

spider ['spaidə] n ragno m. **spider's web** ragnatela f.

spike [spaik] n punta f, chiodo m. v inchiodare; (frustrate) rendere inservibile.

*****spill** [spil] v spandere, versare. **spill over** traboccare.

spilt [spilt] V **spill**.

*****spin** [spin] v (thread) filare; (rotate) (far) girare. **spin-drier** n centrifuga f, idroestrattore m. **spin-dry** v asciugare con la centrifuga. **spin out** prolungare. **spin a yarn** raccontare una frottola. n rotazione f; (phys) spin m invar; (short trip) giro m.

spinach ['spinidʒ] n spinaci m pl.

spindle ['spindl] n fuso m. **spindly** adj esile, affusolato.

spine [spain] n (anat) spina dorsale f; (book) dorso m. **spinal** adj spinale,

vertebrale. **spine-chilling** adj agghiacciante. **spineless** adj smidollato, debole.
spinster ['spinstə] n nubile f; (coll) zitella f.
spiral ['spaiərəl] n spirale f. adj a spirale. **spiral staircase** scala a chiocciola f.
spire ['spaiə] n guglia f.
spirit ['spirit] n spirito m; (drink) superalcolico m. **be in high spirits** avere il morale alto; essere allegro. **spirit-level** n livella a bolla d'aria f. **that's the spirit!** così va bene! **spirited** adj vivace, vigoroso. **spiritless** adj (without vigour) fiacco; (not lively) abbattuto. **spiritual** adj spirituale. **spiritualism** n spiritismo m; (philos) spiritualismo m. **spiritualist** n spiritista m, f.
*spit[1] [spit] v sputare; (rain) piovigginare; (cat) soffiare. **the spitting image of** . . . . . . nato e sputato. n also **spittle** sputo m, saliva f.
spit[2] [spit] n (skewer) spiedo m; (land) lingua di terra f. v (skewer) infilzare.
spite [spait] n dispetto m. **in spite of** nonostante, malgrado. v far dispetto a; (annoy) indispettire. **spiteful** adj dispettoso, maligno.
splash [splaʃ] v (spatter) spruzzare; (mark with colour) macchiare, chiazzare. n spruzzata f; (sound) tonfo m; (liquid splashed) spruzzo m; (patch) macchia f; (showy display) sfoggio m.
spleen [splin] n (med) milza f; (peevishness) malumore m. **vent one's spleen on** sfogarsi su.
splendid ['splendid] adj splendido, stupendo. **splendour** n splendore m.
splice [splais] v (rope) impiombare; (tape) giuntare. n impiombatura f; giuntura f.
splint [splint] n stecca f.
splinter ['splintə] n scheggia f. v frantumarsi.
*split [split] v (cleave) spaccare; dividere, separare. **split hairs** cavillare. **split on** (coll) denunciare. **split up** dividersi, suddividere. n fenditura f; (into fractions) scissione f; separazione f. adj spaccato.
splutter ['splʌtə] v (spit) sputacchiare; (talk confusedly) farfugliare; (splash) spruzzare; (engine) scoppiettare.
*spoil [spɔil] v rovinare, sciupare; (indulge) viziare. **be spoiling for** aver una gran voglia di. **spoil-sport** n guastafeste, m, f invar. **spoils** pl n spoglie f pl.
spoilt [spɔilt] V spoil.

spoke[1] [spouk] V speak.
spoke[2] [spouk] n raggio m; (rung) piolo m. **put a spoke in someone's wheel** mettere un bastone fra le ruote a qualcuno.
spoken ['spoukn] V speak.
spokesman ['spouksmən] n portavoce m, f invar.
sponge [spʌndʒ] n spugna f. **sponge-cake** n pan di Spagna m. **throw in the sponge** gettare la spugna. v lavare con la spugna; (coll: cadge) scroccare. **sponger** n scroccone, -a m, f. **spongy** adj spugnoso.
sponsor ['sponsə] n garante m, f; (TV, etc.) finanziatore, -trice m, f. v essere garante di; rendersi responsabile di; finanziare; (lend support) patrocinare. **sponsorship** n garanzia f; finanziamento m.
spontaneous [spon'teinjəs] adj spontaneo. **spontaneity** n spontaneità f.
spool [spul] n rocchetto m.
spoon [spun] n cucchiaio m. **spoonfeed** v scodellare la pappa a. **spoonful** n cucchiaiata f.
sporadic [spə'radik] adj isolato.
sport [spɔt] n sport m invar; (jesting) scherzo m. **be a sport!** sii bravo! **sportsman** n sportivo m. **sportsmanship** n abilità sportiva f; spirito sportivo m. **sportswoman** n sportiva f. v (display) sfoggiare. **sporting** adj sportivo. **sporting chance** possibilità di successo f.
spot [spot] n (mark) macchia f, puntino m; (pimple) piccolo foruncolo m; (place) posto m, località f. **on the spot** sul posto. **spot check** controllo saltuario m. **spotlight** n riflettore m. v macchiare, punteggiare; (see) riconoscere, scoprire, osservare. **spotless** adj immacolato. **spotter** n osservatore, -trice m, f.
spouse [spaus] n sposo, -a m, f, coniuge m, f.
spout [spaut] n becco m, beccuccio m; (chute) scivolo m; (jet) getto m. **up the spout** (lost) perduto; (in a bad way) ridotto male. v (discharge) scaricare, gettare; (gush out) scaturire; (coll: talk) declamare.
sprain [sprein] v (strain) storcere; (wrench) slogare. n storta f; slogatura f.
sprang [spraŋ] V spring.
sprawl [sprɔl] v stendersi lungo disteso; (spread out) estendersi. **send sprawling** mandare a gambe all'aria.

spray¹ [sprei] n (jet) spruzzo m; (appliance) spray m invar, atomizzatore m; (hail) raffica f. v spruzzare, atomizzare; (scatter) spargere.

spray² [sprei] n (branch) frasca f.

*spread [spred] v (lay out) stendere; (distribute) spargere; (disseminate) diffondere; (apply layer) spalmare. n estensione f, diffusione f; (cover) coperta f; (coll: feast) banchetto m.

spree [spri:] n baldoria f.

sprig [sprig] n ramoscello m.

sprightly ['spraitli] adj vivace.

*spring [spriŋ] v (rise suddenly) saltare, balzare; (move rapidly) scattare. **spring a leak** aprire una falla. **spring from** derivare or provenire da. **spring up** (arise) nascere; (originate) sorgere; (jump up) balzare; (come forth) spuntare. n (beginning) origine f; (source of water) sorgente f; (season) primavera f; (coil) molla f. adj primaverile, giovane. **spring-board** n trampolino m. **spring onion** cipollina f.

sprinkle ['spriŋkl] v spargere, cospargere; (liquid) spruzzare. **sprinkler** n (watering can) annaffiatoio m; (fire) nebulizzatore (antincendio) m. **sprinkling** n (of knowledge) infarinatura f.

sprint [sprint] n (sport) sprint m invar; volata f. v correre di volata, scattare. **sprinter** n sprinter m, f invar, velocista m, f.

sprout [spraut] v germogliare. n germoglio m. **Brussels sprouts** cavolini di Bruxelles m pl.

spruce [spru:s] n abete m.

sprung [sprʌŋ] V **spring**.

spun [spʌn] V **spin**.

spur [spə:] n sprone m. **on the spur of the moment** lì per lì. v **spur on** incitare.

spurious ['spjuəriəs] adj falso, spurio.

spurn [spə:n] v sdegnare; rifiutare.

spurt [spə:t] n (gush) getto improvviso m, zampillo m; (burst) scatto m; (effort) sforzo m. v zampillare.

spy [spai] n spia f. v spiare, fare la spia. **spying** n spionaggio m.

squabble ['skwobl] v litigare, bisticciarsi. n alterco m, bisticcio m, lite f.

squad [skwod] n squadra f.

squadron ['skwodrən] n squadriglia f.

squalid ['skwolid] adj squallido.

squall [skwo:l] n raffica f.

squander ['skwondə] v sprecare, sperperare. **squanderer** n sprecone, -a m, f.

square [skweə] n quadrato m; (street) piazza f; (instrument) squadra f. adj quadro; (math) quadrato; (corner) ad angolo retto; perpendicolare; (settled) saldato; (straightforward) diretto, netto. **square meal** pasto sostanzioso m. v (math) quadrare; (accounts) saldare; (regulate) mettere a punto; (coll: bribe) corrompere. **square up to** affrontare.

squash [skwoʃ] v schiacciare, spremere; (suppress) sopprimere; ridurre al silenzio, umiliare. n (drink) spremuta f; (sport) squash m invar; (crowd) ressa f.

squat [skwot] v rannicchiarsi, accovacciarsi; (occupy illegally) occupare abusivamente. adj tarchiato, tozzo.

squawk [skwo:k] v schiamazzare. n schiamazzo m.

squeak [skwi:k] v stridere, cigolare. n strido m, cigolio m. **have a narrow squeak** scamparla bella.

squeal [skwi:l] v strillare; (coll: complain) protestare. n strillo m.

squeamish ['skwi:miʃ] adj schizzinoso, schifiltoso.

squeeze [skwi:z] v (press) spremere; (force) pigiare; (embrace) stringere; (press together) comprimere. n stretta f; (crowd) calca f; (comm) restrizioni f pl.

squid [skwid] n calamaro m, seppia f.

squiggle ['skwigl] n sgorbio m. v sgorbiare.

squint [skwint] v (be cross-eyed) essere guercio or strabico; (glance sideways) guardare di traverso. n sguardo torto m, strabismo m. **squint-eyed** adj guercio, strabico.

squire ['skwaiə] n gentiluomo m, proprietario di terre m.

squirm [skwə:m] v (wriggle) dimenarsi, contorcersi; (feel embarrassed) essere sulle spine.

squirrel ['skwirəl] n scoiattolo m.

squirt [skwə:t] v schizzare. n (jet) schizzo m; (syringe) schizzetto m; (derog) ometto m, tizio m.

stab [stab] v pugnalare, accoltellare. **stab in the back** pugnalare alle spalle. n pugnalata f, coltellata f. **have a stab at** tentare di.

stabilize ['steibilaiz] v stabilizzare. **stabilization** n stabilizzazione f. **stabilizer** n stabilizzatore m.

stable¹ ['steibl] n stalla f; (racing) scuderia f.

stable² ['steibl] adj stabile; (firm) saldo; permanente. **stability** n stabilità f, fermezza f.

staccato [stə'kɑːtəu] adj staccato.

stack [stak] n (heap) catasta f, mucchio m; (chimney) fumaiolo m. v accatastare, ammucchiare.

stadium ['steidiəm] n stadio m.

staff [stɑːf] n (stick) bastone m; (flag-pole) asta f; (personnel) personale m; (mil) stato maggiore m. v fornire di personale, impiegare.

stag [stag] n cervo m. **stag-beetle** n cervo volante m.

stage [steidʒ] n (phase) fase f; (lap) tappa f; periodo m, momento m; teatro m; (platform) palcoscenico m. **at this stage** a questo punto. **go on the stage** fare l'attore. **stage-coach** n diligenza f. **stage-craft** n scenotecnica f. **stage fright** timor panico m. **stage-manager** n direttore di scena m. v rappresentare, mettere in scena. **staging** n messa in scena f.

stagger ['stagə] v barcollare; (shock) colpire, impressionare; (arrange) scaglionare. **staggering** adj sconcertante.

stagnant ['stagnənt] adj stagnante, inattivo. **stagnate** v ristagnare. **stagnation** n ristagno m.

staid [steid] adj posato, serio.

stain [stein] n macchia f; tinta f, colore m. **stain remover** smacchiatore m. v macchiare; colorire. **stainless steel** acciaio inossidabile m.

stair [steə] n (step) scalino m, gradino m. **staircase** n scala f. **stairs** pl n scale f pl.

stake¹ [steik] n (post) palo m; (execution) rogo m. v (support) palare. **stake out** cintare. **stake out a claim** reclamare.

stake² [steik] n (bet) posta f, scommessa f. **at stake** in gioco. v mettere in gioco, scommettere. **stake one's life** scommettere l'osso del collo.

stale [steil] adj vecchio, stantio; (bread) raffermo.

stalemate ['steilmeit] n stallo m; (deadlock) punto morto m. **reach stalemate** giungere a una posizione di stallo.

stalk¹ [stɔːk] n stelo m, gambo m.

stalk² [stɔːk] v (follow) inseguire furtivamente; (stride haughtily) camminare impettito.

stall¹ [stɔːl] n banco m, chiosco m; (newspapers) edicola f; (theatre) poltrona di platea f. **stalls** pl n (theatre) platea f sing. v (engine) imballare; (aeroplane) picchiare; (stop) fermarsi.

stall² [stɔːl] v (delay) tirar per le lunghe; (act evasively) cercar pretesti.

stallion ['staljən] n stallone m.

stamina ['staminə] n vigore m, capacità di resistenza f.

stammer ['stamə] v balbettare. n balbuzie f. **stammerer** n balbuziente m, f.

stamp [stamp] v marcare, imprimere; (envelope) affrancare; (print on) timbrare; (documents) bollare; (with foot) pestare. **stamp out** domare, annientare. n (impression) impronta f; marchio m; (document) bollo m; (postage) francobollo m; (implement) stampiglia f; (rubber) timbro m. **stamp-collector** n filatelico, -a m, f.

stampede [stam'piːd] n fuga precipitosa f. v fuggire in disordine.

*stand [stand] n posizione f; (platform) tribuna f; (exhibition) stand m invar; (music, etc.) leggio m. v stare, essere; (be upright) stare in piedi; (remain) restare; (tolerate) sopportare, tollerare. **stand by** (wait) rimanere in attesa; (help) aiutare; (remain faithful) restar fedele a. **stand-by** n riserva f, scorta f. **stand for** significare; (support) sostenere. **stand-in** n controfigura f. **stand-offish** adj riservato. **stand out** (project) spiccare; (be conspicuous) risaltare. **standstill** n arresto m, fermata f. **come to a standstill** fermarsi. **stand up** alzarsi. **stand up for** prender la parte di. **stand up to** resistere a.

standard ['standəd] n standard m invar, modello m, campione m; (level) livello m; (flag) stendardo m, bandiera f. adj standard invar, normale. **standard lamp** torciera f, piantana f.

standing ['standiŋ] n posizione f, reputazione f; (period) durata f. adj fermo, fisso; permanente; abituale; (upright) in piedi. **leave standing** abbandonare sul posto.

stank [staŋk] V **stink**.

stanza ['stanzə] n strofa f.

staple¹ ['steipl] n graffa f; (stationery) punto metallico m. v graffare; cucire (con punti metallici). **stapler** n cucitrice f.

staple² ['steipl] n prodotto principale m; (textile) fiocco m. adj principale, base invar.

star [sta:] *n* stella *f*; (*actor*) divo, -a *m, f*.
starfish *n* stella di mare *f*. *adj* principale.
v (*cinema, etc.*) primeggiare. **starry** *adj*
stellato. **starry-eyed** *adj* (*coll*) ingenuo.

starboard ['sta:bəd] *n* dritta *f*.

starch [sta:tʃ] *n* amido *m*, fecola *f*. *v*
inamidare. **starchy** *adj* (*food*) ricco
d'amido; (*manner*) rigido.

stare [steə] *v* fissare; (*gaze fixedly*)
sgranare gli occhi. **stare in the face** (*be
obvious*) saltare agli occhi, essere ovvio. *n*
sguardo fisso *m*.

stark [sta:k] *adj* rigido; (*bleak*) brullo.
stark mad matto da legare. **stark naked**
completamente nudo, nudo nato.

starling ['sta:liŋ] *n* storno *m*, stornello *m*.

start [sta:t] *n* (*beginning*) inizio *m*; (*point
of departure*) partenza *f*; (*sudden movement*) soprassalto *m*; (*lead*) vantaggio *m*.
by fits and starts a sbalzi. *v* iniziare,
cominciare; partire; (*jump*) sussultare;
(*set in motion*) mettere in moto. **to start
with** per cominciare. **starter** *n* starter *m*
invar, motorino d'avviamento *m*.

startle ['sta:tl] *v* (*far*) trasalire, sbigottire.
startling *adj* sorprendente.

starve [sta:v] *v* affamare; (*to death*) (*far*)
morire di fame; (*be very hungry*) soffrire
la fame. **starve of** (*far*) soffrire per mancanza di. **starvation** *n* fame *f*.

state [steit] *n* stato *m*; pompa *f*; (*coll*)
ansietà *f*. **statesman** *n* uomo di stato *m*.
adj statale; solenne. *v* dichiarare,
affermare; specificare; indicare. **stateless**
adj apolide. **stately** *adj* solenne, maestoso. **statement** *n* affermazione *f*, dichiarazione *f*; (*bank, etc.*) estratto conto *m*.

static ['statik] *adj* fisso, statico. **statics** *n*
statica *f*.

station ['steiʃən] *n* stazione *f*; (*headquarters*) sede *f*; (*rank*) condizione sociale *f*.
station-master *n* capostazione (*pl* capistazione) *m*. **station-wagon** *n* (*US*)
giardinetta *f*. *v* appostare, collocare.

stationary ['steiʃənəri] *adj* fermo; costante, fisso.

stationer ['steiʃənə] *n* cartolaio, -a *m, f*.
stationer's *n* cartoleria *f*. **stationery** *n*
oggetti di cancelleria *m pl*.

statistics [stə'tistiks] *n* statistica *f*. **statistical** *adj* statistico. **statistician** *n* statistico,
-a *m, f*.

statue ['statju:] *n* statua *f*.

stature ['statʃə] *n* statura *f*.

status ['steitəs] *n* posizione sociale *f*,
rango *m*, prestigio *m*.

statute ['statju:t] *n* decreto *m*, legge *f*.

staunch [stɔ:ntʃ] *adj* fedele, leale. *v*
stagnare.

stay [stei] *n* soggiorno *m*; arresto *m*; (*law*)
sospensione *f*. *v* (*remain*) restare,
rimanere; (*on holiday, etc.*) soggiornare;
(*at hotel*) alloggiare (in); (*stop*) sostare;
sospendere. **stay in** non uscire, restare a
casa. **stay on** trattenersi. **stay out** rimaner
fuori, non rientrare.

steadfast ['stedfast] *adj* risoluto, saldo.

steady ['stedi] *adj* fermo, stabile; (*responsible*) serio; regolare; costante. *v* reggersi,
tener fermo; calmare.

steak [steik] *n* (*meat*) bistecca *f*; (*fish*)
trancia *f*.

*****steal** [sti:l] *v* rubare. **steal away** andar-
sene di nascosto. **steal a march on**
prevenire.

stealthy ['stelθi] *adj* clandestino. **stealthily**
adv di nascosto or soppiatto.

steam [sti:m] *n* vapore *m*; (*coll: energy*)
carica *f*. **let off steam** (*coll*) sfogarsi. *v*
emettere vapore; (*cook*) cucinare a
vapore. **steam up** appannarsi. **steamer** *n*
(*boat*) piroscafo *m*; (*cookery*) pentola a
vapore *f*. **steamy** *adj* pieno di vapore.

steam-roller *n* rullo compressore *m*;
(*coll*) forza irresistibile *f*. *v* sopraffare.

steel [sti:l] *n* acciaio *m*. *v* indurire. **steely**
adj d'acciaio, inflessibile.

steep¹ [sti:p] *adj* (*sheer*) ripido; (*coll:
unreasonable*) eccessivo.

steep² [sti:p] *v* (*soak*) inzuppare; (*tech*)
macerare.

steeple ['sti:pl] *n* (*spire*) guglia *f*; (*tower*)
campanile *m*.

steer¹ [stiə] *n* (*ox*) manzo *m*.

steer² [stiə] *v* guidare, dirigere. **steer clear
of** evitare. **steering-wheel** *n* volante *m*.

stem¹ [stem] *n* (*stalk*) gambo *m*; (*of pipe*)
cannello; (*branch*) ramo *m*; (*of word*)
radice *f*. **stem from** derivare da.

stem² [stem] *v* contenere, arginare.

stench [stentʃ] *n* puzzo *m*.

stencil ['stensl] *n* (*device*) stampino *m*;
(*duplicating machine*) ciclostile *m*. *v*
stampinare; ciclostilare.

step [step] *n* passo *m*; (*stair*) gradino *m*;
(*measure*) provvedimento *m*. **out of step**
non conforme. **step by step** un poco alla
volta, per gradi. **step-ladder** *n* scala a
libretto *f*, scaleo *m*. **watch one's step**

stare attenti. v fare un passo; (walk) camminare. step down scendere; (retire) ritirarsi. step in entrare; intervenire. step up salire; aumentare; accelerare.

stepbrother ['stepbrʌðə] n fratellastro m.

stepdaughter ['stepdɔːtə] n figliastra f.

stepfather ['stepfaɪðə] n patrigno m.

stepmother ['stepmʌðə] n matrigna f.

stepsister ['stepsistə] n sorellastra f.

stepson ['stepsʌn] n figliastro m.

stereo ['steriou] adj stereo. stereophonic adj stereofonico.

stereotype ['steriətaip] n cliché m; (tech) stereotipia f. stereotyped adj (trite) stereotipato; (tech) stereotipo.

sterile ['sterail] adj sterile. sterility n sterilità f. sterilization n sterilizzazione f. sterilize v sterilizzare.

sterling ['stɜːliŋ] n sterlina f. adj genuino.

stern¹ [stəːn] adj (harsh) severo; (strict) rigoroso.

stern² [stəːn] n (ship) poppa f.

stethoscope ['steθəskoup] n stetoscopio m.

stew [stjuː] n spezzatino m, stufato m. be in a stew essere preoccupato or turbato. v cuocere (a fuoco lento).

steward ['stjuəd] n amministratore, -trice m, f; (ship) cameriere di bordo m, steward m invar. stewardess n stewardess f invar, assistente di volo f. stewardship n gestione f; (office) carica di amministratore f.

stick¹ [stik] n (wood) bastone m; (celery, etc.) gambo m; (small rod) bastoncino m. be in a cleft stick non sapere che pesci pigliare.

*stick² [stik] v attaccare, appiccicare; (stab) ficcare; (remain) rimanere. stick it out tener duro. stick out (be conspicuous) saltare agli occhi; (put out) tirar fuori. stick to (not digress) attenersi a, non divagare da; (remain loyal) restar fedele a. stick up for difendere, battersi per. sticky adj attaccaticcio; adesivo; (weather) requere; (coll; difficult) complesso.

stickler ['stiklə] n pignolo, -a m, f. stickler for ... persona ligia a ...

stiff [stif] adj rigido; (hard to move, difficult) duro; (formal) freddo. adv (coll) a morte. stiffen v irrigidire. stiffness n rigidezza f; durezza f.

stifle ['staifl] v soffocare.

stigma ['stigmə] n segno m, marchio m; (disgrace) stigma m.

stile [stail] n scaletta f.

still¹ [stil] adj (quiet) tranquillo; (motionless) immobile. adv ancora, tuttora. stillborn adj nato morto. n silenzio m; (phot) posa f. v calmare. stillness n silenzio m, tranquillità f.

still² [stil] n distilleria f; (retort) storta f.

stilt [stilt] n trampolo m; (building) palafitta f. stilted adj artificiale; (pompous) ampolloso.

stimulus ['stimjuləs] n pl -li stimolo m. stimulant nm, adj stimolante. stimulate v stimolare. stimulation n stimolo m.

*sting [stiŋ] v (wound) pungere; (incite) spronare; (coll: cheat) truffare. n puntura f; (pang) morso m; (incitement) sprone m.

stingy ['stindʒi] adj tirchio, spilorcio. stinginess n tirchieria f, spilorceria f.

*stink [stiŋk] n puzzo m. v puzzare. stinking adj puzzolente, fetente.

stint [stint] n dovere m, periodo di lavoro m. v risparmiare, fare economia.

stipulate ['stipjuleit] v pattuire, convenire. stipulation n patto m, condizione f, convenzione f.

stir [stəː] v mescolare, agitare; (budge) muoversi. stir up eccitare, incitare. n (excitement) scalpore m; confusione f. stirring adj (touching) commovente, eccitante.

stirrup ['stirəp] n staffa f.

stitch [stitʃ] n (sewing) punto m; (knitting) maglia f. v cucire; (sew on) attaccare; (med) suturare.

stoat [stout] n ermellino m.

stock [stɔk] n (goods) provvista f, stock m invar, riserva f; (standing) credito m; famiglia f; (cookery) brodo m. stockbroker n agente di cambio m. stock exchange borsa valori f. stockholder n azionista m, f. stockpile v far scorta di. stocks and shares titoli m pl. stocktaking n inventario m. v (supply) fornire, rifornire; tenere in magazzino.

stocking ['stɔkiŋ] n calza f.

stocky ['stɔki] adj tarchiato, tozzo.

stodge [stɔdʒ] n (coll) (food) cibo pesante m; (dull matter) mattone m. stodgy adj pesante; (tedious) noioso.

stoical ['stouikl] adj stoico. stoic n stoico, -a m, f.

stoke [stouk] v alimentare. stoke up rimpinzarsi. stoker n fuochista m.

stole[1] [stoul] V steal.

stole[2] [stoul] n stola f.

stolen ['stoulən] V steal.

stomach ['stʌmək] n stomaco m. **stomach-ache** n mal di stomaco m. v (tolerate) sopportare.

stone [stoun] n pietra f; (pebble) sasso m; (fruit) nocciolo m; (med) calcolo m. a **stone's throw from** a due passi da. **stone-deaf** adj sordo come una campana. **stonemason** n muratore m. **stoneware** n gres m invar. v prendere a sassate; (fruit) snocciolare.

stood [stud] V stand.

stool [stuːl] n sgabello m. **stool-pigeon** n spia f.

stoop [stuːp] v curvare, chinarsi; (condescend) abbassarsi. n **walk with a stoop** camminar curvo.

stop [stop] n (halt) sosta f, fermata f; (punctuation) punto m; (organ) registro m. v finire, smettere; (halt) fermare; (prevent) impedire; (withhold) trattenere; (block) turare. **stop-press** n ultimissime f pl. **stop-watch** n cronometro a scatto m. **stoppage** n fermata f, arresto m; (med) blocco m. **stopper** n (bung) tappo m.

store [stoː] n (supply) provvista f, riserva f; (shop) bottega f; (warehouse) magazzino m. **storekeeper** n magazziniere m. v fare provviste di; conservare; accumulare; mettere in magazzino. **storage** n immagazzinamento m; (comm) magazzinaggio m.

storey ['stoːri] n piano m.

stork [stoːk] n cicogna f.

storm [stoːm] n tempesta f; (thunder) temporale m. v (rage) infuriarsi; (rush) precipitarsi; (mil) prendere d'assalto. **stormy** adj burrascoso.

story ['stoːri] n storia f, racconto m; (news) fatto di cronaca m.

stout [staut] adj (fat) grasso; intrepido; robusto.

stove [stouv] n stufa f; (cooker) cucina f.

stow [stou] v stivare; (fill) riempire (di). **stow away** mettere da parte; (on boat, etc.) imbarcarsi clandestinamente. **stowaway** n passeggero clandestino m. **stowage** n stivaggio m.

straddle ['stradl] v stare a cavalcioni, cavalcare.

straggle ['stragl] v disperdersi; (lag behind) rimanere indietro. **straggler** n ritardatario, -a m, f.

straight [streit] adj diritto; (open) franco, aperto. adv diritto, in linea retta; (directly) direttamente. **straight away** subito. **straightforward** adj franco, aperto; onesto; semplice. **straighten** v raddrizzare; (order) assettare.

strain[1] [strein] v filtrare, passare; (force) sforzare; (sprain) storcere. n sforzo m, tensione f; (med) storta f; (tune) melodia f. **strained** adj forzato; filtrato. **strainer** n filtro m, colino m.

strain[2] [strein] n (race) stirpe f, famiglia f.

strait [streit] n (geog) stretto m. **straits** f pl. adj **strait-laced** adj rigoroso, puritano.

strand[1] [strand] n (hair) ciocca f; (rope) fune f.

strand[2] [strand] n (shore) spiaggia f, sponda f. v arenare, incagliarsi.

strange [streindʒ] adj strano, misterioso; (unaccountable) inspiegabile. **stranger** n sconosciuto, -a m, f; estraneo, -a m, f; (foreigner) straniero, -a m, f.

strangle ['strangl] v strangolare. **strangulation** n strangolamento m.

strap [strap] n cinghia f; (on garment) spallina f; (watch) cinturino m. v **strap up** assicurare con cinghia; (med) fissare con cerotto. **strapping** adj robusto.

strategy ['stratədʒi] n strategia f. **strategic** adj strategico.

stratum ['straːtəm] n, pl -ta strato m.

straw [stroː] n paglia f; (drinking) cannuccia f.

strawberry ['stroːbəri] n fragola f.

stray [strei] v (lose one's way) smarrirsi; (roam) vagare. **stray from** deviare or allontanarsi da. adj (animal) randagio; (lost) smarrito; (occasional) isolato.

streak [striːk] n (mark) riga f, striscia f; (vein) vena f; (lightning) lampo m. v striare; venare; (rush) filare.

stream [striːm] n corso d'acqua m; (brook) ruscello m; corrente f. **streamline** v sveltire. **streamlined** adj aerodinamico, svelto. v grondare, riversarsi. **streaming cold** forte raffreddore m.

street [striːt] n strada f, via f. **street-cleaner** n spazzino m. **street-light** n lampione m. **the man in the street** l'uomo qualunque m.

strength [strenθ] n forza f; intensità f;

validità f; (mil) effettivo m. **strengthen** v rinforzare; (give weight to) convalidare.

strenuous ['strenjuəs] adj energico, fervente; (activity) arduo, duro.

stress [stres] n tensione f; pressione f, spinta f; (emphasis) rilievo m; accento m; (med) stress m invar. v mettere in rilievo, sottolineare; accentare; sottoporre a tensione.

stretch [stretʃ] v (pull) tirare; (extend) stendere; (reach) estendersi. **stretch one's legs** sgranchirsi le gambe. **stretch out** allungare, sdraiarsi. n (expanse) tratto m; (time) periodo m. **stretcher** n barella f, lettiga f.

stricken ['strikən] adj colpito.

strict [strikt] adj severo, rigoroso; esatto; (absolute) stretto.

*****stride** [straid] v camminare a grandi passi. n passo m. **take in one's stride** (do easily) superare con facilità; (adjust to) prendersela con calma.

strife [straif] n lotta f, conflitto m.

*****strike** [straik] v colpire; (deal a blow) battere; (match) accendere; (oil) scoprire; (not work) scioperare. **strike home** colpire nel segno. **strike off** radiare. **strike up** (enter upon) stringere. n sciopero m; (discovery) scoperta f. **striking** adj sorprendente, impressionante.

*****string** [striŋ] n spago m, corda f; (series) fila f. **pull strings** manovrare, raccomandare. **strings** pl n (music) strumenti a corda m pl. v (music) incordare; (racket) mettere le corde a; (beads) infilare.

stringent ['strindʒənt] adj rigoroso, severo.

strip¹ [strip] v spogliare, denudare; (car, etc.) smontare; (paint) togliere. **strip of** privare di. **strip-tease** n spogliarello m.

strip² [strip] n striscia f, nastro m; (comic) fumetto m.

stripe [straip] n riga f, striscia f; (mil) gallone m. **striped** adj a righe or strisce.

*****strive** [straiv] v (try hard) sforzarsi, adoperarsi; (struggle) lottare.

striven ['strivn] V strive.

strode [stroud] V stride.

stroke¹ [strouk] n colpo m; (mark) sbarra f; (swimming) bracciata f; (med) colpo apoplettico m; (clock) tocco m; (tech) corsa f. **stroke of genius** lampo di genio m. **stroke of lightning** fulmine m.

stroke² [strouk] v accarezzare, lisciare.

stroll [stroul] n passeggiata f. **go for a stroll** andare a far quattro passi. v girovagare.

strong [stron] adj forte, robusto, resistente. **stronghold** n roccaforte f. **strong language** parole grosse f pl. **strong-minded** adj risoluto. **strong point** forte m.

strove [strouv] V strive.

struck [strʌk] V strike.

structure ['strʌktʃə] n struttura f. **structural** adj strutturale.

struggle ['strʌgl] n (fight) lotta f; (effort) sforzo m. v lottare; sforzarsi.

strum [strʌm] v strimpellare.

strung [strʌŋ] V string.

strut¹ [strʌt] v (prance) camminare impettito.

strut² [strʌt] n (support) puntone m.

stub [stʌb] n (cigarette, pencil, etc.) mozzicone m; (cheque) matrice f; (tree) ceppo m. v urtare. **stub out** spegnere.

stubble ['stʌbl] n stoppia f; (beard) barba ispida f. **stubbly** adj pieno di stoppie; ispido.

stubborn ['stʌbən] adj ostinato, testardo. **stubbornness** n ostinatezza f, testardaggine f.

stuck [stʌk] V stick¹.

stud¹ [stʌd] n (ornament) borchia f; (nail) ribattino m; (button) bottoncino m. v guarnire di borchie; (jewel) tempestare.

stud² [stʌd] n scuderia f. **stud-horse** n stallone m.

student ['stjuːdənt] n (pupil) studente, -essa m, f; (scholar) studioso, -a m, f.

studio ['stjuːdiou] n studio m.

study ['stʌdi] n studio m. v studiare; esaminare attentamente. **studied** adj studiato, premeditato. **studious** adj studioso, attento, premuroso.

stuff [stʌf] n roba f; (substance) sostanza f; (fabric) tessuto m. **know one's stuff** sapere il fatto proprio. v (cookery) farcire; (animal) imbalsamare; (fill) imbottire. **stuffing** n imbottitura f; (cookery) ripieno m. **stuffy** adj soffocante; (tedious) noioso; (blocked up) intasato; (prim) rigido, conservatore.

stumble ['stʌmbl] v inciampare, fare un passo falso; (speech) impaperarsi. **stumbling block** ostacolo m.

stump [stʌmp] n (tree) ceppo m; (limb) moncone m.

stun [stʌn] *v* stordire; *(astound)* sbalordire. **stunning** *adj* sbalorditivo, stupefacente.

stung [stʌŋ] *V* **sting**.

stunk [stʌŋk] *V* **stink**.

stunt[1] [stʌnt] *v* arrestare la crescita di.

stunt[2] [stʌnt] *n* bravata *f*; acrobazia *f*; trovata pubblicitaria *f*.

stupid ['stjuːpid] *adj* stupido, sciocco. **stupidity** *n* stupidità *f*.

stupor ['stjuːpə] *n* stupore *m*, torpore *m*.

sturdy ['stəːdi] *adj* vigoroso, robusto. **sturdiness** *n* vigoria *f*.

sturgeon ['stəːdʒən] *n* storione *m*.

stutter [stʌtə] *n* balbuzie *f*. *v* balbettare. **stutterer** *n* balbuziente *m, f*.

sty [stai] *n* porcile *m*.

stye [stai] *n* orzaiolo *m*.

style [stail] *n* stile *m*. **stylish** *adj* elegante. **stylist** *n* stilista *m, f*.

stylus ['stailəs] *n* puntina *f*.

suave [swɑːv] *adj* cortese, affabile.

subconscious [sʌb'konʃəs] *nm, adj* subcosciente.

subcontract [sʌbkən'trakt] *n* subappalto *m*. *v* dare in subappalto.

subdivision [ˌsʌbdi'viʒən] *n* suddivisione *f*. **subdivide** *v* suddividere.

subdue [səb'djuː] *v* *(conquer)* soggiogare; *(repress)* reprimere; *(reduce intensity)* attenuare. **subdued** *adj* inibito; intimidito; attenuato.

subject [sʌb'dʒikt; *v* səb'dʒekt] *n* soggetto *m*, argomento *m*; *(study)* materia *f*; *(pol)* suddito, -a *m, f. adj* **subject** to soggetto a. *v* *(bring under control)* sottomettere; *(expose)* esporre, sottoporre. **subjective** *adj* soggettivo. **subjectivity** *n* soggettività *f*.

subjunctive [səb'dʒʌŋktiv] *nm, adj* congiuntivo.

*****sublet** [sʌb'let] *v* subaffittare.

sublimate ['sʌblimeit] *v* sublimare. *n* sublimato *m*. **sublimation** *n* sublimazione *f*.

sublime [sə'blaim] *adj* sublime.

submarine ['sʌbməriːn] *n* sottomarino *m*.

submerge [səb'məːdʒ] *v* sommergere. **submersion** *n* sommersione *f*.

submit [səb'mit] *v* *(yield)* sottomettersi, rassegnarsi; deferire; *(present)* sottoporre. **submission** *n* sottomissione *f*, rassegnazione *f*; *(theory)* tesi *f*.

subnormal [sʌb'nɔːməl] *adj* subnormale.

subordinate [sə'bɔːdinət] *adj* subordinato, inferiore. *n* subalterno *m*. *v* subordinare. **subordination** *n* subordinazione *f*.

subscribe [səb'skraib] *v* sottoscrivere, aderire; *(newspapers, etc.)* abbonarsi. **subscriber** *n* abbonato, -a *m, f*. **subscription** *n* abbonamento *m*; *(dues)* quota *f*; *(fund raised)* sottoscrizione *f*.

subsequent ['sʌbsikwənt] *adj* successivo, seguente.

subservient [səb'səːviənt] *adj* subordinato; *(servile)* umile.

subside [səb'said] *v* decrescere, diminuire; *(give way)* cedere, avvallare; *(abate)* quietarsi. **subsidence** *n* avvallamento *m*.

subsidiary [səb'sidiəri] *adj* sussidiario; *(comm)* consociato.

subsidize ['sʌbsidaiz] *v* sovvenzionare. **subsidy** *n* sovvenzione *f*.

subsist [səb'sist] *v* sostentarsi. **subsistence** *n* sostentamento *m*. **subsistence money** *n* acconto paga *m*, trasferta *f*.

substance ['sʌbstəns] *n* sostanza *f*, materia *f*; realtà *f*; *(wealth)* beni *m pl*. **substantial** *adj* sostanziale; *(meal)* sostanzioso; *(considerable)* notevole.

substitute ['sʌbstitjuːt] *n* (p. ..a) sostituto, -a *m, f*; *(thing)* surrogato *m*. *v* sostituire, rimpiazzare. **substitution** *n* sostituzione *f*.

subterfuge ['sʌbtəfjuːdʒ] *n* sotterfugio *m*.

subterranean [sʌbtə'reiniən] *adj* sotterraneo.

subtitle ['sʌbtaitl] *n* sottotitolo *m*.

subtle ['sʌtl] *adj* sottile, delicato; astuto, ingegnoso. **subtlety** *n* sottigliezza *f*, finezza *f*; astuzia *f*.

subtract [səb'trakt] *v* dedurre, sottrarre. **subtraction** *n* sottrazione *f*.

suburb ['sʌbəːb] *n* sobborgo *m*. **suburban** *adj* suburbano.

subvert [səb'vəːt] *v* sovvertire. **subversion** *n* sovversione *f*. **subversive** *n, adj* sovversivo, -a.

subway ['sʌbwei] *n* sottopassaggio *m*; *(US)* metropolitana *f*.

succeed [sək'siːd] *v* riuscire; *(be successful)* aver successo; *(follow)* succedere. **success** *n* successo *m*, buona riuscita *f*. **successful** *adj* *(person)* che ha successo; vittorioso; prospero, arrivato; *(thing)* riuscito. **succession** *n* successione *f*. **successive** *adj* successivo. **successor** *n* successore *m*.

succinct [sək'siŋkt] *adj* succinto.

succulent ['sʌkjulənt] *adj* succulento.
succumb [sə'kʌm] *v* soccombere.
such [sʌtʃ] *adj* tale; *(like)* del genere, simile. *adv* cosi. **such and such** tale dei tali. **such as** come. **such as it is** cosi com'è.
suck [sʌk] *v* succhiare; *(breast)* poppare. **suck up** assorbire; *(slang)* fare il leccapiedi.
sucker ['sʌkə] *n* *(plant)* pollone *m*; *(device)* ventosa *f*; *(slang: fool)* gonzo *m*.
suckle ['sʌkl] *v* allattare.
suction ['sʌkʃən] *n* aspirazione *f*. **suction pump** pompa aspirante *f*.
sudden ['sʌdən] *adj* improvviso, subitaneo. **all of a sudden** ad un tratto, all'improvviso.
suds [sʌdz] *pl n* saponata *f sing*.
sue [suː] *v* *(law)* citare, chiamare in giudizio, querelare. **sue for peace** chiedere *or* sollecitare la pace.
suede [sweid] *nm, adj* scamosciato.
suet ['suit] *n* grasso di rognone *m*.
suffer ['sʌfə] *v* soffrire, patire; tollerare; *(undergo)* subire. **on sufferance** per tacita tolleranza. **suffering** *n* sofferenza *f*, dolore *m*.
sufficient [sə'fiʃənt] *adj* sufficiente. **sufficiency** *n* sufficienza *f*.
suffix ['sʌfiks] *n* suffisso *m*.
suffocate ['sʌfəkeit] *v* soffocare. **suffocation** *n* soffocazione *f*.
sugar ['ʃugə] *n* zucchero *m*. **sugar-beet** *n* barbabietola (da zucchero) *f*. **sugar-cane** *n* canna da zucchero *f*. **sugary** *adj* zuccherino, mellifluo.
suggest [sə'dʒest] *v* suggerire; proporre. **suggestible** *adj* suggestionabile. **suggestion** *n* suggerimento *m*; proposta *f*; *(psych)* suggestione *f*.
suicide ['suisaid] *n* *(deed)* suicidio *m*; *(person)* suicida *m, f*. **commit suicide** suicidarsi. **suicidal** *adj* suicida.
suit [suit] *n* *(garment)* abito *m*; *(law)* causa *f*; *(cards)* seme *m*, colore *m*; *(request)* preghiera *f*. **follow suit** seguire l'esempio; *(cards)* rispondere a colore. **suitcase** *n* valigia *f*. *v* accontentare, convenire a, soddisfare. **suit yourself!** fa come ti pare! **suitable** *adj* adatto, conveniente, opportuno. **suitability** *n* convenienza *f*.
suite [swiːt] *n* *(music)* suite *f invar*; *(retinue)* seguito *m*; *(furniture)* mobilia *f invar*; *(rooms)* fuga di stanze *f*.

sulk [sʌlk] *v* tenere il broncio. **sulky** *adj* imbronciato.
sullen ['sʌlən] *adj* accigliato, imbronciato.
sulphur ['sʌlfə] *n* zolfo *m*.
sultan ['sʌltən] *n* sultano *m*.
sultana [sʌl'tɑːnə] *n* uva sultanina *f*.
sultry ['sʌltri] *adj* afoso; *(person)* eccitante.
sum [sʌm] *n* somma *f*, addizione *f*; *(amount)* importo *m*, totale *m*. **do sums** far calcoli. *v* **sum up** riassumere. **summing-up** *n* riassunto *m*, riepilogo *(pl -ghi)*.
summarize ['sʌməraiz] *v* riassumere. **summary** *nm, adj* sommario.
summer ['sʌmə] *n* estate *f*. *adj* d'estate, estivo.
summit ['sʌmit] *n* cima *f*, vertice *m*.
summon ['sʌmən] *v* convocare; *(law)* citare, chiamare in giudizio. **summon up courage** farsi coraggio.
summons ['sʌmənz] *v* citare in giudizio. *n* citazione *f*. **answer a summons** presentarsi in giudizio.
sumptuous ['sʌmptʃuəs] *adj* sontuoso.
sun [sʌn] *n* sole *m*. *v* **sun oneself** prendere il sole. **sunny** *adj* soleggiato; *(cheerful)* allegro.
sunbathe ['sʌnbeið] *v* fare i bagni di sole. **sunbathing** *n* bagni di sole *m pl*.
sunburn ['sʌnbəm] *n* *(pain)* scottatura solare *f*, eritema solare *m*; *(tan)* abbronzatura *f*. **sunburnt** *adj* scottato dal sole; abbronzato.
Sunday ['sʌndi] *n* domenica *f*.
sundial ['sʌndaiəl] *n* meridiana *f*.
sundry ['sʌndri] *adj* diversi, parecchi. **all and sundry** tutti quanti.
sunflower ['sʌnflauə] *n* girasole *m*.
sung [sʌŋ] *V* **sing**.
sun-glasses ['sʌnglaːsiz] *pl n* occhiali da sole *m pl*.
sunk [sʌŋk] *V* **sink**.
sunlight ['sʌnlait] *n* luce del sole *f*.
sunrise ['sʌnraiz] *n* alba *f*.
sunset ['sʌnset] *n* tramonto *m*.
sunshine ['sʌnʃain] *n* sole *m*; *(good weather)* bel tempo *m*. **sunshine roof** tetto scorrevole *m*.
sunstroke ['sʌnstrouk] *n* colpo di sole *m*, insolazione *f*.
sun-tan ['sʌntan] *n* abbronzatura *f*.
super ['suːpə] *adj (coll)* magnifico.
superannuation [ˌsuːpərənjuˈeiʃən] *n*

(*retirement*) collocamento a riposo *m*; (*pension*) vitalizio *m*.

superb [suːˈpɜːb] *adj* superbo, magnifico.

supercilious [ˌsuːpəˈsiliəs] *adj* altero, borioso.

superficial [ˌsuːpəˈfiʃəl] *adj* superficiale.

superfluous [suˈpɜːfluəs] *adj* superfluo.

superhuman [ˌsuːpəˈhjuːmən] *adj* sovrumano.

superimpose [ˌsuːpərimˈpouz] *v* sovrapporre.

superintendent [ˌsuːpərinˈtendənt] *n* soprintendente *m*; (*police*) commissario *m*.

superior [suˈpiəriə] *adj* superiore. *n* superiore, -a *m, f*. **superiority** *n* superiorità *f*.

superlative [suˈpɜːlətiv] *nm, adj* superlativo.

supermarket [ˈsuːpəˌmaːkit] *n* supermercato *m*.

supernatural [ˌsuːpəˈnatʃərəl] *nm, adj* soprannaturale.

supersede [ˌsuːpəˈsiːd] *v* rimpiazzare, sostituire.

supersonic [ˌsuːpəˈsonik] *adj* supersonico.

superstition [suːpəˈstiʃən] *n* superstizione *f*. **superstitious** *adj* superstizioso.

supervise [ˈsuːpəvaiz] *v* sorvegliare, soprintendere. **supervision** *n* sorveglianza *f*, soprintendenza *f*. **supervisor** *n* soprintendente *m, f*, sorvegliante *m, f*, ispettore, -trice *m, f*.

supper [ˈsʌpə] *n* cena *f*. **have supper** cenare.

supple [ˈsʌpl] *adj* flessibile; agile. **suppleness** *n* flessibilità *f*; agilità *f*.

supplement [ˈsʌpləmənt] *n* supplemento *m*, aggiunta *f*. *v* completare, integrare. **supplementary** *adj* supplementare.

supply [səˈplai] *n* provvista *f*, rifornimento *m*; (*econ*) offerta *f*. *v* provvedere, fornire. **supplier** *n* fornitore *m*.

support [səˈpoːt] *n* appoggio *m*, sostegno *m*. **means of support** mezzi di sostentamento *m pl*. *v* reggere, sostenere; (*keep*) mantenere; (*tolerate*) sopportare.

suppose [səˈpouz] *v* supporre; (*think*) ritenere, pensare. **supposed** *adj* presunto. **be supposed to** dovere. **supposedly** *adv* per supposizione. **supposing** *conj* supponiamo che. **supposition** *n* supposizione *f*.

suppository [səˈpozitri] *n* supposta *f*.

suppress [səˈpres] *v* sopprimere; (*check*) soffocare; (*hide*) nascondere.

supreme [suˈpriːm] *adj* supremo, massimo. **supremacy** *n* supremazia *f*.

surcharge [ˈsɜːtʃaːdʒ] *n* soprattassa *f*.

sure [ʃuə] *adj* certo, sicuro. **make sure** assicurarsi.

surety [ˈʃuərəti] *n* certezza *f*; garanzia *f*. **stand surety for** farsi garante per.

surf [sɜːf] *n* frangente *m*, risacca *f*. **surfing** *n* surfing *m* invar, sport dell'acquaplano *m*.

surface [ˈsɜːfis] *n* superficie *f*, faccia *f*. *adj* superficiale, esterno. *v* venire a galla, affiorare.

surfeit [ˈsɜːfit] *n* eccesso *m*.

surge [sɜːdʒ] *n* ondata *f*, riflusso *m*. *v* fluttuare, rifluire.

surgeon [ˈsɜːdʒən] *n* chirurgo *m*. **surgery** *n* (*subject*) chirurgia *f*; (*consulting room*) gabinetto medico *m*, infermeria *f*. **surgical** *adj* chirurgico.

surly [ˈsɜːli] *adj* scontroso.

surmount [səˈmaunt] *v* superare.

surname [ˈsɜːneim] *n* cognome *m*.

surpass [səˈpaːs] *v* sorpassare, superare.

surplus [ˈsɜːpləs] *n* eccesso *m*, avanzo *m*, residuato *m*.

surprise [səˈpraiz] *n* sorpresa *f*; (*astonishment*) stupore *m*, meraviglia *f*. **take by surprise** (*amaze*) stupire; (*come upon unawares*) cogliere all'improvviso. *adj* (*unexpected*) inaspettato. *v* sorprendere; cogliere all'improvviso; stupire.

surrealism [səˈriəlizəm] *n* surrealismo *m*. **surrealist** *n*(*m*+*f*), *adj* surrealista.

surrender [səˈrendə] *v* cedere; (*mil*) arrendersi. *n* resa *f*.

surreptitious [ˌsʌrəpˈtiʃəs] *adj* furtivo, clandestino.

surround [səˈraund] *v* circondare; (*encircle*) accerchiare. *n* bordura *f*. **surrounding** *adj* circostante. **surroundings** *pl n* dintorni *m pl*; (*environment*) ambiente *m* sing.

survey [ˈsɜːvei; *v* səˈvei] *n* quadro generale *m*; (*official examination*) perizia *f*; rapporto *m*; valutazione *f*; (*of land*) agrimensura *f*; (*geog*) rilievo topografico *m*; (*poll*) sondaggio *m*. *v* esaminare, fare una perizia di; prendere i rilievi di. **surveyor** *n* ispettore, -trice *m, f*; (*land*) agrimensore *m*; (*house*) geometra *m, f*; (*geog*) topografo, -a *m, f*.

survive [sə'vaiv] v sopravvivere. **survival** n sopravvivenza f. **survivor** n superstite m, f.

susceptible [sə'septəbl] adj suscettibile; predisposto. **susceptibility** n suscettibilità f; predisposizione f.

suspect [sə'spekt; n, adj 'sʌspekt] v sospettare; (surmise) dubitare. n persona sospetta adj sospetto.

suspend [sə'spend] v sospendere. **suspense** n incertezza f, apprensione f. **in suspense** in sospeso. **suspension** n sospensione f. **suspension bridge** ponte sospeso m.

suspicion [sə'spiʃən] n sospetto m, dubbio m. **suspicious** adj (distrustful) sospettoso, diffidente; (questionable) sospetto.

sustain [sə'stein] v sostenere; (injury, etc.) subire.

swab [swob] n tampone m; (sample) prelievo m.

swagger ['swagə] v (strut) pavoneggiarsi; (boast) boriarsi, grandeggiare. n boria f, andatura spavalda f.

swallow¹ ['swolou] v inghiottire, ingoiare; (coll: believe) bere; (suppress) reprimere. n gorgata f.

swallow² ['swolou] n (bird) rondine f.

swam [swam] V **swim**.

swamp [swomp] n palude f. v (flood) inondare, allagare; (overwhelm) travolgere.

swan [swon] n cigno m.

swank [swaŋk] (coll) v darsi delle arie. n boria f.

swap or **swop** [swop] n scambio m. v scambiare.

swarm [swoːm] n (bees) sciame m; (crowd) folla f. v sciamare; (throng) accalcarsi; (teem) brulicare.

swarthy ['swoːði] adj di carnagione scura.

swat [swot] v schiacciare.

sway [swei] v oscillare, vacillare; inclinare; influenzare. n oscillazione f. **hold sway** over esercitare potere su.

*__swear__ [sweə] v (declare solemnly) giurare; (curse) bestemmiare. **swear by** giurare su. **swear in** far prestare giuramento, insediare. **swear-word** n, bestemmia f.

sweat [swet] v sudare. n sudore m. **sweatshirt** n argentina f. **sweater** n maglione m.

swede [swiːd] n ravizzone m.

Sweden ['swiːdn] n Svezia f. **Swede** n svedese m, f. **Swedish** nm, adj svedese.

*__sweep__ [swiːp] v spazzare; (view) percorrere. **sweep aside** scartare. **sweep the board** far piazza pulita. **sweep** n spazzata f; curva f; (chimney) spazzacamino m. **sweeping** adj radicale, di lunga portata. **sweeping statement** asserzione f gratuita f.

sweet [swiːt] adj dolce; fresco; (smell) profumato; (sound) armonioso; (temper) amabile, carino. n caramella f; (dessert) dolce m. **sweet-and-sour** adj agrodolce. **sweetbread** n animella f. **sweetheart** n amoroso, -a m, f. **sweet pea** pisello odoroso m. **sweeten** v addolcire; alleviare. **sweetener** n dolcificante m; (bribe) bustarella f. **sweetness** n dolcezza f; (taste) sapore dolce m.

*__swell__ [swel] v aumentare, gonfiarsi. n (sea) ondata f. **swelling** n gonfiore m, tumore m, tumefazione f.

swelter ['sweltə] v soffocare or morire dal caldo. **sweltering** adj soffocante.

swept [swept] V **sweep**.

swerve [swəːv] v (change direction abruptly) scartare; deviare, scostarsi. n scarto m; deviazione f.

swift [swift] adj lesto; (prompt) pronto. n rondone m.

swig [swig] v tracannare. n sorso m.

swill [swil] v (swig) tracannare; (rinse) risciacquare. n (rubbish) rifiuti m pl; (slops) intriglio m; (for pigs) broda (per maiali) f.

*__swim__ [swim] v nuotare. n nuotata f. **go for a swim** andare a nuotare. **in the swim** attivo. **swimmer** n nuotatore, -trice m, f. **swimming** n nuoto m. **swimming costume** costume da bagno m. **swimming pool** or **baths** piscina f. **swimming trunks** calzoncini da bagno m pl.

swindle ['swindl] v truffare, imbrogliare. n truffa f. **swindler** n truffatore, -trice m, f, imbroglione, -a m, f.

swine [swain] n maiale m, porco (pl -ci) m.

*__swing__ [swiŋ] v dondolare, oscillare; (club, etc.) vibrare; influenzare. **swing open** spalancarsi. **swing round** voltarsi di scatto. n oscillazione f, ritmo m; (in playground) altalena f. **in full swing** in piena attività. **swing-door** n porta a due battenti f.

swipe [swaip] (coll) n botta f. v dare una botta (a); (steal) fregare.

swirl [swɜːl] v turbinare. n turbine m.
swish [swɪʃ] v (sound) sibilare; (move) brandire; (rustle) frusciare. n (whip) sferza f; (sound) sibilo m.
Swiss [swɪs] n, adj svizzero, -a.
switch [swɪtʃ] n (elec) interruttore m; (whip) sferza f; (change) svolta f, cambiamento m. **switchback** n montagne russe f pl. **switchboard** n tavolo di controllo m; (phone) centralino m. v spostare, scambiare. **switch off** spegnere. **switch on** accendere. **switch over** commutare.
Switzerland ['switsələnd] n Svizzera f.
swivel ['swivl] n perno m. **swivel chair** sedia girevole f. v girare, rotare.
swollen ['swoulən] V swell. adj gonfio.
swoop [swuːp] v piombare, avventarsi. n calata improvvisa f. **at one fell swoop** d'un sol colpo.
swop V swap.
sword [sɔːd] n spada f. **cross swords** (fight) battersi; (argue) venire alle mani. **swordfish** n pesce spada m.
swore [swɔː] V swear.
sworn [swɔːn] V swear.
swot [swɔt] (coll) v sgobbare. n secchione, -a m, f.
swum [swʌm] V swim.
swung [swʌŋ] V swing.
sycamore ['sikəmɔː] n sicomoro m.
syllable ['siləbl] n sillaba f.
syllabus ['siləbəs] n programma m, prospetto m.
symbol ['simbl] n simbolo m. **symbolic** adj simbolico. **symbolism** n simbolismo m. **symbolize** v simboleggiare.
symmetry ['simitri] n simmetria f. **symmetrical** adj simmetrico.
sympathy ['simpəθi] n simpatia f, comprensione f; compassione f. **sympathetic** adj simpatico, simpatizzante; compassionevole. **sympathetic to** favorevole a, ben disposto verso. **sympathize** v simpatizzare; essere d'accordo; compatire. **sympathizer** n simpatizzante m, f.
symphony ['simfəni] n sinfonia f. **symphony orchestra** orchestra sinfonica f. **symphonic** adj sinfonico.
symposium [sim'pouziəm] n simposio m.
symptom ['simptəm] n sintomo m. **symptomatic** adj sintomatico.
synagogue ['sinəgɔg] n sinagoga f.
synchromesh ['siŋkroumeʃ] n sincronizzatore m.
synchronize ['siŋkrənaiz] v sincronizzare.

syndicate ['sindikit] n sindacato m.
syndrome ['sindroum] n sindrome f.
synod ['sinəd] n sinodo m.
synonym ['sinənim] n sinonimo m. **synonymous** adj sinonimo.
synopsis [si'nopsis] n, pl -ses sinossi f; (film, etc.) sinopsi f. **synoptic** adj sinottico.
syntax ['sintaks] n sintassi f. **syntactic** adj sintattico.
synthesis ['sinθisis] n, pl -ses sintesi f. **synthesize** v sintetizzare. **synthetic** adj sintetico.
syphilis ['sifilis] n sifilide f.
syringe [si'rindʒ] n siringa f. v siringare; (inject) iniettare.
syrup ['sirəp] n sciroppo m; (golden) melassa f. **syrupy** adj sciropposo.
system ['sistəm] n sistema m. **systematic** adj sistematico.

T

tab [tab] n cartellino m, etichetta f. **keep tabs on** tener d'occhio.
tabby ['tabi] n (gatto) soriano or tigrato m.
table ['teibl] n tavola f; (with modifier) tavolo m; (multiplication) tavola pitagorica f; (synopsis) tabella f. **lay/clear the table** apparecchiare/sparecchiare la tavola. **table-cloth** n tovaglia f. **table-mat** n sottopiatto m. **table-napkin** n tovagliolo m. **tablespoon** n cucchiaio da tavola m; (spoonful) cucchiaiata f. **table tennis** tennis da tavolo m. **turn the tables** rovesciare le posizioni. v intavolare.
table d'hôte [taːblə'dout] adj a prezzo fisso.
tablet ['tablit] n tavoletta f; (med) pastiglia f.
taboo [ta'buː] nm, adj tabù.
tabulate ['tabjuleit] v presentare in forma sinottica.
tacit ['tasit] adj tacito.
tack [tak] v (pin) puntina f; (naut) bordata f; (stitch) punto lungo m. **get down to brass tacks** venire ai fatti. v (sewing) imbastire; (sailing) bordeggiare. **tack on** aggiungere. **tacking** n imbastitura f. **tacky** adj appiccicaticcio, appiccicoso.

tackle ['takl] *n* attrezzatura *f*; (*fishing*) arnesi da pesca *m pl*; (*hoisting*) paranco *m*; (*football*) carica *f*; (*rugby*) placcaggio *m*. *v* venire alle prese con, affrontare; caricare; placcare.

tact [takt] *n* tatto *m*, riguardo *m*. **tactful** *adj* riguardoso, diplomatico. **tactless** *adj* mancante di riguardo, senza tatto.

tactics ['taktiks] *pl n* tattica *f sing*. **tactical** *adj* tattico. **tactician** *n* tattico, -a *m*, *f*.

tadpole ['tadpoul] *n* girino *m*.

taffeta ['tafitə] *n* taffettà *m*.

tag [tag] *n* (*stub*) talloncino *m*; (*label*) etichetta *f*, cartellino *m*; (*refrain*) ritornello *m*; (*saying*) locuzione *f*. *v* **tag along** seguire. **tag on** aggiungere.

tail [teil] *n* coda *f*. **tail-board** *n* ribalta *f*. **tail-end** *n* finalino *m*. **tail-light** *n* fanalino *m*. **tails** *pl n* (*dress*) frac *m invar*; (*coin*) croce *f sing*.

tailor ['teilə] *n* sarto, -a *m*, *f*. **tailoring** *n* mestiere del sarto *m*.

taint [teint] *n* tara *f*, traccia di marcio *f*. *v* (*spoil*) guastare, contaminare. **tainted** *adj* tarato.

*take [teik] *v* prendere; (*carry, convey*) portare; (*require*) volerci; (*bath, walk, etc.*) fare. **take after** assomigliare a. **take back** riportare. **take care** badare, far attenzione. **take care of** curarsi di. **take down** tirar giù; (*dictation*) prender nota di. **take in** -(*visitors*) dare alloggio a; (*reduce*) stringere; (*understand*) comprendere; (*deceive*) ingannare. **take off** (*remove*) togliere; (*aero*) decollare; (*mimic*) parodiare. **take-off** *n* decollo *m*; (*caricatura* *f*. **take on** assumere; (*fight*) affrontare. **take out** tirar fuori; accompagnare. **take over** (*assume control*) rilevare. **take-over** *n* rilievo *m*. **take place** accadere, aver luogo. **take to** affezionarsi a; (*addict*) darsi a.

taken ['teikn] *V* **take**.

talcum powder ['talkəm] *n* talco in polvere *m*; borotalco *m*.

tale [teil] *n* storia *f*, racconto *m*; (*gossip*) diceria *f*.

talent ['talənt] *n* talento *m*; (*gift*) dote *f*; (*aptitude*) attitudine *f*. **talented** *adj* dotato.

talk [totk] *n* discorso *m*, conversazione *f*; (*lecture*) conferenza *f*; (*chat*) chiacchierata *f*. *v* parlare; conversare. **talk about** parlare di. **talk nonsense** dire sciocchezze. **talk over** discutere. **talk**

round persuadere. **talk sense** dire cose sensate. **talkative** *adj* loquace.

tall [totl] *adj* alto. **tallboy** *n* canterano *m*. **tall order** impresa difficile *f*. **tall story** storia inverosimile *f*, frottola *f*.

tally ['tali] *n* (*score*) punteggio *m*; (*account*) conto *m*; (*label*) etichetta *f*, scontrino *m*. *v* corrispondere; coincidere (con).

talon ['talən] *n* artiglio *m*.

tambourine [tambə'rim] *n* tamburello *m*.

tame [teim] *adj* docile, domestico. *v* addomesticare, domare.

tamper ['tampə] *v* **tamper with** alterare, falsificare; (*meddle*) ingerirsi in; (*bribe*) subornare.

tampon ['tampon] *n* tampone *m*.

tan [tan] *v* (*leather*) conciare; (*sun*) abbronzare. *n* (*colour*) castano *m*; abbronzatura *f*. *adj* castano.

tandem ['tandəm] *n* tandem *m invar*. **in tandem** in tandem.

tangent ['tandʒənt] *n* tangente *f*. **fly off at a tangent** pigliare un dirizzone.

tangerine [tandʒə'rim] *n* mandarino *m*.

tangible ['tandʒəbl] *adj* tangibile.

tangle ['taŋgl] *n* groviglio *m*, confusione *f*. *v* imbrogliare, imbrogliare. **tangle with** (*fight*) lottare con *or* contro.

tank [taŋk] *n* serbatoio *m*; (*pool*) vasca *f*; (*mil*) carro armato *m*. **tanker** *n* (*ship*) nave cisterna *f*; (*lorry*) autocisterna *f*.

tankard ['taŋkəd] *n* boccale *m*.

tantalize ['tantəlaiz] *v* tormentare.

tantamount ['tantəmaunt] *adj* **be tantamount** to equivalere a, essere come.

tantrum ['tantrəm] *n* accesso d'ira *m*, bizza *f*. **have tantrums** fare le bizze.

tap[1] [tap] *v* (*strike*) picchiare, dare un colpetto a; (*knock*) bussare. *n* colpetto *m*.

tap[2] [tap] *n* rubinetto *m*; (*on cask*) spina *f*, cannella *f*. **on tap** (*beer*) alla spina; (*ready*) a disposizione, pronto. *v* (*draw off*) spillare; (*phone*) intercettare; utilizzare.

tape [teip] *n* nastro *m*. **red tape** burocrazia *f*. **tape-measure** *n* metro *m*. **tape-recorder** *n* registratore a nastro *m*. *v* (*tie*) allacciare; (*record*) registrare.

taper ['teipə] *v* affusolare, assottigliarsi. **taper off** finire a punta. *n* cerino *m*, candela sottile *f*. **tapering** *adj* affusolato, a punta.

tapestry ['tapəstri] n arazzo m, tappezzeria f.

tapioca [tapi'oukə] n tapioca f.

tar [taɪ] n catrame m. v incatramare.

tarantula [tə'rantjulə] n tarantola f.

target ['taɪgit] n bersaglio m, obiettivo m.

tariff ['tarif] n tariffa f.

tarmac ['taɪmak] n macadam al catrame; (runway) pista f.

tarnish ['taɪniʃ] v annerire, offuscare; (stain) macchiare. n annerimento m; macchia f.

tarpaulin [taɪ'pɔɪlin] n copertone m.

tarragon ['tarəgən] n dragoncello m.

tart¹ [taɪt] adj aspro, agro. **tartness** n asprezza f.

tart² [taɪt] n torta f, crostata f; (slang) puttana f.

tartan ['taɪtən] n tartan m invar, tessuto scozzese m.

tartar ['taɪtə] n tartaro m. **cream of tartar** cremor di tartaro m.

task [taɪsk] n compito m, dovere m. **take to task** rimproverare.

tassel ['tasəl] n nappa f, nappina f.

taste [teist] n gusto m, sapore m; (liking) amore m, apprezzamento m; (small sample) assaggio m. v assaggiare, gustare. **taste of** sapere di. **tasteful** adj squisito, di buon gusto. **tasteless** adj insipido; di cattivo gusto. **tasty** adj saporito, appetitoso.

tattered ['tatəd] adj stracciato, a brandelli.

tattoo¹ [tə'tuɪ] n tatuaggio m. v tatuare.

tattoo² [tə'tuɪ] n (mil) ritirata f.

taught [tɔɪt] V **teach**.

taunt [tɔɪnt] v rinfacciare, schernire. n derisione f, scherno m.

Taurus ['tɔɪrəs] n Toro m.

taut [tɔɪt] adj teso.

tavern ['tavən] n osteria f, trattoria f, taverna f.

tawdry ['tɔɪdri] adj vistoso, volgare.

tax [taks] n tassa f, imposta f. **tax-collector** n esattore fiscale m. **tax evasion** evasione fiscale f. **taxpayer** n contribuente m, f. v tassare, imporre una tassa su; (make demands) mettere alla prova. **taxation** n tassazione f, tasse f pl.

taxi ['taksi] n tassì m. **taxi-driver** n tassista m, f. **taxi rank** posteggio (per tassì) m. v (aero) rullare.

tea [tiɪ] n tè m. **teacup** n tazza da tè f. **teapot** n teiera f. **teaspoon** n cucchiaino m. **tea-towel** n canovaccio m.

*

teach [tiɪtʃ] v insegnare. **teacher** n insegnante m, f; (primary school) maestro, -a f; (secondary school, university) professore, -essa m, f. **teaching** n insegnamento m. **teachings** pl n dottrina f sing, precetti m pl.

teak [tiɪk] n tek m.

team [tiɪm] n squadra f; (animals) tiro m. **teamwork** n affiatamento m. v **team up with** mettersi insieme a, collaborare con.

tear¹ [teə] n strappo m. v strappare. **be torn between** dibattersi tra. **tear off** strappar via; (run) scappar via. **tear up** stracciare. **tearing** adj impetuoso, terribile.

tear² [tiə] n lacrima f. **burst into tears** scoppiare in lacrime. **in tears** sciolto in lacrime. **tear-gas** n gas lacrimogeno m. **tearful** adj lacrimoso.

tease [tiɪz] v stuzzicare, canzonare; irritare.

teat [tiɪt] n (nipple) capezzolo m; (rubber) tettarella f.

technical ['teknikəl] adj tecnico. **technicality** n tecnicismo m. **technician** n tecnico, -a m, f. **technique** n tecnica f. **technological** adj tecnologico. **technologist** n tecnologo, -a m, f. **technology** n tecnologia f.

teddy bear ['tedi,beə] n orsacchiotto m.

tedious ['tiɪdiəs] adj noioso. **tedium** n noia f.

tee [tiɪ] n tee m invar. v **tee off** cominciare (dal tee). **tee up** preparare, collocare sul tee.

teem [tiɪm] v (rain) grondare. **teem with** formicolare or brulicare di.

teenage ['tiɪneidʒ] adj adolescente. **teenager** n adolescente m, f.

teeth [tiɪθ] V **tooth**.

teethe [tiɪð] v mettere i denti. **teething** n dentizione f. **teething-ring** n dentaruolo m. **teething troubles** difficiltà iniziali f pl.

teetotal [tiɪ'toutl] adj astemio. **teetotaller** n astemio, -a m, f.

telecommunications [,telikəmjuni'keiʃənz] pl n telecomunicazioni f pl.

telegram ['teligram] n telegramma m.

telegraph ['teligraɪf] n telegrafo m. v telegrafare. **telegraphic** adj telegrafico.

telepathy [tə'lepəθi] n telepatia f. **telepathic** adj telepatico.

terrier

telephone ['telifoun] n telefono m. v telefonare. **telephone box** cabina telefonica f. **telephone call** telefonata f, colpo di telefono m. **telephone exchange** centralino m. **telephone operator** telefonista m, f.
teleprinter ['teliprintə] n telescrivente f.
telescope ['teliskoup] n telescopio m. v incastrare, far scorrere l'uno nell'altro; (shorten) condensare. **telescopic** adj telescopico.
television ['teliviʒən] n televisione f. **television screen** video m. **television set** televisore m. **televise** v teletrasmettere, trasmettere per televisione.
telex ['teleks] n telex m. v trasmettere per telex.
*tell [tel] v dire, raccontare; distinguere. **tell off** (scold) sgridare. **telling-off** n ramanzina f, sgridata f. **telling** adj efficace, indicativo.
temper ['tempə] n (mood) umore m, disposizione f; (metal) tempra f. **keep one's temper** contenersi, rimaner calmo. **lose one's temper** arrabbiarsi, andare in collera. v moderare, temperare; (metal) temprare.
temperament ['tempərəmənt] n temperamento m, indole f. **temperamental** adj capriccioso.
temperate ['tempərət] adj temperato.
temperature ['temprətʃə] n temperatura f. **have a temperature** (med) avere la febbre.
tempestuous [tem'pestjuəs] adj tempestoso, burrascoso.
temple¹ ['templ] n (rel) tempio m.
temple² ['templ] n (anat) tempia f.
tempo ['tempou] n tempo m; ritmo m, andamento m.
temporary ['tempərəri] adj temporaneo.
tempt [tempt] v tentare. **temptation** n tentazione f. **tempter** n tentatore m. **tempting** adj allettante, seducente; (food) appetitoso. **temptress** n tentatrice f.
ten [ten] nm, adj dieci. **tenth** nm, adj decimo.
tenable [tenəbl] adj sostenibile, tenibile.
tenacious [tə'neifəs] adj tenace, ostinato; (persistent) accanito. **tenacity** n tenacia f, ostinazione f; accanimento m.
tenant ['tenənt] n inquilino, -a m, f. **tenancy** n affitto m.
tend¹ [tend] v (be inclined) tendere. **tendency** n tendenza f, inclinazione f. **tendentious** adj tendenzioso.

tend² [tend] v (care for) curare, assistere, soccorrere.
tender¹ ['tendə] adj tenero, delicato; (affectionate) affettuoso; (sensitive) sensibile. **tenderness** n tenerezza f; affettuosità f.
tender² ['tendə] n offerta f; (comm) preventivo m, appalto m. v offrire; appaltare, preventivare. **tender one's resignation** dare or rassegnare le dimissioni.
tendon ['tendən] n tendine m.
tendril ['tendril] n viticcio m.
tenement ['tenəmənt] n casamento m, casa popolare f.
tennis ['tenis] n tennis m. **tennis-ball/racket** n palla/racchetta da tennis f. **tennis-court** n campo da tennis m. **tennis player** giocatore, -trice di tennis m, f.
tenor ['tenə] n tenore m.
tense¹ [tens] adj teso, rigido. **tension** n tensione f; (mech) trazione f.
tense² [tens] n tempo m.
tent [tent] n tenda f.
tentacle ['tentəkl] n tentacolo m.
tentative ['tentətiv] adj di prova, sperimentale; (hesitant) titubante.
tenterhooks ['tentəhuks] pl n **on tenterhooks** sulle spine.
tenuous ['tenjuəs] adj tenue.
tenure ['tenjə] n tenuta f, possesso m, esercizio m.
tepid ['tepid] adj tiepido.
term [təːm] n termine m; durata f; (school) trimestre m. **come to terms with** venire a patti con. **terms** pl n tariffa f sing; condizioni pl; (footing) relazioni f pl.
terminal ['təːminəl] n (elec) terminale m; (aero) terminal m invar. adj finale, estremo.
terminate ['təːmineit] v terminare, porre termine a. **termination** n (act) terminazione f; (end) termine m, conclusione f.
terminology [təːmi'nolədʒi] n terminologia f.
terminus ['təːminəs] n stazione di testa f, capolinea (pl capilinea) m.
terrace ['terəs] n terrazzo m; (row of houses) fila di case f.
terrain [tə'rein] n terreno m.
terrestrial [tə'restriəl] adj terrestre.
terrible ['terəbl] adj terribile, spaventoso.
terrier ['teriə] n terrier m invar.

terrific [tə'rifik] *adj* (*coll*) tremendo, fantastico.

terrify ['terifai] *v* atterrire. **be terrified** avere una paura matta. **terrifying** *adj* spaventoso.

territory ['teritəri] *n* territorio *m*. **territorial** *adj* territoriale.

terror ['terə] *n* terrore *m*. **terror-stricken** *adj* terrorizzato, atterrito. **terrorism** *n* terrorismo *m*. **terrorist** *n* terrorista *m, f*. **terrorize** *v* terrorizzare.

test [test] *n* prova *f*; esame *m*; analisi *f*; (*psych*) test *m invar*; (*industry*) collaudo *m*. **test-tube** *n* provetta *f*. *v* provare; esaminare; analizzare; collaudare.

testament ['testəmənt] *n* testamento *m*.

testicle ['testikl] *n* testicolo *m*.

testify ['testifai] *v* testimoniare, attestare.

testimonial [testi'mouniəl] *n* benservito *m*, attestato di buona condotta *m*.

testimony ['testiməni] *n* testimonianza *f*, deposizione *f*; (*proof*) prova *f*.

tetanus ['tetənəs] *n* tetano *m*.

tether ['teðə] *v* impastoiare. *n* pastoia *f*. **be at the end of one's tether** non poterne più, essere agli sgoccioli.

text [tekst] *n* testo *m*. **textbook** *n* libro di testo *m*. **textual** *adj* testuale.

textile ['tekstail] *nm, adj* tessile.

texture ['tekstjuə] *n* struttura *f*; (*surface*) grana *f*.

Thames [temz] *n* Tamigi *m*.

than [ðən] *conj* di, che.

thank [θaŋk] *v* ringraziare. **thank you** grazie. **thanks** *pl n* grazie *f pl*. **thanks to** grazie a. **thankful** *adj* riconoscente, grato.

that [ðat] *adj, pron* quel(lo), quella. **that is** cioè. **that's all!** ecco tutto! *adv* talmente. *conj* che.

thatch [θatʃ] *n* (copertura di) paglia *f*. *v* coprire di paglia.

thaw [θɔ] *n* disgelo *m*. *v* disgelare.

the [ðə] *art* il or lo, la; (*pl*) i or gli, le.

theatre ['θiətə] *n* teatro *m*; (*hospital*) sala operatoria *f*. **theatrical** *adj* teatrale.

theft [θeft] *n* furto *m*.

their [ðeə] *adj* (il) loro, (la) loro; (*pl*) i loro, (le) loro.

theirs [ðeəz] *pron* il loro, la loro; (*pl*) i loro, le loro.

them [ðem] *pron* (*before verb*) li, le; (*after verb or prep*) loro. **both of them** tutti e due. **none of them** nessuno di loro.

theme [θiim] *n* tema *m*. **theme song** sigla (musicale) *f*. **thematic** *adj* tematico.

themselves [ðəm'selvz] *pron* loro stessi, -e; (*reflexive*) si; (*after prep*) sè stessi, -e.

then [ðen] *adv* (*at that time*) allora; (*next in time*) poi, dopo. **by then** a quel punto. **now and then** di tanto in tanto. *conj* dunque, allora. *adj* di allora.

theology [θi'olədʒi] *n* teologia *f*. **theologian** *n* teologo *m*. **theological** *adj* teologico.

theorem ['θiərəm] *n* teorema *m*.

theory ['θiəri] *n* teoria *f*. **theoretical** *adj* teorico.

therapy ['θerəpi] *n* terapia *f*. **therapeutic** *adj* terapeutico. **therapist** *n* terapista *m, f*.

there [ðeə] *adv* li, là; (*to that place*) ci, vi. **thereabouts** *adv* da quelle parti, all'incirca. **thereafter** *adv* quindi, in seguito. **there are** ci sono. **thereby** *adv* così, in tal modo. **therefore** *adv* dunque, perciò, quindi. **there is** c'è; (*calling attention*) ecco. **there it is!** eccolo! **thereupon** *adv* quindi, subito dopo.

thermal ['θəməl] *adj* termico; (*waters*) termale.

thermodynamics [θəmoudai'namiks] *n* termodinamica *f*.

thermometer [θə'momitə] *n* termometro *m*.

thermonuclear [θəmou'njukliə] *adj* termonucleare.

thermos ® ['θəməs] *n* thermos ® *n invar*.

thermostat ['θəməstat] *n* termostato *m*.

these [ðiiz] *pron, adj* questi, -e.

thesis ['θiisis] *n, pl* **-ses** tesi *f*.

they [ðei] *pron* essi, -e, loro.

thick [θik] *adj* spesso; (*hair*) folto; (*fog*) fitto; stupido. **thick as thieves** amici per la pelle. **thickset** *adj* (*heavily built*) tarchiato; (*dense*) folto, fitto. **thick-skinned** *adj* insensibile. **through thick and thin** nella buona e nella cattiva sorte. **thicken** *v* addensare, ispessire, infittire. **thickness** *n* spessore *m*; (*layer*) strato *m*.

thief [θiif] *n* ladro, -a *m, f*. **thieve** *v* rubare. **thieving** *n* ruberia *f*, il rubare *m*.

thigh [θai] *n* coscia *f*.

thimble ['θimbl] *n* ditale *m*.

thin [θin] *adj* sottile, fine; (*lean*) magro; (*not dense*) rado, sparso; (*weak*) debole. *v* diradare; (*lose weight*) dimagrare; (*dilute*) allungare. **thinner** *n* diluente *m*.

thing [θiŋ] *n* cosa *f*, oggetto *m*. **for one thing ... for another ...** anzitutto ... e poi .... **things** *pl n* (*implements, possessions etc.*) roba *f sing*, cose *f pl*.

think [θiŋk] v pensare; (*believe*) credere, ritenere; (*imagine*) figurarsi. **thinker** n pensatore, -trice m, f.

thinking ['θiŋkiŋ] adj pensante, ragionevole. n pensiero m, il ragionare m. **to my way of thinking** a mio avviso.

third [θəid] nm, adj terzo. **third party** terzi m pl.

thirst [θəist] n sete f. v aver sete. **thirst for** or **after** bramare. **thirsty** adj assetato. **be thirsty** aver sete.

thirteen [θəɪ'tiɪn] nm, adj tredici. **thirteenth** nm, adj tredicesimo.

thirty ['θəɪti] nm, adj trenta. **thirtieth** nm, adj trentesimo.

this [δis] pron, adj questo, -a.

thistle [θisl] n cardo m.

thorn [θoɪn] n spina f; (*shrub*) spino m. **thorny** adj spinoso.

thorough ['θʌrə] adj accurato; profondo; radicale; diligente. **thoroughly** adv a fondo.

thoroughbred [θʌrəbred] n purosangue m. adj di razza, di puro sangue.

thoroughfare ['θʌrəfeə] n via f, passaggio m.

those [δouz] pron, adj quei or quegli, quelle.

though [δou] conj (*in spite of*) sebbene, benché; (*yet, still*) tuttavia, pure. **as though** come se. **even though** anche se. **it looks as though** sembra che.

thought [θoɪt] V **think**. n pensiero m; idea f. **on second thoughts** ripensandoci (su).

thoughtful adj (*reflective*) pensoso; (*thought out*) profondo; (*considerate*) premuroso, sollecito; (*careful*) attento, prudente. **thoughtless** adj (*careless*) imprudente; (*heedless*) sbadato; (*unthinking*) avventato; (*inconsiderate*) irrispettoso.

thousand ['θauzənd] adj mille. n mille m invar, migliaio (pl -a) m. **thousandth** nm, adj millesimo.

thrash [θraʃ] v battere, bastonare. **thrash out** discutere a fondo. **thrashing** n (*defeat*) batosta f; (*beating*) botte f pl.

thread [θred] n filo m; (*screw*) filetto m, passo m. v infilare; filettare. **threadbare** adj logoro.

threat [θret] n minaccia f. **threaten** v minacciare. **threatening** adj minaccioso; (*letter*) minatorio.

three [θriɪ] nm, adj tre. **three-cornered** adj

triangolare, a tre punte. **three-dimensional** adj tridimensionale. **three-ply** adj (*wood*) a tre strati; (*wool*) a tre capi. **three-quarter** adj a tre quarti. **three-speed** adj a tre marce.

thresh [θreʃ] v (*corn, etc.*) trebbiare; battere. **threshing** n trebbiatura f.

threshold ['θreʃould] n soglia f.

threw [θruɪ] V **throw**.

thrift [θrift] n frugalità f, economia f. **thrifty** adj frugale, parsimonioso. **be thrifty** fare economia.

thrill [θril] n brivido m, fremito m; (*excitement*) emozione f. v far rabbrividire; emozionare; entusiasmare. **be thrilled with** essere entusiasta di. **thriller** n (*book, film*) giallo m. **thrilling** adj emozionante, eccitante.

thrive [θraiv] v fiorire, riuscire. **thrive on** approfittare di. **thriving** adj prospero, fiorente.

throat [θrout] n gola f. **have a sore throat** aver mal di gola. **throaty** adj gutturale.

throb [θrob] v battere, palpitare. n battito m, palpito m. **throbbing** adj palpitante, pulsante.

throes [θrouz] pl n **in the throes of** alle prese con.

thrombosis [θrom'bousis] n trombosi f.

throne [θroun] n trono m.

throng [θroŋ] n folla f, calca f. v affollarsi, stiparsi.

throttle ['θrotl] v strozzare; (*suppress*) soffocare; (*mot*) regolare. n (*valve*) valvola a farfalla f.

through [θruɪ] adj diretto, di transito; finito. adv da una parte all'altra; (*to the end*) fino alla fine. prep da, per; (*place*) attraverso; (*time*) durante; (*by means of*) tramite, per mezzo di; (*past*) al di là di. **get through** (*phone*) ottenere la comunicazione; (*finish*) sbrigare. **throughout** adv completamente; (*time*) durante; (*always*) sempre.

throw [θrou] n lancio m, tiro m. v lanciare, gettare; (*coll: confuse*) lasciare perplesso, sconcertare. **throw away** buttar via. **throwaway** adj (*casual*) spigliato; (*remark*) lasciato cadere; (*to be discarded*) da buttar via. **throw in** buttar dentro; (*sport*) rimettere in gioco; (*include*) comprendere. **throw out** buttar fuori, mettere alla porta; (*put forward*) dare. **throw up** lanciare in aria; (*be sick*) rigettare.

thrown [θroun] V throw.

thrush¹ [θrʌʃ] n (bird) tordo m.

thrush² [θrʌʃ] n (med) mughetto m.

*thrust [θrʌst] n spinta f, botta f; (mil) attacco m. v spingere, ficcare, lanciarsi. thrust oneself on imporsi a.

thud [θʌd] n tonfo m.

thug [θʌg] n delinquente m.

thumb [θʌm] n pollice m. thumbmark n impronta digitale f. v thumb a lift fare l'autostop.

thump [θʌmp] n tonfo m. v picchiare, battere.

thunder ['θʌndə] n tuono m. thunderbolt n fulmine m. thunderstorm n temporale m. thunderstruck adj sbalordito. v tuonare. thundering adj (coll) enorme. thundery adj temporalesco; (menacing) minaccioso.

Thursday ['θəːzdi] n giovedì m.

thus [ðʌs] adv così.

thwart [θwɔːt] v frustrare.

thyme [taim] n timo m.

thyroid ['θairoid] n tiroide f.

tiara [tiˈɑːrə] n diadema m.

tick¹ [tik] n (sound) tictac m invar, ticchettio m; (mark) contrassegno m, visto m; (moment) attimo m. v ticchettare, fare tictac; contrassegnare, vistare. tick off (coll: scold) sgridare. ticking-off n (coll) lavata di capo f. tick over (engine) girare in folle.

tick² [tik] n (insect) zecca f, acaro m.

ticket ['tikit] n biglietto m; (label, counterfoil) scontrino m. ticket collector bigliettario, -a m, f. ticket office biglietteria f.

tickle ['tikl] v solleticare; (make itch) fare il solletico; (gratify) lusingare; (amuse) divertire. n irritazione f; (itch) prurito m. ticklish adj (person) che sente il solletico; (tricky) delicato, scabroso.

tide [taid] n marea f; corrente f. tidemark n battigia f. v tide over superare.

tidy ['taidi] adj ordinato; (neat) ben curato or tenuto; (coll: considerable) bello. v mettere in ordine. tidy up far pulizia. tidiness n ordine m.

tie [tai] v legare; (join) attaccare; (lace up) allacciare; (sport) pareggiare. tie down limitare, obbligare. tie up (property, capital etc.) vincolare. n legame m; (neck) cravatta f; (bond) vincolo m; pareggio m; (music) legatura f.

tier [tiə] n (row) fila f; (rank) gradino m; (layer) strato m.

tiger ['taigə] n tigre f.

tight [tait] adj stretto; (fitting closely) aderente; (taut) teso; (coll: drunk) brillo; (coll: mean) tirchio. in a tight corner con le spalle al muro. adv hold tight stringere, tenersi fermo. sit tight non muoversi. tighten v stringere, serrare. tights pl n collant m invar.

tile [tail] n (roof) tegola f; (floor, wall) piastrella f, mattonella f. v coprire con tegole or piastrelle.

till¹ [til] V until.

till² [til] n cassa f.

till³ [til] v coltivare; (plough) arare.

tiller ['tilə] n (rudder) barra del timone f.

tilt [tilt] v inclinare. n inclinazione f. at full tilt di gran carriera, a tutta velocità.

timber ['timbə] n legname m; (beam) trave f. timbered adj costruito in legno, coperto di legno; (wooded) alberato.

time [taim] n tempo m, periodo m; (occasion) volta f; (clock) ora f; epoca f. for a long time (past) da molto tempo; (future) per molto tempo. for the time being per ora. from time to time ogni tanto, di quando in quando. have a good time divertirsi. in time a tempo; (eventually) alla fine. one at a time uno alla volta. on time in orario. take one's time fare con comodo. time bomb bomba a orologeria f. timekeeper n (sport) cronometrista m; (overseer) controllore m. time-signal n segnale orario m. timetable n orario m. v misurare il tempo; (sport) cronometrare; (choose moment) scegliere il momento. timeless adj eterno, permanente. timely adj opportuno, tempestivo.

timid ['timid] adj timido. timidity n timidezza f.

tin [tin] n (metal) stagno m; (can) latta f, scatola f. tin-opener n apriscatole m invar. v inscatolare; stagnare. tinny adj (sound) metallico.

tinge [tindʒ] n sfumatura f, tocco m. v tinged with misto a.

tingle ['tingl] v formicolare. n formicolio m, prurito m.

tinker ['tiŋkə] v (repair) rabberciare, rattoppare; (busy oneself) affaccendarsi.

tinkle ['tiŋkl] v (far) tintinnare, squillare. n tintinnio m, squillo m.

tinsel ['tinsəl] n orpello m.

tint [tint] n tono m, tinta f. v colorire.

tiny ['taini] adj piccino, minuto.

tip¹ [tip] n (end) punta f, estremità f; (summit) cima f. tiptoe v camminare in punta di piedi. on tiptoe in punta di piedi.

tip² [tip] v (topple) rovesciare; (dump) scaricare. n luogo di scarico m.

tip³ [tip] n (money) mancia f; (hint) consiglio m; informazione riservata f. v dare la mancia. tip off avvertire, prevenire.

tipsy ['tipsi] adj (coll) brillo. get tipsy ubriacarsi leggermente.

tire¹ ['taiə] v stancarsi, stancare; (get fed up) stufarsi. tired adj stanco; (fed up) stufo. tireless adj infaticabile; (unceasing) indefesso. tiresome adj noioso, seccante. tiring adj faticoso.

tire² (US) V tyre.

tissue ['tifuː] n tessuto m; (handkerchief) fazzoletto di carta m. tissue paper carta velina f.

tit [tit] n (bird) cincia f.

title ['taitl] n titolo m; (law) diritto m. title-page n frontespizio m. title-role n parte principale f. v intitolare.

to [tuː] prep a, in; (in order to) per; (towards) verso; da. adv to and fro avanti e indietro. to-do n (coll) trambusto m.

toad [toud] n rospo m. toadstool n fungo m.

toast [toust] n (bread) toast m invar; (speech, drink) brindisi m. drink a toast to bere alla salute di. v tostare. toaster n tostapane m invar.

tobacco [tə'bakou] n tabacco m. tobacconist n tabaccaio, -a m, f.

toboggan [tə'bogən] n toboga m invar. v andare in toboga.

today [tə'dei] adv oggi; (nowadays) oggigiorno. a week/fortnight today oggi a otto/quindici. n oggi m.

toddler ['todlə] n bambino, -a m, f, piccino, -a m, f. toddle v sgambettare.

toe [tou] n dito del piede m; (shoe) punta f. tread on someone's toes pestare i piedi a qualcuno.

toffee [tofi] n caramella mou f.

together [tə'geðə] adv insieme, assieme. together with insieme con, assieme a.

toil [toil] n fatica f. v faticare.

toilet ['toilit] n (lavatory) gabinetto m; (dressing, etc.) toilette (pl -s) f, toletta f. toilet-paper n carta igienica f. toilet water acqua da toletta f.

token ['toukən] n segno m, simbolo m; (gift) omaggio m; (coin) gettone m.

Tokyo ['toukiou] n Tokio f.

told [tould] V tell.

tolerate ['toləreit] v tollerare, sopportare. tolerable adj tollerabile. tolerance n tolleranza f. tolerant adj tollerante.

toll¹ [toul] n (money) pedaggio m; (duty) dazio m.

toll² [toul] n (bell) rintocco m. v rintoccare.

tomato [tə'maːtou] n pomodoro m. tomato juice/paste succo/estratto di pomodoro m. tomato sauce salsa di pomodoro f.

tomb [tuːm] n tomba f. tombstone n pietra tombale f.

tomorrow [tə'morou] nm, adv domani. the day after tomorrow dopodomani. tomorrow morning domattina. tomorrow week domani a otto.

ton [tʌn] n tonnellata f. tonnage n tonnellaggio m.

tone [toun] n tono m. v armonizzare. tone down attenuare, smorzare. tonality n tonalità f.

tongs [tongz] pl n pinza f sing; (fire) molle f pl.

tongue [tʌng] n lingua f. hold one's tongue star zitto, tacere. tongue-tied adj ammutolito; (speech defect) scilinguato.

tonic ['tonik] n ricostituente m; (water) acqua brillante f; (music) tonica f. adj tonico.

tonight [tə'nait] adj (evening) stasera; (night) stanotte.

tonsil ['tonsil] n tonsilla f. tonsillitis n tonsillite f.

too [tuː] adv (also) anche, pure; (moreover) inoltre; (more than enough) troppo. too many troppi. too much troppo.

took [tuk] V take.

tool [tuːl] n attrezzo m, arnese m; strumento m. tool-shed n ripostiglio per attrezzi m. tools of the trade ferri del mestiere m pl. v lavorare.

tooth [tuːθ] n, pl teeth dente m. have a sweet tooth essere ghiotto di dolci. have a tooth out farsi cavare un dente. in the teeth of (in defiance of) a dispetto di; (in the presence of) in cospetto di. toothache n mal di denti m. tooth-brush n spazzolino da denti m. toothpaste n dentifricio m. toothpick n stuzzicadenti m. toothless adj sdentato.

top[1] [top] n (*highest point*) cima f, vertice m; (*leading position*) testa f, capo m; (*lid*) coperchio m. **at the top of one's voice** a voce altissima; (*shouting*) a squarciagola. **from top to toe** da capo a piedi. **on top of** (*upon*) sopra, su; (*at the head of*) in testa a; (*following*) dopo, in seguito a. adj (*uppermost*) superiore, ultimo; (*greatest*) più alto; (*foremost*) principale. **at top speed** a velocità massima. **top-heavy** adj sovraccarico (m pl -chi); (*unbalanced*) sbilanciato. **topsoil** n terriccio m. v sorpassare, superare; (*be above*) sovrastare a; (*prune*) scapezzare. **top up** v riempire. **topless** adj (*dress*) a petto scoperto. **topmost** adj il più alto.

top[2] [top] n (*toy*) trottola f.

topaz ['toupæz] n topazio m.

topic ['topik] n argomento m. **topical** adj di attualità.

topography [tə'pogrəfi] n topografia f.

topple ['topl] v (*far*) cadere o crollare.

topsy-turvy [topsi'tɜːvi] adv sottosopra.

torch [tɔːtʃ] n fiaccola f; (*electric*) lampadina tascabile f, torcia elettrica f.

tore [tɔː] V **tear**[1].

torment ['tɔːment; v tɔː'ment] n supplizio m, tortura f. v tormentare, angosciare.

torn [tɔːn] V **tear**[1].

tornado [tɔː'neidou] n tornado m, turbine m.

torpedo [tɔː'piːdou] n siluro m, torpedine f. v silurare. **torpedo-boat** n torpediniera f.

torrent ['torənt] n torrente m. **torrential** adj torrenziale.

torso ['tɔːsou] n torso m.

tortoise ['tɔːtəs] n tartaruga f. **tortoise-shell** nf, adj tartaruga.

tortuous ['tɔːtjuəs] adj tortuoso.

torture ['tɔːtʃə] n tortura f. v torturare.

Tory ['tɔːri] n, adj (*coll*) conservatore, -trice.

toss [tos] v (*throw*) lanciare; (*pitch*) sballottare; (*move restlessly*) agitarsi. **toss aside** buttar via. **toss back** rilanciare. **toss up** (*coin*) far testa o croce; tirare a sorte. **toss-up** n questione di fortuna f. n **toss of the head** scrollata del capo f.

tot[1] [tot] n (*child*) bimbo, -a m, f, piccino, -a m, f; (*drink*) bicchierino m.

tot[2] [tot] v **tot up** sommare, fare la somma di.

total ['toutl] n totale m, ammontare m.

adj totale, globale. v (*add up*) fare la somma di; (*add up to*) ammontare a.

totter ['totə] v barcollare, vacillare. **tottering** adj barcollante; (*shaky*) malsicuro.

touch [tʌtʃ] n (*sense*) tatto m; contatto m; (*music, painting*) tocco m; (*hint*) accenno m; (*med*) attacco leggero m. **touchstone** n pietra di paragone f, criterio m. v toccare; (*lightly*) sfiorare; (*handle*) maneggiare, tastare; (*move*) commuovere. **touch-and-go** adj rischioso. **touch down** (*plane*) atterrare. **touch up** ritoccare, ripassare. **touch wood!** tocca ferro! **touched** adj commosso. **touching** adj commovente; adiacente. **touchy** adj permaloso.

tough [tʌf] adj (*hard*) duro; (*hardy*) tenace; robusto; resistente; difficile. n teppista m. **toughen** v indurire, rinforzare. **toughness** n robustezza f; durezza f; resistenza f.

toupee ['tuːpei] n toupet m invar, parrucca f.

tour [tuə] n giro m, viaggio m; (*theatre, sport*) tournée (pl -s) f. v viaggiare, fare un giro; fare una tournée. **tourism** n turismo m. **tourist** n turista m, f.

tournament ['tuənəmənt] n torneo m.

tow[1] [tou] n (*hemp*) stoppa f.

tow[2] [tou] v rimorchiare. n **in tow a** rimorchio. **tow-rope** n rimorchio m. **tow-path** n alzaia f.

towards [tə'wɔːdz] prep verso, incontro a.

towel ['tauəl] n asciugamano m. v asciugarsi. **towelling** n spugna f.

tower ['tauə] n torre f. v elevarsi. **tower above** dominare. **towering** adj dominante; (*very great*) smisurato; violento.

town [taun] n città f; (*smaller*) cittadina f. **go to town** andare in città; (*do thoroughly*) mettercela tutta. **town clerk** segretario comunale m. **town hall** municipio m. **town planner** urbanista m, f. **town planning** urbanistica f.

toxic ['toksik] adj tossico. **toxicity** n tossicità f.

toy [toi] n giocattolo m. v (*play*) giocherellare; (*trifle*) dilettarsi.

trace [treis] n traccia f. v (*indicate, sketch*) tracciare; (*follow, discover*) rintracciare. **traceable** adj rintracciabile.

track [trak] n (*footpath*) sentiero m; (*mark, trace*) traccia f, orma f; (*sport*) pista f; (*set course*) percorso m; (*record*) banda f. **keep track of** seguire. **off the**

beaten track fuori mano. **on the right track** sulla strada buona. *v* inseguire. **track down** scovare.

tract[1] [trakt] *n* (*region*) zona *f*; (*anat*) apparato *m*.

tract[2] [trakt] *n* (*treatise*) trattato *m*; (*pamphlet*) manifesto *m*.

tractor ['traktə] *n* trattore *m*.

trade [treid] *n* (*work*) mestiere *m*; commercio *m*, traffico *m*; (*business*) affari *m pl*. **trademark** *n* marchio depositato *m*. **tradesman** *n* fornitore *m*, esercente *m*, negoziante *m*. **trade union** sindacato *m*. **trade unionist** sindacalista *m, f. v* fare affari, commerciare. **trade on** approfittare di. **trader** *n* commerciante *m, f*.

trading ['treidiŋ] *n* commercio *m*. *adj* commerciale.

tradition [trə'diʃən] *n* tradizione *f*. **traditional** *adj* tradizionale.

traffic ['trafik] *n* traffico *m*. **traffic jam** intasamento *or* ingorgo (del traffico) *m*. **traffic-light** *n* semaforo *m. v* trafficare.

tragedy ['tradʒədi] *n* tragedia *f*. **tragic** *adj* tragico.

trail [treil] *n* traccia *f*, pista *f. v* (*follow*) inseguire; (*drag*) trascinare. **trailer** *n* rimorchio *m*.

train [trein] *n* (*rail*) treno *m*; (*dress*) strascico *m*; (*following*) seguito *m*; serie *f*. **train of events** svolgimento *m. v* (*teach*) istruire; (*impart skill*) addestrare, ammaestrare; (*sport*) allenare. **trainee** *n* allievo, -a *m, f*; (*apprentice*) apprendista *m, f*. **trainer** *n* allenatore, -trice *m, f*. **training** *n* addestramento *m*; allenamento *m*.

trait [treit] *n* caratteristica *f*.

traitor ['treitə] *n* traditore *m*. **traitress** *n* traditrice *f*. **turn traitor** passare al nemico.

tram [tram] *n* tram *m invar*.

tramp [tramp] *n* (*person*) vagabondo *m*; (*walk*) passeggiata *f*; (*sound*) calpestio *m. v* vagabondare, percorrere a piedi.

trample ['trampl] *v* calpestare. **trample on** pestare.

trampoline ['trampəlin] *n* trampolino *m*.

trance [trans] *n* trance *f invar*; (*daze*) stupore *m*.

tranquil ['traŋkwil] *adj* sereno, calmo. **tranquillity** *n* serenità *f*, calma *f*. **tranquillizer** *n* tranquillante *m*, sedativo *m*.

transact [tran'zakt] *v* **transact business**

trattare, entrare in trattative. **transaction** *n* affare *m*, trattativa *f*.

transcend [tran'send] *v* trascendere, superare. **transcendental** *adj* trascendentale.

transcribe [tran'skraib] *v* trascrivere. **transcript** *or* **transcription** *n* trascrizione *f*.

transept ['transept] *n* transetto *m*.

transfer ['transfə; *v* trans'fə] *n* trasferimento *m*; (*design*) decalcomania *f. v* trasferire; (*drawing*) riportare. **transferable** *adj* trasferibile.

transform [trans'fom] *v* trasformare. **transformation** *n* trasformazione *f*, mutamento *m*; (*phys*) conversione *f*. **transformer** *n* trasformatore *m*.

transfuse [trans'fjuz] *v* trasfondere. **transfusion** *n* trasfusione *f*.

transgress [trans'gres] *v* trasgredire. **transgression** *n* trasgressione *f*, infrazione *f*.

transient ['tranziənt] *adj* transitorio, passeggero; (*phys*) transiente.

transistor [tran'zistə] *n* transistor *m invar*, transistore *m*. **transistorize** *v* transistorizzare.

transit ['transit] *n* passaggio *m*, transito *m*. **in transit** durante il trasporto, in transito. *adj* di passaggio *or* transito.

transition [tran'ziʃən] *n* transizione *f*; (*music*) modulazione *f*.

transitive ['transitiv] *adj* transitivo.

translate [trans'leit] *v* tradurre. **translation** *n* traduzione *f*. **translator** *n* traduttore, -trice *m, f*.

translucent [trans'lusnt] *adj* semitrasparente, traslucido.

transmit [tranz'mit] *v* trasmettere. **transmission** *n* trasmissione *f*. **transmitter** *n* (*radio set*) trasmettitore *m*; (*station*) trasmittente *f*.

transparent [trans'peərənt] *adj* trasparente. **transparency** *n* trasparenza *f*; (*phot*) diapositiva *f*.

transplant [trans'plant; *n* 'transplant] *v* trapiantare. *n* trapianto *m*.

transport ['transpot; *v* trans'pot] *n* trasporto *m. v* trasportare. **transportation** *n* trasporto *m*.

transpose [trans'pouz] *v* trasporre. **transposition** *n* trasposizione *f*.

transverse ['tranzvəs] *adj* traverso, trasversale.

trap [trap] *n* trappola *f*; (*trick*) tranello

m; (vehicle) carrozzetta f. **trapdoor** n trabocchetto m. v prendere in trappola.

trapeze [trə'piːz] n trapezio m.

trash [traʃ] n (rubbish) robaccia f; rifiuti m pl; (nonsense) sciocchezze f pl. **trashy** adj di nessun valore.

trauma ['trɔːmə] n trauma m. **traumatic** adj traumatico.

travel ['travl] n viaggiare m, viaggi m pl. **travel agency** agenzia di viaggi f. v viaggiare. **traveller** n viaggiatore, -trice f. **traveller's cheque** assegno turistico m.

travesty ['travəsti] n travestimento m, parodia f.

trawl [trɔːl] n strascico (pl -chi) m. v pescare con strascico. **trawler** n peschereccio m.

tray [trei] n vassoio m.

treachery ['tretʃəri] n tradimento m, perfidia f. **treacherous** adj traditore, -trice, perfido; (unreliable) falso; (dangerous) pericoloso.

treacle ['triːkl] n melassa f.

*****tread** [tred] v (trample) calcare, calpestare; (walk) camminare. n passo m; (stair) gradino m; (tyre) battistrada m invar.

treason ['triːzn] n tradimento m.

treasure ['treʒə] n tesoro m. v (cherish) aver caro; (prize) apprezzare; (retain carefully) tener caro. **treasurer** n tesoriere, -a m, f. **treasury** n tesoreria f. **Treasury** n Ministero del Tesoro m.

treat [triːt] v trattare; (med) curare. n piacere m. **treatment** n trattamento m.

treatise ['triːtiz] n trattato m, dissertazione f.

treaty ['triːti] n trattato m.

treble ['trebl] adj triplo, triplice; di soprano. n soprano. v triplicare. adv tre volte tanto

tree [triː] n albero m.

trek [trek] v viaggiare (scomodamente). n viaggio (scomodo) m, migrazione f.

trellis ['trelis] n pergolato m, graticcio m.

tremble ['trembl] v tremare; (be agitated) fremere. n tremito m; fremito m.

tremendous [trə'mendəs] adj enorme; (coll) straordinario.

tremor ['tremə] n tremore m.

trench [trentʃ] n (ditch) fosso m; (mil) trincea f. **trenchant** adj tagliente, caustico.

trend [trend] n tendenza f; direzione f; (fashion) moda f. **trendy** adj di moda.

trespass ['trespəs] v trasgredire; (rel) peccare. n trasgressione f; peccato m.

trestle ['tresl] n trespolo m.

trial ['traiəl] n (law) processo m; (test) esame, prova f; esperimento m; (trouble) disperazione f, dolore m. **by trial and error** (a) tentoni.

triangle ['traiaŋgl] n triangolo m. **triangular** adj triangolare.

tribe [traib] n tribù f. **tribal** adj tribale. **tribesman** n membro di tribù m.

tribunal [trai'bjuːnl] n tribunale m.

tributary ['tribjutəri] nm, adj tributario.

tribute ['tribjut] n tributo m, omaggio m. **pay tribute to** rendere omaggio a.

trick [trik] n espediente m; (prank) tiro m; (artifice) trucco m; (cards) bazza f. **confidence trick** truffa all'americana f. **do the trick** ottenere l'effetto voluto. v ingannare, abbindolare. **trickery** n inganno m. **tricky** adj (crafty) furbo; complicato, delicato.

trickle ['trikl] v gocciolare. n gocciolio m; flusso irregolare m. **trickle of water** filo d'acqua m.

tricycle ['traisikl] n triciclo m.

trifle ['traifl] n sciocchezza f, inezia f; (food) zuppa inglese f. **a trifle** (a little) un po', alquanto. v scherzare. **trifling** adj insignificante.

trigger ['trigə] n grilletto m. v **trigger off** far scattare.

trigonometry [trigə'nɔmətri] n trigonometria f.

trill [tril] n trillo m. v trillare; (continuous) trilleggiare.

trilogy ['trilədʒi] n trilogia f.

trim [trim] adj ordinato, ben messo or tenuto, assettato. n assetto m; (ornament) guarnizione f. v (neaten) assettare; guarnire; (hair) spuntare. **trimmings** pl n guarnizioni f pl.

trinket ['triŋkit] n gingillo m.

trio ['triːou] n trio m.

trip [trip] n (excursion) gita f; (journey) viaggio m; (stumble) passo falso m. v (step lightly) saltellare; (stumble) inciampare. **trip up** far cadere, fare lo sgambetto, inciampare. **tripper** n escursionista m, f.

tripe [traip] n trippa f.

triple ['tripl] adj triplo, triplice. v triplicare. **triplet** n trigemino, -a m, f.

tumble

tripod ['traipod] n cavalletto m. treppiede m.

trite [trait] adj banale. comune.

triumph ['traiʌmf] n trionfo m. v trionfare. esultare. **triumphant** adj trionfante.

trivial ['triviəl] adj insignificante. banale. **triviality** n affare di nessuna importanza m.

trod [trod] V tread.

trodden ['trodn] V tread.

trolley ['troli] n carrello m.

trombone [trom'boun] n trombone m.

troop [truːp] n banda f. gruppo m; (mil) truppa f. v troop along sfilare. **troop in/out** entrare/uscire in gruppo.

trophy ['troufi] n trofeo m.

tropic ['tropik] n tropico m. **tropical** adj tropicale.

trot [trot] v trottare. n trotto m. trottata f. **on the trot** (coll) di seguito. **trotter** n (horse) trottatore m; (pig's foot) zampa f.

trouble ['trʌbl] n disturbo m; difficoltà f; (unpleasantness) dispiacere m; preoccupazione f; (annoyance) fastidio m. **make trouble** creare guai. **the trouble is** il guaio è. **troublemaker** n sobillatore. -trice m, f. v disturbare. dare fastidio. **troubled** adj turbato, preoccupato, agitato. **troublesome** adj noioso, fastidioso.

trough [trof] n trogolo m; (drinking) abbeveratoio m.

trousers ['trauzəz] pl n calzoni m pl. pantaloni m pl.

trout [traut] n trota f.

trowel ['trauəl] n (plastering) cazzuola f; (gardening) vanghetto m.

truant ['truːənt] n **play truant** marinare la scuola; (shirk duty) batter la fiacca.

truce [truːs] n tregua f.

truck [trʌk] n autocarro m. camion m.

trudge [trʌdʒ] v trascinarsi. camminare a stento.

true [truː] adj vero; corretto; genuino; (mech) centrato. **come true** avverarsi. **hold true** for valere per.

truffle ['trʌfl] n tartufo m.

trump [trʌmp] n briscola f; (bridge) atout m invar. **trump card** (coll) forte m. v (cards) tagliare; (beat) battere. **trump up** fabbricare.

trumpet ['trʌmpit] n tromba f. **blow one's own trumpet** vantare i propri meriti. v (proclaim loudly) strombazzare; (elephant) barrire.

truncheon ['trʌntʃən] n manganello m. bastone m.

trunk [trʌŋk] n tronco m; (chest) baule m; torso m; (elephant) proboscide f. (car)|portabagagli m **trunk call** telefonata interurbana f. **trunk road** strada maestra or statale f. **trunks** pl n calzoncini m pl.

truss [trʌs] v legare. n (framework) travatura f; (bundle) fastello; (med) cinto erniario m.

trust [trʌst] n fiducia f; (hope) fede f; (law) fedecommesso m; (comm) trust m invar. **trustworthy** adj degno di fiducia, fidato. v fidarsi di, aver fiducia in; (hope) augurarsi. **trustee** n fidecommissario m; curatore, -trice m, f. **trusty** adj fedele, leale.

truth [truːθ] n verità f, vero m. **truthful** adj veritiero, sincero.

try [trai] v tentare; (test) provare; (law) giudicare, processare; (taste) assaggiare. **try on** provare. n tentativo m; (rugby) meta f. **trying** adj difficile; (distressing) penoso; (irritating) seccante.

tsar [zaɪ] n zar m invar.

T-shirt ['tiːʃəɪt] n maglietta f.

tub [tʌb] n tino m; (bath) vasca f. **tubby** adj grassoccio.

tuba ['tjuːbə] n tuba f.

tube [tjuːb] n tubo m; (for toothpaste, etc.) tubetto m; (rail) metropolitana f. **inner tube** n camera d'aria f. **tubing** n tubo m. **tubular** adj tubolare.

tuber ['tjuːbə] n tubero m.

tuberculosis [tjubəːkjuˈlousis] n tubercolosi f.

tuck [tʌk] n piega f, rimbocco m. **tuck-shop** n spaccio di dolciumi m. v (thrust into) stipare; (needlework) rimboccare. **tuck in** ripiegare; (coll: eat) pappare, farsi una mangiata. **tuck up in bed** mettere a letto, coricare.

Tuesday ['tjuːzdi] n martedì m.

tuft [tʌft] n ciuffo m, fiocco m.

tug [tʌg] v (pull) tirare, dare uno strappo a; (drag) trascinare. n strappo m; (boat) rimorchiatore m.

tuition [tjuˈiʃən] n insegnamento m, istruzione f.

tulip ['tjuːlip] n tulipano m.

tumble ['tʌmbl] y cascare, ruzzolare; (somersault) fare un capitombolo. **tumble down** crollare. n caduta f, capitombolo m. **tumbler** n (glass) bicchiere m.

tummy ['tʌmɪ] (coll) n pancia f. **tummy-ache** n mal di pancia m.

tumour ['tjuːmə] n tumore m.

tumult ['tjuːmʌlt] n tumulto m. **tumultuous** adj tumultuoso.

tuna ['tjuːnə] n also **tunny** tonno m.

tune [tjuːn] n motivo m; melodia f, aria f. **call the tune** essere in comando. **in tune** in tono, intonato. **out of tune** fuori tono, stonato. **sing out of tune** stonare. **to the tune of** alla bellezza di. v accordare; (radio) sintonizzare. **tuner** n sintonizzatore m.

tunic ['tjuːnɪk] n tunica f.

tunnel ['tʌnl] n tunnel m invar, traforo m. v traforare.

tunny ['tʌnɪ] V tuna.

turban ['tɜːbən] n turbante m.

turbid ['tɜːbɪd] adj torbido.

turbine ['tɜːbaɪn] n turbina f.

turbot ['tɜːbət] n rombo m.

turbulent ['tɜːbjʊlənt] adj turbolento. **turbulence** n turbolenza f.

tureen [təˈriːn] n zuppiera f.

turf [tɜːf] n zolla erbosa f; (sod) piota f; (peat) torba f; (horse-racing) ippica f. v piotare. **turf out** (coll) buttar fuori.

turkey ['tɜːkɪ] n tacchino m.

Turkey ['tɜːkɪ] n Turchia f. **Turk** n turco, -a m, f. **Turkish** nm, adj turco.

turmeric ['tɜːmərɪk] n curcuma f.

turmoil ['tɜːmɔɪl] n scompiglio m, confusione f.

turn [tɜːn] v girare, voltare; (change) cambiare; (change direction) svoltare. **turn against** alienare, ribellarsi a. **turn away** voltarsi da parte, guardar via; (refuse admission) mandar via. **turncoat** n rinnegato, -a m, f. **turn down** (fold) risvoltare; (lower) abbassare; (reject) rifiutare. **turn into** far diventare, convertire in. **turn off** (stop flow) chiudere; (switch off) spegnere; (change direction) voltare. **turn on** (start flow) aprire; (switch on) accendere; (coll) eccitare; (attack) aggredire. **turn out** (switch off) spegnere; produrre; (send away) cacciar via; (empty) vuotare; risultare; (clothe) vestire. **turn over** rovesciare. **turnover** n (comm) giro d'affari m; (cookery) sfogliata f. **turnstile** n tornello m. **turntable** n (records) giradischi m invar; (rail) piattaforma girevole f. **turn up** (arrive) capitare; (come to light) ricomparire;

(increase intensity) alzare; (occur) succedere. n giro m, rivoluzione f; (change of direction) svolta f; (in rota, game, etc.) turno m. **turning** n curva f, svolta f. **turning point** momento critico or decisivo m.

turnip ['tɜːnɪp] n rapa f.

turpentine ['tɜːpəntaɪn] n trementina f; (oil) essenza di trementina f.

turquoise ['tɜːkwɔɪz] n (stone) turchese f; (colour) turchese m. adj turchese.

turret ['tʌrɪt] n torretta f.

turtle ['tɜːtl] n testuggine f, tartaruga f. **turn turtle** cappottare, capovolgersi. **turtle-dove** n tortora f.

Tuscany ['tʌskənɪ] n Toscana f. **Tuscan** n, adj toscano, -a.

tusk [tʌsk] n zanna f.

tussle ['tʌsl] n zuffa f. v venire alle mani, azzuffarsi.

tutor ['tjuːtə] n insegnante (privato) m; (coach) ripetitore, -trice m, f. **tutorial** n periodo di istruzione (privata) m.

tuxedo [tʌkˈsiːdou] n smoking m invar.

tweed [twiːd] n tweed m invar, tessuto di lana scozzese m.

tweezers ['twiːzəz] pl n pinzette f pl.

twelve [twelv] nm, adj dodici. **twelfth** nm, adj dodicesimo.

twenty ['twentɪ] nm, adj venti. **twentieth** nm, adj ventesimo.

twice [twaɪs] adv due volte; (doubly) il doppio.

twiddle ['twɪdl] v (far) girare. **twiddle one's thumbs** tener le mani in mano.

twig [twɪg] n ramoscello m.

twilight ['twaɪlaɪt] n crepuscolo m, penombra f.

twin [twɪn] n, adj gemello, -a. **twin beds** letti gemelli m pl.

twine [twaɪn] n spago m, corda f. v attorcigliare.

twinge [twɪndʒ] n spasimo m.

twinkle ['twɪŋkl] v scintillare, luccicare; (wink) ammiccare, strizzare l'occhio. n luccichio m; strizzata d'occhio f.

twirl [twɜːl] v girare rapidamente, piroettare.

twist [twɪst] v torcere, intrecciare; (sprain) slogarsi; alterare. **twister** n imbroglione, -a m, f. n movimento rotatorio m; (curve) svolta f; (thread) filo ritorto m.

twit [twɪt] n (coll) scemo, -a m, f.

twitch [twɪtʃ] v (jerk) strappare, dare uno strattone; (body) storcere. n contorsione f, spasimo m. **twitching** adj convulsivo.

twitter ['twitə] v cinguettare. n cinguettio m.

two [tuː] nm, adj due. **in twos** due a due. **two-faced** adj falso. **two-piece** n (garment) duepezzi m invar. **two-seater** adj a due posti. **two-way** adj a doppio senso; (elec) bipolare.

tycoon [tai'kuːn] n magnate m.

type [taip] n tipo m, genere m; (print) carattere m. **typescript** n dattiloscritto m. **typesetter** n compositore m. **typewriter** n macchina da scrivere f. **typewritten** adj scritto a macchina, dattiloscritto. v dattilografare. **typical** adj tipico, caratteristico. **typify** v servire da esempio, simboleggiare. **typist** n dattilografo, -a m, f.

typhoid ['taifoid] n tifo m.

typhoon [tai'fuːn] n tifone m.

typographical [ˌtaipə'grafikl] adj tipografico.

tyrant ['taiərənt] n tiranno m. **tyrannical** adj tirannico. **tyranny** n tirannia f.

tyre or US **tire** ['taiə] n gomma f, copertone m.

U

ubiquitous [juː'bikwitəs] adj onnipresente.

udder ['ʌdə] n mammella f.

ugly ['ʌgli] adj (not pretty) brutto; (not agreeable) antipatico, sgradevole; (vicious) vile. **ugliness** n bruttezza f.

ulcer ['ʌlsə] n ulcera f.

ulterior [ʌl'tiəriə] adj ulteriore. **ulterior motive** secondo fine m.

ultimate ['ʌltimət] adj finale, definitivo, assoluto. **ultimately** adv alla fine. **ultimatum** n ultimatum m invar.

ultraviolet [ʌltrə'vaiələt] adj ultravioletto.

umbilical [ʌm'bilikəl] adj ombilicale.

umbrella [ʌm'brelə] n ombrello m.

umpire ['ʌmpaiə] n arbitro m. v arbitrare.

umpteen [ʌmp'tiːn] (coll) adj innumerevole. **umpteenth** adj ennesimo.

unable [ʌn'eibl] adj incapace. **be unable to** non potere.

unacceptable [ʌnək'septəbl] adj inaccettabile.

unaccompanied [ʌnə'kʌmpənid] adj solo, non accompagnato.

unaccountable [ʌnə'kauntəbl] adj inspiegabile.

unaccustomed [ʌnə'kʌstəmd] adj (not used to) poco abituato; (unusual) insolito.

unadulterated [ʌnə'dʌltəreitid] adj sincero.

unanimous [juː'naniməs] adj unanime.

unapproachable [ʌnə'proutʃəbl] adj inaccessibile.

unarmed [ʌn'aːmd] adj disarmato.

unashamed [ʌnə'ʃeimd] adj svergognato, senza vergogna.

unattainable [ʌnə'teinəbl] adj irraggiungibile.

unattractive [ʌnə'traktiv] adj poco attraente, antipatico.

unauthorized [ʌn'oiθəraizd] adj non autorizzato, illecito.

unavoidable [ʌnə'voidəbl] adj inevitabile.

unaware [ʌnə'weə] adj ignaro. **be unaware of** ignorare. **unawares** adv di sorpresa.

unbalanced [ʌn'balənst] adj squilibrato.

unbearable [ʌn'beərəbl] adj insopportabile.

unbelievable [ʌnbi'liːvəbl] adj incredibile.

*unbend [ʌn'bend] v raddrizzare. **unbending** adj rigido, inflessibile.

unbiased [ʌn'baiəst] adj imparziale.

unbreakable [ʌn'breikəbl] adj infrangibile.

unbridled [ʌn'braidld] adj sfrenato.

unbroken [ʌn'broukn] adj intatto; ininterrotto; (not beaten) imbattuto.

unbutton [ʌn'bʌtn] v sbottonare.

uncalled-for [ʌn'koːldfoː] adj immeritato, gratuito.

uncanny [ʌn'kani] adj strano, misterioso.

uncertain [ʌn'səːtn] adj incerto, dubbio. **uncertainty** n incertezza f.

unchanged [ʌn'tʃeindʒd] adj immutato, invariato.

uncharitable [ʌn'tʃaritəbl] adj aspro, crudele.

uncivilized [ʌn'sivilaizd] adj barbaro.

uncle ['ʌŋkl] n zio m.

uncomfortable [ʌn'kʌmfətəbl] adj scomodo, a disagio. **feel uncomfortable** sentirsi a disagio.

uncommon [ʌn'komən] adj poco comune, insolito.

uncompromising [ʌn'komprəmaiziŋ] adj intrattabile, intransigente.

unconditional [ʌnkən'diʃənl] adj incondizionale, senza riserve, categorico.

unconscious [ʌn'kɔnʃəs] adj (*unaware*) inconscio, inconsapevole; (*med*) privo di coscienza. n inconscio m. **become unconscious** svenire, perdere conoscenza. **be unconscious** of essere ignaro di, non accorgersi di. **unconsciously** adv senza rendersene conto.

uncontrollable [ʌnkən'trouləbl] adj incontrollabile, irreprimibile.

unconventional [ʌnkən'venʃənl] adj anticonformista; non convenzionale.

unconvincing [ʌnkən'vinsiŋ] adj poco convincente. **unconvinced** adj non convinto, poco persuaso.

uncooked [ʌn'kukt] adj crudo, non cotto.

uncouth [ʌn'kuːθ] adj rozzo, grossolano.

uncover [ʌn'kʌvə] v scoprire, rivelare, esporre.

uncut [ʌn'kʌt] adj non tagliato, integro.

undecided [ʌndi'saidid] adj indeciso, irrisoluto.

undeniable [ʌndi'naiəbl] adj innegabile, incontestabile.

under ['ʌndə] adv, prep sotto, al di sotto (di). **be under the weather** sentirsi poco bene. **under age** minorenne. **under lock and key** sottochiave. **under one's breath** sottovoce. **under the circumstances** in queste circostanze.

undercharge [ʌndə'tʃaːdʒ] v far pagare meno del dovuto, non far pagare abbastanza.

underclothes ['ʌndəklouðz] pl n biancheria intima f sing.

undercoat ['ʌndəkout] n (*paint*) prima mano f.

undercover [ʌndə'kʌvə] adj segreto.

*****undercut** [ʌndə'kʌt] v (*comm*) offrire a un prezzo inferiore a.

underdeveloped [ʌndədi'veləpt] adj sottosviluppato.

underdog ['ʌndədog] n vittima f, persona che ha la peggio f.

underdone [ʌndə'dʌn] adj (*meat*) al sangue.

underestimate [ʌndə'estimeit] v sottovalutare.

underexpose [ʌndərik'spouz] v sottoesporre.

underfoot [ʌndə'fut] adv sotto i piedi.

*****undergo** [ʌndə'gou] v subire, supportare.

undergraduate [ʌndə'grædjuət] n studente universitario, studentessa universitaria m, f.

underground ['ʌndəgraund; adv

ʌndə'graund] adj sotterraneo; (*secret*) segreto; clandestino. **underground passage** sottopassaggio m. adv sottoterra. n resistenza f; (*railway*) metropolitana f.

undergrowth ['ʌndəgrouθ] n boscaglia f, macchia f.

underhand [ʌndə'hand] adj clandestino; (*dubious*) losco.

*****underlie** [ʌndə'lai] v sottostare a; essere alla base di.

underline [ʌndə'lain] v sottolineare.

undermine [ʌndə'main] v minare, insidiare.

underneath [ʌndə'niːθ] adv, prep sotto, al di sotto (di).

undernourished [ʌndə'nʌriʃt] adj malnutrito.

underpants ['ʌndəpants] pl n mutande f pl.

underpass ['ʌndəpaːs] n sottopassaggio m.

underprivileged [ʌndə'privilidʒd] adj non privilegiato, derelitto.

underrate [ʌndə'reit] v sottovalutare.

understaffed [ʌndə'staːft] adj a corto di personale or manodopera.

*****understand** [ʌndə'stand] v capire, comprendere; (*realize*) rendersi conto; (*believe*) credere. **understandable** adj comprensibile.

understanding [ʌndə'standiŋ] n comprensione f; (*knowledge*) conoscenza f; (*agreement*) accordo m. **on the understanding that** a condizione or premesso che. adj comprensivo, indulgente.

understate [ʌndə'steit] v minimizzare, attenuare. **understatement** n atto del minimizzare m.

understudy ['ʌndəstʌdi] v sostituire. n sostituto, -a m, f, attore, -trice supplente m, f.

*****undertake** [ʌndə'teik] v intraprendere; (*accept obligation*) impegnarsi; (*warrant*) garantire. **undertaker** n imprenditore di pompe funebri m, becchino m. **undertaking** n impresa f; (*pledge*) impegno m, promessa f.

undertone ['ʌndətoun] n fondo m, senso occulto m. **in an undertone** a bassa voce.

underwear ['ʌndəwɛə] n biancheria or maglieria intima f.

underwater ['ʌndəwɔːtə; adv ʌndə'wɔːtə] adj subacqueo. adv sott'acqua.

underweight [ʌndə'weit] adj di peso insufficiente.

underworld [ˈʌndəwɜːld] n (myth) inferno m; (crime) malavita f.

*__underwrite__ [ʌndəˈraɪt] v sottoscrivere; (support) sostenere; (finance) garantire; (insurance) riassicurare. **underwriter** n riassicuratore m, garante di una emissione m.

undesirable [ʌndɪˈzaɪərəbl] adj indesiderabile, sgradito.

undignified [ʌnˈdɪɡnɪfaɪd] adj poco dignitoso.

*__undo__ [ʌnˈduː] v disfare, sciogliere, annullare; rovinare. **leave undone** tralasciare di fare. **undoing** n rovina f.

undoubted [ʌnˈdautɪd] adj indubbio, incontestato, certo.

undress [ʌnˈdres] v svestire, spogliarsi.

undue [ʌnˈdjuː] adj indebito, eccessivo.

undulate [ˈʌndjuleɪt] v ondeggiare.

unearth [ʌnˈɜːθ] v scoprire, dissotterrare. **unearthly** adj (ghostly) spettrale; (coll) assurdo.

uneasy [ʌnˈiːzɪ] adj turbato, imbarazzato, a disagio.

uneducated [ʌnˈedjukeɪtɪd] adj ignorante, senza coltura.

unemployed [ʌnemˈplɔɪd] adj disoccupato. **the unemployed** i disoccupati m pl. **unemployment** n disoccupazione f.

unending [ʌnˈendɪŋ] adj interminabile, che non finisce più.

unequal [ʌnˈiːkwəl] dj disuguale; (unevenly matched) impari. **unequal to** non all'altezza di. **unequalled** adj senza pari.

uneven [ʌnˈiːvn] adj (not level) irregolare, ineguale; (odd) dispari.

unexpected [ʌneksˈpektɪd] adj inatteso.

unfailing [ʌnˈfeɪlɪŋ] adj infallibile, immancabile.

unfair [ʌnˈfeə] adj ingiusto; (dishonest) sleale; (sport) non sportivo. **unfairness** n ingiustizia f; slealtà f.

unfaithful [ʌnˈfeɪθfəl] adj infedele, disonesto; inesatto. **unfaithfulness** n infedeltà f.

unfamiliar [ʌnfəˈmɪljə] adj (not conversant) poco familiare or pratico; (not well-known) poco conosciuto or noto.

unfasten [ʌnˈfɑːsn] v slegare, sciogliere, disfare.

unfavourable [ʌnˈfeɪvərəbl] adj sfavorevole.

unfit [ʌnˈfɪt] adj (unsuitable) inadatto, non idoneo; (unable) inabile; (unwell) indisposto.

unfold [ʌnˈfould] v (open out) schiudere; (develop) sviluppare; (reveal) rivelare.

unforeseen [ʌnfɔːˈsiːn] adj imprevisto. **unforeseeable** adj imprevedibile.

unfortunate [ʌnˈfɔːtʃənət] adj sfortunato, disgraziato; (unsuitable, unhappy) infelice. **unfortunately** adv purtroppo.

unfriendly [ʌnˈfrendlɪ] adj freddo; ostile.

unfurnished [ʌnˈfɜːnɪʃd] adj non ammobiliato.

ungrateful [ʌnˈɡreɪtfəl] adj ingrato.

unguarded [ʌnˈɡɑːdɪd] adj incustodito, indifeso; imprudente, indiscreto.

unhappy [ʌnˈhapɪ] adj infelice, triste; inopportuno; (infelicitous) poco felice. **unhappily** adv sfortunatamente. **unhappiness** n infelicità f, tristezza f.

unhealthy [ʌnˈhelθɪ] adj malsano; (morbid) morboso.

unhurried [ʌnˈhʌrɪd] adj calmo, senza fretta.

unhurt [ʌnˈhɜːt] adj incolume.

unicorn [ˈjuːnɪkɔːn] n unicorno m.

uniform [ˈjuːnɪfɔːm] adj uniforme, costante. n uniforme f, divisa f. **uniformity** n uniformità f.

unify [ˈjuːnɪfaɪ] v unificare. **unification** n unificazione f.

unilateral [juːnɪˈlatərəl] adj unilaterale.

unimaginable [ʌnɪˈmadʒɪnəbl] adj inconcepibile. **unimaginative** adj poco immaginativo.

unimpaired [ʌnɪmˈpeəd] adj intatto, in pieno vigore.

uninhabited [ʌnɪnˈhabɪtɪd] adj disabitato, deserto. **uninhabitable** adj inabitabile.

unintentional [ʌnɪnˈtenʃənl] adj involontario.

uninterested [ʌnˈɪntrɪstɪd] adj disinteressato. **uninteresting** adj poco interessante, noioso.

union [ˈjuːnjən] n unione f, unificazione f; associazione f; (trade) sindacato f; (tech) collegamento m.

unique [juːˈniːk] adj unico, solo.

unison [ˈjuːnɪsn] n unisono m. **in unison** all'unisono.

unit [ˈjuːnɪt] n unità f; (whole) insieme m.

unite [juːˈnaɪt] v unire, combinare, congiungere. **united** adj unito. **United Kingdom** Regno Unito m. **United Nations** Nazioni Unite f pl. **United States of America** Stati Uniti d'America m pl.

unity ['juːniti] n unità f.
universe ('juːnivəːs) n universo m. **universal** adj universale.
university [juːni'vəːsiti] n università f. adj universitario.
unjust [ʌn'dʒʌst] adj ingiusto.
unkempt [ʌn'kempt] adj spettinato; (untidy) sciatto.
unkind [ʌn'kaind] adj poco gentile; crudele.
unknown [ʌn'noun] adj sconosciuto, ignoto. n ignoto m; (math) incognita f. **unknown to** all'insaputa di.
unlawful [ʌn'lɔːfəl] adj illegale; illecito.
unless [ʌn'les] conj a meno che non, se non.
unlike [ʌn'laik] adj dissimile o diverso (da). **be unlike** non rassomigliarsi. **not unlike** assai simile a. prep a differenza di, all'inverso di.
unlikely [ʌn'laikli] adj improbabile, inverosimile.
unload [ʌn'loud] v scaricare, liberarsi di.
unlock [ʌn'lok] v aprire.
unlucky [ʌn'lʌki] adj sfortunato, disgraziato.
unmarried [ʌn'marid] adj non sposato; (bachelor) celibe; (spinster) nubile. **unmarried mother** ragazza madre f.
unmistakable [ʌnmi'steikəbl] adj inequivocabile, manifesto.
unnatural [ʌn'natʃərəl] adj contro natura; (lacking natural feelings) snaturato, disumano; anormale; forzato.
unnecessary [ʌn'nesəsəri] adj inutile, non necessario.
unnoticed [ʌn'noutist] adj inavvertito.
unobtainable [ʌnəb'teinəbl] adj irreperibile.
unoccupied [ʌn'ɔkjupaid] adj libero, vacante, vuoto.
unofficial [ʌnə'fiʃəl] adj ufficioso.
unopposed [ʌnə'pouzd] adj incontrastato.
unpack [ʌn'pak] v (case) disfare (le valige); (contents) disimballare.
unpaid [ʌn'peid] adj non retribuito o rimunerato; (debt, etc.) non saldato o pagato.
unpardonable [ʌn'paːdnəbl] adj imperdonabile.
unpleasant [ʌn'pleznt] adj spiacevole, sgradevole, antipatico. **unpleasantness** n spiacevolezza f; (disagreement) dissenso m.

unpopular [ʌn'pɔpjulə] adj impopolare. **be unpopular with** esser malvisto da.
unprecedented [ʌn'presidentid] adj inaudito, senza precedenti.
unpredictable [ʌnprə'diktəbl] adj imprevedibile.
unqualified [ʌn'kwɔlifaid] adj non qualificato; senza diploma; categorico, assoluto.
unquestionable [ʌn'kwestʃənəbl] adj indiscutibile, fuori questione. **unquestioned** adj indiscusso, incontestato.
unravel [ʌn'ravəl] v sciogliere, sbrogliare; (clear) chiarire.
unreadable [ʌn'riːdəbl] adj illeggibile; (tedious) noioso.
unreal [ʌn'riəl] adj irreale.
unreasonable [ʌn'riːzənəbl] adj irragionevole.
unrecognizable [ʌn'rekəg'naizəbl] adj irriconoscibile.
unrelenting [ʌnri'lentiŋ] adj inesorabile; (dogged) accanito.
unreliable [ʌnri'laiəbl] adj da non fidarsene; (news) inattendibile.
unrepentant [ʌnri'pentənt] adj impenitente.
unrest [ʌn'rest] n agitazione f, fermento m.
unripe [ʌn'raip] adj immaturo, acerbo.
unruly [ʌn'ruːli] adj indisciplinato, turbolento.
unsafe [ʌn'seif] adj malsicuro, pericoloso.
unsatisfactory [ʌnsatis'faktəri] adj poco soddisfacente, che lascia desiderare.
unsavoury [ʌn'seivəri] adj sgradevole; (coll) disgustoso, poco pulito.
unscrew [ʌn'skruː] v svitare.
unscrupulous [ʌn'skruːpjuləs] adj senza scrupoli.
unselfish [ʌn'selfiʃ] adj altruistico.
unsettle [ʌn'setl] v turbare; disturbare; sconcertare. **unsettled** adj (weather) variabile; (account) non saldato; (not fixed) non sistemato; (uncertain) incerto.
unsightly [ʌn'saitli] adj brutto, spiacevole a vedersi.
unskilled [ʌn'skild] adj inesperto, non qualificato. **unskilled worker** n manovale m.
unsociable [ʌn'souʃəbl] adj poco socievole, scontroso.
unsound [ʌn'saund] adj imperfetto, difettoso; erroneo; (ill-founded) poco profondo.

unspeakable [ʌn'spiːkəbl] *adj* indicibile, inesprimibile; *(very bad)* inqualificabile.

unstable [ʌn'steibl] *adj* instabile.

unsteady [ʌn'stedi] *adj* malfermo, instabile; incostante; *(wavering)* traballante, barcollante.

unsuccessful [ʌnsək'sesfəl] *adj* non or mal riuscito, sfortunato, fallito.

unsuitable [ʌn'suːtəbl] *adj* inadatto; inopportuno; sconveniente. **unsuited** *adj* non idoneo, disadatto, sconvenevole.

unsure [ʌn'ʃuə] *adj* malsicuro, incerto.

untangle [ʌn'taŋgl] *v* districare.

unthinkable [ʌn'θiŋkəbl] *adj* inconcepibile, assurdo.

untidy [ʌn'taidi] *adj* disordinato, trascurato. **untidiness** *n* disordine *m*. trascuratezza *f*.

untie [ʌn'tai] *v* sciogliere, slegare.

until [ən'til] *prep* fino a; *(before)* prima di. *conj* finchè, fino a quando; fino al momento in cui.

untimely [ʌn'taimli] *adj* inopportuno, intempestivo, prematuro.

untoward [ʌntə'wɔːd] *adj* disgraziato.

untrue [ʌn'truː] *adj* non vero, falso, erroneo; infedele; inesatto.

unusual [ʌn'juːʒuəl] *adj* insolito, straordinario, eccezionale.

unwanted [ʌn'wɒntid] *adj* indesiderato, superfluo.

unwelcome [ʌn'welkəm] *adj* *(person)* malaccolto; *(news, etc.)* sgradito, spiacevole.

unwell [ʌn'wel] *adj* indisposto, ammalato.

unwieldy [ʌn'wiːldi] *adj* ingombrante.

unwilling [ʌn'wiliŋ] *adj* restio, riluttante; *(given reluctantly)* dato controvoglia.

***unwind** [ʌn'waind] *v* dipanare; *(relax)* rilassarsi.

unwise [ʌn'waiz] *adj* imprudente, insensato.

unwittingly [ʌn'witiŋli] *adv* senza saperlo, per inavvertenza.

unworthy [ʌn'wɔːði] *adj* indegno. **unworthy of** che non merita.

unwrap [ʌn'rap] *v* disfare.

up [ʌp] *adv* su; *(erect)* in piedi; *(out of bed)* alzato. **be up again** or **be up** *(capable of)* essere all'altezza di; *(mischief)* tramare. **up here** quassù. **up there** lassù. **up to** fino a. **what's up?** cosa succede? *prep* su, per. *n* **ups and downs** alti e bassi *m pl*.

upbringing ['ʌpbriŋiŋ] *n* educazione *f*.

update [ʌp'deit] *v* aggiornare.

upheaval [ʌp'hiːvl] *n* commozione *f*, sconvolgimento *m*.

uphill [ʌp'hil] *adv* in salita, in su. *adj* in salita, ascendente; difficile.

***uphold** [ʌp'hould] *v* sostenere, appoggiare.

upholster [ʌp'houlstə] *v* tappezzare. **upholsterer** *n* tappezziere *m*. **upholstery** *n* tappezzeria *f*.

upkeep ['ʌpkiːp] *n* mantenimento *m*, manutenzione *f*.

uplift [ʌp'lift] *v* edificare, incoraggiare. *n* edificazione *f*. incoraggiamento *m*.

upon [ə'pɒn] *prep* su, sopra.

upper ['ʌpə] *adj* superiore, più alto. **get the upper hand** prevalere. *n* tomaia *f*. **be on one's uppers** essere alle strette. **uppermost** *adj* il più alto.

upright ['ʌprait] *adj* verticale, in piedi; *(righteous)* retto, onesto.

uprising ['ʌpraiziŋ] *n* insurrezione *f*.

uproar ['ʌprɔː] *n* tumulto, fracasso. **uproarious** *adj* tumultuoso, chiassoso. **uproariously funny** da crepar dal ridere.

uproot [ʌp'ruːt] *v* sradicare.

***upset** [ʌp'set] *v* *n* 'ʌpset] *v* sconvolgere, disturbare; *(knock over)* rovesciare. *adj* sconvolto, turbato; rovesciato. *n* disturbo *m*, contrattempo *m*. **upsetting** *adj* turbante, preoccupante.

upshot ['ʌpʃɒt] *n* conclusione *f*, effetto *m*.

upside down [ʌpsai'daun] *adv, adj* sottosopra, in disordine.

upstairs [ʌp'steəz] *adv* di sopra, al piano superiore.

upstream [ʌp'striːm] *adv* a monte, controcorrente.

uptight [ʌp'tait] *adj* *(coll)* nervoso.

up-to-date [ʌptə'deit] *adj* aggiornato, di moda.

upward ['ʌpwəd] *adj* in salita, rivolto in alto. **upwards** *adv* in su, in alto; *(more)* più.

uranium [ju'reiniəm] *n* uranio *m*.

urban ['əːbən] *adj* urbano.

urchin ['əːtʃin] *n* monello, -a *m, f*.

urge [əːdʒ] *n* sprone *m*, impulso *m*. *v* esortare, spingere; insistere.

urgent ['əːdʒənt] *adj* urgente. **urgency** *n* urgenza *f*.

urine ['juːrin] *n* orina *f*. **urinal** *n* orinatoio *m*. **urinary** *adj* urinario. **urinate** *v* orinare.

urn [ɔːn] *n* urna *f*.

us [ʌs] *pron* ci, ce; *(after prep)* noi.

usage [ˈjuːzidʒ] *n* uso *m*, usanza *f*.

use [juːs; *v* juːz] *n* uso *m*, impiego (*pl* -ghi) *m*; utilità *f*. **it's no use!** è inutile! **what's the use?** a cosa serve? *v* usare, impiegare, adoperare. **use up** consumare. **used** *adj* (*car*) d'occasione. **be used to** essere abituato a. **useful** *adj* utile. **useless** *adj* inutile.

usher [ˈʌʃə] *n* usciere *m*. *v* **usher in** far entrare, introdurre. **usherette** *n* maschera *f*.

usual [ˈjuːʒuəl] *adj* solito, usuale. **as usual** come di solito. **usually** *adv* di solito, generalmente.

usurp [juːˈzəːp] *v* usurpare.

utensil [juːˈtensl] *n* utensile *m*, arnese *f*.

uterus [ˈjuːtərəs] *n* utero *m*.

utility [juːˈtiləti] *n* utilità *f*, vantaggio *m*; servizio pubblico *m*. **utilize** *v* utilizzare.

utmost [ˈʌtməust] *adj* massimo, supremo. *n* massimo *m*, possibile *m*. **do one's utmost** fare del proprio meglio.

utter[1] [ˈʌtə] *v* (*say*) pronunciare, emettere.

utter[2] [ˈʌtə] *adj* (*absolute*) completo, assoluto.

U-turn [ˈjuːtəːn] *n* cambio di direzione *m*.

V

vacant [ˈveikənt] *adj* libero, vuoto; vacuo.

vacancy *n* (*job*) posto libero *m*; (*room*) camera libera *f*. **vacate** *v* lasciar libero, sgombrare.

vaccine [ˈvaksiːn] *n* vaccino *m*. **vaccinate** *v* vaccinare. **vaccination** *n* vaccinazione *f*.

vacillate [ˈvasileit] *v* vacillare.

vacuum [ˈvakjum] *n* vuoto *m*. **vacuum cleaner** *n* aspirapolvere *m invar*. **vacuum flask** *n* thermos   *m invar*.

vagina [vəˈdʒainə] *n* vagina *f*. **vaginal** *adj* vaginale.

vagrant [ˈveigrənt] *n, adj* vagabondo, -a. **vagrancy** *n* vagabondaggio *m*.

vague [veig] *adj* vago.

vain [vein] *adj* (*worthless*) vano, inutile; (*conceited*) vanitoso. **in vain** invano.

valiant [ˈvaliənt] *adj* valoroso.

valid [ˈvalid] *adj* (*ticket, etc.*) valevole; (*sound*) valido. **validity** *n* validità *f*.

valley [ˈvali] *n* valle *f*.

value [ˈvaljuː] *n* valore *m*. *v* valutare, stimare; dare importanza a. **valuable** *adj* prezioso, di valore. **valuables** *pl n* valori *m pl*, oggetti di valore *m pl*.

valve [valv] *n* valvola *f*.

vampire [ˈvampaiə] *n* vampiro *m*.

van[1] [van] *n* (*vehicle*) furgone *m*, camion *m*.

van[2] [van] *n* (*forefront*) avanguardia *f*.

vandal [ˈvandl] *n* vandalo *m*. **vandalism** *n* vandalismo *m*.

vanilla [vəˈnilə] *n* vaniglia *f*.

vanish [ˈvaniʃ] *v* sparire.

vanity [ˈvanəti] *n* vanità *f*.

vapour [ˈveipə] *n* vapore *m*. **vaporize** *v* vaporizzare.

variance [ˈveəriəns] *n* variazione *f*. **at variance** in disaccordo.

varicose veins [ˈvarikous] *pl n* vene varicose *f pl*.

variety [vəˈraiəti] *n* varietà *f*, diversità *f*. **various** [ˈveəriəs] *adj* vario, diverso.

varnish [ˈvaːniʃ] *n* vernice *f*, lacca *f*. *v* verniciare, laccare.

vary [ˈveəri] *v* variare; modificare; differire. **variant** *n* variante *f*. **variation** *n* variazione *f*. **varied** *adj* vario, svariato.

vase [vaːz] *n* vaso *m*.

vasectomy [vəˈsektəmi] *n* vasectomia *f*.

vast [vaːst] *adj* vasto, immenso.

vat [vat] *n* tino *m*.

Vatican [ˈvatikən] *n* Vaticano *m*. **Vatican City** la Città del Vaticano *f*.

vault[1] [voːlt] *n* volta *f*; (*cellar*) cantina *f*; (*safe*) camera di sicurezza *f*.

vault[2] [voːlt] *v* saltare, volteggiare. *n* salto *m*.

veal [viːl] *n* vitello *m*.

veer [viə] *v* virare, cambiar direzione.

vegetable [ˈvedʒtəbl] *n* ortaggio *m*, verdura *f*. *adj* vegetale; (*food*) di verdura. **vegetarian** *n, adj* vegetariano, -a. **vegetate** *v* vegetare. **vegetation** *n* vegetazione *f*.

vehement [ˈviːəmənt] *adj* violento, impetuoso.

vehicle [ˈviːikl] *n* veicolo *m*; (*means*) mezzo *m*.

veil [veil] *n* velo *m*. *v* velare; (*hide*) nascondere.

vein [vein] *n* vena *f*; (*leaf, marking*) venatura *f*.

velocity [vəˈlosəti] *n* velocità *f*.

velvet [ˈvelvit] *n* velluto *m*. **velvety** *adj* vellutato.

vending machine ['vendiŋ] n distributore automatico m.

veneer [vəˈniə] n piallaccio m; (*superficial layer*) vernice f.

venerate ['venəreit] v venerare. **venerable** adj venerabile.

venereal disease [vəˈniəriəl] n malattia venerea f.

Venetian blind [vəˈniːʃən] n veneziana f.

vengeance ['vendʒəns] n vendetta f. **with a vengeance** (*unexpectedly*) in modo insospettato; (*with violence*) violentemente.

Venice ['venis] n Venezia f.

venison ['venisn] n cacciagione f.

venom ['venəm] n veleno m; (*spite*) malignità f, cattiveria f. **venomous** adj velenoso; maligno, cattivo.

vent [vent] n (*outlet*) apertura f, sbocco m. **give vent to** sfogare. v esprimere, sfogare.

ventilate ['ventileit] v ventilare. **ventilation** n ventilazione f.

venture ['ventʃə] n impresa (rischiosa) f, avventura f. v azzardare, arrischiare.

venue ['venjuː] n sede f; (*place*) posto m.

verb [vəːb] n verbo m. **verbal** adj verbale. **verbatim** adj parola per parola.

verdict ['vəːdikt] n verdetto m, giudizio m.

verge [vəːdʒ] n orlo m, limite m. **on the verge of** sul punto di. v **verge on** tendere a, avvicinarsi a.

verify ['verifai] v verificare, confermare. **verification** n verifica f.

vermin ['vəːmin] pl n animali nocivi m pl, parassiti m pl; (*scum*) feccia f sing.

vermouth ['vəːməθ] n vermut m invar.

vernacular [vəˈnakjulə] adj indigeno, dialettale; volgare. n **in the vernacular** in volgare.

versatile ['vəːsətail] adj versatile, eclettico.

verse [vəːs] n verso m; (*poem*) poesia f. **in verse** in versi.

version ['vəːʃən] n versione f.

versus ['vəːsəs] prep contro.

vertebra ['vəːtibrə] n, pl **-brae** vertebra f. **vertebral** adj vertebrale. **vertebrate** nm, adj vertebrato.

vertical ['vəːtikl] nf, adj verticale.

vertigo ['vəːtigou] n vertigini f pl.

very ['veri] adv molto, assai. **the very next day** proprio il giorno dopo. adj proprio; esatto; (*same*) stesso; (*mere*) solo.

vessel ['vesl] n (*container*) recipiente m, vaso m; (*ship*) nave f, bastimento m.

vest [vest] n maglia f, maglietta f. v conferire, assegnare.

vestige ['vestidʒ] n vestigio m, traccia f.

vestry ['vestri] n sagrestia f.

vet [vet] (*coll*) v controllare, esaminare. n veterinario, -a m, f.

veteran ['vetərən] n veterano m; (*mil*) reduce m.

veterinary ['vetərinəri] adj veterinario. **veterinary surgeon** v veterinario, -a m, f.

veto ['viːtou] n veto m.

vex [veks] v vessare, irritare. **vexed question** argomento dibattuto m.

via [vaiə] prep per, attraverso, tramite.

viable ['vaiəbl] adj vitale, capace a vivere; (*workable*) praticabile, possibile; (*road*) transitabile. **viability** n praticabilità f; (*biol*) vitalità f.

viaduct ['vaiədʌkt] n viadotto m.

vibrate [vai'breit] v (far) vibrare. **vibration** n vibrazione f.

vicar ['vikə] n parroco m, vicario m. **vicarage** n parrocchia f.

vicarious [viˈkeəriəs] adj vicario.

vice¹ [vais] n (*evil*) vizio m; (*fault*) difetto m.

vice² [vais] n (*tool*) morsa f.

vice-chancellor [vaisˈtʃɑːnsələ] n (*university*) rettore m.

vice-president [vaisˈprezidənt] n vice-presidente m.

vice versa [vaisiˈvəːsə] adv viceversa.

vicinity [viˈsinəti] n vicinanza f, prossimità f; (*neighbourhood*) vicinanze f pl, dintorni m pl.

vicious ['viʃəs] adj (*bad*) cattivo; (*crude*) crudele, maligno. **vicious circle** circolo vizioso m.

victim ['viktim] n vittima f. **fall victim to** essere preda a. **victimize** v perseguitare or punire ingiustamente; sacrificare.

victory ['viktəri] n vittoria f. **victorious** adj vittorioso.

video-tape ['vidiouteip] n video-cassetta f.

vie [vai] v gareggiare.

Vienna [viˈenə] n Vienna f.

view [vjuː] n vista f; (*scene, opinion*) veduta f. **in view of** in vista di; (*considering*) dato; (*on account of*) grazie a, a causa di. **on view** esposto. **viewfinder** n mirino m. **viewpoint** n punto di vista m. **with a view to** allo scopo di. v vedere;

osservare; ispezionare. **viewer** n spettatore, -trice m, f; telespettatore, -trice m, f.

vigil ['vidʒil] n veglia f; vigilia f. **vigilant** adj vigile.

vigour ['vigə] n vigore m. **vigorous** adj vigoroso; robusto.

vile [vail] adj vile, spregevole.

villa ['vilə] n villa f.

village ['vilidʒ] n villaggio m, paese m.

villain ['vilən] n farabutto m, villano m.

vindicate ['vindikeit] v rivendicare, giustificare; (exonerate) discolpare. **vindication** n rivendicazione f, giustificazione f; discolpa f.

vindictive [vin'diktiv] adj vendicativo, malevolo.

vine [vain] n vite f. **vineyard** n vigna f.

vinegar ['vinigə] n aceto m.

vintage ['vintidʒ] n vendemmia f; (year) annata f. adj (wine) pregiato; (car) d'epoca.

vinyl ['vainil] adj vinilico.

viola [vi'oulə] n viola f.

violate ['vaiəleit] v violare, trasgredire. **violation** n violazione f, trasgressione f.

violence ['vaiələns] n violenza f. **violent** adj violento.

violet ['vaiəlit] n (colour) (color) viola m, violetto m; (flower) viola f, violetta f. adj viola invar, violetto.

violin [vaiə'lin] n violino m. **violinist** n violinista m, f.

viper ['vaipə] n vipera f.

virgin ['vəːdʒin] nf, adj vergine f. **virginity** n verginità f.

Virgo ['vəːgou] n Vergine f.

virile ['virail] adj virile. **virility** n virilità f.

virtual ['vəːtʃuəl] adj effettivo, in pratica.

virtue ['vəːtʃuː] n virtù f; (admirable quality) pregio m. **by virtue of** in virtù di, grazie a. **virtuoso** n virtuoso, -a m, f. **virtuous** adj virtuoso.

virulent ['virələnt] adj virulento. **virulence** n virulenza f.

virus ['vaiərəs] n virus m invar. **viral** adj virale.

visa ['viːzə] n visto m.

viscount ['vaikaunt] n visconte m. **viscountess** n viscontessa f.

viscous ['viskəs] adj viscoso. **viscosity** n viscosità f.

visible ['vizəbl] adj visibile; (obvious) evidente. **visibility** n visibilità f.

vision ['viʒən] n visione f; (wisdom) sagacia f. **visionary** n, adj visionario, -a.

visit ['vizit] n visita f. v visitare; (person) fare una visita a, andare a trovare; (place) andare a vedere; (doctor) consultare. **visitor** n visitatore, -trice m, f; (guest) ospite m, f.

visor ['vaizə] n visiera f.

visual ['viʒuəl] adj visivo, visuale. **visualize** v immaginare, concepire.

vital ['vaitl] adj vitale, essenziale; capitale. **vitality** n vitalità f.

vitamin ['vitəmin] n vitamina f.

vivacious [vi'veiʃəs] adj vivace, animato. **vivacity** n vivacità f.

vivid ['vivid] adj vivido, vivace.

vixen ['viksn] n volpe femmina f.

vocabulary [və'kabjuləri] n vocabolario m.

vocal ['voukəl] adj vocale; orale.

vocation [vou'keiʃən] n vocazione f; professione f; (role) funzione f. **vocational** adj vocazionale, professionale.

vociferous [və'sifərəs] adj rumoroso, chiassoso.

vodka ['vodkə] n vodka f.

voice [vois] n voce f. v esprimere, formulare, manifestare.

void [void] nm, adj vuoto. v vuotare; (law) annullare.

volatile ['volətail] adj (chem) volatile; capriccioso; (unpredictable) imprevedibile; esplosivo.

volcano [vol'keinou] n vulcano m. **volcanic** adj vulcanico.

volley ['voli] n raffica f, scarica f; (tennis) volata f. **volleyball** n pallavolo f.

volt [voult] n volt m invar. **voltage** n tensione f, voltaggio m.

volume ['voljum] n volume m. **voluminous** adj voluminoso.

volunteer [volən'tiə] n volontario, -a m, f. v offrirsi volontariamente; (mil) arruolarsi volontario; (offer) dare o offrire spontaneamente. **voluntary** adj volontario.

voluptuous [və'lʌptʃuəs] adj voluttuoso, sensuale.

vomit ['vomit] v vomitare. n vomito m.

voodoo ['vuːduː] n vodù m.

voracious [və'reiʃəs] adj vorace, insaziabile. **voracity** n voracità f.

vote [vout] n voto m, diritto di voto m, suffragio m. v votare, dare il proprio voto; (*agree generally*) convenire. **voter** *n* elettore, -trice *m, f.*

vouch [vautʃ] *v* **vouch for** garantire, attestare. **vouchsafe** *v* degnarsi di dare, concedere.

voucher ['vautʃə] *n* buono *m*, tagliando *m.*

vow [vau] *n* voto *m*, giuramento *m. v* giurare; fare voto di.

vowel ['vauəl] *n* vocale *f.*

voyage ['voiidʒ] *n* viaggio *m*, escursione *f*; (*crossing*) traversata *f. v* viaggiare; attraversare.

vulgar ['vʌlgə] *adj* volgare. **vulgarity** *n* volgarità *f.* **vulgarize** *v* divulgare, volgarizzare; (*debase*) degradare.

vulnerable ['vʌlnərəbl] *adj* vulnerabile.

vulture ['vʌltʃə] *n* avvoltoio *m.*

W

wad [wod] *n* tampone *m*; pacchetto *m*; (*roll*) rotolo *m.* **wadding** *n* (*padding*) imbottitura *f.*

waddle ['wodl] *v* camminare dondolandosi. *n* andatura dondolante *f.*

wade [weid] *v* guadare, avanzare con fatica. **wader** *n* (*bird*) trampoliere *m.*

wafer ['weifə] *n* cialda *f*, wafer *m* invar; (*church*) ostia *f.*

waft [woft] *v* diffondere. *n* zaffata *f.*

wag [wag] *v* agitare, scuotere; (*tail*) dimenare. **set tongues wagging** suscitare pettegolezzi.

wage [weidʒ] *n* salario *m*, paga *f. v* **wage war** muover guerra.

wager ['weidʒə] *n* scommessa *f. v* scommettere.

wagon ['wagən] *n* vagone *m*, carrozza *f.* **be on the wagon** (*coll*) essere astemio.

waif [weif] *n* senzatetto *m* invar; (*foundling*) trovatello, -a *m, f.*

wail [weil] *n* gemito *m*, lamento *m. v* gemere, emettere un lamento.

waist [weist] *n* vita *f.* **waistcoat** *n* gilè *m.* **waistline** *n* misura *or* circonferenza della vita *f.*

wait [weit] *v* aspettare, attendere; servire, sostare. *n* attesa *f*; sosta *f.* **lie in wait** stare in agguato. **waiter** *n* cameriere *m.* **waiting-room** *n* sala d'aspetto *f.* **waitress** *n* cameriera *f.*

waive [weiv] *v* rinunciare. **waiver** *n* rinuncia *f*; (*document*) atto di rinuncia *m.*

*wake¹ [weik] *v* **also wake up** svegliare, svegliarsi. *n* veglia *f.*

wake² [weik] *n* scia *f.* **in the wake of** subito dopo, nella scia di.

Wales [weilz] *n* Galles *m.*

walk [wok] *v* camminare; (*go on foot*) andare a piedi. **walk in** entrare. **walk out on** piantare. **walkover** *n* vittoria incontestata *or* facile *f. n* cammino *m*, passeggiata *f*; (*gait*) passo *m.* **walker** *n* camminatore, -trice *m, f*; (*sport*) podista *m, f.*

wall [wol] *n* muro *m*; (*internal*) parete *f.* **wallpaper** *n* carta da parati *f.*

wallet ['wolit] *n* portafoglio *m.*

wallop ['woləp] (*coll*) *v* (*thrash*) battere, picchiare. *n* (*blow*) colpo violento *m.*

wallow ['wolou] *v* sguazzare.

walnut ['wolnʌt] *n* (*tree*) noce *m*; (*fruit*) noce *f.*

walrus ['wolrəs] *n* tricheco *m.* **walrus moustache** baffi spioventi *m pl.*

waltz [wolts] *n* valzer *m* invar. *v* ballare il valzer. **waltz through** (*coll*) superare facilmente.

wand [wond] *n* bacchetta *f.*

wander ['wondə] *v* vagare, girare; (*stray*) allontanarsi, delirare.

wane [wein] *v* calare, declinare. *n* declino *m*; (*moon*) calare *m.*

wangle ['waŋgl] (*coll*) *n* trucco *m*, intrigo (*pl* -ghi) *m. v* procurare con astuzia.

want [wont] *v* volere, desiderare, aver voglia di; (*lack*) mancare di; (*ought*) dovere. *n* (*need*) bisogno *m*, esigenza *f*; (*deficiency*) mancanza *f.* **wanted** *adj* (*asked for*) richiesto; (*police*) ricercato; (*advertisement*) cercasi.

wanton ['wontən] *adj* deliberato, gratuito, sfrenato. *n* libertino *m*, sgualdrina *f.*

war [wo] *n* guerra *f.* **warfare** *n* guerra *f.* **warmonger** *n* guerrafondaio *m.* **wartime** *n* tempo di guerra *m. v* far guerra, combattere.

warble ['wobl] *n* trillo *m. v* trillare. **warbler** *n* uccello canoro *m.*

ward [wod] *n* (*district*) distretto *m*; (*hospital*) corsia *f*, padiglione *m*; (*law*) pupillo, -a *m, f. v* **ward off** parare, scansare.

warden ['wodn] *n* guardiano, -a *m, f*, custode *m, f.*

warder ['wodə] *n* carceriere, -a *m, f.*

wardrobe ['wɔːdroub] n guardaroba m invar; (cupboard) armadio m.

warehouse ['wɛəhaus] n magazzino m.

warm [wɔːm] adj caldo; cordiale, caloroso; (lively) animato; (enthusiastic) ardente. **be warm** aver caldo. **get warm** scaldarsi. v riscaldare. **warmth** n caldo m; calore m; animazione f; ardore m.

warn [wɔːn] v mettere in guardia, ammonire; (notify) avvertire, preavvisare. **warning** n ammonimento m; preavviso m; allarme m.

warp [wɔːp] v deformare. n ordito m.

warrant ['wɔrənt] n autorizzazione f, diritto m; (law) mandato m. v autorizzare; giustificare; garantire. **warranty** n (comm) garanzia f.

warren ['wɔrən] n (rabbit) garenna f.

warrior ['wɔriə] n guerriero m. **unknown warrior** n milite ignoto m.

Warsaw ['wɔːsɔː] n Varsavia f.

wart [wɔːt] n verruca f.

wary ['wɛəri] adj diffidente, cauto. **be wary of** diffidare di; guardarsi dal.

was [wɔz] V be.

wash [wɔʃ] v lavare. **wash away** portare via; (obliterate) cancellare. **wash-basin** n lavandino m. **wash-out** n (coll) fiasco m. **wash up** lavare i piatti. n lavata f; (clothes, etc.) bucato m; (painting) acquerello m, guazzo m. **have a wash** lavarsi. **washable** adj lavabile. **washing** n bucato m. **washing-machine** n lavatrice automatica f.

washer ['wɔʃə] n rondella f.

wasp [wɔsp] n vespa f.

waste [weist] v sprecare, sciupare. **waste away** deperire. n spreco m; (rubbish) immondizia f; (scrap) scarti m pl, cascami m pl; (geog) deserto m. **waste-paper basket** cestino da rifiuti m. **waste-pipe** n tubo di scarico m. **wasteful** adj dispendioso, sprecone.

watch [wɔtʃ] v guardare, osservare; (as spectator) assistere a; (keep an eye on) tener d'occhio. **watch out** stare attento. **watch over** sorvegliare. n (time) orologio m; osservazione f; guardia f, sorveglianza f. **keep watch** fare la guardia. **watch-dog** n cane da guardia m. **watchful** adj vigile.

water ['wɔtə] n acqua f. v annaffiare, irrigare. **water down** diluire; moderare, attenuare. **watery** adj acquoso; (colour) scialbo.

water-closet n gabinetto m.

water-colour n acquerello m.

watercress ['wɔtəkres] n crescione m.

waterfall ['wɔːtəfɔːl] n cascata f.

waterfront ['wɔːtəfrʌnt] n lungomare m; (wharf) zona portuale f.

watering-can n annaffiatoio m.

water-lily n ninfea f.

waterlogged ['wɔːtəlɔgd] adj saturo d'acqua; (ground) acquitrinoso.

water-melon n cocomero m.

water-mill n mulino ad acqua m.

water polo n pallanuoto f.

waterproof ['wɔːtəpruːf] nm, adj impermeabile. v impermeabilizzare.

watershed ['wɔːtəʃed] n spartiacque m invar.

water-ski n sci nautico m. v fare dello sci nautico. **water-skiing** n sci nautico m.

watertight ['wɔːtətait] adj stagno; (irrefutable) inconfutabile.

water-way n corso navigabile m.

waterworks ['wɔːtəwɜːks] n impianto idrico m. **turn on the waterworks** (coll) mettersi a piangere.

watt [wɔt] n watt m invar. **wattage** n wattaggio m.

wave [weiv] n onda f; (surge) ondata f; (sign) cenno m. **waveband** n gamma di lunghezze d'onda f. v sventolare, far segno con; (hair) ondulare. **wave aside** scartare. **wavy** adj (hair) ondulato; (line) ondeggiante.

waver ['weivə] v (vacillate) titubare, esitare.

wax[1] [waks] n cera f. v dar la cera a, lucidare.

wax[2] [waks] v (increase) crescere; (become) diventare.

way [wei] n (manner) modo m; (respect) rispetto m, particolare m; (street) strada f; passaggio m. **by the way** a proposito. **give way** cedere; (traffic) dare la precedenza. **in a way** in un certo modo. **make way for** fare largo a. **out of the way** (place) fuori strada; (unusual) fuori del comune. **way in** n entrata f. **way out** uscita f.

***waylay** [wei'lei] v abbordare; (ambush) tendere un agguato a.

wayward ['weiwəd] adj capriccioso, ribelle.

we [wiː] pron noi.

weak [wiːk] adj debole. **weaken** v indebolire. **weakling** n persona debole f. **weakness** n debolezza f; (inclination) debole m.

wealth [welθ] n ricchezza f; abbondanza f. **wealthy** adj ricco.

wean [wiːn] v svezzare.

weapon ['wepən] n arma f.

*****wear** [weə] v portare, indossare; (deteriorate) consumare; (last) durare. **wear off** passare, dissiparsi. **wear out** consumare, indebolire; (tire) stancare. n (use) uso m; (clothing) abiti m pl, abbigliamento m; (deterioration) usura f.

weary ['wiəri] adj stanco, stufo. v stancare, stufare.

weasel ['wiːzl] n donnola f.

weather ['weðə] n tempo m. **weather-beaten** adj segnato dalle intemperie. **weather forecast** bollettino meteorologico m. v (expose) esporre all'aria, stagionare; (overcome) superare.

*****weave** [wiːv] v tessere; (devise) ordire. n armatura f. **weaver** n tessitore m. **weaving** n tessitura f.

web [web] n tessuto m; (spider) ragnatela f. **webbed foot** piede palmato m.

wedding ['wediŋ] n matrimonio m; (ceremony) nozze f pl. **wedding-dress** n abito nuziale m. **wedding-ring** n fede f.

wedge [wedʒ] n cuneo m. v incuneare, incastrare.

Wednesday ['wenzdi] n mercoledì m.

weed [wiːd] n erbaccia f, malerba f. **weed-killer** n erbicida m. v diserbare, sarchiare. **weedy** adj coperto di erbacce; (person) sparuto.

week [wiːk] n settimana f. **weekday** n giorno feriale or lavorativo m. **weekend** n fine settimana m. **week-end** n invar.

weekly ['wiːkli] nm, adj settimanale. adv ogni settimana.

*****weep** [wiːp] v piangere. **weeping** n pianto m. **weeping willow** salice piangente m. **weepy** adj (coll) lacrimoso, sentimentale.

weigh [wei] v pesare; (have importance) valere. **weigh anchor** salpare. **weighbridge** n pesa a ponte f, pesa pubblica f. **weigh up** soppesare, valutare. **weight** n peso m. **carry weight** aver peso. **lose weight** dimagrire. **put on weight** ingrassare. **weighty** adj pesante; importante.

weird [wiəd] adj strano, misterioso.

welcome ['welkəm] interj benvenuto! **welcome home!** ben tornato! n benvenuto

m, buona or cordiale accoglienza f. adj benvenuto, gradito. v accogliere; (greet) dare il benvenuto a; (accept gladly) gradire.

weld [weld] v saldare. n saldatura f.

welfare ['welfeə] n benessere m; assistenza sociale f. **welfare worker** n assistente sociale m, f.

well[1] [wel] n pozzo m; (stairs) tromba f.

well[2] [wel] adv bene. interj beh! allora! **as well** (also) anche.

well-behaved adj educato, beneducato.

well-being n benessere m, bene m.

well-bred adj educato, beneducato.

well-built adj ben costruito.

wellingtons ['weliŋtənz] pl n stivali impermeabili m pl, stivali di gomma m pl.

well-known adj ben noto.

well-meaning adj ben intenzionato. **well-meant** adj fatto a fin di bene.

well-off adj benestante, agiato.

well-paid adj ben pagato or retribuito.

well-read adj colto.

well-spoken adj che parla bene.

well-to-do adj benestante, abbiente.

well-worn adj (person) consumato; (hackneyed) trito.

Welsh [welʃ] n(m+f), adj gallese.

went [went] V go.

wept [wept] V weep.

were [wəː] V be.

west [west] n ovest m, occidente m. adv also **westward(s)** verso ovest, in direzione ovest.

western ['westən] adj occidentale, dell'ovest. n (film) western m.

wet [wet] adj bagnato, umido; (rainy) piovoso; (paint, ink, etc.) fresco. **wet blanket** guastafeste m, f invar. **wet through** bagnato fradicio; (person) bagnato fino alle ossa. v bagnare.

whack [wak] (coll) n colpo m; (part) fetta f. v colpire. **be whacked** essere sfinito.

whale [weil] n balena f. **have a whale of a time** (coll) divertirsi un mondo. **whaling** n caccia alla balena f.

wharf [woːf] n banchina f, scalo m.

what [wot] pron (che) cosa; (relative) quello che. adj che, quale. **what a ... !** che ... ! **what for?** perché? **what is the matter?** cosa c'è? cosa succede?

whatever [wot'evə] pron qualsiasi or qualunque cosa. adj qualsiasi, qualunque. **none whatever** nessuno. **nothing whatever** assolutamente nulla.

wheat [wiit] n grano m, frumento m.

wheel [wiil] n ruota f; (pottery) tornio m; (steering) volante m. **wheelbarrow** n carretta f, carriola f. **wheelchair** n sedia a rotelle f. v (make turn) far ruotare; (push) spingere.

wheeze [wiz] v ansimare. n respiro affannoso m.

whelk [welk] n buccino m.

when [wen] adv quando. conj quando; (after which) appena; (whereas) mentre. **whenever** adv qualora, ogni volta che.

where [weə] conj, adv dove. **whereabouts** adv dove, da che parte. **whereas** conj mentre. **whereby** conj, adv onde, per cui. **whereupon** conj dopoché, dal momento che. **wherever** conj dovunque. **wherewithal** n necessario m.

whether [weðə] conj se.

which [witʃ] pron quale; (relative) il quale, la quale; che. adj quale. **which way?** da che parte?

whichever [witʃevə] adj qualunque, qualsiasi. pron quello che; (person) chiunque.

whiff [wif] n buffata f, zaffata f.

while [wail] conj mentre. n momento m. **a long while ago** molto tempo fa.

whim [wim] n capriccio m.

whimper [wimpə] v piagnucolare. n piagnucolio m.

whimsical [wimzikl] adj bizzarro, eccentrico.

whine [wain] v gemere; (complain) uggiolare. n uggiolio m, gemito m.

whip [wip] n frusta f. **whip-round** (coll) colletta f. v frustare; (cookery) frullare. **whipped cream** panna montata f.

whippet [wipit] n levriere inglese m.

whirl [wəil] v turbinare, giro vertiginoso m. **whirlpool** n vortice m. **whirlwind** n turbine m, tromba d'aria f. v girare (rapidamente).

whisk [wisk] v (dust) spolverare; (cookery) frullare. n piumino m; frullino m.

whisker [wiskə] n pelo m. **whiskers** pl n basette f pl; (moustache, cat) baffi m pl.

whisky [wiski] n whisky m invar.

whisper [wispə] v bisbigliare, mormorare. n bisbiglio m, mormorio m.

whist [wist] n whist m invar.

whistle [wisl] v fischiare; (tune) fischiettare. n (sound) fischio m; (instrument) fischietto m.

white [wait] n bianco m. adj bianco.

whitebait pl n bianchetti m pl. **whiten** v imbiancare.

whitewash [waitwoʃ] n intonaco m; (cover-up) riabilitazione f. v imbiancare, intonacare; (cover up) scolpare.

whiting [waitiŋ] n (fish) merlango m.

Whitsun [witsn] n Pentecoste f.

whizz [wiz] v (hum) sibilare; (move) guizzare.

who [hui] pron chi; (relative) che, il quale, la quale. **whoever** pron chiunque.

whole [houl] n totale m, insieme m. **as a whole** nell'insieme. **on the whole** tutto considerato, in fin dei conti. adj intero, tutto; intatto. **wholehearted** adj generoso. **wholemeal** adj integrale. **wholesale** adv all'ingrosso. **wholesaler** n grossista m, f. **wholesome** adj sano.

whom [huim] pron che; (relative) il quale, la quale; (after prep) cui.

whooping cough [huipiŋ] n pertosse f.

whore [hoi] n (derog) puttana f.

whose [huiz] pron di chi. adj di cui; (relative) il cui, la cui.

why [wai] adv, conj perché, per cui.

wick [wik] n stoppino m.

wicked [wikid] adj cattivo, malvagio. **wickedness** n cattiveria f, malvagità f.

wicker [wikə] n vimini m pl.

wicket [wikit] n porta f, sportello m. **a sticky wicket** una situazione scabrosa.

wide [waid] adj largo; (spacious) ampio. adv lontano. **open wide** v spalancare. **wide apart** spaziati. **wide awake** completamente sveglio; (alert) vigilante. **wide open** spalancato. **widespread** adj esteso, diffuso. **widen** v estendere, allargare.

widow [widou] n vedova f. **widower** n vedovo m.

width [widθ] n larghezza f; (cloth) altezza f.

wield [wild] v (weapon) brandire; (power) esercitare.

wife [waif] n moglie f.

wig [wig] n parrucca f.

wiggle [wigl] v dimenare.

wild [waild] adj selvatico; (animal, place) selvaggio; (unrestrained) feroce. **spread like wildfire** divampare. **wild with anger** fuori di sè dalla rabbia. **wild with joy** folle di gioia.

wilderness [wildənəs] n deserto m, solitudine f.

wilful [wilfəl] adj intenzionale; premeditato; ostinato.

will¹ [wil] *aux translated by future tense.*

will² [wil] *n* volontà *f*; *(law)* testamento *m*. **against one's will** malvolentieri, controvoglia. **at will** a piacere.

willing ['wiliŋ] *adj (disposed)* disposto; *(ready)* pronto, volonteroso. **willingness** *n* prontezza *f*; buona volontà *f*.

willow ['wilou] *n* salice *m*.

wilt [wilt] *v* appassire.

*win [win] *v* vincere. **win back** riguadagnare. *n* vittoria *f*; *(games)* vincita *f*. **winner** *n* vincitore *m*.

wince [wins] *v* trasalire. *n* sussulto *m*, trasalimento *m*.

winch [wintʃ] *n* argano *m*. *v* **winch up** sollevare con l'argano.

wind¹ [wind] *n* vento *m*; *(breath)* fiato *m*. **get wind of** aver sentore di, fiutare. *v* sfiatare. **windy** *adj* esposto al vento.

*wind² [waind] *v (twist)* serpeggiare. **wind up** *(roll up)* avvolgere; concludere; *(end up)* andare a finire; *(clock)* caricare; *(business)* liquidare.

wind-cheater *n* giacca a vento *f*.

windfall ['windfoːl] *n* frutto fatto cadere dal vento *m*; fortuna inaspettata *f*.

windlass ['windləs] *n* verricello *m*.

windmill ['wind,mil] *n* mulino a vento *m*.

window ['windou] *n* finestra *f*; *(train)* finestrino *m*; *(car)* cristallo *m*; *(cashier's)* sportello *m*. **French window** *n* portafinestra *f*. **window-dressing** *n* mostra *f*; *(show)* bella mostra *f*, inganno *m*. **window-sill** *n* davanzale *m*.

windpipe ['windpaip] *n* trachea *f*.

windshield ['windʃiːld] *n* parabrezza *m invar*. **windshield wiper** tergicristallo *m*.

windswept ['windswept] *adj* battuto dai venti.

wine [wain] *n* vino *m*. **wineglass** *n* bicchiere da vino *m*. **wine list** carta dei vini *f*.

wing [wiŋ] *n* ala *f*. **in the wings** *(theatre)* tra le quinte. **wingspan** *n* apertura alare *f*.

wink [wiŋk] *v* strizzare l'occhio, ammiccare. *n (signal)* cenno *m*; *(instant)* attimo *m*. **have forty winks** schiacciare un pisolino.

winkle ['wiŋkl] *n* chiocciola di mare *f*.

winter ['wintə] *n* inverno *m*. **wintry** *adj* invernale.

wipe [waip] *v* strofinare; *(dry)* asciugare. **wipe away** *or* **off** cancellare, allontanare. **wipe out** eliminare; *(debts, etc.)*

liquidare; *(annihilate)* annientare. **wiper** *n* strofinaccio *m*; *(windscreen)* tergicristallo *m*.

wire [waiə] *n* filo *m*; telegramma *m*. **wireless** *n* radio *f invar*. *v (elec)* montare; *(fasten)* legare con filo metallico; telegrafare. **wiry** *adj* secco, nerboruto.

wisdom ['wizdəm] *n* saggezza *f*. **wisdom tooth** *n* dente del giudizio *m*.

wise [waiz] *adj* saggio. **wisecrack** *n* battuta *f*.

wish [wiʃ] *n* desiderio *m*, voglia *f*. **wishes** *pl n* auguri *m pl*. *v* desiderare, volere; *(greeting)* augurare. **wishful thinking** pio desiderio *m*.

wisp [wisp] *n (hair)* ciocca *f*; *(smoke)* filo *m*.

wistful ['wistfəl] *adj* pensoso, malinconico.

wit [wit] *n* spirito *m*; arguzia *f*, intelligenza *f*; *(person)* uomo di spirito *m*. **be at one's wits' end** non saper più cosa fare. **live by one's wits** vivere di espedienti.

witch [witʃ] *n* strega *f*. **witchcraft** *n* stregoneria *f*. **witch-doctor** *n* stregone *m*.

with [wið] *prep* con; *(together with)* insieme a; *(because of)* per, a causa di.

*withdraw [wið'droː] *v* ritirare; *(cash)* prelevare. **withdrawal** *n* ritiro *m*; *(mil)* ritirata *f*; prelevamento *m*.

wither ['wiðə] *v (lose freshness)* appassire; atrofizzare; *(decay)* avvizzire.

*withhold [wið'hould] *v* trattenere; *(hide)* nascondere.

within [wi'ðin] *adv* dentro. *prep* entro, in. **within reach** a portata.

without [wi'ðaut] *prep* senza. *adv* fuori. **do without** fare a meno (di).

*withstand [wið'stand] *v* resistere a.

witness ['witnis] *n (evidence)* testimonianza *f*; *(person)* testimone *m*, *f*. *v* testimoniare, attestare.

witty ['witi] *adj* spiritoso, arguto.

wizard ['wizəd] *n* mago *m*.

wobble ['wobl] *v* vacillare, traballare.

woke [wouk] *V* **wake¹**.

woken ['woukn] *V* **wake¹**.

wolf [wulf] *n* lupo *m*. **cry wolf** gridare al lupo. *v* divorare.

woman ['wumən] *n*, *pl* **women** donna *f*. **old woman** *n* vecchia *f*. **young woman** giovane *f*. **womanly** *adj* femminile.

womb [wuːm] *n* utero *m*.

won [wʌn] V win.

wonder ['wʌndə] n meraviglia f; miracolo m. v meravigliarsi; (ask oneself) domandarsi. **wonderful** adj meraviglioso.

wood [wud] n (material) legno m; (as fuel) legna f; (forest) bosco m. **wooden** adj di legno; rigido. **woody** adj (wooded) boscoso; (tough) legnoso.

woodcock ['wudkok] n beccaccia f.

woodcut ['wudkʌt] n silografia f, incisione su legno f.

woodland ['wudlənd] n boscaglia f.

woodpecker ['wudpekə] n picchio m.

wood-pigeon n colombaccio m.

wood-wind n strumenti a fiato m pl.

woodwork ['wudwəːk] n (carpentry) lavoro in legno m, falegnameria f; (wooden parts) parti in legno f pl.

woodworm ['wudwəːm] n tarlo m.

wool [wul] n lana f. **dyed in the wool** adj radicato, convinto. **woollen** adj di lana; (industry) laniero. **woolly** adj di lana, lanoso; confuso.

word [wəːd] n parola f. **in other words** altrimenti detto. **word for word** alla lettera. v esprimere, redigere. **wording** n espressione f, formulazione f.

wore [woː] V wear.

work [wəːk] n lavoro m; (toil) fatica f; (product) opera f. **workman** n operaio m. **works** n (factory) fabbrica f; stabilimento m. **workshop** n officina f. v lavorare; (machine, etc.) (far) funzionare. **work out** risolvere; risultare. **worker** n lavoratore, -trice m, f; operaio, -a m, f. **working** n operazione f, funzionamento m. **working class** classe operaia f. **working order** buon ordine m.

world [wəːld] n mondo m. **world war** guerra mondiale f. **world-wide** adj mondiale, universale. **worldly** adj temporale; mondano.

worm [wəːm] n verme m. v insinuarsi.

worn [woːn] V wear.

worry ['wʌri] n preoccupazione f, ansia f. v preoccupare; molestare. **worrying** adj preoccupante.

worse [wəːs] adj peggio, peggiore. nm, adv peggio. **from bad to worse** di male in peggio. **get worse** peggiorare. **worsen** v peggiorare.

worship ['wəːʃip] n adorazione f, omaggio m; (rel) culto m, servizio religioso m. v adorare; andare a messa, andare in chiesa.

worst [wəːst] adj peggiore, il più brutto. nm, adv peggio.

worsted ['wustid] nm, adj pettinato.

worth [wəːθ] adj **be worth** valere. **be worthless** non valere nulla. **be worthwhile** valere la pena. n merito m, valore m. **worthy** adj degno.

would [wud] aux translated by conditional or imperfect tense.

wound¹ [wuːnd] n ferita f. v ferire; offendere. **wounded** adj ferito.

wound² [waund] V wind².

wove [wouv] V weave.

woven ['wouvn] V weave.

wrangle ['rangl] v litigare, disputare. n lite f, disputa f.

wrap [rap] v (envelop) avvolgere; (cover) coprire; (parcel) incartare. n (shawl) scialle m; (dressing-gown) vestaglia f. **wrapper** n involucro m; (book) copertina f.

wreath [riːθ] n ghirlanda f, corona f. **wreathe** v incoronare. **wreathed in smiles** raggiante.

wreck [rek] n (ship) naufragio m; (ruin) relitto m, rovina f. v rovinare; demolire; naufragare. **wreckage** n rottami m pl.

wren [ren] n scricciolo m.

wrench [rentʃ] v storcere. **wrench open** forzare. n (movement) strappo m; (injury) storta f; (spanner) chiave f.

wrestle ['resl] v lottare. **wrestling** n lotta f.

wretch [retʃ] n (unfortunate) disgraziato, -a m, f; (despicable) incosciente m, f. **wretched** adj disgraziato, miserabile; (pitiful) pietoso.

wriggle ['rigl] v dimenarsi.

*__wring__ [riŋ] v torcere. **wring out** strizzare. **wringer** n strizzatoio m. **wringing wet** fradicio.

wrinkle ['riŋkl] n crespa f; (face) ruga f. v increspare; corrugare.

wrist [rist] n polso m.

writ [rit] n mandato m.

*__write__ [rait] v scrivere. **write down** trascrivere, registrare. **write off** (comm) cancellare. **writer** n scrittore, -trice m, f. **writing** n calligrafia f. **writings** pl n scritti m pl.

writhe [raið] v contorcersi.

written ['ritn] V write.

wrong [roŋ] adv male. adj (not moral) peccato; (incorrect) sbagliato. **be wrong** (person) aver torto, sbagliarsi. n torto m; ingiustizia f; (law) violazione f. v far torto a, maltrattare. **wrongful** adj ingiustificato.

wrote [rout] V **write**:

wrought iron [,rɔtt'aiən] n ferro battuto m.

wrung [rʌŋ] V **wring**.

wry [rai] adj ironico, perverso; (askance) di sbieco.

X

xenophobia [,zenə'foubiə] n xenofobia f. **xenophobic** adj xenofobo.

Xmas ['krisməs] V **Christmas**.

X-ray ['eksrei] n raggio X m; (photo) radiografia f. v radiografare.

xylophone ['zailəfoun] n xilofono m.

Y

yacht [jɔt] n panfilo m. **yachting** n velismo m.

yank [jæŋk] v (coll) dare uno strattone a, tirare con violenza.

yap [jæp] v guaire. n guaito m.

yard [jɑːd] n cortile m; (site) cantiere m; (railway) scalo merci m. **yardstick** n (measure) metro m; (standard) pietra di paragone f.

yarn [jɑːn] n (thread) filo m, filato m; storia f.

yawn [jɔːn] v sbadigliare. n sbadiglio m.

year [jiə] n anno m, annata f. **year-book** n annuario m. **yearly** adj annuo, annuale.

yearn [jəːn] v languire. **yearn for** bramare, desiderare vivamente. **yearning** n vivo desiderio m, brama f.

yeast [jiist] n lievito m.

yell [jel] v gridare, urlare. n grido m, urlo m.

yellow ['jelou] adj giallo; (coll: cowardly) vigliacco. n giallo m. v ingiallire. **yellowy** adj giallastro.

yelp [jelp] v (dog) uggiolare. **yelp with pain** gridare per il dolore. n uggiolio m; grido di dolore m.

yes [jes] nm, adv sì.

yesterday ['jestədi] nm, adv ieri.

yet [jɔt] adv ancora; (already) già. conj ma, tuttavia. **as yet** finora.

yew [juː] n tasso m.

yield [jiːld] v produrre; (surrender) cedere; (profit, interest, etc.) rendere, fruttare. n frutto m, prodotto m; (tech) resa f; (finance) reddito m; (harvest) raccolto m.

yoga ['jougə] n yoga m.

yoghurt ['jogət] m iogurt m.

yoke [jouk] n giogo m; (dress) carrè m.

yolk [jouk] n tuorlo m.

you [juː] pron (subject: fam) tu; (subject: pl) voi; (subject: fml) Lei; (direct object) ti, vi, la; (indirect object) ti or te, vi or ve, le; (after prep) te, voi, Lei. **if I were you** se fossi in te.

young [jʌŋ] adj giovane. **youngster** n (child) bambino, -a m, f; (youth) ragazzo, -a m, f.

your [jɔt] adj (fam) (il) tuo, (la) tua, (i) tuoi, (le) tue; (pl) (il) vostro, (la) vostra, (i) vostri, (le) vostre; (fml) (il) suo, (la) sua, (i) suoi, (le) sue.

yours [jɔtz] pron (fam) il tuo, la tua, i tuoi, le tue; (pl) il vostro, la vostra, i vostri, le vostre; (fml) il suo, la sua, i suoi, le sue.

yourself [jə'self] pron (fam) tu stesso; (fml) Lei stesso; (reflexive) ti, si; (after prep) te stesso, Lei stesso.

yourselves [jə'selvz] pron voi stessi; (reflexive) vi.

youth [juːθ] n gioventù f; (boy) giovane m.

Yugoslavia [juːgou'slɑːvjə] n Iugoslavia f. **Yugoslav** n, adj iugoslavo, -a.

Z

zeal [ziːl] n zelo m. **zealous** adj zelante.

zebra ['zebrə] n zebra f. **zebra crossing** passaggio zebrato m.

zero ['ziərou] n zero m. v mettere a zero, azzerare.

zest [zest] n (enjoyment) gusto m, entusiasmo m; (piquancy) nota piccante f.

zigzag ['zigzag] nm, adj zigzag. v andare a zigzag, serpeggiare.

zinc [ziŋk] n zinco m.

zip [zip] n chiusura or cerniera lampo f. v **zip up** chiudere la (cerniera) lampo.

zodiac ['zoudiak] n zodiaco m.

zone [zoun] n zona f.

zoo [zuː] *n* giardino zoologico *m*, zoo *m invar*. **zoologist** *n* zoologo, -a *m*, *f*. **zoology** *n* zoologia *f*.

zoom [zuːm] *v* (*noise*) ronzare; (*aircraft*) salire in candela; (*film*) zumare. *n* ronzio *m*. **zoom lens** zoom *m invar*, obiettivo zoom *m*.

Italian–Inglese

A

a, ad [a, ad] *prep* to; *(stato in luogo)* at, in; *(prezzo, ora, età)* at. **a 10 metri da** 10 metres away from. **a due a due** two by two. **alle dozzina** by the dozen. **andare a casa** go home. **100 km all'ora** 100 km an hour.
abate [a'bate] *sm* abbot.
abbagliare [abba'ʎare] *v* dazzle.
abbaiare [abba'jare] *v* bark. **abbaiata** *sf* bark.
abbaino [abba'ino] *sm* attic, garret.
abbandonare [abbando'nare] *v* abandon, leave. **abbandonarsi a** *(darsi senza ritegno)* indulge in; give in to. **abbandono** *sm* neglect; desertion.
abbassare [abbas'sare] *v* lower, reduce. **abbasso** *avv* down. **abbasso ... !** *inter* down with ... !
abbastanza [abbas'tantsa] *avv* enough.
abbattere [ab'battere] *v* knock down, fell; *(uccidere)* kill; *(deprimere)* depress. **abbattersi** *v* become disheartened.
abbazia [abba'tsia] *sf* abbey.
abbellire [abbel'lire] *v* embellish, adorn.
abbiente [ab'bjente] *agg* prosperous, well-to-do.
abbigliare [abbi'ʎare] *v* dress. **abbigliamento** *sm* clothes *pl*; *(modo)* dress.
abboccare [abbok'kare] *v* bite. **abboccato** *agg (vino)* medium sweet.
abbonarsi [abbo'narsi] *v* subscribe; take out a season ticket (for). **abbonamento** *sm* subscription; season ticket. **abbonato, -a** *sm, sf* subscriber; ticket-holder.
abbondare [abbon'dare] *v* be plentiful, abound. **abbondante** *agg* plentiful, abundant. **abbondanza** *sf* abundance, plenty.
abbordare [abbor'dare] *v* approach; *(introdurre)* broach.

abborracciare [abborrat'tʃare] *v* botch.
abbottonare [abbotto'nare] *v* button up.
abbozzare [abbot'tsare] *v* sketch, outline. **abbozzare un sorriso** give a faint smile. **abbozzo** *sm* sketch.
abbracciare [abbrat'tʃare] *v* embrace. **abbraccio** *sm* embrace, hug.
abbreviare [abbre'vjare] *v* abbreviate, shorten. **abbreviazione** *sf* abbreviation.
abbronzare [abbron'dzare] *v* tan. **abbronzatura** *sf* (sun-)tan.
abbrustolire [abbrusto'lire] *v* toast.
abbuono [ab'bwɔno] *sm* allowance; *(sport)* handicap.
abdicare [abdi'kare] *v* abdicate. **abdicazione** *sf* abdication.
aberrazione [aberra'tsjone] *sf* aberration.
abete [a'bete] *sm* fir(-tree). **abete rosso** spruce.
abietto [a'bjetto] *agg* abject. **abiezione** *sf* low spirits *pl*.
abile ['abile] *agg* clever, good (at); *(adatto)* suitable. **abilità** *sf* cleverness, skill; *(destrezza)* dexterity.
abilitare [abili'tare] *v* train; *(a una professione)* qualify. **abilitazione** *sf* qualification, diploma.
abisso [a'bisso] *sm* abyss.
abitare [abi'tare] *v* live. **abitante** *s(m+f)* inhabitant. **abitazione** *sf* home, dwelling.
abitato [abi'tato] *agg* inhabited. *sm* built-up area; *(villaggio)* hamlet.
abito ['abito] *sm* suit; dress; *(rel, abitudine)* habit. **abituale** *agg* customary, usual; habitual.
abituarsi [abitu'arsi] *v* **abituarsi a** get used to, become accustomed to.
abitudine [abi'tudine] *sf* habit, custom. **avere l'abitudine di** be in the habit of. **d'abitudine** as a rule.
abolire [abo'lire] *v* abolish. **abolizione** *sf* abolition.

abominevole [abomi'nevole] *agg* abominable.

aborigeno [abo'ridʒeno] *sm* aborigine. *agg* aboriginal.

aborrire [abor'rire] *v* abhor, loathe.

abortire [abor'tire] *v* miscarry; fail. **aborto** *sm* miscarriage. **aborto procurato** abortion.

abrasivo [abra'zivo] *sm, agg* abrasive. **abrasione** *sf* abrasion.

abside ['abside] *sf* apse.

abusare [abu'zare] *v* abuse. **abusivo** *agg* unauthorized, improper. **abuso** *sm* abuse.

accademia [akka'dɛmja] *sf* academy. **accademico** *sm, agg* academic.

*****accadere** [akka'dere] *v* happen. **accaduto** *sm* occurrence.

accampare [akkam'pare] *v* camp; (*avanzare*) put forward. **accampamento** *sm* camp.

accanirsi [akka'nirsi] *v* rage; persist. **accanito** *agg* (*ostinato*) dogged, stubborn; (*spietato*) merciless; (*violento*) fierce.

accanto [ak'kanto] *avv* nearby; (*casa*) next door. **accanto a** next to, near to, beside.

accantonare [akkanto'nare] *v* set aside.

accaparrare [akkapar'rare] *v* corner.

accappatoio [akkappa'tojo] *sm* bathrobe.

accarezzare [akkaret'tsare] *v* caress, stroke.

accasciare [akka'ʃare] *v* crush. **accasciarsi** *v* collapse.

accattone [akkat'tone], **-a** *sm, sf* scrounger.

accavallare [akkaval'lare] *v* (*sovrapporre*) overlap; (*accumulare*) pile up; (*incrociare*) cross.

accecare [attʃe'kare] *v* blind; block up. **accecante** *agg* blinding.

*****accedere** [at'tʃedere] *v* accede.

accelerare [attʃele'rare] *v* accelerate, speed up. **acceleratо** *sm* local train. **acceleratore** *sm* accelerator. **accelerazione** *sf* acceleration.

*****accendere** [at'tʃɛndere] *v* light; (*luce, radio*) switch on, turn on. **accendino** *sm* (*fam*) lighter.

accennare [attʃen'nare] *v* make a sign, nod; hint to, hint at, touch on. **accenno** *sm* indication, mention.

accensione [attʃen'sjone] *sf* ignition.

accento [at'tʃɛnto] *sm* accent, stress; tone. **accentare** *v* accent.

accentrare [attʃen'trare] *v* centralize, concentrate.

accentuare [attʃentu'are] *v* stress; (*aumentare*) heighten.

accerchiare [attʃer'kjare] *v* encircle. **accerchiamento** *sm* encirclement.

accertare [attʃer'tare] *v* verify, ascertain; (*dir*) establish. **accertamento** *sm* verification; establishment.

acceso [at'tʃezo] *agg* alight, switched on; (*colore*) vivid; (*eccitato*) burning.

accessibile [attʃes'sibile] *agg* (*luogo*) accessible; (*persona*) approachable.

accesso [at'tʃɛsso] *sm* access; (*med*) attack, fit.

accessorio [attʃes'sɔrjo] *agg* complementary, secondary. *sm* accessory, fitting.

accetta [at'tʃetta] *sf* hatchet.

accettare [attʃet'tare] *v* accept; admit. **accettabile** *agg* acceptable. **accettazione** *sf* acceptance; (*sala*) reception. **bene accetto** welcome. **male accetto** unwelcome.

acchiappare [akkjap'pare] *v* catch, grab (hold of), seize.

acciaio [at'tʃajo] *sm* steel. **acciaieria** *sf* steelworks.

accidente [attʃi'dɛnte] *sm* accident, mishap. **mandare un accidente a** (*fam*) curse. **non capire un accidente** not understand a thing. **accidenti!** *inter* my goodness! (*ira*) damn it! **accidenti a lui!** blast him! **accidentale** *agg* accidental.

acciglarsi [attʃi'ʎarsi] *v* frown. **accigliato** *agg* frowning.

*****accingersi** [at'tʃindʒersi] *v* **accingersi a** set about; be on the point of.

acciuffare [attʃuf'fare] *v* seize.

acciuga [at'tʃuga] *sf* anchovy.

acclamare [akkla'mare] *v* acclaim. **acclamazione** *sf* acclamation.

acclimatare [akklima'tare] *v* acclimatize.

*****accludere** [ak'kludere] *v* enclose.

accoccolarsi [akkokko'larsi] *v* squat.

*****accogliere** [ak'kɔʎʎere] *v* receive, accept, welcome; contain. **accoglienza** *sf* welcome, reception.

accomodare [akkomo'dare] *v* (*riparare*) mend, fix; (*mettere in ordine*) arrange, tidy; (*sistemare*) settle. **accomodarsi** *v* make oneself comfortable; take a seat; (*mettersi d'accordo*) agree. **accomodamento** *sm* agreement; compromise. **accomodante** *agg* accommodating.

accompagnare [akkompa'ɲare] v accompany. **accompagnatore, -trice** sm, sf escort; (musica) accompanist.

acconciare [akkon'tʃare] v prepare; arrange. **acconciarsi i capelli** do one's hair. **acconciatura** sf hair-style.

*****accondiscendere** [akkondiʃ'ʃendere] v comply (with); condescend.

acconsentire [akkonsen'tire] v consent; acquiesce.

accoppare [akkop'pare] v (fam) kill, slaughter.

accorciare [akkor'tʃare] v shorten.

accordare [akkor'dare] v (uniformare) match; harmonize; (concedere) grant; (musica) tune. **accordarsi** v agree. **accordo** [ak'kɔrdo] sm agreement. **essere** or **andare d'accordo** agree. **d'accordo!** agreed!

*****accorgersi** [ak'kɔrdʒersi] v notice. **accorgimento** sm expedient, stratagem.

*****accorrere** [ak'korrere] v come running, rush.

accorto [ak'kɔrto] agg shrewd. **fare accorto** warn, caution. **stare accorto** be wary. **accortezza** sf shrewdness.

accostare [akkos'tare] v approach. **accostarsi a** v near.

accovacciarsi [akkovat'tʃarsi] v crouch, huddle.

accreditare [akkredi'tare] v accredit.

*****accrescere** [ak'kreʃere] v increase.

accumulare [akkumu'lare] v accumulate, heap. **accumulatore** sm accumulator.

accurato [akku'rato] agg accurate, thorough. **accuratezza** sf thoroughness, care.

accusare [akku'zare] v accuse; (notificare) acknowledge. **accusa** sf accusation, charge.

acerbo [a'tʃerbo] agg (immaturo) unripe; (aspro) sour.

acero [a'tʃero] sm maple.

aceto [a'tʃeto] sm vinegar.

acido [a'tʃido] sm acid. agg acid, sour. **acidità** sf acidity.

acne ['akne] sf acne.

acqua ['akkwa] sf water. **acqua ossigenata** hydrogen peroxide. **acqua in bocca!** keep mum!

acquaforte [akkwa'fɔrte] sf, pl **acqueforti** etching.

acquaio [ak'kwajo] sm kitchen sink.

acquaragia [akkwa'radʒa] sf turpentine, turps.

acquario [ak'kwarjo] sm aquarium.

acquatico [ak'kwatiko] agg aquatic, water.

acquavite [akkwa'vite] sf rough brandy.

acquazzone [akkwat'tsone] sm shower.

acquedotto [akkwe'dotto] sm aqueduct.

acquerello [akkwe'rɛllo] sm water-colour.

acquistare [akkwis'tare] v buy; (ottenere) acquire; (guadagnare) gain. **acquistarsi fama di** gain the reputation of. **acquisto** sm purchase. **buon acquisto** bargain.

acquoso [ak'kwozo] agg watery; (terreno) marshy.

acre ['akre] agg acrid, sharp.

acrilico [a'kriliko] agg acrylic.

acrobata [a'krɔbata] s(m+f) acrobat. **acrobatico** agg acrobatic. **acrobazia** sf acrobatics pl.

aculeo [a'kuleo] sm sting.

acustica [a'kustika] sf acoustics pl. **acustico** agg acoustic. **apparecchio acustico** sm hearing-aid.

acuto [a'kuto] agg acute, intense; (aguzzo) pointed; (perspicace) shrewd. sm (musica) top note.

ad V a.

adagiarsi [ada'dʒarsi] v lie down.

adagio [a'dadʒo] avv slowly; gently. sm (musica) slow movement, adagio.

adattabile [adat'tabile] agg adaptable. **adattabilità** sf adaptability.

adattare [adat'tare] v adapt. **adattarsi** v adapt oneself, resign oneself. **adatto** agg suitable (for); (qualificato) suited (to).

addebitare [addebi'tare] v charge.

addensare [adden'sare] v thicken; (raccogliere) gather.

addestrare [addes'trare] v train. **addestramento** sm training.

addetto [ad'detto] agg employed (in); destined (for), intended (for); assigned. sm (pol) attaché.

addietro [ad'djetro] avv (fa) ago; (prima) before.

addio [ad'dio] inter goodbye, farewell. sm parting, farewell.

addirittura [addirit'tura] avv (persino) even; (direttamente) straight away; absolutely.

additare [addi'tare] v point at; (mostrare) point out, show.

additivo [addi'tivo] sm additive.

addizionare [addittsjo'nare] v add up. **addizionale** agg additional. **addizione** sf addition.

addolcire [addol'tʃire] v sweeten; (*mitigare*) soften.

addolorare [addolo'rare] v distress.

addome [ad'dɔme] *sm* abdomen. **addominale** *agg* abdominal.

addomesticare [addomesti'kare] v tame.

addormentare [addormen'tare] v put to sleep. **addormentarsi** v fall asleep, go to sleep. **addormentato** *agg* sleeping; (*di mente*) dull; (*intorpidito*) numb.

addossare [addos'sare] v lean; (*mettere a carico*) saddle with. **addossarsi** v shoulder.

addosso [ad'dɔsso] *avv*, *prep* on. **d'addosso** off. **essere uno addosso all'altro** be crowded together.

*addurre [ad'durre] v advance, put forward; produce.

adeguare [ade'gware] v adjust.

adempiere [a'dempjere] v *also* **adempire** carry out.

adenoidi [ade'nɔidi] *sf pl* adenoids *pl*.

aderire [ade'rire] v adhere, stick. **aderire a** comply with; accept; (*associarsi*) join. **aderente** *agg* close; (*abito*) close-fitting. **aderenza** *sf* adhesion. **aderenze** *sf pl* (*fam*) contacts *pl*.

adescare [ades'kare] v lure.

adesione [ade'zjone] *sf* adhesion; (*consenso*) assent; support. **adesivo** *sm*, *agg* adhesive.

adesso [a'dɛsso] *avv* now; nowadays; (*poco fa*) just now; (*fra poco*) any minute (now). **per adesso** for the time being.

adiacente [adja'tʃɛnte] *agg* adjacent. **adiacente a** next to.

adibire [adi'bire] v turn (into).

adirarsi [adi'rarsi] v get angry.

adito ['adito] *sm* entry. **dare adito a** give rise to.

adocchiare [adok'kjare] v spot.

adolescente [adole'ʃɛnte] *agg* adolescent. *s*(*m*+*f*) adolescent, teenager. **adolescenza** *sf* adolescence.

adombrare [adom'brare] v shade; (*celare*) hide. **adombrarsi** v take umbrage; (*cavalli*) shy.

adoperare [adope'rare] v use. **adoperarsi** v do one's best.

adorare [ado'rare] v adore, worship. **adorabile** *agg* adorable. **adoratore, -trice** *sm*, *sf* admirer. **adorazione** *sf* worship.

adornare [ador'nare] v adorn, decorate. **adorno** *agg* adorned, decked out.

adottare [adot'tare] v adopt, foster. **adottivo** *agg* adoptive. **adozione** *sf* adoption.

adrenalina [adrena'lina] *sf* adrenaline.

adulazione [adula'tsjone] *sf* flattery. **adulare** v flatter. **adulatore, -trice** *sm*, *sf* flatterer.

adulterare [adulte'rare] v adulterate; (*corrompere*) debase.

adultero [a'dultero], **-a** *sm*, *sf* adulterer. **-ess.** *agg* adulterous. **adulterio** *sm* adultery.

adulto [a'dulto], **-a** *s*, *agg* adult, grown-up.

adunare [adu'nare] v assemble. **adunanza** *sf* assembly. **adunata** *sf* meeting, gathering; (*mil*) parade.

aerare [ae'rare] v air, ventilate. **aeratore** *sm* ventilator.

aereo [a'ɛreo] *agg* aerial, air. *sm* aeroplane.

aerodinamica [aerodi'namika] *sf* aerodynamics. **aerodinamico** *agg* streamlined.

aerodromo [ae'rɔdromo] *sm* aerodrome.

aerolinea [aero'linea] *sf* airline.

aeronautica [aero'nautika] *sf* aeronautics; aviation; (*mil*) air-force. **aeronautico** *agg* aeronautical.

aeroplano [aero'plano] *sm* aeroplane, aircraft. **aeroplano a reazione** jet. **aeroplano di bombardamento** bomber. **aeroplano di combattimento** fighter.

aeroporto [aero'porto] *sm* airport.

aerosol [aero'sɔl] *sm invar* aerosol.

afa ['afa] *sf* oppressive heat.

affabile [af'fabile] *agg* affable. **affabilità** *sf* affability.

affaccendarsi [affattʃen'darsi] v busy oneself. **affaccendato** *agg* busy.

affacciarsi [affat'tʃarsi] v show oneself, appear.

affamato [affa'mato] *agg* starving; (*bramoso*) eager (for). **affamare** v reduce to starvation.

affannare [affan'nare] v worry. **affannarsi** v do one's utmost. **affanno** *sm* (*difficoltà di respiro*) breathlessness; anxiety, worry. **affannoso** *agg* difficult.

affare [af'fare] *sm* affair, business; (*questione*) matter; (*fam*) thing; (*acquisto vantaggioso*) bargain. **affari** *sm pl* (*comm*) business *sing*. **affarista** *s*(*m*+*f*) speculator.

affascinare [affaʃi'nare] v fascinate, charm.

affastellare [affastel'lare] *v* tie in bundles; (*ammucchiare*) pile up; (*frasi, ecc.*) string together.

affaticare [affati'kare] *v* tire, strain.

affatto [af'fatto] *avv* quite; (*con negazione*) at all.

affermare [affer'mare] *v* affirm; assert. **affermarsi** *v* be successful.

afferrare [affer'rare] *v* seize, grab, clutch at.

affettare[1] [affet'tare] *v* affect, pretend. **affettato** *agg* affected; mannered.

affettare[2] [affet'tare] *v* slice. **affettato** *sm* sliced salami *or* ham.

affetto[1] [af'fetto] *sm* affection, feeling. **affettuoso** *agg* affectionate, loving.

affetto[2] [af'fetto] *agg* affected (by); (*med*) suffering (from).

affezionarsi [affetsjo'narsi] *v* become fond (of). **affezionato** *agg* fond, devoted. **affezione** *sf* fondness, affection; (*med*) disorder.

affibbiare [affib'bjare] *v* saddle with.

affidare [affi'dare] *v* entrust. **affidare alla memoria** commit to memory. **affidamento** *sm* trust. **dare affidamento** inspire confidence. **fare affidamento su** rely on.

*__**affiggere** [af'fiddʒere] *v* affix; (*manifesto*) put up.

affilare [affi'lare] *v* sharpen.

affiliare [affi'ljare] *v* (*dir*) foster; (*iscrivere*) enrol.

affinché [affin'ke] *cong* so that, in order that.

affinità [affini'ta] *sf* affinity. **affine** *agg* related. **affini** *sm pl* in-laws *pl*.

affissione [affis'sjone] *sf* bill-posting.

affisso [af'fisso] *agg* exhibited. *sm* poster, bill.

affittare [affit'tare] *v* rent, lease; (*dare in affitto*) let. **affitto** *sm* (*prezzo*) rent; (*locazione*) lease.

*__**affliggere** [af'fliddʒere] *v* afflict. **affliggersi** *v* grieve, worry. **afflizione** *sf* affliction.

*__**affluire** [afflu'ire] *v* flow; (*gente*) flock. **affluente** *sm* (*geog*) tributary. **affluenza** *sf* flow; (*di gente*) influx. **afflusso** *sm* flow.

affogare [affo'gare] *v* drown. **uovo affogato** *sm* poached egg.

affollare [affol'lare] *v* crowd. **affollamento** *sm* (*atto*) crowding; (*folla*) crowd.

affondare [affon'dare] *v* sink.

affrancare [affran'kare] *v* stamp. **affrancatura** *sf* postage.

affranto [af'franto] *agg* distraught.

affresco [af'fresko] *sm* fresco.

affrettare [affret'tare] *v* hurry, speed up.

affrontare [affron'tare] *v* face. **affronto** *sm* affront.

affumicare [affumi'kare] *v* (*annerire*) blacken (with smoke); (*gastr*) smoke; (*snidare*) smoke out. **affumicato** *agg* smoked.

afoso [a'fozo] *agg* sultry.

Africa ['afrika] *sf* Africa. **africano, -a** *s*, *agg* African.

agenda [a'dʒɛnda] *sf* diary.

agente [a'dʒɛnte] *sm* agent. **agente delle tasse** tax inspector. **agente di polizia** police officer.

agenzia [adʒen'tsia] *sf* agency.

agevole [a'dʒevole] *agg* easy. **agevolare** *v* facilitate. **agevolazione** *sf* concession.

agganciare [aggan'tʃare] *v* fasten, hook up.

aggettivo [addʒet'tivo] *sm* adjective.

agghiacciare [aggjat'tʃare] *v* freeze. **far agghiacciare il sangue** make one's blood run cold.

aggiornare [addʒor'nare] *v* bring up to date; (*rinviare*) postpone. **aggiornato** *agg* up-to-date.

aggirarsi [addʒi'rarsi] *v* **aggirarsi su** (*approssimarsi*) be about *or* around.

aggiudicare [addʒudi'kare] *v* award.

*__**aggiungere** [ad'dʒundʒere] *v* add. **aggiungersi** *v* join. **aggiunta** *sf* addition. **aggiuntivo** *agg* additional. **aggiunto** *sm* assistant.

aggiustare [addʒus'tare] *v* repair, adjust; (*ordinare*) tidy, arrange.

aggrappare [aggrap'pare] *v* clutch. **aggrapparsi** *v* cling to.

aggravare [aggra'vare] *v* make worse. **aggravarsi** *v* deteriorate.

aggredire [aggre'dire] *v* attack.

aggregare [aggre'gare] *v* aggregate. **aggregato** *sm*, *agg* aggregate.

aggressione [aggres'sjone] *sf* aggression, attack. **aggressivo** *agg* aggressive. **aggressore** *sm* aggressor, assailant.

aggrottare [aggrot'tare] *v* **aggrottare le ciglia** frown, knit one's brows.

aggruppare [aggrup'pare] *v* group.

agguato [ag'gwato] *sm* ambush, trap. **stare in agguato** lie in wait.

agiato [a'dʒato] *agg* well-off. **agiatezza** *sf* prosperity.

agile ['adʒile] *agg* agile, nimble. **agilità** *sf* agility.

agio ['adʒo] *sm* comfort, ease; (*di tempo*) leisure; (*mec*) play. **sentire a proprio agio** feel at ease.

agire [a'dʒire] *v* act; (*comportarsi*) behave; (*dir*) take legal action.

agitare [adʒi'tare] *v* wave, shake; (*incitare*) stir. **agitato** *agg* agitated, disturbed. **agitatore, -trice** *sm, sf* agitator.

agli [a'ʎi] *prep+art* a gli.

aglio [a'ʎo] *sm* garlic.

agnello [a'ɲello] *sm* lamb.

agnostico [a'ɲostiko], **-a** *s, agg* agnostic.

ago ['ago] *sm* needle. **ago da calza** knitting-needle. **lavoro ad ago** *sm* needlework.

agonia [ago'nia] *sf* agony. **agonizzare** *v* agonize, suffer anguish.

agonismo [ago'nizmo] *sm* fighting spirit.

agopuntura [agopun'tura] *sf* acupuncture.

agosto [a'gosto] *sm* August.

agrario [a'grarjo] *sm* land-owner. *agg* agrarian, agricultural. **riforma agraria** *sf* land reform. **agraria** *sf* agricultural science.

agricoltore [agrikol'tore] *sm* farmer.

agrifoglio [agri'foʎʎo] *sm* holly.

agro ['agro] *agg* sour, sharp, tart.

agrumi [a'grumi] *sm pl* citrus fruit *pl*.

aguzzare [agut'tsare] *v* sharpen.

ahimè [ai'mɛ] *inter* alas!

ai ['ai] *prep+art* a i.

Aia ['aja] *sf* L'Aia The Hague.

airone [ai'rone] *sm* heron.

aiuola [a'jwɔla] *sf* flower-bed.

aiutare [aju'tare] *v* help. **aiuto** *sm* help, aid; assistant.

aizzare [ait'tsare] *v* incite, provoke.

al [al] *prep+art* a il.

ala ['ala] *sf* wing; (*di cappello*) brim. **apertura alare** *sf* wing-span.

alabastro [ala'bastro] *sm* alabaster.

alano [a'lano] *sm* Great Dane.

alba ['alba] *sf* dawn. **albeggiare** *v* dawn.

albatro [al'batro] *sm* albatross.

albergare [alber'gare] *v* give hospitality to; shelter, harbour.

albergo [al'bergo] *sm* hotel. **albergatore** *sm* innkeeper. **alberghiero** *agg* hotel.

albero ['albero] *sm* tree; (*mar*) mast. **albero a camme** camshaft.

albicocca [albi'kɔkka] *sf* apricot. **albicocco** *sm* apricot tree.

albo ['albo] *sm* roll, register; (*tavola*) notice-board. .

album ['album] *sm* album.

alcali [al'kali] *sm* alkali. **alcalino** *agg* alkaline.

alchimia [alki'mia] *sf* alchemy. **alchimista** *sm* alchemist.

alcool ['alkool] *sm* alcohol.

alco(o)lismo [alko(o)'lizmo] *sm* alcoholism. **alco(o)lici** *sm pl* alcoholic drinks *pl*, spirits *pl*. **alco(o)lico** *agg* alcoholic. **alco(o)lizzato, -a** *sm, sf* alcoholic.

alcunché [alkun'ke] *pron* something, anything.

alcuno [al'kuno] *agg* some, any, a few. *pron* anyone, anybody. **alcuni** *pron* some, a few.

alfabeto [alfa'beto] *sm* alphabet.

alfiere¹ [al'fjere] *sm* (*portabandiera*) standard-bearer; (*fig*) forerunner.

alfiere² [al'fjere] *sm* (*scacchi*) bishop.

alfine [al'fine] *avv* in the long run.

alga ['alga] *sf* alga.

algebra ['aldʒebra] *sf* algebra.

aliante [ali'ante] *sm* glider. **aliantista** *s(m+f)* glider-pilot.

alibi ['alibi] *sm* alibi.

alice [a'litʃe] *sf* anchovy.

alienare [alje'nare] *v* alienate. **alienato** *agg* alienated; (*pazzo*) insane. **alienazione** *sf* alienation; (*pazzia*) madness.

alieno [a'ljɛno] *agg* alien, foreign.

alimentare [alimen'tare] *agg* alimentary. *v* feed. **alimentari** *sm pl* foodstuffs *pl*. **alimentazione** *sf* feeding; (*tec*) feed. **alimenti** *sm pl* alimony *sing*. **alimento** *sm* food.

aliquota [a'likwota] *sf* quota, share.

aliscafo [alis'kafo] *sm* hydrofoil.

alito ['alito] *sm* breath.

all' [all] *prep+art* a l'.

alla ['alla] *prep+art* a la.

allacciare [allat'tʃare] *v* tie up, fasten; (*amicizia, relazioni*) establish; (*tec*) connect.

allagare [alla'gare] *v* flood. **allagamento** *sm* flooding.

allargare [allar'gare] *v* broaden; (*sport*) open up.

allarmare [allar'mare] *v* alarm. **allarme** *sm* alarm. **allarmista** *s(m+f)* scaremonger, alarmist. **allarmistico** *agg* alarmist.

alle ['alle] *prep+art* a le.

alleanza [alle'antsa] *sf* alliance. **alleare** *v* ally.

alleato [alle'ato], **-a** *agg* allied. *sm, sf* ally.

allegare¹ [alle'gare] *v* enclose.

allegare² [alle'gare] *v* advance, put forward.

alleggerire [alleddʒe'rire] *v* lighten; (*sofferenza*) ease.

allegoria [allego'ria] *sf* allegory. **allegorico** *agg* allegorical.

allegro [al'legro] *agg* cheerful, merry. *sm* (*musica*) fast movement, allegro. **allegria** *sf* gaiety, fun, cheerfulness.

allenare [alle'nare] *v* train, coach. **allenatore, -trice** *sm, sf* trainer, coach.

allentare [allen'tare] *v* loosen. **allentare il passo** slow down.

allergia [aller'dʒia] *sf* allergy. **allergico** *agg* allergic.

allestire [alles'tire] *v* prepare, get ready; (*teatro*) stage; (*arredare*) fit out, equip. **allestimento** *sm* preparation; staging; fitting out.

allettare [allet'tare] *v* entice, tempt. **allettante** *agg* enticing, tempting.

allevare [alle'vare] *v* (*bambini*) bring up; (*animali*) breed, keep; (*piante*) grow. **allevamento** *sm* bringing up; (*educazione*) upbringing; (*cavalli*) stud farm; (*cani*) kennels *pl*. **allevatore, -trice** *sm, sf* breeder.

alleviare [alle'vjare] *v* relieve, alleviate.

allibratore [allibra'tore] *sm* bookmaker.

allievo [al'ljevo], **-a** *sm, sf* pupil, student; (*apprendista*) trainee. **allievo ufficiale** (*mil*) cadet.

alligatore [alliga'tore] *sm* alligator.

allineare [alline'are] *v* line up; (*adeguare*) adjust. **allineamento** *sm* alignment, coming into line.

allo ['allo] *prep + art* **a lo**.

allocco [al'lokko] *sm* tawny owl.

allodola [al'lɔdola] *sf* lark.

alloggiare [allod'dʒare] *v* house, put up; (*mil*) billet; (*prendere alloggio*) stay, lodge. **alloggio** *sm* accommodation; lodgings *pl*.

allontanare [allonta'nare] *v* move away; (*tener lontano*) keep away; (*pericolo, ecc.*) avert; (*licenziare*) dismiss. **allontanarsi** *v* go away, leave. **allontanamento** *sm* removal.

allora [al'lora] *avv* then; in that case. **da allora** since then, from that time on. **fino allora** until then.

alloro [al'lɔro] *sm* laurel; (*gastr*) bay leaf.

alluce ['allutʃe] *sm* big toe.

allucinazione [allutʃina'tsjone] *sf* hallucination. **allucinare** *v* hallucinate; (*abbagliare*) dazzle.

*alludere [al'ludere] *v* allude, hint (at).

alluminio [allu'minjo] *sm* aluminium.

allungare [allun'gare] *v* lengthen, stretch; (*diluire*) water down; pass. **allungare gli orecchi** strain one's ears. **allungare il muso** (*fam*) make a long face. **allungare la strada** go the long way round. **allungamento** *sm* extension, lengthening.

allusione [allu'zjone] *sf* allusion.

almeno [al'meno] *avv* at least; if only.

Alpi ['alpi] *sf pl* **le Alpi** the Alps *pl*. **alpino** *agg* alpine.

alpinismo [alpi'nizmo] *sm* mountaineering.

alquanto [al'kwanto] *pron, agg* some; a fair amount of. **alquanti** *pron, agg* several; a number of. *avv* somewhat, rather.

alt [alt] *sm, inter* stop.

altalena [alta'lena] *sf* (*sospesa*) swing; (*a bilico*) see-saw; (*fig*) ups and downs *pl*.

altare [al'tare] *sm* altar.

alterare [alte'rare] *v* alter, change; (*falsificare*) forge; (*svisare*) distort; (*turbare*) upset, make angry; (*andare a male*) go off, spoil. **alterazione** *sf* alteration; forgery; deterioration.

alternare [alter'nare] *v* alternate; (*agric*) rotate. **alternarsi** *v* take turns. **alternativa** *sf* alternative. **alternato** *agg* alternating. **alterno** *agg* alternating, alternate.

altero [al'tero] *agg* haughty.

altezza [al'tettsa] *sf* height; (*profondità*) depth; (*di tessuto*) width; (*quota*) altitude; nobility; (*titolo*) Highness. **essere all'altezza di** be equal to, be up to.

altitudine [alti'tudine] *sf* height, altitude.

alto ['alto] *agg* high; (*statura*) tall; (*tessuto*) wide; (*suono forte*) loud; (*suono acuto*) shrill; (*profondo*) deep; (*geog*) northern; (*nobile*) lofty; (*di grado elevato*) high-ranking. *avv* high. *sm* top, upper part. **alti e bassi** ups and downs *pl*.

altoforno [alto'forno] *sm, pl* **altiforni** blast furnace.

altoparlante [altopar'lante] *sm* loudspeaker.

altopiano [alto'pjano] *sm, pl* **altipiani** plateau.

altrettanto [altret'tanto] *pron, agg* as much *or* many (again); (*medesimo*) the same. **altrettanto ... quanto ...** as ... as .... *avv* as, as much.

altri ['altri] *pron* others *pl*, another (person), someone else.

altro ['altro] *agg* other; another; (*in più*) more; (*ulteriore*) further; (*prossimo*) next. *pron* other (one), another (one); (*persona*) somebody else. **cos'altro?** what else? **l'un l'altro** one another, each other. **l'uno e l'altro** both. **nè l'uno nè l'altro** neither. **nessun'altro** nobody else. **nient'altro** nothing else. **non altro** che nothing but. **più che altro** more than anything. **qualcos'altro** something else. **se non altro** at least. **senz'altro** certainly. **tra l'altro** among other things. **tutt'altro!** far from it!

altronde [al'tronde] *avv* **d'altronde** on the other hand, however.

altrove [al'trove] *avv* elsewhere.

altrui [al'trui] *agg invar* other people's, someone else's.

altruista [altru'ista] *s(m+f)* altruist, unselfish person. **altruismo** *sm* altruism, unselfishness. **altruistico** *agg* unselfish, altruistic.

alunno [a'lunno], **-a** *sm, sf* pupil.

alveare [alve'are] *sm* beehive.

alzaia [al'tsaja] *sf* tow-line; (*strada*) tow-path.

alzare [al'tsare] *v* raise, lift; (*raccogliere*) pick up; (*carte da gioco*) cut. **alzarsi** *v* get up, rise. **alzare le spalle** shrug one's shoulders.

amaca [a'maka] *sf* hammock.

amalgamare [amalga'mare] *v* amalgamate, combine. **amalgama** *sm* amalgam.

amante [a'mante] *s(m+f)* lover. *agg* fond (of), keen (on).

amare [a'mare] *v* love, like. **amato** *agg* beloved. **amatore** *sm* lover; (*conoscitore*) connoisseur.

amarena [ama'rɛna] *sf* sour cherry, black cherry.

amaro [a'maro] *agg* bitter; (*doloroso*) painful. *sm* bitterness; (*bibita*) bitters *pl*. **amarezza** *sf* bitterness.

ambasciata [amba'ʃata] *sf* embassy; message. **ambasciatore**, **-trice** *sm, sf* ambassador, ambassadress.

ambedue [ambe'due] *pron, agg* both.

ambidestro [ambi'dɛstro] *agg* ambidextrous.

ambientarsi [ambjen'tarsi] *v* accustom oneself, settle down. **ambiente** *sm* environment, milieu; atmosphere. **temperatura ambiente** *sf* room temperature.

ambiguo [am'biguo] *agg* ambiguous; (*equivoco*) dubious; (*fam*) shady. **ambiguità** *sf* ambiguity; duplicity.

ambito[1] [am'bito] *sm* limits *pl*; sphere.

ambito[2] [am'bito] *agg* longed-for, coveted. **ambire** *v* covet.

ambivalente [ambiva'lɛnte] *agg* ambivalent.

ambizione [ambi'tsjone] *sf* ambition. **ambizioso** *agg* ambitious.

ambo ['ambo] *agg* both.

ambra ['ambra] *sf, agg* amber. **ambra grigia** ambergris.

ambulante [ambu'lante] *agg* wandering. **biblioteca ambulante** *sf* mobile library. **venditore ambulante** *sm* pedlar.

ambulanza [ambu'lantsa] *sf* ambulance; (*infermeria mobile*) field hospital.

ambulatorio [ambula'tɔrjo] *sm* outpatients' department, clinic.

ameba [a'mɛba] *sf* amoeba.

ameno [a'mɛno] *agg* agreeable; (*divertente*) entertaining.

America [a'mɛrika] *sf* America. **americano**, **-a** *s, agg* American.

ametista [ame'tista] *sf* amethyst.

amianto [a'mjanto] *sm* asbestos.

amichevole [ami'kevole] *agg* friendly.

amico [a'miko], **-a** *sm, sf* friend. *agg* friendly. **amicizia** *sf* friendship.

amido ['amido] *sm* starch.

ammaccare [ammak'kare] *v* dent. **ammaccatura** *sf* dent.

ammaestrare [ammaes'trare] *v* teach, train. **ammaestramento** *sm* teaching, training.

ammalarsi [amma'larsi] *v* fall ill.

ammansire [amman'sire] *v* tame, subdue.

ammassare [ammas'sare] *v* amass.

ammazzare [ammat'tsare] *v* kill, murder.

ammenda [am'mɛnda] *sf* (*dir*) fine. **fare ammenda di** make amends for.

***ammettere** [am'mettere] *v* admit; permit; suppose; take for granted. **ammesso che** given that.

ammezzato [ammed'dzato] *agg* mezzanine. *sm* mezzanine floor.

ammiccare [ammik'kare] *v* wink (at).

amministrare [amminis'trare] *v* administer, manage, run. **amministrativo** *agg* administrative. **amministratore**, **-trice** *sm, sf* director. **amministratore delegato** managing director. **amministrazione** *sf* administration, management. **consiglio d'amministrazione** *sm* board of directors.

ammiraglio [ammi'raʎo] *sm* admiral. **ammiragliato** *sm* admiralty.

ammirare [ammi'rare] *v* admire. **ammiratore**, **-trice** *sm*, *sf* admirer, fan. **ammirazione** *sf* admiration. **ammirevole** *agg* admirable.

ammissibile [ammis'sibile] *agg* admissible, acceptable.

ammissione [ammis'sjone] *sf* admission, admittance. **esame d'ammissione** *sm* entrance examination. **tassa d'ammissione** *sf* entrance fee.

ammobiliare [ammobi'ljare] *v* furnish.

ammollare[1] [ammol'lare] *v* soften; (*nell'acqua*) soak.

ammoniaca [ammo'niaka] *sf* ammonia.

ammonire [ammo'nire] *v* warn; reprimand. **ammonimento** *sm* warning; reproof.

ammollare[2] [ammol'lare] *v* let go, slacken.

ammontare [ammon'tare] *sm*, *v* amount.

ammorbidire [ammorbi'dire] *v* soften.

ammortire [ammor'tire] *v* deaden.

ammucchiare [ammuk'kjare] *v* pile up.

ammuffire [ammuf'fire] *v* go mouldy. **ammuffito** *agg* mouldy.

ammutinamento [ammutina'mento] *sm* mutiny.

amnistia [amnis'tia] *sf* amnesty.

amo ['amo] *sm* hook. **abboccare all'amo** swallow the bait.

amorale [amo'rale] *agg* amoral.

amore [a'more] *sm* love; (*persona graziosa*) darling. **amor proprio** self-respect. **per amore di** for the sake of. **amoroso** *agg* loving.

ampère [a'per] *sm invar* ampere, amp.

ampio ['ampjo] *agg* wide, spacious; (*abbondante*) full.

amplificare [amplifi'kare] *v* amplify, enlarge. **amplificatore** *sm* amplifier.

ampolloso [ampol'loso] *agg* pompous.

amputare [ampu'tare] *v* amputate. **amputazione** *sf* amputation.

anacronismo [anakro'nizmo] *sm* anachronism.

anagrafe [a'nagrafe] *sf* register office.

anagramma [ana'gramma] *sm* anagram.

analcolico [anal'kɔliko] *agg* non-alcoholic. *sm* soft drink.

anale [a'nale] *agg* anal.

analfabeta [analfa'bɛta] *agg*, *s*(*m+f*) illiterate. **analfabetismo** *sm* illiteracy.

analgesico [anal'dʒeziko] *agg*, *sm* analgesic.

analizzare [analid'dzare] *v* analyse. **analisi** *sf* analysis (*pl* -ses). **in ultima analisi** when all is said and done. **analista** *s*(*m+f*) analyst. **analitico** *agg* analytic.

analogo [a'nalogo] *agg*, *m pl* -ghi analogous. **analogia** *sf* analogy.

ananas ['ananas] *sm* pineapple.

anarchico [a'narkiko], **-a** *agg* anarchic(al). *sm*, *sf* anarchist. **anarchia** *sf* anarchy.

anatema [ana'tɛma] *sm* anathema.

anatomia [anato'mia] *sf* anatomy. **anatomia patologica** pathology. **anatomico** *agg* anatomical. **anatomista** *s*(*m+f*) anatomist.

anatra ['anatra] *sf* duck. **anatroccolo** *sm* duckling.

anca ['anka] *sf* hip.

anche ['anke] *cong* too, as well, also; (*inoltre*) besides; (*perfino*) even.

ancora[1] [an'kora] *sm* anchor. **ancoraggio** *sm* moorings *pl*. **ancorare** *v* anchor.

ancora[2] [an'kora] *avv* still; (*in frasi negative*) yet; (*di nuovo*) again; (*un altro*) another; (*persino*) even. **ancora un po' a** little more; (*tempo*) a little longer.

***andare** [an'dare] *v* go; (*funzionare*) work, run; (*calzare*) fit; (*essere adatto*) suit; (*dovere*) must be, have to be. **a lungo andare** in the long run. **andare a genio** to one's liking. **andare a piedi** walk. **andare a spasso** go for a walk. **andare avanti** proceed, progress, go on. **andar bene** go well; fit; (*salute*) be well. **andare in bicicletta** cycle. **andare incontro a** go towards, go and meet. **andarsene** go away, leave.

andata [an'data] *sf* **biglietto d'andata** *sm* single ticket.

andirivieni [andiri'vjeni] *sm* coming and going; (*risposta evasiva*) prevarication.

andito ['andito] *sm* passage.

aneddoto [a'nɛddoto] *sm* anecdote.

anelare [ane'lare] *v* pant; (*aspirare*) yearn (for). **anelante** *agg* panting, out of breath.

anello [a'nɛllo] *sm* ring. **anello matrimoniale/di fidanzamento** wedding/engagement ring.

anemia [ane'mia] *sf* anaemia. **anemico** *agg* anaemic.

anemone [a'nɛmone] *sm* anemone.

anestetico [anes'tɛtiko] *agg*, *sm* anaesthetic. **anestesia** *sf* anaesthesia. **anestetista** *s*(*m+f*) anaesthetist.

anfetamina [anfeta'mina] *sf* amphetamine.

anfibio [an'fibjo] *sm*, *agg* amphibian.

angariare [anga'rjare] *v* harass.

angelica [an'dʒelika] *sf* angelica.

angelo ['andʒelo] *sm* angel; (*pesce*) angelfish. **angelo custode** guardian angel. **angelico** *agg* angelic.

anglicano [angli'kano], **-a** *s*, *agg* Anglican. **anglicanesimo** *sm* Anglicanism.

angolo ['angolo] *sm* corner; (*geom, ecc.*) angle. **angolare** *agg* angular. **pietra angolare** *sf* cornerstone.

angoscia [an'goʃa] *sf* anxiety, anguish. **angosciare** *v* distress. **angoscioso** *agg* distressed; distressing.

anguilla [an'gwilla] *sf* eel.

anguria [an'gurja] *sf* water-melon.

anice ['anitʃe] *sm* aniseed.

anima ['anima] *sf* soul; (*parte centrale*) core; (*fervore*) heart; (*di arma da fuoco*) bore. **rodersi l'anima** torment oneself.

animale [ani'male] *sm* animal; (*persona*) brute. *agg* animal.

animare [ani'mare] *v* animate; stimulate. **animato** *agg* animate; (*vivace*) spirited. **disegno** *or* **cartone animato** *sm* cartoon. **essere animato da** be inspired by.

animo ['animo] *sm* mind; (*cuore, coraggio*) heart; (*carattere*) nature. **farsi animo** pluck up courage. **in fondo all'animo** at the back of one's mind. **mettersi l'animo in pace** resign oneself. **stato d'animo** *sm* mood.

animosità [animozi'ta] *sf* animosity, spite.

annacquare [annak'kware] *v* water down.

annaffiare [annaf'fjare] *v* water.

annali [an'nali] *sm pl* annals *pl*.

annata [an'nata] *sf* year; (*raccolto*) crop; (*di vino*) vintage; (*importo*) income.

annebbiare [anneb'bjare] *v* become foggy; (*fig*) dim, cloud.

annegare [anne'gare] *v* drown. **annegamento** *sm* drowning.

*annettere [an'nettere] *v* (*pol*) annex; attach. **annesso** *or* **annexe**, appendage.

annichilare [anniki'lare] *v* annihilate, destroy.

annientare [annjen'tare] *v* annihilate, destroy. **annientamento** *sm* (*total*) destruction.

anniversario [anniver'sarjo] *sm*, *agg* anniversary.

anno ['anno] *sm* year. **anno bisestile** leap-year. **anno luce** light-year.

annodare [anno'dare] *v* knot *or* tie (together).

annoiare [anno'jare] *v* bore.

annotare [anno'tare] *v* note, jot down; (*postillare*) annotate.

annoverare [annove'rare] *v* number; enumerate.

annuale [annu'ale] *agg* annual, yearly.

annuario [annu'arjo] *sm* yearbook.

annuire [annu'ire] *v* nod in agreement; (*acconsentire*) agree.

annullare [annul'lare] *v* cancel; (*matrimonio*) annul; (*legge*) repeal. **annullamento** *sm* cancellation; annulment; repeal.

annunciare [annun'tʃare] *v* announce; (*precorrere*) herald. **annunciatore, -trice** *sm*, *sf* announcer. **annuncio** *sm* announcement, notice; (*pubblicità*) advertisement.

Annunciazione [annuntʃa'tsjone] *sf* Annunciation.

annuo ['annuo] *agg* yearly, annual.

annusare [annu'zare] *v* sniff; (*intuire*) smell.

annuvolare [annuvo'lare] *v* cloud (over).

ano ['ano] *sm* anus.

anodo ['anodo] *sm* anode.

anomalia [anoma'lia] *sf* anomaly. **anomalo** *agg* anomalous.

anonimo [a'nonimo] *agg* anonymous. **società anonima** *sf* limited company.

anormale [anor'male] *agg* abnormal. **anormalità** *sf* abnormality.

ansare [an'sare] *v* puff, pant.

ansia ['ansja] *sf* anxiety; (*angoscia*) dread; (*desiderio*) longing. **ansioso** *agg* anxious; longing; (*impaziente*) restless.

antagonismo [antago'nizmo] *sm* antagonism. **antagonista** *s(m+f)* adversary.

antartico [an'tartiko] *agg* antarctic.

antenato [ante'nato] *sm* forefather, ancestor.

antenna [an'tenna] *sf* (*zool*) antenna; (*radio, TV*) aerial.

anteprima [ante'prima] *sf* preview.

anteriore [ante'rjore] *agg* (*nel tempo*) preceding, previous; (*nello spazio*) front, fore.

antiabbagliante [antiabba'ʎante] *agg* anti-dazzle. **fari antiabbaglianti** *sm pl* dipped headlights *pl*.

antiaereo [antia'ereo] *agg* anti-aircraft.
antibiotico [antibi'ɔtiko] *agg*, *sm* antibiotic.
anticamera [anti'kamera] *sf* lobby, waiting-room. **fare anticamera** be kept waiting. **far fare anticamera** keep waiting.
antichità [antiki'ta] *sf* antiquity; (*oggetto*) antique.
anticiclone [antitʃi'klone] *sm* anticyclone.
anticipare [antitʃi'pare] *v* anticipate; advance; pay in advance. **anticipato** *agg* advanced; (*prima del tempo*) in advance. **anticipazione** *sf* anticipation; (*soldi*) advance.
anticipo [an'titʃipo] *sm* advance, deposit. **in anticipo** early; (*orologio*) fast.
antico [an'tiko] *agg*, *m pl* **-chi** old; ancient; antique. **all'antica** *agg* old-fashioned.
anticoncezionale [antikontʃetsjo'nale] *agg*, *sm* contraceptive.
anticonformista [antikonfor'mista] *agg*, *s(m+f)* non-conformist.
anticongelante [antikondʒe'lante] *sm* anti-freeze.
anticorpo [anti'kɔrpo] *sm* antibody.
antidoto [an'tidoto] *sm* antidote.
antifecondativo [antifekonda'tivo] *sm*, *agg* contraceptive.
antifurto [anti'furto] *sm* burglar alarm.
antilope [an'tilope] *sf* antelope.
antincendio [antin'tʃendjo] *agg* equipaggiamento **antincendio** fire-fighting equipment.
antiorario [antio'rarjo] *agg* anti-clockwise.
antipasto [anti'pasto] *sm* hors d'oeuvre, starter.
antipatia [antipa'tia] *sf* dislike, antipathy. **prendere in antipatia** take a dislike to. **antipatico** *agg* disagreeable, unpleasant.
antiquario [anti'kwarjo] *sm* antique dealer. **antiquariato** *sm* antique trade; (*negozio*) antique shop.
antiquato [anti'kwato] *agg* (*fuori moda*) old-fashioned; (*disusato*) obsolete.
antisemita [antise'mita] *s(m+f)* anti-Semite. *agg* anti-Semitic. **antisemitismo** *sm* anti-Semitism.
antisettico [anti'settiko] *sm*, *agg* antiseptic.
antisociale [antiso'tʃale] *agg* antisocial.
antistaminico [antista'miniko] *sm* antihistamine.
antitesi [an'titezi] *sf* antithesis (*pl* -ses).

antologia [antolo'dʒia] *sf* anthology.
antro ['antro] *sm* cave.
antropologia [antropolo'dʒia] *sf* anthropology. **antropologico** *agg* anthropological. **antropologo**, **-a** *sm*, *sf* anthropologist.
anulare [anu'lare] *agg* annular, ring-shaped. *sm* ring-finger.
anzi ['antsi] *cong* on the contrary; (*invece*) as a matter of fact; (*o meglio*) or better, better still; (*di più*) indeed.
anziano [an'tsjano], **-a** *agg* elderly; aged; senior. *sm*, *sf* elderly person.
anziché [antsi'ke] *cong* (*piuttosto*) rather than; (*invece*) instead of.
anzitutto [antsi'tutto] *avv* above all, first of all.
apatia [apa'tia] *sf* apathy.
ape ['ape] *sf* bee.
aperitivo [aperi'tivo] *sm* aperitif.
aperto [a'perto] *agg* open; (*pronto*) quick. **all'aperto** in the open, outdoors.
apice ['apitʃe] *sm* apex, top.
apocrifo [a'pɔkrifo] *agg* apocryphal.
apolide [a'polide] *agg* stateless.
apostolo [a'postolo] *sm* apostle. **apostolico** *agg* apostolic.
apostrofo [a'postrofo] *sm* apostrophe.
appagare [appa'gare] *v* satisfy.
appalto [ap'palto] *sm* contract.
appannare [appan'nare] *v* (*vista*) dim, blur; (*vetri*) mist up.
apparato [appa'rato] *sm* show, display; (*tec*) machinery; (*biol*) system, apparatus. **apparato scenico** set.
apparecchiare [apparek'kjare] *v* prepare. **apparecchiare la tavola** lay the table. **apparecchio** *sm* set; device, instrument, appliance; (*fam*) (aero)plane; (*fam*) (tele)phone.
apparenza [appa'rentsa] *sf* appearance. **apparente** *agg* apparent. **apparentemente** *avv* apparently; (*a prima vista*) to all appearances.
*****apparire** [appa'rire] *v* appear; (*sembrare*) look, seem. **appariscente** *agg* striking.
appartamento [apparta'mento] *sm* flat, apartment.
appartare [appar'tare] *v* put aside. **appartarsi** *v* withdraw. **appartato** *agg* secluded.
*****appartenere** [apparte'nere] *v* belong.
appassionare [appassjo'nare] *v* move, arouse passion; arouse interest. **appassionarsi per** be very fond of.

appena [ap'pena] *avv* barely, hardly; *(soltanto)* only; *(solo un po')* only just; *(da poco)* just (recently). *cong* **appena ... che ...** no sooner ... than ....

*__appendere__ [ap'pɛndere] *v* hang.

appendice [appen'ditʃe] *sm* appendix. **appendicite** *sf* appendicitis.

appetito [appe'tito] *sm* appetite. **aver appetito** have an appetite, be hungry. **appetitoso** *agg* appetizing; tempting.

appianare [appja'nare] *v* level; *(dissidio, ecc.)* smooth (over), settle.

appiccare [appik'kare] *v (appendere)* hang; *(cominciare)* set off. **appiccar fuoco** a set fire to.

appiccicare [appittʃi'kare] *v* stick. **appiccicaticcio** *agg* sticky.

appigionare [appidʒo'nare] *v* let.

appioppare [appjop'pare] *v* give; *(affibbiare)* saddle with.

appisolarsi [appizo'larsi] *v* doze.

applaudire [applau'dire] *v* applaud. **applauso** *sm* applause.

applicare [appli'kare] *v* apply. **applicazione** *sf* application; concentration; *(dir)* enforcement. **applique** *sf, pl* -s wallbracket.

appoggiare [appod'dʒare] *v* lean; *(posare)* lay; *(fondare)* base; *(favorire)* support. **appoggio** *sm* support.

*__apporre__ [ap'porre] *v* affix, append.

apportare [appor'tare] *v* bring about, produce. **apporto** *sm* contribution.

apposito [ap'pozito] *agg* special; *(adatto)* suitable. **appositamente** *avv* suitably; *(apposta)* deliberately; *(espressamente)* specially.

apposta [ap'posta] *avv* deliberately, on purpose, specially. *agg invar* special.

*__apprendere__ [ap'prɛndere] *v* learn. **apprendista** *s(m + f)* apprentice, learner. **apprendistato** *sm* apprenticeship.

apprensione [appren'sjone] *sf* apprehension, concern. **apprensivo** *agg* apprehensive, uneasy.

appresso [ap'presso] *avv* close by, at hand; *(con sè)* with one; *(in sequito)* later. *prep* close to; *(dietro)* close behind. *agg invar* following.

apprestare [appres'tare] *v* prepare; *(porgere)* bring.

apprezzare [appret'tsare] *v* appreciate. **apprezzamento** *sm* appreciation; *(giudizio)* opinion; *(osservazione)* remark.

approfittare [approfit'tare] *v* profit (by), take advantage (of).

approfondire [approfon'dire] *v* deepen; *(studiare)* probe, go into.

approntare [appron'tare] *v* get ready.

approssimativo [approssima'tivo] *agg* approximate, rough. **approssimare** *v* approximate. **approssimarsi** (a) approach. **approssimazione** *sf* approximation.

approvare [appro'vare] *v* approve (of). **approvazione** *sf* approval.

appuntamento [appunta'mento] *sm* appointment; *(fam)* date.

appunto¹ [ap'punto] *sm* note; *(osservazione)* remark. **muovere** or **fare un appunto** a blame, find fault with.

appunto² [ap'punto] *avv* precisely, just.

appurare [appu'rare] *v* verify.

aprile [a'prile] *sm* April.

*__aprire__ [a'prire] *v* open; *(luce, radio, ecc.)* switch on. **apribottiglie** *sm invar* bottle-opener. **apriscatole** *sm invar* tin-opener.

aquila ['akwila] *sf* eagle. **aquilone** *sm* kite.

Arabia [a'rabja] *sf* Arabia. **arabo, -a** *s*, *agg* Arab; *sm (lingua)* Arabic.

arachide [a'rakide] *sf* ground-nut, peanut.

aragosta [ara'gosta] *sf* lobster.

araldo [a'raldo] *sm* herald. **araldica** *sf* heraldry. **araldico** *agg* heraldic.

arancio [a'rantʃo] *sm* orange tree. *agg invar (colore)* orange. **arancia** *sf* orange. **arancione** *sm, agg invar* orange.

arare [a'rare] *v* plough. **aratro** *sm* plough.

arazzo [a'rattso] *sm* tapestry.

arbitrare [arbi'trare] *v* arbitrate; *(sport)* referee. **arbitro** *sm* referee, umpire.

arbitrio [ar'bitrjo] *sm* will. **arbitrario** *agg* arbitrary.

arbusto [ar'busto] *sm* bush.

arca ['arka] *sf* ark.

arcaico [ar'kaiko] *agg* archaic.

arcata [ar'kata] *sf* arcade; *(di ponte)* span; *(anat)* arch.

archeologia [arkeolo'dʒia] *sf* archaeology. **archeologico** *agg* archaeological. **archeologo, -a** *sm, sf* archaeologist.

archetipo [ar'kɛtipo] *sm* archetype. *agg* archetypal.

archetto [ar'ketto] *sm* bow.

architetto [arki'tetto] *sm* architect. **architettonico** *agg* architectural. **architettura** *sf* architecture.

archivio [ar'kivjo] *sm* archives *pl*; *(comm)* file. **archiviare** *v* (place on) file;

(*questione*, *ecc.*) pigeon-hole. **archivista** s(m + f) archivist; (*comm*) filing clerk.

arciduca [artʃi'duka] sm archduke.

arciere [ar'tʃɛre] sm archer.

arcigno [ar'tʃiɲo] agg sullen.

arcipelago [artʃi'pɛlago] sm, pl -**ghi** archipelago.

arcivescovo [artʃi'veskovo] sm archbishop. **arcivescovado** sm archbishop's palace; (*dignità*) archbishopric.

arco ['arko] sm bow; (*anat*, *arch*) arch; (*geom*) arc. **quartetto d'archi** sm string quartet. **strumenti ad arco** sm pl strings pl. **tiro all'arco** sm archery.

arcobaleno ['arkobaleno] sm rainbow.

arcuato [arku'ato] agg arched. **dalle gambe arcuate** bow-legged.

***ardere** ['ardere] v burn. **ardente** agg burning; (*colore*) fiery; (*appassionato*) ardent.

ardesia [ar'dɛzja] sf slate.

ardire [ar'dire] v dare. **ardito** agg bold, daring; risky. **ardore** sm (*calore*) heat; passion.

arduo ['arduo] agg arduous, laborious; (*ripido*) steep.

area ['area] sf area; (*terreno*) land, ground.

arena[1] [a'rena] sf arena.

arena[2] [a'rena] sf (*sabbia*) sand.

arenaria [are'narja] sf sandstone.

arenarsi [are'narsi] v run aground; (*fermarsi*) come to a standstill.

argano ['argano] sm winch; (*mar*) capstan.

argentina [ardʒen'tina] sf polo-neck sweater.

argento [ar'dʒento] sm silver. **argento vivo** quicksilver. v silver(-plate). **argentare** agg silver-plated; (*colore*) silver. **argenteria** sf silver, silverware.

argilla [ar'dʒilla] sf clay.

argine ['ardʒine] sm embankment; barrier. **arginare** v stem, check.

argomento [argo'mento] sm argument, reason; (*materia*) subject, topic. **argomentare** v discuss, argue.

arguto [ar'guto] agg (*spiritoso*) witty; shrewd. **arguzia** sf wit, humour; shrewdness.

aria ['arja] sf air; (*aspetto*) look; (*musica*) tune; (*opera*) aria. **all'aria aperta** in the open, out-of-doors. **corrente d'aria** sf draught. **darsi delle arie** put on airs.

arido ['arido] agg dry, arid.

arieggiare [arjed'dʒare] v air.

ariete [a'rjɛte] sm ram. **Ariete** sm Aries.

aringa [a'ringa] sf herring.

arioso [a'rjozo] agg airy.

aristocratico [aristo'kratiko], -**a** sm, sf aristocrat. agg aristocratic. **aristocrazia** sf aristocracy.

aritmetica [arit'metika] sf arithmetic. **aritmetico** agg arithmetic(al).

armadio [ar'madjo] sm cupboard; (*per abiti*) wardrobe.

armare [ar'mare] v arm; (*mar*) rig up; reinforce. **armarsi** v take up arms; (*provvedersi*) arm oneself. **arma** sf, pl -**i** weapon, arms pl; (*mil*) force. **armamento** sm armament; (*tec*) equipment.

armata [ar'mata] sf army; (*flotta*) fleet. **armato** [ar'mato] agg armed; equipped.

armatura [arma'tura] sf scaffolding; (*elett*) armature.

armonia [armo'nia] sf harmony. **in armonia con** in keeping with. **armonica** sf harmonics. **armonica a bocca** mouthorgan. **armonico** agg harmonic. **armonioso** agg melodious. **armonizzare** v harmonize; (*colori*, *ecc.*) match.

arnese [ar'neze] sm tool; gadget. **arnese da cucina** kitchen utensil. **bene/male in arnese** in good/poor shape.

arnia ['arnja] sf beehive.

aroma [a'roma] sm aroma; aromatic herb, spice. **aromatico** agg aromatic.

arpa ['arpa] sf harp. **arpeggio** sm arpeggio. **arpista** s(m + f) harpist.

arpione [ar'pjone] sm hook; (*arma*) harpoon; (*cardine*) hinge.

arrabbiarsi [arrab'bjarsi] v become angry or annoyed. **far arrabbiare** annoy, anger. **arrabbiato** agg angry; (*cane*) rabid; (*furioso*) enraged.

arraffare [arraf'fare] v snatch.

arrampicarsi [arrampi'karsi] v climb (up). **arrampicata** sf climbing, climb.

arrangiare [arran'dʒare] v (*aggiustare*) mend; improvise; (*fam*) fix; (*musica*) arrange. **arrangiarsi** v manage; come to an agreement.

arrecare [arre'kare] v cause, bring about.

arredare [arre'dare] v furnish. **arredamento** sm furnishing; (*mobilio*) furniture. **arredatore**, -**trice** sm, sf interior decorator; (*cinema*) set decorator.

***arrendersi** [ar'rendersi] v surrender, give oneself up. **arrendevole** agg yielding.

arrestare [arres'tare] v stop; (dir) arrest. **arresto** sm stop, stoppage; arrest. **arresto cardiaco** heart failure.

arretrato [arre'trato] agg behind; (non fatto) outstanding, overdue; (non sviluppato) backward; (numero di rivista, ecc.) back. **arretrati** sm pl arrears pl; (di paga) back-pay sing.

arricchire [arrik'kire] v enrich. **arricchirsi** become rich.

arricciare [arrit'tʃare] v curl. **arricciare il naso** pull a face. **arricciare il pelo** bristle.

arringa [ar'ringa] sf address.

arrischiare [arris'kjare] v risk, venture. **arrischiato** agg risky; (imprudente) rash.

arrivare [arri'vare] v arrive; succeed; (capitare) happen. **arrivare a** (riuscire) manage to; (giungere) reach, get to; (essere ridotto a) be reduced to. **arrivare fino a** reach, get as far as. **ben arrivato!** welcome! **arrivo** sm arrival.

arrivederci [arrive'dertʃi] inter goodbye! (fam) see you!

arrogante [arro'gante] agg arrogant. **arroganza** sf arrogance.

arrossire [arros'sire] v blush.

arrostire [arros'tire] v roast. **arrosto** sm, agg invar roast.

arrotare [arro'tare] v sharpen. **arrotino** sm knife-grinder.

arrotolare [arroto'lare] v roll up.

arrotondare [arroton'dare] v round off.

arroventato [arroven'tato] agg red-hot.

arruffare [arruf'fare] v ruffle; (confondere) muddle.

arrugginirsi [arruddʒi'nirsi] v rust. **arrugginito** agg rusty.

arruolare [arrwo'lare] v enlist.

arsenale [arse'nale] sm arsenal; (mar) (naval) dockyard.

arsenico [ar'seniko] sm arsenic.

arso [ar'so] agg burnt, parched.

arte ['arte] sf art; (attività) craft; (abilità) skill; (astuzia) cunning. **ad arte** on purpose; (con artifizio) cunningly. **artefice** sm craftsman.

arteria [ar'teria] sf artery. **arteria di traffico** main road, thoroughfare.

artico [ar'tiko] agg arctic.

articolare [artiko'lare] v articulate; (suddividere) split up.

articolo [ar'tikolo] sm article. **articoli** sm pl goods pl. **articolo di cronaca** news item. **articolo di fondo** leading article, leader.

artificiale [artifi'tʃale] agg artificial.

artificio [arti'fitʃo] sm stratagem, device. **fuochi d'artificio** sm pl fireworks pl.

artigiano [arti'dʒano] sm craftsman. **artigianato** sm craftsmanship; (prodotti) handicraft; (classe) craftsmen pl.

artiglieria [artiʎe'ria] sf artillery.

artiglio [ar'tiʎo] sm claw, talon. **cadere negli artigli di** fall into the clutches of.

artista [ar'tista] s(m+f) artist. **artistico** artistic.

arto ['arto] sm limb.

artrite [ar'trite] sf arthritis.

asbesto [az'besto] sm asbestos.

ascella [a'ʃella] sf armpit.

*ascendere [a'ʃendere] v rise.

ascensore [aʃen'sore] sm elevator.

ascesa [a'ʃeza] sf also **ascensione** ascent, climb.

ascesso [a'ʃesso] sm abscess.

asceta [a'ʃeta] s(m+f) ascetic. **ascetico** agg ascetic. **ascetismo** sm asceticism.

ascia ['aʃa] sf axe.

asciugare [aʃu'gare] v dry. **asciugamano** sm towel. **asciugatoio** sm bath towel. **carta asciugante** sf blotting-paper.

asciutto [a'ʃutto] agg dry. **essere all'asciutto** (salvo) be safe; (al verde) be broke. **pasta asciutta** sf pasta.

ascoltare [askol'tare] v listen (to); heed, pay attention (to); (lezioni, messa, ecc.) attend. **ascoltatore, -trice** sm, sf listener. **dare ascolto a** pay attention to.

asfalto [as'falto] sm asphalt. **asfaltare** v asphalt.

Asia ['azja] sf Asia. **asiatico** sm, agg Asian, Asiatic.

asilo [a'zilo] sm refuge, shelter; (pol) asylum. **asilo infantile** kindergarten, nursery school. **dare asilo a** shelter.

asino ['azino] sm ass, donkey. **asineria** sf stupidity. **asinino** agg asinine. **tosse asinina** sf whooping cough.

asma ['azma] sm asthma. **asmatico** agg asthmatic.

asola ['azola] sf buttonhole.

asparago [as'parago] sm asparagus.

aspettare [aspet'tare] v await, wait (for). **aspettare con desiderio** look forward to. **aspettare un bambino** be expecting a baby. **aspettativa** sf expectation; (licenza) leave of absence.

aspetto¹ [as'petto] sm appearance, look. **sotto questo aspetto** from this point of view.

aspetto² [as'petto] *sm* waiting. **sala d'aspetto** *sf* waiting-room.

aspirare [aspi'rare] *v* inhale, breathe in; (*desiderare*) aspire. **aspirapolvere** *sm invar* vacuum cleaner.

aspirina [aspi'rina] *sf* aspirin.

asportare [aspor'tare] *v* remove, take away.

aspro ['aspro] *agg* sour, tart; (*vino*) rough; (*suono*) harsh; (*clima*) raw; (*fig*) hard. **asprezza** *sf* sourness; harshness.

assaggiare [assad'dʒare] *v* taste, try. **assaggio** *sm* taste; (*campione*) sample.

assai [as'sai] *avv* very; (*very*) much; (*abbastanza*) enough.

assalire [assa'lire] *v* assail, attack.

assalto [as'salto] *sm* attack.

assassinare [assassi'nare] *v* murder. **assassinio** *sm* murder. **assassino, -a** *sm, sf* murderer, murderess.

asse¹ [asse] *sm* axis; (*mec*) axle.

asse² ['asse] *sf* (*tavola*) board, plank. **asse da stiro** ironing-board.

assediare [asse'djare] *v* besiege. **assedio** *sm* siege. **stato d'assedio** *sm* state of emergency.

assegnare [asse'ɲare] *v* assign, allot. **assegnazione** *sf* allocation.

assegno [as'seɲo] *sm* check. **assegno circolare** banker's draft. **assegno in bianco** blank check. **assegno sbarrato** crossed check. **assegno turistico** traveller's check.

assemblea [assem'blɛa] *sf* assembly, meeting.

assenso [as'sɛnso] *sm* assent, agreement.

assente [as'sɛnte] *agg* absent. **assentarsi** *v* absent oneself, stay away. **assenteismo** *sm* absenteeism. **assenza** *sf* absence; (*mancanza*) lack.

assentire [assen'tire] *v* assent, approve.

asserire [asse'rire] *v* assert, affirm. **asserzione** *sf* assertion, statement.

assessore [asses'sore] *sm* (*dir*) assessor; (*comunale*) councillor.

assestare [asses'tare] *v* arrange, settle.

assetato [asse'tato] *agg* thirsty.

assettare [asset'tare] *v* tidy, put in order.

assicurare [assiku'rare] *v* assure; (*dir*) insure; (*rendere certo*) ensure; (*procurare*) secure; (*lettera*) register. **assicurarsi** *v* take out insurance. **assicuratore** *sm* underwriter. **assicurazione** *sf* insurance.

assiduo [as'siduo] *agg* assiduous.

assieme [as'sjeme] *avv* together.

assieparsi [assje'parsi] *v* crowd (round).

assillare [assil'lare] *v* pester.

assimilare [assimi'lare] *v* assimilate. **assimilazione** *sf* assimilation.

Assise [as'size] *sf* **corte d'Assise** *sf* Assizes *pl*.

assistente [assis'tɛnte] *s(m+f)* assistant; (*universitario*) lecturer; (*di volo*) steward, stewardess. **assistente sociale** social worker. **assistenza** *sf* assistance; (*sociale*) welfare.

***assistere** [as'sistere] *v* (*aiutare*) assist, help; be present at; (*sport*) watch; (*lezione*) attend.

asso ['asso] *sm* ace; champion. **piantare in asso** leave in the lurch.

associare [asso'tʃare] *v* associate, join. **associarsi** *v* join; become a partner *or* member. **associazione** *sf* association, society; (*comm*) partnership.

assoggettare [assodʒet'tare] *v* subject.

assoluto [asso'luto] *agg* absolute, complete.

***assolvere** [as'sɔlvere] *v* (*rel*) absolve; (*dir*) discharge, acquit. **assoluzione** *sf* absolution; discharge, acquittal. **assolvimento** *sm* fulfilment.

assomigliare [assomiʎ'ʎare] *v* resemble.

assonnato [asson'nato] *agg* sleepy; (*torpido*) sluggish.

assopirsi [asso'pirsi] *v* nod off; calm *or* cool down.

assorbire [assor'bire] *v* absorb. **assorbente** *agg* absorbent. **assorbente (igienico)** *sm* sanitary towel. **carta assorbente** *sf* blotting-paper.

assordare [assor'dare] *v* deafen; (*attutire un suono*) muffle.

assortire [assor'tire] *v* sort out. **assortimento** *sm* assortment.

***assuefare** [assue'fare] *v* accustom.

***assumere** [as'sumere] *v* assume; (*personale*) take on, engage; (*procurarsi*) obtain.

assunzione [assun'tsjone] *sf* engagement; (*di un obbligo*) undertaking; (*elevazione*) ascent; (*filos*) assumption. **Assunzione** *sf* (*rel*) Assumption.

assurdo [as'surdo] *agg* absurd, preposterous. *sm* absurdity.

asta ['asta] *sf* pole; (*mec*) rod; (*scrittura*) stroke. **a mezz'asta** at half-mast. **vendita all'asta** *sf* auction.

astante [as'tante] *s(m+f)* bystander.

astemio [as'tɛmjo], **-a** *sm, sf* teetotaller. *agg* teetotal.

*°**astenersi** [aste'nersi] *v* abstain, refrain.

asterisco [aste'risko] *sm* asterisk.

astinenza [asti'nɛntsa] *sf* abstinence.

astio [l'astjo] *sm* rancour, resentment. **portar astio** bear a grudge.

*°**astrarre** [as'trarre] *v* abstract. **astratto** *sm, agg* abstract. **astrazione** *sf* abstraction.

astro [l'astro] *sm* star.

astrologia [astrolo'dʒia] *sf* astrology. **astrologico** *agg* astrological. **astrologo, -a** *sm, sf* astrologer.

astronauta [astro'nauta] *s(m+f)* astronaut.

astronomia [astrono'mia] *sf* astronomy. **astronomico** *agg* astronomic(al). **astronomo, -a** *sm, sf* astronomer.

astuccio [as'tuttʃo] *sm* case.

astuto [as'tuto] *agg* astute, shrewd. **astuzia** *sf* shrewdness, cunning; *(azione)* trick.

Atene [a'tɛne] *sf* Athens. **ateniese** *s(m+f)*, *agg* Athenian.

ateo ['ateo], **-a** *sm, sf* atheist. *agg* atheistic.

atlante [at'lante] *sm* atlas.

atlantico [at'lantiko] *agg* Atlantic.

atleta [at'lɛta] *s(m+f)* athlete. **atletica** *sf* athletics. **atletico** *agg* athletic.

atmosfera [atmos'fɛra] *sf* atmosphere. **atmosferico** *agg* atmospheric.

atomo ['atomo] *sm* atom. **atomico** *agg* atomic.

atrio ['atrjo] *sm* (entrance) hall, lobby.

atroce [a'trotʃe] *agg* dreadful, terrible; *(feroce)* cruel. **atrocità** *sf* atrocity.

attaccare [attak'kare] *v* attach, fasten; *(appendere)* hang (up); *(incollare)* stick (on); apply; pass on; *(assalire, corrodere)* attack; *(iniziare)* begin. **attaccabottoni** *s(m+f) invar (fam)* bore. **attaccabrighe** *s(m+f) invar (fam)* troublemaker. **attaccapanni** *sm (gruccia)* coat-hanger; *(mobilia)* coat-rack. **attaccar briga** *or* **lite** pick a quarrel. **attaccaticcio** *agg* sticky. **attacco** *sm* attack; *(inizio)* opening; *(giuntura)* joint, fastening; *(elett)* plug.

attecchire [attek'kire] *v (radicare)* take root; *(diffondersi)* catch on.

atteggiare [atted'dʒare] *v* assume. **atteggiarsi** *v* pose. **atteggiamento** *sm* attitude, expression.

*°**attendere** [at'tɛndere] *v* await, wait (for); *(dedicarsi)* devote oneself to, look after. **attendibile** *agg* reliable, trustworthy.

*°**attenersi** [atte'nersi] *v* **attenersi a** keep to.

attentato [atten'tato] *sm* attack; attempted murder *or* assassination.

attento [at'tɛnto] *agg* attentive, alert; careful. **stare attento** pay attention to, mind. *inter* careful! mind! look out!

attenzione [atten'tsjone] *sf* attention, care. **fare attenzione a** pay attention to.

atterrare [atter'rare] *v (di aereo)* land; *(gettare a terra)* knock down. **atterraggio** *sm* landing.

attesa [at'teza] *sf* wait; *(aspettativa)* expectation.

attestare [attes'tare] *v* certify, attest. **attestato** *sm* certificate, testimonial.

attiguo [at'tiguo] *agg* adjoining.

attimo [l'attimo] *sm* instant, moment.

attirare [atti'rare] *v* attract, draw.

attitudine¹ [atti'tudine] *sf (disposizione)* aptitude, bent.

attitudine² [atti'tudine] *sf* attitude.

attivare [atti'vare] *v* activate, bring into action.

attivo [at'tivo] *agg* active; *(diligente)* busy. **bilancio attivo** *sm* credit balance. *sm* asset.

attizzare [attit'tsare] *v* poke; *(fig)* stir up.

atto¹ ['atto] *agg* suitable, fit.

atto² ['atto] *sm* action, act; gesture; *(dir)* deed. **atto di accusa** indictment. **atto di citazione** summons. **atto di nascita/morte** birth/death certificate. **atto matrimoniale** marriage certificate. **dare atto** give notice. **in atto** in progress.

attonito [at'tonito] *agg* astonished.

attorcigliare [attortʃiʎare] *v* twist.

attore [at'tore] *sm* actor; *(dir)* plaintiff.

attorniare [attor'njare] *v* surround.

attorno [at'torno] *avv* round, around, about. **guardarsi attorno** look round; *(fig)* be wary. **qui attorno** hereabouts.

*°**attrarre** [at'trarre] *v* attract. **attrattiva** *sf* attraction, fascination. **attrazione** *sf* attraction.

attraversare [attraver'sare] *v* cross; go through. **attraversamento** *sm* crossing.

attrezzo [at'trettso] *sm* tool, appliance. **attrezzi** *sm pl* equipment; kitchen utensils *pl*; *(teatro)* props *pl*. **attrezzare** *v* equip; furnish. **attrezzatura** *sf* equipment.

attribuire [attribu'ire] *v* ascribe, attribute; (*assegnare*) award. **attributo** *sm* attribute.

attrice [at'tritʃe] *sf* actress.

attrito [at'trito] *sm* friction.

attuale [attu'ale] *agg* present, current; (*valido*) topical; (*filos*) actual. **attualmente** *avv* at present.

attualità [attuali'ta] *sf* topicality. *sf pl* news *sing*, current events *pl*. **di attualità** topical; (*di moda*) fashionable. **tornare di attualità** come back into fashion.

attuare [attu'are] *v* carry out, put into effect. **attuarsi** *v* come true, be fulfilled.

attutire [attu'tire] *v* mitigate; (*suono*) muffle.

audace [au'datʃe] *agg* daring, bold; risky, rash. **audacia** *sf* boldness, daring.

audiovisivo [audjovi'zivo] *agg* audio-visual.

auditorio [audi'tɔrjo] *sm* auditorium, studio.

audizione [audi'tsjone] *sf* audition; (*dir*) hearing.

augurare [augu'rare] *v* wish. **augurarsi** *v* hope. **augurio** *sm* wish; (*presagio*) omen.

aula ['aula] *sf* classroom; (*università*) lecture theatre; courtroom.

aumentare [aumen'tare] *v* increase. **aumentare di peso** put on weight. **aumento** *sm* increase.

aureo ['aureo] *agg* golden.

aureola [au'rɛola] *sf* halo.

aurora [au'rora] *sf* dawn.

ausiliare [auzi'ljare] *sm*, *agg also* **ausiliario** auxiliary.

austero [aus'tɛro] *agg* austere.

Australia [aus'tralja] *sf* Australia. **australiano**, **-a** *s*, *agg* Australian.

Austria ['austrja] *sf* Austria. **austriaco**, **-a** *s*, *agg* Austrian.

autarchia [autar'kia] *sf* self-sufficiency. **autarchico** *agg* self-sufficient.

autentico [au'tɛntiko] *agg* authentic, genuine. **autenticare** *v* authenticate.

autista[1] [au'tista] *s(m+f)* driver. **autista di piazza** taxi-driver.

autista[2] [au'tista] *agg* autistic.

auto ['auto] *sf* (*fam*) car.

autobiografia [autobiogra'fia] *sf* autobiography. **autobiografico** *agg* autobiographical.

autoblinda [auto'blinda] *sf* armoured car.

autobus ['autobus] *sm* bus.

autocarro [auto'karro] *sm* truck.

autocolonna [autoko'lonna] *sf* convoy.

autocontrollo [autokon'trɔllo] *sm* self-control.

autocratico [auto'kratiko] *agg* autocratic.

autodidatta [autodi'datta] *s(m+f)* self-taught person.

autofurgone [autofur'gone] *sm* van.

autolettiga [autolet'tiga] *sf* ambulance.

autolinea [auto'linea] *sf* bus route.

automa [au'tɔma] *sm* automaton, robot.

automatico [auto'matiko] *agg* automatic. **distributore automatico** slot-machine. **automatizzare** *v* automate.

automezzo [auto'mɛddzo] *sm* motor vehicle.

automobile [auto'mobile] *sf* car. **automobilismo** *sm* motoring. **automobilista** *s(m+f)* motorist. **automobilistico** *agg* motor.

autonomo [au'tɔnomo] *agg* autonomous. **autonomia** *sf* autonomy.

autopsia [autop'sia] *sf* post-mortem, autopsy.

autore [au'tore], **-trice** *sm*, *sf* author; artist.

autorevole [auto'revole] *agg* authoritative.

autorimessa [autori'messa] *sf* garage.

autorità [autori'ta] *sf* authority. **autoritario** *agg* authoritarian.

autoritratto [autori'tratto] *sm* self-portrait.

autorizzare [autorid'dzare] *v* authorize. **autorizzazione** *sf* authorization; permit.

autostop [autos'tɔp] *sm invar* hitch-hiking. **fare l'autostop** hitch-hike.

autostrada [autos'trada] *sf* expressway.

autosufficiente [autosuffi'tʃɛnte] *agg* self-sufficient.

autotreno [auto'treno] *sm* articulated lorry.

autoveicolo [autove'ikolo] *sm* motor vehicle.

autunno [au'tunno] *sm* autumn. **autunnale** *agg* autumnal.

avambraccio [avam'brattʃo] *sm* forearm.

avanguardia [avan'gwardja] *sf* forefront; (*mil*) vanguard; (*arte*) avant-garde.

avanti [a'vanti] *avv* forward, ahead; (*prima*) before. **andare avanti** go forward, proceed. **avanti** a before, in front of. **avanti e indietro** backwards and forwards, to and fro. **d'ora in avanti** from now on. **tirare avanti** (*fam*) scrape along, get by. *inter* come in! (*andiamo*) come now!

avantieri [avan'tjɛri] *avv* the day before yesterday.

avanzare[1] [avan'tsare] *v* advance; (*presentare*) put forward. **avanzata** *sf* advance.

avanzare[2] [avan'tsare] *v* be owed; remain, be left over. **avanzo** *sm* remainder; (*cibo*) left-overs *pl*.

avaro [a'varo], **-a** *agg* mean. *sm*, *sf* miser. **avarizia** *sf* meanness, stinginess.

avena [a'vena] *sf* oats *pl*. **farina d'avena** *sf* oatmeal.

***avere** [a'vere] *v* have; get. **aver caldo/freddo** be hot/cold. **aver fame/sete** be hungry/thirsty. **aver fretta** be in a hurry. **aver paura/sonno** be afraid/sleepy. *sm* (*comm*) credit; belongings *pl*; property.

aviazione [avja'tsjone] *sf* aviation, flying; (*arma*) air-force. **aviatore**, **-trice** *sm*, *sf* aviator, pilot.

avido ['avido] *agg* avid, eager.

aviolinea [avjo'linea] *sf* airline.

avo ['avo] *sm* (*nonno*) grandfather; (*antenato*) forefather, ancestor. **avito** *agg* ancestral.

avocado [avo'kado] *sm* avocado.

avorio [a'vɔrjo] *sm* ivory.

avvampare [avvam'pare] *v* blaze, flare up.

avvantaggiare [avvantad'dʒare] *v* profit, benefit.

***avvedersi** [avve'dersi] *v* become aware.

avvelenare [avvele'nare] *v* poison. **avvelenamento** *sm* poisoning. **avvelenatore**, **-trice** *sm*, *sf* poisoner.

***avvenire** [avve'nire] *v* happen. *sm* future. **avvenimento** *sm* event, occurrence.

avventato [avven'tato] *agg* rash, reckless. **avventare** *v* hurl; (*azzardare*) venture.

avventore [avven'tore], **-a** *sm*, *sf* patron, regular customer.

avventurare [avventu'rare] *v* venture, risk. **avventura** *sf* adventure; (*amorosa*) love affair. **avventuriere** *sm* adventurer.

avverbio [av'vɛrbjo] *sm* adverb.

avversario [avver'sarjo], **-a** *sm*, *sf* adversary, opponent. *agg* opposing.

avversione [avver'sjone] *sf* dislike, aversion.

avversità [avversi'ta] *sf* adversity.

avverso [av'vɛrso] *agg* adverse; opposing.

avvertire [avver'tire] *v* (*osservare*) notice; (*percepire*) feel; (*ammonire*) warn; (*avvisare*) inform. **avvertenza** *sf* warning, notice; (*attenzione*) care; (*istruzioni*) directions *pl*.

avvezzare [avvet'tsare] *v* (*educare*) train; (*abituare*) accustom.

avviare [avvi'are] *v* start (up), set going; (*comm*) set up; direct. **scuola d'avviamento** *sf* training college, technical college. **avviato** *agg* under way; (*prospero*) thriving.

avvicinare [avvitʃi'nare] *v* approach; (*portar vicino*) bring near.

avvilire [avvi'lire] *v* disgrace; (*scoraggiare*) dishearten; humiliate. **avvilito** *agg* downhearted; demoralized.

avviluppare [avvilup'pare] *v* entangle; (*avvolgere*) wrap up.

avvincente [avvin'tʃɛnte] *agg* fascinating.

avvisare [avvi'zare] *v* let know, advise; (*ammonire*) warn. **avviso** *sm* notice, note; announcement; (*pubblicità*) advertisement; opinion. **avviso circolare** circular. **come d'avviso** as advised.

avvizzire [avvit'tsire] *v* wither.

avvocato [avvo'kato] *sm* lawyer, barrister, solicitor; advocate, champion. **avvocatura** *sf* legal profession.

***avvolgere** [av'vɔldʒere] *v* envelop, wrap up; (*arrotolare*) roll up, wind.

avvoltoio [avvol'tojo] *sm* vulture.

azalea [adza'lɛa] *sf* azalea.

azienda [a'dzjenda] *sf* firm, business, company; (*impresa*) undertaking. **azienda agricola** farm. **aziendale** *agg* business.

azione [a'tsjone] *sf* action, (*atto*) deed; (*mec*) movement, motion; (*dir*) lawsuit; (*comm*) share. **azionista** *s(m+f)* shareholder.

azoto [a'dzɔto] *sm* nitrogen.

azzardare [addzar'dare] *v* risk, venture. **azzardarsi** *v* dare. **azzardato** *agg* risky, rash. **azzardo** *sm* risk.

azzuffarsi [addzuf'farsi] *v* brawl, come to blows.

azzurro [ad'dzurro] *agg*, *sm* (sky) blue.

B

banda

babbo ['babbo] sm (fam) dad, daddy.
babbuino [babbu'ino] sm baboon.
babordo [ba'bordo] sm port.
bacca ['bakka] sf berry.
baccalà [bakka'la] sm dried salt cod.
baccano [bak'kano] sm row, din, uproar.
baccello [bat'tʃɛllo] sm pod.
bacchetta [bak'ketta] sf rod, stick; (musica) baton.
baciare [ba'tʃare] v kiss. **bacio** sm kiss.
bacino [ba'tʃino] sm basin; (anat) pelvis.
baco ['bako] sm larva; (da seta) silkworm.
bada ['bada] sf **tenere a bada** hold at bay.
badare [ba'dare] v **badare a** pay attention to, take care to. **badare di** be careful to. **senza badare a** regardless of.
badessa [ba'dessa] sf abbess.
badia [ba'dia] sf abbey.
badile [ba'dile] sm spade.
baffo ['baffo] sm **farsene un baffo** not care a damn. **baffi** sm pl moustache sing. **leccarsi i baffi** lick one's lips. **ridere sotto i baffi** laugh up one's sleeve.
bagaglio [ba'gaʎo] sm baggage. **bagagliaio** sm (ferr) luggage van; (auto) boot. **deposito bagagli** sm left luggage.
bagattella [bagat'tɛlla] sf (gioco) bagatelle; (inezia) trifle.
bagliore [ba'ʎore] sm flash.
bagnare [ba'ɲare] v wet. **bagnato** agg wet.
bagnino [ba'ɲino] sm beach attendant, lifeguard.
bagno ['baɲo] sm bath; (locale) bathroom. **fare il bagno** take a bath. **bagnante** s(m+f) bather. **bagnomaria** sm bainmarie.
baia ['baja] sf (geog) bay.
baionetta [bajo'netta] sf bayonet.
balbettare [balbet'tare] v stammer.
balbuziente [balbut'tsjɛnte] s(m+f) stammerer.
balcone [bal'kone] sm balcony. **balconata** sf (teatro, ecc.) gallery.
baldacchino [baldak'kino] sm canopy; (rel) baldachin.
baldanza [bal'dantsa] sf self-confidence; audacity. **baldanzoso** agg self-confident; audacious.
baldoria [bal'dɔrja] sf merrymaking. **far baldoria** make merry.
balena [ba'lena] sf whale.
balenare [bale'nare] v flash (with lightning); (apparire subitamente) come in a flash. **baleno** sm flash.

balia¹ ['balja] sf nurse.
balia² [ba'lia] sf **in balia di** in the power of, at the mercy of.
balistica [ba'listika] sf ballistics. **balistico** agg ballistic.
balla ['balla] sf (involto) bale; (frottola) fib, lie.
ballare [bal'lare] v dance.
ballata [bal'lata] sf ballad.
ballerino [balle'rino], **-a** sm, sf balletdancer.
balletto [bal'letto] sm ballet.
ballo ['ballo] sm ball; dance. **essere in ballo** be at stake.
ballottaggio [ballot'taddʒo] sm ballot. **ballottare** v ballot.
balneare [balne'are] agg bathing.
balocco [ba'lokko] sm toy, plaything.
balordo [ba'lordo] agg senseless, absurd; (tonto) dull.
balsamo ['balsamo] sm balsam; (lenimento) balm.
balza ['baltsa] sf (rupe) cliff; (frangia) fringe.
balzare [bal'tsare] v bounce, leap.
bambagia [bam'badʒa] sf cotton wool. **tenere nella bambagia** pamper, spoil.
bambinaia [bambi'naja] sf (children's) nurse, nanny.
bambino [bam'bino], **-a** sm, sf child (pl -ren). **bambinata** sf childishness. **bambinesco** adj puerile.
bamboccio [bam'bottʃo] sm (scioccone) simpleton; (fantoccio) rag-doll; (bambino) bonny child.
bambola ['bambola] sf doll.
bambù [bam'bu] sm bamboo.
banale [ba'nale] adj banal.
banana [ba'nana] sf banana. **banano** sm banana tree.
banca ['banka] sf bank. **bancario** agg bank, banking. **banchiere** sm banker.
bancarella [banka'rɛlla] sf barrow, stall.
bancarotta [banka'rotta] sf bankruptcy.
banchetto [ban'ketto] sm banquet. **banchettare** v banquet, feast.
banchina [ban'kina] sf (porto) wharf, quay; (stazione) platform.
banco ['banko] sm bench; (di vendita) counter; (banca) bank. **bancogiro** sm giro. **banconota** sf banknote.
banda¹ ['banda] sf (lato) side.
banda² ['banda] sf (striscia) stripe; (radio) band. **banda sonora** sound-track.

banda 234

banda¹ ['banda] *sf* group, band; *(delinquenti)* gang.

bandiera [ban'djera] *sf* flag, banner. **bandiera di comodo** flag of convenience.

banderuola *sf* pennant; *(ventaruola)* weather-vane; *(girella)* fickle person.

bandire [ban'dire] *v* proclaim; *(esiliare)* banish. **bandito** *sm* bandit. **banditore** *sm* town-crier. **bando** *sm* proclamation, banishment.

bangio ['bandʒo] *sm invar* banjo.

bar [bar] *sm invar* bar, café.

bara ['bara] *sf* bier, coffin. **aver un piede nella bara** have one foot in the grave.

baracca [ba'rakka] *sf* hut. **mandare avanti la baracca** carry on. **piantare baracca e burattini** abandon everything. **baraccone** *sm* stall, stand.

baraonda [bara'onda] *sf* hubbub, confusion.

barare [ba'rare] *v* cheat. **baro** *sm* cheat.

barattare [barat'tare] *v* barter. **baratto** *sm* barter, exchange.

barattolo [ba'rattolo] *sm* jar, tin.

barba ['barba] *sf* beard. **che barba!** what a bore! **barbuto** *adj* bearded.

barbabietola [barba'bjetola] *sf* beetroot.

barbaro ['barbaro] *sm* barbarian. *adj* barbarous.

barbiere [bar'bjere] *sm* barber.

barbiturato [barbitu'rato] *sm* barbiturate.

barca ['barka] *sf* boat. **barca a remi** rowing-boat. **barca a vela** sailing-boat. **barca a motore** motor boat. **barcamenarsi** *v* manage.

barcollare [barkol'lare] *v* totter, stagger.

bardare [bar'dare] *v* harness.

barella [ba'rella] *sf* stretcher. **barelliere** *sm* stretcher-bearer.

barile [ba'rile] *sm* barrel, cask.

barista [ba'rista] *sm* barman. *sf* barmaid.

baritono [ba'ritono] *sm* baritone.

barlume [bar'lume] *sm* glimmer.

barocco [ba'rokko] *sm, agg* baroque.

barometro [ba'rometro] *sm* barometer.

barone [ba'rone] *sm* baron; *(dell'industria)* tycoon. **baronessa** *sf* baroness.

barra ['barra] *sf* bar, rod.

barricare [barri'kare] *v* barricade. **barricata** *sf* barricade.

barriera [bar'rjera] *sf* barrier.

baruffa [ba'ruffa] *sf* brawl.

barzelletta [bardzel'letta] *sf* joke, funny story.

bascula ['baskula] *sf* weighing machine.

base ['baze] *sf* basis *(pl -ses)*; *(tec)* base. **a base di** made up of. **in base a** on the basis of. **basamento** *sm* pedestal; foundation. **basare** *v* base, found.

basetta [ba'zetta] *sf* sideburn.

basilica [ba'zilika] *sf* basilica.

basilico [ba'ziliko] *sm* basil.

basso ['basso] *agg* low, low-lying; *(poco profondo)* shallow. *avv* low, low down. *sm (musica)* bass. **a basso ...!** down with ...!

bassofondo [basso'fondo] *sm* shallows *pl*. **bassifondi** *sm pl (quartieri)* slums *pl*; *(strati sociali)* underworld *sing*.

bassotto [bas'sotto] *sm* dachshund.

bastardo [bas'tardo], **-a** *s, agg* bastard; *(non di razza)* mongrel.

bastare [bas'tare] *v* suffice, be enough. **basta!** *inter* enough! *(silenzio)* quiet! **basta che** provided that.

bastimento [basti'mento] *sm* ship.

bastonare [basto'nare] *v* beat, cane. **bastonata** *sf* caning, beating.

bastone [bas'tone] *sm* stick, cane; golf-club. **bastone da passeggio** walking stick.

battaglia [bat'taʎa] *sf* battle; campaign. **cavallo di battaglia** hobby-horse.

battaglio [bat'taʎʎo] *sm (campana)* clapper; *(porta)* door-knocker.

battaglione [battaʎ'ʎone] *sm* battalion.

battello [bat'tello] *sm* boat.

battere ['battere] *v* beat. **battere a macchina** type. **battere le mani** clap (one's hands). **in un batter d'occhio** in a flash. **senza batter ciglio** without batting an eyelid.

batteria [batte'ria] *sf* battery; *(sport)* heat; *(insieme)* set.

batterio [bat'terjo] *sm* bacterium *(pl -a)*. **batteriologia** *sf* bacteriology. **batteriologo, -a** *sm, sf* bacteriologist.

battesimo [bat'tezimo] *sm* baptism, christening. **battesimale** *adj* baptismal. **battezzare** *v* baptize, christen.

battibecco [batti'bekko] *sm* quarrel.

batticuore [batti'kwore] *sm* **avere il batticuore** have palpitations. **far venire il batticuore** make anxious.

battimani [batti'mani] *sm* applause.

battistero [battis'tero] *sm* baptistry.

battito [bat'tito] *sm* beat, pulsation.

battitore [batti'tore] *sm (sport)* server, striker; *(caccia)* beater.

battuta [bat'tuta] *sf (colpo)* blow; *(spiritosaggine)* witty remark; *(musica)* beat; *(sport)* service.

batuffolo [ba'tuffolo] *sm* wad.

baule [ba'ule] *sm* trunk. **fare i bauli** *(fam)* go away.

bava ['bava] *sf* dribble.

bavaglino [bava'ʎino] *sm* bib.

bavaglio [ba'vaʎo] *sm* gag. **mettere il bavaglio a** gag.

bavero ['bavero] *sm* collar.

bazzicare [battsi'kare] *v* associate with; frequent.

beatitudine [beati'tudine] *sf* beatitude.

beato [be'ato] *agg* blessed. **beato te!** lucky you!

bebè [be'bɛ] *sm* baby.

beccaccia [bek'kattʃa] *sf* woodcock. **beccaccino** *sm* snipe.

beccare [bek'kare] *v* peck; *(fam)* catch, collar.

becchino [bek'kino] *sm* undertaker; gravedigger.

becco[1] ['bekko] *sm* beak; *(bruciatore)* burner.

becco[2] ['bekko] *sm (caprone)* goat; *(cornuto)* cuckold.

Befana [be'fana] *sf* Epiphany.

beffare [beffare] *v* mock. **beffarsi di** make fun of. **beffa** *sf* jest, practical joke.

begli ['beʎi] *V* **bello**.

bei ['bei] *V* **bello**.

bel ['bel] *V* **bello**.

belare [be'lare] *v* bleat.

Belgio ['bɛldʒo] *sm* Belgium. **belga** *s(m+f), agg, m pl* -**gi** Belgian.

belletto [bel'letto] *sm* make-up, rouge.

bellezza [bel'lettsa] *sf* beauty. **che bellezza!** fiow lovely!

bello ['bɛllo] *agg* beautiful; fine; fair. **il bello è che** the odd thing is (that). **nel bel mezzo** right in the middle. **oh bella!** you don't say! **questa à bella!** *(ironico)* that's a good one! **sul più bello** at the crucial moment.

belva ['belva] *sf* wild animal.

bemolle [be'molle] *sm (musica)* flat.

benché [ben'ke] *cong* although.

bendare [ben'dare] *v (fasciare)* bandage; *(coprire gli occhi)* blindfold. **benda** *sf* bandage; blindfold.

bene ['bɛne] *avv* well. **star bene** feel well; *(abito)* suit. **va bene** all right. *sm* good; *(amore)* love; wealth, property. **beni di consumo** consumer goods *pl*. **voler bene a** be fond of. **benino** *avv* fairly well, reasonably.

*****benedire** [bene'dire] *v* bless, consecrate. **benedetto** *agg* blessed. **benedetti voi!** lucky you!

beneducato [benedu'kato] *agg* well-mannered.

beneficenza [benefi'tʃentsa] *sf* charity.

beneficio [bene'fitʃo] *sm* profit; advantage. **benefico** *agg* beneficial.

benessere [be'nɛssere] *sm* well-being, welfare.

benestante [bene'stante] *agg* comfortably off, well-to-do. **benestare** *sm* well-being; *(autorizzazione)* consent.

benevolo [be'nɛvolo] *agg* kindly, well-disposed.

beninteso [benin'tezo] *avv* naturally, of course.

benvenuto [benve'nuto] *sm, agg* welcome. **dare il benvenuto a** welcome.

benzina [ben'dzina] *sf* gasoline. **far benzina** fill up. **distributore di benzina** *sm* gasoline station or pump.

*****bere** ['bere] *v* drink.

bernoccolo [ber'nokkolo] *sm* bump; *(disposizione)* flair.

berretto [ber'retto] *sm* cap, hat.

bersaglio [ber'saʎo] *sm* target.

bestemmia [bes'temmja] *sf* swear-word, curse. **bestemmiare** *v* swear, curse.

bestia ['bɛstja] *sf* animal, beast; ignoramus. **bestiale** *agg* bestial, brutal; *(fam: intenso)* beastly.

bestiame [bes'tjame] *sm* livestock.

betoniera [beto'njera] *sf* cement-mixer.

bettola ['bettola] *sf* low dive.

betulla [be'tulla] *sf* birch.

bevanda [be'vanda] *sf* drink, beverage. **bevibile** *agg* drinkable.

biada ['bjada] *sf* fodder, forage.

biancheria [bjanke'ria] *sf (indumenti intimi)* underwear; *(da casa)* linen.

bianchetti [bjan'ketti] *sm pl* whitebait *pl.*

bianchetto [bjan'ketto] *sm* whitewash.

bianco ['bjanko] *agg* white; *(non scritto)* blank. *sm* white.

biancospino [bjanko'spino] *sm* hawthorn.

biascicare [bjaʃi'kare] *v (cibo)* munch; *(parole)* mumble.

biasimare [bjazi'mare] *v* blame. **biasimo** *sm* blame.

Bibbia ['bibbja] *sf* Bible. **biblico** *agg* biblical.

bibita ['bibita] *sf* (soft) drink, beverage.

bibliografia [bibljogra'fia] *sf* bibliography. **bibliografico** *agg* bibliographical. **bibliografo, -a** *sm, sf* bibliographer.

biblioteca [bibljo'tɛka] *sf* library. **bibliotecario, -a** *sm, sf* librarian.

bicchiere [bik'kjɛre] *sm* glass, tumbler.

bicicletta [bitʃi'kletta] *sf* bicycle. **andare in bicicletta** cycle.

bicipite [bi'tʃipite] *sm* biceps.

bidè [bi'dɛ] *sm* bidet.

bidone [bi'done] *sm* drum, can.

bieco ['bjɛko] *agg* **guardare con occhio bieco** look askance at.

biennale [bien'nale] *agg* biennial. *sf* biennial event.

bietta ['bjetta] *sf* wedge.

biforcarsi [bifor'karsi] *v* branch off, fork. **biforcazione** *sf* fork, junction.

bigamia [biga'mia] *sf* bigamy. **bigamo** *sm* bigamist.

bighellonare [bigello'nare] *v* idle; (*girellare*) saunter.

bigio ['bidʒo] *agg* grey; (*tempo*) dull.

bigliardo [bi'ʎardo] *sm* billiards.

biglietto [bi'ʎetto] *sm* ticket; note; card. **bigliettaio, -a** *sm, sf* conductor. **biglietteria** *sf* booking-office.

bigodino [bigo'dino] *sm* curler, roller.

bigotto [bi'gɔtto], **-a** *sm, sf* bigot. *agg* bigoted.

bilancia [bi'lantʃa] *sf* scales *pl*; (*comm*) balance. **Bilancia** *sf* Libra. **bilanciare** *v* balance; (*pesare*) weigh.

bilancio [bi'lantʃo] *sm* balance sheet; budget.

bile ['bile] *sf* bile.

bilico [bi'liko] *sm* **in bilico** in the balance.

bilingue [bi'lingwe] *agg* bilingual.

bilione [bi'ljone] *sm* a thousand millions.

bimbo ['bimbo], **-a** *sm, sf* child (*pl* -ren).

bimensile [bimen'sile] *agg* fortnightly.

binario [bi'narjo] *agg* binary. *sm* rails *pl*, railway line.

binocolo [bi'nɔkolo] *sm* binoculars *pl*.

biochimico [bio'kimiko], **-a** *agg* biochemical. *sm, sf* biochemist. *sf* (*scienza*) biochemistry.

biografia [biogra'fia] *sf* biography. **biografico** *agg* biographical. **biografo, -a** *sm, sf* biographer.

biologia [biolo'dʒia] *sf* biology. **biologico** *agg* biological. **biologo, -a** *sm, sf* biologist.

biondo ['bjondo] *agg* blond, fair-haired.

birbante [bir'bante] *sm* rascal, knave.

birbone [bir'bone] *sm* rogue, scamp.

birichino [biri'kino], **-a** *sm, sf* imp, mischievous child. *agg* impish, cheeky. **birichinata** *sf* childish prank.

birillo [bi'rillo] *sm* skittle.

birra ['birra] *sf* beer. **birreria** *sf* public house.

bis [bis] *inter* encore! **dare il bis** give an encore.

bisaccia [bi'zattʃa] *sf* knapsack, saddle-bag.

bisbetico [biz'bɛtiko] *agg* cantankerous, peevish.

bisbigliare [bizbi'ʎare] *v* whisper. **bisbiglio** *sm* whisper.

biscia ['biʃa] *sf* snake.

biscotto [bis'kɔtto] *sm* biscuit.

bisestile [bizes'tile] *agg* **anno bisestile** leap-year.

bisognare [bizo'nare] *v* be necessary. **bisogno** *sm* need, requirement. **aver bisogno di** need. **non c'è bisogno** there is no need. **bisognoso** *agg* needy.

bistecca [bis'tekka] *sf* steak.

bisticciare [bistit'tʃare] *v* quarrel. **bisticcio** *sm* quarrel.

bistrattare [bistrat'tare] *v* ill-treat.

bitorzolo [bi'tortsolo] *sf* pimple.

bivio ['bivjo] *sm* junction, fork.

bizzarro [bid'dzarro] *agg* strange, odd.

bizzeffe [bid'dzeffe] *avv* **a bizzeffe** galore.

blandire [blan'dire] *v* caress, entice. **blandizie** *sf pl* flattery *sing*.

blando ['blando] *agg* bland, mellow.

blasfemo [blas'femo] *agg* blasphemous.

blatta ['blatta] *sf* cockroach.

blesità [blezi'ta] *sf* lisp. **parlar bleso** lisp.

bloccare [blok'kare] *v* block, blockade. **blocco** *sm* block; (*massa*) lump; blockade; (*ostruzione*) blockage. **in blocco** in bulk.

blu [blu] *agg* blue. **bluastro** *agg* bluish.

blusa ['bluza] *sf* blouse.

boa[1] ['bɔa] *sm invar* (*zool*) boa.

boa[2] *sf* (*mar*) buoy.

boato [bo'ato] *sm* roar, rumble. **boato sonico** sonic bang.

bobina [bo'bina] *sf* bobbin, reel.

bocca ['bokka] *sf* mouth; (*apertura*) opening. **in bocca al lupo!** good luck!

boccale [bok'kale] *sm* tankard.

boccata [bok'kata] *sf* mouthful.

bocchino [bok'kino] *sm* mouthpiece; cigarette-holder.

boccia ['bɔttʃa] *sf* (*sport*) bowl; (*vaso*) decanter; (*bot*) bud.

bocciare [bot'tʃare] *v* (*dir*) repeal; (*esami*) fail.

boccio ['bɔttʃo] *sm also* **bocciolo** bud.

boccone [bok'kone] *sm* mouthful.

bocconi [bok'koni] *avv* prone, flat on one's face.

bofonchiare [bofon'kjare] *v* snort.

boia ['bɔja] *sm invar* executioner. **boiata** *sf* (*fam*) rubbish.

boicottare [boikot'tare] *v* boycott. **boicottaggio** *sm* boycott.

bolide ['bolide] *sm* fire-ball. **andare come un bolide** go like a bomb. **passare come un bolide** flash past.

bolla¹ ['bolla] *sf* bubble; (*med*) blister.

bolla² ['bolla] *sf* (*sigillo*) seal; (*papale*) bull; (*comm*) bill.

bollare [bol'lare] *v* seal, stamp.

bolletta [bol'letta] *sf* (*comm*) bill, receipt. **essere in bolletta** (*fam*) be broke. **bollettino** *sm* bulletin, list.

bollire [bol'lire] *v* boil. **bollente** *agg* boiling. **bollito** *sm* boiled meat. **bollitore** *sm* kettle.

bollo ['bollo] *sm* stamp, seal. **bollo di circolazione** tax disc.

bomba ['bomba] *sf* bomb.

bombardare [bombar'dare] *v* bomb, shell. **bombardamento** *sm* bombardment, shelling.

bombetta [bom'betta] *sf* bowler hat.

bombola [bom'bola] *sf* gas cylinder.

bonario [bo'narjo] *agg* good-natured.

bontà [bon'ta] *sf* goodness.

borbottare [borbot'tare] *v* mutter; rumble.

bordello [bor'dello] *sm* brothel; (*confusione*) uproar.

bordo ['bordo] *sm* (*mar*) side; (*orlo*) border, edge. **a bordo** on board. **giornale di bordo** *sm* (ship's) log. **virare di bordo** (*mar*) tack.

borghese [bor'geze] *agg* bourgeois, middle-class; civilian. *s(m+f)* middle-class person; civilian. **in borghese** in civilian or plain clothes. **borghesia** *sf* middle class, bourgeoisie.

borgo ['borgo] *sm* (*paesello*) hamlet; (*sobborgo*) suburb.

boria ['bɔrja] *sf* conceit, arrogance. **metter**

su **boria** put on airs. **borioso** arrogant, conceited.

borotalco [boro'talko] *sm invar* talcum powder.

borsa¹ ['borsa] *sf* bag; (*della spesa*) shopping bag; (*per documenti*) brief-case; (*diplomatica*) attaché case; (*dell'acqua*) hot-water bottle. **borsa di studio** scholarship, grant. **borsaiolo** *sm* pickpocket. **borsetta** *sf* handbag. **borsista** *s(m+f)* scholarship-holder.

borsa² ['borsa] *sf* (*comm*) stock exchange. **borsa nera** black market. **borsista** *sm* stockbroker.

bosco ['bɔsko] *sm* wood, forest. **boscaglia** *sf* thicket. **boscereccio** *agg* woody. **boschetto** *sm* grove. **boscoso** *agg* wooded.

botanico [bo'taniko], **-a** *agg* botanical. *sm, sf* botanist. *sf* botany.

botta ['bɔtta] *sf* blow. **fare a botte** come to blows. **dare le botte** a spank, slap.

botte ['bɔtte] *sf* cask, barrel.

bottega [bot'tega] *sf* shop; (*laboratorio*) workshop. **bottegaio**, **-a** *sm*, *sf* shopkeeper. **botteghino** *sm* small shop; (*teatro*) box-office.

bottiglia [bot'tiʎa] *sf* bottle.

bottone [bot'tone] *sm* button. **attaccare un bottone a** (*fam*) buttonhole. **bottoni gemelli** cuff-links *pl*.

bozza ['bɔttsa] *sf* draft, sketch; (*stampa*) galley proof. **bozzetto** *sm* sketch.

bozzolo [bot'tsolo] *sm* cocoon.

braccetto [brat'tʃetto] *sm* **a braccetto** arm in arm.

braccialetto [brattʃa'letto] *sm* bracelet.

bracciante [brat'tʃante] *sm* labourer.

bracciata [brat'tʃata] *sf* armful.

braccio [brat'tʃo] *sm, pl* **-a** *f in anat sense* arm. **prendere in braccio** take into one's arms. **bracciolo** *sm* (*sedia*) arm.

braciola [bra'tʃɔla] *sf* chop.

bramare [bra'mare] *v* yearn *or* long for. **brama** *sf* longing, strong desire.

branchia ['brankja] *sf* gill.

branco ['branko] *sm* flock, drove, herd.

brancolare [branko'lare] *v* grope.

branda ['branda] *sf* camp-bed.

brandello [bran'dello] *sm* shred, tatter.

brandire [bran'dire] *v* brandish.

brano ['brano] *sm* (*pezzo*) shred, piece; (*frammento di opera*) passage, extract.

branzino [bran'dzino] *sm* sea bass.

brasare [bra'zare] *v* braise. **brasato** *sm* braised beef.

bravo ['bravo] *agg* good; capable; (*dabbene*) decent. *inter* well done! **bravura** *sf* skill.

breccia ['brettʃa] *sf* breach.

bretelle [bre'telle] *sf pl* braces *pl.*

breve ['breve] *agg* brief, short. *sf* breve. **per farla breve** to cut a long story short. **tra breve** shortly. **brevità** *sf* brevity.

brevetto [bre'vetto] *sm* patent. **brevettare** *v* patent.

brezza ['brettsa] *sf* breeze.

bricco ['brikko] *sm* jug, pot.

briccone [brik'kone] *sm* knave, rascal. *agg* knavish, mischievous.

briciola ['britʃola] *sf* crumb. **briciolo** *sm* tiny piece, morsel.

bridge ['bridʒ] *sm invar* (*carte*) bridge.

briga ['briga] *sf* trouble. **attaccar briga** pick a quarrel. **darsi** or **prendersi la briga di** go to the trouble of.

brigadiere [briga'djere] *sm* sergeant-major; (*generale*) brigadier.

brigante [bri'gante] *sm* brigand, bandit.

brigata [bri'gata] *sf* company, group; (*mil*) brigade; (*uccelli*) flock.

briglia ['briʎa] *sf* bridle. **tenere in briglia** rein in, restrain.

brillare [bril'lare] *v* shine, sparkle, glitter. **brillante** *agg* sparkling, brilliant. **brillo** *agg* tipsy.

brina ['brina] *sf* rime, hoar-frost.

brindare [brin'dare] *v* **brindare a drink to**, toast.

brindello [brin'dello] *sm* shred, tatter.

brindisi [brin'dizi] *sm* toast. **fare un brindisi a** drink to, toast.

brio ['brio] *sm* liveliness, vivacity.

britannico [bri'tanniko], **-a** *agg* British. *sm, sf* Briton, British person.

brivido ['brivido] *sm* shudder, shiver. **aver dei brividi** shudder, shiver.

brocca ['brokka] *sf* jug, pitcher.

broccolo ['brɔkkolo] *sm* broccoli.

brodo ['brɔdo] *sm* broth, soup. **tutto fa brodo** it is all grist to the mill.

broglio ['brɔʎo] *sm* malpractice, racket.

bronchite [bron'kite] *sf* bronchitis.

broncio ['brontʃo] *sm* **tenere** or **portare il broncio** sulk.

brontolare [bronto'lare] *v* mutter, grumble. **brontolone**, **-a** *sm, sf* grumbler.

bronzo ['brondzo] *sm* bronze.

bruciapelo [brutʃa'pelo] *sm* **a bruciapelo** point-blank.

bruciare [bru'tʃare] *v* burn, scorch. **bruciare le tappe** hurry. **bruciatura** *sf* burn, scald. **bruciore** *sm* burning sensation, intense desire.

bruco ['bruko] *sm* larva, caterpillar.

brufolo ['brufolo] *sm* pimple.

brughiera [bru'gjera] *sf* heath, moor.

brulicare [bruli'kare] *v* swarm, crawl, teem. **brulichio** *sm* swarming, teeming.

brullo ['brullo] *agg* bleak; barren.

bruno ['bruno] *agg* brown; dark.

brusco ['brusko] *agg* sharp; brusque, harsh; (*improvviso*) sudden.

brusio [bru'zio] *sm* bustle, hum.

bruto ['bruto] *sm, agg* brute. **brutale** *agg* brutal.

brutto ['brutto] *agg* ugly, plain; (*non buono*) bad. **avere brutta cera** look poorly. **far brutta figura** cut a sorry figure, disgrace oneself. **il brutto è che** the worst is (that), the difficulty is (that).

buca ['buka] *sf* hole, pit. **buca delle lettere** *sf* letter-box. **bucare** *v* make a hole in; (*biglietto*) punch; (*gomma*) puncture. **bucatura** *sf* puncture.

bucaneve [buka'neve] *sm invar* snowdrop.

bucato [bu'kato] *sm* washing. **fare il bucato** do the washing.

buccia ['buttʃa] *sf* peel, skin, rind.

buco ['buko] *sm* hole. **buco nell'acqua** failure.

buddismo [bud'dizmo] *sm* Buddhism. **buddista** *s*(*m+f*), *agg* Buddhist.

budello [bu'dello] *sm* gut.

budino [bu'dino] *sm* pudding.

bue ['bue] *sm, pl* **buoi** ox (*pl* -en); (*carne*) beef.

bufalo ['bufalo], **-a** *sm, sf* buffalo.

bufera [bu'fera] *sf* gale, blizzard.

buffè [buf'fe] *sm invar* (*credenza*) sideboard; (*gastr*) buffet.

buffo ['buffo] *agg* comic(al), amusing. *sm* (*teatro*) comic. **il buffo è che** the odd thing is (that).

bugia¹ [bu'dʒia] *sf* lie. **dire bugie** tell lies. **bugiardo**, **-a** *sm, sf* liar.

bugia² [bu'dʒia] *sf* candlestick.

buio ['bujo] *sm, agg* dark. **al buio** in the dark. **buio pesto** pitch-dark.

bulbo ['bulbo] *sm* bulb. **bulbo oculare** eyeball.

Bulgaria [bulga'ria] *sf* Bulgaria. **bulgaro**, **-a** *s, agg* Bulgarian.

bullone [bul'lone] *sm* bolt.

buono¹ ['bwɔno], **-a** agg good; kind; (giusto) right. **a buon conto** apropos. **a buon mercato** cheap(ly). **alla buona** simply. **buoncostume** sm good conduct. **buongustaio, -a** sm, sf gourmet. **buongusto** sm good taste. **buono a nulla** sm, agg good-for-nothing. **buonsenso** sm good sense. **con le buone o con le cattive** by hook or by crook. sm, sf good person.

buono² ['bwɔno], sm (documento) bond, coupon, voucher.

buonora [bwo'nora] sf **alla buonora!** at last! **di buonora** early.

burattino [burat'tino] sm puppet.

burbero ['burbero], **-a** agg grumpy, gruff. sm, sf grumpy person.

burlare [bur'lare] v make a fool of; (scherzare) joke. **burlarsi di** make fun of. **burla** sf joke, jest.

burocrate [bu'rokrate] sm bureaucrat. **burocratico** agg bureaucratic. **burocrazia** sf bureaucracy; (fam) red tape.

burrasca [bur'raska] sf blizzard, storm. **burrascoso** agg stormy.

burro ['burro] sm butter.

burrone [bur'rone] sm ravine.

bussare [bus'sare] v knock.

bussola ['bussola] sf compass.

busta ['busta] sf envelope.

bustarella [busta'rella] sf bribe.

busto ['busto] sm bust; (indumento) corset.

buttare [but'tare] throw. **buttar giù** (cibo) gulp down; (scritto) jot down; (gastr) put in boiling water.

C

cabina [ka'bina] sf (aero, mar) cabin; (telefono, ecc.) booth; (ascensore) cage.

cablogramma [kablo'gramma] sm cable.

cacao [ka'kao] sm cocoa.

cacare [ka'kare] v (volg) shit.

caccia¹ ['kattʃa] sf hunt, chase; (ricerca) pursuit, search. **a caccia di** in search of. **caccia grossa** big game. **dar la caccia** pursue.

caccia² ['kattʃa] sm invar (aero) fighter; (mar) destroyer.

cacciagione [kattʃa'dʒone] sf game.

cacciare [kat'tʃare] v hunt; (espellere) throw or drive out; (introdurre) thrust; (mettere) stick, put.

cacciavite [kattʃa'vite] sm screwdriver.

cachi ['kaki] agg, sm khaki.

cacio ['katʃo] sm cheese.

cactus ['kaktus] sm cactus.

cadauno [kada'uno] agg, pron each.

cadavere [ka'davere] sm corpse.

***cadere** [ka'dere] v fall; (aero) crash. **cader dalle nuvole** be dumbfounded. **lasciar cadere** drop. **caduta** sf fall; (aero) crash.

cadetto [ka'detto] sm younger son; (mil) cadet.

caffè [kaf'fɛ] sm coffee; (locale) café. **caffettiera** sf coffee-pot; (macchina) coffee-maker.

caffeina [kaffe'ina] sf caffeine.

cafone [ka'fone] sm (fam) lout.

cagionare [kadʒo'nare] v cause. **cagione** sf cause, reason. **a cagion di** on account of, owing to.

cagna ['kaɲa] sf bitch.

cagnara [ka'ɲara] sf (fam) row, uproar.

calabrone [kala'brone] sm hornet.

calamaio [kala'majo] sm inkstand, inkwell.

calamaro [kala'maro] sm squid.

calamita [kala'mita] sf magnet.

calamità [kalami'ta] sf calamity.

calare [ka'lare] v lower, let down; (maglia) decrease, cast off; (scendere) go down; (abbassarsi) drop. **calata** sf descent; (banchina) quay.

calcagno [kal'kaɲo] sm heel. **stare alle calcagna di** follow closely.

calcare¹ [kal'kare] v press (hard); (disegno) trace. **calco** sm (impronta di rilievo) cast; (disegno) tracing.

calcare² [kal'kare] sm limestone.

calce ['kaltʃe] sf lime.

calcestruzzo [kaltʃes'truttso] sm concrete.

calcio¹ ['kaltʃo] sm (chim) calcium.

calcio² ['kaltʃo] sm (fucile) (rifle) butt.

calcio² ['kaltʃo] sm kick; (sport) football. **calcio di rigore** penalty (kick). **dare un calcio** kick.

calcolare [kalko'lare] v calculate, consider. **calcolatore, -trice** sm, sf calculator, computer.

calcolo¹ ['kalkolo] sm calculation; (congettura) reckoning; (mat) calculus. **a calcoli fatti** all things considered.

calcolo² ['kalkolo] sm (med) calculus, stone.

caldaia [kal'daja] *sf* boiler.
caldo ['kaldo] *agg* warm; (*molto*) hot. *sm* warmth; heat. **aver** o **far caldo** be hot.
caleidoscopio [kaleido'skɔpjo] *sm* kaleidoscope.
calendario [kalen'darjo] *sm* calendar.
calibro ['kalibro] *sm* calibre; (*mec*) gauge; (*strumento*) callipers *pl*.
calice ['kalitʃe] *sm* goblet; (*rel*) chalice; (*bot*) calyx.
caligine [ka'lidʒine] *sf* fog.
calligrafia [kalligra'fia] *sf* handwriting.
callo ['kallo] *sm* corn. **callifugo** *sm, pl* **-ghi** corn-plaster.
calmare [kal'mare] *v* calm; ease. **calmarsi** *v* calm down. **calma** *sf* calm, tranquillity. **perdere la calma** lose one's temper. **prendersela con calma** take it easy. **calmante** *sm* sedative. **calmo** *agg* calm.
calore [ka'lore] *sm* heat; (*cordialità*) warmth.
caloria [kalo'ria] *sf* calorie.
calorifero [kalo'nifero] *sm* radiator.
caloroso [kalo'rozo] *agg* warm.
calpestare [kalpes'tare] *v* trample on.
calunnia [ka'lunnja] *sf* calumny; (*diffamazione orale*) slander; (*scritta*) libel. **calunniare** *v* slander; libel.
calvo ['kalvo] *agg* bald. **calvizie** *sf* baldness.
calza ['kaltsa] *sf* (*corta*) sock; (*lunga*) stocking. **fare la calza** knit. **ferro da calza** *sm* knitting-needle.
calzare [kal'tsare] *v* put on; (*portare*) wear; (*convenire*) fit. **calzatura** *sf* footwear.
calzolaio [kaltso'lajo] *sm* shoemaker. **calzoleria** *sf* shoe shop.
calzoni [kal'tsoni] *sm pl* trousers *pl*.
camaleonte [kamale'onte] *sm* chameleon.
cambiale [kam'bjale] *sf* bill of exchange.
cambiare [kam'bjare] *v* change. **cambiar casa** move. **tanto per cambiare** just for a change. **cambiamento** *sm* change.
cambio [kam'bjo] *sm* change; (*econ*) exchange; (*auto*) transmission, gearbox.
camera ['kamera] *sf* room; (*da letto*) bedroom; (*assemblea, tec*) chamber. **camera d'aria** (*pneumatico*) inner tube. **musica da camera** chamber music.
camerata[1] [kame'rata] *sf* dormitory.
camerata[2] [kame'rata] *s(m+f)* comrade; (*fam*) mate.

cameriera [kame'rjɛra] *sf* (*albergo*) chamber-maid; (*ristorante*) waitress; (*domestica*) maid.
cameriere [kame'rjɛre] *sm* (*ristorante*) waiter; servant.
camicia [ka'mitʃa] *sf* shirt; (*da donna*) blouse; (*tec*) jacket. **camicia da notte** night-gown. **camicia di forza** strait-jacket. **camiciola** *sf* (*maglia*) vest; T-shirt.
camino [ka'mino] *sm* fireplace; chimney.
camion [ka'mjon] *sm invar* truck **camioncino** *sm* van.
cammello [kam'mɛllo] *sm* camel.
camminare [kammi'nare] *v* walk; (*procedere*) go. **camminata** *sf* walk.
cammino [kam'mino] *sm* way; (*percorso*) journey; (*sentiero*) path. **mettersi in cammino** set out.
camorra [ka'morra] *sf* racket. **camorrista** *s(m+f)* racketeer.
camoscio [ka'mɔʃo] *sm* chamois; (*pelle*) chamois leather.
campagna [kam'paɲa] *sf* country; (*paesaggio*) countryside; (*terreno*) land; (*villeggiatura*) holidays *pl*; (*mil, propaganda, ecc.*) campaign. **campagnolo** *agg* rural, country.
campana [kam'pana] *sf* bell; (*di lampada*) lampshade. **campanello** *sm* bell. **campanile** *sm* bell tower.
campare [kam'pare] *v* live.
campeggiare [kamped'dʒare] *v* camp. **campeggio** *sm* camping; (*terreno*) campsite.
campestre [kam'pɛstre] *agg* rural, country.
campione [kam'pjone] *sm* (*sport, difensore*) champion; (*piccola quantità*) sample; (*di tessuto*) pattern. **campionario** *sm* sample collection; pattern book. **campionessa** *sf* champion.
campo ['kampo] *sm* field. **campo di golf** golf-course. **campo di tennis** tennis court.
camposanto [kampo'santo] *sm* cemetery.
camuffamento [kamuffa'mento] *sm* disguise; (*mil*) camouflage. **camuffare** *v* disguise; camouflage.
camuso [ka'muzo] *agg* snub-nosed.
Canada [ka'nada] *sm* Canada. **Canadese** *s(m+f), agg* Canadian.
canaglia [ka'naʎa] *sf* scoundrel; (*marmaglia*) rabble.
canale [ka'nale] *sm* canal; (*radio, TV*) channel. **Canale della Manica** (English)

Channel. **canale di scarico** drain. **canale di scolo** gutter.

canapa [ka'napa] *sf* hemp.

canapè [kana'pε] *sm* (*mobile*) settee; (*tartina*) canapé.

canarino [kana'rino] *sm* canary. *agg* canary yellow.

cancellare [kantʃel'lare] *v* cancel, wipe out; (*con gomma*) rub out; (*con penna*) cross out.

cancelliere [kantʃel'ljere] *sm* chancellor. **cancelleria** *sf* chancellery, chancery; (*cartoleria*) stationery.

cancello [kan'tʃεllo] *sm* gate. **cancellata** *sf* railings *pl*.

cancro [kan'kro] *sm* cancer. **Cancro** *sm* Cancer.

cancrena [kan'krεna] *sf* gangrene.

candeggiare [kanded'dʒare] *v* bleach. **candeggina** *sf* bleach.

candela [kan'dela] *sf* candle; (*auto*) sparking-plug. **precipitare in candela** do a nose-dive. **candelabro** *sm* candlestick; (*a bracci*) candelabra.

candidato [kandi'dato], **-a** *sm*, *sf* candidate. **candidatura** *sf* candidature.

candido ['kandido] *agg* spotless, snow-white; (*sincero*) candid.

candito [kan'dito] *agg* candied, crystallized.

cane ['kane] *sm* dog. **cane bastardo** mongrel. **cane da guardia** watch-dog. **cane da salotto** lap-dog.

canestro [ka'nεstro] *sm* basket.

canguro [kan'guro] *sm* kangaroo.

canicola [ka'nikola] *sf* heat-wave.

canile [ka'nile] *sm* kennel.

canino [ka'nino] *agg* canine.

canna ['kanna] *sf* cane; (*pianta*) reed; (*fucile*) barrel; (*bicicletta*) cross-bar; (*pesca*) rod; (*tubo, organo*) pipe. **cannello** *sm* tube; (*per saldare*) blowpipe.

cannella [kan'nεlla] *sf* cinnamon.

cannibale [kan'nibale] *sm* cannibal.

cannocchiale [kannok'kjale] *sm* telescope.

cannone [kan'none] *sm* cannon. **cannonata** *sf* cannon shot. **è una cannonata!** (*fam*) it's terrific!

cannuccia [kan'nuttʃa] ·*sf* (*per bibite*) (drinking) straw; (*di pipa*) stem.

canoa [ka'nɔa] *sf* canoe.

canone ['kanone] *sm* canon; (*soldi dovuti*) fee; (*per affitto*) rent.

canonico [ka'nɔniko] *agg* canonical. **diritto canonico** *sm* canon law. **canonica** *sf* rectory.

canonizzare [kanonid'dzare] *v* canonize.

canottaggio [kanot'taddʒo] *sm* rowing. **canottiere** *sm* oarsman.

canottiera [kanot'tjera] *sf* T-shirt.

canotto [ka'nɔtto] *sm* rowing-boat; (*di salvataggio*) lifeboat.

canovaccio [kano'vattʃo] *sm* (*per stoviglie*) dishcloth; (*teatro*) plot.

cantare [kan'tare] *v* sing; (*del gallo*) crow; (*cinguettare*) chirp; (*fam: fare la spia*) squeal. **cantata** *sf* singsong; (*musica*) cantata. **canterellare** *or* **canticchiare** *v* hum.

cantiere [kan'tjere] *sm* yard; (*mar*) ship-yard, dockyard.

cantilena [kanti'lena] *sf* singsong.

cantina [kan'tina] *sf* cellar.

canto[1] ['kanto] *sm* song; (*poesia*) lyric; (*liturgia*) chant. **canto popolare** folk-song.

canto[2] ['kanto] *sm* (*angolo*) corner; (*parte*) side. **da canto** aside. **d'altro canto** on the other hand. **in un canto** in a way.

cantone[1] [kan'tone] *sm* corner. **cantonata** *sf* (street-)corner; (*errore*) blunder. **prendere una cantonata** blunder.

cantone[2] [kan'tone] *sm* (*geog*) canton.

cantoniere [kanto'njere] *sm* (*ferr*) signal-man.

canuto [ka'nuto] *agg* white-haired.

canzonare [kantso'nare] *v* make fun of, tease, mock. **canzonatore, -trice** *sm, sf* mocker. **canzonatura** *sf* mockery.

canzone [kan'tsone] *sf* song; (*discorso noioso*) old story. **canzonetta** *sf* pop song.

caos [ka'ɔs] *sm* chaos. **caotico** *agg* chaotic.

capace [ka'patʃe] *agg* (*abile*) capable; (*in grado di*) able. **capacità** *sf* capacity; ability.

capanna [ka'panna] *sf* hut. **capannone** *sm* shed; (*aero*) hangar.

caparbio [ka'parbjo] *agg* stubborn.

caparra [ka'parra] *sf* deposit.

capello [ka'pello] *sm* hair. **capelli** *sm pl* hair *sing*. **averne fin sopra i capelli** (*di*) be heartily sick (of). **capelluto** *agg* hairy. **cuoio capelluto** *sm* scalp.

capezzale [kapet'tsale] *sm* **al capezzale** at the bedside.

capezzolo [ka'pettsolo] *sm* nipple.

capire [ka'pire] *v* understand; (*rendersi*

conto) realize. **farsi capire** make oneself understood. **si capisce** naturally.

capitale [kapi'tale] *sm* (*econ*) capital. *sf* capital (city). *agg* capital. fundamental; (*principale*) main. **capitalismo** *sm* capitalism. **capitalista** *s*(*m*+*f*), *agg* capitalist.

capitano [kapi'tano] *sm* captain.

capitare [kapi'tare] *v* (*giungere*) turn up; (*presentarsi*) arise, come up; (*accadere*) happen. **capitar bene** strike lucky. **dove capita** anywhere.

capitello [kapi'tɛllo] *sm* capital.

capitolo [ka'pitolo] *sm* chapter. **aver voce in capitolo** have a say in the matter.

capo ['kapo] *sm* head; (*pezzo*) item; (*geog*) cape. **da capo** again, from the beginning. **da capo a fondo** from top to bottom. **da un capo all'altro** from one end to the other. **in capo a** within. **per sommi capi** briefly, in short. **venire a capo di** get to the bottom of.

capobanda [kapo'banda] *sm invar* ring-leader; (*musica*) bandmaster.

capodanno [kapo'danno] *sm* New Year's Day.

capofitto [kapo'fitto] *agg* **a capofitto** headlong; (*con massimo impegno*) whole-heartedly.

capogiro [kapo'dʒiro] *sm* giddiness, dizzy spell. **fare venire il capogiro a** make dizzy.

capolavoro [kapola'voro] *sm* masterpiece.

capolinea [kapo'linea] *sm*, *pl* **capilinea** terminus.

capoluogo [kapo'lwɔgo] *sm*, *pl* **-ghi** main town, capital.

capomastro [kapo'mastro] *sm* foreman.

capoofficina [kapoofi'tʃina] *sm*, *pl* **capioffi-cina** foreman.

caporale [kapo'rale] *sm* corporal.

caposala [kapo'sala] *s*(*m*+*f*), *pl* **capisala**, **caposala** (*fabbrica*) foreman; (*albergo*) head-waiter; (*ospedale*) ward sister.

capostazione [kaposta'tsjone] *sm*, *pl* **capistazione** station-master.

capotare [kapo'tare] *v* (*auto*) overturn; (*mar*) capsize.

capote [ka'pɔt] *sf*, *pl* **-s** (*auto*) hood.

capotreno [kapo'trɛno] *sm* guard.

°capovolgere [kapo'vɔldʒere] *v* overturn; (*fig*) turn upside down, reverse; (*mar*) capsize. **capovolgimento** *sm* reversal.

cappa ['kappa] *sf* cloak; (*di camino*) hood.

cappella¹ [kap'pɛlla] *sf* chapel. **cappellano** *sm* chaplain.

cappella² [kap'pɛlla] *sf* (*di fungo*) cap.

cappello [kap'pɛllo] *sm* hat. **cappellaio** *sm* hatter.

cappero ['kappero] *sm* caper. **capperi!** *inter* gosh! good heavens!

cappotta [kap'pɔtta] *sf* (*auto*) hood.

cappotto [kap'pɔtto] *sm* coat; (*bridge*) slam.

cappuccino [kapput'tʃino] *sm* coffee with milk, cappuccino; (*rel*) Capuchin friar.

cappuccio [kap'puttʃo] *sm* hood; (*tec*) cap; (*rel*) cowl.

capra ['kapra] *sf* goat. **capretto** *sm* kid. **capro** *sm* he-goat. **capro espiatorio** scape-goat.

capriccio [ka'prittʃo] *sm* whim, fancy. **fare i capricci** have tantrums.

Capricorno [kapri'kɔrno] *sm* Capricorn.

caprifoglio [kapri'fɔʎʎo] *sm* honeysuckle.

capriola¹ [kapri'ɔla] *sf* somersault, jump.

capriola² [kapri'ɔla] *sf* (*zool*) roe deer. **capriolo** *sm* roebuck.

capsico [kap'siko] *sm* capsicum.

capsula ['kapsula] *sf* capsule; (*di dente*) crown.

carabiniere [karabi'njɛre] *sm* policeman, soldier in police corps.

caraffa [ka'raffa] *sf* carafe, jug.

caramella [kara'mɛlla] *sf* sweet. **caramel-lato** *agg* candied; (*zucchero*) caramelized.

carato [ka'rato] *sm* carat.

carattere [ka'rattere] *sm* (*indole*) nature; (*forza, lettera*) character; characteristic; (*teatro*) role; type. **caratteristica** *sf* characteristic, (*distintiva*) feature; (*tec*) specification. **caratteristico** *agg* typical, distinctive.

carboidrato [karboi'drato] *sm* carbohydrate.

carbonchio [kar'bonkjo] *sm* carbuncle; (*vet*) anthrax; (*agric*) blight.

carbone [kar'bone] *sm* coal. **carbone coke** coke. **carbone di legna** charcoal. **carboncino** *sm* (*disegno*) charcoal.

carbonio [kar'bonjo] *sm* carbon.

carburante [karbu'rante] *sm* fuel.

carburatore [karbura'tore] *sm* carburet-tor.

carcassa [kar'kassa] *sf* carcass; (*fam*) wreck.

carcere ['kartʃere] *sm* prison, jail. **carcer-ato, -a** *sm*, *sf* prisoner. **carceriere, -a** *sm*, *sf* jailer.

carciofo [kar'tʃɔfo] *sm* artichoke.

cardiaco [kar'diako] *agg* cardiac. **attacco cardiaco** *sm* heart attack. **cardiologo, -a** *sm, sf* heart specialist, cardiologist.

cardinale [kardi'nale] *sm, agg* cardinal.

cardine ['kardine] *sm* hinge; (*fig*) cornerstone.

cardo ['kardo] *sm* (*bot*) thistle.

carena [ka'rɛna] *sf* hull. (**bacino di**) **carenaggio** *sm* dry dock.

carestia [kares'tia] *sf* famine.

carezzare [karet'tsare] *v* stroke, caress. **carezza** *sf* caress. **fare le carezze** a pat, stroke.

cariarsi [ka'rjarsi] *v* decay.

carica ['karika] *sf* (*impiego*) position; (*ufficio pubblico*) office; (*mil, elett*) charge; (*sport*) tackle.

caricare [kari'kare] *v* load; (*riempire*) fill; (*mil, elett*) charge; (*sport*) tackle; (*orologio, molla*) wind up.

caricatura [karika'tura] *sf* caricature.

carico ['kariko] *sm, pl* **-chi** (*di nave*) cargo; (*peso*) burden; (*tec*) load. **a carico di** (*contro*) against; (*a spese di*) at the expense of, chargeable to. **testimone a carico** witness for the prosecution. *agg* loaded, filled (with), full (of).

carie ['karje] *sf* (*dentaria*) tooth decay; (*di legno, cereali, ecc.*) rot.

carino [ka'rino] *agg* lovely, charming.

carità [kari'ta] *sf* charity; (*misericordia*) compassion. **aver carità di** take pity on. **fare la carità** give alms. **per carità!** God forbid!

carlinga [kar'linga] *sf* fuselage.

carnagione [karna'dʒone] *sf* complexion, skin.

carne ['karne] *sf* flesh; (*alimento*) meat. **carne di manzo/maiale/vitello** beef/pork/veal. **carnale** *agg* carnal. **carnoso** *agg* fleshy.

carneficina [karnefi'tʃina] *sf* slaughter. **carnefice** *sm* executioner.

carnevale [karne'vale] *sm* carnival.

carnivoro [kar'nivoro] **-a** *sm, sf* carnivore. *agg* carnivorous.

caro [ka'ro] *agg* dear. **aver caro** hold dear. **pagar caro** pay a lot for; (*fig*) pay dearly for. **cari** *sm pl* loved ones *pl*.

carogna [ka'rona] *sf* carrion; (*fam*) bastard, sod.

carosello [karo'zɛllo] *sm* merry-go-round.

carota [ka'rɔta] *sf* carrot.

carovana [karo'vana] *sf* caravan; procession.

carpione [kar'pjone] *sm* **in carpione** soused.

carponi [kar'poni] *avv* on all fours.

carrabile [kar'rabile] *agg* **passo carrabile** *sm* passageway.

carreggiata [karred'dʒata] *sf* carriageway, track. **rimettersi in carreggiata** catch up. **uscire di carreggiata** go off the road; (*fig*) go astray.

carrello [kar'rɛllo] *sm* (*vagoncino*) trolley; (*mec*) (under-)carriage.

carretta [kar'retta] *sf* cart.

carriera [kar'rjɛra] *sf* career; (*velocità*) full speed. **fare carriera** get on, make good.

carriola [kar'rjɔla] *sf* wheelbarrow.

carro ['karro] *sm* (*a quattro ruote*) wagon; (*a due ruote*) cart. **carro armato** armoured vehicle, tank. **carro attrezzi** breakdown van. **carro funebre** hearse. **carro merci** goods wagon.

carrozza [kar'rɔttsa] *sf* coach. **carrozza letto** sleeping-car, sleeper. **in carrozza!** all aboard!

carrucola [kar'rukola] *sf* pulley.

carta ['karta] *sf* paper; (*geog*) map; (*da gioco, documento*) card; (*statuto*) charter. **carta asciugante** *or* **assorbente** blotting paper. **carta carbone** carbon paper. **carta da parati** wallpaper. **cartapecora** *sf* parchment. **cartapesta** *sf* papier mâché.

cartastraccia *sf* waste paper.

cartella [kar'tɛlla] *sf* (*custodia per fogli*) folder; (*busta di pelle*) brief-case; (*per scolari*) satchel; (*scheda*) card, file.

cartellino [kartel'lino] *sm* tag.

cartello [kar'tɛllo] *sm* (*insegna*) sign; (*indicatore*) signpost, road sign; (*avviso*) notice, poster. **cartellone** *sm* poster.

cartilagine [karti'ladʒine] *sf* cartilage.

cartolaio [karto'lajo], **-a** *sm, sf* stationer. **cartoleria** *sf* stationer's (shop).

cartolina [karto'lina] *sf* postcard.

cartone [kar'tone] *sm* cardboard; (*disegno*) cartoon. **cartoni animati** (*cinema*) cartoons *pl*. **cartoncino** *sm* card.

cartuccia [kar'tuttʃa] *sf* cartridge.

casa ['kaza] *sf* home; (*edificio, dinastia*) house; (*comm*) firm. **a casa** (*stato in' luogo*) at home; (*moto a luogo*) home. **a casa del diavolo** off the beaten track. **cambiar casa** move house. **casa di cura** nursing home. **casa popolare** council house.

casalinga [kaza'linga] *sf* housewife. **casalinghi** *sm pl* household goods *pl.* **casalingo** *agg* domestic; (*semplice*) homely, plain.

cascame [kas'kame] *sm* waste.

cascare [kas'kare] *v* fall; (*capelli, denti*) fall out; (*muri, ecc.*) fall down. **cascata** *sf* fall; (*d'acqua*) waterfall; (*perle, ecc.*) cascade.

cascina [ka'ʃina] *sf* dairy farm; (*casa colonica*) farmhouse.

casco ['kasko] *sm* helmet; (*parrucchieri*) hair-drier.

caseggiato [kazed'dʒato] *sm* block of buildings.

casella [ka'zɛlla] *sf* (*riquadro*) square; (*scompartimento*) compartment. **casella postale** post-office box. **casellario** *sm* (*mobile*) filing cabinet; (*ufficio*) registry.

casello [ka'zɛllo] *sm* (*ferr*) signal-box; (*autostrada*) toll-booth.

caserma [ka'zɛrma] *sm* barracks *pl.*

casino [ka'zino] *sm* (*fam: confusione*) row, racket; (*postribolo*) brothel; (*casa signorile*) lodge.

casinò [kazi'nɔ] *sm* casino.

caso ['kazo] *sm* case; (*affare*) matter; (*combinazione, destino*) chance; possibility. **a caso** at random. **fare caso a** heed, attach importance to. **in caso** in case. **in caso diverso** *or* **contrario** otherwise. **in ogni caso** in any case, at any rate. **per caso** by chance. **poniamo il caso** let us suppose.

cassa ['kassa] *sf* case, box; (*istituzione*) fund; (*dove si paga*) cash desk. **cassa da morto** coffin. **cassa pronta** ready cash. **libro di cassa** cash-book.

casseruola [kasse'rwɔla] *sf* casserole, saucepan.

cassetta [kas'setta] *sf* box; (*teatro*) takings *pl.* **cassetto** *sm* drawer. **cassettone** *sm* chest of drawers.

cassiere [kas'sjere], **-a** *sm, sf* cashier.

casta ['kasta] *sf* caste.

castagno [kas'taɲo] *sm* chestnut tree; (*colore*) chestnut. *agg* chestnut. **castagna** *sf* chestnut. **castagnola** *sf* (*petardo*) cracker.

castello [kas'tɛllo] *sm* castle; (*impalcatura*) scaffolding. **castello di poppa** quarterdeck. **castello di prua** forecastle.

castigare [kasti'gare] *v* punish. **castigo** *sm, pl* **-ghi** punishment.

casto ['kasto] *agg* chaste. **castità** *sf* chastity.

castoro [kas'tɔro] *sm* beaver.

castrare [kas'trare] *v* castrate, geld. **castrato** *sm* (*carne*) lamb.

casuale [kazu'ale] *agg* fortuitous, accidental; (*dir*) contingent. **casualmente** *avv* by chance.

catacomba [kata'komba] *sf* catacomb.

catafascio [kata'faʃo] *sm* **andare a catafascio** go to rack and ruin.

catalizzatore [kataliddza'tore] *sm* catalyst. *agg* catalytic.

catalogo [ka'talogo] *sm, pl* **-ghi** catalogue, list. **catalogare** *v* catalogue.

catapulta [kata'pulta] *sf* catapult; (*missili*) launcher. **catapultare** *v* launch.

catarifrangente [katarifran'dʒɛnte] *sm* reflector.

catarro [ka'tarro] *sm* catarrh.

catasta [ka'tasta] *sf* pile.

catastrofe [ka'tastrofe] *sf* catastrophe. **catastrofico** *agg* catastrophic.

catechismo [kate'kizmo] *sm* catechism.

categoria [katego'ria] *sf* category, class. **categorico** *agg* categorical, absolute, explicit.

catena [ka'tena] *sf* chain. **catena di montaggio** assembly line. **catenaccio** *sm* bolt; (*fam: macchina vecchia*) old crock; (*sport*) defensive tactics *pl.*

cateratta [kate'ratta] *sf* cataract; (*chiusa*) floodgate.

catetere [kate'tɛre] *sm* catheter.

catino [ka'tino] *sm* basin. **piovere a catinelle** rain cats and dogs.

catodo ['katodo] *sm* cathode.

catrame [ka'trame] *sm* tar.

cattedra ['kattedra] *sf* (*tavola*) desk; (*ufficio di insegnante*) teaching post; (*carica universitaria*) chair.

cattedrale [katte'drale] *sf* cathedral.

cattivarsi [katti'varsi] *v* win, gain.

cattivo [kat'tivo] *agg* bad; (*in senso morale*) wicked; (*scortese*) nasty; (*capriccioso*) naughty. **cattiveria** *sf* wickedness, naughtiness; (*parole cattive*) spiteful remark.

cattolico [kat'tɔliko], **-a** *s, agg* Catholic. **Cattolicesimo** *sm* Catholicism.

catturare [kattu'rare] *v* capture, arrest. **cattura** *sf* capture, arrest.

caucciù [kaut'tʃu] *sm* rubber.

causa ['kauza] *sf* cause; (*dir*) lawsuit,

action. **a causa di** because of, on account of. **fare causa a** sue. **causale** *agg* causal.

causare [kau'zare] *v* cause, give rise to, bring about.

caustico ['kaustiko] *agg* caustic.

cauto ['kauto] *agg* cautious, careful. **cautela** *sf* caution; *(precauzione)* care.

cauzione [kau'tsjone] *sf (caparra)* security, bail. **rilasciare su cauzione** release on bail. **cauzionare** *v* pay a deposit.

cava ['kava] *sf* quarry.

cavalcare [kaval'kare] *v* ride; *(ponte)* span. **cavalcata** *sf* ride. **cavalcavia** *sm invar* flyover. **a cavalcioni** astride. **cavaliere** [kava'ljɛre] *sm* knight; *(chi cavalca)* rider.

cavalleria [kavalle'ria] *sf (mil)* cavalry; *(medievale, cortesia)* chivalry. **cavalleresco** *agg* chivalrous. **cavallerizza** *sf* horsewoman; *(maneggio)* riding school. **cavallerizzo** *sm* horseman; *(chi insegna)* riding master.

cavalletta [kaval'letta] *sf* grasshopper. **cavalletto** [kaval'letto] *sm (sostegno)* trestle, stand; *(da pittore)* easel.

cavallo [ka'vallo] *sm* horse; *(scacchi)* knight. **a cavallo** on horseback. **a cavallo di** astride, straddling. **andare a cavallo** ride. **cavallo dei pantaloni** crotch. **cavalla** *sf* mare. **cavallina** *sf* filly. **correre la cavallina** sow one's wild oats.

cavare [ka'vare] *v* draw *or* pull out. **cavarsela** *v* get by, manage. **cavarsi** *v (togliersi)* take off. **cavatappi** *sm invar* corkscrew.

caverna [ka'vɛrna] *sf* cave. **cavernoso** *agg* cavernous, hollow.

cavia ['kavja] *sf* guinea pig.

caviale [ka'vjale] *sm* caviar.

caviglia [ka'viʎa] *sf* ankle.

cavillare [kavil'lare] *v* quibble.

cavo¹ ['kavo] *sm*, *agg (vuoto)* hollow.

cavo² ['kavo] *sm* cable.

cavolo ['kavolo] *sm* cabbage. **cavoli di Bruxelles** Brussels sprouts *pl*. **cavolfiore** *sm* cauliflower. **testa di cavolo** *(fam)* clot.

cazzo ['kattso] *sm (volg)* prick.

cazzotto [kat'tsɔtto] *sm (fam)* punch. **fare a cazzotti** fight.

ce [tʃe] *V* ci.

cece ['tʃetʃe] *sm* chick-pea.

cecità [tʃetʃi'ta] *sf* blindness.

Cecoslovacchia [tʃekozlo'vakkja] *sf* Czechoslovakia. **ceco(slovacco)** -a *s, agg* Czech(oslovak).

cedere ['tʃedere] *v* yield; *(trasferire)* hand

over; *(piegarsi)* give way. **cedere il passo** make way. **cedere il posto** give up one's seat.

cedola ['tʃedola] *sf (scontrino)* coupon; *(di titolo)* dividend voucher.

cedro¹ [tʃedro] *sm (agrume)* citron.

cedro² [tʃedro] *sm (conifera)* cedar.

ceffone [tʃef'fone] *sm* slap (in the face).

celare [tʃe'lare] *v* conceal, hide.

celebrare [tʃele'brare] *v* celebrate.

celebre ['tʃelebre] *agg* famous. **celebrità** *sf* fame; *(persona)* celebrity.

celere ['tʃelere] *agg* rapid. *sf* flying squad.

celeste [tʃe'lɛste] *agg, sm* sky-blue.

celibe ['tʃelibe] *agg* single. *sm* bachelor.

cella ['tʃella] *sf* cell. **cella frigorifera** cold storage.

cellula ['tʃellula] *sf* cell.

cellulosa [tʃellu'loza] *sf* cellulose.

cemento [tʃe'mento] *sm* cement. **cemento armato** reinforced concrete. **cementare** *v* cement.

cena ['tʃena] *sf* supper, dinner. **cenare** *v* have supper *or* dinner.

cencio ['tʃentʃo] *sm* rag; *(per stoviglie)* dishcloth; *(per spolverare)* duster. **cencioso** *agg* ragged, tattered.

cenere ['tʃenere] *sf* ash. **Ceneri** *sf pl* Ash Wednesday *sing*.

cenno ['tʃenno] *sm* sign, gesture; *(col capo)* nod; *(con gli occhi)* wink; *(con la mano)* wave; *(allusione)* mention.

censimento [tʃensi'mento] *sm* census.

censurare [tʃensu'rare] *v (biasimare)* censure; *(sottoporre a censura)* censor. **censura** *sf* censorship; *(riprovazione)* censure.

centenario [tʃente'narjo], -a *sm, sf* centenarian. *sm (ricorrenza)* centenary. *agg* hundred-year-old.

centesimo [tʃen'tezimo] *sm* hundredth; *(soldo)* cent. *agg* hundredth.

centigrado [tʃen'tigrado] *agg* centigrade.

centimetro [tʃen'timetro] *sm* centimetre; *(nastro per misurare)* tape-measure.

cento ['tʃento] *agg, sm* hundred. **per cento** per cent. **centinaio** *sm, pl* **-a** *f* hundred; *(circa cento)* about a hundred. **a centinaia** by the hundred, in hundreds.

centrale [tʃen'trale] *agg* central, principal. *sf (deposito)* main depot; *(del telefono)* exchange; *(di energia)* power station; *(di amministrazione)* head office. **centralino** *sm* switchboard. **centralinista** *s(m+f)* switchboard operator.

centro ['tʃentro] sm centre; (mezzo) middle; (luogo di soggiorno) resort; (fam: colpo centrato) bull's-eye.

ceppo ['tʃeppo] sm (razza) stock; (base di albero) stump; (pezzo di legno) block; (auto) brake-block. **ceppi** sm pl fetters pl.

cera¹ ['tʃera] sf wax; (per lucidare) polish. **dare la cera** wax. **ceralacca** sf sealing-wax.

cera² ['tʃera] sf (aspetto) air, expression. **aver buona/brutta cera** look well/ill. **far buona cera** a welcome heartily.

ceramica [tʃe'ramika] sf (oggetto) piece of pottery; (materiale) earthenware; (arte) pottery. **ceramiche** sf pl pottery sing. **ceramista** s(m+f) potter.

cercare [tʃer'kare] v look for, search for; (nei libri) look up; (tentare) try; (volere) want. **cerca di** search; (questua) beg.

cerchia ['tʃerkja] sf circle.

cerchio ['tʃerkjo] sm circle; (giocattolo, di botte) hoop. **fare cerchio intorno** a circle round.

cereale [tʃere'ale] sm, agg cereal.

cerebrale [tʃere'brale] agg cerebral.

cerimonia [tʃeri'mɔnja] sf ceremony. **far cerimonie** stand on ceremony. **senza cerimonie** without fuss. **cerimoniale** sm, agg ceremonial.

cerino [tʃe'rino] sm (candela) taper; (fiammifero) wax match.

cerniera [tʃer'njera] sf hinge; (di borsetta) clasp. **cerniera lampo** zip fastener.

cernita ['tʃernita] sf choice.

cero ['tʃero] sm (church) candle.

cerotto [tʃe'rɔtto] sm plaster.

certezza [tʃer'tettsa] sf certainty.

certificare [tʃertifi'kare] v certify. **certificato** sm certificate.

certo ['tʃerto] agg certain. avv certainly. **dare or sapere per certo** know for a fact. **tenere per certo** have no doubts about.

certuni [tʃer'tuni] pron some (people).

cervello [tʃer'vɛllo] sm brain; (intelligenza, cibo) brains pl. **dare al cervello** go to one's head.

cervo ['tʃervo] sm deer, stag. **cervo volante** (insetto) stag beetle; (aquilone) kite. **cerva** sf deer, doe, hind.

cesello [tʃe'zɛllo] sm (strumento) engraving tool, small chisel. **cesellare** v engrave, chisel; (fare con cura) polish.

cesoie [tʃe'zɔje] sf pl shears pl.

cespo ['tʃespo] sm (di erbe) tuft; (di fiori) cluster. **cespo di lattuga** head of lettuce.

cespuglio [tʃes'puʎo] sm shrub, bush.

cessare [tʃes'sare] v cease, stop. **cessate il fuoco** sm cease-fire. **cessazione** sf cessation; (comm) termination, stoppage.

cessione [tʃes'sjone] sf relinquishment; (dir) transfer, assignment.

cesso ['tʃesso] sm (fam) loo, lavatory.

cesta ['tʃesta] sf basket.

cestino [tʃes'tino] sm waste-paper basket; (da lavoro) work-basket. **cestino da viaggio** packed lunch. **cestinare** v throw away; (scritti) reject.

cesto ['tʃesto] sm basket.

ceto ['tʃeto] sm class.

cetriolo [tʃetri'ɔlo] sm cucumber. **cetriolino** sm gherkin.

che¹ [ke] pron (persone: soggetto) who; (persone: oggetto) whom, that; (cose) which, that; (quando) when; (dove) where; (interrogativo) what; (indefinito) something. inter what! (come) how! agg (quale) what; (numero limitato) which. **non è un gran che** it's nothing much.

che² [ke] cong that; (comparativa) than; (quando) when; (dopo) after; (eccettuativa) but.

checché [ke'ke] pron whatever.

chi [ki] pron (soggetto) who; (oggetto) whom; (colui che) he who; (colei che) she who; (coloro che) those who; (chiunque) whoever. **chi ... chi ...** some ... others .... **di chi** whose.

chiacchierare [kjakkje'rare] v chat. **chiacchiera** sf chat; (discorso inutile) idle talk. **far due or quattro chiacchiere** chat. **chiacchierata** sf chat.

chiacchierone [kjakkje'rone], -a agg talkative; (pettegolo) gossipy. sm, sf chatterbox, gossip.

chiamare [kja'mare] v call; (far venire) send for; (al telefono) ring (up). **chiamare in giudizio** sue. **chiamare sotto le armi** call up. **chiamata** sf call. **chiamata in giudizio** summons. **chiamata urbana/interurbana** local/trunk call.

chiarire [kja'rire] v clarify; (spiegare) explain.

chiaro ['kjaro] agg clear; (luminoso) bright; (non scuro) light. sm light. avv clearly, distinctly. **chiaro e tondo** blunt. **mettere in chiaro** clear up.

chiasso ['kjasso] sm noise, racket, row. **far chiasso** kick up a row. **chiassoso** agg rowdy, noisy; (colore) loud.

chiavare [kja'vare] v (volg) screw, fuck.

chiave ['kjave] sf key; (tec) spanner; (segno musicale) clef. **chiave apritutto** master key. **chiave inglese** adjustable spanner.

chiavistello [kjavis'tello] sm bolt, latch.

chiazzare [kjat'tsare] v spot; (con colori diversi) mottle. **chiazza** sf spot; (sulla pelle) patch, blotch. **chiazzato** agg spotty; blotchy; mottled.

chicco ['kikko] sm grain; (di caffè) bean; (d'uva) grape; (di grandine) hailstone; (del rosario) bead.

***chiedere** ['kjɛdere] v ask; (per avere) ask for; (di diritto) demand; (vivamente) beg; (richiedere) require; (prezzo) charge. **chiedersi** v wonder.

chiesa ['kjɛza] sf church.

chiglia ['kiʎa] sf keel.

chilo ['kilo] sm kilo.

chilometro [ki'lɔmetro] sm kilometre.

chimera [ki'mɛra] sf chimera.

chimico [kimiko] agg chemical. sm chemist. **chimica** sf (scienza) chemistry; (persona) chemist.

china[1] ['kina] sf slope; decline.

china[2] ['kina] sf **inchiostro di china** sm Indian ink.

chinare [ki'nare] v bend; (occhi) lower. **chinarsi** v stoop.

chincaglieria [kinkaʎe'ria] sf fancy goods pl.

chiocciare [kjot'tʃare] v cluck; (covare) brood. **chioccia** sf broody hen.

chiocciola ['kjɔttʃola] sf snail; (anat) cochlea. **scala a chiocciola** sf spiral staircase.

chiodo ['kjɔdo] sm nail; fixed idea; (fam) debt. **chiodato** agg nailed; (scarpe) hobnailed.

chioma ['kjɔma] sf hair.

chiosco ['kjɔsko] sm kiosk, stall.

chiostro ['kjɔstro] sm cloister.

chiromante [kiro'mante] s(m+f) fortuneteller. **chiromanzia** sf fortune-telling.

chirurgia [kirur'dʒia] sf surgery. **chirurgico** agg surgical. **chirurgo** sm surgeon.

chissà [kis'sa] avv who knows, goodness knows; (forse) perhaps.

chitarra [ki'tarra] sf guitar.

***chiudere** [kjudere] v close, shut; (a chiave) lock (up); (sbattendo) slam; (spegnere) turn or switch off; (tappare)

stop up; (recingere) enclose. **chiudere bottega** shut up shop. **chiuder dentro** shut in. **chiudere in attivo/perdita** show a profit/loss.

chiunque [ki'unkwe] pron whoever; (qualunque persona) anyone.

chiusa ['kjuza] sf (parte finale) close; (recinto) enclosure; (sbarramento artificiale) lock; (diga) dam.

chiuso ['kjuzo] agg closed, shut.

chiusura [kju'zura] sf (termine) end; (serratura) fastener; (il chiudere) closing, shut-down.

ci [tʃi], **ce** pron (to) us; (riflessivo) ourselves; (reciproco) each other; (impersonale) one; (di ciò) about it or that. **ci conto su** I'm counting on it. **ci penso io** I'll think about it. avv (li) there; (qui) here.

ciabatta [tʃa'batta] sf slipper.

cialda ['tʃalda] sf waffle; (cialdino) wafer.

ciambella [tʃam'bella] sf (pasta) doughnut; (cuscino) rubber ring; (di salvataggio) lifebuoy.

ciambellano [tʃambel'lano] sm chamberlain.

cianciare [tʃan'tʃare] v prattle away, talk idly.

cianfrusaglia [tʃanfru'zaʎa] sf knickknack, junk.

cianuro [tʃa'nuro] sm cyanide.

ciao ['tʃao] inter (incontrandosi) hello! (congedandosi) cheerio! goodbye!

ciarlare [tʃar'lare] v chatter, chat. **ciarla** sf (chiacchiera) chat; (pettegolezzo) gossip.

ciarlatano [tʃarla'tano] sm charlatan.

ciascuno [tʃas'kuno] agg each; (ogni) every. pron each one; (ognuno) everyone.

cibare [tʃi'bare] v feed. **cibo** sm food.

cicala [tʃi'kala] sf cicada.

cicalino [tʃika'lino] sm buzzer.

cicatrice [tʃika'tritʃe] sf scar.

cicca ['tʃikka] sf (mozzicone) fag end. **non valere una cicca** be not worth a thing.

cicchetto [tʃik'ketto] sm (bicchierino) nip; (rimprovero) dressing-down.

cicerone [tʃitʃe'rone] sm (tourist) guide.

ciclamino [tʃikla'mino] sm cyclamen.

ciclismo [tʃi'klizmo] sm cycling. **ciclista** s(m+f) cyclist.

ciclo ['tʃiklo] sm cycle. **ciclico** agg cyclical.

ciclomotore [tʃiklomo'tore] sm moped.

ciclone [tʃi'klone] sm cyclone.

cicogna [tʃi'koɲa] sf stork.

cicoria [tʃi'kɔrja] sf chicory. **cicoria belga** endive.

cicuta [tʃi'kuta] sf hemlock.

cieco [tʃɛko], **-a** agg blind. sm, sf blind person.

cielo [tʃɛlo] sm sky; (sede divina) heaven. **a cielo aperto** in the open. **per amor del cielo!** for heaven's sake!

cifra [tʃifra] sf figure, number; (somma) amount; (codice segreto) cipher.

ciglio [tʃiʎo] sm, pl **-a** f in anat sense eyelash; (bordo) edge. **non batter ciglio** not bat an eyelid.

cigno [tʃiɲo] sm swan.

cigolare [tʃigo'lare] v creak, squeak. **cigolio** sm creaking, squeaking.

cilecca [tʃi'lekka] sf **far cilecca** misfire.

ciliegia [tʃi'ljedʒa] sf cherry. **ciliegio** sm cherry tree.

cilindro [tʃi'lindro] sm cylinder; (rullo) roller; (cappello) top hat.

cima [tʃima] sf top, summit. **da cima a fondo** from top to bottom. **cimare** v (piante) trim, clip; (tessuti) shear.

cimelio [tʃi'mɛljo] sm (oggetto prezioso) treasure; (ricordo) relic, memento.

cimice [tʃimitʃe] sf bedbug.

ciminiera [tʃimi'njɛra] sf chimney.

cimitero [tʃimi'tɛro] sm cemetery.

cimurro [tʃi'murro] sm distemper.

Cina [tʃina] sf China. **cinese** agg, s(m+f) Chinese.

cincia [tʃintʃa] sf tit(mouse). **cinciallegra** sf (great) tit.

cincin [tʃin'tʃin] inter cheers!

cinema [tʃinema] sm invar cinema. **cinematografico** agg film. **cinematografo** sm cinema.

cinetico [tʃi'nɛtiko] agg kinetic. **cinetica** sf kinetics.

*cingere [tʃindʒere] v surround, encircle. **cingere d'assedio** besiege.

cinghia [tʃingja] sf belt.

cinghiale [tʃin'gjale] sm (wild) boar; (pelle) pigskin.

cinguettare [tʃingwet'tare] v twitter. **cinguettio** sm twittering.

cinico [tʃiniko], **-a** agg cynical. sm, sf cynic. **cinismo** sm cynicism.

cinquanta [tʃin'kwanta] sm, agg fifty. **cinquantesimo** sm, agg fiftieth.

cinque [tʃinkwe] sm, agg five.

cintura [tʃin'tura] sf belt; (giro della vita)

waist. **cintura di sicurezza** safety-belt. **cinturino** sm strap.

ciò [tʃɔ] pron this, that. **ciò che** what. **ciò detto** having said this. **ciònondimeno** or **ciònonostante** nevertheless, just the same. **con ciò** therefore. **e con ciò?** so what?

cioccolata [tʃokko'lata] sf chocolate; (bevanda) (drinking) chocolate. **cioccolatino** sm (piece of) chocolate. **cioccolato** sm chocolate.

cioè [tʃo'ɛ] avv that is; (o piuttosto) or better.

ciondolo [tʃondolo] sm pendant. **ciondolare** v dangle; (bighellonare) hang about.

ciotola [tʃotola] sf bowl.

ciottolo [tʃottolo] sm pebble.

cipiglio [tʃi'piʎo] sm frown.

cipolla [tʃi'polla] sf onion.

cipresso [tʃi'presso] sm cypress.

cipria [tʃiprja] sf powder.

Cipro [tʃipro] sm Cyprus. **cipriota** agg, s(m+f) Cypriot.

circa [tʃirka] prep (riguardo a) about, concerning. avv (pressappoco) about, approximately.

circo [tʃirko] sm circus.

circolare¹ [tʃirko'lare] sf, agg circular. **assegno circolare** sm banker's draft.

circolare² [tʃirko'lare] v circulate. **circolatorio** agg circulatory. **circolazione** sf circulation.

circolo [tʃirkolo] sm circle.

*circoncidere [tʃirkon'tʃidere] v circumcise. **circoncisione** sf circumcision.

circondare [tʃirkon'dare] v surround.

circonferenza [tʃirkonfe'rɛntsa] sf circumference.

circonvallazione [tʃirkonvalla'tsjone] sf ring-road.

*circoscrivere [tʃirkos'krivere] v circumscribe.

circostante [tʃirkos'tante] agg surrounding.

circostanza [tʃirkos'tantsa] sf circumstances pl; (condizione particolare) occurrence. **di circostanza** fitting.

circuito [tʃir'kuito] sm circuit; (sport) (race-)track.

cisterna [tʃis'tɛrna] sf cistern; (serbatoio) tank. **nave cisterna** sf tanker.

citare [tʃi'tare] v (riportare parole) quote; (nominare) cite; (dir: convocare) summon(s). **citazione** sf quotation; summons.

citofono [tʃi'tɔfono] *sm* (*fam*) intercom.

città [tʃit'ta] *sf* town, city. **cittadina** *sf* small town; (*persona*) citizen. **cittadinanza** *sf* citizenship, nationality; (*popolazione*) people. **cittadino** *sm* citizen.

ciuco ['tʃuko] *sm* donkey.

ciuffo ['tʃuffo] *sm* tuft.

ciurma ['tʃurma] *sf* crew; (*ciurmaglia*) riffraff.

civetta [tʃi'vetta] *sf* (*uccello*) owl; (*donna*) flirt. **civettare** *v* flirt.

civico ['tʃiviko] *agg* civic.

civile [tʃi'vile] *agg* civil; (*non militare*) civilian; (*incivilito*) civilized. **civilizzare** *v* civilize. **civismo** *sm* public spirit.

civiltà [tʃivil'ta] *sf* civilization; (*cortesia*) good breeding.

clacson ['klakson] *sm invar* horn, hooter.

clamore [kla'more] *sm* clamour; (*fig*) outcry, sensation. **clamoroso** *agg* noisy, sensational.

clandestino [klandes'tino] *agg* clandestine.

clarinetto [klari'netto] *sm* clarinet.

classe ['klasse] *sf* class; (*scuola*) form.

classico ['klassiko] *agg* classic, classical; typical. *sm* classic.

classificare [klassifi'kare] *v* classify. **classificatore** *sm* file. **classificazione** *sf* classification.

classismo [klas'sizmo] *sm* class-consciousness. **classista** *agg* class-conscious.

clausola ['klauzola] *sf* clause.

claustrofobia [klaustrofo'bia] *sf* claustrophobia.

clavicembalo [klavi'tʃembalo] *sm* harpsichord.

clavicola [kla'vikola] *sf* collar-bone.

clemenza [kle'mɛntsa] *sf* clemency; (*tempo*) mildness. **clemente** *agg* mild, clement.

cleptomane [klep'tomane] *s(m+f)*, *agg* kleptomaniac. **cleptomania** *sf* kleptomania.

clero ['klɛro] *sm* clergy. **clericale** *agg* clerical.

cliché [kli'ʃe] *sm* (*stampa*) block; (*luogo comune*) cliché.

cliente [kli'ɛnte] *s(m+f)* (*di negozio*) customer; (*di professionista*) client; (*di albergo*) guest. **cliente abituale** patron. **clientela** *sf* customers *pl*, clientele; (*di professionista*) practice.

clima ['klima] *sm* climate. **climatico** *agg* climatic.

clinica ['klinika] *sf* clinic. **clinico** *agg* clinical.

cloro ['klɔro] *sm* chlorine.

clorofilla [kloro'filla] *sf* chlorophyll.

cloroformio [kloro'fɔrmjo] *sm* chloroform.

cloruro [klo'ruro] *sm* chloride.

coabitare [koabi'tare] *v* cohabit.

coagulare [koagu'lare] *v* coagulate; (*latte*) curdle; (*sangue*) clot. **coagulazione** *sf* coagulation; curdling; clotting.

coalizione [koali'tsjone] *sf* coalition. **coalizzarsi** *v* unite.

coatto [ko'atto] *agg* compulsory.

cobalto [ko'balto] *sm* cobalt.

cobra ['kɔbra] *sm invar* cobra.

cocaina [koka'ina] *sf* cocaine. **cocainomane** *s(m+f)* cocaine addict.

coccarda [kok'karda] *sf* rosette.

cocchio ['kɔkkjo] *sm* carriage, coach. **cocchiere** *sm* coachman.

coccinella [kottʃi'nella] *sf* ladybird.

coccio ['kɔttʃo] *sm* (*terracotta*) earthenware; (*rottame*) piece, crock.

cocciuto [kot'tʃuto] *agg* stubborn, pigheaded. **cocciutaggine** *sf* stubbornness, pig-headedness.

cocco[1] ['kɔkko], **-a** *sm*, *sf* (*fam*: *amore*) pet, darling.

cocco[2] ['kɔkko] *sm* coconut tree *or* palm. **noce di cocco** *sf* coconut.

coccodrillo [kokko'drillo] *sm* crocodile.

cocente [ko'tʃɛnte] *agg* burning, scorching.

cocomero [ko'komero] *sm* water-melon.

cocuzzolo [ko'kuttsolo] *sm* tip.

coda ['koda] *sf* tail; (*fila*) queue; (*musica*) coda. **con la coda dell'occhio** out of the corner of one's eye. **fare la coda** queue (up).

codardo [ko'dardo] *agg* cowardly.

codeina [kode'ina] *sf* codeine.

codesto [ko'desto] *agg* that. *pron* that (one).

codice ['kɔditʃe] *sm* code. **codice della strada** highway code.

coefficiente [koeffi'tʃɛnte] *sm* coefficient; (*causa*) contributory factor.

coerente [koe'rɛnte] *agg* coherent; (*fig*) consistent.

coesistere [koe'zistere] *v* coexist. **coesistenza** *sf* coexistence.

coetaneo [koe'taneo], **-a** *s*, *agg* contemporary.

cofano ['kɔfano] *sm* (*auto*) bonnet; (*forziere*) chest.

*cogliere ['kɔʎere] *v* (*staccare*) pick; (*sorprendere, capire*) catch; (*colpire*) hit. **cogliere la palla al balzo** seize the opportunity.

coglione [koʎ'ʎone] (*volg*) *sm* testicle; (*sciocco*) fool. **coglioneria** *sf* foolishness.

cognato [koɲ'ɲato] *sm* brother-in-law. **cognata** *sf* sister-in-law.

cognizione [koɲ'ɲittsjone] *sf* knowledge; (*dir*) cognizance.

cognome [koɲ'ɲome] *sm* surname.

coi ['kɔi] *prep+art* con i.

*coincidere [koin'tʃidere] *v* coincide. **coincidenza** *sf* coincidence; (*treno, ecc.*) connection.

*coinvolgere [koin'vɔldʒere] *v* involve.

coito ['kɔito] *sm* coitus, sexual intercourse.

col [kol] *prep+art* con il.

colare [ko'lare] *v* (*filtrare*) sieve, strain; (*gocciolare*) drip, trickle; (*fondere*) melt, cast; (*a picco*) sink. **colabrodo** or **colapasta** *sm invar* strainer, colander. **colatoio** *sm* strainer. **colino** *sm* sieve.

colazione [kola'tsjone] *sf* (*del mattino*) breakfast; (*di mezzogiorno*) lunch. **far colazione** (have) breakfast; (have) lunch.

colei [ko'lei] *pron* (*soggetto*) she; (*oggetto*) her. **colei che** (she) who.

colera [ko'lɛra] *sm invar* cholera.

colesterolo [koleste'rɔlo] *sm* cholesterol.

coll' [koll] *prep+art* con l'.

colla ['kɔlla] *sf* glue, paste.

collaborare [kollabo'rare] *v* collaborate; (*giornale*) contribute. **collaboratore, -trice** *sm, sf* collaborator; contributor. **collaborazione** *sf* collaboration; contribution.

collana [kol'lana] *sf* necklace; (*raccolta*) collection.

collants [kol'lã] *sm pl* tights *pl*.

collare [kol'lare] *sm* collar.

collasso [kol'lasso] *sm* collapse. **collasso cardiaco** heart failure.

collaterale [kollate'rale] *agg* collateral.

collaudare [kollau'dare] *v* test. **collaudo** *sm* test.

colle¹ ['kɔlle] *sm* (*altura*) hill.

colle² ['kɔlle] *sm* (*valico*) pass.

collega [kol'lɛga] *s(m+f)*, *m pl* -ghi colleague.

collegare [kolle'gare] *v* connect, link (up).

collegarsi *v* (*telefono*) get through. **collegamento** *sm* connection, link; (*mil*) liaison.

collegio [kol'lɛdʒo] *sm* college; (*convitto*) boarding school; (*consiglio*) board. **collegio di difesa** counsel for the defence. **collegio elettorale** constituency.

collegiale [kolle'dʒale] *s(m+f)* boarder. *agg* (*collettivo*) corporate, collective; (*di collegio*) college, boarding-school.

collera ['kɔllera] *sf* anger, rage.

colletta [kol'letta] *sf* collection.

collettivo [kollet'tivo] *agg* collective.

colletto [kol'letto] *sm* collar.

collettore [kollet'tore] *sm* collector; (*tec*) manifold.

collezionare [kollettsjo'nare] *v* collect. **collezione** *sf* collection.

collina [kol'lina] *sf* hill.

collisione [kolli'zjone] *sf* collision.

collo¹ ['kɔllo] *sm* neck. **collo del piede** instep.

collo² ['kɔllo] *sm* (*pacco*) parcel, package; (*bagaglio*) item of luggage.

collocare [kollo'kare] *v* place. **collocare a riposo** retire, pension off. **collocamento** *sm* (*occupazione*) employment, job; (*il collocare*) placing, setting; (*vendita*) sale. **collocamento a riposo** retirement. **ufficio di collocamento** *sm* employment exchange.

colloide [kol'lɔide] *sm* colloid. *agg* colloidal.

colloquio [kol'lɔkwjo] *sm* conversation, talk; (*intervista*) interview; (*esame*) oral (examination).

colmare [kol'mare] *v* fill; (*fino all'orlo*) fill to the brim; (*coprire di*) shower. **colmo** *sm* top, summit; (*culmine*) height; (*situazione paradossale*) last straw, limit.

colombo [ko'lombo], -a *sm, sf* dove, pigeon. **colombaia** *sf* dovecote.

colonia [ko'lɔnja] *sf* colony; (*per bambini*) holiday camp; (*per lavoro*) settlement. **coloniale** *agg* colonial.

colonna [ko'lonna] *sf* column; (*sostegno*) pillar; (*fila*) line, queue. **colonna vertebrale** spinal column, backbone.

colonnello [kolon'nello] *sm* colonel.

colore [ko'lore] *sm* colour; (*sostanza colorante*) paint, dye, tint; (*carte da gioco*) suit. **farne di tutti i colori** get up to all sorts of mischief. **colorante** *sm* dye. **colorare** *v* colour.

commuovere

colorire [kolo'rire] v colour; *(arrossire)* blush.

colorito [kolo'rito] sm *(carnagione)* complexion; *(tinta)* colour(ing). agg colourful.

coloro [ko'loro] pron *(soggetto)* they; *(oggetto)* them. **coloro che** (those) who.

colossale [kolos'sale] agg colossal, tremendous. **colosso** sm *(statua)* colossus; *(uomo)* giant.

colpa ['kolpa] sf fault; *(colpevolezza)* guilt; *(peccato)* sin. **dare la colpa a** blame. **per colpa di** through, because of. **prendersi la colpa** take the blame.

colpevole [kol'pevole] agg *(persona)* guilty; *(azione)* culpable. s(m+f) culprit. **dichiararsi colpevole** plead guilty.

colpire [kol'pire] v hit, strike.

colpo ['kolpo] sm stroke, blow; *(arma da fuoco)* shot; *(impresa)* move, raid. **colpo d'aria** draught. **far colpo** impress, cause a stir, make a hit.

coltello [kol'tello] sm knife. **coltellata** sf stab.

coltivare [kolti'vare] v cultivate; *(far crescere)* grow. **coltivatore** sm grower. **coltivazione** sf cultivation; growing. **colto¹** ['kolto] agg cultivated, cultured.

coltura [kol'tura] sf cultivation; *(allevamento)* breeding; *(med)* culture.

colui [ko'lui] pron *(soggetto)* he; *(oggetto)* him. **colui che** (he) who.

coma ['kɔma] sm invar coma. **comatoso** agg comatose.

comandare [koman'dare] v *(reggere comando)* be in command, command; *(chiedere)* order; *(mec)* control. **comandamento** sm commandment. **comandante** sm commander. **comando** sm command; *(sede)* headquarters; *(mec)* control, drive. **comando a distanza** remote control.

combaciare [komba'tʃare] v coincide.

combattere [kom'battere] v fight. **combattente** sm serviceman. **combattimento** sm fight. **combattivo** agg pugnacious. **combattuto** agg undecided, torn.

combinare [kombi'nare] v combine; *(mettere d'accordo)* agree; *(concludere)* arrange, bring off, achieve. **combinazione** sf combination; *(caso)* chance.

combustibile [kombus'tibile] sm fuel. agg combustible.

combustione [kombus'tjone] sf combustion.

come ['kome] avv as; *(somiglianza)* like; *(in qual modo)* how.

comedone [kome'done] sm blackhead.

cometa [ko'meta] sf comet.

comico ['komiko], -a sm, sf comic, comedian. agg comic(al), funny; *(commedia)* dramatic.

comignolo [ko'miɲolo] sm chimney-pot.

cominciare [komin'tʃare] v begin, start. **a cominciare da** from.

comitato [komi'tato] sm committee.

comitiva [komi'tiva] sf party.

comizio [ko'mitsjo] sm meeting.

commedia [kom'mɛdja] sf play, comedy; *(finzione)* play-acting, sham; *(scena comica)* farce. **commediante** s(m+f) *(fam)* ham; *(ipocrita)* humbug. **commediografo** sm playwright.

commemorare [kommemo'rare] v commemorate. **commemorativo** agg memorial.

commentare [kommen'tare] v comment (on). **commentario** sm commentary. **commentatore, -trice** sm, sf commentator. **commento** sm comment; *(radio)* commentary.

commercio [kom'mertʃo] sm trade, commerce. **commercio all'ingrosso/al minuto** wholesale/retail trade. **mettere in commercio** put on sale.

commesso [kom'messo], -a sm, sf *(di negozio)* (shop) assistant; *(d'ufficio)* clerk. **commesso viaggiatore** travelling salesman.

commestibile [kommes'tibile] agg edible. **commestibili** sm pl foodstuffs pl, provisions pl.

*****committere** [kom'mettere] v *(fare)* commit; *(mettere insieme)* fit together, join; *(ordinare)* commission.

commissariato [kommissa'rjato] sm *(polizia)* police station. **commissario** sm *(polizia)* police inspector; *(sovietico)* commissar; *(amministratore)* commissioner.

commissione [kommis'sjone] sf commission; *(incombenza)* errand; *(ordinazione)* order; *(comitato)* board. **fare delle commissioni** go shopping.

commosso [kom'mosso] agg moved, touched.

commozione [kommo'tsjone] sf deep feelings pl; *(med)* concussion.

*****commuovere** [kom'mwɔvere] v move,

touch. **commovente** *agg* moving, touching.

commutare [kommu'tare] *v* commute.

comò [ko'mɔ] *sm* chest of drawers.

comodino [komo'dino] *sm* bedside table.

comodo ['kɔmodo] *sm* convenience. *agg* comfortable; (*opportuno*) convenient; (*utile*) useful, handy. **far comodo** be useful *or* handy; (*garbare*) please, suit. **fare con comodo** take one's time. **comodare** *v* suit. **comodità** *sf* comfort.

compagnia [kompa'ɲia] *sf* company.

compagno [kom'paɲo], **-a** *sm, sf* companion, mate, friend. **compagno d'armi** fellow-soldier. **compagno di prigionia/viaggio** fellow-prisoner/traveller. **compagno di scuola** classmate.

*****comparire** [kompa'rire] *v* appear. **comparsa** *sf* appearance; (*film*) extra.

compartimento [komparti'mento] *sm* compartment.

compassione [kompas'sjone] *sf* pity. **far compassione** arouse pity. **per compassione** out of pity. **compassionevole** *agg* (*che fa compassione*) pitiful; (*che ha compassione*) compassionate.

compasso [kom'passo] *sm* compasses *pl*.

compatire [kompa'tire] *v* be sorry for. **compatibile** *agg* compatible; (*perdonabile*) excusable.

compatriota [kompatri'ɔta] *s(m+f)* compatriot.

compatto [kom'patto] *agg* compact, dense; (*fig*) united. **compattezza** *sf* compactness; unity.

compendio [kom'pendjo] *sm* (*riassunto*) summary; (*trattato*) outline. **compendioso** *agg* brief.

compensare [kompen'sare] *v* compensate; (*ricompensare*) reward. (**legno**) **compensato** *sm* plywood. **compensazione** *sf* compensation; (*econ*) clearing. **compenso** *sm* compensation; reward. **in compenso** in return, in exchange.

competente [kompe'tɛnte] *agg* competent, qualified; (*adeguato*) fair. **competenza** *sf* experience, authority; (*dir*) competence.

competere [kom'pɛtere] *v* (*spettare*) be due; (*gareggiare*) compete, rival. **competitivo** *agg* competitive.

*****compiacere** [kompja'tʃere] *v* please. **compiacersi** *v* be pleased, rejoice; congratulate; (*degnarsi*) be good enough. **compiaciuto** *agg* pleased, satisfied.

*****compiangere** [kom'pjandʒere] *v* pity; (*rimpiangere*) mourn. **compianto** *sm* grief.

compiere [kom'pjere] *v* (*finire*) complete; (*adempiere*) carry out, fulfil. **compiere ... anni** be ... years old. **compimento** *sm* fulfilment.

compilare [kompi'lare] *v* compile, draw up.

compito ['kompito] *sm* task; (*dovere*) duty; (*scuola*) homework.

compleanno [komple'anno] *sm* birthday.

complementare [komplemen'tare] *agg* complementary; (*secondario*) subsidiary. **complemento** *sm* complement; (*gramm*) object.

complesso [kom'plɛsso] *agg* complex; complicated. *sm* (*insieme*) whole; (*industria*) combine, group; (*psic*) complex; (*musica*) ensemble, band. **in complesso** (*tutto sommato*) on the whole; (*in tutto*) in all, altogether. **nel complesso as a** whole.

completo [kom'plɛto] *agg* complete; (*pieno*) full up; (*assoluto*) total. *sm* (*abito*) suit; (*di maglia*) twin set; (*in generale*) outfit. **al completo** (*pieno*) full up; (*esaurito*) sold out; (*tutti presenti*) in full force. **completare** *v* complete, finish.

complicare [kompli'kare] *v* complicate; (*aggravare*) worsen. **complicato** *agg* complicated, complex; (*intricato*) involved. **complicazione** *sf* complication.

complice ['komplitʃe] *s(m+f)* accomplice; (*dir*) accessory. **complice in adulterio** correspondent. **essere complice in** be a party to. **complicità** *sf* complicity.

complimento [kompli'mento] *sm* compliment. **complimenti** *sm pl* (*cerimonie*) ceremony *sing*; (*ossequi*) regards *pl*; (*auguri*) congratulations *pl*. **far complimenti** stand on ceremony. **complimentare** *v* compliment.

complotto [kom'plɔtto] *sm* plot. **complottare** *v* plot.

componente [kompo'nɛnte] *agg* component. *s(m+f)* component, member.

*****comporre** [kom'porre] *v* (*costituire*) make up; (*assestare*) tidy; (*mettere assieme*) assemble, put together; (*musica*) compose; (*atteggiare*) put on. **comporre una lite** settle a quarrel.

comportare [kompor'tare] *v* (*richiedere*) involve; (*portare con sè*) imply; (*consentire*) permit. **comportarsi** *v* behave. **comportamento** *sm* behaviour.

compositore [kompozi'tore], **-trice** *sm, sf* (*musica*) composer; type-setter.

composizione [kompozi'tsjone] *sf* composition.

composto [kom'posto] *sm* compound, mixture. *agg* (*decoroso*) dignified; (*assestato*) neat; (*costituito*) made up (of), consisting (of); (*mat*) compound. **compostezza** *sf* self-possession; decorum; neatness.

comprare [komp'rare] *v* buy; (*corrompere*) bribe. **comprare all'ingrosso** buy wholesale. **compratore, -trice** *sm, sf* buyer.

***comprendere** [kom'prendere] *v* include; (*capire*) understand. **comprensibile** *agg* understandable, intelligible. **comprensione** *sf* understanding. **comprensivo** *agg* (*che include*) inclusive, comprehensive; (*tollerante*) understanding. **compreso** *agg* inclusive; (*capito*) understood.

compressa [kom'pressa] *sf* tablet, pill; (*garza*) compress.

compressore [kompres'sore] *sm* compressor.

***comprimere** [kom'primere] *v* compress; (*reprimere*) suppress.

***compromettere** [kompro'mettere] *v* compromise. **compromesso** *sm* compromise. **compromettente** *agg* compromising.

comprovare [kompro'vare] *v* confirm.

compunto [kom'punto] *agg* contrite.

comune [ko'mune] *agg* common. *sm* commune, municipality; (*autorità*) town council. **avere in comune** share. **fuori del comune** uncommon, unusual.

comunicare [komuni'kare] *v* communicate, announce; (*malattia*) pass on; (*rel*) administer Communion. **comunicarsi** *v* spread; receive Communion. **comunicato** *sm* communiqué, bulletin. **comunicato stampa** press release.

comunione [komu'njone] *sf* community; (*rel*) (Holy) Communion.

comunismo [komu'nizmo] *sm* communism. **comunista** *s(m+f)*, *agg* communist.

comunità [komuni'ta] *sf* community.

comunque [ko'munkwe] *avv* (*in ogni modo*) anyhow, at any rate. *cong* however, no matter how.

con [kon] *prep* with; (*mezzo*) with, by.

conca ['konka] *sf* basin; (*valle*) depression.

concavo [kon'kavo] *agg* concave.

***concedere** [kon'tʃedere] *v* grant, award; (*permettere*) allow.

concentrare [kontʃen'trare] *v* concentrate. **concentramento** *sm* concentration. **concentrato** *sm* concentrate.

concentrico [kon'tʃentriko] *agg* concentric.

concepire [kontʃe'pire] *v* conceive; (*capire*) understand; (*nutrire*) entertain, cherish. **concepibile** *agg* conceivable.

conceria [kontʃe'ria] *sf* tannery.

concernere [kon'tʃernere] *v* concern, regard. **per quanto mi concerne** as far as I am concerned.

concerto [kon'tʃerto] *sm* concert.

concessione [kontʃes'sjone] *sf* concession.

concetto [kon'tʃetto] *sm* concept, notion, idea.

concezione [kontʃe'tsjone] *sf* conception; (*pensiero*) concept.

conchiglia [kon'kiʎa] *sf* shell.

conciare [kon'tʃare] *v* (*pelli*) tan; (*tabacco*) cure; (*ridurre male*) get into a mess; spoil. **conciare per le feste** (*fam*) give a thrashing.

conciliare [kontʃi'ljare] *v* reconcile.

concilio [kon'tʃiljo] *sm* council.

concime [kon'tʃime] *sm* manure; (*artificiale*) fertilizer.

conciso [kon'tʃizo] *agg* concise, to the point.

concittadino [kontʃitta'dino], **-a** *sm, sf* fellow-citizen.

conclave [kon'klave] *sm* conclave.

***concludere** [kon'kludere] *v* conclude; (*operare con profitto*) achieve. **conclusione** *sf* conclusion, result. **in conclusione** to sum up, in short. **conclusivo** *agg* final, conclusive; (*determinante*) decisive.

concordare [konkor'dare] *v* agree, fix. **concordato** *sm* agreement.

concorrente [konkor'rente] *agg* concurrent; (*rivale*) competing. *s(m+f)* competitor; (*a un concorso*) candidate, applicant. **concorrenza** *sf* competition. **far concorrenza** compete (with).

***concorrere** [kon'korrere] *v* contribute; (*gareggiare*) compete (for); (*convergere*) come together.

concorso [kon'korso] *sm* (*affluire*) concourse, gathering; contribution; contest, competition; (*esame*) competitive examination.

concreto [kon'kreto] *sm, agg* concrete. **concretare** *v* get done.

condannare [kondan'nare] v condemn; (*dichiarare colpevole*) sentence. condanna *sf* conviction, sentence. condannato, -a *sm, sf* condemned person.

condensazione [kondensa'tsjone] *sf* condensation. condensare *v* condense.

condire [kon'dire] *v* season; (*insalata*) dress. condimento *sm* seasoning, dressing.

*condividere [kondi'videre] *v* share.

condizione [kondi'tsjone] *sf* condition. condizioni *sf pl* state *sing*; (*comm*) terms *pl*. condizioni di vita standard of living *sing*. essere in condizione di be able to. mettere in condizione di enable to. condizionale *sm, agg* conditional.

condoglianza [kondo'ʎantsa] *sf* condolence. fare le condoglianze express one's sympathy.

condonare [kondo'nare] *v* remit, condone. condono *sm* remission.

condotta [kon'dotta] *sm* (*comportamento*) conduct, behaviour; (*di un'azione, ecc.*) handling; (*tubazione*) piping.

*condurre [kon'durre] *v* (*portare*) lead; (*accompagnare*) take; (*auto*) drive; (*dirigere*) manage, run; (*eseguire, fis*) conduct; (*ridurre*) reduce. condursi *v* behave.

conduttore [kondut'tore] *agg* conducting. *sm* (*fis*) conductor; (*conducente*) driver. conduttura *sf* (*tubazione*) piping; (*condotto*) pipe.

confederazione [konfedera'tsjone] *sf* federation.

conferenza [konfe'rentsa] *sf* (*congresso*) conference; (*discorso*) lecture. conferenza stampa press conference. conferenziere, -a *sm, sf* lecturer, speaker.

conferire [konfe'rire] *v* award, confer; (*dare*) give.

confermare [konfer'mare] *v* confirm, conferma *sf* confirmation.

confessare [konfes'sare] *v* confess. confessione *sf* confession. confessore *sm* confessor.

confetto [kon'fetto] *sm* sugared almond.

confettura [konfet'tura] *sf* preserve.

confezionare [konfetsjo'nare] *v* make up. confezione *sf* (*involucro*) wrapping; (*lavorazione*) manufacture. confezioni *sf pl* (*abiti pronti*) ready-made clothes *pl*.

confidare [konfi'dare] *v* trust, confide. confidenza *sf* confidence. dar confidenza a be familiar with. prendersi la confidenza take the liberty. confidenziale *agg* confidential.

confinare [konfi'nare] *v* border (on); (*relegare*) confine; (*pol*) intern, banish. confine *sm* border.

confiscare [konfis'kare] *v* seize, confiscate. confisca *sf* seizure, confiscation.

conflitto [kon'flitto] *sm* conflict.

*confondere [kon'fondere] *v* confuse; (*scambiare*) mistake for; (*mettere in imbarazzo*) embarrass. confondersi *v* become mixed up.

conformare [konfor'mare] *v* conform, adapt. conforme a *agg* in conformity with, true to. conformista *s(m+f)* conformist.

confortare [konfor'tare] *v* comfort, console. confortevole *agg* comforting; (*comodo*) comfortable. conforto *sm* comfort.

confrontare [konfron'tare] *v* compare; (*dir*) confront. confronto *sm* comparison; (*dir*) confrontation. a confronto di compared with. senza confronto far and away.

confusione [konfu'zjone] *sf* confusion; (*ressa*) bustle; (*chiasso*) din, turmoil. confusione mentale mental aberration. confuso *agg* confused, muddled; vague; (*turbato*) bewildered.

congedare [kondʒe'dare] *v* dismiss; (*mil*) discharge. congedarsi *v* say goodbye (to); take leave (of). congedo *sm* (*commiato*) leave; discharge.

congegno [kon'dʒeɲo] *sm* device, gadget. congegnare *v* plan, devise.

congelare [kondʒe'lare] *v* freeze. congelatore *sm* freezer.

congenito [kon'dʒenito] *agg* congenital.

congestionato [kondʒestjo'nato] *agg* congested; (*traffico*) blocked; (*viso*) flushed. congestione *sf* congestion; (*traffico*) jam.

*congiungere [kon'dʒundʒere] *v* (*unire*) join; (*collegare*) connect, link (up). congiuntivite *sf* conjunctivitis. congiuntivo *sm* subjunctive. congiuntura *sf* (*punto di unione*) joint; (*circostanza*) juncture; economic situation. congiunzione *sf* conjunction.

congiura [kon'dʒura] *sf* plot, conspiracy. congiurato, -a *sm, sf* plotter, conspirator.

congratularsi [kongratu'larsi] *v* congratulate.

congregare [kongre'gare] v congregate, gather. **congrega** sf band. **congregazione** sf congregation.

congresso [kon'gresso] sm congress.

congruo ['kongruo] agg adequate, fair.

coniare [ko'njare] v coin. **conio** sm coining; (impronta, qualità) stamp; (matrice) minting die.

conico ['koniko] agg conical.

conifero [ko'nifero] agg coniferous. **conifera** sf conifer.

coniglio [ko'niʎo] sm rabbit.

coniugare [konju'gare] v conjugate. **coniuge** ['konjudʒe] s(m+f) spouse. **coniugale** agg conjugal.

*****connettere** [kon'nɛttere] v connect, link; associate; (ragionare) think straight. **connessione** sf connection.

connotati [konno'tati] sm pl description sing, distinguishing features pl.

cono ['kono] sm cone.

*****conoscere** [ko'noʃere] v know; (fare la conoscenza) meet. **conoscere di fama/vista** know by reputation/sight. **conoscente** s(m+f) acquaintance. **conoscenza** sf knowledge; (conoscente) acquaintance; (coscienza) consciousness, senses pl. **conoscitore**, **-trice** sm, sf expert, connoisseur. **conosciuto** agg (well-)known, renowned.

conquistare [konkwis'tare] v conquer; (fig) gain. **conquista** sf conquest. **conquistatore**, **-trice** sm, sf conqueror.

consacrare [konsa'krare] v consecrate, dedicate.

consanguineo [konsan'gwineo], **-a** agg related (by blood). sm, sf blood relation.

consapevole [konsa'pevole] agg aware, conscious. **consapevolezza** sf awareness, consciousness.

consecutivo [konseku'tivo] agg consecutive; (seguente) following.

consegnare [konse'ɲare] v deliver, hand over; (mil) confine to barracks. **consegna** sf delivery; (merce ordinata) consignment; (custodia) care; (deposito) (safe) custody; (mil: ordine) order; (mil: punizione) confinement.

conseguire [konse'gwire] v · (ottenere) obtain, get; (raggiungere) achieve; (risultare) follow, ensue. **conseguenza** sf consequence, result; (malattia) aftereffect. **di conseguenza** consequently, as a result.

consenso [kon'sɛnso] sm approval; (accordo) agreement; (permesso) consent.

consentire [konsen'tire] v (essere d'accordo) agree; (accondiscendere) consent; (permettere) allow. **consenziente** agg consenting.

conservare [konser'vare] v keep, preserve. **conserva** sf preserve. **mettere in conserva** preserve; (in scatola) tin; (in bottiglia) bottle. **conservatore**, **-trice** s, agg conservative. **conservazione** sf preservation.

considerare [conside'rare] v consider; (guardare) examine; (stimare) esteem, think highly of; (tener conto) bear in mind. **consideratezza** sf caution. **considerato** agg careful, wary. **considerazione** sf (prudenza) caution; (risguardo) consideration; (stima) esteem, regard. **considerevole** agg considerable.

consigliare [konsiʎ'Aare] v advise, recommend. **consigliere** sm counsellor. **consigliere comunale** town councillor. **consigliere delegato** managing director. **consiglio** sm advice; (organo amministrativo) board; (ente pubblico) council; (colloquio) meeting. **consiglio d'amministrazione** board of directors.

*****consistere** [kon'sistere] v consist. **consistente** agg substantial; (convincente) sound. **consistenza** sf consistency; (fondamento) basis. **consistenza di cassa/magazzino** cash/stock in hand.

consolare [konso'lare] v console, comfort; (rallegrare) cheer (up). **consolazione** sf consolation, comfort; (piacere) delight.

console ['konsole] sm consul. **consolare** agg consular. **consolato** sm consulate.

consolidare [konsoli'dare] v consolidate; (rinforzare) reinforce.

consonante [konso'nante] sf consonant.

consono ['konsono] agg **consono a** in keeping with; in accordance with.

consorte [kon'sorte] s(m+f), agg consort.

consorzio [kon'sortsjo] sm partnership; (impresa commerciale, banca) consortium, trust; (imprese riunite) syndicate, cooperative.

constare [kon'stare] v consist. **a quanto mi consta** to my knowledge, as far as I know.

constatare [konsta'tare] v (notare) see; (accertare) ascertain, verify; (riconoscere) recognize. **constatazione** sf verification; recognition.

consueto [konsu'eto] *agg* (*solito*) usual; (*abituato*) used. **come di consueto** as usual. **di consueto** usually. **consuetudine** *sf* habit, custom.

consulente [konsu'lɛnte] *s(m+f)*, *agg* consultant. **consulenza** *sf* advice. **consultare** *v* consult. **consultazione** *sf* consultation; (*biblioteca*) reference. **consultivo** *agg* consultative, advisory.

consumare[1] [konsu'mare] *v* consume, use up; (*logorare*) wear out; (*dissipare*) squander; (*mangiare*) eat. **consumazione** *sf* (*bibita*) drink; (*spuntino*) snack. **consumismo** *sm* consumer society. **consumo** *sm* consumption; (*spreco*) waste. **articoli di consumo** *sm pl* consumer goods *pl*.

consumare[2] [konsu'mare] *v* (*portare a compimento*) consummate. **consumazione** *sf* consummation.

consuntivo [konsun'tivo] *sm* balance sheet.

contabile [kon'tabile] *s(m+f)* bookkeeper; (*ragioniere*) accountant. **valore contabile** *sm* book value. **contabilità** *sf* bookkeeping; accountancy. **tenere la contabilità** keep the books.

contachilometri [kontaki'lɔmetri] *sm invar* mileometer; (*tachimetro*) speedometer.

contadino [konta'dino], **-a** *agg* (*della campagna*) rustic; (*dei contadini*) peasant. *sm*, *sf* peasant; (*agricoltore*) farmer.

contagioso [konta'dʒozo] *agg* contagious, catching. **contagiare** *v* infect, contaminate.

contagiri [konta'dʒiri] *sm invar* rev(olution) counter.

contaminare [kontami'nare] *v* contaminate.

contanti [kon'tanti] *sm pl* cash *sing*, ready money *sing*.

contare [kon'tare] *v* count; (*proporsi*) think. **contato** *agg* limited. **ho i giorni contati** my days are numbered. **ho i minuti contati** I have no time to waste. **contatore** *sm* meter.

contatto [kon'tatto] *sm* contact. **essere/mantenersi/mettersi in contatto** be/keep/get in touch.

conte ['konte] *sm* count. **contea** *sf* (*suddivisione amministrativa*) county; (*titolo, dominio di conti*) earldom. **contessa** *sf* countess.

conteggio [kon'teddʒo] *sm* count, counting. **conteggiare** *v* (*calcolare*) count; (*far pagare*) charge.

contegno [kon'teɲo] *sm* bearing, behaviour. **darsi** *or* **assumere un contegno** strike an attitude. **contegnoso** *agg* dignified, reserved.

contemplare [kontem'plare] *v* contemplate; consider, provide for. **contemplazione** *sf* contemplation.

contempo [kon'tempo] *sm* **nel contempo** in the meantime, meanwhile.

contemporaneo [kontempo'raneo], **-a** *sm*, *sf* contemporary. *agg* contemporary; simultaneous.

*contendere [kon'tendere] *v* dispute; (*litigarsi*) quarrel (over); oppose. **contendente** *s(m+f)* competitor.

*contenere [konte'nere] *v* contain, hold; (*trattenere*) hold back. **contenersi** *v* (*dominarsi*) restrain oneself; (*comportarsi*) act. **contenitore** *sm* container.

contentare [konten'tare] *v* (*appagare*) satisfy; (*far contento*) please. **contentarsi** *v* be satisfied. **contentezza** *sf* satisfaction, contentment; (*gioia*) joy. **contento** *agg* (*soddisfatto*) pleased, satisfied; (*felice*) happy; (*allegro*) cheerful.

contenuto [konte'nuto] *sm* (*recipiente*) contents *pl*; (*argomento*) content. *agg* reserved, restrained.

contestare [kontes'tare] *v* contest; (*dir*) charge (with); (*impugnare*) challenge. **contestazione** *sf* dispute; notification.

contiguo [kon'tiguo] *agg* neighbouring, adjoining.

continente [konti'nɛnte] *sm*, *agg* continent. **continentale** *agg* continental. **continenza** *sf* continence.

contingente [kontin'dʒɛnte] *sm* quota; (*mil*) contingent. **contingenza** *sf* circumstance; contingency. **indennità di contingenza** *sf* cost of living allowance.

continuare [kontinu'are] *v* continue, carry on; (*riprendere*) resume; (*insistere*) keep on. **continuazione** *sf* continuation. **continuità** *sf* continuity. **continuo** *agg* endless; (*costante*) continual; (*ininterrotto*) continuous.

conto ['kɔnto] *sm* account; (*somma da pagare*) bill; calculation. **a conti fatti** all things considered. **a (ogni) buon conto** in any case. **far conto che** *or* **di** suppose, imagine; (*proporsi*) intend. **fare conto su** rely on. **per conto di** on behalf of. **per**

conto mio as far as I'm concerned; (*da solo*) on my own. **tener conto di** make a note of; consider, take into account.

*contorcere [kon'tortʃere] *v* twist. **contorcersi** *v* writhe. **contorsione** *sf* contortion. **contorsionista** *s(m+f)* contortionist.

contorno [kon'torno] *sm* (*linea*) outline; (*gastr*) vegetables *pl*, side-dish; (*ornamento*) surround, border.

contrabbandare [kontrabban'dare] *v* smuggle. **contrabbando** *sm* contraband, smuggling. **merce di contrabbando** *sf* smuggled goods *pl*.

contrabbasso [kontrab'basso] *sm* double-bass.

contraccambiare [kontrakkam'bjare] *v* reciprocate. **in contraccambio di** in return for.

contraccolpo [kontrak'kolpo] *sm* counter-blow; (*fig*) repercussion.

*contraddire [kontrad'dire] *v* contradict. **contraddizione** *sf* contradiction. **spirito di contraddizione** *sm* contrariness.

contraddittorio [kontraddit'torjo] *agg* contradictory. *sm* (*dir*) cross-examination.

contraente [kontra'ɛnte] *agg* contracting.

contraereo [kontra'ɛreo] *agg* anti-aircraft.

*contraffare [kontraf'fare] *v* imitate; (*falsificare*) forge, counterfeit. **contraffattore, -trice** *sm*, *sf* counterfeiter, forger; imitator. **contraffazione** *sf* forgery.

contralto [kon'tralto] *sm* contralto. *agg* alto.

*contrapporre [kontrap'porre] *v* oppose, contrast. **contrapposizione** *sf* opposition, contrast.

contrariare [kontra'rjare] *v* irritate, oppose.

contrario [kon'trarjo] *agg* opposite, contrary; (*avverso*) unfavourable. *sm* contrary, opposite. **al contrario** on the contrary. **al contrario di** unlike. **essere contrario a** be opposed to.

*contrarre [kon'trarre] *v* contract.

contrassegnare [kontrasse'ɲare] *v* mark. **contrassegno** *sm* mark.

contrastare [kontras'tare] *v* (*ostacolare*) bar, oppose; (*essere in conflitto*) clash; dispute. **contrasto** *sm* contrast; conflict.

contrattaccare [kontrattak'kare] *v* counter-attack. **contrattacco** *sm* counter-attack.

contrattempo [kontrat'tɛmpo] *sm* hitch.

contratto [kon'tratto] *sm* contract. **contrattare** *v* negotiate; (*mercanteggiare*) haggle.

contravvenzione [kontravven'tsjone] *sf* (*violazione*) infringement; (*multa*) fine. **contravventore, -trice** *sm*, *sf* offender.

contrazione [kontra'tsjone] *sf* contraction.

contribuire [kontribu'ire] *v* contribute. **contribuente** *sm*, *sf* taxpayer. **contributo** *sm* contribution; (*dir*) tax.

contristare [kontris'tare] *v* sadden.

contrito [kon'trito] *agg* contrite.

contro ['kontro] *prep*, *avv* against.

controbattere [kontro'battere] *v* rebut.

controbilanciare [kontrobilan'tʃare] *v* counterbalance.

controfirmare [kontrofir'mare] *v* countersign. **controfirma** *sf* countersignature.

controllare [kontrol'lare] *v* control; (*esaminare*) check. **controllo** *sm* control; (*verifica*) check; inspection. **controllo delle nascite** birth-control. **controllore** *sm* inspector.

contromano [kontro'mano] *avv* in the opposite direction.

contromarcia [kontro'martʃa] *sf* reverse (gear).

contropelo [kontro'pelo] *avv* against the grain.

controproducente [kontroprodu'tʃɛnte] *agg* self-defeating, counter-productive.

contrordine [kon'trordine] *sm* countermand. **dare un contrordine** countermand.

controsenso [kontro'sɛnso] *sm* nonsense, contradiction in terms.

controversia [kontro'vɛrsja] *sf* controversy. **controverso** *agg* controversial.

controvoglia [kontro'vɔʎa] *avv* unwillingly.

conturbare [kontur'bare] *v* perturb.

contusione [kontu'zjone] *sf* bruise. **contuso** *agg* bruised.

convalescenza [konvale'ʃentsa] *sf* convalescence. **convalescente** *s(m+f)*, *agg* convalescent. **convalescenziario** *sm* convalescent home.

convalidare [konvali'dare] *v* confirm. **convalida** or **convalidazione** *sf* confirmation.

convegno [kon'veɲo] *sm* meeting, rendez-vous. **darsi convegno** make a meeting.

*convenire [konve'nire] *v* (*venire insieme*) come together, meet; (*essere d'accordo*) agree; (*ammettere*) admit; (*essere vantaggioso*) suit, pay, be worth it. **conveniente**

agg (*vantaggioso*) favourable, reasonable; (*adatto*, *adeguato*) suitable. **convenienza** *sf* (*utilità*) convenience; (*decoro*) propriety; (*l'essere adatto*) suitability.

convento [kon'vɛnto] *sm* convent.

convenzione [konven'tsjone] *sf* (*patto*) agreement; (*uso*) custom, convention.

***convergere** [kon'verdʒere] *v* converge. **convergente** *agg* converging.

conversare [konver'sare] *v* converse. **conversazione** *sf* conversation, talk.

conversione [konver'sjone] *sf* conversion; (*trasformazione*) change, turn(ing).

convertire [konver'tire] *v* convert, turn. **convertibile** *agg* convertible. **convertito, -a** *sm, sf* convert.

convesso [kon'vɛsso] *agg* convex.

***convincere** [kon'vintʃere] *v* convince. **convincente** *agg* convincing. **convinto** *agg* (*persuaso*) convinced; (*dimostrato colpevole*) convicted; (*fedele*) staunch. **convinzione** *sf* conviction.

convitato [konvi'tato] *sm* guest.

convito [kon'vito] *sm* banquet.

convitto [kon'vitto] *sm* boarding-school.

convocare [konvo'kare] *v* convoke, convene; (*radunare*) call together, rally.

convoglio [kon'vɔʎo] *sm* convoy. **convoglio funebre** funeral procession. **convogliare** *v* (*scortare*) convoy; (*condurre*, *trasportare*) convey.

convulsione [konvul'sjone] *sf* convulsion. **convulsivo** *agg* convulsive. **convulso** *agg* convulsed.

cooperare [koope'rare] *v* cooperate, collaborate; (*contribuire*) contribute. **cooperativa** *sf* cooperative. **cooperazione** *sf* cooperation, collaboration.

coordinare [koordi'nare] *v* coordinate, coordinate. **coordinata** *sf* coordinate.

coperchio [ko'perkjo] *sm* lid, cover.

coperta [ko'perta] *sf* (*drappo*) blanket; (*riparo*) cover. **copertina** *sf* (*quaderno*) cover; (*libro*) dust-jacket.

coperto[1] [ko'perto] *agg* covered; (*riparato*) sheltered; (*chiuso*) closed; (*nuvoloso*) overcast; (*nascosto*) concealed. **sm al coperto** under cover. **mettersi al coperto** shelter.

coperto[2] [ko'perto] *sm* (*a tavola*) place (-setting); (*prezzo*) cover charge.

copertone [koper'tone] *sm* (*pneumatico*) tyre; (*telone*) tarpaulin.

copia [ˈkɔpja] *sf* copy; (*fig*) image. **bella/brutta copia** fair/rough copy. **copiare**

v copy. **carta copiativa** *sf* carbon paper. **matita copiativa** *sf* indelible pencil. **copiatura** *sf* copy; (*trascrizione*) copying.

copioso [ko'pjozo] *agg* copious.

coppa [ˈkɔppa] *sf* cup; (*auto*) sump.

coppia [ˈkɔppja] *sf* couple. **a coppie** in pairs, in twos.

***coprire** [ko'prire] *v* cover; (*nascondere*) hide. **coprire un rumore** drown a noise.

coraggio [ko'raddʒo] *sm* courage, bravery; (*sfacciataggine*) nerve; (*cuore*) heart. **farsi coraggio** pluck up courage. **perdere coraggio** lose heart. **coraggioso** *agg* courageous, brave; (*ardito*) bold.

corallo [ko'rallo] *sm* coral.

corazzare [korat'tsare] *v* armour. **corazza** *sf* armour. **corazzata** *sf* battleship.

corbelleria [korbelle'ria] *sf* (*detto*) nonsense; (*atto*) foolery.

corda [ˈkɔrda] *sf* cord; (*cordicella*, *musica*) string; (*fune*) rope; (*geom*) chord. **avere la corda al collo** have one's back to the wall. **essere giù di corda** feel low. **tagliar la corda** (*andarsene di soppiatto*) sneak off; (*fuggire*) cut and run.

cordiale [kor'djale] *agg* cordial, warm. **cordiali saluti** kind regards *pl*. **cordialità** *sf* friendliness.

cordoglio [kor'dɔʎo] *sm* grief. **esprimere il proprio cordoglio** offer one's condolences.

cordone [kor'done] *sm* cord; (*schieramento*) cordon.

coreografo [kore'ɔgrafo] *sm* choreographer. **coreografia** *sf* choreography.

coriandoli [ko'rjandoli] *sm pl* confetti *sing*.

coricare [kori'kare] *v* lay down, (*mettere a letto*) put to bed. **coricarsi** *v* lie down; go to bed.

cornacchia [kor'nakkja] *sf* crow.

cornamusa [korna'muza] *sf* bagpipes *pl*.

cornetto [kor'netto] *sm* (*musica*) cornet; (*telefono*) receiver.

cornice [kor'nitʃe] *sf* frame; (*ambiente*) setting; (*arch*) cornice.

corno [ˈkɔrno] *sm, pl* **-a** *f in zool sense* horn; (*ramificato*) antler; (*musica*) French horn. **corno da caccia** bugle. **corno inglese** cor anglais. **dire corna di** run down. **fare le corna** (*non essere fedele*) be unfaithful; (*gesto*) make a V-sign. **non capire un corno** not understand a thing. **non valere un corno** not be worth a brass farthing. **cornuto** agg horned.

coro ['kɔro] sm choir; (canto) chorus. **in coro** in chorus, all together.

corpo ['kɔrpo] sm body; (mil, ecc.) corps. **a corpo morto** headlong, whole-heartedly. **corpo a corpo** hand to hand. **corporatura** sf build. **corporeo** agg bodily.

corporazione [korpora'tsjone] sf guild, association.

corpulento [korpu'lɛnto] agg stout.

corpuscolo [kor'puskolo] sm corpuscle.

corredo [kor'redo] sm outfit; (mil) equipment. **corredare** v fit out, equip; (fig) furnish (with).

*****correggere** [kor'reddʒere] v correct; (bevanda) lace.

corrente [kor'rɛnte] agg current; (che scorre) running; (andante) common or garden. **essere/tenere al corrente** be/keep informed or up-to-date. **mettere al corrente** acquaint, inform. sf current, stream; (tendenza, moda) trend. **corrente d'aria** draught.

*****correre** [kor'rerere] v run; (veicoli) go; (circolare) circulate. **correre dietro** a run after.

corretto [kor'retto] agg correct, right, exact. **correttezza** sf fairness; (educazione) propriety.

correzione [korre'tsjone] sf correction. **correzione di bozze** proof-reading.

corridoio [korri'dojo] sm passage, corridor.

corridore [korri'dore] sm runner; (automobilista) racing-driver; (ciclista) racing-cyclist. **cavallo corridore** sm racehorse.

corriera [kor'rjera] sf coach.

corriere [kor'rjere] sm messenger, courier; (merci) carrier; (posta) mail.

corrimano [korri'mano] sm handrail.

*****corrispondere** [korris'pondere] v correspond; (accordarsi) agree; (pagare) pay; (ricambiare) reciprocate. **corrispondente** s(m+f) correspondent. **corrispondenza** sf correspondence; (posta) mail; (conformità) relation; (somiglianza) likeness.

corroborare [korrobo'rare] v corroborate; (rinforzare) strengthen.

*****corrodere** [kor'rodere] v corrode. **corrosione** sf corrosion.

*****corrompere** [kor'rompere] v corrupt;

(con denaro) bribe; (guastare) spoil. **corrotto** agg corrupt.

corrucciarsi [korrut'tʃarsi] v be angered and upset (by).

corrugare [korru'gare] v crease, wrinkle. **corrugare la fronte** knit one's brow.

corruzione [korru'tsjone] sf corruption; (con denaro) bribery.

corsa ['korsa] sf (gara) race; (azione) racing; (atletica) running; (percorso) run. **andare di corsa** (be in a) hurry. **di gran corsa** in a great hurry, in great haste. **fare una corsa** (da) (fam) pop over or round (to).

corsia [kor'sia] sf (teatro, ecc.) gangway; (ospedale) ward; (autostrada) lane; (tappeto) runner.

corsivo [kor'sivo] agg italic. sm italics pl.

corso[1] ['korso] sm course; (econ) circulation; (quotazione) rate; (strada principale) high street. **in corso** in progress; (in sospeso) pending; (corrente) present.

corso[2] ['korso], -a s, agg Corsican.

corte ['korte] sf court; (cortile) courtyard. **corte marziale** court-martial. **fare la corte (a)** (ragazza) court; (lusingare) play up (to). **corteggiare** v court. **corteggio** sm retinue.

corteccia [kor'tettʃa] sf (albero) bark; (frutto) rind; (anat) cortex.

corteo [kor'tɛo] sm procession.

cortese [kor'teze] agg polite, courteous; (gentile) kind. **cortesia** sf politeness, courtesy; kindness. **avere la cortesia di** be so kind as to. **per cortesia** (per favore) please, kindly; (per ragioni di cortesia) out of politeness.

cortile [kor'tile] sm courtyard; (casa colonica) farmyard. **animali da cortile** sm pl farmyard animals pl.

cortina [kor'tina] sf curtain. **cortina di ferro** iron curtain. **cortina di fumo** smoke-screen.

corto ['korto] agg short. **a farla corta** to come to the point. **essere a corto di** be short of.

corvo ['korvo] sm (imperiale) raven; (comune) rook.

cosa ['kɔza] pron what. **a cosa serve?** what is it for? sf thing; (qualcosa) something; (faccenda) matter. **a cose fatte** after the event. **cosa da nulla** nothing. **cosa da poco** trifle. **gran cosa** much. **qualsiasi** or **qualunque cosa** anything. **tante cose** (augurio) best wishes pl.

coscia ['kɔʃa] *sf* thigh; (*gastr*) leg.

cosciente [koˈʃɛnte] *agg* aware. **coscienza** *sf* conscience; (*conoscenza*) consciousness; (*impegno*) conscientiousness. **avere la coscienza pulita/sporca** have a clear/guilty conscience. **in coscienza** morally, honestly. **coscienzioso** *agg* conscientious.

coscrizione [koskriˈtsjone] *sf* draft, conscription. **coscritto** *sm* conscript, recruit.

così [koˈzi] *avv* (*in questo modo*) like this or that; (*tanto*) so; (*con agg qualificante un sostantivo*) such. **cong** so. **così ... come ...** as ... as .... **così così** so-so. **cosiddetto** *agg* so-called.

cosmetico [kozˈmetiko] *sm, agg* cosmetic. **cosmesi** *or* **cosmetica** *sf* beauty culture.

cosmo ['kɔzmo] *sm* cosmos. **cosmonauta** *s(m+f)* astronaut. **cosmonautica** *sf* astronautics.

cosmopolita [kozmoˈpɔlita] *s(m+f)*, *agg* cosmopolitan.

coso ['kɔzo] *sm* (*fam*) thingummy.

***cospargere** [kosˈpardʒere] *v* strew.

cospicuo [kosˈpikuo] *agg* conspicuous; (*grande*) considerable.

cospirare [kospiˈrare] *v* plot.

costa ['kɔsta] *sf* coast, coastline; (*litorale*) shore; (*coltello, libro*) back; (*costola*) rib.

costà [kosˈta] *avv* (*over*) there.

costante [kosˈtante] *agg* constant, firm; (*saldo*) steady. *sf* constant. **costanza** *sf* steadfastness, firmness.

costare [kosˈtare] *v* cost. **costar caro** be expensive. **mi è costato caro** I have paid dearly for it.

costeggiare [kostedˈdʒare] *v* skirt; (*costa*) follow the coast.

costei [kosˈtɛi] *pron* this woman.

***costellare** [kostelˈlare] *v* stud.

costellazione [kostellaˈtsjone] *sf* constellation.

costernare [kosterˈnare] *v* dismay.

costiero [kosˈtjɛra] *agg* coastal.

costipato [kostiˈpato] *agg* (*stitico*) constipated; (*fam: raffreddato*) having a bad cold.

costituire [kostituˈire] *v* (*formare*) set up, form; (*dar luogo*) constitute; (*dichiarare*) appoint. **costituirsi** *v* (*presentarsi spontaneamente*) give oneself up. **costituirsi parte civile** take legal proceedings. **costituzione** *sf* constitution.

costo ['kɔsto] *sm* cost, price. **costoso** *agg* costly, dear.

costola ['kɔstola] *sf* rib.

costoro [kosˈtoro] *pron* these people.

***costringere** [kosˈtrindʒere] *v* force, compel.

***costruire** [kostruˈire] *v* build, construct. **costruzione** *sf* construction; (*edificio*) building.

costui [kosˈtui] *pron* this man.

costume [kosˈtume] *sm* (*usanza*) custom, use; (*condotta*) behaviour; (*indumento*) costume; (*abitudine personale*) habit. **il buon costume** morality.

costura [kosˈtura] *sf* seam.

cotogna [koˈtoɲa] *sf* quince.

cotoletta [kotoˈletta] *sf* cutlet.

cotone [koˈtone] *sm* cotton. **cotone idrofilo** cotton-wool. **cotoniero** *agg* cotton. **cotonificio** *sm* cotton mill.

cotta ['kɔtta] *sf* **prendere una cotta** (*fam*) fall in love.

cottimo ['kɔttimo] *sm* piece-work.

cotto ['kɔtto] *agg* cooked; (*carne*) done; (*in forno*) baked. **farne di cotte e di crude** be up to all sorts of tricks. **nè cotto nè crudo** neither one thing nor the other.

cottura [kotˈtura] *sf* cooking; (*in forno*) baking.

covare [koˈvare] *v* hatch; (*fig*) brood over; (*sotto la cenere*) smoulder. **covata** *sf* brood.

covo ['kovo] *sm* lair, den.

cozza ['kɔttsa] *sf* mussel.

cozzare [kotˈtsare] *v* collide *or* clash (with); (*con le corna*) butt. **cozzo** *sm* collision, clash; butt.

crampo ['krampo] *sm* cramp.

cranio ['kranjo] *sm* skull.

cratere [kraˈtere] *sm* crater.

cravatta [kraˈvatta] *sf* tie.

creanza [kreˈantsa] *sf* (good) manners *pl*, breeding.

creare [kreˈare] *v* create, give rise to; (*eleggere*) appoint. **creatore** *sm* maker, creator. **creatura** *sf* creature. **creazione** *sf* creation.

credenza[1] [kreˈdɛntsa] *sf* belief (*pl* -s), opinion; (*fede*) faith; (*comm*) credit.

credenza[2] [kreˈdɛntsa] *sf* (*mobile*) sideboard.

credere ['krɛdere] *v* believe; (*pensare*) think; (*aver fiducia*) trust. **credibile** *agg* credible, believable. **credibilità** *sf* credibility.

credito ['kredito] *sm* credit; (*stima*) esteem. **creditore** *sm* creditor.

credulo ['kredulo] *agg* credulous. **credulone, -a** *sm, sf* gullible person.

crema ['krɛma] *sf* cream. **cremoso** *agg* creamy.

cremare [kre'mare] *v* cremate. **crematorio** *sm* crematorium. **cremazione** *sf* cremation.

cremisi ['krɛmizi] *agg, sm* crimson.

cren ['krɛn] *sm* horse-radish.

crepare [kre'pare] *v* burst, crack; (*fam: morire*) die, kick the bucket. **crepacuore** *sm* heartbreak.

crepitare [krepi'tare] *v* crackle. **crepitio** *sm* crackle, crackling.

crepuscolo [kre'puskolo] *sm* twilight, dusk; decline.

*****crescere** [kreʃere] *v* grow; (*maturarsi*) grow up; (*aumentare*) rise; (*sovrabbondare*) be left over. **crescita** *sf* growth.

crescione [kreʃone] *sm* (*d'acqua*) watercress; (*inglese*) mustard and cress.

cresima ['krɛzima] *sf* confirmation. **cresimare** *v* confirm.

crespa ['krɛspa] *sf* (*ruga*) wrinkle; (*stoffa*) crease; (*piccola ondulazione*) ripple. **crespo** ['krɛspo] *agg* frizzy. *sm* crepe.

cresta ['krɛsta] *sf* crest.

creta ['krɛta] *sf* clay.

cretino [kre'tino], **-a** *sm, sf* idiot, fool. *agg* idiotic, foolish. **cretineria** *sf* stupidity; (*discorso, azione*) foolish thing.

cricca ['krikka] *sf* clique, gang.

cricco ['krikko] *sm* jack.

criceto [kri'tʃeto] *sm* hamster.

criminale [krimi'nale] *agg, s(m+f)* criminal. **crimine** *sm* crime. **criminoso** *agg* criminal.

criniera [kri'njɛra] *sf* mane.

cripta ['kripta] *sf* crypt.

crisalide [kri'zalide] *sf* chrysalis.

crisantemo [krizan'tɛmo] *sm* chrysanthemum.

crisi ['krizi] *sf* crisis (*pl* -ses); (*med*) fit, attack.

cristallizzare [kristallid'dzare] *v* crystallize.

cristallo [kris'tallo] *sm* crystal; (*vetro*) plate-glass, (window) pane. **cristallino** *agg* crystalline; pure, limpid.

cristiano [kris'tjano], **-a** *agg* Christian. *sm, sf* Christian; (*essere umano*) soul.

Cristo ['kristo] *sm* Christ. **non c'è cristo**

(*possibilità*) there isn't a chance. **povero cristo** poor devil.

criterio [kri'tɛrjo] *sm* criterion (*pl* -a), norm; sense.

critico ['kritiko] *agg* critical. *sm* critic. **critica** *sf* criticism; (*scritto*) review; (*persona*) critic. **criticare** *v* criticize; review; (*biasimare*) blame.

crivellare [krivel'lare] *v* riddle. **crivello** *sm* sieve.

croccante [krok'kante] *agg* crisp. *sm* (*dolce*) praline.

crocchia ['krɔkkja] *sf* bun, chignon.

crocchio ['krɔkkjo] *sm* cluster.

croce ['krotʃe] *sf* cross. **a occhio e croce** roughly. **croce uncinata** swastika. **crocevia** *sm invar* crossroads. **fare a testa e croce** toss a coin. **punto a croce** *sm* cross-stitch.

crociare [kro'tʃare] *v* cross.

crociata [kro'tʃata] *sf* crusade. **crociato** *sm* crusader.

crocicchio [kro'tʃikkjo] *sm* crossroads.

crociera [kro'tʃera] *sf* cruise.

*****crocifiggere** [krotʃifid'dʒere] *v* crucify. **crocifisso** [krotʃi'fisso] *sm* crucifix. *agg* crucified.

croco ['krɔko] *sm* crocus.

crogiolarsi [krodʒo'larsi] *v* bask. **crogiolo** *sm* crucible; (*fig*) melting-pot.

crollare [krol'lare] *v* (*cadere*) collapse, slump; (*spalle*) shrug. **crollo** *sm* collapse, slump.

croma ['krɔma] *sf* quaver.

cromo ['krɔmo] *sm* (*metallo*) chromium. **giallo cromo** chrome yellow. **cromatura** *sf* chromium-plating.

cromosoma [kromo'sɔma] *sm* chromosome.

cronaca ['krɔnaka] *sf* (*narrazione*) chronicle; (*radio, TV, stampa*) news, review.

cronico ['krɔniko] *agg* chronic. *sm* chronic invalid.

cronista [kro'nista] *s(m+f)* reporter.

cronologico [krono'lɔdʒiko] *agg* chronological.

cronometro [kro'nɔmetro] *sm* chronometer, stop-watch. **cronometrare** *v* time.

crosta ['krɔsta] *sf* crust; (*ferita*) scab. **crostata** *sf* tart.

crostacei [kros'tatʃei] *sm pl* crustaceans *pl*, shellfish *pl*.

crucciare [krut'tʃare] *v* distress, worry.

cruciale [kru'tʃale] *agg* crucial.

cruciverba [krutʃi'vɛrba] *sm invar* crossword.

crudele [kru'dɛle] *agg* cruel; (*duro, aspro*) harsh; (*doloroso*) bitter. **crudeltà** *sf* cruelty; (*asprezza*) harshness.

crudo ['krudo] *agg* raw; (*rigido*) harsh; (*brusco*) crude; (*volgare*) coarse.

crumiro [kru'miro], **-a** *sm, sf* blackleg.

cruna ['kruna] *sf* eye (of a needle).

crusca ['kruska] *sf* bran.

cruscotto [krus'kɔtto] *sm* instrument panel; (*auto*) dashboard.

cubo ['kubo] *sm* cube. **cubico** *agg* cubic. **cubismo** *sm* cubism.

cuccagna [kuk'kaɲa] *sf* (*abbondanza*) plenty; (*allegria*) fun.

cuccetta [kut'tʃetta] *sf* couchette.

cucchiaio [kuk'kjajo] *sm* spoon; (*contenuto*) spoonful; (*da tavola*) tablespoon. **cucchiaino** *sm* teaspoon.

cucciolo [kuttʃolo] *sm* puppy.

cucina [ku'tʃina] *sf* (*luogo*) kitchen; (*atto del cucinare*) cooking; (*cibo*) food; (*apparecchio*) cooker. **cucina casalinga** home cooking. **cucinare** *v* cook.

cucire [ku'tʃire] *v* sew, stitch; (*con cucitrice*) staple. **cucirino** *sm* sewing thread. **cucito** *sm* sewing, needlework. **cucitrice** *sf* (*persona*) seamstress; (*apparecchio*) stapler. **cucitura** *sf* seam.

cuculo ['kukulo] *sm* cuckoo.

cuffia ['kuffja] *sf* cap; bonnet; (*telefono, radio*) earphones *pl*, headphones *pl*.

cugino [ku'dʒino], **-a** *sm, sf* cousin.

cui ['kui] *pron* (*persone*) whom; (*cose*) which. **il cui, la cui,** ecc. whose. **in cui** (*quando*) when; (*dove*) where.

culla ['kulla] *sf* cradle. **cullare** *v* rock, lull. **cullarsi** *v* (*illudersi*) delude oneself.

culmine ['kulmine] *sm* summit, height. **culminare** *v* culminate.

culo ['kulo] *sm* (*fam*) bottom; (*volg*) arse.

culto ['kulto] *sm* worship; (*religione*) cult.

cultura [kul'tura] *sf* culture, learning; cultivation. **culturale** *agg* cultural.

cumulo ['kumulo] *sm* pile, heap.

cuneo ['kuneo] *sm* wedge.

cunetta [ku'netta] *sf* gutter.

*****cuocere** ['kwɔtʃere] *v* (*cucinare*) cook; (*al forno*) bake; (*a lesso*) boil; (*alla griglia*) grill; (*arrosto*) roast; (*in umido*) stew; (*ceramica, ecc.*) fire. **cuocere a fuoco lento** simmer. **cuoco, -a** *sm, sf* cook.

cuoio ['kwɔjo] *sm* leather; (*pelle*) hide.

cuoio capelluto scalp. **cuoio scamosciato** chamois leather, suede.

cuore ['kwɔre] *sm* heart. **di cuore** heartily. **di tutto cuore** with all one's heart. **mettersi il cuore in pace** set one's mind at rest. **nel cuore di** at the height of; (*notte*) at dead of. **senza cuore** heartless.

cupido ['kupido] *agg* greedy. **cupidigia** *sf* greed.

cupo ['kupo] *agg* (*profondo, suono*) deep; (*privo di luce, colore*) dark.

cupola ['kupola] *sf* dome.

cura ['kura] *sf* care; (*med*) cure, treatment. **curare** *v* look after, take care of; cure, treat. **curarsi** *v* mind *or* care about. **curativo** *agg* curative.

curatore [kura'tore], **-trice** *sm, sf* guardian. **curatela** *sf* guardianship.

curioso [ku'rjozo] *agg* curious; (*strano*) odd. **curiosità** *sf* curiosity. **curiosare** *v* pry.

curvare [kur'vare] *v* bend. **curvare il capo** bow one's head. **curva** *sf* bend, curve. **curvatura** *sf* curvature, sweep. **curvo** *agg* curved, bent.

cuscino [ku'ʃino] *sm* cushion; (*guanciale*) pillow. **cuscinetto** *sm* (*a sfere*) ball-bearing; (*a rulli*) roller-bearing. **stato cuscinetto** *sm* buffer state.

custode [kus'tɔde] *s*(*m+f*) keeper, caretaker. **custodia** *sf* custody, care, safe keeping; (*astuccio*) case. **custodire** *v* keep; look after; (*sorvegliare*) guard.

cutaneo [ku'taneo] *agg* cutaneous, skin.

D

da [da] *prep* from; (*moto a luogo*) to; (*stato in luogo*) at; (*durata*) for; (*fin da*) since; (*causa*) of, from; (*segno distintivo*) with; (*come*) as, like. **da allora** since then. **da allora in poi** ever since. **da lontano** from afar. **da molto** for a long time. **da noi** at home; (*al mio paese*) in my country.

dabbasso [dab'basso] *avv* downstairs.

dabbene [dab'bene] *agg* decent, honest.

daccapo [dak'kapo] *avv* (*di nuovo*) again, once more; (*da principio*) from the beginning, all over again.

dacché [dak'ke] *cong* since.

dado ['dado] *sm* die (*pl* dice); (*gastr*) cube; (*mec*) nut.

daffare [daf'fare] *sm invar* work, business.

dagli¹ ['daʎi] *prep* + *art* da gli.

dagli² ['daʎi] *inter* (*forza*) go on! come on! (*noioso*) not again! pack it in!

dai ['dai] *prep* + *art* da i.

daino ['daino] *sm* (*fallow*) deer. **daina** *sf* doe. **pelle di daino** *sf* buckskin.

dal [dal] *prep* + *art* da il.

dalia ['dalja] *sf* dahlia.

dall' [dall] *prep* + *art* da l'.

dalla ['dalla] *prep* + *art* da la.

dalle ['dalle] *prep* + *art* da le.

dallo ['dallo] *prep* + *art* da lo.

daltonismo [dalto'nizmo] *sm* colour-blindness. **daltonico** *agg* colour-blind.

dama ['dama] *sf* lady, noblewoman; (*gioco*) draughts; (*carta*) queen.

damasco [da'masko] *sm* damask.

dancing ['damsin] *sm invar* dance-hall.

Danimarca [dani'marka] *sf* Denmark. **danese** *sm*, *agg* Danish; *s(m+f)* Dane.

dannare [dan'nare] *v* damn. **dannato, -a** *s*, *agg* damned. **dannazione** *sf* damnation; (*tormento*) trial.

danneggiare [danned'dʒare] *v* (*guastare*) damage; (*nuocere*) injure, harm. **danno** *sm* damage; injury, harm; (*pregiudizio*) detriment. **danno doloso** wilful damage. **dannoso** *agg* harmful.

danzare [dan'tsare] *v* dance. **danza** *sf* dancing; (*ballo*) dance. **danzatore, -trice** *sm*, *sf* dancer.

dappertutto [dapper'tutto] *avv* everywhere, all over the place.

dappoco [dap'pɔko] *agg invar* worthless; (*inetto*) good-for-nothing.

dappresso [dap'presso] *avv* close to, close up.

dapprima [dap'prima] *avv* at first.

dardeggiare [darded'dʒare] *v* dart. **dardo** *sm* dart.

*****dare** ['dare] *v* give; (*avere come risultato*) make, come to; (*esame*) take; apply; (*colpire*) hit; (*fruttare*) yield. **dare ai o sui nervi a qualcuno** get on someone's nerves. **dare alla luce** give birth to. **dar da fare** a keep busy. **dar fine** a put an end to. **dare nell'occhio** catch the eye. **dare per scontato** take for granted. **dar retta** a listen to. **dare su** look out on to; (*affacciare*) face. **darsi a** (*dedicarsi*) devote oneself to; (*applicarsi*) go in for.

darsena ['darsena] *sf* dock.

data ['data] *sf* date. **di fresca data** recent. **di vecchia data** of long standing. **in che data?** when? **datare** *v* date; (*risalire*) go back (to).

dato ['dato] *agg* given; (*in vista*) considering, in view of. **dato che** supposing that, as, since. *sm* data. **dato di fatto** fact. **datore di lavoro** *sm* employer.

dattero ['dattero] *sm* (*frutto*) date; (*albero*) date-palm.

dattilografo [datti'lografo], **-a** *sm*, *sf* typist. **dattilografare** *v* type.

davanti [da'vanti] *avv* in front. *sm*, *agg* front. **davanti a** in front of; (*dirimpetto*) facing; (*in presenza di*) before.

davanzale [davan'tsale] *sm* window-sill.

davvero [dav'vero] *avv* really. **dici davvero?** do you (really) mean it?

dazio ['datsjo] *sm* (*imposta*) duty; (*ufficio*) customs (office).

dea ['dɛa] *sf* goddess.

debito¹ ['debito] *agg* due.

debito² ['debito] *sm* debt; (*comm*) debit; (*dovere*) duty. **estinguere/fare un debito** settle/incur a debt. **sentirsi in debito** be indebted. **debitore** *sm* debtor.

debole ['debole] *agg* weak, feeble; (*luce, suono, speranza*) faint. *sm* (*persona*) weakling; (*punto*) weak point; (*inclinazione*) weakness, foible. **debolezza** *sf* weakness; (*difetto*) failing.

debuttare [debut'tare] *v* make one's debut. **debutto** *sm* debut.

decade ['dɛkade] *sf* ten days *pl*.

*****decadere** [deka'dere] *v* decline. **decadere da** (*dir*) forfeit. **decadente** *agg* decadent. **decadenza** *sf* decline; (*dir*) forfeiture, lapse. **decaduto** *agg* impoverished; (*scaduto*) fallen into disuse.

decalcomania [dekalkoma'nia] *sf* transfer.

decano [de'kano] *sm* dean; (*diplomatico*) doyen.

decantare¹ [dekan'tare] *v* (*lodare*) sing the praises of.

decantare² [dekan'tare] *v* (*liquido*) decant.

decapitare [dekapi'tare] *v* behead.

deceduto [detʃe'duto] *agg* deceased.

decennio [de'tʃennjo] *sm* decade.

decente [de'tʃɛnte] *agg* decent. **decenza** *sf* decency, propriety.

decentrare [detʃen'trare] *v* decentralize. **decentramento** *sm* decentralization.

decesso [de'tʃɛsso] *sm* death.

decibel [detʃi'bɛl] *sm invar* decibel.

*****decidere** [de'tʃidere] *v* decide (on); (*risolvere, determinare*) settle. **decidersi**

make up one's mind; (*indursi*) bring oneself to.

deciduo [de'tʃiduo] *agg* deciduous.

decifrare [detʃi'frare] *v* decipher; (*fam*) make out.

decimale [detʃi'male] *agg*, *sm* decimal.

decimo [de'tʃimo] *sm*, *agg* tenth.

decina [de'tʃina] *sf* ten; (*circa dieci*) ten or so. **a decine** (*fig*) by the dozen.

decisione [detʃi'zjone] *sf* decision, resolution; (*dir*) ruling. **decisivo** *agg* decisive; (*prova*) conclusive; (*voto*) casting.

deciso [de'tʃizo] *agg* (*fermo*) decided, firm, resolute; (*definito, risolto*) settled, resolved; (*spiccato*) marked. **decisamente** *avv* decidedly; definitely.

declamare [dekla'mare] *v* declaim; (*protestare*) rail.

declinare [dekli'nare] *v* decline. **declinazione** *sf* (*fis*) declination; (*gramm*) declension. **declino** *sm* decline.

declivio [de'klivjo] *sm* slope.

decollare [dekol'lare] *v* take off. **decollo** *sm* take-off.

***decomporsi** [dekom'porsi] *v* disintegrate, decompose. **decomposizione** *sf* disintegration, decomposition.

decorare [deko'rare] *v* decorate. **decorazione** *sf* decoration.

decoro [de'kɔro] *sm* dignity; (*orgoglio*) pride. **decoroso** *agg* proper.

decorrere [de'korrere] *v* elapse. **con decorrenza da ...** with effect from. **decorso** *sm* (*svolgimento*) course; (*periodo*) lapse.

decrepito [de'krɛpito] *agg* decrepit.

decrescente [dekre'ʃɛnte] *agg* decreasing, diminishing; (*luna*) on the wane.

decreto [de'kreto] *sm* decree, order. **decreto di citazione** writ; (*testimone*) subpoena. **decretare** *v* decree, order; (*concedere*) award.

dedalo ['dɛdalo] *sm* maze.

dedicare [dedi'kare] *v* dedicate, devote; consecrate; (*intitolare*) name after. **dedicarsi a** (*occuparsi di*) take up, go in for. **dedica** *sf* dedication.

dedito ['dɛdito] *agg* devoted to; (*assorbito*) engrossed in (*in*); (*vizio*) addicted.

***dedurre** [de'durre] *v* deduce; (*desumere*) infer; (*prendere, derivare*) take, draw; (*sottrarre*) deduct. **deduzione** *sf* deduction.

defalcare [defal'kare] *v* deduct.

deferire [defe'rire] *v* defer, refer. **deferire al tribunale** sue. **deferente** *agg* deferential.

deficiente [defi'tʃɛnte] *agg* deficient; insufficient; (*inferiore alla media*) backward; (*fam*) moronic. *s*(*m*+*f*) moron, half-wit. **deficienza** *sf* deficiency, lack; (*scarsità*) shortage; (*idiozia*) mental deficiency.

deficit ['dɛfitʃit] *sm invar* deficit. **bilancio deficitario** *sm* debit balance.

definire [defi'nire] *v* define; (*risolvere*) settle. **definitivo** *agg* definitive. **in definitiva** (*dopo tutto*) after all; to sum up; (*in fin dei conti*) all things considered. **definizione** *sf* definition; settlement.

deflazione [defla'tsjone] *sf* deflation. **deflazionare** *v* deflate. **deflazionistico** *agg* deflationary.

***deflettere** [de'flettere] *v* deviate. **deflessione** *sf* deflection; deviation.

deformare [defor'mare] *v* deform, distort; (*mec*) warp; (*senso*) twist. **deformazione** *sf* deformation, distortion; warping. **deforme** *agg* deformed, misshapen; (*viso*) disfigured.

defunto [de'funto], **-a** *s*, *agg* deceased.

degenerare [dedʒene'rare] *v* degenerate. **degenerato, -a** *s*, *agg* degenerate.

degente [de'dʒɛnte] *agg* bedridden. **degenza** *sf* (*a letto*) stay in bed; (*in ospedale*) stay in hospital.

degli ['deʎi] *prep* + *art* = gli.

degnare [de'ɲare] *v* deign; deem or consider worthy. **degnarsi di** condescend to. **degno** *agg* worthy, deserving. **degno di fiducia** trustworthy. **degno di lode** praiseworthy. **degno di nota** noteworthy.

degradare [degra'dare] *v* degrade. **degradazione** *sf* degradation.

degustare [degus'tare] *v* taste, sample.

dei[1] ['dei] *prep* + *art* = di i.

dei[2] ['dei] *V* dio.

deificare [deifi'kare] *v* deify.

del [del] *prep* + *art* = di il.

delatore [dela'tore], **-trice** *sm*, *sf* informer. **delazione** *sf* denouncement; (*fam*) tip-off.

delegare [dele'gare] *v* delegate. **delega** *sf* (*procura*) proxy; (*dir*) power of attorney. **delegato, -a** *sm*, *sf* delegate. **delegazione** *sf* delegation.

deleterio [dele'tɛrjo] *agg* harmful.

delfino [del'fino] *sm* dolphin.

deliberare [delibe'rare] *v* deliberate;

(*decidere*) resolve. **deliberato** *agg* determined, resolved. **deliberazione** *sf* deliberation, decision.

delicato [deli'kato] *agg* delicate; (*gusto*) refined. **delicatezza** *sf* delicacy; (*tatto*) tact; refinement.

delimitare [delimi'tare] *v* define, circumscribe. **delimitazione** *sf* demarcation.

delineare [deline'are] *v* sketch, outline. **delinearsi** *v* (*presentarsi*) appear, emerge; (*apparire*) loom up, take shape.

delinquente [delin'kwɛnte] *s(m+f)* delinquent, criminal; (*mascalzone*) rascal. **delinquenza** *sf* criminality.

deliquio [de'likwjo] *sm* **cadere in deliquio** faint. **essere in deliquio** be in a faint.

delirare [deli'rare] *v* be delirious; (*farneticare*) rave. **delirio** *sm* delirium; (*follia*) frenzy.

delitto [de'litto] *sm* crime; (*reato*) offence; (*grave*) felony; (*lieve*) misdemeanour. **delittuoso** *agg* criminal.

delizia [de'litsja] *sf* delight. **delizioso** *agg* delightful; (*sapore*) delicious.

dell' [dell] *prep* + *art* di l'.

della [della] *prep* + *art* di la.

delle [delle] *prep* + *art* di le.

dello [dello] *prep* + *art* di lo.

delta [delta] *sm invar* delta.

*****deludere** [de'ludere] *v* disappoint; (*render vano*) frustrate.

delusione [delu'zjone] *sf* disappointment. **deluso** *agg* disappointed.

demente [de'mente] *agg* insane. *s(m+f)* lunatic. **demenza** *sf* madness, insanity; (*med*) dementia.

democratico [demo'kratiko], **-a** *sm*, *sf* democrat. *agg* democratic. **democrazia** *sf* democracy.

democristiano [demokris'tjano], **-a** *sm*, *sf* Christian Democrat. *agg* Christian Democratic.

demografia [demogra'fia] *sf* demography. **demografico** *agg* demographic.

demolire [demo'lire] *v* demolish. **demolizione** *sf* demolition.

demone ['dɛmone] *sm* demon; (*potenza ispiratrice*) genius; passion. **demonico** *agg* demonic.

demonio [de'monjo] *sm* devil. **brutto come il demonio** as ugly as sin. **demoniaco** *agg* demoniacal, devilish.

demoralizzare [demoralid'dzare] *v* demoralize. **demoralizzarsi** *v* lose heart.

denaro [de'naro] *sm* money; (*grossezza di filo*) denier. **denaro spicciolo** small change.

denigrare [deni'grare] *v* denigrate; (*fam*) run down. **denigratorio** *agg* disparaging. **denigrazione** *sf* denigration, disparagement.

denominatore [denomina'tore] *sm* denominator. **denominare** *v* name. **denominazione** *sf* naming; (*nome*) name.

denotare [deno'tare] *v* denote, show.

denso ['dɛnso] *agg* dense, thick. **densità** *sf* density; (*spessore*) thickness.

dente ['dɛnte] *sm* tooth (*pl* teeth); (*ruota*) cog; (*forchetta*) prong. **a denti stretti** tight-lipped. **avere il dente avvelenato contro** have it in for. **dente del giudizio** wisdom tooth. **dente di latte** milk-tooth. **dente finto** false tooth. **dente sporgente** buck-tooth. **mettere i denti teethe**, cut one's teeth. **restare a denti asciutti** go hungry; (*fig*) go away empty-handed. **dentario** *agg* dental. **dentato** *agg* toothed.

dentellare [dentel'lare] *v* indent, notch. **dentellatura** *sf* indentation.

dentice ['dentitʃe] *sm* sea bream.

dentiera [den'tjɛra] *sf* denture.

dentifricio [denti'fritʃo] *sm* toothpaste.

dentista [den'tista] *s(m+f)* dentist.

dentro ['dentro] *avv* in; (*all'interno*) inside. *prep* in, inside; (*in casa*) indoors. **andar dentro** (*fam*) go to jail.

denunziare [denun'tsjare] *v* also **denunciare** denounce; (*riferire*) report; (*dichiarare*) declare; (*disdire*) terminate; (*rendere palese*) show. **denunzia** or **denuncia** *sf* report; (*accusa*) charge; declaration; notice of termination.

deodorante [deodo'rante] *agg*, *sm* deodorant.

deperire [depe'rire] *v* (*piante*) wither; (*animali*) waste away; (*persone*) get run down; (*cibi*) perish. **deperibile** *agg* perishable.

depilatorio [depila'torjo] *agg* depilatory. *sm* hair-remover.

dépliant [depli'ã] *sm*, *pl* **-s** leaflet.

deplorare [deplo'rare] *v* (*compiangere*) lament, regret; (*biasimare*) deplore, regret. **deplorevole** *agg* deplorable.

*****deporre** [de'porre] *v* put or set down, deposit, lay; (*testimoniare*) (bear) witness. **deporre in giudizio** give evidence. **deposizione** *sf* deposition, testimony.

deportare [depor'tare] v deport. **deportato, -a** sm, sf deportee. **deportazione** sf deportation.

deposito [de'pozito] sm deposit; (*magazzino*) warehouse, store. **deposito bagagli** left-luggage office. **depositare** v deposit. **depositario** sm trustee.

depravare [depra'vare] v deprave.

depredare [depre'dare] v plunder.

depresso [de'presso] agg depressed. **depressione** sf depression. **depressivo** agg depressive, depressant.

deprezzare [depret'tsare] v depreciate. **deprezzamento** sm depreciation.

*deprimere [de'primere] v depress. **deprimente** agg depressing.

depurare [depu'rare] v purify. **depuratore** sm purifier. **depurazione** sf purification.

deputare [depu'tare] v delegate. **deputato, -a** sm, sf deputy; delegate; Member of Parliament.

deragliare [dera'ʎare] v be derailed, go off the rails. **deragliamento** sm derailment.

derapare [dera'pare] v skid.

derelitto [dere'litto], **-a** agg forsaken. sm, sf down-and-out; (*trovatello*) foundling.

deretano [dere'tano] sm behind.

*deridere [de'ridere] v laugh at, mock, deride. **derisione** sf derision, ridicule. **derisorio** agg derisory, laughable.

deriva [de'riva] sf **alla deriva** adrift. **andare alla deriva** drift.

derivare [deri'vare] v derive; (*conseguire*) follow, result; (*sviare*) divert. **derivata** sf (*mat*) derivative. **derivato, -a** (*chim*) derivative; (*sottoprodotto*) by-product. **derivazione** sf derivation, origin. **collegare in derivazione** (*elett, radio*) shunt.

dermatite [derma'tite] sf dermatitis. **dermatologo, -a** sm, sf dermatologist.

derogare [dero'gare] v deviate (from), depart (from); (*non osservare*) not comply (with); (*dir*) waive. **deroga** sf departure. **in deroga a** notwithstanding; (*dir*) waiving. **derogabile** agg not binding.

derrate [der'rate] sf pl provisions pl; (*alimentari*) foodstuffs pl.

derubare [deru'bare] v rob.

*descrivere [de'skrivere] v describe. **descrittivo** agg descriptive. **non descrivibile** indescribable. **descrizione** sf description, account.

deserto [de'zɛrto] sm desert, wilderness.

agg (*vuoto*) deserted; (*disabitato*) uninhabited.

desiderare [dezide'rare] v wish; (*volere*) want; (*bramare*) long for, desire. **lasciare a desiderare** leave to be desired. **desiderabile** agg desirable.

desiderio [dezi'dɛrjo] sm wish; (*brama, rimpianto*) longing, desire. **aver desiderio di** wish or want to. **pio desiderio** wishful thinking.

designare [dezi'ɲare] v designate; (*denominare*) call; (*nominare, stabilire*) appoint.

desinare [dezi'nare] sm lunch, dinner. v lunch, dine.

desinenza [dezi'nentsa] sf ending.

*desistere [de'zistere] v desist. **desistere da** give up.

desolato [dezo'lato] agg (*afflitto*) distressed; (*deserto*) desolate; (*devastato*) desolated. **desolante** agg distressing. **desolazione** sf desolation; distress.

despota ['dɛspota] sm despot.

destare [des'tare] v awake, rouse; (*suscitare*) arouse, awaken. **destar meraviglia** cause wonder.

destinare [desti'nare] v destine; (*assegnare*) intend, assign; (*dedicare*) devote; (*riservare*) set aside; (*indirizzare*) address; decide. **destinatario, -a** sm, sf (*lettera*) addressee; (*merci*) consignee. **esser destinato a** (*decretato dalla sorte*) be bound or destined to; (*condannato*) be doomed to. **destinazione** sf destination. **destino** sm destiny, fate.

destituire [destitu'ire] v dismiss. **destituito** agg dismissed; (*privo*) devoid. **destituzione** sf dismissal.

desto ['dɛsto] agg (*sveglio*) (wide-)awake; (*vivace*) lively.

destra ['dɛstra] sf (*lato*) right, right-hand side; (*mano*) right hand; (*pol*) right (wing). **a destra** on or to the right. **tenere la destra** keep to the right.

destro ['dɛstro] agg (*lato*) right(-hand); (*abile*) skilful, dextrous; (*accorto*) clever. **destrezza** sf ability, skill, dexterity. **destrorso** agg from left to right; (*in senso orario*) clockwise.

detenere [dete'nere] v hold; (*trattenere in prigione*) detain. **detenuto, -a** sm, sf detainee. **detenzione** sf detention. **detenzione abusiva** unlawful possession.

detergente [deter'dʒɛnte] sm, agg detergent.

deteriorare [deterjo'rare] v deteriorate. **deterioramento** sm deterioration.

determinare [determi'nare] v determine; (causare) bring about. **determinante** agg determining, decisive. **determinato** agg (preciso) definite, distinct; (stabilito) appointed; (noto) given; (particolare) special; (deciso) determined. **determinazione** sf determination.

deterrente [deter'rɛnte] sm, agg deterrent.

detersivo [deter'sivo] sm, agg detergent.

detestare [detes'tare] v detest, loathe. **detestabile** agg hateful, odious.

detonatore [detona'tore] sm detonator. **detonante** sm, agg explosive. **capsula detonante** sf percussion cap.

*****detrarre** [det'rarre] v deduct, take away; (nuocere a) detract (from).

detrimento [detri'mento] sm detriment, prejudice.

detrito [de'trito] sm debris; (geol) detritus.

dettagliare [detta'ʎare] v (particolareggiare) detail; (vendere al minuto) retail. **dettagliante** s(m+f) retailer. **dettaglio** sm detail; retail.

dettare [det'tare] v dictate. **dettar legge** lay down the law. **dettato** sm dictation.

detto ['detto] agg (già citato) above-mentioned, aforesaid; (chiamato) known as, alias. **detto fatto** no sooner said than done. **detto fra noi** between you and me. sm saying.

deturpare [detur'pare] v disfigure, deface.

devastare [devas'tare] v ravage, devastate. **devastazione** sf devastation, destruction. **devastatore** [devasta'tore] agg devastating, destructive. sm devastator, destroyer.

deviare [devi'are] v deviate; (spostare in altra direzione) divert. **deviazione** sf deviation; (fis) deflection; (traffico) diversion, detour.

devolvere [de'volvere] v devolve, assign.

devoto [de'voto] agg (rel) devout; (dedicato, affezionato) devoted. **devozione** sf devotion; devoutness.

di [di] prep of; (partitivo) some, any; (moto da luogo) from; (paragone) than.

diabete [dia'bɛte] sm diabetes. **diabetico, -a** s, agg diabetic.

diacono [di'akono] sm deacon.

diadema [dia'dɛma] sm diadem, tiara.

diaframma [dia'framma] sm diaphragm; (divisione) partition.

diagnosi [di'aɲozi] sf diagnosis (pl -ses). **fare la diagnosi di** diagnose.

diagonale [djago'nale] sf, agg diagonal.

diagramma [dia'gramma] sm diagram; (grafico) chart, curve.

dialetto [dia'lɛtto] sm dialect. **dialettale** agg dialect.

dialogo ['djalogo] sm, pl -ghi dialogue; (trattativa) negotiations pl; (colloquio) conversation, talk.

diamante [dia'mante] sm diamond.

diametro [di'ametro] sm diameter. **diametrale** agg diametrical.

diamine ['djamine] inter heavens! che diamine ... ! what on earth ... !

diapason [di'apazon] sm tuning fork; (tono) pitch; (estensione di voce) range.

diapositiva [diapozi'tiva] sf transparency, slide.

diario [di'arjo] sm diary, journal. **diario di bordo** log-book.

diarrea [diar'rɛa] sf diarrhoea.

diavolo ['djavolo] sm devil. **che diavolo ... !** what the devil ... ! **un buon diavolo** a good chap. **diavoleria** sf mischief. **diavoletto** sm imp; (bigodino) roller, curler.

dibattere [di'battere] v debate. **dibattersi** v struggle. **dibattimento** sm hearing. **dibattito** sm debate. **dibattuto** agg (discusso) controversial, vexed; (tormentato) troubled.

dicastero [dikas'tɛro] sm ministry.

dicembre [di'tʃɛmbre] sm December.

diceria [ditʃe'ria] sf rumour, gossip.

dichiarare [dikja'rare] v declare; (gioco di carte) bid. **dichiarazione** sf declaration; bid; (attestazione) statement; (amore) proposal. **dichiarazione dei redditi** tax return.

diciannove [ditʃan'nɔve] agg, sm nineteen. **diciannovesimo** sm, agg nineteenth.

diciassette [ditʃas'sɛtte] agg, sm seventeen. **diciassettesimo** sm, agg seventeenth.

diciotto [di'tʃɔtto] agg, sm eighteen. **diciottesimo** sm, agg eighteenth.

dicitura [ditʃi'tura] sf caption.

didascalia [didaska'lia] sf caption; (cinema) subtitle; (teatro) stage directions pl.

didattico [di'dattiko] agg didactic.

didentro [di'dentro] **al/dal didentro** on/from the inside.

didietro [di'djɛtro] *sm* behind.

dieci ['djɛtʃi] *sm, agg* ten.

diesis [di'ɛzis] *sm* (*musica*) sharp.

dieta ['djɛta] *sf* diet. **essere a dieta** be on a diet.

dietro ['djɛtro] *avv* behind. *prep* (*luogo*) behind; (*tempo*) after; (*su, in seguito a*) on. **dietro front** about turn.

difatti [di'fatti] *cong* in fact.

*****difendere** [di'fɛndere] *v* defend.

difensiva [difen'siva] *sf* defensive. **difensivo** *agg* defensive.

difensore [difen'sore] *sm* defender. **avvocato difensore** *sm* counsel for the defence.

difesa [di'fesa] *sf* defence. **difesa legittima** self-defence. **senza difesa** defenceless. **stare sulla difesa** be on the defensive.

difeso [di'fezo] *agg* (*riparato*) sheltered; (*fortificato*) defended, protected.

difetto [di'fetto] *sm* (*mancanza*) lack; (*imperfezione*) defect, fault. **difettare** *v also* **far difetto** lack; (*venir meno*) fail; (*essere difettoso*) be defective *or* faulty. **difettoso** *agg* defective, faulty.

diffamare [diffa'mare] *v* denigrate; (*a voce*) slander; (*per iscritto*) libel. **diffamatorio** *agg* defamatory; slanderous; libellous. **diffamatore, -trice** *sm, sf* libeller; slanderer.

differente [diffe'rɛnte] *agg* different, unlike.

differenza [diffe'rɛntsa] *sf* difference. **a differenza di** unlike. **differenziale** *sm, agg* differential. **differenziare** *v* differentiate.

differire [diffe'rire] *v* (*rimandare*) defer; (*esser diverso*) differ, be different.

difficile [dif'fitʃile] *agg* difficult; (*improbabile*) unlikely; (*duro*) hard. *sm* difficulty. *s(m+f)* difficult person.

difficoltà [diffikol'ta] *sf* difficulty; (*ostacolo*) trouble. **difficoltoso** *agg* difficult.

diffidare [diffi'dare] *v* (*non fidarsi*) mistrust, be suspicious of; (*avvisare*) warn, caution. **diffida** *sf* warning, notice. **diffidente** *agg* suspicious. **diffidenza** *sf* suspicion.

*****diffondere** [dif'fondere] *v* spread; (*luce, calore, ecc.*) diffuse; (*dilungarsi*) dwell; (*comm*) promote.

diffusione [diffu'zjone] *sf* spreading, diffusion; (*giornali*) circulation. **diffuso** *agg* widespread; diffused; widely circulated; (*prolisso*) long-winded.

diga ['diga] *sf* dam, barrier.

digerire [didʒe'rire] *v* digest; (*assimilare*) take in; (*tollerare*) stand, bear; (*credere*) swallow. **digeribile** *agg* digestible. **digestione** *sf* digestion. **digestivo** *sm, agg* digestive.

digitale [didʒi'tale] *agg* **impronta digitale** *sf* finger-print.

digiunare [didʒu'nare] *v also* **stare a digiuno** fast. **digiuno** *sm* fast. **a digiuno** on an empty stomach. **essere a digiuno di** (*fig*) be without.

dignità [diɲi'ta] *sf* dignity; (*ufficio*) high rank. *sf pl* dignitaries *pl*. **dignitoso** *agg* dignified.

digredire [digre'dire] *v* digress.

digressione [digres'sjone] *sf* digression.

digrignare [digri'ɲare] *v* **digrignare i denti** gnash one's teeth; (*animali*) bare the teeth.

dilagare [dila'gare] *v* flood, spread. **dilagamento** *sm* flooding.

dilaniare [dila'njare] *v* rend.

dilapidare [dilapi'dare] *v* squander.

dilatare [dila'tare] *v* dilate, open (wide). **dilatazione** *sf* dilation.

dilatorio [dila'torjo] *agg* dilatory. **dilazione** *sf* delay, deferment.

dileguare [dile'gware] *v* dispel. **dileguarsi** *v* disappear, fade.

dilemma [di'lemma] *sm* dilemma.

dilettante [dilet'tante] *agg, s(m+f)* amateur. **dilettantesco** *agg* amateurish.

dilettare [dilet'tare] *v* delight; (*far divertire*) amuse. **dilettarsi** *v* delight in, enjoy.

diletto¹ [di'letto] *sm* (*piacere*) delight, pleasure; (*godimento*) enjoyment.

diletto² [di'letto] *agg* beloved; (*preferito*) favourite.

diligente [dili'dʒɛnte] *agg* (*che lavora*) industrious; (*accurato*) conscientious; painstaking.

diligenza¹ [dili'dʒɛntsa] *sf* industry, conscientiousness. **con diligenza** conscientiously.

diligenza² [dili'dʒɛntsa] *sf* (*carrozza*) stage-coach.

diluire [dilu'ire] *v* dilute; (*allungare con acqua*) water down; (*vernice, ecc.*) thin (down).

dilungarsi [dilun'garsi] *v* (*andar per le lunghe*) talk at length, dwell.

diluvio [di'luvjo] *sm* flood, deluge.

dimagrire [dima'grire] v also **dimagrare** lose weight; (di proposito) slim; (far sembrare snello) make look slimmer.

dimenare [dime'nare] v wave (about); (coda) wag. **dimenarsi** v fidget, toss about.

dimensione [dimen'sjone] sf dimension. **a due/tre dimensioni** two-/three-dimensional.

dimenticare [dimenti'kare] v forget; (perdonare) forget about; (trascurare) neglect. **dimenticarsi** (di) forget (about). **dimentico** agg, m pl -chi forgetful; (noncurante) oblivious.

dimestichezza [dimesti'kettsa] sf familiarity. **aver dimestichezza con** be familiar with.

dimettere [di'mettere] v discharge; (licenziare) dismiss. **dimettersi** v resign.

dimezzare [dimed'dzare] v halve.

diminuire [diminu'ire] v diminish, reduce; (calare) drop; (lavoro a maglia) cast off, decrease. **diminuire di peso** lose weight. **diminuire di prezzo** cost less. **diminuire di valore** fall in value, be worth less. **diminutivo** agg diminutive. **diminuzione** sf decrease; drop, cut, fall.

dimissione [dimis'sjone] sf resignation. **dare** or **rassegnare le dimissioni** resign. **dimissionario** agg outgoing.

dimorare [dimo'rare] v stay, live. **dimora** sf (abitazione) home, abode; (soggiorno) stay, residence.

dimostrare [dimos'trare] v demonstrate; (manifestare) show, display; prove. **dimostrabile** agg demonstrable. **dimostrante** s(m+f) demonstrator. **dimostrativo** agg demonstrative. **dimostratore, -trice** sm, sf demonstrator. **dimostrazione** sf demonstration; (prova) proof.

dinamica [di'namika] sf dynamics. **dinamico** agg dynamic, forceful.

dinamite [dina'mite] sf dynamite.

dinamo ['dinamo] sf invar dynamo.

dinanzi [di'nantsi] avv ahead, forward. **agg** invar (dirimpetto) facing; (precedente) previous. **prep dinanzi a** (davanti a) in front of; (dirimpetto) opposite; in the presence of, before.

dinastia [dinas'tia] sf dynasty. **dinastico** agg dynastic.

dinoccolato [dinokko'lato] agg shambling. **camminare dinoccolato** v slouch.

dinosauro [dino'sauro] sm dinosaur.

dintorno [din'torno] avv around, about.

dintorni sm pl outskirts pl, surroundings pl.

dio ['dio] sm, pl **dei** god. **come un dio** wonderfully, beautifully.

diocesi ['djot∫ezi] sf diocese.

diodo ['diodo] sm diode.

dipanare [dipa'nare] v unravel.

dipartimento [diparti'mento] sm department, district.

dipendente [dipen'dɛnte] s(m+f) (impiegato) employee. agg dependent, subordinate. **dipendenza** sf dependence; (edificio) annexe; (filiale) branch. **essere alle dipendenze di** be in the employ of.

***dipendere** [di'pɛndere] v depend (on); (derivare) be due (to), be caused (by). **dipende!** that depends! **dipende da te!** it is up to you!

***dipingere** [di'pindʒere] v paint; (rappresentare) depict. **dipingersi** v (truccarsi) make up. **dipinto** sm painting.

diploma [di'plɔma] sm diploma, certificate, qualification. **diplomarsi** v obtain a certificate, qualify.

diplomatico [diplo'matiko], -a agg diplomatic. sm, sf diplomat. **diplomazia** sf diplomacy.

diporto [di'porto] sm pleasure, pastime.

diradare [dira'dare] v thin; (nebbia) clear.

diramare [dira'mare] v issue, broadcast. **diramarsi** v branch out or off. **diramazione** sf branch; (comunicato, ecc.) broadcasting, circulation.

***dire** ['dire] v say; (raccontare, ordinare) tell; (significare) mean. **a chi lo dici!** don't I know! **aver da dire su** find fault with. **è tutto dire** which is saying a lot. **inutile dire** it goes without saying. sm speech, words pl. **a dire di tutti** by all accounts. **oltre ogni dire** beyond all description.

diretto [di'rɛtto] agg direct; (inteso) meant, destined; (guidato) conducted. sm (ferr) through train. **direttissimo** sm (ferr) express train. **direttiva** sf directive; (condotta) policy. **direttivo** agg (che dirige) guiding; (proprio alla direzione) managerial. **direttore** sm manager; (scuola) headmaster; (giornale) editor; (orchestra) conductor. **direttrice** sf manageress; headmistress.

direzione [dire'tsjone] sf direction; (il dirigere) management, administration; (sede) head office. **assumere la direzione**

take charge. **in che direzione?** which way?

*dirigere [di'ridʒere] v direct; (*rivolgere*) address; (*guidare*) lead; (*amministrare*) manage; (*giornale*) edit; (*orchestra*) conduct. **dirigersi verso** go towards, head for. **dirigibile** sm airship.

dirimpetto [dirim'petto] agg invar, avv opposite.

diritto[1] [di'ritto] agg (*non curvo*) straight; (*eretto, onesto*) upright; (*fam: astuto*) crafty; (*fam: accorto*) shrewd; (*destro*) right(-hand). avv straight. **andar diritto** go straight ahead or on. sm (*moneta*) obverse; (*lato buono*) good side; (*tennis*) forehand.

diritto[2] [di'ritto] sm (*legge*) law; (*pretesa*) right; (*tassa*) due, duty. **a buon diritto** with good cause. **diritti d'autore** copyright sing; (*compenso*) royalties pl. **diritto acquisito** vested interest.

diroccato [dirok'kato] agg dilapidated.

dirottare [dirot'tare] v divert; change course.

dirotto [di'rotto] agg (*pianto*) copious; (*pioggia*) pouring.

disabitato [dizabi'tato] agg uninhabited.

disabituare [dizabitu'are] v wean.

disaccordo [dizak'kɔrdo] sm disagreement; variance. **essere o trovarsi in disaccordo su** disagree on, be at variance over.

disadatto [diza'datto] agg ill-suited.

disadorno [diza'dorno] agg bare.

disagevole [diza'dʒevole] agg uncomfortable.

disagio [di'zadʒo] sm (*imbarazzo*) uneasiness; (*mancanza di comodità*) discomfort. **essere a disagio** be ill at ease. **sentirsi a disagio** feel uneasy. **disagiato** agg uncomfortable; (*duro*) hard.

disamorarsi [dizamo'rarsi] v become estranged (from), cease to care (for).

disapprovare [dizappro'vare] v disapprove. **disapprovazione** sf disapproval.

disappunto [dizap'punto] sm disappointment.

disarmare [dizar'mare] v disarm; (*smantellare*) dismantle; (*edificio*) remove the scaffolding from. **disarmo** sm disarmament.

disarmonia [dizarmo'nia] sf discord.

disastro [di'zastro] sm disaster; (*incidente*) crash; (*fam: insuccesso*) utter failure.

combinare un disastro (*fam*) make a mess. **disastroso** agg disastrous.

disattento [dizat'tento] agg inattentive; (*sbadato*) careless. **disattenzione** sf carelessness; (*errore*) slip. **per disattenzione** through an oversight.

disavanzo [diza'vantso] sm deficit.

disavventura [dizavven'tura] sf misfortune.

disbrigo [diz'brigo] sm, pl -ghi settlement, dispatch.

discapito [dis'kapito] sm **a discapito di** at the cost of, to the prejudice of.

*discendere [di'ʃendere] v descend; (*andar giù*) go down; (*venir giù*) come down. **discendente** s(m+f) descendant. **discendenza** sf descent; (*collettivo*) offspring. **discensore** sm lift.

discepolo [di'ʃepolo] sm disciple.

discernere [di'ʃernere] v discern; distinguish.

discesa [di'ʃesa] sf descent; (*declivio*) slope. **discesa in picchiata** nose-dive. **in discesa** downhill.

*dischiudere [dis'kjudere] v open; (*svelare*) disclose.

*disciogliere [di'ʃɔʎere] v dissolve; (*liquefare*) melt.

disciplinare [diʃipli'nare] v discipline, control. agg disciplinary. **disciplina** sf discipline. **disciplinato** agg (well-)disciplined, orderly.

disco ['disko] sm disc; (*grammofono*) record; (*sport*) discus; (*hockey*) puck; (*telefono*) dial. **disco rosso/verde** red/green light.

discolo ['diskolo] agg mischievous.

discolpare [diskol'pare] v clear. **discolpa** sf justification, defence.

*disconoscere [disko'noʃere] v refuse to acknowledge.

discontinuo [diskon'tinuo] agg discontinuous; (*non regolare*) erratic.

discorde [dis'kɔrde] agg also **discordante** discordant; (*contrastante*) conflicting; (*stonante*) clashing. **discordare** v disagree; conflict; clash. **discordia** sf disagreement.

*discorrere [dis'korrere] v talk. **discorrere del più e del meno** talk about this and that. **e via discorrendo** and so on.

discorso [dis'korso] sm conversation, talk; (*in pubblico, gramm*) speech. **cambiare discorso** change the subject. **senza tanti discorsi** quite frankly. **tenere**

un discorso make a speech, give an address.

discoteca [disko'tɛka] *sf* (*locale*) discotheque; record collection.

discreto [dis'krɛto] *agg* fair, reasonable; (*non importuno*) tactful, discreet; (*separato*) discrete. **discretamente** *avv* moderately well. **discrezionale** *agg* discretionary. **discrezione** *sf* discretion, moderation, tact.

discriminazione [diskrimina'tsjone] *sf* discrimination. **discriminare** *v* discriminate; (*dir*) extenuate.

discussione [diskus'sjone] *sf* discussion, debate; (*litigio*) argument. **mettere in discussione** discuss, debate; (*in dubbio*) question.

discusso [dis'kusso] *agg* discussed, controversial.

*****discutere** [dis'kutere] *v* discuss, debate; (*litigare*) argue. **discutibile** *agg* debatable, questionable.

disdegnare [dizde'ɲare] *v* disdain, scorn. **disdegno** *sm* disdain, scorn.

*****disdire** [diz'dire] *v* (*annullare*) cancel; (*negare*) deny; (*ritrattare*) withdraw, take back; (*mentire*) refute. **disdetta** *sf* notice; (*sfortuna*) bad luck; cancellation.

disegnare [dize'ɲare] *v* draw; (*progettare*) design, sketch; (*delineare*) outline. **disegnatore** *sm* draughtsman. **disegno** *sm* drawing; (*schizzo*) sketch; (*progetto*) design, plan; (*abbozzo*) outline. **a disegni** patterned. **disegno animato** (*cinema*) cartoon. **disegno di legge** bill.

diseredare [dizere'dare] *v* disinherit. **diseredato, -a** *s, agg* destitute.

disertare [dizer'tare] *v* desert. **disertore** *sm* deserter. **diserzione** *sf* desertion.

*****disfare** [dis'fare] *v* undo; (*smontare*) take to pieces; (*valigia*) unpack; (*sciogliere*) melt. **disfatta** *sf* defeat. **disfattismo** *sm* defeatism. **disfattista** *s(m+f), agg* defeatist.

disgelare [dizdʒe'lare] *v* thaw (out); (*frigorifero*) defrost. **disgelo** *sm* thaw.

*****disgiungere** [diz'dʒundʒere] *v* detach, separate.

disgraziato [dizgra'tsjato], **-a** *agg* unfortunate, unlucky; (*infelice*) wretched. *sm, agg* (*sventurato*) wretch; (*sciagurato*) scoundrel. **disgrazia** *sf* misfortune; (*incidente*) accident, mishap; (*sfavore*) disgrace; (*sfortuna*) bad luck.

disgregare [dizgre'gare] *v* break up. **disgregazione** *sf* break-up.

disguido [diz'gwido] *sm* (*equivoco*) misunderstanding; (*errore nel recapito*) mistake in delivery.

disgustare [dizgus'tare] *v* disgust. **disgusto** *sm* disgust, revulsion, loathing. **disgustoso** *agg* disgusting, loathsome, revolting.

disidratare [dizidra'tare] *v* dehydrate.

*****disilludere** [dizil'ludere] *v* disillusion, disenchant. **disillusione** *sf* disenchantment, disillusion.

disimpegnare [dizimpe'ɲare] *v* free, release; (*oggetto dato in pegno*) redeem; (*mil*) relieve. **disimpegnarsi** *v* (*cavarsela*) acquit oneself, manage. **disimpegno** *sm* (*adempimento*) fulfilment; (*politica*) disengagement.

disinfettare [dizinfet'tare] *v* disinfect. **disinfettante** *sm* disinfectant. **disinfezione** *sf* disinfection.

disintegrare [dizinte'grare] *v* disintegrate; (*fis*) split, decay.

disinteressarsi [dizinteres'sarsi] *v* take no interest (in). **disinteressato** *agg* disinterested; (*altruistico*) unselfish.

disinvolto [dizin'vɔlto] *agg* unconstrained, self-possessed; (*spigliato*) free and easy, casual; (*senza ritegno*) uninhibited. **disinvoltura** *sf* ease, casualness; self-possession.

disistima [dizis'tima] *sf* lack of esteem; (*disprezzo*) contempt.

dislivello [dizli'vɛllo] *sm* difference (in level); (*fig*) inequality.

dislocare [dizlo'kare] *v* displace; (*mil*) detach.

dismisura [dizmi'zura] *sf* **a dismisura** excessively.

disoccupato [dizokku'pato], **-a** *s, agg* unemployed. **disoccupazione** *sf* unemployment. **sussidio di disoccupazione** *sm* unemployment benefit; (*fam*) dole.

disonesto [dizo'nɛsto] *agg* dishonest; (*immorale*) dishonourable; (*impudico*) shameless. **disonestà** *sf* dishonesty; dishonourable behaviour; shamelessness.

disonorare [dizono'rare] *v* dishonour, disgrace. **disonore** *sm* dishonour, disgrace. **disonorevole** *agg* dishonourable, disgraceful, shameful.

disopra [di'sopra] *avv* above; (*al piano superiore*) upstairs. *agg invar* (*superiore*) upper; (*posto più in alto*) higher up;

upstairs. *sm invar* top, upper part. **al disopra di** (*più di*) more than; (*superiore a*) above all; (*più alto di*) above. **dal disopra** from above.

disordinare [dizordi'nare] *v* upset, turn upside down. **disordinato** *agg* untidy; confuso; (*sregolato*) disorderly. **disordine** *sm* disorder; (*confusione*) muddle.

disorientare [dizorjen'tare] *v* (*confondere*) confuse, bewilder. **disorientarsi** *v* lose one's bearings, become confused.

disossare [dizos'sare] *v* bone.

disotto [di'sotto] *avv* below, underneath; (*al piano inferiore*) downstairs. *agg invar* below; (*tra due*) lower; (*in fondo*) bottom; downstairs.

dispaccio [dis'pattʃo] *sm* dispatch.

disparato [dispa'rato] *agg* dissimilar, different.

dispari ['dispari] *agg* odd.

disparte [dis'parte] *avv* **in disparte** aside, to one side. **tenersi in disparte** keep at a distance.

dispensa [dis'pensa] *sf* distribution; (*mobile*) cupboard; (*locale*) pantry, larder; (*fascicolo*) number, issue; (*esonero*) exemption. **a dispense** in instalments. **dispensa ecclesiastica** dispensation. **dispensa universitaria** lecture notes *pl*. **dispensare** *v* dispense. **dispensario** *sm* clinic.

disperare [dispe'rare] *v* despair. **disperato** *agg* desperate. **disperazione** *sf* despair.

disperdere [dis'perdere] *v* disperse, scatter; dissipate; (*sprecare*) waste. **dispersione** *sf* dispersion; waste.

dispetto [dis'petto] *sm* spite; (*irritazione*) annoyance. **a dispetto di** despite. **fare un dispetto** annoy. **per dispetto** out of spite. **dispettoso** *agg* spiteful, annoying.

dispiacere [dispja'tʃere] *v* displease. **mi dispiace ...** (*non mi piace*) I don't like ... ; (*sono spiacente*) I'm sorry ... . **ti dispiace ...?** do you mind ...? *sm* (*rammarico*) regret; (*noia*) displeasure; (*fastidio*) trouble, worry.

disponibile [dispo'nibile] *agg* available; (*libero*) vacant. **posto disponibile** *sm* vacancy.

disponibilità [disponibili'ta] *sf* availability. *sf pl* assets *pl*.

disporre [dis'porre] *v* dispose; (*collocare in ordine, stabilire*) arrange; prepare; induce; order. **disporre di** have available,

have at one's disposal; (*avere*) have. **disporsi** *v* prepare, get ready; (*in fila*) line up.

dispositivo [dispozi'tivo] *sm* device.

disposizione [dispozi'tsjone] *sf* arrangement, layout; (*stato d'animo*) disposition; (*inclinazione*) bent; (*norma*) provision; (*comando*) order. **a disposizione** available.

disposto [dis'posto] *agg* arranged, laid out; (*pronto*) ready, willing; (*stabilito*) laid down.

disprezzare [dispret'tsare] *v* despise, scorn. **disprezzo** *sm* scorn, contempt.

disputare [dispu'tare] *v* dispute; (*litigare*) argue; (*contendere*) fight (over), strive (for); (*incontro*) play; (*corsa*) run. **disputa** *sf* dispute; (*lite*) argument.

dissanguare [dissan'gware] *v* bleed.

disseccare [dissek'kare] *v* dry up.

disseminare [dissemi'nare] *v* scatter; (*diffondere*) spread.

dissenteria [dissente'ria] *sf* dysentery.

dissentire [dissen'tire] *v* dissent, disagree.

disseppellire [disseppel'lire] *v* unearth; (*esumare*) exhume.

dissertazione [disserta'tsjone] *sf* dissertation.

dissestare [disses'tare] *v* upset, unbalance. **dissestato** *agg* ruined; (*strada*) in poor condition; (*bilancio*) adverse.

dissetarsi [disse'tarsi] *v* quench one's thirst. **dissetante** *agg* thirst-quenching.

dissidente [dissi'dente] *s(m+f)*, *agg* dissident; (*rel*) non-conformist.

dissidio [dis'sidjo] *sm* disagreement; (*lite*) quarrel.

dissimile [dis'simile] *agg* different, unlike.

dissimulare [dissimu'lare] *v* dissimulate; (*fingere*) pretend; (*nascondere*) hide.

dissipare [dissi'pare] *v* dissipate; (*sospetti, dubbi, ecc.*) dispel; (*sprecare*) squander.

dissociare [disso'tʃare] *v* dissociate. **dissociazione** *sf* dissociation.

dissoluto [disso'luto] *agg* dissolute.

dissoluzione [dissolu'tsjone] *sf* dissolution, break-up.

dissolvere [dis'solvere] *v* dispel; (*sciogliere*) dissolve.

dissotterrare [dissotter'rare] *v* unearth; (*esumare*) exhume.

dissuadere [dissua'dere] *v* dissuade, deter.

distaccare [distak'kare] *v* detach; (*sport:*

lasciar dietro) leave behind. **distaccarsi** v (*spiccare*) stand out; (*allontanarsi*) withdraw. **distaccamento** sm (*mil*) detachment. **distacco** sm detachment; (*separazione*) parting, separation; (*sport: vantaggio*) lead.

distante [dis'tante] agg distant, remote, far. avv far, far off. **distanza** sf distance; (*tempo*) interval.

*****distare** [dis'tare] v be far (from).

*****distendere** [dis'tendere] v spread; (*allungare*) stretch; (*appendere*) hang (up); (*mettere giù*) lay; (*rilassare*) relax. **distendersi** v lie down, relax.

distensione [disten'sjone] sf stretching; relaxation; (*pol*) détente. **distensivo** agg relaxing.

distesa [dis'teza] sf expanse; (*fila*) row.

disteso [dis'tezo] agg (*teso*) stretched; (*coricato*) lying down; (*braccio*) outstretched; (*spiegato*) spread out; relaxed.

distillare [distil'lare] v distil. **distilleria** sf distillery.

*****distinguere** [dis'tingwere] v distinguish, tell; (*contrassegnare*) mark; draw a distinction; (*riconoscere*) recognize. **distinguibile** agg distinguishable; recognizable.

distinta [dis'tinta] sf list. **distinta delle spese** statement of expenses.

distintivo [distin'tivo] agg distinctive; (*atto a distinguere*) distinguishing. sm badge.

distinto [dis'tinto] agg distinct, different, separate; (*scelto, raffinato*) distinguished. **ben distinto** precise. **distinti saluti** yours faithfully.

distinzione [distin'tsjone] sf distinction. **fare una distinzione** make a distinction, discriminate. **senza distinzione** (*senza merito*) undistinguished; (*senza criterio*) indiscriminately; (*in modo equo*) impartially.

*****distogliere** [dis'tɔʎere] v divert, turn away.

distorsione [distor'sjone] sf distortion; (*med*) sprain.

*****distrarre** [dis'trarre] v distract; (*divertire*) amuse. **distrarsi** v amuse oneself; (*essere disattento*) be inattentive. **distratto** agg inattentive; (*assente*) absent-minded; (*sbadato*) careless. **distrazione** sf (*svago*) distraction, relaxation; (*sbadataggine*) carelessness; absent-mindedness; lack of attention.

distretto [dis'tretto] sm district.

distribuire [distribu'ire] v distribute; (*disporre*) arrange; (*assegnare*) hand out; (*le carte*) deal; (*posta*) deliver. **distributore** sm (*di accensione*) distributor; (*di benzina*) petrol pump, service station. **distribuzione** sf distribution; (*fornitura*) supply; arrangement; delivery. **distribuzione dei premi** prize-giving. **distribuzione dei ruoli** (*cinema*) casting.

districare [distri'kare] v disentangle; (*fig*) sort out. **districarsi** v extricate oneself.

*****distruggere** [dis'truddʒere] v destroy, ruin. **distruttivo** agg destructive. **distrutto** agg destroyed, ruined; (*fig*) broken. **distruzione** sf destruction, ruin.

disturbare [distur'bare] v disturb; (*molestare, seccare*) trouble, bother; (*recar fastidio*) inconvenience; (*radio*) jam. **disturbo** sm trouble; (*incomodo*) nuisance, inconvenience; (*indisposizione*) upset, disorder; (*radio*) jamming; atmospherics pl, interference. **recar disturbo** trouble, inconvenience.

disubbidire [dizubbi'dire] v disobey.

disuguale [dizu'gwale] agg unequal; (*non regolare*) irregular. **disuguaglianza** sf difference, disparity.

disunire [dizu'nire] v separate, divide.

disuso [di'zuzo] sm disuse. **andare** or **cadere in disuso** fall into disuse, become obsolete. **disusato** agg obsolete, out-of-date; (*fuori moda*) old-fashioned.

dito ['dito] sm, pl -a f finger. **dito anulare/indice/medio/mignolo** ring/index/middle/little finger. **dito del piede** toe. **ditale** sm (*cucire*) thimble; (*guanto*) finger-stall.

ditta [ditta] sf firm, company.

dittatore [ditta'tore] sm dictator. **dittatorio** agg dictatorial. **dittatura** sf dictatorship.

dittico ['dittiko] sm diptych.

dittongo [dit'tongo] sm diphthong.

diurno [di'urno] agg day(-time). **spettacolo diurno** sm matinee.

diva ['diva] sf (film-)star.

divagare [diva'gare] v digress, wander; (*distrarre*) distract.

divampare [divam'pare] v flare up, blaze.

divano [di'vano] sm divan, settee, couch.

diventare [diven'tare] v also **divenire** become, turn or grow (into). **diventar matto** go mad. **diventar pallido/rosso** go or turn pale/red.

divergere [di'vɛrdʒere] v diverge; *(essere diverso)* differ. **divergenza** sf divergence; difference.

diversi [di'vɛrsi] agg several. pron *(parecchi)* several (people); *(alcuni)* some (people).

diversivo [diver'sivo] agg diverting; distracting. sm diversion; distraction.

diverso [di'vɛrso] agg different; distinct, separate; *(di genere diverso)* various; *(comm)* sundry. **in caso diverso** otherwise. **diversamente** avv differently; *(se no)* otherwise. **diversità** sf difference; diversity.

divertente [diver'tɛnte] agg amusing, enjoyable. **divertimento** sm entertainment, amusement. **buon divertimento!** enjoy yourself! have a good time!

divertire [diver'tire] v amuse; *(ricreare)* entertain. **divertirsi** v enjoy oneself.

dividendo [divi'dɛndo] sm dividend.

*dividere [di'videre] v divide; *(condividere)* share. **dividersi** v separate, part, split (up).

divieto [di'vjɛto] sm prohibition. **divieto di sorpasso/sosta/transito** no overtaking/stopping/thoroughfare.

divinare [divi'nare] v divine; *(prevedere)* foretell.

divincolarsi [divinko'larsi] v wriggle.

divino [di'vino] agg sacred, holy; *(sublime)* divine, heavenly. **divinità** sf divinity.

divisa [di'viza] sf uniform; motto. **divisa estera** foreign currency.

divisibile [divi'zibile] agg divisible. **divisibilità** sf divisibility.

divisione [divi'zjone] sf division; *(reparto)* department.

diviso [di'vizo] agg divided, separated; *(condiviso)* shared. **divisore** sm divisor.

divisorio [divi'zɔrjo] sm partition. agg dividing.

divo ['divo] sm (film-)star.

divorare [divo'rare] v devour, eat up.

divorzio [di'vɔrtsjo] sm divorce. **divorziare** v divorce.

divulgare [divul'gare] v spread; *(rivelare)* divulge; *(rendere accessibile)* popularize. **divulgazione** sf spreading; *(notizie)* broadcasting; popularization.

dizionario [ditsjo'narjo] sm dictionary.

dizione [di'tsjone] sf diction.

doccia ['dottʃa] sf shower; *(grondaia)* gutter.

docente [do'tʃɛnte] s(m+f) lecturer, teacher.

docile [do'tʃile] agg docile, mild; *(materiale)* easily worked. **docilità** sf mildness, submissiveness; workability.

documento [doku'mento] sm document, paper. **documentare** v document. **documentario** agg, sm documentary. **documentazione** sf documentation; *(dir)* evidence.

dodici ['doditʃi] agg, sm twelve. **dodicesimo** sm, agg twelfth.

dogana [do'gana] sf customs. **doganale** agg customs. **doganiere** sm customs officer.

doge ['dɔdʒe] sm doge.

doglie ['dɔʎʎe] sf pl **doglie del parto** labour pains pl.

dogma ['dɔgma] sm dogma. **dogmatico** agg dogmatic.

dolce ['doltʃe] agg sweet; *(mite)* mild; *(morbido)* soft. sm sweet. **dolcezza** sf sweetness; mildness; softness.

*dolere [do'lere] v *(far male)* ache, hurt. **mi duole di** or **che . . .** I regret that . . . , I'm sorry that . . . .

dollaro ['dɔllaro] sm dollar.

dolo ['dɔlo] sm *(dir)* malice; *(inganno)* fraud.

dolore [do'lore] sm pain; *(male fisico)* ache; *(sofferenza morale)* sorrow; *(rincrescimento)* regret. **doloroso** agg painful; sorrowful.

domanda [do'manda] sf question; *(richiesta)* request; *(scritta)* application; *(econ)* demand; *(dir)* petition. **domandare** v *(per sapere)* ask; *(per avere)* ask for; *(esigere)* demand. **domandarsi** v wonder.

domani [do'mani] avv tomorrow. **a domani!** see you tomorrow! **domani a otto** tomorrow week. **domani l'altro** the day after tomorrow. sm tomorrow; future. **un domani** one day.

domare [do'mare] v tame; *(sedare)* put down; *(spegnere)* put out; *(frenare)* curb. **domatore** sm tamer.

domattina [domat'tina] avv tomorrow morning.

domenica [do'menika] sf Sunday.

domestico [do'mɛstiko] agg domestic; *(della casa)* household, home. **apparecchio domestico** household appliance. sm servant. **domestica** sf maid. **domestichezza** sf familiarity.

domiciliarsi [domitʃi'ljarsi] v settle.

domicilio [domi'tʃiljo] sm domicile, home.

dominare [domi'nare] v dominate; (predominare) prevail; (frenare) control; (aver potestà) rule. **dominio** sm domination; rule; (territorio) domain; (proprietà) possession. **pubblico dominio** (proprietà) common property; (noto a tutti) common knowledge.

domino ['domino] sm (gioco) dominoes.

donare [do'nare] v give, present; (star bene) suit, become. **donatore, -trice** sm, sf donor. **donazione** sf donation, gift.

donde ['donde] avv (da dove) whence, from where; (di che) with which.

dondolare [dondo'lare] v swing, rock. **cavallo a dondolo** sm rocking-horse. **sedia a dondolo** sf rocking-chair.

donna ['donna] sf woman (pl women); (domestica) maid, servant; (giochi) queen. **donnaiolo** sm philanderer. **donnesco** agg feminine. **donnola** ['donnola] sf weasel.

dono ['dono] sm gift.

dopo ['dopo] avv after; (poi) then, afterwards; (più tardi) later (on); (prossimo) next. **a dopo!** see you later! **dopobarba** agg, sm invar after-shave. **dopo che** since. **dopo di che** whereupon. **dopodomani** sm, avv the day after tomorrow. **dopotutto** avv after all. **molto tempo dopo** long after.

dopopranzo [dopo'prantso] avv after lunch. sm afternoon.

doppiare[1] [dop'pjare] v (cinema) dub. **doppiaggio** sm dubbing.

doppiare[2] [dop'pjare] v double; (sport) lap.

doppio ['doppjo] agg double; (insincero) two-faced; (duplice) dual, twofold. **a doppio petto** double-breasted. **fare il doppio gioco** double-cross. sm double, twice as much or many. **doppione** sm duplicate.

dorare [do'rare] v gild; (gastr) coat with egg. **doratura** sf gilding, gold-plating.

dormicchiare [dormik'kjare] v doze, snooze.

dormire [dor'mire] v sleep; (esser fermo) lie dormant. **dormita** sf good sleep.

dormitorio [dormi'tɔrjo] sm dormitory.

dormiveglia [dormi'veʎa] sm **essere nel dormiveglia** be half-asleep.

dorso ['dorso] sm back; (nuoto) back-stroke.

dose ['dɔze] sf dose; quantity. **dose eccessiva** overdose. **rincarare la dose** (fam) pile it on. **dosaggio** sm dosage.

dosso ['dɔsso] sm back. **togliersi un peso di dosso** take a weight off one's mind.

dotare [do'tare] v endow, provide. **dotato** agg gifted; endowed or provided (with); (munito) equipped (with). **dotazione** sf equipment; (rendita) endowment. **dote** sf (matrimonio) dowry; (donazione) endowment; (qualità) gift.

dotto[1] ['dotto] agg scholarly, learned. sm scholar.

dotto[2] ['dotto] sm (condotto) duct.

dottore [dot'tore], **-essa** sm, sf doctor.

dottrina [dot'trina] sf (cultura) learning; (teoria, insieme di principi) doctrine.

dove ['dove] avv where. cong (se) if; (mentre) whereas. **fin dove** as far as.

*dovere [do'vere] v must, have to; (esser lecito) may; (essere inevitabile) be bound to; (esser causato da) be due to; (al condizionale) should, ought to. **come si deve** properly; (persona) proper, decent. sm duty. **doveroso** agg right and proper; (obbligato) (duty-)bound. **dovuto** agg, sm due.

dovunque [do'vunkwe] avv (dappertutto) everywhere; (in qualsiasi luogo) anywhere. cong wherever.

dozzina [dod'dzina] sf dozen. **a dozzine** by the dozen. **da dozzina** cheap, poor.

dragare [dra'gare] v dredge; (mine) sweep. **draga** sf dredge, dredger. **dragamine** sm invar minesweeper.

drago ['drago] sm dragon; (aquilone) kite. **dragone** sm dragon; (mil) dragoon.

dramma ['dramma] sm play; tragedy. **drammatico** agg dramatic; (esagerato) theatrical. **drammatizzare** v dramatize. **drammaturgo** sm playwright, dramatist.

drappello [drap'pello] sm squad, band.

drappo ['drappo] sm cloth; (funebre) pall. **drappeggiare** v drape.

drastico ['drastiko] agg drastic.

drenare [dre'nare] v drain. **drenaggio** sm drainage.

dritta ['dritta] sf (mano) right (hand); (parte) right(-hand side); (mar) starboard.

dritto ['dritto] agg (fam) astute. sm (non rovescio) right side; (fam) crafty person, fast worker.

drizzare [drit'tsare] v (raddrizzare)

straighten; (*erigere*) erect. **drizzare le orecchie** prick up one's ears.

droga ['drɔga] *sf* drug; (*sostanza aromatica*) spice. **drogare** *v* drug, dope; spice. **drogarsi** *v* take drugs.

droghiere [dro'gjere], **-a** *sm*, *sf* grocer. **drogheria** *sf* grocer's shop. **articoli di drogheria** *sm pl* groceries *pl*.

dromedario [drome'darjo] *sm* dromedary.

dualismo [dua'lizmo] *sm* dualism.

dubbio ['dubbjo] *sm* doubt. **essere in dubbio** be in doubt, be uncertain. **mettere in dubbio** doubt, call in question. **due volte** no doubt, doubtless. *agg also* **dubbioso** doubtful, uncertain; (*ambiguo*) dubious.

dubitare [dubi'tare] *v* doubt; (*essere in dubbio*) be in doubt; (*diffidare*) distrust. **non dubitare!** don't worry!

duca ['duka] *sm* duke.

duce ['dutʃe] *sm* leader.

duchessa [du'kessa] *sf* duchess.

due ['due] *sm*, *agg* two. **a due a due** two by two, in twos. **duepezzi** *sm invar* two-piece. **due punti** colon. **due volte** twice. **due volte tanto** twice as much *or* many. **nessuno dei due** neither of them. **tutti e due** both of them.

duello [du'ɛllo] *sm* duel. **duellare** *v* duel. **duellista** *or* **duellante** *sm* duellist.

duetto [du'etto] *sm* duet.

duna ['duna] *sf* dune.

dunque ['dunkwe] *cong* (*nel discorso*) well, now then; (*perciò*) so, therefore, hence; (*rafforzativo*) then. **trovarsi al dunque** come to the crunch. **venire al dunque** come to the point.

duo ['duo] *sm invar* duo.

duodeno [duo'dɛno] *sm* duodenum. **duodenale** *agg* duodenal.

duomo ['dwɔmo] *sm* cathedral.

duplex ['dupleks] *sm invar* (*telefono*) party-line.

duplicare [dupli'kare] *v* duplicate. **duplicato** *agg*, *sm* duplicate. **duplicatore** *sm* duplicator, copier. **duplice** *agg* double.

durare [du'rare] *v* last; (*cibo*) keep; (*abiti*) wear; (*sopportare*) endure. **durata** [du'rata] *sf* length (of time), duration. **di breve durata** short-lived, not lasting. **di lunga durata** lasting. **durata di una carica** term of office. **durevole** *agg* lasting.

duro ['duro] *agg* hard, tough. **aver la pelle dura** be thick-skinned. **aver la testa dura**

be stubborn. **tener duro** hold out. **durezza** *sf* hardness. **durone** *sm* callus.

duttile ['duttile] *agg* ductile.

E

e [e], **ed** *cong* and; (*invece*) and then. **e ... e ...** both ... and .... **tutti e due** both (of them). **tutti e tre** all three (of them).

ebano ['ebano] *sm* ebony. **d'ebano** (*colore*) jet-black. **ebanista** *sm* cabinet-maker.

ebbene [eb'bɛne] *cong* well (then).

ebbro ['ebbro] *agg* intoxicated, drunk. **ebbrezza** *sf* intoxication; (*fig*) rapture, elation.

ebdomadario [ebdoma'darjo] *agg*, *sm* weekly.

ebete ['ebete] *agg* dull-witted.

ebollizione [ebolli'tsjone] *sf* boiling. **punto di ebollizione** *sm* boiling point.

ebraico [e'braiko] *agg* Jewish, Hebrew. *sm* (*lingua*) Hebrew.

ebreo [e'brɛo], **-a** *sm*, *sf* Jew. *agg* Jewish.

eccedere [et'tʃedere] *v* exceed; surpass. **eccedere i limiti** go too far.

****eccellere** [et'tʃɛllere] *v* excel, be outstanding. **eccellente** *agg* excellent. **eccellenza** *sf* excellence; (*titolo*) Excellency. **per eccellenza** par excellence.

eccentrico [et'tʃentriko] *agg*, *sm* eccentric. **eccentricità** *sf* eccentricity.

eccepibile [ettʃe'pibile] *agg* objectionable. **eccepire** *v* take exception (to), object (to).

eccesso [et'tʃɛsso] *sm* excess. **all'eccesso** excessively, to a fault. **eccesso di velocità** speeding. **eccessivo** *agg* excessive, exaggerated.

eccetera [et'tʃetera] etcetera, and so forth *or* on.

eccetto [et'tʃetto] *prep* except. **eccetto che** (*tranne che*) except for, but for; (*a meno che*) unless.

eccettuare [ettʃettu'are] *v* except, leave out.

eccezione [ettʃe'tsjone] *sf* exception. **ad eccezione di** except for. **eccezionale** *agg* exceptional.

eccidio [et'tʃidjo] *sm* slaughter.

eccitare [ettʃi'tare] *v* excite, stimulate; (*provocare*) stir up, rouse. **eccitamento** *sm* excitement; *(stimolo)* incitement. **eccitante** *sm* stimulant. **eccitazione** *sf* excitement.

ecclesiastico [ekkle'zjastiko] *agg* clerical, ecclesiastic(al). *sm* clergyman.

ecco ['ekko] *avv* this or that is; *(qui)* here is; *(li)* there is. **ecco fatto** that is that. **ecco tutto** that is all.

eccome [ek'kome] *avv*, *inter* and how, certainly.

echeggiare [eked'dʒare] *v* echo; *(risonare)* resound.

eclettico [e'klettiko] *agg* eclectic.

eclissare [eklis'sare] *v* eclipse. **eclisse** *or* **eclissi** *sf* eclipse.

eco ['ɛko] *s(m+f)*, *pl* -i *m* echo. **echi di cronaca** gossip (column) *sing*. **far eco a** echo.

ecologia [ekolo'dʒia] *sf* ecology. **ecologico** *agg* ecological. **ecologo, -a** *sm*, *sf* ecologist.

economia [ekono'mia] *sf* economy; *(risparmio)* thrift, saving; *(scienza)* economics. **fare economie** economize, save. **economico** *agg* economic; *(a bassa spesa)* economical, cheap.

economizzare [ekonomid'dzare] *v* economize, save.

economo [e'kɔnomo] *sm* steward, supply officer.

ed [ed] *V* e.

edera ['edera] *sf* ivy.

edibile [e'dibile] *agg* edible.

edicola [e'dikola] *sf* bookstall.

edificare [edifi'kare] *v* *(erigere)* construct; *(stimolare al bene)* edify. **edificante** *agg* edifying. **edificio** *sm* building; *(fig)* structure.

edile [e'dile] *agg* building. *sm* builder. **edilizia** *sf* building trade. **edilizio** *agg* building.

Edimburgo [edim'burgo] *sf* Edinburgh.

editore [edi'tore], **-trice** *sm*, *sf* publisher. *agg* publishing. **edito** *agg* published.

editto [e'ditto] *sm* edict.

edizione [edi'tsjone] *sf* edition; *(tiratura)* issue.

educare [edu'kare] *v* educate; *(ammaestrare)* train. **educativo** *agg* educational. **educato** *agg* *(cortese)* polite. **bene/male educato** well-/ill-mannered. **educazione** *sf* education, upbringing; training; *(comportamento)* manners *pl*; breeding.

effeminato [effemi'nato] *agg* effeminate. **effeminatezza** *sf* effeminacy.

effervescente [efferve'ʃɛnte] *agg* effervescent, sparkling.

effetto [ef'fetto] *sm* effect; *(conseguenza)* result; impression; *(comm)* bill. **aver effetto** take effect. **dare effetto a** carry out. **fare effetto** work. **fare l'effetto di** give the impression of.

effettuare [effettu'are] *v* effect, bring about; *(realizzare)* carry out; *(fare)* make. **effettuabile** *agg* feasible. **effettuazione** *sf* execution.

efficace [effi'katʃe] *agg* effective, efficient. **efficacia** *sf* efficacy, effectiveness; force.

efficiente [effi'tʃɛnte] *agg* efficient. **efficienza** *sf* efficiency, effectiveness; *(mec)* working order.

effigie [ef'fidʒe] *sf* effigy; image.

effimero [ef'fimero] *agg* ephemeral.

effluente [efflu'ɛnte] *sm* effluent, sewage. **efflusso** *sm* outflow.

egida ['ɛdʒida] *sf* aegis.

Egitto [e'dʒitto] *sm* Egypt. **egiziano, -a** *s*, *agg* Egyptian. **egizio, -a** *s*, *agg* (ancient) Egyptian.

egli ['eʎi] *pron* he.

egocentrico [ego'tʃɛntriko] *agg* egocentric, self-centred.

egoista [ego'ista] *s(m+f)* egoist, selfish person. **egoistico** *agg* egoistic(al), selfish.

egotista [ego'tista] *s(m+f)* egotist, boaster. **egotistico** *agg* egotistic(al).

egregio [e'grɛdʒo] *agg* distinguished; *(in lettere)* dear.

eguale [e'gwale] *V* **uguale**.

egualitario [egwali'tarjo], **-a** *s*, *agg* egalitarian.

eiettore [ejet'tore] *sm* ejector. **sedile eiettore** *sm* ejector seat.

elaborare [elabo'rare] *v* elaborate, devise; *(dati)* process. **elaborato** *agg* elaborate. **elaboratore** *sm* *(elettronico)* ,computer; *(dati)* processor. **elaborazione** *sf* preparation, formulation; *(dati)* processing.

elargire [elar'dʒire] *v* lavish.

elastico [e'lastiko] *agg* elastic; *(molleggiante)* springy; *(fig)* flexible; *(agile)* nimble. *sm* elastic; *(anello)* elastic band; *(materasso)* spring.

elefante [ele'fante] *sm* elephant. **elefantesco** *agg* elephantine.

elegante [ele'gante] *agg* elegant; *(vestito)* smart; *(fine)* graceful; *(ingegnoso)* neat. **eleganza** *sf* elegance; smartness, stylishness.

*eleggere [e'leddʒere] v elect, nominate. **eleggibile** agg eligible. **eleggibilità** sf eligibility.

elegia [ele'dʒia] sf elegy. **elegiaco** agg elegiac.

elemento [ele'mento] sm element; (individuo) fellow, individual. **elementare** agg elementary; (naturale) elemental.

elemosina [ele'mɔzina] sf alms, charity. **chiedere l'elemosina** beg. **fare l'elemosina** give alms.

elenco [e'lenko] sm list; (telefonico) directory; (iscritti) register. **elencare** v list; enumerate.

eletto [e'letto] agg chosen; (scelto) select; (nominato) elected.

elettorale [eletto'rale] agg electoral, election. **collegio elettorale** sm constituency. **propaganda elettorale** sf electioneering. **scheda/urna elettorale** sf ballot-paper/box. **elettorato** sm electorate; (diritto di eleggere) franchise.

elettore [elet'tore], **-trice** sm, sf elector, voter; (di collegio elettorale) constituent.

elettrico [e'lettriko] agg electric(al). **elettricista** sm electrician. **elettricità** sf electricity.

elettrificare [elettrifi'kare] v electrify. **elettrificazione** sf electrification.

elettrizzare [elettrid'dzare] v electrify; (fig) thrill.

elettrodo [e'lettrodo] sm electrode.

elettrodomestico [elettrodo'mestiko] sm electric appliance.

elettrodotto [elettro'dotto] sm power line, mains.

elettrolisi [elet'trɔlizi] sf electrolysis. **elettrolitico** agg electrolytic.

elettrone [elet'trone] sm electron. **elettronica** sf electronics. **elettronico** agg electronic.

elettrotecnico [elettro'tekniko] sm electrical engineer.

elevare [ele'vare] v raise. **elevato** agg high; (fig) lofty. **elevazione** sf elevation; (atto di alzare) raising.

elezione [ele'tsjone] sf election. **elezioni politiche** general election sing.

elica ['elika] sf propeller. **elicottero** sm helicopter.

eliminare [elimi'nare] v eliminate; (escludere) rule out. **eliminatoria** sf (sport) qualifying round. **eliminazione** sf elimination; exclusion.

elio ['eljo] sm helium.

ella ['ella] pron she; (formula di cortesia) you.

ellisse [el'lisse] sf ellipse. **ellittico** agg elliptical.

elmetto [el'metto] sm also **elmo** helmet.

elogio [e'lɔdʒo] sm praise. **elogiare** v praise.

eloquente [elo'kwente] agg eloquent; (significativo) meaningful. **eloquenza** sf eloquence.

elsa ['elsa] sf hilt.

*eludere [e'ludere] v elude, dodge, evade.

emaciato [ema'tʃato] agg emaciated.

emanare [ema'nare] v emanate; (diffondere) give off, send out; (promulgare) issue. **emanazione** sf emanation; promulgation.

emancipare [emantʃi'pare] v emancipate. **emancipazione** sf emancipation.

embargo [em'bargo] sm embargo.

emblema [em'blema] sm emblem; symbol, model. **emblematico** agg emblematic, symbolic.

embolia [embo'lia] sf embolism. **embolo** sm embolus.

embrione [embri'one] sm embryo. **embrionale** agg embryonic.

emendare [emen'dare] v amend. **emendamento** sm amendment.

emergenza [emer'dʒentsa] sf emergency.

*emergere [e'mɛrdʒere] v emerge; (distinguersi) stand out; (apparire) appear.

*emettere [e'mettere] v emit, give out; (ordine, azioni) issue; (giudizio) deliver; (grido) utter.

emicrania [emi'krania] sf migraine.

emigrare [emi'grare] v emigrate; (animali) migrate. **emigrante** s(m+f) emigrant. **emigrato, -a** sm, sf emigrant; (pol) exile. **emigrazione** sf emigration, migration; (econ) flight.

eminente [emi'nɛnte] agg eminent, distinguished; (elevato) high. **eminenza** sf eminence.

emisfero [emis'fero] sm hemisphere. **emisferico** agg hemispheric(al).

emissario¹ [emis'sarjo] sm (mandatario) emissary.

emissario² [emis'sarjo] sm (canale, ecc.) outlet.

emissione [emis'sjone] sf emission; (econ) issue. **emittente** agg issuing; (radio) transmitting.

emolliente [emol'ljente] *sm, agg* emollient.

emorragia [emorra'dʒia] *sf* haemorrhage, bleeding.

emorroidi [emor'rɔidi] *sf pl* piles *pl*.

emotivo [emo'tivo] *agg* emotional; *(impressionabile)* excitable; *(che provoca emozione)* emotive, thrilling.

emozione [emo'tsjone] *sf* emotion; excitement. **emozionante** *agg* exciting. **emozionare** *v* excite; *(commuovere)* move.

empio ['empjo] *agg* impious; *(crudele)* cruel.

empire [em'pire] *v* fill.

empirico [em'piriko] *agg* empirical.

emporio [em'pɔrjo] *sm* store.

emù [e'mu] *sm* emu.

emulare [emu'lare] *v* emulate. **emulazione** *sf* rivalry; *(dir)* nuisance.

emulsione [emul'sjone] *sf* emulsion.

enciclopedia [entʃiklope'dia] *sf* encyclopaedia. **enciclopedico** *agg* encyclopaedic.

encomio [en'kɔmjo] *sm* praise. **encomiabile** *agg* praiseworthy.

endemico [en'dɛmiko] *agg* endemic.

energia [ener'dʒia] *sf* energy. **energetico** *sm, agg* tonic. **energico** *agg* energetic; *(forte)* forceful, strong.

enfasi ['enfazi] *sf* emphasis *(pl* -ses*)*. **enfatico** *agg* emphatic.

enfiare [en'fjare] *v* swell, inflate.

enigma [e'nigma] *sm* puzzle, riddle; *(mistero, persona misteriosa)* enigma, mystery. **enigmatico** *agg* puzzling; mysterious.

ennesimo [en'nɛzimo] *agg* nth; *(fam)* umpteenth.

enorme [e'norme] *agg* enormous, huge. **enormità** *sf (causa di indignazione)* enormity; *(errore)* blunder.

ente ['ente] *sm (filos)* being; *(azienda)* undertaking, concern; authority; *(istituzione)* body.

enteroclisi [entero'klizi] *sm* enema.

entità [enti'ta] *sf* entity; importance; *(consistenza)* extent.

entrambi [en'trambi] *agg, pron* both.

entrare [en'trare] *v* enter; *(andar dentro)* go in(to); *(con difficoltà)* get in(to); *(venir dentro)* come in(to); *(associarsi)* join. **entrare in ballo** come into play. **entrare in vigore** come into effect.

entrata [en'trata] *sf* entrance, entry; *(accesso)* admission. **entrate** *sf pl (redditi)*

income *sing*, earnings *pl*; *(incassi)* receipts *pl*; *(di enti pubblici)* revenue *sing*.

entro ['entro] *prep* within; *(ora/data precisata)* by. **entro oggi** before the day is out.

entusiasmo [entu'zjazmo] *sm* enthusiasm. **entusiasmare** *v* thrill, excite. **entusiasta** *s(m+f)* enthusiast. **entusiastico** *agg* enthusiastic.

enumerare [enume'rare] *v* list. **enumerazione** *sf* listing; list.

enunciare [enun'tʃare] *v* enunciate; *(esprimere)* express; formulate.

enzima [en'dzima] *sm* enzyme.

epatite [epa'tite] *sf* hepatitis.

epico ['epiko] *agg* epic, heroic. **epica** *sf* epic poetry.

epidemia [epide'mia] *sf* epidemic. **epidemico** *agg* epidemic.

Epifania [epifa'nia] *sf* Epiphany; *(festa)* Twelfth Night.

epigramma [epi'gramma] *sm* epigram. **epigrammatico** *agg* epigrammatic.

epilessia [epiles'sia] *sf* epilepsy. **epilettico, -a** *s, agg* epileptic.

epilogo [e'pilogo] *sm, pl* **-ghi** epilogue; *(fig)* end, conclusion.

episodio [epi'zɔdjo] *sm* episode. **episodico** *agg* episodic; *(frammentario)* bitty; *(accidentale)* incidental; isolated.

epistola [e'pistola] *sf* epistle. **epistolare** *agg* epistolary.

epitaffio [epi'taffjo] *sm* epitaph.

epiteto [e'piteto] *sm* epithet.

epoca ['epoka] *sf* period; *(tempo)* time. **a quell'epoca** at that time. **che fa epoca** epoch-making. **da quell'epoca** from that time on, since then.

eppure [ep'pure] *cong* and yet.

epurare [epu'rare] *v* purge. **epurazione** *sf* purging; purge.

equanime [e'kwanime] *agg (imparziale)* fair; *(sereno)* even-tempered. **equanimità** *sf* fairness, equanimity.

equatore [ekwa'tore] *sm* equator. **equatoriale** *agg* equatorial.

equazione [ekwa'tsjone] *sf* equation.

equestre [e'kwestre] *agg* equestrian.

equilibrare [ekwili'brare] *v* balance. **equilibrio** *sm* balance, equilibrium; moderation, common sense; *(padronanza di sé)* poise. **perdere l'equilibrio** lose one's balance. **tenere in equilibrio** balance. **tenersi in equilibrio** keep one's balance. **equilibrista** *s(m+f)* acrobat.

equinozio [ekwi'nɔtsjo] *sm* equinox.

equipaggiare [ekwipad'dʒare] *v* (*fornire*) equip; (*nave*) man. **equipaggiamento** *sm* kit. **equipaggio** *sm* crew.

equiparare [ekwipa'rare] *v* level.

equitazione [ekwita'tsjone] *sf* (horse-)riding.

***equivalere** [ekwiva'lere] *v* be equivalent, correspond. **equivalente** *sm*, *agg* equivalent.

equivoco [e'kwivoko] *sm* (*errore*) mistake; (*malinteso*) misunderstanding. **a scanso di equivoci** to avoid misunderstandings. *agg* ambiguous; (*di dubbia moralità*) questionable, shady. **non equivoco** unambiguous, straightforward.

equo ['ekwo] *agg* fair.

era ['era] *sf* era, age.

erario [e'rarjo] *sm* Treasury. **erariale** *agg* fiscal.

erba ['erba] *sf* grass; (*gastr*) herb. **in erba** green; (*fig*) budding. **erbaceo** *agg* herbaceous.

erbaccia [er'battʃa] *sf* weed.

erbicida [erbi'tʃida] *sm* herbicide, weedkiller.

erbivendolo [erbi'vendolo], **-a** *sm*, *sf* greengrocer.

erbivoro [er'bivoro] *sm* herbivore. *agg* herbivorous.

erede [e'rɛde] *s(m+f)* heir, heiress. **erede apparente** heir presumptive. **erede universale** sole heir.

eredità [eredi'ta] *sf* inheritance, heritage. **ereditare** *v* inherit. **ereditario** *agg* inherited, hereditary. **principe ereditario** *sm* crown prince. **ereditiera** *sf* heiress.

eremita [ere'mita] *sm* hermit. **eremitaggio** *sm* hermitage.

eretico [e'rɛtiko], **-a** *sm*, *sf* heretic. *agg* heretical. **eresia** *sf* heresy; (*fam*: *sproposito*) rubbish.

eretto [e'rɛtto] *agg* erect, upright. **erettile** *agg* erectile.

erezione [ere'tsjone] *sf* erection.

ergastolo [er'gastolo] *sm* life imprisonment *or* sentence.

erica ['erika] *sf* heather.

***erigere** [e'ridʒere] *v* raise, erect; (*fondare*, *considerare*) set up.

ermellino [ermel'lino] *sm* ermine; (*bruno*) stoat.

ermetico [er'metiko] *agg* (*aria*) air-tight; (*acqua*) water-tight; obscure.

ernia ['ɛrnja] *sf* hernia, rupture.

***erodere** [e'rodere] *v* erode.

eroe [e'rɔe] *sm* hero. **eroico** *agg* heroic. **eroina** *sf* heroine. **eroismo** *sm* heroism; (*atto*) heroic deed.

erogare [ero'gare] *v* distribute, deliver; (*in donazione*) donate. **erogazione** *sf* distribution, delivery; donation.

eroina [ero'ina] *sf* (*stupefacente*) heroin.

erosione [ero'zjone] *sf* erosion.

erotico [e'rɔtiko] *agg* erotic. **erotismo** *sm* eroticism.

erpete ['ɛrpete] *sm* herpes.

erpice ['erpitʃe] *sm* harrow.

errare [er'rare] *v* (*andare senza meta*) roam, wander; (*sbagliare*) err, be mistaken. **erratico** *agg* erratic. **errato** *agg* incorrect. **se non vado errato** if I am not mistaken.

erroneo [er'rɔneo] *agg* erroneous, wrong.

errore [er'rore] *sm* mistake, error. **errore giudiziario** miscarriage of justice. **per errore** by mistake, in error.

erudito [eru'dito] *agg* erudite, learned. **erudizione** *sf* learning.

eruttare [erut'tare] *v* (*ruttare*) belch; (*vulcano*) erupt; (*fig*) spew out. **eruzione** *sf* eruption.

esacerbare [ezatʃer'bare] *v* exacerbate.

esagerare [ezadʒe'rare] *v* exaggerate; (*caricare*) overdo. **esagerazione** *sf* exaggeration.

esagono [e'zagono] *sm* hexagon. **esagonale** *agg* hexagonal.

esalare [eza'lare] *v* exhale, give off. **esalazione** *sf* exhalation.

esaltare [ezal'tare] *v* exalt; (*lodare*) extol; (*entusiasmare*) thrill, stir. **esaltato**, **-a** *sm*, *sf* fanatic, hot-head.

esame [e'zame] *sm* examination, test; (*controllo*) inspection, check. **dare un esame** take an examination. **prendere in esame** consider, take into consideration.

esaminare [ezami'nare] *v* examine, test, check.

esanime [e'zanime] *agg* lifeless.

esasperare [ezaspe'rare] *v* (*irritare*) exasperate; (*inasprire*) sharpen, increase. **esasperazione** *sf* exasperation; sharpening, increase.

esatto [e'zatto] *agg* exact; correct; accurate; punctual. *avv* (*in punto*) exactly. **esattezza** *sf* exactness; accuracy, precision.

esattore [ezat'tore] *sm* (*tassa*) collector. **esattoria** *sf* tax office.

esaudire [ezau'dire] *v* grant.

esaurire [ezau'rire] *v* exhaust, use up; (*vendere completamente*) sell out; (*condurre a termine*) complete. **esaurirsi** *v* (*debilitarsi*) wear oneself out.

esca ['eska] *sf* bait; (*fig*) lure; (*per accendere*) tinder. **dar esca a** fan, stir up.

escandescenza [eskande'fentsa] *sf* **dare in escandescenze** flare up; (*fam*) fly off the handle.

eschimese [eski'meze] *s(m+f)*, *agg* Eskimo.

esclamare [eskla'mare] *v* exclaim, cry out. **punto esclamativo** *sm* exclamation mark. **esclamazione** *sf* exclamation.

*****escludere** [es'kludere] *v* exclude. **esclusione** *sf* exclusion. **ad esclusione di** except.

esclusivo [esklu'zivo] *agg* exclusive. **esclusiva** *sf* (*comm*) exclusive *or* sole right; (*rappresentanza*) sole agency. **escluso** *agg* excluded, impossible; (*eccettuato*) except; (*non compreso*) exclusive of, not including.

escogitare [eskodʒi'tare] *v* devise, think up.

escursione [eskur'sjone] *v* excursion, trip; (*a macchina*) drive; (*a piedi*) hike. **escursionista** *s(m+f)* tripper; hiker.

esecutivo [ezeku'tivo] *sm*, *agg* executive.

esecutore [ezeku'tore], **-trice** *sm*, *sf* (*dir*) executor; (*musica*) performer; (*carnefice*) executioner.

esecuzione [ezeku'tsjone] *sf* execution, performance.

eseguire [eze'gwire] *v* carry out; (*musica, teatro*) perform; (*dir*) execute.

esempio [e'zɛmpjo] *sm* example; model. **ad** *or* **per esempio** for instance. **dare l'esempio** set an example.

esemplare [ezem'plare] *agg* exemplary. *sm* example, model; (*tipico*) specimen. **esemplificare** *v* exemplify, illustrate.

esentare [ezen'tare] *v* exempt. **esentarsi da** get out of. **esente** *agg* exempt, free. **esenzione** *sf* exemption.

esequie [e'zɛkwje] *sf pl* (*cerimonie*) funeral rites *pl*; funeral *sing*.

esercente [ezer'tʃɛnte] *s(m+f)* retailer; (*negoziante*) shopkeeper. **esercire** *v* manage, run.

esercitare [ezertʃi'tare] *v* practise; (*usare*)

exercise. **esercitazione** *sf* practice; exercise; (*mil*) drill. **esercizio** *sm* exercise; (*attività*) practice; (*azienda*) concern.

esibire [ezi'bire] *v* exhibit. **esibirsi** *v* (*dar spettacolo*) perform; (*mettersi in mostra*) show off. **esibizione** *sf* exhibition, show, display. **esibizionismo** *sm* exhibitionism. **esibizionista** *s(m+f)* exhibitionist.

*****esigere** [e'zidʒere] *v* require, need, demand. **esigente** *agg* exacting. **esigenza** *sf* requirement; (*necessità*) need; (*pretesa*) demand. **esiguo** *agg* meagre.

esilarante [ezila'rante] *agg* exhilarating. **esile** ['ɛzile] *agg* slender; (*debole*) feeble.

esiliare [ezi'ljare] *v* exile. **esiliarsi** *v* go into exile. **esiliato, -a** *sm*, *sf* exile. **esilio** *sm* exile.

*****esimere** [e'zimere] *v* exempt, free. **esimio** [e'zimjo] *agg* distinguished, outstanding.

esistenzialismo [ezistentsja'lizmo] *sm* existentialism. **esistenzialista** *s(m+f)*, *agg* existentialist.

esistere [e'zistere] *v* exist, be. **esistente** *agg* existing. **esistenza** *sf* existence. **esistenza di cassa/magazzino** (*comm*) cash/stock in hand.

esitare [ezi'tare] *v* hesitate. **esitazione** *sf* hesitation.

esito ['ɛzito] *sm* outcome; (*dramma*) denouement. **buon esito** success.

esodo ['ɛzɔdo] *sm* exodus.

esofago [e'zɔfago] *sm* oesophagus; gullet.

esonerare [ezone'rare] *v* exempt. **esonero** *sm* exemption.

esorbitante [ezorbi'tante] *agg* exorbitant.

esorcizzare [ezortʃid'dzare] *v* exorcise. **esorcismo** *sm* exorcism.

esordire [ezor'dire] *v* start out; (*artista*) make one's debut. **esordio** *sm* start, debut.

esortare [ezor'tare] *v* urge. **esortazione** *sf* exhortation, encouragement.

esoso [e'zɔzo] *agg* (*avido*) greedy; exorbitant; odious.

esoterico [ezo'teriko] *agg* esoteric.

esotico [e'zɔtiko] *agg* exotic.

*****espandere** [es'pandere] *v* expand, extend. **espandersi** *v* spread. **espansione** *sf* expansion; (*effusione d'affetto*) effusiveness. **espansivo** *agg* effusive; (*forza*) expansive.

espatriare [espa'trjare] *v* emigrate. **espatrio** *sm* expatriation.

espediente [espe'djɛnte] sm expedient, device; (soluzione) way out. **vivere di espedienti** live on one's wits.

*****espellere** [es'pellere] v expel.

esperienza [espe'rjɛntsa] sf experience; experiment; (conoscenza) familiarity. **fare esperienza** of experience. **senza esperienza** inexperienced.

esperimento [esperi'mento] sm experiment; (tentativo) trial, test.

esperto [es'perto], -a sm, sf expert, authority. agg expert (in); (abile) skilful (at); experienced (in).

espiare [espi'are] v expiate, atone. **capro espiatorio** sm scapegoat.

espletare [esple'tare] v accomplish.

esplicito [es'plitʃito] agg explicit. **esplicativo** agg explanatory.

*****esplodere** [es'plɔdere] v explode. **far esplodere** explode, blow up.

esplorare [esplo'rare] v explore; (investigare) probe. **esploratore, -trice** sm, sf explorer; (mil) scout. **giovani esploratori** Boy Scouts pl. **esplorazione** sf exploration; (mil) reconnaissance.

esplosione [esplo'zjone] sf explosion.

esplosivo [esplo'zivo] sm, agg explosive.

esponente [espo'nɛnte] sm exponent; representative. **esponenziale** agg exponential.

*****esporre** [es'porre] v expose; (arrischiare) risk; (spiegare) expound; (mostrare) exhibit, display.

esportare [espor'tare] v export. **esportatore, -trice** sm, sf exporter. **esportazione** sf export.

esposizione [espozi'tsjone] sf exhibition, show; (spiegazione) explanation; (posizione, foto) exposure.

esposto [es'posto] agg exhibited, displayed; exposed. sm statement.

espressione [espres'sjone] sf expression. **espressivo** agg expressive, eloquent.

espresso [es'prɛsso] agg express; (manifestato) expressed; (dichiarato) avowed, declared. **piatto espresso** sm specially prepared dish. sm (lettera) express letter; (caffè) espresso; (ferr) express train.

*****esprimere** [es'primere] v express.

espulsione [espul'sjone] sf expulsion.

essa [ˈessa] pron (persona: soggetto) she; (persona: oggetto) her; (cosa, animale) it.

esse [ˈesse] pron (soggetto) they; (oggetto) them.

essenza [es'sɛntsa] sf essence. **essenziale** agg essential.

*****essere** [ˈɛssere] v be; (ausiliare con forma attiva) have. sm being; (fam) person, creature; (condizione) existence.

essi [ˈessi] pron (soggetto) they; (oggetto) them.

essiccare [essik'kare] v dry. **essiccatoio** sm dryer.

esso [ˈesso] pron (persona: soggetto) he; (persona: oggetto) him; (cosa, animale) it.

est [est] sm east. **dell'est** east, eastern.

estasi [ˈɛstazi] sf ecstasy. **estatico** agg ecstatic.

estate [es'tate] sf summer. **estate di San Martino** Indian summer.

*****estendere** [es'tɛndere] v extend, stretch; (ampliare) broaden. **estendersi** v (stendersi) stretch; (diffondersi) spread.

estensione [esten'sjone] sf extension; (dimensione) extent; (distesa) expanse; (fig, musica) range; (significato) wider sense.

estenuare [estenu'are] v exhaust. **estenuante** agg exhausting, wearing.

esteriore [este'rjore] agg outer, exterior, external. sm (parte esterna) outside; (apparenze) appearances pl.

esterno [es'tɛrno] agg external, outer, exterior. sm outside; (scolaro) day-boy; (film) exterior.

estero [ˈɛstero] agg foreign. sm foreign countries pl. **all'estero** abroad.

esterrefatto [esterre'fatto] agg (atterrito) aghast, horrified; (sbigottito) amazed.

esteso [es'tezo] agg large, wide-ranging; (fig) thorough. **per esteso** in full.

estetica [es'tɛtika] sf aesthetics. **estetico** agg aesthetic.

estetista [este'tista] s(m+f) beauty specialist, beautician.

*****estinguere** [es'tingwere] v put out; (far svanire) extinguish; (econ) wipe out; (debito) pay off; (sete) quench. **estinguersi** v die out. **estinto** agg extinguished; (scomparso) extinct. **estinzione** sf extinction; (sete) quenching; (econ) discharge.

estirpare [estir'pare] v eradicate.

estivo [es'tivo] agg summer.

*****estorcere** [es'tɔrtʃere] v extort. **estorsione** sf extortion.

estradare [estra'dare] v extradite. **estradizione** sf extradition.

estraneo [es'traneo] *agg* extraneous, unrelated (to), unconnected (with); *(alieno)* foreign. **essere estraneo a** have no part in. **mantenersi estraneo a** have nothing to do with, keep clear of. *sm* stranger; unauthorized person. **estraniare** *v* estrange.

****estrarre** [es'trarre] *v* extract, draw (out); *(miniera)* mine; *(cava)* quarry. **estratto** *sm* extract; *(compendio)* abstract; *(stralcio)* excerpt. **estrazione** *sf* extraction.

estremo [es'tremo] *agg* extreme; *(ultimo)* final; *(grandissimo)* utmost. *sm* extreme; *(colmo)* height; *(estremità)* end, tip. **estremi** *sm pl* particulars *pl*; *(dir)* essential elements *pl*. **estremismo** *sm* extremism. **estremista** *s(m+f)* extremist.

estro ['estro] *sm (ghiribizzo)* whim, fancy; *(impulso)* inspiration; *(venereo)* heat. **estroso** *agg* whimsical, capricious; inspired.

estrogeno [es'trɔdʒeno] *sm* oestrogen.

estroverso [estro'verso], **-a** *sm, sf* extrovert. *agg* extroverted.

estuario [estu'arjo] *sm* estuary.

esuberante [ezube'rante] *agg* exuberant. **esuberanza** *sf* exuberance.

esule ['ezule] *s(m+f)* exile. **esulare** *v* lie outside, be beyond.

esultare [ezul'tare] *v* rejoice. **esultante** *agg* exultant.

esumare [ezu'mare] *v* exhume; *(fig)* unearth.

età [e'ta] *sf* age. **all'età di dieci anni** at the age of) ten. **età della ragione** age of discretion.

etere ['etere] *sm* ether.

eterno [e'tɛrno] *agg* eternal, everlasting; *(lunghissimo)* interminable. **eternità** *sf* eternity; *(molto tempo)* ages *pl*.

eterodosso [etero'dɔsso] *agg* heterodox.

eterogeneo [etero'dʒɛneo] *agg* heterogeneous.

etica ['etika] *sf* ethics. **etico** *agg* ethical.

etichetta[1] [eti'ketta] *sf (cartellino)* label.

etichetta[2] [eti'ketta] *sf (regole)* etiquette.

etimologia [etimolo'dʒia] *sf* etymology. **etimologico** *agg* etymological.

etnico ['etniko] *agg* ethnic.

ettaro ['ettaro] *sm* hectare.

etto ['etto] *sm* hundred grams.

eucalipto [euka'lipto] *sm* eucalyptus.

eufemismo [eufe'mizmo] *sm* euphemism. **eufemistico** *agg* euphemistic.

eunuco [eu'nuko] *sm, pl* **-chi** eunuch.

Europa [eu'rɔpa] *sf* Europe. **europeo, -a** *s, agg* European.

eutanasia [eutana'zia] *sf* euthanasia.

evacuare [evaku'are] *v* evacuate.

****evadere** [e'vadere] *v* escape (from); *(sbrigare)* dispatch; *(fattura)* settle; *(ordini)* execute; *(fisco)* avoid.

evanescente [evane'ʃɛnte] *agg (suono)* fading; *(fugace)* fleeting; *(crema)* vanishing.

evangelista [evandʒe'lista] *sm* evangelist. **evangelico** *agg* evangelical.

evaporare [evapo'rare] *v* evaporate. **evaporatore** *sm* humidifier. **evaporazione** *sf* evaporation.

evasione [eva'zjone] *sf* escape; *(fisco)* evasion; *(comm)* execution.

evasivo [eva'zivo] *agg* evasive.

evaso [e'vazo], **-a** *agg* escaped; *(comm)* dispatched, dealt with. *sm, sf* fugitive, escaped convict.

evento [e'vento] *sm* event; *(eventualità)* eventuality. **in ogni evento** in any case, at all events.

eventuale [eventu'ale] *agg* possible, any. **eventualità** *sf* eventuality. **nell'eventualità di** *or* **che** in the event of. **eventualmente** *cong* if, in case.

evidente [evi'dɛnte] *agg* obvious, manifest, clear; *(irrefutabile)* unmistakable. **evidenza** *sf (chiarezza)* clarity, obviousness. **mettere in evidenza** stress, emphasize. **mettersi in evidenza** make oneself conspicuous, draw attention to oneself. **tenere un'evidenza** *(comm)* keep pending.

evitare [evi'tare] *v* avoid; *(non arrecare)* spare, save.

evo ['evo] *sm* **Medio Evo** Middle Ages *pl*.

evocare [evo'kare] *v* evoke.

evoluzione [evolu'tsjone] *sf* evolution. **evoluto** *agg* evolved, fully developed; advanced, progressive.

evviva [ev'viva] *inter* hurrah! **evviva ... !** long live ... !

extra ['ekstra] *agg invar (qualità)* first-rate; *(fuori del previsto)* additional. *sm invar* extra.

F

fa [fa] *avv* ago.

fabbisogno [fabbi'zoɲo] *sm* requirements *pl.*

fabbrica ['fabbrika] *sf* factory; (*officina*) works; (*edificio*) building. **fabbricante** *sm* manufacturer. **fabbricare** *v* manufacture, produce; (*costruire*) build; (*inventare*) make up. **fabbricato** *sm* building. **fabbricazione** *sf* manufacture, production.

fabbro ['fabbro] *sm* (*ferraio*) (black)smith.

faccenda [fat'tʃɛnda] *sf* matter; (*caso, circostanza*) business. **faccende domestiche** housework *sing.*

facchino [fak'kino] *sm* porter. **facchinaggio** *sm* porterage. **facchinata** *sf* (*lavoro*) drudgery.

faccia ['fattʃa] *sf* face; (*lato*) side. **avere una bella/brutta faccia** look well/unwell. **di faccia** opposite. **faccia tosta** (*fam*) cheek, nerve. **in faccia** a opposite. **facciata** *sf* front; (*pagina*) side.

facezia [fa'tʃɛtsja] *sf* pleasantry; (*detto spiritoso*) witticism. **faceto** *agg* facetious, witty.

facile ['fatʃile] *agg* easy; (*incline*) easily moved, prone. **facilità** *sf* ease, facility; (*l'esser facile*) easiness; (*capacità*) aptitude. **con facilità** with ease, readily; (*lingua*) fluently.

facilitare [fatʃili'tare] *v* facilitate; (*aiutare*) help. **facilitazione** *sf* facilitation, making easy. **facilitazioni di pagamento** easy terms *pl.*

facoltà [fakol'ta] *sf* faculty; (*potere*) power. **facoltativo** *agg* optional. **facoltoso** *agg* wealthy.

faggio ['faddʒo] *sm* beech.

fagiano [fa'dʒano] *sm* pheasant.

fagiolo [fa'dʒɔlo] *sm* bean. **andare a fagiolo** (*fam*) suit. **fagiolino** *sm* French bean.

fagotto [fa'gɔtto] *sm* bundle, (*musica*) bassoon. **far fagotto** pack up.

falcata [fal'kata] *sf* step.

falce ['faltʃe] *sf* sickle; (*manico lungo*) scythe.

falciare [fal'tʃare] *v* mow; (*fig*) mow down. **falciatrice** *sf* mower.

falco ['falko] *sm* hawk. **falcone** *sm* falcon; (*tec*) derrick.

falda ['falda] *sf* (*strato*) layer, sheet; (*di pendio*) foot; (*di cappello*) brim; (*di vestito*) skirt; (*di marsina*) tail.

falegname [fale'ɲame] *sm* joiner, carpenter. **falegnameria** *sf* (*arte*) joinery, carpentry; (*bottega*) joiner's shop.

falena [fa'lɛna] *sf* moth; (*cenere*) ash; (*persona fatua*) flighty person.

falla ['falla] *sf* leak. **aprire/chiudere una falla** spring/stop a leak.

fallace [fal'latʃe] *agg* fallacious.

fallire [fal'lire] *v* fail; (*non colpire*) miss; (*dir, comm*) go bankrupt. **fallimento** *sm* failure; bankruptcy.

fallito [fal'lito], **-a** *agg* unsuccessful. *sm, sf* bankrupt; (*fig*) failure.

fallo¹ ['fallo] *sm* (*errore*) fault; (*sport*) foul. **cogliere in fallo** find out. **essere in fallo** be at fault. **senza fallo** without fail, certainly.

fallo² ['fallo] *sm* (*membro virile*) phallus.

falò [fa'lɔ] *sm* bonfire.

falsare [fal'sare] *v* falsify; (*alterare*) distort. **falsario** *sm* (*documenti*) forger; (*monete*) counterfeiter.

falsariga [falsa'riga] *sf* (*modello*) pattern; (*norma*) lines *pl.*

falsificare [falsifi'kare] *v* falsify; (*arte*) fake. **falsificazione** *sf* falsification, faking; forgery, fake.

falso ['falso] *agg* false; (*falsificato*) counterfeit, faked, forged; (*fam*) bogus. *sm* (*non vero*) falsehood; (*reato*) forgery. **giurare il falso** commit perjury.

fama ['fama] *sf* fame, reputation.

fame ['fame] *sf* hunger; (*carestia*) famine. **aver fame** be hungry. **aver fame di** (*fig*) hunger for. **aver una fame da lupo** be ravenous. **fare la fame** go hungry. **morir di fame** starve to death; (*fig*) be starving.

famelico [fa'meliko] *agg* ravenous.

famigerato [famidʒe'rato] *agg* notorious.

famiglia [fa'miʎa] *sf* family. **in famiglia** at home.

familiare [fami'ljare] *agg* domestic; (*consueto, intimo*) familiar; (*semplice*) informal. *s(m+f)* (*parente*) relative. **familiarità** *sf* familiarity. **familiarizzarsi** *v* familiarize oneself.

famoso [fa'moso] *agg* famous, well-known; memorable.

fanale [fa'nale] *sm* lamp; (*auto*) light. **fanale anteriore** headlight. **fanale di coda** tail-light.

fanatico [fa'natiko], **-a** *agg* fanatical; (*fam: entusiasta*) wild (about). *sm, sf* fanatic; (*tifoso*) fan. **fanatismo** *sm* fanaticism.

fanciullo [fan'tʃullo], **-a** *sm, sf* child (*pl* -ren). **fanciullaggine** *sf* childish behaviour. **fanciullesco** *agg* childish, puerile;

(*innocente*) child-like. **fanciullezza** *sf* childhood.

fandonia [fan'dɔnja] *sf* nonsense.

fanfara [fan'fara] *sf* (brass-)band; (*composizione*) fanfare. **fanfaronata** *sf* boasting. **fanfarone, -a** *sm*, *sf* boaster.

fango ['fango] *sm* mud. **fare i fanghi** take mud-baths. **fangoso** *agg* muddy.

fannullone [fannul'lone], **-a** *sm*, *sf* idler, loafer.

fantascienza [fantaʃ'ʃɛntsa] *sf* science fiction.

fantasia [fanta'zia] *sf* fantasy; (*capriccio*) fancy; imagination. *agg* (*moda*) fancy, patterned.

fantasma [fan'tazma] *sm* ghost, phantom.

fantasticare [fantasti'kare] *v* daydream, dream up. **fantastico** *agg* fantastic; (*non reale*) fanciful, strange.

fante ['fante] *sm* (*mil*) infantryman; (*carte*) knave, jack. **fanteria** *sf* infantry. **fantino** *sm* jockey.

fantoccio [fan'tɔttʃo] *sm* puppet.

farabutto [fara'butto] *sm* rascal, rogue.

faraona [fara'ona] *sf* guinea-fowl.

farcire [far'tʃire] *v* stuff.

fardello [far'dɛllo] *sm* burden.

*fare ['fare] *v* (*agire*) do; (*produrre*) make; (*essere*) be; (*avere*) have; (*un mestiere, ecc.*) go in for, practise; (*comportarsi*) play; (*orologio*) say. **farcela** *v* (*riuscire*) manage; (*resistere*) be able to go on. **far attenzione** pay attention. **far bene** do good. **far bene a** be good for. **far chiamare** send for. **far entrare** let in. **fare il pieno** (*auto*) fill up. **far male** (*dolere*) hurt, ache; (*nuocere*) be bad for; (*agire male*) do the wrong thing. **far notare** point out. **fare per** be about to. **far vedere** show. **farsi** *v* (*diventare*) become, grow into; (*convertirsi*) turn into; (*tempo*) get.

farfalla [far'falla] *sf* butterfly; (*falena*) moth. **nuoto a farfalla** *sm* butterfly stroke.

farina [fa'rina] *sf* flour. **farina gialla** maize meal. **farina integrale** wholemeal. **farinaceo** *agg* floury, starchy. **farinoso** *agg* floury, mealy; (*neve*) powdery.

faringe [fa'rindʒe] *sf* pharynx. **faringite** *sf* pharyngitis.

farmacia [farma'tʃia] *sf* (*negozio*) chemist's (shop); (*scienza*) pharmacy. **farmacista** *s(m+f)* chemist. **farmaco** *sm* medicine.

farneticare [farneti'kare] *v* rave.

faro ['faro] *sm* ligh.house; (*lume, fig*) beacon; (*auto*) headlight.

farragine [far'radʒine] *sf* muddle, jumble.

farsa ['farsa] *sf* farce.

fascia ['faʃa] *sf* band; (*benda*) bandage; (*uniforme*) sash; (*postale*) wrapper; (*zona*) strip.

fasciare [fa'ʃare] *v* wrap; (*bambini*) swaddle; (*ferita*) dress, bandage.

fascicolo [fa'ʃikolo] *sm* (*opuscolo*) pamphlet, booklet; (*numero*) issue.

fascino ['faʃino] *sm* charm, fascination.

fascio ['faʃo] *sm* bundle, bunch.

fascismo [fa'ʃizmo] *sm* fascism. **fascista** *s(m+f)*, *agg* fascist.

fase ['faze] *sf* phase; (*auto*) stroke.

fastidio [fas'tidjo] *sm* trouble; (*avversione*) dislike; (*cosa fastidiosa*) bother, inconvenience. **dar fastidio** trouble; (*molestare*) annoy, bother. **darsi fastidio** put oneself out. **fastidioso** *agg* troublesome, annoying.

fasto ['fasto] *sm* pomp.

fasullo [fa'zullo] *agg* (*fam*) bogus, phoney.

fata ['fata] *sf* fairy.

fatale [fa'tale] *agg* inevitable; (*funesto*) fatal; (*decisivo*) fateful; irresistible.

fatica [fa'tika] *sf* (*sforzo*) effort, labour; (*stanchezza, tec*) fatigue. **a fatica** with difficulty. **costar fatica** require an effort. **durare fatica** find it difficult. **reggere alla fatica** stand the strain. **faticare** *v* labour; (*stentare*) have difficulty. **faticoso** *agg* tiring.

fatta ['fatta] *sf* kind.

fattezze [fat'tettse] *sf pl* features *pl*.

fattibile [fat'tibile] *agg* feasible.

fatto¹ ['fatto] *agg* made, done. **a conti fatti** all things considered. **detto fatto** no sooner said than done. **fatto a macchina/mano** machine-/hand-made. **fatto su misura** tailor-made.

fatto² ['fatto] *sm* fact; (*avvenimento*) event; (*azione*) deed; (*affare*) business. **cogliere sul fatto** catch in the act. **dire il fatto suo** have one's say. **fatto compiuto** fait accompli. **fatto sta** the fact remains. **in fatto di** regarding.

fattore [fat'tore] *sm* factor; (*capo di fattoria*) steward.

fattoria [fatto'ria] *sf* farm, estate.

fattorino [fatto'rino] *sm* messenger; (*di negozio*) errand-boy; (*di autobus*) conductor.

fattura [fat'tura] *sf* (*confezione*) making; (*lavorazione*) construction, workmanship; (*conto*) bill; (*comm*) invoice. **fatturare** *v* (*comm*) invoice; (*manipolare*) doctor. **fatturato** *sm* turnover.

fatuo ['fatuo] *agg* foolish, fatuous.

fauci ['fautʃi] *sf pl* jaws *pl*; (*fig*) clutches *pl*.

fauna ['fauna] *sf* fauna.

fausto ['fausto] *agg* propitious.

fautore [fau'tore], **-trice** *sm, sf* supporter.

fava ['fava] *sf* broad bean.

favilla [fa'villa] *sf* spark. **far faville** sparkle, shine.

favo ['favo] *sm* honeycomb.

favola ['favola] *sf* fable, story. **favoloso** *agg* fabulous.

favore [fa'vore] *sm* favour; (*appoggio*) support. **di favore** (*biglietto*) complimentary; (*prezzo*) special. **per favore** please.

favoreggiare [favored'dʒare] *v* favour; (*dir*) aid and abet.

favorevole [favo'revole] *agg* favourable, in favour.

favorire [favo'rire] *v* favour; (*sostenere*) support; (*promuovere*) promote, foster. **favorito, -a** *s, agg* favourite. **favoritismo** *sm* favouritism.

fazione [fa'tsjone] *sf* faction, party. **fazioso** *agg* subversive.

fazzoletto [fattso'letto] *sm* handkerchief; (*da testa*) headsquare.

febbraio [feb'brajo] *sm* February.

febbre ['febbre] *sf* temperature, fever; (*fam: sulle labbra*) cold sore; (*brama*) lust, passion. **febbre da fieno** hay fever. **febbricitante** *agg* feverish.

feccia ['fettʃa] *sf* dregs *pl*.

feci ['fetʃi] *sf pl* faeces *pl*.

fecola ['fekola] *sf* starch.

fecondare [fekon'dare] *v* fertilize. **fecondazione** *sf* fertilization. **fecondazione artificiale** artificial insemination. **fecondità** *sf* fertility. **fecondo** *agg* fertile, prolific, fruitful.

fede ['fede] *sf* faith; (*fiducia*) confidence, trust; (*anello*) wedding ring; (*attestazione*) proof.

fedele [fe'dele] *agg* faithful, true. *s(m+f)* believer; (*seguace*) follower. **fedeltà** *sf* faithfulness, fidelity.

federa ['federa] *sf* pillow-case.

federale [fede'rale] *agg* federal.

federazione [federa'tsjone] *sf* federation, association.

fedina [fe'dina] *sf* police *or* criminal record.

fedine [fe'dine] *sf pl* side-whiskers *pl*.

fegato ['fegato] *sm* liver; (*coraggio*) guts *pl*. **mangiarsi il fegato** eat one's heart out.

felce [feltʃe] *sf* fern; (*comune*) bracken.

felice [fe'litʃe] *agg* happy; (*fortunato*) lucky. **felicità** *sf* happiness, bliss. **felicitarsi con** congratulate. **felicitazioni** *sf pl* congratulations *pl*.

felino [fe'lino] *agg* feline.

felpa ['felpa] *sf* plush.

feltro ['feltro] *sm* felt.

femmina ['femmina] *sf* female; (*figlia*) daughter. *agg* female, womanly; (*gramm*) feminine. **scuola femminile** girls' school. *sm* feminine (gender). **femminilità** *sf* femininity.

femore ['femore] *sm* femur.

*** fendere** ['fendere] *v* split, pierce; (*solcare*) plough (through). **fenditura** *sf* cleft; (*fessura*) crack.

fenicottero [feni'kɔttero] *sm* flamingo.

fenomeno [fe'nɔmeno] *sm* phenomenon (*pl* -a); (*prodigio*) marvel. **fenomenale** *agg* phenomenal; (*eccezionale*) extraordinary, remarkable.

feretro ['feretro] *sm* coffin.

ferie ['fɛrje] *sf pl* holidays *pl*. **giorno feriale** *sm* weekday.

ferire [fe'rire] *v* wound, injure, hurt. **ferita** *sf* wound, injury; (*persona*) casualty. **ferito** *sm* casualty.

fermacarte [ferma'karte] *sm invar* (*a molla*) paper-clip; (*pesante*) paperweight.

fermaglio [fer'maʎo] *sm* clasp, clip.

fermare [fer'mare] *v* stop; (*arrestare*) check; (*fissare*) secure, fasten; (*prenotare*) book. **fermarsi** stop; (*rimanere*) stay. **fermata** *sf* stop; (*tappa*) stay; (*veicoli*) halt. **fermata facoltativa** request stop.

fermentare [fermen'tare] *v* ferment. **fermentazione** *sf* fermentation. **fermento** *sm* ferment; (*fig*) unrest.

fermo ['fermo] *agg* still; (*non in moto*) stationary; (*saldo*) firm, steady. **restar fermo** stand still; (*fig*) hold good. *sm* *(mec)* catch, fastener, lock; *(dir)* detention; *(sospensione)* stop.

feroce [fe'rotʃe] *agg* wild; *(crudele)* savage, ferocious; *(fig)* fierce. **ferocia** *sf* cruelty, ferocity.

ferragosto [ferra'gosto] *sm* mid-August holiday.

ferramenta [ferra'menta] *sf pl* ironmongery *sing.*

ferreo ['fɛrreo] *agg* iron.

ferro ['fɛrro] *sf* iron. **essere ai ferri corti** be at loggerheads. **ferro battuto** wrought iron. **ferro da calza** knitting needle. **ferro di cavallo** horseshoe. **tocca ferro!** touch wood!

ferrovia [ferro'via] *sf* railway. **ferroviario** *agg* rail(way), train. **ferroviere** *sm* railwayman.

fertile ['fɛrtile] *agg* fertile, fruitful. **fertilità** *sf* fertility, fruitfulness. **fertilizzante** *sm* fertilizer. **fertilizzare** *v* fertilize.

fervore [fer'vore] *sm* fervour. **fervente** *agg* fervent. **fervido** *agg* ardent; *(caloroso)* heartfelt; *(vivace)* lively.

fesso ['fesso] *(volg) agg, sm* idiot, fool. **fesseria** *sf (azione)* foolishness; *(parole)* nonsense; *(inezia)* trifle.

fessura [fes'sura] *sf* crack, slit; *(gettone, moneta)* slot.

festa ['festa] *sf* holiday; *(compleanno)* birthday; *(onomastico)* saint's day; *(festeggiamento)* celebration; *(ricevimento)* party. **far festa** *(non lavorare)* take a holiday, take time off; *(smettere il lavoro)* stop work; *(divertirsi)* make merry. **far festa a** give a warm welcome to).

festeggiare [fested'dʒare] *v* celebrate; *(far festa)* give a hearty welcome (to). **festeggiamenti** *sm pl* festivities *pl.* **festeggiamento** *sm* celebration.

festività [festivi'ta] *sf* festivity, holiday. **festivo** *agg (della domenica)* Sunday; *(non-feriale)* holiday.

festone [fes'tone] *sm* festoon; *(ricamo)* scallop.

fetente [fe'tɛnte] *sm (volg)* stinker, scoundrel. *agg also* **fetido** stinking, foul. **fetore** *sm* stench.

feticcio [fe'tittʃo] *sm* fetish.

feto ['fɛto] *sm* foetus.

fetta ['fetta] *sf* slice. **tagliare a fette** slice, cut into slices. **fettuccia** *sf (nastro)* tape, ribbon. **fettuccine** *sf pl* noodles *pl.*

feudale [feu'dale] *agg* feudal. **feudalesimo**

sm feudalism. **feudo** *sm* feud; *(proprietà terriera)* lands *pl;* *(fig)* domain.

fiaba ['fjaba] *sf* story, (fairy) tale.

fiacca ['fjakka] *sf (stanchezza)* weariness; *(pigrizia)* laziness; *(svogliatezza)* listlessness. **battere la fiacca** *(fam: stare in ozio)* kick one's heels; *(agire svogliatamente)* be sluggish. **fiaccare** *v (indebolire)* weaken; *(spossare)* wear out; *(spezzare)* break. **fiacco** *agg (debole)* weak; *(stanco)* exhausted, weary.

fiaccola ['fjakkola] *sf* torch. **alla luce di fiaccole** by torchlight.

fiala ['fjala] *sf* phial, medicine bottle.

fiamma ['fjamma] *sf* flame; *(improvvisa, irregolare)* flare; *(molto viva)* blaze. **in fiamme** on fire. **nuovo fiammante** brandnew. **fiammata** *sf* blaze, flare.

fiammeggiare [fjammed'dʒare] *v* blaze, flame.

fiammifero [fjam'mifero] *sm* match.

fiammingo [fjam'mingo] *agg* Flemish.

fiancheggiare [fjanked'dʒare] *v* flank; *(sostenere)* help.

fianco ['fjanko] *sm* side; *(mil)* flank. **di fianco a** *(vicino)* next to, by; *(lungo)* alongside.

fiasco ['fjasko] *sm* flask, (straw-covered) bottle; *(insuccesso)* flop. **far fiasco** flop.

fiatare [fja'tare] *v* breathe. **fiato** *sm* breath. **fiati** *sm pl* woodwind *pl.* **senza fiato** out of breath. **strumenti a fiato** *sm pl* wind instruments *pl.* **tutto d'un fiato** in one go.

fibbia ['fibbja] *sf* buckle.

fibra ['fibra] *sf* fibre; *(fig)* constitution.

ficcare [fik'kare] *v* poke, stick; *(fam: mettere)* put. **ficcanaso** *sm* busybody.

fico ['fiko] *sm* fig. **fico d'India** prickly pear. **non m'importa un fico** *(secco)* *(fam)* I couldn't care less. **non valere un fico** be worthless.

fidanzarsi [fidan'tsarsi] *v* get engaged. **fidanzamento** *sm* engagement. **fidanzato, -a** *sm, sf* fiancé, -e.

fidarsi [fi'darsi] *v (aver fiducia)* rely (on), trust; *(osare)* trust oneself, dare.

fido ['fido] *sm (econ)* credit.

fiducia [fi'dutʃa] *sf* trust, confidence. **aver fiducia in** trust. **di fiducia** *(fidato)* reliable, trustworthy; responsible. **fiduciario** *sm* (official) representative; *(dir)* trustee. **fiducioso** *agg* trusting.

fiele ['fjɛle] *sm* bile; *(fig)* ill-will.

fieno ['fjɛno] *sm* hay.

fiera ['fjɛra] *sf* fair; (*mostra*) exhibition; (*di beneficienza*) bazaar.

fiero ['fjɛro] *agg* (*orgoglioso*) proud; (*audace*) bold, spirited; (*feroce, violento*) fierce; (*austero*) severe. **fierezza** *sf* pride; boldness.

fifa ['fifa] (*fam*) *sf* fear. **aver fifa** be afraid. **fifone, -a** *sm, sf* coward.

figliastro [fiʎ'ʎastro] *sm* stepson. **figliastra** *sf* stepdaughter.

figlio ['fiʎo] *sm* son; (*fig: frutto*) result, product. **figli** *sm pl* children *pl*. **figlia** *sf* daughter; (*comm*) counterfoil. **figliare** *v* give birth. **figliata** *sf* litter.

figlioccio [fiʎ'ʎottʃo] *sm* godson. **figlioccia** *sf* goddaughter.

figliolo [fiʎ'ʎolo] *sm* (*figlio*) son; (*ragazzo*) boy, young man; (*fam*) chap. **figliola** *sf* (*figlia*) daughter; (*ragazza*) girl. **figliolanza** *sf* offspring.

figura [fi'gura] *sf* figure; (*aspetto*) shape; (*illustrazione*) picture; (*tavola*) plate. **far bella figura** show up to advantage; make a good impression; (*riuscir bene*) do well. **far brutta figura** cut a sorry figure, disgrace oneself.

figurare [figu'rare] *v* represent, portray; (*simboleggiare*) stand for; (*mostrare*) pretend; (*risultare*) appear; (*far figura*) look smart. **figurarsi** *v* imagine. **figurati!** *inter* (*altro che*) of course! you bet! **figurina** *sf* figurine; (*cartoncino*) card. **figurino** *sm* fashion-plate; (*giornale*) fashion magazine. **figuro** *sm* shady character.

fila ['fila] *sf* row, line; (*coda*) queue; (*serie*) string. **di fila** (*di seguito*) in succession, in a row; (*senza interruzione*) on end, non-stop. **in fila indiana** in single file. **mettere in fila** line up. **mettersi in fila** queue up.

filantropo [fi'lantropo], **-a** *sm, sf* philanthropist. **filantropico** *agg* philanthropic.

filare [fi'lare] *v* spin; (*cavo, catena*) pay out; (*correre*) run, speed along.

filarmonico [filar'moniko] *agg* philharmonic.

filastrocca [filas'trɔkka] *sf* (*per bambini*) nursery rhyme; (*storia lunga*) tedious list, rigmarole.

filatelia [filate'lia] *sf* stamp-collecting, philately. **filatelico** *agg* stamp. **filatelista** *s(m+f)* stamp collector.

filatura [fila'tura] *sf* (*industria*) spinning; (*filanda*) spinning mill.

filetto [fi'letto] *sm* (*gastr*) fillet; border; (*filo sottile, mec*) thread; (*tipografia*) rule.

filettare [filet'tare] *v* (*ornare*) decorate; (*bordare*) edge; (*mec*) thread. **filettatura** *sf* edging, braid; threading.

filiale [fi'ljale] *sf* branch. *agg* filial.

filibustiere [filibus'tjɛre] *sm* pirate; (*imbroglione*) rogue.

filigrana [fili'grana] *sf* filigree; (*carta*) watermark.

film [film] *sm invar* film. **filmare** *v* film.

filo ['filo] *sm* thread; (*filato*) yarn; (*metallico*) wire; (*coltello*) edge; (*elettrico*) flex. **filo d'erba** blade of grass. **filo spinato** barbed wire. **lana a due/tre fili** *sf* two-/three-ply wool. **perdere il filo** (*discorso*) lose track; (*taglio*) become blunt. **per filo e per segno** in detail.

filodrammatico [filodram'matiko], **-a** *sm, sf* amateur actor, amateur actress. *agg* amateur theatrical.

filologo [fi'lologo], **-a** *sm, sf* philologist. **filologia** *sf* philology. **filologico** *agg* philological.

filone [fi'lone] *sm* seam, vein; (*pane*) French loaf; (*fig*) current, line.

filosofia [filozo'fia] *sf* philosophy. **filosofico** *agg* philosophical. **filosofo, -a** *sm, sf* philosopher.

filtrare [fil'trare] *v* filter. **filtro** *sm* filter; (*colino*) strainer.

filza [fil'tsa] *sf* string.

finale [fi'nale] *agg* final; (*ultimo*) last. *sf* (*sport*) final; (*gramm*) ending. *sm* (*musica*) finale. **finalista** *s(m+f)* finalist. **finalità** *sf* (*scopo*) purpose, aim; (*filosofia*) finality.

finanza [fi'nantsa] *sf* finance; (*fam: risorse economiche*) finances *pl*. **finanze** *sf pl* (*entrate dello Stato*) public revenue *sing*. **guardia di finanza** *sf* customs officer.

finanziare [finan'tsjare] *v* finance. **finanziamento** *sm* financing; (*fondi*) funds *pl*. **finanziario** *agg* financial. **finanziatore, -trice** *sm, sf* backer. **finanziera** *sf* frock-coat.

finché [fin'ke] *cong* (*per tutto il tempo che*) as long as; (*fino a quando*) until, till.

fine¹ ['fine] *sf* end; (*libro, film, ecc.*) ending. *sm* end; (*scopo*) aim; (*esito*) conclusion. **alla fine** (*luogo*) at the end; (*tempo*) in the end; (*finalmente*) at last. **in fin dei conti** when all is said and done, in the end. **secondo fine** ulterior motive, hidden purpose. **senza fine** endless.

fine² ['fine] *agg* fine; (*signorile*) refined; (*acuto*) sharp; (*penetrante*) subtle. **finezza** *sf* fineness; (*raffinatezza*) finesse, polish; (*minuzie*) nicety.

fine-settimana [finesetti'mana] *s(m+f) invar* weekend.

finestra [fi'nɛstra] *sf* window.

*fingere ['findʒere] *v* pretend. **fingersi** *v* pretend to be.

finire [fi'nire] *v* finish; (*smettere*) stop; (*terminare, sboccare*) end; (*capitare*) end up. **andare a finire** (*capitare*) get to; (*concludersi*) turn out, end up. **finimondo** *sm* pandemonium. **finissaggio** *sm* finish. **finitura** *sf* finishing off; finishing touches *pl*.

Finlandia [fin'landja] *sf* Finland. **finlandese** *sm, agg* Finnish; *s(m+f)* (*abitante*) Finn.

fino¹ ['fino] *agg* fine, delicate; (*acuto*) subtle.

fino² ['fino] *avv* (*persino*) even. **fino a** (*tempo*) until, up to; (*luogo*) as far as. **fino a che punto?** how far? **fin da** (*passato*) since, as far back as; (*presente, futuro*) (as) from. **fin dove?** how far? **fino in fondo** right down, to the (very) end.

finocchio [fi'nɔkkjo] *sm* (*bot*) fennel; (*volg*) queer, gay.

finora [fi'nora] *avv* up to now, so far.

finta ['finta] *sf* pretence, sham; (*sport*) feint. **far finta di** pretend.

finto ['finto] *agg* false; (*simulato*) bogus; (*non reale*) mock; artificial. **fintapelle** *sf* imitation leather.

finzione [fin'tsjone] *sf* pretence; (*falsità*) falsehood; (*illusione*) fiction.

fio ['fio] *sm* **pagare il fio** pay the price.

fioccare [fjok'kare] *v* (*neve*) fall; (*fig*) come down thick and fast.

fiocco [fjɔkko] *sm* flake; (*batuffolo*) flock; (*fibra tessile*) staple; (*nastro*) bow. **coi fiocchi** first-class, magnificent. **fiocchi d'avena** oatflakes *pl*. **fiocco di neve** snowflake.

fioco ['fjɔko] *agg* faint; (*luce*) dim.

fionda ['fjonda] *sf* catapult, sling.

fiordo ['fjɔrdo] *sm* fjord.

fiore ['fjore] *sm* flower; (*di albero*) blossom; (*meglio*) cream; (*carte da gioco*) club. **a fiori** floral. **fior di quattrini** pots of money *pl*. **in fiore** in bloom, in blossom. **fiorente** *agg* (*di fiore*) flowering; (*fig*) thriving, flourishing.

fiorentino [fjoren'tino], **-a** *s, agg* Florentine.

fioretto [fjo'retto] *sm* (*sport*) foil; (*musica, discorso*) embellishment.

fiorire [fjo'rire] *v* flower, bloom, blossom. **fioritura** *sf* flowering, blossoming; (*fiori*) bloom, blossom.

Firenze [fi'rɛntse] *sf* Florence.

firma ['firma] *sf* signature. **firmare** *v* sign. **firmatario** *sm* signatory.

fisarmonica [fizar'mɔnika] *sf* accordion.

fiscale [fis'kale] *agg* fiscal, tax. **fisco** *sm* treasury, tax authorities *pl*.

fischiare [fis'kjare] *v* whistle; (*disapprovare*) boo, hiss. **fischiata** *sf* booing, hissing. **fischiettare** *v* whistle (softly). **fischietto** *sm* whistle. **fischio** *sm* whistle, boo, hiss.

fisica ['fizika] *sf* physics; (*scienziata*) physicist.

fisico ['fiziko] *agg* physical. *sm* (*corpo*) body; (*costituzione*) make-up; (*scienziato*) physicist.

fisima ['fizima] *sf* whim, fancy.

fisiologia [fizjolo'dʒia] *sf* physiology. **fisiologico** *agg* physiological. **fisiologo, -a** *sm, sf* physiologist.

fisionomia [fizjono'mia] *sf* expression.

fisioterapia [fizjotera'pia] *sf* physiotherapy. **fisioterapista** *s(m+f)* physiotherapist.

fissare [fis'sare] *v* fix; (*attaccare*) fasten; (*guardare fissamente*) stare (at), gaze (at); (*prenotare*) book. **fissarsi di** be set on. **fissazione** *sf* fixation.

fissato [fis'sato] *agg* obsessed. *sm* (*fam*) fanatic, maniac. **essere fissato** have a bee in one's bonnet.

fissione [fis'sjone] *sf* fission.

fitta ['fitta] *sf* (*dolore*) twinge, sharp pain.

fittizio [fit'titsjo] *agg* fictitious.

fitto¹ ['fitto] *agg* thick, dense; (*conficcato*) stuck, driven in; (*tessuto, ecc.*) close. *sm* thick, middle. **a capo fitto** headlong. **buio fitto** pitch dark.

fitto² ['fitto] *sm* (*affitto*) rent.

fiume ['fjume] *sm* river; (*fig*) flood, stream. **fiumana** *sf* torrent.

fiutare [fju'tare] *v* smell; (*annusare rumorosamente*) sniff; (*intuire*) scent. **fiutare un inganno** (*fam*) smell a rat. **fiuto** *sm* scent, nose. **al fiuto** straight off, instinctively. **aver fiuto di** get wind of.

flaccido ['flattʃido] *agg* flabby, limp.

flacone [fla'kone] *sm* small bottle.

flagellare [fladʒel'lare] v flagellate, whip. **flagello** sm scourge, whip.

flagrante [fla'grante] agg flagrant. **cogliere in flagrante** catch in the act, catch red-handed.

flanella [fla'nɛlla] sf flannel.

flauto ['flauto] sm flute. **flauto dolce** recorder. **flautista** s(m+f) flautist.

flebile ['flɛbile] agg (debole) faint, feeble; (lamentevole) mournful, melancholy.

flemma ['flɛmma] sf coolness, imperturbability. **flemmatico** agg cool, self-possessed, phlegmatic.

flessibile [fles'sibile] agg flexible, pliable; versatile. **flessibilità** sf flexibility, pliability; versatility. **flessione** sf bending; (diminuzione graduale) drop, fall; (ginnastica) bend.

flessuoso [flessu'ozo] agg supple, lithe. **flessuosità** sf suppleness.

*fflettere** ['flɛttere] v bend, bow; (membra) flex.

flipper ['flipper] sm invar pin-table.

flirt [flɔrt] sm invar (amore superficiale) flirtation; (persona) boy-friend, girl-friend. **flirtare** v flirt.

flora ['flɔra] sf flora.

florido ['flɔrido] agg (prospero) flourishing, thriving; (colorito) ruddy, glowing with health.

floscio ['flɔʃo] agg floppy, limp.

flotta ['flɔtta] sf fleet. **flottiglia** sf flotilla.

fluido ['fluido] sm, agg fluid. **fluidità** sf fluidity; (scorrevolezza) fluency; instability.

fluire [flu'ire] v flow.

fluorescente [fluore'ʃɛnte] agg fluorescent. **fluorescenza** sf fluorescence.

fluoro ['fluɔro] sm fluorine.

flusso ['flusso] sm flow, stream. **flusso e riflusso** ebb and flow. **flusso di sangue dal naso** nosebleed.

fluttuare [fluttu'are] v fluctuate.

fobia [fo'bia] sf phobia; (fam) (pet) aversion.

foca ['fɔka] sf seal.

focaccia [fo'kattʃa] sf bun. **rendere pan per focaccia** give as good as one gets.

focale [fo'kale] agg focal.

foce ['fotʃe] sf mouth, outlet.

focena [fo'tʃena] sf porpoise.

focolaio [foko'lajo] sm (med) focus; (centro di diffusione) hotbed, breeding ground.

focolare [foko'lare] sm hearth; (fig) fireside, home.

focoso [fo'kozo] agg fiery; (ardente) burning.

fodera ['fɔdera] sf lining; (rivestimento) cover. **foderare** v line; cover. **fodero** sm sheath.

foga ['fɔga] sf rush; (ardore) heat.

foggia ['fɔddʒa] sf fashion; (forma) shape. **foggiare** v shape, form, fashion.

foglia ['fɔʎʎa] sf leaf. **mettere le foglie** come into leaf. **fogliame** sm foliage.

foglio ['fɔʎʎo] sm sheet; (giornale) paper; (banconota) note. **foglio di via** travel-warrant. **foglio volante** leaflet.

fogna ['fɔɲa] sf sewer. **fognatura** sf sewerage.

foia ['fɔja] sf heat. **essere in foia** be on heat.

foiata [fo'jata] sf gust.

folclore [fol'klɔre] sm folklore. **folcloristico** agg folk.

folgorare [folgo'rare] v flash; (inveire) rail; (colpire con fulmine) strike with lightning. **folgorare con lo sguardo** wither with a glance.

folla ['fɔlla] sf crowd; (gran quantità) host.

folle ['fɔlle] agg crazy; (pazzo) mad; (sciocco) foolish; (auto) neutral. **andare in folle** coast. **folletto** sm imp. **follia** sf madness, folly.

follicolo [fol'likolo] sm follicle.

folto ['folto] sm, agg thick.

fomentare [fomen'tare] v encourage; (eccitare) rouse. **fomento** sm (impacco caldo) poultice; (sprone) spur.

fonda ['fɔnda] sf anchorage.

fondamento [fonda'mento] sm, pl -a f in literal sense foundation. **fondamentale** agg fundamental, basic.

fondare [fon'dare] v found; (istituire) establish; base. **fondarsi su** be based on; (fare assegnamento) rely on. **fondatore, -trice** sm sf founder. **fondazione** sf foundation, establishment.

*ffondere** ['fɔndere] v melt, fuse; (in una forma) cast, mould; (unire) blend, merge.

fonderia [fonde'ria] sf foundry.

fondiario [fon'djarjo] agg land. **proprietà fondiaria** sf real estate.

fondina¹ [fon'dina] sf (di pistola) holster.

fondina² [fon'dina] sf (piatto) soup plate.

fondista [fon'dista] s(m+f) (sport) long

distance runner; (*giornalista*) leader writer.

fondo ['fondo] *agg* deep. *sm* bottom; (*feccia*) dregs *pl*; (*caffè*) grounds *pl*; (*estremità*) end; (*sfondo*) background; (*pittura*) primer; (*denaro*) fund; (*terreno*) estate. **a fondo** (*profondamente*) thoroughly; (*con tutte le forze*) wholeheartedly. **andare a fondo** sink. **andare a fondo di** get to the bottom of. **articolo di fondo** *sm* leading article. **dar fondo a** (*consumare*) use up. **fino in fondo** to the end. **fondo (di) cassa/magazzino** cash/stock in hand. **fondo stradale** road surface. **in fondo** (*sotto*) at *or* to the bottom; (*dietro*) at *or* to the back; (*in conclusione*) after all. **mandare a fondo** sink.

fonetica [fo'nɛtika] *sf* phonetics. **fonetico** *agg* phonetic.

fontana [fon'tana] *sf* fountain.

fonte ['fonte] *sf* spring; (*fig*) source. *sm* (*battesimale*) font.

foraggiare [forad'dʒare] *v* forage. **foraggio** *sm* forage.

forare [fo'rare] *v* perforate; (*gomma*) puncture; (*al trapano*) bore. **foratura** *sf* perforation; puncture.

forbici ['fɔrbitʃi] *sf pl* scissors *pl*; (*da siepe, cesoie*) shears *pl*; (*da potatura*) secateurs *pl*. **forbicina** *sf* earwig.

forbire [for'bire] *v* clean; (*fig*) polish.

forca ['fɔrka] *sf* pitchfork; (*patibolo*) gallows. **va alla** *or* **sulla forca!** (*fam*) get stuffed! **forcella** *sf* fork; (*volatili*) wishbone.

forchetta [for'ketta] *sf* fork. **una buona forchetta** a hearty eater. **forchettata** *sf* forkful.

forcina [for'tʃina] *sf* hairpin.

forcipe ['fɔrtʃipe] *sm* forceps *pl*.

forense [fo'rɛnse] *agg* forensic.

foresta [fo'resta] *sf* forest.

forestiero [fores'tjɛro], **-a** *agg* foreign. *sm*, *sf* foreigner.

forfait¹ [for'fɛ] *sm invar* (*contratto*) flat rate. **a forfait** all-in.

forfait² [for'fɛ] *sm invar* (*sport*) withdrawal. **dichiarare forfait** scratch.

forfora [for'fora] *sf* dandruff.

forma ['forma] *sf* form, shape; (*stampo*) mould; (*del calzolaio*) last. **a forma di X** X-shaped.

formaggio [for'maddʒo] *sm* cheese.

formale [for'male] *agg* formal. **formalità** *sf* formality.

formare [for'mare] *v* form; (*modellare*) shape; (*costituire*) make up; (*numero telefonico*) dial. **formarsi un'idea** get an idea. **formato** *sm* format, size. **formazione** *sf* formation; (*addestramento*) training.

formica [for'mika] *sf* ant. **formicaio** *sm* antheap; (*fig*) teeming crowd.

formicolare [formiko'lare] *v* swarm; (*provare sensazione*) tingle. **formicolio** *sm* swarming; (*sensazione*) pins and needles.

formidabile [formi'dabile] *agg* remarkable; (*molto forte*) powerful, formidable.

formula ['fɔrmula] *sf* formula (*pl* -ae).

formulare [formu'lare] *v* formulate; (*avanzare*) put forward; (*esprimere*) express. **formulario** *sm* (*modulo*) form.

fornace [for'natʃe] *sf* kiln, furnace.

fornaio [for'najo], **-a** *sm*, *sf* baker.

fornire [for'nire] *v* supply, furnish. **ben fornito** well-stocked. **fornitore** *sm* supplier. **fornitura** *sf* supply.

forno ['forno] *sm* oven. **fornello** *sm* cooker.

foro¹ ['foro] *sm* (*buco*) hole.

foro² ['foro] *sm* (*tribunale*) (law-)court; (*gli avvocati*) the bar; (*Roma*) forum.

forse ['forse] *avv* perhaps, maybe; (*circa*) about. **in forse** in doubt.

forsennato [forsen'nato] *agg* crazy, mad.

forte ['fɔrte] *agg* strong; (*grande*) large; (*bravo*) good; (*suono*) loud; (*intenso*) heavy. *avv* (*con forza*) hard; (*assai*) very much; (*velocemente*) fast; (*a voce alta*) loud. *sm* (*specialità*) strong point; (*persona*) powerful person; (*mil*) fort.

fortezza [for'tettsa] *sf* (*mil*) fortress; (*forza morale*) strength.

fortificare [fortifi'kare] *v* strengthen, fortify. **fortificazione** *sf* fortification.

fortuito [for'tuito] *agg* fortuitous, chance.

fortuna [for'tuna] *sf* fortune; (*buona sorte*) luck; success. **di fortuna** (*improvvisato*) makeshift; emergency. **fortuna che** fortunately. **fortunato** *agg* fortunate, lucky.

foruncolo [fo'runkolo] *sm* boil.

forza ['fɔrtsa] *sf* strength; (*potere, potenza*) power; (*fis, mil*) force. **a forza di** through, by dint of. **a tutta forza** with all one's strength. **bella forza!** there's nothing to it! **farsi forza** (*coraggio*) pluck up courage. **forza maggiore** force majeure, circumstances beyond one's control. **per forza** necessarily; (*controvoglia*) unwillingly. **per forza di cose** of necessity.

forzare [for'tsare] v force. **forzato** sm convict.

foschia [fos'kia] sf haze, mist.

fosco ['fosko] agg (scuro) dark; (tetro) gloomy.

fosfato [fos'fato] sm phosphate.

fosforescente [fosfore'ʃɛnte] agg phosphorescent. **fosforo** sm phosphorus.

fossa ['fossa] sf pit, hole; (cimitero) grave. **fossato** sm ditch; (mil) moat. **fossetta** sf dimple.

fossile ['fossile] sm, agg fossil.

fosso ['fosso] sm ditch. **saltare il fosso** (fig) take the plunge.

foto ['foto] sf invar (fam) snap, photo. **fotocopia** [foto'kɔpja] sf photocopy. **fotogenico** [foto'dʒɛniko] agg photogenic. **fotografare** [fotogra'fare] v photograph. **fotografia** sf (tecnica) photography; (copia) photograph. **fotografico** agg photographic. **apparecchio fotografico** sm camera. **fotografo, -a** sm, sf photographer.

fottere ['fottere] (volg) v fuck. **fottuto** agg (spacciato) ruined, buggered.

fra [fra] prep (fra due) between; (fra più di due) among(st); (entro) in, within; (partitivo) of. **detto fra (di) noi** between ourselves. **fra l'altro** among other things; (inoltre) besides. **fra tutti** (tutti insieme) altogether, in all.

frac [frak] sm invar (fam) tails pl.

fracassare [frakas'sare] v smash. **fracassarsi** v break. **fracasso** sm (chiasso) racket, din, row; (scalpore) uproar.

fradicio ['fradiʧo] agg (inzuppato) sopping (wet), wet through; (guasto) rotten. **ubriaco fradicio** dead drunk.

fragile ['fradʒile] agg fragile; (delicato) frail

fragola ['fragola] sf strawberry.

fragore [fra'gore] sm din. **fragoroso** agg roaring, resounding.

fragrante [fra'grante] agg fragrant.

***fraintendere** [frain'tɛndere] v misunderstand, misconstrue.

frammassone [frammas'sone] sm freemason. **frammassoneria** sf freemasonry.

frammento [fram'mento] sm fragment; (scheggia) splinter. **frammentario** agg fragmentary.

***frammettersi** [fram'mettersi] v (interporsi) come between; (immischiarsi) meddle.

frammezzo [fram'mɛddzo] avv **frammezzo a** in the midst of.

frana ['frana] sf landslide. **franare** v slide down; (crollare) cave in.

francamente [franka'mente] avv frankly.

franchezza [fran'kettsa] sf frankness.

franchigia [fran'kidʒa] sf exemption. **in franchigia** (posta) post-free; (tassa) tax-free.

Francia ['franʧa] sf France. **francese** sm, agg French; s(m+f) French person.

franco[1] ['franko] agg (schietto) frank, open; (disinvolto) (self-)confident; (libero) free (of), exempt (from). **in porto franco** (comm) carriage paid.

franco[2] ['franko] sm (moneta) franc.

francobollo [franko'bollo] sm (postage) stamp.

***frangersi** ['frandʒersi] v break. **frangente** sm (ondata) breaker; (crisi) spot, predicament.

frangia ['frandʒa] sf fringe.

frantumare [frantu'mare] v crush. **in frantumi** in or to pieces.

***frapporre** [frap'porre] v interpose.

frase ['fraze] sf phrase; (periodo) sentence. **frase fatta** stock phrase.

frassino ['frassino] sm ash.

frastagliare [frasta'ʎare] v indent.

frastornato [frastor'nato] agg dizzy.

frastuono [fras'twono] sm din, uproar.

frate ['frate] sm friar.

fratello [fra'tɛllo] sm brother. **fratellanza** sf brotherhood. **fratellastro** sm stepbrother.

fraterno [fra'tɛrno] agg brotherly, fraternal. **fraternizzare** v fraternize.

frattaglie [frat'taʎe] sf pl offal sing; (di pollame) giblets pl.

frattanto [frat'tanto] avv also **nel frattempo** meanwhile, in the meantime.

frattura [frat'tura] sf fracture; (fig) break. **fratturare** v fracture, break.

frazione [fra'tsjone] sf fraction; (borgata) hamlet. **frazionare** v split up.

freccia ['frettʃa] sf arrow; (auto) indicator. **frecciata** sf shaft.

freddo ['freddo] agg cold; (fig) cool, chilly. sm cold. **aver freddo** be cold, feel cold. **fa freddo** it is cold. **fa un freddo cane** it is bitterly cold. **morir di freddo** be dying of cold. **soffrire il freddo** feel the cold.

freddura [fred'dura] sf pun.

fregare [fre'gare] v rub; (per lucidare) polish; (per lavare) scrub; (fam: rubare) pinch, swipe; (volg: imbrogliare) cheat. **fregata** sf rub(bing). **fregatura** sf (volg: imbroglio) swindle; (fam: contrattempo) wash-out, flop.

fregio ['fredʒo] sm ornament; (arch) frieze. **fregiare** v decorate.

fremere ['frɛmere] v quiver.

fremito ['frɛmito] sm quiver; (di emozione) thrill; (brivido) shudder.

frenare [fre'nare] v brake; (fig) restrain, control, check.

frenesia [frene'zia] sf frenzy. **frenetico** agg frenzied, raving.

freno ['freno] sm brake; (fig) check, restraint; (cavallo) bit. **allentare il freno** (fig) slacken the reins. **mordere il freno** champ at the bit. **stringere i freni** (fig) clamp down.

frequentare [frekwen'tare] v frequent, go to often; (scuola, ecc.) attend; (persone) mix with. **frequentatore, -trice** sm, sf regular. **frequente** agg frequent. **frequenza** sf frequency. **con frequenza** frequently.

fresa ['freza] sf also **fresatrice** cutter, milling machine.

fresco ['fresko] agg fresh; (leggermente freddo) cool. sm cool(ness); freshness; (pittura) fresco. **al fresco** in the cool; (prigione) in the cooler. **star fresco** (nei guai) be in a mess; (sbagliarsi) kid oneself.

fretta ['fretta] sf hurry. **aver fretta** be in a hurry. **far fretta** a hurry. **fatto in fretta** rushed, hurried. **frettoloso** agg rushed, hasty.

*friggere ['friddʒere] v fry; (scoppiettare bollendo) sizzle.

frigido ['fridʒido] agg cold, frigid. **frigidità** sf coldness, frigidity.

frigorifero [frigo'rifero] sm refrigerator. **frigo** sm invar (fam) fridge.

fringuello [frin'gwello] sm chaffinch.

frittata [frit'tata] sf omelette. **frittella** sf pancake.

fritto ['fritto] agg fried. sm fried food. **star fritto** (fam) be in trouble, be in for it. **frittura** sf (vivanda) fried food; (atto del friggere) frying.

frivolo ['frivolo] agg frivolous. **frivolezze** sf frivolity, trifle.

frizione [frit'tsjone] sf (massaggio) rubdown; (auto) clutch; (attrito) friction.

frizzare [frit'tsare] v tingle; (bevande) sparkle; (metallo rovente) hiss.

frodare [fro'dare] v defraud. **frode** sf fraud. **frodo** sm smuggling. **cacciare** or **pescare di frodo** poach. **cacciatore** or **pescatore di frodo** poacher.

frollare [frol'lare] v ripen. **frollo** agg ripe; (carne) tender; (selvaggina) high; (pasta) short.

fronda ['fronda] sf (leafy) branch; (fig) embellishment.

fronte ['fronte] sf (testa) forehead; (faccia) face; (parte anteriore) front; (arch) façade. sm (mil) front. **a fronte** (in faccia) facing. **di fronte** (dirimpetto) opposite; (da davanti) from the front. **far fronte a** face.

fronteggiare [fronted'dʒare] v face, stand up to.

frontespizio [frontes'pitsjo] sm title-page.

frontiera [fron'tjera] sf frontier, border.

fronzoli ['frondzoli] sm pl frills pl.

frotta ['frotta] sf flock, swarm.

frottola ['frottola] sf fib.

frugale [fru'gale] agg frugal.

frugare [fru'gare] v rummage, go through; (perquisire) search.

frullare [frul'lare] v whisk; (fig) whirl. **frullino** sm whisk.

frumento [fru'mento] sm wheat.

frusciare [fruʃ'ʃare] v rustle.

frustare [frus'tare] v whip. **frusta** sf whip. **frustata** sf lash.

frustrazione [frustra'tsjone] sf frustration. **frustrare** v frustrate, thwart.

frutta ['frutta] sf fruit. **frutta cotta** stewed fruit. **fruttare** v bear fruit; yield; (rendere) bring in; (procurare) earn.

frutteto [frut'teto] sm orchard.

fruttifero [frut'tifero] agg fruitful; (redditizio) profitable.

fruttivendolo [frutti'vendolo], -a sm, sf fruiterer, greengrocer.

frutto ['frutto] sm fruit; (interesse) yield; (rendita) income; profit. **frutti di mare** seafood sing.

fu [fu] agg invar late, deceased.

fucilare [futʃi'lare] v shoot. **fucilata** sf shot. **fucilazione** sf execution. **fucile** sm rifle; (da caccia) shotgun.

fucina [fu'tʃina] sf forge.

fuco[1] ['fuko] sm (ape) drone.

fuco[2] ['fuko] sm (alga) fucus.

fucsia ['fuksja] sf fuchsia.

fuga ['fuga] *sf* escape; *(musica)* fugue; *(serie)* suite. **mettere in fuga** put to flight. **prendere la fuga** take flight, flee, escape. **fugace** *agg* transient.

fuggire [fud'dʒire] *v* flee, escape, run away. **fuggiasco** *sm*, *agg* fugitive; *(profugo)* refugee.

fulcro ['fulkro] *sm* fulcrum; *(fig)* heart.

fuliggine [fu'liddʒine] *sf* soot. **fuligginoso** *agg* sooty.

fulminare [fulmi'nare] *v (dal fulmine)* strike (by lightning); *(dalla corrente)* electrocute; *(con uno sguardo)* wither; *(allibire)* dumbfound. **fulmine** *sm* lightning, thunderbolt. **un fulmine a ciel sereno** a bolt from the blue.

fumaiolo [fuma'jɔlo] *sm (casa)* chimney-pot; *(nave)* funnel, smoke-stack.

fumare [fu'mare] *v* smoke; *(emettere vapore)* steam. **fumata** *sf* smoke. **fumatore, -trice** *sm, sf* smoker.

fumetto [fu'metto] *sm* comic-strip. **fumettista** *s(m+f)* comic-strip writer.

fumo ['fumo] *sm* smoke. **andare in fumo** go up in smoke.

funambolo [fu'nambolo], **-a** *sm, sf* tight-rope walker.

fune ['fune] *sf* rope, cable; *(per bucato)* washing line.

funebre ['funebre] *agg* funeral; *(lugubre)* funereal.

funerale [fune'rale] *sm* funeral. **funereo** *agg* funereal.

funesto [fu'nesto] *agg* fatal; *(doloroso)* distressing.

fungo ['fungo] *sm* mushroom; *(non mangereccio)* toadstool; *(bot)* fungus *(pl -gi)*.

funicolare [funiko'lare] *sf* funicular railway.

funivia [funi'via] *sf* cable-car.

funzionare [funtsjo'nare] *v* function, work. **funzionale** *agg* functional, practical. **funzionamento** *sm* operation, working.

funzionario [funtsjo'narjo] *sm* official; *(impiegato statale)* civil servant.

funzione [fun'tsjone] *sf* function; *(carica)* office; *(compito)* duty. **entrare in funzione** come into operation. **essere in funzione di** ... act as ....

fuochista [fwo'kista] *sm* stoker.

fuoco ['fwɔko] *sm* fire; *(fis, mat, foto)* focus. **appiccare** or **dare fuoco** a set fire

to. **a prova di fuoco** fireproof. **fuoco di Sant'Antonio** *(med)* shingles. **mettere a fuoco** *(foto)* focus. **prendere fuoco** catch fire.

fuorché [fwor'ke] *prep, cong* except.

fuori ['fwɔri] *avv out; (all'esterno)* outside. *prep also* **fuori di** or **da** out of. **esser fuori di sè** be beside oneself. **fuoribordo** *sm (motore)* outboard motor; *(barca)* motor boat. **fuori strada** *(veicoli)* off the road; *(fig)* on the wrong track. **mettere fuori combattimento** *(sport)* knock out; *(fig)* put out of the running.

furbo ['furbo] *agg* cunning, crafty. **furbacchione** *sm* cunning fellow. **furberia** *sf* cunning.

furetto [fu'retto] *sm* ferret.

furfante [fur'fante] *sm* rascal.

furgone [fur'gone] *sm (delivery)* van. **furgoncino** *sm* small (delivery) van.

furia ['furja] *sf (collera)* rage, fury; *(fretta)* rush, haste. **a furia di** ... by dint of ....

furibondo [furi'bondo] *agg* furious.

furioso [fu'rjozo] *agg* violent, furious.

furore [fu'rore] *sm* fury, rage.

furtivo [fur'tivo] *agg* furtive, stealthy.

furto ['furto] *sm* theft. **furto con scasso** burglary. **piccolo furto** petty theft, petty larceny.

fusa ['fuza] *sf pl* **fare le fusa** purr.

fuscello [fu'ʃello] *sm* twig.

fusibile [fu'zibile] *agg* fusible. *sm (elett)* fuse.

fusione [fu'zjone] *sf* fusion; *(colata)* casting; *(scioglimento)* melting; *(fig)* merging; *(comm)* merger.

fuso[1] ['fuzo] *agg (liquefatto)* melted, molten; *(colato)* cast.

fuso[2] ['fuzo] *sm* spindle; *(ancora)* shank. **diritto come un fuso** *(eretto)* straight as a ramrod; *(difilato)* like a shot. **fuso orario** time zone.

fusoliera [fuzo'ljera] *sf* fuselage.

fustagno [fus'taɲo] *sm* fustian; *(a coste)* corduroy.

fustella [fus'tella] *sf (tec)* die.

fustigare [fusti'gare] *v* flog; *(fig)* lash out at.

fusto ['fusto] *sm* trunk; *(ossatura)* frame; *(barile)* barrel, cask; *(recipiente di metallo)* drum.

futile ['futile] *agg* futile; *(meschino)* petty.

futuro [fu'turo] *agg, sm* future.

G

gabbare [gab'bare] *v* cheat.

gabbia ['gabbja] *sf* cage. **gabbia degli imputati** dock.

gabbiano [gab'bjano] *sm* seagull.

gabinetto [gabi'netto] *sm* study, office; *(di medico)* surgery; *(WC)* toilet, lavatory; *(pol)* cabinet; *(di scienze)* laboratory.

gaffe ['gaf] *sf, pl* -s blunder. **fare una gaffe** *(fam)* put one's foot in it.

gagà [ga'ga] *sm (fam)* dandy.

gagliardo [ga'ʎardo] *agg* vigorous; *(robusto)* strapping; *(coraggioso)* brave. **gagliardetto** *sm* pennant, flag.

gaio ['gajo] *agg* cheerful.

gala ['gala] *sf (ricevimento)* feast. *sm (mar)* flags *pl. sf (stoffa)* frill; *(cravatta)* bow-tie.

galantuomo [galan'twɔmo] *sm* (true) gentleman, man of honour. **galante** *agg* gallant, courteous.

galassia [ga'lassja] *sf* galaxy.

galateo [gala'tɛo] *sm* etiquette, good manners *pl.*

galea [ga'lɛa] *sf* galley.

galeotto [gale'ɔtto] *sm (carcerato)* convict; *(furfante)* scoundrel; *(vogatore forzato)* galley slave.

galera [ga'lɛra] *sf* prison.

galla ['galla] *sf* **stare** *or* **rimanere a galla** float, keep afloat. **tenersi a galla** keep afloat; *(fig)* keep one's head above water. **venire a galla** come to the surface; *(fig)* come to light, emerge.

galleggiare [galled'dʒare] *v* float. **galleggiante** *agg* floating. *sm* float; *(tec)* ballcock.

galleria [galle'ria] *sf* gallery; *(traforo)* tunnel; *(passaggio sotterraneo)* subway; *(cinema, ecc.)* circle, balcony.

Galles ['galles] *sm* Wales. **gallese** *sm, agg* Welsh; *s(m+f)* Welshman.

gallo ['gallo] *sm* cock. **galletto** *sm* cockerel; *(tec)* wing-nut. **gallina** *sf* hen.

gallone¹ [gal'lone] *sm (misura)* gallon.

gallone² [gal'lone] *sm* braid; *(mil)* stripe.

galoppare [galop'pare] *v* gallop. **galoppata** *sf* gallop; *(lavoro faticoso)* hard work. **galoppo** *sm* gallop.

galvanizzare [galvanid'dzare] *v* galvanize.

gamba ['gamba] *sf* leg. **andare a gambe**

all'aria fall flat on one's back; *(fallire)* fail. **a tre gambe** three-legged. **darsela a gambe** take to one's heels. **gambe storte** bandy *or* bow legs *pl.* **in gamba** *(valente)* smart. *inter* take care!

gambero ['gambero] *sm (di acqua dolce)* crayfish; *(gamberetto)* shrimp; *(gamberone)* prawn. **rosso come un gambero** as red as a lobster.

gambo ['gambo] *sm (pianta)* stem, stalk; *(tec)* shank.

gamma ['gamma] *sf* range; *(lunghezza d'onda)* wave-band.

ganascia [ga'naʃa] *sf* jaw; *(freno)* brake-shoe.

gancio ['gantʃo] *sm* hook.

ganghero ['gangero] *sm* hinge. **essere fuori dai gangheri** be beside oneself. **uscire dai gangheri** lose one's head.

gara ['gara] *sf* competition; *(corsa)* race; *(comm)* tender.

garage [ga'raʒ] *sm, pl* -s garage.

garantire [garan'tire] *v* guarantee; *(rendersi garante)* vouch for; *(assicurare)* assure. **essere garante per** *or* **di** vouch for. **rendersi garante per** *(dir)* stand bail for.

garanzia [garan'tsia] *sf* guarantee.

garbare [gar'bare] *v* please, suit. **garbato** *agg* polite, well-mannered. **garbo** *sm (maniera)* good manners *pl,* politeness; *(gentilezza)* charm.

garbuglio [gar'buʎo] *sm* muddle.

gareggiare [gared'dʒare] *v* compete.

gargarismo [garga'rizmo] *sm* gargle. **fare i gargarismi** gargle.

garitta [ga'ritta] *sf* cabin; *(mil)* sentry-box.

garofano [ga'rɔfano] *sm* carnation. **chiodo di garofano** *sm* clove.

garrire [gar'rire] *v* twitter. **garrito** *sm* twitter.

garrulo ['garrulo] *agg (uccello)* twittering; *(persona loquace)* garrulous.

garza ['gardza] *sf* gauze.

garzone [gar'dzone] *sm* boy, mate.

gas ['gas] *sm* gas. **a gas** gas. **gas asfissiante/esilarante** poison/laughing gas. **gassoso** *agg* gaseous.

gasolio [ga'zɔljo] *sm* fuel oil, diesel fuel.

gassosa [gas'soza] *sf* fizzy drink, lemonade.

gastrico ['gastriko] *agg* gastric.

gastronomia [gastrono'mia] *sf* gastronomy, cooking. **gastronomico** *agg* gastronomic(al). **gastronomo** *sm* (*buongustaio*) gourmet.

gattabuia [gatta'buja] *sf* (*fam*) clink.

gatto ['gatto] *sm* cat. **gatta** *sf* she-cat. **comprare una gatta nel sacco** buy a pig in a poke. **gatta ci cova!** I smell a rat! **una gatta da pelare** a tricky job to do. **gattino** *sm* kitten; (*bot*) catkin.

gazza ['gaddza] *sf* magpie.

gazzarra [gad'dzarra] *sf* uproar, row.

gazzella [gad'dzɛlla] *sf* gazelle.

gazzetta [gad'dzetta] *sf* gazette.

gelare [dʒe'lare] *v* freeze. **gelata** *sf* (hard) frost.

gelatina [dʒela'tina] *sf* gelatine.

gelato [dʒe'lato] *agg* frozen. *sm* ice-cream. **gelataio** *sm* ice-cream vendor. **gelateria** *sf* ice-cream shop *or* parlour.

gelido ['dʒɛlido] *agg* icy.

gelo ['dʒɛlo] *sm* frost; intense cold; (*sensazione*) chill.

gelone [dʒe'lone] *sm* chilblain.

gelosia[1] [dʒelo'zia] *sf* jealousy; (*cura attenta*) great care.

gelosia[2] [dʒelo'zia] *sf* (*finestra*) blind.

geloso [dʒe'lozo] *agg* jealous.

gelso ['dʒɛlso] *sm* (*mora*) mulberry; (*albero*) mulberry-tree.

gelsomino [dʒelso'mino] *sm* jasmine.

gemello [dʒe'mɛllo] *sm*, *agg* twin. **gemelli** *sm pl* (*di polsino*) cuff-links *pl*. **Gemelli** *sm pl* Gemini *sing*.

gemere ['dʒɛmere] *v* groan; (*colare*) drip, ooze; (*tubare*) coo. **gemito** *sm* groan.

gemma [dʒe'mma] *sf* gem; (*bot*) bud.

gene ['dʒɛne] *sm* gene.

genealogia [dʒenealo'dʒia] *sf* (*scienza*) genealogy; (*stirpe*) pedigree. **albero genealogico** *sm* family tree.

generale [dʒene'rale] *sm*, *agg* general. **in generale** in general; (*di solito*) as a rule. **generalizzare** [dʒeneralid'dzare] *v* generalize. **generalizzazione** *sf* generalization.

generare [dʒene'rare] *v* generate, produce. **generazione** *sf* generation.

genere [dʒɛnere] *sm* kind, type; (*tipo di merce*) product, article; (*stile*) genre; (*gramm*) gender. **d'ogni genere** of all kinds. **il genere umano** mankind. **nel suo genere** in his way.

generico [dʒe'nɛriko] *agg* generic; general.

genero ['dʒɛnero] *sm* son-in-law.

generoso [dʒene'rozo] *agg* generous; (*vino*) full-bodied; (*cavallo*) thoroughbred.

genetica [dʒe'nɛtika] *sf* genetics. **genetico** *agg* genetic. **genetista** *s*(*m+f*) geneticist.

gengiva [dʒen'dʒiva] *sf* gum. **gengivite** *sf* gingivitis.

geniale [dʒe'njale] *agg* ingenious, clever. **genialità** *sf* brilliance.

genio[1] [dʒɛnjo] *sm* genius; (*disposizione*) talent, gift; (*inclinazione*) taste. **andare a genio** be to one's liking, suit.

genio[2] [dʒɛnjo] *sm* (*mil*) engineers *pl*.

genitali [dʒeni'tali] *sm pl* genitals *pl*.

genitore [dʒeni'tore] *sm* parent.

gennaio [dʒen'najo] *sm* January.

Genova ['dʒɛnova] *sf* Genoa. **genovese** *agg*, *s*(*m+f*) Genoese.

gente ['dʒɛnte] *sf* people *pl*.

gentile [dʒen'tile] *agg* kind; (*cortese*) polite; delicate. **gentilezza** *sf* kindness; politeness; (*atto gentile*) favour. **gentiluomo** *sm* (*nobile*) nobleman; (*persona retta*) gentleman.

genuino [dʒenu'ino] *agg* genuine, natural; authentic. **genuinità** *sf* authenticity, naturalness, spontaneity.

genziana [dʒen'tsjana] *sf* gentian.

geografia [dʒeogra'fia] *sf* geography. **geografico** *agg* geographical. **atlante geografico** *sm* atlas. **carta geografica** *sf* map. **geografo, -a** *sm*, *sf* geographer.

geologia [dʒeolo'dʒia] *sf* geology. **geologico** *agg* geological. **geologo, -a** *sm*, *sf* geologist.

geometra [dʒe'ɔmetra] *s*(*m+f*) surveyor. **geometria** [dʒeome'tria] *sf* geometry. **geometrico** *agg* geometrical.

geranio [dʒe'ranjo] *sm* geranium.

gerarchia [dʒerar'kia] *sf* hierarchy. **gerarca** *sm* (*rel*) hierarch; (*capo*) leader. **gerarchico** *agg* hierarchical. **per via gerarchica** through official channels.

gerente [dʒe'rɛnte] *sm* manager.

gergo ['dʒɛrgo] *sm* slang, jargon.

geriatria [dʒerja'tria] *sf* geriatrics. **geriatrico** *agg* geriatric.

Germania [dʒer'manja] *sf* Germany. **germanico** *agg* German.

germe ['dʒɛrme] *sm* germ. **germinare** *v* germinate.

germogliare [dʒermo'ʎare] *v* bud, sprout; (*fig*) germinate. **germoglio** *sm* shoot; (*origine*) germ.

gesso ['dʒɛsso] *sm (minerale)* gypsum; *(da disegno)* chalk; *(a pronta presa)* plaster (of Paris); *(opera)* plaster cast.

gesta ['dʒɛsta] *sf pl (noble)* deeds *pl*, feats *pl*.

gesticolare [dʒestiko'lare] *v* gesticulate.

gestire [dʒes'tire] *v* manage, run. **gestione** *sf* management.

gesto ['dʒɛsto] *sm* gesture; *(azione)* deed; *(del capo)* nod; *(della mano)* wave.

Gesù [dʒe'zu] *sm* Jesus.

gesuita [dʒezu'ita] *sm* Jesuit. **gesuitico** *agg* Jesuitical.

gettare [dʒet'tare] *v* throw; *(emettere)* let out; *(tec)* cast. **gettare i soldi dalla finestra** throw money down the drain. **gettare le fondamenta** lay the foundations. **gettar luce su ...** cast light on .... **gettata** *sf* cast; *(di reti)* casting.

getto ['dʒɛtto] *sm (lancio)* throw; *(di liquido o gas)* jet; *(metallo, ecc.)* casting.

gettone [dʒet'tone] *sm* counter, token.

ghermire [ger'mire] *v* clutch, grab.

ghetto ['gɛtto] *sm* ghetto.

ghiacciaia [gjat'tʃaja] *sf* ice-box.

ghiacciaio [gjat'tʃajo] *sm* glacier.

ghiacciare [gjat'tʃare] *v* freeze. **ghiacciata** *sf* drink with crushed ice.

ghiaccio ['gjattʃo] *sm* ice. **di ghiaccio** *(freddissimo)* ice-cold, frozen; *(fig)* icy. **ghiacciolo** *sm* icicle; *(gelato)* ice lolly.

ghiaia ['gjaja] *sf* gravel.

ghianda ['gjanda] *sf* acorn.

ghiandaia [gjan'daja] *sf* jay.

ghiandola ['gjandola] *sf* gland. **ghiandolare** *agg* glandular.

ghigliottina [giʎot'tina] *sf* guillotine. **ghigliottinare** *v* guillotine.

ghignare [gi'ɲare] *v* sneer. **ghigno** *sm* sneer, smirk.

ghiotto ['gjotto] *agg* greedy; *(appetitoso)* inviting. **ghiottone, -a** *sm, sf* glutton, greedy person. **ghiottoneria** *sf (golosità)* gluttony; *(cibo ghiotto)* titbit.

ghiribizzo [giri'bittso] *sm* fancy, whim.

ghirigoro [giri'goro] *sm* flourish.

ghirlanda [gir'landa] *sf* garland, wreath.

ghiro ['giro] *sm* dormouse. **dormire come un ghiro** sleep like a log.

ghisa ['giza] *sf* cast iron.

già ['dʒa] *avv* already; *(un tempo)* once; *(ex)* formerly.

giacca ['dʒakka] *sf* coat; *(giacchetta)* jacket.

giacché [dʒak'ke] *cong* as, since.

giacchetta [dʒak'ketta] *sf* jacket.

*giacere [dʒa'tʃere] *v* lie; *(in sospeso)* be in abeyance. **mettersi a giacere** lie down. **giacenza** *sf* abeyance; *(merce)* (unsold) stock; *(econ)* deposit. **giacimento** *sm* deposit.

giacinto [dʒa'tʃinto] *sm* hyacinth.

giada ['dʒada] *sf* jade.

giaggiolo [dʒad'dʒolo] *sm* iris.

giaguaro [dʒa'gwaro] *sm* jaguar.

giallo ['dʒallo] *agg* yellow. *sm (colore)* yellow; *(libro, film)* thriller. **giallo d'uovo** (egg) yolk. **giallastro** *agg* yellowish, sallow. **giallognolo** *agg* pale yellow, yellowish.

giammai [dʒam'mai] *avv* never. **se giammai** if ever.

Giappone [dʒap'pone] *sm* Japan. **giapponese** *s(m+f)*, *agg* Japanese.

giardinetta [dʒardi'netta] *sf* estate car.

giardino [dʒar'dino] *sm* garden. **giardino d'infanzia** kindergarten, nursery school. **giardino zoologico** zoo. **giardinaggio** *sm* gardening. **giardiniere, -a** *sm, sf* gardener.

giarrettiera [dʒarret'tjera] *sf* suspender, garter.

giavellotto [dʒavel'lotto] *sm* javelin.

Gibilterra [dʒibil'terra] *sf* Gibraltar.

gigante [dʒi'gante] *sm*, *agg* giant. **gigantesco** *agg* gigantic, huge.

gigione [dʒi'dʒone] *sm* ham (actor). **fare il gigione** ham.

giglio ['dʒiʎo] *sm* lily.

gilè [dʒi'le] *sm* waistcoat.

ginecologo [dʒine'kologo] *-a sm, sf* gynaecologist. **ginecologia** *sm* gynaecology. **ginecologico** *agg* gynaecological.

ginepro [dʒi'nepro] *sm* juniper.

ginestra [dʒi'nestra] *sf* broom. **ginestrone** *sm* furze, gorse.

Ginevra [dʒi'nevra] *sf* Geneva.

gingillarsi [dʒindʒil'larsi] *v (divertirsi)* amuse oneself; *(perder tempo)* hang about.

ginnasio [dʒin'nazjo] *sm* secondary school.

ginnastica [dʒin'nastika] *sf (sport)* gymnastics; *(esercizi)* physical exercises *pl*.

ginocchio [dʒi'nokkjo] *sm pl -a f* knee. **ginocchioni** *avv also* in ginocchio on one's knees.

giocare [dʒo'kare] *v* play; *(in borsa)* gamble (on the Stock Exchange); *(scommettere)* bet. **giocata** *sf (partita)* game;

(*puntata*) stake, bet. **giocatore, -trice** *sm, sf* player; (*d'azzardo*) gambler.

giocattolo [dʒo'kattolo] *sm* toy.

giocherellare [dʒokerel'lare] *v* toy.

giochetto [dʒo'ketto] *sm* (*passatempo*) pastime; (*tranello*) trick; (*lavoro facile*) child's play.

gioco ['dʒɔko] *sm* (*divertimento, tec*) play; (*con regole, partita*) game; (*vizio*) gambling; (*combinazione di carte*) hand; (*posta*) stake; (*beffa*) trick. **entrare in gioco** come into play. **fare il doppio gioco** double-cross. **mettere in gioco** (*far agire*) bring into action; (*rischiare*) stake.

giocoliere [dʒoko'ljere] *sm* juggler.

giocondo [dʒo'kondo] *agg* cheerful, merry.

giogo ['dʒogo] *sm* yoke; (*valico*) pass; (*cima allungata*) ridge.

gioia[1] ['dʒɔja] *sf* joy, delight.

gioia[2] ['dʒɔja] *sf* (*gemma*) jewel.

gioire [dʒo'ire] *v* rejoice. **gioioso** *agg* joyful.

giornalaio [dʒorna'lajo], **-a** *sm, sf* newsagent.

giornale [dʒor'nale] *sm* (*quotidiano*) newspaper; (*registro*) journal; diary. **giornale di bordo** log(-book). **giornale radio** news (bulletin).

giornaliero [dʒorna'ljero] *agg* daily.

giornalismo [dʒorna'lizmo] *sm* journalism. **giornalista** *s*(*m+f*) journalist.

giornata [dʒor'nata] *sf* day. **a giornata** by the day. **di giornata** (*fresco*) fresh; (*di turno*) on duty. **donna a giornata** daily (woman). **vivere alla giornata** live from day to day.

giorno ['dʒorno] *sm* day. **a giorni** (*tra breve*) soon; (*a intervalli*) sometimes. **al giorno** a day. **al giorno d'oggi** nowadays. **che giorno è?** (*data*) what is the date? (*della settimana*) what day (of the week) is it? **da un giorno all'altro** (*improvvisamente*) suddenly; (*tra poco*) any day now. **di giorno** by day. **giorno festivo** holiday. **giorno libero** day off. **punto a giorno** *sm* hem-stitch. **un giorno o l'altro** one of these days.

giostra ['dʒɔstra] *sf* (*fiera*) merry-go-round; (*torneo*) tournament.

giovane ['dʒovane] *agg* young; (*giovanile*) youthful; (*non stagionato*) new. *sm* (*giovanotto*) young man, youth. *sf* young woman, girl. **giovanile** *agg* youthful, juvenile.

giovare [dʒo'vare] *v* help, do good.

giovedì [dʒove'di] *sm* Thursday.

giovenca [dʒo'venka] *sf* heifer.

gioventù [dʒoven'tu] *sf* youth; (*i giovani*) young people *pl*.

giovevole [dʒo'vevole] *agg* useful.

gioviale [dʒo'vjale] *agg* genial, jolly.

giovinezza [dʒovi'nettsa] *sf* (*gioventù*) youth; (*qualità*) youthfulness. **seconda giovinezza** second childhood.

giradischi [dʒira'diski] *sm invar* record player.

giradito [dʒira'dito] *sm* whitlow.

giraffa [dʒi'raffa] *sf* giraffe.

giramento [dʒira'mento] *sm* **giramento di capo** dizzy spell; (*fit of*) dizziness.

girandola [dʒi'randola] *sf* (*fuochi d'artificio*) Catherine wheel; (*giocattolo*) toy windmill; (*fig*) fickle person.

girare [dʒi'rare] *v* turn; (*scansare*) get round, avoid; (*percorrere viaggiando*) travel, tour; (*andare da un posto all'altro*) go around; (*comm*) endorse; (*cinema*) shoot, take; (*camminare senza meta*) wander about; circulate. **girare a vuoto** (*mec*) idle. **mi gira la testa** I feel dizzy or giddy.

girarrosto [dʒirar'rosto] *sm* spit.

girasole [dʒira'sole] *sm* sunflower.

girino [dʒi'rino] *sm* tadpole.

giro ['dʒiro] *sm* turn; (*pista*) lap; (*percorso*) round; (*viaggio*) tour; (*passeggiata a piedi*) stroll, walk; (*in macchina*) drive; (*in bicicletta, a cavallo*) ride; (*periodo*) course, space; circulation; (*mec*) revolution. **andare in giro** go round. **essere in giro** (*fuori*) be out; (*in qualche posto*) be somewhere. **giro collo** neck. **giro d'affari** turnover. **giro d'orizzonte** survey. **giro manica** armhole. **guardarsi in giro** look around. **prendere in giro** make fun of.

gironzolare [dʒirondzo'lare] *v* stroll, wander (about).

girovago [dʒi'rovago] *sm, pl* **-ghi** vagabond, tramp. *agg* wandering. **girovagare** *v* stroll, wander (about).

gita ['dʒita] *sf* excursion, trip. **fare una gita** make an excursion, go on a trip.

giù [dʒu] *avv* down; (*dabbasso*) downstairs. **andare su e giù** (*salire e scendere*) go up and down; (*avanti e indietro*) go to and fro. **giù di lì** thereabouts. **in giù** (*moto*) down; (*stato*) low; (*in meno*) under. **su per giù** thereabouts.

giubba ['dʒubba] *sf* jacket; (*mil*) tunic. **giubbotto di salvataggio** *sm* life-jacket.

giubilare [dʒubi'lare] *v* rejoice.

giubileo [dʒubi'lɛo] *sm* jubilee.

giudaismo [dʒuda'izmo] *sm* Judaism.

giudicare [dʒudi'kare] *v* judge; (*ritenere*) consider. **a giudicare da** judging by. **passare in giudicato** be beyond recall, be final.

giudice ['dʒuditʃe] *sm* judge. **giudice istruttore** examining magistrate.

giudiziario [dʒudi'tsjarjo] *agg* judicial.

giudizio [dʒu'ditsjo] *sm* judgment; (*parere*) opinion; (*dir*) sentence, verdict; (*buon senso*) common sense. **aver giudizio** be sensible. **citare in giudizio** summon. **comparire in giudizio** appear before a court. **dente del giudizio** *sm* wisdom tooth. **far giudizio** behave oneself. **rinviare a giudizio** commit for trial. **giudizioso** *agg* sensible.

giugno ['dʒuɲo] *sm* June.

giulivo [dʒu'livo] *agg* merry.

giullare [dʒul'lare] *sm* (*cantastorie*) minstrel; (*buffone*) clown.

giunco ['dʒunko] *sm* rush.

*****giungere** ['dʒundʒere] *v* arrive (at), reach; (*riuscire*) manage; (*arrivare al punto di*) go so far as. **mi è giunto** I have received. **mi giunge nuovo** it is news to me.

giungla ['dʒungla] *sf* jungle.

giunta[1] ['dʒunta] *sf* addition; (*peso*) makeweight; (*sartoria*) insert. **giuntare** *v* (*unire*) join; (*cucire*) sew together; (*cinema, nastro*) splice.

giunta[2] ['dʒunta] *sf* (*comitato*) council; (*mil*) junta.

giunto ['dʒunto] *sm* joint.

giuntura [dʒun'tura] *sf* joint; (*accoppiamento*) coupling.

giunzione [dʒun'tsjone] *sf* junction; (*giunto*) joint.

giurare [dʒu'rare] *v* swear. **giuramento** *sm* oath. **giuramento falso** (*spergiuro*) perjury. **mancare al giuramento** break an oath. **prestar giuramento** swear, take an oath. **giurato** [dʒu'rato], **-a** *sm*, *sf* juror. *agg* sworn.

giuria [dʒu'ria] *sf* jury.

giuridico [dʒu'ridiko] *agg* legal.

giurisdizione [dʒurizdi'tsjone] *sf* jurisdiction.

*****giustapporre** [dʒustap'porre] *v* juxtapose. **giustapposizione** *sf* juxtaposition.

giustezza [dʒus'tettsa] *sf* correctness; (*esattezza*) precision.

giustificare [dʒustifi'kare] *v* justify. **giustificazione** *sf* justification; (*scusa*) excuse.

giustizia [dʒus'titsja] *sf* justice; (*equità*) fairness. **assicurare alla giustizia** bring to justice. **fare** *or* **rendere giustizia** do justice.

giusto ['dʒusto] *agg* just; (*equo*) fair; (*legittimo*) rightful; (*corretto*) right. *avv* (*proprio, appena*) just; (*esattamente*) correctly. *sm* (*persona*) righteous man.

glaciale [gla'tʃale] *agg* glacial; (*fig*) icy.

gladiolo [gla'diolo] *sm* gladiolus.

glassa ['glassa] *sf* of icing. **glassare** *v* ice.

gli[1] [ʎi] *art* the.

gli[2] [ʎi] *pron* (*persona*) (to) him; (*cosa, animale*) (to) it.

glicerina [glitʃe'rina] *sf* glycerine.

glicine ['glitʃine] *sm* wisteria.

globo ['globo] *sm* globe. **globo oculare** eyeball.

globulo ['globulo] *sm* globule; (*med*) corpuscle. **globulare** *agg* globular.

gloria ['glorja] *sf* glory; (*vanto*) pride. **gloriarsi** *v* glory (in); (*vantarsi*) boast (of).

glorificare [glorifi'kare] *v* glorify.

glucosio [glu'kozjo] *sm* glucose.

gnomo ['ɲomo] *sm* gnome.

gnomone [ɲo'mone] *sm* sundial.

gobba ['gobba] *sf* hump.

gobbo ['gobbo], **-a** *sm*, *sf* hunchback. *agg* hunchbacked.

goccia ['gottʃa] *sf* drop. **goccia a goccia** drop by drop; (*fig*) little by little. **una goccia nel mare** a drop in the ocean. **gocciolare** *v* drip.

*****godere** [go'dere] *v* enjoy; (*rallegrarsi*) rejoice. **godimento** *sm* enjoyment; (*piacere*) pleasure.

goffo ['goffo] *agg* awkward, clumsy. **goffaggine** *sf* awkwardness, clumsiness; (*atto*) clumsy action; (*parola*) blunder.

gol [gol] *sm invar* goal.

gola ['gola] *sf* throat; (*golosità*) greed, gluttony. **aver l'acqua alla gola** be in deep water. **far gola** tempt.

golf[1] [golf] *sm invar* (*sport*) golf.

golf[2] [golf] *sm invar* (*maglione*) sweater, jumper; (*con bottoni*) cardigan.

golfo ['golfo] *sm* gulf.

goliardo [go'ljardo] *sm* (university) student. **goliardico** *agg* university.

goloso [go'lozo] *agg* greedy. **golosità** *sf* greediness, gluttony.

golpe[1] ['golpe] *sf* smut, blight.

golpe[2] ['golpe] *sm* coup (d'état).

gomito ['gomito] *sm* elbow. **gomitata** *sf* dig with the elbow. **farsi avanti a (forza di) gomitate** elbow one's way forward.

gomitolo [go'mitolo] *sm* ball.

gomma ['gomma] *sf* rubber; (*colla*) gum; (*pneumatico*) tyre. **gommapiuma** *sf* foam rubber. **gommato** *agg* rubberized; gummed. **gommoso** *agg* rubbery.

gondola ['gondola] *sf* gondola. **gondoliere** *sm* gondolier.

gonfalone [gonfa'lone] *sm* banner, standard.

gonfiare [gon'fjare] *v* swell (up); (*riempire di gas, ecc.*) inflate, blow up; (*montare*) puff up; exaggerate. **gonfiatura** *sf* blowing up, swelling up; (*gonfiore*) swelling; exaggeration. **gonfio** *agg* swollen, inflated. **gonfiore** *sm* swelling.

gong ['gɔŋ] *sm invar* gong.

gonna ['gonna] *sf also* **gonnella** skirt.

gonorrea [gonor'rɛa] *sf* gonorrhea.

gonzo ['gondzo] *sm* simpleton.

gorgheggiare [gorged'dʒare] *v* trill, warble. **gorgheggio** *sm* trill, warble; (*di uccello*) warbling.

gorgo ['gorgo] *sm* whirlpool.

gorgogliare [gorgoʎʎare] *v* gurgle; (*intestino*) rumble. **gorgoglio** *sm* rumble; gurgle.

gorilla [go'rilla] *sm invar* gorilla.

gotico ['gɔtiko] *agg* Gothic.

gotta ['gotta] *sf* gout.

governante [gover'nante] *sf* (*incaricata della casa*) housekeeper; (*istitutrice*) governess.

governare [gover'nare] *v* govern; (*dirigere*) run; (*dominare*) rule; (*pilotare*) steer. **governativo** *agg* government, governmental. **governatore** *sm* governor. **governo** *sm* government; (*dominio*) rule; (*amministrazione*) management. **governo della casa** housekeeping.

gozzo ['goddzo] *sm* crop; (*med*) goitre. **averla nel or sul gozzo** be unable to swallow.

gozzovigliare [goddzoviʎʎare] *v* revel, go on a spree.

gracchiare [grak'kjare] *v* croak.

gracidare [gratʃi'dare] *v* croak.

gracile ['gratʃile] *agg* frail. **gracilità** *sf* frailty.

gradasso [gra'dasso] *sm* boaster, braggart. **fare il gradasso** boast, brag.

gradazione [grada'tsjone] *sf* gradation; (*sfumatura*) shade. **gradazione alcolica** alcoholic strength.

gradevole [gra'devole] *agg* agreeable.

gradiente [gra'djɛnte] *sm* gradient.

gradimento [gradi'mento] *sm* (*approvazione*) liking; (*piacere*) pleasure.

gradino [gra'dino] *sm* step. **gradinata** *sf* flight of steps.

gradire [gra'dire] *v* (*trovar piacevole*) find agreeable; (*accogliere con gioia*) welcome; (*accettare*) accept; (*nelle richieste*) like.

grado[1] ['grado] *sm* degree; (*mil, rango*) rank. **a gradi** step by step. **avanzare di grado** be promoted. **essere in grado di** be able to.

grado[2] ['grado] *sm* **di buon grado** willingly.

graduale [gradu'ale] *agg* gradual.

graduare [gradu'are] *v* graduate. **graduatoria** *sf* (*elenco*) list; (*ordine*) classification.

graffa ['graffa] *sf* bracket; (*fermaglio*) (paper-)clip.

graffiare [graf'fjare] *v* scratch. **graffiatura** *sf* scratch. **graffio** *sm* scratch.

grafico [gra'fico] *agg* graphic. *sm* (*diagramma*) chart, graph; (*persona*) graphic artist.

grafologo [gra'fɔlogo], **-a** *sm, sf* graphologist.

gramigna [gra'miɲa] *sf* couch-grass; (*malerba*) weed. **attaccarsi come la gramigna** cling like a leech.

grammatico [gram'matiko] *agg* grammatical. *sm* grammarian. **grammatica** *sm* grammar; (*persona*) grammarian.

grammo ['grammo] *sm* gram.

grammofono [gram'mofono] *sm* gramophone.

grana[1] ['grana] *sf* (*struttura*) grain. *sm* (*formaggio*) Parmesan (cheese).

grana[2] ['grana] *sf* (*seccatura*) nuisance. **piantare una grana** make trouble.

granaglie [gra'naʎe] *sf pl* cereals *pl*.

granaio [gra'najo] *sm* barn; (*zona produttrice di grano*) granary; (*locale sottotetto*) loft.

granata[1] [gra'nata] *sf* (*scopa*) broom.

granata[2] [gra'nata] *sf* (*mil*) grenade.

granata[3] [gra'nata] *sf* (*frutto*) pomegranate; (*pietra*) garnet.

Gran Bretagna ·[gran bre'taɲa] *sf* Great Britain.

grancassa [gran'kassa] *sf* (*musica*) bass drum. **batter la grancassa** blow one's own trumpet.

granchio [grankjo] *sm* crab. **prendere un granchio** make a blunder.

grande ['grande] *agg* big; (*ampio, numeroso*) large; (*largo*) wide; (*fig*) great; (*adulto*) grown-up. **in grande** on a large scale. **in gran parte** largely. **non ... un gran che** not ... much.

grandeggiare [granded'dʒare] *v* (*emergere*) tower, stand out; (*darsi arie*) show off.

grandezza [gran'dettsa] *sf* (*dimensione, taglia*) size; (*altezza*) height; (*larghezza*) width; (*ampiezza*) breadth; (*fig*) greatness; (*mat, fis*) magnitude.

grandinare [grandi'nare] *v* hail. **grandine** *sf* hail. **chicco di grandine** *sm* hailstone.

grandioso [gran'djozo] *agg* grand.

granduca [gran'duka] *sm, pl* -**chi** grand duke. **granducato** *sm* grand duchy. **granduchessa** *sf* grand duchess.

granello [gra'nɛllo] *sm* grain; (*di frutta*) pip. **granello di pepe** peppercorn.

granita [gra'nita] *sf* crushed-ice drink.

granito [gra'nito] *sm* granite.

grano ['grano] *sm* (*granello*) grain; (*frumento*) wheat; (*cereale in genere*) corn, cereal.

granturco [gran'turko] *sm* maize.

granulo ['granulo] *sm* granule. **granulare** *agg* granular.

grappolo ['grappolo] *sm* bunch.

grasso ['grasso] *agg* fat; (*unto*) greasy, oily; (*che contiene grasso*) fatty. *sm* fat; (*sostanza untuosa*) grease. **grassoccio** *agg* plump.

grata ['grata] *sf* grating, grille. **gratella** *sf* grill.

graticcio [gra'tittʃo] *sm* trellis.

graticola [gra'tikola] *sf* grill.

gratifica [gra'tifika] *sf* bonus.

gratis ['gratis] *agg* free. *avv* for nothing, for love.

gratitudine [grati'tudine] *sf* gratitude.

grato ['grato] *agg* grateful, obliged; (*gradevole*) pleasant; (*gradito*) welcome.

grattacapo [gratta'kapo] *sm* worry, headache.

grattacielo [gratta'tʃɛlo] *sm* skyscraper.

grattare [grat'tare] *v* scratch; (*grattugiare*)

grate; (*raschiare*) scrape; (*fam: rubare*) pinch.

grattugiare [grattu'dʒare] *v* grate. **grattugia** *sf* grater.

gratuito [gra'tuito] *agg* free; (*non retribuito*) unpaid; (*ingiustificato*) gratuitous; (*infondato*) unfounded.

gravare [gra'vare] *v* burden.

grave ['grave] *agg* (*serio*) grave; (*pesante*) heavy; (*malattia*) serious; (*perdita*) grievous. **gravità** *sf* gravity. **gravoso** *agg* hard, onerous.

gravido ['gravido] *agg* pregnant. **gravidanza** *sf* pregnancy.

grazia ['gratsja] *sf* grace; (*fascino*) charm; (*clemenza*) pardon; (*favore*) favour. **grazie** *sm pl, inter* thanks. **grazie a** thanks to.

Grecia ['grɛtʃa] *sf* Greece. **greco, -a** *s, agg, m pl* -**ci** Greek. **naso greco** sm Grecian nose.

gregge ['greddʒe] *sm* flock, herd.

greggio ['greddʒo] *agg* raw, crude.

grembiule [grem'bjule] *sm* apron; (*con petto*) pinafore; (*con maniche*) overall.

grembo ['grembo] *sm* lap.

gremire [gre'mire] *v* fill (up). **gremirsi** *v* get crowded.

gres [grɛs] *sm* stoneware.

gretto ['gretto] *agg* mean; (*idea, animo*) narrow-minded. **grettezza** *sf* meanness; narrow-mindedness.

gridare [gri'dare] *v* shout; (*strillare*) yell, scream. **gridare aiuto** call for help. **grido** *sm, pl* -**a** *f* shout; cry; scream, yell. **di grido** (*noto*) famous; (*di moda*) fashionable. **l'ultimo grido** the latest fashion, the last word.

griffa ['griffa] *sf* claw.

grigio ['gridʒo] *agg* grey; (*fig*) drab. *sm* grey. **grigiastro** *agg* greyish. **grigiore** *sm* greyness; (*fig*) drabness. **grigioverde** *sm, agg* grey-green, khaki.

griglia ['griʎa] *sf* grill; (*saracinesca*) shutter; (*schermo*) grille; (*radio*) grid; (*focolare*) grate.

grilletto [gril'letto] *sm* trigger.

grillo ['grillo] *sm* cricket; (*capriccio*) whim. **gli è saltato il grillo di** he got it into his head to.

grimaldello [grimal'dello] *sm* jemmy.

grinza ['grintsa] *sf* crease; (*ruga*) wrinkle. **non fare una grinza** (*calzare bene*) fit perfectly; (*filare bene*) be flawless.

gripparsi [grip'parsi] *v* (*auto*) seize up.

grondaia [gron'daja] sf gutter.

grondare [gron'dare] v drip; (abbondantemente) pour.

groppa [grɔppa] sf back.

grossa [grɔssa] sf (comm) gross. **dormire della grossa** sleep like a log.

grossezza [gros'settsa] sf (volume) bulk, size; (spessore) thickness.

grossista [gros'sista] s(m+f) wholesaler.

grosso [grɔsso] agg large, big; (spesso) thick; (non raffinato) coarse; serious. **dirle grosse** tell fibs. **farne di grosse** cause all sorts of trouble. **grossolano** agg coarse, rough.

grotta [grɔtta] sf cave; grotto.

grottesco [grot'tesko] agg grotesque.

groviera [gro'vjɛra] s(m+f) also **gruviera** (formaggio) gruyère.

groviglio [gro'viʎo] sm tangle; (confusione) mess.

gru [gru] sf crane.

gruccia [gruttʃa] sf crutch; (attaccapanni) coat-hanger.

grugnire [gru'ɲire] v grunt. **grugnito** sm grunt.

grugno ['gruɲo] sm (maiale) snout; (fam: muso) mug.

grullo ['grullo] agg foolish.

grumo ['grumo] sm clot.

gruppo ['gruppo] sm group; (mec) unit.

gruviera [gru'vjɛra] V **groviera**.

gruzzolo ['gruttsolo] sm pile; (risparmi) nest-egg.

guadagnare [gwada'ɲare] v earn; (ottenere) gain; (vincere) win; (raggiungere) reach; (risparmiare) save.

guadagno [gwa'daɲo] sm (retribuzione) earnings pl; profit; advantage.

guado ['gwado] sm ford. **guadare** v wade.

guaina [gwa'ina] sf sheath.

guaio ['gwajo] sm trouble. **guai** inter woe betide you, us, etc.

guaire [gwa'ire] v whine, yelp. **guaito** sm whine, yelp.

guancia [gwantʃa] sf cheek. **guanciale** sm pillow.

guanto ['gwanto] sm glove. **calzare come un guanto** fit like a glove. **gettare il guanto** throw down the gauntlet. **trattare coi guanti** treat with kid gloves.

guardaboschi [gwarda'boski] sm forester.

guardacaccia [gwarda'kattʃa] sm invar gamekeeper.

guardacoste [gwarda'kɔste] sm invar coastguard.

guardalinee [gwarda'linee] sm invar (sport) linesman.

guardamano [gwarda'mano] sm invar (sciabola) hilt; (fucile) guard; (guanto) protective glove.

guardare [gwar'dare] v look (at); (affacciarsi) look out; face; (dare un'occhiata) have a look; (custodire) look after, mind; (stare a vedere) watch; (considerare) view; (cercare) try to, be careful to. **andare a guardare** have a look. **Dio ne guardi!** God forbid! **guarda che roba!** just look at that! **guardar di sbieco** or **traverso** look askance (at). **guardare fisso** stare, gaze (at). **guarda un po'!** well, well!

guardaroba [gwarda'rɔba] sm invar (luogo) cloakroom; (armadio) wardrobe. **guardarobiera** sf cloakroom attendant.

guardarsi [gwar'darsi] v look at oneself. **guardarsi intorno** look around. **guardarsi da** (fare attenzione a) beware of; (astenersi da) refrain from. **me ne guardo bene!** heaven forbid!

guardata [gwar'data] sf look, glance.

guardavia [gwarda'via] sm invar guardrail.

guardia ['gwardja] sf (custodia) watch, guard; (turno) duty; (custode) keeper, watchman; (sentinella) sentry; (sport) guard. **essere di guardia** be on duty; (mil) be on guard duty. **fare la guardia** (sorvegliare) guard, watch; (badare) watch over. **guardia di finanza** (corpo) Customs pl; (singolo) Customs officer. **mettere in guardia** warn. **guardiano** sm keeper, guardian.

guardingo [gwar'dingo] agg cautious, wary.

guarire [gwa'rire] v cure; (rimettersi in salute) recover; (ferita) heal. **guarigione** sf recovery; healing.

guarnigione [gwarni'dʒone] sf garrison.

guarnire [gwar'nire] v decorate; (vestiario) trim; (gastr) garnish; (corredare) equip; (mil) garrison. **guarnizione** sf decoration, trimming, garnish; (tec) packing; (auto) gasket.

guastafeste [gwasta'feste] s(m+f) invar spoilsport.

guastamestieri [gwastames'tieri] s(m+f) invar bungler; (fam) menace.

guastare [gwas'tare] v spoil; (rovinare) ruin, damage. **guastarsi** v (cibi) go bad; (mec) break down; (tempo) change for the worse. **guasto** agg (cibo) bad, rotten; (mec) broken; (salute, ecc.) bad.

guazzabuglio [gwattsa'buʎo] sm hotchpotch, jumble.

guazzare [gwat'tsare] v splash about; (fig) wallow. **guazzo** sm pool; (pittura) gouache.

guercio ['gwertʃo] agg cross-eyed.

guerra ['gwɛrra] sf war; (il guerreggiare) warfare. **far guerra** wage war. **guerra mondiale** world war. **guerrafondaio** sm, sf warmonger.

guerreggiare [gwerred'dʒare] v fight.

guerresco [gwer'resko] agg (bellicoso) warlike; (di guerra) war.

guerriero [gwer'rjɛro] agg (bellicoso) warlike; (combattivo) aggressive. sm warrior.

guerriglia [gwer'riʎa] sf guerrilla warfare. **guerrigliero** sm guerrilla.

gufo ['gufo] sm owl.

guglia ['guʎa] sf (arch) spire; (geog) pinnacle.

guida ['gwida] sf guide; (direzione, comando) guidance, leadership; (tappeto) runner; (elenco) directory; (auto) drive, driving; (comandi) controls pl. **esame (di) guida** sm driving test. **guida a destra/sinistra** right-/left-hand drive. **scuola (di) guida** sf driving school.

guidare [gwi'dare] v guide; (dirigere, comandare) lead; (auto) drive; (aero) fly; (nave) steer; (moto) ride. **guidatore, -trice** sm, sf driver.

guinzaglio [gwin'tsaʎo] sm leash, lead. **mettere il guinzaglio** (fig) keep a tight rein (on). **tenere al guinzaglio** keep on a leash.

guisa ['gwiza] sf **a** or **in guisa di** in the manner of, like.

guizzare [gwit'tsare] v (lampo) flash; (pesci) dart; (sfuggire) wriggle; (fiamma) flicker. **guizzo** sm flash; dart; flicker.

guscio ['guʃo] sm shell; (legumi) pod.

gustare [gus'tare] v taste; (trovar buono) enjoy. **gusto** sm taste; (piacere) enjoyment. **con gusto** tastefully. **di gusto** heartily. **non aver gusto** be tasteless. **prenderci gusto** take a liking (to). **senza gusto** tasteless.

gutturale [guttu'rale] agg guttural.

H

hascisc [a'ʃiʃ] sm hashish.
hockey ['hɔki] sm hockey.

I

i [i] art the.
iattanza [jat'tantsa] sf arrogance.
ibernazione [iberna'tsjone] sf hibernation. **ibernare** v hibernate.
ibrido ['ibrido] sm, agg hybrid.
Iddio [id'dio] sm God.
idea [i'dɛa] sf idea; opinion; (proposito) intention. **cambiare idea** change one's mind. **dare l'idea** give the impression.
ideale [ide'ale] sm, agg ideal. **idealismo** sm idealism. **idealista** s(m+f) idealist. **idealistico** agg idealistic.
identico [i'dɛntiko] agg identical.
identificare [identifi'kare] v identify. **identificazione** sf identification.
identità [identi'ta] sf identity.
ideologia [ideolo'dʒia] sf ideology. **ideologico** agg ideological.
idillio [i'dilljo] sm idyll. **idillico** agg idyllic.
idioma [i'djɔma] sm language. **frase idiomatica** sf idiom.
idiota [i'kjɔta] s(m+f) idiot, fool. agg idiotic, stupid.
idiotismo [idjo'tizmo] sm (lingua) idiom; (med) idiocy.
idiozia [idjo'tsia] sf idiocy; stupidity.
idolo ['idolo] sm idol. **idoleggiare** v idolize.
idoneo [i'dɔneo] agg fit, suitable; (capace) able. **non idoneo** unfit, unsuitable. **idoneità** sf ability, suitability.
idrante [i'drante] sm hydrant. **idratante** agg (crema) moisturizing.
idraulico [i'drauliko] agg hydraulic. sm plumber. **idraulica** sf hydraulics.
idroelettrico [idroe'lettriko] agg hydroelectric.
idroestrattore [idroestrat'tore] sm spindrier.
idrofilo [i'drɔfilo] agg **cotone idrofilo** sm cotton-wool.

idrofobia [i'drɔfobia] *sf* rabies, hydrophobia. **idrofobo** *agg* rabid, hydrophobic.

idrogeno [i'drɔdʒɛːo] *sm* hydrogen.

idrosci [idro'ʃi] *sm* water-skiing.

idrovolante [idrovo'lante] *sm* seaplane.

iena ['jɛna] *sf* hyena.

ieri ['jɛri] *avv, sm* yesterday. **ieri l'altro** the day before yesterday. **tutto ieri** all day yesterday.

iettatore [jetta'tore] *sm* jinx. **iettatura** *sf* bad luck; (*malocchio*) evil eye.

igiene [i'dʒɛne] *sf* hygiene. **igienico** *agg* hygienic; (*sano*) healthy. **assorbente igienico** *sm* sanitary towel. **carta igienica** *sf* toilet paper.

iglù [i'glu] *sm* igloo.

ignaro [i'ɲaro] *agg* unaware, ignorant.

ignobile [i'ɲɔbile] *agg* mean, base.

ignominia [iɲo'minja] *sf* disgrace.

ignorante [iɲo'rante] *agg* ignorant; (*non colto*) uneducated. *s(m+f)* ignoramus. **ignoranza** *sf* ignorance.

ignorare [iɲo'rare] *v* (*non sapere*) not know; (*trascurare, fingere di non conoscere*) ignore.

ignoto [i'ɲɔto] *agg* unknown. *sm* (*concetto*) unknown; (*persona*) unknown person.

ignudo [i'ɲudo] *agg* naked.

il [il] *art* the.

ilare ['ilare] *agg* cheerful. **ilarità** *sf* (*allegria*) cheerfulness; (*riso*) hilarity.

illecito [il'letʃito] *agg* illicit, unlawful.

illegale [ille'gale] *agg* illegal, unlawful. **illegalità** *sf* illegality.

illeggibile [illed'dʒibile] *agg* illegible; (*fig*) unreadable.

illegittimo [ille'dʒittimo] *agg* illegitimate. **illegittimità** *sf* illegitimacy.

illeso [il'lezo] *agg* unhurt.

illibato [illi'bato] *agg* pure, chaste.

illimitato [illimi'tato] *agg* unlimited, boundless.

illogico [il'lɔdʒiko] *agg* illogical, unsound. **illogicità** *sf* illogicality.

*****illudere** [il'ludere] *v* deceive, fool. **illudersi** *v* delude oneself.

illuminare [illumi'nare] *v* light, illuminate; (*rischiarare*) light up; (*mostrare la verità*) enlighten; (*a giorno*) floodlight. **illuminazione** *sf* illumination, lighting. **illuminismo** *sm* Enlightenment.

illusione [illu'zjone] *sf* illusion; impression. **farsi (delle) illusioni** delude oneself;

(*fam*) kid oneself. **non farsi (delle) illusioni** have no illusions. **illusionista** *s(m+f)* conjurer.

illusorio [illu'zɔrjo] *agg* illusory, vain.

illustrare [illus'trare] *v* illustrate; (*spiegare*) explain. **illustrativo** *agg* explanatory. **illustrato** *agg* illustrated. **illustratore, -trice** *sm, sf* illustrator. **illustrazione** *sf* illustration, explanation.

illustre [il'lustre] *agg* famous, illustrious. **illustre ignoto** *sm* nobody.

imbaccuccare [imbakuk'kare] *v* wrap up.

imballare[1] [imbal'lare] *v* pack; (*involucro*) wrap; (*in scatole*) box; (*in casse*) crate. **imballaggio** *sm* packing; wrapping; boxing; crating.

imballare[2] [imbal'lare] *v* (*auto*) race.

imbalsamare [imbalsa'mare] *v* embalm. **imbalsamatore, -trice** *sm, sf* embalmer; (*di animali*) taxidermist.

imbambolato [imbambo'lato] *agg* bewildered.

imbandierare [imbandje'rare] *v* deck with flags.

imbandire [imban'dire] *v* prepare.

imbarazzare [imbarat'tsare] *v* embarrass; (*impedire*) hamper; (*ostacolare*) block, hinder. **imbarazzo** *sm* embarrassment; (*impaccio*) hindrance, trouble. **essere in imbarazzo** be in a difficult situation, be in a fix; (*scelta difficile*) be in a quandary. **mettere in imbarazzo** (*in situazione difficile*) put in a spot; (*a disagio*) make ill at ease.

imbarcare [imbar'kare] *v* take aboard. **imbarcarsi** *v* embark. **imbarcazione** *sf* craft, boat. **imbarco** *sm* embarkation; (*merci*) shipment.

imbastire [imbas'tire] *v* (*cucire*) tack; (*tracciare sommariamente*) draw up, outline.

imbattersi [im'battersi] *v* come across; (*fam*) bump into.

imbattibile [imbat'tibile] *agg* invincible, unbeatable.

imbavagliare [imbava'ʎare] *v* gag.

imbecille [imbe'tʃille] *agg* stupid, idiotic. *s(m+f)* fool, idiot; (*med*) imbecile.

imbellettare [imbellet'tare] *v* make up; (*fig*) embellish.

imbellire [imbel'lire] *v* beautify.

imbevuto [imbe'vuto] *agg* steeped (in), imbued (with).

imbiancare [imbjan'kare] *v* whiten; (*muri*

whitewash; (candeggiare) bleach. **imbianchino** sm house-painter.

imbizzarrirsi [imbiddzar'rirsi] v get excited.

imboccare [imbok'kare] v (cibo) feed; (suggerire) prompt; enter; (portare alla bocca) put to one's mouth. **imboccatura** sf mouth; entrance; (bocchino) mouthpiece.

imbonire [imbo'nire] v entice, talk into buying. **imbonimento** sm (discorso) salestalk; (elogio immeritato) build-up.

imboscata [imbos'kata] sf ambush. **imboscato** sm shirker, (draft-)dodger.

imbottigliare [imbotti'ʎare] v bottle; (mil) blockade; (traffico) jam.

imbottire [imbot'tire] v stuff; (sarto) pad, wad. **coperta imbottita** sf quilt. **panino imbottito** sm (discorso) sandwich. **imbottitura** sf stuffing; padding; wadding.

imbrattare [imbrat'tare] v soil, dirty.

imbrigliare [imbri'ʎare] v build-up.

imbroccare [imbrok'kare] v (azzeccare) get right.

imbrogliare [imbro'ʎare] v (gabbare) cheat; (mettere in disordine) mix up, muddle up; (ingarbugliare) tangle (up). **imbroglio** sm (faccenda confusa) muddle, mess; (groviglio) tangle; (raggiro) trick, swindle. **imbroglione, -a** sm, sf cheat, trickster, swindler.

imbronciarsi [imbron'tʃarsi] v sulk; (cielo) cloud over.

imbrunire [imbru'nire] v darken, get dark. sm nightfall.

imbruttire [imbrut'tire] v spoil.

imbucare [imbu'kare] v post.

imburrare [imbur'rare] v butter.

imbuto [im'buto] sm funnel.

imitare [imi'tare] v imitate. **imitazione** sf imitation.

immagazzinare [immagaddzi'nare] v store.

immaginare [immadʒi'nare] v imagine. **s'immagini!** (tutt'altro) not in the least! (certamente) by all means! **immaginario** agg imaginary. **immaginazione** sf imagination.

immagine [im'madʒine] sf image; (figura, ritratto) picture. **immagine reflessa** reflection.

immancabile [imman'kabile] agg unfailing, certain.

immangiabile [imman'dʒabile] agg inedible, uneatable.

immatricolarsi [immatriko'larsi] v register, enrol.

immaturo [imma'turo] agg unripe; (fig) immature; (prematuro) untimely.

immedesimarsi [immedezi'marsi] v identify oneself (with).

immediato [imme'djato] agg immediate. **immediatamente** avv immediately; directly; (subito) at once.

immemorabile [immemo'rabile] agg immemorial.

immemore [im'mɛmore] agg heedless, forgetful.

immenso [im'mɛnso] agg huge, vast; enormous. **immensità** sf hugeness, immensity; (gran numero) mass, enormous number.

*****immergere** [im'mɛrdʒere] v immerse; (intingere) dip; (con forza, tuffare) plunge; (sottomarino) submerge. **immersione** sf immersion; (tuffo) dive.

immeritato [immeri'tato] agg undeserved.

immeritevole agg undeserving.

*****immettere** [im'mettere] v admit, introduce.

immigrare [immi'grare] v immigrate. **immigrante** s(m+f), agg immigrant. **immigrato, -a** s, agg immigrant. **immigrazione** sf immigration.

imminente [immi'nɛnte] agg imminent. **imminenza** sf imminence.

immischiare [immis'kjare] v involve, mix up. **immischiarsi** v get involved, interfere.

immobile [im'mobile] agg (che non si muove) motionless, still; (che non si può muovere) immovable. **società immobiliare** sf building society. **immobilità** sf immobility, stillness. **beni immobili** sm pl real estate sing.

immobilizzare [immobilid'dzare] v immobilize; (econ) tie up.

immoderato [immode'rato] agg excessive. **immoderatezza** sf excessiveness; (smoderatezza) lack of moderation.

immodesto [immo'desto] agg conceited, immodest.

immolare [immo'lare] v sacrifice.

immondo [im'mondo] agg filthy. **immondezzaio** sm rubbish dump. **immondizia** sf (sporcizia) filth; (spazzatura) rubbish, garbage.

immorale [immo'rale] agg immoral.

immortale [immor'tale] agg immortal. **immortalare** v immortalize. **immortalità** sf immortality.

immune [im'mune] *agg* immune, free. **immunità** *sf* immunity. **immunizzare** *v* immunize.

immutabile [immu'tabile] *agg* immutable, unchangeable; *(costante)* unswerving. **immutabilità** *sf* immutability; firmness. **immutato** *agg* unchanged, unfailing.

impacchettare [impakket'tare] *v* parcel up, package.

impacciare [impat'tfare] *v* hamper, hinder. **impaccio** *sm* obstacle, hindrance; *(situazione imbarazzante)* fix, predicament. **impacciato** *agg* awkward; *(imbarazzato)* ill at ease; *(goffo)* clumsy.

impadronirsi [impadro'nirsi] *v* **impadronirsi di** seize, take possession of; *(imparare a fondo)* master.

impagabile [impa'gabile] *agg* invaluable, priceless.

impalcatura [impalka'tura] *sf* *(struttura provvisoria)* scaffolding; *(struttura di sostegno)* framework; *(cervo)* antlers *pl*.

impallidire [impalli'dire] *v* turn pale; *(fig)* fade; *(offuscarsi)* grow dim.

impanare[1] [impa'nare] *v* *(mec)* thread.

impanare[2] [impa'nare] *v* *(gastr)* dip in breadcrumbs.

impannata [impan'nata] *sf* window-frame.

impantanarsi [impanta'narsi] *v* get bogged down.

imparare [impa'rare] *v* learn. **imparare a memoria** learn by heart.

impareggiabile [impared'dʒabile] *agg* incomparable.

impartire [impar'tire] *v* give, impart.

imparziale [impar'tsjale] *agg* impartial, unbiased; *(giusto)* fair.

impassibile [impas'sibile] *agg* impassive, unmoved.

impastare [impas'tare] *v* *(pane)* knead; *(lavorare)* mix; *(incollare)* paste. **impastatrice** *sf* mixer. **impasto** *sm* mixture.

impatto [im'patto] *sm* impact.

impaurire [impau'rire] *v* frighten.

impaziente [impa'tsjente] *agg* impatient; *(desideroso)* anxious. **impazientirsi** *v* lose one's patience.

impazzare [impat'tsare] *v* be in full swing; *(gastr)* curdle. **all'impazzata** wildly.

impazzire [impat'tsire] *v* go mad. **far impazzire** drive mad.

impeccabile [impek'kabile] *agg* impeccable.

impedire [impe'dire] *v* prevent; *(sbarrare)* block; *(impacciare)* hinder. **impedimento** *sm* impediment; obstacle; *(l'impedire)* prevention.

impegnare [impe'nare] *v* *(dare in pegno)* pledge; *(tenere impegnato)* engage; *(obbligare)* bind; *(tenere occupato)* take up; *(prenotare)* book. **impegnarsi** *v* undertake, strive. **impegnativo** *agg* *(lavoro)* exacting, demanding; *(promessa)* binding. **impegnato** *agg* engaged; *(vincolato)* pledged; *(pol)* committed. **impegno** *sm* engagement; obligation; commitment; *(zelo)* eagerness, enthusiasm.

impenetrabile [impene'trabile] *agg* impenetrable, impervious.

impenitente [impeni'tɛnte] *agg* unrepentant. **scapolo impenitente** *sm* confirmed bachelor.

impennarsi [impen'narsi] *v* flare up; *(cavallo)* rear (up); *(aereo)* go into a climb.

impensabile [impen'sabile] *agg* unthinkable.

impensato [impen'sato] *agg* unforeseen.

impensierirsi [impensje'rirsi] *v* worry.

imperativo [impera'tivo] *sm*, *agg* imperative. **imperare** *v* rule.

imperatore [impera'tore] *sm* emperor. **imperatrice** *sf* empress.

impercettibile [impertʃet'tibile] *agg* imperceptible.

imperdonabile [imperdo'nabile] *agg* unforgivable.

imperfetto [imper'fetto] *agg* faulty, defective. *sm* imperfect (tense). **imperfezione** *sf* defect.

imperioso [impe'rjozo] *agg* imperious; *(ineluttabile)* pressing, impelling.

impermalirsi [imperma'lirsi] *v* take umbrage, take offence.

impermeabile [imperme'abile] *sm* raincoat. *agg* impervious; *(all'acqua)* waterproof; *(all'aria)* airtight. **impermeabilizzare** *v* waterproof.

imperniare [imper'njare] *v* hinge; *(fondare)* base.

impero [im'pero] *sm* *(territorio)* empire; *(autorità)* rule.

imperscrutabile [imperskru'tabile] *agg* inscrutable.

impersonale [imperso'nale] *agg* impersonal.

impersonare [imperso'nare] v (*simboleggiare*) personify; (*attore*) impersonate. **impersonarsi** v be the personification (of).

imperterrito [imper'territo] agg undaunted; unperturbed.

impertinente [imperti'nente] agg impertinent, cheeky.

imperturbabile [impertur'babile] agg unruffled, imperturbable, calm. **imperturbato** agg unperturbed, unruffled.

impeto ['impeto] sm impetus, force; (*accesso*) outburst. **agire d'impeto** act on impulse.

impettito [impet'tito] agg stiff, erect. **camminare impettito** strut.

impetuoso [impetu'wozo] agg impetuous.

impiallacciato [impjallat'tʃato] agg veneered. **impiallacciatura** sf veneer.

impiantare [impjan'tare] v set up; (*fondare*) establish; (*tec*) install. **impianto** sm plant, installation; (*fondazione*) establishment.

impiantito [impjan'tito] sm flooring.

impiastrare [impjas'trare] v smear. **impiastro** sm (*cataplasma*) poultice; (*persona uggiosa*) bore.

impiccare [impik'kare] v hang. **impiccato** sm hanged man.

impicciare [impit'tʃare] v be in the way, hamper. **impicciarsi** v meddle, interfere. **impiccio** [im'pittʃo] sm (*ostacolo*) hindrance; (*guaio*) mess, trouble. **essere d'impiccio** v be in the way.

impiegare [impje'gare] v employ; spend. **impiegatizio** agg clerical. **impiegato, -a** sm, sf employee; (*funzionario*) official. **impiegati** pl (*collettivo*) staff sing, personnel sing.

impiego [im'pjɛgo] sm, pl **-ghi** use; (*denaro*) investment; (*posto, occupazione*) employment, job.

impietrito [impje'trito] agg petrified.

impigliarsi [impiʎ'ʎarsi] v get entangled, get mixed up.

impiparsi [impi'parsi] v (*fam*) not care a damn.

implacabile [impla'kabile] agg implacable.

implicare [impli'kare] v (*coinvolgere*) involve; (*comportare*) imply, entail.

implicito [im'plitʃito] agg implicit.

implorare [implo'rare] v implore, entreat.

impolverare [impolve'rare] v cover with dust.

imponderabile [imponde'rabile] agg imponderable.

imponente [impo'nente] agg imposing, impressive.

imponibile [impo'nibile] agg taxable. sm taxable income.

impopolare [impopo'lare] agg unpopular. **impopolarità** sf unpopularity.

*****imporre** [im'porre] v impose; (*costringere*) oblige; (*ordinare*) order; (*comportare*) involve. **imporsi** v (*farsi valere*) assert oneself; (*incontrar favore*) go down well; (*rendersi necessario*) become necessary.

importante [impor'tante] agg important. sm important thing, main point. **importanza** sf importance. **di nessuna importanza** unimportant.

importare [impor'tare] v (*aver peso*) matter; (*comportare*) involve; (*introdurre dall'estero*) import. **non importa!** it doesn't matter! never mind! **non me ne importa niente!** (*fam*) I couldn't care less!

importazione [importa'tsjone] sf import; (*atto*) importation.

importo [im'porto] sm amount.

importunare [importu'nare] v trouble, bother. **importuno** agg troublesome, tiresome, boring.

imposizione [impozi'tsjone] sf imposition.

impossessarsi [imposses'sarsi] v get hold of, seize.

impossibile [impos'sibile] agg impossible. **fare l'impossibile** do all one can. **impossibilità** sf impossibility.

imposta[1] [im'posta] sf (*finestra*) shutter.

imposta[2] [im'posta] sf (*econ*) tax, duty.

impostare[1] [impos'tare] v (*spedire*) post.

impostare[2] [impos'tare] v (*avviare*) get under way; (*questione, ecc.*) set out, state; (*nave*) lay down; (*voce*) pitch. **impostazione** sf approach.

impostore [impos'tore] sm imposter.

impotente [impo'tente] agg powerless; (*med*) impotent. **impotenza** sf powerlessness; impotence.

impoverire [impove'rire] v impoverish. **impoverimento** sm impoverishment.

impraticabile [imprati'kabile] agg (*strada*) impassable; (*campo sportivo*) unfit for play.

impratichirsi [imprati'kirsi] v practise.

imprecare [impre'kare] v curse. **imprecazione** sf curse.

impreciso [impre't∫izo] agg (inesatto) inaccurate; (indeterminato) imprecise, vague. **imprecisabile** agg indefinable. **imprecisione** sf inaccuracy; vagueness.

impregnare [impre'nare] v impregnate; (fig) imbue; (inzuppare) soak.

imprenditore [imprendi'tore] sm contractor; entrepreneur. **imprenditore di pompe funebri** undertaker. **imprenditore edile** building contractor. **piccolo imprenditore** tradesman.

impreparato [imprepa'rato] agg unprepared; (lavoro) untrained. **impreparazione** sf unpreparedness; lack of training.

impresa [im'preza] sf undertaking, enterprise; (azienda) concern, firm; (azione) deed; (azione pericolosa) exploit. **impresario** sm entrepreneur; (theatre) manager, impresario.

imprescindibile [impreʃin'dibile] agg that cannot be disregarded.

impressionare [impressjo'nare] v make an impression; (spaventare) frighten; (turbare) shock, upset; (foto) expose. **impressionarsi** v be upset, be shocked; be affected. **impressionabile** agg impressionable, easily affected; easily frightened. **impressionante** agg striking, impressive; frightening; upsetting. **impressione** sf impression; sensation.

imprestare [impres'tare] v lend.

imprevidenza [imprevi'dentsa] sf lack of foresight. **imprevedibile** agg unforeseeable. **imprevidente** agg heedless.

imprevisto [impre'visto] agg unforeseen. **salvo imprevisti** if all goes well.

imprigionare [impridʒo'nare] v imprison.

*__imprimere__ [im'primere] v imprint, impress; (dare) impart; (pittura) prime.

improbabile [impro'babile] agg unlikely, improbable. **improbabilità** sf unlikelihood.

improduttivo [improdut'tivo] agg unproductive.

impronta [im'pronta] sf impression, mark, stamp. **impronta del piede** footprint. **impronta digitale** fingerprint. **improntare** v stamp. **all'impronto** at sight.

improprio [im'proprjo] agg (inadatto) inappropriate; (inopportuno) out of place; (mat) improper.

improrogabile [improro'gabile] agg termine **improrogabile** sm deadline.

improvvisare [improvvi'zare] v improvise. **improvvisamente** avv suddenly, all of a sudden. **improvvisata** sf surprise. **improvvisazione** sf improvisation.

imprudente [impru'dente] agg rash, imprudent. **Imprudenza** sf imprudence. **commettere un'imprudenza** do something rash.

impudente [impu'dente] agg impudent.

impudico [impu'diko] agg, m pl -chi immodest.

impugnare[1] [impu'nare] v (contestare) challenge; (dir) contest.

impugnare[2] [impu'nare] v (afferrare) grasp. **impugnare le armi** take up arms. **impugnatura** sf handle; (spada) hilt; (racchetta) grip.

impulso [im'pulso] sm impulse. **dare impulso** boost. **impulsivo** agg impulsive.

impunemente [impune'mente] avv with impunity.

impunito [impu'nito] agg (delitto) unpunished.

impuntarsi [impun'tarsi] v refuse to budge, dig one's heels in.

impuro [im'puro] agg impure. **impurità** sf impurity.

imputare [impu'tare] v impute, attribute, ascribe; (dir) charge. **imputabile** agg attributable. **imputato, -a** sm, sf defendant, accused. **imputazione** sf charge.

imputridire [imputri'dire] v rot.

in [in] prep in; (su, sopra) on; (moto a luogo) to; (dentro) into; (moto per luogo) round, through; (entro) within; (durante) during.

inabile [in'abile] agg (non capace) unable, incapable; (non idoneo) unfit; (per infortunio) disabled; (dir) ineligible.

inabitabile [inabi'tabile] agg uninhabitable. **inabitato** agg uninhabited.

inaccessibile [inattʃes'sibile] agg inaccessible.

inaccettabile [inattʃet'tabile] agg unacceptable.

inadatto [ina'datto] agg unsuitable (for); (incapace) unfit (for).

inadeguato [inade'gwato] agg insufficient, inadequate.

inalare [ina'lare] v inhale.

inalienabile [inalje'nabile] agg inalienable.

inalterabile [inalte'rabile] *agg* unchangeable. **inalterato** *agg* unchanged.

inamidare [inami'dare] *v* starch.

inammissibile [innammis'sibile] *agg* inadmissible.

inanimato [inani'mato] *agg* inanimate, lifeless.

inappagabile [inappa'gabile] *agg* insatiable. **inappagato** *agg* unsatisfied.

inapplicabile [inappli'kabile] *agg* inapplicable.

inarcare [inar'kare] *v* arch, bend. **inarcare le sopracciglia** raise one's eyebrows.

inargentare [inardʒen'tare] *v* silver.

inaridire [inari'dire] *v* dry up.

inaspettato [inaspet'tato] *agg* unexpected.

inasprire [inas'prire] *v* exacerbate, make worse.

inattendibile [inatten'dibile] *agg* unreliable.

inatteso [inat'tezo] *agg* unexpected.

inattivo [inat'tivo] *agg* idle.

inattuabile [inat'twabile] *agg* impracticable.

inaudito [inau'dito] *agg* (*non udito prima*) unheard of; incredible, extraordinary.

inaugurare [inaugu'rare] *v* inaugurate, open. **inaugurazione** *sf* inauguration, opening.

inavveduto [inavve'duto] *agg* thoughtless, careless.

inavvertenza [inavver'tɛntsa] *sf* carelessness, oversight.

incagliarsi [inka'ʎarsi] *v* (*mar*) run aground; (*fig*) get stuck.

incalcolabile [inkalko'labile] *agg* incalculable.

incalzare [inkal'tsare] *v* follow closely; (*fig*) press.

incamminare [inkammi'nare] *v* start (off). **incamminarsi** *v* set off; (*avviarsi*) be on the way (to).

incanalare [inkana'lare] *v* channel.

incantare [inkan'tare] *v* enchant, charm. **incantarsi** *v* (*rimanere intontito*) be in a daze; (*mec*) jam, break down. **incantato** *agg* enchanted; (*intontito*) dazed, spellbound. **incantatore, -trice** *sm, f* charmer. **incantesimo** *sm* charm, spell. **incantevole** *agg* charming, enchanting.

incanto[1] [in'kanto] *sm* spell, magic. **stare d'incanto** suit perfectly.

incanto[2] [in'kanto] *sm* (*vendita*) auction.

incapace [inka'patʃe] *agg* incapable.

incapacità *sf* inability; (*fisica*) disability; (*dir*) incapacity.

incappare [inkap'pare] *v* run into, come up against.

incarcerare [inkartʃe'rare] *v* imprison, jail.

incaricare [inkari'kare] *v* charge, entrust; order. **incaricarsi** *v* take charge. **incaricato, -a** *sm, sf* person in charge; (*università*) lecturer; (*funzionario*) official.

incarico [in'kariko] *sm, pl* **-chi** task, assignment, charge.

incarnare [inkar'nare] *v* embody; (*personaggio*) impersonate.

incartare [inkar'tare] *v* wrap (up).

incasellare [inkazel'lare] *v* pigeon-hole.

incassare [inkas'sare] *v* (*riscuotere*) collect, cash; (*sport*) take; (*inserire*) embed. **incasso** *sm* collection; (*entrata*) takings *pl*.

incastellatura [inkastella'tura] *sf* (*impalcatura*) scaffolding; (*mec*) casing.

incastonare [inkasto'nare] *v* set, mount. **incastonatura** *sf* setting, mounting.

incastrare [inkas'trare] *v* wedge, drive; (*imprigionare*) jam, sandwich; (*falegnameria*) mortise. **incastro** *sm* joint; (*cavità*) hollow, recess; mortise.

incatenare [inkate'nare] *v* chain; (*fig*) tie. **incatramare** [inkatra'mare] *v* tar.

incauto [in'kauto] *agg* incautious.

incavare [inka'vare] *v* hollow out. **incavo** *sm* hollow; (*scanalatura*) groove.

incendiare [intʃen'djare] *v* set on fire; (*fig*) fire.

incendiario [intʃen'djarjo] *agg* incendiary. *sm* arsonist, fire-raiser.

incendio [in'tʃendjo] *sm* fire. **bocca d'incendio** *sf* (fire) hydrant. **incendio doloso** arson.

incenerire [intʃene'rire] *v* burn down; (*fig*) wither.

incenso [in'tʃenso] *sm* incense.

incensurabile [intʃensu'rabile] *agg* beyond reproach. **essere incensurato** have a clean record.

inceppare [intʃep'pare] *v* obstruct, hamper.

incertezza [intʃer'tettsa] *sf* uncertainty; (*dubbio*) doubt; (*indecisione*) hesitation.

incerto [in'tʃerto] *agg* uncertain; dubious; (*indeciso*) hesitant; (*malsicuro*) unsure. *sm* uncertainty.

incespicare [intʃespi'kare] *v* stumble, trip up.

incessante [intʃes'sante] *agg* ceaseless, constant.

incesto [in'tʃesto] *sm* incest. **incestuoso** *agg* incestuous.

incettare [intʃet'tare] *v also* fare incetto di corner, buy up. **incetta** *sf* cornering.

inchiesta [in'kjesta] *sf* inquiry, investigation; (*giornalismo*) report; (*scandalo*) probe.

inchinare [inki'nare] *v* (*abbassare*) lower. **inchinarsi** *v* bend down, bow; (*donna*) curtsey. **inchino** *sm* bow, curtsey.

inchiodare [inkjo'dare] *v* nail.

inchiostro [in'kjostro] *sm* ink. **inchiostro di china** Indian ink.

inciampare [intʃam'pare] *v* stumble (over), trip up. **inciampo** *sm* obstacle, stumbling block.

incidente [intʃi'dente] *sm* (*episodio*) incident; (*infortunio*) accident; (*disputa*) argument.

incidenza [intʃi'dentsa] *sf* incidence.

*incidere¹ [intʃi'dere] *v* cut (into); carve; (*intagliare*) engrave; (*ad acquaforte*) etch; (*registrare*) record; (*med*) incise, lance. **incisione** *sf* incision; cut; engraving; etching; recording. **incisivo** *agg* incisive. **per inciso** by the way, incidentally. **incisore** *sm* engraver.

*incidere² [intʃi'dere] *v* **incidere su** affect.

incinta [in'tʃinta] *agg* pregnant.

incipriare [intʃi'prjare] *v* powder.

incitare [intʃi'tare] *v* incite. **incitamento** *sm* incitement, spur.

incivile [intʃi'vile] *agg* uncivilized; (*villano*) boorish, uncivil.

incivilire [intʃivi'lire] *v* civilize.

inclemente [inkle'mente] *agg* harsh.

inclinare [inkli'nare] *v* incline; (*propendere*) tend, be inclined. **inclinazione** *sf* inclination; (*pendenza*) slope; (*disposizione d'animo*) leaning; (*simpatia*) liking; (*strada*) gradient. **incline** *agg* prone.

*includere [in'kludere] *v* (*comprendere*) include; (*accludere*) enclose; (*implicare*) imply. **inclusione** *sf* inclusion. **incluso** *agg* included; (*comm*) inclusive.

incoerente [inkoe'rente] *agg* incoherent; (*fig*) inconsistent.

incognita [in'kɔnita] *sf* (*matematica*) unknown; (*fatto imprevedibile*) unknown factor, uncertainty; (*persona*) mystery, dark horse.

incognito [in'kɔnito] *agg* unknown. *sm* incognito; (*ignoto*) unknown.

incollare [inkol'lare] *v* (*attaccare*) glue; (*spalmare*) paste.

incolore [inko'lore] *agg* colourless.

incolpare [inkol'pare] *v* blame.

incolto [in'kolto] *agg* (*non coltivato*) uncultivated; (*trascurato*) untidy; (*privo di coltura*) uncultured.

incolume [in'kɔlume] *agg* unharmed.

incombente [inkom'bente] *agg* (*imminente*) impending; (*spettante*) incumbent.

incominciare [inkomin'tʃare] *v* begin, start. (*tanto*) **per cominciare** to begin with.

incomodo [in'kɔmodo] *agg* (*disagevole*) uncomfortable; (*inopportuno*) inconvenient. *sm* trouble, inconvenience. **il terzo incomodo** the odd man out. **incomodare** *v* inconvenience, trouble.

incomparabile [inkompa'rabile] *agg* incomparable.

incompatibile [inkompa'tibile] *agg* incompatible. **incompatibilità** *sf* incompatibility.

incompetente [inkompe'tente] *agg* incompetent. *s(m+f)* incompetent person.

incompiuto [inkom'pjuto] *agg* unfinished.

incompleto [inkom'pleto] *agg* incomplete.

incomprensibile [inkompren'sibile] *agg* incomprehensible. **incomprensibilità** *sf* incomprehensibility.

incompreso [inkom'prezo] *agg* misunderstood.

inconcepibile [inkontʃe'pibile] *agg* inconceivable.

inconciliabile [inkontʃi'ljabile] *agg* irreconcilable.

inconcludente [inkonklu'dente] *agg* inconclusive.

incondizionato [inkonditsjo'nato] *agg* unconditional; (*pieno*) complete.

inconsapevole [inkonsa'pevole] *agg* unaware, unconscious.

inconscio [in'kɔnʃo] *agg* unconscious; (*persona*) unaware. *sm invar* unconscious.

inconsiderabile [inkonside'rabile] *agg* negligible. **inconsiderato** *agg* thoughtless. **inconsideratezza** *sf* thoughtlessness.

inconsistente [inkonsis'tente] *agg* flimsy; (*infondato*) groundless.

inconsolabile [inkonso'labile] *agg* inconsolable.

inconsueto [inkonsu'eto] *agg* unusual.

incontenibile [inkonte'nibile] *agg* uncontrollable.

incontentabile [inkonten'tabile] *agg* hard to please, exacting.

incontrare [inkon'trare] *v* meet; (*esser popolare*) be a success. **incontrar favore** find favour. **incontrarsi per caso** run into.

incontrario [inkon'trarjo] *sm* **all'incontrario** (*a rovescio*) the wrong way round.

incontrastato [inkontras'tato] *agg* unopposed.

incontro[1] [in'kontro] *sm* meeting; (*partita*) match; (*gioco*) game; (*favore*) reception, success. **incontro alla pari** (*sport*) tie, draw.

incontro[2] [in'kontro] *avv* towards. **all'incontro** on the contrary. **andare incontro a** go towards, approach; (*fig*) meet halfway.

incontrollabile [inkontrol'labile] *agg* uncontrollable.

inconveniente [inkonve'njente] *sm* drawback, snag.

incoraggiare [inkorad'dʒare] *v* encourage.

incorniciare [inkorni'tʃare] *v* frame.

incoronare [inkoro'nare] *v* crown. **incoronazione** *sf* coronation.

incorporare [inkorpo'rare] *v* incorporate; annex.

incorreggibile [inkorred'dʒibile] *agg* incorrigible.

*incorrere [in'korrere] *v* incur.

incorruttibile [inkorrut'tibile] *agg* incorruptible.

incosciente [inko'ʃente] *agg* unconscious; (*sconsiderato*) irresponsible.

incredibile [inkre'dibile] *agg* incredible, unbelievable.

incredulo [in'kredulo] *agg* incredulous, disbelieving.

incremento [inkre'mento] *sm* (*aumento*) increase; (*sviluppo*) growth, expansion; (*mat*) increment. **incrementare** *v* increase; (*far prosperare*) promote.

increspare [inkres'pare] *v* (*acqua*) ripple; (*capelli*) curl. **increspare la fronte** frown.

incrinare [inkri'nare] *v* crack.

incrociare [inkro'tʃare] *v* cross. **incrociatore** *sm* cruiser. **incrocio** *sm*

crossing; (*accoppiamento*) cross-breeding; (*frutto*) cross, hybrid.

incrostato [inkros'tato] *agg* encrusted.

incubatrice [inkuba'tritʃe] *sf* incubator. **incubazione** *sf* incubation.

incubo ['inkubo] *sm* nightmare.

incudine [in'kudine] *sf* anvil.

inculcare [inkul'kare] *v* inculcate.

incuneare [inkune'are] *v* wedge.

incurabile [inku'rabile] *agg* incurable.

incurante [inku'rante] *agg* heedless, unconcerned.

incuriosire [inkurjo'zire] *v* arouse curiosity.

incursione [inkur'sjone] *sf* incursion, raid. **incursione aerea** air-raid.

incustodito [inkusto'dito] *agg* unattended.

indagare [inda'gare] *v* investigate, inquire into. **indagine** *sf* inquiry, investigation; (*scientifica*) research; (*studio*) survey.

indebitamente [indebita'mente] *avv* unduly; (*ingiustamente*) unlawfully.

indebitarsi [indebi'tarsi] *v* run into debt. **indebitato** *agg* indebted.

indebolire [indebo'lire] *v* weaken. **indebolimento** *sm* weakening; (*debolezza*) weakness.

indecente [inde'tʃente] *agg* indecent. **indecenza** *sf* indecency; (*vergogna*) disgrace.

indecifrabile [indetʃi'frabile] *agg* illegible.

indecisione [indetʃi'zjone] *sf* indecision.

indeciso [inde'tʃizo] *agg* undecided; (*non risolto, instabile*) unsettled.

indefesso [inde'fesso] *agg* tireless.

indefinibile [indefi'nibile] *agg* indefinable.

indefinito [indefi'nito] *agg* indefinite; (*non risolto*) unsettled.

indegno [in'deɲo] *agg* unworthy. **indegnità** *sf* base action.

indelicato [indeli'kato] *agg* tactless; indiscreet.

indemagliabile [indema'ʎabile] *agg* nonrun, ladder-proof.

indenne [in'denne] *agg* unharmed, unscathed.

indennità [indenni'ta] *sf* (*risarcimento*) allowance; (*dir*) indemnity. **indennizzare** *v* compensate. **indennizzo** *sm* compensation.

inderogabile [indero'gabile] *agg* binding, irrevocable.

indescrivibile [indeskri'vibile] *agg* indescribable.

indesiderabile [indezide'rabile] *agg* undesirable.

indeterminabile [indetermi'nabile] *agg* indeterminate, imprecise.

indi ['indi] *avv* (*dopo*) then; (*da quel luogo*) from there. **indi a poco** soon after.

India ['indja] *sf* India. **indiano, -a** *s*, *agg* Indian.

indiavolato [indjavo'lato] *agg* (*molto agitato*) wild; (*eccessivo*) awful; (*indemoniato*) frenzied.

indicare [indi'kare] *v* indicate, show; (*significare*) mean. **indicativo** *agg* indicative. **indicato** *agg* indicated; (*adatto*) suitable.

indicatore [indika'tore] *sm* indicator; (*tec*) gauge; (*stradale*) signpost.

indicazione [indika'tsjone] *sf* indication; (*dato, notizia*) information; (*istruzione per l'uso*) direction.

indice ['inditʃe] *sm* index; (*dito*) index finger; (*tec*) pointer.

indietreggiare [indjetred'dʒare] *v* draw back, withdraw.

indietro [in'djetro] *avv* (*in arretrato*) in arrears; (*debole*) weak; (*moto*) back(wards).

indifeso [indi'fezo] *agg* undefended; (*fig*) defenceless.

indifferente [indiffe'rɛnte] *agg* indifferent; (*lo stesso*) all the same; (*che non interessa*) unimportant. **indifferenza** *sf* indifference, lack of interest.

indigeno [in'didʒeno] *sm*, *agg* native.

indigesto [indi'dʒɛsto] *agg* indigestible; (*non digerito*) undigested.

indignare [indi'ɲare] *v* fill with indignation.

indimenticabile [indimenti'kabile] *agg* unforgettable.

indipendente [indipen'dɛnte] *agg* independent. **indipendenza** *sf* independence.

*indire [in'dire] *v* announce; (*radunare*) call.

indiretto [indi'rɛtto] *agg* indirect.

indirizzare [indirit'tsare] *v* address; (*rivolgere*) direct. **indirizzo** *sm* address; (*tendenza*) trend; direction.

indisciplinato [indiʃipli'nato] *agg* undisciplined.

indiscreto [indis'kreto] *agg* indiscreet.

indiscusso [indis'kusso] *agg* beyond dispute, incontrovertible.

indispensabile [indispen'sabile] *agg* indispensable, essential.

indispettire [indispet'tire] *v* irritate.

indisposizione [indispozi'tsjone] *sf* indisposition, slight illness. **indisposto** *agg* indisposed, unwell.

indistinto [indis'tinto] *agg* indistinct. **indistinguibile** *agg* indistinguishable.

indivia [in'divja] *sf* endive.

individuale [individu'ale] *agg* individual.

individuare [individu'are] *v* (*determinare*) locate; (*riconoscere*) single out; (*scoprire*) discover, recognize.

individuo [indi'viduo] *sm* person; (*spreg*) fellow, character.

indivisibile [indivi'zibile] *agg* indivisible. **indiviso** *agg* undivided.

indizio [in'ditsjo] *sm* sign, indication; (*dir*) (circumstantial) evidence.

indole ['indole] *sf* nature, character.

indolenzire [indolen'tsire] *v* make sore, make ache. **indolenzito** *agg* sore, aching.

indomani [indo'mani] *sm* **l'indomani** the following day.

indossare [indos'sare] *v* (*mettersi indosso*) put on; (*portare*) wear. **indossatrice** *sf* model. **indosso** *avv* on.

indotto [in'dotto] *agg* induced.

indovinare [indovi'nare] *v* guess. **indovinato** *agg* (*riuscito*) successful; (*che sta bene*) becoming. **indovinello** *sm* puzzle, riddle. **indovino, -a** *sm*, *sf* fortuneteller.

indù [in'du] *s*(*m+f*), *agg* Hindu.

indubbio [in'dubbjo] *agg* certain, unmistakable.

indubitabile [indubi'tabile] *agg* unquestionable. **indubitato** *agg* certain, unquestioned.

indugiare [indu'dʒare] *v* delay; (*soffermarsi*) linger (over). **indugio** *sm* delay.

indulgente [indul'dʒɛnte] *agg* lenient. **indulgenza** *sf* indulgence.

indumento [indu'mento] *sm* garment.

indurire [indu'rire] *v* harden. **indurimento** *sm* hardening.

*indurre [in'durre] *v* induce. **indurre in errore** mislead; (*fig*) lead astray. **indurre in tentazione** lead into temptation.

industria [in'dustrja] *sf* industry; (*attività industriale*) business.

industriale [indus'trjale] *agg* industrial. *sm* industrialist, manufacturer. **industrializzare** *v* industrialize. **industrializzazione** *sf* industrialization.

inebriare [inebri'are] v intoxicate.

inedito [in'edito] agg unpublished.

ineducato [inedu'kato] agg ill-mannered.

ineguale [ine'gwale] agg unequal; (non uniforme) uneven.

ineluttabile [inelut'tabile] agg relentless; (inevitabile) unavoidable.

inerente [ine'rεnte] agg (riferentesi) concerning; (implicito) inherent.

inerme [i'nεrme] agg unarmed; (senza difesa) defenceless.

inerpicarsi [inerpi'karsi] v scramble up.

inerte [i'nεrte] agg inert. **inerzia** sf sluggishness; (fis) inertia.

inesatto [ine'zatto] agg (sbagliato) wrong, incorrect; (imprecise) inaccurate.

inesistente [inezis'tεnte] agg non-existent.

inesorabile [inezo'rabile] agg inexorable.

inesperienza [insper'jεntsa] sf inexperience.

inesperto [ines'pεrto] agg inexperienced.

inesplicabile [inespli'kabile] agg inexplicable.

inespressivo [inespres'sivo] agg expressionless.

inesprimibile [inespri'mibile] agg indescribable.

inetto [i'nεtto] agg inept, inadequate; (incapace) unsuited (to), incapable (of).

inevaso [ine'vazo] agg outstanding.

inevitabile [inevi'tabile] agg unavoidable.

inezia [i'nεtsja] sf trifle.

infagottare [infagot'tare] v bundle up, wrap up.

infallibile [infal'libile] agg infallible. **infallibilità** sf infallibility.

infame [in'fame] agg infamous, vile. **infamia** sf infamy, disgrace.

infangare [infan'gare] v muddy.

infante [in'fante] s(m+f) infant, newborn baby. **infantile** agg childlike; (puerile) childish, infantile. **asilo infantile** sm nursery school. **infanzia** sf infancy, childhood.

infarcire [infar'tʃire] v stuff.

infarinare [infari'nare] v (dip in) flour. **infarinatura** sf coating of flour; (fig) smattering.

infastidire [infasti'dire] v bother, trouble.

infaticabile [infati'kabile] agg tireless.

infatti [in'fatti] cong in fact, as a matter of fact, indeed.

infatuarsi [infatu'arsi] v become infatuated (with); fall (for).

infausto [in'fausto] agg inauspicious, unlucky.

infedele [infe'dele] agg unfaithful.

infelice [infe'litʃe] agg unhappy; (inopportuno) unfortunate; (disgraziato) wretched, unlucky; (cattivo) bad. s(m+f) unhappy person, wretch.

inferiore [infe'rjore] agg lower; (di grado più basso) inferior; (numeri) below, less than. **inferiorità** sf inferiority.

inferire [infe'rire] v (arrecare) inflict, cause; (dedurre) infer.

infermeria [inferme'ria] sf infirmary. **infermiere, -a** sm, sf nurse. **infermità** sf illness. **infermo** sm, agg invalid.

inferno [in'fεrno] sm hell. **infernale** agg infernal, hellish.

inferriata [infer'rjata] sf grille.

infestare [infes'tare] v infest.

infettare [infet'tare] v infect; (fig) taint. **infettivo** agg infectious, catching. **infezione** sf infection.

infiacchire [infjak'kire] v weaken.

infiammare [infjam'mare] v set on fire; (eccitare, med) inflame. **infiammabile** agg inflammable. **infiammazione** sf inflammation.

infido [in'fido] agg untrustworthy.

inferire [infje'rire] v rage.

infilare [infi'lare] v thread, string; (introdurre) insert; (imboccare) turn into, take. **infilata** sf row, string.

infiltrarsi [infilt'rarsi] v infiltrate.

infimo ['infimo] agg (the) lowest.

infine [in'fine] avv in the end, finally.

infinito [infi'nito] agg infinite; (interminabile) endless; (innumerevole) countless. sm infinity; (gramm) infinitive. **infinità** sf infinity; (gran numero) large number, crowd.

infischiarsi [infis'kjarsi] v not give a damn.

infisso [in'fisso] sm frame.

inflazione [infla'tsjone] sf inflation.

inflessibile [infles'sibile] agg inflexible. **inflessione** sf inflection.

***infliggere** [in'fliddʒere] v inflict.

influenza [influ'εntsa] sf influence; (med) influenza, flu. **influenzare** v influence.

influire [influ'ire] v have an influence. **influire su** affect, influence. **influsso** sm influence.

infondato [infon'dato] agg groundless, unfounded.

*infondere [in'fondere] v instil, inspire.

informare [infor'mare] v inform, tell; (plasmare) form, shape. **informarsi** v inquire, find out. **informazione** sf information.

informe [in'forme] agg shapeless.

informicolirsi [informiko'lirsi] v have pins and needles.

infortunio [infor'tunjo] sm accident.

infossato [infos'sato] agg hollow.

*inframmettersi [infram'mettersi] v interfere.

*infrangere [in'frandʒere] v break. **infrangibile** agg unbreakable.

infrazione [infra'tsjone] sf infringement, breach.

infreddarsi [infred'darsi] v catch a cold. **infreddatura** sf cold.

infrequente [infre'kwente] agg infrequent.

infuori [in'fwori] avv **all'infuori di** apart from, except.

infuriare [infu'rjare] v rage. **infuriarsi** v fly into a temper.

ingannare [ingan'nare] v deceive; (truffare) cheat; (essere infedele) be unfaithful. **inganno** sm deceit, deception, trick.

ingarbugliarsi [ingarbuʎʎarsi] v get entangled.

ingegnarsi [indʒe'narsi] v get by, manage.

ingegnere [indʒe'nere] sm engineer. **ingegneria** sf engineering.

ingegno [in'dʒeno] sm genius, talent. **ingegnoso** agg ingenious, clever.

ingenuo [in'dʒenwo] agg ingenuous, naive. sm naive person. **fare l'ingenuo** feign innocence; pretend not to understand.

ingerirsi [indʒe'rirsi] v meddle, interfere.

ingessare [indʒes'sare] v put in plaster.

Inghilterra [ingil'terra] sf England.

inghiottire [ingjot'tire] v swallow.

inginocchiarsi [indʒinok'kjarsi] v kneel (down).

ingiuria [in'dʒurja] sf offence; insult; (fig) damage. **ingiuriare** v insult; (oltraggiare) offend. **ingiurioso** agg insulting, offensive.

ingiusto [in'dʒusto] agg unjust; unfair.

inglese [in'gleze] sm (persona) Englishman; (lingua) English. sf Englishwoman. agg English. **filare all'inglese** take French leave. **zuppa inglese** sf trifle.

ingoiare [ingo'jare] v gulp (down), swallow (down).

ingolfarsi [ingol'farsi] v (auto) flood; (debiti) be swamped.

ingombrare [ingomb'rare] v obstruct, get in the way.

ingombro [in'gombro] agg cluttered (with). sm obstruction; (spazio) space.

ingommare [ingom'mare] v stick.

ingordo [in'gordo] agg greedy. **ingordigia** sf greed.

ingorgarsi [ingor'garsi] v be blocked up. **ingorgo** sm obstruction; (traffic) jam.

ingranare [ingra'nare] v engage; (fam) get on. **ingranaggio** sm (mec) gear; (fig) works pl, mechanism.

ingrandire [ingran'dire] v enlarge, magnify. **ingrandimento** sm enlargement.

ingrassare [ingras'sare] v fatten, make fat; (ungere) grease. **ingrassarsi** v put on weight, get fat; (arricchirsi) profit.

ingrato [in'grato] agg ungrateful; (sgradevole) thankless. **ingratitudine** sf ingratitude.

ingrediente [ingre'djente] sm ingredient.

ingresso [in'gresso] sm entrance; admission.

ingrossare [ingros'sare] v swell.

ingrosso [in'grosso] avv **all'ingrosso** wholesale.

inguaicibile [ingwal'tʃibile] agg creaseresistant.

inguaribile [ingwa'ribile] agg incurable.

inguine ['ingwine] sm groin.

inibire [ini'bire] v inhibit, forbid. **inibizione** sf inhibition.

inlettare [injet'tare] v inject. **iniezione** sf injection.

inimicizia [inimi'tsitsja] sf enmity, hostility.

inimitabile [inimi'tabile] agg inimitable.

inimmaginabile [inimmadʒi'nabile] agg unimaginable.

inintelligibile [ininteli'dʒibile] agg unintelligible.

ininterrotto [ininter'rotto] agg uninterrupted, continuous.

iniziale [ini'tsjale] agg initial. sf initial (letter).

iniziare [ini'tsjare] v start, begin; (avviare) initiate. **iniziativa** sf initiative, enterprise. **inizio** sm beginning.

innaffiare [innaf'fjare] v water.

innalzare [innal'tsare] v raise.

innamorarsi [innamo'rarsi] v fall in love (with).

innanzi [in'nantsi] *prep* before. **innanzi tutto** first of all; (*sopratutto*) above all. *avv* (*prima*) before; (*avanti*) on, ahead. **d'ora innanzi** from now on, henceforth.

innato [in'nato] *agg* innate.

innegabile [inne'gabile] *agg* undeniable.

innestare [innes'tare] *v* (*piante*) graft; insert; (*med*) inoculate. **innestare una marcia** (*auto*) put into gear. **innesto** *sm* graft; (*auto*) clutch; (*med*) inoculation.

inno ['inno] *sm* hymn. **inno nazionale** national anthem.

innocente [inno'tʃente] *agg* innocent. **dichiararsi innocente** (*dir*) plead not guilty. **innocenza** *sf* innocence.

innocuo [in'nɔkuo] *agg* innocuous, harmless.

innominabile [innomi'nabile] *agg* unmentionable.

innovare [inno'vare] *v* innovate. **innovatore, -trice** *sm, sf* innovator. **innovazione** *sf* innovation.

innumerevole [innume'revole] *agg* innumerable.

inoculare [inoku'lare] *v* inoculate.

inoffensivo [inoffen'sivo] *agg* inoffensive, harmless.

inoltrare [inol'trare] *v* send on, forward. **inoltrarsi** *v* advance.

inoltre [i'noltre] *avv* besides, furthermore.

inondare [inon'dare] *v* flood. **inondazione** *sf* flood.

inoperoso [inope'rozo] *agg* idle; (*econ*) unemployed.

inopportuno [inoppor'tuno] *agg* untimely; inopportune. **inopportunità** *sf* unsuitability; inappropriateness.

inorridire [inorri'dire] *v* horrify; be horrified.

inospitale [inospi'tale] *agg* inhospitable.

inosservato [inosser'vato] *agg* unobserved.

inossidabile [inossi'dabile] *agg* stainless.

inquadrare [inkwa'drare] *v* (*mettere in cornice*) frame; (*fig*) set; (*mil*) organize. **inquadratura** *sf* (*cine*, *TV*) shot.

inquietare [inkwje'tare] *v* worry. **inquietante** *agg* worrying. **inquieto** *agg* restless; (*preoccupato*) uneasy. **inquietudine** *sf* restlessness, worry.

inquilino [inkwi'lino], **-a** *sm, sf* tenant.

inquinare [inkwi'nare] *v* pollute. **inquinamento** *sm* pollution.

insabbiare [insab'biare] *v* (*pratica*) shelve.

insalata [insa'lata] *sf* salad; (*confusione*) muddle. **insalatiera** *sf* salad-bowl.

insalubre [insa'lubre] *agg* unhealthy.

insanabile [insa'nabile] *agg* incurable.

insanguinare [insangwi'nare] *v* stain with blood.

insaputa [insa'puta] *sf* **all'insaputa di** without the knowledge of.

insaziabile [insa'tsjabile] *agg* insatiable.

inscatolare [inskato'lare] *v* tin, can.

inscenare [inʃe'nare] *v* stage.

insegna [in'seɲa] *sf* (*emblema*) insignia *pl*; (*stemma*) coat of arms; motto; (*cartello*) sign.

insegnare [inse'ɲare] *v* teach. **insegnamento** *sm* teaching, education. **insegnante** *s(m+f)* teacher.

inseguire [inse'gwire] *v* pursue, chase. **inseguimento** *sm* pursuit, chase.

insensato [insen'sato] *agg* senseless, foolish.

insensibile [insen'sibile] *agg* (*leggerissimo*) imperceptible, very slight; (*indifferente*) insensitive, unfeeling.

inseparabile [insepa'rabile] *agg* inseparable.

inserire [inse'rire] *v* insert. **inserirsi** *v* introduce oneself, appear. **inserto** *sm* supplement. **inserzione** *sf* insertion; (*pubblicitaria*) advertisement.

inservibile [inser'vibile] *agg* useless.

inserviente [inser'vjente] *s(m+f)* attendant.

insetto [in'setto] *sm* insect. **insetticida** *sm* insecticide.

insicuro [insi'kuro] *agg* insecure.

insidia [in'sidja] *sf* snare, trap; (*pericolo*) danger. **insidioso** *agg* insidious.

insieme [in'sjeme] *avv* together; (*allo stesso tempo*) at the same time. *sm* whole; (*abbigliamento*) outfit.

insigne [in'siɲe] *agg* notable, illustrious.

insignificante [insiɲifi'kante] *agg* insignificant, trivial.

insignire [insi'ɲire] *v* decorate, honour.

insincero [insin'tʃero] *agg* insincere.

insinuare [insinu'are] *v* insinuate, creep. **insinuazione** *sf* insinuation.

insipido [in'sipido] *agg* insipid, tasteless.

*insistere [in'sistere] *v* insist (on). **insistente** *agg* insistent; (*incessante*) persistent, ceaseless. **insistenza** *sf* insistence.

insocievole [inso'tʃevole] *agg* unsociable.

insoddisfatto [insoddis'fatto] *agg* dissatisfied.

insofferente [insoffe'rɛnte] *agg* intolerant, impatient.

insoffribile [insof'fribile] *agg* unbearable.

insolazione [insola'tsjone] *sf* sunstroke.

insolente [inso'lɛnte] *agg* insolent. **insolenza** *sf* insolence.

insolito [in'sɔlito] *agg* unusual, strange.

insolubile [inso'lubile] *agg* insoluble. **insoluto** *agg* unsolved; (*non pagato*) outstanding.

insomma [in'somma] *inter* well! now then! *avv* (*in conclusione*) in short, in other words.

insonnia [in'sɔnnja] *sf* insomnia, sleeplessness. **insonne** *agg* sleepless; (*fig*) indefatigable.

insopportabile [insoppor'tabile] *agg* unbearable, intolerable.

*****insorgere** [in'sɔrdʒere] *v* rebel, rise (up against); protest.

insormontabile [insormon'tabile] *agg* insurmountable.

insospettato [insospet'tato] *agg* unexpected, unsuspected.

insostenibile [insoste'nibile] *agg* (*non difensibile*) untenable; (*non sopportabile*) unbearable.

insostituibile [insostitu'ibile] *agg* irreplaceable.

insperato [inspe'rato] *agg* undreamt of, unexpected.

inspiegabile [inspje'gabile] *agg* inexplicable.

installare [instal'lare] *v* install, establish. **installarsi** *v* settle (down). **installazione** *sf* installation.

insù [in'su] *avv* up.

insubordinato [insubordi'nato] *agg* insubordinate.

insuccesso [insut'tʃɛsso] *sm* failure.

insudiciare [insudi'tʃare] *v* soil, dirty.

insufficiente [insuffi'tʃɛnte] *agg* insufficient, inadequate. **insufficienza** *sf* insufficiency; (*mancanza*) shortage.

insulina [insu'lina] *sf* insulin.

insultare [insul'tare] *v* insult. **insulto** *sm* insult, abuse; (*accesso*) fit.

insuperabile [insupe'rabile] *agg* insuperable, insurmountable; (*imbattibile*) unbeatable.

insurrezione [insurre'tsjone] *sf* insurrection.

insussistente [insussis'tɛnte] *agg* nonexistent, baseless.

intaccare [intak'kare] *v* attack; (*far tacche*) notch, nick; (*consumare*) eat into.

intagliare [inta'ʎare] *v* carve, cut.

intangibile [intan'dʒibile] *agg* intangible.

intanto [in'tanto] *avv* meanwhile, in the meantime; (*fam: invece*) but, whereas, while.

intasare [inta'zare] *v* clog, block. **intasamento** *sm* obstruction, blockage.

intascare [intas'kare] *v* pocket.

intatto [in'tatto] *agg* intact.

intavolare [intavo'lare] *v* (*iniziare*) begin.

integrale [inte'grale] *agg* complete, total. **calcolo integrale** *sm* integral calculus. **pane integrale** *sm* wholemeal bread.

integrare [inte'grare] *v* integrate.

integro [in'tegro] *agg* complete; (*onesto*) upright. **integrità** *sf* integrity.

intelletto [intel'lɛtto] *sm* intellect. **intellettuale** s(*m* + *f*), *agg* intellectual.

intelligente [intelli'dʒɛnte] *agg* intelligent. **intelligenza** *sf* intelligence. **intelligibile** *agg* intelligible.

intemperie [intem'perje] *sf pl* bad weather *sing*.

intempestivo [intempes'tivo] *agg* untimely. **intempestività** *sf* untimeliness.

intendente [inten'dɛnte] *sm* superintendent, administrator. **intendenza** *sf* administration.

*****intendere** [in'tɛndere] *v* (*udire*) hear; (*comprendere*) understand; (*aver intenzione, volere*) intend; (*significare*) mean. **intendersi** *v* (*andar d'accordo*) agree, get on; (*essere competente*) be knowledgeable (about). **s'intende** of course, it goes without saying.

intenditore [intendi'tore], **-trice** *sm, sf* connoisseur, good judge.

intenso [in'tɛnso] *agg* intense. **intensificare** *v* intensify. **intensità** *sf* intensity.

intento [in'tɛnto] *agg* busy. *sm* object, end.

intenzione [inten'tsjone] *sf* intention. **aver l'intenzione di** intend to. **bene/male intenzionato** *agg* well-/ill-disposed.

intercettare [intertʃet'tare] *v* intercept.

*****interdire** [inter'dire] *v* (*proibire*) forbid; (*dir*) disqualify. **interdizione** *sf* ban, disqualification.

interessare [interes'sare] *v* interest; (*riguardare*) concern; (*stare a cuore*) matter. **interessarsi** *v* take an interest (in); (*prendersi cura*) look after, take care (of). **interessato** *agg* interested, concerned;

(*oppportunistico*) self-interested. **interesse** *sm* interest; (*tornaconto*) profit.

interferire [interfe'rire] *v* interfere. **interferenza** *sf* interference.

interiore [inte'rjore] *agg* inner, interior.

intermedio [inter'mɛdjo] *agg* intermediate. **intermediario, -a** *agg* intermediary.

interminabile [intermi'nabile] *agg* endless, never-ending.

internare [inter'nare] *v* intern; (*med*) commit. **internamento** *sm* internment; commitment. **internato** *sm* (*convitto*) boarding school; (*scolaro*) boarder.

internazionale [internatsjo'nale] *agg* international.

interno [in'tɛrno] *agg* inner, internal. *sm* inside, interior; (*telefono*) extension.

intero [in'tero] *sm, agg* whole. **per intero** in full.

interpellare [interpel'lare] *v* ask, consult.

interpretare [interpre'tare] *v* interpret, explain; (*teatro, ecc.*) play. **interpretazione** *sf* interpretation. **interprete** *s(m+f)* interpreter; (*teatro, ecc.*) actor, performer; (*cantante*) singer.

interrare [inter'rare] *v* inter, bury.

interrogare [interro'gare] *v* interrogate, question; examine, test; consult. **interrogatorio** *sm* examination; questioning. **interrogazione** *sf* interrogation; (*domanda*) question; (*dir*) questioning, examination.

*****interrompere** [inter'rompere] *v* interrupt, break (off).

interruttore [interrut'tore] *sm* switch. **interruzione** [interru'tsjone] *sf* interruption, break.

interurbano [interur'bano] *agg* **chiamata** *or* **telefonata interurbana** *sf* trunk-call.

intervallo [inter'vallo] *sm* interval, break.

*****intervenire** [interve'nire] *v* intervene; (*assistere*) take part, attend; (*med*) operate. **intervento** *sm* intervention; operation.

intervista [inter'vista] *sf* interview. **intervistare** *v* interview. **intervistatore, -trice** *sm, sf* interviewer.

intesa [in'teza] *sf* agreement, understanding; (*pol*) entente. **inteso** *agg* (*volto a un fine*) intended, meant; (*compreso*) understood; (*convenuto*) agreed. **ben inteso** understood.

intestare [intes'tare] *v* head; (*mettere a nome di*) make out to. **intestatario, -a** *sm, sf* holder.

intestino [intes'tino] *sm* intestine.

intimare [inti'mare] *v* order; (*dichiarare*) declare.

intimidire [intimi'dire] *v* intimidate.

intimità [intimi'ta] *sf* intimacy; (*ambiente intimo, fig*) privacy.

intimo ['intimo] *agg* intimate; (*interno*) innermost. *sm* (*amico*) close friend; (*anima*) heart of hearts. **biancheria intima** *sf* underwear.

intimorire [intimo'rire] *v* intimidate, frighten.

*****intingere** [in'tindʒere] *v* dip.

intingolo [in'tingolo] *sm* (*piatto*) stew; (*salsa*) sauce, gravy.

intirizzire [intirit'tsire] *v* grow numb. **intirizzito** *agg* numb.

intitolare [intito'lare] *v* entitle; dedicate.

intollerabile [intolle'rabile] *agg* intolerable, unbearable.

intollerante [intolle'rante] *agg* intolerant.

intonaco [in'tɔnako] *sm* plaster. **intonacare** *v* plaster, whitewash.

intonare [into'nare] *v* (*accordare*) tune, (*cominciare a cantare*) intone, strike up; (*armonizzare*) match.

intontire [inton'tire] *v* daze.

intorno [in'torno] *avv* around; (*circa*) about; (*argomento*) on, about.

intorpidire [intorpi'dire] *v* grow numb.

intossicante [intossi'kante] *agg* poisoning. **intossicazione** *sf* poisoning.

intraducibile [intradu'tʃibile] *agg* untranslatable.

intralciare [intral'tʃare] *v* hold up, hinder. **intralcio** *sm* hindrance, obstacle.

intransigente [intransi'dʒɛnte] *agg* intransigent.

intransitivo [intransi'tivo] *agg* intransitive.

*****intraprendere** [intra'prendere] *v* undertake, take on, begin. **intraprendente** *agg* enterprising. **intraprendenza** *sf* enterprise, initiative.

intrattabile [intrat'tabile] *agg* intractable; (*fam*) impossible, difficult.

*****intrattenere** [intratte'nere] *v* entertain. **intrattenersi** *v* linger; (*indugiare su*) dwell (on).

*****intravedere** [intrave'dere] *v* catch a glimpse (of); (*intuire*) sense.

intreccio [in'trettʃo] *sm* plaiting; (*trama*) plot. **intrecciare** *v* intertwine; (*capelli*) braid.

intrepido [in'trepido] agg intrepid, brave.

intrigo [in'trigo] sm, pl **-ghi** plot, intrigue. **intrigare** v plot, intrigue.

intrinseco [in'trinseko] agg intrinsic.

intriso [in'trizo] agg soaked.

*__introdurre__ [intro'durre] v introduce; (inserire) insert; (far entrare) show in. **introdotto** agg (conosciuto) well-known, well-established; (esperto) well up in. **introduzione** sf introduction.

introito [in'trɔito] sm income; (incasso) takings pl.

*__intromettersi__ [intro'mettersi] v meddle, intervene.

intronare [intro'nare] v deafen.

introspettivo [introspet'tivo] agg introspective.

introvabile [intro'vabile] agg unobtainable, not to be found.

introverso [intro'verso], **-a** s, agg introvert.

intrusione [intru'zjone] sf intrusion. **intruso**, **-a** sm, sf intruder.

intuitivo [intui'tivo] agg intuitive. **intuire** v sense. **intuito** sm intuition, instinct, insight.

inumano [inu'mano] agg inhuman.

inumidire [inumi'dire] v moisten.

inusitato [inuzi'tato] agg uncommon.

inutile [i'nutile] agg useless; (non necessario) unnecessary.

invadente [inva'dente] agg intrusive. s(m+f) busybody.

*__invadere__ [inva'vadere] v invade, flood.

invalido [in'valido], **-a** agg invalid; (privo di valore) null and void; (mutilato) disabled. sm, sf invalid; disabled person. **invalidare** v (dir) invalidate.

invano [in'vano] avv in vain. agg vain, useless.

invariabile [inva'rjabile] agg invariable, even. **invariato** agg unchanged.

invasione [inva'zjone] sf invasion.

invecchiare [invek'kjare] v age. **invecchiamento** sm ageing.

invece [in'vetʃe] avv instead (of); (mentre) whereas, while.

invendibile [inven'dibile] agg unsaleable. **invenduto** agg unsold.

inventare [inven'tare] v invent. **inventore** sm inventor. **invenzione** sf invention.

inventario [inven'tarjo] sm inventory.

inverno [in'verno] sm winter. **invernale** agg winter, wintry.

inverosimile [invero'simile] agg unlikely.

inverso [in'verso] agg contrary, opposite; (mat) inverse. sm contrary, opposite. **inversione** sf inversion; (tec) reversal.

invertebrato [inverte'brato] agg, sm invertebrate.

investigare [investi'gare] v investigate.

investire [inves'tire] v (comm) invest; (scontrare) collide, hit; (scontrare persone) hit, run down. **investimento** sm investment; collision, crash.

invetriata [invetri'ata] sf (porta) glassdoor; (finestra) window.

invettiva [invet'tiva] sf invective.

inviare [invi'are] v dispatch, send (off). **inviato**, **-a** sm, sf (diplomatico) envoy; (giornale) correspondent. **invio** sm dispatch.

invidiare [invi'djare] v envy. **invidia** sf envy. **invidioso** agg envious.

invigorire [invigo'rire] v invigorate, strengthen.

invincibile [invin'tʃibile] agg invincible.

invisibile [invi'zibile] agg invisible.

invitare [invi'tare] v invite. **invitato**, **-a** sm, sf guest. **invito** sm invitation.

invocare [invo'kare] v invoke, call for.

invogliare [invo'ʎare] v tempt.

*__involgere__ [in'voldʒere] v wrap (up).

involontario [involon'tarjo] agg involuntary.

involtino [invol'tino] sm (gastr) roulade, olive.

involto [in'vɔlto] sm bundle, package.

involucro [in'volukro] sm covering, wrapper.

invulnerabile [invulne'rabile] agg invulnerable.

inzaccherare [indzakke'rare] v spatter with mud.

inzuppare [indzup'pare] v soak.

io ['io] pron I. sm self.

iodio ['jɔdjo] sm iodine.

ione ['jone] sm ion.

iperbole [i'perbole] sf hyperbole. **iperbolico** agg exaggerated; (mat) hyperbolic.

ipertensione [iperten'sjone] sf hypertension. **iperteso** agg hypertensive.

ipnosi [ip'nɔzi] sf hypnosis. **ipnotico** agg hypnotic. **ipnotismo** sm hypnotism. **ipnotizzare** [ipnotid'dzare] v hypnotize. **ipnotizzatore**, **-trice** sm, sf hypnotist.

ipocondriaco [ipokon'driako], **-a** s, agg hypochondriac. **ipocondria** sf hypochondria.

ipocrita [i'pɔkrita] *s(m+f)* hypocrite. **agg** hypocritical. **ipocrisìa** *sf* hypocrisy.

ipoteca [ipo'tɛka] *sf* mortgage. **ipotecare** *v* mortgage.

ipotenusa [ipote'nuza] *sf* hypotenuse.

ipotesi [i'pɔtezi] *sf* hypothesis (*pl* -ses). **nella migliore delle ipotesi** at best. **nella peggiore delle ipotesi** if the worst comes to the worst. **ipotetico** *agg* hypothetical.

ippica ['ippika] *sf* horse-racing. **ippico** *agg* horse.

ippocampo [ippo'kampo] *sm* sea-horse.

ippocastano [ippokas'tano] *sm* horse-chestnut.

ippodromo [ip'pɔdromo] *sm* racecourse.

ippopotamo [ippo'pɔtamo] *sm* hippopotamus.

ira ['ira] *sf* rage, anger. **irascibile** *agg* irascible.

iride ['iride] *sf* iris; (*arcobaleno*) rainbow.

Irlanda [ir'landa] *sf* Ireland. **irlandese** *sm*, *agg* Irish. **gli irlandesi** the Irish.

ironia [iro'nia] *sf* irony. **ironico** *agg* ironic(al).

irradiare [irra'djare] *v* radiate; (*fig*) irradiate.

irraggiungibile [irraddʒun'dʒibile] *agg* unattainable.

irragionevole [irradʒo'nevole] *agg* unreasonable.

irrazionale [irratsjo'nale] *agg* irrational.

irreale [irre'ale] *agg* unreal.

irregolare [irrego'lare] *agg* irregular. **irregolarità** *sf* irregularity.

irreperibile [irrepe'ribile] *agg* that cannot be found.

irrequieto [irre'kwjeto] *agg* restless.

irresistibile [irrezis'tibile] *agg* irresistible.

irresoluto [irrezo'luto] *agg* wavering, undecided. **irresolutezza** *sf* indecision, wavering.

irresponsabile [irrespon'sabile] *agg* irresponsible. **irresponsabilità** *sf* irresponsibility.

irrigare [irri'gare] *v* irrigate. **irrigazione** *sf* irrigation.

irrigidire [irridʒi'dire] *v* stiffen. **irrigidimento** *sm* stiffening; (*fig*) obstinacy.

irrimediabile [irrime'djabile] *agg* irreparable.

irrisorio [irri'zɔrjo] *agg* derisory, ridiculous.

irritare [irri'tare] *v* irritate; (*dar fastidio*) annoy. **irritabile** *agg* irritable. **irritante**

agg irritating; (*med*) irritant. **irritazione** *sf* irritation.

irriverenza [irrive'rɛntsa] *sf* disrespect.

*irrompere [ir'rompere] *v* burst into; (*riversarsi*) pour into.

irsuto [ir'suto] *agg* shaggy, hairy.

irto ['irto] *agg* bristling (with).

*iscrivere [is'krivere] *v* enrol, register; (*diventar socio*) join. **iscritto** *sm* member. **iscrizione** *sf* registration, enrolment; (*scritta*) inscription.

Islanda [is'landa] *sf* Iceland. **islandese** *sm*, *agg* Icelandic; *s(m+f)* Icelander.

isola ['izola] *sf* island.

isolare [izo'lare] *v* isolate; (*fis*) insulate. **isolamento** *sm* isolation; insulation.

ispettore [ispet'tore], **-trice** *sm*, *sf* inspector.

ispezionare [ispetsjo'nare] *v* inspect. **ispezione** *sf* inspection.

ispirare [ispi'rare] *v* inspire.

issare [is'sare] *v* hoist.

istamina [ista'mina] *sf* histamine.

istante [is'tante] *sm* instant, moment. **istantanea** *sf* snapshot. **istantaneo** *agg* instantaneous.

istanza [is'tantsa] *sf* (*domanda*) application, petition.

isterico [is'tɛriko] *agg* hysterical. **attacco isterico** *sm* hysterics *pl*. **isteria** *sf* hysteria.

istigare [isti'gare] *v* instigate.

istillare [istil'lare] *v* instil.

istinto [is'tinto] *sm* instinct.

istituire [istitu'ire] *v* institute, establish. **istituto** [isti'tuto] *sm* institute; (*ente*) institution, organization. **istituzione** *sf* institution.

istrice ['istritʃe] *sm* porcupine; (*persona scontrosa*) touchy person.

*istruire [istru'ire] *v* instruct, educate. **istruire un processo** (*dir*) prepare a case. **istruttore**, **-trice** *sm*, *sf* instructor, **-tress**, teacher. **giudice istruttore** *sm* examining magistrate. **istruttoria** *sf* (*dir*) examination. **istruttorio** *agg* preliminary. **istruzione** *sf* instruction, education, tuition.

Italia [i'talja] *sf* Italy. **italiano**, **-a** *s*, *agg* Italian.

itinerario [itine'rarjo] *sm* itinerary, route.

itterizia [itte'ritsja] *sf* jaundice.

Iugoslavia [jugo'slavja] *sf* Yugoslavia. **iugoslavo**, **-a** *s*, *agg* Yugoslav.

iuta ['juta] *sf* jute.

L

la¹ [la] *art* the.

la² [la] *pron* (*cosa, animale*) it; (*persona*) her; (*formula di cortesia*) you.

là [la] *avv* there. **di là** (*nell'altra stanza*) in the other room; (*da quella parte*) that way. **in là** (*oltre*) further. **va là!** come off it!

labbro ['labbro] *sm, pl* **-a** *f in anat sense* lip; (*orlo*) brim.

labirinto [labi'rinto] *sm* labyrinth, maze.

laboratorio [labora'torjo] *sm* laboratory; (*industria*) workshop.

laborioso [labo'rjozo] *agg* laborious.

laburista [labu'rista] *agg* Labour.

lacca ['lakka] *sf* lacquer.

laccio ['lattʃo] *sm* noose; (*trappola*) snare, trap; (*legame*) tie. **laccio da scarpe** shoelace.

lacerare [latʃe'rare] *v* lacerate, tear.

lacrima ['lakrima] *sf* tear.

lacrimogeno [lakri'mɔdʒeno] *agg* **gas lacrimogeno** *sm* tear-gas.

lacuna [la'kuna] *sf* gap.

ladro ['ladro] *sm* thief. **al ladro!** stop thief! **vestito come un ladro** dressed like a tramp.

laggiù [lad'dʒu] *avv* down there.

lagnarsi [la'narsi] *v* complain. **lagna** *sf* bore.

lago ['lago] *sm* lake.

laico ['laiko] *agg* lay. *sm* layman.

lama¹ ['lama] *sf* blade. **lametta** *sf* razor-blade.

lama² ['lama] *sm invar* (*zool*) llama.

lambiccarsi [lambik'karsi] *v* **lambiccarsi il cervello** rack one's brains.

lambire [lam'bire] *v* lick, lap.

lamentare [lamen'tare] *v* lament. **lamentarsi (di)** complain (about). **lamentela** *sf* complaint. **lamentevole** *agg* pitiful. **lamento** *sm* lament. **lamentoso** *agg* plaintive.

lamiera [la'mjera] *sf* sheet.

lamina ['lamina] *sf* thin layer; (*metallo*) foil. **laminare** *v* (*ridurre in lamine*) roll; (*coprire con lamine*) laminate. **laminato** *sm* laminate. **laminatoio** *sm* rolling-mill.

lampada ['lampada] *sf* lamp. **lampadario** *sm* chandelier. **lampadina** *sf* (light) bulb. **lampadina tascabile** torch.

lampeggiare [lamped'dʒare] *v* flash.

lampione [lam'pjone] *sm* lamp-post.

lampo ['lampo] *sm* flash; (*temporale*) lightning. **cerniera lampo** *sf* zip.

lampone [lam'pone] *sm* raspberry.

lampreda [lam'preda] *sf* lamprey.

lana ['lana] *sf* wool. **di lana** woollen. **industria laniera** *sf* wool industry. **lanificio** *sm* woollen mill.

lancetta [lan'tʃetta] *sf* hand.

lancia¹ [lantʃa] *sf* (*arma*) lance.

lancia² [lantʃa] *sf* (*barca*) launch. **lancia di salvataggio** lifeboat.

lanciare [lan'tʃare] *v* throw, fling; (*diffondere*) launch; (*bombe*) drop. **lanciafiamme** *sm invar* flame-thrower. **lanciamissili** *sm invar* rocket-launcher. **lanciare un grido** utter a cry. **lancio** *sm* throw, fling; launching.

languire [lan'gwire] *v* languish; (*diminuire di forza*) flag. **languido** *agg* languid.

lanterna [lan'tɛrna] *sf* lantern.

lanugine [la'nudʒine] *sf* down.

lapide ['lapide] *sf* (*sepolcrale*) tombstone; (*commemorativa*) memorial tablet.

lapis ['lapis] *sm* pencil.

lardo ['lardo] *sm* lard, dripping.

largo ['largo] *agg* wide, broad. **al largo di** away from, off. **far largo a** make room for. **larghezza** *sf* width, breadth; (*fig*) generosity.

larice ['laritʃe] *sm* larch.

laringe [la'rindʒe] *sf* larynx. **laringite** *sf* laryngitis.

larva ['larva] *sf* larva; (*spettro*) shadow.

lasciare [la'ʃare] *v* leave; (*permettere*) let. **lascito** *sm* legacy.

lascivo [la'ʃivo] *agg* lascivious.

laser ['lazer] *sm invar* laser.

lassativo [lassa'tivo] *sm, agg* laxative.

lasso ['lasso] *sm* (*periodo*) lapse. *agg* (*rilassato*) loose.

lassù [las'su] *avv* up there.

lastra ['lastra] *sf* plate; sheet.

lastricare [lastri'kare] *v* pave. **lastrico** *sm* pavement; (*miseria*) poverty.

latente [la'tɛnte] *agg* latent.

laterale [late'rale] *agg* lateral, side.

laterizi [late'ritsi] *sm pl* bricks *pl*, tiles *pl*.

latice [la'titʃe] *sm* latex.

latino [la'tino] *sm, agg* Latin.

latitante [lati'tante] *agg* fugitive. **rendersi latitante** abscond.

latitudine [lati'tudine] *sf* latitude.

lato¹ ['lato] *sm* side. **da un lato ... dall'altro ...** on the one hand ... on the other .... **d'altro lato** on the other hand.

lato² ['lato] *agg* **in senso lato** in a broad sense.

latrare [la'trare] *v* bark.

latrina [la'trina] *sf* latrine.

latta ['latta] *sf* (*lamiera*) tin, tinplate; (*recipiente*) tin, can.

lattaio [lat'tajo] *sm* milkman.

latte ['latte] *sm* milk. **latte magro** skimmed milk. **latteo** *agg* milky. **latteria** *sf* dairy. **lattiera** *sf* milk jug.

lattuga [lat'tuga] *sf* lettuce.

laurea ['laurea] *sf* degree. **laurearsi** *v* graduate. **laureato, -a** *sm, sf* graduate. **essere laureato in ...** have a degree in ....

lauro ['lauro] *sm* laurel.

lauto ['lauto] *agg* generous, sumptuous.

lava ['lava] *sf* lava.

lavabo [la'vabo] *sm* wash-basin.

lavaggio [la'vaddʒo] *sm* washing. **lavaggio a secco** dry-cleaning. **lavaggio del cervello** brain-washing.

lavagna [la'vaɲa] *sf* slate; (*scolastica*) blackboard.

lavanda¹ [la'vanda] *sf* (*bot*) lavender.

lavanda² [la'vanda] *sf* wash(ing).

lavandaia [lavan'daja] *sf* laundress, washer-woman.

lavanderia [lavande'ria] *sf* laundry; (*a gettoni*) launderette.

lavandino [lavan'dino] *sm* sink.

lavapiatti [lava'pjatti] *sm also* **lavastoviglie** *invar* dishwasher.

lavatrice [lava'tritʃe] *sf* washing machine.

lavare [la'vare] *v* wash. **lavare a secco** *v* dry-clean. **lavare il capo a** tell off. **lavarsi** *v* (have a) wash. **lavata di capo** *sf* telling-off. **lavatura** *sf* washing; (*acqua sporca*) dishwater.

lavativo [lava'tivo] *sm* (*fam*) bore, pain in the neck.

lavorare [lavo'rare] *v* work; (*con fatica*) labour; (*aziende, negozi, ecc.*) do business; (*il terreno*) till; (*teatro, ecc.*) act, play. **lavorativo** *agg* working. **lavorato** *agg* finished; (*metallo*) wrought; (*a macchina*) machined.

lavoratore [lavora'tore], **-trice** *sm, sf* worker. **lavoratore a cottimo** piece-worker.

lavorazione [lavora'tsjone] *sf* manufacture; (*fattura*) workmanship; work. **lavorazione in serie** mass-production.

lavoro [la'voro] *sm* work; (*occupazione*) job; (*teatro, ecc.*) play. **lavori di casa** *sm pl* housework *sing*. **lavoro a cottimo** *sm* piece-work. **lavoro straordinario** *sm* overtime.

lazzarone [laddza'rone] *sm* scoundrel.

le¹ [le] *art* the.

le² [le] *pron* (*persona*) (to) her; (*cosa, animale*) (to) it; (*formula di cortesia*) (to) you; (*pl*) them.

leale [le'ale] *agg* sincere; (*onesto*) fair. **lealtà** *sf* loyalty, fairness.

lebbroso [leb'brozo], **-a** *agg* leprous. *sm, sf* leper. **lebbra** *sf* leprosy.

leccare [lek'kare] *v* lick. **leccalecca** *sm invar* (*fam*) lollipop. **leccapiedi** *sm invar* (*fam*) bootlicker. **leccare i piedi a** lick the boots of. **leccornia** *sf* titbit, tasty morsel.

lecito [le'tʃito] *agg* (*dir*) lawful; (*permesso*) allowed.

lega ['lega] *sf* league, alliance; (*metalli*) alloy.

legale [le'gale] *agg* legal; (*legittimo*) lawful. **medicina legale** *sf* forensic medicine. **numero legale** *sm* quorum. **ora legale** *sf* summer-time. **legalizzare** *v* legalize, certify.

legame [le'game] *sm* tie, bond; (*fig*) link; (*amoroso*) liaison.

legare [le'gare] *v* tie (up), bind; (*assicurare*) fasten. **matto da legare** crazy, mad as a hatter.

legato [le'gato] *agg* tied (up); (*libro*) bound; (*impacciato*) stiff. *sm* (*papale*) legate; (*testamento*) legacy.

legatura [lega'tura] *sf* binding.

legge ['leddʒe] *sf* law; (*votata dal parlamento*) act (of parliament); (*norma di condotta*) rule. **progetto di legge** *sm* bill. **proposta di legge** *sf* draft bill.

leggenda [led'dʒenda] *sf* legend; (*didascalia*) caption. **leggendario** *agg* legendary.

*****leggere** [leddʒere] *v* read.

leggero [led'dʒero] *agg* light; (*lieve*) slight. **leggerezza** *sf* lightness; (*frivolezza*) levity; (*sconsideratezza*) thoughtlessness.

leggiadro [led'dʒadro] *agg* graceful, lovely.

leggibile [led'dʒibile] *agg* readable, legible.

leggio [led'dʒio] *sm* music stand; (*chiesa*) lectern.

legione [le'dʒone] *sf* legion.

legislazione [ledʒizla'tsjone] *sf* legislation. **legislatore** *sm* legislator.

legittimo [le'dʒittimo] *agg* lawful; (*tale per legge*) legitimate; proper; justifiable.

legna [ˈleɲa] *sf invar* firewood. **mettere legna al fuoco** add fuel to the fire.

legname [leˈɲame] *sm* timber; (*in tronchi*) logs *pl*.

legnata [leˈɲata] *sf* blow. **un sacco di legnate** *sm* (*fam*) a good hiding.

legno [ˈleɲo] *sm* wood. **di legno** wooden, wood. **lavoro in legno** *sm* woodwork; (*edilizia*) timberwork. **legno compensato** plywood. **legno impiallacciato** veneer.

lei [ˈlɛi] *pron* (*soggetto*) she; (*oggetto*) her; (*formula di cortesia*) you.

lembo [ˈlembo] *sm* (*orlo*) edge, border; (*striscia*) strip.

lemme lemme [ˈlɛmme ˈlɛmme] *avv* (*fam*) very leisurely.

lena [ˈlena] *sf* vigour. **lavorare di buona lena** (*fam*) put one's back into it.

lente [ˈlɛnte] *sf* lens. **lente a contatto** contact lens. **lente d'ingrandimento** magnifying glass. **lenti** *sf pl* glasses *pl*.

lenticchia [lenˈtikkja] *sf* lentil.

lentiggine [lenˈtiddʒine] *sf* freckle. **lentigginoso** *agg* freckled.

lento [ˈlento] *agg* slow; (*allentato*) loose. **lento a capire** slow in the uptake.

lenza [ˈlentsa] *sf* (fishing-)line.

lenzuolo [lenˈtswɔlo] *sm, pl* **-a** *f when referring to a pair* sheet.

leone [leˈone] *sm* lion. **leonessa** *sf* lioness.

leopardo [leoˈpardo] *sm* leopard.

lepido [ˈlɛpido] *agg* witty.

lepre [ˈlɛpre] *sf* hare. **lepre in salmì** jugged hare. **labbro leporino** *sm* hare-lip.

lesbico [ˈlɛzbiko] *agg* lesbian. **lesbica** *sf* lesbian.

lesina [ˈlezina] *sf* awl; (*taccagneria*) (*fam*) meanness. **lesinare** *v* skimp.

lesione [leˈzjone] *sf* injury; (*med*) lesion; (*danno*) damage. **parte lesa** *sf* injured party. -

lessare [lesˈsare] *v* boil. **lesso** *sm* boiled meat.

lessico [ˈlɛssiko] *sm* lexicon; vocabulary.

lesto [ˈlɛsto] *agg* swift, quick. **lesto di lingua** glib. **lesto di mano** light-fingered. **lestofante** *sm* swindler.

letale [leˈtale] *agg* lethal, deadly.

letame [leˈtame] *sm* manure, dung; (*fig*)

filth. **letamaio** *sm* dung-heap; (*luogo sudicio*) pigsty.

letargico [leˈtardʒiko] *agg* lethargic. **letargo** *sm* (*zool*) hibernation; (*med, torpore*) lethargy.

letizia [leˈtitsja] *sf* joy, gladness.

lettera [ˈlettera] *sf* letter. **alla lettera** literally; verbatim. **lettera d'accompagnamento/raccomandata** covering/registered letter. **lettera di sollecitazione** reminder. **lettera maiuscola/minuscola** capital/small letter. **letterario** [letteˈrarjo] *agg* literary. **letteratura** [letteraˈtura] *sf* literature.

lettiga [letˈtiga] *sf* litter; (*barella*) stretcher.

letto [ˈletto] *sm* bed.

lettore [letˈtore] *sf* reader; (*universitario*) modern language lecturer.

lettura [letˈtura] *sf* reading.

leucemia [leutʃeˈmia] *sf* leukaemia.

leva[1] [ˈleva] *sf* (*mec*) lever; (*fig*) incentive. **far leva** lever. **far leva su** exploit, play on.

leva[2] [ˈleva] *sf* call-up; conscripts *pl*.

levante [leˈvante] *sm* east.

levare [leˈvare] *v* (*alzare*) raise, lift; (*togliere*) take away *or* off; (*estrarre*) pull out. **levare di mezzo** get rid of, remove. **levarsi** *v* (*alzarsi*) rise; (*dal letto*) get up. **levarsi la fame** satisfy one's hunger. **levarsi la sete** quench one's thirst. **levata della posta** *sf* mail collection. **levata del sole** *sf* sunrise.

levatoio [levaˈtojo] *agg* **ponte levatoio** *sm* drawbridge.

levatrice [levaˈtritʃe] *sf* midwife.

levigare [leviˈgare] *v* smooth; polish; (*pomiciare*) rub down; (*con carta vetrata*) sand down.

levriere [leˈvrjere] *sm* greyhound.

lezione [leˈtsjone] *sf* lesson; class; (*durata*) period; (*universitario*) lecture.

lezioso [leˈtsjozo] *agg* affected, mannered.

lezzo [ˈlettso] *sm* stench; (*sudiciume*) filth.

li [li] *pron* them.

lì [li] *avv* there. **giù di lì** thereabouts. **lì per lì** (*sul momento*) there and then; (*dapprima*) at first.

libbra [ˈlibbra] *sf* pound.

libellula [liˈbellula] *sf* dragonfly.

liberale [libeˈrale] *s(m+f)*, *agg* liberal.

liberare [libeˈrare] *v* free, liberate; (*salvare*) save, rescue. **liberazione** *sf* liberation; release.

libero ['libero] *agg* free; *(sgombro)* clear; exempt. **aria libera** *sf* open air. **libero pensatore** *sm* freethinker. **tempo libero** *sm* time off.

libertà [liber'ta] *sf* freedom, liberty. **giorno di libertà** *sm* day off. **libertà condizionata** probation. **libertà provvisoria** bail. **mettere in libertà** set free.

Libra ['libra] *sf* Libra.

libraio [li'brajo] *sm* bookseller. **libreria** *sf* *(negozio)* bookshop; *(raccolta di libri)* library; *(casa editrice)* publishers *pl*.

libro ['libro] *sm* book. **a libro** hinged. **libro di cassa** cash register. **libro giallo** thriller. **libro mastro** ledger. **libro nero** blacklist.

licenza [li'tʃɛntsa] *sf* licence, permission; *(scuola)* leaving certificate.

licenziare [litʃen'tsjare] *v* dismiss. **licenziamento** *sm* dismissal.

liceo [li'tʃɛo] *sm* secondary school, high school.

lichene [li'kene] *sm* lichen.

lido ['lido] *sm* shore.

lieto ['ljɛto] *agg* glad, happy.

lieve ['ljɛve] *agg* slight, light.

lievito ['ljɛvito] *sm* yeast; *(fig)* ferment.

lignaggio [liɲ'naddʒo] *sm* lineage, pedigree.

ligustro [li'gustro] *sm* privet.

lilla ['lilla] *agg, sm invar* lilac.

lima ['lima] *sf* file. **limare** *v* file. **limatura** *sf* filing; *(polvere)* filings *pl*.

limitare [limi'tare] *v* limit, restrict. **limitazione** *sf* limitation, restraint.

limite ['limite] *sm* limit; *(confine)* boundary. **caso limite** borderline case. **limitrofo** *agg* bordering.

limo ['limo] *sm* mud, slime.

limone [li'mone] *sm* *(albero)* lemon-tree; *(frutto)* lemon. **limonata** *sf* lemonade.

limpido ['limpido] *agg* clear.

lince ['lintʃe] *sf* lynx.

linciare [lin'tʃare] *v* lynch. **linciaggio** *sm* lynching.

lindo ['lindo] *agg* clean, tidy.

linea ['linea] *sf* line; *(corpo umano)* figure. **lineetta** *sf* dash.

lineamenti [linea'menti] *sm pl* features *pl*; *(elementi essenziali)* outlines *pl*.

lineare [line'are] *agg* linear; coherent; *(di indirizzo stabile)* unswerving.

linfa ['linfa] *sf* lymph; *(bot)* sap.

lingua ['lingwa] *sf* tongue; *(linguaggio)* language. **linguaggio** *sm* language.

linguista *s(m + f)* linguist. **linguistico** *agg* linguistic.

lino ['lino] *sm* *(pianta)* flax; *(tessuto)* linen. **olio di lino** *sm* linseed oil.

liocorno [lio'kɔrno] *sm* unicorn.

liquefare [likwe'fare] *v* liquefy, melt. **liquefazione** *sf* liquefaction.

liquidare [likwi'dare] *v* liquidate; *(conti)* settle; *(merci)* sell off; *(sciogliere)* wind up. **liquidazione** *sf* liquidation, settlement; *(svendita)* clearance sale; winding-up; *(indennità)* leaving bonus. **liquidatore** *sm* receiver.

liquido ['likwido] *sm, agg* liquid, fluid.

liquirizia [likwi'ritsja] *sf* liquorice.

liquore [li'kwore] *sm* liqueur.

lira¹ ['lira] *sf* *(moneta)* lira. **lira sterlina** pound sterling.

lira² ['lira] *sf* *(musica)* lyre.

lirico ['liriko] *agg* lyrical; opera. **cantante lirico** *s(m + f)* opera singer. **dramma lirico** *sm* opera. **teatro lirico** *sm* opera house. **lirica** *sf* lyric poetry.

lisca ['liska] *sf* fish-bone.

lisciare [li'ʃare] *v* smooth. **liscio** *agg* smooth; *(bevanda)* neat. **andar liscio** go smoothly. **passarla liscia** get off scot-free.

liseuse [li'zøz] *sf, pl* **-s** bed-jacket.

liso ['lizo] *agg* worn.

lista ['lista] *sf* *(striscia)* strip; *(elenco)* list. **lista elettorale** electoral register. **listare** *v* border. **listino** *sm* list.

litania [lita'nia] *sf* litany.

lite ['lite] *sf* quarrel; *(dir)* (law)suit.

litigare [liti'gare] *v* quarrel. **litigio** *sm* quarrel, row. **litigioso** *agg* quarrelsome; *(dir)* contentious.

litorale [lito'rale] *agg* coastal. *sm* shore.

litro ['litro] *sm* litre.

liturgia [litur'dʒia] *sf* liturgy. **liturgico** *agg* liturgical.

liuto [li'uto] *sm* lute.

livellare [livel'lare] *v* level. **livella** *sf* level. **livellatore, -trice** *sm, sf* leveller. **livello** [li'vɛllo] *sm* level. **livello del mare** sea-level. **passaggio a livello** *sm* level crossing.

livido ['livido] *agg* livid. *sm* bruise.

Livorno [li'vorno] *sf* Leghorn.

livrea [li'vrea] *sf* livery.

lizza ['littsa] *sf* **entrare in lizza** compete.

lo¹ [lo] *art* the.

lo² [lo] *pron* *(persona)* him; *(cosa, animale)* it.

lobo ['lɔbo] *sm* lobe.

locale¹ [lo'kale] *agg* local.

locale² [lo'kale] *sm* room, spot. **locale notturno** night-club. **località** *sf* locality.

localizzare [lokalid'dzare] *v* (*individuare*) locate; (*circoscrivere*) localize.

locanda [lo'kanda] *sf* inn. **locandiere, -a** *sm, sf* innkeeper.

locatario [loka'tarjo] *sm* tenant.

locatore [loka'tore] *sm* landlord.

locazione [lokat'tsjone] *sf* lease, tenancy.

locomotiva [lokomo'tiva] *sf* locomotive, engine.

lodare [lo'dare] *v* praise. **lode** *sf* praise. **lodevole** *agg* praiseworthy.

logaritmo [loga'ritmo] *sm* logarithm.

loggia ['lɔddʒa] *sf* loggia; (*massone*) lodge. **loggione** *sm* gallery.

logica ['lɔdʒika] *sf* logic. **logico** *agg* logical.

logistica [lo'dʒistika] *sf* logistics. **logistico** *agg* logistic(al).

logorare [logo'rare] *v* wear out. **logoramento** *sm* wear; (*mentale*) strain. **logorio** *sm* wear and tear. **logoro** *agg* worn out.

Londra ['londra] *sf* London. **londinese** *s(m+f)* Londoner.

longevo [lon'dʒɛvo] *agg* long-lived. **longevità** *sf* longevity.

longitudine [londʒi'tudine] *sf* longitude. **longitudinale** *agg* longitudinal.

lontano [lon'tano] *agg* far, far away; (*assente*) absent; distant; vague. *avv* far. **lontananza** *sf* distance.

lontra ['lontra] *sf* otter.

loquace [lo'kwatʃe] *agg* loquacious.

lordo ['lordo] *agg* (*peso*) gross; (*sporco*) filthy.

loro ['loro] *pron* (*soggetto*) they; (*oggetto*) them; (*formula di cortesia*) you; (*di essi*) theirs. *agg* their.

losco ['losko] *agg* sinister.

loto ['lɔto] *sm* lotus.

lotta ['lɔtta] *sf* struggle, fight; (*sport*) wrestling. **lottare** *v* struggle, fight; wrestle.

lotteria [lotte'ria] *sf* lottery.

lotto ['lɔtto] *sm* portion; (*comm*) lot; lottery.

lozione [lo'tsjone] *sf* lotion.

lubrificante [lubrifi'kante] *agg* lubricating. *sm* lubricant. **lubrificare** *v* lubricate. **lubrificazione** *sf* lubrication.

lucchetto [luk'ketto] *sm* padlock.

luccicare [luttʃi'kare] *v* shine, sparkle.

luccio ['luttʃo] *sm* pike.

lucciola ['luttʃola] *sf* firefly.

luce ['lutʃe] *sf* light.

lucernario [lutʃer'narjo] *sm* skylight.

lucertola [lu'tʃertola] *sf* lizard.

lucidare [lutʃi'dare] *v* polish.

lucido [lu'tʃido] *agg* shiny, glossy; (*fig*) lucid. *sm* polish.

luglio ['luʎo] *sm* July.

lugubre ['lugubre] *agg* lugubrious.

lui ['lui] *pron* (*soggetto*) he; (*oggetto*) him.

lumaca [lu'maka] *sf* snail; (*persona*) slowcoach.

lume ['lume] *sm* light; lamp. **far lume su** throw light on.

luminoso [lumi'nozo] *agg* bright, shining.

luna ['luna] *sf* moon. **avere la luna** to be in a bad mood. **luna di miele** honeymoon. **luna-park** *sm invar* fun-fair. **lunare** *agg* lunar. **sbarcare il lunario** make ends meet.

lunedì [lune'di] *sm* Monday.

lungo¹ ['lungo] *agg* long; (*alto*) tall; (*lento*) slow; (*diluito*) weak. **alla lunga** in the long run. **a lungo** (for) long. **di gran lunga** by far. **lunghezza** *sf* length.

lungo² ['lungo] *prep* along. **lungomare** *sm* seashore.

luogo ['lwɔgo] *sm* place. **aver luogo** take place. **fuori luogo** out of place. **in luogo di** instead of. **luogotenente** *sm* lieutenant.

lupo ['lupo] *sm* wolf. **lupa** *sf* she-wolf.

luppolo ['luppolo] *sm* hop.

lurido ['lurido] *agg* filthy.

lusingare [luzin'gare] *v* flatter; (*illudere*) delude. **lusinga** *sf* flattery; delusion. **lusinghiero** *agg* flattering, alluring.

Lussemburgo [lussem'burgo] *sm* Luxembourg.

lusso ['lusso] *sm* luxury. **di lusso** luxury, de luxe. **lussuoso** *agg* luxurious.

lustrare [lus'trare] *v* polish. **lustrino** *sm* sequin. **lustro** *sm* polish, sheen; lustre.

lutto ['lutto] *sm* mourning; (*dolore*) grief.

M

ma [ma] *cong* but. **macché!** *inter* (*neanche per sogno*) of course not! not on your life! **ma davvero?** really? **ma no!** of course not! **ma sì!** of course!

macabro ['makabro] *agg* macabre.

maccheroni [makke'roni] *sm pl* macaroni *sing.*

macchia¹ ['makkja] *sf* spot; stain.

macchia² ['makkja] *sf* (*arbusti*) bush.

macchiare [mak'kjare] *v* stain. **caffè macchiato** *sm* coffee with a dash of milk.

macchietta [mak'kjetta] *sf* (*persona*) character.

macchina ['makkina] *sf* machine; (*automobile*) car. **macchina da scrivere** typewriter. **macchina fotografica** camera.

macchinare [makki'nare] *v* plot.

macchinario [makki'narjo] *sm* machinery.

macchinista [makki'nista] *s(m + f)* machinist; (*ferr*) engine driver.

macedonia [matʃe'donja] *sf* fruit salad.

macellare [matʃel'lare] *v* slaughter. **macelleria** *sf* butcher's shop. **macellaio** *sm* butcher. **macello** *sm* slaughterhouse; (*fig*) shambles.

macerare [matʃe'rare] *v* soak; macerate.

macerie [ma'tʃerje] *sf pl* ruins *pl.*

macina ['matʃina] *sf* millstone, grindstone. **macinare** *v* grind. **macinino** *sm* (*da caffè*) coffee-mill; (*da pepe*) pepper-mill.

madido ['madido] *agg* soaking wet.

Madonna [ma'donna] *sf* **la Madonna** the Virgin Mary.

madornale [mador'nale] *agg* gross.

madre ['madre] *sf* mother; (*comm*) counterfoil. **madreperla** *sf* mother-of-pearl.

madrigale [madri'gale] *sm* madrigal.

maestà [mae'sta] *sf* majesty. **maestoso** *agg* majestic; imposing.

maestro [ma'estro] *sm* master; teacher. *agg* principal, main. **colpo maestro** *sm* master-stroke. **maestra** *sf* mistress; teacher. **maestranze** *sf pl* work force *sing.*

mafia ['mafja] *sf* mafia. **mafioso, -a** *sm, sf* member of the Mafia.

magagna [ma'gaɲa] *sf* flaw, fault.

magari [ma'gari] *inter* most certainly! (*oh se ...*) if only .... *avv* (*forse*) perhaps; (*perfino*) even.

magazzino [magad'dzino] *sm* store, warehouse. **magazzinaggio** *sm* warehousing. **magazziniere** *sm* warehouseman.

maggio ['maddʒo] *sm* May.

maggiorana [maddʒo'rana] *sf* marjoram.

maggioranza [maddʒo'rantsa] *sf* majority.

maggiore [mad'dʒore] *s(m + f)*, *agg* major; (*più grande*) greater, larger; (*più vecchio*) older; (*di due fratelli*) elder;

(*superlativo*) greatest, oldest, eldest. *sm* major. **andare per la maggiore** be a hit.

maggiorenne [maddʒo'renne] *agg* of age. *s(m + f)* major.

maggiormente [maddʒor'mente] *avv* (all the) more; (*di più*) most.

magia [ma'dʒia] *sf* magic. **magico** *agg* magic(al).

magistero [madʒis'tero] *sm* teaching (profession). **scuola di magistero** *sf* college of education. **magistrale** *agg* (*di maestro*) magisterial; (*da maestro*) masterly.

magistrato [madʒis'trato] *sm* magistrate.

maglia ['maʎa] *sf* stitch; (*rete*) mesh; (*indumento intimo*) vest; T-shirt; (*maglione*) jersey. **fare la maglia** knit. **lavoro a maglia** *sm* knitting. **maglieria** *sf* knitwear. **maglione** *sm* jersey, pullover.

magnanimo [ma'ɲanimo] *agg* magnanimous.

magnete [ma'ɲete] *sm* (*auto*) magneto; (*calamita*) magnet. **magnetismo** *sm* magnetism.

magnetofono [maɲe'tɔfono] *sm* tape-recorder.

magnifico [ma'ɲifiko] *agg* magnificent, splendid. **magnificenza** *sf* magnificence.

magnolia [ma'ɲɔlja] *sf* magnolia.

mago ['mago] *sm* (*stregone*) sorcerer; (*illusionista*) magician.

magro ['magro] *agg* thin; (*fig*) meagre; (*povero di grasso*) lean. **magra** *sf* (*fiume*) low level; (*fig*) shortage.

mai ['mai] *avv* never, ever. **caso o se mai** in case, if ever. **come mai** how (on earth).

maiale [ma'jale] *sm* pig; (*carne*) pork.

maionese [majo'neze] *sf* mayonnaise.

mais ['mais] *sm* maize.

maiuscolo [ma'juskolo] *agg* capital. **maiuscola** *sf* capital (letter).

malaccorto [malak'kɔrto] *agg* ill-advised.

malafede [mala'fede] *sf* bad faith.

malandato [malan'dato] *agg* in bad condition.

malanno [ma'lanno] *sm* misfortune, trouble.

malapena [mala'pena] *sf* **a malapena** scarcely.

malaria [ma'larja] *sf* malaria.

malato, -a [ma'lato] *agg* sick, ill. *sm, sf* sick person, patient. **malattia** *sf* illness, disease.

malavita [mala'vita] *sf* underworld.

malavoglia [mala'voʎa] *sf* reluctance.

malavveduto [malavve'duto] *agg* unwise.

malconcio [mal'kontʃo] *agg* shabby.

malcontento [malkon'tento] *agg* dissatisfied. *sm* dissatisfaction.

maldestro [mal'destro] *agg* awkward.

maldicente [maldi'tʃente] *agg* slanderous.

male [ˈmale] *avv* (*non bene*) badly; (*in modo non buono*) ill; (*in modo imperfetto*) not well; (*indisposto*) unwell. **sentirsi male** feel unwell or ill. **far male** hurt. **mal di denti** toothache. **mal di gola** sore throat. **mal di mare** sea-sickness. **mal di testa** headache.

maledire [male'dire] *v* curse, damn. **maledizione** *sf* curse.

maleducato [maledu'kato] *agg* ill-mannered, rude.

malefico [ma'lɛfiko] *agg* harmful.

malerba [ma'lɛrba] *sf* weed.

malessere [ma'lessere] *sm* malaise.

malevolo [ma'levolo] *agg* hostile.

malfamato [malfa'mato] *agg* ill-famed.

malfatto [mal'fatto] *agg* badly made.

malfattore [malfat'tore] *sm* evil-doer.

malfermo [mal'fermo] *agg* unsteady.

malfido [mal'fido] *agg* unreliable.

malgrado [mal'grado] *prep* notwithstanding, in spite of.

malia [ma'lia] *sf* charm. **maliardo** *agg* bewitching.

maligno [ma'liɲo] *agg* spiteful; (*med*) malignant.

malinconia [malinko'nia] *sf* melancholy, gloom. **malinconico** *agg* gloomy, dismal.

malincuore [malin'kwore] *avv* **a malincuore** reluctantly, half-heartedly.

malinteso [malin'tezo] *agg* misunderstood, mistaken. *sm* misunderstanding.

malizia [ma'litsja] *sf* cunning, malice. **malizioso** *agg* malicious, cunning.

mallevadore [malleva'dore] *sm* guarantor, surety.

malmenare [malme'nare] *v* manhandle.

malnutrito [malnu'trito] *agg* undernourished.

malora [ma'lora] *sf* ruin. **andare in malora** (*fam*) go to the dogs. **va in malora!** (*al diavolo*) go to hell!

malsano [mal'sano] *agg* unhealthy.

malsicuro [malsi'kuro] *agg* unsafe.

malta [ˈmalta] *sf* mortar.

maltempo [mal'tempo] *sm* bad weather.

malto [ˈmalto] *sm* malt.

maltrattare [maltrat'tare] *v* ill-treat. **maltrattamento** *sm* ill-treatment.

malumore [malu'more] *sm* bad temper.

malva [ˈmalva] *sm invar* (*colore*) mauve. *sf* (*bot*) mallow.

malvagio [mal'vadʒo] *agg* wicked.

malversare [malver'sare] *v* embezzle. **malversatore, -trice** *sm, sf* embezzler. **malversazione** *sf* embezzlement.

malvisto [mal'visto] *agg* unpopular.

malvivente [malvi'vente] *sm* crook.

malvolentieri [malvolen'tjeri] *avv* reluctantly.

mamma [ˈmamma] *sf* mother, mum(my). **mamma mia!** good gracious!

mammella [mam'mella] *sf* breast.

mammifero [mam'mifero] *sm* mammal.

mammola [ˈmammola] *sf* violet.

manata [ma'nata] *sf* handful.

mancare [man'kare] *v* (*aver difetto*) lack; (*essere assente*) be missing; (*fallire, sentire la mancanza*) miss. **ci mancherebbe altro!** that would be the limit! **mancare alla parola** not keep one's word. **sentirsi mancare** feel faint.

mancia [ˈmantʃa] *sf* tip. **dar la mancia** tip.

mancino [man'tʃino], **-a** *sm, sf* left-hander. *agg* left-handed, left. **colpo mancino** *sm* underhand trick.

mandare [man'dare] *v* send. **mandare a fondo** sink. **mandare avanti** run. **mandar giù** (*cibo*) swallow. **mandar via** dismiss.

mandarino[1] [manda'rino] *sm* (*cinese*) mandarin.

mandarino[2] [manda'rino] *sm* (*albero*) mandarin tree; (*frutto*) mandarin, tangerine.

mandato [man'dato] *sm* commission; (*pol*) mandate; (*dir*) warrant.

mandibola [man'dibola] *sf* jaw.

mandolino [mando'lino] *sm* mandolin.

mandorla [ˈmandorla] *sf* almond. **mandorlo** *sm* almond-tree.

mandria [ˈmandrja] *sf* herd, flock.

mandrino [man'drino] *sm* (*tec*) spindle, mandrel.

maneggiare [maned'dʒare] *v* handle. **maneggio** *sm* handling; (*addestramento cavalli*) riding-school; (*intrigo*) plot.

manette [ma'nette] *sf pl* handcuffs *pl*.

mangano [ˈmangano] *sm* mangle.

mangereccio [mandʒe'rettʃo] *agg* edible.

mangiare [man'dʒare] *v* eat; (*corrodere*) eat into; (*dissipare*) squander; (*carte, scacchi, ecc.*) take. **dar da mangiare a**

feed. **far da mangiare** prepare a meal. **mangiare la foglia** smell a rat. **mangiarsi il fegato** fret. *sm* food.
mangiatoia [mandʒaˈtoja] *sf* manger.
mangime [manˈdʒime] *sm* fodder.
maniaco [maˈniako], **-a** *agg* maniacal. *sm*, *sf* maniac. **mania** *sf* mania.
manica [ˈmanika] *sf* sleeve. **senza maniche** sleeveless.
manichino [maniˈkino] *sm* mannequin, (tailor's) dummy.
manico [ˈmaniko] *sm* handle; (*violino*, *ecc.*) neck.
manicomio [maniˈkɔmjo] *sm* lunatic asylum.
maniera [maˈnjɛra] *sf* manner.
manifattura [manifatˈtura] *sf* manufacture.
manifestare [manifesˈtare] *v* show; express; (*pol*) demonstrate. **manifestazione** *sf* display, show; expression; demonstration.
manifesto[1] [maniˈfesto] *sm* poster, bill; (*pol*) manifesto. **manifestino** *sm* leaflet.
manifesto[2] [maniˈfesto] *agg* clear, manifest.
maniglia [maˈniʎa] *sf* handle.
manipolare [manipoˈlare] *v* manipulate.
mano [ˈmano] *sf*, *pl* **-i** hand; (*strato*) coat. **alla mano** ready, to hand. **a portata di mano** within reach. **dar** *or* **stringere la mano** a shake hands with. **di prima/seconda mano** first-/second-hand. **far man bassa** make a clean sweep. **fuori mano** outlying, off the beaten track. **man mano che** as. **mettere le mani avanti** take precautions. **sotto mano** handy.
manodopera [manoˈdɔpera] *sf invar* labour, workforce.
*****manomettere** [manoˈmettere] *v* tamper with, violate.
manopola [maˈnɔpola] *sf* (*manubrio*) hand-grip; (*guanto*) mitten; (*radio*, *ecc.*) knob.
manoscritto [manoˈskritto] *sm* manuscript. *agg* handwritten.
manovale [manoˈvale] *sm* labourer.
manovella [manoˈvella] *sf* handle, crank.
manovrare [manovˈrare] *v* handle, manoeuvre. **manovra** *sf* manoeuvre.
mansione [manˈsjone] *sf* function, duty.
mansueto [mansuˈeto] *agg* gentle, meek.
mantello [manˈtɛllo] *sm* coat, cloak.
*****mantenere** [manteˈnere] *v* maintain, keep. **mantenimento** *sm* maintenance.

mantice [ˈmantitʃe] *sm* bellows *pl*.
manto [ˈmanto] *sm* cloak, mantle.
manuale [manuˈale] *agg*, *sm* manual.
manubrio [maˈnubrjo] *sm* handlebar.
manutenzione [manutenˈtsjone] *sf* maintenance, upkeep; (*auto*) servicing.
manzo [ˈmandzo] *sm* (*animale*) steer; (*carne*) beef.
mappa [ˈmappa] *sf* map. **mappamondo** *sm* globe.
maratona [maraˈtona] *sf* marathon.
marca [ˈmarka] *sf* brand.
marcare [marˈkare] *v* mark; (*sport*) score; accentuate.
marchese [marˈkeze] *sm* marquis. **marchesa** *sf* marchioness.
marchio [ˈmarkjo] *sm* mark; (*comm*) trade-mark. **marchio depositato** registered trade-mark.
marcia[1] [ˈmartʃa] *sf* march; (*auto*) gear; (*sport*) walking. **fare marcia indietro** reverse; (*fig*) back out. **mettere in marcia** get going, set off.
marcia[2] [ˈmartʃa] *sf* (*materia*) pus.
marciapiede [martʃaˈpjɛde] *sm* pavement.
marciare [marˈtʃare] *v* march; (*sport*) walk; (*fam: funzionare*) work.
marcio [ˈmartʃo] *agg* rotten; (*fig*) corrupt. *sm* rottenness; rotten part.
marcire [marˈtʃire] *v* rot, go bad. **marciume** *sm* rot.
marco[1] [ˈmarko] *sm* mark.
mare [ˈmare] *sm* sea; (*grande quantità*) host. **alto mare** high sea. **essere in alto mare** (*fig*) be floundering, be at sea. **mare agitato** *or* **mosso** rough sea. **maretta** *sf* choppy sea.
marea [maˈrea] *sf* tide.
maresciallo [mareˈʃallo] *sm* (*sottufficiale*) sergeant major; (*ufficiale*) field-marshal.
margarina [margaˈrina] *sf* margarine.
margherita [margeˈrita] *sf* daisy.
margine [ˈmardʒine] *sm* edge, border; (*fig*) margin.
marina [maˈrina] *sf* navy. **marinaio** *sm* sailor.
marinare [mariˈnare] *v* marinate. **marinare la scuola** play truant.
marionetta [marjoˈnetta] *sf* puppet.
maritare [mariˈtare] *v* marry; (*mescolare*) mix. **maritarsi** *v* get married.
marito [maˈrito] *sm* husband.
marittimo [maˈrittimo] *agg* sea; maritime.

marmaglia [mar'maʎa] *sf* rabble.

marmellata [marmel'lata] *sf* jam; *(di agrumi)* marmalade.

marmo ['marmo] *sm* marble.

marra ['marra] *sf* hoe.

marrone [mar'rone] *sm* chestnut. *agg* brown.

marsupiale [marsu'pjale] *sm*, *agg* marsupial.

martedì [marte'di] *sm* Tuesday.

martellare [martel'lare] *v* hammer; *(fig)* pound. **martellata** *sf* hammer-blow; *(fig)* heavy blow. **martello** *sm* hammer; *(porta)* knocker; *(orologio)* striker.

martinetto [marti'netto] *sm* jack.

martin pescatore [mar'tin peska'tore] *sm* kingfisher.

martire ['martire] *s(m+f)* martyr. **martirio** *sm* martyrdom. **martoriare** *v* torture.

marxismo [mar'ksizmo] *sm* Marxism. **marxista** *s(m+f)*, *agg* Marxist.

marzapane [martsa'pane] *sm* marzipan.

marziale [mar'tsjale] *agg* martial.

marzo ['martso] *sm* march.

mascalzone [maskal'tsone] *sm* rascal, scoundrel. **mascalzonata** *sf* nasty trick.

mascara [mas'kara] *sm* mascara.

mascella [ma'ʃella] *sf* jaw.

maschera [ˈmaskera] *sf* mask; *(travestimento)* disguise; *(cinema, teatro)* usherette. **mascherare** *v* mask; *(con costumi)* dress up; *(celare)* disguise; *(schermare)* screen; *(mimetizzare)* camouflage.

maschile [mas'kile] *agg* male; *(gramm)* masculine; *(per ragazzi)* boys'; *(per uomini)* men's.

maschio ['maskjo] *sm* male; *(ragazzo)* boy.

masochismo [mazo'kizmo] *sm* masochism. **masochista** *s(m+f)* masochist.

massa ['massa] *sf* mass; *(gran numero)* heap, lot; *(elett)* earth.

massacrare [massa'krare] *v* massacre. **massacro** *sm* massacre.

massaggiare [massad'dʒare] *v* massage. **massaggio** *sm* massage.

massaia [mas'saja] *sf* housewife.

masserizie [masse'ritsje] *sf pl* fixtures and fittings *pl*.

massiccio [mas'sittʃo] *agg* solid.

massima ['massima] *sf* maxim; *(norma)* rule. **di massima** general, informal. **in linea di massima** as a general rule, on the whole.

massimo ['massimo] *agg* greatest;

(estremo) utmost; *(il più alto)* highest; *(il migliore)* best; *(fis)* maximum. *sm* maximum; *(tutto ciò che)* most; *(meglio)* best.

massone [mas'sone] *sm* freemason. **massoneria** *sf* freemasonry.

masticare [masti'kare] *v* chew; *(borbottare)* mutter. **gomma da masticare** *sf* chewing gum.

mastice ['mastitʃe] *sm* mastic; *(per vetri)* putty.

mastino [mas'tino] *sm* mastiff.

mastro ['mastro] *sm* ledger.

matassa [ma'tassa] *sf* skein, hank.

matematico [mate'matiko] **-a** *agg* mathematical. *sm*, *sf* mathematician. *sf* mathematics.

materasso [mate'rasso] *sm* mattress. **materassino** *(pneumatico)* *sm* air-bed.

materia [ma'tɛrja] *sf* matter; substance; *(argomento, disciplina)* subject; *(fam: marcia)* pus. **entrare in materia** broach a subject. **materia prima** raw material.

materiale [mate'rjale] *sm*, *agg* material. **materialismo** *sm* materialism. **materialista** *s(m+f)* materialist.

materno [ma'tɛrno] *agg* maternal, motherly. **scuola materna** *sf* nursery school. **maternità** *sf* motherhood; *(ospedale)* maternity hospital.

matita [ma'tita] *sf* pencil.

matriarcale [matriar'kale] *agg* matriarchal.

matrice [ma'tritʃe] *sf* matrix; *(modulo)* counterfoil.

matricola [ma'trikola] *sf* register; *(numero)* serial number; *(studente)* freshman. **matricolare** *v* register.

matrigna [ma'trina] *sf* stepmother.

matrimonio [matri'mɔnjo] *sm* marriage, matrimony; *(festa nuziale)* wedding. **matrimoniale** *agg* matrimonial. **letto matrimoniale** *sm* double bed.

matta ['matta] *sf* *(carte)* joker.

mattatoio [matta'tɔjo] *sm* slaughterhouse.

matterello [matte'rello] *sm* rolling-pin.

mattina [mat'tina] *sf* morning. **mattinata** *sf* morning; *(teatro)* matinée. **mattiniero** *agg* early rising.

matto ['matto] *agg* mad. **andar matto per** be crazy about. **matto da legare** mad as a hatter. **scacco matto** checkmate.

mattone [mat'tone] *sm* brick; *(fam: noioso)* bore. **mattonella** *sf* tile; *(biliardo)* cushion.

menta

mattutino [mattu'tino] *agg* morning.

maturare [matu'rare] *v* mature, ripen; *(med)* come to a head. **maturazione** *sf* ripening. **maturità** *sf* maturity. **esame di maturità** *sm* school-leaving examination, A level(s). **maturo** *agg* ripe; mature.

mausoleo [mauzo'lɛo] *sm* mausoleum.

mazza ['mattsa] *sf* club; *(martello)* sledge-hammer. **mazzata** *sf* heavy blow.

mazzo ['mattso] *sm* bunch; *(carte)* pack. **fare il mazzo** shuffle the cards or pack.

me [me] *pron* me. *V* **mi**.

meccanico [mek'kaniko] *agg* mechanical. *sm* mechanic. **meccanica** *sf* mechanics. **meccanismo** *sm* mechanism, works. **meccanizzare** *v* mechanize. **meccanizzazione** *sf* mechanization.

meccanografico [mekkano'grafiko] *agg* data processing.

medaglia [me'daʎa] *sf* medal. **medaglione** *sm* medallion; *(gioiello)* locket.

medesimo [me'dezimo] *agg* same.

media ['mɛdja] *sf* mean, average; *(scuola)* secondary school. **fare la media di** average.

mediana [me'djana] *sf* median. **mediano** *agg* median, medial.

mediante [me'djante] *prep* through, by (means of).

mediatore [medja'tore], **-trice** *sm, sf* intermediary; *(comm)* broker. **mediazione** *sf* mediation; brokerage.

medicare [medi'kare] *v* treat; *(ferita)* dress. **medicina** *sf* medicine.

medicinale [meditʃi'nale] *agg* medicinal. *sm* medicine.

medico ['mɛdiko] *sm* doctor, physician. *agg* medical. **medico chirurgo** surgeon. **medico condotto** medical officer. **medico generico** general practitioner.

medievale [medje'vale] *agg* medieval.

medio ['mɛdjo] *agg* middle; average; *(scuola)* secondary. *sm* middle finger.

mediocre [me'djɔkre] *agg* mediocre, poor.

meditare [medi'tare] *v* meditate, ponder. **meditazione** *sf* meditation.

mediterraneo [mediter'raneo] *sm, agg* Mediterranean.

medium ['mɛdjum] *s(m+f)* *invar* medium.

medusa [me'duza] *sf* jelly-fish.

megafono [me'gafono] *sm* loudspeaker.

megera [me'dʒɛra] *sf* harridan.

meglio ['mɛʎo] *agg, avv (comparativo)* better; *(superlativo)* best. *sm* best. **alla**

meglio as well as possible. **tanto meglio!** so much the better!

mela ['mela] *sf* apple. **mela cotogna** quince. **melo** *sm* apple-tree.

melagrana [mela'grana] *sf* pomegranate. **melograno** *sm* pomegranate tree.

melanzana [melan'dzana] *sf* aubergine, egg-plant.

melassa [me'lassa] *sf* treacle, molasses.

melma ['melma] *sf* slime.

melodia [melo'dia] *sf* melody. **melodico** *agg* melodious. **melodioso** *agg* melodious, sweet-sounding.

melodramma [melo'dramma] *sm* melo-drama.

melone [me'lone] *sm* melon.

membrana [mem'brana] *sf* membrane; *(acustica)* diaphragm.

membro ['membro] *sm, pl* **-a** *f* in collective sense member; *(anat)* limb.

memoria [me'mɔrja] *sf* memory; *(oggetto ricordo)* souvenir; *(scritto)* memoir. **a memoria** by heart. **prendere memoria di** make a note of. **memoriale** *sm* memorial; petition; *(raccolta di documenti)* record. **memorizzare** *v* memorize.

menare [me'nare] *v* lead; *(portare)* take, bring; *(assestare)* strike. **a menadito** at one's fingertips.

mendicare [mendi'kare] *v* beg. **mendicante** *s(m+f)* beggar.

meno ['meno] *avv (comparativo)* less; *(superlativo)* least; *(mat)* minus. *agg invar (minore)* less; *(in minor numero)* fewer. *prep (eccetto)* but (for), except (for). **a meno che** unless. **fare a meno di** do without. **meno male!** thank goodness! **o meno** *(o no)* or not. **tanto meno** let alone. **venir meno** *(svenire)* faint; *(mancare)* fail. **venir meno alla parola** break one's word. *sm invar* (the) least. **i meno** *sm pl* (the) minority *sing*.

menomare [meno'mare] *v* diminish; *(danneggiare)* injure, disable. **menomato, -a** *s, agg* disabled.

menopausa [meno'pauza] *sf* menopause.

mensa ['mɛnsa] *sf* table; refectory; *(mil)* mess.

mensile [men'sile] *agg* monthly. *sm (giornale)* monthly; *(paga)* monthly pay.

mensola ['mɛnsola] *sf* bracket, shelf; *(caminetto)* mantelpiece.

menta ['menta] *sf* mint; *(peperina)* peppermint; *(romana)* spearmint.

mente ['mente] *sf* mind; intellect. **venire in mente** occur; come to mind. **mentale** *agg* mental. **mentalità** *sf* mentality.

mentire [men'tire] *v* lie. **mentito** *agg* false.

mento ['mento] *sm* chin.

mentre ['mentre] *cong* while, as; *(laddove)* whereas.

menu [mə'ny] *sm* menu.

menzionare [mentsjo'nare] *v* mention. **menzione** *sf* mention.

menzogna [men'dzoɲa] *sf* lie. **menzognero** *agg* lying, false.

meraviglia [mera'viʎa] *sf* wonder, marvel; *(stupore)* surprise. **a meraviglia** wonderfully. **meravigliare** *v* surprise, amaze. **meraviglioso** *agg* marvellous, wonderful.

mercante [mer'kante] *sm* merchant, trader. **mercanteggiare** *v* trade, deal; *(contrattare)* haggle, bargain. **mercantile** *agg* mercantile. **nave mercantile** *sf* merchant ship.

mercanzia [merkan'tsia] *sf* merchandise, goods *pl*.

mercato [mer'kato] *sm* market. **a buon mercato** cheap, inexpensive.

merce ['mertʃe] *sf* merchandise, goods *pl*; *(in magazzino)* stock.

mercenario [mertʃe'narjo] *agg*, *sm* mercenary.

merciaio [mer'tʃajo], **-a** *sm*, *sf* haberdasher. **merceria** *sf* haberdashery.

mercoledì [mercole'di] *sm* Wednesday.

mercurio [mer'kurjo] *sm* mercury.

merda ['merda] *sf* *(volg)* shit.

merenda [me'renda] *sf* *(afternoon)* snack, tea.

meridiano [meri'djano] *sf* *(geog)* meridian. *agg* *(di mezzogiorno)* midday. **meridiana** *sf* *(geog)* meridian line; *(orologio solare)* sundial.

meridionale [meridjo'nale] *agg* southern, south. *s(m+f)* southerner. **meridione** *sm* south.

meringa [me'ringa] *sf* meringue.

meritare [meri'tare] *v* deserve, merit. **meritevole** *agg* deserving, worthy.

merito ['merito] *sm* merit. **a pari merito** equal. **in merito a** regarding, as to, about. **per merito di** thanks to.

merletto [mer'letto] *sm* lace.

merlo ['merlo] *sm* blackbird; *(sempliciotto)* fool.

merluzzo [mer'luttso] *sm* cod; *(nasello)* hake.

mero ['mɛro] *agg* mere.

meschino [mes'kino] *agg* wretched, mean.

mescolare [mesko'lare] *v* mix; *(unire)* blend. **mescolatore, -trice** *sm*, *sf* mixer.

mese ['meze] *sm* month.

messa[1] ['messa] *sf* *(rel)* Mass. **messale** *sm* missal.

messa[2] ['messa] *sf* *(il mettere)* placing, putting.

messaggio [mes'saddʒo] *sm* message. **messaggero** *sm* messenger; *(fig)* herald.

messo ['messo] *sm* usher.

mestiere [mes'tjere] *sm* job, trade; *(manuale)* craft; profession. **di mestiere** by profession. **essere del mestiere** be an expert. **ferri del mestiere** *sm pl* tools of the trade *pl*.

mesto ['mɛsto] *agg* sad, mournful. **mestizia** *sf* sadness.

mestolo ['mestolo], **-a** *sm*, *sf* ladle, kitchen spoon.

mestruazione [mestrua'tsjone] *sf* menstruation; *(fam)* period. **mestruale** *agg* menstrual.

meta ['meta] *sf* goal, aim; destination; *(rugby)* try.

metà [me'ta] *sf* half; *(centro)* middle. **a metà strada** half-way. **fare a metà** halve; *(fam)* go halves.

metabolismo [metabo'lizmo] *sm* metabolism. **metabolico** *agg* metabolic.

metafisico [meta'fiziko], **-a** *agg* metaphysical. *sm*, *sf* metaphysician. **metafisica** *sf* metaphysics.

metafora [me'tafora] *sf* metaphor, figure of speech. **metaforico** *agg* metaphorical.

metallo [me'tallo] *sm* metal. **metallico** *agg* metallic. **metallurgia** *sf* metallurgy.

metamorfosi [meta'morfozi] *sf* metamorphosis, transformation.

metano [me'tano] *sm* methane.

meteora [me'tɛora] *sf* meteor. **meteorico** *agg* meteoric.

meteorologia [meteorolo'dʒia] *sf* meteorology. **meteorologico** *agg* meteorological, weather. **bollettino meteorologico** *sm* weather report. **previsioni meteorologiche** *sf pl* weather forecast *sing*.

meticcio [me'tittʃo], **-a** *s*, *agg* half-caste.

meticoloso [metiko'lozo] *agg* meticulous.

metodista [meto'dista] *s(m+f)*, *agg* methodist.

metodo ['mɛtodo] *sm* method. **metodico** *agg* methodical.

metro ['mɛtro] *sm* metre; (*per misurare*) rule; (*a nastro*) tape-measure. **metrico** *agg* (*misura*) metric; (*poesia*) metrical.

metropoli [me'trɔpoli] *sf* metropolis. **metropolitana** *sf* underground (railway).

*****mettere** ['mettere] *v* put; place; lay (down); (*indossare*) put on, wear; (*supporre*) suppose. **mettersi sotto** get down to it.

mezzo [mɛddzo] *agg* half; (*medio*) middle. **mezzogiorno** *sm* noon, midday; (*geog*) south. *sm* half; (*centro*) middle; (*strumento*) means. **a** or **per mezzo di** by, through. **mezzi** *pl* means *pl*. *avv* half; (*quasi*) nearly. **andarci di mezzo** (*avere la peggio*) suffer for it; (*essere in gioco*) be at stake. **togliere di mezzo** get rid of.

mi [mi], **me** *pron* (to) me; (*riflessivo*) myself.

miagolare [mjago'lare] *v* mew, miaow. **miagolio** *sm* mewing.

mica¹ ['mika] *avv* (*fam*) at all.

mica² ['mika] *sf* mica.

miccia ['mittʃa] *sf* fuse.

microbo ['mikrobo] *sm* microbe.

microcosmo [mikro'kɔzmo] *sm* microcosm.

microfilm [mikro'film] *sm invar* microfilm.

microfono [mi'krɔfono] *sm* microphone; (*telefono*) mouthpiece.

microscopio [mikro'skɔpjo] *sm* microscope. **microscopico** *agg* microscopic.

microsolco [mikro'solko] *sm* microgroove; (*disco a 33 giri*) LP; (*disco a 45 giri*) EP.

midollo [mi'dollo] *sm* marrow; (*bot*) pith. **bagnato fino al midollo** soaked to the skin. **fino al midollo** to the core. **midollo spinale** spinal cord.

miele ['mjɛle] *sm* honey.

mietere ['mjɛtere] *v* reap, harvest; (*uccidere*) mow down. **mietitore, -trice** *sm*, *sf* reaper, harvester. **mietitrebbiatrice** *sf* combine harvester. **mietitura** *sf* reaping, harvesting; (*periodo, messe*) harvest.

migliaio [mi'ʎajo] *sm*, *pl* **-a** *f* thousand; (*circa mille*) about a thousand.

miglio¹ [mi'ʎo] *sm*, *pl* **-a** *f* mile.

miglio² [mi'ʎo] *sm* (*bot*) millet.

migliore [mi'ʎore] *agg* (*comparativo*) better; (*superlativo*) best. *sm* best.

mignolo [mi'ɲolo] *sm* (*della mano*) little finger; (*del piede*) little toe.

migrare [mi'grare] *v* migrate. **migratorio** *agg* migratory. **migrazione** *sf* migration.

milione [mi'ljone] *sm* million. **milionesimo** *sm*, *agg* millionth.

militare [mili'tare] *agg* military. *sm* soldier. *v* militate. **militarismo** *sm* militarism. **militarista** *s(m+f)*, *agg* militarist.

milite ['milite] *sm* soldier, warrior. **milizia** *sf* (*corpo armato*) militia.

millantare [millan'tare] *v* boast. **millantato credito** *sm* false pretences *pl*. **millantatore, -trice** *sm*, *sf* braggart, show-off. **millanteria** *sf* boasting.

mille ['mille] *agg*, *sm* thousand. **millennio** *sm* millennium. **millesimo** *agg*, *sm* thousandth.

milligrammo [milli'grammo] *sm* milligram.

millimetro [mil'limetro] *sm* millimetre.

mimetizzare [mimetid'dzare] *v* camouflage. **mimetizzazione** *sf* camouflage.

mimica ['mimika] *sf* mime. **mimico** *agg* mimic. **mimo** *sm* mime; (*uccello*) mocking-bird.

mina ['mina] *sf* mine; (*di matita*) lead. **minare** *v* mine; (*insidiare*) undermine. **minatore** *sm* miner.

minaccia [mi'nattʃa] *sf* threat. **minacciare** *v* threaten. **minaccioso** *agg* threatening.

minareto [mina'rɛto] *sm* minaret.

minerale [mine'rale] *agg*, *sm* mineral.

minerario [mine'rarjo] *agg* mining.

minestra [mi'nɛstra] *sf* soup.

mingherlino [minger'lino] *agg* skinny.

miniatura [minja'tura] *sf* miniature.

miniera [mi'njɛra] *sf* mine.

minimo ['minimo] *agg* (*il più piccolo*) least, smallest, slightest; (*più basso*) minimum; (*piccolissimo*) very small, very slight; (*molto basso*) very low. *sm* minimum; (*la minima cosa*) least.

ministero [mini'stɛro] *sm* (*pol*) ministry. **pubblico ministero** public prosecutor.

ministro [mi'nistro] *sm* minister.

minore [mi'nore] *s(m+f)*, *agg* (*più piccolo*) less, smaller; (*più basso*) lower; (*più giovane*) younger; (*superlativo*) least, lowest, youngest; (*mat, musica*) minor. **minorità** *sf* minority.

minorenne [mino'renne] *s(m+f)* minor. *agg* under age.

minuetto [minu'etto] *sm* minuet.

minuscolo [mi'nuskolo] *agg* small, diminutive. **minuscola** *sf* small letter.

minuta [mi'nuta] *sf* draft.

minuto[1] [mi'nuto] *agg* small, minute; detailed. **al minuto** retail. **vendere al minuto** retail.

minuto[2] [mi'nuto] *sm* (*primo*) minute. **minuto secondo** second. **spaccare il minuto** be dead on time.

mio ['mio], *m pl* **miei** *agg* my. *pron* mine.

miope ['miope] *agg* short-sighted. **miopia** *sf* short-sightedness.

mira ['mira] *sf* aim.

miracolo [mi'rakolo] *sm* miracle. **miracoloso** *agg* miraculous.

miraggio [mi'raddʒo] *sm* mirage.

mirare [mi'rare] *v* aim; (*prendere mira*) take aim. **mirino** *sm* sight; (*foto*) viewfinder.

mirtillo [mir'tillo] *sm* bilberry. **mirtillo rosso** cranberry.

miscela [mi'ʃela] *sf* mixture; (*caffè, tè, tabacco*) blend. **miscelare** *v* mix, blend.

mischia ['miskja] *sf* fray.

mischiare [mis'kjare] *v* mix; (*carte*) shuffle.

miscuglio [mis'kuʎo] *sm* mixture.

miseria [mi'zerja] *sm* poverty; (*inezia*) pittance; squalor. **miserabile** *agg* miserable, wretched. **misero** ['mizero] *agg* poor, wretched.

misericordia [mizeri'kɔrdja] *sf* mercy. **senza misericordia** merciless; (*spietato*) ruthless.

missile ['missile] *sm* missile.

missione [mis'sjone] *sf* mission. **missionario, -a** *s, agg* missionary.

mistero [mis'tero] *sm* mystery. **misterioso** *agg* mysterious.

mistico ['mistiko], **-a** *agg* mystical. *sm, sf* mystic. *sf* mysticism. **misticismo** *sm* mysticism.

misto ['misto] *agg* mixed.

misura [mi'zura] *sf* measure; (*taglia, dimensione*) size; (*atto e modo del misurare*) measurement; moderation. **fatto su misura** made to measure. **prendere delle misure** take steps.

misurare [mizu'rare] *v* measure; limit; (*indumenti*) try on. **misurato** *agg* measured, moderate.

mite ['mite] *agg* mild, moderate.

mito ['mito] *sm* myth. **mitico** *agg* mythical. **mitologia** *sf* mythology. **mitologico** *agg* mythological.

mitra[1] ['mitra] *sf* (*rel*) mitre.

mitra[2] ['mitra] *sm invar* tommy-gun.

mitragliatrice [mitraʎa'tritʃe] *sf* machine-gun. **mitragliamento** *sm* machine-gun fire; (*fig*) bombarding. **mitragliare** *v* machine-gun; (*fig*) bombard.

mittente [mit'tɛnte] *s(m+f)* sender.

mobile ['mɔbile] *agg* mobile, moving; movable. **squadra mobile** *sf* flying squad. *sm* piece of furniture. **mobili** *sm pl* furniture *sing*.

mobilia [mo'bilja] *sf* furnishings *pl*; (*mobili*) furniture.

mobiliare [mobi'ljare] *agg* movable. *v* furnish.

mobilitare [mobili'tare] *v* mobilize. **mobilitazione** *sf* mobilization.

mocassino [mokas'sino] *sm* moccasin.

moccolo ['mɔkkolo] *sm* candle-end. **reggere il moccolo** play gooseberry. **tirare dei moccoli** (*fam*) swear.

moda ['mɔda] *sf* fashion. **di** *or* **alla moda** in fashion, fashionable. **fuori moda** out of fashion. **passare di moda** go out of fashion.

modalità [modali'ta] *sf* procedure, formality.

modellare [model'lare] *v* model. **modella** *sf* model. **modello** *sm* model; (*disegno*) pattern.

moderare [mode'rare] *v* moderate, lower; control. **moderatore** *sm* moderator; (*TV, radio*) chairman. **moderazione** *sf* moderation, restraint.

moderno [mo'dɛrno] *agg* modern; (*al passo coi tempi*) up-to-date. **modernizzare** *v* modernize, bring up-to-date.

modestia [mo'dɛstja] *sf* modesty. **modesto** *agg* modest, unassuming; (*umile*) humble.

modificare [modifi'kare] *v* modify, alter. **modifica** *sf* alteration, modification.

modista [mo'dista] *sf* milliner.

modo ['mɔdo] *sm* manner, way; opportunity; (*gramm*) mood. **ad ogni modo** anyhow, in any case. **di modo che** (*affinché*) so that; (*e così*) and so. **in modo da** so that. **in qualche modo** somehow. **modo di dire** expression, idiom. **modo di fare** manner. **per modo di dire** so to speak.

modulare [modu'lare] *v* modulate.

modulo ['mɔdulo] *sm* form; (*mat, tec*) modulus.

mogano ['mɔgano] *sm* mahogany.

moglio ['mɔdʒo] *agg* downhearted.

moglie ['moλe] *sf* wife.

moina [mo'ina] *sf* fare moine coax.

molare [mo'lare] *v* grind. *agg* molar. **pietra molare** *sf* millstone. **mola** *sf* grinding wheel.

mole ['mole] *sf* pile, mass; *(grandezza)* size.

molecola [mo'lεkola] *sf* molecule.

molesto [mo'lεsto] *agg* troublesome, annoying. **molestare** *v* trouble, annoy. **molestia** *sf* annoyance, nuisance.

molla ['molla] *sf* spring; *(stimolo)* mainspring. **molle** *sf pl* tongs *pl*. **mollare** *v* *(lasciar andare)* let go; *(allentare)* loosen, slacken. **molleggiato** *agg* sprung. **molletta** *sf* *(biancheria)* (clothes-)peg; *(capelli)* hair-pin.

molle ['molle] *agg* soft; *(bagnato)* wet; *(debole)* weak. **mettere in molle** steep.

mollusco [mol'lusko] *sm* mollusc.

molo ['molo] *sm* jetty; *(banchina)* wharf.

molteplice [mol'teplitʃe] *agg* manifold; varied.

moltiplicare [moltipli'kare] *v* multiply.

moltitudine [molti'tudine] *sm* multitude, host.

molto ['molto] *agg* a lot of, lots of, much; *(pl)* many; *(tempo)* long. *avv* much, a lot; *(con agg e avv positivi)* very. *pron.* a lot, much; *(pl)* many.

momento [mo'mento] *sm* moment. **a momenti** *(tra poco)* shortly; *(quasi)* almost. **al momento d'oggi** nowadays. **dal momento che** since.

monaca ['monaka] *sf* nun. **monaco** *sm* monk.

Monaco ['monako] *sf* *(principato)* Monaco; *(di Baviera)* Munich.

monarca [mo'narka] *sm* monarch, king. **monarchia** *sf* monarchy. **monarchico, -a** *sm, sf* monarchist.

monastero [monas'tεro] *sm* monastery. **monastico** *agg* monastic.

monco ['monko] *agg* maimed. **essere monco di ... have ... missing. moncherino** *sm* stump.

mondezzaio [mondet'tsajo] *sm* rubbish heap; *(ambiente sudicio)* pigsty. **mondare** *v* *(sbucciare)* peel; *(togliere erbacce)* weed.

mondo ['mondo] *sm* world. **mandare all'altro mondo** *(fam)* send to hell. **mettere al mondo** give birth to. **vivere nel mondo della luna** have one's head in the clouds. **mondiale** *agg* world; *(diffuso)* world-wide.

monello [mo'nεllo] *sm* urchin. **monelleria** *sf* prank.

moneta [mo'neta] *sf* coin; *(denaro)* money; *(spicciola)* (small) change. **monetario** *agg* monetary.

monito ['monito] *sm* warning.

monocolore [monoko'lore] *agg* plain; *(pol)* one-party.

monocromo [mo'nokromo] *agg, sm* monochrome.

monogamo [mo'nogamo], **-a** *agg* monogamous. *sm, sf* monogamist. **monogamia** *sf* monogamy.

monolitico [mono'litiko] *agg* monolithic.

monologo [mo'nologo] *sm, pl* **-ghi** monologue.

monopolio [mono'poljo] *sm* monopoly. **monopolizzare** *v* monopolize.

monoteismo [monote'izmo] *sm* monotheism.

monotono [mo'notono] *agg* monotonous. **monotonia** *sf* monotony.

monsone [mon'sone] *sm* monsoon.

monta ['monta] *sf* *(accoppiamento)* mounting; *(luogo)* stud-farm; *(modo di cavalcare)* riding.

montacarichi [monta'kariki] *sm* goods lift.

montaggio [mon'taddʒo] *sm* assembly; *(cinema)* editing.

montagna [mon'taɲa] *sf* mountain. **montagne russe** switchback *sing*.

montare [mon'tare] *v* *(salire)* climb; *(tec)* assemble; *(incorniciare)* mount; *(film)* edit; *(macchina)* get in(to). **montare a cavallo** get on a horse; *(cavalcare)* ride. **montatura** *sf* assembly; *(occhiali)* frame; *(pubblicitaria)* stunt.

monte ['monte] *sm* mountain; *(davanti a nome)* Mount. **a monte** above, upstream. **andare a monte** fall through. **mandare a monte** upset; *(disdire)* cancel. **monte di pietà** pawnshop. **monte premi** jackpot. **montuoso** *agg* mountainous.

montone [mon'tone] *sm* ram; *(carne)* mutton.

monumento [monu'mento] *sm* monument. **monumentale** *agg* monumental.

mora ['mora] *sf* *(gelso)* mulberry; *(rovo)* blackberry.

morale [mo'rale] *agg* moral. *sf* *(dottrina)* ethics *pl*; morality, morals *pl*; *(insegnamento)* moral. *sm* morale. essere su/giù

di morale be cheerful/depressed. **moralizzare** v moralize.

morbido ['mɔrbido] agg soft.

morbillo [mor'billo] sm measles.

morbo ['mɔrbo] sm disease. **morboso** agg morbid; pathological.

*****mordere** ['mɔrdere] v bite; (afferrare) grip. **mordere il freno** strain at the leash. **mordace** agg biting, caustic.

morfina [mor'fina] sf morphine.

morigerato [moridʒe'rato] agg sober, clean-living.

*****morire** [mo'rire] v die. **avere una fame/sete da morire** be terribly hungry/thirsty.

mormorare [mormo'rare] v murmur. **mormorio** sm murmur.

moro[1] ['mɔro] agg dark; (nero) black; (carnagione) swarthy; (capelli) brown.

moro[2] ['mɔro] sm (gelso) mulberry.

morsa ['mɔrsa] sf vice. **morsetto** sm clamp; (elett) terminal.

morsicare [morsi'kare] v gnaw, bite. **morso** sm bite; (fig) sting; (cavallo) bit.

mortaio [mor'tajo] sm mortar.

mortale [mor'tale] agg mortal; (implacabile) deadly. **mortalità** sf mortality.

morte ['mɔrte] sf death.

morto ['mɔrto] agg dead. sm dead person; (carte) dummy. **fare il morto** float (on one's back).

mosaico [mo'zaiko] sm mosaic.

mosca ['moska] sf fly; (barbetta) goatee. **mosca cieca** blindman's buff. **moscerino** sm small fly.

Mosca ['moska] sf Moscow.

moscato[1] [mos'kato] agg muscat(el). **noce moscata** sf nutmeg.

moscato[2] [mos'kato] agg (cavallo) dappled.

moschea [mos'kɛa] sf mosque.

moschetto [mos'ketto] sm musket. **moschettiere** sm musketeer.

mossa ['mɔssa] sf movement; (fig) move.

mosso ['mɔsso] agg (mare) rough; (capelli) wavy.

mostarda [mos'tarda] sf mustard.

mostrare [mos'trare] v show. **mostra** sf show, exhibition; ostentation; (campione) sample. **mettere in mostra** display.

mostro ['mɔstro] sm monster. **mostruosità** sf monstrosity. **mostruoso** agg monstrous.

motivo [mo'tivo] sm ground, reason; (disegno, musica) motif. **motivare** v motivate. **motivazione** sf motivation.

moto[1] ['mɔto] sm motion; (sommossa) rebellion. **mettere in moto** set in motion, start (up).

moto[2] ['mɔto] sf (fam) motor-bike.

motocicletta [mototʃik'letta] sf motorcycle. **motociclista** s(m+f) motor-cyclist.

motore [mo'tore] sm engine. agg motor. **albero motore** sm crankshaft. **motorino d'avviamento** sm starter (motor).

motoscafo [moto'skafo] sm motor-boat.

motto ['mɔtto] sm motto; (detto) saying.

movimento [movi'mento] sm movement; activity. **movimentato** agg lively, busy.

mozione [mo'tsjone] sf motion.

mozzare [mot'tsare] v cut off; (coda) dock. **mozzare il fiato** take one's breath away.

mozzicone [mottsi'kone] sm butt.

mucca ['mukka] sf cow.

mucchio ['mukkjo] sm heap.

muco ['muko] sm mucus. **mucosa** sf mucous membrane.

muda ['muda] sf moulting.

muffa ['muffa] sf mould. **muffoso** agg mouldy.

muggire [mud'dʒire] v also **mugghiare** bellow; (mare) roar; (vento) howl.

mughetto [mu'getto] sm lily of the valley.

mugnaio [mu'najo] sm miller.

mugolare [mugo'lare] v howl, whine.

mulattiera [mulat'tjera] sf (mule-)track.

mulino [mu'lino] sm mill; (a vento) windmill. **mulinello** sm whirlpool; (pesca) reel.

mulo ['mulo] sm mule.

multa ['multa] sf fine.

multicolore [multiko'lore] agg multicoloured.

multiplo ['multiplo] agg, sm multiple.

mummia ['mummja] sf mummy. **mummificare** v mummify.

*****mungere** ['mundʒere] v milk.

municipio [muni'tʃipjo] sm (comune) municipality; (sede) town hall. **municipale** agg municipal.

munire [mu'nire] v supply; fortify.

munizione [muni'tsjone] sf munitions pl; (military) stores pl. **munizioni** sf pl ammunition sing.

*****muovere** ['mwɔvere] v move.

muraglia [mu'raʎa] sf wall.

muratore [mura'tore] sm bricklayer.

muro ['muro] sm wall. **mura** sf pl city

walls *pl*. **parlare al muro** talk to a brick wall.

musa ['muza] *sf* muse.

muschio[1] ['muskjo] *sm* (*bot*) moss. **muscoso** *agg* mossy.

muschio[2] ['muskjo] *sm* (*odore*) musk.

muscolo ['muskolo] *sm* muscle.

museo [mu'zɛo] *sm* museum.

museruola [muze'rwɔla] *sf* muzzle.

musica ['muzika] *sf* music. **musicale** *agg* musical, music. **musicista** *s(m+f)* musician.

muso ['muzo] *sm* snout; (*spreg*) mug. **mettere il muso lungo** pull a long face.

mussolina [musso'lina] *sf* muslin.

mutande [mu'tande] *sf pl also* **mutandine** (*da donna*) panties *pl*; (*da uomo*) underpants *pl*; (*da bagno*) swimming trunks *pl*.

mutare [mu'tare] *v* change; (*fare la muta*) shed. **mutabile** *or* **mutevole** *agg* changeable; (*fig*) fickle. **mutamento** *sm* change. **mutazione** *sf* mutation.

mutilare [muti'lare] *v* maim, mutilate. **mutilato, -a** *sm, sf* disabled person.

muto ['muto], **-a** *agg* silent; (*affetto da mutismo*) dumb. *sm, sf* mute. **linguaggio dei muti** *sm* deaf-and-dumb language.

mutuo ['mutuo] *agg* mutual. *sm* loan. **mutuo ipotecario** mortgage. **mutua** *sf* insurance.

N

nafta ['nafta] *sf* fuel oil.

nailon ['nailon] *sm invar* nylon.

nanna ['nanna] *sf* **fare la nanna** (*fam*) sleep.

nano ['nano], **-a** *s, agg* dwarf.

Napoli ['napoli] *sf* Naples. **napoletano, -a** *s, agg* Neapolitan.

nappa ['nappa] *sf* tassel; (*fam: naso*) conk; (*pelle*) nappa.

narciso [nar'tʃizo] *sm* narcissus; (*giunchiglia*) daffodil.

narcotico [nar'kɔtiko] *agg, sm* narcotic. **narcosi** *sf* narcosis.

narice [na'ritʃe] *sf* nostril.

narrare [nar'rare] *v* tell. **narrativa** *sf* fiction. **narrazione** *sf* tale.

*nascere [na'ʃere] *v* be born; (*fig*) (a)rise, start (up). **far nascere** give rise to. **nascita** *sf* birth. **atto di nascita** *sm* birth certificate.

*nascondere [nas'kondere] *v* hide. **nascondiglio** *sm* hide-out. **nascondino** *sm* hide-and-seek.

nascosto [nas'kosto] *agg* hidden.

nasello [na'zɛllo] *sm* hake.

naso ['nazo] *sm* nose. **cacciare** *or* **ficcare il naso (in)** poke one's nose (into).

nastro ['nastro] *sm* ribbon; (*tec*) tape. **nastro sonoro** sound-track. **nastro trasportatore** conveyor belt.

nasturzio [nas'turtsjo] *sm* nasturtium.

natale [na'tale] *agg* native. **Natale** *sm* Christmas. **natalizio** *agg* Christmas. **giorno natalizio** *sm* birthday.

natatoia [nata'toja] *sf* flipper, fin.

natica [na'tika] *sf* buttock.

nativo [na'tivo] *agg* native.

nato ['nato] *agg* born. **appena nato** newborn. **... nato e sputato** the (spitting) image of ... **nato morto** stillborn.

natura [na'tura] *sf* nature. **naturale** *agg* natural. **naturalezza** *sf* spontaneity; simplicity. **naturalistico** *agg* naturalistic.

naturalizzare [naturalid'dzare] *v* naturalize. **naturalizzazione** *sf* naturalization.

naufragio [nau'fradʒo] *sm* shipwreck; (*fig*) wreck. **naufragare** *v* be shipwrecked; (*fig*) come to grief. **naufrago, -a** *sm, sf* survivor.

nausea ['nauzea] *sf* nausea. **dare la nausea a** make sick. **provar nausea** feel sick. **nauseante** *agg* nauseating, sickening. **nauseato** *agg* nauseated, sickened.

nautico ['nautiko] *agg* nautical. **sport nautici** *sm pl* water sports *pl*.

navata [na'vata] *sf* (*centrale*) nave; (*laterale*) aisle.

nave ['nave] *sf* ship. **nave cisterna** tanker. **nave di salvataggio** lifeboat. **nave traghetto** ferry. **navale** *agg* naval. **navalmeccanica** *sf* shipbuilding. **navalmeccanico** *sm* shipyard worker.

navetta [na'vetta] *sf* shuttle.

navigare [navi'gare] *v* sail, navigate. **navigatore** *sm* navigator. **navigazione** *sf* navigation.

nazionalizzare [natsjonalid'dzare] *v* nationalize. **nazionalizzazione** *sf* nationalization.

nazione [na'tsjone] *sf* nation. **nazionale** *agg* national; (*econ*) domestic. **nazionalismo** *sm* nationalism. **nazionalista** *s(m+f)*, *agg* nationalist. **nazionalità** *sf* nationality.

nazismo [na'dzizmo] *sm* Nazism, National Socialism. **nazista** *s(m+f)*, *agg* Nazi.

ne [ne] *pron* of it or them, about it or them; (*partitivo*) some, any. *avv* from there.

nè [ne] *cong* neither, nor; (*con altra negazione*) either. **nè ... nè ...** neither ... nor ... .

neanche [ne'anke] *avv*, *cong*, *also* **nemmeno, neppure** neither; either; (*rafforzativo*) not even.

nebbia ['nebbja] *sf* fog; (*foschia*) haze, mist. **nebbioso** *agg* foggy.

necessario [netʃes'sarjo] *agg* necessary, needed (for). *sm* necessary. **lo stretto necessario** the bare necessities *pl*.

necessità [netʃessi'ta] *sf* necessity, need. **di prima necessità** essential. **in caso di necessità** if necessary. **trovarsi nella necessità di** be obliged to.

negare [ne'gare] *v* deny. **negato** *agg* denied; (*senza disposizione*) hopeless (at). **negazione** *sf* denial.

negativa [nega'tiva] *sf* negative. **negativo** *agg* negative.

negli ['neʎi] *prep+art* in **gli**.

negligente [negli'dʒɛnte] *agg* negligent. **negligenza** *sf* negligence.

negoziare [nego'tsjare] *v* negotiate.

negozio [ne'gotsjo] *sm* shop; (*affare*) deal. **negoziante** *s(m+f)* shopkeeper; dealer; (*all'ingrosso*) wholesaler; (*al minuto*) retailer.

negro ['negro], **-a** *agg* Negro, black. *sm*, *sf* Negro, black person. **negriere** *sm* slaver; (*fig*) slave-driver.

nei ['nei] *prep+art* in **i**.

nel [nel] *prep+art* in **il**.

nell' [nell] *prep+art* in **l'**.

nella ['nella] *prep+art* in **la**.

nelle ['nelle] *prep+art* in **le**.

nello ['nello] *prep+art* in **lo**.

nemico [ne'miko], **-a** *agg* enemy, hostile; (*dannoso*) bad. *sm*, *sf* enemy.

nemmeno [nem'meno] *V* **neanche**.

neo ['nɛo] *sm* mole; (*posticcio*) beauty-spot.

neon [nɛon] *sm* neon.

neonato [neo'nato], **-a** *agg* new-born. *sm*, *sf* new-born baby.

neozelandese [neodzelan'deze] *agg* New Zealand. *sm*, *sf* New Zealander.

nepotismo [nepo'tizmo] *sm* nepotism.

neppure [nep'pure] *V* **neanche**.

nerbo ['nɛrbo] *sm* whip; (*fig*) force.

nero ['nero] *agg*, *sm* black. **bestia nera** *sf* bugbear. **borsa nera** *sf* black market. **nerastro** *agg* blackish.

nervo ['nɛrvo] *sm* nerve; (*bot*) rib, vein; (*corda*) string. **avere i nervi** be on edge, be irritable. **dare ai** *or* **sui nervi a qualcuno** get on somebody's nerves. **nervoso** *agg* nervous; irritable; (*eccitabile*) highly strung. **esaurimento nervoso** *sm* nervous breakdown.

nesso ['nɛsso] *sm* connection.

nessuno [nes'suno] *agg* no. *pron* (*persone*) nobody, no-one; (*cose*) none; (*qualcuno*) anybody.

nettare [net'tare] *sm* nectar.

netto ['netto] *agg* clean; (*fig*) clear, sharp; (*peso*, *comm*) net. **nettezza** *sf* cleanliness; (*precisione*) clarity. **nettezza urbana** *sf* street-cleaning; refuse collection.

neutrale [neu'trale] *s(m+f)*, *agg* neutral. **neutralità** *sf* neutrality. **neutralizzare** *v* neutralize; (*fig*) counteract.

neutro ['nɛutro] *agg*, *sm* neutral; (*gramm*, *sesso*) neuter. **neutrone** *sm* neutron.

neve ['neve] *sf* snow. **cumulo di neve** *sm* snowdrift. **pupazzo di neve** *sm* snowman. **nevato** *or* **nevoso** *agg* snowy. **nevicare** [nevi'kare] *v* snow. **nevicata** *sf* snowfall.

nevischio [ne'viskjo] *sm* sleet.

nevralgia [nevral'dʒia] *sf* neuralgia.

nevrosi [ne'vrozi] *sf* neurosis. **nevrotico, -a** *s*, *agg* neurotic.

nibbio ['nibbjo] *sm* kite.

nicchia ['nikkja] *sf* niche, recess.

nichel ['nikel] *sm* nickel. **nichelare** *v* nickel-plate. **nichelatura** *sf* nickel-plating.

nichilismo [niki'lizmo] *sm* nihilism. **nichilista** *s(m+f)* nihilist.

nicotina [niko'tina] *sf* nicotine.

nido ['nido] *sm* nest. **nido d'ape** honeycomb. **nido d'infanzia** crèche, day nursery. **nidiata** *sf* brood.

niente ['njɛnte] *pron* nothing; (*con altra negazione*) anything. *sm* nothing; (*cosa da poco*) slightest thing. **da niente** unimportant. **niente paura!** don't be afraid! **non fa niente** (*non importa*) it doesn't matter.

ninfa ['ninfa] *sf* nymph. **ninfomane** *sf*, *agg* nymphomaniac.

ninfea [nin'fea] *sf* water lily.

ninna-nanna [ninna'nanna] *sm* lullaby.

ninnolo ['ninnolo] *sm* (*balocco*) toy; (*gingillo*) knick-knack.

nipote [ni'pote] *sm* (*di nonni*) grandson; (*di zii*) nephew. *sf* (*di nonni*) grand-daughter; (*di zii*) niece.

nitido ['nitido] *agg* neat; (*fig*) clear.

nitrire [ni'trire] *v* neigh. **nitrito** *sm* neigh.

no [nɔ] *avv* no. *sm* no; (*rifiuto*) refusal. **come no!** of course! and how! **se no** otherwise, or else. **uno sì e uno no** every other one.

nobile ['nɔbile] *agg* noble. *sm* nobleman. *sf* noblewoman. **nobiltà** *sf* nobility.

nocca ['nɔkka] *sf* knuckle; (*del cavallo*) fetlock.

nocciola [not'tʃɔla] *sf* hazel-nut. *agg, sm invar* (*colore*) hazel. **nocciolina** (**americana**) *sf* peanut. **nocciolo** *sm* (*pianta*) hazel.

nocciolo [not'tʃɔlo] *sm* (*bot*) stone, kernel; (*fig*) heart, point; (*tec*) core.

noce ['nɔtʃe] *sm* (*albero*) walnut(-tree); (*legno*) walnut. *sf* (*frutto*) walnut. **noce di burro** pat of butter. **noce di cocco** coconut. **noce moscata** nutmeg. **nocepesca** *sf* nectarine.

nocivo [no'tʃivo] *agg* harmful.

nodo ['nɔdo] *sm* knot; (*incrocio*) junction; (*trama*) plot. **avere un nodo alla gola** have a lump in one's throat. **nodo scorsoio** slip-knot. **nodoso** *agg* knotty.

noi ['noi] *pron* (*soggetto*) we; (*oggetto*) us.

noia ['nɔja] *sf* (*tedio*) boredom; (*fastidio*) nuisance; (*fam*) bore. **avere delle noie con** have trouble with. **dare noia (a)** trouble, bother. **noioso** *agg* boring; (*fastidioso*) troublesome.

noleggiare [noled'dʒare] *v* hire, rent. **noleggio** *sm* hire; (*prezzo*) rental. **nolo** *sm* freight. **dare a nolo** hire (out). **prendere a nolo** hire, rent.

nomade ['nɔmade] *agg* nomadic. *s*(*m+f*) nomad.

nome ['nome] *sm* name; (*gramm*) noun. **a nome di** on behalf of. **conoscere di nome** know by name. **fare il nome di** mention; (*proporre*) propose. **nome di battaglia** pseudonym. **nomignolo** *sm* nickname.

nomina ['nɔmina] *sf* appointment. **nominare** *v* mention; name; (*eleggere*) appoint.

non [non] *avv* not. **non ... affatto** not at all. **non ... mai** never. **non ... nessuno** nobody. **non ... niente** *or* **nulla** nothing. **nonché** *cong* as well as.

noncurante [nonku'rante] *agg* heedless.

nondimeno [nondi'meno] *cong* nevertheless.

nonno ['nɔnno] *sm* grandfather; (*fam*) grand-dad. **nonna** *sf* grandmother; (*fam*) grandma, granny. **nonni** *sm pl* grandparents *pl*.

nono ['nɔno] *sm, agg* ninth.

nonostante [nonos'tante] *prep* notwithstanding, in spite of. *cong* al(though).

nontiscordardimè [nontiskordardi'me] *sm* forget-me-not.

nord [nɔrd] *sm* north. **a nord** north. **del nord** north, northern. **nord-est** *sm* north-east. **nord-ovest** *sm* north-west.

norma ['nɔrma] *sf* rule, standard; (*istruzione*) direction; regulation. **a norma di legge** according to the law.

normale [nor'male] *agg* normal, regular; standard. *sf* perpendicular. **normalmente** *avv* as a rule.

Norvegia [nor'vedʒa] *sf* Norway. **norvegese** *s*(*m+f*), *agg* Norwegian.

nostalgia [nostal'dʒia] *sf* nostalgia; (*della casa*) homesickness. **avere nostalgia di** miss. **nostalgico** *agg* nostalgic, homesick.

nostro ['nɔstro] *agg* our. *pron* ours. **nostrano** *agg* local, home-grown.

nota ['nɔta] *sf* note; list.

notaio [no'tajo] *sm* notary.

notare [no'tare] *v* note; (*osservare*) notice. **far notare** point out.

notificare [notifi'kare] *v* notify; inform. **notificazione** *sf* notification; (*avviso*) notice.

notizia [no'titsja] *sf* news (item), information. **notiziario** *sm* news (bulletin).

noto ['nɔto] *agg* well-known, renowned. **render noto** make known.

notorio [no'tɔrjo] *agg* renowned; (*spreg*) notorious. **notorietà** *sf* renown.

notte ['nɔtte] *sf* night. **buona notte!** goodnight! **dare la buona notte** bid goodnight. **nottata** *sf* night.

notturno [not'turno] *agg* night, nocturnal. *sm* (*musica*) nocturne.

novanta [no'vanta] *sm, agg* ninety. **novantesimo** *sm, agg* ninetieth.

nove ['nɔve] *sm, agg* nine.

novella [no'vella] *sf* short story. **novellista** *s*(*m+f*) short-story writer.

novello [no'vello] *agg* new.

novembre [no'vembre] *sm* November.

novità [novi'ta] *sf* novelty; (*notizie*) news.

novizio [no'vitsjo] *sm* beginner, novice.

nozione [no'tsjone] *sf* notion, idea.

nozze ['nɔttse] *sf pl* wedding *sing*. **viaggio di nozze** *sm* honeymoon.

nube ['nube] *sf* cloud. **nubifragio** *sm* cloudburst.

nubile ['nubile] *agg* unmarried, single.

nuca ['nuka] *sf* nape of the neck.

nucleo ['nukleo] *sm* nucleus. **nucleo familiare** family. **nucleare** *agg* nuclear.

nudo ['nudo] *agg* bare, naked. **a piedi nudi** barefoot. **nudismo** *sm* nudism. **nudista** *s(m+f)* nudist. **nudità** *sf* nudity, nakedness.

nulla ['nulla] *pron* nothing; (*con altra negazione*) anything. *sm* nothing; (*cosa da poco*) slightest thing. **da nulla** unimportant. **non fa nulla!** (*non importa*) it doesn't matter!

nullo ['nullo] *agg* null. **dichiarar nullo** annul. **nullaosta** *sm invar* clearance. **nullità** *sf* cipher.

numero ['numero] *sm* number; (*segno*) numeral. **numero chiuso** quota. **numero legale** quorum.

numismatica [numiz'matika] *sf* numismatics. **numismatico, -a** *sm, sf* numismatist.

*****nuocere** ['nwɔtʃere] *v* harm.

nuora ['nwɔra] *sf* daughter-in-law.

nuotare [nwo'tare] *v* swim. **nuotatore, -trice** *sm, sf* swimmer. **nuoto** *sm* swimming.

nuovo ['nwɔvo] *agg* new. **Nuova York** *sf* New York. **Nuova Zelanda** *sf* New Zealand.

nutrire [nu'trire] *v* feed, nourish. **nutrire affetto per** feel affection for. **nutriente** *agg* nourishing. **nutrimento** *sm* nourishment.

nuvola ['nuvola] *sf* cloud. **senza nuvole** cloudless. **nuvoloso** *agg* cloudy; (*cielo*) overcast.

nuziale [nu'tsjale] *agg* wedding.

O

o [o] *cong* or. **o . . . o . . .** either . . . or . . . **o l'uno o l'altro** either.

oasi ['ɔazi] *sf* oasis (*pl* -es).

*****obbedire** [obbe'dire] *v* obey. **obbedienza** *sf* obedience.

obbligare *v* bind, force. **obbligarsi** *v* undertake. **obbligato** *agg* fixed, set; (*riconoscente*) obliged. **obbligatorio** *agg* compulsory. **obbligazione** *sf* (*dir*) obligation; (*comm*) bond, debenture. **obbligo** *sm, pl* -ghi duty, obligation. **essere d'obbligo** be compulsory *or* obligatory.

obbrobrio [ob'brɔbrjo] *sm* disgrace.

obeso [o'bɛzo] *agg* obese. **obesità** *sf* obesity.

obiettare [objet'tare] *v* object. **obiezione** *sf* objection.

obiettivo [objet'tivo] *sm* objective; (*scope*) aim; (*foto, ecc.*) lens. *agg* objective.

obitorio [obi'tɔrjo] *sm* morgue.

oblazione [obla'tsjone] *sf* offering.

oblio [o'blio] *sm* oblivion.

obliquo [o'blikwo] *agg* oblique.

oblò [o'blɔ] *sm* porthole.

oblungo [o'blungo] *agg* oblong.

oboe ['ɔboe] *sm* oboe.

oca ['ɔka] *sf* goose (*pl* geese); (*maschio*) gander.

occasionale [okkazjo'nale] *agg* (*fortuito*) chance; immediate; (*saltuario*) occasional.

occasione [okka'zjone] *sf* chance, opportunity; (*buon affare*) bargain; (*circostanza*) occasion.

occhiali [ok'kjali] *sm pl* glasses *pl*, spectacles *pl*. **occhiali da sole** sun-glasses *pl*. **occhialuto** *agg* bespectacled.

occhio ['ɔkkjo] *sm* eye; (*bot*) bud. **a occhi chiusi** blindly. **a occhio** by sight. **a occhio nudo** with the naked eye. **a quattr'occhi** in private. **costare un occhio della testa** cost the earth. **dare nell'occhio** catch the eye. **tenere d'occhio** keep an eye on.

occidente [ottʃi'dɛnte] *sm* west. **occidentale** *agg* west, western.

*****occorrere** [ok'korrere] *v* be necessary. **all'occorrenza** in case of need.

occulto [ok'kulto] *agg* occult; (*nascosto*) hidden.

occupare [okku'pare] *v* occupy; (*far lavorare*) employ; (*tempo*) spend; (*carica*) hold; (*tener occupato*) keep busy. **occuparsi di** concern oneself with. **occupato** *agg* engaged; (*indaffarato*) busy. **occupazione** *sf* occupation.

oceano [o'tʃeano] *sm* ocean.

ocra ['ɔkra] *sf* ochre.

oculare [oku'lare] *agg* **testimonio oculare** *sm* eye-witness.

oculista [oku'lista] *s(m+f)* oculist.

ode ['ɔde] *sf* ode.

odiare [o'djare] *v* hate, loathe. **odio** *sm* hatred, hate, loathing. **avere in odio** hate, detest. **odioso** *agg* hateful.

odierno [o'djerno] *agg* of today; modern.

odissea [odis'sɛa] *sf* odyssey.

odontoiatria [odontoja'tria] *sf* dentistry.

odorare [odo'rare] *v* smell. **odorato** *sm* sense of smell. **odore** *sm* smell, odour. **sentir un odore di** smell. **odoroso** *agg* sweet-smelling.

*****offendere** [offendere] *v* offend; (*ledere*) injure, hurt. **offendere la legge** break the law. **offendersi** *v* take offence. **offensiva** *sf* offensive. **offensivo** *agg* offensive. **offensore** *sm* attacker; (*dir*) offender.

offerta [offerta] *sf* offer; (*comm*) bid; (*econ*) supply. **offerente** *s(m+f)* bidder.

offesa [offeza] *sf* offence; insult; (*danno*) harm.

officina [offi'tʃina] *sf* works, workshop. **capo officina** *sm* (works) foreman.

*****offrire** [offrire] *v* offer; (*comm*) bid. **offrirsi** *v* offer; present oneself.

offuscare [offus'kare] *v* dim; (*foto, ecc.*) blur; (*fig*) obscure.

oggetto [od'dʒetto] *sm* object; (*argomento*) subject; (*cosa*) thing. **oggettività** *sf* objectivity. **oggettivo** *agg* objective.

oggi ['oddʒi] *avv, sm* today. **al giorno d'oggi** nowadays. **oggi a otto** a week today.

ogni ['oɲi] *agg* every, each. **ad** or **in ogni modo** in any case. **ogni tanto** every so often, now and then.

Ognissanti [oɲis'santi] *sm* All Saints' Day.

ognuno [o'ɲuno] *pron* everybody, everyone; (*ciascuno*) each.

ohimè [oi'mɛ] *inter* alas!

Olanda [o'landa] *sf* Holland. **olandese** *agg* Dutch. **gli olandesi** the Dutch.

oleodotto [oleo'dotto] *sm* (*oil*) pipeline.

oleoso [ole'ozo] *agg* oily.

olfatto [olfatto] *sm* sense of smell.

olimpiade [olim'piade] *sf* Olympic games *pl*. **olimpico** [o'limpiko] *agg* Olympian. **olimpionico** *agg* Olympic.

olio ['ɔljo] *sm* oil. **olio combustibile** (*gasolio*) fuel oil.

oliva [o'liva] *sf* olive. **oliveto** olive grove. **olivo** olive-tree.

olmo ['olmo] *sm* elm-tree.

olocausto [olo'kausto] *sm* holocaust, sacrifice.

oltraggiare [oltrad'dʒare] *v* outrage. **oltraggio** *sm* outrage. **oltraggio al pudore** indecent behaviour. **oltraggioso** *agg* outrageous.

oltranza [ol'trantsa] *sf* **ad oltranza** to the (bitter) end.

oltre ['oltre] *avv* (*luogo*) further, farther; (*tempo*) beyond. *prep* beyond; (*più di*) more than, over. **oltre a** besides, apart from.

oltremare [oltre'mare] *avv* overseas.

oltremodo [oltre'mɔdo] *avv* exceedingly.

oltrepassare [oltrepas'sare] *v* exceed; surpass.

omaggio [o'maddʒo] *sm* (*dono*) (complimentary) gift. **porgere omaggi a** pay respects to. **rendere omaggio a** pay homage to.

ombelico [ombe'liko] *sm, pl* **-chi** navel. **ombelicale** *agg* umbilical.

ombra ['ombra] *sf* shadow; (*opposto di luce*) shade. **ombretto** *sm* eye-shadow.

ombrello [om'brello] *sm* umbrella.

omero ['ɔmero] *sm* humerus.

*****omettere** [o'mettere] *v* omit, leave out.

omicida [omi'tʃida] *agg* murderous. *s(m+f)* murderer, murderess. **omicidio** *sm* homicide, murder. **omicidio colposo** manslaughter.

omissione [omis'sjone] *sf* omission.

omogeneo [omo'dʒɛneo] *agg* homogeneous. **omogeneità** *sf* homogeneity.

omologare [omolo'gare] *v* ratify.

omonimo [o'mɔnimo] *agg* homonymous. *nm* namesake; (*parola*) homonym.

omosessuale [omosessu'ale] *s(m+f), agg* homosexual. **omosessualità** *sf* homosexuality.

oncia ['ontʃa] *sf* ounce.

onda ['onda] *sf* wave. **a onde** wavy. **ondata** *sf* wave, surge.

onde ['onde] *avv* whence. *cong* so that.

ondeggiare [onded'dʒare] *v* wave, sway, roll; (*fig*) waver.

ondulare [ondu'lare] *v* (*capelli*) wave. **ondulato** *agg* wavy; (*lastra, cartone*) corrugated.

onere ['ɔnere] *sm* burden. **oneroso** *agg* burdensome.

onesto [o'nɛsto] *agg* honest; (*prezzo*) fair. **onestà** *sf* honesty, integrity.

onice ['ɔnitʃe] *sm* onyx.

onnipotente [onnipo'tɛnte] *agg* omnipotent.

onnivoro [on'nivoro] *agg* omnivorous.

onomastico [ono'mastiko] *sm* saint's day.

onorare [ono'rare] *v* honour.

onorario [ono'rarjo] *agg* honorary. *sm* fee.

onore [o'nore] *sm* honour. **a onor del vero** to tell the truth. **fare onore a** honour; do credit *or* justice to. **farsi onore** distinguish oneself. **onorevole** *agg* honourable.

onorificenza [onorifi'tʃɛntsa] *sf* honour. **onorifico** *agg* honorary.

onta ['onta] *sf* shame.

ontano [on'tano] *sm* alder.

opaco [o'pako] *agg*, *m pl* -**chi** opaque, dull.

opale [o'pale] *sm* opal.

opera ['ɔpera] *sf* work; (*teatro*) opera; (*azione*) deed; institution. **mettere in opera** put into practice; instal. **per opera di** thanks to. **operetta** *sf* operetta, light opera. **operoso** *agg* active.

operaio [ope'rajo], -**a** *sm*, *sf* worker. *agg* working.

operare [ope'rare] *v* function, work; (*med*) operate. **farsi operare** have an operation. **operatore** (*cinema*) cameraman; (*di borsa*) stockbroker. **operatorio** *agg* operating. **operazione** *sf* operation.

opinione [opi'njone] *sf* opinion.

oppio ['ɔppjo] *sm* opium.

opponente [oppo'nɛnte] *agg* opposing. *s(m+f)* adversary.

*opporre [op'porre] *v* oppose. **opporre resistenza** offer resistance. **opporsi a** set oneself against; object to.

opportuno [oppor'tuno] *agg* opportune. **opportunismo** *sm* opportunism. **opportunista** *s(m+f)* opportunist. **opportunità** *sf* opportunity.

opposizione [oppozi'tsjone] *sf* opposition.

opposto [op'posto], -**a** *s*, *agg* opposite. **all'opposto** on the contrary.

oppressione [oppres'sjone] *sf* oppression. **oppresso** *agg* oppressed. **oppressore** *sm* oppressor.

*opprimere [op'primere] *v* oppress, burden.

oppure [op'pure] *cong* or, or else.

opulento [opu'lɛnto] *agg* opulent.

opuscolo [o'puskolo] *sm* pamphlet, booklet.

ora[1] ['ora] *sf* hour; (*tempo*) time. **alla**

buon'ora! at last! **all'ora** (*velocità*) per hour. **di buon'ora** early. **ora di punta** rush-hour. **ora legale** summer-time. **ora straordinaria** overtime.

ora[2] ['ora] *avv* (*adesso*) now; (*appena*) just. **d'ora in poi** from now on, henceforth. **or ora** just (now).

orale [o'rale] *agg* oral. *sm* (*esame*) viva.

orario [o'rarjo] *agg* (*all'ora*) per hour; time. **in senso orario** clockwise. **segnale orario** time-signal. *sm* (*ore*) hours *pl*; (*tabella*) timetable. **in orario** on time.

orazione [ora'tsjone] *sf* speech. **oratore** *sm* orator. **oratorio** *sm* (*chiesa*) oratory; (*musica*) oratorio.

orbene [or'bɛne] *avv* well (now).

orbita ['ɔrbita] *sf* orbit. **orbitare** *v* orbit.

orchestra [or'kɛstra] *sf* orchestra. **orchestrare** *v* orchestrate. **orchestrazione** *sf* orchestration.

orchidea [orki'dɛa] *sf* orchid.

orco ['ɔrko] *sm* ogre.

orda ['ɔrda] *sf* horde.

ordigno [or'diɲo] *sm* device.

ordinare [ordi'nare] *v* order; (*mettere in ordine*) tidy up; (*sistemare*) arrange; (*rel*) ordain. **ordinamento** *sm* order; arrangement; system. **ordinazione** *sf* order; (*rel*) ordination.

ordinario [ordi'narjo] *agg*, *sm* ordinary.

ordine ['ordine] *sm* order. **ordine del giorno** agenda.

ordire [or'dire] *v* (*tessile*) warp; (*fig*) hatch. **ordito** *sm* warp; (*fig*) plot.

orecchio [o'rekkjo] *sm* ear. **a orecchio** by ear. **a portato d'orecchio** within earshot. **orecchino** *sm* ear-ring. **orecchioni** *sm pl* mumps *sing*.

orefice [o'refitʃe] *sm* goldsmith, jeweller. **oreficeria** *sf* jewellery; (*negozio*) jeweller's (shop).

orfano ['ɔrfano], -**a** *s*, *agg* orphan. **orfanotrofio** *sm* orphanage.

organico [or'ganiko] *agg* organic. *sm* personnel. **organismo** *sm* organism; (*fig*) body.

organizzare [organid'dzare] *v* organize, arrange. **organizzazione** *sf* organization, body. **organizzatore**, -**trice** *sm*, *sf* organizer.

organo ['ɔrgano] *sm* organ. **organetto** *sm* barrel-organ.

orgasmo [or'gazmo] *sm* orgasm.

orgia ['ɔrdʒa] *sf* orgy.

orgoglio [or'goʎo] *sm* pride. **orgoglioso** *agg* proud.

orientare [orjen'tare] *v* orient(ate); direct. **orientarsi** *v* find one's bearings; tend. **orientamento** *sm* orientation; (*direzione*) trend. **senso d'orientamento** *sm* sense of direction.

oriente [o'rjɛnte] *sm* East. **orientale** *agg* oriental, eastern, east.

orifizio [ori'fitsjo] *sm* orifice, opening.

origano [o'rigano] *sm* oregano.

originare [oridʒi'nare] *v* (*avere origini*) originate; (*dare origini*) give rise to.

origine [o'ridʒine] *sf* origin; (*inizio*) beginning. **originale** *sm*, *agg* original; eccentric. **originalità** *sf* originality; eccentricity. **originario** *agg* native.

origliare [ori'ʎare] *v* eavesdrop.

orina [o'rina] *sf* urine. **orinare** *v* urinate. **orinatorio** *agg* urinary.

oriundo [o'rjundo] *agg* native.

orizzonte [orid'dzonte] *sm* horizon. **giro d'orizzonte** *sm* general survey. **orizzontale** *agg* horizontal. **orizzontarsi** *v* find one's bearings.

orlo [orlo] *sm* edge; (*abisso*) brink; (*bicchiere*) rim; (*tessuto*) hem. **orlare** *v* hem; (*bordare*) trim.

orma [orma] *sf* footprint; track.

ormai [or'mai] *avv* by now; (*passato*) by then.

ormeggiare [ormed'dʒare] *v* moor. **ormeggio** *sm* mooring.

ormone [or'mone] *sm* hormone.

ornare [or'nare] *v* adorn, decorate. **ornamentale** *agg* ornamental. **ornamento** *sm* ornament, decoration.

ornitologia [ornitolo'dʒia] *sf* ornithology. **ornitologo** *-a sm*, *sf* ornithologist.

oro [ɔro] *sm* gold. **d'oro** *agg* gold, golden.

orologio [oro'lɔdʒo] *sm* clock; (*da polso o tasca*) watch. **orologeria** *sf* clockwork; (*negozio*) watchmaker's (shop). **bomba ad orologeria** *sf* time-bomb. **orologiaio** *sm* watchmaker.

oroscopo [o'rɔskopo] *sm* horoscope.

orpello [or'pɛllo] *sm* tinsel.

orrendo [or'rɛndo] *agg* hideous, horrifying.

orribile [or'ribile] *agg* horrible, dreadful.

orrore [or'rore] *sm* horror, dread, loathing. **avere orrore di** loathe.

orso [orso] *-a sm*, *sf* bear. **orsacchiotto** *sm* bear-cub; (*giocattolo*) teddy-bear.

ortica [or'tika] *sf* nettle. **orticaria** *sf* nettle-rash.

orto [ɔrto] *sm* kitchen garden. **ortaggi** *sm pl* vegetables *pl*. **orticoltore** *sm* horticulturist. **orticoltura** *sf* horticulture. **ortolano** *sm* greengrocer.

ortodosso [orto'dɔsso] *agg* orthodox. **ortodossia** *sf* orthodoxy.

ortografia [ortogra'fia] *sf* spelling. **errore ortografico** *sm* spelling mistake.

ortopedia [ortope'dia] *sf* orthopaedics. **ortopedico** *agg* orthopaedic.

orzaiolo [ordza'jolo] *sm* stye.

orzo [ɔrdzo] *sm* barley.

osare [o'zare] *v* dare; risk.

osceno [o'ʃɛno] *agg* obscene. **oscenità** *sf* obscenity.

oscillare [oʃil'lare] *v* swing, oscillate.

oscurare [osku'rare] *v* darken; (*fig*) obscure. **oscuramento** *sm* darkening; (*guerra*) black-out. **oscurità** *sf* dark; (*fig*) obscurity.

ospedale [ospe'dale] *sm* hospital. **ospedaliero** *agg* hospital.

ospitare [ospi'tare] *v* offer hospitality (to); (*albergare*) put up. **ospitale** *agg* hospitable.

ospite [ɔspite] *sm+f*) (*persona ospitata*) guest; (*persona che ospita*) host, hostess.

ospizio [os'pitsjo] *sm* hostel.

ossatura [ossa'tura] *sf* (*arch*) framework; (*anat*) bone structure.

ossequio [os'sɛkwjo] *sm* homage. **ossequi** *sm pl* (*saluti*) regards *pl*. **ossequioso** *agg* respectful.

osservare [osser'vare] *v* obscure; (*notare*) notice. **osservanza** *sf* observance. **osservatore**, **-trice** *sm*, *sf* observer. **osservatorio** *sm* observatory. **osservazione** *sf* observation; (*nota*) remark. **fare un'osservazione** comment; criticize.

ossessionare [ossessjo'nare] *v* haunt. **ossessionante** *agg* haunting. **ossessione** *sf* obsession. **ossesso** *agg* possessed.

ossia [os'sia] *cong* or rather, in other words.

ossigeno [os'sidʒeno] *sm* oxygen. **ossidare** *v* oxidize. **ossido** *sm* oxide.

osso [ɔsso] *sm*, *pl* -a *f in collective sense* bone. **ossuto** *agg* bony.

ostacolare [ostako'lare] *v* hinder, obstruct. **ostacolo** *sm* obstacle, hindrance; (*atletica*) hurdle. **corsa a ostacoli** *sf* obstacle race; hurdling.

ostaggio [os'taddʒo] sm hostage.
oste ['ɔste] sm host, innkeeper.
ostello [os'tɛllo] sm refuge; (*per la gioventù*) (youth-)hostel.
ostentare [osten'tare] v show off. **ostentato** agg ostentatious.
osteria [oste'ria] sf inn.
ostetrico [os'tetriko] sm obstetrician. **ostetrica** sf obstetrician; (*levatrice*) midwife. **ostetricia** sf obstetrics; midwifery.
ostia ['ɔstja] sf (*rel*) host; (*cialda*) wafer.
ostile [os'tile] agg hostile. **ostilità** sf hostility.
ostinarsi [osti'narsi] v persist. **ostinatezza** sf obstinacy, stubbornness. **ostinato** agg obstinate, stubborn.
ostrica ['ɔstrika] sf oyster.
ostruire [ostru'ire] v obstruct, block. **ostruzione** sf obstruction.
otite [o'tite] sf otitis.
otorinolaringoiatra [otorinolaringo'jatra] s(m+f) ear, nose, and throat specialist.
ottagono [ot'tagono] sm octagon.
ottano [ot'tano] sm octane.
ottanta [ot'tanta] sm, agg eighty. **ottantesimo** agg, sm eightieth.
ottava [ot'tava] sf octave. **ottavo** sm, agg eighth.
*ottenere** [otte'nere] v obtain, get. **ottenibile** agg obtainable.
ottico ['ɔttiko] agg optic. sm optician. **ottica** sf (*persona*) optician; (*scienza*) optics.
ottimismo [otti'mizmo] sm optimistic.
ottimo ['ɔttimo] agg excellent, very good.
otto ['ɔtto] agg, sm eight.
ottobre [ot'tobre] sm October.
ottone [ot'tone] sm brass. **ottoni** sm pl (*musica*) brass pl.
otturare [ottu'rare] v plug; (*dente*) fill. **otturatore** sm (*foto*) shutter.
ottuso [ot'tuzo] agg dull; (*non tagliente*) blunt; (*angolo*) obtuse.
ovaia [o'vaja] sf ovary.
ovale [o'vale] agg, sm oval.
ovatta [o'vatta] sf wadding; (*cotone idrofilo*) cotton wool.
ovazione [ova'tsjone] sf ovation.
ovest ['ɔvest] sm west. **a ovest di** (to the) west of. **dell'ovest** west, western.
ovile [o'vile] sm sheepfold.
ovulo ['ɔvulo] sm ovum; (*bot*) ovule. **ovulazione** sf ovulation.
ovunque [o'vunkwe] avv everywhere. cong wherever.

ovvero [ov'vero] cong or (rather).
ovvio ['ɔvvjo] agg obvious.
oziare [o'tsjare] v (*pigrizia*) idleness; (*tempo libero*) leisure, spare time. **ozioso** agg idle.

P

pacato [pa'kato] agg calm.
pacchia ['pakkja] sf godsend.
pacco ['pakko] sm parcel. **pacchetto** sm packet, small parcel.
pace ['patʃe] sf peace.
pacificare [patʃifi'kare] v pacify, appease; reconcile. **pacifico** agg peaceful; (*ovvio*) self-evident.
pacifismo [patʃi'fizmo] sm pacifism. **pacifista** s(m+f) pacifist.
padella [pa'dɛlla] sf frying pan.
padiglione [padi'ʎone] sm pavilion.
Padova ['padova] sf Padua.
padre ['padre] sm father. **padre adottivo** foster-father. **padrino** sm godfather.
padrone [pa'drone] -a sm, sf master, mistress; owner; (*fam*) boss. **padronale** agg private; (*non di servizio*) owner's. **padronanza** sf mastery. **padroneggiarsi** v control oneself.
paesaggio [pae'zaddʒo] sm landscape.
paese [pa'eze] sm country; village; (*città*) town. **paesano** agg rural, country.
paffuto [paf'futo] agg plump.
paga ['paga] sf pay, wages pl.
pagaia [pa'gaja] sf paddle.
pagano [pa'gano] -a s, agg pagan, heathen.
pagare [pa'gare] v pay. **pagamento** sm payment.
pagella [pa'dʒɛlla] sf school report.
paggio ['paddʒo] sm page(-boy).
pagina ['padʒina] sf page.
paglia ['paʎa] sf straw. **pagliericcio** sm palliasse. **paglietta** sf steel wool; (*cappello*) straw hat.
pagliaccio [pa'ʎattʃo] sm clown. **pagliacciata** sf buffoonery.
pagnotta [pa'ɲɔtta] sf loaf (of bread).
pago ['pago] agg contented (with).
pagoda [pa'gɔda] sf pagoda.
paio ['pajo] sm, pl -a f pair; (*due o circa due*) couple.

pala ['pala] *sf* shovel; *(di remo)* blade. **palata** *sf* shovel(ful). **soldi a palate** *sm pl* pots *or* bags of money *pl*.

palato [pa'lato] *sm* palate.

palazzo [pa'lattso] *sm (edificio)* building; *(appartamenti)* block of flats; *(casa di principe, ecc.)* palace. **palazzina** *sf* villa.

palco ['palko] *sm* platform, stand; *(teatro)* box. **palcoscenico** *sm* stage.

palese [pa'leze] *agg* obvious, clear. **palesare** *v* reveal.

palestra [pa'lɛstra] *sf* gymnasium.

paletto [pa'letto] *sm* bolt.

palio ['paljo] *sm* **mettere in palio** offer as a prize.

palla ['palla] *sf* ball. **pallacanestro** *sf* basketball. **pallanuoto** *sf* water polo.

palleggiare [palled'dʒare] *v (tennis)* knock up; *(calcio)* dribble. **palleggio** *sm* knock-up, dribbling.

pallido ['pallido] *agg* pale; *(fig)* faint.

pallino [pal'lino] *sm (bocce)* jack; *(fig)* craze. **a pallini** with polka dots.

pallone [pal'lone] *sm* ball; *(calcio)* football; *(aerostato)* balloon.

pallottola [pal'lɔttola] *sf* pellet; *(rivoltella)* bullet.

palma¹ ['palma] *sf (albero)* palm(-tree).

palma² ['palma] *sf (anat)* palm. **piede palmato** *sm* webbed foot.

palmo ['palmo] *sm* palm.

palo ['palo] *sm* pole; *(di porta)* post.

palombaro [palom'baro] *sm* diver.

palpare [pal'pare] *v* feel; *pat.* **palpabile** *agg* palpable.

palpebra ['palpebra] *sf* eyelid. **battere le palpebre** blink.

palpitare [palpi'tare] *v* throb.

paltò [pal'tɔ] *sm invar* overcoat.

palude [pa'lude] *sf* marsh, swamp. **terreno paludoso** *sm* marshland.

panca ['panka] *sf* bench. **panchetto** *sm* (foot)stool. **panchina** *sf* bench, garden seat. **pancone** *sm* work-bench.

pancetta [pan'tʃetta] *sf* bacon.

pancia ['pantʃa] *sf* belly; *(fam)* tummy. **mal di pancia** *sm (fam)* tummy-ache. **panciotto** *sm* waistcoat. **panciuto** *agg (persona)* pot-bellied; *(cosa)* bulging.

pancreas ['pankreas] *sm invar* pancreas.

panda ['panda] *sm invar* panda.

pandemonio [pande'mɔnjo] *sm* uproar.

pane ['pane] *sm* bread; *(forma)* loaf. **buono come il pane** as good as gold.

guadagnarsi il pane earn one's living. **pan grattato** breadcrumbs *pl*. **pan tostato** toast. **panettiere** *sm* baker. **panificio** *sm* bakery.

panfilo ['panfilo] *sm* yacht.

panico ['paniko] *sm* panic.

paniere [pa'njɛre] *sm* basket.

panino [pa'nino] *sm* roll. **panino imbottito** sandwich.

panna¹ ['panna] *sf* cream. **panna montata** whipped cream.

panna² ['panna] *sf (mec)* breakdown.

pannello [pan'nɛllo] *sm* panel.

panno ['panno] *sm* cloth. **panni** *sm pl (vestiti)* clothes *pl*. **pannolino** *sm* nappy.

panorama [pano'rama] *sm* panorama, view.

pantaloni [panta'loni] *sm pl* trousers *pl*; *(corti)* shorts *pl*.

pantano [pan'tano] *sm* bog.

pantera [pan'tɛra] *sf* panther.

pantofola [pan'tɔfola] *sf* slipper.

pantomima [panto'mima] *sf* play-acting.

paonazzo [pao'nattso] *agg* purple.

papa ['papa] *sm* pope. **ogni morte di papa** once in a blue moon. **vivere come un papa** live like a lord. **papale** *agg* papal.

papà [pa'pa] *sm (fam)* dad(dy).

papavero [pa'pavero] *sm* poppy.

papera ['papera] *sf* slip, blunder. **prendere una papera** slip up.

papero ['papero] *-a sm, sf* gosling.

papiro [pa'piro] *sm* papyrus; *(fam)* paper.

pappa ['pappa] *sm* mush. **pappare** *v* gobble up.

pappagallo [pappa'gallo] *sm* parrot.

paprica ['paprika] *sf* paprika.

parabola [pa'rabola] *sf (storia)* parable; *(mat)* parabola.

parabrezza [para'brettsa] *sm invar* windshield.

paracadute [paraka'dute] *sm invar* parachute. **paracadutista** *s(m + f)* parachutist; *(mil)* paratrooper.

paradiso [para'dizo] *sm* paradise, heaven.

paradosso [para'dɔsso] *sm* paradox. **paradossale** *agg* paradoxical.

parafango [para'fango] *sm* mudguard.

paraffina [paraf'fina] *sf* paraffin.

parafrasi [pa'rafrazi] *sf* paraphrase.

parafulmine [para'fulmine] *sm* lightning conductor.

parafuoco [para'fwɔko] *sm, pl -chi* fireguard, firescreen.

paragonare [parago'nare] v compare. **paragonabile** agg comparable. **paragone** sm comparison. **senza paragone** without equal.

paragrafo [pa'ragrafo] sm paragraph.

paralisi [pa'ralizi] sf paralysis (pl -ses). **paralitico, -a** sm, sf cripple. **paralizzare** v paralyse.

parallelo [paral'lɛlo] agg, sm parallel. **parallela** sf parallel (line). **parallelogrammo** sm parallelogram.

paralume [para'lume] sm lampshade.

paranoia [para'nɔja] sf paranoia. **paranoico** agg paranoid.

parapetto [para'petto] sm parapet.

parare [pa'rare] v adorn; (evitare) ward off; (sport) save.

parasole [para'sole] sm sunshade.

parassita [paras'sita] agg parasitic. s(m+f) parasite.

parata[1] [pa'rata] sf (sfilata) parade.

parata[2] [pa'rata] sf (scherma) parry; (calcio, ecc.) save.

parato [pa'rato] sm **carta da parati** sf wallpaper.

paraurti [para'urti] sm invar bumper.

paravento [para'vɛnto] sm screen.

parcheggiare [parked'dʒare] v park. **parcheggio** sm parking; (luogo) car park.

parchimetro [par'kimetro] sm parking meter.

parco[1] [ˈparko] sm park; (industriale) depot; (auto) fleet.

parco[2] [ˈparko] agg frugal, moderate.

parecchio [pa'rekkjo] agg quite a lot of, several. **parecchio tempo** quite a long time. pron quite a lot, several. avv quite a lot.

pareggiare [pared'dʒare] v equal; (sport) draw; (comm) balance. **pareggio** sm balance; draw.

parente [pa'rɛnte] s(m+f) relative, relation. **parentela** sf relationship; (parenti) relations pl.

parentesi [pa'rɛntezi] sf bracket, parenthesis (pl -ses). **fra parentesi** incidentally.

*****parere** [pa'rere] v seem, appear; (suono) sound; (fatto) feel. **faccio come mi pare I** do as I like. sm opinion.

parete [pa'rete] sf wall; (monte) face.

pari [ˈpari] agg equal, same; (non dispari) even; equivalent. **alla pari** (in famiglia) au pair. **essere pari** be quits; (forze) be equal or level. s(m+f) equal, peer.

Parigi [pa'ridʒi] sf Paris. **parigino, -a** s, agg Parisian.

parità [pari'ta] sf parity. **a parità di condizioni** all things being equal.

parlamento [parla'mento] sm parliament. **parlamentare** agg parliamentary.

parlare [par'lare] v speak, talk. **parlar chiaro** speak clearly; (fig) speak one's mind. sm talk; (parlata) way of speaking, dialect.

parmigiano [parmi'dʒano] agg Parmesan. sm Parmesan cheese.

parodia [paro'dia] sf parody.

parola [pa'rɔla] sf word. **parola d'ordine** password. **parole crociate** sf pl crossword sing.

parolacce [paro'lattʃe] sf pl bad language sing.

parrocchia [par'rɔkkja] sf parish. **parroco** sm, pl -chi parish priest.

parrucca [par'rukka] sf wig.

parrucchiere [parruk'kjɛre] sm hairdresser.

parte [ˈparte] sf part; (porzione) share; (lato) side; (dir) party. **a parte** apart; extra. **dall'altra parte** on the other hand. **da parte** aside. **da parte mia** from me. **da queste parti** round here. **per parte mia** as far as I am concerned.

partecipare [partetʃi'pare] v participate, take part; (condividere) share; announce. **partecipazione** sf sharing; announcement; presence.

partenza [par'tɛntsa] sf departure; (sport) start.

participio [parti'tʃipjo] sm participle.

particolare [partiko'lare] agg particular, special. sm detail.

partigiano [parti'dʒano], **-a** s, agg partisan.

partire [par'tire] v leave; go away; start.

partita [par'tita] sf game; (incontro) match; (contabilità) entry; (merci) lot.

partito [par'tito] sm party; condition; decision. **mal partito** predicament. **per partito preso** having made up one's mind.

partitura [parti'tura] sf score.

parto [ˈparto] sm birth; (umano) childbirth; (atto) delivery. **partorire** v give birth (to).

parziale [par'tsjale] agg partial; (predisposto) biased.

pascere [ˈpaʃere] v feed (on). **ben pasciuto** well-fed, plump.

pascolare [pasko'lare] v graze. **pascolo** sm pasture.

Pasqua ['paskwa] sf Easter. **Pasqua degli ebrei** Passover.

passabile [pas'sabile] agg fair.

passaggio [pas'saddʒo] sm passage; (traversata) crossing. **dare un passaggio** give a lift. **diritto di passaggio** sm right of way. **essere di passaggio** be on the way through. **vietato il passaggio** no thoroughfare.

passaporto [passa'porto] sm passport.

passare [pas'sare] v pass; go past; (gastr) strain.

passatempo [passa'tempo] sm pastime.

passato [pas'sato] agg past; (scorso) last. sm past.

passatoia [passa'toja] sf runner.

passeggero [passed'dʒero], -a agg passing, transient. sm, sf passenger.

passeggiare [passed'dʒare] v go for a walk or stroll. **passeggiata** sf walk, stroll; (non a piedi) ride.

passerella [passe'rella] sf footbridge.

passero ['passero] sm sparrow.

passibile [pas'sibile] agg liable (to).

passione [pas'sjone] sf passion.

passivo [pas'sivo] agg passive; (comm) debit. sm (gramm) passive; (comm) liability.

passo ['passo] sm step; (andatura) pace; (velocità) rate; (geog) pass; (di vite) thread. **cedere il passo** give way. **fare due passi** go for a stroll. **sbarrare il passo** block the way. **segnare il passo** mark time.

pasta ['pasta] sf dough; (minestra) pasta; (impasto) paste; (dolce) pastry. **pasta frolla** shortcrust pastry. **pasta sfoglia** puff pastry.

pastello [pas'tello] sm pastel.

pastica [pas'tikka] sf lozenge.

pasticceria [pastittʃe'ria] sf (negozio) confectioner's (shop); (pasticcini) pastries pl. **pasticciere** sm confectioner.

pasticciare [pastit'tʃare] v bungle, mess up. **pasticcio** sm mess; (gastr) pie.

pastiglia [pas'tiʎa] sf tablet.

pasto ['pasto] sm meal. **vino da pasto** sm table wine.

pastore [pas'tore] sm shepherd; (prete) minister. **cane pastore** sm sheepdog. **pastorale** agg pastoral.

pastorizzare [pastorid'dzare] v pasteurize. **pastorizzazione** sf pasteurization.

pastoso [pas'tozo] agg mellow.

pastrano [pas'trano] sm overcoat.

pastura [pas'tura] sf pasture.

patata [pa'tata] sf potato.

patella [pa'tella] sf (anat) knee-cap; (zool) limpet.

patente[1] [pa'tente] agg patent.

patente[2] [pa'tente] sf licence.

paterno [pa'terno] agg paternal. **paternale** sf lecture. **paternità** sf paternity.

patetico [pa'tetiko] agg pathetic, moving.

patibolo [pa'tibolo] sm gallows.

patina ['patina] sf coat.

patire [pa'tire] v suffer. **patimento** sm suffering, pain. **patito** sm (fam) fan.

patologico [pato'lodʒiko] agg pathological.

patria ['patria] sf country; home.

patrigno [pa'triɲo] sm stepfather.

patrimonio [patri'mɔnjo] sm estate; fortune. **patrimonio pubblico** public heritage.

patriota [patri'ɔta] s(m+f) patriot. **patriottico** agg patriotic. **patriottismo** sm patriotism.

patrocinio [patro'tʃinjo] sm defence. **patrocinare** v defend.

patrono [pa'trono] sm patron. **patronato** sm patronage; institution.

pattinare [patti'nare] v skate. **pattinaggio** sm skating. **pattino** sm skate; (mec) shoe.

patto ['patto] sm pact, agreement; condition, term. **pattuire** v agree.

pattuglia [pat'tuʎa] sf patrol.

pattumiera [pattu'mjera] sf dustbin.

paura [pa'ura] sf fear; (spavento) fright. **aver paura** be afraid of, fear. **far paura** scare. **pauroso** agg (che fa paura) frightening; (che ha paura) timid, afraid.

pausa ['pauza] sf pause, interval.

pavimento [pavi'mento] sm floor.

pavone [pa'vone] sm peacock. **pavonessa** sf peahen.

pavoneggiarsi [pavoned'dʒarsi] v show off.

paziente [pa'tsjente] s(m+f), agg patient. **pazientare** v wait patiently. **pazienza** sf patience.

pazzo ['pattso], -a agg crazy, insane. sm, sf lunatic. **pazzesco** agg mad; incredible. **pazzia** sf madness, folly.

peccare [pek'kare] v sin. **pecca** sf fault. **peccato** sm sin. **che peccato!** what a pity! **peccatore, -trice** sm, sf sinner.

pece ['petʃe] *sf* pitch.

pecora ['pɛkora] *sf* sheep; *(femmina)* ewe.

peculiare [peku'ljare] *agg* peculiar.

pedaggio [pe'daddʒo] *sm* toll.

pedale [pe'dale] *sm* pedal. **pedalare** *v* pedal.

pedana [pe'dana] *sf* platform; *(sport)* springboard.

pedante [pe'dante] *agg* pedantic. *s(m+f)* pedant.

pedata [pe'data] *sf* kick; *(orma)* footprint.

pedestre [pe'destre] *agg* pedestrian.

pediatria [pedja'tria] *sf* paediatrics. **pediatra** *s(m+f)* paediatrician. **pediatrico** *agg* paediatric.

pedicure [pedi'kure] *sf (cura)* pedicure. *s(m+f) invar* chiropodist.

pedina [pe'dina] *sf* piece; *(scacchi)* pawn. **muovere una pedina** make a move; *(fig)* pull strings.

pedinare [pedi'nare] *v* shadow.

pedone [pe'done] *s(m+f)* pedestrian. **pedonale** *agg* pedestrian.

peggio ['peddʒo] *agg (comparativo)* worse; *(superlativo)* the worst. *sm* the worst. **alla peggio** if the worst comes to the worst.

peggiorare [peddʒo'rare] *v (stare)* get worse; *(rendere)* make worse. **peggioramento** *sm* worsening.

peggiore [ped'dʒore] *agg (comparativo)* worse; *(superlativo)* the worst. *s(m+f)* the worst.

pegno ['peɲo] *sm* pledge, pawn.

pelare [pe'lare] *v* peel, skin; *(fig)* fleece. **pelarsi** *v (fam)* go bald.

pelle ['pelle] *sf* skin; *(cuoio)* hide; *(frutta)* peel; *(carnagione)* complexion. **rimetterci la pelle** lose one's life.

pellegrino [pelle'grino] *sm* pilgrim. **pellegrinaggio** *sm* pilgrimage.

pellicano [pelli'kano] *sm* pelican.

pelliccia [pel'littʃa] *sf* fur; *(mantello)* fur coat. **pellicciaio** *sm* furrier.

pellicola [pel'likola] *sf* film; membrane.

pelo ['pelo] *sm* hair; *(pelame)* coat. **cercare il pelo nell'uovo** split hairs. **contro pelo** against the grain. **per un pelo** by a whisker.

peltro ['peltro] *sm* pewter.

peluria [pe'lurja] *sf* down.

pelvi ['pɛlvi] *sf* pelvis.

pena ['pena] *sf (dolore)* pain; *(disturbo)* trouble; punishment. **valere la pena** be worth it, be worthwhile.

penale [pe'nale] *agg* criminal, penal. *sf* fine.

penare [pe'nare] *v* find difficult, be hardly able to.

pendente [pen'dɛnte] *agg* hanging; *(dir, comm)* pending; *(torre)* leaning. *sm* pendant. **pendenza** *sf* slope, incline.

pendere ['pendere] *v* hang (down); incline, slope; *(dir)* be pending.

pendio [pen'dio] *sm* slope.

pendolare [pendo'lare] *v* swing. *s(m+f)* commuter. **pendolo** *sm* pendulum.

pene ['pene] *sm* penis.

penetrare [pene'trare] *v* penetrate, pierce. **penetrante** *agg* penetrating, piercing; acute. **penetrazione** *sf* penetration.

penicillina [penitʃil'lina] *sf* penicillin.

penisola [pe'nizola] *sf* peninsula.

penitente [peni'tɛnte] *s(m+f)*, *agg* penitent. **penitenza** *sf* penance; *(gioco)* forfeit. **penitenziario** *sm* jail.

penna ['penna] *sf* feather; *(da scrivere)* pen. **penna a sfera** ball-point pen. **penna stilografica** fountain pen. **pennuto** *agg* feathered.

pennello [pen'nello] *sm* brush.

penombra [pe'nombra] *sf* twilight.

penoso [pe'nozo] *agg* painful.

pensare [pen'sare] *v* think; intend. **pensarci** *v* think about it. **pensarci sopra** think it over. **pensatore, -trice** *sm, sf* thinker.

pensiero [pen'sjɛro] *sm* thought; *(mente, parere)* mind. **essere in pensiero** worry. **pensieroso** *agg* thoughtful; pensive.

pensile ['pensile] *agg* hanging.

pensionare [pensjo'nare] *v* pension off. **pensionato** *sm* pensioner; *(collegio)* boarding-school. **pensione** *sf* pension. **essere in pensione** be retired. **mezza pensione** half board. **pensione completa** full board.

pentagono [pen'tagono] *sm* pentagon. **pentagonale** *agg* pentagonal.

Pentecoste [pente'kɔste] *sf* Whitsun.

pentirsi [pen'tirsi] *v* regret, be sorry for; *(rel)* repent. **pentimento** *sm* regret; repentance.

pentola [pen'tola] *sf* pot.

penultimo [pe'nultimo] *agg* penultimate.

penzolare [pendzo'lare] *v* dangle. **penzoloni** *avv* dangling.

pepe ['pepe] *sm* pepper. **pepare** *v* pepper. **pepato** *agg* peppery, hot. **peperone** *sm* capsicum; (*frutto*) pepper; (*peperoncino*) chili.

pepita [pe'pita] *sf* nugget.

per ['per] *prep* for; (*attraverso*) through; (*mat, entro, tramite*) by. **per caso** by chance. **per cento** per cent. **per di più** in addition. **per lo meno** at least. **per ora** for the present. **per terra** on the floor. **per volta** at a time. **stare per** be about to, be on the point of.

pera ['pera] *sf* pear. **pero** *sm* pear-tree.

perbacco [per'bakko] *inter* by Jove!

perbene [per'bene] *agg invar* respectable, nice. *avv* well, nicely.

percentuale [pertʃentu'ale] *agg* per cent. *sf* percentage.

percepire [pertʃe'pire] *v* notice, be aware (of); (*riscuotere*) receive. **percepibile** *agg* noticeable; (*comm*) due. **percettibile** *agg* perceptible. **percezione** *sf* perception.

perché [per'ke] *avv* why. *cong* because, as; (*affinché*) so that. *sm* reason.

perciò [per'tʃɔ] *cong* so, therefore.

***percorrere** [per'korrere] *v* cover.

percorso [per'korso] *sm* trip, run.

percossa [per'kɔssa] *sf* blow, impact.

***percuotere** [per'kwɔtere] *v* strike, hit.

percussione [perkus'sjone] *sf* percussion.

***perdere** ['perdere] *v* lose; (*colare*) leak; (*sprecare*) waste. **lascia perdere**! skip it! **perdere di vista** lose sight of. **perdersi** *v* get lost. **perdita** *sf* loss; leak; waste.

perdonare [perdo'nare] *v* forgive. **perdono** *sm* forgiveness, pardon.

perenne [pe'renne] *agg* perpetual.

perfetto [per'fetto] *agg* perfect.

perfezionare [perfetsjo'nare] *v* (*migliorare*) improve; make perfect. **perfezionarsi** *v* specialize. **perfezionamento** *sm* specialization. **perfezione** *sf* perfection. **perfezionista** *s(m+f)* perfectionist.

perfidia [per'fidja] *sf* treachery, wickedness. **perfido** *agg* treacherous, wicked.

perfino [per'fino] *avv* even.

perforare [perfo'rare] *v* pierce, perforate.

pergamena [perga'mena] *sf* parchment.

pericolo [pe'rikolo] *sm* danger; risk. **pericolante** *agg* unsafe. **pericoloso** *agg* dangerous; risky.

periferia [perife'ria] *sf* periphery; (*città*) suburbs *pl*. **periferico** *agg* suburban; peripheral.

perimetro [pe'rimetro] *sm* perimeter.

periodico [peri'ɔdiko] *agg* periodic. *sm* periodical.

periodo [pe'riodo] *sm* period.

peripezia [peripe'tsia] *sf* vicissitude.

perire [pe'rire] *v* perish, die.

periscopio [peri'skɔpjo] *sm* periscope.

perito [pe'rito], **-a** *s, agg* expert. **perizia** *sf* (*bravura*) skill, expertise; (*pratica*) experience; (*valutazione*) examination, expert opinion.

perla ['perla] *sf* pearl.

perlomeno [perlo'meno] *avv* at least.

perlustrare [perlus'trare] *v* patrol; (*mil*) reconnoitre. **perlustrazione** *sf* patrol; reconnaissance.

permaloso [perma'lozo] *agg* touchy.

permanente [perma'nɛnte] *agg* permanent, lasting. *sf* (*fam*) perm. **permanenza** *sf* (*soggiorno*) stay. **in permanenza** permanently. **permanere** *v* remain.

permeare [perme'are] *v* permeate. **permeabile** *agg* permeable.

permesso [per'messo] *sm* permission; licence; (*congedo*) leave, pass. **(con) permesso?** may I? (*inter*) allow me!

***permettere** [per'mettere] *v* allow, permit.

pernice [per'nitʃe] *sf* partridge.

perno ['pɛrno] *sm* pivot, pin. **far perno su** hinge on.

pernottare [pernot'tare] *v* spend the night.

pero [pero] *sm* pear-tree. **pera** *sf* pear.

però [pe'rɔ] *cong* but; (*tuttavia*) still, yet, however.

perossido [pe'rɔssido] *sm* peroxide.

perpendicolare [perpendiko'lare] *agg, sf* perpendicular.

perpetuo [per'petuo] *agg* perpetual.

perplesso [per'plesso] *agg* puzzled; (*incerto*) undecided. **perplessità** *sf* perplexity; indecision.

perquisire [perkwi'zire] *v* search. **perquisizione** *sf* search.

perseguire [perse'gwire] *v* pursue. **perseguimento** *sm* pursuit.

perseguitare [persegwi'tare] *v* persecute. **persecuzione** *sf* persecution.

perseverare [perseve'rare] *v* persevere. **perseveranza** *sf* perseverance.

persiana [per'sjana] *sf* shutter, blind.

persiano [per'sjano] *agg* Persian.

persico [per'siko] *agg* Persian. **(pesce) persico** *sm* perch.

persino [per'sino] *avv* even.

*persistere [per'sistere] v persist. persistenza sf persistence.

perso ['pɛrso] agg lost. a tempo perso in one's spare time.

persona [per'sona] sf person; (qualcuno) somebody. di or in persona in person, personally; (personificato) personified. persona di servizio domestic (help).

personaggio [perso'naddʒo] sm (teatro, ecc.) character; celebrity.

personale [perso'nale] agg personal. sm (aspetto) figure; (dipendenti) staff. sf (mostra) one-man show. personale di direzione management. personale qualificato skilled workers pl.

personalità [personali'ta] sf personality.

personificare [personifi'kare] v personify. personificazione sf personification.

perspicace [perspi'katʃe] agg keen, shrewd.

*persuadere [persua'dere] v persuade; convince. persuasione sf persuasion; conviction. persuasivo agg convincing. persuaso agg convinced.

pertanto [per'tanto] cong thus, therefore, so.

pertica ['pɛrtika] sf pole.

pertinace [perti'natʃe] agg stubborn; (deciso) determined.

pertinente [perti'nɛnte] agg pertaining (to); (domanda) relevant.

pertosse [per'tosse] sf whooping cough.

*pervadere [per'vadere] v pervade.

*pervenire [perve'nire] v arrive (at).

pervertire [perver'tire] v corrupt, pervert. perverso agg perverse. pervertito, -a sm, sf pervert.

pesare [pe'zare] v weigh. pesa sf (pesatura) weighing; (basculla) weighbridge. pesante agg heavy; (aria) stuffy; (duro) rough. peso sm weight; (onere) burden.

pesca¹ ['pɛska] sf (bot) peach. pesco sm peach-tree.

pesca² ['peska] sf fishing; (industria) fishery; (quantità) catch. pescare v fish; (trovare) pick up, get hold of; (acciuffare) catch. pescatore sm fisherman; (con lenza) angler.

pesce ['peʃe] sm fish. buttarsi a pesce su make a dive for. pesce d'aprile April fool. sano come un pesce fit as a fiddle. pescivendolo, -a sm, sf fishmonger.

pessimismo [pessi'mizmo] sm pessimism.

pessimista s(m+f) pessimist. pessimistico agg pessimistic.

pessimo ['pɛssimo] agg very bad; (scadente, incapace) very poor.

pestare [pes'tare] v crush; (fam: picchiare) give a (good) hiding. pestare i piedi a qualcuno tread on someone's toes. pestello sm pestle.

peste ['pɛste] sf plague; (fig) pest, curse.

pesto ['pesto] agg crushed. essere buio pesto be pitch dark.

petalo ['pɛtalo] sm petal.

petizione [peti'tsjone] sf petition.

petrolifero [petro'lifero] agg oil.

petrolio [pe'trɔljo] sm oil. lampada a petrolio sf paraffin lamp. petroliera sf (oil-)tanker.

pettegolo [pet'tegolo], -a sm, sf gossip. agg gossipy. pettegolezzo sm gossip.

pettinare [petti'nare] v comb. pettinarsi v comb one's hair. pettinato (tessuto) worsted. pettinatura sf combing; (acconciatura) hair-style. pettine sm comb.

petto ['pɛtto] sm breast; (torace) chest. a doppio/un petto double-/single-breasted.

petulante [petu'lante] agg pert.

pezza ['pɛttsa] sf rag; (toppa) patch; (pannolino) napkin. pezza da piedi doormat. pezza di tessuto roll of cloth. pezzato agg spotted. pezzente s(m+f) beggar.

pezzo ['pɛttso] sm piece; (tempo) period; (giornale) article. pezzo di ricambio spare part. pezzo di terreno plot of land. pezzo grosso (fig) VIP, big shot.

*piacere [pja'tʃere] v please. mi piace ... I like .... sm pleasure; favour. a piacere ad lib, freely. far piacere a please. per piacere please, if you please. piacevole agg pleasant.

piaga ['pjaga] sf sore; (fig) wound.

piagnucolare [pjanuko'lare] v whine, whimper. piagnucolio sm whining, whimpering. piagnucolone, -a sm, sf (fam) crybaby.

pialla ['pjalla] sf plane. piallare v plane.

pianella [pja'nɛlla] sf (mattonella) tile; (pantofola) mule, slipper.

pianerottolo [pjane'rɔttolo] sm landing.

pianeta [pja'neta] sm planet.

*piangere ['pjandʒere] v weep, cry. far piangere v move to tears; (ironico) be pathetic.

pianificare [pjanifi'kare] v plan. pianificatore, -trice sm, sf planner. pianificazione sf planning.

pianista [pja'nista] *s(m+f)* pianist.

piano¹ ['pjano] *agg* flat, level; (*chiaro*) clear. *avv* (*adagio*) slow, slowly; (*con cautela*) carefully; (*a voce bassa*) softly. **pian piano** very slowly, very softly; (*poco alla volta*) little by little.

piano² ['pjano] *sm* plane, level; (*casa*) floor, storey; (*autobus*) deck. **primo piano** foreground. **secondo piano** background.

piano³ ['pjano] *sm* (*progetto*) plan. **piano di studi** syllabus. **piano regolatore** town plan.

pianoforte [pjano'fɔrte] *sm* pianoforte; (*fam*) piano. **pianoforte a coda** grand piano.

pianta ['pjanta] *sf* (*bot*) plant; (*disegno*) plan; (*carta di città*) map. **di sana pianta** from scratch. **in pianta stabile** on the permanent staff. **pianta del piede** sole.

piantagione [pjanta'dʒone] *sf* plantation.

piantare [pjan'tare] *v* plant; (*conficcare*) drive; (*tenda*) pitch; (*abbandonare*) quit. **piantare grave** (*fam*) make trouble. **piantare in asso** leave in the lurch.

pianterreno [pjanter'rɛno] *sm* ground floor.

pianto ['pjanto] *sm* crying; tears *pl*.

pianura [pja'nura] *sf* plain.

piastra ['pjastra] *sf* plate. **piastrella** *sf* tile. **piastrellare** *v* tile.

piattaforma [pjatta'fɔrma] *sf* platform. **piattaforma di lancio** launching pad. **piattaforma girevole** turntable.

piatto ['pjatto] *agg* flat. *sm* plate; (*portata*) dish, course; (*bilancia*) pan. **lavare i piatti** wash up.

piazza ['pjattsa] *sf* square; (*comm*) market; (*posto*) place; (*fam: calvizie*) bald patch. **a due piazze** (*letto, ecc.*) double. **a una piazza** single. **far piazza pulita** make a clean sweep. **scendere in piazza** demonstrate. **piazzaforte** *sf* stronghold. **piazzale** *sm* square. **piazzare** *v* place. **piazzista** *sm* salesman, commercial traveller.

picca ['pikka] *sf* pike. **picche** *sf pl* (*carte*) spades *pl*. **rispondere picche** turn down flat.

piccante [pik'kante] *agg* sharp, spicy; (*arguto*) spirited; (*licenzioso*) racy.

picchiare [pik'kjare] *v* hit, strike; (*colpire*) beat; (*bussare*) knock. **picchiata** *sf* (*aereo*) (nose-)dive.

picchio ['pikkjo] *sm* woodpecker.

piccino [pit'tʃino] *agg* tiny. *sm* child (*pl* -ren).

piccione [pit'tʃone] *sm* pigeon, dove. **piccionaia** *sf* dovecot; (*fam: teatro*) (the) gods.

picco ['pikko] *sm* peak. **a picco** sheer. **colare** *or* **mandare a picco** sink.

piccolo ['pikkolo], **-a** *agg* small, little. *sm*, *sf* little one, child (*pl* -ren). **da piccolo** as a child. **fin da piccolo** since childhood. **in piccolo** on a small scale. **piccolezza** *sf* (*inezia*) trifle.

piccone [pik'kone] *sm* pick-axe.

pidocchio [pi'dɔkkjo] *sm* louse (*pl* lice). **pidocchioso** *agg* lousy; (*fig*) mean.

piede ['pjɛde] *sm* foot (*pl* feet). **a piedi** on foot. **a piedi nudi** barefoot. **essere tra i piedi** be in the way. **fatto con i piedi** (*fam*) slipshod. **in piedi** standing. **togliersi dai piedi** get out of the way. **piedistallo** *sm* pedestal.

piega ['pjɛga] *sf* fold; crease; (*ornamento*) pleat. **messa in piega** *sf* set. **mettere in piega** *v* set. **prendere una brutta piega** take a turn for the worse.

piegare [pje'gare] *v* bend; (*foglio, tessuto*) fold.

pieghettare [pjeget'tare] *v* pleat.

pieghevole [pje'gevole] *agg* folding; flexible.

piena ['pjɛna] *sf* flood, spate; (*folla*) crowd.

pieno ['pjɛno] *agg* full. **in pieno** completely; exactly. (*nel mezzo*) in the middle of. **pieno zeppo** full up, chock full. **fare il pieno** (*auto*) fill up.

pietà [pje'ta] *sf* pity, compassion; (*devozione*) piety. **fare pietà** arouse pity. **pietoso** *agg* pitiful.

pietanza [pje'tantsa] *sf* dish, course.

pietra ['pjɛtra] *sf* stone. **pietra dura** semiprecious stone. **pietra di paragone** touchstone. **pietrina** *sf* flint.

piffero ['piffero] *sm* pipe; (*sonatore*) piper.

pigiama [pi'dʒama] *sm* pyjamas *pl*.

pigiare [pi'dʒare] *v* press, squeeze. **pigiatura** *sf* pressing.

pigione [pi'dʒone] *sf* rent.

pigliare [pi'ʎare] (*fam*) *V* **prendere**.

pigmento [pig'mento] *sm* pigment. **pigmentazione** *sf* pigmentation.

pigmeo [pig'mɛo] *sm* pygmy.

pigna ['piɲa] *sf* pine-cone.

pignatta [pi'ɲatta] *sf* pot.

pignolo [pi'ɲɔlo], **-a** agg fussy, pedantic. sm, sf pedant.

pigolare [pigo'lare] v peep, chirp. **pigolio** sm peeping, chirping.

pigro ['pigro], **-a** agg idle, lazy. sm, sf lazy person, loafer. **pigrizia** sf laziness, idleness.

pila ['pila] sf pile; (elett) battery.

pilastro [pi'lastro] sm pillar, column.

pillola ['pillola] sf pill.

pilone [pi'lone] sm pillar; (ponte) pier; (elett) pylon.

pilotare [pilo'tare] v pilot; (auto) drive. **pilota** sm pilot.

pinacoteca [pinako'tɛka] sf picture gallery.

pineta [pi'neta] sf pine forest.

pingue ['pingwe] agg fat.

pinguino [pin'gwino] sm penguin.

pinna ['pinna] sf fin.

pinnacolo [pin'nakolo] sm pinnacle.

pino ['pino] sm pine (tree). **pinolo** sm pine-seed.

pinza ['pintsa] sf pliers pl; (zool) pincer. **pinzetta** sf tweezers pl.

pio ['pio] agg pious.

pioggia ['pjɔddʒa] sf rain. **pioggerella** sf also **pioggia fine** drizzle.

piolo [pi'ɔlo] sm peg; (scala) rung.

piombare¹ [pjom'bare] v hurtle, plunge; (avventarsi) pounce.

piombare² [pjom'bare] v fill; (otturare) seal (with lead); (sigillare) seal (with lead). **piombo** sm lead; (piombino) plummet.

pioniere [pjo'njere], **-a** sm, sf pioneer.

pioppo ['pjoppo] sm poplar.

*****piovere** ['pjovere] v rain; (fig) pour (in). **piovere a catinelle** rain cats and dogs. **piovigginare** v drizzle. **piovoso** agg rainy.

piovra ['pjovra] sf (giant) squid; (persona) blood-sucker.

pipa ['pipa] sf pipe.

pipistrello [pipi'strello] sm bat.

pira ['pira] sf pyre.

piramide [pi'ramide] sf pyramid.

pirata [pi'rata] sm pirate. **pirata della strada** hit-and-run driver. **pirateria** sf piracy.

piroscafo [pi'roskafo] sm steamer; (da carico) freighter; (di linea) liner.

piscia ['piʃa] (volg) sf piss. **pisciare** v piss.

piscina [pi'ʃina] sf swimming pool.

pisello [pi'zɛllo] sm pea. **pisello odoroso** sweet pea.

pisolino [pizo'lino] sm **fare** or **schiacciare un pisolino** take a nap.

pista ['pista] sf track; (aero) runway.

pistola [pis'tola] sf pistol. **pistola a spruzzo** spray-gun. **pistolettata** sf pistol-shot.

pistone [pis'tone] sm piston.

pitocco [pi'tɔkko], **-a** sm, sf beggar; (avaro) miser.

pitone [pi'tone] sm python.

pittore [pit'tore] sm painter.

pittoresco [pitto'resko] agg picturesque.

pittura [pit'tura] sf painting; (descrizione) picture; (vernice) paint. **pitturare** v paint.

più [pju] avv (comparativo) more; (superlativo) most. **al più presto** as soon as possible. **il più che** possible. **il più la maggioranza** the majority. **il più possibile** as much as possible. **più volte** several times. **sempre più** .... more and more .... **tanto più** especially. **tutt'al più** at most.

piuma ['pjuma] sf feather. **piumino** sm down; (per cipria) powder-puff; (letto) eiderdown, duvet.

piuttosto [pjut'tosto] avv rather.

piviere [pi'vjere] sm plover.

pizzicare [pittsi'kare] v pinch; (pungere) sting; (musica) pluck. **pizzico** sm, pl **-chi** pinch, dash. **pizzicore** sm itch. **pizzicotto** sm pinch.

pizzo [pittso] sm (merletto) lace; (barba) goatee.

placare [pla'kare] v calm down, placate.

placca ['plakka] sf plate; (ornamento) plaque; (med) patch.

placenta [pla'tʃɛnta] sf placenta.

placido [pla'ʃido] agg placid.

plagiare [pla'dʒare] v plagiarize. **plagiario**, **-a** sm, sf plagiarist.

planare [pla'nare] v glide. **planata** sf glide.

plasmare [plaz'mare] v mould. **plasma** sm plasma.

plastica ['plastika] sf (arte) modelling; (med) plastic surgery; (materia) plastic. **plasticare** v model. **plastico** agg plastic.

platano ['platano] sm plane-tree.

platea [pla'tɛa] sf stalls pl.

platino ['platino] sm platinum.

platonico [pla'tɔniko] agg platonic.

plausibile [plau'zibile] agg plausible.

plebe ['plɛbe] sf plebs pl; (plebaglia) mob, riff-raff. **plebeo** agg plebeian; common.

plebiscito [plebi'ʃito] sm plebiscite.

pleurite [pleu'rite] sf pleurisy.

plico ['pliko] sm parcel.

plotone [plo'tone] *sm* platoon.

plumbeo ['plumbeo] *agg* leaden.

plurale [plu'rale] *agg, sm* plural.

plutocratico [pluto'kratiko] *agg* plutocratic. **plutocrate** *sm* plutocrat. **plutocrazia** *sf* plutocracy.

pneumatico [pneu'matiko] *sm* tyre. *agg* (*mec*) pneumatic; (*gonfiabile*) inflatable.

po' [po] *V* poco.

pochino [po'kino] *agg* not much *or* many. *avv, pron* very little *or* few. *sm* bit.

poco ['poko] *agg* little; (*tempo*) short. *avv* little, not very. *pron* little, not much. **a poco a poco** little by little. **da poco** unimportant. **fra poco** soon. **pochi** *pron, agg* few *pl.* **poco dopo** not long after. **poco fa** a short while ago. **poco male!** never mind! **un poco** *or* **po'** a little.

podere ['podere] *sm* estate.

podestà [podes'ta] *sm* mayor.

podio ['podjo] *sm* platform.

podismo [po'dizmo] *sm* track events *pl*; (*corsa*) running. **podista** *s(m+f)* track athlete; runner.

poema [po'ema] *sm* poem.

poi ['poi] *avv* then; (*più tardi*) later. *sm* future. **da ... in poi** from ... onwards. **il senno di poi** hindsight.

poiché [poi'ke] *cong, as*, since.

polacco [po'lakko], **-a** *agg* Polish. *sm, sf* Pole. *sm* (*lingua*) Polish.

polarizzare [polarid'dzare] *v* polarize. **polare** *agg* polar. **stella polare** *sf* pole star.

polca ['polka] *sf* polka.

polemica [po'lemika] *sf* polemic; controversy. **polemico** *agg* contentious, polemical.

polenta [po'lenta] *sf* (*gastr*) maize porridge; (*fam: persona lenta*) slow-coach.

policlinico [poli'kliniko] *sm* hospital.

poligamo [po'ligamo], **-a** *agg* polygamous. *sm, sf* polygamist. **poligamia** *sf* polygamy.

poligono [po'ligono] *sm* polygon.

polimero [po'limero] *sm* polymer.

polistirolo [polisti'rɔlo] *sm* polystyrene.

politecnico [poli'tɛkniko] *sm* polytechnic.

politene [poli'tɛne] *sm* polythene.

politico [po'litiko] *agg* political. *sm* politician. **politica** *sf* politics; (*linea di condotta*) policy.

polizia [poli'tsia] *sf* police. **poliziesco** *agg* police. **romanzo** *o* **film poliziesco** thriller. **poliziotto** *sm* policeman.

polizza ['polittsa] *sf* policy; (*ricevuta*) voucher.

pollame [pol'lame] *sm* poultry. **pollaio** *sm* chicken coop. **pollastra** *sf* pullet; (*fam*) lass, chick. **pollastro** cockerel; (*fam*) gullible person, mug.

pollice ['pollitʃe] *sm* thumb; (*del piede*) big toe.

polline ['polline] *sm* pollen.

pollo ['pollo] *sm* chicken. **far ridere i polli** be ridiculous.

polmone [pol'mone] *sm* lung. **polmonare** *agg* pulmonary. **polmonite** *sf* pneumonia.

polo ['polo] *sm* pole. **essere ai poli opposti** be poles apart.

Polonia [po'lɔnja] *sf* Poland.

polpa ['polpa] *sf* flesh; (*carne*) meat; (*fig*) substance. **polpetta** *sf* meatball. **polposo** *agg* fleshy.

polpaccio [pol'pattʃo] *sm* (*anat*) calf.

polso ['polso] *sm* wrist; (*med*) pulse; (*polsino*) cuff.

poltiglia [pol'tiʎa] *sf* mush; mixture.

poltrona [pol'trona] *sf* easy chair, armchair; (*teatro*) stall.

poltrone [pol'trone], **-a** *sm, sf* idler, loafer.

polvere ['polvere] *sf* dust; powder. **polveriera** *sf* powder-keg. **polverizzare** *v* pulverize. **polveroso** *agg* dusty.

pomata [po'mata] *sf* ointment.

pomeriggio [pome'riddʒo] *sm* afternoon. **pomeridiano** *agg* afternoon.

pomice ['pomitʃe] *sf* pumice-stone.

pomo ['pomo] *sm* (*frutto*) apple; (*albero*) apple-tree.

pomodoro [pomo'dɔro] *sm* tomato.

pompa[1] ['pompa] *sf* pump. **pompa antincendio** fire-engine. **pompare** *v* pump (up).

pompa[2] ['pompa] *sf* pomp. **far pompa di** show off. **impresario di pompe funebri** *sm* undertaker. **pomposo** *agg* pompous.

pompelmo [pom'pelmo] *sm* grapefruit.

pompiere [pom'pjere] *sm* fireman.

ponderare [ponde'rare] *v* consider. **ponderato** *agg* careful. **ponderoso** *agg* ponderous.

ponente [po'nɛnte] *sm* west.

ponte ['ponte] *sm* bridge; (*impalcatura*) scaffolding. **ponte aereo** air-lift. **ponte radio** radio link. **ponte sospeso** suspension bridge.

pontefice [pon'tefitʃe] *sm* pontiff. **pontificare** *v* pontificate. **pontificio** *agg* papal.

pontile [pon'tile] *sm* pier; (*da sbarco*) landing stage.

popolare [popo'lare] *agg* popular; working-class; (*tradizionale*) folk. **casa popolare** *sf* council house. *v* populate. **popolarità** *sf* popularity. **popolarizzare** *v* popularize.

popolo ['popolo] *sm* people; common people. **popolazione** *sf* population.

popone [po'pone] *sm* melon.

poppa¹ ['poppa] *sf* (*mar*) stern. **avere il vento in poppa** sail before the wind.

poppa² ['poppa] *sf* (*anat*) breast. **poppare** *v* suck.

porcellana [portʃel'lana] *sf* porcelain, china.

porco ['pɔrko] *sm, pl* **-ci** pig. *agg* (*volg*) bloody. **porcaio** *sm* pig-sty. **porcellino d'India** *sm* guinea-pig. **porcheria** *sf* muck, filth; (*cibo*) disgusting stuff; (*cosa malfatta*) rubbish. **porcospino** *sm* porcupine.

*porgere ['pɔrdʒere] *v* give, hand. **porgere aiuto** offer help.

pornografia [pornogra'fia] *sf* pornography. **pornografico** *agg* pornographic.

poro ['pɔro] *sm* pore. **poroso** *agg* porous.

porpora ['porpora] *agg invar, sf* purple.

*porre ['porre] *v* put; set, place. **porre in dubbio** question. **porre in evidenza** stress. **porre rimedio** set right.

porro ['pɔrro] *sm* leek.

porta ['pɔrta] *sf* door. **a porte chiuse** behind closed doors; (*dir*) in camera. **mettere alla porta** (*fig*) throw out. **porta di sicurezza** emergency exit.

portabagagli [portaba'gaʎi] *sm invar* luggage-rack; (*facchino*) porter.

portabile [por'tabile] *agg* portable.

portacenere [porta'tʃenere] *sm invar* ashtray.

portachiavi [porta'kjavi] *sm invar* keyring.

portaerei [porta'ɛrei] *sf* aircraft-carrier.

portafinestra [portafi'nestra] *sf, pl* **portefinestre** French window.

portafoglio [porta'fɔʎʎo] *sm* wallet; (*borsa*) briefcase; (*pol*) portfolio.

portalettere [porta'lettere] *sm invar* postman.

portamonete [portamo'nete] *sm invar* purse.

portare [por'tare] *v* bring; (*prendere*) take; (*trasportare*) carry; (*indossare*) wear; (*addurre*) put forward. **essere portato** have a gift (for). **portatore** *sm* carrier; (*comm*) bearer.

portasapone [portasa'pone] *sm invar* soap-dish.

portasigarette [portasiga'rette] *sm invar* cigarette-case.

portaspilli [porta'spilli] *sm invar* pincushion.

portauovo [portauovo] *sm invar* egg-cup.

portavoce [porta'votʃe] *sm invar* spokesman, mouthpiece.

portento [por'tɛnto] *sm* portent; (*persona*) prodigy.

portico ['pɔrtiko] *sm* arcade; (*di casa*) porch.

portinaio [porti'najo], **-a** *sm, sf* doorkeeper; caretaker. **portineria** *sf* caretaker's lodge.

porto¹ ['pɔrto] *sm* port, harbour.

porto² ['pɔrto] *sm* (*comm*) carriage. **porto d'armi** gun licence.

porto³ ['pɔrto] *sm* (*vino*) port.

Portogallo [porto'gallo] *sm* Portugal. **portoghese** *agg, s(m+f)* Portuguese; *sm* (*lingua*) Portuguese. **fare il portoghese** gate-crash.

portone [por'tone] *sm* front door.

porzione [por'tsjone] *sf* portion, share.

posa ['pɔza] *sf* (*atteggiamento*) pose; (*foto*) exposure.

posare [po'zare] *v* put *or* lay down; rest; (*ritratto*) pose.

poscritto [pos'kritto] *sm* postscript.

positivo [pozi'tivo] *agg* positive; affirmative; practical. **positiva** *sf* (*foto*) positive.

posizione [pozi'tsjone] *sf* position.

*posporre [pos'porre] *v* postpone; (*mettere dopo*) place after. **posposizione** *sf* postponement.

*possedere [posse'dere] *v* possess, own. **possedimento** *sm also* **possesso** possession. **possessore** *sm* owner.

possibile [pos'sibile] *agg* possible. **fare il possibile** do one's best. **possibilità** *sf* possibility; (*capacità*) means. **possibilmente** *avv* if possible.

posta¹ ['pɔsta] *sf* post, mail; (*ufficio*) post office. **a giro di posta** by return of post. **mettersi alla posta (di)** be on the lookout (for). **posta aerea** air mail. **postale** *agg* postal.

posta² ['pɔsta] *sf* (*gioco*) bet, stake.

post-bellico [post'bɛlliko] *agg* post-war.

posteggiare [posted'dʒare] *v* park. **posteggio** *sm* parking; (*spazio*) parking space.

posteriore [poste'rjore] *agg* back, rear; (*tempo*) later.

posterità [posteri'ta] *sf* posterity.

posticcio [pos'tittʃo] *agg* artificial. *sm* hairpiece.

posticipare [postitʃi'pare] *v* defer.

postino [pos'tino] *sm* postman.

posto ['posto] *sm* (*luogo*) place; (*spazio*) room; (*impiego*) position; (*da sedere*) seat. **essere a posto** be in order; (*star bene*) be well, be content. **mettere a posto** tidy up; repair. **sul posto** on the spot.

postumo ['postumo] *agg* posthumous.

potabile [po'tabile] *agg* (*spreg*) drinkable. **acqua potabile** *sf* drinking water.

potare [po'tare] *v* prune.

potassio [po'tassjo] *sm* potassium. **potassa** *sf* potash.

potente [po'tɛnte] *agg* powerful; (*efficace*) potent; (*valido*) forceful. **potenza** *sf* power; (*forza*) strength; (*efficacia*) potency.

potenziale [poten'tsjale] *agg, sm* potential. **potenzialità** *sf* capacity.

potenziare [poten'tsjare] *v* strengthen, expand. **potenziamento** *sm* strengthening, expansion.

*potere[1] [po'tere] *v* can, be able; (*possibilità, permesso*) may. **non poterne più** (*essere sfinito*) be exhausted; (*essere al limite della sopportazione*) be unable to stand it any longer. **può darsi** maybe.

potere[2] [po'tere] *sm* power.

povero ['povero], **-a** *agg* poor. *sm, sf* poor person. **povero di** lacking in. **povertà** *sf* poverty; (*scarsità*) want, lack.

pozza ['pottsa] *sf* pool. **pozzanghera** *sf* puddle.

pozzo ['pottso] *sm* well; (*cavità*) shaft. **pozzo nero** cesspool.

pranzare [pran'tsare] *v* have dinner; (*a mezzogiorno*) have lunch. **pranzo** *sm* dinner; lunch. **dopo pranzo** (*nel pomeriggio*) in the afternoon. **sala da pranzo** *sf* dining room.

pratica ['pratika] *sf* practice; experience; (*incartamento*) file. **praticante** *s(m+f)* apprentice; (*rel*) churchgoer. **praticare** *v* practise; (*fare*) make; frequent; associate (with).

pratico [pratiko] *agg* practical; (*esperto*) skilled; (*funzionale*) useful, handy.

all'atto pratico in practice. **essere pratico di** be familiar with.

prato ['prato] *sm* meadow; (*giardino*) lawn. **pratolina** *sf* daisy.

preavvisare [preavvi'zare] *v* also **preavvertire** inform in advance; (*ammonire*) warn. **preavviso** *sm* (advance) notice; warning.

pre-bellico [pre'bɛlliko] *agg* pre-war.

precario [pre'karjo] *agg* precarious.

precauzione [prekau'tsjone] *sf* (*cautela*) caution, care; (*provvedimento*) precaution. **precauzionale** *agg* precautionary.

precedente [pretʃe'dɛnte] *agg* previous, preceding, former. *sm* (*dir*) precedent. **precedenti (penali)** *sm pl* (criminal) record *sing*. **precedentemente** *avv* before. **precedenza** *sf* priority. **in precedenza** previously.

precedere [pre'tʃedere] *v* precede.

precipitare [pretʃipi'tare] *v* hurl (down); (*affrettare*) hasten; (*chim*) precipitate; (*cadere*) crash; (*piombare*) plunge. **precipitoso** *agg* hurried; (*fig*) rash.

precipizio [pretʃi'pitsjo] *sm* precipice.

precisare [pretʃi'zare] *v* specify; (*fam*) spell out. **precisazione** *sf* clarification. **precisione** *sf* precision. **preciso** *agg* precise, exact; identical.

precoce [pre'kɔtʃe] *agg* precocious; premature, untimely.

preconcetto [prekon'tʃetto] *sm* preconceived idea, prejudice.

precursore [prekur'sore] *sm* forerunner.

preda ['prɛda] *sf* prey; (*bottino*) booty. **essere in preda a** be a struck by. **in preda alle fiamme** in flames. **predare** *v* plunder.

predecessore [predetʃes'sore] *sm* predecessor.

predestinare [predesti'nare] *v* preordain.

predetto [pre'detto] *agg* aforesaid.

predica ['prɛdika] *sf* sermon; (*ramanzina*) telling-off. **predicare** *v* preach.

prediletto [predi'lɛtto], **-a** *s, agg* favourite.

*predire [pre'dire] *v* predict, foretell.

*predisporre [predis'porre] *v* arrange (in advance); predispose.

predominare [predomi'nare] *v* prevail. **predominio** *sm* sway.

prefabbricato [prefabbri'kato] *agg* prefabricated.

prefazione [prefa'tsjone] *sf* preface, foreword.

preferire [prefe'rire] *v* prefer. **preferenza** *sf* preference. **preferibile** *agg* preferable.

prefetto [pre'fetto] *sm* prefect. **prefettura** *sf* prefecture.

*prefiggere [pre'fiddʒere] *v* fix (in advance); (*gramm*) prefix. **prefiggersi** *v* resolve.

prefisso [pre'fisso] *sm* (*gramm*) prefix; (*telefono*) (area) code.

pregare [pre'gare] *v* pray. **prego** *inter* (*per favore*) please! (*risposta*) don't mention it!

pregevole [pre'dʒevole] *agg* valuable.

preghiera [pre'gjera] *sf* prayer; (*domanda*) request.

pregiato [pre'dʒato] *agg* valued. **pregio** *sm* regard; merit. **di nessun pregio** worthless.

pregiudicare [predʒudi'kare] *v* prejudice; (*danneggiare*) harm. **pregiudicato** *sm* ex-convict.

pregiudizio [predʒu'ditsjo] *sm* prejudice, bias.

pregustare [pregus'tare] *v* look forward to.

preistorico [preis'tɔriko] *agg* prehistoric.

prelato [pre'lato] *sm* prelate.

prelevare [prele'vare] *v* withdraw.

prelibato [preli'bato] *agg* exquisite.

preliminare [prelimi'nare] *agg* preliminary. *sm* element.

preludio [pre'ludjo] *sm* prelude.

prematuro [prema'turo] *agg* premature.

premeditato [premedi'tato] *agg* premeditated.

premere ['premere] *v* press. **mi preme (di) sapere** I am anxious to know.

premiare [pre'mjare] *v* award a prize to; (*ricompensare*) reward. **premio** *sm* prize; reward; (*comm*) premium.

preminente [premi'nente] *agg* pre-eminent.

premura [pre'mura] *sf* (*fretta*) haste; (*riguardo*) solicitude, attention. **fare premura a** hurry up. **farsi premura** take care. **premuroso** *agg* thoughtful, solicitous.

*prendere ['prendere] *v* take; (*cogliere, subire, catturare*) catch; (*ricevere*) receive; (*ritirare*) pick up; (*occupare*) take up; (*assumere*) take on; (*ottenere*) get. **andare a prendere** fetch. **prendere alla lettera** take literally. **prendere per il naso** mock. **prendere qualcuno per il bavero** pull someone's leg. **prendere un**

granchio (*fig*) make a blunder. **prendersela** *v* take it amiss; (*con qualcuno*) get angry with; (*a cuore*) take to heart.

prenotare [preno'tare] *v* book, reserve. **prenotazione** *sf* booking, reservation.

preoccupare [preokku'pare] *v* worry. **preoccupazione** *sf* worry.

preparare [prepa'rare] *v* prepare; (*tavola*) lay; (*letto*) make. **preparare la strada** pave the way. **preparativo** *sm* arrangement. **preparazione** *sf* preparation.

preposizione [preposi'tsjone] *sf* preposition.

prepotente [prepo'tente] *agg* overbearing. *s(m+f)* (*fam*) bully.

prerogativa [preroga'tiva] *sf* privilege.

presa ['preza] *sf* hold; (*stretta*) grasp; (*elett*) socket; (*carte*) trick; (*cattura*) capture. **cane da presa** sm retriever. **essere alle prese con** wrestle with. **far presa** set. **macchina da presa** *sf* cine-camera. **presa di posizione** taking sides. **presa in giro** leg-pull. **venire alle prese** come to grips.

presbite ['prezbite] *agg* long-sighted.

prescindere [pre'ʃindere] *v* **a prescindere da** apart from.

*prescrivere [pre'skrivere] *v* prescribe. **prescrizione** *sf* ordinance. **prescrizione medica** doctor's orders *pl*; (*ricetta*) prescription.

presentare [prezen'tare] *v* present; (*far conoscere*) introduce; (*mostrare*) show; offer. **presentatore, -trice** *sm, sf* compere, question-master.

presente [pre'zente] *agg* present; in the presence of; (*questo*) this. *sm* present. **i presenti** those present *pl*. **tener presente** keep in mind.

presentimento [presenti'mento] *sm* presentiment, foreboding.

presenza [pre'zentsa] *sf* presence; appearance. **di presenza** personally. **fare atto di presenza** put in an appearance. **presenziare (a)** *v* attend.

preservare [prezer'vare] *v* preserve; protect. **preservativo** *sm* preservative; (*guaina profilattica*) condom. **preservazione** *sf* preservation.

preside ['prezide] *sm* headmaster; (*di facoltà*) dean. *sf* headmistress.

presidente [prezi'dente] *sm* president; (*di assemblea*) chairman. **presidente della camera** (*pol*) speaker. **presidente del Consiglio** (*pol*) Prime Minister. **presidenza** *sf* (*pol*) presidency; chairmanship. **assumere la presidenza** take the chair.

presidio [pre'zidjo] *sm* garrison; (*fig*) protection. **presidiare** *v* garrison; protect.

*presiedere [pre'sjɛdere] *v* be in charge (of).

pressa ['prɛssa] *sf* press. **pressare** *v* press.

pressappoco [pressap'poko] *avv* about, roughly.

pressione [pres'sjone] *sf* pressure.

presso ['prɛsso] *prep* near; (*insieme a, fra*) with; (*accanto a*) by; (*indirizzo*) care of, c/o. *avv* nearby. **pressoché** *avv* almost.

prestabilire [prestabi'lire] *v* prearrange.

prestare [pres'tare] *v* lend. **prestare aiuto** help. **prestar fede** believe. **prestar giuramento** take an oath. **prestazione** *sf* (*rendimento*) performance. **prestazioni** *sf pl* services *pl*.

prestigio [pres'tidʒo] *sm* prestige. **gioco di prestigio** *sm* conjuring trick. **prestigiatore, -trice** *sm, sf* conjurer. **prestigioso** *agg* prestigious.

prestito ['prɛstito] *sm* loan. **dare in prestito** lend. **prendere in prestito** borrow.

presto ['prɛsto] *avv* (*tra poco*) soon; (*in fretta*) quickly; (*di buon'ora*) early. **si fa presto** (*facilmente*) it's easy.

*presumere [pre'zumere] *v* imagine. **presunto** *agg* presumed; (*erede*) presumptive. **presuntuoso** *agg* presumptuous. **presunzione** *sf* presumption.

*presupporre [presup'porre] *v* presuppose, assume; (*richiedere*) require. **presupposizione** *sf* assumption.

prete ['prɛte] *sm* priest.

*pretendere [pre'tendere] *v* (*esigere, presumere*) expect; (*sostenere*) claim. **pretensioso** *agg* pretentious.

pretesa [pre'teza] *sf* claim; (*presunzione*) pretention. **aver poche/molte pretese** easy/difficult to please.

pretesto [pre'testo] *sm* pretext; (*occasione*) opportunity.

prettamente [pretta'mente] *avv* typically.

*prevalere [preva'lere] *v* prevail.

*prevedere [preve'dere] *v* foresee; (*considerare*) provide for. **prevedibile** *agg* foreseeable.

*prevenire [preve'nire] *v* (*precedere*) arrive before; (*fig*) anticipate; (*evitare*) avert; (*avvertire*) warn. **prevenuto** *agg* (*maldisposto*) biased.

preventivo [preven'tivo] *agg* precautionary; (*dir*) preventive. *sm* estimate. **preventivare** *v* estimate. **prevenzione** *sf* (*ostilità*) bias; (*provvedimento*) prevention.

previdente [previ'dɛnte] *agg* far-sighted, provident. **previdenza** *sf* foresight. **previdenza sociale** social security.

previo ['prɛvjo] *agg* prior.

previsione [previ'zjone] *sf* forecast; (*aspettativa*) anticipation; (*comm*) estimate. **previsto** *agg* foreseen; (*dir*) provided for. **meno/più del previsto** less/more than anticipated.

prezioso [pre'tsjozo] *agg* precious, valuable.

prezzemolo [pret'tsemolo] *sm* parsley.

prezzo [prettso] *sm* price; (*tariffa*) rate; (*trasporto pubblico*) fare. **a buon prezzo** cheaply.

prigione [pri'dʒone] *sf* prison, jail. **prigionia** *sf* captivity. **prigioniero, -a** *sm, sf* prisoner.

prima ['prima] *avv* (*in anticipo*) first, in advance; (*precedentemente*) before; (*più presto*) earlier; (*una volta*) once; (*in primo luogo*) first. *sf* (*teatro*) première; (*auto*) first gear; (*treno*) first class.

primario [pri'marjo] *agg* primary; (*med*) consultant.

primato [pri'mato] *sm* supremacy; record.

primavera [prima'vera] *sf* spring. **primaverile** *agg* spring.

primitivo [primi'tivo] *agg* primitive; original.

primizia [pri'mitsja] *sf* early produce; (*notizia*) latest news.

primo ['primo] *agg* first; (*precedente*) former; (*principale*) main. **per primo** first.

primula ['primula] *sf* primrose.

principale [printʃi'pale] *agg* principal, main. *sm* principal; (*fam*) boss.

principe ['printʃipe] *sm* prince. **principato** *sm* principality. **principesco** *agg* princely. **principessa** *sf* princess.

principio [prin'tʃipjo] *sm* beginning; (*fondamento*) principle; origin. **da or in principio** at first. **per principio** on principle.

priorità [priori'ta] *sf* priority.

prisma ['prizma] *sm* prism.

privare [pri'vare] *v* deprive.

privato [pri'vato], **-a** *agg* private; personal. *sm, sf* private citizen. **privatista** *s(m+f)* (*scolaro*) private school pupil;

(*candidato*) external student. **privativa** *sf* monopoly. **privazione** *sf* privation, loss.

privilegio [privi'lɛdʒo] *sm* privilege. **privilegiato** *agg* privileged.

privo ['privo] *agg* devoid (of), without. **privo di denaro** penniless. **privo di sensi** (*svenuto*) unconscious.

probabile [pro'babile] *agg* probable, likely. **poco probabile** unlikely. **probabilità** *sf* probability, likelihood; (*possibilità*) chance.

problema ['problema] *sm* problem. **problematico** *agg* problematic; doubtful.

proboscide [pro'bɔʃide] *sf* trunk.

procedere [pro't∫edere] *v* proceed; (*comportarsi*) behave. **procedimento** *sm* (*svolgimento*) course; (*tec*) process; (*dir*) proceedings *pl*.

processione [prot∫es'sjone] *sf* procession.

processo [pro't∫esso] *sm* process; (*dir*) trial, lawsuit. **essere sotto processo** be on trial. **processo verbale** minutes *pl*.

procinto [pro't∫into] *sm* **essere in procinto di** be on the point of, be about to.

proclamare [prokla'mare] *v* proclaim. **proclamazione** *sf* proclamation.

proclive [pro'klive] *agg* prone (to).

procreare [prokre'are] *v* procreate. **procreazione** *sf* procreation.

procurare [proku'rare] *v* get; (*dare, causare*) give. **procura** *sf* power of attorney. **per procura** by proxy. **procuratore** *sm* proxy; (*magistrato*) attorney; (*comm*) agent.

proda ['prɔda] *sf* bank.

prode ['prɔde] *agg* valiant.

prodigare [prodi'gare] *v* lavish. **prodigo** *agg*, *m pl* -**ghi** prodigal, lavish.

prodigio [pro'didʒo] *sm* prodigy. **prodigioso** *agg* wonderful, marvellous.

prodotto [pro'dotto] *sm* product; (*alimentare*) foodstuff; (*chimico*) chemical.

***produrre** [pro'durre] *v* produce; cause; (*mostrare*) show; (*fare*) make. **produrre un testimonio** call a witness. **produttivo** *agg* productive. **produttività** *sf* productivity. **produttore** *sm* producer. **produzione** *sf* production; (*fabbricazione*) manufacture; (*quantità*) output.

profanare [profa'nare] *v* desecrate; (*contaminare*) debase. **profano** *agg* profane; (*empio*) sacrilegious; (*inesperto*) ignorant.

***proferire** [profe'rire] *v* utter, pronounce.

professare [profes'sare] *v* profess. **professionale** *agg* professional; vocational;

(*connesso alla professione*) occupational. **professione** *sf* profession; (*mestiere*) trade. **di professione** by profession. **professionista** *s(m+f)* professional (person).

professore [profes'sore], -**essa** *sm, sf* teacher. **professore titolare/incaricato** university professor/lecturer.

profeta [pro'fɛta] *sm* prophet. **profetico** *agg* prophetic. **profezia** *sf* prophecy.

proficuo [pro'fikuo] *agg* useful.

profilo [pro'filo] *sm* profile; (*contorno*) outline. **profilare** *v* outline; (*mec*) profile. **profilato** *sm* (*mec*) section.

profittare [profit'tare] *v* profit; (*approfittare*) take advantage; (*progredire*) make progress. **profittatore** *sm* profiteer. **profitto** *sm* profit; advantage. **trarre profitto** benefit.

profondo [pro'fondo] *agg* deep; (*radicato*) deep-rooted. *sm* depth. **profondare** *v* sink. **profondità** *sf* depth.

profugo ['prɔfugo], -**a** *sm, pl* -**ghi**, *sf* refugee.

profumare [profu'mare] *v* perfume. **profumato** *agg* perfumed; fragrant. **profumeria** *sf* perfumery. **profumo** *sm* fragrance, scent.

profusione [profu'zjone] *sf* profusion.

progettare [prodʒet'tare] *v* plan; (*tec*) design. **progettazione** *sf* planning. **progetto** *sm* project, plan. **progetto di legge** bill. **progetto di massima** preliminary plan.

prognosi ['prɔɲɔzi] *sf* prognosis.

programma [pro'gramma] *sm* programme; prospectus; (*scuola*) syllabus. **programmare** *v* programme. **programmatore**, -**trice** *sm, sf* programmer. **programmazione** *sf* programming.

progredire [progre'dire] *v* make progress, get on. **progressione** *sf* progression. **progressivo** *agg* progressive. **progresso** *sm* progress. **fare progressi** improve, make progress.

proibire [proi'bire] *v* forbid, prohibit. **proibito** *agg* forbidden. **proibizionismo** *sm* prohibition.

proiettare [projet'tare] *v* project; (*gettar fuori*) eject; (*cine*) screen. **proiettile** *sm* projectile; (*mil*) shell. **a prova di proiettile** bullet-proof. **proiettore** *sm* projector.

prole ['prɔle] *sf* offspring.

proletario [prole'tarjo], -**a** *s, agg* proletarian. **proletariato** *sm* proletariat.

prolifico [proˈlifiko] *agg* prolific.

prolisso [proˈlisso] *agg* long-winded.

prologo [ˈprɔlogo] *sm, pl* -ghi prologue.

prolungare [prolunˈgare] *v* extend; (*tempo*) prolong; (*spazio*) lengthen. **prolungarsi** *v* (*dilungarsi*) dwell (on). **prolunga** *sf* extension. **prolungamento** *sm* extension.

promemoria [promeˈmɔrja] *sm invar* memorandum.

***promettere** [proˈmettere] *v* promise. **promessa** *sf* promise. **promesso** *agg* promised. **promettente** *agg* promising.

prominente [promiˈnɛnte] *agg* prominent, jutting (out). **prominenza** *sf* prominence, projection.

promiscuo [proˈmiskuo] *agg* mixed; (*scuola*) co-educational; (*relazioni*) promiscuous.

promontorio [promonˈtɔrjo] *sm* headland.

promozione [promoˈtsjone] *sf* promotion.

***promuovere** [proˈmwɔvere] *v* promote; provoke.

pronome [proˈnome] *sm* pronoun.

pronosticare [pronostiˈkare] *v* forecast. **pronostico** *sm* forecast.

pronto [ˈpronto] *agg* ready; (*rapido*) prompt; (*vivace*) lively. *inter* (*telefono*) hello!

prontuario [pronˈtwarjo] *sm* handbook.

pronunciare [pronunˈtʃare] *v* pronounce. **pronunciarsi a favore di** declare oneself in favour of. **pronuncia** *sf* pronunciation.

propaganda [propaˈganda] *sf* propaganda. **propagandista** *s(m+f)* propagandist.

propagare [propaˈgare] *v* propagate.

propenso [proˈpɛnso] *agg* inclined; favourable.

propizio [proˈpitsjo] *agg* propitious; favourable.

proponimento [proponiˈmento] *sm* resolution.

***proporre** [proˈporre] *v* propose; intend; suggest.

proporzione [proporˈtsjone] *sf* proportion; (*mat*) ratio. **in proporzione a** compared with. **proporzionale** *agg* proportional.

proposito [proˈpɔzito] *sm* purpose; intention; (*scopo*) aim; (*progetto*) plan. **a proposito** (*opportunamente*) at the right time; (*inter*) by the way; (*opportuno*) to the point. **a proposito di** with regard to. **cambiare proposito** change one's mind.

proposizione [propoziˈtsjone] *sf* proposition; clause.

proposta [proˈposta] *sf* proposal.

proprietà [proprjeˈta] *sf* property; (*precisione*, *decoro*) propriety; (*possesso*) ownership. **essere di proprietà di** belong to. **proprietà letteraria** copyright.

proprio [ˈprɔprjo] *agg* one's (own); (*mat*, *gramm*) proper, characteristic. *avv* exactly, just; (*veramente*) really.

propulsione [propulˈsjone] *sf* propulsion.

prora [ˈprɔra] *sf* prow.

prorogare [proroˈgare] *v* (*rinviare*) put off, adjourn; (*prolungare*) extend. **proroga** *sf* adjournment; extension.

***prorompere** [proˈrompere] *v* burst out.

prosa [ˈprɔza] *sf* prose; theatre. **prosaico** *agg* prosaic.

prosciugare [proʃuˈgare] *v* drain.

prosciutto [proˈʃutto] *sm* ham.

***proscrivere** [proˈskrivere] *v* proscribe.

proseguire [proseˈgwire] *v* continue, go on. **proseguimento** *sm* continuation.

prosperare [prospeˈrare] *v* prosper, thrive. **prosperità** *sf* prosperity. **prospero** *agg* prosperous, thriving.

prospettiva [prospetˈtiva] *sf* (*tec*) perspective; (*previsione*) prospect, outlook. **prospettare** *v* (*esporre*) show; (*guardare*) look out (on). **prospettarsi** *v* (*essere in vista*) be in sight.

prospetto [prosˈpetto] *sm* (*tabella*) list; (*pubblicità*) prospectus.

prossimo [ˈprɔssimo] *agg* near; (*seguente*) next; (*vicino nel passato*, *stretto*) close. **passato/trapassato prossimo** *sm* (*gramm*) present/past perfect. *sm* neighbour. **prossimità** *sf* proximity.

prostituire [prostituˈire] *v* prostitute. **prostituta** *sf* prostitute. **prostituzione** *sf* prostitution.

protagonista [protagoˈnista] *s(m+f)* protagonist, chief character.

***proteggere** [proˈteddʒere] *v* protect, shelter; favour.

proteina [proteˈina] *sf* protein.

protesi [ˈprɔtezi] *sf* prosthesis.

protesta [proˈtesta] *sf* protest. **protestare** *v* protest; (*dichiarare*) declare. **protesto** *sm* protest.

protestante [protesˈtante] *s(m+f)*, *agg* Protestant.

protetto [proˈtetto], -a *agg* protected; favourite. *sm*, *sf* protégé; favourite. **protettorato** *sm* protectorate. **protettore** *sm* protector, defender. **santo protettore** patron saint.

protezione [prote'tsjone] *sf* protection; (*mecenatismo*) patronage. **protezione antincendio** fireproofing.

protocollo [proto'kɔllo] *sm* protocol; register. **carta protocollo** *sf* foolscap (paper).

protone [pro'tone] *sm* proton.

prototipo [pro'tɔtipo] *sm* prototype.

***protrarre** [pro'trarre] *v* protract; (*prorogare*) put off.

prova ['prɔva] *sf* proof; evidence; (*esame, testimonianza*) test; (*cimento*) trial; (*tentativo*) try; (*sarto*) fitting; (*teatro*) rehearsal. **a prova di acqua** waterproof. **a prova di fuoco** fireproof. **dar buona prova di sé** give a good account of oneself. **reggere alla prova** stand the test.

provare [pro'vare] *v* try (out); (*collaudare*) test; (*spettacolo*) rehearse; (*assaggiare*) taste; (*dimostrare*) prove; (*mettere alla prova*) put to the test; (*abito, ecc.*) try on.

***provenire** [prove'nire] *v* come (from); (*fig*) spring (from), be caused (by). **provenienza** *sf* origin, source.

proverbio [pro'vɛrbjo] *sm* proverb, saying. **proverbiale** *agg* proverbial.

provetta [pro'vetta] *sf* test-tube.

provincia [pro'vintʃa] *sf* province. **di provincia** provincial.

provocare [provo'kare] *v* provoke, cause. **provocatorio** *agg* provocative. **provocazione** *sf* provocation.

***provvedere** [provve'dere] *v* make provision for, provide for; (*prendere provvedimenti*) take steps; (*badare a*) see to; (*procurare*) provide. **provvedimento** *sm* step, measure. **provveditore** *sm* administrator; (*agli studi*) education officer.

provvidenza [provvi'dentsa] *sf* providence; (*fam*) godsend. **provvidenziale** *agg* providential.

provvigione [provvi'dʒone] *sf* commission.

provvisorio [provvi'zɔrjo] *agg* provisional.

provvista [prov'vista] *sf* provisions *pl*, stock. **provvisto di** supplied, provided.

prua ['prua] *sf* prow.

prudente [pru'dɛnte] *agg* prudent, careful, cautious. **prudenza** *sf* care, caution.

***prudere** ['prudere] *v* itch. **prurito** *sm* itch.

prugna ['pruɲa] *sf* plum; (*secca*) prune. **prugno** *sm* plum-tree.

pseudonimo [pseu'dɔnimo] *sm* pseudonym.

psicanalisi [psika'nalizi] *sf* psycho-analysis. **psicanalista** *s(m+f)* psycho-analyst. **psicanalitico** *agg* psycho-analytical.

psichiatra [psi'kjatra] *s(m+f)* psychiatrist. **psichiatria** *sf* psychiatry.

psichico ['psikiko] *agg* psychic.

psicologo [psi'kɔlogo], -a *sm*, *sf* psychologist. **psicologia** *sf* psychology. **psicologico** *agg* psychological.

psicopatico [psiko'patiko], -a *agg* psychopathic. *sm*, *sf* psychopath.

psicosi [psi'kɔzi] *sf* psychosis. **psicotico**, -a *s*, *agg* psychotic.

psicosomatico [psikoso'matiko] *agg* psychosomatic.

psicoterapia [psikotera'pia] *sf* psychotherapy. **psicoterapista** *s(m+f)* psychotherapist.

pubblicare [pubbli'kare] *v* publish. **pubblicazione** *sf* publication, issue. **pubblicista** *s(m+f)* (freelance) journalist.

pubblicità [pubblitʃi'ta] *sf* publicity; advertising. **fare pubblicità** advertise. **piccola pubblicità** classified advertisements *pl*. **pubblicitario** *agg* advertising, publicity.

pubblico ['pubbliko] *agg* public. *sm* public; (*teatro*) audience.

pubertà [puber'ta] *sf* puberty.

pudico [pu'diko] *agg*, *m pl* -chi modest; (*vergognoso*) bashful.

pudore [pu'dore] *sm* modesty; (*vergogna*) shame. **oltraggio al pudore** *sm* indecent behaviour. **senza pudore** shameless.

puerile [pue'rile] *agg* puerile.

pugilato [pudʒi'lato] *sm* boxing. **fare del pugilato** box. **pugile** *sm* boxer. **pugilistico** *agg* boxing.

pugnalare [puɲa'lare] *v* stab. **pugnalata** *sf* stab. **pugnale** *sm* dagger.

pugno ['puɲo] *sm* fist; (*colpo*) punch; (*piccola quantità*) fistful. **essere un pugno in un occhio** be an eyesore. **fare a pugni** fight; (*fig*) clash. **prendere a pugni** punch. **tenere in pugno** clutch; (*fig*) control.

pulce ['pultʃe] *sf* flea. **gioco della pulce** tiddly-winks.

pulcino [pul'tʃino] *sm* chick. **bagnato come un pulcino** wet through.

puledro [pu'ledro] *sm* colt. **puledra** *sf* filly.

puleggia [pu'leddʒa] *sf* pulley.

pulire [pu'lire] *v* clean; (*lavando*) wash; (*con strofinaccio, ecc.*) wipe (clean); (*con* spazzola) brush; (sfregando) scour; (lucidare) polish. **pulirsi il naso** blow one's nose. **pulito** agg clean.

pulizia [puli'tsia] sf (il pulire) cleaning; (l'essere pulito) cleanliness. **le pulizie** do the cleaning. **far pulizia** clean; (sgombrare) clear out.

pullman ['pullman] sm invar coach.

pullover [pul'lover] sm invar pullover.

pullulare [pullu'lare] v swarm.

pulpito ['pulpito] sm pulpit. **montare in pulpito** preach.

pulsare [pul'sare] v throb, beat. **pulsante** sm button; (campanello) buzzer.

*****pungere** ['pundʒere] v sting; (morsicare) bite; (con spillo) prick. **pungente** agg pungent; (fig) sharp; (ispido) prickly. **pungiglione** sm sting. **pungolo** sm goad.

punire [pu'nire] v punish. **punibile** agg punishable. **punitivo** agg punitive. **punizione** sf punishment; (sport) penalty.

punta ['punta] sf point; (estremità) tip. **ora di punta** sf rush hour. **prendere di punta** clash (with).

puntare [pun'tare] v point, direct; (scommettere) bet.

puntata [pun'tata] sf (scritto) instalment, part.

punteggiare [punted'dʒare] v punctuate. **punteggiatura** sf punctuation.

punteggio [pun'teddʒo] sm score.

puntellare [puntel'lare] v prop up. **puntello** sm prop; (fig) support.

puntiglioso [puntiʎ'ʎozo] agg stubborn. **puntiglio** sm stubbornness.

puntina [pun'tina] sf (da disegno) drawing pin; (grammofono) stylus.

punto ['punto] sm point; (segno) d t; (med, ricamo, maglia) stitch. **avv** (affatto) at all. **di punto in bianco** point-blank. **due punti** colon. **in punto** (tempo) on the dot, sharp. **mettere a punto** put right; (auto) tune; (fig) clarify. **punto esclamativo/interrogativo** exclamation/question mark. **punto e virgola** semicolon. **punto fermo** full stop.

puntuale [puntu'ale] agg punctual, on time.

puntualizzare [puntualid'dzare] v define, precisely.

puntura [pun'tura] sf sting, bite; (di spillo, ecc.) prick; (med) injection, puncture; (dolore) stitch.

punzecchiare [pundzek'kjare] v sting, bite, prick; (stuzzicare) tease.

punzonare [puntso'nare] v punch. **punzonatrice** sf punch. **punzone** sm punch, die.

pupa ['pupa] sf (fam) baby; (bambola) doll. **pupattola** sf doll. **pupazzo** sm puppet. **pupo** (fam) baby, little boy.

pupilla [pu'pilla] sf pupil.

purché [pur'ke] cong provided that, as long as.

pure ['pure] avv also, too. cong even (though); (tuttavia) yet.

purè [pu're] sm invar purée. **purè di patate** mashed potatoes pl.

purgare [pur'gare] v purge; purify. **purga** sf purge; (il purgare) purging, cleansing; (purgante) laxative; (gastr) soaking.

purgatorio [purga'tɔrjo] sm purgatory.

purificare [purifi'kare] v purify.

puritano [puri'tano], -a s, agg puritan.

puro ['puro] agg pure. **purezza** sf purity. **purosangue** agg, sm invar thoroughbred.

purpureo [pur'pureo] agg purple.

purtroppo [pur'trɔppo] avv unfortunately.

pus [pus] sm invar pus.

*****putrefare** [putre'fare] v putrefy, rot. **putrefazione** or **putrido** agg putrid, rotten.

puttana [put'tana] sf whore; (fam) tart.

puzzare [put'tsare] v stink, smell. **puzzo** sm stench, smell. **puzzolente** agg stinking.

Q

qua [kwa] avv here. (al) **di qua di** on this side of. **di qua** (stato in luogo) here; (moto a luogo) over here; (da qui) from here. **fin qua** (spazio) up to here; (tempo) so far. **per di qua** this way. **qua sopra/sotto/vicino** up/down/near here. **quacchero** ['kwakkero], -a sm, sf Quaker.

quaderno [kwa'derno] sm exercise-book.

quadrante [kwa'drante] sm (mat, astron) quadrant; (orologio) dial; (solare) sundial.

quadrato [kwa'drato] agg square; (sensibile) level-headed. sm square. **quadrare** v square; (far senso) make sense; (garbare) please.

quadretto [kwa'dretto] sm small square; (fig) scene. **a quadretti** check(ed), chequered.

quadrifoglio [kwadri'fɔʎʎo] *sm* four-leafed clover; (*autostrada*) clover-leaf.

quadro¹ ['kwadro] *agg* square.

quadro² ['kwadro] *sm* (*dipinto*) picture; (*ambito*) scope; (*tabella*) table. **quadri** *sm pl* (*carte*) diamonds *pl*. **a quadri** check(ed), chequered.

quadrupede [kwa'drupede] *agg*, *sm* quadruped.

quaggiù [kwad'dʒu] *avv* down here.

quaglia ['kwaʎʎa] *sf* quail.

qualche ['kwalke] *agg* some, any; (*alcuni*) a few. **in qualche luogo** somewhere. **in qualche modo** somehow. **qualcosa** *pron* *also* **qualche cosa** something, anything. **qualcuno** *pron* somebody, anybody.

quale ['kwale] *agg*, *pron* what; (*fra numero limitato*) which; (*come*) as. **tale e quale** just like. **inter** what? *avv* as.

qualificare [kwalifi'kare] *v* qualify. **qualifica** *sf* title; position; (*doti professionali*) qualification; (*giudizio*) report. **qualificativo** *agg* qualifying. **qualificato** *agg* skilled.

qualità [kwali'ta] *sf* quality; (*specie*) sort, kind. **qualitativo** *agg* qualitative.

qualora [kwa'lora] *cong* in case.

qualunque [kwa'lunkwe] *agg invar also* **qualsiasi** any; (*ogni*) every; (*non importa quale*) whatever, whichever. **l'uomo qualunque** the man in the street.

quando ['kwando] *avv* when. *cong* when; (*ogniqualvolta*) whenever; (*mentre*) whereas; (*giacché*) since. **da quando** (*dacché*) (ever) since; (*da quanto tempo*) since when. **di quando in quando** from time to time. **fino a quando** until; (*interrogativo*) until when; (*per quanto tempo*) how long.

quantità [kwanti'ta] *sf* quantity **quantitativo** *sm* amount.

quanto ['kwanto] *agg* how much *or* many; (*esclamativo*) what (a lot of); (*relativo*) as much *or* many . . . as. *pron* how much *or* many; as much *or* many; (*quello che*) what. *avv* how (much *or* many); (*tempo*) how long; (*distanza*) how far; (*come*) as; (*nella misura che*) as much as. **da quanto** (*tempo*) how long; (*per ciò che*) as far as. **per quanto** however; (*per ciò che*) as far as. **quanto a** as for. **quanto fa?** how much is it? **quanto mai** very much indeed. **quanto prima** soon. **quanto tempo** how long.

quaranta [kwa'ranta] *agg*, *sm* forty.

quarantena *sf* quarantine. **quarantesimo** *sm*, *agg* fortieth.

quaresima [kwa'rezima] *sf* Lent.

quarta ['kwarta] *sf* (*auto*) fourth *or* top gear; (*musica*) fourth. **partire in quarta** (*fam*) be off like a shot.

quartetto [kwar'tetto] *sm* quartet.

quartiere [kwar'tjere] *sm* district, quarter. **quartieri bassi** slums *pl*.

quarto ['kwarto] *agg* fourth. *sm* quarter. **sono le due e/meno un quarto** it is a quarter past/to two.

quarzo ['kwartso] *sm* quartz.

quasi ['kwazi] *avv* nearly, almost; (*con valore negativo*) hardly. *cong* (*come se*) as if.

quassù [kwas'su] *avv* up here.

quatto quatto ['kwatto 'kwatto] *avv* very quickly.

quattordici [kwat'torditʃi] *agg*, *sm* fourteen. **quattordicesimo** *agg*, *sm* fourteenth.

quattrini [kwat'trini] *sm pl* money *sing*; (*fam*) cash *sing*. **quattrini a palate** loads of money *sing*. **senza quattrini** penniless.

quattro ['kwattro] *sm*, *agg* four. **dirne quattro a qualcuno** give someone a piece of one's mind. **far quattro passi** go for a stroll. **farsi in quattro** go out of one's way.

quegli ['kweʎi] *V* quello.

quei ['kwei] *V* quello.

quel [kwel] *V* quello.

quello ['kwello] *agg* that (*pl* those). *pron* that (one) (*pl* those); (*lo stesso*) the same. **di quello che** than. **quello che** the one who (*pl* those who); (*ciò che*) what.

quercia ['kwertʃa] *sf* oak.

querela [kwe'rela] *sf* lawsuit, action. **presentare** *or* **sporgere querela** bring an action. **querelante** *s(m+f)* plaintiff.

questionario [kwestjo'narjo] *sm* questionnaire.

questione [kwes'tjone] *sf* question; (*affare*) matter; problem; (*disputa*) argument. **fare una questione** make an issue. **mettere in questione** question.

questo ['kwesto] *agg* this (*pl* these). *pron* this (one) (*pl* these). **con questo** (*con queste parole*) with these words; (*ciònonostante*) in spite of this.

questura [kwes'tura] *sf* police station.

qui ['kwi] *avv* here. **di qui** from here; (*moto a luogo*) here; (*tempo*) from now (on). **fin qui** up to here; (tempo) up to now.

quietanza [kwje'tantsa] sf receipt.

quietare [kwje'tare] v calm. **quiete** sf calm; (assenza di moto) rest.

quindi ['kwindi] cong so. avv afterwards.

quindici ['kwinditʃi] agg, sm fifteen. **quindici giorni** a fortnight. **quindicesimo** agg, sm fifteenth. **quindicinale** sm fortnightly.

quinta ['kwinta] sf (teatro) wing. **dietro le quinte** behind the scenes.

quintessenza [kwintes'sɛntsa] sf quintessence.

quintetto [kwin'tetto] sm quintet.

quinto ['kwinto] sm, agg fifth.

quota ['kwɔta] sf (porzione) share; (altitudine) height; (livello) level; (econ) quota. **quota zero** square one. **quotare** v appreciate; (borsa) quote. **quotazione** sf quotation.

quotidiano [kwoti'djano] agg, sm daily.

quoziente [kwo'tsjɛnte] sm quotient.

R

rabarbaro [ra'barbaro] sm rhubarb.

rabberciare [rabber'tʃare] v patch, mend; (scritto) re-hash.

rabbia ['rabbja] sf fury, rage; (idrofobia) rabies. **che rabbia!** how infuriating! **far rabbia a** make angry. **rabbioso** agg furious; (idrofobo) rabid.

rabbino [rab'bino] sm rabbi. **rabbinico** agg rabbinical.

rabbonire [rabbo'nire] v calm down, soothe.

rabbrividire [rabbrivi'dire] v shiver; (fig) shudder.

rabbuffare [rabbuf'fare] v (scompigliare) ruffle; (sgridare) scold. **rabbuffo** sm telling-off, scolding.

rabbuiarsi [rabbu'jarsi] v darken.

raccapezzare [rakkapet'tsare] v scrape together. **raccapezzarsi** v make out.

raccapricciare [rakkaprit'tʃare] v be horrified. **raccapricciante** agg horrifying.

raccattare [rakkat'tare] v pick up, collect.

racchetta [rak'ketta] sf racket; (ping-pong) bat.

***raccogliere** [rak'kɔʎere] v pick; (riprendere da terra) pick up; (riunire)

collect; (fare il raccolto) gather, harvest. **raccoglimento** sm attention. **raccoglitore** sm (cartella) binder.

raccolta [rak'kɔlta] sf collecting; collection; (agric) harvesting. **fare la raccolta** (di) collect.

raccolto [rak'kɔlto] agg (concentrato nei pensieri) deep in thought; (rannicchiato) crouching. sm harvest, crop.

raccomandare [rakkoman'dare] v recommend; (esortare) urge. **mi raccomando!** please do! **raccomandarsi a** rely on. (lettera) **raccomandata** sf registered letter. **raccomandato, -a** sm, sf protégé. **raccomandazione** sf recommendation.

raccomodare [rakkomo'dare] v also **racconciare** repair, mend.

raccontare [rakkon'tare] v tell. **racconto** sm story, tale; (resoconto) account.

raccorciare [rakkor'tʃare] v shorten.

raccordare [rakkor'dare] v connect. **raccordo** sm connection; (strada, ecc.) junction.

racimolare [ratʃimo'lare] v scrape together.

radar ['radar] sm invar radar.

raddolcire [raddol'tʃire] v sweeten; (acqua) soften.

raddoppiare [raddop'pjare] v double; (fig) redouble.

raddrizzare [raddrit'tsare] v straighten; (elett) rectify. **raddrizzatore** sm rectifier.

***radere** ['radere] v (sbarbare) shave; (sfiorare) graze. **radere al suolo** raze to the ground.

radiale [ra'djale] agg radial.

radiare [ra'djare] v expel; (mil) cashier; cancel. **radiare dall'albo** strike off the register.

radiatore [radja'tore] sm radiator.

radiazione[1] [radja'tsjone] sf (fis) radiation.

radiazione[2] [radja'tsjone] sf expulsion; cancellation.

radica ['radika] sf briar.

radicale [radi'kale] agg radical. sm (chim) radical; (mat) root.

radicare [radi'kare] v (take) root. **radicato** agg deep-rooted.

radicchio [ra'dikkjo] sm chicory.

radice [ra'ditʃe] sf root. **mettere radici** take root. **radice quadrata/cubica** square/cube root.

radio[1] ['radjo] sm invar radium.

radio² ['radjo] *sf invar* radio. **giornale radio** *sm* news (broadcast). **segnale radio** *sm* time signal.

radioattivo [radjoat'tivo] *agg* radioactive. **radioattività** *sf* radioactivity.

radiocontrollato [radjokontrol'lato] *agg* radio-controlled.

radiodiffusione [radjodiffu'zjone] *sf also* radiotrasmissione broadcast. **radiodiffuso** *agg* broadcast.

radiografare [radjogra'fare] *v* X-ray. **radiografia** *sf* (*immagine*) X-ray; (*procedimento*) radiography.

radiologo [ra'djologo], **-a** *sm, pl* **-ghi**, *sf* radiologist.

rado ['rado] *agg* sparse. **di rado** rarely. **radura** *sf* clearing.

radunare [radu'nare] *v* gather. **radunarsi** *v* assemble. **radunata** *sf* assembly, meeting. **raduno** *sm* meeting.

rafano ['rafano] *sm* radish.

raffica ['raffika] *sf* (*vento*) gust; (*colpi*) volley.

raffigurare [raffigu'rare] *v* represent.

raffinare [raffi'nare] *v* refine. **raffinatezza** *sf* refinement. **raffinazione** *sf* refining. **raffineria** *sf* refinery.

rafforzare [raffor'tsare] *v* reinforce.

raffreddare [raffred'dare] *v* cool. **raffreddarsi** *v* (*diventar freddo*) cool down; (*fam: prendersi un raffreddore*) catch a cold. **raffreddamento** *sm* cooling (down or off). **raffreddore** *sm* cold.

raffrenare [raffre'nare] *v* restrain.

raffrontare [raffron'tare] *v* compare. **raffronto** *sm* comparison.

rafia ['rafia] *sf* raffia.

raganella [raga'nɛlla] *sf* rattle.

ragazza [ra'gattsa] *sf* girl; (*innamorata*) girl-friend. **da ragazza** as a girl. **nome da ragazza** *sm* maiden name. **ragazza madre** unmarried mother.

ragazzo [ra'gattso] *sm* boy, lad; (*fam*) fellow, chap; (*innamorato*) boy-friend. **da ragazzo** as a boy. **fin da ragazzo** since childhood.

raggiare [rad'dʒare] *v* radiate.

raggio [rad'dʒo] *sm* ray; (*geom*) radius; (*ambito*) range; (*ruota*) spoke. **raggio d'azione** range; (*fig*) scope. **fare i raggi** X-ray.

raggirare [raddʒi'rare] *v* trick. **raggiro** *sm* trick.

***raggiungere** [rad'dʒundʒere] *v* reach; (*riunirsi*) join; (*allinearsi*) catch up

(with); (*conseguire*) attain. **raggiungibile** *agg* within reach; attainable.

raggiustare [raddʒus'tare] *v* mend; (*fig*) set right.

raggomitolare [raggomito'lare] *v* roll up. **raggomitolarsi** *v* curl up.

raggrinzare [raggrin'tsare] *v also* **raggrinzire** wrinkle, crease.

raggrumare [raggru'mare] *v* clot.

raggruppare [raggrup'pare] *v* group (together). **raggrupparsi** *v* assemble. **raggruppamento** *sm* grouping; (*gruppo*) group; (*mil*) unit.

ragguagliare [raggwa'ʎare] *v* level; (*paragonare*) compare; inform; (*mat*) convert. **ragguaglio** *sm* comparison; information; (*resoconto*) report; conversion.

ragia ['radʒa] *sf* **acqua ragia** *sf* turpentine.

ragionare [radʒo'nare] *v* reason; discuss. **ragionamento** *sm* reasoning; discussion.

ragione [ra'dʒone] *sf* reason; (*diritto*) right; (*rapporto*) rate; (*spiegazione*) account; (*mat*) ratio. **a ragione** rightly, with reason. **ragion veduta** after due consideration. **aver ragione** be right. **dar ragione a qualcuno** admit that someone is right. **rendersi ragione (di)** account (for).

ragioneria [radʒone'ria] *sf* accountancy. **ragioniere**, **-a** *sm, sf* accountant.

ragionevole [radʒo'nevole] *agg* reasonable.

ragliare [ra'ʎare] *v* bray. **raglio** *sm* bray.

ragno [ra'ɲo] *sm* spider. **ragnatela** *sf* cobweb.

ragù [ra'gu] *sm* meat sauce.

raid [reid] *sm invar* (*mil*) raid; (*sport*) rally.

raion ['rajon] *sm invar* rayon.

rallegrare [alleg'rare] *v* cheer up. **rallegrarsi** *v* be delighted; congratulate. **rallegramenti** *sm pl* congratulations *pl*.

rallentare [rallen'tare] *v* slacken, slow down. **rallentamento** *sm* slackening, slowing down.

rame ['rame] *sm* copper. **ramaiolo** *sm* ladle.

ramengo [ra'mengo] *sm* **andare a ramengo** (*fam*) go to the dogs.

ramificare [ramifi'kare] *v* ramify. **ramificazione** *sf* ramification.

ramino [ra'mino] *sm* rummy.

rammaricarsi [rammari'karsi] *v* regret; (*lamentarsi*) complain. **rammarico** *sm, pl* **-chi** regret.

rammendare [rammen'dare] v darn. **rammendo** sm (atto) darning; (parte rammendata) darn.

rammentare [rammen'tare] v (ricordare) recall; (richiamare alla memoria) call to mind.

rammollire [rammol'lire] v soften. **rammollito** agg soft; (rimbambito) doddering.

ramo ['ramo] sm branch. **ramoscello** sm twig.

rampa ['rampa] sf ramp; (scala) flight. **rampante** agg rampant.

rampicante [rampi'kante] agg climbing. sm (pianta) creeper.

rampino [ram'pino] sm hook.

rampollo [ram'pollo] sm offspring; (pianta) shoot; (acqua) spring.

rampone [ram'pone] sm (pesca) harpoon; (alpinismo) crampon.

rana ['rana] sf frog; (nuoto a rana) breaststroke. **uomo rana** sm frogman.

rancido ['rantʃido] agg rancid.

rancio ['rantʃo] sm meal.

rancore [ran'kore] sm grudge.

randagio [ran'dadʒo] agg stray.

randello [ran'dello] sm club.

rango ['rango] sm rank; (posizione sociale) standing.

rannicchiarsi [rannik'kjarsi] v crouch, huddle.

rannuvolarsi [rannuvo'larsi] v cloud over; (fig) darken.

ranocchio [ra'nokkjo] sm frog.

rantolare [ranto'lare] v wheeze.

ranuncolo [ra'nunkolo] sm buttercup.

rapa ['rapa] sf turnip.

rapace [ra'patʃe] agg rapacious. **uccello rapace** sm bird of prey.

rapare [ra'pare] v crop.

rapido ['rapido] agg quick, rapid. sm express (train).

rapina [ra'pina] sf robbery. **rapinare** v rob.

rapire [ra'pire] v (rapinare) rob; (persone) kidnap, abduct; (estasiare) enrapture. **rapimento** sm kidnapping; (estasi) rapture.

rappezzare [rappet'tsare] v patch.

rapporto [rap'porto] sm (legame) connection; relationship; (resoconto) report; (mec, mat) ratio.

*rapprendersi [rap'prendersi] v coagulate; (latte) curdle.

rappresaglia [rappre'zaʎa] sf reprisal.

rappresentare [rappresen'tare] v represent; (significare) mean; (teatro) show. **rappresentante** s(m+f) representative, agent. **rappresentanza** sf agency. **rappresentativo** agg representative. **rappresentazione** sf representation; description; (teatro, cine) performance.

raro ['raro] agg rare; exceptional. **rarità** sf rarity.

rasare [ra'zare] v shave; (erba, ecc.) cut. **rasoio** sm razor.

raschiare [ras'kjare] v scrape; (cancellare) scratch out. **raschiatura** sf scratching; scratch. **raschietto** sm scraper.

rasentare [razen'tare] v go close (to); (fig) come close (to).

raso ['razo] agg (liscio) smooth; (sbarbato) shaved. sm (tessuto) satin.

raspa ['raspa] sf rasp. **raspare** v rasp.

rassegnare [rasse'ɲare] v **rassegnare le dimissioni** resign. **rassegnarsi** v resign oneself. **rassegna** sf review; inspection; (resoconto) survey.

rasserenarsi [rassere'narsi] v clear up; (fig) cheer up.

rassettare [rasset'tare] v tidy up; (accomodare) repair.

rassicurare [rassiku'rare] v reassure.

rassomigliare [rassomi'ʎare] v resemble. **rassomigliarsi** v look alike.

rastrello [ras'trello] sm rake. **rastrellamento** sm (polizia) round-up. **rastrellare** v rake; (fig) comb. **rastrelliera** sf rack.

rata ['rata] sf instalment.

ratificare [ratifi'kare] v ratify. **ratifica** sf ratification.

ratto[1] ['ratto] sm (zool) rat.

ratto[2] ['ratto] sm (rapimento) rape.

rattoppare [rattop'pare] v patch. **rattoppo** sm (toppa) patch.

rattrappire [rattrap'pire] v make numb.

rattristare [rattris'tare] v sadden. **rattristarsi** v become sad, grieve.

rauco ['rauko] agg hoarse.

ravanello [rava'nello] sm radish.

*ravvedersi [ravve'dersi] v mend one's ways.

ravviare [ravvi'are] v tidy (up).

ravvicinare [ravvitʃi'nare] v bring near; reconcile. **ravvicinamento** sm (pol) rapprochement.

ravvisare [ravvi'zare] v recognize.

ravvivare [ravvi'vare] v revive.

*ravvolgere [rav'voldʒere] v wrap (up).

raziocinio [ratsjo'tʃinjo] *sm* reason; common sense.

razionale [ratsjo'nale] *agg* rational. **razionalizzare** *v* rationalize. **razionalizzazione** *sf* rationalization.

razionare [ratsjo'nare] *v* ration. **razionamento** *sm* rationing. **razione** *sf* ration.

razza¹ ['rattsa] *sf* race; (*specie*) kind; (*stirpe*) descent; (*animali*) breed. **di ogni razza** of all sorts. **di razza incrociata** crossbred. **di razza (pura)** (*animali*) pedigree, thoroughbred. **razziale** *agg* racial. **razzismo** *sm* racialism, racism. **razzista** *agg. s(m+f)* racist, racialist.

razza² ['rattsa] *sf* (*pesce*) ray, skate.

razzia [rat'tsia] *sf* raid.

razzo ['rattso] *sm* rocket.

re [re] *sm* king.

reagire [rea'dʒire] *v* react. **reagente** *sm* reagent.

reale¹ [re'ale] *agg* real. **realismo** *sm* realism. **realista** *s(m+f)* realist. **realistico** *agg* realistic. **realtà** *sf* reality. **in realtà** in (actual) fact.

reale² [re'ale] *agg* (*regale*) royal. **realista** *agg. s(m+f)* royalist.

realizzare [realid'dzare] *v* realize; (*effettuare*) put into effect; (*sport*) score. **realizzabile** *agg* feasible. **realizzazione** *sf* realization; (*teatro, ecc.*) production. **prezzo di realizzo** cost price.

reato [re'ato] *sm* offence; (*grave*) crime.

reattivo [reat'tivo] *agg* reactive. *sm* (*chim*) reagent; (*psic*) test.

reattore [reat'tore] *sm* reactor; (*aereo*) jet.

reazione [rea'tsjone] *sf* reaction. **motore a reazione** jet engine. **reazionario, -a** *s, agg* reactionary.

rebbio ['rebbjo] *sm* prong.

recapito [re'kapito] *sm* (*indirizzo*) address; (*consegna*) delivery. **recapitare** *v* deliver.

recare [re'kare] *v* (*portare*) bear; (*arrecare*) cause.

recensire [retʃen'sire] *v* review. **recensione** *sf* review. **recensore, -a** *sm, sf* reviewer.

recente [re'tʃente] *agg* recent. **recentissime** *sf pl* latest news *sing*.

recessione [retʃes'sjone] *sf* recession.

recinto [re'tʃinto] *sm* enclosure; (*per animali*) pen. **recintare** *v* enclose.

recipiente [retʃi'pjente] *sm* container.

reciproco [re'tʃiproko] *agg* reciprocal, mutual. **reciprocare** *v* reciprocate. **reciprocità** *sf* reciprocity.

recitare [retʃi'tare] *v* (*versi, ecc.*) recite; (*una parte*) play; (*sostenere un ruolo*) act; (*fingere*) put on an act. **recita** *sf* performance. **recital** *sm invar* recital. **recitazione** *sf* recitation.

reclamare [rekla'mare] *v* complain; (*richiedere*) demand; protest. **reclamo** *sm* complaint.

reclame [re'klam] *sf invar* advertisement. **fare (della) reclame** advertise.

reclusione [reklu'zjone] *sf* confinement; imprisonment.

reclutare [reklu'tare] *v* recruit. **recluta** *sf* recruit.

record ['rekord] *sm invar* record.

recriminare [rekrimi'nare] *v* recriminate.

redarguire [redargu'ire] *v* rebuke.

redattore [redat'tore], **-trice** *sm, sf* editor. **redazione** *sf* editorial staff; (*ufficio*) editor's office; (*atto del redigere*) editing, compiling.

reddito ['reddito] *sm* income; (*statale*) revenue; (*utile*) return. **imposta sul reddito** *sf* income tax. **reddito imponibile** taxable income.

redentore [reden'tore] *agg* redeeming. *sm* redeemer.

*redigere [re'didʒere] *v* (*compilare*) draw up; (*scrivere*) write; (*giornale*) edit.

*redimere [re'dimere] *v* redeem. **redimibile** *agg* redeemable.

redini ['redini] *sf pl* reins *pl*.

redivivo [redi'vivo] *agg* (*fig*) another.

reduce ['redutʃe] *agg* returning. *sm* (*mil*) veteran; (*superstite*) survivor.

refe ['refe] *sm* thread.

referendum [refe'rendum] *sm invar* referendum.

referenza [refe'rentsa] *sf* reference.

refettorio [refet'tɔrjo] *sm* refectory.

refrattario [refrat'tarjo] *agg* refractory; (*fig*) unmoved (by).

refrigerare [refridʒe'rare] *v* refresh, cool.

regalare [rega'lare] *v* give (away). **regalo** *sm* gift, present.

regale [re'gale] *agg* regal.

regata [re'gata] *sf* regatta.

reggente [red'dʒente] *sm* ruler. *agg* ruling.

*reggere ['reddʒere] *v* (*sostenere*) hold; support; (*resistere*) stand; (*dirigere*) run; (*gramm*) govern; (*durare*) last. **reggere al confronto con** bear comparison with. **reggere alla prova** stand the test. **reggersi** *v* stand.

reggia ['reddʒa] *sf* royal palace.

reggimento [reddʒi'mento] *sm* regiment.

reggipetto [reddʒi'petto] *sm* bra.

regia [re'dʒia] *sf* (*cinema*) direction; (*teatro*) production.

regime [re'dʒime] *sm* regime. **essere a regime** be on a diet. **regime di vita** way of life.

regina [re'dʒina] *sf* queen.

regio [re'dʒo] *agg* royal.

regione [re'dʒone] *sf* region. **regionale** *agg* regional.

regista [re'dʒista] *sf* (*cine*) director; (*teatro, TV*) producer.

registrare [redʒis'trare] *v* record; (*in registro*) register; (*mettere a punto*) adjust. **registratore** *sm* recorder; register. **registrazione** *sf* record; registration; adjustment; (*radio, TV*) recording. **registro** *sm* register. **cambiar registro** (*fam*) change one's tune.

regnare [re'ɲare] *v* rule, reign. **regno** *sm* (*territorio*) kingdom, realm; (*periodo, potere*) reign.

regola ['regola] *sf* rule; norm. **di regola** normally. **in regola** in order. **per vostra regola** for your information. **regolamentare** *agg* prescribed. **regolamento** *sm* (*il regolare*) regulation; (*norme*) rules *pl*; (*comm*) settlement.

regolare [rego'lare] *v* regulate; (*mettere a punto*) adjust; (*comm*) settle. **regolarsi** *v* act; control oneself. *agg* regular. **regolarità** *sf* regularity. **regolarizzare** *v* regularize.

regolo ['regolo] *sm* ruler; (*calcolatore*) slide-rule.

reincarnazione [reinkarna'tsjone] *sf* reincarnation.

reintegrare [reinte'grare] *v* reinstate. **reintegrazione** *sf* reinstatement.

relativo [rela'tivo] *agg* relative; concerning; (*corrispondente*) relevant. **relativamente a** regarding. **relatività** *sf* relativity.

relazione [rela'tsjone] *sf* relation(ship), connection; (*resoconto*) report. **essere in buone relazioni** be on good terms. **in relazione a** as regards. **mettere in relazione** relate.

relegare [rele'gare] *v* relegate.

religione [reli'dʒone] *sf* religion. **religiosa** *sf* nun. **religioso** *agg* religious.

reliquia [re'likwja] *sf* relic. **reliquiario** *sf* reliquary.

relitto [re'litto] *sm* wreck; (*rottame*) wreckage.

remare [re'mare] *v* row. **remata** *sf* stroke. **fare una remata** go for a row.

reminiscenza [remini'ʃentsa] *sf* recollection.

remissivo [remis'sivo] *agg* meek.

remoto [re'mɔto] *agg* remote.

*rendere ['rendere] *v* return; (*fruttare*) bring in; (*far diventare*) make; be efficient. **render conto di** account for. **render l'idea** make oneself clear. **rendere omaggio** pay homage. **rendersi conto** (*spiegare*) explain; (*capire*) realize. **rendere un servizio** do a favour.

rendimento [rendi'mento] *sm* (*utile*) yield; (*resa*) output; (*fis, mec*) efficiency.

rendita ['rendita] *sf* income; (*econ*) revenue; (*reddito*) yield.

rene ['rene] *sm* kidney. **reni** *sf pl* (*fam*) back *sing*.

renna ['renna] *sf* reindeer.

reparto [re'parto] *sm* department; (*mil*) unit. **capo reparto** departmental head; (*maestranza*) foreman; (*negozio*) supervisor.

repellente [repel'lente] *agg* repellent; (*ripugnante*) repulsive.

repentaglio [repen'taʎo] *sm* **mettere a repentaglio** jeopardize.

reperibile [repe'ribile] *agg* to be found; (*disponibile*) available.

repertorio [reper'tɔrjo] *sm* repertoire; (*elenco*) list.

replica ['replika] *sf* repetition; (*risposta*) reply; (*teatro*) performance; objection; copy. **replicare** *v* repeat; reply; perform again; object.

repressione [repres'sjone] *sf* repression. **represso** *agg* repressed.

*reprimere [re'primere] *v* repress, control.

repubblica [re'pubblika] *sf* republic. **repubblicano** *agg* republican.

reputare [repu'tare] *v* consider. **reputazione** *sf* reputation.

requisire [rekwi'zire] *v* requisition. **requisito** *sm* requirement. **requisitoria** *sf* (*dir*) indictment; (*rimprovero*) reproof.

resa ['reza] *sf* (*l'arrendersi*) surrender; (*restituzione*) return; (*rendimento*) yield. **resa dei conti** statement (of accounts); (*fig*) reckoning.

*rescindere [re'ʃindere] *v* rescind.

residente [rezi'dɛnte] *s(m+f)*, *agg* resident. **residenza** *sf* residence; (*permanenza*) stay.

residuo [re'ziduo] *agg* residual. *sm* residue; (*fig*) trace. **residuato** *sm* surplus.

resina ['rɛzina] *sf* resin.

resistere [re'zistere] *v* resist; (*sopportare*) bear; (*non essere danneggiato*) be resistant (to). **resistente** *agg* resistant, proof (against). **resistenza** *sf* resistance; (*capacità di resistere*) endurance.

resoconto [rezo'konto] *sm* report.

***respingere** [res'pindʒere] *v* push back, repel; (*rifiutare*) reject; (*bocciare*) fail. **respingente** *sm* buffer.

respirare [respi'rare] *v* breathe. **respiratore** *sm* respirator. **respiratorio** *agg* respiratory. **respirazione** *sf* respiration. **respiro** *sm* breath; (*fig*) breathing space. **sentirsi mancare il respiro** feel breathless.

responsabile [respon'sabile] *agg* responsible. *s(m+f)* person responsible. **responsabilità** *sf* responsibility. **prendersi la responsabilità** take the responsibility.

ressa ['rɛssa] *sf* crowd.

restare [res'tare] *v* remain; (*avanzare*) be left (over). **restarci male** (*delusi*) be disappointed; (*offesi*) be offended. **restare d'accordo** agree. **restante** *sm* remainder.

restaurare [restau'rare] *v* restore. **restauro** *sm* restoration; (*riparazione*) repair.

restio [res'tio] *agg* restive; (*bambini*) fractious.

restituire [restitu'ire] *v* return; (*fig*) restore. **restituzione** *sf* return.

resto ['rɛsto] *sm* remainder; (*di denaro*) change. **del resto** (*d'altronde*) on the other hand; (*inoltre*) besides.

***restringere** [res'trindʒere] *v* (*limitare*) restrict; (*ridurre di larghezza*) narrow; (*vestiario*) take in; (*tessuto*) shrink. **restringimento** *sm* shrinkage, narrowing. **restrizione** *sf* restriction.

rete ['rete] *sf* net; (*sistema, tec*) network; (*calcio*) goal; (*inganno*) trap. **rete metallica** wire netting.

reticente [reti'tʃɛnte] *agg* reticent.

reticolato [retiko'lato] *sm* (*disegno*) grid; (*graticcio*) grating. **reticolo** *sm* lattice, grating.

retina ['rɛtina] *sf* retina.

retorica [re'tɔrika] *sf* rhetoric. **retorico** *agg* rhetorical.

retribuire [retribu'ire] *v* reward. **retribuzione** *sf* reward; (*paga*) payment.

retro ['rɛtro] *sm* back.

retroattivo [retroat'tivo] *agg* retrospective.

***retrocedere** [retro'tʃɛdere] *v* recede; (*ritirarsi*) retreat; (*mil*) demote; (*sport*) move down.

retrodatare [retroda'tare] *v* back-date.

retrogrado [re'trɔgrado] *agg* retrograde; (*fig*) backward, reactionary.

retroguardia [retro'gwardja] *sf* rearguard.

retromarcia [retro'martʃa] *sf* reverse.

retroscena [retro'ʃɛna] *sm invar* backstage; (*fig*) background.

retrospettivo [retrospet'tivo] *agg* retrospective.

retrovisore [retrovi'zore] *sm* rear-view mirror.

retta[1] ['rɛtta] *sf* (*geom*) straight line.

retta[2] ['rɛtta] *sf* **dar retta a** listen to, pay attention to.

retta[3] ['rɛtta] *sf* fee for board and lodging.

rettangolo [ret'tangolo] *sm* rectangle. **rettangolare** *agg* right-angled, rectangular.

rettificare [rettifi'kare] *v* rectify, correct; (*mec*) grind. **rettifica** *sf* rectification, correction; grinding.

rettile ['rɛttile] *sm* reptile.

rettilineo [retti'lineo] *agg* straight.

retto ['rɛtto] *agg* straight; (*leale*) upright, straightforward; correct; (*geom*) right.

rettore [ret'tore] *sm* rector.

reumatismo [reuma'tizmo] *sm* rheumatism. **reumatico** *agg* rheumatic.

reverendo [reve'rɛndo] *agg* reverend. *sm* (*fam*) priest.

reversibile [rever'sibile] *agg* reversible.

revisione [revi'zjone] *sf* (*tec*) overhaul; (*dei conti*) audit; (*dir*) review. **revisore** *sm* auditor; (*di bozze*) proofreader.

revocare [revo'kare] *v* revoke.

riabbassare [riabbas'sare] *v* lower again.

riabbottonare [riabbotto'nare] *v* button up.

riabbracciare [riabbrat'tʃare] *v* embrace again.

riabilitare [riabili'tare] *v* rehabilitate. **riabilitazione** *sf* rehabilitation.

riaccompagnare [riakkompa'nare] *v* take back.

riacquistare [riakkwis'tare] *v* (*ricomprare*) buy back; (*ricuperare*) recover.

riaddormentarsi [riaddormen'tarsi] *v* fall asleep again.

riaffermare [riaffer'mare] *v* reaffirm.

riallacciare [riallat'tʃare] *v* re-tie; (*fig*) renew.

rialto [ri'alto] *sm* rise.

rialzare [rial'tsare] *v* raise (again). **rialzo** *sm* rise.

*****riammettere** [riam'mettere] *v* re-admit. **riammissione** *sf* re-admission.

riammogliarsi [riammoʎ'ʎarsi] *v* remarry.

rianimare [riani'mare] *v* revive; (*fig*) cheer (up).

*****riapparire** [riappa'rire] *v* reappear.

*****riaprire** [riap'rire] *v* reopen; (*riprendere*) resume. **riapertura** *sf* reopening; resumption.

riarmare [riar'mare] *v* rearm; (*nave*) refit; (*edificio*) reinforce. **riarmamento** *sf* rearmament.

riassestare [riasses'tare] *v* rearrange.

riassettare [riasset'tare] *v* tidy up.

riassicurare [riassiku'rare] *v* reassure; (*dir*) reinsure. **riassicurazione** *sf* reassurance; reinsurance.

*****riassumere** [rias'sumere] *v* take on again; (*compendiare*) sum up; (*condensare*) summarize. **riassunto** *sm* summary. **riassunzione** *sf* re-employment; (*dir*) resumption.

riattaccare [riattak'kare] *v* (*con filo*) sew on again; (*con colla*) stick on again; (*riprendere*) resume.

riattivare [riatti'vare] *v* reactivate; put back into service; (*strada*) reopen.

*****riavere** [ria'vere] *v* have again; (*ricuperare*) recover.

riavvicinare [riavvitʃi'nare] *v* approach again; (*fig*) reconcile. **riavvicinamento** *sm* (*pol*) rapprochement.

ribadire [riba'dire] *v* rivet; (*fig*) confirm.

ribaldo [ri'baldo] *sm* rogue.

ribaltare [ribal'tare] *v* turn over; (*mandar sottosopra*) overturn. **ribalta** *sf* (*asse*) flap; (*teatro*) proscenium; (*fig*) limelight. **tornare alla ribalta** (*questione*) come up again. **venire alla ribalta** come on to the scene. **ribaltabile** *agg* folding; (*tavolo*) drop-leaf; (*camion*) tip-up.

ribassare [ribas'sare] *v* reduce. **ribasso** *sm* reduction. **essere in ribasso** drop.

ribattere [ri'battere] *v* hit back; (*chiodo*) rivet; (*sport*) return; (*confutare*) refute; (*replicare*) answer back.

ribelle [ri'belle] *agg* rebellious. *s(m+f)*

rebel. **ribellarsi** *v* revolt. **ribellione** *sf* rebellion.

ribes ['ribes] *sm* (red)currant. **ribes nero** blackcurrant.

riboccare [ribok'kare] *v* overflow.

ribollire [ribol'lire] *v* boil (again); ferment; (*fig*) seethe.

ribrezzo [ri'brettso] *sm* disgust. **far ribrezzo** disgust. **provar ribrezzo** be disgusted (by).

ributtare [ribut'tare] *v* throw again; (*buttar fuori*) throw out; vomit; (*rifiutare*) reject.

ricacciare [rikat'tʃare] *v* turn out (again); (*rimettere*) push back.

*****ricadere** [rika'dere] *v* fall (back); (*pendere*) hang (down). **ricaduta** *sf* relapse.

ricalcare [rikal'kare] *v* (*disegno*) trace; (*fig*) follow faithfully. **ricalco** *sm* tracing.

ricamare [rika'mare] *v* embroider. **ricamo** *sm* embroidery.

ricambiare [rikam'bjare] *v* (*sostituire*) change; (*scambiare*) exchange; (*di nuovo*) change again. **di ricambio** spare.

ricapitolare [rikapito'lare] *v* sum up.

ricaricare [rikari'kare] *v* recharge; (*armi*) reload; (*orologio*) wind up again; (*pipa*) refill.

ricattare [rikat'tare] *v* blackmail. **ricattatore, -trice** *sm, sf* blackmailer. **ricatto** *sm* blackmail.

ricavare [rika'vare] *v* obtain; get; (*dedurre*) deduce. **ricavato** or **ricavo** *sm* proceeds *pl*.

ricchezza [rik'kettsa] *sf* wealth.

riccio[1] ['rittʃo] *agg* curly. *sm* curl; (*voluta*) scroll. **riccioluto** or **ricciuto** *agg* curly.

riccio[2] ['rittʃo] *sm* (*zool*) hedgehog; (*castagna*) (chestnut) husk. **riccio di mare** sea-urchin.

ricco ['rikko], **-a** *agg* rich. *sm, sf* rich person.

ricerca [ri'tʃerka] *sf* search; (*scientifica*) research; (*indagine*) investigation. **ricercare** *v* search (for); investigate. **ricercato** *agg* (much-)wanted; in (great) demand; (*affettato*) precious; (*raffinato*) refined. **ricercatezza** *sf* affectation; refinement. **ricercatore, -trice** *sm, sf* (*persona*) research worker; (*apparecchio*) detector.

ricetta [ri'tʃetta] *sf* recipe.

ricettare [ritʃet'tare] *v* receive. **ricettatore** *sm* receiver (of stolen goods).

ricettivo [ritʃet'tivo] *agg* receptive. **ricettività** *sf* receptivity.

*ricevere [ri'tʃevere] *v* receive; *(accogliere)* welcome. **ricevimento** *sm* reception; *(ricevuta)* receipt. **ricevitore** *sm* receiver; *(impiegato)* collector. **ricevuta** *sf* receipt. **ricezione** *sf* reception.

richiamare [rikja'mare] *v* call back; *(far tornare, ricordare)* recall; *(rimproverare)* rebuke. **richiamare in vita** revive. **richiamo** *sm* call; recall; rebuke. **far da richiamo** act as a decoy.

*richiedere [ri'kjedere] *v* *(aver bisogno)* require; *(per sapere)* ask; *(per ottenere)* ask for. **richiesta** *sf* request; *(econ)* demand; *(burocratica)* application. **richiesto** *agg* in (great) demand; necessary.

ricino ['ritʃino] *sm* **olio di ricino** *sm* castor-oil.

ricominciare [rikomin'tʃare] *v* start again.

ricompensa [rikom'pensa] *sf* reward. **ricompensare** *v* *(contraccambiare)* repay; *(premiare)* reward.

riconciliare [rikontʃi'ljare] *v* reconcile; *(procurare di nuovo)* win back. **riconciliarsi** *v* make it up.

ricondurre [rikon'durre] *v* take back; *(di nuovo)* take again.

*riconoscere [riko'noʃere] *v* recognize; *(ammettere)* admit. **riconoscente** *agg* grateful. **riconoscenza** *sf* gratitude. **riconoscibile** *agg* recognizable. **riconoscimento** *sm* recognition; admission; identification.

riconquistare [rikonkwis'tare] *v* win back.

ricopiare [riko'pjare] *v* copy.

*ricoprire [riko'prire] *v* cover (again); *(occupare)* hold; *(rivestire)* coat; *(colmare)* smother.

*ricordare [rikor'dare] *v* remember; *(richiamare alla memoria)* recall; *(far ricordare)* remind. **ricordo** *sm* recollection; *(oggetto)* souvenir. **ricordo di famiglia** heirloom. **ricordo d'infanzia** childhood memory. **ricordi** *sm pl* *(libro)* memoirs *pl*.

*ricorrere [ri'korrere] *v* resort; *(dir)* appeal; *(ripetersi)* recur. **ricorso** *sm* resort, recourse; *(dir)* appeal.

ricostituente [rikostitu'ente] *sm* tonic. **ricostituire** *v* reconstitute.

*ricostruire [rikostru'ire] *v* rebuild; *(fig)* reconstruct. **ricostruzione** *sf* reconstruction.

ricotta [ri'kɔtta] *sf* cottage cheese.

ricoverare [rikove'rare] *v* take in; *(all'ospedale)* send to hospital. **ricoverato, -a** *sm, sf* *(ospedale)* patient; *(ospizio)* inmate. **ricovero** *sm* shelter; *(ospizio)* home; *(in ospedale)* admission to hospital.

ricrearsi [rikre'arsi] *v* amuse oneself. **ricreazione** *sf* recreation; *(scuola)* playtime; *(pausa)* break.

ricredersi [ri'kredersi] *v* change one's mind.

ricuperare [rikupe'rare] *v* recover; *(mar)* salvage. **ricupero** *sm* recovery; salvage.

ricurvo [ri'kurvo] *agg* bent.

ricusare [riku'zare] *v* decline.

*ridare [ri'dare] *v* *(dare nuovamente)* give again; *(restituire)* give back.

*ridere ['ridere] *v* laugh. **(cosa) da ridere** *(divertente)* funny; *(inezia)* of no importance. **far ridere** be funny; be ridiculous. *sm* laughter.

ridicolo [ri'dikolo] *agg* ridiculous. *sm* absurdity; *(derisione)* ridicule.

ridimensionare [ridimensjo'nare] *v* reorganize; *(ridurre)* cut down; *(fig)* reappraise.

*ridire [ri'dire] *v* *(riferire)* tell; *(criticare)* find fault with; *(dire di nuovo)* repeat.

ridosso [ri'dɔsso] *sm* **a ridosso di** close to; *(dietro)* behind.

*ridurre [ri'durre] *v* reduce; *(trasformare)* turn. **riduzione** *sf* reduction; cut; adaptation.

rielaborare [rielabo'rare] *v* work out again; modify.

*riempire [riem'pire] *v* fill; *(compilare)* fill in; *(gastr)* stuff. **riempitivo** *sm* filler; *(fig)* stopgap.

rientrare [rien'trare] *v* *(tornare)* return; *(rincasare)* come or go home; *(far parte)* come within, form part of; *(entrare nuovamente)* re-enter. **rientro** *sm* return; re-entry; *(rientranza)* recess.

riepilogare [riepilo'gare] *v* summarize. **riepilogo** *sm, pl* -ghi recapitulation.

riesumare [riezu'mare] *v* exhume; *(fig)* unearth.

rievocare [rievo'kare] *v* recall; commemorate.

*rifare [ri'fare] *v* make or do again; *(ricostruire)* rebuild; imitate.

riferire [rife'rire] *v* relate; report. **riferimento** *sm* reference. **punto di riferimento** *sm* landmark.

rifilare [rifi'lare] (*fam*) v palm off; (*dire d'un fiato*) reel off.

rifinire [rifi'nire] v (*dare l'ultima mano*) give the finishing touch; (*ritoccare*) touch up. **rifinitura** *sf* finishing touches *pl*; (*guarnizione*) fittings *pl*.

rifiutare [rifju'tare] v refuse; decline. **rifiuto** *sm* refusal; (*scarto*) refuse, rubbish.

riflessione [rifles'sjone] *sf* reflection; (*osservazione*) remark.

riflessivo [rifles'sivo] *agg* thoughtful; (*gramm*) relexive.

riflesso [ri'flesso] *sm* reflection; (*med*) reflex. **di riflesso** indirectly.

*****riflettere** [ri'flettere] v reflect; (*pensarci su*) think (over or about). **riflettersi su** (*ripercuotersi*) affect. **riflettore** *sm* reflector; (*cinema, ecc.*) floodlight.

*****rifondere** [ri'fondere] v recast; (*ricomporre*) recompose; (*risarcire*) refund.

riformare [rifor'mare] v reform; (*formare di nuovo*) re-form. **riforma** *sf* reform.

rifornire [rifor'nire] v supply (with). **rifornirsi di benzina** (*auto*) fill up. **rifornimento** *sm* supply.

rifuggire [rifud'dʒire] v escape (again); (*fig*) shrink (from).

rifugiarsi [rifu'dʒarsi] v (take) shelter. **rifugiato, -a** *sm, sf* refugee.

rifugio [ri'fudʒo] *sm* shelter. **rifugio antiaereo** air-raid shelter. **rifugio fiscale** tax-haven.

*****rifulgere** [ri'fuldʒere] v glow.

riga ['riga] *sf* line; (*fila*) row; (*righello*) ruler. **a righe** striped. **riga a T** T-square.

rigare [ri'gare] v rule; (*tracciar strisce*) stripe; (*scalfire*) score.

rigaglie [ri'gaʎe] *sf pl* giblets *pl*.

rigettare [ridʒet'tare] v (*buttar fuori*) throw out; (*fig*) reject; vomit; (*gettare indietro*) throw back.

rigido [ri'dʒido] *agg* rigid, stiff; (*freddo*) severe. **rigidezza** or **rigidità** *sf* rigidity; (*fig*) rigour, severity.

rigirare [ridʒi'rare] v turn round; (*fig*) twist round. **rigiro** *sm* twist. **giri e rigiri** *sm pl* twists and turns *pl*.

rigo ['rigo] *sm* line; (*musica*) stave.

rigoglioso [rigoʎ'ʎozo] *agg* blooming.

rigonfio [ri'gonfjo] *agg* swollen.

rigore [ri'gore] *sm* rigour; (*calcio*) penalty (kick). **a rigor di logica** strictly speaking. **a rigore** in point of fact. **di rigore** compulsory. **rigoroso** *agg* rigorous.

rigovernare [rigover'nare] v (*i piatti*) wash up; (*animali*) tend.

riguardare [rigwar'dare] v regard. **riguardo** *sm* regard; (*cautela*) care; consideration. **di riguardo** of consequence. **riguardo a** regarding. **riguardo a me** as for me. **senza riguardo** inconsiderate. **riguardoso** *agg* thoughtful, respectful.

rilanciare [rilan'tʃare] v launch; (*asta, carte*) raise.

rilasciare [rila'ʃare] v (*liberare*) release; (*consegnare*) issue.

rilassare [rilas'sare] v relax; (*allentare*) slacken. **rilassamento** *sm* relaxation.

rilegare [rile'gare] v bind; (*incastonare*) set. **rilegatura** *sf* binding.

*****rileggere** [ri'leddʒere] v re-read.

rilevare [rile'vare] v (*notare*) notice; (*comm*) take over; (*topografia*) survey.

rilievo [ri'ljevo] *sm* relief; importance; (*osservazione*) remark; survey. **mettere in rilievo** stress, emphasize.

riluttante [rilut'tante] *agg* reluctant.

rima ['rima] *sf* rhyme.

rimandare [riman'dare] v send back; (*posporre*) defer.

*****rimanere** [rima'nere] v remain; (*essere*) be. **rimanere d'accordo** agree. **rimanere in dubbio** be left in doubt. **rimaner male** be put out; (*deluso*) be disappointed; (*offeso*) be hurt.

rimasugli [rima'zuʎi] *sm pl* left-overs *pl*.

rimbalzare [rimbal'tsare] v bounce; (*proiettile*) ricochet.

rimbambire [rimbam'bire] v become childish. **rimbambito** *agg* (*fam*) gaga.

rimbeccare [rimbek'kare] v retort. **di rimbecco** sharply.

rimboccare [rimbok'kare] v turn down. **rimboccarsi le maniche** roll up one's sleeves.

rimbombare [rimbom'bare] v resound.

rimborsare [rimbor'sare] v reimburse. **rimborso** *sm* refund.

rimediare [rime'djare] v remedy; (*fam: racimolare*) scrape together; (*accomodare*) patch; (*provvedere*) take care. **rimedio** *sm* remedy.

rimescolare [rimesko'lare] v stir; (*carte*) shuffle.

rimessa [ri'messa] *sf* (*deposito*) depot; garage; (*trasferimento*) remittance; (*perdita*) loss. **rimessa in gioco** (*calcio*) throw-in.

*rimettere [ri'mettere] v put back; (*indossare*) put back on; (*spedire*) send; (*denaro*) remit. **rimetterci** v lose. **rimettersi** v (*riaversi*) recover; (*affidarsi*) trust.

rimodernare [rimoder'nare] v modernize.

rimontare [rimon'tare] v (*mettere insieme*) reassemble; (*sport*) catch up; (*risalire*) go up; (*a cavallo*) remount; (*auto*) get back in.

rimorchiare [rimor'kjare] v (have in) tow. **rimorchio** sm trailer. **cavo da rimorchio** sm tow-rope.

rimorso [ri'morso] sm remorse. **rimorso di coscienza** pangs of conscience pl.

rimostrare [rimos'trare] v remonstrate.

rimpasto [rim'pasto] sm (*fig*) reshuffle.

rimpatriare [rimpa'trjare] v repatriate. **rimpatrio** sm repatriation.

*rimpiangere [rim'pjandʒere] v regret. **rimpianto** sm regret.

rimpiattino [rimpjat'tino] sm hide-and-seek.

rimpiazzare [rimpjat'tsare] v replace.

rimpiccolire [rimpikko'lire] v make smaller.

rimpinzarsi [rimpin'tsarsi] v stuff oneself, gorge.

rimproverare [rimprove'rare] v reproach; (*sgridare*) scold; (*fam*) tell off; (*biasimare*) blame. **rimprovero** sm reproach; blame.

*rimuovere [ri'mwovere] v remove; (*distogliere*) dissuade.

Rinascimento [rinaʃi'mento] sm Renaissance.

rinascita [ri'naʃita] sf rebirth; (*fig*) revival.

rincagnato [rinka'nato] agg **naso rincagnato** sm pug nose, snub nose.

rincalzare [rinkal'tsare] v (*sorreggere*) prop up; (*lenzuola*) tuck in.

rincarare [rinka'rare] v (*rendere più caro*) raise (the price of); (*essere più caro*) rise, become more expensive.

rincasare [rinka'zare] v return home.

*rinchiudere [rin'kjudere] v shut in. **rinchiuso** agg shut in; (*aria*) stale, fusty. **saper di rinchiuso** smell fusty or musty.

*rincorrere [rin'korrere] v run after, chase. **rincorsa** sf run-up.

*rincrescere [rin'kreʃere] v cause regret or sorrow. **mi rincresce di** ... I'm sorry to .... **ti rincresce** ...? do you mind...? **rincrescimento** sm regret.

rinculare [rinku'lare] v recoil.

rinforzare [rinfor'tsare] v reinforce, strengthen. **rinforzo** sm reinforcement.

rinfrescare [rinfres'kare] v cool; (*pulire*) freshen up; (*memoria*) refresh; (*ravvivare*) brush up. **rinfrescata** sf cooling. **darsi una rinfrescata** freshen up. **rinfreschi** sm pl refreshments pl. **rinfresco** sm (*ricevimento*) party.

rinfusa [rin'fuza] sf **alla rinfusa** higgledy-piggledy.

ringhiare [rin'gjare] v growl, snarl.

ringhiera [rin'gjera] sf railing; (*delle scale*) banister.

ringiovanire [rindʒova'nire] v rejuvenate; (*nell'aspetto*) make look younger.

ringraziare [ringra'tsjare] v thank. **ringraziamento** sm thanks pl. **lettera di ringraziamento** sf thank-you letter.

rinnegare [rinne'gare] v deny. **rinnegato**, **-a** s, agg renegade.

rinnovare [rinno'vare] v renew. **rinnovamento** sm renewal; (*rimodernamento*) renovation. **rinnovazione** sf renewal; renovation.

rinoceronte [rinotʃe'ronte] sm rhinoceros.

rinomato [rino'mato] agg renowned. **rinomanza** sf renown.

rinsaldare [rinsal'dare] v consolidate; (*inamidare*) starch.

rintoccare [rintok'kare] v (*campana*) toll; (*orologio*) strike. **rintocco** sm toll; stroke.

rintracciare [rintrat'tʃare] v trace; track down.

rintronare [rintro'nare] v thunder; (*assordare*) deafen.

rintuzzare [rintut'tsare] v (*rendere ottuso*) blunt; (*respingere*) repel; (*ribattere*) refute; (*frenare*) check.

rinunciare [rinun'tʃare] v give up; (*fare a meno*) forgo; (*dir*) renounce; (*non voler fare*) refrain (from). **rinunce** sf pl (*privazioni*) hardship sing. **rinuncia** sf abandonment; renunciation.

*rinvenire[1] [rinve'nire] v (*ritrovare*) recover.

*rinvenire[2] [rinve'nire] v (*ritornare in sè*) come to; (*riprendere freschezza*) revive.

rinviare [rinvi'are] v (*mandare indietro*) send back; (*posporre*) put off; (*dir*) adjourn; (*indirizzare*) refer. **rinvio** sm postponement; adjournment; (*testo*) (cross-)reference.

rinvigorire [rinvigo'rire] *v* invigorate; (*ritornar vigoroso*) regain strength.

rione [ri'one] *sm* district. **rionale** *agg* local.

riordinare [riordi'nare] *v* rearrange; (*comm*) reorder.

riorganizzare [riorganid'dzare] *v* reorganize. **riorganizzazione** *sf* reorganization.

ripagare [ripa'gare] *v* pay back.

riparare [ripa'rare] *v* (*aggiustare*) repair; (*porre rimedio*) make up (for), redress; protect; (*esame*) repeat. **ripararsi** *v* take shelter. **riparazione** *sf* repair; redress.

riparo [ri'paro] *sm* shelter; (*protezione*) cover; (*mec*) guard. **mettersi al riparo (da)** shelter (from).

ripartire¹ [ripar'tire] *v* (*partire di nuovo*) leave *o* start (up) again.

ripartire² [ripar'tire] *v* (*dividere*) split up; distribute.

ripassare [ripas'sare] *v* (*tornare*) pass again; (*visitare*) call back; (*attraversare*) cross again; (*rivedere*) review; (*mec*) overhaul. **ripassata** *sf* (*pittura*) fresh coat of paint; revision, overhaul; (*stirata*) press.

ripensare [ripen'sare] *v* think (over); (*mutare pensiero*) reconsider. **ripensare a** (*tornare col pensiero*) recall.

ripentirsi [ripen'tirsi] *v* repent; (*cambiar pensiero*) have second thoughts.

*ripercuotersi [riper'kwɔtersi] *v* (*suono*) reverberate; (*fig*) have an effect. **ripercussione** [riperkus'sjone] *sf* repercussion.

ripetere [ri'petere] *v* repeat. **ripetizione** *sf* repetition; (*studio*) coaching.

ripiano [ri'pjano] *sm* terrace; (*scomparto*) shelf.

ripido ['ripido] *agg* steep.

ripiegare [ripje'gare] *v* fold again; (*fig*) make do. **di ripiego** makeshift.

ripieno [ri'pjɛno] *agg* filled, stuffed. *sm* filling, stuffing.

*riporre [ri'porre] *v* put (back).

riportare [ripor'tare] *v* (*portare indietro*) bring back; (*ricondurre*) take again; (*riferire*) report; (*ricevere*) get; (*mat*) carry forward. **riporto** *sm* carrying forward; amount carried forward.

riposare [ripo'zare] *v* rest. **riposarsi** *v* take a rest. **riposo** *sm* rest. **andare a riposo** retire. **mettere a riposo** pension off. **senza riposo** without interruption.

ripostiglio [ripos'tiʎo] *sm* cubby-hole.

*riprendere [ri'prɛndere] *v* take again; (*recuperare*) recover; (*ricominciare*) resume. **riprendersi (da)** get over.

ripresa [ri'preza] *sf* resumption; (*innovamento*) renewal; (*calcio*) second half; (*boxe*) round; (*auto*) acceleration; (*cine*) shot.

ripristinare [ripristi'nare] *v* restore. **ripristino** *sm* restoration.

*riprodurre [ripro'durre] *v* reproduce. **riproduzione** *sf* reproduction.

riprova [ri'prɔva] *sf* fresh proof; confirmation. **riprovare** *v* blame; (*esame*) fail.

ripudiare [ripu'djare] *v* repudiate.

ripugnante [ripuɲ'ɲante] *agg* repugnant. **ripugnare** *v* disgust.

ripulsione [ripul'sjone] *sf* repulsion.

risaia [ri'zaja] *sf* rice-field.

risalire [risa'lire] *v* (*andar su*) go up (again); (*nel tempo*) go back.

risaltare [risal'tare] *v* (*distinguersi*) stand out; (*sporgere*) project. **far risaltare** bring out. **risalto** *sm* emphasis; projection.

risanare [risa'nare] *v* heal; (*fig*) improve; (*bonificare*) reclaim.

risaputo [risa'puto] *agg* well-known.

risarcire [rizar't͡ʃire] *v* compensate. **risarcimento** *sm* compensation.

risata [ri'zata] *sf* laugh. **fare** *o* **farsi una bella risata** have a good laugh. **scoppiare in una risata** burst out laughing.

riscaldare [riskal'dare] *v* heat, warm up. **riscaldamento** *sm* heating; (*impianto*) heating system.

riscatto [ris'katto] *sm* ransom; (*econ*) redemption. **riscattare** *v* ransom; redeem.

rischiarare [riskja'rare] *v* illuminate.

rischiare [ris'kjare] *v* risk. **rischiare di** run the risk of. **rischio** *sm* risk. **rischioso** *agg* risky.

risciacquare [riʃak'kware] *v* rinse. **risciacquatura** *sf* (*atto*) rinsing; (*acqua*) dishwater. **risciacquo** *sm* mouthwash.

riscontrare [riskon'trare] *v* (*rilevare*) find; (*confrontare*) compare; (*controllare*) check. **riscontro** *sm* finding; comparison; check; (*lettera*) reply.

riscossa [ris'kɔssa] *sf* (*riconquista*) recovery; (*insurrezione*) revolt.

*riscuotere [ris'kwɔtere] *v* (*ritirare denaro*) draw; (*riportare*) win, earn; (*scuotere*) shake.

risentire [risen'tire] *v* (*provare*) feel; (*mostrare*) show; (*udire di nuovo*) hear again; (*soffrire*) feel the effects of. **risentirsi** *v* resent. **risentimento** *sm* resentment; consequence.

riserbo [ri'sɛrbo] *sm* reserve.

riserva [ri'sɛrva] *sf* (*provvista*) supply; (*scorta*, *sport*) reserve; (*dubbio*) reservation. **riservare** *v* reserve, keep; (*prenotare*) book; (*dimostrare*) show. **riservatezza** *sf* discretion; (*segretezza*) confidential nature; (*carattere*) reserve. **riservato** *agg* reserved; confidential.

risibile [ri'zibile] *agg* laughable.

risiedere [ri'sjedere] *v* reside.

risma ['rizma] *sf* (*carta*) ream; (*spreg*) kind.

riso[1] ['rizo] *sm* (*bot*) rice.

riso[2] ['rizo] *sm*, *pl* **-a** *f* laughter; (*risata*) laugh; ridicule.

risoluto [riso'luto] *agg* resolute. **risolutezza** *sf* decisiveness.

risoluzione [risolu'tsjone] *sf* resolution; (*mat*) solution; (*dir*) cancellation.

*risolvere [ri'sɔlvere] *v* resolve; (*mat*, *indovinello*) solve; (*dir*) cancel; (*scomporre*) break down. **risolversi** *v* (*fig*) turn out; decide.

risonare [riso'nare] *v* also **risuonare** ring; (*echeggiare*) resound.

*risorgere [ri'sɔrdʒere] *v* rise again. **far risorgere** revive. **risorgimento** *sm* revival.

risorsa [ri'sorsa] *sf* resource.

risparmiare [rispar'mjare] *v* spare; (*economizzare*, *mettere da parte*) save. **risparmiatore, -trice** *sm*, *sf* saver. **risparmio** *sm* saving; (*denaro*) savings *pl*. **fare risparmio (di)** save.

rispecchiare [rispek'kjare] *v* reflect.

rispettare [rispet'tare] *v* respect; (*mantenere*) keep.

rispettivo [rispet'tivo] *agg* respective.

rispetto [ris'petto] *sm* respect. **rispetto a** (*in relazione a*) with respect to, as to; (*in confronto*) compared to. **rispettoso** *agg* respectful.

risplendere [ris'plendere] *v* shine.

*rispondere [ris'pondere] *v* answer; (*rimbeccare*) answer back; (*obbedire*) respond; (*carte*) follow suit. **rispondere di no/sì** say no/yes. **rispondere male** give a wrong answer; (*sgarbatamente*) answer back. **rispondere picche** give a flat refusal.

risposta [ris'posta] *sf* answer, reply. **botta e risposta** tit for tat. **per tutta risposta** merely. **senza risposta** unanswered.

rissa ['rissa] *sf* brawl.

ristabilire [ristabi'lire] *v* restore.

ristagnare [rista'nare] *v* stagnate; (*fig*) come to a standstill; (*comm*) be slack. **ristagno** *sm* stagnation; (*econ*) slump.

ristampare [ristam'pare] *v* reprint. **ristampa** *sf* reprint.

ristorante [risto'rante] *sm* restaurant. **vagone ristorante** *sm* dining car.

ristorare [risto'rare] *v* restore. **ristorarsi** *v* refresh oneself. **ristoro** *sm* refreshment.

ristretto [ris'tretto] *agg* (*limitato*) restricted; (*angusto*) narrow; (*caffè*) very strong. **brodo ristretto** *sm* consommè.

risultare [rizul'tare] *v* appear; gather; (*conseguire*) ensue. **mi risulta che ...** I gather that ....

risultato [rizul'tato] *sm* result.

risuonare [riswo'nare] *V* **risonare**.

risurrezione [rizurre'tsjone] *sf* resurrection.

risuscitare [risuʃi'tare] *v* revive; (*rel*) resurrect.

risvegliare [rizve'ʎare] *v* wake (up); (*fig*) awaken, revive.

ritaglio [ri'taʎo] *sm* cutting.

ritardare [ritar'dare] *v* be late; (*orologio*) be slow; (*differire*) delay. **ritardatario, -a** *sm*, *sf* latecomer. **ritardo** *sm* delay. **in ritardo** late.

ritegno [ri'teɲo] *sm* reserve; (*freno*) restraint.

*ritenere [rite'nere] *v* think; consider; (*trattenere*) hold.

ritirare [riti'rare] *v* withdraw; (*ottenere in consegna*) collect. **ritirarsi** *v* withdraw; (*interrompere un'attività*) retire. **ritirata** *sf* retreat. **ritiro** *sm* withdrawal; (*il prendere*) collection; (*luogo appartato*) retreat.

ritmo ['ritmo] *sm* rhythm. **ritmico** *agg* rhythmic(al).

rito ['rito] *sm* rite; (*usanza*) custom. **di rito** customary.

ritoccare [ritok'kare] *v* touch up.

ritornare [ritor'nare] *v* return; (*andare indietro*) go back. **biglietto di andata e ritorno** return ticket. **di ritorno** back. **viaggio di andata e ritorno** round trip. **ritornello** *sm* refrain.

*ritrarre [ri'trarre] *v* (*tirare indietro*) draw back; (*rappresentare*) portray.

ritratto [ri'tratto] *sm* portrait. **ritrattista** *s*(*m+f*) portrait-painter.

ritroso [ri'trozo] *agg* (*scontroso*) contrary; (*restio*) unwilling. **a ritroso** (*indietro*) backwards; (*controcorrente*) against the stream.

ritrovare [ritro'vare] *v* find (again); (*recuperare*) recover; (*incontrare*) meet again. **ritrovarsi** *v* meet (again); (*orientarsi*) get one's bearings; (*essere a proprio agio*) feel at ease. **ritrovato** *sm* invention; expedient. **ritrovo** *sm* meeting-place; club.

ritto ['ritto] *agg* upright.

rituale [ritu'ale] *agg*, *sm* ritual.

riunire [riu'nire] *v* gather; (*ricongiungere*) reunite; (*convocare*) call. **riunione** *sf* meeting.

*****riuscire** [riu'ʃire] *v* succeed; (*andare a finire*) turn out; (*aver capacità*) be good (at). **mi riesce antipatico/simpatico** I dislike/like him. **riuscita** *sf* result; success.

riva ['riva] *sf* shore; (*fiume*) bank.

rivale [ri'vale] *s(m+f)*, *agg* rival. **rivalità** *sf* rivalry.

rivalutare [rivalu'tare] *v* (*econ*) revalue; (*fig*) reappraise. **rivalutazione** *sf* revaluation; reappraisal.

*****rivedere** [rive'dere] *v* see again; (*incontrare*) meet again; (*ripassare*) go over. **rivedere i conti** audit (the accounts).

rivelare [rive'lare] *v* reveal. **rivelatore** *sm* (*tec*) detector. **rivelazione** *sf* revelation.

rivendere [ri'vendere] *v* resell; (*al dettaglio*) retail. **rivendita** *sf* resale; (*negozio*) shop.

rivendicare [rivendi'kare] *v* claim.

riverberare [riverbe'rare] *v* reverberate.

riverire [rive'rire] *v* revere; respect; (*salutare*) pay one's respects (to). **riverenza** *sf* reverence; respect; (*inchino*) bow; (*di donna*) curtsy.

rivestire [rives'tire] *v* cover; (*vernice*) coat; (*fodera*) line. **rivestire una carica** hold an office; (*conferire*) confer an office. **rivestirsi** *v* dress again, change (clothes). **rivestimento** *sm* covering; coating; lining.

rivetto [ri'vetto] *sm* rivet.

riviera [ri'vjɛra] *sf* coastal region. **Riviera** *sf* Riviera.

rivincita [ri'vintʃita] *sf* return match. **prendersi la rivincita** take one's revenge.

rivista [ri'vista] *sf* review; (*periodico*) magazine; (*teatro*) revue.

*****rivolgere** [ri'voldʒere] *v* turn. **rivolgersi** *v*

(*indirizzare*) address; (*ricorrere*) turn to; (*per domandare, ecc.*) apply.

rivolta [ri'volta] *sf* revolt; (*mar, mil*) mutiny.

rivoltare [rivol'tare] *v* turn; (*ripugnare*) revolt; (*insalata*) toss. **rivoltarsi** *v* (*ribellarsi*) revolt.

rivoltella [rivol'tella] *sf* revolver. **rivoltellata** *sf* shot.

rivoluzione [rivolu'tsjone] *sf* revolution. **rivoluzionario, -a** *s*, *agg* revolutionary.

rivulsione [rivul'sjone] *sf* revulsion.

rizzare [rit'tsare] *v* raise; erect. **far rizzare i capelli** make one's hair stand on end. **rizzare le orecchie** prick up one's ears.

roba ['rɔba] *sf* stuff, things *pl*. **bella roba!** that's a fine thing! **robaccia** *sf* rubbish.

robusto [ro'busto] *agg* sturdy; solid. **robustezza** *sf* sturdiness; (*fig*) vigour.

rocca[1] ['rɔkka] *sf* fortress. **cristallo di rocca** *sm* rock-crystal.

rocca[2] ['rɔkka] *sf* (*conocchia*) distaff; (*bobina*) reel. **rocchetto** *sm* reel; (*elett*) coil.

roccia ['rɔttʃa] *sf* rock; (*sport*) rock-climbing. **roccioso** *agg* rocky.

rodaggio [ro'daddʒo] *sm* running-in.

*****rodere** ['rɔdere] *v* gnaw. **rodersi il fegato** (*fig*) be eaten up. **roditore** *sm* rodent.

rododendro [rodo'dɛndro] *sm* rhododendron.

rogna ['rɔɲa] *sf* (*animali*) mange; (*agric*) scab; (*fam*) pain in the neck. **rognoso** *agg* mangy; (*noioso*) boring.

rognone [ro'ɲone] *sm* kidney.

rogo ['rɔgo] *sm* stake; (*incendio*) fire.

Roma ['roma] *sf* Rome. **romano, -a** *s*, *agg* Roman. **fare alla romana** go Dutch.

Romania [roma'nia] *sf* Romania. **romeno, -a** *s*, *agg* Romanian.

romanico [ro'maniko] *agg* Romanesque.

romantico [ro'mantiko] *agg* romantic. **romanticismo** *sm* romanticism; sentimentalism.

romanza [ro'mandza] *sf* romance.

romanzo[1] [ro'mandzo] *sm* novel; (*storia inventata*) fiction. **romanzo a fumetti** comic strip. **romanzo d'appendice** serial story. **romanzo fiume** saga. **romanzesco** *agg* romantic; fantastic.

romanzo[2] [ro'mandzo] *agg* (*lingua*) Romance.

rombo[1] ['rombo] *sm* (*geom*) rhombus; (*pesce*) turbot.

rombo² ['rombo] *sm* roar. **rombare** *v* roar.

*rompere ['rompere] *v* break; (*spezzare*) break off. **rompere l'anima** (*volg*) pester. **rompicapo** *sm* (*fam*) headache; (*indovinello*) puzzle. **a rompicollo** at breakneck speed. **rompiscatole** *s(m+f)* (*fam*) pain in the neck.

ronda ['ronda] *sf* **fare la ronda** (*mil*) be on watch; (*polizia*) be on the beat.

rondella [ron'della] *sf* washer.

rondine ['rondine] *sf* swallow.

rondò¹ [ron'do] *sm* (*musica*) rondo.

rondò² [ron'do] *sm* (*incrocio*) roundabout.

rondone [ron'done] *sm* swift.

ronfare [ron'fare] *v* (*fam*) snore.

ronzare [ron'dzare] *v* buzz. **ronzio** *sm* buzz(ing).

ronzino [ron'dzino] *sm* nag.

rosa ['roza] *sf* rose. **all'acqua di rose** (*fam*) watered-down. *agg invar* pink. **veder tutto rosa** see everything through rose-coloured spectacles. **rosato** *agg* (*vino*) rosé. **roseo** *agg* rosy. **rosetta** *sf* (*coccarda*) rosette; (*mec*) washer.

rosario [ro'zarjo] *sm* rosary.

rosbif [roz'bif] *sm invar* roast beef.

rosicare [rozi'kare] *v* also **rosicchiare** nibble; (*rodere*) gnaw.

rosmarino [rozma'rino] *sm* rosemary.

rosolare [rozo'lare] *v* brown.

rosolia [rozo'lia] *sf* German measles.

rospo ['rospo] *sm* toad.

rossetto [ros'setto] *sm* lipstick; (*belletto*) rouge.

rosso ['rosso] *agg* red. *sm* red; (*l'essere rosso*) redness. **rosso d'uovo** egg-yolk. **rossastro** *or* **rossiccio** *agg* reddish. **rossore** *sm* blush.

rosticceria [rostitt∫e'ria] *sf* rotisserie.

rostro ['rostro] *sm* rostrum.

rotaia [ro'taja] *sf* rail.

rotare [ro'tare] *v* rotate. **rotatorio** *agg* rotatory. **rotazione** *sf* rotation.

roteare [rote'are] *v* wheel; (*occhi*) roll.

rotella [ro'tella] *sf* small wheel; (*mobili*) castor; (*ginocchio*) knee-cap. **gli manca una rotella** (*fam*) he has a screw loose. **pattino a rotelle** *sm* roller-skate.

rotolare [roto'lare] *v* roll. **rotolo** *sm* roll. **andare a fotoli** *or* **rotoloni** go to rack and ruin. **rotoloni** *avv* rolling (over and over).

rotondo [ro'tondo] *agg* round.

rotta¹ ['rotta] *sf* route. **cambiar rotta** change course.

rotta² ['rotta] *sf* (*disfatta*) rout; (*breccia*)

breach. **a rotta di collo** at breakneck speed. **mettere in rotta** (put to) rout.

rotto ['rotto] *agg* broken. **per il rotto della cuffia** by the skin of one's teeth. **rottame** *sm* fragment. **rottami** *sm pl* scrap sing.

rottura *sf* break; (*violazione*) breach; (*interruzione*) breakdown.

rovente [ro'vente] *agg* red-hot.

rovere ['rovere] *sm* oak.

rovesciare [rove∫'∫are] *v* upset; (*abbattere*) overthrow; (*gettare*) throw (back). **rovesciarsi** *v* overturn; (*barca, ecc.*) capsize; (*affluire*) pour. **rovescio** *sm* shower; (*retro*) back; (*danno*) setback; (*sport*) backhand. **andare a rovescio** go wrong. **a rovescio** the wrong way round; (*capovolto*) upside-down; (*col dentro fuori*) inside out.

rovinare [rovi'nare] *v* ruin. **rovina** *sf* ruin. **andare in rovina** collapse. **mandare in rovina** ruin. **rovinoso** *agg* ruinous.

rovistare [rovis'tare] *v* ransack.

rovo ['rovo] *sm* bramble.

rozzo ['roddzo] *agg* rough; (*fig*) coarse.

ruba ['ruba] *sf* **andare a ruba** sell like hot cakes.

rubacchiare [rubak'kjare] *v* pilfer.

rubare [ru'bare] *v* steal. **rubacuori** *s(m+f)* charmer. **rubare il tempo a qualcuno** take up someone's time. **ruberia** *sf* theft.

rubinetto [rubi'netto] *sm* tap. **rubinetto di chiusura** stopcock.

rubino [ru'bino] *sm* ruby.

rubrica [ru'brika] *sf* (*indirizzi*) address-book; (*telefonica*) directory; (*quaderno*) index-book; (*giornale*) feature.

rude ['rude] *agg* rough.

rudere ['rudere] *sm* ruin; (*persona*) wreck.

ruffiano [ruf'fjano] *sm* pimp; (*adulatore*) bootlicker.

ruga ['ruga] *sf* wrinkle. **rugoso** *agg* wrinkled.

ruggine ['ruddzine] *sf* rust; (*astio*) ill-feeling. **rugginoso** *agg* rusty.

ruggire [rud'dzire] *v* roar. **ruggito** *sm* roar.

rugiada [ru'dzada] *sf* dew. **goccia di rugiada** *sf* dewdrop.

rullare [rul'lare] *v* roll; (*aereo*) taxi. **rullio** *sm* rolling. **rullo** *sm* roll; (*tec*) roller.

rum [rum] *sm* rum.

ruminare [rumi'nare] *v* ruminate.

rumore [ru'more] *sm* noise; (*diceria*) rumour; sensation. **rumoreggiare** *v* make a noise; rumble. **rumoroso** *agg* noisy.

ruolo ['rwɔlo] *sm* roll; (*teatro, funzione*) role. **insegnante non di ruolo** supply teacher. **personale di ruolo** permanent staff.

ruota ['rwɔta] *sf* wheel. **andare a ruota libera** free-wheel. **a ruota** circular. **far la ruota** (*pavoneggiarsi*) show off. **seguire a ruota** follow close behind.

rupe ['rupe] *sf* cliff.

rupia [ru'pia] *sf* rupee.

rurale [ru'rale] *agg* rural.

ruscello [ru'ʃɛllo] *sm* stream.

ruspa ['ruspa] *sf* bulldozer. (**pollo**) **ruspante** *sm* free-range chicken.

russare [rus'sare] *v* snore.

Russia ['russja] *sf* Russia. **russo, -a** *s, agg* Russian.

rustico [ru'stiko] *agg* rustic; (*contadino*) rural; (*rozzo*) rough.

ruttare [rut'tare] *v* belch. **rutto** *sm* belch.

ruvido ['ruvido] *agg* rough. **ruvidezza** *sf* roughness.

ruzzare [rut'tsare] *v* romp.

ruzzolare [ruttso'lare] *v* tumble; (*rotolare*) roll (down). **ruzzolone** *sm* tumble. **fare un ruzzolone** (*fam*) come a cropper.

S

sabato ['sabato] *sm* Saturday. **il** *or* **di sabato** on Saturdays.

sabbia ['sabbja] *sf* sand. **sabbie mobili** quicksand *sing*. **sabbiare** *v* sand-blast. **sabbioso** *agg* sandy.

sabotaggio [sabo'taddʒo] *sm* sabotage. **sabotare** *v* sabotage. **sabotatore, -trice** *sm, sf* saboteur.

sacca ['sakka] *sf* bag; (*fig*) pocket.

saccarina [sakka'rina] *sf* saccharine.

saccente [sat'tʃɛnte] *s(m+f)*, *agg* know-all.

saccheggiare [sakked'dʒare] *v* sack, loot. **saccheggiatore** *sm* plunderer, looter. **saccheggio** *sm* sacking, looting.

sacco ['sakko] *sm* sack. **cogliere con le mani nel sacco** catch red-handed. **sacco a pelo** sleeping-bag. **sacco da montagna** rucksack. **sacco postale** mail-bag. **un sacco di** lots of.

sacerdote [satʃer'dɔte] *sm* priest. **sacerdozio** *sm* priesthood.

sacramento [sakra'mento] *sm* sacrament.

sacrificare [sakrifi'kare] *v* sacrifice; (*rinunciare*) give up; (*non valorizzare*) waste. **sacrificio** *sm* sacrifice; (*di sé*) self-sacrifice.

sacrilegio [sakri'ledʒo] *sm* sacrilege; (*fig*) crime. **sacrilego** *agg, m pl* **-ghi** sacrilegious; criminal.

sacro ['sakro] *agg* sacred. *sm* (*osso*) sacrum. **sacrosanto** *agg* sacrosanct.

sadico ['sadiko], **-a** *agg* sadistic. *sm, sf* sadist. **sadismo** *sm* sadism.

saetta [sa'etta] *sf* flash (of lightning); (*mec*) bit; (*freccia*) arrow.

sagace [sa'gatʃe] *agg* sagacious. **sagacia** *sf* sagacity.

saggio¹ [sadd'ʒo], **-a** *agg* wise; (*sapiente*) sage. *sm, sf* sage. **saggezza** *sf* wisdom.

saggio² [sadd'ʒo] *sm* (*metalli preziosi*) assay; (*prova*) proof; (*dimostrazione pubblica*) display; (*scritto critico*) essay. **saggiare** *v* test; assay. **saggiatura** *sf* assay; (*segno*) hallmark. **saggista** *s(m+f)* essayist.

Sagittario [sadʒit'tarjo] *sm* Sagittarius.

sagoma ['sagoma] *sf* outline; (*forma, modello*) pattern. **sagomare** *v* shape.

sagra ['sagra] *sf* feast.

sagrestano [sagres'tano] *sm* sacristan. **sagrestia** *sf* vestry.

sala ['sala] *sf* room, hall. **sala da pranzo** dining-room. **sala d'aspetto** waiting-room. **sala di lettura/macchine** reading-/engine-room. **sala operatoria** operating theatre.

salace [sa'latʃe] *agg* salacious.

salamandra [sala'mandra] *sf* salamander.

salame [sa'lame] *sm* salami; (*fig*) fool.

salamoia [sala'mɔja] *sf* brine. **mettere in salamoia** pickle.

salare [sa'lare] *v* salt. **salato** *agg* salty; (*conservato*) salted; (*caro*) dear.

salario [sa'larjo] *sm* pay; (*settimanale*) wages *pl*; (*mensile*) salary. **salariale** *agg* pay.

salassare [salas'sare] *v* bleed.

salda ['salda] *sf* size, sizing. **dare la salda a** size; (*inamidare*) starch.

saldare [sal'dare] *v* (*tec*) solder; (*autogeno*) weld; (*econ*) settle. pay. **saldatore** *sm* (*operaio*) solderer, welder; (*utensile*) soldering iron. **saldatrice** *sf* welder. **saldatura** *sf* welding; soldering.

saldo¹ [saldo] *agg* solid; firm. **saldezza** *sf* solidity; firmness.

saldo² ['saldo] sm settlement; (somma da pagare) balance. **saldi** sm pl (merce) remnants pl.

sale ['sale] sm salt. **non aver sale in zucca** be stupid. **restar di sale** be dumbfounded. **salgemma** sm rock-salt. **salino** agg saline.

salice ['salitʃe] sm willow(-tree). **salice piangente** weeping willow.

saliente [sa'ljɛnte] agg, sm salient.

*****salire** [sa'lire] v climb, go up; (autobus, treno) board, get on; (auto) get in; (alzarsi, crescere) rise. **far salire** send up.

saliscendi sm invar (chiusura) latch; (fig) ups and downs pl. **salita** sf climb; entrance; (tratto che sale) slope. **in salita** uphill; (che aumenta) rising.

saliva [sa'liva] sf saliva. **salivale** agg salivary. **salivare** v salivate.

salma ['salma] sf corpse.

salmo ['salmo] sm psalm.

salmone [sal'mone] sm salmon.

salone [sa'lone] sm living-room; (esposizione) show; (parrucchiere) salon.

salotto [sa'lɔtto] sm drawing-room, lounge.

salpare [sal'pare] v weigh anchor.

salsa ['salsa] sf sauce; (a base di carne) gravy. **in tutte le salse** in all kinds of ways. **salsiera** sf sauce-boat; gravy-boat.

salsiccia [sal'sittʃa] sf sausage.

salso ['salso] agg salt(y). **salsedine** sf saltiness.

saltare [sal'tare] v jump; (balzare) leap; (tralasciare) skip; (bottone, etc.) come off; (esplodere) blow up; (serratura) force; (governo) bring down. **far saltare** destroy, blow up; (serratura) force; (governo) bring down. **saltare di palo in frasca** switch from one subject to another. **saltare (in aria)** (esplodere) blow up. **saltare in bestia** fly into a rage. **saltare in mente** cross one's mind, get into one's head.

saltellare [saltel'lare] v also **salterellare** skip or hop about.

saltimbanco [saltim'banko] sm acrobat; (spreg) charlatan.

salto ['salto] sm jump, leap; (omissione) gap. **in un salto** in a jiffy. **salto con l'asta** pole-vault. **salto in alto/lungo** high-/long-jump. **saltuario** agg intermittent, occasional.

salubre ['salubre] agg healthy.

salumeria [salume'ria] sf delicatessen.

salumi sm pl cold meats pl. **salumiere, -a** sm, sf pork-butcher; grocer.

salutare [salu'tare] v greet; (mil) salute. **salutami tuo fratello** remember me to your brother. **saluto** sm greeting; salute. **cordiali/distinti saluti** yours sincerely/faithfully.

salute [sa'lute] sf health; (benessere) welfare. **inter (a chi starnutisce) bless you! (nei brindisi) cheers!

salvare [sal'vare] v save; (trarre in salvo) rescue; protect. **salvacondotto** sm pass. **salvadanaio** sm money-box. **salvagente** sm (ciambella) lifebelt; (giacca) life-jacket; (strada) traffic island. **salvaguardare** v safeguard. **salvaguardia** sf safeguard. **salvataggio** sm rescue.

salve ['salve] inter hello! (salute) bless you!

salvia ['salvja] sf sage.

salvietta [sal'vjetta] sf (tovagliolo) napkin; (asciugamano) towel.

salvo ['salvo] agg safe. **mettere in salvo** save, put aside. **prep** except (for), bar(ring). **salvo che** except that; (a meno che) unless. **salvezza** sf salvation; (sicurezza) safety.

sambuco [sam'buko] sm, pl **-chi** elder.

sanare [sa'nare] v heal; (porre rimedio) rectify; (bonificare) reclaim. **sanatorio** sm sanatorium.

sancire [san'tʃire] v sanction; ratify.

sandalo¹ ['sandalo] sm sandal.

sandalo² ['sandalo] sm (legno) sandalwood.

sangue ['sangwe] sm blood. **al sangue** (gastr) rare. **a sangue caldo/freddo** warm-/cold-blooded. **farsi cattivo sangue** get worked up. **puro sangue** thoroughbred. **sangue freddo** sang-froid, composure. **sanguemisto** sm half-breed.

sanguigno [san'gwiɲo] agg blood; (colore) blood-red; (costituzione) sanguine.

sanguinare [sangwi'nare] v bleed. **sanguinario** agg bloodthirsty. **sanguinolento** agg bleeding; (insanguinato) bloody. **sanguinoso** agg bloody.

sanguisuga [sangwi'suga] sf leech.

sanità [sani'ta] sf health; (salubrità) wholesomeness. **sanità mentale** sanity. **sanitario** agg sanitary; (di medicina) medical.

sano ['sano] agg healthy; (integro) sound; (salubre) wholesome; (di mente) sane;

intact. **sano come un pesce** sound as a bell. **sano e salvo** safe and sound.

santo ['santo], **-a** *agg* holy; (*seguito da nome*) Saint; pious; sacred; (*rafforzativo*) blessed. *sm, sf* saint. **santerello, -a** *sm, sf* (*fam*) goody-goody. **santificare** *v* sanctify; (*venerare*) hallow; canonize. **santità** *sf* holiness; (*fig*) sanctity. **santuario** *sm* sanctuary.

sanzione [san'tsjone] *sf* sanction. **sanzionare** *v* sanction.

****sapere** [sa'pere] *v* know; (*essere capace, aver imparato*) can, know how (to); (*aver odore*) smell (of); (*aver sapore*) taste (of). **buono a sapersi** worth knowing. **far sapere** let know, inform. **non ne voglio sapere** I don't want to have anything to do with it. **non si sa mai** you never can tell. **per quanto ne sappia** as far as I know. **saperla lunga** know a thing or two. **venire a sapere** learn, gather. *sm* knowledge, learning.

sapienza [sa'pjɛntsa] *sf* wisdom; learning. **sapiente** *agg* wise; learned. **sapientone, -a** *sm, sf* (*fam*) know-all.

sapone [sa'pone] *sm* soap. **sapone in polvere** soap-powder. **saponetta** *sf* bar of soap. **saponiera** *sf* soap-dish. **saponoso** *agg* soapy.

sapore [sa'pore] *sm* taste, flavour. **saporito** *agg* tasty; (*salato*) rather salty; (*arguto*) witty.

saracinesca [saratʃi'neska] *sf* roller-blind; (*di chiusa*) floodgate.

sarcasmo [sar'kazmo] *sm* sarcasm. **sarcastico** *agg* sarcastic.

sarchio ['sarkjo] *sm* hoe. **sarchiare** *v* hoe.

sarda ['sarda] *sf also* **sardina** pilchard, sardine.

Sardegna [sar'deɲa] *sf* Sardinia. **sardo, -a** *s, agg* Sardinian.

sardonico [sar'dɔniko] *agg* sardonic.

sarta ['sarta] *sf* dressmaker. **sarto** *sm* tailor. **sartoria** *sf* (*laboratorio*) dressmaker's or tailor's workshop; (*tecnica*) dressmaking, tailoring.

sasso ['sasso] *sm* stone; (*ciottolo*) pebble; (*roccia*) rock. **prendere a sassate** pelt with stones, stone. **sassoso** *agg* stony.

sassofono [sas'sɔfono] *sm* saxophone. **sassofonista** *s(m+f)* saxophonist.

Satana ['satana] *sm* Satan. **satanico** *agg* satanic.

satellite [sa'tɛllite] *agg, sm* satellite.

satirico [sa'tiriko] *agg* satirical. **satira** *sf*

satire. **satireggiare** *v also* **mettere in satira** satirize.

satiro ['satiro] *sm* satyr.

satollo [sa'tollo] *agg* full up.

saturare [satu'rare] *v* saturate; (*fig*) cram. **saturazione** *sf* saturation. **saturo** *agg* saturated; crammed, full.

savio ['savjo] *agg* wise; prudent.

saziare [sa'tsjare] *v* satisfy; (*riempire presto*) be filling. **saziarsi** *v* have one's fill; (*stancarsi*) tire. **sazietà** *sf* surfeit. **a sazietà** more than enough. **mangiare a sazietà** eat or have one's fill. **sazio** *agg* satisfied; (*fam*) full up; (*stanco*) tired.

sbadato [zba'dato] *agg* careless, thoughtless. **sbadataggine** *sf* carelessness, thoughtlessness.

sbadigliare [zbadi'ʎare] *v* yawn. **sbadiglio** *sm* yawn.

sbafare [zba'fare] *v* (*scroccare*) scrounge; (*mangiare avidamente*) gobble up. **mangiare/vivere a sbafo** scrounge a meal/living.

sbagliare [zba'ʎare] *v* make a mistake; (*scambiare*) mistake. **sbagliare i calcoli** miscalculate; (*fig*) make a (big) mistake. **sbagliar il passo** stumble; (*mil*) be out of step. **sbagliar numero** get the wrong number. **sbagliar ortografia** spell incorrectly. **sbagliarsi sul conto di** be wrong about. **sbagliato** *agg* wrong, mistaken. **calcolo sbagliato** *sm* miscalculation. **pronuncia sbagliata** *sf* mispronunciation. **sbaglio** *sm* mistake.

sbalestrato [zbales'trato] *agg* unsettled; (*smarrito*) lost.

sballare [zbal'lare] *v* (*merce*) unpack. **sballato** *agg* wild.

sballottare [zballot'tare] *v* toss about. **sballottamento** *sm* tossing.

sbalordire [zbalor'dire] *v* astonish; (*turbare*) bewilder, shock. **sbalordimento** *sm* astonishment; shock, bewilderment. **sbalorditivo** *agg* amazing; (*incredibile*) staggering.

sbalzare[1] [zbal'tsare] *v* throw, fling. **sbalzo** *sm* jerk, jolt; (*fig*) jump. **a sbalzi** jerkily; (*fig*) by fits and starts.

sbalzare[2] [zbal'tsare] *v* (*metallo*) emboss. **lavoro a sbalzo** *sm* embossing.

sbandare [zban'dare] *v* (*auto*) skid; (*mar*) list; (*aero*) bank; (*disperdere*) break or split up. **sbandata** *sf* skid. **prendere una sbandata per** have a crush on. **sbandato** *agg* scattered; (*fig*) bewildered.

sbaragliare [zbara'ʎare] v (put to) rout. **andare** or **buttarsi allo sbaraglio** risk everything. **mettere allo sbaraglio** jeopardize.

sbarazzarsi [zbarat'tsarsi] v get rid of.

sbarbare [zbar'bare] v shave. **sbarbatello** sm novice.

sbarcare [zbar'kare] v land; (*merce*) unload. **sbarco** sm landing; unloading.

sbarra ['zbarra] sf bar, barrier; (*segno grafico*) stroke. **sbarramento** sm barrage; block(age). **sbarrare** v bar, block; (*porta*) bolt; (*assegno*) cross; (*occhi*) open wide.

sbatacchiare [zbatak'kjare] v slam; (*ali*) flap.

sbattere ['zbattere] v (*scaraventare*) fling; (*chiudere violentemente*) slam; (*urtare*) bash; (*ali*) flap; (*gastr*) whip, beat. **non saper dove sbattere la testa** not know which way to turn. **sbatter fuori** (*fam*) chuck out.

sbavare [zba'vare] v (*emettere bava*) dribble; (*colore, ecc.*) smudge. **sbavatura** sf dribble; smudge.

sberla ['zberla] sf slap.

sbiadire [zbja'dire] v fade. **sbiadito** agg faded; (*fig*) dull.

sbiancare [zbjan'kare] v whiten.

sbianchire [zbjan'kire] v whiten; (*gastr*) blanch.

sbieco ['zbjɛko] agg crooked. **guardar di sbieco** look askance at. **tagliar di sbieco** cut on the bias.

sbigottire [zbigot'tire] v astonish; (*turbare*) dismay. **sbigottimento** sm astonishment; dismay.

sbilancio [zbi'lantʃo] sm (*squilibrio*) lack of equilibrium; (*econ*) deficit. **sbilanciare** v unbalance.

sbilenco [zbi'lɛnko] agg crooked.

sbloccare [zblok'kare] v free, release; (*prezzi*) unfreeze.

sboccare [zbok'kare] v come out; (*condurre*) lead; (*fiume*) flow (into). **sbocco** sm outlet.

sbocciare [zbot'tʃare] v bloom, blossom.

sbollentare [zbollen'tare] v blanch.

sbornia [zbornja] sf postumi di una **sbornia** sm pl hangover sing. **prendere una sbornia** get drunk.

sborsare [zbor'sare] v pay out, disburse. **sborso** sm disbursement.

sbottare [zbot'tare] v burst out.

sbottonare [zbotto'nare] v unbutton.

sbozzare [zbot'tsare] v sketch; (*fig*) outline.

sbracciarsi [zbrat'tʃarsi] v gesticulate; (*rimboccarsi le maniche*) roll up one's sleeves; (*fig*) do one's utmost. **sbracciato** agg (*abito*) sleeveless.

sbraitare [zbrai'tare] v yell; protest.

sbranare [zbra'nare] v tear to pieces.

sbrattare [zbrat'tare] v tidy up. **stanza di sbratto** sf lumber-room.

sbriciolare [zbritʃo'lare] v crumble.

sbrigare [zbri'gare] v get done, finish (off); (*risolvere*) settle. **sbrigarsi** v (*far presto*) hurry up; (*liberarsi*) get rid (of). **sbrigativo** agg quick; (*superficiale*) hasty.

sbrigliare [zbri'ʎare] v unbridle, give free rein (to). **sbrigliatezza** sf unruliness. **sbrigliato** agg unruly, wild.

sbrindellare [zbrindel'lare] v tear to shreds. **sbrindellato** agg in rags or tatters.

sbrodolare [zbrodo'lare] v (*insudiciare*) soil; (*fig*) spin out; (*fam*) waffle.

sbrogliare [zbro'ʎare] v disentangle. **sbrogliarsi** v extricate oneself.

sbronzo [zbrondzo] agg drunk. **prendersi una sbronza** get drunk.

sbruffare [zbruf'fare] v spurt; (*fig*) brag.

sbucare [zbu'kare] v come out, emerge; (*fig*) spring up.

sbucciare [zbut'tʃare] v peel; (*escoriare*) scrape. **sbucciapatate** sm invar potato-peeler. **sbucciatura** sf scrape, graze.

sbudellare [zbudel'lare] v disembowel; (*gastr*) gut. **sbudellarsi dal ridere** split one's sides laughing.

sbuffare [zbuf'fare] v puff, pant; (*rabbia*) snort.

scabbia ['skabbia] sf scabies. **scabbiosa** sf (*bot*) scabious.

scabroso [ska'brozo] agg also **scabro** rough; (*problema*) thorny, knotty.

scacciare [skat'tʃare] v drive out or away; (*fig*) dispel; expel.

scacco ['skakko] sm (*quadretto*) check; (*figurina del gioco*) chessman. **scacchi** sm pl (*gioco*) chess sing. **scacco matto** checkmate. **subire uno scacco** suffer a setback. **scacchiera** sf chess-board; (*per dama*) draught-board.

*****scadere** [ska'dere] v expire; (*perdere valore*) decline; (*econ*) fall due. **scadente** agg poor. **scadenza** sf expiry; (*effetti*) maturity. **a breve/lunga scadenza** short-/long-term. **scadimento** sm decline.

scafandro [ska'fandro] *sm* diving-suit; (*astronauta*) space-suit.

scaffale [skaf'fale] *sm* shelf. **scaffalatura** *sf* shelving.

scafo ['skafo] *sm* hull.

scagionare [skadʒo'nare] *v* exonerate.

scaglia ['skaʎa] *sf* scale; (*sapone*) flake. **scagliare** *v* flake.

scagliare [ska'ʎare] *v* (*lanciare*) fling, hurl.

scaglione [ska'ʎone] *sm* group; (*mil*) echelon. **scaglionare** *v* stagger; (*mil*) range. **scaglionamento** *sm* staggering.

scala ['skala] *sf* stairs *pl*, staircase; (*piano*) level; (*misura*, *rapporto*) scale; (*apparecchio*) ladder. **far le scale** climb the stairs; (*musica*) practise scales. **scala a chiocciola** spiral staircase. **scala di corda** rope-ladder. **scala portatile** steps *pl*, step-ladder. **scalinata** *sf* flight of stairs.

scalare [ska'lare] *v* scale. *agg* graduated; (*fis*) scalar. **scalata** *sf* climb. **scalatore**, **-trice** *sm*, *sf* climber.

scalcagnato [skalka'nato] *agg* shabby.

scaldare [skal'dare] *v* warm (up); (*a temperatura più elevata*) heat (up). **scaldabagno** *sm* water-heater.

scalfire [skal'fire] *v* scratch.

scalmanato [skalma'nato] *agg* flustered. *sm*, *sf* hothead. **scalmana** *sf* chill; (*fig*) craze.

scalo ['skalo] *sm* (*banchina*) pier; (*porto d'approdo*) port of call; (*aero*) stopover. **far scalo** (*mar*) call; (*aero*) land, stop. **scalo merci** (*mar*) wharf; (*ferr*) goods yard. **senza scalo** non-stop.

scalogna [ska'loɲa] *sf* bad luck. **scalognato** *agg* unlucky.

scaloppa [ska'loppa] *sf* cutlet. **scaloppina** *sf* escalope.

scalpello [skal'pello] *sm* chisel; (*chirurgia*) scalpel. **scalpellare** *v* chisel; cut away.

scalpore [skal'pore] *sm* sensation.

scaltro ['skaltro] *agg* shrewd.

scalzo ['skaltso] *agg* barefoot.

scambiare [skam'bjare] *v* (*dare in cambio*) exchange; (*confondere*) mistake, mix up. **scambievole** *agg* mutual. **scambio** *sm* exchange; (*ferr*) points *pl*. **libero scambio** free trade.

scamosciato [skamoʃ'ʃato] *agg* suede.

scampagnata [skampa'ɲata] *sf* outing.

scampanato [skampa'nato] *agg* flared.

scampare [skam'pare] *v* escape; (*evitare*) avoid. **Dio ce ne scampi!** God forbid!

scamparla bella have a narrow escape. **scampato**, **-a** *sm*, *sf* (*superstite*) survivor. **scampo** *sm* way out.

scampo ['skampo] *sm* prawn.

scampolo ['skampolo] *sm* remnant.

scanalare [skana'lare] *v* groove; (*colonna*) flute. **scanalatura** *sf* groove; flute.

scandagliare [skanda'ʎare] *v* sound (out). **scandaglio** *sm* sounding.

scandalizzare [skandalid'dzare] *v* shock; (*dar scandalo*) scandalize. **scandalo** *sm* scandal. **scandaloso** *agg* scandalous.

scandire [skan'dire] *v* (*pronuciare*) articulate; (*versi*) scan.

scanno ['skanno] *sm* stall.

scansare [skan'sare] *v* dodge, shirk; (*spostare*) shift. **scansarsi** *v* get out of the way. **scansafatiche** *s(m+f)* *invar* loafer.

scapaccione [skapat'tʃone] *sm* slap.

scapestrato [skapes'trato], **-a** *agg* wild, unruly. *sm*, *sf* madcap, daredevil.

scapigliato [skapi'ʎato] *agg* dishevelled; (*fig*) reckless.

scapitare [skapi'tare] *sm* loss; (*danno*) injury. **a scapito di** to the detriment of.

scapola ['skapola] *sf* shoulder-blade.

scapolo ['skapolo] *agg* single. *sm* bachelor.

scappamento [skappa'mento] *sm* (*auto*) exhaust.

scappare [skap'pare] *v* run away; escape, flee. **devo scappare** (*ho fretta*) I must rush. **lasciarsi scappar di bocca** blurt out. **scappare di mente** slip one's mind. **scappatella** *sf* escapade. **scappatoia** *sf* way out; (*fig*) loophole.

scappellotto [skapel'lotto] *sm* smack. **passare a scappellotti** (*fam*) scrape through.

scarabocchio [skara'bokkjo] *sm* (*macchia*) blot; (*sgorbio*) scrawl; (*disegno*) doodle. **scarabocchiare** *v* scrawl; doodle.

scarafaggio [skara'faddʒo] *sm* cockroach.

scaramanzia [skaraman'tsia] *sf* spell. **per scaramanzia** for luck.

scaramuccia [skara'muttʃa] *sf* skirmish.

scaraventare [skaraven'tare] *v* hurl, fling.

scarcerare [skartʃe'rare] *v* release (from prison). **scarceramento** *sm* release.

scardinare [skardi'nare] *v* unhinge.

scaricare [skari'kare] *v* discharge; (*deporre un carico*) unload; (*sfogare*) vent; (*liquido*) empty; (*gas*) let out. **scaricare la colpa** shift the blame. **scarica** *sf* discharge; (*raffica*) volley. **scaricalasino** *sm invar* piggy-bank.

scarico ['skariko] *sm, pl* **-chi** discharge; unloading; *(di rifiuti)* dumping; *(i rifiuti stessi)* rubbish; *(deposito di rifiuti)* dump; *(auto)* exhaust. **a mio scarico** in my defence. **a scarico di coscienza** to clear one's conscience. *agg (vuoto)* empty; *(batteria)* flat.

scarlattina [skarlat'tina] *sf* scarlet fever.

scarlatto [skar'latto] *agg, sm* scarlet.

scarno ['skarno] *agg* skinny; *(spoglio)* bare; *(povero)* scanty.

scarpa ['skarpa] *sf* shoe. **scarpe da ginnastica** *or* **tennis** plimsolls *pl.* **scarpone** *sm* boot. **scarponi da calciatore/sci** football-/ski-boots *pl.*

scarso ['skarso] *agg* poor; *(manchevole)* lacking (in); *(insufficiente)* short. **un chilo scarso** just under a kilo. **scarseggiare** *v* be scarce; be short (of); *(fig)* lack (in). **scarsezza** *or* **scarsità** *sf* shortage; lack.

scartabellare [skartabel'lare] *v* skim or flip through.

scartare[1] [skar'tare] *v (togliere dalla carta)* unwrap; *(respingere)* discard, reject. **scarto** *sm (cosa scartata)* reject; *(alle carte)* discard. **merci di scarto** *sf pl* inferior goods *pl,* rejects *pl.*

scartare[2] [skar'tare] *v (spostarsi lateralmente)* swerve. **scarto** *sm* swerve, skid; difference.

scassare [skas'sare] *v (fam: guastare)* smash, bust; *(il terreno)* break up. **furto con scasso** *sm* burglary.

scassinare [skassi'nare] *v* force (open). **scassinatore, -trice** *sm, sf* burglar; *(di banche)* bank-robber.

scatenare [skate'nare] *v* unleash; cause. **scatenarsi** *v* break out.

scatola ['skatola] *sf* box; carton; *(di latta)* can. **averne piene le scatole** *(fam)* be fed up to the back teeth (with). **cibo in scatola** *sm* tinned food. **rompere le scatole** *(fam)* be a nuisance. **scatolame** *sm* tinned goods *pl.*

scattare [skat'tare] *v* spring; *(rilasciarsi)* spring up; *(armi)* go off; *(aprirsi)* spring open; *(chiudersi)* snap shut. **far scattare** release. **scattare a vuoto** misfire. **scatto** *sm* release; *(rumore)* click; *(sport)* spurt; *(accesso)* outburst. **a scatti** jerkily. **di scatto** suddenly.

scaturire [skatu'rire] *v* gush; *(fig)* arise.

scavalcare [skaval'kare] *v* step *or* climb over; *(saltando)* jump over; *(sbalzare di sella)* throw; *(superare)* overtake.

scavare [ska'vare] *v* dig; mine; *(pozzo)* sink; *(trovare)* dig up; *(sartoria)* widen. **scavatore** *sm* digger. **scavatura** *sf* excavation. **scavo** *sm* excavation.

***scegliere** ['ʃeʎere] *v* choose. **c'è (molto) da scegliere** there is plenty to choose from. **c'è poco da scegliere** there is little choice.

scellerato [felle'rato], **-a** *agg* wicked. *sm, sf* wicked person. **scelleratezza** *sf* wickedness; *(atto)* misdeed.

scelta ['ʃelta] *sf* choice, selection; quality. **a scelta** according to preference. **non aver possibilità di scelta** have no choice. **scelto** *agg* chosen, picked; *(eccellente)* choice.

scemare [ʃe'mare] *v* diminish.

scemo ['ʃemo], **-a** *agg* stupid, idiotic; *(sciocco)* foolish. *sm, sf* fool, idiot. **scemenza** *sf (azione)* idiocy, foolishness; *(parole)* nonsense.

scena ['ʃena] *sf* scene; *(palcoscenico)* stage. **mettere in scena** stage, produce. **scenario** *sm (teatro)* set; *(cinema)* scenario, script; *(fig)* setting. **scenata** *sf* scene, row. **sceneggiare** *v* adapt, dramatize. **sceneggiatura** *sf* script. **scenico** *agg* scenic.

***scendere** ['ʃendere] *v (andar giù)* go down; *(venir giù)* come down; *(autobus, treno)* get off; *(auto)* get out; *(calare)* drop; *(sostare)* stop. **scendere a un accordo** reach an agreement. **scendere dal letto** get up. **scendiletto** *sm invar (tappetino)* bedside rug; *(vestaglia)* dressing-gown.

sceriffo [ʃe'riffo] *sm* sheriff.

scervellarsi [ʃervel'larsi] *v* rack one's brains. **scervellato** *agg* hare-brained.

scettico ['ʃettiko], **-a** *agg* sceptical. *sm, sf* sceptic. **scetticismo** *sm* scepticism.

scettro ['ʃettro] *sm* sceptre.

scheda ['skeda] *sf* card; *(di schedario)* index-card; *(elettorale)* ballot(-paper). **schedare** *v* catalogue; *(archiviare)* file. **schedario** *sm* file; *(mobile)* filing cabinet; *(elenco)* list. **schedina** *sf* coupon.

scheggia ['skeddʒa] *sf* splinter. **scheggiare** *v* splinter, chip.

scheletro ['skeletro] *sm* skeleton; *(tec)* framework. **scheletrico** *agg* skeletal; *(fig)* bare.

schema ['skema] *sm* scheme; *(abbozzo)* outline; *(modello)* pattern. **schema di legge** bill. **schematico** *agg* schematic.

scherma ['skerma] *sf* fencing. **tirare di scherma** fence. **schermaglia** *sf* skirmish. **schermitore, -trice** *sm, sf* fencer.

schermo ['skermo] *sm* screen; *(difesa)* shield. **schermare** *v* screen, shield. **schermire** *v* protect.

schernire [sker'nire] *v* scorn, mock. **schernitore, -trice** *agg* scornful, mocking. **scherno** *sm* mockery, derision; *(oggetto di scherno)* laughing-stock.

scherzare [sker'tsare] *v* joke; *(prendere alla leggera)* trifle (with); *(giocare)* play. **c'è poco da scherzare** it is not a laughing matter. **scherzi!** *inter* you must be joking! **scherzo** *sm* joke; *(tiro)* trick; *(musica)* scherzo. **per scherzo** for fun, as a joke. **scherzoso** *agg* playful; *(giocoso)* jocular.

schettinare [sketti'nare] *v* roller-skate. **schettinaggio** *sm* roller-skating. **schettino** *sm* roller-skate.

schiacciare [skjat'tʃare] *v* *(spiaccicare)* squash; *(frantumare)* crush; *(noci)* crack. **schiacciare un pisolino** have a nap. **schiacciante** *agg* crushing. **schiaccianoci** *sm* nutcrackers *pl*. **schiacciasassi** *sm* steam-roller.

schiaffare [skjaf'fare] *v* *(fam)* chuck. **schiaffo** ['skjaffo] *sm* slap. **schiaffeggiare** *v* slap.

schiamazzare [skjamat'tsare] *v* cackle; *(far baccano)* make a row. **schiamazzo** *sm* cackle; row.

schiantare [skjan'tare] *v* shatter, burst. **schianto** *sm* crash.

schiappa ['skjappa] *sf* *(fam)* washout.

schiarire [skja'rire] *v* clear (up). **schiarimento** *sm* clearing up; *(spiegazione)* explanation; information.

schiavo ['skjavo], -a *s, agg* slave. **schiavitù** *sf* slavery.

schiena ['skjɛna] *sf* back. **colpire alla schiena** stab in the back. **mal di schiena** *sm* backache. **schienale** *sm* back.

schiera ['skjɛra] *sf* band; *(moltitudine)* mass, crowd. **schieramento** *sm* formation; line-up. **schierare** *v* line up; *(mil)* deploy. **schierarsi contro** take sides against. **schierarsi dalla parte di** side with.

schietto ['skjetto] *agg* sincere; genuine; frank. **a dirla schietta** (to speak) frankly. **schiettezza** *sf* genuineness; frankness.

schifo ['skifo] *sm* disgust. **avere a schifo** loathe. **far schifo** *v* *(essere disgustoso)* be disgusting; *(disgustare)* (fill with) disgust. **schifare** *v* disgust. **schifezza** *sf* rubbish, muck. **schifiltoso** *agg* fussy; *(esigente)* fastidious. **schifoso** *agg* disgusting.

schioccare [skjok'kare] *v* crack; *(dita)* snap.

schioppo ['skjoppo] *sm* gun; *(da caccia)* shotgun. **schioppettata** *sf* (gun)shot.

schiudersi ['skjudersi] *v* open (up).

schiuma ['skjuma] *sf* foam; *(birra)* froth; *(sapone)* lather; *(feccia)* scum. **aver la schiuma alla bocca** foam at the mouth. **schiumare** *v* skim. **schiumoso** *agg* foamy; frothy; lathery.

schivare [ski'vare] *v* avoid; *(fam)* dodge; *(boxe)* duck.

schizofrenia [skitsofre'nia] *sf* schizophrenia. **schizofrenico, -a** *s, agg* schizophrenic.

schizzare [skit'tsare] *v* *(zampillare)* spurt; *(spruzzare)* squirt; *(sporcare)* splash; *(disegnare)* sketch. **schizzar via** dash off. **schizzetto** *sm* spray; syringe; *(giocattolo)* water-pistol. **schizzo** *sm* spurt; squirt; splash; sketch.

schizzinoso [skittsi'nozo] *agg* fastidious; squeamish.

sci [ʃi] *sm* *(attrezzo)* ski; *(attività)* skiing. **fare dello sci** ski, go skiing. **sci nautico** water-ski; water-skiing. **sciare** *v* ski. **sciatore, -trice** *sm, sf* skier.

scia ['ʃia] *sf* wake; *(traccia)* trail. **seguire la scia di** follow in the footsteps of. **sciabola** ['ʃabola] *sf* sabre.

sciacallo [ʃa'kallo] *sm* jackal.

sciacquare [ʃak'kware] *v* rinse (out). **sciacquata** *sf* rinse. **sciacquatura** *sf* *(azione)* rinsing; *(acqua)* dishwater. **sciacquo** *sm* rinsing; *(liquido)* mouthwash.

sciagura [ʃa'gura] *sf* disaster; *(incidente)* accident, crash. **sciagurato** *agg* *(sfortunato)* unlucky, wretched; *(malvagio)* wicked.

scialacquare [ʃalak'kware] *v* squander. **scialacquatore, -trice** *sm, sf* spendthrift.

scialbo ['ʃalbo] *agg* pale; faint; *(fig)* dull.

scialle ['ʃalle] *sm* shawl.

scialo ['ʃalo] *sm* waste.

sciame ['ʃame] *sm* swarm. **sciamare** *v* swarm.

sciancato [ʃan'kato] *agg* lame; *(sedia, ecc.)* shaky, rickety.

sciarada [ʃa'rada] *sf* charade.

sciarpa ['ʃarpa] sf scarf.

sciatica ['ʃatika] sf sciatica. **scia.co** agg sciatic.

sciatto ['ʃatto] agg slovenly; (fam) sloppy.

scientifico [ʃen'tifiko] agg scientific.

scienza ['ʃɛntsa] sf science. **scienziato, -a** sm, sf scientist; (studioso) scholar.

scimmia ['ʃimmja] sf monkey; (senza coda) ape. **brutto come una scimmia** as ugly as sin. **scimmiottare** v also **fare la scimmia** a ape.

scimpanzè [ʃimpan'tse] sm chimpanzee.

scimunito [ʃimu'nito], **-a** agg foolish. sm, sf fool.

*****scindere** ['ʃindere] v separate; divide.

scintilla [ʃin'tilla] sf spark. **dare** or **emettere scintille** spark. **scintillare** v sparkle; (lampeggiare) flash.

sciocco ['ʃɔkko], **-a** agg foolish. sm, sf fool. **sciocchezza** sf foolish thing; (cosa da niente) trifle; (l'essere sciocco) foolishness. **dire sciocchezze** talk nonsense.

*****sciogliere** ['ʃɔʎere] v (fondere) melt; dissolve; (porre fine) break up; (disfare) undo; (allentare) loosen; (slegare) untie; (società) wind up. **scioglimento** sm dissolution; breaking up; melting.

sciolto ['ʃɔlto] agg loose; (agile) nimble. **aver la lingua sciolta** have the gift of the gab. **versi sciolti** sm pl blank verse sing. **scioltezza** sf nimbleness; (fig) fluency.

scioperare [ʃope'rare] v (go on) strike. **scioperante** s(m+f) striker. **scioperato** agg lazy. **sciopero** sm strike. **entrare in sciopero** go on strike. **far sciopero** strike. **sciopero bianco/lampo** sit-down/wildcat strike.

sciorinare [ʃori'nare] v (bucato) hang out; (fig) show off; (spreg) dash off. **sciorinare bugie** tell a string of lies.

sciovinismo [ʃovi'nizmo] sm chauvinism. **sciovinista** s(m+f) chauvinist.

scipito [ʃi'pito] agg insipid.

scippare [ʃip'pare] v snatch. **scippatore, -trice** sm, sf bag-snatcher.

scirocco [ʃi'rokko] sm sirocco.

sciroppo [ʃi'roppo] sm syrup. **sciroppato** agg in syrup. **sciropposo** agg syrupy.

scisma ['ʃizma] sm schism. **scismatico** agg schismatic.

scissione [ʃis'sjone] sf split. **scisso** agg split.

sciupare [ʃu'pare] v (rovinare) ruin, spoil; (perdere) waste. **sciuparsi** v (salute) ruin

one's health; (sgualcirsi) get creased. **sciupato** agg ruined; wasted; (di aspetto) haggard. **sciupìo** sm waste. **sciupone, -a** sm, sf wastrel.

scivolare [ʃivo'lare] v slide; (sfuggire, sdrucciolare) slip; (aero) glide. **scivolata** sf slide; glide. **scivolo** sm chute; (mar) slipway. **scivolone** sm slip; (caduta) tumble. **scivoloso** agg slippery.

sclerosi [skle'rɔzi] sf sclerosis. **sclerotico** agg sclerotic.

scoccare [skok'kare] v (orologio) strike; (scagliare) fling.

scocciare [skot'tʃare] v bother. **scocciarsi** v get bored. **scocciatore, -trice** sm, sf bore; (fam) pest. **scocciatura** sf bore.

scodella [sko'della] sf bowl. **scodellare** v serve; (minestra) ladle out; (fig) come out with.

scoglio ['skɔʎo] sm rock; (fig) stumbling block. **scogliera** sf cliff; (a fior d'acqua) reef. **scoglioso** agg rocky.

scoiattolo [sko'jattolo] sm squirrel.

scolare [sko'lare] v drain; (gastr) strain. **scolapiatti** sm invar draining-board. **scolo** sm drainage; (condotto) drain.

scolaro [sco'laro], **-a** sm, sf pupil; disciple. **scolastico** agg (della scuola) school; (spreg) bookish; (filosofia) scholastic.

scollato [skol'lato] agg low-necked.

scolorire [skolo'rire] v also **scolorare** discolour, fade. **scolorito** agg faded.

scolpire [skol'pire] v sculpt; (incidere) carve; (fig) impress.

scombinare [skombi'nare] v upset. **scombinato** agg (mal combinato) badly arranged; confused.

scombro ['skombro] sm also **sgombro** mackerel.

scombussolare [skombusso'lare] v upset; (stordire) stun.

*****scommettere** [skom'mettere] v bet. **scommessa** sf bet. **scommettitore, -trice** sm, sf punter.

scomodare [skomo'dare] v trouble, inconvenience. **scomodità** sf discomfort; (disagio) inconvenience. **scomodo** agg (non comodo) uncomfortable; inconvenient.

scompaginare [skompadʒi'nare] v throw into disarray; (fig) upset.

*****scomparire** [skompa'rire] v disappear; (fig) look insignificant.

scomparso [skom'parso], **-a** agg vanished. sm, sf deceased. **scomparsa** sf disappearance.

scompartimento [skomparti'mento] *sm* compartment. **scomparto** *sm* compartment; (*parete*) partition.

scompigliare [skompi'ʎare] *v* upset; confuse; (*capelli*) ruffle. **scompiglio** *sm* confusion.

*scomporre [skom'porre] *v* take apart; resolve; decompose; (*turbare*) perturb. senza scomporsi unperturbed. **scomposto** *agg* broken down; (*in disordine*) untidy; (*indecoroso*) unseemly.

scomunicare [skomuni'kare] *v* excommunicate. **scomunica** *sf* excommunication.

sconcertare [skontʃer'tare] *v* baffle. **sconcertato** *agg* bewildered.

sconcio [skontʃo] *agg* indecent; obscene. *sm* disgrace. **sconcezza** *sf* obscenity. **dire sconcezze** use foul language. **sconciare** *v* spoil.

sconfessare [skonfes'sare] *v* repudiate.

*sconfiggere [skon'fiddʒere] *v* defeat. **sconfitta** *sf* defeat. **sconfitto** *agg* defeated, beaten. **dichiararsi sconfitto** acknowledge defeat.

sconfortante [skonfor'tante] *agg* disheartening. **sconforto** *sm* discouragement; depression.

scongelare [skondʒe'lare] *v* defrost.

scongiurare [skondʒu'rare] *v* beseech; (*evitare*) avoid; (*rel*) exorcise. **scongiuro** *sm* exorcism.

*sconnettere [skon'nettere] *v* disconnect. **sconnesso** *agg* (*fig*) disjointed.

sconosciuto [skono'ʃuto], **-a** *agg* unknown. *sm*, *sf* stranger.

sconquassare [skonkwas'sare] *v* smash; shake (up). **sconquassato** *agg* shattered.

sconsiderato [skonside'rato] *agg* thoughtless. **sconsideratezza** *sf* thoughtlessness.

sconsigliare [skonsi'ʎare] *v* advise against; dissuade.

sconsolato [skonso'lato] *agg* disconsolate.

scontare [skon'tare] *v* (*detrarre*) deduct; (*econ*) discount; (*debito*) pay off. **sconto** *sm* discount.

scontentare [skonten'tare] *v* dissatisfy; (*lasciare scontento*) disappoint. **scontentezza** *sf* dissatisfaction; disappointment. **scontento** *agg* displeased; disappointed.

scontrarsi [skon'trarsi] *v* meet; (*veicoli*) crash. **scontro** *sm* encounter; (*discussione*) argument; (*violento*) clash; crash.

scontrino [skon'trino] *sm* check.

scontroso [skon'trozo] *agg* surly. **scontrosità** *sf* surliness.

*sconvenire [skonve'nire] *v* be unsuitable; (*non essere decoroso*) be unbecoming. **sconveniente** *agg* unfavourable; unbecoming.

*sconvolgere [skon'vɔldʒere] *v* upset. **sconvolgimento** *sm* upset; confusion. **sconvolto** *agg* upset.

scopa ['skopa] *sf* broom. **scopare** *v* sweep; (*volg*) screw.

scoperchiare [skoper'kjare] *v* take the lid off.

scoperto [sko'pɛrto] *agg* uncovered; (*aperto*) open; (*nudo*) bare. *sm* open; (*conto*) overdraft. **allo scoperto** outdoors, in the open (air). **scoperta** *sf* discovery.

scopo ['skɔpo] *sm* purpose. **a** *or* **allo scopo di** in order to. **senza scopo** pointless.

scoppiare [skop'pjare] *v* burst; explode; (*manifestarsi*) break out. **scoppiettare** *v* crackle. **scoppio** *sm* explosion; outbreak; (*rumore*) bang.

*scoprire [sko'prire] *v* (*fatti, cose nuove*) discover; (*togliere copertura*) uncover, bare; (*esporre*) expose; (*manifestare*) show. **scoprire le (proprie) carte** lay one's cards on the table.

scoraggiare [skorad'dʒare] *v* discourage, dishearten.

scorbuto [skor'buto] *sm* scurvy. **scorbutico** *agg* (*fig*) cantankerous.

scorciare [skor'tʃare] *v* shorten. **scorciatoia** *sf* short cut.

scordare [skor'dare] *v* *also* **scordarsi** forget.

scordato [skor'dato] *agg* (*musica*) out of tune.

scoreggia [sko'reddʒa] (*volg*) *sf* fart. **scoreggiare** *v* fart.

*scorgere [skɔrdʒere] *v* notice.

scoria ['skɔrja] *sf* slag; (*fig*) dross.

scorno ['skɔrno] *sm* humiliation.

scorpione [skor'pjone] *sm* scorpion. **Scorpione** *sm* Scorpio.

scorrazzare [skorrat'tsare] *v* run about. **scorrazzata** *sf* trip.

*scorrere ['skorrere] *v* (*liquido*) run, flow; (*tempo*) pass (by); (*scivolare*) glide; (*leggere in fretta*) run through. **scorrevole** *agg* flowing. **scorrevolezza** *sf* fluidity; (*fig*) fluency.

scorretto [skor'rɛtto] *agg* incorrect; (*sgarbato*) impolite; (*non leale*) unfair.

scorrettezza sf incorrectness, lack of manners; unfairness.

scorsa ['skɔrsa] sf glance.

scorso ['skɔrso] agg last. **l'anno scorso** last year.

scorsoio [skor'sojo] agg **nodo scorsoio** sm slip-knot.

scorta ['skɔrta] sf escort; (provvista) stock, supply; reserve. **di scorta** spare. **fare la scorta a** escort. **fare una scorta (di)** stock up (on). **sotto la scorta di** under the guidance of. **sulla scorta di** on the basis of.

scortare v escort.

scortese [skor'teze] agg rude. **scortesia** sf rudeness.

scorticare [skorti'kare] v skin; (escoriare) graze.

scorza ['skɔrtsa] sf skin; (corteccia) bark.

scosceso [skoʃ'ezo] agg steep.

scossa ['skɔssa] sf shock; (scatto, sbalzo) jerk; (tremore) shake. **a scosse** jerkily. **scosso** agg shaken.

scostare [skos'tare] v shift. **scostarsi** v move aside; (deviare) stray. **scostamento** sm shifting; (mat) deviation. **scostante** agg unpleasant.

scostumato [skostu'mato] agg dissolute, licentious. **scostumatezza** sf licentiousness.

scotennare [skoten'nare] v skin; (di cuoio capelluto) scalp.

scottare [skot'tare] v burn; (con liquido bollente) scald; (causare bruciatura) scorch; (essere caldo) be hot. **scottatura** sf burning; scalding; scorching; (ustione) burn, scald.

scovare [sko'vare] v (stanare) flush out; (rintracciare) track down; (trovare) find.

Scozia ['skɔtsja] sf Scotland. **scozzese** agg Scottish, Scotch; s(m+f) Scot.

screanzato [skrean'tsato] agg rude.

screditare [skredi'tare] v discredit.

scremare [skre'mare] v skim.

screpolare [skrepo'lare] v crack. **screpolatura** sf crack.

screziato [skre'tsjato] agg variegated.

scribacchiare [skribak'kjare] v scribble.

scricchiolare [skrikkjo'lare] v creak. **scricchiolio** sm creaking noise.

scricciolo [skrit'tʃolo] sm wren.

scrigno ['skriɲo] sm casket.

scriminatura [skrimina'tura] sf parting.

scritta ['skritta] sf inscription; (dir) document.

scritto ['skritto] agg written. sm writing; letter; document. **scrittoio** sm (writing-) desk. **scrittore, -trice** sm, sf writer.

scrittura [skrit'tura] sf writing; (contratto) engagement; (calligrafia) handwriting. **(Sacra) Scrittura** (Holy) Scripture. **scritturare** v engage.

scrivania [skriva'nia] sf (writing-)desk.

*scrivere ['skrivere] v write; (compitando) spell. **scrivere bene/male** (calligrafia) have a good/bad handwriting; (stile) write well/badly; (compitare) spell correctly/incorrectly.

scroccare [skrok'kare] v scrounge. **vivere a scrocco** scrounge a living. **scroccone, -a** sm, sf scrounger.

scrocco ['skrɔkko] sm **coltello a scrocco** sm clasp-knife. **serratura a scrocco** sf spring-lock, latch.

scrofa ['skrɔfa] sf sow.

scrollare [skrol'lare] v shake; (spalle) shrug.

scrosciare [skroʃ'ʃare] v thunder; (pioggia) pelt down. **scroscio** sm (pioggia) downpour. **scroscio di applausi** thunderous applause. **scroscio di risa** roar of laughter.

scrostare [skros'tare] v scrape (off).

scroto ['skrɔto] sm scrotum.

scrupolo ['skrupolo] sm scruple, qualm. **avere or farsi scrupoli (di)** have qualms (about). **essere onesto fino allo scrupolo** be scrupulously honest. **senza scrupoli** unscrupulous. **scrupoloso** agg scrupulous, meticulous.

scrutare [skru'tare] v scan; (indagare) delve into. **scrutatore, -trice** sm, sf scrutineer. **scrutinare** v scrutinize. **scrutinio** sm scrutiny; (elezioni) poll.

scucire [sku'tʃire] v unstitch. **scucitura** sf rip.

scudo ['skudo] sm shield. **farsi scudo** shield oneself. **scuderia** sf (ricovero) stable; (allevamento) stud; (auto) racing team. **scudetto** sm (calcio) league championship.

scugnizzo [sku'nittso] sm urchin.

sculacciare [skulat'tʃare] v spank. **sculacciata** sf spanking.

scultore [skul'tore] sm sculptor. **scultrice** sf sculptress. **scultura** sf sculpture.

scuola ['skwola] sf school. **scuola dell'obbligo** compulsory schooling. **scuola guida** driving school. **scuola materna** nursery school. **scuola pubblica** state school.

*scuotere ['skwɔtere] v shake; (le spalle) shrug. **scuotersi di dosso** shrug off.

scure ['skure] sf axe.

scuro ['skuro] agg dark. sm dark, darkness. **scuretto** sm (window-)shutter. **scurire** v darken.

scusa ['skuza] sf excuse; apology. **chiedere scusa a qualcuno** beg someone's pardon. **scusabile** agg excusable; justifiable. **scusante** sf excuse; justification. **scusare** v excuse; pardon. **scusarsi** v apologize; justify oneself. **mi scusi!** (I'm) sorry! I beg your pardon!

sdegnare [zde'nare] v (disprezzare) scorn; irritate. **sdegnato** agg indignant; irritated. **sdegno** sm indignation. **sdegnoso** agg disdainful.

sdoppiare [zdop'pjare] v split (in two). **sdoppiamento** sm split. **sdoppiamento della personalità** split personality.

sdraiarsi [zdra'jarsi] v (stendersi) stretch out; (mettersi a giacere) lie down. **sdraia** sf also **sedia a sdraio** deck-chair.

sdrucciolare [zdruttʃo'lare] v slip. **sdrucciolevole** agg slippery. **sdrucciolone** sm slip.

sdrucire [zdru'tʃire] v rip.

se¹ [se] cong if; whether; (se solo) if only. **come se** as though. **se non altro** if nothing else, at least.

se² [se] V si.

sè [sɛ] pron one(self); (lui) him(self); (lei) her(self); (cosa, animale) it(self); (loro) them(selves). **da sè** on one's own. **di per sè** in itself. **fra sè e sè** to oneself. **va da sè** it goes without saying.

sebbene [seb'bɛne] cong (al)though.

seccare [sek'kare] v dry (up); (importunare) bother. **seccarsi** v (diventar secco) dry up; (annoiarsi) get bored; (infastidirsi) get annoyed. **secca** sf shallow; (fig) fix. **seccante** boring; annoying. **seccato** agg annoyed; (fam) fed up. **seccatore, -trice** sm, sf nuisance. **seccatura** sf nuisance. **secco** agg dry; (essiccato) dried; (fig) sharp. **lavare a secco** dry-clean. **rimanere in secco** be left high and dry.

secchia ['sekkja] sf bucket. **secchio** sm pail; (per carbone) coal-scuttle. **secchione** sm (fam: sgobbone) swot.

*secernere [se'tʃɛrnere] v secrete.

secessione [setʃes'sjone] sf secession.

secolo ['sɛkolo] sm century; (periodo) age. **al secolo** alias. **secolare** agg centuries old; (laico) secular.

secondino [sekon'dino] sm warder.

secondo¹ [se'kondo] sm, agg second. **in un secondo tempo** on a later occasion. **secondo fine** sm ulterior motive.

secondo² [se'kondo] prep according to; depending on. **inter** it depends!

secrezione [sekre'tsjone] sf secretion.

sedano ['sɛdano] sm celery. **sedano rapa** celeriac.

sedare [se'dare] v calm; (reprimere) quell. **sedativo** agg, sm sedative.

sede ['sɛde] sf seat; (comm) office; residence; (seduta) sitting. **in altra sede** (luogo) elsewhere; (tempo) some other time. **Santa Sede** Holy See. **sede centrale** headquarters. **sede legale** registered office.

*sedere [se'dere] v sit (down). **dar da sedere** offer a seat. **sedersi** v sit down, take a seat. **tirarsi su a sedere** sit up. sm (deretano) bottom. **sedentario** agg sedentary.

sedia ['sɛdja] sf chair.

sedicente [sedi'tʃɛnte] agg so-called; would-be.

sedici ['sed.itʃi] agg, sm sixteen. **sedicesimo** sm, agg sixteenth.

sedile [se'dile] sm seat.

sedimento [sedi'mento] sm sediment. **sedimentazione** sf sedimentation.

sedizione [sedi'tsjone] sf sedition; rebellion. **sedizioso** agg seditious.

*sedurre [se'durre] v seduce; (attrarre) entice. **seducente** agg alluring, tempting. **seduttore, -trice** agg seductive. **seduzione** sf seduction; temptation.

seduta [se'duta] sf session; (pasto, posa) sitting; (riunione) meeting. **seduta spiritica** seance. **seduta stante** forthwith.

sega ['sega] sf saw. **a sega** saw-toothed. **sega a catena** chain-saw. **sega da traforo** fretsaw. **segare** v saw. **segatrice** sf saw. **segatura** sf (azione) sawing; (frammenti) sawdust.

segale ['segale] sf rye.

seggio ['sɛddʒo] sm seat; (carica) chair. **seggiola** sf chair. **seggiolino** sm seat. **seggiolone** sm armchair; (per bambini) high chair.

seggiovia [seddʒo'via] sf chair-lift.

seghettare [seget'tare] v serrate.

segmento [seg'mento] sm segment. **segmentare** v divide up. **segmentazione** sf segmentation; (fig) breaking up.

segnalare [seɲaˈlare] v signal; (*indicare*) point out; (*render noto*) report. **segnalato** *agg* announced, reported; (*straordinario*) outstanding. **segnalatore** *sm* (*persona*) signaller; indicator; alarm. **segnalazione** *sf* signalling; report; notification; (*nota informativa*) notice. **segnalazione stradale** road sign. **segnale** *sm* signal; (*cartello*) sign; (*telefono*) tone. **segnaletica** *sf* road signs *pl*.

segnalibro [seɲaˈlibro] *sm* bookmark.

segnapunti [seɲaˈpunti] *sm invar* (*tabellone*) score-board; (*libretto*) score-book.

segnare [seˈɲare] v mark; (*marchiare*) brand. **segnare i punti** keep the score. **segnare le ore** tell the time.

segno [ˈseɲo] *sm* sign; (*traccia*) mark. **come** o **in segno di** as a sign of, in token of. **essere in segno che** mean. **tiro a segno** *sm* target practice.

sego [ˈsego] *sm* fallow.

segregare [segreˈgare] v segregate, set apart. **segregazione** *sf* segregation; isolation. **segregazione cellulare** solitary confinement.

segretario [segreˈtarjo], **-a** *sm*, *sf* secretary; (*chi redige verbali, ecc.*) clerk. **segretariato** *sm* secretariat. **segreteria** *sf* secretary's office; (*enti pubblici*) secretariat.

segreto [seˈgreto] *agg* secret. *sm* secret; (*intimità*) depth; (*segretezza*) secrecy. **in segreto** in secret; (*riservatamente*) confidentially. **nel segreto più assoluto** in utmost secrecy. **segreti dei mestieri** tricks of the trade *pl*. **segreto di Pulcinella** open secret. **segreta** *sf* dungeon. **segretezza** *sf* secrecy.

seguace [seˈgwatʃe] *s(m+f)* follower; disciple.

seguente [seˈgwɛnte] *agg* following; (*futuro*) next.

segugio [seˈgudʒo] *sm* bloodhound; (*fig*) sleuth.

seguire [seˈgwire] v follow; (*frequentare*) attend. **segue a tergo** continued overleaf, PTO. **seguitare** v continue. **seguito** *sm* following; succession; favour; continuation; consequence. **di seguito** on end, non-stop. **in seguito** later (on). **in seguito a** as a result of, because of.

sei [ˈsɛi] *agg*, *sm* six.

selce [ˈseltʃe] *sf* flint; (*strada*) pavingstone. **selciato** *sm* paving.

selettivo [seletˈtivo] *agg* selective. **selettività** *sf* selectivity. **selettore**, **-trice** *sm*, *sf* selector.

selezionare [seletsjoˈnare] v select; grade. **selezionamento** *sm* selection. **selezione** *sf* selection; (*scelta*) choice. **selezione automatica** (*telefono*) automatic dialling, STD.

sella [ˈsella] *sf* saddle. **sellare** v saddle.

seltz [ˈselts] *sm invar* soda-water.

selva [ˈselva] *sf* forest. **selvoso** *agg* wooded.

selvaggio [selˈvaddʒo], **-a** *agg* wild; (*incivile*) savage. *sm*, *sf* savage. **selvaggina** *sf* game. **selvatico** *agg* wild; (*scontroso*) uncouth.

semaforo [seˈmaforo] *sm* traffic lights *pl*.

semantica [seˈmantika] *sf* semantics. **semantico** *agg* semantic.

sembrare [semˈbrare] v seem. **cosa te ne sembra?** what do you think of it?

seme [ˈseme] *sm* seed; (*di mele, pere, ecc.*) pip; (*carte da gioco*) suit. **sementa** *sf* (*operazione*) sowing; (*semente*) seed. **semente** *sf* seed. **semenza** *sf* seed; (*perle*) seed-pearls *pl*.

semestre [seˈmɛstre] *sm* half-year. **semestrale** *agg* half-yearly.

semibreve [semiˈbrɛve] *sf* semibreve.

semicerchio [semiˈtʃerkjo] *sm* semicircle. **semicircolare** [semitʃirkoˈlare] *agg* semicircular.

semicroma [semiˈkrɔma] *sf* semiquaver.

semidio [semiˈdio] *sm* demi-god.

semifinale [semifiˈnale] *sf* semifinal. **semifinalista** *s(m+f)* semifinalist.

semiminima [semiˈminima] *sf* crotchet.

seminare [semiˈnare] v sow; (*fig*) scatter, strew. **semina** *sf* sowing. **seminale** *agg* seminal. **uscire dal seminato** digress.

seminario [semiˈnarjo] *sm* (*rel*) seminary; (*università*) seminar. **seminarista** *sm* seminarist.

seminterrato [seminterˈrato] *sm* basement.

seminudo [semiˈnudo] *agg* half-naked.

semita [seˈmita] *s(m+f)* Semite. *agg also* **semitico** Semitic.

semitono [semiˈtono] *sm* semitone.

semivivo [semiˈvivo] *agg* half-dead.

semola [ˈsemola] *sf* (*crusca*) bran. **semolino** *sm* semolina.

semovente [semoˈvɛnte] *agg* self-propelled.

semplice ['semplitʃe] *agg* simple; (*di un solo elemento*) single; (*senza affettazione*) plain. **semplicemente** *avv* simply; (*soltanto*) only. **semplicione** *sm* simpleton. **semplicità** *sf* simplicity. **semplificare** *v* simplify; facilitate. **semplificazione** *sf* simplification.

sempre ['sempre] *avv* always; (*ancora*) still. **da sempre** from the beginning. **per sempre** for ever. **sempre che** (*purché*) as long as, provided that; (*ammesso che*) supposing that. **sempre più** more and more. **sempreverde** *s(m+f)*, *agg* evergreen. **una volta per sempre** once and for all.

senape ['senape] *sf* mustard.

senato [se'nato] *sm* senate. **senatore** *sm* senator.

senile [se'nile] *agg* senile. **senilità** *sf* senility.

senno ['senno] *sm* wits *pl*; (*sensatezza*) (common) sense. **con senno** sensibly. **senno di poi** hindsight. **uscir di senno** go out of one's mind.

seno ['seno] *sm* bosom, breast; (*grembo*) womb; (*anat*) sinus; (*mat*) sine; (*geog*) inlet. **allattare al seno** breast-feed. **in seno a** (*nel mezzo di*) within; (*tra le braccia*) in the arms of.

sensale [sen'sale] *sm* broker.

sensato [sen'sato] *agg* sensible. **sensatezza** *sf* good sense.

sensazione [sensa'tsjone] *sf* feeling, sensation. **sensazionale** *agg* sensational.

sensibile [sen'sibile] *agg* (*che sente*) sensitive; (*notevole*) appreciable; perceptible; susceptible. **sensibilità** *sf* sensitivity. **sensibilizzare** *v* sensitize.

sensitivo [sensi'tivo] *agg* (*funzione*) sensory; (*sensibile*) sensitive. **sensitività** *sf* sensitivity.

senso ['senso] *sm* sense; (*significato*) meaning; (*direzione, modo*) way. **a senso** in one's own words; (*tradurre*) freely. **far senso** (*ripugnare*) disgust. **in senso antiorario** anticlockwise. **in senso orario** clockwise. **non aver senso** not make sense; be pointless. **senso proibito** no entry. **senso unico** one-way. **sensorio** *agg* sensory. **sensuale** *agg* sensual; sensuous. **sensualità** *sf* sensuality; sensuousness.

sentenza [sen'tentsa] *sf* sentence, judgment; (*massima*) saying. **sputare sentenze** be sententious. **sentenziare** *v* pass judgment *or* sentence; rule; decree. **sentenzioso** *agg* sententious.

sentiero [sen'tjero] *sm* path.

sentimento [senti'mento] *sm* feeling; (*concetto*) sense. **sentimenti** *sm pl* (*modo di sentire*) sentiments *pl*.

sentinella [senti'nella] *sf* sentry.

sentire [sen'tire] *v* feel; (*col gusto*) taste; (*con l'udito*) hear; (*con l'olfatto*) smell; (*dare ascolto*) listen to; (*aver notizia*) gather. **al mio modo di sentire** to my way of thinking. **sentirsela** *v* feel like. **sentirsi** *v* feel.

sentito [sen'tito] *agg* (*udito*) heard; sincere. **per sentito dire** by hearsay.

sentore [sen'tore] *sm* inkling.

senza ['sentsa] *prep* without. **rimanere senza** run out of. **senza contare** apart from; over and above. **senza dire** not to mention. **senza fallo** certainly. **senz'altro** definitely. **senza soldi** penniless. **senzatetto** *s(m+f)* *invar* homeless person.

separare [sepa'rare] *v* separate, divide. **separarsi** *v* part; (*coniugi*) separate. **separazione** *sf* separation, division; parting.

sepolcro [se'polkro] *sm* tomb. **sepolcrale** *agg* sepulchral.

sepolto [se'polto] *agg* buried. **sepoltura** *sf* burial.

*****seppellire** [seppel'lire] *v* bury.

seppia ['seppja] *sf* (*zool*) cuttlefish. *agg*, *sm invar* (*colore*) sepia.

seppure [sep'pure] *cong* even though, even if.

sequela [se'kwela] *sf* succession.

sequestrare [sekwes'trare] *v* seize, confiscate; (*persona*) imprison unlawfully; (*rapire*) kidnap. **sequestro** *sm* seizure, confiscation; kidnapping; illegal confinement.

sera ['sera] *sf* evening, night. **buona sera!** (*di pomeriggio*) good afternoon! (*di sera*) good evening! **si fa sera** it is getting dark. **serale** *agg* evening, night. **serata** *sf* evening, night; (*ricevimento*) party; (*teatro*) performance.

serbare [ser'bare] *v* (*mantenere*) keep; (*metter da parte*) put aside. **serbare gratitudine verso** be grateful to. **serbatoio** *sm* tank; (*penna*) barrel; (*fucile, ecc.*) magazine.

serbo ['serbo] *sm* **dare in serbo** put into

custody. **mettere in serbo** put by or aside. **tenere in serbo** keep in store.

serenata [sere'nata] *sf* serenade.

serenella [sere'nɛlla] *sf* lilac.

sereno [se'reno] *agg* calm, serene; (*cielo*) clear; (*senza preoccupazioni*) carefree; objective. *sm* clear sky; (*aperto*) open air. **serenità** *sf* serenity; objectivity.

sergente [ser'dʒɛnte] *sm* sergeant.

serico ['sɛriko] *agg* silk.

serie ['sɛrje] *sf invar* series; (*assortimento*) set; (*sport*) division. **fuori serie** (*auto*) custom-built. **modello di serie** *sm* production model. **prodotto in serie** mass-produced. **produzione in serie** *sf* mass-production.

serio ['sɛrjo] *agg* serious; (*degno di fiducia*) trustworthy; (*comm*) reputable. *sm* seriousness. **sul serio** (*seriamente*) seriously; (*davvero*) really. **serietà** *sf* seriousness; (*fidatezza*) reliability.

sermone [ser'mone] *sm* sermon; (*rimprovero*) lecture.

serpeggiare [serped'dʒare] *v* wind.

serpente [ser'pɛnte] *sm* snake, serpent. **serpente a sonagli** rattlesnake. **serpentino** *agg* snake-like.

serra ['sɛrra] *sf* greenhouse, hothouse.

serraglio [ser'raʎo] *sm* menagerie.

serrare [ser'rare] *v* close; (*a chiave*) lock; (*stringere*) tighten; (*denti, pugni*) clench. **serrare al cuore** embrace. **serramento** *sm* (*di finestra*) window-frame; (*di porta*) door-frame. **serrata** *sf* lock-out. **serrato** *agg* closed; (*fila*) serried; (*fig*) to the point. **serratura** [serra'tura] *sf* lock. **buco della serratura** *sm* keyhole. **serratura a cilindro** Yale lock ®. **serratura a lucchetto** padlock. **serratura a scatto** latch.

servire [ser'vire] *v* serve; (*fam: occorrere*) be useful; (*carte da gioco*) deal. **a cosa serve?** what is the use? **cosa ti serve?** what do you need? **posso servirti?** can I help you? **servirsi** *v* use; make use; (*di cibo*) help oneself. **servile** *agg* servile; (*fig*) slavish. **servitore** *sm* servant. **servitù** *sf* (*schiavitù*) slavery; (*personale di servizio*) servants *pl*. **ridurre in servitù** enslave.

servizio [ser'vitsjo] *sm* service; (*lavoro*) work; favour; (*giornale*) report; (*turno*) duty. **a mezzo servizio** part-time. **donna di servizio** *sf* maid. **fare servizio** (*trasporto*) run; (*negozio*) be open. **fuori servizio** off duty; (*che non funziona*) out of order. **in servizio** on duty. **servizievole** *agg* obliging.

servo ['servo], **-a** *sm*, *sf* servant.

sesamo ['sɛzamo] *sm* sesame.

sessanta [ses'santa] *agg*, *sm* sixty. **sessantesimo** *agg*, *sm* sixtieth.

sessione [ses'sjone] *sf* session.

sesso ['sɛsso] *sm* sex. **sessuale** *agg* sexual. **sessualità** *sf* sexuality.

sestetto [ses'tetto] *sm* sextet.

sesto[1] ['sesto] *sm*, *agg* sixth.

sesto[2] ['sesto] *sm* order; (*di arco*) curve. **mettere in sesto** tidy up. **rimettersi in sesto** get back on one's feet again.

seta ['seta] *sf* silk.

setaccio [se'tattʃo] *sm* sieve. **setacciare** *v* also **passare al setaccio** sift, sieve.

sete ['sete] *sf* thirst. **aver sete** be thirsty. **mettere la seta** make thirsty.

setola ['setola] *sf* bristle.

setta ['setta] *sf* sect. *agg*, *sm* sectarian.

settanta [set'tanta] *agg*, *sm* seventy. **settantesimo** *agg*, *sm* seventieth.

sette ['sɛtte] *agg*, *sm* seven. **settimo** *agg*, *sm* seventh.

settembre [set'tɛmbre] *sm* September.

settentrione [setten'trjone] *sm* north. **settentrionale** *agg* northern, north.

settico ['sɛttiko] *agg* septic. **setticemia** *sf* blood-poisoning.

settimana [setti'mana] *sf* week; (*paga*) week's wages. **a metà settimana** mid-week. **a settimane** by the week; (*una sì e una no*) every other week. **fine settimana** *sf* week-end. **settimanale** *agg*, *sm* weekly.

settore [set'tore] *sm* sector; (*campo*) field.

severo [se'vero] *agg* severe, strict; (*grave*) serious. **severità** *sf* severity.

seviziare [sevi'tsjare] *v* torture; (*violentare*) rape. **sevizie** *sf pl* torture sing.

sezione [se'tsjone] *sf* section; (*tribunale*) division; (*sezionamento*) dissection. **sezionare** *v* dissect; (*dividere in sezioni*) section.

sfaccendato [sfattʃen'dato], **-a** *agg* idle. *sm*, *sf* loafer.

sfaccettare [sfattʃet'tare] *v* cut.

sfacchinare [sfakki'nare] *v* slave. **sfacchinata** *sf* heavy work.

sfacciato [sfat'tʃato], **-a** *agg* impudent; (*svergognato*) shameless; (*vistoso*) gaudy. *sm*, *sf* impudent or shameless person.

sfacciataggine sf impudence; shamelessness.

sfacelo [sfa'tʃɛlo] sm ruin; (disfacimento) decay. **andare in sfacelo** break up; (fam) go to rack and ruin.

sfaldarsi [sfal'darsi] v flake; (sbriciolarsi) crumble. **sfaldatura** sf flaking; crumbling.

sfalsare [sfal'sare] v stagger.

sfamare [sfa'mare] v feed. **sfamarsi** v satisfy one's hunger.

sfarfallare [sfarfal'lare] v (svolazzare) flutter; (esser volubile) flirt; (auto) wobble.

sfarzo ['sfartso] sm magnificence, pomp. **senza sfarzo** simply. **sfarzosità** sf sumptuousness; ostentation. **sfarzoso** agg sumptuous; ostentatious.

sfasciare [sfa'ʃare] v (rompere) smash.

sfatare [sfa'tare] v refute.

sfavillante [sfavil'lante] agg glittering, sparkling.

sfavore [sfa'vore] sm disfavour, discredit. **andare a sfavore di** go against. **sfavorevole** agg unfavourable; (contrario) adverse.

sfegatato [sfega'tato] agg passionate.

sfera ['sfɛra] sf sphere; (ambiente) circle; (campo) field. **cuscinetto a sfere** sm ball-bearing. **penna a sfera** sf ball-point pen. **sferico** agg spherical.

sferrare [sfer'rare] v (attacco) launch; (pugno) deal. **sferrare un calcio** kick.

sferza ['sfɛrtsa] sf whip. **sferzare** v whip; lash.

sfiatato [sfia'tato] agg breathless; (strumento musicale) cracked; (fam) hoarse.

sfibrare [sfi'brare] v (indebolire) weaken. **sfibrante** agg enervating. **sfibrato** agg exhausted.

sfida ['sfida] sf challenge. **sfidare** v challenge; (invitare) defy; (fig) brave.

sfiducia [sfi'dutʃa] sf distrust. **avere sfiducia di** distrust; lack confidence in. **sfiduciarsi** v lose confidence. **sfiduciato** agg distrustful; (di sè stesso) diffident; (scoraggiato) disheartened.

sfigurare [sfigu'rare] v disfigure; make a bad impression.

sfilacciare [sfilat'tʃare] v fray.

sfilare¹ [sfi'lare] v (togliere di dosso) take off; (ago) unthread.

sfilare² [sfi'lare] v parade. **sfilata** sf parade; (lunga fila) long row.

sfilza ['sfiltsa] sf string.

sfinge ['sfindʒe] sf sphinx.

sfinire [sfi'nire] v wear out. **sfinimento** sm exhaustion.

sfiorare [sfjo'rare] v skim (over); (toccando) graze, barely touch; (successo, ecc.) be on the verge of.

sfiorito [sfjo'rito] agg withered.

sfitto ['sfitto] agg vacant.

sfocato [sfo'kato] agg (foto) out of focus; (fig) hazy.

sfociare [sfo'tʃare] v flow (into); (fig) result. **sfocio** sm outlet.

sfogare [sfo'gare] v let out; (fig) give vent to. **sfogarsi** v (sfogar l'ira) give vent to one's anger; (confidarsi) pour out one's heart; (bambino) run wild. **sfogo** sm outlet; (sollievo) relief.

sfoggiare [sfod'dʒare] v show off. **sfoggio** sm display; ostentation.

sfogliare¹ [sfo'ʎare] v also **dare una sfogliata a** (pagine) leaf or skim through.

sfogliare² [sfo'ʎare] v (levar le foglie) strip (of leaves). **sfoglia** sf leaf; (gastr) puff pastry.

sfolgorare [sfolgo'rare] v blaze; (occhi) shine.

sfollare [sfol'lare] v disperse; evacuate. **sfollamento** sm evacuation. **sfollato, -a** sm, sf evacuee.

sfondare [sfon'dare] v break through; (schiantare) smash; (logorare) wear out. **sfondato** agg (senza fondo) bottomless; (logoro) worn out. **ricco sfondato** rolling in money. **sfondo** sm background, setting.

sformare [sfor'mare] v pull out of shape; (estrarre dalla forma) turn out. **sformato** sm (gastr) pie.

sfornito [sfor'nito] agg **sfornito di** lacking in, without.

sfortuna [sfor'tuna] sf bad luck; (contrattempo) misfortune. **sfortunato** agg unlucky; (senza successo) unfortunate.

sforzare [sfor'tsare] v force, strain. **sforzarsi di** try hard to. **sforzo** sm effort.

sfottere [sfot'tere] v (fam) take the mickey (out of). **sfottimento** sm teasing, ridicule.

sfracellare [sfratʃel'lare] v shatter.

sfrangiato [sfran'dʒato] agg fringed.

sfrattare [sfrat'tare] v turn out, evict. **sfratto** sm eviction.

sfregare [sfre'gare] v rub; (lucidando) polish; (lavando) scrub. **sfregamento** sm rubbing; polishing; scrubbing.

sfrenare [sfre'nare] v let loose. **sfrenatezza** sf lack of restraint; wild behaviour. **sfrenato** agg unbridled; (senza ritegno) immoderate.

***sfriggere** ['sfriddʒere] v also **sfrigolare** sizzle.

sfrondare [sfron'dare] v prune.

sfrontato [sfron'tato] agg impudent, brazen; (fam) cheeky. **sfrontatezza** sf effrontery; (fam) cheek.

sfruttare [sfrut'tare] v exploit. **sfruttamento** sm exploitation; utilization. **sfruttatore, -trice** sm, sf exploiter.

sfuggire [sfud'dʒire] v shun; (scappare) escape from. **lasciarsi sfuggire** let slip; (occasione) let go by. **sfuggire di mano** slip out of one's hand. **sfuggire di mente** slip one's mind. **sfuggente** agg (mento, fronte) receding. **di sfuggita** fleetingly.

sfumare [sfu'mare] v (svanire) disappear; (colori, suoni) fade away, tone down. **sfumato** agg (pittura) shaded; (fig) vague. **sfumatura** sf nuance.

sfuriata [sfu'rjata] sf outburst; (tempesta) storm; (rabbuffo) telling-off.

sfuso ['sfuzo] agg (sciolto) loose; (liquefatto) melted.

sgabello [zga'bɛllo] sm stool.

sgabuzzino [zgabut'tsino] sm cubby-hole.

sgambettare [zgambet'tare] v (camminare a piccoli passi) toddle (along); (fare lo sgambetto) trip up.

sganciare [zgan'tʃare] v unhook; (bombe) release; (fam: sborsare) fork out.

sgangherato [zgange'rato] agg (sfasciato) rickety; (sconnesso) incoherent; (esagerato) boisterous.

sgarbato [zgar'bato] agg rude, discourteous. **sgarbatezza** sf rudeness, discourtesy.

sgarbugliare [zgarbu'ʎare] v disentangle.

sgargiante [zgar'dʒante] agg showy.

sgarrare [zgar'rare] v be or go wrong.

sgelare [zdʒe'lare] v thaw out; (surgelati) defrost.

sghembo ['zgembo] agg crooked. **di sghembo** askew.

sgherro ['zgɛrro] sm thug.

sghignazzare [zgiɲat'tsare] v laugh sarcastically, sneer; (sguaiatamente) guffaw. **sghignazzata** sf sarcastic laughter; guffaw.

sghiribizzo [zgiri'bittso] sm whim.

sgobbare [zgob'bare] v slave. **sgobbata** sf grind. **sgobbone, -a** s, sf slogger; (studente) swot.

sgocciolare [zgottʃo'lare] v drip; (vuotare) drain. **sgocciolatura** sf dripping; (macchie) drips pl. **essere agli sgoccioli** be or have nearly finished.

sgolarsi [zgo'larsi] v shout oneself hoarse.

sgombrare [zgom'brare] v also **sgomberare** clear; (vuotare) empty; (portar via) clear away; evacuate; (lasciar libero) vacate.

sgombro[1] [zgombro] sm also **sgombero** (trasloco) move; clearing (away); evacuation. agg clear; empty.

sgombro[2] [zgombro] V **scombro**.

sgomentare [zgomen'tare] v dismay. **sgomento** sm dismay.

sgonfiare [zgon'fjare] v deflate; (fam) annoy. **sgonfiarsi** v go down; (pneumatico) go flat; (fig) be deflated. **sgonfio** agg deflated, flat.

sgorbia ['zgɔrbja] sf gouge.

sgorbio ['zgɔrbjo] sm (macchia) blot; (scarabocchio) scrawl.

sgorgare [zgor'gare] v gush (out); (uscire) spring.

sgradevole [zgra'devole] agg disagreeable, unpleasant. **sgradito** agg disagreeable; (non gradito) unwelcome.

sgrammaticato [zgrammati'kato] agg ungrammatical.

sgranare [zgra'nare] v shell; (occhi) open wide.

sgranchire [zgran'kire] v stretch.

sgravare [zgra'vare] v relieve; (partorire) give birth.

sgraziato [zgra'tsjato] agg ungainly, awkward.

sgretolare [zgreto'lare] v break up. **sgretolarsi** v crumble. **sgretolato** agg crumbling.

sgridare [zgri'dare] v scold; (fam) tell off. **sgridata** sf scolding; (fam) telling-off.

sguaiato [zgwa'jato] agg unseemly; vulgar; (grossolano) coarse. **sguaiataggine** sf vulgarity; coarseness.

sgualcire [zgwal'tʃire] v crease, crumple.

sgualdrina [zgwal'drina] sf (spreg) tart.

sguardo ['zgwardo] sm look; (occhiata) glance; (fisso) stare; (prolungato) gaze. **al primo sguardo** at first sight. **fissare lo sguardo su** stare at. **gettare uno sguardo su** glance at.

sguarnire [zgwar'nire] v strip.

sguattero ['zgwattero], **-a** sm, sf skivvy.

sguazzare [zgwat'tsare] v splash about; (fig) wallow.

sguinzagliare [zgwintsa'ʎare] v let loose.

sgusciare[1] [zgu'ʃare] v (scivolare) slip.

sgusciare[2] [zgu'ʃare] v shell; (uova, noci) crack.

shampoo [ʃam'pu] sm invar shampoo.

si [si] pron (lui) himself; (lei) herself; (cosa, animale) itself; (loro) themselves; (reciproco) each other; (riflessivo) oneself; (indefinito) one.

sì [si] avv yes. **credo di sì** I think so. **dire di sì** say yes. **far cenno di sì** nod. **spero di sì** I hope so. **un giorno sì e uno no** every other day.

sia ['sia] cong **sia ... sia ...** whether ... or ... ; (entrambi) both.

siamese [sia'meze] agg, s(m+f) Siamese.

sibilare [sibi'lare] v hiss. **sibilo** sm hiss.

sicario [si'karjo] sm hired assassin.

sicché [sik'ke] cong (di modo che) and so; (e perciò) so that.

siccità [sittʃi'ta] sf drought.

siccome [sik'kome] cong as, since.

Sicilia [si'tʃilja] sf Sicily. **siciliano, -a** s, agg Sicilian.

sicomoro [siko'mɔro] sm sycamore.

sicura [si'kura] sf safety catch.

sicurezza [siku'rettsa] sf safety; certainty; (garanzia) security; (confidenza) self-assurance. **di sicurezza** safety. **per maggior sicurezza** to be on the safe side. **pubblica sicurezza** police. **sicurezza sociale** social security; welfare.

sicuro [si'kuro] agg safe; (tranquillo) secure; certain, sure; (fidato) reliable; (saldo) steady. sm safety; safe place. **andar sul sicuro** take no chances. **dare per sicuro** be certain about. **di sicuro** certainly. **star sicuro** not worry.

sidro [sidro] sm cider.

siepe ['sjɛpe] sf hedge.

siero ['sjɛro] sm serum.

siesta ['sjɛsta] sf siesta; (fam) nap. **fare la siesta** take a nap.

sifilide [si'filide] sf syphilis.

sifone [si'fone] sm siphon.

sigaretta [siga'retta] sf cigarette. **sigaro** sm cigar.

sigillare [sidʒil'lare] v seal. **sigillatura** sf sealing, seal. **sigillo** sm seal. **anello con sigillo** sm signet-ring.

sigla ['sigla] sf initials pl; (auto) registration number. **sigla musicale** signature tune. **siglare** v initial.

significare [siɲifi'kare] v mean; (simboleggiare) stand for. **significativo** agg meaningful, significant; important. **significato** sm meaning; importance.

signora [siɲ'ora] sf lady; (donna) woman (pl women); (cortesia) madam; (seguito dal cognome) Mrs; (padrona) mistress; (moglie) wife. **fare la signora** live like a lady.

signore [siɲ'ore] sm gentleman; (uomo) man (pl men); (cortesia) sir; (seguito dal cognome) Mr; (padrone) master.

signoreggiare [siɲored'dʒare] v rule.

signoria [siɲo'ria] sf domination.

signorile [siɲo'rile] agg elegant, high-class; (uomo) gentlemanly; (donna) lady-like. **signorilità** sf elegance; refinement.

signorina [siɲo'rina] sf young lady or woman; (cortesia) madam; (seguito dal cognome) Miss; (non sposata) unmarried woman. **nome da signorina** sm maiden name.

silenzio [si'lentsjo] sm silence. **far silenzio** be quiet. **silenziare** v muffle. **silenziatore** sm silencer. **silenzioso** agg silent, quiet.

silicio [si'litʃo] sm silicon. **silice** sf silica. **silicone** sm silicone. **silicosi** sf silicosis.

sillaba ['sillaba] sf syllable. **sillabare** v (gramm) syllabify; (fig) spell out. **sillabario** sm spelling book.

silo ['silo] sm silo.

silofono [si'lofono] sm xylophone.

silurare [silu'rare] v torpedo; (far fallire) wreck; (destituire) dismiss. **siluramento** sm torpedoing; wrecking; dismissal. **siluro** sm torpedo.

silvestre [sil'vɛstre] agg woody; (selvaggio) wild.

silvia ['silvja] sf (bot) wood anemone; (zool) warbler.

simbolo ['simbolo] sm symbol; (rel) creed. **simboleggiare** v symbolize. **simbolico** agg symbolic.

simile ['simile] agg like, similar; (predicato) alike; (tale) such. **similitudine** sf simile.

simmetria [simme'tria] sf symmetry. **simmetrico** agg symmetrical.

simpatia [simpa'tia] sf (sentimento di attrazione) liking; (qualità) likeableness; (affinità) sympathy. **avere** or **provare simpatia per** like, take to. **simpatico** agg nice, likeable; (piacevole) agreeable; (anat) sympathetic. **simpatizzare** v sympathize.

simposio [sim'pɔzjo] *sm* symposium.

simulare [simu'lare] *v* feign; (*imitare*) simulate. **simulacro** *sm* image; (*fig*) semblance. **simulazione** *sf* simulation.

simultaneo [simul'taneo] *agg* simultaneous. **simultaneità** *sf* simultaneity.

sinagoga [sina'gɔga] *sf* synagogue.

sincero [sin'tʃero] *agg* sincere, true; (*non artefatto*) genuine. **sincerità** *sf* sincerity.

sincopare [sinko'pare] *v* syncopate. **sincope** *sf* syncope; (*musica*) syncopation.

sincronizzare [sinkronid'dzare] *v* synchronize. **sincronizzatore** *sm* synchronizer. **sincronizzazione** *sf* synchronization.

sindacale [sinda'kale] *agg* (*di sindacato*) (trade) union. **sindacalismo** *sm* trade unionism. **sindacalista** *s(m+f)* trade unionist.

sindacare [sinda'kare] *v* check; (*contabilità*) audit; (*fig*) criticize.

sindacato [sinda'kato] *sm* (*operaio*) trade union; (*padronale, d'impresa*) consortium; (*finanziario*) syndicate.

sindaco ['sindako] *sm* mayor; (*comm*) auditor.

sindrome ['sindrome] *sf* syndrome.

sinfonia [sinfo'nia] *sf* symphony. **sinfonico** *agg* symphonic. **orchestra sinfonica** *sf* symphony orchestra.

singhiozzare [singjot'tsare] *v* (*avere il singhiozzo*) hiccup; (*piangere*) sob. **singhiozzo** *sm* sob; hiccup. **a singhiozzi** by fits and starts.

singolare [singo'lare] *agg* singular; (*strano*) strange. *sm* singular. **singolarità** *sf* singularity; strangeness.

singolo ['singolo] *agg* single, individual. *sm* (*persona*) individual; (*telefono*) private line; (*tennis*) singles; (*canottaggio*) skiff.

sinistra [si'nistra] *sf* left(-hand side); (*mano*) left hand. **a sinistra** on *or* to the left. **tenere la sinistra** keep to the left. **uomo di sinistra** *sm* left-winger.

sinistrare [sinis'trare] *v* damage. **sinistrato, -a** *sm, sf* victim. **zona sinistrata** *sf* disaster area.

sinistro [si'nistro] *agg* left; (*lato*) lefthand; (*fig*) sinister. *sm* accident; (*pugilato*) left.

sino ['sino] *cong* **sino a** (*tempo*) until; (*luogo*) as far as. *avv* (*persino*) even. **sinora** *avv* (*per ora*) so far; (*fino ad ora*) up to now.

sinossi [si'nɔssi] *sf* synopsis (*pl* -ses). **sinottico** *agg* synoptic.

sintassi [sin'tassi] *sf* syntax. **sintattico** *agg* syntactic(al).

sintesi ['sintezi] *sf* synthesis (*pl* -ses). **in sintesi** (*in poche parole*) in short; (*sommariamente*) summing up. **sintetico** *agg* synthetic; (*fig*) concise. **sintetizzare** *v* synthesize; (*riassumere*) summarize.

sintomo ['sintomo] *sm* symptom. **sintomatico** *agg* symptomatic.

sintonizzare [sintonid'dzare] *v* tune in.

sinuoso [sinu'ozo] *agg* sinuous, winding.

sinusite [sinu'zite] *sf* sinusitis.

sipario [si'parjo] *sm* curtain.

sirena [si'rena] *sf* siren; (*creatura*) mermaid.

siringa [si'ringa] *sf* syringe; (*bot*) lilac; catheter. **siringare** *v* syringe; catheterize.

sismico ['sizmiko] *agg* seismic. **sismografo** *sm* seismograph.

sistema [sis'tema] *sm* system; (*modo di fare*) way; method. **sistemare** *v* (*mettere a posto*) arrange; (*put in*) order; (*risolvere*) settle; organize; (*collocare*) install. **sistemarsi** *v* settle (down); (*lavoro*) get a job. **sistematico** *agg* systematic; methodical. **sistemazione** *sf* arrangement; (*composizione*) settlement; (*alloggio*) accommodation; (*lavoro*) job.

situare [situ'are] *v* place; (*collocare*) locate. **situazione** *sf* situation. **situazione di fatto** state of affairs.

slabbrare [zlab'brare] *v* (*vasellame*) chip; (*tessuto*) tear.

slacciare [zlat'tʃare] *v* undo, untie.

slanciare [zlan'tʃare] *v* hurl. **slanciato** *agg* slender, slim. **slancio** *sm* swing; (*di passione, ecc.*) burst. **di slancio** in a rush; (*fig*) on impulse.

slattare [zlat'tare] *v* wean.

slavato [zla'vato] *agg* washed out; (*fig*) dull.

sleale [zle'ale] *agg* disloyal; (*fatto senza lealtà*) unfair. **gioco sleale** *sm* foul play. **slealtà** *sf* disloyalty; unfairness.

slegare [zle'gare] *v* untie. **slegato** *agg* untied; (*non rilegato*) unbound; (*fig*) disjointed.

slip [zlip] *sm invar* (*mutande*) briefs *pl*; (*da bagno*) swimming trunks *pl*.

slitta ['zlitta] *sf* sleigh, sledge; (*tec*) slide. **slittare** *v* slip; (*ruote*) skid; (*scivolare*) slide.

slogan ['zlɔgan] *sm invar* slogan.

slogare [zlo'gare] *v* dislocate. **slogatura** *sf* dislocation.

sloggiare [zlod'dʒare] *v* dislodge.

smacchiare [zmak'kjare] *v* clean. **smacchiatore** *sm* stain-remover. **smacchiatura** *sf* cleaning.

smacco ['zmakko] *sm* defeat.

smagliante [zma'ʎante] *agg* dazzling.

smagliarsi [zma'ʎarsi] *v* (*calze*) ladder; (*pelle*) stretch.

smagrire [zma'grire] *v* slim.

smaltare [zmal'tare] *v* enamel; (*unghie*) paint; (*ceramica*) glaze. **smalto** *sm* enamel; glaze; (*per le unghie*) nail-varnish.

smaltire [zmal'tire] *v* digest; (*fig*) swallow; (*comm*) dispose of.

smanceroso [zmantʃe'rozo] *agg* affected; (*smorfioso*) mawkish. **smanceria** *sf* affectation.

smania ['zmanja] *sf* craving; (*agitazione*) frenzy. **aver la smania addosso** fidget. **smaniare** *v* (*essere agitato*) fret; (*essere furioso*) rave; (*desiderare*) crave (for).

smantellare [zmantel'lare] *v* dismantle; (*fig*) pull to pieces.

smargiassata [zmardʒas'sata] *sf* brag; bravado. **smargiasso, -a** *sm, sf* braggart. **fare lo smargiasso** brag.

smarrire [zmar'rire] *v* lose; (*non riuscire a trovare*) mislay. **smarrirsi** *v* (*persone*) lose one's way; (*cose*) be mislaid, go astray. **smarrimento** *sm* loss; (*svenimento*) fainting-fit; (*turbamento*) bewilderment.

smascherare [zmaske'rare] *v* unmask, reveal. **smascheramento** *sm* unmasking.

smembrare [zmem'brare] *v* dismember.

smemorato [zmemo'rato], **-a** *agg* forgetful; (*distratto*) absent-minded. *sm, sf* forgetful *or* absent-minded person. **smemoratagine** *sf* forgetfulness; (*dimenticanza*) lapse of memory. **smemoratezza** *sf* forgetfulness; absent-mindedness.

smentire [zmen'tire] *v* deny; (*ritrattare*) retract; (*dimostrare la falsità*) belie. **smentita** *sf* denial.

smeraldo [zme'raldo] *sm* emerald. *agg invar* (*colore*) emerald-green.

smerciare [zmer'tʃare] *v* sell. **smercio** *sf* sale.

smerigliare [zmeri'ʎare] *v* (*mec*) grind; (*vetro*) frost. **carta smerigliata** *sf* (*grossa*) emery paper; (*fine*) sandpaper. **vetro smerigliato** *sm* frosted glass. **smeriglio** *sm* emery.

smerlare [zmer'lare] *v* scallop. **smerlo** *sm* scallop.

***smettere** ['zmettere] *v* stop.

smidollato [zmidol'lato] *agg* spineless.

militarizzare [zmilitarid'dzare] *v* demilitarize. **smilitarizzazione** *sf* demilitarization.

smilzo ['zmiltso] *agg* lean.

sminuire [zminu'ire] *v* diminish; (*fig*) belittle.

sminuzzare [zminut'tsare] *v* break into small pieces; (*sbriciolare*) crumble.

smistare [zmis'tare] *v* sort (out); (*ferr*) shunt.

smisurato [zmizu'rato] *agg* boundless; enormous.

smobilitare [zmobili'tare] *v* demobilize. **smobilitazione** *sf* demobilization.

smoderato [zmode'rato] *agg also* **smodato** immoderate. **smoderatezza** *sf* lack of moderation; excess.

smoking ['zmɔkin] *sm invar* dinner-jacket.

smontare [zmon'tare] *v* (*scomporre*) dismantle, take apart; (*totalmente*) strip; (*da veicoli*) get out *or* off. **smontaggio** *sm* dismantling; stripping.

smorfia ['zmɔrfja] *sf* wry face. **fare una smorfia** pull a face; (*di dolore*) wince with pain. **smorfioso** *agg* simpering.

smorto ['zmɔrto] *agg* pale, wan; (*fig*) colourless.

smorzare [zmor'tsare] *v* (*colori*) tone down; (*suoni*) muffle; (*luce*) dim; (*fig*) dampen. **smorzata** *sf* (*tennis*) drop-shot.

smunto ['zmunto] *agg* emaciated.

***smuovere** ['zmwɔvere] *v* shift; (*commuovere*) touch; dissuade.

smussare [zmus'sare] *v* smooth; (*angolo*) round off; (*fig*) soften. **smussarsi** *v* become blunt.

snaturare [znatu'rare] *v* distort. **snaturato** *agg* unnatural; degenerate.

snazionalizzare [znatsjonalid'dzare] *v* denationalize. **snazionalizzazione** *sf* denationalization.

snellire [znel'lire] *v* slim (down); simplify; speed up. **snellezza** *sf* slimness. **snello** *agg* slim; (*agile*) nimble; simple, easy.

snervare [zner'vare] *v* exhaust.

snidare [zni'dare] *v* drive out.

snob ['znɔb] *agg, s(m+f) invar* snob. **snobbare** *v* snub. **snobismo** *sm* snobbery.

snocciolare [znottʃo'lare] *v* stone; (*fam: spendere*) shell out; (*fam: spiattellare*) rattle off.

snodare [zno'dare] v unknot; (*articolare meglio*) loosen (up); (*piegare*) bend. **snodabile** agg (*tec*) articulated. **snodato** agg flexible, loose.

soave [so'ave] agg delicate, sweet. **soavità** sf sweetness, delicacy.

sobbalzare [sobbal'tsare] v jolt; (*trasalire*) jump. **di sobbalzo** with a start.

sobbarcarsi [sobbar'karsi] v undertake.

sobbollire [sobbol'lire] v simmer.

sobborgo [sob'borgo] sm suburb.

sobillare [sobil'lare] v incite, stir up. **sobillatore, -trice** sm, sf trouble-maker.

sobrio ['sɔbrjo] agg sober. **sobrietà** sf sobriety.

*****socchiudere** [sok'kjudere] v half-close. **socchiuso** agg half-closed; (*porta*) ajar.

soccombere [sok'kombere] v succumb.

*****soccorrere** [sok'korrere] v assist; come to the aid of; (*salvare*) rescue.

soccorritore [sokkorri'tore], **-trice** agg helping, aid. sm, sf helper.

soccorso [sok'korso] sm help, assistance; rescue. **pronto soccorso** first aid; (*all'ospedale*) casualty ward. **soccorsi** sm pl (*rinforzi*) reinforcements pl; (*rifornimenti*) supplies pl.

socialdemocratico [sotʃaldemo'kratiko], **-a** sm, sf social democrat. **socialdemocrazia** sf social democracy.

sociale [so'tʃale] agg social; (*benessere*) welfare; (*comm*) relating to a firm, company. **assistente sociale** s(m+f) welfare officer, social worker. **assistenza sociale** sf welfare. **tessera sociale** sf membership card.

socialismo [sotʃa'lizmo] sm socialism. **socialista** agg, s(m+f) socialist.

società [sotʃe'ta] sf society; (*comm*) company, partnership; association. **gioco di società** sm parlour game. **mettersi in società** go into partnership. **società anonima** limited company. **società dei consumi** consumer society. **società per azioni** limited company.

socievole [so'tʃevole] agg social; (*persona*) sociable. **socievolezza** sf sociability.

socio ['sɔtʃo], **-a** sm, sf partner; member.

sociologia [sotʃolo'dʒia] sf sociology. **sociologico** agg sociological. **sociologo, -a** sm, sf sociologist.

soda ['sɔda] sf soda.

sodalizio [soda'litsjo] sm brotherhood; (*amicizia*) fellowship.

*****soddisfare** [soddis'fare] v satisfy; (*appagare*) gratify; (*riparare*) make amends for. **soddisfacente** agg satisfactory; satisfying. **soddisfatto** agg satisfied; (*contento*) pleased. **soddisfazione** sf satisfaction. **bella satisfazione!** big deal!

sodio ['sɔdjo] sm sodium.

sodo ['sɔdo] agg firm; (*fig*) sound. **uovo sodo** sm hard-boiled egg. avv hard; (*profondamente*) soundly.

sofà [so'fa] sf sofa, settee.

sofferente [soffe'rɛnte] agg suffering. **sofferenza** sf suffering.

soffermarsi [soffer'marsi] v linger (over).

soffiare [sof'fjare] v blow; (*sbuffare*) puff; (*dama, scacchi*) huff. **soffiare di rabbia** fume (with rage). **soffio** sm puff; (*med*) murmur. **in un soffio** in a flash. **per un soffio** by a whisker.

soffice ['soffitʃe] agg soft.

soffietto [sof'fjetto] sm bellows pl; (*fam: articoletto*) plug. **a soffietto** folding. **lavorar di soffietto** (*fam*) tell tales.

soffitta [sof'fitta] sf attic.

soffitto [sof'fitto] sm ceiling.

soffocare [soffo'kare] v suffocate, choke; (*reprimere*) suppress, stifle. **soffocamento** sm suffocation.

*****soffriggere** [sof'friddʒere] v brown.

*****soffrire** [sof'frire] v suffer (from); (*sopportare*) bear, stand; (*consentire*) allow. **soffrire la fame** go hungry. **soffrir di (mal di) cuore** have heart trouble.

sofisma [so'fizma] sm sophistry. **sofisticare** v (*sottilizzare*) quibble; (*fam*) split hairs; (*adulterare*) doctor.

soggetto [sod'dʒetto] sm subject; (*argomento*) topic; person. **recitare a soggetto** improvise. agg subject, liable; (*sottomesso*) subjected; (*predisposto*) prone. **soggettivo** agg subjective. **soggezione** sf subjection; embarrassment; (*timore*) awe. **aver soggezione di** (*sentirsi imbarazzato*) feel uneasy in the presence of; (*averne timore*) be overawed by. **ispirare soggezione a** make uneasy; overawe.

sogghignare [soggi'ɲare] v sneer.

*****soggiacere** [soddʒa'tʃere] v be subjected; succumb.

soggiorno [sod'dʒorno] sm stay; (*luogo*) resort; (*stanza*) living room. **permesso di soggiorno** sm residence permit. **soggiornare** v stay.

*****soggiungere** [sod'dʒundʒere] v add.

soglia ['sɔʎa] *sf* threshold.

sogliola ['sɔʎola] *sf* sole.

sognare [so'nare] *v* dream; (*ad occhi aperti*) daydream. **sognatore, -trice** *sm, sf* dreamer. **sogno** *sm* dream. **fare un sogno** have a dream. **neanche per sogno!** not likely!

soia ['sɔja] *sf* soya (bean).

solaio [so'lajo] *sm* (*soffitta*) loft; (*piano di edificio*) floor.

solare [so'lare] *agg* solar. **luce solare** *sf* sunlight.

solco ['solko] *sm* (*agric*) furrow; (*traccia*) track; (*lampo*) streak; (*disco*) groove.

soldato [sol'dato] *sm* soldier. **andare soldato** join up. **fare il soldato** be in the army.

soldo ['sɔldo] *sm* penny. **soldi** *sm pl* (*denaro*) money *sing*. **essere al soldo di** be in the pay of. **essere senza soldi** be penniless.

sole ['sole] *sm* sun. **al sole** in the sun. **chiaro come il sole** clear as daylight. **fare un bagno di sole** sunbathe. **occhiali da sole** *sm pl* sun-glasses *pl*. **soleggiato** *agg* sunny.

solenne [so'lenne] *agg* solemn; (*fig*) tremendous. **solennità** *sf* solemnity; (*festa*) holiday. **solennizzare** *v* solemnize.

*****solere** [so'lere] *v* be in the habit of.

soletta [so'letta] *sf* sole; (*suola interna*) insole.

solfato [sol'fato] *sm* sulphate. **solforico** *agg* sulphuric. **solfuro** *sm* sulphide.

solidale [soli'dale] *agg* (*tec*) integral; (*d'accordo*) in agreement (with); (*dir*) joint. **solidarietà** *sf* solidarity.

solidificare [solidifi'kare] *v* harden. **solidificarsi** *v* set. **solidificazione** *sf* hardening; setting.

solido ['sɔlido] *agg* solid; stable; (*robusto*, *valido*) sound; (*colori*) fast. *sm* solid. **solidità** *sf* solidity; stability; soundness; fastness.

soliloquio [soli'lɔkwjo] *sm* soliloquy.

solista [so'lista] *s*(*m+f*) soloist.

solitario [soli'tarjo], **-a** *agg* solitary. *sm, sf* loner. *sm* (*brillante*, *gioco*) solitaire.

solito ['sɔlito], **-a** *agg* usual. *pron* same. *sm* (*abitudine*) habit; (*cosa*) usual. **come al solito** as usual. **di solito** usually, as a rule. **essere solito a fare** be used to doing.

solitudine [soli'tudine] *sf* solitude.

sollazzare [sollat'tsare] *v* amuse.

sollecitare [solletʃi'tare] *v* press for; (*affrettare*) speed up; (*mec*) stress; (*chiedere con insistenza*) solicit. **sollecitazione** *sf* solicitation, entreaty; (*mec*) stress. **lettera di sollecitazione** *sf* reminder.

sollecito [sol'letʃito] *agg* (*fatto con premura*) prompt; (*premuroso*) solicitous. **sollecitudine** *sm* (*prontezza*) dispatch; (*preoccupazione*) solicitude.

solleticare [solleti'kare] *v* tickle; (*fig*) arouse. **solletico** *sm* tickle. **fare il solletico** tickle. **sentire** *or* **soffrire il solletico** be ticklish.

sollevare [solle'vare] *v* raise; (*tirar su*) lift (up). **sollevarsi** *v* rise; (*riprendersi*) recover.

sollievo [sol'ljevo] *sm* relief.

solo ['solo] *agg* alone; by oneself; (*unico*) only, sole; (*semplice*) mere; (*musica*) unaccompanied. *avv* (*soltanto*) only; (*ma*) but. **da solo** alone, by oneself. **solo che** only. **solo soletto** quite alone. **una sola volta** once only. **un solo** just one, only one.

solstizio [sol'stitsjo] *sm* solstice.

soltanto [sol'tanto] *avv* only.

solubile [so'lubile] *agg* soluble. **solubilità** *sf* solubility. **soluzione** *sf* solution.

solvente [sol'vɛnte] *agg, sm* solvent. **solvibile** *agg* (*comm*) solvent. **solvibilità** *sm* (*comm*) solvency.

soma ['soma] *sf* burden.

somaro [so'maro] *sm* donkey.

somigliare [somi'ʎare] *v* resemble, be like. **somigliante** *agg* similar. **somiglianza** *sf* resemblance.

somma ['somma] *sf* sum. **fare la somma** add up. **tirare le somme** sum up. **sommare** *v* add *or* sum up. **tutto sommato** all things considered.

sommario [som'marjo] *agg* brief; (*dir*) summary. *sm* summary, outline.

*****sommergere** [som'mɛrdʒere] *v* submerge. **sommergibile** *sm* submarine.

sommesso [som'messo] *agg* meek.

somministrare [somminis'trare] *v* administer.

sommità [sommi'ta] *sf* peak, summit.

sommo ['sommo] *agg* highest; (*fig*) supreme. *sm* peak.

sommossa [som'mɔssa] *sf* riot.

sommozzatore [sommottsa'tore] *sm* skin-diver; (*mil*) frogman.

sonaglio [so'naʎo] *sm* bell. **serpente a sonagli** *sm* rattlesnake.

sonare [so'nare] *v also* **suonare** sound; (*campanello*) ring; (*musica*) play; (*orologio*) strike; (*fam: imbrogliare*) cheat. **sonata** *sf* (*musica*) sonata; (*fam: bastonatura*) caning; (*fam: fregatura*) swindle. **prendersi una sonata** be taken in. **sonato** *agg* (*compiuto*) past; (*rimbambito*) gaga.

sonda ['sonda] *sf* probe. **sondaggio** *sm* probing, sounding; (*indagine*) poll. **sondare** *v* sound, probe.

sonnambulo [son'nambulo], **-a** *sm, sf* sleep-walker.

sonnecchiare [sonnek'kjare] *v* doze.

sonnifero [son'nifero] *agg* soporific. *sm* sleeping pill.

sonno ['sonno] *sm* sleep; (*senso di torpore*) drowsiness. **aver sonno** be sleepy. **fare un bel sonno** have a good sleep. **sonnolento** *agg* sleepy, drowsy. **sonnolenza** *sf* drowsiness.

sonoro [so'nɔro] *agg* sound; (*che risona*) resonant; (*consonanti*) voiced. **sonorità** *sf* resonance; (*fis*) acoustics *pl*.

sontuoso [sontu'ozo] *agg* sumptuous. **sontuosità** *sf* sumptuousness.

soporifero [sopo'rifero] *agg, sm* soporific.

sopperire [soppe'rire] *v* provide for.

soppesare [soppe'zare] *v* weigh up.

soppiantare [soppjan'tare] *v* supplant.

soppiatto [sop'pjatto] *agg* di **soppiatto** stealthily. **entrare/uscire di soppiatto** steal in/away.

sopportare [soppor'tare] *v* (*reggere*) support; (*fig*) bear, stand. **sopportabile** *agg* bearable. **sopportazione** *sf* endurance.

***sopprimere** [sop'primere] *v* suppress; abolish. **soppressione** *sf* suppression; abolition.

sopra ['sopra] *prep* on, upon; (*senza contatto diretto*) over, above. **al di sopra di** above; (*oltre*) beyond. *avv* on; (*più in su*) above; (*al piano superiore*) upstairs. **come/vedi sopra** (*nei rinvii*) as/see above.

soprabito [so'prabito] *sm* overcoat.

sopracciglio [soprat'tʃiʎo] *sm* eyebrow.

sopraccitato [soprattʃi'tato] *agg* abovementioned.

sopraccoperta [soprakko'perta] *sf* (*letto*) counterpane; (*libro*) dust-jacket.

***sopraffare** [sopraf'fare] *v* overcome; dominate.

sopraffino [sopraf'fino] *agg* excellent; highly refined.

sopraggiungere [soprad'dʒundʒere] *v* turn up; (*accadere improvvisamente*) happen, arise.

sopralluogo [sopral'lwɔgo] *sm, pl* **-ghi** (on the spot) inspection; (*statistica*) poll.

sopralzo [so'praltso] *sm* extension.

soprammobile [sopram'mɔbile] *sm* knickknack.

soprannaturale [soprannatu'rale] *agg, sm* supernatural.

soprannome [sopran'nome] *sm* nickname. **soprannominare** *v* call.

soprannumero [sopran'numero] *sm* excess.

soprano [so'prano], **-a** *sm, sf* soprano.

soprappensiero [soprappen'sjero] *avv* lost in thought.

soprappiù [soprap'pju] *sm* surplus; (*aggiunta*) addition. **di** *or* **per soprappiù** in addition, besides.

soprapprezzo [soprap'prettso] *sm* (*econ*) premium; (*maggiorazione*) increase in price.

soprassalto [sopras'salto] *sm* sudden start. **di soprassalto** suddenly.

soprassedere [soprasse'dere] *v* put off.

soprattassa [soprat'tassa] *sf* additional charge.

soprattutto [soprat'tutto] *avv* above all; (*per la maggior parte*) mainly.

sopravanzare [sopravan'tsare] *v* be left over.

sopravvalutare [sopravvalu'tare] *v* overrate. **sopravvalutazione** *sf* overestimate.

***sopravvenire** [sopravve'nire] *v* turn up; (*accadere d'improvviso*) happen, arise.

sopravvento [soprav'vento] *agg, avv* windward; (*fig*) upper hand.

***sopravvivere** [soprav'vivere] *v* survive. **sopravvissuto, -a** *sm, sf* survivor. **sopravvivenza** *sf* survival.

soprelevare [soprele'vare] *v* raise.

***soprintendere** [soprin'tendere] *v* supervise; be in charge of. **soprintendente** *s(m+f)* superintendent. **soprintendenza** *sf* (*atto*) supervision; (*ufficio*) superintendence.

sopruso [so'pruzo] *sm* outrage.

soqquadro [sok'kwadro] *sm* **mettere a soqquadro** turn upside down.

sorbetto [sor'betto] *sm* sorbet, water ice.

sorbire [sor'bire] *v* sip. **sorbirsi** *v* (*sopportare*) put up with.

sorcio [sor'tʃo] *sm* mouse (*pl* mice).

sordido ['sordido] *agg* sordid. **sordidezza** *sf* sordidness.

sordina [sor'dina] *sf* (*musica*) mute. **in sordina** (*fig*) on the quiet.

sordo ['sordo], -**a** *agg* deaf; (*smorzato*) dull; (*fig*) hidden. **sordo come una campana** deaf as a post. *sm*, *sf* deaf person. **fare il sordo** feign deafness. **sordità** *sf* deafness.

sordomuto [sordo'muto], -**a** *agg* deaf and dumb. *sm*, *sf* deaf-mute.

sorella [so'rella] *sf* sister. **sorellastra** *sf* step-sister, half-sister.

sorgere ['sordʒere] *v* rise; (*aver origine*) arise. **sorgente** *sf* source. **acqua sorgiva** *sf* spring water.

soriano [so'rjano] *sm*, *agg* tabby.

sormontare [sormon'tare] *v* surmount; (*stoffa*) overlap.

sornione [sor'njone] *agg* sly.

sorpassare [sorpas'sare] *v* (*oltrepassare*) overtake; (*eccedere*) exceed. **sorpassare in altezza/lunghezza** be higher/longer. **sorpassato** *agg* (*non più attuale*) out of date. **sorpasso** *sm* overtaking. **divieto di sorpasso** *sm* no overtaking.

sorprendere [sor'prendere] *v* surprise; (*cogliere all'improvviso*) catch. **sorprendente** *agg* surprising. **sorpresa** *sf* surprise.

sorreggere [sor'reddʒere] *v* hold up; sustain. **sorreggersi** *v* stand upright.

sorridere [sor'ridere] *v* smile; (*destar piacere*) appeal. **sorridente** *agg* smiling. **sorriso** *sm* smile.

sorso ['sorso] *sm* (*sorsata*) sip; (*d'un fiato*) gulp; (*piccola quantità*) drop. **sorseggiare** *v also* **bere a piccoli sorsi** sip.

sorta ['sorta] *sf* kind, sort. **di sorta** (*di nessun tipo*) whatever.

sorte ['sorte] *sf* fate; fortune; (*condizione propria*) lot. **sorteggiare** *v also* **tirare a sorte** draw lots. **sorteggio** *sm* draw.

sortilegio [sorti'ledʒo] *sm* spell.

sorvegliare [sorve'ʎare] *v* watch; (*sovrintendere*) oversee; (*vigilare*) keep an eye on. **sorvegliante** *s(m+f)* overseer; (*custode*) caretaker; (*guardiano*) watchman. **sorveglianza** *sf* surveillance, watch.

sorvolare [sorvo'lare] *v* fly over; (*fig*) skip.

sosia ['sɔzja] *sm invar* double.

sospendere [sos'pendere] *v* suspend; (*attaccare in alto*) hang; interrupt; (*seduta*) adjourn; defer. **sospendere il lavoro** stop work. **sospensione** *sf* suspension; interruption; (*cessazione*) stoppage. **sospeso** *agg* hanging; (*non definito*) outstanding. **col fiato sospeso** with bated breath. **in sospeso** in suspense; (*non risolto*) pending.

sospettare [sospet'tare] *v* suspect; (*diffidare*) distrust, be suspicious (of).

sospetto [sos'petto] *agg* suspect, suspicious. **persona sospetta** *sf* suspect. *sm* suspicion. **sospettoso** *agg* distrustful.

sospingere [sos'pindʒere] *v* push; (*fig*) drive. **a ogni piè sospinto** at every step.

sospirare [sospi'rare] *v* sigh; (*aspettare con ansia*) long *or* yearn for. **sospiro** *sm* sigh.

sosta ['sɔsta] *sf* stop; pause; (*riposo*) rest; (*aspettare*) wait. **divieto di sosta** no waiting. **senza sosta** ceaselessly; without stopping. **sostare** *v* stop; pause; wait; rest.

sostantivo [sostan'tivo] *agg* substantive. *sm* noun.

sostanza [sos'tantsa] *sf* matter; (*parte utile*) substance; (*parte nutritiva*) nourishment; (*patrimonio*) property. **cibo di sostanza** nourishing food. **in sostanza** essentially. **sostanza alimentare** foodstuff. **sostanziale** *agg* substantial; essential. **sostanzioso** *agg* nourishing.

sostegno [sos'teɲo] *sm* support.

sostenere [soste'nere] *v* support; (*asserire*) maintain; (*tenere alto*) keep up; (*tollerare*) stand. **sostenere una carica** hold an office. **sostenere una parte** act a part. **sostenersi** *v* (*star su*) hold oneself up, stand up; (*fig*) hold water. **sostenibile** *agg* tenable.

sostenitore [sosteni'tore], -**trice** *agg* supporting. *sm*, *sf* supporter.

sostentare [sosten'tare] *v* support; maintain. **sostentamento** *sm* support; maintenance.

sostenuto [soste'nuto] *agg* (*contegnoso*) reserved; (*musica*) sostenuto. **sostenutezza** *sf* reserve.

sostituire [sostitu'ire] *v* substitute; (*rimpiazzare*) replace. **sostituto**, -**a** *sm*, *sf* deputy, substitute. **sostituzione** *sf* substitution; replacement.

sottaceto [sotta't∫eto] *avv* **mettere sottaceto** pickle. **sottaceti** *sm pl* pickles *pl*.

sottalimentazione [sottalimenta'tsjone] *sf* undernourishment.

sottana [sot'tana] *sf* skirt; (*sottoveste*) slip, underskirt; (*rel*) cassock.

sottecchi [sot'tekki] *avv* **di sottecchi** stealthily.

sottentrare [sotten'trare] *v* replace.

sotterfugio [sotter'fudʒo] *sm* subterfuge.

sotterraneo [sotter'raneo] *agg* underground. *sm* basement. **sotterranea** *sf* underground (railway); (*fam*) tube.

sotterrare [sotter'rare] *v* bury. **sotterra** *avv* underground.

sottile [sot'tile] *agg* thin; fine; (*acuto*) sharp. **sottigliezza** *sf* thinness; sharpness; (*sofisticheria*) nicety.

sottinsù [sottin'su] *avv* **di sottinsù** from below.

*sottintendere [sottin'tendere] *v* imply, infer; (*non esprimere*) leave out. **sottinteso** *agg* implied; (*chiaro da sè*) understood. *sm* allusion. **senza sottintesi** plainly.

sotto ['sotto] *prep* under; (*al di sotto di*) below, beneath; (*in cambio di*) on. *avv* underneath, below; (*al piano di sotto*) downstairs. **andar sotto le armi** join up. **metter sotto** (*investire*) run down. **mettersi sotto** get down to. **sotto la pioggia** in the rain. **sotto questo punto di vista** from this point of view. **sotto questo riguardo** in this respect. **sotto sotto** deep down.

sottobanco [sotto'banko] *avv* under the counter.

sottobicchiere [sottobik'kjere] *sm* mat, coaster.

sottobraccio [sotto'brattʃo] *avv* arm-in-arm. **prendere sottobraccio qualcuno** take someone's arm.

sottocchio [sot'tokkjo] *avv* **tenere sottocchio** keep an eye on.

sottocommissione [sottokommis'sjone] *sf* subcommittee; subcommission.

sottocoppa [sotto'kɔppa] *sm invar* mat; (*piattino*) saucer.

*sottoesporre [sottoes'pɔrre] *v* underexpose.

sottofondo [sotto'fondo] *sm* foundation; (*suono*) background noise. **musica in sottofondo** *sf* background music.

sottolineare [sottoline'are] *v* underline; (*fig*) stress.

sottomano [sotto'mano] *avv* (*a portata di mano*) within (easy) reach, on hand; (*di nascosto*) on the quiet; (*sport*) underhand.

*sottomettere [sotto'mettere] *v* (*assoggettare*) subject; (*costringere a sottostare*) subdue; subordinate. **sottomettersi** *v* submit. **sottomesso** *agg* subdued; (*obbediente*) submissive.

sottopassaggio [sottopas'saddʒo] *sm* underpass.

*sottoporre [sotto'pɔrre] *v* (*presentare*) submit; (*costringere*) subject, expose. **sottoporsi a un'operazione** undergo an operation. **sottoposto, -a** *sm*, *sf* subordinate.

sottoprodotto [sottopro'dotto] *sm* by-product.

sottordine [sot'tordine] *sm* suborder. **in sottordine** of minor importance.

*sottoscrivere [sotto'skrivere] *v* sign; (*fig*) support; (*econ*) underwrite, subscribe. **sottoscritto, -a** *sm*, *sf* undersigned; (*fam*) yours truly. **sottoscrizione** *sf* subscription.

sottosopra [sotto'sopra] *avv* upside down.

*sottostare [sotto'stare] *v* be under; (*sottomettersi*) give in. **sottostante** *agg* (down) below.

sottosuolo [sotto'swɔlo] *sm* subsoil.

sottoterra [sotto'tɛrra] *avv* underground.

sottotitolo [sotto'titolo] *sm* subtitle.

sottovalutare [sottovalu'tare] *v* underestimate.

sottoveste [sotto'vɛste] *sf* slip.

sottovoce [sotto'votʃe] *avv* in a low voice, softly.

*sottrarre [sot'trarre] *v* remove; (*mat*) subtract; (*salvare*) save (from). **sottrarsi a** escape; (*evitare*) avoid. **sottrazione** *sf* subtraction; removal.

sottufficiale [sottuffi'tʃale] *sm* non-commissioned officer; (*mar*) petty officer.

sovente [so'vɛnte] *avv* also **di sovente** frequently.

soverchio [so'verkjo] *agg* excessive. **soverchieria** *sf* bullying; (*sopruso*) outrage.

sovietico [so'vjetiko], **-a** *s*, *agg* Soviet.

sovrabbondante [sovrabbon'dante] *agg* plentiful; excessive. **sovrabbondanza** *sf* plenty; excess.

sovraccaricare [sovrakkari'kare] *v* overburden; (*tec*) overload. **sovraccarica** *sf* overcharge. **sovraccarico** *agg*, *m pl* **-chi** overloaded.

*sovr(a)esporre [sovr(a)es'porre] v over-expose. **sovresposizione** sf over-exposure.

sovraffollato [sovraffol'lato] agg over-crowded.

sovrano [so'vrano], **-a** agg sovereign, supreme. sm, sf sovereign. **sovranità** sf sovereignty; (fig) supremacy.

sovrappopolato [sovrap'popo'lato] agg overpopulated.

*sovrapporre [sovrap'porre] v superimpose; (fig) set over; (accavallare) overlap.

sovrastante [sovra'stante] agg towering; (imminente) impending.

sovreccitare [sovrettʃi'tare] v over-excite. **sovreccitarsi** v become over-excited. **sovreccitazione** sf over-excitement.

sovrumano [sovru'mano] agg superhuman.

sovvenzione [sovven'tsjone] sf subsidy. **sovvenzionare** v subsidize.

sovversione [sovver'sjone] sf subversion. **sovversivo** -a -s, agg subversive. **sovvertire** v subvert.

sozzo ['sottso] agg filthy; (fig) loathsome. **sozzura** sf filth; loathsomeness.

spaccare ['spakkare] v (fendere) split; (rompere) break; (legna) chop. **spaccarsi** v split (open); break (up). **spaccare il minuto** be dead on time. **fare la spaccata** do the splits. **spacco** sm split; (strappo) tear; (giacca) vent.

spacciare ['spattʃare] v (vendere) sell off; (mettere in circolazione) peddle; (dichiarar inguaribile) give up. **spacciato** agg (fam: rovinato) done for. **spacciatore, -trice** sm, sf pedlar; (di droghe) pusher; (di notizie false) rumour-monger. **spaccio** sm sale; (negozio) shop; (mil, fabbrica) canteen.

spaccone [spak'kone] sm braggart. **fare lo spaccone** brag.

spada ['spada] sf sword; (sport) épée. a **spada tratta** vigorously. **pesce spada** sm sword-fish. **tirar di spada** fence. **spadaccino** sm swordsman. **spadista** s(m+f) fencer.

spadroneggiare [spadroned'dʒare] v be bossy.

spaesato [spae'zato] agg lost.

Spagna ['spaɲa] sf Spain. **spagnolo, -a** agg, sm Spanish; sm, sf (abitante) Spaniard.

spago ['spago] sm string, twine.

spalancare [spalan'kare] v open wide.

spalancare gli orecchi prick up one's ears. **spalancato** agg wide open.

spalare [spa'lare] v shovel.

spalla ['spalla] sf shoulder; (dorso) back. **alle spalle di** (stato) behind; (moto) from behind. **aver le spalle grosse** be broad-shouldered. **aver sulle spalle** (fig) be responsible for. **alzar le spalle** shrug one's shoulders. **ridere alle spalle di qualcuno** laugh behind someone's back. **vivere alle spalle di** live off. **spallata** sf (spinta) push with the shoulder; (alzata di spalle) shrug. **spalletta** sf parapet.

spalmare [spal'mare] v spread.

spanare [spa'nare] v strip.

spanciare [span'tʃare] v bulge. **spanciarsi dalle risa** split one's sides laughing.

*spandere [spandere] v (versare) shed; (involontariamente) spill; (stendere, divulgare) spread.

spanna ['spanna] sf span.

spappolare [spappo'lare] v crush.

sparare [spa'rare] v fire; (tirare) shoot. **spararle grosse** (fam) shoot a line; tell tall stories. **sparata** sf volley. **sparo** sm shot.

sparecchiare [sparek'kjare] v clear (away).

spareggio [spa'reddʒo] sm (sport) decider.

*spargere ['spardʒere] v scatter; (versare) shed; (involontariamente) spill; (sale, pepe, ecc.) sprinkle; (diffondere) spread.

*sparire [spa'rire] v disappear. **far sparire** (nascondere) hide; (fam: rubare) pinch.

sparlare [spar'lare] v speak ill (of).

sparo ['sparo] sm shot.

sparpagliare [sparpa'ʎare] v scatter.

spartire [spar'tire] v divide; (in parti) share out; (musica) score. **spartiacque** sm invar watershed. **spartineve** sm invar snow-plough. **spartitraffico** sm traffic island. **spartito** sm score.

sparuto [spa'ruto] agg gaunt; (esiguo) scanty.

sparviere [spar'vjere] sm sparrow-hawk.

spasimare [spazi'mare] v suffer agonies; (fig) crave, long (for). **spasimo** sm pang; (med) spasm. **spasmodico** agg spasmodic.

spassarsela [spas'sarsela] v enjoy oneself. **spassionato** [spassjo'nato] agg dispassionate.

spasso ['spasso] sm fun. **andare a spasso** go for a walk. **mandare a spasso** (fam: licenziare) sack; (fam: liberarsene) get rid of. **portare a spasso** take for a walk. **quel**

ragazzo è uno spasso! that boy is a scream! **spassoso** agg amusing.

spastico [spas'tiko], **-a** s, agg spastic. **spasticità** sf spasticity.

spatola ['spatola] sf spatula; (di pittore) palette-knife; (zool) spoonbill.

spatriare [spatri'are] v expatriate.

spaurire [spau'rire] v scare. **spauracchio** sm scarecrow.

spavaldo [spa'valdo] agg defiant; (baldanzoso) bold; (arrogante) cocky. **spavalderia** sf defiance; boldness; cockiness.

spaventare [spaven'tare] v frighten, scare. **spaventarsi** v get frightened, get scared. **spaventapasseri** sm scarecrow. **spaventevole** agg terrifying. **spavento** sm fright. **fare spavento** frighten, scare. **prenderci uno spavento** have a fright. **spaventoso** agg frightful; (terribile) dreadful; (enorme) tremendous.

spazientirsi [spatsjen'tirsi] v lose one's patience.

spazio ['spatsjo] sm space; (estensione limitata) room; distance. **spaziale** agg space, spatial. **spaziare** v space; (fig) range. **spazioso** agg roomy.

spazzare [spat'tsare] v sweep; (spazzar via) sweep away. **spazzacamino** sm chimney-sweep. **spazzaneve** sm invar snowplough. **spazzatura** sf cleaning; sweeping; (rifiuti) rubbish. **spazzaturaio** sm dustman. **spazzino** sm road sweeper.

spazzola ['spattsola] sf brush. **capelli a spazzola** crew-cut. **spazzola per capelli** hairbrush. **spazzolare** v brush. **spazzolino da denti/unghie** sm tooth-/nail-brush. **spazzolone** (per lavare) scrubbing brush.

specchio ['spekkjo] sm mirror; model; (prospetto) table; summary. **specchio d'acqua** sheet of water. **specchio retrovisore** driving mirror. **specchiarsi** v (guardarsi) look at oneself in the mirror; (riflettersi) be reflected. **specchiato** agg (fig) exemplary. **specchiera** sf large mirror; (toletta) dressing-table. **specchietto** sm small mirror; (tavola) table, summary.

speciale [spe'tʃale] agg special; particular; (fuori del solito) peculiar. **specialista** s(m + f) specialist. **specialità** sf speciality; (prodotto speciale) specialty; (farmaceutica) proprietary medicine. **specializzarsi** v specialize. **specializzato** agg specialized;

(operaio) skilled; (medico) specialist. **specializzazione** sf specialization.

specie ['spetʃe] sf invar kind, sort; (bot, zool) species; surprise. **mi fa specie** it surprises me. **sotto specie di** in the form of.

specificare [spetʃifi'kare] v specify. **specifica** sf detailed list. **specificazione** sf specification. **specifico** agg specific.

speculare [speku'lare] v speculate. **speculativo** agg speculative. **speculatore, -trice** sm, sf speculator; (di borsa) stockbroker. **speculazione** sf speculation.

spedalità [spedali'ta] sf hospitalization.

spedire [spe'dire] v send; post; (inoltrare) forward. **spedire all'altro mondo** (fam) bump off. **spedito** agg (veloce) quick; (corrente) fluent. **speditore, -trice** sm, sf sender; (comm) shipper. **spedizione** sf dispatch; (trasporto) shipment; (cosa spedita) consignment. **casa di spedizione** forwarding or shipping agents pl. **fare una spedizione** send a consignment. **spedizioniere** sm shipping or forwarding agent.

****spegnere** ['speɲere] v extinguish, put out; (con interruttore) switch or turn off; (sete) quench. **spegnersi** v go out; (motore) stall.

spelacchiato [spelak'kjato] agg (con pochi peli) mangy; (logoro) threadbare.

spellare [spel'lare] v skin; (escoriare) graze. **spellarsi** v peel. **spellatura** sf skinning; grazing; peeling.

spelonca [spe'lonka] sf hovel.

****spendere** ['spendere] v spend. **senza spender fatica** effortlessly. **spendere bene/male** use one's money wisely/unwisely. **spendereccio** agg extravagant.

spennacchiare [spennak'kjare] v also **spennare** pluck; (fig) fleece.

spensierato [spensje'rato] agg carefree. **spensierataggine** sf thoughtlessness; irresponsibility. **spensieratezza** sf lightheartedness.

spento ['spento] agg out, off; (fig) dull.

spenzolare [spendzo'lare] v dangle.

speranza [spe'rantsa] sf hope. **avere buone speranze** have high hopes. **avere una speranza** have a chance. **filo di speranza** sm glimmer of hope. **senza speranza** hopeless.

sperare [spe'rare] v hope; (aspettarsi) expect. **sperare (in) bene** hope for the best. **sperare in Dio** trust in God. **spero di no/sì** I hope not/so.

*   **sperdersi** [sper'dersi] v get lost. **sperduto** agg lost; (*fuori mano*) out-of-the-way; (*solo*) lonely.

spergiurare [sperdʒu'rare] v commit perjury, perjure oneself. **spergiuro** sm perjury; (*persona*) perjurer.

spericolato [speriko'lato] agg reckless.

sperimentare [sperimen'tare] v experiment (with); (*mettere alla prova*) try out, test; (*farne esperienza*) experience. **sperimentale** agg experimental.

sperma ['sperma] sm sperm.

sperone [spe'rone] sm spur; (*mar*) ram. **sperone di cavaliere** larkspur. **speronare** v ram.

sperperare [sperpe'rare] v squander. **sperpero** sm waste.

sperticato [sperti'kato] agg (*fig*) excessive.

spesa ['speza] sf expenditure; (*costo*) expense; (*acquisto*) purchase; (*compra*) shopping. **a spese di** at the expense of. **con poca spesa** cheaply; (*fig*) easily. **contro spese** on expense account. **far la spesa** go shopping. **non badare a spese** spare no expense. **senza spesa** free. **spese** sf pl cost sing, charges pl. **spese generali** overheads pl. **essere spesato** have one's expenses paid.

spesso ['spesso] agg thick. avv often, frequently. **spesse volte** very often, frequently. **spessore** sm thickness.

spettacolo [spet'takolo] sm show; (*rappresentazione*) performance; (*vista*) sight. **dare spettacolo di sè** make an exhibition of oneself. **spettacolo pomeridiano** matinée. **spettacoloso** agg spectacular.

spettare [spet'tare] v (*competere per dovere*) be up (to); (*appartenere per diritto*) be due (to); (*essere di pertinenza*) be the concern (of).

spettatore [spetta'tore], -**trice** sm, sf spectator; (*testimone*) witness. **spettatori** sm pl audience sing.

spettinare [spetti'nare] v ruffle the hair of. **spettinato** agg unkempt, dishevelled.

spettro ['spettro] sm ghost; (*fig*) spectrum.

spezie ['spetsje] sf pl spices pl.

spezzare [spet'tsare] v break; (*staccando*) break off; (*fare a pezzi*) break up; (*gastr*) cut up. **spezzatino** sm stew. **spezzettare** v chop (up). **spezzone incendiario** sm incendiary bomb.

spia ['spia] sf spy, informer; (*indizio*) sign; (*apertura*) spy-hole; (*tec*) warning light. **fare la spia** be a spy; (*polizia*) inform; (*riportare*) tell tales.

spiacciare [spjatt'ʃikare] v squash.

*   **spiacere** [spja'tʃere] v displease. **mi spiace . . .** I dislike . . . . **mi spiace di . . .** (*rammarico*) I'm sorry . . . . **se non ti spiace** if you don't mind. **spiacevole** agg unpleasant, disagreeable; (*increscioso*) regrettable.

spiaggia ['spjaddʒa] sf (*sea-*)shore, beach.

spianare [spja'nare] v level; (*render liscio*) smooth; (*radere al suolo*) flatten, raze (to the ground); (*fig*) iron out. **spianato** agg smooth. **spianatoia** sf pastry board. **spianatoio** sm rolling-pin. **a tutto spiano** flat out.

spiantare [spjan'tare] v uproot; (*rovinare*) ruin.

spiare [spi'are] v spy (on); (*aspettare*) look out for; explore.

spiazzo ['spjattso] sm open space; (*radura*) clearing.

spiccare [spik'kare] v pick; (*pronunciare distintamente*) spell out; (*dir*) issue; (*comm*) draw; (*risaltare*) stand out. **spiccare il volo** take off. **spiccato** agg distinct, marked; (*notevole*) striking. **spicco** sm prominence. **far spicco** catch the eye.

spicchio ['spikkjo] sm segment; (*aglio*) clove.

spicciare [spit'tʃare] v dispatch. **spicciarsi** v hurry up. **spicciativo** agg quick; (*brusco*) abrupt. **spiccio** agg swift. **alla spicciolata** in dribs and drabs. **spiccioli** sm pl (small) change sing. **spicciolo** agg small.

spiedo ['spjedo] sm spit. **spiedino** sm skewer.

spiegare [spje'gare] v (*distendere*) unfold; (*ali*) spread; (*vele*) unfurl; (*render chiaro*) explain. **spiegarsi** v (*capire*) understand; (*diventar comprensibile*) explain oneself, make oneself understood. **spieghiamoci!** let's get it straight! **spiegabile** agg explicable.

spiegazione [spjega'tsjone] sf explanation; (*ragione*) reason.

spiegazzare [spjegat'tsare] v crumple (up), crease.

spietato [spje'tato] agg (*senza pietà*) pitiless; (*accanito*) relentless.

spifferare [spiffe'rare] v blab, blurt out. **spiffero** sm (*fam*) draught.

spiga ['spiga] sf ear. **disegno a spiga** sm herringbone pattern.

spigliato [spi'ʎato] agg (free and) easy; (padrone di sè) self-possessed. **spigliatezza** sf ease.

spigola ['spigola] sf bass.

spigolare [spigo'lare] v glean. **spigolature** sf pl tit-bits pl.

spigolo ['spigolo] sm corner; edge.

spilla ['spilla] sf brooch. **spilla da cravatta** tie-pin.

spillare [spil'lare] v tap; (attingere) draw. **spillo** ['spillo] sm pin. **spillo di sicurezza** safety-pin.

spilluzzicare [spilluttsi'kare] v nibble.

spilorcio [spi'lortʃo], -a agg stingy. sm, sf miser. **spilorceria** sf meanness.

spina ['spina] sf (bot) thorn; (aculeo) sting; (riccio) quill; (elett) plug. **birra alla spina** sf draught beer. **spina di pesce** fishbone. **spina dorsale** backbone. **star sulle spine** be on tenterhooks. **spinare** v bone. **spinato** agg (pesce) filleted; (filo) barbed.

spinacio [spi'natʃo] sm (bot) spinach. **spinaci** sm pl (gastr) spinach sing.

*spingere ['spindʒere] v push; drive; (stimolare) urge; (premere) press.

spino ['spino] sm (bot) blackthorn, bramble. **spineto** sm bramble bush. **spinoso** agg prickly, thorny.

spinta ['spinta] sf push; pressure; (aiuto) (helping) hand; (stimolo) boost; (fis) thrust. **spinto** agg pushed; disposed; (fam) extremist. **spintone** sm hard push, shove; (raccomandazione) good word.

spionaggio [spio'naddʒo] sm espionage. **spione** sm (fam) tell-tale.

spiovente [spjo'vɛnte] agg (baffi) drooping; (spalle) stooping; (tetto) sloping.

spira ['spira] sf coil. **spirale** agg, sf spiral.

spiraglio [spi'raʎo] sm chink; (di luce, speranza) glimmer; (aria) breath of air).

spirare[1] [spi'rare] v (soffiare) blow; (emettere) give off or out; (emanare) be given off or out.

spirare[2] [spi'rare] v (morire) expire.

spirito ['spirito] sm spirit; (animo) mind; sense of humour. **bello spirito** wit. **condizioni di spirito** sm pl mood sing. **con spirito** wittily. **pieno di spirito** (vivace) lively; (arguto) witty.

spiritosaggine [spirito'zaddʒine] sf witticism.

spiritoso [spiri'tozo], -a agg witty. sm, sf funny person.

spirituale [spiritu'ale] agg spiritual. **spiritualismo** sm spiritualism. **spiritualista** s(m+f) spiritualist.

spiumare [spju'mare] v pluck.

spizzicare [spittsi'kare] v nibble. **a spizzico** or **spizzichi** in dribs and drabs.

*splendere ['splɛndere] v shine. **splendido** agg brilliant; (meraviglioso) splendid. **splendore** sm brilliance; splendour.

spodestare [spodes'tare] v (cacciare) oust; (privare di beni) dispossess.

spogliare [spo'ʎare] v strip; (svestire) undress; (esaminare) go through; sort out. **spogliarsi** v undress. **spogliarello** sm strip-tease. **spogliatoio** sm changing-room. **spoglie** sf pl (bottino) spoils pl; (mortali) mortal remains pl. **spoglio** agg (nudo) bare; (privo) devoid (of); (libero) free (from). **fare lo spoglio** (corrispondenza) sort out; (dati) extract; (voti) scrutinize.

spola ['spola] sf shuttle; (macchina da cucire) spool, bobbin. **far la spola** shuttle, ply. **spoletta** sf bobbin; (tec, mil) fuse.

spolmonarsi [spolmo'narsi] v shout oneself hoarse.

spolverare [spolve'rare] v dust. **spolverat(ur)a** sf dusting.

sponda ['sponda] sf (mare, lago) shore; (fiume) bank; (bordo) edge; (biliardo) cushion.

spontaneo [spon'taneo] agg spontaneous. **di mia spontanea volontà** of my own free will. **spontaneità** sf spontaneity.

spopolare [spopo'lare] v depopulate; (vuotare) empty; (aver successo) be a hit.

spora ['spora] sf spore.

sporadico [spo'radiko] agg sporadic.

sporco ['sporko] agg dirty; dishonest. **aver la coscienza sporca** have a guilty conscience. **sporcizia** sf dirt, filth; (fam) muck.

*sporgere ['spordʒere] v stick out, project, protrude. **sporgersi** v lean out. **sporgere querela contro sue. sporgente** agg jutting out; (dente) protruding; (occhio) bulging. **sporgenza** sf projection.

sport [sport] sm invar sport. **fare per sport** do for fun.

sporta ['sporta] sf (sacca) shopping-bag; (quantità) bagful. **una sporta di legnate** a good hiding. **un sacco e una sporta** a lot.

sportello [spor'tello] sm counter; (per biglietti) ticket office; (porta) door.

sportivo [spor'tivo] *agg* sports; (*interessato*) sporty, sporting; (*leale*) sportsmanlike, sporting. *sm* sportsman. **sportiva** *sf* sportswoman.

sposa ['spɔza] *sf* bride. **sposalizio** *sm* wedding. **sposare** *v* marry; (*fig*) wed. **sposarsi** *v* get married. **sposata** *sf* married woman. **sposato** *sm* married man. **sposino, -a** *sm*, *sf* newly-wed. **sposo** *sm* bridegroom.

spossare [spos'sare] *v* exhaust. **spossatezza** *sf* exhaustion; (*stanchezza*) weariness. **spossato** *agg* worn out, weary.

spossessare [sposses'sare] *v* dispossess.

spostare [spos'tare] *v* shift; (*rimuovere*) displace; (*turbare*) upset; transfer. **spostamento** *sm* shift; displacement; transfer. **spostato** [spos'tato], **-a** *agg* (*fuori posto*) out of place; (*fig*) unsettled. *sm*, *sf* misfit.

spranga ['spranga] *sf* crossbar; (*chiavistello*) bolt. **sprangare** *v* bolt.

sprazzo ['sprattso] *sm* flash.

sprecare [spre'kare] *v* waste. **è tempo/fiato sprecato** it is a waste of breath/time. **spreco** *sm* waste. **sprecone, -a** *sm*, *sf* spendthrift.

spregevole [spre'dʒevole] *agg* despicable. **spregiare** *v* despise, spurn. **spregiativo** *agg* disparaging; (*gramm*) pejorative.

spregiudicato [spredʒudi'kato], **-a** *agg* (*senza pregiudizi*) open-minded; (*senza scrupoli*) unscrupulous. *sm*, *sf* unscrupulous person. **spregiudicatezza** *sf* open-mindedness; unscrupulousness.

spremere ['spremere] *v* squeeze. **spremersi il cervello** rack one's brains. **spremilimoni** *sm* lemon squeezer. **spremuta** *sf* (*bevanda*) juice.

sprezzare [spret'tsare] *v* despise. **sprezzante** *agg* contemptuous. **sprezzo** *sm* scorn.

sprigionare [spridʒo'nare] *v* give off.

sprint [sprint] *sm invar* (*sport*) sprint; (*auto*) pick-up, *sf* sports car.

sprizzare [sprit'tsare] *v* (*acqua*) squirt; (*sangue*) spurt; (*fig*) burst with.

sprofondare [sprofon'dare] *v* collapse; (*affondare*) sink; (*lasciarsi sopraffare*) be overwhelmed (by). **sprofondarsi** *v* sink; (*fig*) immerse oneself. **sprofondamento** *sm* collapse. **sprofondato** *agg* (*fig*) immersed, engrossed.

spronare [spro'nare] *v* spur (on). **spronata** *sf* spur. **sprone** *sm* spur.

sproporzionato [sproportsjo'nato] *agg*

out of proportion; disproportionate. **sproporzione** *sf* lack of proportion.

sproposito [spro'pɔzito] *sm* blunder; (*strafalcione*) howler. **a sproposito** (*inopportunamente*) at the wrong time; (*fuori luogo*) in the wrong place. **commettere uno sproposito** do something silly. **costare uno sproposito** cost the earth. **spropositato** *agg* excessive.

sprovvisto [sprov'visto] *agg also* **sprovveduto** shorn (of); (*privo*) lacking (in). **alla sprovvista** unawares.

spruzzare [sprut'tsare] *v* spray; (*senza intenderlo*) splash. **spruzzata** *sf* sprinkling. **spruzzatore** *sm* sprinkler; (*profumi*) atomizer. **spruzzo** *sm* spray; (*schizzo*) spurt; splash.

spudorato [spudo'rato] *agg* shameless. **spudoratezza** *sf* shamelessness.

spugna ['spuɲa] *sf* sponge; (*tessuto*) towelling; (*fam*) boozer. **bere come una spugna** drink like a fish. **spugnatura** *sf* sponging down. **spugnoso** *agg* spongy.

spuma ['spuma] *sf* froth. **spumante** *sm* sparkling wine. **spumare** *v* (*bevande gassate*) fizz; (*vino*) sparkle. **spumare dalla rabbia** (*fam*) foam at the mouth. **spumeggiare** *v* froth. **spumoso** *agg* frothy.

spuntare [spun'tare] *v* (*germogliare*) sprout; (*apparire improvvisamente*) emerge; (*sorgere*) rise; (*fig*) overcome; (*capelli, ecc.*) trim. **spuntato** *agg* (*matita*) blunt; (*vino*) sour.

spuntino [spun'tino] *sm* snack.

spunto ['spunto] *sm* cue; idea; (*sport*) spurt. **prendere lo spunto da** start (off) from.

spuntone [spun'tone] *sm* spike.

spurgare [spur'gare] *v* clear out. **spurgarsi** *v* clear one's throat.

spurio ['spurjo] *agg* spurious.

sputacchiare [sputak'kjare] *v* splutter. **sputacchiera** *sf* spitoon.

sputare [spu'tare] *v* spit. **sputa fuori!** spit it out! **sputar sentenze** lecture. **sputar veleno** speak spitefully. **sputo** *sm* spit(tle), saliva; (*espettorato*) sputum.

squadernare [skwader'nare] *v* leaf through.

squadra¹ ['skwadra] *sf* (*strumento*) square. **a squadra** at right angles. **fuori squadra** crooked; (*fuori posto*) out of place; (*disordinato*) disorderly. **squadrare** *v* square; (*fig*) eye.

squadra² ['skwadra] *sf* (*mil*) section, squad; (*aero*) squadron; (*gruppo*) gang; (*sport*) team. **squadra mobile** flying squad. **squadriglia** *sf* band; (*mar*, *aero*) squadron.

squadro [skwadro] *sm* angel-fish.

squagliarsi [skwaʎˈʎarsi] *v* melt. **squagliar-sela** *v* sneak off.

squalificare [skwalifiˈkare] *v* disqualify. **squalifica** *sf* disqualification.

squallido ['skwallido] *agg* dismal; (*fig*) squalid. **squallore** *sm* dreariness, squalor.

squalo ['skwalo] *sm* dog-fish; (*pescecane*) shark.

squama ['skwama] *sf* scale. **squamare** *v* scale. **squamoso** *agg* scaly.

squarciare [skwarˈtʃare] *v* tear (to pieces), rend. **a squarciagola** at the top of one's voice. **squarcio** *sm* (*stoffa*) tear; (*ferita*) gash; (*fig*) passage.

squartare [skwarˈtare] *v* quarter. **squartatoio** *sm* cleaver.

squassare [skwasˈsare] *v* shake violently.

squattrinato [skwattriˈnato] *agg* penniless.

squilibrare [skwiliˈbrare] *v* unbalance. **squilibrarsi** *v* lose one's balance. **squilibrato** *agg* (mentally) unbalanced. **squilibrio** *sm* lack of equilibrium; (*econ*) imbalance; disproportion; (*mentale*) derangement.

squillare [skwilˈlare] *v* ring; (*tromba*) sound; (*voce*) be shrill. **squillo** *sm* ring; (*suono*) squeal; (*tromba*) sound. **ragazza squillo** *sf* call-girl.

squinternare [skwinterˈnare] *v* take to pieces; (*fig*) upset.

squisito [skwiˈzito] *agg* excellent; delicious; (*raffinato*) exquisite. **squisitezza** *sf* deliciousness; delicacy.

squittire [skwitˈtire] *v* (*uccelli*) chirp; (*topi*) squeak.

sradicare [sradiˈkare] *v* (*divellere*) uproot; (*fig*) root out, eradicate.

sregolato [sregoˈlato] *agg* (*smodato*) immoderate; (*scapestrato*) wild.

stabbio ['stabbjo] *sm* pen; (*porcile*) pigsty; (*letame*) dung.

stabile ['stabile] *agg* stable; (*che non oscilla*) steady; permanent; (*durevole*) lasting. **stabilimento** [stabiliˈmento] *sm* establishment; (*fabbrica*) factory, works; (*edificio*) building.

stabilire [stabiˈlire] *v* establish; decide. **stabilirsi** *v* settle. **stabilità** *sf* stability.

stabilito *agg* (*istituito*) established; (*fissato*) fixed; (*convenuto*) agreed. **stabilizzare** *v* stabilize. **stabilizzarsi** *v* settle. **stabilizzazione** *sf* stabilization.

staccare [stakˈkare] *v* (*togliere*) take off; (*separare*) detach; (*tagliando*) cut off; (*strappando*) pluck; (*sganciare*) unhook; (*risaltare*) stand out. **staccare il lavoro** (*fam*) knock off work. **staccarsi** *v* move away; (*venir via*) come off; separate. **staccato** *agg* detached; separate; (*musica*) staccato.

stadio ['stadjo] *sm* (*sport*) stadium; (*tec*, *fase*) stage.

staffa ['staffa] *sf* stirrup; (*mec*) bracket; (*calza*) heel. **perdere le staffe** (*fig*) lose one's temper. **staffetta** *sf* courier; (*sport*) relay(-race).

staffilare [staffiˈlare] *v* lash; (*fig*) lash out (at). **staffilata** *sf* lash; (*fig*) lashing criticism. **staffile** *sm* stirrup-strap; (*sferza*) lash.

stagione [staˈdʒone] *sf* season; (*condizioni atmosferiche*) weather. **fuori stagione** out of season; (*fig*) untimely. **stagionale** *agg* seasonal. **stagionare** *v* season; (*invecchiare*) age; mature. **stagionatura** *sf* ageing; maturing; seasoning.

stagno¹ ['staɲo] *sm* (*metallo*) tin. **stagnare** *v* tin; (*saldare*) solder; (*chiudere*) seal. **stagnola** *sf* tin foil.

stagno² ['staɲo] *sm* (*bacino d'acqua*) pool. *agg* (*a tenuta d'acqua*) watertight. **stagnare** *v* stagnate; (*sangue*) stanch; (*fermare*) stop.

stalagmite [stalagˈmite] *sf* stalagmite.

stalattite [stalatˈtite] *sf* stalactite.

stalla ['stalla] *sf* stable; (*bovini*) cow-shed; (*fig*) pigsty. **stallaggio** *sm* stabling. **stallone** *sm* stallion.

stallo ['stallo] *sm* seat; (*scacchi*) stalemate. **andare in stallo** (*aero*) stall.

stamattina [stamatˈtina] *avv* also **stamani** this morning.

stamberga [stamˈberga] *sf* hovel.

stambugio [stamˈbudʒo] *sm* cubby-hole.

stame ['stame] *sm* (*bot*) stamen; (*tessile*) fine yarn.

stamigna [staˈmiɲa] *sf* bunting.

stampa ['stampa] *sf* printing; (*giornali*) press; (*immagine*, *foto*) print. **errore di stampa** *sm* misprint. **stampe** *sf pl* (*posta*) printed matter *sing*. **stampaggio** (*foto*) printing; (*metallo*) forging; (*plastici*) moulding. **stampare** *v* print; publish;

(*con pressa*) press; forge; mould.
stampatello *sm* block letters *pl.* **stampato** *sm* printed matter; (*modulo*) form; (*disegno*) print. **stampatore, -trice** *sm, sf* printer.

stampella [stam'pɛlla] *sf* crutch.

stampiglia [stam'piʎa] *sf* stamp. **stampigliare** *v* stamp.

stampino [stam'pino] *sm* stencil; (*punzone*) punch.

stampo [stampo] *sm* mould; (*matrice*) die; (*fig*) kind, sort.

stanare [sta'nare] *v* drive out.

stancare [stan'kare] *v* tire; (*annoiare*) bore. **stancarsi** *v* get tired, tire. **stanchezza** *sf* tiredness; (*fiacchezza*) fatigue. **stanco** *agg* tired; bored.

standard ['standard] *sm invar* standard. **standardizzare** *v* standardize. **standardizzazione** *sf* standardization.

stanga ['stanga] *sf* bar. **stangare** *v* (*colpire*) thrash; (*bocciare*) fail; (*scuola*) give a bad mark; (*far pagare troppo*) rob. **stangata** *sf* blow.

stanotte [sta'nɔtte] *avv* tonight.

stante ['stante] *agg* a sè **stante** apart. **seduta stante** straight away. **prep** (*a causa di*) on account of.

stantio [stan'tio] *agg* stale.

stantuffo [stan'tuffo] *sm* piston; (*di pressa idraulica*) plunger.

stanza ['stantsa] *sf* room; (*poesia*) stanza. **stanza da bagno** bathroom. **stanza da pranzo** dining-room.

stanziare [stan'tsjare] *v* allocate; deliberate.

stappare [stap'pare] *v* uncork.

****stare** ['stare] *v* stay, remain; (*abitare*) live; (*essere*) be; (*vestiario*) suit; (*spettare*) be up to. **come stai?** how are you? **lasciar stare** leave alone. **non poter stare senza** be unable to do without. **stare a dieta** be on a diet. **stare in guardia** be on one's guard. **stare per** be about to. **sto bene** I am well. **sto male** I am not well.

starna ['starna] *sf* partridge.

starnutire [starnu'tire] *v* sneeze. **starnuto** *sm* sneeze.

stasera [sta'sera] *avv* this evening.

stasi ['stazi] *sf* standstill.

statale [sta'tale] *agg* state. **strada statale** *sf* trunk road. *s(m+f)* civil servant.

statica ['statika] *sf* statics. **statico** *agg* static; (*senza movimento*) motionless.

statista [sta'tista] *sm* statesman.

statistica [sta'tistika] *sf* statistics. **statistico** *agg* statistical.

stato ['stato] *sm* state; condition; (*posizione sociale*) status. **colpo di stato** *sm* coup d'état. **Stati Uniti** *sm pl* United States *pl.* **stato d'animo** mood. **ufficio di stato civile** *sm* register office. **statunitense** *s(m+f)*, *agg* American.

statua ['statua] *sf* statue. **statuario** *agg* statuary.

statura [sta'tura] *sf* (*altezza*) height; (*fig*) stature.

statuto [sta'tuto] *sm* statute; constitution. **statutario** statutory.

stavolta [sta'vɔlta] *avv* this time.

stazione [sta'tsjone] *sf* station; (*località di soggiorno*) resort. **stazionamento** *sm* parking. **stazionare** *v* stop; park. **stazionario** *agg* stationary.

stecca ['stekka] *sf* small stick; (*biliardo*) cue; (*persiane*) slat; (*sigarette*) carton; (*hockey*) stick. **steccare** *v* fence (in); (*sonare*) play a wrong note. **steccato** *sm* fence. **a stecchetto** (*senza soldi*) hard up; (*senza cibo*) on short rations. **stecchito** *agg* (*rinsecchito*) dried up; (*magrissimo*) skinny. **morto stecchito** stone dead. **stecco** *sm* dry twig. **steccone** *sm* post.

stella ['stella] *sf* star. **alle stelle** (*prezzi*) sky-high. **stella alpina** edelweiss. **stella cadente** *or* **filante** shooting star; (*di carta*) streamer. **stella di mare** starfish. **stellare** *agg* (*astron*) stellar; (*forma*) star-shaped; (*bot*) stellate. **stellato** *agg* starry; (*fig*) studded. **stelletta** (*mil*) star; (*fam*) pip.

stelo ['stelo] *sm* stem; (*fiore*) stalk; (*gambo di utensile*) shank.

stemma ['stɛmma] *sm* coat of arms.

stemp(e)rare [stemp(e)'rare] *v* dissolve.

stendardo [sten'dardo] *sm* standard.

****stendere** ['stɛndere] *v* (*allungare*) stretch (out); (*distendere*) spread (out); (*bucato*) hang out; (*contratto*) draw up. **stendersi** *v* stretch out.

stenodattilografia [stenodattilogra'fia] *sf* shorthand typing. **stenodattilografo, -a** *sm, sf* shorthand typist. **stenografare** *v* take down in shorthand. **stenografia** *sf* shorthand. **stenografo, -a** *sm, sf* stenographer.

stentare [sten'tare] *v* find it hard, have difficulty. **stentatezza** *sf* difficulty. **stentato** *agg* laboured; (*di crescita arrestata*) stunted; (*pieno di stenti*) hard.

stento *sm* hardship; difficulty. **a stento** barely.

steppa ['steppa] *sf* steppe.

sterco ['stɛrko] *sm* excrement; (*letame*) dung.

stereo ['stereo] *agg*, *sm* stereo.

stereofonico [stereo'fɔniko] *agg* stereophonic; (*fam*) stereo.

stereotipato [stereoti'pato] *agg* stereotyped; (*fisso*) frozen. **concezione stereotipata** *sf* stereotype.

sterile ['sterile] *agg* sterile; (*fig*) vain. **sterilire** *v* sterilize. **sterilità** *sf* sterility; (*fig*) uselessness. **sterilizzare** *v* sterilize. **sterilizzatore** *sm* sterilizer. **sterilizzazione** *sf* sterilization.

sterlina [ster'lina] *sf* pound (sterling).

sterminare [stermi'nare] *v* exterminate. **sterminato** *agg* boundless. **sterminio** *sm* extermination.

sterna ['stɛrna] *sf* tern.

sterno ['stɛrno] *sm* breastbone.

sterzo ['stertso] *sm* (*auto*) steering; (*bicicletta*) handlebars *pl*. **sterzare** *v* (*auto*) steer; (*fig*) swerve. **sterzata** *sf* steering; swerve. **fare una sterzata** make a sharp turn.

stesso ['stesso] *agg* same; (*proprio*) very; (*personificato*) itself; (*in persona*) personally; (*rafforzativo*, *riflessivo*) myself, yourself, etc.

stesura [ste'zura] *sf* drafting; draft.

stetoscopio [stetos'kɔpjo] *sm* stethoscope.

stia ['stia] *sf* chicken coop. **essere (pigiati) come in una stia** be cooped up.

stigma ['stigma] *sm* stigma. **stigmatizzare** *v* stigmatize.

stilare [sti'lare] *v* draw up.

stile ['stile] *sm* style; (*eleganza*) stylishness. **di stile** stylish. **in grande stile** in style. **stilista** *s(m+f)* stylist. **stilistico** *agg* stylistic. **stilizzare** *v* stylize.

stilla ['stilla] *sf* drop. **a stilla a stilla** drop by drop. **stillare** *v* (*trasudare*) ooze, exude; (*gocciolare*) drip. **stillarsi il cervello** rack one's brains. **stillicidio** *sm* constant trickle.

stilo ['stilo] *sm* (*per scrivere*) stylus; (*stadera*) beam. **stilografica** *sf* fountain-pen.

stima ['stima] *sf* (*buona opinione*) esteem, regard; (*giudizio*) estimation; (*valutazione*) estimate. **a mia stima** in my estimation. **aver stima di** hold in high

esteem. **con (la massima) stima** (*in lettere*) yours faithfully.

stimare [sti'mare] *v* estimate; (*apprezzare*) value, esteem; consider. **stimatore, -trice** *sm*, *sf* (*perito*) valuer; (*ammiratore*) admirer.

stimolare [stimo'lare] *v* stimulate; (*fig*) arouse; (*appetito*) whet. **stimolante** *sm* stimulant. **stimolatore cardiaco** *sm* pacemaker. **stimolazione** *sf* (*med*) stimulation; (*fig*) arousal. **stimolo** *sm* stimulus (*pl* -li).

stinco ['stinko] *sm* shin. **stincata** *sf* blow on the shin.

***stingere** ['stindʒere] *v* (*macchiare*) run; (*sbiadire*) fade.

stipare [sti'pare] *v* pack, cram.

stipendio [sti'pɛndjo] *sm* salary. **stipendio arretrato** back pay.

stipite ['stipite] *sm* doorpost.

stipulare [stipu'lare] *v* stipulate. **stipulazione** *sf* stipulation.

stiracchiare [stirak'kjare] *v* stretch; (*lesinare*) skimp. **stiracchiare sul prezzo** haggle. **stiracchiamento** *sm* stretching; haggling. **stiracchiatura** *sf* distortion.

stirare [sti'rare] *v* (*col ferro*) iron, press. **stirarsi** *v* stretch. **stiro** *sm* ironing; pressing. **ferro da stiro** *sm* iron. **tavolo da stiro** *sm* ironing-board.

stirpe ['stirpe] *sf* (*origine*) descent, extraction; (*razza*) race; family; (*discendenti*) offspring.

stitico ['stitiko] *agg* constipated; (*fig*) stingy. **stitichezza** *sf* constipation.

stiva ['stiva] *sf* hold. **stivaggio** *sm* stowage.

stivale [sti'vale] *sm* boot. **lustrar gli stivali a** (*fig*) lick the boots of. **rompere gli stivali a** (*fig*) pester.

stivaletto [stiva'letto] *sm* bootee.

stizza ['stittsa] *sf* anger. **avere** *or* **provare stizza per** be angry about. **stizzire** *v* anger. **stizzirsi** *v* get angry. **stizzito** *agg* angry. **stizzoso** *agg* irritable.

stoccafisso [stokka'fisso] *sm* dried cod.

stoccata [stok'kata] *sf* stab; (*scherma*) thrust; (*battuta*) gibe. **stocco** *sm* rapier.

Stoccolma [stok'kolma] *sf* Stockholm.

stoffa ['stɔffa] *sf* fabric, material; (*dote*) makings *pl*. **ha della stoffa** he has what it takes.

stoico ['stɔiko], **-a** *agg* stoical. *sm*, *sf* stoic.

stoino [sto'ino] *sm* doormat.

stola ['stɔla] *sf* stole.

stolto ['stolto], -a *agg* foolish. *sm, sf* fool.

stoltezza *sf* foolishness; (*azione*) foolish action; (*parole*) nonsense.

stomaco ['stɔmako] *sm* stomach; (*fam*) tummy; (*fam: coraggio*) guts. **mal di stomaco** *sm* stomach-ache. **... mi sta** *or* **rimane sullo stomaco** I cannot stomach .... **stomacare** *v* nauseate. **stomachevole** *agg* revolting.

stonare [sto'nare] *v* (*cantare*) sing out of tune; (*sonare*) play out of tune; (*contrastare*) clash. **stonata** *sf* wrong note. **stonato** *agg* out of tune; clashing; (*turbato*) upset.

stoppa ['stoppa] *sf* tow. **stoppare** *v* (*otturare*) block; (*sport*) stop. **stoppaccio** *sm* wad. **stoppie** *sf pl* stubble *sing*. **stoppino** *sm* wick.

***storcere** [stor'tfere] *v* twist; (*piegare*) bend. **storcersi il naso** turn up one's nose. **storcersi la bocca** make a wry face. **storcersi per il dolore** writhe in pain. **storcimento** *sm* twisting; wrench.

stordire [stor'dire] *v* stun; (*rumore*) deafen. **stordimento** *sm* (*stato d'animo*) bewilderment. **stordito** *agg* stunned; bewildered; (*distratto*) scatter-brained.

storia ['stɔrja] *sf* history; (*racconto*) story, tale; (*frottola*) fib, lie; (*faccenda*) business. **la solita storia** the same old story. **libro di storia** history book. **storie** *sf pl* (*trambusto*) fuss *sing*. **storiella** *sf* little story; (*barzelletta*) joke; (*fandonia*) fib.

storico ['stɔriko], -a *agg* (*della storia*) historical; (*famoso*) historic. *sm, sf* historian.

storione [sto'rjone] *sm* sturgeon.

stormo ['stormo] *sm* (*uccelli*) flock; (*cani*) pack; (*persone*) crowd; (*fig*) mess. **sonare a stormo** sound the alarm.

stornare [stor'nare] *v* (*allontanare*) avert; dissuade; transfer; annul. **storno** *sm* transfer.

stornello [stor'nɛllo] *sm also* **storno** (*uccello*) starling.

storno ['storno] *agg* dapple-grey.

storpio ['stɔrpjo], -a *agg* crippled. *sm, sf* cripple. **storpiare** *v* cripple; mispronounce.

storto ['storto] *agg* crooked; (*sbagliato*) wrong. **aver gli occhi storti** squint. **aver le gambe storte** be bandy-legged. **storta** *sf* twist, sprain; (*recipiente*) retort. **prendersi una storta alla caviglia** twist one's ankle.

stoviglie [sto'viʎe] *sf pl* crockery *sing*. **lavar le stoviglie** wash the dishes, wash up.

strabico ['strabiko] *agg* cross-eyed. **strabismo** *sm* squint. **essere affetto da strabismo** have a squint.

strabiliante [strabi'ʎante] *agg* amazing.

straboccare [strabok'kare] *v* overflow. **straboccchevole** *agg* excessive.

stracarico [stra'kariko] *agg, m pl* -**chi** overloaded; (*fig*) overburdened.

stracciare [strat'tfare] *v* tear; (*facendo a pezzi*) tear up.

straccio ['strattfo] *sm* rag. *agg* waste. **straccione, -a** *sm, sf* ragamuffin; beggar.

stracco ['strakko] (*fam*) *agg* worn out, done in. **stracco morto** dead beat.

stracotto [stra'kotto] *agg* overcooked. **cotto e stracotto** overdone. *sm* (*gastr*) stew, casserole.

strada ['strada] *sf* road, street; (*percorso*) way; (*itinerario*) route; (*cammino*) journey; (*varco*) path. **a mezza strada** halfway. **che strada fai?** which way are you going? **far strada a qualcuno** show someone the way. **farsi strada** (*aprirsi un passaggio*) clear a way for oneself; (*ottener successo*) do well for oneself. **fuori strada** off the road; (*fig*) on the wrong track. **lungo** *or* **per la strada** on the way. **strada facendo** on the way. **stradale** *agg* road. **codice stradale** *sm* highway code. **lavori stradali** *sm pl* roadworks *pl*.

strafalcione [strafal'tfone] *sm* blunder.

***strafare** [stra'fare] *v* overdo it.

straforo [stra'foro] *sm* **di straforo** indirectly; (*di nascosto*) on the quiet; (*di sfuggita*) in passing.

strage ['stradʒe] *sf* slaughter; (*distruzione*) havoc; (*fam*) mass.

stragrande [stra'grande] *agg* huge. **stragrande maggioranza** *sf* great majority.

stralciare [stral'tfare] *v* take out; (*dedurre*) deduct; (*mettere in liquidazione*) wind up. **stralcio** *sm* removal; extract; liquidation. **vendere a stralcio** sell off.

stralunare [stralu'nare] *v* roll one's eyes. **stralunato** *agg* (*fig*) distraught.

stramazzare [stramat'tsare] *v* fall to the ground.

strambo ['strambo] *agg* odd; eccentric. **stramberia** *sf* oddity; eccentricity.

strampalato [strampa'lato] *agg* weird.

strangolare [strango'lare] *v* strangle. **strangolarsi** *v* choke. **strangolamento** *sm* strangulation.

straniero [stra'njɛro], -**a** *agg* foreign. *sm, sf* foreigner; (*termine burocratico*) alien.

strano ['strano] *agg* strange, odd. *sm* strange *or* odd thing. **strano a dirsi** oddly enough. **stranezza** *sf* peculiarity; (*atteggiamento*) odd behaviour.

straordinario [straordi'narjo] *agg* extraordinary; (*insolito*) unusual; special. **lavoro straordinario** *sm* overtime. *sm* unusual thing; overtime.

strapagare [strapa'gare] *v* (*fam*) pay through the nose.

strapazzare [strapat'tsare] *v* wear out; (*trattar male*) ill-treat. **uova strapazzate** *sf pl* scrambled eggs *pl*. **strapazzata** *sf* (*sgridata*) dressing-down; (*faticata*) strain. **strapazzo** *sm* strain; ill-treatment. **vestiti da strapazzo** *sm pl* working clothes *pl*.

strapieno [stra'pjɛno] *agg* full up.

strapiombare [strapjom'bare] *v* overhang, jut out. **a strapiombo** sheer, overhanging.

strappare [strap'pare] *v* snatch; (*portar via*) pull off *or* out; (*rompendo*) tear (off *or* out); (*in più pezzi*) tear up. **strappata** *sf* tug. **strappo** *sm* pull, tug; (*strattone*) jerk; tear. **strappo muscolare** pulled *or* torn muscle.

straripare [strari'pare] *v* overflow. **straripamento** *sm* overflowing.

strascicare [straʃʃi'kare] *v* trail; (*con fatica*) drag; (*fig*) drag out; (*pronuncia*) drawl. **strascico** *sm, pl* -**chi** (*fig*) aftereffect; (*vestito*) train.

strascinare [straʃʃi'nare] *v* drag along.

stratagemma [strata'dʒɛmma] *sm* stragem; (*fig*) trick.

strategia [strate'dʒia] *sf* strategy. **strategico** *agg* strategic. **stratego**, -**a** *sm, sf* strategist.

strato ['strato] *sm* layer; (*vernice*) coat; (*geol, classe*) stratum (*pl* -**a**). **stratificato** *agg* stratified.

strattone [strat'tone] *sm* pull, jerk. **a strattoni** jerkily.

stravagante [strava'gante] *agg* extravagant. **stravaganza** *sf* extravagance.

stravecchio [stra'vɛkkjo] *agg* very old.

*****stravincere** [stra'vintʃere] *v* win hands down; (*battere*) beat hollow.

straviziare [stravi'tsjare] *v* over-indulge. **stravizio** *sm* over-indulgence.

*****stravolgere** [stra'vɔldʒere] *v* twist; (*fig*) affect deeply. **stravolgere gli occhi** roll one's eyes. **stravolgimento** *sm* twisting; contortion. **stravolto** *agg* twisted; (*fig*) deeply upset.

straziare [stra'tsjare] *v* torture, torment. **straziare il cuore a qualcuno** break someone's heart. **cuore straziato** *sm* broken heart. **strazio** *sm* torment, agony. **far strazio di** (*fig*) play havoc with.

strega ['strega] *sf* witch. **stregare** *v* bewitch. **stregone** *sm* wizard; (*mago*) sorcerer; (*popoli primitivi*) witch-doctor. **stregoneria** *sf* witchcraft; sorcery. **fare stregonerie** cast spells.

stregua [stre'gwa] *sf* **alla stregua di** in the same way as. **a questa stregua** at this rate.

stremato [stre'mato] *agg* exhausted.

stremo ['strɛmo] *sm* limit.

strenna ['strɛnna] *sf* gift.

strenuo ['strɛnuo] *agg* valiant; (*fig*) untiring.

strepitare [strepi'tare] *v* make a din; (*gridando*) shout. **strepito** *sm* clamour, uproar. **fare strepito** cause a stir. **strepitoso** *agg* noisy; (*fragoroso*) resounding; (*fig*) tremendous.

streptococco [strepto'kɔkko] *sm* streptococcus. **streptomicina** *sf* streptomycin.

stretta ['stretta] *sf* hold; (*abbraccio*) embrace; (*presa*) grip; critical point; (*situazione difficile*) predicament. **essere** *or* **trovarsi alle strette** be in a tight corner. **stretta alla gola** lump in the throat. **stretta di mano** handshake.

stretto ['stretto] *agg* narrow; (*vestiario*) tight; (*rigoroso*) strict; (*denti, pugni*) clenched. *sm* strait. **strettoia** *sf* (*strada*) narrowing of the road; (*fig*) tight spot.

striato [stri'ato] *agg* striped.

stricnina [strik'nina] *sf* strychnine.

stridere ['stridere] *v* (*stridare*) shriek, screech; (*insetti*) chirp; (*cigolare*) squeak; (*fig*) clash. **stridente** *agg* strident; clashing. **strido** *sm, pl* -**a** *f* shriek, screech: squeak; chirp.

strigliata [stri'ʎata] *sf* dressing-down.

strillare [stril'lare] *v* scream; (*parlare ad alta voce*) shout. **strillo** *sm* scream. **strillone** *sm* news-vendor.

striminzito [strimin'tsito] *agg* skimpy; (*magro*) skinny.

strimpellare [strimpel'lare] v strum.

strinare [stri'nare] v scorch.

stringa ['stringa] sf lace. **stringare** v lace (up); (fig) condense.

*stringere ['strindʒere] v (avvicinare) squeeze or press (together); (serrare) clasp, clutch; (vestiario) pinch; (concludere) make; (denti, pugni) clench. **il tempo stringe** time is getting short. **stringere i tempi** speed things up; (musica) quicken the tempo. **stringere la cinghia** (fig) tighten one's belt. **stringere la mano** a shake hands with. **stringere un'amicizia** strike up a friendship. **stringi stringi** when all is said and done.

striscia ['striʃa] sf strip; (riga larga) stripe; (traccia) streak. **a strisce** striped. **strisce pedonali** sf pl zebra crossing sing.

strisciare v creep, crawl; (sfiorando) slide; (sfiorare) graze. **strisciare i piedi** drag one's feet. **colpire di striscio** graze. **striscione** sm banner.

stritolare [strito'lare] v crush.

strizzare [strit'tsare] v wring out; (spremere) squeeze. **strizzar l'occhio** wink. **strizzata** sf squeeze; wink.

strofinare [strofi'nare] v rub. **strofinaccio** sm rag. **strofinata** sf quick rub. **strofinio** sm prolonged rubbing.

strombazzare [strombat'tsare] v shout from the roof-tops. **strombazzare i propri meriti** blow one's own trumpet.

strombettare [strombet'tare] v blare; (auto) blow the horn.

stroncare [stron'kare] v break off; (tagliando) cut off; (fig) cut short; (criticare) slate. **stroncatura** sf slating.

stronzo ['strontso] sm (volg) turd; (fig) idiot.

stropicciare [stropit'tʃare] v rub. **stropicciarsene** v (fam) not care a damn.

strozzare [strot'tsare] v strangle, choke; (med) strangulate. **strozzatura** sf narrowing; (occlusione) bottle-neck; strangling. **strozzino, -a** sm, sf usurer.

*struggere [strud'dʒere] v melt; (fig) eat up. **struggersi** v be consumed.

strumento [stru'mento] sm instrument; (arnese) tool. **strumento ad arco** stringed instrument. **strumento a fiato** woodwind instrument. **strumentale** agg instrumental. **strumentare** v orchestrate.

strusciare [stru'ʃare] v scrape.

strutto ['strutto] sm lard.

struttura [strut'tura] sf structure. **strutturale** agg structural. **strutturare** v structure. **strutturazione** sf organization.

struzzo ['struttso] sm ostrich. **fare lo struzzo** bury one's head in the sand.

stuccare[1] [stuk'kare] v plaster; (decorare) stucco. **stuccatore** sm plasterer; stucco-worker. **stucco** sm plaster; (per finestre) putty; (arte) stucco. **rimaner di stucco** be dumbfounded.

stuccare[2] [stuk'kare] v (nauseare) make sick; (annoiare) bore. **stucchevole** agg sickly; boring. **stucco** agg sick (of).

studente [stu'dente], **-essa** sm, sf student. **studentesco** agg (di scuola) school; university.

studiare [stu'djare] v study; (cercar di trovare) try and find. **studiare a memoria** learn by heart. **studiato** agg studied; affected.

studio ['studjo] sm study; (progetto) plan; (di avvocato) office; (di medico) surgery; (di artista, fotografo, ecc.) studio. **allo studio** under consideration. **fare gli studi** study.

studioso [stu'djozo], **-a** agg studious. sm, sf scholar.

stufa ['stufa] sf stove, heater. **stufare** v (gastr) stew; (fam: annoiare) bore. **stufarsi di** get sick and tired of. **stufato** sm stew. **stufo** agg fed up (with).

stuoia [stu'ɔja] sf mat. **stuoino** sm doormat.

stuolo ['stwɔlo] sm crowd.

*stupefare [stupe'fare] v astound. **stupefacente** sm drug, narcotic. **stupefatto** agg astonished, amazed.

stupendo [stu'pendo] agg stupendous.

stupido ['stupido] agg stupid; (sciocco) foolish. **stupidaggine** sf stupidity; (atto) foolish thing; (parole) nonsense; (inezia) trifle. **dir stupidaggini** talk nonsense. **stupidità** sf stupidity.

stupire [stu'pire] v amaze, astonish. **stupirsi** v be amazed or astonished (at). **stupore** sm astonishment, amazement; (med) stupor.

stuprare [stu'prare] v rape. **stupro** sm rape.

sturare [stu'rare] v uncork. **sturabottiglie** sm invar corkscrew. **sturalavandini** sm invar plunger.

stuzzicare [stuttsi'kare] v prod; (*molestare*) annoy; (*punzecchiare*) tease; (*stimolare*) excite. **stuzzicadenti** sm invar toothpick. **stuzzicar l'appetito** whet the appetite. **stuzzicante** agg exciting; appetizing.

su [su] prep on; (*senza contatto*) over; (*più in alto di*) above; (*vicino*) by; (*verso*) towards; (*intorno a, circa*) about; (*oltre*) after. **dare su** look out over. **novanta volte su cento** (*fig*) nine times out of ten. avv (*in alto*) up; (*indosso*) on; (*al piano superiore*) upstairs. **avercela su con** (*fam*) be cross with. **in su** up; (*età, numero*) upwards. **su per giù** roughly. inter come on!

subacqueo [su'bakkweo] agg underwater.

subaffittare [subaffit'tare] v sublet. **dare in subaffitto** sublet.

subalterno [subal'terno], **-a** s, agg subordinate.

subappaltare [subappal'tare] v subcontract. **subappalto** sm subcontract.

subbia ['subbja] sf chisel.

subbio ['subbjo] sm beam.

subbuglio [sub'buʎo] sm turmoil; confusion.

subconscio [sub'kɔnʃo] sm, agg subconscious.

subdolo ['subdolo] agg underhand.

subentrare [suben'trare] v take the place of; succeed.

subire [su'bire] v suffer; (*sottoporsi a*) undergo.

subissare [subis'sare] v (*fig*) overwhelm. **subisso** sm (*fam*) load; (*rovina*) ruin.

subito ['subito] avv at once, immediately. **subito prima** just before. **subitaneità** sf suddenness. **subitaneo** agg sudden.

sublimare [subli'mare] v sublimate. **sublimato** sm sublimate. **sublimazione** sf sublimation.

sublime [sub'lime] agg, sm sublime.

subnormale [subnor'male] agg, sm subnormal.

subodorare [subodo'rare] v **subodorare un inganno** smell a rat.

subordinare [subordi'nare] v subordinate. **subordinato**, **-a** agg, s subordinate. **subordinazione** sf subordination.

subornare [subor'nare] v suborn. **subornazione** sf subornation.

suburbano [subur'bano] agg suburban.

*succedere [sut'tʃedere] v follow; succeed; (*capitare*) happen. **cosa sta succedendo?** what is happening? **cosa ti succede?** what is the matter with you? **sono cose che succedono** these things will happen.

successione [suttʃes'sjone] sf succession. **successione delle colture** crop rotation. **tasse di successione** sf pl death duties pl. **successivamente** avv subsequently. **successivo** agg (*seguente*) following; (*uno dopo l'altro*) consecutive. **successore** sm successor.

successo [sut'tʃɛsso] sm success. **aver cattivo successo** be unsuccessful. **aver successo** be successful.

succhiare [suk'kjare] v suck. **succhietto** or **succhiotto** sm dummy. **succhione** sm sucker.

succhiello [suk'kjɛllo] sm gimlet.

succinto [sut'tʃinto] agg scanty; (*fig*) succinct.

succitato [suttʃi'tato] agg above-mentioned.

succo ['sukko] sm juice; (*fig*) essence, gist. **succoso** agg juicy; (*fig*) meaty. **succulento** agg succulent, juicy; (*pasto*) tasty.

succube ['sukkube] s(m+f) slave.

succursale [sukkur'sale] sf branch.

sud [sud] sm south. **abitante del sud** s(m+f) southerner. **al sud** (*stato*) in the south; (*moto*) to the south. **del sud** south, southern. **Sudafrica** sf South Africa. **sudafricano**, **-a** s, agg South African. **Sudamerica** sf South America. **sudamericano**, **-a** s, agg South American.

sudare [su'dare] v sweat, perspire; (*lavorar molto*) toil. **sudar freddo** be in a cold sweat. **sudata** sf sweat. **sudaticcio** agg sweaty.

suddetto [sud'detto] agg above-mentioned.

suddito ['suddito], **-a** sm, sf subject.

*suddividere [suddi'videre] v subdivide, divide. **suddivisione** sf division, subdivision.

sud-est [sud'ɛst] sm south-east. **del sud-est** south-east(ern).

sudicio ['suditʃo] agg dirty; (*molto sporco*) filthy. sm invar filth. **sudiciume** sm filth.

sudore [su'dore] sm sweat, perspiration.

sud-ovest [sud'ɔvest] sm south-west. **del sud-ovest** south-west(ern).

sufficiente [suffi'tʃɛnte] agg enough;

(adeguato) sufficient; presumptuous. **sufficiente a se stesso** self-sufficient. *sm* enough. **avere il sufficiente per vivere** have enough to live on. **sufficienza** *sf* sufficiency. **a sufficienza** more than enough.

suffisso [suf'fisso] *sm* suffix.

suffragio [suf'fradʒo] *sm* suffrage. **suffragetta** *sf* suffragette.

suffumicare [suffumi'kare] *v* fumigate. **suffumicazione** *sf* fumigation.

suga ['suga] *agg* **carta suga** *or* **sugante** *sf* blotting paper.

suggello [sud'dʒɛllo] *sm* seal. **suggellare** *v* seal.

suggerire [suddʒe'rire] *v* suggest; *(consigliare)* advise; *(richiamare)* bring to mind; *(teatro)* prompt. **suggerimento** *sm* suggestion; piece of advice. **suggeritore, -trice** *sm, sf* prompter.

suggestione [suddʒes'tjone] *sf* suggestion; impression; *(fascino)* charm. **suggestionabile** *agg* easily influenced, impressionable. **suggestionabilità** *sf* suggestibility. **suggestionare** *v* influence; *(persuadere)* induce. **suggestivo** *agg* suggestive; evocative. **domanda suggestiva** *sf* leading question.

sughero ['sugero] *sm* cork.

sugli ['suʎi] *prep + art* **su gli**.

sugna ['suɲa] *sf* pork fat.

sugo ['sugo] *sm* *(succo)* juice; *(salsa)* sauce; *(fig)* (main) point. **senza sugo** *(fig)* pointless. **sugoso** *agg* juicy; *(fig)* meaty.

sui ['sui] *prep + art* **su i**.

suicida [sui'tʃida] *agg* suicidal. *s(m+f)* suicide. **suicidarsi** *v* commit suicide. **suicidio** *sm* suicide.

suino [su'ino] *sm* pig, swine. *agg* pig. **carne suina** *sf* pork.

sul [sul] *prep + art* **su il**.

sulfureo [sul'fureo] *agg* sulphurous.

sull' [sull] *prep + art* **su l'**.

sulla ['sulla] *prep + art* **su la**.

sulle ['sulle] *prep + art* **su le**.

sullo ['sullo] *prep + art* **su lo**.

sultano [sul'tano] *sm* sultan. **(uva) sultanina** *sf* sultana.

sunto ['sunto] *sm* summary. **sunteggiare** *v* *also* **fare il sunto** sum up, summarize.

suo ['suo], *m pl* **suoi** *agg* *(uomo)* his; *(donna)* her; *(cosa, animale)* its; *(riflessivo)* one's. *pron* his; hers. **a ciascuno il suo** to each his own.

suocera ['swɔtʃera] *sf* mother-in-law;

(spreg) battle-axe. **suocero** *sm* father-in-law.

suola ['swɔla] *sf* sole. **suolare** *v* *(mettere la suola)* sole.

suolo ['swɔlo] *sm* ground; *(terreno)* soil.

suonare [swo'nare] *V* **sonare**.

suono ['swɔno] *sm* sound; tone. **suono falso** discord; *(fig)* false ring.

suora ['swɔra] *sf* nun, sister.

super ['super] *agg* *(benzina)* four-star.

superare [supe'rare] *v* *(dimensione, quantità)* exceed; *(oltrepassare)* go beyond, surpass; *(di passaggio)* pass, overtake; *(sostenere)* get over *or* through. **superato** *agg* *(antiquato)* old-fashioned; *(non più valido)* obsolete.

superbo [su'pɛrbo] *agg* haughty; *(fiero)* proud; *(fig)* magnificent, superb. **superbia** *sf* haughtiness. **senza superbia** modestly.

supercongelato [superkondʒe'lato] *agg* deep-frozen.

superficie [super'fitʃe] *sf* surface; area. **alla superficie** on the surface. **superficiale** *agg* superficial; *(geom)* plane. **tensione superficiale** *sf* surface tension.

superfluo [su'pɛrfluo] *agg* *(eccessivo)* superfluous; *(inutile)* unnecessary. *sm* surplus.

superiore [supe'rjore] *agg* *(più in alto)* upper; *(maggiore)* higher; *(fig)* superior; *(di grado)* senior; advanced. **superiore alla media** above average. **superiorità** *sf* superiority.

superlativo [superla'tivo] *sm, agg* superlative.

supermercato [supermer'kato] *sm* supermarket.

supero ['supero] *sm* surplus.

supersonico [super'sɔniko] *agg* supersonic.

superstite [su'pɛrstite] *agg* surviving. *s(m+f)* survivor.

superstizione [supersti'tsjone] *sf* superstition. **superstizioso** *agg* superstitious.

superuomo [super'wɔmo] *sm* superman.

supervisione [supervi'zjone] *sf* supervision. **supervisore** *sm* supervisor.

supino [su'pino] *agg* supine. **giacere supino** lie on one's back.

suppellettili [suppel'lettili] *sf pl* furnishings *pl*; *(di casa)* household goods *pl*.

suppergiù [supper'dʒu] *avv* roughly, more or less.

supplemento [supple'mento] *sm* supplement; (*prezzo*) additional charge; (*biglietto*) excess fare. **supplementare** *agg* additional, extra; (*econ, mat*) supplementary.

supplicare [suppli'kare] *v* implore. **supplica** *sf* plea. **in atto di supplica** imploringly. **supplicante** *s(m+f)* supplicant. **supplichevole** *agg* imploring.

supplire [sup'plire] *v* make up for; (*fare le veci*) stand in for. **supplente** *s(m+f)* supply teacher.

supplizio [sup'plitsjo] *sm* torture; (*pena di morte*) capital punishment. **suppliziare** *v* torture.

*supporre [sup'porre] *v* suppose; imagine. **supposizione** *sf* supposition. **supposto che** assuming that, supposing.

supporto [sup'porto] *sm* support; (*mec*) bearing; (*sostegno*) stand.

supposta [sup'posta] *sf* suppository.

suppurare [suppu'rare] *v* fester. **suppurazione** *sf* festering.

supremo [su'premo] *agg* supreme; (*massimo*) highest. **supremazia** *sf* supremacy.

surgelare [surdʒe'lare] *v* freeze. **surgelato** *sm* frozen food.

surreale [surre'ale] *agg* unreal. **surrealismo** *sm* surrealism. **surrealista** *s(m+f)*, *agg* surrealist.

surriscaldare [surriskal'dare] *v* overheat. **surriscaldamento** *sm* overheating.

surrogare [surro'gare] *v* substitute. **surrogato** *sm*, *agg* substitute. **surrogazione** *sf* surrogation.

suscettibile [suʃet'tibile] *agg* capable (of), susceptible; (*facile a risentirsi*) touchy. **suscettibilità** *sf* susceptibility. **offendere la suscettibilità di qualcuno** hurt someone's feelings.

suscitare [suʃi'tare] *v* provoke, give rise to.

susina [su'zina] *sf* plum, damson. **susino** *sm* plum-tree, damson-tree.

susseguirsi [susse'gwirsi] *v* follow (each other). **susseguente** *agg* following, subsequent.

sussidiare [sussi'djare] *v* subsidize. **sussidiario** *agg* subsidiary. **sussidio** *sm* aid; (*di denaro*) subsidy.

sussistere [sus'sistere] *v* exist; (*esser fondato*) subsist. **sussistenza** *sf* subsistence; (*mil*) catering.

sussultare [sussul'tare] *v* (give a) start. **far sussultare** startle. **sussulto** *sm* start.

sussurrare [sussur'rare] *v* murmur; (*dire a bassa voce*) whisper. **sussurro** *sm* murmur; whisper.

sutura [su'tura] *sf* suture. **suturare** *v* suture.

suvvia [suv'via] *inter* come on!

svago ['zvago] *sm* diversion; (*divertimento*) amusement. **svagare** *v* distract. **svagarsi** *v* amuse oneself. **svagatezza** *sf* absent-mindedness. **svagato** *agg* absent-minded.

svaligiare [zvali'dʒare] *v* ransack. **svaligiatore**, **-trice** *sm*, *sf* burglar.

svalutare [zvalu'tare] *v* devalue. **svalutazione** *sf* devaluation.

svanire [zva'nire] *v* vanish; (*fig*) fade away; (*esaurirsi*) lose strength. **svanito** *agg* (*odore*) evaporated; (*mente*) feeble-minded.

svantaggio [zvan'taddʒo] *sm* disadvantage; (*pregiudizio*) drawback; (*danno*) detriment. **svantaggiato** *agg* handicapped. **svantaggioso** *agg* disadvantageous; detrimental.

svariare [zva'rjare] *v* vary; diversify. **svariato** *agg* various.

svasato [zva'zato] *v* flared. **svasatura** *sf* flare.

svastica ['zvastika] *sf* swastika.

svecchiare [zvek'kjare] *v* renew.

svedese [zve'deze] *agg* Swedish. *sm* (*lingua*) Swedish; (*fiammifero*) safety match. *s(m+f)* (*persona*) Swede.

svegliare [zve'ʎare] *v* wake up; (*fig*) arouse. **svegliarsi** *v* wake up. **sveglia** *sf* call; (*mil*) reveille; (*orologio*) alarm-clock. **sveglio** *agg* awake; (*fig*) quick (-witted).

svelare [zve'lare] *v* reveal.

svelto ['zvɛlto] *agg* quick; intelligent; (*slanciato*) slim. **svelto di mano** light-fingered. **sveltezza** *sf* quickness; (*rapidità*) speed; slimness. **sveltire** *v* quicken; (*render disinvolto*) smarten *or* liven up; make (more) slender.

svendere ['zvendere] *v* sell off. **svendita** *sf* sale.

*svenire [zve'nire] *v* faint. **svenevole** *agg* mawkish. **svenimento** *sm* fainting fit.

sventare [zven'tare] *v* foil. **sventatezza** *sf* thoughtlessness. **sventato** *agg* thoughtless.

sventola ['zventola] *sf* fan; (*pugilato*) hook; (*schiaffo*) slap. **sventolare** *v* flutter; (*arieggiare*) air.

T

sventrare [zven'trare] v rip open; (*animale*) disembowel; (*fig*) demolish. **sventramento** sm demolition.

sventura [zven'tura] sf misfortune; (*mala sorte*) bad luck. **per colmo di sventura** to crown it all. **per mia sventura** unluckily for me. **sventurato** agg unlucky.

svergognare [zvergo'ɲare] v (put to) shame. **svergognatezza** sf impudence. **svergognato, -a** sm, sf shameless or impudent person.

svernare [zver'nare] v winter.

sverza ['zvertsa] sf splinter. **sverzare** v splinter.

svestire [zves'tire] v undress.

Svezia ['zvetsja] sf Sweden.

svezzare [zvet'tsare] v wean. **svezzamento** sm weaning.

sviare [zvi'are] v divert; (*fig*) lead astray. **sviare il discorso** change the subject. **sviamento** sm diversion. **sviato** agg misguided.

svignarsela [zvi'ɲarsela] v sneak away.

svigorire [zvigo'rire] v weaken.

sviluppo [zvi'luppo] sm development; (*crescita*) growth. **età dello sviluppo** of puberty. **sviluppare** v develop; (*produrre*) generate; (*estendersi*) grow.

svincolare [zvinko'lare] v release; (*riscattare*) redeem. **svincolarsi** v free oneself (from). **svincolo** sm release; (*comm*) clearance; (*autostrada*) exit.

svisare [zvi'zare] v twist.

sviscerare [zviʃe'rare] v disembowel; (*fig*) exhaust. **sviscerarsi per dote** on. **sviscerato** agg passionate; (*spreg*) obsequious.

svista ['zvista] sf oversight.

svitare [zvi'tare] v unscrew. **svitato, -a** sm, sf (*fam*) nut.

Svizzera ['zvittsera] sf Switzerland. **svizzero, -a** s, agg Swiss.

svogliato [zvo'ʎato] agg listless; unenthusiastic; (*indolente*) slack. **svogliatezza** sf listlessness.

svolazzare [zvolat'tsare] v flutter. **svolazzo** sm flourish.

***svolgere** ['zvoldʒere] v develop. **svolgersi** v proceed, go; (*distendersi*) unfold; (*voltarsi*) turn. **svolgimento** sm development. **svolta** sf turning; (*fig*) turning point; curve.

svuotare [zvwo'tare] v empty.

tabacco [ta'bakko] sm tobacco. **tabaccaio, -a** sm, sf tobacconist. **tabaccheria** sf tobacconist's (shop).

tabella [ta'bella] sf table; list. **tabellone** sm notice-board; (*per affissioni murali*) hoarding; (*sport*) score-board.

tabù [ta'bu] agg, sm taboo.

tabulatore [tabula'tore], **-trice** sm, sf tabulator.

tacca ['takka] sf nick; (*macchia*) blotch; (*qualità*) kind; (*difetto*) fault.

taccagno [tak'kaɲo] agg stingy. **taccagneria** sf stinginess.

taccheggiatore [takkeddʒa'tore], **-trice** sm, sf shop-lifter. **taccheggio** sm shoplifting.

tacchino [tak'kino] sm turkey.

taccia ['tattʃa] sf (bad) reputation. **tacciare** v accuse.

tacco ['takko] sm heel. **battere i tacchi** click one's heels.

taccuino [takku'ino] sm note-book.

***tacere** [ta'tʃere] v be or keep quiet; (*fam*) shut up; (*non dir nulla*) say nothing. **far tacere** hush.

tachimetro [ta'kimetro] sm speedometer.

tacito ['tatʃito] agg tacit; (*silenzioso*) silent. **taciturno** agg taciturn.

tafano [ta'fano] sm horsefly.

tafferuglio [taffe'ruʎo] sm brawl.

taglia ['taʎa] sf (*premio*) reward; (*statura*) size.

tagliando [ta'ʎando] sm coupon; (*scontrino*) voucher.

tagliare [ta'ʎare] v cut; (*staccare, interrompere*) cut off; (*trinciare*) carve; (*in più parti*) cut up; (*vino*) blend. **tagliaboschi** sm invar woodcutter. **tagliacarte** sm invar paper-knife. **tagliapietre** sm invar stonemason. **tagliare la testa al toro** settle a matter once and for all.

tagliente [ta'ʎente] agg cutting.

tagliere [ta'ʎere] sm chopping board.

taglio ['taʎo] sm cut; (*parte staccata*) piece; (*parte tagliente*) (cutting) edge; (*importo*) denomination.

tagliola [ta'ʎola] sf trap.

tagliuzzare [taʎut'tsare] v chop up; (*a strisce*) cut to shreds.

tailleur [ta'jœr] sm suit.

talco ['talko] sm talc.

tale ['tale] *agg* such; certain. **tal dei tali** so-and-so. **tale quale** exactly like. **tale ... tale ... like ... like ... un (certo) tale** a certain person.

talento [ta'lɛnto] *sm* talent.

talismano [taliz'mano] *sm* talisman, charm.

talloncino [tallon'tʃino] *sm* counterfoil.

tallone [tal'lone] *sm* heel. **tallonare** *v* shadow; (*sport*) mark.

talora [ta'lora] *avv* at times.

talpa ['talpa] *sf* mole.

taluni [ta'luni] *pron, agg* some.

talvolta [tal'vɔlta] *avv* sometimes.

tamburo [tam'buro] *sm* drum; (*sonatore*) drummer; (*mec*) barrel, drum. **tamburellare** *v* drum. **tamburello** *sm* tambourine.

Tamigi [ta'midʒi] *sm* Thames.

tamponare [tampo'nare] *v* plug; (*auto*) bump into. **tamponare una falla** stop a leak. **tampone** *sm* plug; tampon.

tana ['tana] *sf* den.

tanfo ['tanfo] *sm* musty smell.

tangente [tan'dʒɛnte] *sf* tangent. **tangenziale** *sf* (*strada*) ring road.

tangibile [tan'dʒibile] *agg* tangible.

tango ['tango] *sm* tango.

tanto ['tanto] *agg* (so) much *or* many; (*altrettanto*) as much *or* many; (*molto*) a lot (of). **tanto ... quanto ...** as much ... as ... *pron* a lot; much *or* many. **tanti** *pron* (*persone*) so many (people). **tanto per so much for.** *avv* so (much); (*soltanto*) just. **da tanto** (*tempo*) for such a long time. **di tanto in tanto** from time to time. **ogni tanto** from time to time. **tanti auguri!** best wishes! congratulations! **tanto meglio** so much the better. **tanto più che** especially as.

tappa ['tappa] *sf* stage; (*sosta*) stop.

tappare [tap'pare] *v* shut; (*con tappo*) bung (up). **tapparsi il naso** hold one's nose. **tapparsi le orecchie** close one's ears.

tapparella [tappa'rɛlla] *sf* blind.

tappeto [tap'peto] *sm* carpet; (*piccolo*) rug; (*sport, tec*) mat. **mettere al tappeto** knock down.

tappezzare [tappet'tsare] *v* (*di carta*) paper; (*di legno*) panel; (*di stoffa*) cover, upholster. **tappezzeria** *sf* (*carta*) wallpaper; (*stoffa*) tapestry; (*legno*) panelling; (*mobili*) upholstery. **tappezziere** *sm* decorator; upholsterer.

tappo ['tappo] *sm* stopper, plug; (*sughero*) cork; (*a vite*) screw-cap.

tara ['tara] *sf* tare; defect. **tarato** *agg* (*tec*) calibrated; (*difettoso*) tainted.

tarantola [ta'rantola] *sf* tarantula.

tarchiato [tar'kjato] *agg* sturdy.

tardare [tar'dare] *v* be late. **tardi** *avv* late. **tardivo** *agg* late; retarded. **tardo** *agg* (*lento*) slow; (*tempo*) late; (*età*) ripe old.

targa ['targa] *sf* plate; (*auto*) number-plate. **targare** *v* (*auto*) register.

tariffa [ta'riffa] *sf* rate; (*trasporto pubblico*) fare; (*dogana*) tariff.

tarlo ['tarlo] *sm* woodworm. **tarlo del dubbio** gnawing doubt. **tarlato** *agg* worm-eaten.

tarma ['tarma] *sf* moth.

tarpare [tar'pare] *v* **tarpare le ali a** clip the wings of.

tartagliare [tarta'ʎare] *v* stammer.

tartaro [tar'taro] *sm* tartar.

tartaruga [tarta'ruga] *sf* tortoise.

tartassare [tartas'sare] *v* ill-treat.

tartina [tar'tina] *sf* canapé.

tartufo [tar'tufo] *sm* truffle.

tasca ['taska] *sf* pocket. **avere le tasche piene (di)** (*fam*) be sick and tired (of). **conoscere come le proprie tasche** know like the back of one's hand. **tascabile** *agg* pocket.

tassa ['tassa] *sf* tax; (*imposta*) duty; (*giudiziaria, scolastica*) fee. **tassametro** *sm* meter.

tassare [tas'sare] *v* tax. **tassare troppo** (*fig*) overtax. **tassabile** *agg* taxable; subject to duty. **tassativo** *agg* express; definite.

tassello [tas'sɛllo] *sm* dowel; (*prelievo*) wedge; (*indumento*) gusset.

tassì [tas'si] *sm* taxi. **tassista** *sm* taxi-driver.

tasso¹ ['tasso] *sm* (*zool*) badger.

tasso² ['tasso] *sm* (*bot*) yew(-tree).

tasso³ ['tasso] *sm* (*rapporto*) rate.

tastare [tas'tare] *v* feel. **tastare il terreno** (*fig*) see how the land lies. **tastiera** *sf* keyboard. **tasto** *sm* key; (*argomento*) subject; (*tatto*) touch. **a tastoni** feeling one's way.

tattica ['tattika] *sf* tactics *pl.* **tattico** *agg* tactical.

tatto ['tatto] *sm* touch; (*fig*) tact. **con tatto** tactfully. **mancare di tatto** be tactless. **senza tatto** tactlessly.

tatuaggio [tatu'addʒo] *sm* tattoo. **tatuare** *v* tattoo.

tautologia [tautolo'dʒia] *sf* tautology. **tautologico** *agg* tautological.

taverna [ta'vɛrna] *sf* inn, pub.

tavola ['tavola] *sf* table; (*asse*) board. **tavola calda** snack-bar. **tavola da disegno/stiro** drawing/ironing board. **tavola di comando** console. **tavola nera** blackboard. **tavola reale** (*gioco*) backgammon.

tavolato [tavo'lato] *sm* (*pavimento*) flooring; (*assito*) partition; (*geog*) plateau.

tavolo ['tavolo] *sm* table; (*ufficio, studio*) desk.

tavolozza [tavo'lɔttsa] *sf* palette.

tazza ['tattsa] *sf* cup; (*gabinetto*) lavatory pan; (*fontana*) basin.

te [te] *pron* you. *V* **ti**.

tè [tɛ] *sm* tea.

teatro [te'atro] *sm* theatre; (*attività professionale*) stage; (*complesso di opere*) plays *pl.* **teatro lirico** (*edificio*) opera house; (*genere*) opera. **teatrale** *agg* theatrical.

tecnica ['tɛknika] *sf* technique; technology.

tecnico ['tɛkniko], **-a** *agg* technical. *sm, sf* technician, engineer; expert. **tecnicismo** *sm* technicality.

tecnologia [teknolo'dʒia] *sf* technology. **tecnologico** *agg* technological.

tedesco [te'desko], **-a** *s, agg* German.

tedio ['tɛdjo] *sm* tediousness. **tedioso** *agg* tedious.

tegame [te'game] *sm* (frying-)pan. **uova al tegame** *sf pl* fried eggs *pl.*

teglia ['teʎa] *sf* baking tin.

tegola ['tegola] *sf* (roofing-)tile. **coprire di tegole** tile. **tetto di tegole** *sm* tiled roof.

tela ['tela] *sf* cloth; (*pittura*) canvas; (*teatro*) curtain. **tela cerata** oilcloth. **tela di lenzuola** sheeting. **tela di lino** linen.

telaio [te'lajo] *sm* loom; (*auto*) chassis; (*tec*) frame.

telecabina [teleka'bina] *sf* cable-car.

telecomando [teleko'mando] *sm* remote control. **telecomandare** *v* operate by remote control.

telecronaca [tele'krɔnaka] *sf* news bulletin. **telecronista** *s(m + f)* television commentator.

telefonare [telefo'nare] *v* telephone; (*fam*) phone. **telefonata** *sf* telephone call. **telefonata urbana/interurbana/con preavviso** local/trunk/personal call. **telefonico** *agg* telephone. **telefonista** *s(m + f)* telephonist. **telefono** *sm* telephone.

telegiornale [teledʒor'nale] *sm* television news.

telegrafare [telegra'fare] *v* telegraph. **telegrafico** *agg* telegraph; (*conciso*) telegraphic. **telegrafista** *s(m + f)* telegraph operator.

telegramma [tele'gramma] *sm* telegram.

telepatia [telepa'tia] *sf* telepathy. **telepatico** *agg* telepathic.

teleschermo [tele'skɛrmo] *sm* television screen.

telescopio [tele'skɔpjo] *sm* telescope.

telespettatore [telespetta'tore], **-trice** *sm, sf* viewer.

teletrasmissione [teletrazmis'sjone] *sf* television programme.

televisione [televi'zjone] *sf* televison; (*fam*) TV. **televisore** *sm* television set.

telone [te'lone] *sm* tarpaulin.

tema ['tɛma] *sm* theme, subject; (*scolastico*) essay. **fuori tema** off the point.

temerario [teme'rarjo] *agg* reckless; (*avventato*) rash. **temerità** *sf* temerity.

temere [te'mere] *v* fear, be afraid. **non temere!** don't worry!

temperamento [tempera'mento] *sm* temperament.

temperare [tempe'rare] *v* temper; (*matita*) sharpen. **temperato** *agg* temperate. **temperino** *sm* pen-knife.

temperatura [tempera'tura] *sf* temperature.

tempesta [tem'pesta] *sf* storm. **tempestare** *v* storm; (*ornare*) stud; (*importunare*) bombard. **tempestoso** *agg* stormy.

tempestivo [tempes'tivo] *agg* timely. **tempestività** *sf* timeliness.

tempia ['tempja] *sf* temple.

tempio ['tempjo] *sm* temple.

tempista [tem'pista] *s(m + f)* opportunist.

tempo ['tɛmpo] *sm* time; (*atmosferico*) weather; (*gramm*) tense; (*musica*) movement. **a suo tempo** (*passato*) originally; (*futuro*) in due course; (*al momento giusto*) at the right time. **a tempo debito** in due course. **a tempo perso** in one's spare time. **da tempo** for some time. **in un primo tempo** at first. **tempo da cani** foul weather.

temporale¹ [tempo'rale] *agg* temporal.

temporale² [tempo'rale] *sm* (thunder)storm. **temporalesco** *agg* stormy.

temporaneo [tempo'raneo] *sm* temporary.

temporeggiare [tempored'dʒare] *v* mark time, temporize.

temprare [tem'prare] *v* temper. **tempra** *sf* (*tec*) tempering, temper; (*fig*) fibre; (*voce*) timbre.

tenace [te'natʃe] *agg* firm; (*fig*) tenacious. **tenacia** *sf* tenacity. **tenacità** *sf* tenacity, firmness.

tenaglie [te'naʎe] *sf pl* pincers *pl*; (*pinze*) pliers *pl*; (*molle*) tongs *pl*.

tenda ['tɛnda] *sf* (*drappo*) curtain; (*da campo*) tent; (*tendone da sole*) awning. **tenda alla veneziana** Venetian blind. **tendina** *sf* net curtain.

tendenza [ten'dentsa] *sf* tendency; (*attitudine*) bent; (*orientamento, econ*) trend. **tendenziale** *agg* potential. **tendenzioso** *agg* tendentious.

*tendere ['tɛndere] *v* (*mettere in tensione*) stretch; (*porgere*) hold out; (*reti*) cast. **tendere a** (*mirare*) aim at; be inclined to; (*volgersi verso*) tend towards. **tendere un tranello** set a trap.

tendine ['tɛndine] *sm* tendon.

tenebre ['tɛnebre] *sf pl* darkness *sing*. **tenebroso** *agg* dark; (*fig*) mysterious.

tenente [te'nɛnte] *sm* lieutenant.

*tenere [te'nere] *v* hold; (*mantenere, trattenere*) keep; (*seguire una direzione*) keep to. **tenerci a** attach great importance to. **tenere a** (*volere*) want. **tener d'occhio** keep an eye on. **tener presente** bear in mind.

tenero ['tɛnero] *agg* tender. **tenerezza** *sf* tenderness.

tenia ['tɛnja] *sf* tapeworm.

tennis ['tɛnnis] *sm* tennis. **tennista** *s(m+f)* tennis player.

tenore [te'nore] *sm* tenor; content. **a tenore di** in accordance with. **tenore di vita** living standard.

tensione [ten'sjone] *sf* tension.

tentacolo [ten'takolo] *sm* tentacle.

tentare [ten'tare] *v* (*cercare*) try; (*sperimentare*) try out; (*cercare di dare*) attempt; (*invogliare*) tempt. **tentativo** *sm* attempt. **tentatore** *sm* tempter. **tentatrice** *sf* temptress. **tentazione** *sf* temptation. **aver la tentazione (di)** be tempted (to).

tentennare [tenten'nare] *v* wobble; hesitate.

tentoni [ten'toni] *avv* **a tentoni** groping one's way.

tenue ['tɛnue] *agg* slender; (*debole*) faint; (*fig*) slight.

tenuta [te'nuta] *sf* (*divisa*) uniform; (*possedimento fondiario*) estate; capacity; (*auto*) road-holding; (*tec*) seal. **a tenuta d'acqua** water-tight. **a tenuta d'aria** air-tight.

teologia [teolo'dʒia] *sf* theology. **teologico** theological. **teologo, -a** *sm, sf* theologist.

teorema [teo'rɛma] *sm* theorem.

teoria [teo'ria] *sf* theory. **in teoria** theoretically.

teorico [te'ɔriko], **-a** *agg* theoretical. *sm, sf* theorist.

tepore [te'pore] *sm* warmth.

teppa ['teppa] *sf* *also* **teppaglia** rabble. **teppismo** *sm* hooliganism. **teppista** *s(m+f)* hooligan.

terapia [tera'pia] *sf* therapy. **terapeutico** *agg* therapeutic. **terapista** *s(m+f)* therapist.

tergicristallo [terdʒikris'tallo] *sm* windshield-wiper.

tergiversare [terdʒiver'sare] *v* prevaricate.

tergo ['tɛrgo] *sm* **a tergo** (*di dietro*) behind. **vedi a tergo** (*nei rinvii*) please turn over, PTO.

terme ['tɛrme] *sf pl* (thermal) baths *pl*. **termale** *or* **termico** *agg* thermal.

terminare [termi'nare] *v* end. **terminazione** *sf* ending. **termine** *sm* term; limit; (*punto estremo*) end; (*comm*) expiry (date). **a breve/lungo termine** short-/long-term. **ai termini di legge** by law. **a rigor di termini** strictly speaking. **terminologia** *sf* terminology.

termodinamica [termodi'namika] *sf* thermodynamics.

termometro [ter'mɔmetro] *sm* thermometer.

termonucleare [termonukle'are] *agg* thermonuclear.

termos *V* **thermos**.

termosifone [termosi'fone] *sm* radiator.

termostato [ter'mɔstato] *sm* thermostat. **termostatico** *agg* thermostatic.

terra ['tɛrra] *sf* earth; (*estensione di terreno, paese*) land; (*suolo*) soil. **a terra** (*senza soldi*) broke; (*depresso*) in low spirits; (*gomma*) flat. **collegare** *or* **mettere a terra** (*elett*) earth. **raso terra** close to the ground.

terraglia [ter'raʎa] *sf* earthenware. **terraglie** *sf pl* (*vasellame*) crockery *sing*.

terrapieno [terra'pjɛno] *sm* embankment.
terrazza [ter'rattsa] *sf* terrace. **terrazzo** *sm* terrace; (*alpinismo*) ledge.
terremoto [terre'mɔto] *sm* earthquake. **terremotato, -a** *sm*, *sf* earthquake victim.
terreno[1] [ter'reno] *agg* earthly, worldly. **piano terreno** ground floor.
terreno[2] [ter'reno] *sm* land; (*suolo*) ground; (*podere*) plot (of land); (*fig*) field.
terreo ['tɛrreo] *agg* earthy; (*colorito*) deathly pale.
terrestre [ter'rɛstre] *agg* terrestrial.
terribile [ter'ribile] *agg* terrible.
territorio [terri'tɔrjo] *sm* territory. **territoriale** *agg* territorial.
terrore [ter'rore] *sm* terror. **aver terrore (di)** be terrified (of). **terrorismo** *sm* terrorism. **terrorista** *s(m+f)* terrorist. **terroristico** *agg* terrorist. **terrorizzare** *v* terrorize.
terzo ['tɛrtso] *agg*, *sm* third. **terzi** *sm pl* (*comm*, *dir*) third party *sing*. **terzina** *sf* triplet.
tesa ['teza] *sf* (*cappello*) brim; (*reti*) spreading.
teschio ['tɛskjo] *sm* skull.
tesi ['tɛzi] *sf* thesis (*pl* -ses).
teso ['tezo] *agg* taut; (*nervoso*) tense. **stare con le orecchie tese** prick up one's ears.
tesoro [te'zɔro] *sm* treasure; (*tesoreria*, *pol*) treasury. **far tesoro (di)** treasure. **tesoriere** *sm* treasurer.
tessera ['tɛssera] *sf* card; (*lasciapassare*) pass; (*ferr*) season-ticket. **tesseramento** *sm* rationing. **tesserare** *v* give a membership card; ration.
tessere ['tɛssere] *v* weave. **tessitura** *sf* weaving; (*stabilimento*) (weaving) mill; (*trama*) plot. **tessuto** *sm* fabric; (*bot*, *zool*, *fig*) tissue.
tessile ['tɛssile] *agg* textile. *sm* textile; (*operaio*) textile worker.
testa ['tɛsta] *sf* head. **a testa** (*ciascuno*) each, per head. **colpo di testa** *sm* (*sport*) header; (*fig*) whim. **essere in testa** be in the lead. **fare a testa e croce** toss up. **passare in testa** take the lead. **rompersi la testa** rack one's brains.
testamento [testa'mento] *sm* will; (*bibbia*) testament.
testardo [tes'tardo] *agg* stubborn. **testardaggine** *sf* stubbornness.
testata [tes'tata] *sf* (*intestazione*) heading;

(*colpo di testa*) butt; (*auto*) cylinder head; (*parte anteriore*) head.
testicolo [tes'tikolo] *sm* testicle.
testimone [testi'mone] *s(m+f)* witness. **testimoniale** *agg* evidence. **testimonianza** *sf* testimony; (*prova*) evidence. **testimoniare** *v* testify; (*deporre in giudizio*) (bear) witness.
testo ['tɛsto] *sm* text; (*libro*) text-book. **far testo** be an authority. **testuale** *agg* exact.
testone [tes'tone] *sm* (*stupido*) blockhead; (*testardo*) pig-headed person.
testuggine [tes'tuddʒine] *sf* tortoise; (*di mare*) turtle.
tetano ['tɛtano] *sm* tetanus.
tetro ['tɛtro] *agg* gloomy.
tetta ['tɛtta] *sf* (*fam*) breast. **tettarella** *sf* dummy.
tetto ['tɛtto] *sm* roof (*pl* -s). **essere senza tetto** be homeless. **tettoia** *sf* roofing, canopy.
Tevere ['tevere] *sm* Tiber.
thermos ® *or* **termos** ['tɛrmos] *sm invar* thermos (flask) ®.
ti [ti], **te** *pron* (to) you; (*riflessivo*) yourself.
tiara ['tjara] *sf* tiara.
tic [tik] *sm invar* tic.
ticchettare [tikket'tare] *v* click; (*pioggia*) patter; (*orologio*) tick.
ticchio ['tikkjo] *sm* whim.
tictac [tik'tak] *sm* tick.
tiepido ['tjɛpido] *agg* lukewarm.
tifo ['tifo] *sm* (*med*) typhus; (*fam*: *sport*) fanaticism. **fare il tifo per** be a fan of.
tifoidea [tifoi'dɛa] *sf* (*febbre*) **tifoide** *agg* typhoid (fever).
tifone [ti'fone] *sm* typhoon.
tifoso [ti'fozo], **-a** *sm*, *sf* fan.
tiglio ['tiʎo] *sm* lime(-tree); (*fibra*) bast.
tigna ['tina] *sf* ringworm.
tignola [ti'nola] *sf* moth.
tigre ['tigre] *sf* tiger.
timbrare [tim'brare] *v* stamp; (*posta*) postmark. **timbro** *sm* stamp; postmark; (*suono*) timbre.
timido ['timido] *agg* shy; (*timoroso*) timid.
timo ['timo] *sm* (*bot*) thyme.
timone [ti'mone] *sm* rudder; (*fig*) helm. **timoniere** *sm* helmsman; (*canottaggio*) cox.
timore [ti'more] *sm* fear. **senza timore** fearless. **timoroso** *agg* fearful; (*preoccupato*) anxious.
timpano ['timpano] *sm* (*anat*) ear-drum;

(*musica*) kettle-drum. **timpani** *sm pl* timpani *pl.*

tinca ['tinka] *sf* tench.

***tingere** ['tindʒere] *v* dye; (*macchiare*) spot.

tino ['tino] *sm* tub, vat.

tinta *sf* colour; (*sfumatura*) shade. **tintarella** *sf* tan. **tinto** *agg* dyed; (*macchiato*) tinged. **tintore** *sm* dyer. **tintoria** *sf* cleaners. **tintura** *sf* dyeing; (*med*) tincture.

tipo ['tipo] *sm* type; (*genere*) sort, kind. **tipico** *agg* typical.

tipografia [tipogra'fia] *sf* typography; (*stamperia*) press. **tipografico** *agg* typographical. **tipografo, -a** *sm, sf* printer.

tiranneggiare [tiranned'dʒare] *v* tyrannize. **tirannia** *sf* tyranny. **tirannico** *agg* tyrannical. **tiranno** *sm* tyrant.

tirante [ti'rante] *sm* (connecting) rod; brace.

tirapiedi [tira'pjedi] *sm invar* hanger-on.

tirare [ti'rare] *v* pull, draw; (*lanciare*) throw; (*sparare*) shoot. **tirare avanti** keep going. **tirar fuori** pull out; (*estrarre*) take out. **tirare in lungo** draw out. **tirarsi indietro** draw back. **tirarsi su** draw oneself up; (*fam*) get back on one's feet. **tirata** *sf* pull; (*discorso*) tirade. **tiratura** *sf* printing; (*numero*) run.

tirchio ['tirkjo] *agg* stingy.

tiritera [tiri'tera] *sf* rigmarole.

tiro ['tiro] *sm* (*lancio*) throw; (*arma*) shot. **fuori tiro** out of range.

tirocinio [tiro'tʃinjo] *sm* apprenticeship.

tiroide [ti'roide] *sf* thyroid.

titolare [tito'lare] *agg* titular, regular. *s(m+f)* proprietor.

titolo ['titolo] *sm* title; (*comm*) share; (*obbligazione*) bond; (*filato*) count. **a titolo di** out of.

titubare [titu'bare] *v* hesitate.

tizio ['titsjo] *sm* fellow. **Tizio, Caio, e Sempronio** Tom, Dick, and Harry.

tizzo ['tittso] *sm* ember.

toboga [to'boga] *sm invar* toboggan.

toccare [tok'kare] *v* touch; (*riguardare*) concern. **tocca a me** it's my turn; (*spettare di diritto*) I am entitled; (*spettare di dovere*) it is up to me. **toccasana** *sm invar* panacea.

tocco¹ ['tokko] *sm* touch; (*campana*) stroke; (*l'una*) one o'clock.

tocco² ['tokko] *sm* (*pezzo*) hunk.

toga ['tɔga] *sf* toga.

***togliere** ['tɔʎere] *v* take away; (*indumenti*) take off. **ciò non toglie che** it does not alter the fact that. **togliere di mezzo** get out of the way. **togliersi** *v* (*levarsi*) take off; (*soddisfare*) satisfy.

toletta [to'letta] *sf* also **toilette** toilet; (*mobile*) dressing table; (*acconciatura*) toilette; (*abito*) outfit.

tollerare [tolle'rare] *v* tolerate, stand; (*permettere*) allow. **tollerabile** *agg* bearable. **tollerante** *agg* tolerant. **tolleranza** *sf* tolerance.

tomaia [to'maja] *sf* upper.

tomba ['tomba] *sf* tomb.

tombola¹ ['tombola] *sf* (*gioco*) tombola; bingo.

tombola² ['tombola] *sf* (*caduta*) fall.

tomo ['tɔmo] *sm* tome; (*tipo strano*) odd type.

tonaca ['tɔnaka] *sf* (*frati, monache*) habit; (*preti*) cassock.

tonalità [tonali'ta] *sf* tonality; (*colore*) shade.

tonare [to'nare] *v* thunder.

tonchio ['tonkjo] *sm* weevil.

tondo ['tondo] *agg* round. *sm* round plate; (*forma*) circle. **parlar chiaro e tondo** speak bluntly.

tonfo ['tonfo] *sm* thud; (*nell'acqua*) splash.

tonico ['tɔniko] *agg* tonic. **tonica** *sf* (*musica*) tonic.

tonnellata [tonnel'lata] *sf* ton. **tonnellaggio** *sm* tonnage.

tonno ['tonno] *sm* tuna, tunny.

tono ['tɔno] *sm* tone. **cambiar tono** change (one's) tune. **fuori tono** out of tune. **giù di tono** out of sorts. **in tono** in tune; (*fisicamente*) fit.

tonsilla [ton'silla] *sf* tonsil. **tonsillite** *sf* tonsillitis.

tonto ['tonto], **-a** *agg* silly. *sm, sf* fool.

topazio [to'patsjo] *sm* topaz.

topico ['tɔpiko] *agg* local; (*fig*) topical.

topo ['tɔpo] *sm* mouse (*pl* mice); (*campagnolo*) fieldmouse. **topo di biblioteca** bookworm.

topografia [topogra'fia] *sf* topography. **topografico** *agg* topographical.

toporagno [topo'raɲo] *sm* shrew.

toppa ['tɔppa] *sf* patch; (*serratura*) keyhole.

torace [to'ratʃe] *sm* chest.

torba ['tɔrba] sf peat.

torbido ['tɔrbido] agg turbid, muddy. **c'è del torbido** there's something fishy going on.

*****torcere** ['tɔrtʃere] v twist; (strizzare) wring out. **torcere il collo a qualcuno** wring someone's neck. **torcere il naso** turn up one's nose. **torcersi il collo** crane one's neck. **torcicollo** sm crick in the neck.

torchio ['tɔrkjo] sm press. **torchiare** v press.

torcia ['tɔrtʃa] sf torch.

tordo ['tɔrdo] sm thrush.

Torino [to'rino] sf Turin.

torma ['tɔrma] sf herd; (persone) throng.

tormentare [tormen'tare] v torment. **tormento** sm torment; (infastidire) plague.

tornaconto [torna'konto] sm advantage.

tornante [tor'nante] sm hairpin bend.

tornare [tor'nare] v return; (andare di nuovo) go back; (venire di nuovo) come back; (ricominciare) start again. **ben tornato!** welcome back! **qualcosa non torna** something is not quite right.

torneo [tor'nɛo] sm tournament.

tornio ['tɔrnjo] sm lathe. **tornire** v turn. **tornitore** sm (tec) lathe operator; (di legno) wood turner.

toro ['tɔro] sm bull. **Toro** sm Taurus.

torpedine [tor'pedine] sf torpedo.

torpedone [torpe'done] sm coach.

torpido ['tɔrpido] agg sluggish. **torpore** sm sluggishness.

torre ['torre] sf tower; (scacchi) rook, castle. **torretta** sf turret.

torrefare [torre'fare] v roast. **torrefazione** sf roasting.

torrente [tor'rɛnte] sm torrent. **torrenziale** agg torrential.

torrido ['tɔrrido] agg torrid.

torrone [tor'rone] sm nougat.

torso ['tɔrso] sm stalk; (frutta) core; (anat) torso. **a torso nudo** bare-chested.

torsolo ['tɔrsolo] sm stalk; (frutta) core.

torta ['tɔrta] sf cake; (di frutta) tart; (pasticcio) pie.

tortiglione [torti'ʎone] sm spiral. **a tortiglione** spiral.

torto[1] ['tɔrto] sm wrong; (colpa) fault. **a torta** wrongfully. **aver torto** be wrong. **dar torto a** prove wrong.

torto[2] ['tɔrto] agg twisted.

tortora ['tɔrtora] sf turtle-dove.

tortuoso [tortu'ozo] agg tortuous.

torturare [tortu'rare] v torture. **tortura** sf torture.

torvo ['tɔrvo] agg surly.

tosare [to'zare] v shear; (cani) clip; (fig) fleece. **tosatrice** sf (capelli) hair-clippers pl; (erba) lawn-mower. **tosatura** sf shearing; clipping.

Toscana [tos'kana] sf Tuscany. **toscano, -a** s, agg Tuscan.

tosse ['tosse] sf cough. **tossire** v cough.

tossico ['tɔssiko] agg poisonous. sm poison. **tossicità** sf toxicity. **tossicomane** s(m+f) drug addict. **tossicomania** sf drug addiction. **tossina** sf toxin.

tostare [tos'tare] v roast; (pane) toast. **tostapane** sm invar toaster.

tosto ['tɔsto] agg **faccia tosta** sf (fam) cheek.

totale [to'tale] agg, sm total. **totalità** sf entirety.

totalitario [totali'tarjo] agg (pol) totalitarian.

totano ['tɔtano] sm squid.

totocalcio [toto'kaltʃo] sm football pools pl.

tovaglia [to'vaʎa] sf table-cloth. **tovagliolo** sm napkin, serviette.

tozzo[1] ['tottso] agg squat; (persone) stocky.

tozzo[2] ['tottso] sm piece.

tra [tra] prep among(st); (tra due) between; (nel mezzo) in the midst of; (tempo) in. **tra breve** or **poco** soon. **tra l'altro** among other things; (inoltre) besides.

traballare [trabal'lare] v wobble; (persone, fig) totter.

traboccare [trabok'kare] v overflow. **trabocchetto** sm trap.

tracannare [trakan'nare] v gulp down.

traccia ['trattʃa] sf track, trail; (orma) footprint; (indizio) trace. **tracciare** v trace; (abbozzare) sketch (out); (a grandi linee) outline. **tracciato** sm layout.

trachea [tra'kɛa] sf windpipe.

tracolla [tra'kɔlla] sf shoulder-strap. **a tracolla** over one's shoulder. **borsetta a tracolla** sf shoulder-bag.

tradire [tra'dire] v betray; (coniugi) be unfaithful (to). **tradimento** sm treachery; (dir) treason. **a tradimento** by surprise. **traditore** sm traitor. **traditrice** sf traitress.

tradizione [tradi'tsjone] sf tradition. **tradizionale** agg traditional.

*tradurre [tra'durre] v translate; (condurre) convey. **traduttore, -trice** sm, sf translator. **traduzione** sf translation.

trafelato [trafe'lato] agg out of breath.

trafficare [traffi'kare] v (commerciare) trade, deal; (spreg) traffic; (darsi da fare) busy oneself. **traffico** sm traffic.

*trafiggere [tra'fiddʒere] v pierce.

trafila [tra'fila] sf (operazione) (lengthy) procedure. **trafilare** v draw. **trafiletto** sm paragraph.

traforare [trafo'rare] v bore, drill; (legno) cut with a fretsaw. **traforatrice** sf drill; (sega) fretsaw. **traforo** sm tunnel; fretsaw.

tragedia [tra'dʒɛdja] sf tragedy.

traghetto [tra'getto] sm ferry. **traghettare** v ferry (across).

tragico ['tradʒiko] agg tragic. sm tragedy; (autore) tragedian; (attore) tragic actor. **prendere sul tragico** dramatize.

tragitto [tra'dʒitto] sm journey; (traversata) crossing.

traguardo [tra'gwardo] sm finish; (sport) winning-post; (fig) goal.

traiettoria [trajet'tɔrja] sf trajectory; (di volo) flight-path.

trainare [trai'nare] v pull or haul along; (rimorchiare) tow. **traino** sm haulage; (rimorchio) trailer; (con pattini) sledge.

tralasciare [trala'ʃare] v leave out; interrupt; (trascurare) neglect.

tralcio ['traltʃo] sm shoot.

traliccio [tra'littʃo] sm (tessuto) ticking; (struttura) truss; (graticcio) trellis.

tram [tram] sm invar tram.

trama ['trama] sf (tessile) weft; (fig) plot. **tramare** v plot.

tramandare [traman'dare] v hand down.

trambusto [tram'busto] sm turmoil.

*tramezzare [tramed'dzare] v interpose; (dividere un locale) partition (off). **tramezzo** sm partition.

tramite ['tramite] sm means pl; intermediary. prep (per mezzo di) through.

tramontana [tramon'tana] sf (nord) north; (vento) north wind.

tramontare [tramon'tare] v set; (aver fine) come to an end; (dileguarsi) wane. **tramonto** sm sunset; (fig) decline.

tramortire [tramor'tire] v stun.

trampolino [trampo'lino] sm springboard; (piscina) diving-board; (palestra) trampoline; (sci) ski-jump.

trampolo ['trampolo] sm stilt.

tramutare [tramu'tare] v transform.

trancia ['trantʃa] sf (taglierina) cutter; (gastr) slice.

tranello [tra'nɛllo] sm trap; (fig) catch.

trangugiare [trangu'dʒare] v gulp down; (fig) swallow.

tranne ['tranne] prep except or but (for).

tranquillo [tran'kwillo] agg quiet, calm. **stare tranquillo** keep quiet or calm; (non turbarsi) not worry. **tranquillità** sf calm. **tranquillante** sm tranquillizer.

transatlantico [transat'lantiko] agg transatlantic. sm ocean liner.

transazione [transa'tsjone] sf (comm) transaction; (dir) settlement.

transistor [tran'sistor] sm invar transistor.

transitivo [transi'tivo] agg transitive.

transito ['transito] sm transit. **transito interrotto** road closed. **transitabile** agg practicable. **transitorio** agg transitory; (fis) transient.

transizione [transi'tsjone] sf transition.

tranvai [tran'vaj] sm tram. **tranvia** sf tramway.

trapanare [trapa'nare] v drill. **trapanatrice** sf drill. **trapanatura** sf drilling. **trapano** sm drill.

trapassare [trapas'sare] v run through; pass. **trapassato** sm past perfect. **trapasso** sm passing; transition; (dir) transfer.

trapelare [trape'lare] v leak out.

trapezio [tra'pɛtsjo] sm (geom) trapezium; (sport) trapeze. **trapezista** s(m+f) trapeze artist.

trapiantare [trapjan'tare] v transplant. **trapianto** sm transplant; (agric) transplantation.

trappola ['trappola] sf trap, snare.

trapuntare [trapun'tare] v quilt; (ricamare) embroider. **trapunta** sf quilt.

*trarre ['trarre] v draw. **trarre in inganno** deceive. **trarre in tentazione** lead into temptation.

trasalire [trasa'lire] v jump.

trasandato [trazan'dato] agg untidy.

*trascendere [tra'ʃendere] v transcend.

trascinare [traʃi'nare] v drag; (fig) carry away.

*trascorrere [tras'korrere] v spend; (tempo) pass.

*trascrivere [tras'krivere] v transcribe. **trascrizione** sf transcription.

trascurare [trasku'rare] v neglect; (omettere) fail. **trascurato** agg neglected; (noncurante) careless; (sciatto) slovenly.

trasferire [trasfe'rire] v transfer. **trasferirsi** v (traslocare) move. **trasferibile** agg transferable. **trasferimento** sm transfer. **trasferta** sf (sport) away match; (viaggio) business trip; (indennità) travelling expenses pl.

trasformare [trasfor'mare] v transform; (cambiare) change. **trasformare in turn** into. **trasformatore** sm transformer. **trasformazione** sf transformation.

trasfusione [trasfu'zjone] sf (med) transfusion.

trasgredire [trazgre'dire] v disobey; (legge) infringe. **trasgressione** sf infringement.

traslocare [trazlo'kare] v move; (impiegato) transfer. **trasloco** sm, pl -chi move; transfer.

*__trasmettere__ [traz'mettere] v transmit; (communicare, dir) convey; (radio) broadcast. **trasmettitore** sm transmitter; (malattia) carrier. **trasmissione** sf transmission; broadcast. **trasmittente** sf transmitter.

trasmodato [trazmo'dato] agg excessive. **trasognato** [traso'ɲato] agg dreamy.

trasparente [traspa'rɛnte] agg transparent. sm transparency. **trasparenza** sf transparency.

trasparire [traspa'rire] v show through; (alla luce) shine through; (palesarsi) appear.

traspirare [traspi'rare] v transpire.

trasportare [traspor'tare] v carry; (trascinare) transport, carry away. **trasportatore** sm carrier; (tec) conveyor. **trasporto** sm transport; (comm) carriage; (inoltro) forwarding; (per nave) shipping.

trastullare [trastul'lare] v amuse. **trastullo** sm amusement; (fig) plaything.

trasudare [trasu'dare] v ooze.

trasversale [trazver'sale] agg transverse.

trasvolare [trazvo'lare] v fly across; (fig) barely touch.

tratta [ˈtratta] sf (comm) draft; (traffico illecito) trade.

trattare [trat'tare] v treat, deal with, handle. **si tratta di** ... it is about ..., it is a question of .... **trattabile** agg negotiable; (persona) tractable. **trattamento** sm treatment. **trattativa** sf negotiation. **trattato** sm (opera) treatise; (dir) treaty.

tratteggiare [tratted'dʒare] v hatch; (abbozzare) outline.

*__trattenere__ [tratte'nere] v (far rimanere) keep (back); (frenare) restrain, hold back; (detrarre) withhold. **trattenersi** v (restare) stay; restrain oneself. **trattenimento** sm reception; (spettacolo) show.

tratto ['tratto] agg drawn. sm stroke; (elemento caratteristico) feature; (frazione) stretch; (brano) passage. **a tratti** at times. **di tratto in tratto** every now and then. **d'un tratto** all of a sudden.

trattore [trat'tore] sm tractor.

trattoria [tratto'ria] sf restaurant.

traudire [trau'dire] v mishear.

trauma ['trauma] sm trauma. **traumatico** agg traumatic.

travagliare [trava'ʎare] v torment. **travaglio** sm torment; (angoscia) distress. **travaglio di parto** labour.

travasare [trava'zare] v decant.

trave ['trave] sf beam; (di tetto) rafter; (di soffitto) joist. **fare una trave di ogni fuscello** make a mountain out of a molehill.

traversare [traver'sare] v cross; (da parte a parte) go through. **traversata** sf crossing. **traversina** sf sleeper.

traverso [tra'vɛrso] agg cross, transverse. sm breadth, width. **andare di traverso** (cibo) go down the wrong way. **a traverso** sideways on. **guardare di traverso** look askance at. **prendere di traverso** take the wrong way.

travestire [traves'tire] v disguise. **travestito, -a** sm, sf (psic) transvestite.

traviare [travi'are] v lead astray. **traviamento** sm straying; corruption.

travisare [travi'zare] v distort. **travisamento** sm distortion.

*__travolgere__ [tra'vɔldʒere] v sweep away; (investire) knock down; (fig) overwhelm. **travolgente** agg sweeping; overwhelming.

trazione [tra'tsjone] sf traction; (auto) drive.

tre [tre] agg, sm three.

trebbiare [treb'bjare] v thresh. **trebbia** or **trebbiatrice** sf threshing machine. **trebbiatura** sf threshing.

treccia ['trettʃa] sf braid, plait. **farsi le trecce** plait one's hair.

tredici ['treditʃi] agg, sm thirteen. **tredicesimo** sm, agg thirteenth.

tregua ['trɛgwa] sf truce; (riposo) rest. **senza tregua** unremitting; without respite; (senza sosta) non-stop.

tremare [tre'mare] v tremble; (di freddo) shiver; (per emozioni) shudder. **la tremarella** sf (fam) the shivers pl.

tremendo [tre'mɛndo] *agg* terrible, dreadful.

trementina [tremen'tina] *sf* turpentine.

tremito ['trɛmito] *sm* shaking, shudder(ing).

tremolare [tremo'lare] *v* quiver; (*stelle*) twinkle; (*luce*) flicker.

tremore [tre'more] *sm* tremor; (*agitazione*) trembling.

treno ['trɛno] *sm* train. **treno accelerato/diretto/direttissimo/rapido** slow/fast/through/express train. **treno di gomme/ruote** set of tyres/wheels.

trenta ['trenta] *sm*, *agg* thirty. **trentesimo** *sm*, *agg* thirtieth.

trepidare [trepi'dare] *v* be anxious.

trespolo ['trɛspolo] *sm* trestle; (*sgabello*) stool.

triangolo [tri'angolo] *sm* triangle. **triangolare** *agg* triangular.

tribolare [tribo'lare] *v* suffer; (*far soffrire*) torment. **vita tribolata** *sf* hard life.

tribordo [tri'bordo] *sm* starboard.

tribù [tri'bu] *sf* tribe. **membro di tribù** *sm* tribesman.

tribuna [tri'buna] *sf* platform; (*palco riservato*) gallery; (*campo sportivo*) stand; (*coperta*) grandstand.

tribunale [tribu'nale] *sm* court.

tributo [tri'buto] *sm* tribute. **tributare** *v* render. **tributario** *agg* (*tributi*) tax; (*fiume*) tributary.

tricheco [tri'kɛko] *sm* walrus.

triciclo [tri'tʃiklo] *sm* tricycle.

tricolore [triko'lore] *sm*, *agg* tricolour.

tric-trac ['tric'trac] *sm invar* backgammon.

tridimensionale [tridimensjo'nale] *agg* three-dimensional.

trifoglio [tri'fɔʎʎo] *sm* clover.

triglia ['triʎa] *sf* red mullet. **far l'occhio di triglia** (*fam*) make sheep's eyes.

trigonometria [trigonome'tria] *sf* trigonometry.

trillare [tril'lare] *v* trill. **trillo** *sm* trill.

trilogia [trilo'dʒia] *sf* trilogy.

trimestre [tri'mɛstre] *sm* quarter; (*scolastico*) term. **trimestrale** *agg* quarterly.

trina ['trina] *sf* lace.

trincare [trin'kare] *v* drink.

trincea [trin'tʃɛa] *sf* (*mil*) trench; (*ferr*) cutting. **trincerare** *v* entrench. **trinceramento** *sm* entrenchment.

trinciare [trin'tʃare] *v* cut up; (*pollo, ecc.*) carve; (*in strisce sottili*) shred. **trinciato** *sm* (*tabacco*) shag.

trinità [trini'ta] *sf* trinity.

trio ['trio] *sm* trio.

trionfare [trion'fare] *v* triumph. **trionfale** *agg* triumphal. **trionfante** *agg* triumphant. **trionfo** *sm* triumph; success.

triplice ['triplitʃe] *agg* threefold. **in triplice copia** in triplicate. **triplo** *agg* treble, triple; (*di tre parti*) threefold. **il triplo** three times as much.

tripode ['tripode] *sm* tripod.

trippa ['trippa] *sf* tripe.

tripudiare [tripu'djare] *v* rejoice. **tripudio** *sm* jubilation.

triste ['triste] *agg* sad. **tristezza** *sf* sadness. **tristo** ['tristo] *agg* (*malvagio*) wicked; (*meschino*) mean.

tritare [tri'tare] *v* grind; (*carne*) mince. **carne tritata** *sf* mince. **tritacarne** *sm invar* mincer. **trito** *agg* chopped, ground, minced; (*fig*) trite.

trittico ['trittiko] *sm* triptych.

trivellare [trivel'lare] *v* drill, bore. **trivella** *sf* auger; (*succhiello*) gimlet; (*miniera*) drill. **trivellazione** *sf* drilling, boring.

triviale [tri'vjale] *agg* vulgar; (*banale*) trivial. **trivialità** *sf* vulgarity; triviality.

trofeo [tro'fɛo] *sm* trophy.

trogolo ['trɔgolo] *sm* trough.

troia ['trɔja] (*volg*) *sf* (*scrofa*) sow; (*prostituta*) whore. **troiaio** *sm* pigsty. **troiata** *sf* (*lavoro mal fatto*) awful mess; (*azione sudicia*) dirty trick.

tromba ['tromba] *sf* trumpet; (*mil*) bugle; (*auto*) horn; (*ascensore, scale*) well; (*anat*) tube. **tromba d'aria** tornado. **trombetta** *sm* trumpeter; (*trombettiere*) bugler. **trombone** *sm* trombone. **trombonista** *s(m+f)* trombonist.

trombosi [trom'bɔzi] *sf* thrombosis.

troncare [tron'kare] *v* cut off; (*spezzare, fig*) break off.

tronco¹ [tronko] *agg* cut off, broken off; (*mat, parole*) truncated.

tronco² [tronko] *sm* trunk; (*tratto*) section; (*arch*) shaft.

tronfio ['tronfjo] *agg* puffed up, pompous.

trono ['trɔno] *sm* throne.

tropico ['trɔpiko] *sm* tropic. **tropicale** *agg* tropical.

troppo ['trɔppo] *agg* too much; (*pl*) too many. *avv* too much; (*con agg e avv*) too.

trota ['trɔta] *sf* trout.

trottare [trot'tare] v trot. **trotto** sm trot; (*andatura svelta*) brisk pace. **andare al piccolo trotto** jog-trot. **rompere il trotto** break into a gallop. **trotterellare** v jog (along); (*bambini*) toddle (along).

trottola ['trɔttola] sf (spinning) top.

trovare [tro'vare] v find. **andare a trovare** go to see, call on. **trovare in fallo** catch red-handed. **trovarsi** v (*essere*) be; (*per caso*) happen to be; (*sentirsi*) get on; (*incontrarsi*) meet; (*pensare*) think. **trovata** sf good idea; expedient. **trovata pubblicitaria** publicity stunt. **trovatello, -a** sm, sf foundling.

truccare [truk'kare] v make up; (*falsificare*) doctor; (*auto*) soup up; (*sport*) fix. **truccarsi** v disguise oneself; (*imbellettarsi*) put make-up on. **truccatore, -trice** sm, sf make-up artist. **truccatura** sf (*teatro*) making-up; (*belletto, ecc.*) make-up. **trucco** sm make-up; (*inganno*) trick.

truce ['trutʃe] agg grim.

truciolo ['trutʃolo] sm (wood) chip, shaving.

truffare [truf'fare] v cheat, swindle; (*dir*) defraud. **truffa** sf swindle; (*dir*) fraud. **truffatore, -trice** sm, sf swindler, cheat.

truppa ['truppa] sf troop; (*fig*) horde.

tu [tu] pron you. **a tu per tu** face to face.

tuba ['tuba] sf (*musica*) tuba; (*cappello*) top-hat; (*anat*) tube.

tubare [tu'bare] v coo.

tubercolosi [tuberko'lɔzi] sf tuberculosis.

tubo ['tubo] sm pipe, tube; (*flessibile*) hose(-pipe); (*anat*) canal. **tubazione** sf piping. **tubetto** sm tube. **tubolare** agg tubular.

tuffare [tuf'fare] v plunge, dip. **tuffarsi** v plunge; (*fare un tuffo*) dive. **tuffo** sm dive.

tulipano [tuli'pano] sm tulip.

tumefatto [tume'fatto] agg swollen.

tumore [tu'more] sm tumour.

tumulto [tu'multo] sm uproar; (*sommossa*) riot. **tumultuoso** agg tumultuous; (*chiassoso*) rowdy.

tunica ['tunika] sf tunic.

tuo ['tuo], m pl **tuoi** agg your. pron yours.

tuono ['twono] sm thunder. **tuonare** v thunder.

tuorlo ['twɔrlo] sm yolk.

turare [tu'rare] v plug; (*con sughero*) cork. **turarsi il naso** hold one's nose. **turacciolo**

sm stopper; (*di sughero*) cork; (*botte*) bung.

turba ['turba] sf mob.

turbante [tur'bante] sm turban.

turbare [tur'bare] v trouble; disturb; (*sconvolgere*) upset. **turbarsi** v get upset. **turbamento** sm disturbance, anxiety.

turbina [tur'bina] sf turbine.

turbine ['turbine] sm whirl; (*neve, sabbia*) storm; (*fig*) seething) horde. **turbine di vento** whirlwind. **turbolento** agg turbulent; (*inquieto*) unruly.

turchese [tur'keze] s(m+f), agg turquoise.

Turchia [tur'kia] sf Turkey. **turco, -a** sm, agg Turkish; sm, sf (*persona*) Turk. **bestemmiare come un turco** swear like a trooper. **fumare come un turco** smoke like a chimney. **parlare (in) turco** (*fam*) talk double Dutch.

turchino [tur'kino] agg, sm deep blue.

turismo [tu'rizmo] sm tourism; (*culturale*) sight-seeing. **fare del turismo** tour, travel. **turista** s(m+f) tourist; sightseer.

turlupinare [turlupi'nare] v swindle; (*fam*) take in.

turno ['turno] sm (*volta*) turn; (*lavoro*) shift; (*mil*) guard. **essere di turno** be on duty. **fare a turno** take turns. **lavoro a turni** sm shift-work.

turpe ['turpe] agg foul. **turpiloquio** sm foul language.

tuta ['tuta] sf overalls pl; (*sport*) track-suit.

tutela [tu'tɛla] sf defence; (*dir*) guardianship, protection. **tutelare** v protect; (*salvaguardare*) safeguard.

tuttavia [tutta'via] cong nevertheless.

tutto ['tutto] agg all; (*intero*) the whole (of); (*pl*) every. pron everything; (*pl*) everybody *sing*. avv completely. **a tutta velocità** at full speed. **il tutto** the whole (thing), everything. **innanzi tutto** first of all. **in tutti i modi** anyhow. **noi tutti** all of us. **tutt'ad un tratto** all of a sudden. **tutt'altro** anything but. **tutti e due** both (of them). **tutti i giorni** every day. **una volta per tutte** once and for all.

tuttora [tut'tora] avv still.

U

ubbia [ub'bia] *sf* silly idea; prejudice.
ubbidire [ubbi'dire] *v* obey; (*essere ubbidiente*) be obedient; (*dar retta*) listen (to). **ubbidiente** *agg* obedient. **ubbidienza** *sf* obedience.
ubriacare [ubria'kare] *v* make drunk, intoxicate. **ubriacarsi** *v* get drunk. **ubriachezza** *sf* drunkenness. **ubriaco, -a** *s, agg, m pl* **-chi** drunk. **ubriaco fradicio** dead drunk.
uccello [ut'tʃɛllo] *sm* bird.
*uccidere [ut'tʃidere] *v* kill; (*assassinare*) murder. **uccisione** *sf* killing; murder. **ucciso** *agg* killed; murdered. **uccisore** *sm* killer; murderer.
*udire [u'dire] *v* hear. **udibile** *agg* audible.
udienza *sf* hearing; (*formale*) audience. **uditivo** *agg* (*fis*) audible; (*med*) auditory. **udito** *sm* hearing. **uditore, -trice** *sm, sf* listener. **uditorio** *sm* audience.
uffa ['uffa] *inter* **uffa, che noia!** what a bore!
ufficiale [uffi'tʃale] *agg* official. *sm* officer. **ufficiale di stato civile** registrar.
ufficio [uf'fitʃo] *sm* office; (*dovere, compito*) duty. **d'ufficio** official; (*ufficialmente*) officially; (*in veste ufficiale*) ex officio. **ufficio di collocamento** employment exchange. **ufficioso** *agg* unofficial.
ufo ['ufo] *avv* **a ufo** for nothing. **mangiare a ufo** scrounge a meal.
uggia ['uddʒa] *sf* boredom. **avere in uggia** dislike. **prendere in uggia** take a dislike to. **uggioso** *agg* boring.
uggiolare [uddʒo'lare] *v* whine.
ugola ['ugola] *sf* (*anat*) uvula; (*fig*) voice.
uguagliare [ugwa'ʎare] *v* (*essere uguale*) equal; (*rendere uguale*) equalize, even out; (*livellare*) level. **uguaglianza** *sf* equality.
uguale [u'gwale] *agg also* **eguale** the same; uniform; (*mat*) equal. *sm* equal. **ugualmente** *avv* equally; uniformly; (*tuttavia*) just *or* all the same.
ulcera ['ultʃera] *sf* ulcer.
uliva [u'liva] *V* **oliva**.
ulteriore [ulte'rjore] *agg* further. **ulteriormente** *avv* further; (*più avanti*) farther on; (*in seguito*) subsequently.
ultimo ['ultimo], **-a** *agg* last; (*più recente*) latest; (*fondamentale*) ultimate. *sm, sf* last. **all'ultimo** at the end; (*in fine*) finally. **fino all'ultimo** to the very end. **ultimamente** *avv* also **negli ultimi tempi** lately.

ultimare *v* finish. **ultimatum** *sm invar* ultimatum. **ultimazione** *sf* completion.
ultrasensibile [ultrasen'sibile] *agg* hypersensitive.
ultrasonico [ultra'soniko] *agg* supersonic.
ultravioletto [ultravio'letto] *agg* ultraviolet.
ululare [ulu'lare] *v* howl. **ululato** *sm* howling; (*urlo*) howl.
umanesimo [uma'nezimo] *sm* humanism. **umanista** *s(m+f)* humanist. **umanistico** *agg* humanist.
umano [u'mano] *agg* human; (*compassionevole*) humane; (*comprensivo*) understanding. **umanità** *sf* humanity. **umanitario** *agg* humanitarian.
umettare [umet'tare] *v* moisten.
umido ['umido] *agg* damp; (*clima*) humid. *sm* dampness; humidity; (*gastr*) stew. **cucire in umido** stew. **umidità** *sf* dampness; humidity.
umile ['umile] *agg* humble. **umiltà** *sf* (*virtù, sentimento*) humility; (*qualità*) humbleness.
umiliare [umi'ljare] *v* humiliate, humble. **umiliazione** *sf* humiliation.
umore [u'more] *sm* (*disposizione*) mood; (*indole*) temperament; (*liquido*) humour. **essere di buon/cattivo umore** be in a good/bad mood; (*abitualmente*) be good-/bad-tempered. **umorismo** *sm* humour. **umorista** *s(m+f)* humorist. **umoristico** *agg* humorous; (*spiritoso*) witty.
un [un] *V* **uno**.
unanime [u'nanime] *agg* unanimous. **unanimità** *sf* unanimity. **all'unanimità** unanimously.
uncino [un'tʃino] *sm* hook. **uncinare** *v* hook. **croce uncinata** *sf* swastika. **uncinetto** *sm* crochet-hook. **lavorare all'uncinetto** crochet.
undici ['unditʃi] *agg, sm* eleven. **undicesimo** *sm, agg* eleventh.
*ungere [un'dʒere] *v* grease; (*rel*) anoint.
Ungheria [unge'ria] *sf* Hungary. **ungherese** *s(m+f)*, *agg* Hungarian.
unghia ['ungja] *sf* nail; (*artiglio*) claw; (*minima distanza*) hair's breadth. **unghie** *sf pl* (*fig*) clutches *pl*. **unghiata** *sf* scratch; (*temperino*) indentation.
unguento [un'gwento] *sm* ointment.
unico ['uniko] *agg* only; (*esclusivo*) sole; (*senza pari*) unique; (*enfatico*) one and only. **unicamente** *avv* only.

unicorno [uni'kɔrno] *sm* unicorn.

unificare [unifi'kare] *v* (*fondere*) merge; standardize. **unificazione** *sf* union; merger; standardization.

uniforme [uni'forme] *sf, agg* uniform. **uniformare** *v* (*adattare*) bring into line (with); (*render piano*) level out; standardize. **uniformarsi** *v* comply (with); adapt (to). **uniformità** *sf* uniformity; (*di superficie*) evenness; (*accordo*) agreement.

unione [u'njone] *sf* union; (*concordia*) unity.

unire [u'nire] *v* join; (*fig*) unite. **unirsi** *v* join; (*insieme con altri*) join up with.

unità [uni'ta] *sf* unity; (*misura, mil*) unit. **unità di misura** measure.

unito [u'nito] *agg* united; (*tinta*) plain. **unitamente** *a* together with.

università [universi'ta] *sf* university. **universitario, -a** *sm, sf* university student. **universo** [uni'verso] *sm* universe. **universale** *agg* universal.

uno ['uno] *agg* one, a. *art* a, an. *pron* one; (*qualcuno*) someone. **fare un po' per uno** share equally. **nè l'uno nè l'altro** neither. **non me ne va bene una!** I can't get one thing right! **tutt'uno** the same thing. **uno a uno** one by one.

unto ['unto] *agg* (*cosparso di grasso*) greasy, oily; (*spalmato*) greased, oiled; (*sporco*) dirty. *sm* grease; (*gastr*) fat. **untuoso** *agg* greasy; (*fig*) unctuous.

uomo ['wɔmo] *sm, pl* **uomini** man (*pl* men). **l'uomo qualunque** the man in the street. **uomo d'affari** businessman. **uomo di fiducia** right-hand man. **uomo di spirito** wit.

uopo ['wɔpo] *sm* **all'uopo** (*a tale scopo*) for this purpose; (*al momento opportuno*) at the right moment. **essere d'uopo** be necessary.

uovo ['wɔvo] *sm, pl* **-a f** egg. **uovo al burro** *or* **tegame** fried egg. **uovo alla coque** boiled egg. **uovo in camicia** poached egg. **uovo sodo/strapazzato** hardboiled/scrambled egg.

uragano [ura'gano] *sm* hurricane; (*tempesta*) storm.

uranio [u'ranjo] *sm* uranium.

urbano [ur'bano] *agg* (*di città*) town, urban; (*cortese*) urbane. **nettezza urbana** refuse collection. **urbanistica** *sf* town-planning. **urbanista** *s(m+f)* town-planner.

urgente [ur'dʒɛnte] *agg* urgent. **urgenza** *sf* urgency. **aver urgenza di** need urgently. **chiamata d'urgenza** *sf* emergency call.

urgere ['urdʒere] *v* (*sollecitare*) urge; (*abbisognare*) be required urgently.

urina [u'rina] *sf* urine. **urinare** *v* urinate. **urinario** *agg* urinary.

urlare [ur'lare] *v* scream; (*animali*) howl; (*dire ad alta voce*) shout. **urlo** *sm, pl* **-a f** shout; howl; scream.

urna ['urna] *sf* urn. **andare alle urne** go to the polls.

urrà [ur'ra] *inter* hurrah!

urtare [ur'tare] *v* knock *or* bump (into); (*dare uno spintone*) jostle; (*fig*) annoy. **urtarsi** *v* (*scontrarsi*) clash; (*auto*) collide; (*fig*) get irritated. **urto** *sm* (*spinta*) push; (*scontro*) clash, collision.

usare [u'zare] *v* use; (*essere solito a*) be accustomed to; (*essere di moda*) be fashionable; (*servirsi di*) make use of; (*fig*) exercise. **usanza** *sf* custom; habit.

uscio ['uʃo] *sm* door. **mettere fuori dell'uscio** turn out (of the house). **uscio di casa** front door.

***uscire** [u'ʃire] *v* leave; (*andar fuori*) go out; (*venir fuori*) come out; (*scendere*) get off; (*sboccare*) lead. **uscir di mente** slip one's mind. **uscir di strada** go off the road. **uscire in macchina** go for a drive. **uscita** *sf* (*passaggio*) exit, way out; (*sbocco*) outlet; (*motto di spirito*) witty remark; (*spesa*) outlay; (*a carte*) lead. **essere in libera uscita** be off duty. **giorno di libera uscita** *sm* day off. **uscita di sicurezza** emergency exit.

usignolo [uzi'ɲolo] *sm* nightingale.

uso ['uzo] *sm* use; (*usanza*) custom; (*voga*) fashion. **c'è l'uso** it is customary. **uso e consumo** wear and tear. **usuale** *agg* usual; customary; common.

ustionare [ustjo'nare] *v* scald. **ustione** *sf* scald.

usufruire [uzufru'ire] *v* benefit (from).

usura[1] [u'zura] *sf* usury. **a usura** with interest. **usuraio, -a** *sm, sf* usurer.

usura[2] [u'zura] *sf* (*tec*) wear. **resistente all'usura** hard-wearing.

usurpare [uzur'pare] *v* usurp. **usurpatore, -trice** *sm, sf* usurper.

utensile [u'tensile] *sm* tool, utensil. **macchina utensile** *sf* machine tool.

utente [u'tɛnte] *s(m+f)* user.

utero ['utero] *sm* womb.

utile ['utile] *agg* useful; (*persona di aiuto*) helpful. **in tempo utile** in good time. **tornar utile** come in handy. *sm* profit. **utili** *sm pl* (*reddito*) income *sing*. **utilità** *sf* usefulness; use; profit. **utilizzare** *v* utilize. **utilizzazione** *sf* utilization.

utopia [uto'pia] *sf* utopia.

uva ['uva] *sf* grapes *pl*. **acino d'uva** *sm* grape. **uva secca** *or* **passa** raisins *pl*. **uva spina** gooseberry.

V

vacanza [va'kantsa] *sf* holiday; (*l'essere vacante*) vacancy. **vacante** *agg* vacant.

vacca ['vakka] *sf* cow. **vaccata** *sf* (*volg*) rubbish. **vacchetta** *sf* (*cuoio*) cowhide.

vaccinare [vattʃi'nare] *v* vaccinate. **vaccinazione** *sf* vaccination. **vaccino** *sm* vaccine.

vacillare [vatʃil'lare] *v* totter; (*essere incerto*) waver.

vagabondo [vaga'bondo] -**a** *agg* roving, *sm*, *sf* vagrant; (*spreg*) loafer. **vagabondare** *v* wander (about).

vagare [va'gare] *v* stray.

vagina [va'dʒina] *sf* vagina.

vagire [va'dʒire] *v* wail. **vagito** *sm* wail(ing).

vaglia ['vaʎa] *sm invar* money order. **vaglia postale** postal order.

vaglia[2] ['vaʎa] *sf di* **vaglia** of note.

vagliare [va'ʎare] *v* sift; (*argomenti, ecc.*) weigh (up). **vagliatura** *sf* sifting; (*esame attento*) careful consideration. **vaglio** *sm* sieve; close examination.

vago ['vago] *agg* vague. **vaghezza** *sf* vagueness.

vagone [va'gone] *sm* (*per passeggeri*) carriage; (*per merci*) wagon. **vagone letto/ristorante** sleeping-/dining-car.

vaiolo [va'jolo] *sm* smallpox.

valanga [va'langa] *sf* avalanche; (*fig*) shower.

valente [va'lente] *agg* skilled, clever.

*valere [va'lere] *v* (*aver valore*) be worth; (*aver merito*) be good; (*aver forza legale*) apply; (*esser regolare*) be valid; (*contare*) count; (*essere utile*) be of use; (*importare*) matter. **far valere** assert. **farsi valere** demand respect; (*imporsi*) assert

oneself. **vale a dire** that is to say. **tanto vale** one might as well. **valere la pena** be worth it. **valere un occhio della testa** be worth a fortune.

valevole [va'levole] *agg* valid.

valicare [vali'kare] *v* cross. **valico** *sm, pl* -**chi** pass; crossing.

valido ['valido] *agg* valid; (*efficace*) effective; (*forte*) strong. **validità** *sf* validity.

valigia [va'lidʒa] *sf* suitcase. **far le valigie** pack. **valigeria** *sf* (*merce*) travel goods *pl*.

valle ['valle] *sf also* **vallata** valley. **a valle di** below. **scendere a valle** go downhill. **vallone** *sm* deep valley; (*depressione*) gorge.

valletto [val'letto] *sm* page; assistant.

valore [va'lore] *sm* value; (*pregio*) worth; validity; (*significato*) meaning; (*coraggio*) valour. **aver valore di** amount to. **carte valori** *pl* securities *pl*. **di valore** of value, valuable; (*professionista*) leading. **imposta di valore aggiunto (IVA)** valued added tax (VAT). **privo di valore** worthless; of no value. **valori** *sm pl* valuables *pl*.

valorizzare [valorid'dzare] *v* exploit; (*mettere in evidenza*) make the most of. **valorizzazione** *sf* exploitation.

valuta [va'luta] *sf* currency.

valutare [valu'tare] *v* value; (*calcolare*) estimate; (*tenere in considerazione*) rate; (*vagliare*) weigh. **valutazione** *sf* evaluation; estimation; (*calcolo approssimativo*) estimate.

valvola ['valvola] *sf* valve; (*elett*) fuse. **valvola di sicurezza** safety-valve.

valzer [val'tser] *sm invar* waltz.

vampa ['vampa] *sf* blaze; (*arrossamento*) flush. **vampata** *sf* blaze; (*fig*) burst; flush; (*al viso*) blush.

vampiro [vam'piro] *sm* vampire.

vandalo ['vandalo] *sm* vandal. **vandalismo** *sm* vandalism.

vaneggiare [vaned'dʒare] *v* rave.

vanesio [va'nezjo] *agg* fatuous, vain.

vangare [van'gare] *v* dig (over). **vanga** *sf* spade.

vangelo [van'dʒelo] *sm* gospel.

vaniglia [va'niʎa] *sf* vanilla.

vanità [vani'ta] *sf* vanity. **vanitoso** *agg* vain.

vano ['vano] *agg* vain. *sm* (*locale*) room; (*spazio*) space. **rendere vano** make useless. **riuscir vano** be unsuccessful.

vantaggio [van'taddʒo] *sm* advantage; (*sport*) lead, handicap; profit. **vantaggiare** *v* favour. **vantaggioso** *agg* advantageous.

vantare [van'tare] *v* boast (of). **vantarsi** *v* boast, brag. **vantatore, -trice** *sm*, *sf* boaster, braggart. **vanteria** *sf* boasting, bragging. **vanto** *sm* (*vanteria*) boasting, bragging; (*atto*) boast.

vanvera ['vanvera] *sf* **a vanvera** (*senza riflettere*) without thinking; (*a casaccio*) at random.

vapore [va'pore] *sm* steam; (*nave*) steamer. **a tutto vapore** full steam ahead. **vaporizzare** *v* vaporize. **vaporizzatore** *sm* vaporizer; (*profumi*) atomizer.

varare [va'rare] *v* launch. **varo** *sm* launch(ing).

varcare [var'kare] *v* cross; (*eccedere*) go beyond. **varco** *sm* opening. **aspettare al varco** lie in wait (for).

variare [va'rjare] *v* change; (*esser diverso*) vary. (**tanto**) **per variare** (just) for a change. **variare d'aspetto** look different. **variabile** *sf*, *agg* variable. **variabilità** *sf* variability. **variante** *sf* variant. **variato** *agg* varied. **variazione** *sf* variátion.

varicella [vari'tʃella] *sf* chicken-pox.

varicoso [vari'kozo] *agg* varicose.

varietà [varje'ta] *sf* variety. *sm* (*teatro*) variety.

vario ['varjo] *agg* (*variato*) varied; (*diverso*) various, different; (*non regolare*) variable. **variopinto** *agg* multicoloured. **vari** *pron pl* various people *pl*, several people *pl*.

vasca ['vaska] *sf* basin; (*da bagno*) bathtub; (*tino*) vat; (*piscina*) (swimming-)pool. **fare una vasca** (*sport*) swim a length.

vascello [va'ʃello] *sm* vessel, warship. **ufficiale di vascello** *sm* naval officer.

vasellame [vazel'lame] *sm* crockery; (*di metallo prezioso*) plate; (*di porcellana*) china; (*di vetro*) glassware.

vaso ['vazo] *sm* pot; (*per fiori recisi*) vase; (*anat*) vessel. **vaso da fiori** flower-pot. **vaso da notte** chamber-pot. **vasaio, -a** *sm*, *sf* potter.

vassoio [vas'sojo] *sm* tray; (*del muratore*) mortar-board.

vasto ['vasto] *agg* wide, vast. **vastità** *sf* vastness.

Vaticano [vati'kano] *sm* Vatican. **città del Vaticano** *sf* Vatican City.

vaticinio [vati'tʃinjo] *sm* prediction. **vaticinare** *v* predict.

ve [ve] *V* vi.

vecchio ['vekkjo] *agg* old. *sm* old man. **vecchia** *sf* old woman. **vecchiaia** *sf* old age. **vecchiotto** *agg* oldish, fairly old; (*fuori moda*) out-of-date.

vece ['vetʃe] *sf* **fare le veci di** take the place of. **in mia vece** in my place.

*****vedere** [ve'dere] *v* see. **avere a che vedere con** have to do with. **dare a vedere** let it be understood. **far vedere** show. **non vederci più** (*fam*) be furious. **non veder l'ora di** look forward to. **stare a vedere** (*attendere*) see; (*guardare*) watch; (*scommettere*) bet. **vedere di buon occhio** approve (of). **vediamo un po'** let's see *sm*. **a mio vedere** in my opinion.

vedetta [ve'detta] *sf* look-out.

vedova ['vedova] *sf* widow. **vedovo** *sm* widower. **rimaner vedova** or **vedovo** be widowed. **vedovanza** *sf* widowhood.

veemente [vee'mɛnte] *agg* vehement.

vegetale [vedʒe'tale] *agg*, *sm* vegetable. **vegetariano, -a** *s*, *agg* vegetarian. **vegetativo** *agg* vegetative. **vegetazione** *sf* vegetation.

vegetare [vedʒe'tare] *v* vegetate. **vegeto** *agg* flourishing. **vivo e vegeto** alive and kicking.

vegliare [ve'ʎare] *v* (*vigilare*) watch; (*fare la veglia*) keep watch; (*star sveglio*) stay up. **veglia** *sf* watch, vigil; (*lo star desto*) wakefulness; (*festa*) party; (*funebre*) wake. **veglione** *sm* ball, party.

veicolo [ve'ikolo] *sm* vehicle; (*malattia*) carrier.

vela ['vela] *sf* sail; (*sport*) sailing. **a gonfie vele** booming. **barca a vela** *sf* sailing-boat. **volo a vela** *sm* gliding. **veleggiare** *v* sail; (*velivolo*) glide. **veliero** *sm* sailing-ship.

velare [ve'lare] *v* veil; cover; (*offuscare*) cloud, dim; (*suono*) muffle.

veleno [ve'leno] *sm* poison. **avere il veleno in corpo** (*fam*) have a chip on one's shoulder. **sputare veleno** (*fig*) vent one's spleen. **velenoso** *agg* poisonous; (*fig*) venomous.

velino [ve'lino] *agg* **carta velina** *sf* flimsy (paper). **velina** *sf* (*copia*) carbon copy.

velivolo [ve'livolo] *sm* aircraft; (*aliante*) glider.

velleità [velle'ita] *sf* vain ambition.

vellicare [velli'kare] v titillate.

vello ['vɛllo] sm fleece.

velluto [vel'luto] sm velvet. **di velluto** velvet. **vellutato** agg velvety.

veloce [ve'lotʃe] agg quick, fast. **velocista** s(m+f) sprinter. **velocità** sf speed; (fis) velocity. **eccedere la velocità** (auto) speed.

velodromo [ve'lɔdromo] sm cycle-track.

veltro ['vɛltro] sm greyhound.

vena ['vena] sf vein; (fig) talent; inspiration. **essere in vena** be in the mood.

venale [ve'nale] agg saleable; (spreg) mercenary.

vendemmiare [vendem'mjare] v harvest (grapes). **vendemmia** sf grape harvest.

vendere ['vendere] v sell. **aver ... da vendere** have ... to spare; have plenty of ... **vendere a contanti** sell for cash. **vendere al dettaglio** or **minuto** retail. **vendere all'asta** auction. **vendere all'ingrosso** sell wholesale. **vendere fumo** bluff. **vendibile** agg saleable; (messo in vendita) for sale.

vendetta [ven'detta] sf revenge; (castigo meritato) vengeance.

vendicare [vendi'kare] v avenge. **vendicarsi** take revenge. **vendicativo** agg vindictive.

vendita [vendita] sf sale. **vendita a rate** hire-purchase. **venditore, -trice** sm, sf vendor; (negoziante) shopkeeper.

venerare [vene'rare] v revere; (rel) worship. **venerabile** agg venerable. **venerazione** sf veneration.

venerdì [vener'di] sm Friday. **Venerdi Santo** Good Friday.

venereo [ve'nɛreo] agg venereal.

Venezia [ve'nɛtsja] sf Venice. **veneziana** sf Venetian blind. **veneziano, -a** s, agg Venetian.

veniale [ve'njale] agg venial.

*__venire__ [ve'nire] v come; (riuscire) come out; (essere) be. **far venire** (mandare a chiamare) call, send for. **mi viene da ...** I feel like .... **venire alle mani** come to blows. **venire incontro** come towards; (incontrare) meet; (fig) meet halfway. **venir meno** (mancare) be lacking; (svenire) pass out.

ventaglio [ven'taʎo] sm fan.

venti ['venti] agg, sm twenty. **ventesimo** agg, sm twentieth.

ventilare [venti'lare] v air; (agric) winnow. **ventilato** agg airy, ventilated. **ventilazione** sf ventilation.

vento ['vɛnto] sm wind.

ventosa [ven'toza] sf sucker.

ventre ['vɛntre] sm stomach; abdomen; (forma) belly; (grembo materno) womb. **ventrale** agg ventral.

ventricolo [ven'trikolo] sm ventricle.

ventriloquo [ven'trilokwo], -a sm, sf ventriloquist.

ventura [ven'tura] sf fortune. **alla ventura** at random. **andare** or **mettersi alla ventura** trust to luck; take a chance. **soldato di ventura** sm mercenary.

venturo [ven'turo] agg next.

vera ['vera] sf wedding ring.

verace [ve'ratʃe] agg (veritiero) truthful; (vero) true, real. **veracità** sf truthfulness.

veranda [ve'randa] sf veranda.

verbale [ver'bale] sm record, minutes pl. **mettere a verbale** put on record. agg verbal.

verbo ['vɛrbo] sm verb; (parola) word. **verboso** agg verbose, long-winded.

verde ['verde] agg green. sm green; (natura) greenery; (zona) green belt. **essere** or **trovarsi al verde** be broke. **verdastro** agg greenish. **verdeggiare** v be verdant; (diventar verde) turn green.

verdetto [ver'detto] sm verdict.

verdura [ver'dura] sf greens pl, vegetables pl.

verga ['verga] sf rod. **verga magica** magic wand. **vergare** v line; (scrivere) write.

vergine ['verdʒine] sf, agg virgin. **Vergine** sf Virgo. **verginale** agg virginal. **verginità** sf virginity.

vergogna [ver'goɲa] sf shame; (disonore) disgrace. **fare vergogna** shame. inter shame on you! **vergognarsi** v be or feel ashamed (of); (non osare) be too shy (to). **vergognoso** agg shameful; shy.

verificare [verifi'kare] v check. **verificarsi** v (avvenire) occur; (avverarsi) come true. **verifica** sf control; verification; (dei conti) audit. **verificabile** agg verifiable. **verificazione** sf verification, check; audit.

verità [veri'ta] sf truth; (giustezza) truthfulness. **veritiero** agg truthful.

verme ['vɛrme] sm worm; (larva di insetto) maggot.

vermiglio [ver'miʎo] agg, sm vermilion.

vermut ['vɛrmut] sm invar vermouth.

verniciare [verni'tʃare] v paint; (con vernice trasparente) varnish; (a smalto) enamel. **vernice** sf varnish, lacquer; (apparenza) veneer; (strato sottile) film. **verniciata** sf coat of paint. **verniciatura** sf painting; varnishing.

vero ['vero] agg true; real. sm truth. **a onor del vero** to tell the truth. **di vero cuore** from the bottom of one's heart. **vero e proprio** out and out.

verosimile [vero'simile] agg likely. **aver del verosimile** be likely.

verricello [verri'tʃɛllo] sm winch.

verro ['vɛrro] sm boar.

verruca [ver'ruka] sf wart.

versare [ver'sare] v pour (out); (rovesciare) spill; (spargere) shed; (pagare) pay; (trovarsi) find oneself. **versamento** sm payment, deposit. **versante** sm side. **versato** agg paid (up); (pratico) skilled.

versatile [ver'satile] agg versatile. **versatilità** sf versatility.

versione [ver'sjone] sf version; (traduzione) translation.

verso¹ ['vɛrso] prep towards; (circa) about. **verso il basso** down(wards). **verso l'alto** up(wards).

verso² ['vɛrso] sm (metrica) verse; (suono particolare) sound; gesture; direction; (modo) means. **in verso antiorario** anticlockwise. **in verso orario** clockwise. **per un verso o per un altro** in one way or another.

vertebra ['vɛrtebra] sf vertebra (pl -brae). **vertebrato** agg, sm vertebrate.

vertenza [ver'tentsa] sf dispute; (dir) lawsuit.

verticale [verti'kale] agg, sf vertical.

vertice ['vɛrtitʃe] sm summit; (mat) vertex.

vertigini [ver'tidʒini] sf pl dizziness sing; (attacco) dizzy spell sing; (med) vertigo sing. **aver le vertigini** feel dizzy or giddy. **vertiginoso** agg dizzy.

vescica [ve'ʃika] sf bladder; (bolla cutanea) blister.

vescovo ['veskovo] sm bishop. **vescovado** sm (dignità) bishopric; (territorio) diocese; (palazzo) bishop's palace. **vescovile** agg episcopal.

vespa ['vespa] sf wasp. **vespaio** sm wasps' nest.

vestaglia [ves'taʎa] sf dressing-gown; (vestaglietta) housecoat.

veste ['vɛste] sf dress; (rel) vestment; (fig) capacity. **in veste di amico** as a friend. **in veste ufficiale** in an official capacity. **vestiario** sm wardrobe; (indumenti) clothes pl. **capo di vestiario** sm item of clothing. **vestibolo** [ves'tibolo] sm vestibule, lobby.

vestigio [ves'tidʒo] sm trace.

vestire [ves'tire] v dress; (indossare) wear; (detto di abiti) fit. **vestirsi** v dress. **vestito** sm dress.

veterano [vete'rano], -a s, agg veteran.

veterinario [veteri'narjo] agg veterinary. sm veterinary surgeon, vet. **veterinaria** sf veterinary science.

veto ['veto] sm invar veto.

vetro ['vetro] sm glass; (di finestra) pane. **vetro smerigliato** frosted glass. **vetraio** sm glazier. **vetrata** sf (porta) glass door; (finestra) stained-glass window.

vetta ['vetta] sf top.

vettore [vet'tore] sm vector; (comm) carrier.

vettovaglie [vetto'vaʎe] sf pl provisions pl.

vettura [vet'tura] sf carriage; (auto) car. **biglietto di vettura** sm (comm) bill of lading.

vezzeggiare [veddzed'dʒare] v fondle.

vi [vi], ve pron (to) you; (riflessivo) yourselves; (reciproco) each other. avv (qui) here; (lì) there.

via¹ ['via] sf way; (strada) street; (sentiero) path. **in via di costruzione** under construction. **in via eccezionale** exceptionally. **per via aerea** by air. **per via di** (a causa di) because of. **via mare/terra** by sea/land.

via² ['via] avv away; (suvvia) come on. sm invar starting signal. **e così via** and so on. **va via!** go on! **via le mani!** hands off! **via via** gradually; (a mano a mano) as.

viabilità [viabili'ta] sf road conditions pl.

viadotto [via'dotto] sm viaduct.

viaggiare [viad'dʒare] v travel; (veicoli) run; (essere trasportato) be carried. **viaggiatore, -trice** sm, sf traveller; passenger. **piccione viaggiatore** sm carrier pigeon.

viaggio [vi'addʒo] sm journey, trip. **mettersi in viaggio** set out or off. **viaggio d'andata/di ritorno** outward/return journey. **viaggio d'andata e ritorno** round trip. **viaggio di nozze** honeymoon.

viale [vi'ale] sm avenue.

viandante [vian'dante] s(m+f) wayfarer.

viavai [via'vaj] *sm* coming and going.

vibrare [vib'rare] *v* vibrate; *(fig)* quiver; *(assestare)* hurl. **vibrare un colpo** deal a blow. **vibrazione** *sf* vibration; *(fremito)* quiver.

vicario [vi'karjo] *sm* vicar.

viceconsole [vitʃe'kɔnsole] *s(m+f)* vice-consul.

vicedirettore [vitʃediret'tore], **-trice** *sm, sf* assistant manager; *(scuola)* deputy head.

vicenda [vi'tʃɛnda] *sf* event; succession. **vicendevolmente** *avv* also **a vicenda** *(a turno)* in turns; *(scambievolmente)* each other, one another.

vicepresidente [vitʃeprezi'dɛnte], **-essa** *sm, sf* vice-president, vice-chairman.

viceversa [vitʃe'vɛrsa] *avv* vice versa; *(invece)* but.

vicinanza [vitʃi'nantsa] *sf* vicinity.

vicinato [vitʃi'nato] *sm* neighbourhood.

vicino [vi'tʃino], **-a** *agg* near; *(accanto)* next; *(confinante)* neighbouring; *(fig)* close. *avv* close (by); near (by); *(accanto a)* beside, by. **da vicino** at close quarters. *sm, sf* neighbour. **vicino di casa** next-door neighbour.

vicolo [vikolo] *sm* alley.

video ['video] *sm invar* (television) screen.

vidimare [vidi'mare] *v* certify. **vidimazione** *sf* certification.

vietare [vje'tare] *v* prohibit; *(impedire)* prevent. **vietato** *agg* forbidden. **ingresso vietato** no admission. **sosta vietata** no parking.

vigente [vi'dʒɛnte] *agg* current; *(dir)* in force.

vigilare [vidʒi'lare] *v* watch (over); keep a watch (on). **vigilante** *agg* watchful. **vigilanza** *sf* vigilance; *(controllo)* supervision; *(urbana)* police.

vigile [vi'dʒile] *agg* watchful. *sm* policeman. **vigile del fuoco** fireman.

vigilia [vi'dʒilja] *sf* eve; *(rel)* vigil. **vigilia di Natale/Capodanno** Christmas/New Year's Eve.

vigliacco [vi'ʎakko] *agg* cowardly. *sm, sf* coward. **vigliaccheria** *sf* cowardice; cowardly action.

vigna ['viɲa] *sf* vineyard.

vignetta [vi'ɲetta] *sf* sketch; *(umoristica)* cartoon.

vigore [vi'gore] *sm* force; *(forza vitale)* vigour. **entrare in vigore** *(dir)* come into force. **vigoria** *sf* energy.

vile ['vile] *agg (vigliacco)* cowardly; *(basso)* base, low. *s(m+f)* coward. **vilipendio** *sm* contempt.

villa ['villa] *sf* villa. **villa di campagna** country house.

villaggio [vil'laddʒo] *sm* village.

villano [vil'lano], **-a** *agg* rude; *(rozzo)* uncouth; offensive. *sm, sf* lout, boor. **villania** *sf* rudeness.

villeggiare [villed'dʒare] *v* spend a holiday. **villeggiatura** *sf* holidays *pl*.

viltà [vil'ta] *sf* cowardice; cowardly action.

viluppo [vi'luppo] *sm* tangle.

vimini ['vimini] *sm pl* wicker *sing*. **di vimini** wicker. **lavoro in vimini** *sm* wickerwork.

*vincere ['vintʃere] *v* win; *(battere)* beat; *(sopraffare)* overcome; *(sconfiggere)* defeat. **lasciarsi vincere (da)** yield (to). **vincita** *sf* win.

vincitore [vintʃi'tore], **-trice** *sm, sf* winner; *(di battaglia)* victor. *agg* winning, victorious.

vincolare [vinko'lare] *v* bind; *(comm)* tie up. **vincolo** *sm* tie.

vino ['vino] *sm* wine. **vino di mele** cider. **vinicolo** *agg* wine.

viola¹ [vi'ɔla] *sf (bot)* violet. *agg, sm invar (colore)* violet. **viola del pensiero** pansy. **violacciocca** *sf* stock; *(gialla)* wallflower. **violaceo** *agg* violet.

viola² [vi'ɔla] *sf (musica)* viola.

violare [vio'lare] *v* violate; *(una donna)* rape; *(domicilio)* break into. **violare l'ordine pubblico** cause a breach of the peace. **violazione** *sf* violation. **violazione carnale** rape. **violazione della pace** breach of the peace. **violazione di domicilio** house-breaking.

violentare [violen'tare] *v* force; *(una donna)* rape. **violentatore** *sm* rapist. **violento** *agg* violent. **violenza** *sf* violence.

violetta [vio'letta] *sf* violet. **violetto** *agg, sm invar* violet.

violino [vio'lino] *sm* violin. **violinista** *s(m+f)* violinist.

violoncello [violon'tʃɛllo] *sm* (violon)cello. **violoncellista** *s(m+f)* (violon)cellist.

viottolo [vi'ɔttolo] *sm* path.

vipera ['vipera] *sf* viper.

virale [vi'rale] *agg* viral.

virare [vi'rare] *v (alare)* haul (in); *(mutar*

direzione) veer, change course; (*aero*) turn.

virgola ['virgola] *sf* comma; (*mat*) point. **tra virgolette** in inverted commas.

virile [vi'rile] *agg* virile; masculine; (*fig*) manly. **virilità** *sf* virility.

virtù [vir'tu] *sf* virtue; faculty. **in virtù di** by virtue of, in accordance with. **virtuale** *agg* virtual.

virtuoso [virtu'ozo], -a *agg* virtuous. *sm*, *sf* virtuoso.

virulento [viru'lento] *agg* virulent.

virus [virus] *sm invar* virus.

viscere ['viʃere] *sm* internal organ. *sf pl* intestines *pl*; (*di animali*) entrails *pl*. **le viscere della terra** the bowels of the earth *pl*.

vischio ['viskjo] *sm* mistletoe; (*estratto*) bird-lime; (*fig*) snare. **viscido** *agg* slimy.

visconte [vis'konte] *sm* viscount.

viscoso [vis'kozo] *agg* viscous. **viscosa** *sf* viscose. **viscosità** *sf* viscosity.

visibile [vi'zibile] *agg* visible. **andare/mandare in visibilio** go/send into raptures. **visibilità** *sf* visibility.

visiera [vi'zjera] *sf* visor; (*berretto*) peak; (*scherma*) mask.

visione [vi'zjone] *sf* sight; (*apparizione*) vision; idea; (*cinema*) showing. **prendere in visione** inspect. **ricevere in visione** receive on approval. **visionario**, -a *sm*, *sf* visionary.

visita ['vizita] *sf* visit; (*persona*) visitor; (*esame*) examination. **visita domiciliare** domiciliary visit; (*perquisizione*) house search. **visitare** *v* visit; (*andare a trovare*) call on; (*med*) examine. **visitatore**, -trice *sm*, *sf* visitor.

visivo [vi'zivo] *agg* visual. **campo visivo** *sm* field of vision.

viso ['vizo] *sm* face. **a viso aperto** openly. **far buon viso a cattiva sorte** make the best of it. **fare il viso lungo** sulk.

visone [vi'zone] *sm* mink.

vispo ['vispo] *agg* lively; (*svelto*) brisk.

vista ['vista] *sf* sight; (*spettacolo*) view. **avere in vista** have in mind. **a vista** on sight. **a vista d'occhio** before one's very eyes. **conoscere di vista** know by sight. **perdere di vista** lose sight (of).

visto ['visto] *sm* visa. **visto di soggiorno** tourist visa.

vistoso [vis'tozo] *agg* showy; (*notevole*) considerable.

visuale [vizu'ale] *agg* visual. *sf* view; line of vision. **visualizzare** *v* visualize.

vita¹ ['vita] *sf* life; (*durata*) lifetime. **a vita** for life. **condanna a vita** *sf* life sentence. **essere in fin di vita** be at death's door. **guadagnarsi la vita** earn one's living.

vita² ['vita] *sf* (*corpo*) waist.

vitale [vi'tale] *agg* vital. **vitalità** *sf* vitality.

vitalizio [vita'litsjo] *agg* life(long). *sm* (*rendita*) annuity.

vitamina [vita'mina] *sf* vitamin.

vite¹ ['vite] *sf* (*bot*) vine. **viticcio** *sm* tendril. **viticoltura** *sf* viticulture.

vite² ['vite] *sf* (*mec*) screw. **cadere in vite** (*aero*) go into a spin.

vitello [vi'tello] *sm* calf; (*gastr*) veal. **vitellone** *sm* bullock; (*fig*) loafer.

vitreo ['vitreo] *agg* glassy, vitreous.

vittima ['vittima] *sf* victim; (*chi subisce danni*) casualty. **essere vittima di un incidente** be involved in an accident. **fare la vittima** (*fig*) be a martyr.

vitto ['vitto] *sm* food; (*nutrimento giornaliero*) board. **vitto e alloggio** board and lodging.

vittoria [vit'torja] *sf* victory; (*sport*) win. **vittorioso** *agg* victorious.

vituperare [vitupe'rare] *v* berate. **vituperio** *sm* insult; (*causa*) disgrace.

viva ['viva] *inter* hurrah! **viva ... !** long live ... !

vivacchiare [vivak'kjare] *v* manage.

vivace [vi'vatʃe] *agg* lively; (*intenso*) bright. **vivacità** *sf* liveliness; brightness.

vivaio [vi'vajo] *sm* nursery; (*pesci*) fishpond.

vivanda [vi'vanda] *sf* food; (*piatto*) dish.

***vivere** ['vivere] *v* live; (*trascorrere*) spend. **avere di che vivere** have enough to live on. **lasciar vivere** leave in peace. **vivere alla giornata** live from hand to mouth. *sm* life; (*modo di vivere*) living.

viveri ['viveri] *sm pl* provisions *pl*.

vivido ['vivido] *agg* vivid.

vivisezione [vivise'tsjone] *sf* vivisection.

vivo ['vivo] *agg* living; (*vivace*) lively; (*intenso*) bright. **a viva forza** by force. **farsi vivo** show up; (*mettersi in contatto*) get in touch. *sm* living person; (*fig*) heart. **ferire nel vivo** wound to the quick.

viziare [vi'tsjare] *v* spoil; (*fin*) vitiate.

vizio ['vitsjo] *sm* vice; bad habit; defect; (*peccato*) sin. **vizio parziale (di mente)** diminished responsibility. **vizioso** *agg* depraved.

vizzo ['vittso] *agg* withered.

vocabolo [vo'kabolo] *sm* word. **vocabolario** *sm* vocabulary; dictionary.

vocale [vo'kale] *agg* vocal. *sf* vowel.

vocazione [voka'tsjone] *sf* vocation; *(inclinazione naturale)* leaning. **vocazionale** *agg* vocational.

voce ['votʃe] *sf* voice; expression; *(elemento di elenco)* heading; opinion. **a bassa voce** softly. **ad alta voce** out loud. **aver voce in capitolo** have a say in the matter. **corre voce** rumour has it. **dire a (viva) voce** tell personally. **sotto voce** in an undertone.

vociare [vo'tʃare] *v* bawl.

vociferare [votʃife'rare] *v* talk at the top of one's voice; *(fig)* rumour.

vodka ['vodka] *sf* vodka.

vogare [vo'gare] *v* row. **vogatore** *sm* oarsman.

voglia ['voʎa] *sf* wish; *(disposizione)* will; *(capriccio)* fancy; *(med)* birthmark. **avere una gran voglia di** be dying to. **aver voglia di (fare)** feel like (doing), want to (do). **di buona voglia** willingly. **di cattiva** *or* **mala voglia** unwillingly.

voi ['voi] *pron* you.

volano [vo'lano] *sm (mec)* flywheel; *(sport)* shuttlecock.

volare [vo'lare] *v* fly. **volar giù** hurtle down. **volata** *sf (sport)* sprint; *(corsa rapida)* dash. **di volata** in a rush. **fare una volata** make a dash.

volatile [vo'latile] *agg* volatile.

volentieri [volen'tjɛri] *avv* willingly; with pleasure. **fare volentieri** like doing.

***volere** [vo'lere] *v* want; *(desiderare)* wish; *(comando)* will; *(intendere)* mean; *(cortesia)* like. **l'hai voluto tu!** you've asked for it! **neanche a volere** not even if you try. **non vuol dire** *(non ha importanza)* it doesn't matter. **se Dio vuole** God willing. **senza volere** without meaning to. **volerci** *v* take. **voler bene a** *(aver affetto)* be fond of; *(amare)* love. **voler dire** mean.

volgare [vol'gare] *agg* vulgar; common. *sm (lingua)* vernacular. **volgarità** *sf* vulgarity. **volgarizzare** *v* popularize.

***volgere** ['vɔldʒere] *v* turn. **col volgere degli anni** with the passing of time. **volgere alla fine** near the end. **volgere la parola a** address.

volgoₙ['volgo] *sm* common people *pl*.

volo ['volo] *sm* flight. **cogliere al volo** seize. **volo a vela** gliding. **volo in picchiata** nose-dive.

volontà [volon'ta] *sf* will. **di mia spontanea** *or* **propria volontà** of my own free will.

volontario [volon'tarjo], **-a** voluntary. *sm*, *sf* volunteer. **volontario del sangue** blood donor. **volontariato** *sm* voluntary service.

volonteroso [volonte'rozo] *agg* willing.

volpe ['volpe] *sf* fox; *(femmina)* vixen.

volta¹ ['vɔlta] *sf* time; turn. **alla volta** at a time. **alla volta di** towards. **a volte** sometimes. **spesse volte** often. **una buona volta** once and for all. **una volta** once; *(nelle fiabe)* once upon a time.

volta² ['vɔlta] *sf (arch)* vault.

voltare [vol'tare] *v* turn. **voltagabbana** *s(m+f)* *invar* fickle person.

volto ['volto] *sm* face.

volubile [vo'lubile] *agg* fickle.

volume [vo'lume] *sm* volume; *(mole)* size. **voluminoso** *agg* voluminous; *(ingombrante)* bulky.

voluta [vo'luta] *sf* scroll.

voluttuoso [voluttu'ozo] *agg* voluptuous. **voluttà** *sf* voluptuousness.

vomitare [vomi'tare] *v* vomit, be sick. **aver voglia di vomitare** feel sick. **vomito** *sm (atto)* vomiting; *(materia)* vomit. **mi viene il vomito** I feel sick.

vongola ['vongola] *sf* clam.

vorace [vo'ratʃe] *agg* greedy.

voragine [vo'radʒine] *sf* chasm, gulf.

vortice ['vortitʃe] *sm* vortex; *(gorgo)* whirlpool; *(fig)* whirl.

vostro ['vostro] *agg* your. *pron* yours.

votare [vo'tare] *v* vote; *(approvare)* pass; put to the vote; *(dedicare)* devote. **votazione** *sf* voting; *(scrutinio)* ballot; *(scuola)* marks *pl*. **voto** *sm* vote; *(promessa)* vow; *(scuola)* mark. **a pieni voti** with full marks. **pronunciare i voti** take one's vows.

vulcano [vul'kano] *sm* volcano. **vulcanico** *agg* volcanic; *(fig)* brilliant.

vulnerabile [vulne'rabile] *agg* vulnerable. **vulnerabilità** *sf* vulnerability.

vuotare [vwo'tare] *v* empty. **vuotare il sacco** *(fig)* spill the beans.

vuoto ['vwoto] *agg* empty. *sm* void; *(fis)* vacuum; *(fig)* emptiness, gap. **andare a vuoto** fail. **a vuoto** in vain. **girare a vuoto** *(mec)* idle.

X

xenofobo [kse'nɔfobo], **-a** agg xenophobic. sm, sf xenophobe. **xenofobia** sf xenophobia.

xerocopiare [kseroko'pjare] v Xerox ®.

xilofono [ksi'lɔfono] sm xylophone.

Y

yoga ['jɔga] sm invar yoga.

yoghurt ['jɔgurt] sm invar yoghurt.

Z

zacchera ['dzakkera] sf splash (of mud).

zaffata [dzaf'fata] sf whiff; (getto di liquido) splash.

zafferano [dzaffe'rano] sm saffron.

zaffiro [dzaf'firo] sm sapphire.

zaino ['dzajno] sm kit-bag; (alpinisti) rucksack.

zampa ['dzampa] sf leg; (con unghie) paw; (maiale) trotter. **a quattro zampe** on all fours. **zampe di gallina** sf pl (rughe) crow's-feet pl; (scrittura) scrawl sing.

zampare v paw (the ground). **aver lo zampino in** have a hand in. **mettere lo zampino** interfere.

zampillare [dzampil'lare] v spurt, gush. **zampillo** sm spurt.

zampogna [dzam'poɲa] sf bagpipes pl.

zangola ['dzangola] sf churn. **zangolare** v churn.

zanna ['dzanna] sf fang; (di elefante, cinghiale) tusk.

zanzara [dzan'dzara] sf mosquito. **zanzariera** sf mosquito-net.

zappare [dzap'pare] v hoe. **zappa** sf hoe.

zattera [dzat'tera] sf raft.

zazzera [dzad'dzera] sf mop of hair.

zebra ['dzɛbra] sf zebra. **zebre** sf pl (passaggio) zebra crossing sing. **zebrato** agg striped.

zecca[1] ['dzekka] sf mint. **nuovo di zecca** brand-new. **zecchino** sm gold coin.

zecca[2] ['dzekka] sf (zool) tick.

zelo ['dzelo] sm zeal. **zelante** agg keen, zealous.

zenzero ['dzendzero] sm ginger.

zeppa ['dzeppa] sf wedge. **zeppare** v

wedge.

zeppo ['dzeppo] agg (pieno) **zeppo** packed, cram-full.

zerbino [dzer'bino] sm (door-)mat.

zero ['dzero] sm nought; (fig, mat) zero; (sport) nil; (tennis) love.

zia ['dzia] sf aunt.

zibellino [dzibel'lino] sm sable.

zibetto [dzi'betto] sm civet.

zigzag [dzig'dzag] sm zigzag. **andare a zigzag** zigzag.

zimbello [dzim'bello] sm decoy; (oggetto di scherno) laughing-stock. **zimbellare** v lure.

zinco ['dzinko] sm zinc.

zingaro ['dzingaro], **-a** s, agg gipsy.

zio ['dzio] sm uncle.

zirlare [dzir'lare] v chirp.

zitella [dzi'tella] sf spinster. **vecchia zitella** (spreg) old maid.

zittire [dzit'tire] v (far tacere) hush; (disapprovazione) hiss.

zitto ['dzitto] agg quiet. **star zitto** keep quiet; (fam) shut up.

zoccolo ['dzɔkkolo] sm clog; (zool) hoof; base; (parete) skirting-board.

zodiaco [dzo'diako] sm zodiac.

zolfo ['dzolfo] sm sulphur.

zolla ['dzolla] sf clod.

zona ['dzona] sf zone; area. **zona pedonale** pedestrian precinct. **zona verde** (periferica) green belt.

zonzo ['dzondzo] avv **andare a zonzo** wander about.

zoo [dzo] sm invar zoo.

zoologia [dzoolo'dʒia] sf zoology. **zoologico** agg zoological. **zoologo, -a** sm, sf zoologist.

zoppicare [dzoppi'kare] v limp; (tavolo, ecc.) be rickety; (fig) be shaky. **zoppo** agg lame; rickety; shaky.

zotico ['dzɔtiko], **-a** agg boorish. sm, sf boor.

zucca ['dzukka] sf pumpkin; (fam: testa) nut. **zuccone** sm (fam) blockhead.

zucchero ['dzukkero] sm sugar. **zucchero a velo** icing sugar. **zucchero semolato** castor sugar. **zuccherare** v sweeten.

zucchino [dzuk'kino], **-a** sm, sf courgette.

zuffa ['dzuffa] sf scuffle, brawl.

zuppa ['dzuppa] sf soup. **zuppa inglese** trifle. **zuppiera** sf tureen. **zuppo** agg drenched.